THE OXFORD

Essential Dictionary of Foreign Terms in English

AMERICAN EDITION

Also Available

THE OXFORD DESK DICTIONARY AND THESAURUS
THE OXFORD ESSENTIAL BIOGRAPHICAL DICTIONARY
THE OXFORD ESSENTIAL DICTIONARY
THE OXFORD ESSENTIAL GEOGRAPHICAL DICTIONARY
THE OXFORD ESSENTIAL SPELLING DICTIONARY
THE OXFORD ESSENTIAL THESAURUS
THE OXFORD FRENCH DICTIONARY
THE OXFORD GERMAN DICTIONARY
THE OXFORD ITALIAN DICTIONARY
THE OXFORD PORTUGUESE DICTIONARY
THE OXFORD RUSSIAN DICTIONARY
THE OXFORD NEW SPANISH DICTIONARY

THE OXFORD Essential Dictionary of Foreign Terms in English

AMERICAN EDITION

EDITED BY
Jennifer Speake

AMERICAN EDITOR
Mark LaFlaur

BERKLEY BOOKS, NEW YORK

Editor:	Jennifer Speake
American Editor:	Mark LaFlaur
Assistant Editor:	Deborah Argosy
Data Entry:	Karen Fisher, Kimberly Roberts
Proofreaders:	Linda Costa, Laurie H. Ongley
Editor in Chief:	Frank Abate
Managing Editor:	Elizabeth J. Jewell

THE OXFORD ESSENTIAL DICTIONARY OF FOREIGN TERMS IN ENGLISH

A Berkley Book / published in mass market paperback by arrangement with Oxford University Press, Inc.

PRINTING HISTORY
Berkley edition / August 1999

The Penguin Putnam Inc. World Wide Web site address is
http://www.penguinputnam.com

ISBN: 0-425-16995-2

BERKLEY®
Berkley Books are published by
The Berkley Publishing Group, a division of Penguin Putnam Inc.,
375 Hudson Street, New York, New York 10014.
BERKLEY and the "B" design are trademarks
belonging to Penguin Putnam Inc.

PRINTED IN THE UNITED STATES OF AMERICA

10 9 8 7 6 5 4 3 2 1

Contents

Preface

The Oxford Essential Dictionary of Foreign Terms in English records the influx of words from a variety of other languages into both American and British English, concentrating especially on those introduced during the course of the twentieth century. Older dictionaries in this field tend to have a preponderance of French and Latin expressions; many of these are indeed still current and are represented in the present work, but the English language is now open to new words on a worldwide basis. Many recent introductions reflect an unprecedented cultural eclecticism, particularly in what might be called "lifestyle" words—those dealing with areas such as fashion, cuisine, ethnic music, and recreation.

There is nothing new about sources for foreign words being indicative of historical or cultural events. The influx of French military terms in the early eighteenth century, for instance, can be linked to the Continental campaigns of the Duke of Marlborough. More recently, the British rule of India spawned a large number of Anglo-Indian terms for the various functionaries and institutions necessary to keep the wheels of empire turning. However, neither of these two categories is heavily represented in late twentieth-century speech, *nouvelle cuisine* being more fashionable than fortification and *karma* having a higher profile than imperial administration.

The criterion for currency that has been applied in the selection of entries favors words first introduced during the twentieth century. An exception to this is the large category of words, particularly from the classical languages, that are recent introductions or revivals with exclusively scientific senses; these are excluded on the grounds that they do not fulfill another criterion, that the word may be encountered in non-specialist literature. However, many other words have both technical and more general senses, and in such cases the technical senses are generally included or mentioned in the entry, as the evolution of the various senses once they have entered the language is often interesting in itself. For instance, *flèche*, which occurs in Middle English with its basic French meaning of 'arrow,' soon became obsolete after its first introduction (most probably because it duplicated an already established word); but reintroduced from Modern French with a variety of special applications, it has fared better. Terms that are used in particular sports or other fields of activity and have remained so (or have not had time to move beyond their restricted area) have been excluded; admitting terms for bull-fighting passes or judo throws would have considerably increased the proportion of, respectively, Spanish and Japanese entries.

Introduced expressions have met with varying fortunes in English, but certain patterns can be seen. On the whole, phrases tend to be more resistant to naturalization than single words. At one end of the scale of naturalization, many words, especially those from Old French and Latin, have become totally assimilated in spelling, pronunciation, and plural form, and are thus no longer thought of as foreign in any sense other than the purely etymological. Others (such as *restaurant*) are nearing the end of this process of assimilation, with only some slight variation in standard pronunciation (in the UK) as a gesture towards an alien origin. Others, particularly Latin and French phrases, have remained obstinately "foreign" over several centuries.

Italicization is a helpful but not infallible clue to the extent of assimilation, the rule of thumb being that the more "foreign" a word is felt to be the more likely it is to be distinguished in this way. However, italics are generally retained in practice even for well-established words where there might be any possibility of confusion with an English word, as between *pace* (Latin ablative singular of *pax* used as a preposition) and "pace," the English noun and verb.

Practice regarding italics, however, varies between British and American English and between publisher and publisher. For this reason, no attempt has been made to distinguish between italic and non-italic in the headwords in this dictionary.

Retention of accent marks is another indicator of awareness of the foreign origin of a word, since the native English writer has a strong tendency to drop them. In this respect the spelling *detour*, to take a common example, is well down the route to total assimilation, but the pronunciation still has a faint echo of the original *détour*.

How far spelling can move away from the original before a word can be said to be wholly Anglicized is not only a matter of the dropping or retention of accents. Various words from the Romance languages have doubled or single consonants in the original and the opposite in the usual English spelling: examples are *concessionnaire* in French, but *concessionaire* in English, *improvvisatore* in Italian, but *improvisatore* in English; on the other hand it is *commando* in English, but *comando* in Portuguese. However, in none of these cases does the fluctuation in spelling seriously affect the perception of the word as "foreign."

More latitude is seen in the case of words transcribed from non-Roman alphabets, and significant variants have been noted. For instance, the Greek letter *kappa*, formerly often transcribed as *c*, is now more frequently rendered *k*, particularly in specialist contexts. Variation between *s* and *sh* and between *c* and *ch* occurs in the transliterations from various languages of the Indian subcontinent. Attempts by users to make transliterations conform to English spelling norms generally do not disguise the alien origin of the word itself.

To keep the dictionary within reasonable bounds, several whole categories of words have been excluded, unless there is some strong reason to make an exception for a particular member of the class. If a word has a transferred meaning in English or is sufficiently at home to be used figuratively, it is generally included; thus, made-up words, even those with impeccable classical Greek or Latin elements such as *homophobia* and *megalomania*, are usually not admitted, but *utopia* is included. A very few other words such as *braggadocio* that are not genuine foreign words at all have been allowed in on the basis of their being so easily mistaken for a genuine borrowing. Also in are Latin phrases such as *infra dig.* that are seldom or never given their full form in English usage. Currencies, obsolete coins, weights and measures, and scientific units are excluded, but exceptions are made for *shekel* and *sou* on account of their metaphorical uses. Plant and animal names do not have entries unless they are also the names of a commodity that is widely traded or used; thus *jojoba* and *vicuña* are both in.

Evidence for use in the latter part of the twentieth century almost always guarantees inclusion, although some items that duplicate good English expressions and that are therefore unlikely to move beyond an entirely literary ambience have been omitted (e.g., *dialogue des sourds* smacks of affectation as an alternative to 'dialogue of the deaf'). Sometimes a foreign expression fulfils a valid function as a euphemism: *faux marbre* sounds considerably more chic than *fake* (or *false*) *marble*. Words that are current but used only in the context of the country of origin have been looked at individually on the basis of likelihood of applications outside the particular national context; for example, *ragazza* as a word for 'girl' is most unlikely to be encountered anywhere except in a text specifically about or set in Italy, while *wagon-lit*, on the other hand, is much less country-specific. Greetings and polite forms of address have generally been excluded on similar grounds, *gnädige Frau* and such expressions belonging more properly in a foreign language phrase book.

Dates are given in abbreviated form, following the method used for the *New Shorter Oxford English Dictionary*:

OE	Old English	pre-1149
ME	Middle English	1150–1349
LME	late Middle English	1350–1469
L15	late fifteenth century	1470–1499
E16	early sixteenth centur	1500–1529
M16	mid sixteenth century	1530–1569
L16	late sixteenth century	1570–1599
E17	early seventeenth century	1600–1629
M17	mid seventeenth century	1630–1669
L17	late seventeenth century	1670–1699
E18	early eighteenth century	1700–1729
M18	mid eighteenth century	1730–1769
L18	late eighteenth century	1770–1799
E19	early nineteenth century	1800–1829
M19	mid nineteenth century	1830–1869
L19	late nineteenth century	1870–1899
E20	early twentieth century	1900–1929
M20	mid twentieth century	1930–1969
L20	late twentieth century	1970–1999

Usage Notes

Some entries feature usage notes, indicated by a ■ symbol, giving further information, usually of historical background, to assist the reader in correct usage. Meanings specific to particular professions or sciences are indicated by inclusion of such terms as *Computing*, *Medicine*, or *Philosophy*. Words or meanings restricted in formality, tone, or history, have such indicators as *colloquial*, *literary*, and *derogatory*. And many entries contain italicized terms, such as *especially*, *specifically*, and *transferred*, that further specify or qualify the term's meanings.

Abbreviations include *Brit.* (British), *c.* (*circa* = "about," for approximate dates), *pass.* (passive), and *sc.* (*scilicet* = "namely").

aa *noun* M19 **Hawaiian** (*'a-'a*). *Geology* Rough, scoriaceous lava. Cf. PAHOEHOE.

aba *noun* (also **abba**) E19 **Arabic** (*'abā'*). A sleeveless outer garment of various forms, worn by Arabs. Cf. ABAYA.

abacus *noun* plural **abaci**, **abacuses** M16 **Latin** (from Greek *abakos*, *abax* slab, originally drawing board covered with dust, from Semitic: cf. Hebrew *'ābāq* dust). **1** M16 *Architecture* The upper member of a capital, supporting the architrave. **2** L17 A calculating frame, *especially* one with balls sliding on wires. **3** L18 *Classical Antiquities* A sideboard.

■ The word was first introduced (LME) in its antique sense of 'a board strewn with sand, for drawing figures, etc.', but this sense is not found after the medieval period.

à bas *interjection* M19 **French**. Down with . . . !

■ Always followed by the name of a person or thing.

abatis *noun* (also **abattis**) plural **abat(t)is**, **abatises** M18 **French** (from Old French *abatre*, ultimately from Latin *batt(u)ere* to beat). *Military* A defense formed by placing felled trees lengthwise one over the other with their branches toward the enemy line. Also, a barricade of barbed wire.

abattoir *noun* E19 **French** (from *abattre* to fell). A slaughterhouse.

abaya *noun* M19 **Arabic**. An ABA.

Abba *noun* LME **ecclesiastical Latin** (from New Testament Greek, from Aramaic *'abbā* father). *Christian Church* **1** LME *Abba, father*: an invocation to God as Father (Mark 14:36, etc.). **2** M17 A title given to bishops and patriarchs in the Syrian Orthodox and Coptic churches.

abba see ABA.

abbé *noun* M16 **French** (from ecclesiastical Latin *abbat-* abbot). In France: an abbot, a secular priest, or *loosely* anyone, with or without official duties, who is entitled to wear ecclesiastical dress.

ab extra *adverb phrase* M17 **Late Latin**. From outside.

ab initio *adverb phrase* E17 **Latin**. From the beginning.

ab intra *adverb phrase* L17 **Modern Latin**. From inside.

Abitur *noun* (also **abitur**) M20 **German** (abbreviation of *Abiturientenexamen* leavers' examination). In Germany: a set of examinations taken in the final year of secondary school (success in which formerly ensured a university place).

Abiturient *noun* (also **abiturient**) plural **Abiturienten** M19 **German** (from Modern Latin *abiturire* to wish to leave). A candidate for the ABITUR.

ablaut *noun* M19 **German** (from *ab* off + *Laut* sound). *Philology* Vowel change in related words, *especially* that in Indo-European, which survives in English in, e.g., *sing, sang, sung, song*.

abonné *noun* L19 **French** (past participle of *abonner* to subscribe). A subscriber; a season-ticket holder.

abonnement *noun* L19 **French** (from *abonner* to subscribe). A subscription, as for a newspaper, etc.; a season ticket.

ab origine *adverb phrase* M16 **Latin** (from *ab* from + *origine* ablative of *origo* beginning, source). From the beginning; from the creation of the world.

abortus *noun* plural **aborti**, **abortuses** M19 **Latin** (= miscarriage). *Medicine* **1** M19 Abortion. **2** E20 An aborted fetus.

ab ovo *adverb phrase* L16 **Latin** (= from the egg). From the (very) beginning.

abrazo *noun* plural **abrazos** E20 **Spanish**. An embrace, a hug, especially as a salutation.

abri *noun* E19 **French**. A shelter; *specifically* in *Archaeology*, an overhanging rock affording shelter.

abscissa *noun* plural **abscissae, abscissas** L17 **Modern Latin** (*abscissa* use as noun (sc. *linea* line) of feminine past participle of *abscindere* to cut asunder). **1** L17 *Mathematics* Originally, the portion of a line between a fixed point on it and the point of intersection with an ordinate. Now, the distance of a point from the *y*-axis measured parallel to the *x*-axis. **2** L19 *Botany abscciss layer*, a distinctive layer of cells at which separation occurs on leaf-fall.

abseil, *noun & intransitive verb* M20 **German** (*abseilen*, from *ab* down + *Seil* rope). **1** M20 *Mountaineering* Rappel (make a descent) down a steep rock-face by means of a doubled rope coiled around the body and fixed at a higher point. **2** L20 (Make) a similar descent from a helicopter.

absinth *noun* (also (in sense 2 usually) **absinthe**) LME **French** (*absinthe* from Latin *absinthium* from Greek *apsinthion* wormwood). **1** LME Wormwood, the plant *Artemisia absinthium* or its essence; *figuratively* bitterness, sorrow. **2** M19 A green liqueur made (at least originally) from wine and wormwood. **b** L19 A green color resembling that of the liqueur.

absit omen *interjection* L16 **Latin** (= may this (ill) omen be absent). May this evil foreboding not become fact.

absurdum *noun* plural **absurda** M19 **Latin** (neuter singular of *absurdus* absurd, used as noun). An absurd or illogical conclusion or condition. See also REDUCTIO AD ABSURDUM.

ab urbe condita *adverbial phrase* E17 **Latin** (= since the founding of the city). (In the Roman annual dating system) since the founding of Rome.

■ The traditional date of the founding of Rome was 753 BC.

AC abbreviation of APPELLATION CONTRÔLÉE.

academia *noun* M20 **Latin** (from Greek *akadem(e)ia*, adjective from *Akademos*). The world of higher learning; the university environment or community.

■ Akademos was the man or demigod who gave his name to the garden just outside ancient Athens where Plato conducted his philosophical school.

acanthus *noun* M16 **Latin** (from Greek *akanthos*, from *akantha* thorn, perhaps from *akē* sharp point). **1** M16 Any of several erect herbaceous plants belonging to the genus *Acanthus* (family Acanthaceae), having decorative spiny leaves; especially *Acanthus spinosus*, native to the Mediterranean region. **2** M18 *Architecture* A conventionalized form of the leaf of *Acanthus spinosus*, used to decorate Corinthian and Composite capitals; hence, a similar decorative motif used on furniture and fabrics.

a cappella, *adjective & adverb phrase* (also **a capella**) L19 **Italian** (= in chapel style). Of choral music: unaccompanied. Cf. ALLA CAPPELLA.

accelerando *adverb, adjective, & noun* E19 **Italian**. *Music* E19 **A** *adverb & adjective* (A direction:) with gradual increase of speed. **B** *noun* L19 plural **accelerandos, accelerandi**. A gradual increase of speed; a passage (to be) played with a gradual increase of speed; also *figurative*.

acciaccatura *noun* plural **acciaccaturas, acciaccature** E19 **Italian** (from *acciaccare* to crush). *Music* A grace note performed quickly before an essential note of a melody.

accidie *noun* ME **Anglo-Norman** (= Old French *accide* from medieval Latin *accidia*, alteration of late Latin ACEDIA). Sloth, torpor, apathy. Now also, despair.

■ Became obsolete (E16), but subsequently revived (L19).

accouchement *noun* L18 **French** (from *accoucher* to give birth). Childbirth.

accoucheur *noun* M18 French (from *accoucher* to give birth). A man (formerly also a woman) who acts as midwife. The feminine **accoucheuse** is now usually used for a woman.

accra *noun* (also **akkra**, **akara**, and other variants) L19 Yoruba (*àkàrà* bean cake). A West African and West Indian fritter made with black-eyed peas or a similar pulse. Also, a West Indian fritter made with mashed fish.

acedia *noun* E17 Late Latin (*acedia* from Greek *akēdia*, from *a-* not + *kēdos* care, concern). ACCIDIE.

Aceldama *noun* M17 Greek (*Akeldama* from Aramaic *ḥăqel dĕmā* field of blood). A scene of bloodshed; a place of slaughter.

achar *noun* L16 Hindustani (ultimately from Persian *āchār*). Pickles, as prepared in the Indian subcontinent.

acharnement *noun* M18 French (from *acharner* to give a taste of flesh (to dogs, etc.)). Bloodthirsty fury; ferocity, gusto.

acharya *noun* E19 Sanskrit (*ācārya* master, teacher). In the Indian subcontinent: (a title given to) a spiritual teacher or leader; *transferred* an influential mentor.

à cheval *adverb phrase* M19 French (= on horseback). With one foot on each side; in command of two lines of communication; with a stake risked equally on two chances.

achkan *noun* E20 Hindustani (*ackan*). A knee-length coat, buttoned in front, worn by men in the Indian subcontinent.

acme *noun* L16 Greek (*akmē* highest point). The highest point; the point or period of perfection.

■ Long after its introduction into English it was consciously used as a Greek word and written in Greek letters. It was formerly also used in the specific senses of 'the period of full growth; the flower or full bloom of life' (L16–M19) and 'the crisis of an illness' (M17–M19).

à contrecœur *adverb phrase* E19 French (literally, 'against the heart'). Against one's will, reluctantly.

acropolis *noun* E17 Greek (*akropolis*, from *akros* tip, peak + *polis* city). The citadel or elevated fortified part of a Greek city, especially of Athens.

acroterion *noun* plural **acroteria** (also **acroter**, plural **acroters**; **acroterium**, **acroteria**; **akroterion**, **akroteria**) M17 Greek (*akrōtērion* extremity. Variants from French *acrotère* and (its source) Latin *acroterium* from Greek). *Architecture* **1** *collectively singular* and (usually) in *plural* Ornaments in ranges on roofs of classical buildings. **2** E18 A pedestal for a statue or the like on the center or side of a pediment.

acte gratuit *noun phrase* plural **actes gratuits** M20 French. A gratuitous, random, or inconsequent action performed on impulse.

■ The concept of the *acte gratuit* was given currency by the works of the French novelist and essayist André Gide (1869–1951) and explored in such works as *Les Caves du Vatican* (1914).

actio in distans M19 Latin (= action on something apart). Action at a distance, the exertion of force by one body upon another separated from it by space; *figurative* the exertion of influence from afar.

acumen *noun* L16 Latin (= point, acuteness, from *acuere* to sharpen, from *acus* needle). **1** L16 Sharpness of wit; penetration of perception; keenness of discrimination. **2** L18 *Botany* A tapering point.

AD abbreviation of ANNO DOMINI.

adage *noun 1* M16 French (from Latin *adagium*, from *ad* to + an early form of *aio* I say). A saying expressing common experience; a folk maxim.

adage *noun 2* M20 French (from Italian, as next). ADAGIO noun 2.

adagio *adverb, adjective, & noun* L17 Italian (from *ad agio* at ease). *Music* **A** *adverb & adjective* L17 In slow time, leisurely. **B** *noun* plural **adagios**. **1** M18 A musical piece or movement in slow time. **2** M18 A dance or ballet movement in slow time.

adat *noun* L18 **Malay** (from Arabic *'āda*). Custom, or customary law, in the Islamic regions of Southeast Asia, especially in contrast to Islamic religious law.

■ Also in the phrase *adat law.*

ADC abbreviation of AIDE-DE-CAMP.

ad captandum vulgus *adverb & adjective phrase* M18 **Latin** (= for alluring the crowd). (Designed) to appeal to the emotions (of the rabble).

■ Also used in the abbreviated form *ad captandum.*

addendum *noun* plural **addenda** L17 **Latin** (neuter gerundive of *addere* to add). A thing to be added, especially because of omission; an appendix, an addition; *singular* and (especially) in *plural* (occasionally treated as *singular*), additional matter at the end of a book.

addio *interjection* L18 **Italian** (from *a* to + *Dio* god: cf. ADIEU, ADIOS). Goodbye.

■ Formerly in general use in the subscription of letters, etc.

ad eundem *adverb phrase* E18 **Latin** (= to the same (degree)). (Admitted) to the same degree or rank at another university or institution.

à deux *adverb & adjective phrase* L19 **French**. Of, for, or between two. Cf. FOLIE À DEUX, MÉNAGE.

ad hoc *adverb & adjective phrase* M17 **Latin** (literally, 'to this'). For this particular purpose; especial(ly).

ad hominem *adverb & adjective phrase* L16 **Latin** (= to the person). Of an argument, etc.: directed to the individual, personal; appealing to an opponent's known personal views rather than reason.

■ Such an argument, which plays upon an opponent's own premises, seeking to draw from them a conclusion that is rejected by that same opponent, is a legitimate debating tactic, unlike the kind of ARGUMENTUM AD HOMINEM that is really no more than a personal attack.

ad idem *adverb phrase* L16 **Latin** (= to the same thing). On the same point, in agreement.

adieu *interjection & noun* LME **French** (Anglo-Norman *adeu*, Old French *adieu*, from *à* to + *Dieu* god: cf. ADDIO, ADIOS). **A** *interjection* LME Goodbye. *Archaic.* **B** *noun* LME plural **adieus**, **adieux**. A leave-taking; a parting word; a farewell.

ad infinitum *adverb & adjective phrase* E17 **Latin** (literally, 'to infinity'). Without limit, forever.

ad interim *adverb & adjective phrase* L18 **Latin** (*ad* to + *interim* adverb 'meanwhile' used as noun). For the meantime.

adios *interjection* M19 **Spanish** (*adiós*, from *a* to + *Dios* god: cf. ADIEU, ADDIO). Goodbye.

ad lib *adverb, adjective, verb & noun* (also **ad-lib**, when used as attributive adjective or verb) E19 **Latin** (abbreviation of next). **A** *adverb* E19 AD LIBITUM. **B** *adjective* E20 Extemporized; spontaneous. **C** *transitive & intransitive verb* E20 To speak extempore, to improvise. **D** *noun* M20 Something extemporized; an ad-lib remark.

ad libitum *adverb & adjective phrase* E17 **Latin**. According to pleasure; to any desired extent.

■ Often used in the abbreviated form AD LIB.

ad litem *adverb & adjective phrase* M18 **Latin** (= for the lawsuit). *Law* Of a guardian, etc.: appointed to act, in a lawsuit, on behalf of a child or other incapable person.

ad nauseam *adverb phrase* M17 **Latin** (literally, 'to sickness'). To a disgusting or tiresome extent.

■ The phrase was earlier (E17) introduced in the form *ad nauseam usque* (right up to sickness), and also occurs as *usque ad nauseam*, but these have been superseded by the shorter form.

adobe *noun* M18 **Spanish** (from *adobar* to plaster, from Arabic *aṭ-ṭūb*, from *al* the + *ṭūb* bricks). **1** M18 An unfired brick dried in the sun. **b** E19 A house built of such bricks. **2** L18 Clay or earth prepared for making into such bricks or suitable for this purpose.

ad personam *adverb & adjective phrase* M20 Latin (literally, 'to the person'). Personal(ly); on an individual basis.

ad referendum *adverb phrase* L18 Modern Latin (literally, 'for reference'). Subject to the assent of a higher authority.

ad rem *adverb & adjective phrase* L16 Latin (literally, 'to the matter'). To the point; to the purpose.

adsuki variant of ADZUKI.

adsum *interjection* L16 Latin (1st singular present indicative of *adesse* to be present). I am present.

■ As an answer to a roll call, etc.

ad usum Delphini *adjective phrase* L18 Latin (= for the use of the Dauphin). Originally, designating or pertaining to an edition of the classics prepared for the use of the son of Louis XIV of France; hence, expurgated.

ad valorem *adverb & adjective phrase* L17 Latin (= according to the value). Of taxes: in proportion to the estimated value of goods.

adversaria *noun plural* E18 Latin (use as noun of neuter plural (sc. *scripta* writings) of *adversarius* facing one). Miscellaneous remarks and observations; *collectively singular* a commonplace book; a journal.

ad vivum *adverb & adjective phrase* M17 Latin (= according to the living (model)). (Painted) from life.

advocatus diaboli *noun phrase* E19 Modern Latin (literally, 'devil's advocate'). *Roman Catholic Church* The official whose function is to put the case against a person's beatification or canonization; *transferred* a person who provokes argument or debate by supporting the opposing side or by pointing out the weaknesses in his or her own case.

■ The phrase, particularly in its transferred sense, is now much more familiar in its English form: 'devil's advocate'.

adytum *noun* plural **adyta** E17 Latin (from Greek *aduton* use as noun of neuter singular of *adutos* impenetrable). The innermost part of a temple; a private chamber, a sanctum.

adzuki *noun* (also **adsuki**, **azuki**) E18 Japanese (*azuki*). A bushy leguminous plant, *Vigna angularis*, cultivated in China and Japan; the edible bean of this plant.

■ Also in the phrase *adzuki bean*.

aegis *noun* (also **egis**) E17 Latin (from Greek *aigis* shield of Zeus). **1** E17 A shield, defensive armor, *especially* that of Jupiter or Minerva. **2** L18 *figurative* Protection; an impregnable defense.

■ Most frequently in the phrase *under the aegis of* 'under the protection of'.

aegrotat *noun* L18 Latin (*aegrotat* 3rd singular present indicative of *aegrotare* to be ill, from *aeger* sick, ill). In universities, a certificate that a student is too ill to attend an examination, etc.; a passing grade on an examination or a credit awarded to a student having such a certificate.

aetatis *adjective* (usually abbreviated as **aet.** or **aetat**) E19 Latin. Of or at the age of.

■ The formula *aetatis*, *aetatis suae*, or one of the abbreviations, plus a figure, is found much earlier, in England and elsewhere, inscribed on portraits to give the age of the sitter. The full formula *anno aetatis suae* is also occasionally found.

affaire *noun* E19 French. A temporary sexual relationship outside marriage; a love affair. Also *generally* a sensational event, case, or scandal.

■ Originally more usual in its full form *affaire de* (or *du*) *cœur* (literally, 'affair of the heart'). In its more general sense, used with the definite article (either French or English), followed by the name of the person(s) involved.

affairé *adjective* E20 French. Busy; involved.

affaire de (or **du**) **cœur** see AFFAIRE.

affiche *noun* E19 French. A notice affixed to a wall, etc.; a poster.

affidavit *noun* M16 **Medieval Latin** (= he/she has affirmed, 3rd person singular perfect indicative of *affidare* to declare on oath). *Law* A written statement, confirmed by oath, to be used as evidence.

■ In legal phraseology a deponent *swears* an affidavit, the judge *takes* it; in popular use, however, the deponent *takes* or *makes* it.

afflatus *noun* M17 **Latin** (from *afflat-* past participial stem of *afflare*, from *ad* on + *flare* to blow). The communication of supernatural knowledge; divine impulse; (especially poetic) inspiration.

aficionado *noun* plural **aficionados** M19 **Spanish** (= amateur, use as noun of past participle of *aficioner* to become fond of, from *afición* from Latin *affectio* favorable disposition). **1** M19 A devotee of bullfighting. **2** L19 An ardent follower of any activity or interest.

à fond *adverb phrase* E19 **French** (literally, 'to bottom'). Thoroughly, fully.

a fortiori *adverb phrase* E17 **Latin**. With yet stronger reason; more conclusively; even more so.

afreet *noun* (also **afrit**, **efreet**) L18 **Arabic** (*'ifrīt*, colloquial *'afrīt*). A powerful jinnee in Arabian stories and Muslim mythology.

aga *noun* (also **agha**) M16 **Turkish** (*ağa* master, lord from Mongolian *aqa*). An Ottoman title, now abolished, for (originally) a military commander and (later) officials of various ranks. Now, a title of respect for landowners among Turkish village people.

agal *noun* M19 **Arabic** (representing Bedouin pronunciation of Arabic *'iḳāl* bond, rope for hobbling a camel). A fillet worn around the head by Bedouin Arabs to keep the KEFFIYEH in position.

agape *noun* plural **agapae**, **agapes** E17 **Greek** (*agapē* brotherly love). **1** E17 A love feast held by early Christians in connection with the Eucharist; *transferred* a parochial feast at a festival time. **2** M19 Christian love, charity.

agapemone *noun* M19 **Greek** (irregular formation from *agapē* love + *monē* abode). An abode of love; an establishment where free love is practiced.

■ Originally with capital initial, the name of a community founded in Somerset, England, *c.*1850 by H. J. Prince.

agar-agar *noun* (in sense 2 usually simply **agar**) E19 **Malay**. **1** E19 Any of certain Southeast Asian seaweeds from which a gelatinous substance is extracted. **2** M19 The substance itself, used especially to make soups and to form biological culture media.

agenda *noun plural*, also used as *singular* (less commonly in singular **agendum**; **agend**) E17 **Latin** (plural of *agendum*, use as noun of gerundive of *agere* to do). **1** E17 *plural* Things to be done; matters of practice. **2** M18 *collective singular* A memorandum book. *archaic*. **3** L19 As *plural*, items of business to be considered at a meeting or to be otherwise attended to. As *singular*, a list of such items.

agent provocateur *noun phrase* plural **agents provocateurs** L19 **French** (= provocative agent). An agent employed to tempt suspected persons into committing an incriminating act.

aggiornamento *noun* M20 **Italian**. Bringing up to date, especially of Roman Catholic church policy by and after the Second Vatican Council (1962–65).

agio *noun* plural **agios** L17 **Italian** (*ag(g)io*). **1** L17 The percentage charged for changing paper money into cash, or an inferior for a more valuable currency; the excess value of one currency over another. **2** E19 *loosely*. Money-changing.

agiotage *noun* L18 **French** (from *agioter* to speculate, from Italian *ag(g)io* from as preceding). Money-changing business; speculation in stocks; stockjobbing.

agitato *adverb, adjective, & noun* E19 **Italian.** *Music* **A** *adverb & adjective* E19 (A direction:) in an agitated manner. **B** *noun* E19 plural **agitati, agitatos.** A passage (to be) played or sung in an agitated manner. *rare.*

agitprop *noun* (also **Agitprop**) E20 **Russian** (from *agit(atsiya)* agitation + *prop(aganda)* propaganda). *History* Soviet Communist propaganda; the system or activity of disseminating this.

agloo, aglu see IGLOO.

agnolotti *noun plural* L20 **Italian.** Pasta made into cases with meat or other stuffing. Cf. RAVIOLI.

agnomen *noun* M17 **Latin** (*agnomen*, from *ad* to + *(g)nomen* name). A name given or acquired during the course of one's life, a nickname; *Roman History* a fourth name occasionally given as an honor.

Agnus Dei *noun phrase* LME **Latin** (= Lamb of God). *Christian Church* **1** LME Part of the Mass beginning with the words *Agnus Dei*; a musical setting of this. **2** LME A figure of a lamb bearing a cross or flag, as an emblem of Christ. **b** L16 A cake of wax stamped with such a figure and blessed by the Pope.

■ In sense 2 the Agnus Dei is the emblem of St. John the Baptist in art, who is very often depicted with it and holding a scroll with the words *ECCE AGNUS DEI* 'Behold the Lamb of God'.

a gogo *adverb & postpositive adjective phrase* M20 **French** (*à gogo*). In abundance, galore. *colloquial.*

agon *noun* plural **agones** E17 **Greek** (*agōn* contest). *Greek History* **1** E17 A public celebration comprising athletic games; a contest for the prize at such games or *transferred* elsewhere. **2** L19 A verbal contest between two characters in a play.

agonistes *postpositive adjective* L17 **Greek** (= contestant). One who is engaged in a struggle.

■ First used in the title of John Milton's *Samson Agonistes* (1671) and imitated by later authors.

agora *noun* plural **agorae, agorai, agoras** L16 **Greek.** *Greek History* An assembly; a place of assembly, *especially* a marketplace.

agoraphobia *noun* L19 **pseudo-Greek** (from AGORA + -PHOBIA). Irrational terror of open spaces.

■ Coined by the German psychologist Carl Westphal in 1871.

agraphon *noun* plural **agrapha** L19 **Greek** (neuter of *agraphos* unwritten). A saying attributed to Jesus but not in the canonical Gospels. Usually in *plural.*

agrément *noun* plural **agréments, agrémens** E18 **French.** **1** E18 In *plural* Agreeable qualities, circumstances, etc. **2** L18 *Music* In *plural* Grace notes; embellishments. **3** E20 Official approval given to a diplomatic representative of another country.

aguardiente *noun* E19 **Spanish** (from *agua* water + *ardiente* fiery). Coarse Spanish brandy; a similar distilled liquor, *especially* one made from sugar cane.

AH see under HEGIRA.

ahimsa *noun* L19 **Sanskrit** (from *a* non- + *hiṃsā* violence). The doctrine in Hindu, Buddhist, and Jain philosophy that there should be no violence or killing of any living creature, however humble.

à huis clos *adverb phrase* E17 **French.** In secret, IN CAMERA.

aide-de-camp *noun* (also **aid-de-camp, aide de camp**) plural **aides-de-camp, aids-de-camp** L17 **French** (= camp adjutant). *Military* An officer acting as a confidential assistant to a senior officer, or assisting on a ceremonial occasion; *transferred* anyone acting in a similar capacity to a more senior person.

■ Often abbreviated in military use to ADC.

aide-mémoire *noun* M19 **French.** (A book or document serving as) an aid to the memory; (in diplomats' use) a memorandum.

aigre-doux *adjective* (also **aigre-douce**) LME **French**. Compounded of sweet and sour; bittersweet.

aigrette *noun* M18 **French**. An egret's plume; a tuft of feathers or hair; a spray of gems, etc., worn on the head.

aiguille *noun* M18 **French** (= needle). A sharply pointed peak of rock, especially in the Alps.

aikido *noun* M20 **Japanese** (*aikidō*, from *ai* together, unify + *ki* spirit + *dō* way). A Japanese form of self-defense and martial art, developed from jujitsu and involving holds and throws.

aileron *noun* E20 **French** (diminutive of *aile* wing). A movable airfoil used to control the balance of an aircraft in flight, usually a hinged flap in the trailing edge of a wing.

aioli *noun* E20 **French** (from Provençal *ai* garlic + *oli* oil). Mayonnaise seasoned with garlic.

akara, **akkra** variants of ACCRA.

akroterion variant of ACROTERION.

akvavit variant of AQUAVIT.

à la *prepositional phrase* L16 **French** (abbreviation of À LA MODE). In the manner, method, or style of.

■ Followed by a French noun in standard phrases (see following entries), but also often with an English noun.

à la bonne femme see BONNE FEMME.

à la broche *adverb & adjective phrase* E20 **French**. (Cooked) on a spit; spit-roasted. Cf. À LA BROCHETTE.

à la brochette *adverb & adjective phrase* M19 **French**. (Cooked) on a skewer. Cf. À LA BROCHE.

à la carte *adverb & adjective phrase* E19 **French**. By the bill of fare; ordered as separately priced item(s) from a menu, not as part of a set meal.

à la daube *adverb & adjective phrase* E18 **French**. (Of poultry, meat, or game) stewed, braised.

à la Florentine *adverb & adjective phrase* E20 **French** (= in the Florentine manner). (Of eggs, fish, etc.) served on a bed of spinach or with a spinach sauce.

■ Now generally just 'Florentine'.

à la fourchette *adverb & adjective phrase* E19 **French**. (Of a meal) requiring the use (only) of a fork.

à la lanterne *interjection* L18 **French** (= to the lantern). Away with (them)!

■ The phrase is a quotation from the refrain of the French Revolutionary song "Ça ira." It records the Revolutionary mobs' practice of hanging their victims from the street lamps.

alameda *noun* L18 **Spanish**. In Spain and Spanish-speaking areas: a public walk, shaded with trees; an ALLÉE.

à la mode *adverb & adjective phrase* L16 **French** (= in the fashion). **1** L16 In or according to the fashion; fashionable. **2** *Cooking* **a** E20 Of food: served with ice cream. **b** M17 Of beef: braised or made into a rich stew, usually with wine.

■ Also in use (M–L17) as a noun (phrase), usually as one word, meaning 'a fashion, a temporary mood' or (M17) 'a thin glossy usually black silk'.

à la page *adverb & adjective phrase* M20 **French** (literally, 'at the page'). Up to date, up to the minute.

à la russe *adverb & adjective phrase* (also **à la Russe**) E19 **French**. In the Russian manner.

■ In the mid–nineteenth century *à la russe* often alluded to the then newfangled custom in fashionable society of serving meals on a table decorated with flowers and dessert, with the individual courses brought in from another room or served from side tables.

alba *noun* E19 **Provençal** (ultimately from Latin *albus* white). A medieval Provençal song at dawn. Cf. AUBADE.

albarello *noun* plural **albarelli** L19 **Italian** (*alberello* pot, vial). A majolica jar used especially as a container for drugs.

albedo *noun* plural **albedos** M19 **ecclesiastical Latin** (= whiteness, from Latin *albus* white). The proportion of incident radiation reflected by a surface, especially of a planet or moon.

albergo *noun* plural **alberghi** E17 **Italian**. An Italian inn. Cf. AUBERGE.

albino *noun & adjective* E18 **Spanish and Portuguese** (from *albo* white). **A** *noun* plural **albinos** **1** E18 A human being having a congenital deficiency of pigmentation in the skin and hair, which are white, and the eyes, which are usually pink. **2** E19 An abnormally white animal or plant. **B** *adjective* E19 Congenitally lacking in pigmentation; abnormally white.

■ Originally applied by the Portuguese to albinos among African blacks.

album *noun* E17 **Latin** (= blank tablet, use as noun of neuter of *albus* white). **I** A blank book for the insertion of collected items. **1** E17 A blank book in which people other than the owner insert autographs, memorial verses, etc. **2** M19 A blank book for the insertion of stamps, photographs, etc. **II** **3** E20 A holder for a set of recordings; an integral set of recordings; a recording comprising several pieces of music, etc.

■ First taken into English from the German use of the Latin phrase *album amicorum* album of friends, i.e., an autograph book.

albumen *noun* (also **albumin** in sense 3) L16 **Latin** (from *albus* white). **1** L16 The white of an egg. **2** L17 *Botany* The nutritive material surrounding the embryo in some plant seeds; the endosperm. **3** E19 Soluble protein, such as that in egg white.

alcade variant of ALCALDE.

alcaide *noun* (also **alcaid, alcayde**) E16 **Spanish** (from Arabic *al-ḳā'id* the leader, the commander). The governor of a Spanish, Portuguese, Moorish, etc., fortress; a jailer.

alcalde *noun* (also **alcade**) M16 **Spanish** (*alcalde* (French *alcade*) from Arabic *al-ḳāḍī* the judge). A mayor, magistrate, or similar administrative officer in Spain, Portugal, and parts of South America and the southwestern United States.

alcayde variant of ALCAIDE.

alcazar *noun* plural **alcazars, alcazares** E17 **Spanish** (*alcázar* from Arabic *al-ḳaṣr* the castle). A Spanish palace or fortress.

alcheringa *noun* L19 **Aranda** (= in the dreamtime). A golden age in the mythology of some Australian Aborigine groups.

aldea *noun* E17 **Portuguese** (*aldeia*, Spanish *aldea* from Arabic *al-ḍay'a*, from *al* the + *ḍay'a* agricultural village, farm). A small village or a farm in Portugal, Spain, or one of their former territories.

al dente *adverb & adjective phrase* M20 **Italian** (literally, 'to the tooth'). Of pasta, vegetables, etc.: (cooked) so as to be still slightly firm when bitten.

aleatico *noun* (also **Aleatico**) E19 **Italian**. A sweet Italian red wine.

aleph *noun* ME **Hebrew** (*'ālep*, literally, 'ox'; cf. ALPHA). **1** ME The first letter of the Hebrew, Phoenician, and other Semitic alphabets. **2** E20 *Mathematics* A transfinite cardinal numeral.

alfa *noun* (also **halfa**) M19 **Arabic** (*ḥalfā'*, colloquial *ḥalfa*). Esparto grass.

alfalfa *noun* M19 **Spanish** (from Arabic *al-fasfaṣa* a green fodder). A leguminous plant, *Medicago sativa*, cultivated for green fodder.

alfilaria *noun* M19 **Mexican Spanish** (from Spanish *alfiler* pin, with reference to the long-beaked carpels). The common stork's-bill, *Erodium cicutarium*, grown as fodder; pin clover.

alforja *noun* Also formerly written **alforge** E17 **Spanish** (*alforja*, Portuguese *alforge* from Arabic *al-ḳurj* the saddlebag). In Spain, Portugal, Latin

America, and other areas of Spanish influence (as the southwestern United States): a wallet, a saddlebag.

alfresco *adverb & adjective* (also **al fresco**) M18 **Italian** (*al fresco*). **A** *adverb* **1** M18 In the open air. **2** M18 *Art* In fresco. **B** *adjective* E19 Open-air.

alga *noun* plural **algae** M16 **Latin** (= seaweed). Originally, seaweed; now, any of a large group of nonvascular mainly aquatic cryptogams capable of photosynthesis, including seaweeds and many unicellular and filamentous organisms. Also *collectively*, the mass formed by such organisms.

alguacil *noun* plural **alguacils, alguaciles** (also **alguazil** plural **alguazils, alguaziles**) E16 **Spanish** ((earlier *alguazil*) from Arabic *al-wazīr*, from *al* the + *wazīr* vizier). **1** E16 In Spain: an officer of justice, a warrant officer, a sergeant. In Latin America or other areas of Spanish influence: a sheriff, a police officer. **2** *Bullfighting* E20 A mounted official at a bullfight.

alhaji *noun* (also as a title **Alhaji**) M20 **Hausa** (from Arabic *al* the + *ḥajj* pilgrimage). In West Africa: a Muslim who has been to Mecca as a pilgrim.

alias *adverb & noun* LME **Latin** (= at another time, otherwise). **A** *adverb* LME Otherwise called or named; called at other times. **B** *noun* E17 A name by which a person is or has been called on other occasions; an assumed name.

alibi *adverb, noun, & verb* L17 **Latin** (= elsewhere). **A** *noun* L18 A plea by the person accused of an act that he or she was elsewhere when it took place; evidence to support such a plea; *colloquially* an excuse of any kind. **B** *transitive & intransitive verb* E20 Provide an alibi, offer an excuse, (for).

■ *Alibi* was originally used in English as an adverb, following the Latin, but during the late eighteenth century this usage became obsolete and was superseded by the modern noun usage.

aliquot *adjective & noun* L16 **French** (*aliquote* from Latin *aliquot* some, several, from *alius* one of two + *quot* how many). Originally *Mathematics*. **A** *adjective* L16 That is contained in the whole an integral number of times. Chiefly in *aliquot part*. **B** *noun* E17 An aliquot part, integral factor; *loosely* any fraction of a whole, a sample.

alla breve *adverb, adjective, & noun phrase* M18 **Italian** (= according to the breve). *Music* A time signature indicating two or four half note beats in a bar; such a tempo or time signature.

alla cappella *adverb & adjective phrase* M18 **Italian**. Of choral music or choirs: unaccompanied.

■ Introduced earlier than A CAPPELLA.

alla marcia *adverb, adjective, & noun phrase* L19 **Italian**. *Music* (A piece, movement, etc.) in the style of a march.

allargando *adverb, adjective, & noun* L19 **Italian** (= broadening). *Music* **A** *adverb & adjective* L19 (A direction:) getting slower and slower and often also fuller in tone. **B** *noun* M20 plural **allargandi, allargandos**. A passage (to be) so played.

allée *noun* M18 **French**. A walk or passage in a garden, park, etc., usually flanked and shaded by trees or shrubs; an alley.

allegretto *adverb, adjective, & noun* M18 **Italian** (diminutive of ALLEGRO). *Music* **A** *adverb & adjective* M18 (A direction:) in fairly quick time, but not as quick(ly) as allegro. **B** *noun* L19 plural **allegrettos, allegretti**. A movement or piece in fairly quick time. Also, a short movement or piece in quick time.

allegro *adverb, adjective, & noun* L17 **Italian** (= lively, gay). *Music* **A** *adverb & adjective* L17 (A direction:) in quick time; *transferred* (of forms of words and phrases) used in speech and shortened (e.g., *we'll* for *we will*). **B** *noun* M18 plural **allegros, allegri**. A movement or piece in quick time.

allemande *noun* L17 **French** (= German (feminine)). **1** L17 A piece of music for a German dance or in its rhythm, *especially* one that forms a movement of a suite. **2** E18 Any of various German dances. **b** E19 A figure in square dancing in which adjacent dancers link arms or join hands and make a full or partial turn. Also used as a call to dancers to execute this figure turning in the specified direction. **3** *Cooking* E19 A rich velouté sauce thickened with egg yolks.

■ The earliest sense (M17) in which *Allemande* was used in English was 'a German woman', but this is not attested outside this period.

allumette *noun* E17 French (from *allumer* to set light to). A match for lighting or setting things alight.

■ Rare before the nineteenth century.

alluvium *noun* plural (now *rare*) **alluvia**, **alluviums** M17 Latin (neuter of *alluvius* washed against, from *ad* to + *luere* to wash). A deposit of clay, silt, sand, etc., left by flowing water, as in a river valley or delta.

Alma Mater *noun phrase* (also **alma mater**) plural **Alma Maters**, (*rare*) **Almae Matres** M17 Latin (= bounteous mother, a title given to various Roman goddesses, especially Ceres and Cybele). **1** M17 Someone or something providing nourishment and care. **2** L17 *especially* A university or school as regarded by its past and present members. **3** The official song or hymn of a school, college, or university.

aloe vera *noun phrase* L20 Latin (= true aloe). A plant resembling a cactus from which an extract used in skin care and other health products is obtained.

aloha *interjection & noun* E19 Hawaiian. Used in Hawaii especially at greeting or parting: love, affection; an utterance of this.

à l'outrance variant of À OUTRANCE.

alpaca *noun* L18 Spanish (from Aymara *allpaca*). A domesticated Peruvian animal, *Lama pacos*, resembling the llama, with long fine woolly hair and usually brown and white coloring; the wool of the alpaca; fabric or a garment made from this.

alpargata *noun* E19 Spanish. An ESPADRILLE.

alpenhorn *noun* L19 German (= Alphorn). A long wooden horn used by Alpine herdsmen.

alpenstock *noun* E19 German (= Alp stick). A long iron-tipped staff used in mountain climbing.

alpha *noun* ME Latin (from Greek). **1** ME The first letter (*A, a*) of the Greek alphabet; the beginning of anything. **2** E17 Denoting the first in a numerical or other sequence. **3** *attributive Science* M18 First, most important; as in *Astronomy* (preceding the genitive of the Latin name of the constellation) designating the chief star in a constellation; thus *Alpha Centauri* is the brightest star in the constellation Centaurus. **4** E20 Brit. (A person gaining) a top mark in an examination, etc.

■ In sense 1 *alpha* often appears in the phrase *the alpha and (the) omega*, which originally referred to God (see Revelation 1:8), but now is also used in the transferred sense of 'the beginning and the end'. In scientific terminology *alpha* has specialist applications in chemistry, medicine, and computing, as well as astronomy.

al segno *adverb phrase* L18 Italian (= to the sign). *Music* (A direction:) go back (= DAL SEGNO) or continue to the point indicated by the sign.

alter ego *noun phrase* plural **alter egos** M16 Latin (= other self). A person's second self; an intimate friend; a representative of another person.

althorn *noun* M19 German (*alt* alto + *horn* horn). *Music* A wind instrument of the saxhorn family.

altiplano *noun* E20 Spanish. The high tableland of central South America.

alto *noun & adjective* L16 Italian (= high (sc. song) from Latin *altus* high). *Music* **A** *noun* plural **altos** **1a** L16 The highest adult male voice, with range above the tenor, the countertenor voice; a part written for such a voice. **b** E19 A female voice of similar range, a contralto voice; a part written for such a voice. **2** L18 A person who has a countertenor or contralto voice. **3** L19 An alto wind instrument (see **B**). **B** *adjective* E18 Designating, pertaining to, or intended for a countertenor or contralto voice. Also, designating that member of a group of similar instruments with a range or relative pitch comparable to an alto voice (among wind instruments usually the second or third highest member of the family).

alto-relievo *noun* (also **alto-rilievo**) plural **alto-relievos** M17 **Italian** (*alto-rilievo*). (A sculpture, molding, carving, etc., in) high relief.

alumna *noun* plural **alumnae** L19 **Latin** (feminine of next). A female graduate or former student of a school, college, university, or other educational institution.

alumnus *noun* plural **alumni** M17 **Latin** (= nursling, pupil, from *alere* to nourish). Formerly, a pupil. Now *specifically*, a (male) graduate or former student of a school, college, university, or other educational institution.

a.m. abbreviation of ANTE MERIDIEM.

ama *noun* plural same M20 **Japanese**. A Japanese woman who dives for shellfish and edible seaweed.

amah *noun* M19 **Portuguese** (*ama* nurse). In parts of the Indian subcontinent and the Far East: a wet nurse, a children's nurse, a house servant.

amanuensis *noun* plural **amanuenses** E17 **Latin** (from *a manu* in *servus a manu* slave at hand + *-ensis* belonging to). A person who writes from dictation or copies manuscripts; a literary assistant.

■ The Latin phrase *servus a manu* was used by Suetonius (*Life of Julius Caesar*: 74) and by the Latin legal writers to denote a slave who acted as a secretary.

amateur *noun & adjective* L18 **French** (from Italian *amatore* from Latin *amator* lover). **A** *noun* **1** L18 A person who is fond *of* something; a person who has a taste for something. **2** L18 A person who practices something, especially an art or game, only as a pastime; an unpaid player, performer, etc. (opposed *professional*); also (*depreciative*), a dabbler. **B** E19 *attributive* or as *adjective* Done by amateurs, not professional; also (*depreciative*), unskillful.

ambiance *noun* M20 **French** (from *ambiant* from Latin *ambire* to go around). Environment, ambience; also *specifically*, the combination of the accessory elements of a painting to support the main effect of a piece.

■ The Anglicized *ambience* tends to be used in general contexts, with *ambiance* suggesting a more contrived or specially created atmosphere, as in the *ambiance* of a club or restaurant.

ambiente *noun* E20 **Italian and Spanish**. Surroundings, ambience.

ambo *noun* plural **ambos** also written in Latin form **ambones** M17 **Medieval Latin** (from Greek *ambōn* rim, edge of a cup). The pulpit or reading desk in early Christian churches; an oblong enclosure with steps at both ends.

ambrosia *noun* M16 **Latin** (from Greek = immortality, elixir of life, from *ambrotos* immortal; in Dioscurides and Pliny applied to one or more herbs). **I** **1** M16 *Classical Mythology* The food, drink, or unguent of the gods. **2** E17 (Honey and) pollen used as food by bees, bee-bread. **3** M17 Something divinely sweet to taste or smell. **4** L17 Water, oil, and fruits mixed as a libation; also, a perfumed or flavored drink. **5** L19 A fungal product that forms the food of the pinhole borer. **II** **6** M16 Wood-sage and certain other plants. Now only as Modern Latin name of a genus of plants of the Compositae family.

ameba variant of AMOEBA.

âme damnée *noun phrase* plural **âmes damnées** E19 **French** (= damned soul). A devoted adherent; a stooge.

ameer mainly US variant of AMIR.

amende honorable *noun phrase* plural **amendes honorables** E17 French (= honorable reparation). Public or open apology and reparation; an instance of this.

a mensa et thoro *adverb & adjective phrase* E17 Latin (= from table and bed). *Law*. Formerly (before 1857) of a divorce: decreed by an ecclesiastical court on grounds sanctioned by law (having the effect of a modern judicial separation).

à merveille *adverb phrase* M18 French (= to a marvel). Admirably, wonderfully.

âmes damnées plural of ÂME DAMNÉE.

amicus curiae *noun phrase* plural **amici curiae** E17 Modern Latin (= friend of the court). *Law* A disinterested adviser who assists the court by drawing attention to points that might otherwise fail to be mentioned.

amigo *noun* plural **amigos** M19 Spanish. A friend, a comrade.

■ Frequently used as a colloquial form of address.

amir *noun* (also **ameer**) L16 Persian and Urdu (from Arabic *'amīr* commander, governor, prince, from *amara* to command; cf. EMIR). A title of various Muslim rulers.

amnesia *noun* L18 Greek (*amnēsia* forgetfulness). Loss of memory.

amoeba *noun* (also **ameba**) plural **amoebas, amoebae** M19 Modern Latin (from Greek *amoibē* change, alternation). A single-celled aquatic protozoan, characterized by a constantly changing shape.

amok *adjective, noun, & adverb* (also **amuck**, (earliest) **am(o)uco**) E16 Portuguese (*am(o)uco* from Malay *amuk* fighting furiously, in a homicidal frenzy). **A** *adjective* E16 In a homicidal frenzy. *rare*. Only in E16. **B** *noun* **1** M17 A Malay in a homicidal frenzy. **2** M19 A homicidal frenzy; an act of running amok. **C** *adverb* L17 *run amok*, run about in a frenzied thirst for blood; go on a destructive rampage; rush wildly and heedlessly.

amole *noun* M19 Mexican Spanish. The root of any of several plants of Mexico and the southern United States, used as a detergent; any of these plants.

amontillado *noun* (also **Amontillado**) plural **amontillados** E19 Spanish (from *Montilla* a town in southern Spain). Formerly, a wine of the sherry type produced in Montilla. Now, a medium sherry of a matured type. Also, a drink or glass of either of these wines.

amoretto *noun* plural **amoretti, amoretto(e)s** L16 Italian (diminutive of *amore* love). **1** L16–E18 A sweetheart; a love poem. **2** E17 A cupid.

amorino *noun* plural **amorini, amorinos** M19 Italian (diminutive of *amore* love). A cupid.

amoroso *noun, adverb, & adjective* E17 Spanish and Italian (from medieval Latin *amorosus* amorous). **A** *noun* plural **amorosi, amorosos** **1** E17–E19 A lover; a gallant. **2** L19 A type of sweetened oloroso sherry. **B** *adverb & adjective* L18 *Music* (A direction:) tender(ly).

amour *noun* ME Old and Modern French (from Latin *amor*). **1** ME Love; affection. Now *rare* except in AMOUR COURTOIS, AMOUR PROPRE. **2** LME–E18 In *plural*. Sexual or romantic love. **3** L16 A love affair, especially a secret one.

amour courtois *noun phrase* L19 French (= courtly love). A highly conventionalized medieval code of love and etiquette first developed by the troubadours among the chivalric aristocracy of southern France.

amourette *noun* E19 French. **1** E19 A brief or unimportant love affair. **2** M19 A cupid, an amoretto.

amour propre *noun phrase* (also **amour-propre**) L18 French. Self-esteem; vanity.

amphisbaena *noun* LME Latin (from Greek *amphisbaina*, from *amphis* both ways + *bainein* to go, walk). **1** LME A fabled serpent with a head at each end and able to move in either direction. **2** M19 A wormlike burrowing lizard of the genus *Amphisbaena.*

■ Pliny describes the mythical serpent in the eighth book of his *Natural History*, and Lucan (*Pharsalia* ix.719) lists it among the poisonous monsters of Libya that sprang from the dripping blood of the gorgon Medusa's severed head.

amphora *noun* plural **amphorae, amphoras** ME **Latin** (from Greek *amphoreus*, or French *amphore*). **1** ME A Greek or Roman two-handled vessel. **2** LME A Greek or Roman liquid measure of varying capacity.

ampoule *noun* M17 **Modern French. 1** M17 An AMPULLA 2. *rare.* **2** E20 A small sealed glass vessel for holding sterilized materials for injection, poisons, air-sensitive chemicals, etc.

ampulla *noun* plural **ampullae** LME **Latin** (diminutive of *ampora* variant of AMPHORA). **1** LME *Roman Antiquities* A small two-handled globular flask or bottle. **2** L16 A vessel for holding consecrated oil or for other sacred uses. **3** M19 *Anatomy* A vessel or cavity shaped like the ancient ampulla.

amuck variant of AMOK.

amuse-gueule *noun* L20 **French** (literally, 'amusement for the mouth'). A snack, an appetizer.

anabasis *noun literary* plural **anabases** E18 **Greek** (= going up, from *ana-* up + *basis* going). A military advance, an up-country march.

■ The original *anabasis* was that of ten thousand Greek auxiliaries under the Persian Cyrus the Younger into Asia in 401 BC. The Athenian writer Xenophon narrated the story of the ill-fated expedition, which turned into a *katabasis* or retreat in which he played a conspicuous role, in his *Anabasis.*

anacoluthon *noun* plural **anacolutha** E18 **Late Latin** (from Greek *anakolouthon* neuter singular of adjective = lacking sequence, from as *an-* not + *akolouthos* following). A sentence or construction lacking grammatical sequence.

anacrusis *noun* plural **anacruses** M19 **Modern Latin** (from Greek *anakrousis* prelude, from *anakrouein*, from as *ana-* not + *krouein* to strike). **1** M19 *Prosody* An unstressed syllable at the beginning of a verse. **2** E20 *Music* An unstressed note or unstressed notes before the first strong beat of a phrase.

anagnorisis *noun* plural **anagnorises** L18 **Greek** (*anagnōrisis*). *Recognition; the denouement in a drama.*

analemma *noun* plural **analemmae, analemmas** M17 **Latin** ((Vitruvius) = sundial, from Greek *analēmma* support, (base of a) sundial). **1** M17 (An astronomical instrument incorporating) an orthographic projection of the sphere on the plane of the meridian. **2** M19 A figure representing the sun's daily declination and the difference between the right ascension of the mean sun and that of the true sun, drawn especially on terrestrial globes.

analgesia *noun* E18 **Greek** (*analgēsia* painlessness, ultimately from *an-* not + *algeein* to feel pain). *Medicine* Absence or reduction of ability to feel pain; relief of pain, especially by drugs.

anamnesis *noun* plural **anamneses** L16 **Greek** (*anamnēsis* remembrance). **1** L16 The recalling of things past; reminiscence. **2** L19 *Christian Church* That part of the Eucharistic canon in which the sacrifice of Christ is recalled. **3** L19 A patient's account of his or her medical history.

anamorphosis *noun* plural **anamorphoses** E18 **Greek** (*anamorphōsis* transformation). **1** E18 A distorted projection or drawing of anything, which appears normal when viewed from a particular point or by means of a suitable mirror. **2** M19 *Botany* and *Zoology* Progression to a higher type. Now *specifically* development of the adult form through a series of small changes.

anaphora *noun* L16 **Latin and Greek** (branch I, Latin from Greek = repetition, from as *ana-* back, again + *pherein* carry; branch II Late Greek). **I 1** L16 *Rhetoric* The repetition of the same word or phrase in several successive clauses. **2** M20 *Linguistics* The use of an expression that refers to or stands for an earlier word or group of words. **II 3** M18 *Christian Church* The part of the Eucharist at which the oblation is made.

anastrophe *noun* **M16 Greek** (*anastrophē* turning back, from as *ana-* back + *strephein* to turn). *Rhetoric* Inversion or unusual order of words or clauses.

anathema *noun* plural **anathemas**, in sense 3 also **anathemata** E16 **ecclesiastical Latin** ((as senses 1 and 2) from Greek originally 'a thing devoted' (sense 3), later 'an accursed thing', originally variant of *anathēma* votive offering, from *anatithenai* to set up). **1** E16 Something or someone accursed or assigned to damnation; something or someone detested. **2** L16 The formal act or formula of consigning to damnation; the curse of God; the curse of the church, excommunicating a person or denouncing a doctrine, etc.; a denunciation of alleged impiety, heresy, etc.; an imprecation. **3** L16 Something devoted or consecrated to divine use. Now *rare*.

anchoveta *noun* **M20 Spanish** (diminutive of *anchova*). A Pacific anchovy, *Cetengraulis mysticetus*, used as bait or to make fish meal.

ancien régime *noun phrase* **L18 French** (= former regime). The system of government in France before the Revolution of 1789. Also *transferred*, the old system or style of things.

ancona *noun* plural **ancone** **L19 Italian** (from medieval Latin, of uncertain origin: perhaps alteration of Greek *eikona* accusative of *eikōn* icon). An altarpiece, *especially* one consisting of a group of paintings connected by architectural structure.

andante *adverb, adjective, & noun* **E18 Italian** (present participle of *andare* to go). *Music* **A** *adverb & adjective* E18 (A direction:) (originally) distinct(ly); (now) moderately slow(ly). **B** *noun* L18 A moderately slow movement or piece.

andantino *adverb, adjective, & noun* **E19 Italian** (diminutive of preceding). *Music* **A** *adverb & adjective* E19 (A direction:) (originally) somewhat slower than andante; (now usually) with less of andante, i.e., somewhat quicker than andante. **B** *noun* M19 plural **andantinos**. A movement or piece somewhat quicker (originally slower) than an andante.

andouille *noun* **E17 Old and Modern French** (of unknown origin). A kind of pork sausage, usually served as an hors d'oeuvre.

andouillette *noun* (also **andouillet**) **E17 French** (diminutive of preceding). A sausage made from a paste of ground veal, bacon, and other ingredients.

angekok *noun* **M18 Eskimo** ((Greenlandic) *angakkoq*). An Eskimo sorcerer or medicine man.

angelus *noun* **M17 Latin** (from the opening words *Angelus domini* the angel of the Lord). **1** M17 A devotional exercise commemorating the Incarnation, said by Roman Catholics at morning, noon, and sunset. **2** M19 The bell rung at the times for the angelus. More fully *angelus bell*.

anesthesia *noun* (also **anaesthesia**) **E18 Modern Latin** (from Greek *anaisthēsia*, from as *an-* not + *aisthēsis* sensation). Absence of sensation; *especially* artificially induced inability to feel pain.

angina pectoris *noun* **M18 Latin** (*angina* quinsy (from Greek *agkhonē* strangling, assimilated to Latin *angere* to squeeze) + *pectoris* of the chest). *Medicine* Severe pain in the chest, and often also the arms and neck, due to inadequate blood supply to the heart muscles.

■ *Angina* alone was earlier (M16) used of any condition marked by a suffocating, oppressive pain or discomfort, especially quinsy. It is now rare in this sense and is current only as a shortened form of *angina pectoris*.

anglice *adverb* (also **Anglice**) E17 **Medieval Latin** (from Latin *Anglus* English). In (plain) English.

angst *noun* E20 **German**. Anxiety, neurotic fear; guilt, remorse.

an-hua *noun & adjective* E20 **Chinese** (*ànhuā*, from *àn* obscure + *huā* flower). (Of) a type of decoration of Chinese porcelain or fabrics that is visible only by transmitted light.

anima *noun* E20 **Latin** (= (i) air, breath, life; (ii) mind, soul). *Psychoanalysis* The inner self (opposed to PERSONA). Also, the source of the feminine component of a personality. Cf. ANIMUS.

anima mundi *noun phrase* L16 **Medieval Latin** (= soul of the world; apparently formed to render Greek *psukhē tou kosmou*). A power supposed to organize the whole universe and to coordinate its parts.

■ The concept is first found in the writings of the French philosopher and theologian Peter Abelard (1079–1142), who was accused in 1140 by his detractors of identifying it with the Holy Spirit. The phrase was introduced into English philosophical discourse in the seventeenth century by the alchemist Thomas Vaughan in *Anima Magica Abscondita* (1650), who defined it as 'the universal spirit of Nature', and given wider currency by the Cambridge Platonist Ralph Cudworth (1617–88) in *The True Intellectual System of the Universe* (1678) and by the writings of John Locke.

animus *noun* E19 **Latin** (= spirit, mind). **1** E19 Actuating feeling, animating spirit, usually hostile; animosity shown in speech or action. **2** E20 *Psychoanalysis* The source of the masculine component of a personality. Cf. ANIMA.

anis *noun* L19 **French**. A liqueur or aperitif flavored with aniseed; occasionally, aniseed.

ankh *noun* L19 **Egyptian** (= life, soul). An object resembling a cross, but with a loop in place of the upper limb, used in ancient Egyptian art as a symbol of life.

■ Also called CRUX ANSATA.

ankus *noun* L19 **Hindustani** (*aṅkas* from Sanskrit *aṅkuśa*). In the Indian subcontinent: an elephant-goad.

anlaut *noun* L19 **German** (from *an* on + *Laut* sound). *Philology* The initial sound of a word.

anno aetatis suae see under AETATIS.

Anno Domini *adverb & noun phrase* M16 **Latin** (= in the year of the Lord). **A** *adverb* M16 Of the Christian era. Usually written AD. **B** *noun* **1** L17 A particular year. **2** L19 Advanced or advancing age. *colloquial.*

annulus *noun* plural **annuli** M16 **Latin** (late form of *anulus* diminutive of *anus* ring). Chiefly *Mathematics* and *Botany* A ring, a circle that is not filled in; *specifically* a partial veil forming a collar around the stalk in some agarics.

annus horribilis *noun phrase* L20 **Modern Latin** (= horrible year; formed after ANNUS MIRABILIS). A dreadful or miserable year.

■ The phrase leapt into circulation after H.M. the Queen used it with reference to 1992, a year of much-publicized matrimonial troubles within the British royal family and a serious fire at Windsor Castle.

annus mirabilis *noun phrase* M17 **Modern Latin** (= wonderful year). A remarkable or auspicious year.

■ The origin of the phrase is the title of Dryden's poem *Annus Mirabilis: The Year of Wonders* (1667), which chronicled events in 1666, including British naval battles against the Dutch and the Great Fire of London. Dryden's use of *mirabilis* as 'remarkable in both good and bad senses' has tended to be superseded by the more positive sense of 'marvelous', a tendency reinforced by the currency of ANNUS HORRIBILIS in the 1990s.

anomie *noun* (also **anomy**) M20 **French** (from Greek *anomia*, from *anomos* lawless). Lack of the usual social standards in a group or person.

■ The term was resurrected in its current sense by the French sociologist Émile Durkheim in *Suicide* (1897). It occurs in English in technical sociological contexts, but also more generally.

anonym *noun* (also **anonyme**) E19 **French** (*anonyme* from Greek *anōnumos* anonymous). **1** E19 An anonymous person or publication. **2** M19 A pseudonym.

anorak *noun* E20 **Eskimo** (Greenlandic *annoraaq*). **1** A hooded jacket made of skin or cloth and worn by Eskimos and so by others in polar regions; a parka; a similar weatherproof garment worn elsewhere. **2** A person who wears an anorak; an obsessive hobbyist. *derogatory*.

anorexia *noun* M17 **Late Latin** (from Greek *an-* no + *orexis* appetite). *Medicine* Absence of appetite.

■ First introduced in 1598 in the French form *anorexie*, which, like the Anglicized form *anorexy*, is now obsolete. *Anorexia* now very often refers to the specific complaint of ANOREXIA NERVOSA.

anorexia nervosa *noun phrase* L19 **Late Latin** (= nervous anorexia) Chronic anorexia induced by emotional disturbance.

Anschauung *noun* plural **Anschauungen** M19 **German** (= looking at). **1** M19 *Philosophy* (especially *Kantian*) A sense perception, an intuition, an immediate apprehension by sense. **2** E20 An outlook, an attitude, a point of view. Cf. WELTANSCHAUUNG.

Anschluss *noun* E20 **German** (from *anschliessen* to join, annex). Union, annexation; *specifically* the annexation of Austria by Germany in 1938.

an sich *adjective & adverb phrase* M19 **German**. In itself; in the abstract; not in relation to anything else. See also DING AN SICH.

anta *noun* plural **antae**, **antas** L16 **Latin**. *Architecture* A square pilaster at either side of a door or at the corner of a building. Cf. ANTES, IN ANTIS.

ante *noun* E19 **Latin** (= before). **1** E19 In poker and similar games: a stake put up by a player before drawing cards. **2** L19 *transferred* An advance payment; a sum of money for a payment.

■ Often in the phrase *upping (*or *to up) the ante*, that is, 'raising the stakes'.

antebellum *adjective* (also **ante-bellum**) M19 **Latin** (*ante bellum* before the war). Occurring or existing before a particular war, especially the American Civil War. Opposed to POST-BELLUM.

antefix *noun* (also in Latin form **antefixum**, plural **antefixa**) M19 **Latin** (*antefixum*, from as *ante-* before + noun use of *fixus* fixed). *Classical Architecture* An ornament on an eave or cornice to conceal the ends of tiles; also, as ornamental head, etc., making a spout from a gutter. Usually in *plural*.

ante meridiem *adjective & adverb phrase* M16 **Latin**. Before midday; between midnight and the following noon.

■ Abbreviated to *a.m.*

antemortem *adjective* L19 **Latin** (*ante mortem* before death). Made before death. Cf. POSTMORTEM.

antenna *noun* plural **antennae** (especially sense 4) **antennas** M17 **Latin** (alteration of *antemna* sailyard, used in plural as translation of Aristotle's *keraioi* 'horns' of insects). **1** M17 *Zoology* Either of a pair of sensory appendages on the heads of insects, crustaceans, and some other arthropods; a feeler. **2** M19 *figurative* In *plural*. Receptive senses, means of exploration. **3** M19 *Botany* Either of a pair of projections on the male flowers of certain orchids. **4** E20 A metal wire, rod, or other structure used to transmit or receive radio or other electromagnetic waves; an antenna. Chiefly *in technical use*.

antependium *noun* L16 **Medieval Latin** (from as *ante-* before + Latin *pendere* to hang). A veil or hanging for the front of an altar, podium, etc.

antepenultima *noun* plural **antepenultimae**, **antepenultimas** L16 **Late Latin** ((*syllaba*) *antepaenultima*, from as *ante-* before + *penultima* feminine of *paenultimus* last but one). *Prosody* The third syllable from the end of a word or verse.

ante rem *adjective & adverb phrase* L19 **Medieval Latin** (= before the thing). *Philosophy* Prior to the existence of something else; *specifically* (of a universal) prior to the particular; of or pertaining to the theory that the universal is logically prior to the particular. Cf. IN RE 2, POST REM.

■ The phrase occurs in the writings of the thirteenth-century scholastic philosopher Albertus Magnus.

antes *noun plural* L16 **French** (representing Latin *antae* plural of ANTA). *Architecture* Square pilasters.

anthemion *noun* plural **anthemia** M19 **Greek** (= flower). A figure or ornament resembling a stylized honeysuckle.

anthrax *noun* L19 **Latin** (= carbuncle, from Greek *anthrax*, *anthrak-* coal, carbuncle). *Medicine* Infection with the bacterium *Bacillus anthracis*, which in animals usually takes the form of a fatal acute septicemia, and in humans usually affects the skin, causing development of a pustule, or the lungs, causing a form of pneumonia.

■ Originally (LME) with its Latin sense, but this is now rare or obsolete.

anthropophagi *noun plural* M16 **Latin** (*anthropophagus* from Greek *anthrōpophagos* man-eating). Cannibals.

■ The singular *anthropophagus* is rare.

anti *noun & adjective* L18 **Greek** (*anti-* = opposite, against). **A** *noun* L18 Someone who is opposed to someone or something as a particular policy or movement, etc. **B** *adjective* M19 Against or antagonistic to someone or something.

■ The use of *anti-* as a prefix in words adopted (ultimately) from Greek, and in English words modeled on these, long predates the use of *anti* as an independent word, and as a prefix *anti-* has been freely used with nouns and adjectives in the twentieth century with the sense 'opposite, against, preventing'.

antipasto *noun* plural **antipasti**, **antipastos** E17 **Italian**. An appetizer, an hors d'oeuvre.

■ Rare before the mid-twentieth century. Also used figuratively.

antipodes *noun plural* (sense 3 also treated as *singular*) (also **Antipodes**) LME **French** (or late Latin from Greek plural of *antipous* having the feet opposite, from as *anti-* opposite + *pous*, *pod-* foot). **1** LME–M19 Those who live on the opposite side of the earth to each other or to oneself. **2** M16 Places on the surface of the earth directly or diametrically opposite to each other; a place diametrically opposite to another, *especially* Australasia as the region on the opposite side of the earth to Europe. **3** E17 Exact opposites. Also as *singular*. (Followed by *of*, *to*.)

antistrophe *noun* M16 **Late Latin** (from Greek *antistrophē*, from *antistrephein* to turn against). **1** M16 *Rhetoric* The repetition of words in inverse order. **2** E17 The returning movement, from left to right, in Greek choruses and dances, answering to the strophe; the lines of choral song recited during this movement; *transferred* any choral response. **3** E17 An inverse correspondence.

antithesis *noun* plural **antitheses** LME **Late Latin** (from Greek, from *antitithenai*, from as *anti-* against + *tithenai* to set, place: cf. THESIS). **1** *Grammar* **a** The substitution of one case for another. Only in LME. **b** L16–M17 The substitution of one sound for another. **2** E16 *Rhetoric* (An) opposition or contrast of ideas, expressed by parallelism of words that are the opposites of, or strongly contrasted with, each other. Also, repetition of the same word at the end of successive clauses. **3** M16 The second of two opposed clauses or sentences; a counterthesis. **4** E17 Direct or striking opposition of character or function (*of, between* two things). **5** M17 The direct opposite, a complete contrast, (*of, to*). **6** L19 In Hegelian philosophy: the negation of the THESIS as the second stage in the process of dialectical reasoning. Cf. SYNTHESIS 2.

antonomasia *noun* M16 **Latin** (from Greek, from *antonomazein* to name instead, from as *anti-* instead + *onoma* name). The substitution of an epithet, etc., or the name of an office or dignity, for a proper name (e.g., *the Gipper* for Ronald Reagan). Also, conversely, use of a proper name to express a general idea (e.g., *Jezebel* for 'a wicked woman').

AOC see under APPELLATION CONTRÔLÉE.

à outrance *adverb phrase* Also **à l'outrance**, **à toute outrance** E17 **French** (= to beyond bounds). To the death; to the bitter end.

Apache *noun & adjective* (senses A.2, B.2 also written **apache**) M18 **Mexican Spanish** (probably from Zuñi *Ápachu*, literally, 'enemy'; senses A.2, B.2 through French). **A** *noun* plural **Apaches**, same. **1** M18 A member of an Athapaskan Indian people of New Mexico and Arizona; the language of this people. **2** E20 A violent street ruffian, originally in Paris. **B** *attributive* or as *adjective* **1** M19 Of or pertaining to the Apache or their language. **2** E20 Designating a vigorous dance for two associated with street ruffians or apaches.

aparejo *noun* plural **aparejos** M19 **Spanish** (= preparation, harness, tackle). A packsaddle.

apartheid *noun* M20 **Afrikaans** (literally, 'separateness', from Dutch *apart* apart + *-heid* -hood). The former South African policy or system of racial segregation. Also *transferred* and *figurative*, any other form of segregation.

aperçu *noun* E19 **French**. A summary, a conspectus; an insight, a revealing glimpse.

aperitif *noun* (also **apéritif**) L19 **French** (*apéritif* (noun and adjective) from medieval Latin *aperitivus* (adjective) variant of late Latin *apertivus*, from *apertus* open). An alcoholic drink taken as an appetizer. Also *figurative*.

apex *noun* plural **apexes**, **apices** E17 **Latin**. **1** The tip, top, peak, or pointed end of anything; the vertex of a triangle, cone, etc.; *Botany* the growing point of a shoot, etc. **2** L18 *Astronomy* The point on the celestial sphere toward which the sun is moving. Also *solar apex*.

apfelstrudel *noun* M20 **German** (from *Apfel* apple + STRUDEL). A flaky pastry with a spicy apple filling.

■ Also very frequently in partially Anglicized form *apple strudel*.

aphasia *noun* M19 **Greek** (from *aphatos* speechless, from *a-* without + *phanai* to speak). Loss or impairment of the faculty of speech or of understanding of language (or both), due to cerebral disease or damage.

aplomb *noun* L18 **French** (from *à plomb* according to the plummet). **1** L18 Perpendicularity; steadiness. Now *rare* or *obsolete*. **2** E19 Self-possession, coolness; assurance.

apocatastasis variant of APOKATASTASIS.

Apocrypha *noun* (usually treated as *singular*; rarely as *plural*, with *singular* **Apocryphon**) (also **apocrypha**) LME **ecclesiastical Latin** (neuter plural (sc. *scripta* writings) of *apocryphus* from Greek *apokruphos* hidden, from *apokruptein* to hide). A writing or statement of doubtful authorship or authenticity; *specifically* **a** those Old Testament books included in the Septuagint and Vulgate that are not included in the Hebrew Scriptures, and that were excluded from the Protestant canon at the Reformation; **b** *New Testament Apocrypha*, various early Christian writings parallel to but excluded from the New Testament canon.

apodyterium *noun* plural **apodyteria** E17 **Latin** (from Greek *apodutērion*, from *apoduein* to strip). *Classical History* A room adjacent to a bath or palaestra where clothes were deposited.

à point *adverb phrase* E20 **French** (= to the point). Especially *Cooking*. At or to exactly the right point; just enough, without overcooking or undercooking.

apokatastasis *noun* (also **apocatastasis**) L17 **Greek** (= reestablishment). Restoration, renewal; *specifically* in *Theology* the ultimate salvation of all moral beings.

apo koinou *adjective & adverb phrase* L19 **Greek** (literally, 'in common'). *Grammar* Designating a construction comprising two clauses having an unrepeated word or phrase in common; so as to form such a construction.

apologia *noun* L18 **Latin**. A written defense of one's own (or someone else's) opinions or conduct.

■ The currency of *apologia* is largely due to the impact of John Henry Newman's *Apologia pro Vita Sua* (1864), charting his intellectual and spiritual progress from Anglicanism to Roman Catholicism. The complete phrase is sometimes used of an autobiography, especially one by a controversial figure.

aporia *noun* M16 **Late Latin** (from Greek, from *aporos* impassable). **1** M16 *Rhetoric* The expression of doubt. **2** L19 A doubtful matter, a perplexing difficulty.

a posteriori *adverb & adjective phrase* E17 **Latin** (= from what comes after). **1** E17 Of reasoning: (by) proceeding from effects to causes; inductive(ly), empirical(ly). Opposed (to) A PRIORI. **2** M18 From behind; on the buttocks. *facetious*.

apotheosis *noun* plural **apotheoses** L16 **ecclesiastical Latin** (from Greek *apotheōsis*, from *apotheoun* to deify, from *apo-* + *theos* god). **1** L16 (Elevation to) divine status. **2** E17 Glorification or exaltation of a person, principle, or practice; canonization; idealization. **3** M17 Ascension to glory, resurrection, triumph; highest development, culmination.

apparat *noun* M20 **Russian** (through German from Latin *apparatus* from *apparare* to make ready). The Communist Party machine in the former USSR and other countries.

apparatchik *noun* plural **apparatchiki**, **apparatchiks** M20 **Russian** (from preceding). **1** M20 A member of the APPARAT; a Communist agent. **2** L20 *transferred* An implementer of party or official policy; an executive officer.

apparatus criticus *noun phrase* plural **apparatus critici** M19 **Modern Latin**. A collection of material, as variant readings and other paleographical and critical matter, for the textual study of a document.

appellation contrôlée *noun phrase* M20 **French** (= controlled appellation). (A guarantee of) the description of a bottle of French wine (or other item of food) in conformity with statutory regulations as to its origin.

■ Abbreviated to AC. Also *appellation d'origine contrôlée*, abbreviated to AOC.

appliqué *noun & verb* M18 **French** (noun use of past participle of *appliquer* from Latin *applicare* to apply (to)). Chiefly *Needlework*. **A** *noun* M18 (A piece of) ornamental work cut out from one material and affixed to the surface of another; the technique of ornamenting in this way. **B** *transitive verb* L19 Decorate in this way. Chiefly as *appliquéd* participial adjective.

appoggiatura *noun* plural **appogiature** M18 **Italian** (from *appoggiare* to lean upon, rest). *Music* A grace note performed before an essential note of a melody and normally taking half or less than half its time value; the use of such notes.

après *preposition* M20 **French**. After.

■ Combined with English words in (jocular) imitation of APRÈS-SKI, as *après-bath*, *après-sex*, etc.

après coup *adverb phrase* M19 **French** (literally, 'after stroke'). After the event; as an afterthought.

après nous le déluge *adverb phrase* M19 **French** (literally, 'after us the flood'). (Used to express the feeling that) the present state of affairs or order of things will not long survive us.

■ Attributed in the *Mémoires* of Mme de Hausset (1824) to Mme de Pompadour (1721–64), mistress of King Louis XV of France, who had premonitions of catastrophe after the French defeat by the Prussians at Rossbach in 1757. It is very often quoted by English speakers in the version *après moi le déluge*.

après-ski *noun & adjective* M20 **French**. (Worn, done, etc., at) the time when skiing is over for the day at a resort.

a priori *adverb & adjective phrase* L16 **Latin** (*a priori* from what is before). **1** L16 Of reasoning: (by) proceeding from causes to effects; deductive(ly). Opposed to A POSTERIORI. **2** E19 *loosely* Presumptive(ly); without previous investigation; as far as one knows. **3** M19 *Philosophy* Of knowledge or concepts: not derived from sensory experience; innate(ly).

apropos *adverb, adjective, & preposition* (also **à propos**) M17 **French** (*à propos*, from *à* to + *propos* purpose). **A** *adverb* **1** M17 To the point; fitly, opportunely. **2** M18 In respect or as a relevant association *of* (now less commonly, *to*). **b** M18 *absolutely* Incidentally, by the way. **B** *adjective* M17 Pertinent, appropriate, opportune. (Followed by *of*, *to*.) **C** *preposition* M20 Concerning, with regard to. *colloquial*.

à propos de bottes *adverb phrase* M18 **French** (= with regard to boots, i.e., to something quite irrelevant). Without rhyme or reason, motiveless.

apsara *noun* (also **upsara**) M19 **Hindi** (*apsarā* from Sanskrit *apsarās*). *Hindu Mythology* Any of a class of celestial nymphs, frequently regarded as the wives of the gandharvas or heavenly musicians.

aqua fortis *noun phrase* (also **aquafortis**) L15 **Latin** (= strong water). Nitric acid; originally, any powerful solvent. Now *archaic*.

aqua regia *noun phrase* (also formerly **aqua regis**) E17 **Latin** (= royal water). *Chemistry* A concentrated mixture of nitric and hydrochloric acids, able to dissolve gold, platinum, etc.

aquarelle *noun* M19 **French** (from Italian *acquarella* watercolor, from *acqua* from Latin *aqua* water). A style of painting in thin, usually transparent, watercolors; a painting in this style.

aquarium *noun* plural **aquaria**, **aquariums** M19 **Modern Latin** (use as noun of neuter singular of *aquarius* pertaining to water, after VIVARIUM). An artificial pond or tank (usually with transparent sides) for keeping live aquatic plants and animals; a place containing such tanks.

aquavit *noun* (also **akvavit**) L19 **Norwegian, Swedish, Danish** (*akvavit* AQUA VITAE). An alcoholic spirit distilled from potatoes or other starch-containing plants and usually flavored with caraway seeds.

aqua vitae *noun phrase* (also **aqua-vitae**) LME **Latin** (= water of life: cf. French *eau de vie*). Alcoholic spirits, especially of the first distillation, especially brandy.

arabesque *noun & adjective* M17 **French** (from Italian *arabesco*, from *arabo* Arabic). **A** *noun* **1** M17 Decorative work of a kind that originated in Arabic or Moorish art, consisting of flowing lines of branches, leaves, scrollwork, etc., fancifully intertwined; an ornamental design of this kind. **2** M19 *Ballet* A posture in which the body is bent forward and supported on one leg with the other leg extended horizontally backward, with the arms extended one forward and one backward. **3** M19

Music A passage or composition with fanciful ornamentation of the melody. **B** *adjective* L18 Of ornamental design: decorated with arabesques (sense 1).

arak *noun* (also **arrack**) E17 **Arabic** (*'araḳ* sweat, especially in *'araḳ at-tamr* fermented and distilled juice of dates). In Eastern countries: an alcoholic spirit of local manufacture, especially distilled from the sap of the coco palm or from rice.

arbiter elegantiae E19 **Latin** (= judge of elegance). An authority on matters of taste or etiquette.

■ First introduced in the form *arbiter elegantiarum* 'judge in matters of taste', which was current in English in the nineteenth century, but the singular form of the genitive, *elegantiae*, is now usual. It has classical sanction in being applied by Tacitus (*Annales* xvi.18) to Titus Petronius, *elegantiae arbiter* at the court of Nero.

arboretum *noun* plural **arboreta, arboretums** E19 **Latin** (= place with trees, from *arbor* tree). A place devoted to the cultivation and exhibition of rare trees; a botanical tree garden.

arbor vitae *noun phrase* (also (especially in sense 1) **arborvitae** E17 **Latin** (= tree of life). E17 Any of a number of North American or Far Eastern evergreen conifers, belonging chiefly to the genus *Thuja*.

Arcades ambo *noun phrase* E19 **Latin** (= both Arcadians, i.e., both pastoral poet-musicians). Two people of the same (often literary or aesthetic) tastes, profession, or character.

■ The phrase is a quotation from Virgil (*Eclogues* vii. 4) and, following Byron, is frequently used derogatorily with overtones of 'idle layabouts' or worse.

arcanum *noun* plural **arcana** L16 **Latin** (noun use of neuter singular of *arcanus* concealed). Usually in *plural*. **1** L16 A hidden thing; a mystery, a profound secret. **2** E17 *specifically* Any of the supposed secrets of nature sought by alchemists; a marvelous remedy, an elixir. *archaic*.

archi plural of ARCO.

archon *noun* plural **archons, archontes** L16 **Greek** (*arkhōn, arkhont-* ruler, noun use of present participle of *arkhein* to rule). **1** L16 The chief magistrate, or, after the time of Solon, each of the nine chief magistrates, of ancient Athens. **2** M18 A ruler, a president. **3** M18 A power subordinate to God, held by some of the Gnostics to have created the world.

arco *noun, adverb & adjective* M18 **Italian.** *Music* **A** *noun* M18 plural **archi, arcos**. A bow for a stringed instrument. **B** *adverb & adjective* E19 (A direction:) resuming use of the bow after a pizzicato passage.

à rebours *adverb phrase* E20 **Old French** (*à* from + *rebors* (modern *rebours*) rough, perverse, the wrong side, etc., from popular Latin *rebursum*, Latin *reburrum* rough-haired, bristly). In the wrong way, against the grain; through perversity.

■ *Rebours* was formerly naturalized in the Scottish phrase *at rebours*. The adoption of the phrase in its modern form may be on account of its having been the title of an influential book (1884) by the French novelist Joris-Karl Huysmans.

areg plural of ERG.

arête *noun* E19 **French** (from Latin *arista* ear of corn, fish-bone or -spine). A sharp mountain ridge with steep sides.

argot *noun* M19 **French** (of unknown origin). The jargon, slang, or peculiar phraseology of a social class or group; originally, rogues' and thieves' cant.

argumentum ad hominem *noun phrase* M17 **Latin.** An argument, usually disparaging or abusive, attacking the personal circumstances or character of an opponent rather than employing sound reasoning to make the point. Cf. AD HOMINEM.

■ In attributive use often shortened to *ad hominem*.

argumentum e silentio *noun phrase* (also **argumentum ex silentio**) M20 **Latin** (= argument from silence). A conclusion based on silence, i.e., on lack of contrary evidence.

■ The more (classically) correct *argumentum ex silentio* is also found.

Arhat *noun* (also **Arahat, arahat**) L19 **Sanskrit** (*arhat*, Pali *arahat* meritorious). *Buddhism* and *Jainism* A saint of one of the highest ranks.

aria *noun* E18 **Italian** (from Latin *aera* accusative of *aer* from Greek *aēr* air). *Music* A long song for one voice usually with accompaniment; *especially* such a song in an opera, oratorio, etc.

arietta *noun* E18 **Italian** (diminutive of ARIA). *Music* A short tune or song.

arioso *adjective, adverb, & noun* E18 **Italian** (from ARIA). *Music* **A** *adjective* E18 Melodious, songlike, cantabile; having something of the quality of an aria. Also as *adverb* as a direction. **B** *noun* L19 plural **ariosos**. A piece of vocal or instrumental music of this kind.

armada *noun* (also **armado** and in sense 1b **Armada**) M16 **Spanish** (from Proto-Romance *armata* army). **1** M16 A fleet of warships. **b** L16 *specifically* The Spanish Armada, the fleet sent by Philip II of Spain to attack England in 1588. **2** L16–M17 A single warship. **3** E18 *transferred* and *figurative* A large army or airborne force; a large fleet of vessels of any kind.

armamentarium *noun* plural **armamentaria** L19 **Latin** (= arsenal, armory). The medicines, equipment, and techniques available to a medical practitioner.

arme blanche *noun phrase* plural **armes blanches** L19 **French** (literally, 'white arm'). A cavalry sword or lance; the cavalry.

armiger *noun* M16 **Latin** (= bearing arms, from *arma* arms + *gerere* to carry). An esquire: originally, a person who attended a knight to bear his shield; now, a person entitled to heraldic arms.

armilla *noun* plural **armillae, armillas** M17 **Latin** (diminutive of *armus* shoulder). **1** M17 An ancient astronomical instrument consisting of a graduated ring or hoop fixed in the plane of the equator (*equinoctial armilla*), sometimes crossed by another in the plane of the meridian (*solstitial armilla*). **2** L17 A coronation stole; an armil. **3** E18 Chiefly *Archaeology*. A bracelet, an armlet.

armoire *noun* L16 **French**. A cupboard, a wardrobe; *especially* one that is ornate or antique.

arpeggio *noun* plural **arpeggios** E18 **Italian** (from *arpeggiare* to play on the harp, from *arpa* harp). *Music* The sounding of the notes of a chord in (usually rapid upward) succession, not simultaneously; a chord so sounded.

arrack variant of ARAK.

arrêt *noun* M17 **French**. An authoritative sentence or decision, *specifically* of the monarch (*historical*) or parliament of France.

arrière-pensée *noun* E19 **French** (literally, 'behind-thought'). A concealed thought or intention; an ulterior motive; a mental reservation.

arrivisme *noun* (also in Anglicized form **arrivism**) M20 **French** (from Old French *ariver* to arrive, ultimately from Latin *ad* to + *ripa* shore). The behavior or character of an ARRIVISTE.

arriviste *noun* (also in Anglicized form **arrivist**) E20 **French** (from as preceding). An ambitious or self-seeking person.

arrondissement *noun* E19 **French** (from *arrondiss-* lengthened stem of *arrondir* make round). In France: an administrative subdivision of a city or department.

arroyo *noun* plural **arroyos** M19 **Spanish**. A steep gully, a watercourse.

arsis *noun* plural **arses** LME **Late Latin** (from Greek = lifting, raising, from *airein* to raise). The syllable or part of a metrical foot that is stressed (originally, *Classical Prosody*, by raised pitch or volume); the unstressed beat in barred music. Opposed to THESIS I sense 1.

art brut *noun phrase* **M20 French** (literally, 'raw art'). Primitive or pseudo-primitive art.

■ *L'Art brut* was the title of an exhibition of paintings in Paris in 1949 that included works by children and psychiatric patients.

artel *noun* **L19 Russian** (*artel'*). A Russian or Soviet collective enterprise of craftsmen or skilled workers.

artiste *noun* **E19 French**. A performing artist; a professional singer, dancer, actor, etc.

art nouveau *noun phrase* **E20 French** (literally, 'new art'). A decorative style in French and English art of the late nineteenth century characterized by ornamented and flowing lines. Cf. JUGENDSTIL.

aryballos *noun* **M19 Greek** (*aruballos* bag, purse, oil-flask). *Greek Antiquities* A globular flask with a narrow neck used to hold oil or unguent.

ascesis *noun* (also **askesis**) **L19 Greek** (*askēsis* exercise, training, from *askein* to exercise). The practice of self-discipline.

ashram *noun* **E20 Sanskrit** (*āśrama* hermitage). **1** E20 In the Indian subcontinent: a hermitage, a place of religious retreat. **2** M20 *transferred* Any group with shared spiritual or social aims living together.

askari *noun* plural **askaris** **L19 Arabic** (*'askarī* soldier). An East African soldier or police officer.

askesis variant of ASCESIS.

asphyxia *noun* **M19 Modern Latin** (from Greek *asphuxia*, from *a-* without + *sphuxis* pulsation). *Medicine* The condition of defective aeration of the blood caused by failure of the oxygen supply; suffocation.

■ Earlier (E18) in the sense of 'stoppage of the pulse', but there is no apparent evidence of this outside dictionaries.

assai *adverb* **E18 Italian**. *Music* (In directions:) very.

assegai *noun* (also **assagai**) **E17 French** (*azagaie* (now *zagaie*, *sagaie*)) or Portuguese (*azagaia*, Spanish *azagaya* from colloquial Arabic *az-zaġāya from al* the + Berber *zaġāya* spear). An iron-bladed spear with a hardwood shaft used for stabbing or as a missile by South African indigenous peoples.

assemblé *noun* **L18 French** (past participle of *assembler* to bring together). *Ballet* A leap in which the feet are brought together before landing.

assemblée *noun* **E18 French**. An assembly; *especially* a gathering of polite society for recreational purposes.

assiette *noun* **M18 French** (= plate, course of a meal; seat, site; bed, foundation). A prepared dish of food.

■ Usually with qualifying word or phrase, as in *assiette anglaise* 'a platter of assorted cold meats'.

ataman *noun* **M19 Russian**. A Cossack leader. Cf. HETMAN.

ataraxia *noun* **M19 Greek** (= impassiveness, from *a-* not + *tarassein* to disturb). Imperturbability; ataraxy.

atelier *noun* **L17 French**. A workshop or studio, especially of an artist or couturier.

a tempo *adverb phrase* **M18 Italian** (= in time). *Music* (A direction:) in the tempo indicated previously, before the direction to deviate from it.

à terre *adverb & adjective phrase* **E20 French**. Chiefly *Ballet*. On the ground.

atlantes *noun plural* **E17 Greek** (*Atlas, Atlant-*, the Titan supposed to hold up the pillars of the universe, and a mountain range in western North Africa also regarded mythically as supporting the heavens). *Architecture* Male figures used as pillars to support an entablature.

■ The singular form of the word, meaning 'a person who supports a great burden' was introduced via Latin (L16) and soon afterward (M17) became the name for 'a collection of maps or charts bound in a volume'.

In this sense, and in other senses derived from it, *atlas* has long been entirely naturalized. The connection between the world-supporting Titan and the book of maps was first made in the mid–sixteenth century, when Antonio Lafreri, a French publisher working in Rome, put together collections of maps to his customers' specifications and bound them with a standard title page depicting Atlas carrying the world on his shoulders. The use of 'Atlas' as a title for a book of maps originated with the Flemish geographers Gerhard and Rumold Mercator, whose complete 107-map *Atlas* was published in 1595. The Mercator *Atlas* in various versions and editions so dominated European cartography in the first half of the seventeenth century (it appeared in English in 1636) that the name became used generically for all such books.

atman *noun* L18 **Sanskrit** (*ātman*). *Hindu Philosophy* The self as the subject of individual consciousness, the soul; the supreme personal principle of life in the universe.

atole *noun* M17 **American Spanish** (from Nahuatl *atolli*). Gruel or porridge made of maize or other meal.

à tort et à travers *adverb phrase* M18 **French** (= wrongly and across). At random, haphazardly.

à toute outrance variant of À OUTRANCE.

atrium *noun* plural **atria**, **atriums** L16 **Latin**. **1** L16 *Architecture* A central court, originally that of an ancient Roman house; a covered court or portico; (a building with) a large light-well; a central hall or glassed-in court in a building. **2** L19 *Anatomy* and *Zoology* Any of various chambers into which one or more passages open; *specifically* (**a**) either of the two upper chambers of the heart into which the veins conduct blood; (**b**) the tympanic chamber of the ear.

à trois *adjective & adverb phrase* L19 **French**. Shared by, or in a group of, three people. Cf. MÉNAGE À TROIS.

attaché *noun* E19 **French** (past participle of *attacher* to attach). A junior official attached to the staff of an ambassador, etc.; a representative of his or her government in a foreign country.

■ Frequently in the combination *attaché case* a small rectangular case, usually with a handle, for carrying documents.

attar *noun* (also (earlier) **otto**) M17 **Persian** (*'itr*, Arabic *'iṭr*, colloquial Arabic *'aṭar* perfume, essence). A fragrant volatile essence, *especially* (more fully *attar of roses*) that obtained from rose petals.

attentat *noun* (also (now only in sense 2) **attentate**) E17 **Old and Modern French** (or medieval Latin *attentatum*, from *attentatum* past participial stem of *attentare* variant of Latin *attemptare* to attempt). **1** E17 An attack; an attempted assassination. **2** E18 *Law* Something wrongfully done by a judge in a proceeding, pending an appeal.

attentisme *noun* M20 **French** (from *attente* wait, waiting). The policy of waiting to see what happens.

attrait *noun* E20 **French** (from *attraire* to attract). *Theology* Vocation; inclination.

aubade *noun* L17 **French** (from Spanish *albada*, from *alba* (= French *aube*) dawn). A piece of music or a poem written to be heard at or appropriate to dawn.

auberge *noun* L16 **French** (from Provençal *alberga* lodging). An inn, *especially* one in France.

aubergine *noun & adjective* L18 **French** (from Catalan *alberginia*, from Arabic *al-bāḏinjān*, from *al-* the + Persian *bādingān*, *bādinjān* from Sanskrit *vātiṃgaṇa*). **A** *noun* **1** L18 The fruit of the eggplant, *Solanum melongena*, eaten as a vegetable; the plant itself. Cf. BRINJAL. **2** L19 A dark purple color typical of the skin of the fruit. **B** *adjective* L19 Of the color aubergine, dark purple.

aubusson *noun* (also more correctly **Aubusson**) E20 **French** (Aubusson =

a town in central France). Tapestry or (especially) a tapestry carpet woven at Aubusson.

AUC abbreviation of AB URBE CONDITA.

au contraire *adverb phrase* M18 **French**. On the contrary.

au courant *adverb & adjective phrase* M18 **French**. In an informed position; aware of current developments.

■ Usually followed by *with*, *of*, but can also be used absolutely.

auditorium *noun* plural **auditoriums, auditoria** E17 **Latin**. **1** E17 *general* A place for hearing. *rare*. **2** M19 *specifically* The part of a theater, lecture hall, or other public building occupied by the audience; such a building as a whole.

au fait *adverb & predicate adjective phrase* M18 **French** (literally, 'to the fact', 'to the point'). Thoroughly conversant (*with*), well instructed (*in*), expert or skillful (*at*).

Aufklärung *noun* E19 **German** (literally, 'clearing up'). The intellectual and philosophical movement in eighteenth-century Europe that promoted reason and individualism against traditional religion and ancient authority; the Enlightenment.

au fond *adverb phrase* L18 **French**. Basically; at bottom.

au grand sérieux *adverb phrase* M19 **French**. In all seriousness. Cf. AU SÉRIEUX.

au gratin *adverb & predicate adjective phrase* E19 **French** (from *au* with the + GRATIN). *Cooking* Sprinkled with breadcrumbs and/or grated cheese and browned.

auguste *noun* E20 **French** (from German *August*, male first name, (*slang*) clown, fool). A circus clown wearing ill-fitting or disheveled clothes.

au mieux *adverb phrase* M19 **French** (= at the best). On the best of, or on very intimate, terms *with* (someone).

aumônière *noun* E19 **French** (feminine of *aumônier* almoner). A purse carried at the waist.

au naturel *adverb phrase* E19 **French**. **1** In the natural state; naked. **2** *Cooking* cooked plainly; uncooked.

au pair *adjective & noun phrase* L19 **French** (= on equal terms). **A** *adjective phrase* L19 Of arrangements between two parties: paid for (entirely or largely) by mutual services. Of a person: party to such an arrangement; *specifically* (of a (usually foreign) girl) undertaking domestic duties in return for room and board. **B** *noun* M20 An au pair girl.

au pied de la lettre *adverb phrase* L18 **French** (= to the foot of the letter). Down to the last detail; literally.

aura *noun* plural **auras**, (*rare*) **aurae** LME **Latin** (from Greek = breath, breeze). **1** LME A gentle breeze, a zephyr. *archaic* and *poetic*. **2** M18 A subtle emanation or exhalation; a surrounding glow; *figurative* an atmosphere diffused by or attending a person, place, etc.; a distinctive impression of character or aspect. **3** L18 A premonitory sensation experienced before an epileptic fit.

aureola *noun* plural **aureolae, aureolas** L15 **Latin** (feminine (sc. *corona* crown) of *aureolus* adjective, diminutive of *aureus* golden, from *aurum* gold). A celestial crown; a halo; an aureole.

au reste *adverb phrase* E17 **French**. As for the rest.

au revoir *interjection & noun phrase* L17 **French** (literally, 'to the seeing again'). (Goodbye) until we meet again; a farewell for the present.

aurora *noun* (also **Aurora**) plural **aurorae, auroras** LME **Latin** (*Aurora* the Roman goddess of the dawn). **1** LME The rising light of the morning; the dawn. **b** *figurative* M19 The beginning, the early period. **2** M17 A rich orange color, as of the sky at sunrise. **3** E18 A luminous phenomenon, often taking the form of variable streamers or resembling drapery, seen in the upper atmosphere of high northern (*borealis*) and southern (*australis)* latitudes.

aurora australis M18 Latin (= southern dawn). The aurora of the southern polar regions, the southern lights.

■ Coined after AURORA BOREALIS.

aurora borealis E18 Latin (= northern dawn). The aurora of the northern polar regions, the northern lights.

■ The phrase was coined to describe the phenomenon in 1621 by the French physicist and philosopher Pierre Gassendi (1592–1655).

au sérieux *adverb phrase* M19 French. Seriously. Cf. AU GRAND SÉRIEUX.

Auslese *noun* (also **auslese**) plural **Auslesen**, **Ausleses** M19 German (from *aus* out + *lese* picking, vintage). A white wine made (especially in Germany) from selected bunches of grapes picked later than the general harvest.

auteur *noun* M20 French (= author). *Cinema* A director who so greatly influences the movies directed as to be able to rank as their author.

auto *noun* plural **autos** M16 Spanish and Portuguese (from Latin *actus* act). **1** M16 An AUTO-DA-FÉ. **2** L18 A play (by a Spanish or Portuguese author).

autobahn *noun* plural **autobahns**, **autobahnen** M20 German (from *Auto* automobile + *Bahn* road). In Germany, Switzerland, or Austria: a highway.

auto-da-fé *noun* plural **autos-da-fé**, **auto-da-fés** E18 Portuguese (= act of the faith (Spanish *auto de fe*)). (The execution of) a judicial sentence of the Inquisition; *especially* the public burning of a heretic; *transferred* a public burning.

autogiro *noun* (also **autogyro**) plural **autogiros** E20 Spanish (from as *auto-* self + *giro* gyration). A type of aircraft having a propeller and freely rotating horizontal vanes.

automat *noun* L17 German (from French *automate* from Latin AUTOMATON). L AN AUTOMATON E A CAFETERIA IN WHICH FOOD IS OBTAINED FROM A SLOT MACHINE; A SLOT MACHINE.

automaton *noun* plural **automatons**, **automata** E17 Latin ((also *automatum*) from Greek, noun use of neuter of *automatos* acting of itself). **1** E17 Something having the power of spontaneous motion; *especially* a living being viewed as a machine. **2** M17 A piece of mechanism with concealed motive power, *especially* one simulating a living being; a robot. **3** L17 A living being whose actions are purely involuntary or mechanical; a person behaving without active intelligence or mechanically in a set pattern or routine. **4** M20 *Computing* A machine whose responses to all possible inputs are specified in advance.

autopista *noun* M20 Spanish (from *auto* automobile + *pista* track, PISTE). In Spain and Spanish-speaking countries: a highway.

autoroute *noun* M20 French (from *auto* automobile + *route* road). In France: a highway.

autostrada *noun* plural **autostradas**, **autostrade** E20 Italian (from *auto* automobile + *strada* road from Latin STRATUM). In Italy: a highway.

avalanche *noun & verb* L18 French (from Romansh, alteration of Alpine French dialect *lavanche* (of unknown origin), by blending with *avaler* descend: cf. Provençal *lavanca*, Italian *valanga*). **A** *noun* **1** L18 A large mass of snow, rocks, and ice, moving swiftly down a mountainside. **2** *transferred* and *figurative* M19 A sudden onrush or descent; a rapidly descending mass. **b** *Physics* M20 A process of cumulative ionization in which each electron and ion generates further charged particles. Also more fully *Townsend avalanche*. Frequently *attributive*. **B** *intransitive verb* L19 Descend in or like an avalanche.

avant-garde *noun & adjective* LME French (from *avant* forward, before + *garde* guard). **A** *noun* **1** LME The vanguard of an army. Now *archaic* or *historical*. **2** E20 The pioneering or innovative writers, artists, etc., in a particular period. **B** *adjective* E20 Of or pertaining to the artistic avant-garde; progressive, ultramodern.

avant la lettre *adverb phrase* M20 **French** (literally, 'before the letter'). Before the word, definition, etc., was invented.

avatar *noun* L18 **Sanskrit** (*avatāra* descent, from *ava* off, away, down + *tar-* to pass over). **1** L18 *Hindu Mythology* The descent of a god to earth in incarnate form. **2** E19 An incarnation or embodiment (of another person, an idea, etc.). **3** E19 A manifestation to the world as a ruling power or as an object of worship; *generally* a manifestation, a phase.

ave *noun & interjection* (also **Ave** in sense A.1) ME **Latin** (as imperative singular of *avere* to be or fare well, used as an expression of greeting or farewell). **A** *noun* **1** ME An AVE MARIA. **b** ME A bead on a rosary (as used for counting the number of aves recited). **2** E17 A shout of welcome or farewell. **B** *interjection* LME Hail! Farewell!

■ The earliest use of the noun was short for AVE MARIA.

ave atque vale *interjection* M19 **Latin** (= hail and farewell). Hello and goodbye, hail and farewell.

■ The concluding words of Catullus's graveside address to his dead brother (*Carmina* ci.10), the exclamation is now sometimes used jocularly as a greeting to someone whom one has seen or will see for only a short time.

Ave Maria *interjection & noun phrase* (also **Ave Mary**) ME **Latin** (= hail, Mary!). **1** ME The angel's greeting to the Virgin Mary combined with that of Elizabeth (cf. Luke 1:28, 42), used as a devotional recitation; the prayer to the Virgin as Mother of God beginning with these words; a recitation of this devotional phrase or prayer (often shortened to AVE). **2** L16 (The time of) the ave-bell.

avoirdupois *noun* ME **Old French** (*aveir de peis* goods of weight, from *ave(i)r* (modern *avoir*) noun use of *avoir* to have (from Latin *habere*) + *de* of + *peis, pois* (modern *poids* weight). **1** ME–L17 Merchandise sold by weight. **2** L15 A system of weights based on a pound (the *avoirdupois pound*) of 16 ounces or 7,000 grains. More fully *avoirdupois weight*. **3** L16 Weight, heaviness; *colloquially* excess bodily weight.

■ The substitution of *du* for the earlier *de* was established in the seventeenth century.

avoué *noun* E19 **French**. **1** E19 A person who holds the advowson of an ecclesiastical house or benefice; an advowee. **2** E19 A French attorney.

awabi *noun* E18 **Japanese**. The Japanese abalone, *Haliotis gigantea*.

axiomata media *noun phrase plural* M19 **Modern Latin** (= middle principles). *Philosophy* Principles above simple empirical laws but below the highest generalizations or fundamental laws.

■ The phrase is Francis Bacon's in his *Novum Organum* (I.xix), published in Latin in 1620. It was introduced into English philosophical discourse by J. S. Mill in the mid–nineteenth century.

ayah *noun* L18 **Portuguese** (*aia* feminine of *aio* tutor). A nurse or maidservant, especially of Europeans in India, Southeast Asia, etc.

ayahuasca *noun* L20 **South American Spanish** (From Quechua *ayawáskha* from *aya* corpse + *waskha* rope). A hallucinogenic drug made from the bark of a tropical vine found in the Amazon basin; the vine itself. Also called *yagé*.

ayatollah *noun* (also (as a title) **Ayatollah**) M20 **Persian** (from Arabic *'āyatullāh* miraculous sign of God). A Shiite religious leader in Iran; *figurative* a dogmatic leader, an influential or powerful person.

ayurveda *noun* (also **Ayurveda**) E20 **Sanskrit** (*āyur-veda* science of life, medicine). An ancient Indian health system.

azan *noun* M19 **Arabic** (*'adān* announcement). The Muslim call to ritual prayer, often made by a muezzin or broadcast through loudspeakers from the minaret of a mosque.

azotea *noun* E19 **Spanish.** In Spain and Spanish-speaking countries: the flat roof of a house used as a terrace.

azuki variant of ADZUKI.

azulejo *noun* plural **azulejos** M19 **Spanish** (from *azul* blue). A kind of colored glazed tile used in Spanish buildings.

baas *noun* L18 **Dutch.** In South Africa: a (usually white) employer, master, overseer, etc.

■ The word was first used in English in 1625 (*Purchas his Pilgrimes* I. ii. 117) for a sea captain: "Our Baase (for so a Dutch capitaine is called)." It traveled to South Africa with the Dutch settlers of that country and became, in both Afrikaans and South African English, the normal form of address used by black or Colored South Africans for those in authority (hence BAASSKAP).

baasskap *noun* M20 **Afrikaans** (from Dutch *baasschap*, from BAAS + *-schap* -ship). Domination, especially of nonwhites by whites.

baba *noun* E19 **French** (from Polish, literally, 'married (peasant) woman'). A rich spongecake; *specifically* one served in a rum syrup. More fully *rum baba* or *baba au rhum*.

babiche *noun* E19 **Canadian French** (from Micmac *a:papi:č*). Thongs or thread made of rawhide, sinew, etc.

babu *noun* (also **baboo** or (as title) **Babu**) L18 **Hindustani** (*bābū*). **1** L18–E19 Originally, a Hindu title of respect. Later, a Hindu gentleman. **2** M19 *History* An Indian clerk or official who could write English; *derogatory* an Indian, especially in Bengal, who had had a superficial English education; *attributive* the ornate and often unidiomatic English written by such a person.

babushka *noun* M20 **Russian** (= grandmother). **1** M20 In Russia: a grandmother, an old woman. **2** M20 A head-scarf folded diagonally and tied under the chin.

bac abbreviation of BACCALAUREATE or BACCARAT.

bacalao *noun* (also **bacalhau**) M16 **Spanish** (*bacal(l)ao*, Portuguese *bacalhau*). Codfish, especially dried or salted.

baccalaureate *noun* M17 **French** (*baccalauréat* or medieval Latin *baccalaureatus*, from *baccalaureus*, originally with reference to *bacca lauri* laurel berry). **1** M17 The university degree of bachelor. **2** L20 An examination intended to qualify successful candidates for higher education. **3** A religious service held for a graduating class.

■ *Bac* or *bachot*, the colloquial French abbreviations of *baccalauréat*, are also found.

baccarat *noun* (also **baccara**) M19 **French** (*baccara*, of unknown origin). A gambling card game, played between a banker and one punter, or several punters in turn, in which the best one- or two-card hand is that yielding the highest remainder when its total face value is divided by 10.

bach *noun* L19 **Welsh** ((dialect) literally, 'little'). Dear, beloved; little one; friend.

■ Chiefly vocative and often placed appositionally after personal names.

bachot abbreviation of BACCALAUREATE.

bacillus *noun* plural **bacilli** L19 **Late Latin** (= little rod, diminutive of *baculus* rod, stick). Any rod-shaped bacterium; *loosely* any pathogenic bacterium.

backfisch *noun* plural **backfische** L19 **German** (literally, 'fish for frying'). A girl in late adolescence, a teenage girl.

backsheesh variant of BAKSHEESH.

bacterium *noun* plural **bacteria** M19 **Modern Latin** (from Greek *baktērion* diminutive of *baktēria* staff, cane). Any of the very widely distributed group *Bacteria* of microscopic prokaryotic mainly single-celled organisms, many of which are symbiotic or pathogenic in animals and plants.

badigeon *noun* M18 **French** (of unknown origin). A composition used to fill up gaps in stone or wood.

badinage *noun & verb* M17 **French** (from *badiner* to joke, from *badin* fool from Provençal, from *badar* to gape, from Proto-Romance). **A** *noun* M17 Humorous banter or ridicule. **B** *verb* E19 Banter playfully.

badmash *noun* M19 **Urdu** (from Persian, from *bad* evil + Arabic *ma'āš* means of livelihood). In the Indian subcontinent: a rascal, a hooligan.

bagarre *noun* L19 **French**. A tumult; a scuffle, a brawl.

bagasse *noun* E19 **French** (from Spanish *bagazo*). The residue left after the extraction of juice from sugar cane or sugar beet.

bagatelle *noun* M17 **French** (from Italian *bagatella* perhaps diminutive of Latin *baca* berry, or from Italian *baga* baggage). **1** M17 A trifle, a thing of no value or importance; a negligible amount. **2** M18 A piece of verse or music in a light style. **3** E19 A game in which small balls are struck (usually by a mechanical striker operated by the player) toward numbered holes on a board with a semicircular end.

bagel *noun* (also **beigel**) E20 **Yiddish** (*beygel*). A usually hard ring-shaped roll of bread.

bagnio *noun* plural **bagnios** L16 **Italian** (*bagno* from Latin *balneum* bath). **1** L16 An oriental prison; slave quarters. Now only *historical*. **2** E17–E19 A bath, a bathhouse. **3** E17 A brothel.

baguette *noun* E18 **French** (from Italian *bacchetto* diminutive of *bacchio* from Latin *baculum* staff). **1** E18 *Architecture* A small molding of semicircular section, like an astragal. **2** E20 A gem, usually a diamond, cut in a long rectangular shape. **3** M20 A long narrow French loaf.

bahada variant of BAJADA.

bahut *noun* M19 **French**. An ornamental chest or cabinet.

baignoire *noun* M19 **French** (= bathtub). A box at a theater on the same level as the orchestra seats.

bain-marie *noun* plural **bains-marie** E18 **French** (translation of medieval Latin *balneum Mariae* translation of medieval Greek *kaminos Marias* furnace of Maria, a supposed Jewish alchemist). A vessel of hot water in which cooking pans and their contents are slowly heated; a double saucepan. Also, a dish prepared in this.

bajada *noun* (also **bahada**) M19 **Spanish** (= descent, slope). A broad slope of alluvial material at the foot of an escarpment.

baklava *noun* M17 **Turkish**. An originally eastern Mediterranean dessert made of thin pieces of flaky pastry, honey or syrup, and nuts.

baksheesh *noun* (also **backsheesh**) M18 **Persian** (ultimately from *bakšīš* from *bakšīdan* to give). In Eastern countries: a gratuity, a tip.

balafon *noun* L20 **African**. A West African musical instrument similar to a xylophone.

balalaika *noun* L18 **Russian** (of Tartar origin). A guitar-like musical instrument with a triangular body and from two to four strings, popular in Slavonic countries.

balancé *noun* L18 **French** (= balanced (sc. *pas* step)). *Dancing* A swaying step from one foot to the other.

bal costumé *noun phrase* plural **bals costumés** E19 **French**. A fancy dress ball.

baldachin *noun* (also **baldaquin**) M17 **Italian** (*baldacchino*, ultimately from *Baldacco* Italian form of *Baghdad*). A canopy supported on columns or fixed to a roof or wall, and placed over an altar, throne, or doorway.

■ When first introduced into English (L16), *baldacchino* denoted rich brocade of a type that had originally been made in Baghdad. It was later (M17) transferred to describe a canopy made out of this material, and in current usage the canopy can be of any material.

ballabile *noun* plural **ballabili** M19 **Italian** (from *ballare* to dance). A dance by the *corps de ballet* or by the chorus in an opera; a piece of music for this; any piece of instrumental music suggestive of a dance.

ballade *noun* LME **French** (from Provençal *balada* dance, song, or poem to dance to, from *balar* to dance). **A** *noun* **1** LME A poem (originally for singing with accompaniment) of one or more triplets of stanzas having 7, 8, or 10 lines, each usually ending with the same refrain line, and an envoy; more *generally*, a poem divided into stanzas of equal length, usually of 7 or 8 lines. Also *collectively*, poetry of this form. **2** M19 *Music* An extended, usually dramatic, piece usually for the piano.

ballerina *noun* plural **ballerinas** L18 **Italian** (feminine of *ballerino* dancing master, from *ballare* to dance). *Ballet* A female dancer, *especially* one who undertakes a leading role in classical ballet.

ballet *noun* M17 **French** (from Italian *balletto* diminutive of *ballo* ball). (A theatrical performance of) dancing and mime to music; a company performing this.

ballet blanc *noun phrase* M20 **French** (= white ballet). A ballet in which the female dancers wear long white tutus.

ballista *noun* plural **ballistae**, **ballistas** E16 **Latin** (ultimately from Greek *ballein* to throw). A large military engine used in antiquity for hurling stones and other missiles.

ballon *noun* M19 **French**. **1** M19 Elasticity and buoyancy in dancing; smooth passage from step to step. **2** M20 A spherical glass for brandy, a brandy balloon.

ballon d'essai *noun phrase* plural **ballons d'essai** L19 **French** (= trial balloon). An experiment to see how a new policy or project will be received; a tentative proposal.

ballonné *noun* L18 **French** (past participle of *ballonner* to swell or puff out, distend). A bouncing step in dancing.

bal masqué *noun phrase* plural **bals masqués** M18 **French**. A masked ball.

bal musette *noun phrase* plural **bals musettes** E20 **French**. In France: a popular dancehall (with an accordion band).

balsa *noun* E17 **Spanish** (= raft). **1** E17 A raft or fishing boat, used chiefly on the Pacific coasts of South America. **2** M19 A tropical American tree, *Ochroma pyramidale* (more fully *balsa tree*); its strong, very light wood, used for rafts, floats, etc. (more fully *balsa wood*).

balti *noun* L20 **Urdu** (*bālṭī* bucket). A type of Indian cuisine apparently originating in Northern Pakistan and served in metal pans.

bambino *noun* plural **bambini**, **bambinos** E18 **Italian** (diminutive of *bambo* silly). In Italy: a young child or baby; *specifically* an image of the infant Jesus in swaddling clothes.

banco *interjection* L18 **French** (from Italian). In baccarat, etc.: expressing a player's willingness to meet single-handedly the banker's whole stake. Cf. VA BANQUE.

bandar-log L19 **Hindustani** (*bāndar*, from Sanskrit *vānara* rhesus monkey + *log* people, from Sanskrit *loka*). The monkeys collectively; *figurative* a group of irresponsible chatterers.

bandeau *noun* plural **bandeaux** E18 **French** (from Old French *bandel* diminutive of *bande*). A band or strip of material, *especially* one used for binding a woman's hair.

banderilla *noun* plural **banderillas** L18 **Spanish** (diminutive of *bandera* banner). *Bullfighting* A decorated dart thrust into a bull's neck or shoulders during a bullfight.

banderillero *noun* plural **banderilleros** L18 **Spanish** (from BANDERILLA). *Bullfighting* A bullfighter who uses banderillas. Also called PEON.

banderole *noun* (also **banderol**; (especially in sense 2, earlier form) **bannerol**) M16 **French** (*ban(n)erole*, later *banderole*, from Italian *banderuola* diminutive of *bandiera* banner). **1** M16 A long narrow flag with a cleft end, flown from the masthead of a ship. **2** M16 A rectangular banner borne at the funerals of public figures and placed over the tomb. **3** L16 An ornamental streamer of the kind attached to a knight's lance. **4** E17 A ribbon-like scroll bearing a device or inscription.

bandobast variant of BUNDOBUST.

bandolero *noun* plural **bandoleros** M17 **Spanish**. A Spanish bandit.

bania *noun* L18 **Hindustani** (*baniyā* from Sanskrit *vāṇija*). A Hindu trader or merchant.

banian variant of BANYAN.

bannerol variant of BANDEROLE.

banquette *noun* E17 **French** (from Italian *banchetta* diminutive of *banca* bench, shelf). **1** E17 A raised step or way running along the inside of a rampart, at the bottom of a trench, etc., on which soldiers stand to fire at the enemy. **2** M19 A long upholstered seat along a wall.

banyan *noun* (also **banian**) L16 **Portuguese** (from Gujarati *vāṇiyo* man of the trading caste, from Sanskrit *vāṇija* merchant). **I 1** L16 A BANIA. **2** M17 An Indian broker or steward attached to a company or individual. **3** E18 In full *banyan shirt*, etc. A loose flannel shirt or jacket. **II 4** M17 In full *banyan tree*. An Indian fig tree, *Ficus benghalensis*, the branches of which root themselves over a wide area.

■ *Banyan* has tended this century to supersede the generally preferred earlier spelling *banian*. In sense 4 the word was originally applied by Europeans to a particular tree of the species growing in a port on the Persian Gulf, under which Hindu merchants had set up a shrine; in 1634 Sir Thomas Herbert wrote of 'A tree . . . named by us the Bannyan Tree, from their adorning and adoring it with ribbons and streamers of varicoloured Taffata' (*Travels* II (1638)). The tree is not known by this name in any Indian language.

banzai *interjection & adjective* L19 **Japanese** (= ten thousand years (of life to you)). **A** L19 *interjection* A form of acclamation used by the Japanese especially to their Emperor, a cheer used in battle, etc. **B** E20 *attributive* or as *adjective* (As if) shouting 'banzai'; uproarious; (of an attack by Japanese) reckless. *slang*.

banzuke *noun* L20 **Japanese**. The ranking list of sumo wrestlers.

baragouin *noun* E17 **French**. Gibberish; unintelligible jargon.

baraza *noun* L19 **Kiswahili**. In East Africa: a place of public audience or reception; a meeting, a reception.

barbette *noun* L18 **French** (from *barbe* beard + diminutive *-ette*). A platform in a fort or ship from which guns fire over a parapet, etc., and not through an embrasure.

barbotine *noun* M19 **French**. (Pottery ornamented with) a slip of kaolin clay.

barcarole *noun* (also **barcarolle**) L18 **French** (*barcarolle* from Venetian Italian *barcarola* related to *barcarolo* gondolier, from *barca* boat). A song sung by Venetian gondoliers; a piece of music in imitation of such songs or suggestive of the rocking motion of a boat.

barchan *noun* (also **barchane, barkhan, barkan**) L19 **Turkic** (*barkhan*). A shifting crescent-shaped sand dune, concave on the leeward side.

barège *noun & adjective* E19 **French** (from *Barèges* a village in southwest France). **A** *noun* E19 (A garment made of) a gauzelike fabric of silk and wool. **B** *adjective* M19 Made of barège.

barkan, barkhan variants of BARCHAN.

bar mitzvah *noun phrase* (also **Bar mitzvah**) M19 **Hebrew** (*bar miṣwāh* son of commandment). (A religious initiation ceremony for) a Jewish boy aged thirteen, regarded as liable to observe the religious precepts and eligible to take part in public worship. Cf. BAT MITZVAH.

barouche *noun* E19 **German** (dialect *Barutsche* from Italian *baroccio* (Spanish *barrocho*) two-wheeled, ultimately from Latin *birotus*, from *bi-* two + *rota* wheel). A four-wheeled horse-drawn carriage with a collapsible half-hood, a seat in front for the driver, and seats facing each other for passengers. Chiefly *historical*.

barre *noun* E20 **French**. **1** E20 *Music* (A finger used as) a CAPOTASTO. **2** M20 A waist-level horizontal bar to help dancers keep their balance during some exercises.

barré *adjective & noun* L19 **French** (past participle of *barrer* to bar). *Music* (A chord) played with strings stopped by a CAPOTASTO or finger.

barrera *noun* E20 **Spanish** (= barrier). *Bullfighting* (The row of seats nearest to) the barrier encircling a bullring.

barrette *noun* E20 **French** (diminutive of BARRE). A bar-shaped clip or ornament for a woman's or girl's hair.

barrio *noun* plural **barrios** M19 **Spanish** (perhaps from Arabic). A ward or quarter of a town or city in Spain and Spanish-speaking countries; a Spanish-speaking quarter of a town or city.

bas bleu *noun phrase* plural **bas bleus** L18 **French** (translation from English). A bluestocking; a serious-minded and learned woman.

bascule *noun* L17 **French** ((earlier *bacule*) = seesaw, from stem of *battre* to beat + *cul* buttocks). A lever apparatus of which one end is raised when the other is lowered.

basha, bashaw variants of PASHA.

basho *noun* plural **bashos** L20 **Japanese**. A sumo wrestling tournament.

basilica *noun* M16 **Latin** (branch I, literally, 'royal palace' from Greek *basilikē* noun use of feminine of *basilikos* royal, from *basileus* king; branch II from Greek *basilika* neuter plural of *basilikos*). **I** *singular* (pl. **basilicas**, (*rare*) [illegible]**e**) **1** M16 *History* A large oblong [illegible] or building, with double colonna[illegible] and a semicircular apse, used for courts of law and public assemblies. **2** M16 A building of this form used as a Christian church. Also, used as the title of certain churches granted privileges by the Pope. **II** *plural* **3** M17 *History* (**Basilica**) *The* 9th-century Byzantine legal code initiated by the emperor Basil I.

basmati *noun* M19 **Hindustani** (*bāsmatī* literally, 'fragrant'). A kind of rice with very long thin grains and a delicate fragrance. More fully *basmati rice*.

basse-taille *noun* L19 **French** (from *basse* feminine of *bas* low + *taille* cut). A technique of applying translucent enamels to metal reliefs so that the shade of the enamel is darkest where the relief is most deeply cut.

bassetto *noun* plural **bassettos** E18 **Italian** (diminutive of BASSO). A violoncello.

bassinet *noun* (also **bassinette**) M19 **French** (diminutive of *bassin* basin). A cradle or baby carriage, often made of wicker, with a curved hood.

■ A buttercup is called a bassinet in Normandy, and *bacinetz* occurs in a

1509 French list of vernacular flower names. In English too, *bassinet* was for a long time (L16–E18) used solely in a botanical context, with Lyte's 1578 herbal referring to the marsh marigold as the 'Brave Bassinet'; later herbalists recorded it as a dialect name for a geranium or various species of ranunculus.

basso *noun & adjective* plural **bassos, bassi** E18 **Italian** (= low, from Latin *bassus*). *Music* Bass.

basso buffo plural **bassi buffi, bassos buffos** E20 **Italian** (BASSO + *buffo* buffoon). *Music* A bass singer who takes comic parts in opera.

basso cantante plural **bassi cantanti** L19 **Italian** (BASSO + *cantant*[illegible] literally, 'singing'). *Music* (A sing[illegible]ith) a voice in the upper re[illegible]f the bass range.

basso continuo plural **ba**[illegible]**tinuos** E18 **Italian** (BASSO + CONT[illegible]). *Music* A figured bass, a thorou[illegible] bass.

basso ostinato plural **basso ostinatos** L19 **Italian** (BASSO + OSTINATO). *Music* A short passage usually in the bass, constantly repeated with varying melody and harmony, a ground bass.

basso profundo (occasionally **profondo**) plural **bassi profundi, bassos profundos** M19 **Italian** (BASSO + *profundo*, literally, 'deep'). *Music* (A singer with) a very deep and rich voice.

basso-relievo *noun* (also **basso-rilievo**) plural **basso-relievos** M17 **Italian** (*basso-rilievo*). (A sculpture, carving, etc., in) low relief; bas-relief.

basta *interjection* L16 **Italian**. Enough! No matter!

bastide *noun* E16 **Old French** (Provençal *bastida* (medieval Latin *bastida*) noun use of feminine past participle of *bastir* to build). **1** E16 *History* A fortified village or town. **2** E18 A country house in southern France.

basuco *noun* (also **basuko, bazuco, bazuko**) L20 **Colombian Spanish** (perhaps connected with Spanish *basura* waste; or with Spanish *bazucar* to shake violently). A cheap form of impure cocaine made from adulterated coca paste and highly addictive when smoked as a drug.

■ The explosive effect of *basuco* has led to an alternative suggestion for the etymology, linking it with the English word *bazooka*, adopted in Spanish and applied figuratively to the drug and then borrowed back into English in a slightly altered form. Other names for the drug, which first appeared in the English-speaking world in the mid-1980s, are *little devil* and *Suzuki*.

batardeau *noun* plural **batardeaux** M18 **French** (earlier *bastardeau* diminutive of Old French *bastard* of unknown origin). A cofferdam. Also, a wall built across the moat or ditch surrounding a fortification.

batata *noun* M16 **Spanish** (from Taino). Sweet potato.

bateau *noun* plural **bateaux** E18 **French** (= boat). A light riverboat, especially of a flat-bottomed kind used in Canada and southern Louisiana. Cf. BATEAU-MOUCHE.

■ *Bateau* is also used attributively as an alternative to 'boat' in *bateau neck, bateau-necked*, etc., used of a garment with shallow curved neckline running from shoulder to shoulder.

bateau-mouche plural **bateaux-mouches** E20 **French**. A riverboat that takes sightseers on the Seine in Paris.

bathos *noun* E18 **Greek** (= depth). **1** E18 *Rhetoric* Ludicrous descent from the elevated to the commonplace; anticlimax. **2** E19 A comedown; a performance absurdly unequal to the occasion.

■ First introduced (M17) with its original Greek meaning of 'depth, lowest phase, bottom', *bathos* is now rare or obsolete in this sense, which has been superseded by the two senses above. Alexander Pope was primarily responsible for sense 1 in *Peri Bathous: or the Art of Sinking in Poetry* (1727), a parody of the work by the ancient Greek rhetorician Longinus, *On the Sublime*.

batik *noun & adjective* L19 **Javanese** (literally, 'painted'). **A** L19 *noun* A method (originally used in Java) of making colored designs on textiles by waxing the parts not to be dyed; (a garment made of) a fabric dyed by this method. **B** E20 *attributive* or as *adjective* Executed or ornamented by this method.

batiste *noun & adjective* E19 **French** ((earlier *batiche*) perhaps from base of *battre* to beat). (Of) a fine light cotton or linen fabric like cambric.

bat mitzvah *noun phrase* (also **Bat mitzvah**) M20 **Hebrew** (*bat miṣwāh* daughter of commandment, after BAR MITZVAH). (A religious initiation ceremony for) a Jewish girl aged twelve years and one day, regarded as the age of religious maturity.

baton *noun* E16 **French** (*bâton* (earlier *baston*) = Provençal, Spanish *baston* Italian *bastone* from Proto-Romance, from late Latin *bastum* stick). **1** E16 A stick or staff used as a weapon. **b** L19 A police officer's cudgel, *especially* a relatively long one. **2** L16 A staff carried as symbol of office, *especially* that of a field marshal. **3** *Heraldry* M18 A narrow truncated bend. **4** *Music* L18 A conductor's wand; a drum major's stick. **5** M19 A long loaf or stick of bread. **6** E20 A short stick carried in a relay race and passed from one participant to the next.

■ Although *baton* or *batton* was used by Scots writers in the sixteenth century, the commoner spelling in England until the nineteenth century was *batoon*. *Baton* in the general sense 1 is now much less common than in its various specialized senses.

battement *noun* M19 **French** (= beating). *Dancing* Any of a number of beating leg movements. Cf. GRAND BATTEMENT, PETIT BATTEMENT.

batterie *noun* E18 **French**. **1** *Dancing* E18 A movement in which the feet or calves are beaten together during a leap. **2** L18 Abbreviation of BATTERIE DE CUISINE. **3** *Music* M20 Percussion instruments in an orchestra or band.

■ French *batterie* in its commoner senses (electrical or military) has been fully assimilated in English as *battery*, but it is retained in more specialist meanings, such as 'drum kit' (see sense 3).

batterie de cuisine *noun phrase* L18 **French** (= articles for cooking). Apparatus or utensils for preparing or serving a meal.

battue *noun* E19 **French** (noun use of feminine past participle of *battre* to beat). **1** E19 A driving of game toward the guns by beaters; a shooting party on this plan. **2** *transferred* **a** M19 A thorough search. **b** M19 A wholesale slaughter.

batture *noun* E19 **French**. **1** E19 A stretch of river shore, usually formed by deposition, between the natural embankment and the low-water mark. **2** E19 A sandbar in a river.

■ Sense 2 Canadian.

battuta *noun* E18 **Italian** (from *battere* to beat). *Music* The beating of time; a strong beat; the regular beat.

Bauhaus *noun* E20 **German** (*Bau* building + *Haus* house). (The principles of) a German school of architecture and design founded in 1919 by Walter Gropius and closed in 1933.

bavaroise *noun* (also **bavarois**) M19 **French** (noun use of feminine adjective *bavaroise* Bavarian). A dessert containing gelatin and whipped cream, served cold.

bayadère *noun* L16 **French** (from Portuguese *bailadeira*, from *bailar* to dance, related to medieval Latin *ballare* to dance). **1** L16 A Hindu dancing girl (especially at a southern Indian temple). **2** M19 A striped textile fabric.

bayou *noun* M18 **American French** (from Choctaw *bayuk*). A marshy offshoot of a river, lake, etc.

bazaar *noun* L16 **Italian** (*bazarro* from Turkish from Persian *bāzār* market). **1** L16 An oriental market. **2** E19 A large shop, or arcade of shops, selling ornamental items, bric-à-brac, etc. **3** E19 A sale of miscellaneous new or secondhand goods in aid of charity.

bazuco, bazuko variants of BASUCO.

béarnaise *adjective* (also **Béarnaise**) L19 **French** (feminine of *béarnais* of Béarn, a region of southwest France). A rich white sauce flavored with tarragon. In full, *béarnaise sauce* (also *sauce béarnaise*).

beau *noun* plural **beaux, beaus** L17 **French** (noun use of adjective, ultimately from Latin *bellus* fine, beautiful). **1** L17 A fashionable man, a ladies' man; a fop, a dandy. **2** E18 A lady's male companion, a suitor; a boyfriend, a lover.

beau geste *noun phrase* plural **beaux gestes** E20 **French** (= splendid gesture). A display of magnanimity; a generous act.

beau ideal *noun phrase* E19 **French** (*beau idéal* = ideal beauty). One's highest or ideal type of excellence or beauty; the perfect model.

■ Now often misunderstood to mean 'beautiful ideal'.

Beaujolais nouveau L20 **French** (= new Beaujolais). A light, usually red, burgundy wine of the latest vintage produced in the Beaujolais district of France.

beau monde *noun phrase* L17 **French** (= fine world). (The world of) fashionable society.

beau rôle *noun phrase* plural **beaux rôles** L19 **French** (= fine role). A fine acting part; the leading part.

beau sabreur *noun phrase* plural **beaux sabreurs** M19 **French** (= fine (or handsome) swordsman). A gallant warrior, a handsome or dashing adventurer.

■ Originally a sobriquet of Joachim Murat (1767–1815), French cavalry officer and brother-in-law of Napoleon.

beauté du diable *noun phrase* M19 **French** (= devil's beauty). Superficial attractiveness; captivating charm.

beaux arts *noun & adjective phrase* (also **beaux-arts**) E19 **French** (*beaux-arts*). **A** *noun phrase plural* E19 Fine arts. Also *elliptical*, the *École des Beaux-Arts* in Paris. **B** *adjective phrase* E20 Of or pertaining to the classical decorative style maintained by the *École des Beaux-Arts* especially in the nineteenth century.

beaux esprits plural of BEL ESPRIT.

beaux gestes plural of BEAU GESTE.

beaux yeux *noun phrase* E19 **French**. Beautiful eyes; admiring glances; favorable regard.

bebung *noun* L19 **German** (= trembling). *Music* A pulsating or trembling effect given to a sustained note; *specifically* such an effect produced on the clavichord by rocking the fingertip.

beccafico *noun* plural **beccaficos** E17 **Italian** (from *beccare* to peck + *fico* fig). Any of a number of small birds (warblers, etc.) esteemed as a delicacy in the Mediterranean region.

béchamel *noun* M18 **French**. *Cooking* A fine savory white sauce, frequently made with added cream or milk. More fully *béchamel sauce*.

■ Called after the Marquis de *Béchamel*, steward of Louis XIV.

bêche-de-mer *noun* plural **bêches-de-mer** L18 **pseudo-French** (from Portuguese *bicho do mar*, literally, 'worm of the sea'). **1** L18 A sea cucumber eaten as a Chinese delicacy. **2** L19 An English-based pidgin used formerly as a trade language and contact vernacular in the southwest Pacific. Also *bêche-de-mer English* or *beach-la-mar*.

Bedouin *noun & adjective* (also **Beduin, beduin**) LME **Old French** (*beduin* (modern *bédouin*) ultimately (through medieval Latin *beduini* plural) from Arabic *badawī*, plural *badawīn* (from *badw* desert) nomadic desert tribes). **A** *noun* **1** LME An Arab of the desert. **2** M19 A person living a nomadic life. **B** *adjective* M19 Of the desert or Bedouins; nomadic, wandering.

Bedu *noun & adjective* plural of noun same E20 **Arabic** (*badw*). (Of) a Bedouin; *collective* (of) Bedouins.

beebee variant of BIBI.

Beerenauslese *noun* (also **beerenauslese**) plural **Beerenauslesen**, **Beerenausleses** E20 **German** (from *Beeren* berries, grapes + AUSLESE). A white wine made (especially in Germany) from selected individual grapes picked later than the general harvest.

béguin *noun* E20 **French**. An infatuation, a fancy.

■ *Avoir le béguin de* (or *pour*) is 'to have a crush on' in colloquial French.

beguine *noun 1* (also **béguine**) LME **Old and Modern French** (*béguine* (Middle Dutch, Middle High German *begīne*), medieval Latin *Beguina*, perhaps ultimately from Middle Dutch verb meaning 'to mutter (prayers)'). A member of a lay sisterhood in the Low Countries, formed in the twelfth century and not bound by vows.

beguine *noun 2* E20 **American French** (from French BÉGUIN). (The distinctive rhythm of) a dance of West Indian origin.

begum *noun* (also (as title) **Begum**) M17 **Urdu** (*begam* from Early Turkic *begim*, from *beg* bey + 1st person singular possessive suffix *-im*). In the Indian subcontinent: a Muslim noblewoman or lady of high rank. Also (**Begum**), a title given to a married Muslim woman (= Mrs).

beignet *noun* M19 **French**. A fritter; *specifically* a square of fried dough sprinkled with powdered sugar and eaten hot. Usually in *plural*.

bel canto *noun phrase* L19 **Italian** (= fine song). (A style of) singing characterized by full rich broad tone, legato phrasing, and accomplished technique.

bel esprit *noun phrase* plural **beaux esprits** M17 **French** (= fine mind). A brilliant or witty person.

belle *noun* E17 **French** (feminine of *bel*, BEAU, from Latin *bella* feminine of *bellus* beautiful). A beautiful woman, *especially* the outstanding beauty of a place, time, etc.

belle époque *noun phrase* (also **belle epoque**, **Belle Epoque**) plural **belles époques** M20 **French** (= fine period). A period of settled comfort and prosperity.

■ Originally and specifically used of the period in France from the late nineteenth century to the war of 1914–18.

belle laide *noun phrase* (also **belle-laide**) plural **belles laides** E20 **French** (from feminine adjectives *belle* beautiful + *laide* ugly). An attractive though ugly woman. Cf. JOLIE LAIDE.

belles-lettres *noun plural* (occasionally treated as *singular*) M17 **French** (literally, 'fine letters'). Studies or writings of a purely literary character, *especially* essays, criticism, etc. Originally more widely, literature generally, the humanities.

belote *noun* (also **belotte**) M20 **French**. A card game like pinochle, played with a 32-card deck, popular in France.

■ Perhaps from F. Belot, a Frenchman said to have developed the game.

bema *noun* plural **bemas**, **bemata** L17 **Greek** (*bēma* a step, a raised place to speak from). **1** L17 *Christian Church* The altar part or sanctuary in ancient and Orthodox churches; the chancel. **2** E19 *Greek Antiquities* The platform from which Athenian orators spoke.

benedicite *interjection & noun* ME **Latin** (2nd person plural imperative of *benedicere* to wish well to, bless, from *bene* well + *dicere* to say). **A** *interjection* **1** ME Expressing a wish: God bless you! **2** ME Expression of astonishment: Good gracious! **B** *noun* **1** ME An invocation of a blessing; *especially* a grace at table. **2** M17 *Christian Church the Benedicite*, the canticle beginning *Benedicite, omnia opera* 'O all ye works [of the Lord], bless ye [the Lord]', known also as "The Song of the Three Children," which is an alternative to the *Te Deum* at matins in the *Book of Common Prayer*.

bene esse *noun phrase* E17 **Modern Latin.** Well-being, welfare, especially opposed to ESSE.

benthos *noun* L19 **Greek** (= depth of the sea). The flora and fauna of the bottom of the sea (or of a lake).

ben trovato *adjective phrase* L19 **Italian** (literally, 'well found'). Of a story, etc.: happily invented; appropriate though untrue.

■ *Se non è vero, è molto ben trovato* 'if it is not true, it is a happy invention' was apparently a well-known saying in sixteenth-century Italy, being found for example in the writings of Giordano Bruno. Smollett used the phrase in 1771 in the form *ben trovata.*

berceau *noun* plural **berceaux** L17 **French** (literally, 'cradle'). An arbor; a shaded or leafy walk.

berceuse *noun* L19 **French** (from *bercer* to rock + feminine agent-suffix *-euse*). *Music* A lullaby; an instrumental piece with a gently rocking rhythm.

beret *noun* E19 **French** (*béret* from southwest French dialect and Old Provençal *berret*). A round felt or cloth cap that lies flat on the head, covering it closely (as traditionally worn by Basque peasantry); such a cap forming part of military uniform.

beretta variant of BIRETTA.

berg *noun* E19 **Afrikaans** (from Dutch (= Old English *beorg* barrow, hill)). A mountain; a mountain range.

bergère *noun* M18 **French** (= shepherdess). A long-seated upholstered armchair fashionable in the eighteenth century. Also, a chair with canework seat, back, and sides.

bergerette *noun* LME **French** (from *berger* shepherd). A pastoral or rustic song about shepherds, for dancing to.

bergschrund *noun* M19 **German** (from *Berg* mountain + *schrund* cleft). A crevasse or gap at the junction of a glacier or snowfield with a steep upper slope.

bersaglieri *noun plural* M19 **Italian** (from *bersaglio* target). Highly trained Italian infantry, originally riflemen or sharpshooters.

bertillonage *noun* L19 **French** (*bertillonnage*). The system of identification of criminals by anthropometric measurements, etc.

■ The system is named after its inventor, the French criminologist Alphonse Bertillon (1853–1914), who introduced it in 1882. It was soon supplemented, and in the early years of the twentieth century superseded, by fingerprinting.

beta *noun* ME **Latin** (from Greek). **1** ME The second letter (*B, β*) of the Greek alphabet. **2** L17 Denoting the second in a numerical sequence. **3** *attributive Science* L19 (Frequently written β); as in *Astronomy* (preceding the genitive of the Latin name of the constellation) designating the second brightest star in a constellation. **4** E20 **Brit.** A second-class mark in an examination, etc.

■ Like *alpha, beta* has a number of specialist applications in scientific terminology and often appears in the same context to designate the entity secondary to the *alpha* one.

betel *noun* M16 **Portuguese** (from Malayalam *verrila*). The leaf of a climbing evergreen shrub, *Piper betle,* which is chewed in the East with acreca nut parings and a little lime. Also (more fully *betel pepper*), the plant itself.

bête noire *noun phrase* plural **bêtes noires** M19 **French** (literally, 'black beast'). The bane of someone's life; an insufferable person or thing; an object of strong or obsessive aversion.

bethel *noun* E17 **Hebrew** (*bēt, ēl* from *bēt* house of + *'ēl* god). **1** E17 A place where God is worshiped. **2** E19 *transferred* A Nonconformist chapel; a seamen's church.

bêtise *noun* (also **betise**) E19 **French** (= stupidity, from *bête* foolish, from Old French *beste* beast). An ill-judged or ill-timed remark or action; a piece of folly.

beur *noun* L20 **French**. In France: a child of immigrant parents, born in France.

beurre manié *noun phrase* M20 **French** (= handled butter). *Cooking* A mixture of flour and butter used for thickening sauces or soups.

beurre noir *noun phrase* M19 **French** (= dark butter). *Cooking* A sauce made by heating butter until it is brown, usually mixing it with vinegar.

bévue *noun* L17 **French**. A blunder.

bey *noun* (also (as title) **Bey**) L16 **Turkish** (modern form of *beg* governor). The governor of a district or province in the Ottoman Empire. Also (**Bey** following name) formerly used in Turkey and Egypt as a courtesy title.

bezesteen *noun* M17 **Turkish** ((perhaps through French or Italian, from Turkish) *bezesten* (now *bedesten*) covered market for fine cloth and valuables, from Persian *bazistān*, from *baz* (Turkish *bez*) from Arabic *bazz* cloth + suffix of place *-istān*). An exchange, bazaar, or marketplace in the Middle East.

bhajan *noun* E20 **Sanskrit** (*bhajana*). *Hinduism* A devotional song.

bhaji *noun* L20 **Hindi** (*bhāji* fried vegetables from Sanskrit *bhrajj* to fry). In Indian cooking, a fritter, generally made with onions, but also with other vegetables.

bhakta *noun* E19 **Sanskrit**. *Hinduism* A religious devotee.

bhakti *noun* M19 **Sanskrit**. *Hinduism* Religious devotion or piety as a means of salvation.

bhang *noun* (also **bang**) L16 **Persian and Urdu** (*bang* (through Portuguese *bangue*), later assimilated to Hindustani *bhāṅ* from Sanskrit *bhaṅg*). A preparation of the cannabis or Indian hemp plant (*Cannabis sativa*) used as an intoxicating or hallucinogenic drug or for medicinal purposes.

bhangra *noun* M20 **Panjabi** (*bhāngrā*). **1** M20 A type of Punjabi folk dance for men associated with the harvest. **2** L20 A style of popular (especially dance) music combining Punjabi folk music with rock and roll or disco music.

■ In Britain *bhangra* (also known as *bhangra beat*) originated in the Asian communities in the 1980s, but by the end of the decade had won a wider following.

bhikkhu *noun* (also **bhikku**) M19 **Pali** (*bhikkhu* from as BHIKSHU). A Buddhist mendicant or religious devotee.

bhikshu *noun* plural **bhikshus**, same E19 **Sanskrit** (*bhikṣu* beggar, from *bhikṣ* beg). A brahminical or Buddhist mendicant or religious devotee. Cf. BHIKKHU.

bianco sopra bianco *noun phrase* L19 **Italian** (literally, 'white upon white'). A form of white decoration upon white porcelain.

■ Earlier in English (M19) in the elliptical form *sopra bianco*.

bibelot *noun* L19 **French** (from reduplication of *bel* beautiful). A small curio or artistic trinket.

biberon *noun* M19 **French**. A drinking vessel with elongated spout, formerly used by travelers, invalids, and children.

bibi *noun* (also **beebee**) E19 **Urdu** (*bībī* from Persian). In the Indian subcontinent: a mistress of a household; a non-European female consort.

bibliotheca *noun* E18 **Latin** (from Greek *bibliothēkē* library, from *biblion* book + *thēkē* repository). A collection of books or treatises; a library; a bibliographer's catalog.

■ Following St. Jerome, *bibliotheca* was used in both medieval Latin and Old English to mean 'the Bible'. In Anglo-Latin it occurs interchangeably with *biblia* in an eleventh-century catalog of the library of Lindisfarne, but by time of the compilation of the thirteenth-century Durham catalog only *biblia* appears. By the end of that century the Middle English *bibul* and its many variants, from which Modern English *bible* derives, had replaced *bibliotheca* in the vernacular. The modern reintroduction into English of *bibliotheca* in a bibliographical sense is thus entirely separate from the earlier biblical sense and relies on learned Latin usage. *Bibliotheca annua* (1700–1704), an annual catalog of English and Latin books published in England, was an early example. Since the nineteenth century *bibliotheca* has been used in titles of series (e.g., *Bryophytorum bibliotheca*; *Bibliotheca Americana Vetustissima*) or individual bibliographies (e.g., *Bibliotheca arcana* (1885), a catalog of banned erotica; *Bibliotheca chemica* (1906), a catalog of alchemical works).

bibliothèque *noun* M16 **French** (from as BIBLIOTHECA). A library.

■ Formerly naturalized, but now treated as French.

bidet *noun* M17 **French** (from earlier sense 'pony', from *bider* to trot, of unknown origin). **1** M17 A small horse. *archaic.* **2** L18 A shallow oval basin on a low stand used for washing especially the genital area.

■ The evolution of sense 2 from sense 1 is explained in Grose's definition of *bidet* in his *Dictionary of the Vulgar Tongue* (1785): "commonly pronounced biddy, a kind of tub, contrived for ladies to wash themselves, for which purpose they bestride it like a little French poney, . . . called in France bidets."

bidon *noun* M19 **French**. A container for liquids; a gas or oil can, etc.

bidonville *noun* M20 **French** (from BIDON + *ville* town). A shantytown built of oil drums, etc., *especially* a slum on the outskirts of a French or North African city.

bien entendu *adverb phrase* M19 **French** (from *bien* well + *entendu* past participle of *entendre* to hear, understand). Of course; that goes without saying.

bien-être *noun* M19 **French** (from *bien* well + *être* to be). A state of well-being.

biennale *noun* M20 **Italian** (from Latin *biennis* of two years). A large art exhibition or music festival, especially one held every two years.

■ Originally a specific festival, the Biennale, held biennially in Venice, Italy.

biennium *noun* plural **bienniums**, **biennia** E20 **Latin** (from as *bi-* two + *annus* year). A period of two years.

bien pensant *adjective & noun phrase* Also **bien-pensant** E20 **French** (*bien* well, *pensant* present participle of *penser* to think). (A person who is) right-thinking.

■ Often with a derogatory implication of timorous or mindless compliance with current intellectual or moral fashion.

bienséance *noun* L17 **French** (from *bien* well + *séant*, from *seoir* to befit). Decorum.

bierhaus *noun* plural **bierhäuser** M20 **German** (from *Bier* beer + *Haus* house). In a German-speaking country: a tavern or alehouse.

Bierstube, *noun* plural **Bierstuben**, **Bierstubes** E20 **German** (from *Bier* beer + *Stube* room). A German tavern, taproom, or bar. Cf. WEINSTUBE.

bigarade *noun* E18 **French** (from Provençal *bigarrado*). The Spanish bitter orange.

bigarreau *noun* plural **bigarreaus**, **bigareaux** E17 **French** (from *bigarré* variegated). A variety of sweet cherry, usually heart-shaped and with firm flesh. In full *bigarreau cherry*.

bijou *noun & adjective* M17 **French** (from Breton *bizoù* finger ring, from *biz* finger). **A** *noun* M17 plural **bijoux**. A jewel, a trinket. **B** *adjective* M19 Small and elegant.

bijouterie *noun* E19 **French**. Jewelry, trinkets, etc.

Bildungsroman *noun* plural **Bildungsromane** E20 **German** (from *Bildung* education + *Roman* novel). A novel dealing with one person's formative years or spiritual education.

billabong *noun* M19 **Aboriginal** (*Billibang* Bell River, from *billa* water + *bang* channel dry except after rain). In Australia: a branch of a river, forming a blind channel, backwater, or stagnant pool.

billet-doux *noun* plural **billets-doux** L17 **French** (literally, 'sweet note'). A love letter.

■ Now chiefly jocular.

biltong *noun* E19 **Afrikaans** (from Dutch *bil* buttock + *tong* tongue). In South Africa: lean meat cut into strips and dried.

bimbo *noun* plural **bimbos, bimboes** E20 **Italian** (= small child, baby). **1** E20 A man, *especially* a young and foolish one. **2** E20 A young woman, *especially* one who is sexually attractive but empty-headed.

■ Now used in a slang and almost always derogatory sense, *bimbo* was originally a direct borrowing from Italian. P. G. Wodehouse used it in sense 1, but it was already current in the 1920s with the sense of a pretty but brainless tart. *Bimbo* was revived in the 1980s media to designate a young woman who has an affair with a rich or famous man and then sells the "revelations" to the popular press. The word has also spawned a number of derivatives: *bimbette* (a teenage bimbo), *bimboy* (a male bimbo), *bimboland*, etc.

binghi *noun* M19 **Aboriginal**. An Aborigine.

■ Originally a neutral word (R. Dawson in *Present State of Australia* (1831) mentions having been greeted by Aborigines as "bingeye, or brother"), *binghi* has become an Australian slang term and usually derogatory.

bint *noun* M19 **Arabic** (= daughter, girl). A girl, a woman; (formerly) a girlfriend.

■ Mainly servicemen's slang, used by personnel stationed in Egypt and elsewhere in the Middle East during the two world wars; usually derogatory.

biretta *noun* (also **beretta, birretta**) L16 **Italian** (*berretta* or Spanish *birreta*, feminine diminutives corresponding to Old Provençal *berret* beret, based on late Latin *birrus, birettum* hooded cape or cloak, perhaps of Celtic origin). A square cap worn by Roman Catholic ecclesiastics (black by priests, purple by bishops, red by cardinals) or by other clergymen.

biriani variant of BIRYANI.

birretta variant of BIRETTA.

biryani *noun* (also **biriani** and other variants) M20 **Urdu** (from Persian *biryānī*, from *biriyān* fried, grilled). A dish of the Indian subcontinent consisting of spiced meat or vegetables and cooked rice.

bis *adverb* E17 **French and Italian** (from Latin *bis* twice). Encore; again; twice; *specifically* as a direction in a musical score indicating that a passage is to be repeated.

bismillah *interjection & noun* L18 **Arabic** (*bi-smi-llāh(i)*, the first word of the Koran). (The exclamation) in the name of God: used by Muslims at the beginning of any undertaking.

bisque *noun 1* M17 **French** (of unknown origin). In various games, especially tennis, croquet, and golf, (the allowing of) a point or stroke to be scored or taken when desired as a handicapping advantage.

bisque *noun 2* M17 **French** (from Old French *bescuit, besquit*, ultimately from Latin *bis* twice + *coctus* past participle of *coquere* to cook). A variety of unglazed white porcelain used for statuettes, etc. Also porcelain that has undergone firing but no other treatment; biscuit.

bisque *noun 3* (also **bisk**) M17 **French** (= crayfish soup). A rich soup usually made from shellfish but also from birds, etc.

bister *noun* (also **bistre**) E18 **French** (of unknown origin). (The color of) a brown pigment prepared from soot.

bistro *noun* (also **bistrot**) plural **bistros** E20 **French**. A small wine bar or restaurant.

bivouac *noun & verb* E18 **French** (probably from Swiss German *Bîwacht*, literally, 'extra watch'). **A** *noun* E18 Originally, a night watch by a whole army. Later, a temporary encampment, usually for the night, without tents; the place of such an encampment. **B** *intransitive & intransitive verb* E19 in *pass*. Inflected **bivouack**. Remain in the open air (especially during the night) without tents, etc.

■ The Swiss word is said to have been used in Aargau and Zürich to denote a patrol of citizens to assist the ordinary town watch.

bizarre *adjective & noun* M17 **French** (from Italian *bizzarro* angry, of unknown origin. Cf. Spanish and Portuguese *bizarro* handsome, brave). **A** *adjective* **1** M17 Eccentric, fantastic, grotesque. **2** M18 Designating variegated forms of garden flowers, as carnations, tulips, etc. **B** *noun* **1** L18 A bizarre carnation, tulip, etc. **2** M19 *absolutely* The bizarre quality of things; bizarre things.

blague *noun* M19 **French**. Humbug, claptrap.

blagueur *noun* L19 **French** (from BLAGUE). A pretentious talker; a joker, a teller of tall stories.

blanc *noun* M18 **French** (= white). **1** M18 White paint, especially for the face. Now *archaic* or *historical*. **2** M19 A type of light-colored stock or gravy.

blancbec *noun* M19 **French** (literally, 'white beak'). A raw youngster, a greenhorn.

blanc de blanc *noun phrase* M20 **French**. A (usually sparkling) white wine made from white grapes only.

blanc de chine *noun phrase* L19 **French**. A white glazed Chinese porcelain, especially of the Ming period. Also called Dehua after its place of origin.

blanc de perle *adjective phrase* L19 **French**. Pearl-white.

blanc fixe *noun phrase* M19 **French**. Barium sulfate, especially as used in paints.

blancmange *noun* (also (earlier) **blancmanger**) LME **Old French** (*blanc mangier* (modern *blancmanger*), from *blanc* white + *mang(i)er* food, noun use of *mang(i)er* to eat). **1** LME–L15 A dish of white meat or fish in a cream sauce. **2** M16 An opaque jelly made with isinglass or gelatin and milk or (now usually) cornstarch and milk, often flavored and sweetened.

■ The terminal 'r' was dropped in the eighteenth century.

blanquette *noun* M18 **French** (from Old French *blanchet* from *blanc*, *blanche* white). A dish of light meat, especially veal, cooked in a white sauce.

blasé *adjective* E19 **French**. Cloyed with or tired of pleasure; bored or unimpressed by things from having seen or experienced them too often.

bled *noun* M20 **French** (from colloquial (Algerian) Arabic, corresponding to classical Arabic *balad* vast stretch of country, *bilād* land, country). In northwest Africa: uncultivated land behind a fertile populated area.

bleu-du-roi *noun & adjective* (also **bleu-de-roi**) M19 **French** (= king's blue). (Of) the ultramarine blue of Sèvres porcelain.

blin *noun* plural **blini**, **bliny**, **blinis** L19 **Russian**. A kind of pancake, frequently stuffed. Cf. BLINTZE.

blintze *noun* E20 **Yiddish** (*blintse* from Russian *blinets* diminutive of *blin*). A BLIN.

blitzkrieg *noun* (also **Blitzkrieg**) M20 **German** (from *Blitz* lightning + *Krieg* war). A violent campaign intended to bring about speedy victory.

■ Used specifically of the German military campaigns in World War II, *Blitzkrieg* is usually found in the abbreviated form *Blitz* with reference to the Luftwaffe's bombardment of British cities. Both *blitzkrieg* and *blitz* are in general metaphorical use.

bloc *noun* E20 **French** (= block, from Middle Dutch *blok*, Middle and Modern Low German *block*, of unknown origin). A combination of nation-states, parties, groups, or people, formed to promote a particular interest.

blond *adjective & noun* (also **blonde**) L15 **Old and Modern French** (from medieval Latin *blundus*, *blondus* yellow, perhaps of Germanic origin). **A** *adjective* L15 (Especially of the hair) of a light golden-brown color, flaxen, fair; (of the complexion) light-colored with fair hair. **B** *noun* M18 A person (especially a woman) with blond hair and complexion.

■ The feminine form of the adjective *blonde* was introduced from French in the seventeenth century, but the masculine/feminine distinction is often not observed in English usage, with *blonde* being used of both men and women.

blouson *noun* E20 **French**. A short jacket fitting loosely on the body like a blouse.

blutwurst *noun* M19 **German** (from *Blut* blood + *Wurst* sausage). (A) blood sausage.

bocage *noun* L16 **French**. **1** L16 Wooded country interspersed with pasture (in France); a thicket, a wood. **2** *Ceramics* E20 (A, the) representation of silvan scenery (especially a leafy tree stump or flowery arbor) as a decorative element but also as a support for a figure during firing. Frequently *attributive*.

boccaro *noun* (also **bucaro**, **buccaro**) plural **boccaros** L19 **Spanish** (*búcaro* from Portuguese *púcaro* clay cup, ultimately from Latin *poculum* cup). A scented red unglazed earthenware of a type originally made in Mexico and imitated in Spain and Portugal.

bodega *noun* M19 **Spanish** (from Latin *apotheca* from Greek *apothēkē* storehouse; cf. BOUTIQUE). (Originally in Spain) a shop selling wine.

bodegón *noun* plural **bodegones** M19 **Spanish** (from BODEGA, as originally representing a bodega scene). A Spanish picture representing still life or a genre subject.

Boer *noun & adjective* (also **boer**) M19 **Dutch** (*boer* farmer). **A** *noun* M19 A South African of Dutch descent, an Afrikaner; *History* an early Dutch inhabitant of the Cape. **B** *attributive* or as *adjective* Of, made by, or typical of Boers.

boerewors *noun* M20 **Afrikaans** (from *boer* farmer + wors *sausage*). (A) coarse sausage made with beef and pork.

bœuf *noun* E20 **French** (= beef). *Cooking* Used in the names of various beef dishes.

bœuf bourguignon *noun phrase* E20 **French** (= beef of Burgundy). *Cooking* A casserole of beef cooked slowly in red wine.

bois brûlé *noun phrase* plural **bois brûlés** E19 **French** (= burnt wood). In North America: a half-breed, especially one of French and American Indian descent.

boiserie *noun* M19 **French**. Wainscoting, wooden paneling.

boîte *noun* E20 **French** (= box). A small (French) restaurant or nightclub.

bolas *noun singular* (with plural **bolases**) or *plural* (also *singular* **bola**) E19 **Spanish and Portuguese** (plural of *bola* ball). A missile (chiefly South American) consisting of balls connected by a strong cord, which is thrown to entangle the legs of a quarry.

bolero *noun* plural **boleros** L18 **Spanish**. **1** L18 A lively Spanish dance; a piece of music for this dance. **2** L19 A short jacket just reaching the waist, worn by men in Spain; a woman's short open jacket, with or without sleeves.

boletus *noun* (also Anglicized as **bolet**, **bolete**) E16 **Latin** (*boletus* from Greek *bōlitēs*, perhaps from *bōlos* lump). A mushroom or toadstool of the large genus *Boletus*, having the undersurface of the cap full of pores.

Bolshevik *noun & adjective* (also **bolshevik**) E20 **Russian** (*bol'shevik* = member of the majority, from *bol'she* greater, from *bol'shoĭ* big). **A** *noun* **1** E20 *History* A member of the majority faction of the Russian Social-Democratic Party, which in 1903 favored extreme measures; an advocate of proletarian dictatorship in Russia by soviets; a Russian Communist. **2** E20 *general* A socialist revolutionary. **B** *adjective* E20 Of or pertaining to Bolsheviks or Bolshevism.

bolson *noun* M19 **Spanish** (*bolsón* augmentative of *bolsa* purse). A basin-shaped depression surrounded by mountains, especially in the southern United States and Mexico.

■ Originally United States; cf. Bolsón de Mapimí, the name of a high desert in Mexico.

bolus *noun* M16 **Late Latin** (from Greek *bōlos* clod, lump of earth). **1** M16 A large pill of medicine. Often *contemptuous* or *archaic* except in *Veterinary Medicine*. **2** L18 A small rounded mass of anything, especially of masticated food at the moment of swallowing. **3** M20 *Medicine* A single dose of a pharmaceutical preparation given intravenously.

boma *noun* L19 **Kiswahili**. In East Africa: a defensible enclosure, especially for animals; hence, a police or military post; a magistrate's office.

bombachas *noun plural* M20 **South American Spanish** (from *bombacho* loose-fitting, wide). Baggy pants worn in some South American countries.

bombe *noun* L19 **French** (= bomb). A conical or cup-shaped confection, frequently frozen.

bombé *adjective* E20 **French** (past participle of *bomber* to swell out). Especially of furniture: rounded, convex.

bombilla *noun* M19 **American Spanish** (diminutive of Spanish *bomba* strainer). A tube with a strainer at the end, from which maté is drunk in South America.

bombora *noun* M20 **Aboriginal**. In Australia and New Zealand: a dangerous stretch of water where waves break over a submerged reef.

bon *adjective* L16 **French** (= good (masculine; cf. BONNE)). Good.

■ In various phrases used in English (see entries below).

bona fide *adverb & adjective phrase* M16 **Latin** (= with good faith (ablative of next)). (Acting or done) in good faith; sincere(ly), genuine(ly).

bona fides *noun phrase* L18 **Latin** (= good faith). **1** L18 Good faith, freedom from intent to deceive. **2** M20 (erroneously treated as plural) Guarantees of good faith, credentials.

bonanza *noun & adjective* E19 **Spanish** (= fair weather, prosperity, from Latin *bonus* good). **A** *noun* E19 A run of good luck, an unexpected success; prosperity; a source of great wealth or good fortune. **B** *adjective* L19 Greatly prospering or productive.

■ Originally used among miners for 'a rich find' or 'lucky strike'.

bon appétit *interjection* M19 **French**. Good appetite!

■ Used as a salutation to people about to eat.

bonbon *noun* (also **bon-bon**) L18 **French** (literally, 'good-good'). A piece of confectionery, a candy, *especially* with a chocolate or fondant coating.

bonbonnière *noun* E19 **French**. A fancy box for holding candies.

bond *noun* (also **Bond**) L19 **Afrikaans** (from Dutch (= German *Bund*), from *binden* bind). In South Africa: an Afrikaner league or association, especially the extreme nationalist *Broederbond*.

bondieuserie *noun* M20 **French** (from *bon* good + *Dieu* God). A church ornament or devotional object, *especially* one of little artistic merit; such objects collectively.

■ The French journalist and novelist Jules Vallès (1832–85) is credited with the invention of the term.

bon enfant *noun phrase* M19 **French** (literally, 'good child'). An agreeable companion.

bongo *noun* plural **bongo(e)s** E20 **American Spanish** (*bongó*). *Either of a pair of small drums, usually held between the knees and played with the fingers. Also bongo drum(s).*

bon gré mal gré *adverb phrase* E19 **French** (literally, 'good will, bad will'). (Whether) willingly or unwillingly.

bonheur du jour *noun phrase* plural **bonheurs du jour** L19 **French** (literally, 'happiness of the day'). A small writing table, usually fitted to hold toilet accessories, popular in eighteenth-century France.

bonhomie *noun* (also formerly written **bonhommie**) L18 **French** (from *bonhomme* good man, from medieval Latin *bonus homo* + suffix *-ie*). Good-natured friendliness, geniality.

bonito *noun* plural **bonitos** (also **boneta**) L16 **Spanish**. Any of various striped tuna, especially *Sarda sarda* of the Atlantic and Mediterranean.

bonjour *interjection* L16 **French**. Good day! Hello!

■ Used as a general greeting.

bon mot *noun phrase* plural **bons mots** M18 **French** (literally, 'good word'). A witty remark, a clever saying.

bonne *adjective & noun* E16 **French** (feminine of BON). **A** *adjective* E16 Good. **B** *noun* L18 A (French) nursemaid or personal servant.

■ Adjective use has long been restricted to certain phrases adopted from French (see below) and noun use too is now rare.

bonne bouche *noun phrase* (also **bonne-bouche**) plural **bonnes bouches** M18 **French** (literally, 'good mouth'). A dainty morsel, a tidbit, especially one at the end of a meal; also *figurative*.

■ In French the sense is 'a pleasing taste in the mouth', which has been understood in English as the delicacy that gives this.

bonne femme *adjective phrase* E19 **French** (literally, 'in the manner of a good housewife'). *Cooking* (Of a dish of food) prepared in a particular way.

■ Also in the fuller form *à la bonne femme*, both used postpositively, as in 'sole *bonne femme*'.

bonne fortune *noun phrase* plural **bonnes fortunes** E19 **French** (literally, 'good fortune'). A lady's favors, seen as a cause for self-congratulation on the part of their receipient.

bonsai *noun* E20 **Japanese** (from *bon* tray + *sai* planting). The (Japanese) practice of cultivating artificially dwarfed potted plants or small trees; a plant or tree cultivated by this method.

bon ton *noun phrase* M18 **French** (literally, 'good tone') . The fashionable world.

bon vivant *noun phrase* plural **bons vivants** L17 **French** (literally, '(a person) who lives well'). A gourmand, an epicure.

■ In contemporary usage *bon vivant* and BON VIVEUR appear interchangeably in a general sense of someone with a self-indulgent lifestyle.

bon viveur *noun phrase* plural **bons viveurs** M19 **pseudo-French** (formed after BON VIVANT). A person who indulges a taste for the good things of life.

bon voyage *interjection* L17 **French** (literally, 'good journey'). Pleasant journey!

■ Used as a farewell to a person about to travel.

bonze *noun* L16 **French** (*bonze* or Portuguese *bonzo* probably from Japanese *bonzō*, *bonsō* priest). A Japanese or Chinese Buddhist religious teacher.

boomerang *noun & verb* L18 **Aboriginal** (perhaps modified: cf. Kamilaroi *būmarin*). **A** *noun* **1** L18 A thin curved hardwood missile (of a kind) used by Australian Aborigines as a hunting weapon, *especially* one that can be thrown so as to return to the thrower. **2** M19 *figurative* A scheme, etc., that recoils on its originator. **B** *intransitive verb* L19 Act as a boomerang; *figurative* recoil on the originator.

boondock *noun* M20 **Tagalog** (*bundok* mountain). Rough or isolated country; remote parts.

■ Slang, originally used by service personnel. It appears infrequently in the singular, more usually in the plural, and often in the phrase *(out) in the boondocks*.

bordello *noun* plural **bordellos** L16 **Italian** (from medieval Latin *bordellum*). A brothel.

bordereau *noun* plural **bordereaux** L19 **French** (diminutive of *bord* board). A memorandum of contents, a schedule, a docket.

borné *adjective* L18 **French** (past participle of *borner* to limit). Limited in scope, intellect, outlook, etc.

bortsch *noun* (also **borsch**, **borstch**) E19 **Russian** (*borshch*). A Russian or Polish soup of various ingredients including beetroot and cabbage.

bosquet *noun* (also **bosket**) M18 **French** (from Italian *boschetto* diminutive of *bosco* wood; cf. BOUQUET). A plantation of small trees in a garden, park, etc.; a thicket.

bossage *noun* E18 **French** (from *bosse* boss). *Architecture* Projecting stonework, bosses; *especially* a type of rustic work.

bossa nova *noun phrase* M20 **Portuguese** (*bossa* tendency, *nova* feminine singular of *novo* new). A style of Brazilian music related to the samba; a dance to this music.

botargo *noun* plural **botargo(e)s** L16 **Italian** (from (medieval) Greek *arghotarakho*, perhaps through Pontic dialect *ovotarakho*). A relish made of the roe of the mullet or tuna.

boucan *noun* (also **buccan**) E17 **French** (from Tupi *mukem*, *mocaém*). **1** E17 In South America: a wooden frame for cooking, smoking, or drying meat over an open fire. **2** M19 Meat cooked or cured on such a frame. **3** M19 An open floor on which coffee beans, etc., may be spread out to dry.

bouchée *noun* M19 **French** (= mouthful, from *bouche* mouth). A small baked confection.

■ Usually in plural.

bouclé *adjective & noun* L19 **French** (= buckled, curled). (Fabric) woven with a knotted and curled appearance; (yarn) of looped or curled ply.

boudin *noun* E20 **French**. *Geology* Any of a number of roughly parallel elongated sections resulting from the fracturing of a rock stratum during folding.

■ Although recorded earlier (M19) with its current French meaning of 'a blood sausage', *boudin* has never been entirely naturalized in this sense.

boudoir *noun* L18 **French** (literally, 'place to sulk in', from *bouder* to pout, sulk). A (woman's) small private room.

bouffant *noun & adjective* E19 **French** (present participle of *bouffer* to swell). **A** *noun* E19 A puffed-out part of a dress, etc.; a puffed-out hairstyle. **B** *adjective* L19 Of a dress, hairstyle, etc.: puffed out.

bougie *noun* M18 **French** (from *Bougie* (Arabic *Bijāya*) a town in Algeria which carried on a trade in wax). **1** M18 A wax candle. **2** M18 *Medicine* A rod or tube for exploring or dilating the passages of the body.

bouillabaisse *noun* M19 **French** (from Modern Provençal *bouiabaisso*). A Provençal dish of fish stewed in water or white wine. Also *figurative*.

bouilli *noun* E17 **French** (noun use of past participle of *bouillir* to boil). Boiled or stewed meat, especially beef.

■ Since the mid-eighteenth century often Anglicized as *bully*, especially when referring to beef in the form used for army rations.

bouillon *noun* M17 **French** (from *bouillir* to boil). Broth, thin soup. See also COURT BOUILLON.

boule *noun 1* M19 Greek (*boulē* senate). A legislative body of ancient or modern Greece.

boule *noun 2* plural **boules** E20 French (= bowl). **1** E20 A form of roulette. **2** E20 (*singular* and in *plural*) A French form of lawn bowling played on rough ground, usually with metal balls. **3** M20 A small pear-shaped mass of synthetic sapphire, ruby, etc., made by fusing suitably tinted alumina.

boul(l)e variant of BUHL.

boulevard *noun* M18 French ((originally) = rampart, (later) a promenade on the site of this). A broad street (especially in France) with rows of trees planted along it; a broad main urban road.

boulevardier *noun* L19 French (from *boulevard* + *-ier*). A person who frequents (French) boulevards.

bouleversé *adjective* M19 French (past participle of *bouleverser* to turn as a ball, from as BOULE (*noun 2*) + *verser* to turn). Amazed, upset, completely taken aback.

bouleversement *noun* L18 French (from as preceding). An inversion, *especially* a violent one; an upset, an upheaval.

bouquet *noun* E18 French ((earlier = clump of trees), from dialectal variant of Old French *bos, bois* wood). **1** E18 A bunch of flowers, *especially* a large attractive one for use at a ceremony. **b** E20 *figurative* A compliment. **2** M19 The perfume of wine, etc. **3** M19 A BOUQUET GARNI. **4** L19 A number of rockets, etc., fired together.

bouquet garni *noun phrase* M19 French (literally, 'garnished bouquet'). *Cooking* A bunch of assorted herbs for flavoring.

bouquetier *noun* L18 French. A small holder for a posy of flowers, especially one to be carried in the hand.

bourdon *noun* (also **burdoun**) ME Old and Modern French (= drone, from Proto-Romance, of imitative origin). **1** ME The bass or undersong of a melody. **2** M19 A low-pitched stop in an organ or harmonium; the drone pipe of a bagpipe. **3** E20 The lowest-pitched in a peal of bells.

■ *Bourdon* in sense 1 soon merged with the same sense of *burden* and is now rare or obsolete with its original meaning; sense 2 is a reintroduction.

bourg *noun* LME Old and Modern French (from medieval Latin *burgus* borough). A town or village under the shadow of a castle (*historical*); an ancient town in continental Europe.

bourgade *noun* E17 French (from as preceding + *-ade*). A large village or straggling unwalled town in Europe.

bourgeois *adjective & noun* M16 French. **A** *adjective* **1** M16 Of, pertaining to, characteristic of, or resembling, the bourgeois (see sense B below); middle-class; conventionally respectable and unimaginative, humdrum; selfishly materialistic; capitalistic, reactionary. **2** E20 Of French wine: next in quality to wines classified as the best. **B** *noun* plural same. **1** L17 Originally, a (French) citizen or freeman of a city or burgh, as distinct from a peasant or a gentleman. Now, any member of the middle class. **2** L19 In Communist or socialist writing: a capitalist, an exploiter of the proletariat. *derogatory*. **3** M20 A socially or aesthetically conventional person, a philistine. *derogatory*.

bourgeoise *noun & adjective* L18 French (feminine of preceding). **A** *noun* L18 A female bourgeois. **B** *adjective* M20 Of a female: bourgeois.

bourgeoisie *noun* E18 French (from BOURGEOIS). The bourgeois collectively; the middle class.

bourrée *noun* L17 French. A lively dance of French origin, resembling the gavotte; a piece of music for this dance or in its rhythm, *especially* one that forms a movement of a suite.

■ In a *bourrée step* the dancer moves sideways, with one foot crossing behind or in front of the other.

bourse *noun* L16 **French.** A money market; *especially* (the Bourse) the Paris stock exchange; *transferred* an exchange.

boustrophedon *adverb & adjective* E17 **Greek** (= as the ox turns in plow, from *bous* ox + *strophos* twist + adverbial suffix *-don*). (Written) from right to left and from left to right in alternate lines.

boutade *noun* E17 **French** (from *bouter* to thrust). A sudden outburst or outbreak.

boutique *noun* M18 **French** (from Old Provençal *botica* (Italian *bottega*) from Latin *apotheca* from Greek *apothēkē* storehouse: cf. BODEGA). A small shop. Now usually a shop, or a department in a large store, selling (especially fashionable) clothes or accessories.

bouton *noun* M19 **French** (= button). **1** M19 A round pearl with a flat back. In full *bouton pearl*. **2** M20 *Anatomy* An enlarged part of a nerve fiber or cell, especially an axon, where it forms a synapse.

boutonnière *noun* L19 **French.** A flower or posy worn in a lapel buttonhole.

bouts rimés *noun phrase plural* E18 **French** (= rhymed endings). Rhyming words upon which verses are (to be) composed.

bouzouki *noun* M20 **Modern Greek** (*mpouzouki*: cf. Turkish *bozuk* spoiled, i.e., roughly made (instruments)). In Greece: a form of long-necked lute much used in traditional folk music.

boyar *noun* L16 **Russian** (*boyarin* grandee). *History* A member of an order of Russian aristocracy (abolished by Peter the Great), next in rank to a prince.

braai *noun & verb* M20 **Afrikaans** (abbreviation of next). **A** *noun* M20 In South Africa: a barbecue, a BRAAIVLEIS. **B** *transitive & intransitive verb* M20 Grill (meat) over an open fire.

braaivleis *noun* M20 **Afrikaans** (= grilled meat, from *braai* to grill + *vleis* meat). In South Africa: meat grilled over an open fire; a picnic, barbecue, etc., at which meat is cooked in this way.

braggadocio *noun* plural **braggadocios** L16 **pseudo-Italian** (fictional name formed from *brag* or *braggart* + Italian augmentative suffix *-occio*). **1** L16 A loud-mouthed braggart, an idle boaster. **2** M18 Empty boasting, bluster.

■ *Braggadocchio* is the name of a cowardly braggart in Spenser's *Faerie Queene*, the first part of which was published in 1590: "Proud *Braggadocchio*, that in vaunting vaine / His glory did repose, and credit did maintaine" (III.viii.11).

brahmacharya *noun* E20 **Sanskrit** (*brahmacarya*, from *bráhman* prayer, worship + *carya* conduct). Purity of life, especially regarding sexual matters.

■ Frequently used with reference to the life and teachings of M. K. Gandhi, through whose writings the word entered English.

brahman *noun* (also **brahma**, **brahm**, **Brahman**) L18 **Sanskrit** (*bráhman* sacred utterance). In Hindu philosophy: the ultimate reality underlying all phenomena.

brandade *noun* E19 **French** (from Modern Provençal *brandado*, literally, 'thing that has been moved or shaken'). A Provençal dish made from salt cod.

brasserie *noun* M19 **French** ((originally = brewery), from *brasser* to brew). A (French) saloon selling beer and usually food; *generally* an informal restaurant.

brassière *noun* (also **brassiere**) E20 **French** (= child's reins, camisole, etc.). A woman's shaped undergarment worn to support the breasts.

■ The abbreviation *bra* is almost universal in informal contexts.

bratwurst E20 **German** (from *Brat* a spit (*braten* roast, etc.) + *Wurst* sausage). (A) mild-flavored German pork sausage.

brava *noun & interjection* E19 **Italian** (feminine of *bravo*). (A cry addressed to a woman or girl meaning) excellent, well done!

bravo *noun 1* plural **bravo(e)s** L16 **Italian**. A hired ruffian; a desperado.

bravo *interjection & noun 2* M18 **French** (from as preceding: cf. BRAVA). **A** *interjection* M18 Excellent, well done! **B** *noun* plural **bravos**. M19 A cry of "bravo!", a cheer.

bravura *noun & adjective* M18 **Italian** (from *bravo* brave). **1** *Music* M18 (A passage or style, especially of singing) requiring exceptional powers of execution. **2** E19 (A performance that is) brilliant or ambitious; (a display that is) daring, dash(ing).

breccia *noun* L18 **Italian** (= gravel, rubble, cognate with French *brèche*, German *brechen* from Germanic base of break). *Geology* Rock consisting of angular fragments cemented together, e.g., by lime.

brei *noun* M20 **German** (= pulp, mush, jelly). *Biology* A homogenized pulp of organic tissue prepared for experimental work.

breitschwanz *noun* E20 **German** (= broad tail). The lustrous pelt of a young karakul lamb.

breloque *noun* M19 **French**. A small ornament fastened to a watch chain; a trinket.

bretelle *noun* M19 **French** (= strap, sling, (in plural) trouser suspenders). Each of a pair of ornamental straps extending over the shoulders from the belt on the front of a dress to the belt on the back. Usually in *plural*.

bric-à-brac *noun* (also **bric-a-brac**, **bricabrac**) M19 **French** (from *à bric et à brac* at random). Miscellaneous old ornaments, trinkets, small pieces of furniture, etc.; antiquarian knickknacks.

bricolage *noun* M20 **French** (from *bricoler* to do odd jobs, repair, from as next). Construction or creation from whatever is immediately available for use; something constructed or created in this way, an assemblage of haphazard or incongruous elements.

bricole *noun* E16 **Old and Modern French** (from Provençal *bricola* or Italian *briccola*, of unknown origin). **1** E16 An engine or catapult for discharging stones or bolts. *obsolete* except *historical*. **2** L16 A rebound of the ball from a side wall or cushion in real tennis, billiards, etc.

bricoleur *noun* M20 **French** (= handyman, from *bricoler* to do odd jobs). A person who engages in BRICOLAGE; a constructor or creator of bricolages.

brillante *adverb & adjective* M18 **Italian**. *Music* (A direction:) in a showy or sparkling style.

brinjal *noun* E17 **Anglo-Indian** (ultimately from Portuguese *berinjela*, from as AUBERGINE). Especially in the Indian subcontinent: an eggplant.

brio *noun* M18 **Italian**. Vivacity, liveliness, verve.

brioche *noun* E19 **French**. A small usually round sweet cake made with light yeast dough.

briquette *noun & verb* (also **briquet**) L19 **French** (diminutive of *brique* brick). **A** *noun* L19 A small block or slab, especially of compressed coal dust or other flammable material for use as fuel. **B** *transitive verb* L19 Form into briquettes.

brisé *noun* L18 **French** (past participle of *briser* to break). *Ballet* A movement in which the feet or legs are lightly beaten together in the air.

brise-soleil *noun* M20 **French** (literally, 'sun-breaker'). A device (such as a perforated screen, louver, etc.) for shutting out direct or excessive sunlight.

brocard *noun* M16 **French** (or medieval Latin *brocardus*, appellative use of the Latinized form of the proper name *Burchart*). **1** M16 A cutting speech, a gibe. *rare*. **2** E17 An elementary legal principle or maxim.

■ Burchart was an eleventh-century bishop of Worms and the compiler of volumes of ecclesiastical rules and regulations.

broché *adjective & noun* L19 **French** (past participle of *brocher* to stitch). (A material, especially silk) woven with a pattern on the surface.

brochette *noun* L15 **French** (diminutive of *broche* spit). **1** L15 A small skewer or spit; *specifically* a skewer on which chunks of meat are cooked (cf. À LA BROCHETTE). **2** M19 A pin or bar used to fasten medals, orders, etc., to clothing; a set of decorations worn in this way.

brochure *noun* M18 **French** (literally, 'stitching, stitched work', from *brocher* to stitch + *-ure*). A booklet or pamphlet, especially giving descriptive information.

■ The literal French meaning refers to the fact that, before the days of staplers, such a pamphlet would have been made by stitching a few sheets of paper together.

broderie anglaise *noun phrase* M19 **French** (= English embroidery). Open embroidery on linen, cambric, etc.; fabric so embroidered.

brogan *noun* M19 **Irish** (*brógán*, Gaelic *brógan* diminutive of *bróg* brogue). A coarse stout leather shoe reaching to the ankle.

bronco *noun & adjective* (also **broncho**) M19 **Spanish** (= rough, rude). **A** *noun* M19 plural **broncos**. A wild or half-tamed horse. **B** *adjective* M19. Wild, uncontrollable, rough. *colloquial*.

brouhaha *noun* L19 **French**. A commotion, a sensation; uproar, hubbub.

brouillon *noun* L17 **French**. A rough draft.

bruit *noun* LME **Old and Modern French** (noun use of past participle of *bruire* to roar, from Proto-Romance alteration of Latin *rugire* to roar, by association with Proto-Romance source of 'bray'). **1** LME Noise, clamor. **2** LME Rumor, report. **3** L15–E17 Fame, reputation. **4** M19 *Medicine* Any sound (especially an abnormal one) heard in auscultation.

brunette *noun & adjective* (also (masculine) **brunet**) M16 **French** (*brunet* masculine, *brunette* feminine, diminutive of *brun* brown). (A white person) with a dark complexion or (now usually) brown hair. Of the complexion: dark.

■ The form *brunette*, especially a woman or girl, is far more frequent than the masculine form.

brusque *adjective* (also **brusk**) M17 **French** (= lively, fierce, harsh, from Italian *brusco* sour, tart, adjective use of noun = Spanish, Portuguese *brusco* butcher's broom (a spiny bush) from Proto-Romance). Rough or rude in manner or speech; blunt, offhand, abrupt.

■ Earliest (only in E17) in the sense of 'tart'.

brut *adjective* L19 **French**. Of wine: unsweetened, very dry.

brutum fulmen *noun phrase* plural **bruta fulmina** E17 **Latin** (literally, 'unfeeling thunderbolt'). A mere noise; an ineffective act, an empty threat.

■ The phrase *bruta fulmina et vana* 'insensate and ineffectual thunderbolts' occurs in Pliny's *Natural History* II.xliii.

bubo *noun* plural **buboes** LME **Latin** (from Greek *boubōn* groin, swelling in the groin). A swollen inflamed lymph node especially in the groin or armpit.

bucaro, buccaro variants of BOCCARO.

buccan variant of BOUCAN.

buccra variant of BUCKRA.

bucellas *noun* E19 **Portuguese** (name of a village near Lisbon). A Portuguese white wine; a drink of this.

buckaroo see VAQUERO.

buckling *noun* E20 **German** (*Bückling* bloater). A smoked herring.

buckra *noun* (also **buccra** and other variants) M18 **Ibibio and Efik** (*(m)bakara* European, master). (A black's name for) a white man, a master.

■ Used in the West Indies and southern United States and frequently derogatory.

buffet *noun* E18 **French** (from Old French *buf(f)et*, of unknown origin). **1** E18 A sideboard or recessed cupboard for china, plate, etc. **2** L18 (A place offering) a service of food from a sideboard or counter where guests or customers can help themselves.

buffo *noun & adjective* M18 **Italian** (= puff of wind, buffoon, from *buffare* to puff, from Proto-Romance verb of imitative origin). **A** *noun* M18 plural **buffos**. A comic actor, a singer in OPERA BUFFA. **B** *adjective* L18 Comic, burlesque.

bugaku *noun* L19 **Japanese** (from *bu* dancing + *gaku* music). A Japanese classical dance in which pure dance form and symmetry are emphasized, and masks are used.

buhl *noun & adjective* (also **boul(l)e**, **Buhl**) E19 **German** (*buhl*, French *boule*, from André Charles *Boulle* (1642–1732), French cabinetmaker). (Of) brass, tortoiseshell, etc., worked into ornamental patterns for inlaying; (work) inlaid thus.

bulgur *noun* (also **bulghur**) M20 **Turkish** (= Persian *bulġūr* bruised grain). Cracked wheat, BURGHUL.

bund *noun* (also **Bund**) plural **bunds**, **bunde** M19 **German**. A German league, confederacy, or association. Cf. BOND.

bundobust *noun* (also **bandobast**) L18 **Urdu** (from Persian *band-o-bast* tying and binding). In the Indian subcontinent: arrangements, organization.

Bunraku *noun & adjective* E20 **Japanese**. (Of, pertaining to, or characteristic of) Japanese puppet drama, *specifically* as practiced by the Bunraku-za company.

bunyip *noun* M19 **Aboriginal**. In Australia: a fabulous monster of swamps and lagoons.

bureau *noun* plural **bureaux**, **bureaus** L17 **French** (Old French *burel*, originally = woolen stuff, baize (used for covering writing desks), probably from *bure*, variant of *buire* dark brown, from Proto-Romance alteration of Latin *burrus* fiery red, from Greek *purros* red). **1** L17 A writing desk with drawers for papers, etc. **b** E19 A chest of drawers. **2** L17 An office, especially for the transaction of public business; a department of public administration. **b** E20 An office or business with a specified function; an agency for the coordination of related activities, the distribution of information, etc.

burette *noun* (also **buret**) M19 **French**. A graduated glass tube with tap, used for measuring small quantities of liquid in chemical analysis.

burghul *noun* (also **burgul**) E20 **Arabic** (*burġul* from Persian *burġūl* variant of *bulġūr*). Whole-wheat partially boiled and then dried; a dish made from this.

burin *noun* M17 **French** (related to Italian *burino* (*bulino*), perhaps connected with Old High German *bora* boring-tool). A tool for engraving on copper or wood.

burka *noun* M19 **Urdu** (Persian *burḳa'* from Arabic *burḳu'*). A Muslim woman's long enveloping garment worn in public. Also, a yashmak.

burlesque *adjective, noun, and verb* M17 **French** (from Italian *burlesco*, from *burla* ridicule, joke, fun, of unknown origin). **A** *adjective* **1** M17–M19 Jocular, odd, grotesque. **2** M17 Derisively or amusingly imitative; mock-heroic or mock-pathetic; bombastic. (Now chiefly of literary composition or dramatic representation.) **B** *noun* **1** M17 Derisively or amusingly imitative literary or dramatic composition, bombast; mock-seriousness; an instance or example of this; (a) parody; (a) caricature. **2a** M19 *History* The concluding portion of a blackface minstrel entertainment, containing dialogue and sketches. **b** L19 A variety show, frequently featuring striptease. **C** *transitive verb* L17 Imitate to deride or amuse; parody; caricature.

burnoose *noun* (also **burnous** and other variants) L16 **French** (from Arabic *burnus, burnūs*). An Arab or Moorish hooded cloak; a fashion garment resembling this.

burra *adjective* E19 Hindustani (*baṛā, barā* great, greatest). In the Indian subcontinent: high-ranking, great.

■ Occurs only in phrases such as *burra sahib* and *burra memsahib*, used to refer to important people.

burrito *noun* plural **burritos** M20 American Spanish (diminutive of BURRO). A tortilla rolled around a filling of spiced beef and other ingredients.

burro *noun* plural **burros** E19 Spanish. A small donkey used as a pack animal.

bushido *noun* L19 Japanese (= military knight's way). The code of honor and morals evolved by the samurai.

bustier *noun* L20 French (from *buste* bust). A close-fitting usually strapless bodice or top worn by women.

■ The revival of the *bustier* as a fashion item in the 1980s was closely associated with the rock star Madonna, who frequently wore one for her public appearances.

butoh *noun* L20 Japanese ('dark art'). A Japanese dance style influenced by Western dance.

butte *noun* M19 French. *Physical Geography* An isolated hill with steep sides and a flat top, similar to but narrower than a MESA.

bwana *noun* L19 Kiswahili. In East Africa: master, sir.

■ Frequently used, particularly in colonial times, as a term of respectful address by a black person to a white man.

c., ca. abbreviations of CIRCA.

caba *noun* (also **cabas**) M19 French (*cabas* basket, pannier). A small satchel or handbag.

cabaia variant of KEBAYA.

cabala variant of KABBALAH.

caballada *noun* M19 Spanish (from *caballo* horse). A drove of horses or mules.

■ Earlier in the form CAVAYARD.

caballero *noun* plural **caballeros** M19 Spanish (= French *chevalier*, Italian *cavaliere*). A Spanish gentleman.

cabana *noun* (also **cabaña**) L19 Spanish (*cabaña* from late Latin *capanna, cavana* cabin). A cabin; *specifically* a shelter at a beach or swimming pool.

cabane *noun* M19 French. **1** M19 A hut, a cabin. *French Canadian.* **2** E20 A pyramidal structure supporting the wings of an aircraft.

cabaret *noun* M17 Old and Modern French (originally Walloon and Picard, from Middle Dutch variant of *camaret, cambret* from Old Picard *camberet* little room). **1** M17 A tavern in France, etc. **2** E20 An entertainment provided in a nightclub or restaurant, etc., while customers eat or drink at tables; a restaurant, nightclub, etc., providing such entertainment.

cabas variant of CABA.

cabbala variant of KABBALAH.

cabildo *noun* plural **cabildos** E19 Spanish (from late Latin *capitulum* chapter house). In Spain and Spanish-speaking countries: a town hall or town council.

cabob variant of KEBAB.

cabochon *adjective & noun* M16 **Old and Modern French** (diminutive of *caboche*, Picard variant of Old French *caboce* head, of unknown origin). (A gem) polished but not faceted.

■ Also in the phrase EN CABOCHON.

cabotage *noun* M19 **French** (from *caboter* to coast along (a shore), perhaps ultimately from Spanish *cabo* cape, promontory). **1** M19 Coastal trade. **2** M20 The reservation to a country of (especially air) traffic operation within its territory.

cabotin *noun* (feminine **cabotine**) E20 **French** (= strolling player, perhaps from as preceding from resemblance to vessels traveling from port to port). A third-rate or low-class actor.

cabriole *noun* L18 **French** (from *cabrioler*, earlier *caprioler*, from Italian *capriolare* to leap; cf. CAPRIOLE). **1** L18 A springing dance step in which one leg is extended and the other brought up to it. **2** L18 *History* More fully *cabriole chair*. A kind of small armchair. **3** L18 A CABRIOLET sense 1. Chiefly *historical*. **4** L19 A kind of curved leg characteristic of Chippendale and Queen Anne furniture.

cabriolet *noun* M18 **French** (from as preceding). **1** M18 A light two-wheeled hooded one-horse chaise. Chiefly *historical*. **2** L18 A bonnet or hat shaped like a cabriolet. **3** E20 An automobile with a folding top.

cache *noun & verb* L18 **French** (from *cacher* to hide). **A** *noun* **1** L18 A hiding place for goods, provisions, ammunition, treasure, etc. **2** M19 A hidden store of provisions, etc. **3** M20 An auxiliary computer memory from which high-speed retrieval is possible. Also *cache memory*. **B** *transitive verb* E19 Place or store in a cache.

cache-peigne *noun* L19 **French** (from *cacher* to hide + *peigne* comb). A bow or other trimming for a hat, usually worn at the back.

cache-pot *noun* L19 **French** (from *cacher* to hide + *pot* pot). An ornamental holder for a flowerpot.

cache-sexe *noun* E20 **French** (from *cacher* to hide + *sexe* sex). A covering for the genitals.

cachet *noun* E17 **French** (from *cacher* (in sense 'press', represented now in *écacher* to crush) from Proto-Romance alteration of Latin *coactare* to constrain). **1** E17 A seal for letters, documents, etc. Now *rare* or *obsolete*. **2** M19 A characteristic or distinguishing mark; a characteristic feature or quality conferring prestige or distinction; high status. **3** L19 A small digestible case enclosing a dose of medicine.

cachou *noun* L16 **French** (from Portuguese *cachu* from Malay *kacu*). **1** L16 Catechu, any of various astringent tannin-rich vegetable extracts used especially in tanning. **2** E18 A lozenge taken to sweeten the breath.

cacique *noun* M16 **Spanish or French** (from Taino). **1** M16 A West Indian or South American Indian native chief. **2** L19 In Spain or Latin America: a political boss.

cacodemon *noun* (also **cacodaemon**) L16 **Greek** (*kakodaimōn* from as *kako-* evil + *daimōn* genius). **1** L16 An evil spirit. **2** E18 A malignant or deprecated person.

cacoethes *noun* M16 **Latin** (from Greek *kakoēthes* noun use of adjective *kakoēthes* ill-disposed, from as *kako-* evil + ETHOS). An evil habit; a passion or "itch" for doing something inadvisable.

■ Although also formerly used of a malignant tendency in a medical sense, *cacoethes* mainly occurs in English with reference to the Latin poet Juvenal (*Satire* vii): *tenet insanabile multos / scribendi cacoethes* "the incurable itch to write grips many".

cadastre *noun* L18 **French** (from Modern Provençal *cadastro* from Italian *catast(r)o* earlier *catastico* from late Greek *katastikhon* list, register, from *kata stikhon* line by line). A register of property showing the extent, value, and ownership, of land for taxation.

cadeau *noun* plural **cadeaux** L18 **French**. A gift.

cadenza *noun* M18 Italian. *Music* A (sometimes improvised) flourish or passage for a solo instrument or voice, usually near the close or between the divisions of a movement; *specifically* such a passage in a concerto in which the main themes of the movement (usually the first or last) are developed.

cadet *noun* E17 French (earlier *capdet* from Gascon dialect (= Provençal *capdel*) from Proto-Romance diminutive of Latin *caput* head). **1** E17 A younger son or brother; also occasionally (a member of) a younger branch of a family. **b** M17 *The* youngest son or brother. **2** M17 *History* A gentleman who entered the army without a commission, to learn the profession. **3** L18 A student in a naval, military, or air force college. **4** M19 A young man learning sheep farming. *New Zealand.* **5** L19 A member of a corps receiving elementary military or police training.

cadi *noun* (also **kadi, qadi**) L16 Arabic (*(al-)ḳāḍī*). A civil judge in a Muslim country.

cadre *noun* M19 French (from Italian *quadro* from Latin *quadrus* square). **1** M19 A frame, a framework; a plan. *rare.* **2** M19 *Military* **a** A permanent establishment of trained personnel forming a nucleus for expansion at need. **b** M19 (A list of) the complement of the officers of a regiment, etc. **3** M20 (A member of) a group of workers acting to promote the aims and interests of the Communist Party. **b** M20 In the People's Republic of China: an officeholder in a Party, governmental, or military organization.

caduceus *noun* plural **caducei** L16 Latin (*caduceus, caduceum* from Doric Greek *karuk(e)ion* = Attic *kērukeion* neuter adjective used as noun, from *kērux* herald). *Classical History* A Greek or Roman herald's wand; *specifically* the wand carried by the messenger-god Hermes or Mercury, usually represented with two serpents twined around it.

caesura *noun* M16 Latin (*caesura*, from *caes-* past participial stem of *caedere* to cut). **1** M16 *Prosody* A break or pause between words within a metrical foot in classical prosody or near the middle of a line in English, etc. prosody. **2** L16 *generally* A break, a stop, an interruption.

cafard *noun* M16 French (= cockroach, hypocrite, probably from late Latin *caphardum*). **1** M16–M17 A hypocrite. **2** E20 Melancholia.

café *noun* (also **cafe** and (reflecting slang pronunciation) **caf(f)**) E19 French (= coffee (house)). A coffeehouse; a teashop; an informal restaurant; a bar.

■ Both the 'coffee' and the 'coffeehouse' senses of the French occur in various phrases used in English (see entries below).

café au lait *noun & adjective phrase* M18 French (= coffee with milk). **A** *noun phrase* M18 Coffee with milk, white coffee. **B** *adjective phrase* E20 Of the light brown color of this.

café chantant *noun phrase* plural **cafés chantants** M19 French (literally, 'singing café'). A café with live musical entertainment.

café complet *noun phrase* plural **cafés complets** M20 French (literally, 'complete coffee'). A light breakfast including coffee and usually croissants. Cf. THÉ COMPLET.

café noir *noun phrase* M19 French (= black coffee). Coffee without milk, black coffee.

cafeteria *noun* M19 American Spanish (*cafetería*, from *café* coffee). A coffeehouse; a restaurant; now *especially* a self-service restaurant as part of the facilities in a workplace, institution, or public building.

■ Originally United States, but apparently spread to Europe in the 1920s, when the *Glasgow Herald* (30 July 1925) observed that "Cafeterias, although a commonplace in America, are just beginning to have a hold in Paris."

cafetière *noun* M19 **French** (from *café* coffee). A coffeepot; a coffee maker; a coffee percolator.

cafila *noun* L16 **Arabic** (*ḳāfila*). A company of travelers in the Middle East, a caravan.

■ *Coffle*, an eighteenth-century derivation from *ḳāfila*, refers specifically to a line of slaves or animals fastened together.

caftan *noun* (also **kaftan**) L16 **Turkish** (*kaftan* from Persian *kaftān*, partly through French *cafetan*). **1** L16 An Eastern man's long tunic with a waist girdle. **2** M20 A long loose dress; a loose-fitting shirt.

cagnotte *noun* L19 **French**. Money reserved from the stakes for the bank at certain gambling games.

cagoule *noun* (also **kagoule**) M20 **French** (literally, 'cowl'). A hooded thin waterproof garment pulled on over the head.

caique *noun* E17 **French** (*caïque* from Italian *caicco* from Turkish *kayik*). **1** E17 A light rowing boat or skiff used on the Bosporus. **2** M17 An eastern Mediterranean sailing vessel.

caisson *noun* L17 **French** (= large chest, from Italian *cassone* with assimilation to *caisse* case). **1** L17 A large watertight chamber open at the bottom, from which the water is kept out by air pressure, used in laying foundations under water. **b** M19 A floating vessel used as a dock gate. **2** E18 An ammunition chest; an ammunition wagon.

calabrese *noun* M20 **Italian** (= Calabrian). A variety of usually green sprouting broccoli.

calamari *noun plural* L20 **Italian** (plural of *calamaro* squid). Squid, especially as used in cooking.

calando *adverb* E19 **Italian** (= slackening). *Music* Gradually decreasing in speed and volume.

caldarium *noun* plural **caldaria** M18 **Latin**. *History* A (Roman) hot bath or bathroom.

caldera *noun* L17 **Spanish** (from late Latin *caldaria* pot for boiling). A volcanic crater of great size; *specifically* one whose breadth greatly exceeds that of the vent(s) within it.

calembour *noun* (also **calembourg**) E19 **French**. A pun.

calinda *noun* M18 **American Spanish**. A black American dance found in Latin America and the southern United States.

calliope *noun* M19 **Greek** (*Kalliopē* (literally, 'beautiful-voiced') the Muse of epic poetry). A set of steam whistles producing musical notes, played by a keyboard like that of an organ. Also *steam calliope*.

callus *noun & verb* M16 **Latin** (more commonly *callum*). **A** *noun* **1** M16 A thickened and hardened part of the skin or soft tissue, a callosity. **2** L17 *Medicine* The bony healing tissue that forms around the ends of broken bone. **3** L19 *Botany* A hard formation of tissue; new tissue formed over a wound. **B** *verb intransitive* Form a callus (*over*).

calotte *noun* M17 **French** (perhaps related to *cale* caul). **1** M17 A skullcap, especially as worn by Roman Catholic priests. **2** L19 A snowcap, an ice cap.

caloyer *noun* L16 **French** (from Italian *caloiero* from ecclesiastical Greek *kalogēros*, from *kalos* beautiful + *gērōs* old age). A Greek Orthodox monk.

calque *noun & verb* M20 **French** (= copy, tracing, from *calquer* to trace, from Italian *calcare* from Latin *calcare* to tread). **A** *noun* M20 A loan translation (*of, on*); an expression adopted by one language from another in a more or less literally translated form. **B** *transitive verb* M20 Form as a calque. Usually in *passive* (followed by *on*).

■ A modern example of a calque is "that goes without saying," which is calqued on French *cela va sans dire*.

calumet *noun* L17 **French** (dialectal variant of *chalumeau* from late Latin *calamellus* diminutive of *calamus* reed). An American Indian tobacco pipe with a clay bowl and reed stem, smoked especially as a sign of peace;

transferred and *figurative* a symbol of peace.

calvados *noun* E20 **French** (*Calvados*, a department in Normandy, France). Apple brandy, traditionally made in the Calvados region; a drink of this.

calyx *noun* plural **calyces, calyxes** L17 **Latin** (*calyx, -yc-* from Greek *kalux* shell, husk, pod, from base of *kaluptein* to hide). *Botany* A whorl of leaves (sepals), forming the outer case of a bud or the envelope of a flower.

calzone *noun* L20 **Italian** (literally, 'pants'). In Italian cooking, pizza dough with a stuffing of savory ingredients.

camaieu *noun* L16 **French**. **1** L16–L18 A cameo. **2** E18 A method of monochrome painting.

camaraderie *noun* M19 **French** (from *camarade* comrade). The mutual trust and sociability of comrades.

camarilla *noun* M19 **Spanish** (diminutive of *camara* chamber). A cabal, a clique.

camaron *noun* L19 **Spanish** (*camarón* shrimp). A freshwater shrimp resembling a crayfish.

cambré *adjective* E20 **French** (past participle of *cambrer* to camber, from Old French *cambre* from dialect variant of *chambre* arched, from Latin *camur* curved inward). Curved, arched; *Ballet* (of the body) bent from the waist sideways or backward.

cameo *noun* plural **cameos** LME **Old French** (*came(h)u, camahieu* (modern CAMAIEU): cf. medieval Latin *camahutus*, etc. Later influenced by Italian *cam(m)eo*, corresponding to medieval Latin *cammaeus*). **1** LME A small piece of relief carving in onyx, agate, etc., usually with a background of a different color; a relief design of similar form. **2** M19 A short literary sketch or acted scene; (more fully *cameo part*) a small character part in a play, movie, etc.

camera lucida *noun phrase* plural **camera lucidas** M18 **Latin** (= bright chamber). An instrument by which the rays of light from an object are reflected by a prism and produce an image on paper placed beneath the instrument, traceable with a pencil.

camera obscura *noun phrase* plural **camera obscuras** E18 **Latin** (= dark chamber). A darkened box or enclosure with an aperture for projecting an image of external objects on a screen placed at the focus of the lens; a building containing such a box or enclosure.

camisole *noun* E19 **French** (from Italian *camiciola* or Spanish *camisola*, diminutive of (respectively) *camicia, camisa* from late Latin *camisia*). **1** E19 *History* A type of sleeved short jacket worn by men. **2** M19 *History* A short loose negligee jacket worn by women. **3** M19 A woman's underbodice, usually straight with shoulder straps and embroidered or otherwise ornamentally trimmed.

Camorra *noun* (also **camorra**) M19 **Italian** (perhaps from Spanish *camorra* dispute, quarrel). A secret society akin to the Mafia operating in the Neapolitan district; *generally* any organized body engaged in extortion or other dishonest activities.

camouflage *noun & verb* E20 **French** (from *camoufler* (thieves' slang) to cover up, from Italian *camuffare* disguise, deceive, perhaps associated with French *camouflet* whiff of smoke in the face). **A** *noun* E20 The disguising or concealment of guns, ships, aircraft, etc., by obscuring with splashes of various colors, foliage, netting, smokescreens, etc.; the disguise so used; *generally* any means of disguise or evasion. **B** *verb transitive* E20 Conceal by camouflage.

campagna *noun* (also **campa(g)nia**) L16 **Italian** (from late Latin *campania*). Open country.

■ Now rare except with reference to the Campagna di Roma. In the mid-seventeenth century the word was also briefly used with the sense of 'military campaign'.

campana *noun* E17 **Late Latin** (*campana* bell). **1** E17 A bell; a bell-shaped flower. Now *rare* or *obsolete*. **2** E19 A bell-shaped vase.

campanile *noun* M17 **Italian** (from *campana* bell + *-ile*). A (usually lofty and detached) bell tower, especially in Italy.

campesino *noun* plural **campesinos** M20 **Spanish**. In Spain and Spanish-speaking countries: a peasant farmer.

campo *noun* plural **campos** M19 **American Spanish or Portuguese** (= field, open country, from Latin *campus*). In South America (especially Brazil): a grass plain with occasional stunted trees; a savannah.

■ Frequently in plural.

campus *noun* L18 **Latin**. The grounds and buildings of a college, university, etc., especially where forming a distinct area; a separate part of a university; university or college life.

■ Originally used of the grounds of Princeton University, New Jersey, then of similar open spaces in other United States universities, and now worldwide.

canaille *noun* L16 **French** (from Italian *canaglia*, literally, 'pack of dogs', from *cane* dog). *The* rabble, *the* populace.

canapé *noun* L19 **French**. **1** L19 A piece of bread, toast, etc., with a small savory on top. **2** L19 A sofa, a settee.

■ In sense 2 the history of the Romance word *canapé* is closely linked to that of English *canopy*, both of them deriving from medieval Latin *canopeum* baldachin, a variant of classical Latin *conopeum* bed with net curtains, from Greek *kōnōpeion* Egyptian bed with mosquito curtains, from *kōnōps* mosquito. In English the sense of *canopy* has adhered to the 'curtain' sense of the Latin, while *canapé* in the Romance languages (Spanish and Portuguese as well as French) has retained the primary sense of 'couch, sofa'. By the late eighteenth century sense 1, now by far the more familiar in English, had evolved in French.

canard *noun* M19 **French** (literally, 'duck'). **1** M19 A false report, a hoax. **2** E20 An extra surface attached to an aircraft, hydrofoil, etc., for stability or control. Also, an aircraft fitted with this.

canasta *noun* M20 **Spanish** (= basket, ultimately from Latin *canistrum* bread (or flower) basket). A two-deck card game of the rummy family and of Uruguayan origin, usually played by four in two partnerships; a meld of seven or more cards in this game.

cancan *noun* M19 **French** (reduplication of *canard* duck). A lively dance of French origin, originally a form of quadrille, now performed by a woman and involving high kicks, usually while holding up the front of the skirts.

cancellandum *noun* plural **cancellanda** E20 **Latin** (neuter gerundive of *cancellare* to cancel). *Printing* A leaf for which another is substituted. In full *cancellandum leaf*. Cf. next.

cancellans *noun & adjective* E20 **Latin** (present participle of *cancellare* to cancel). *Printing* **A** *noun* E20 A leaf that replaces another. Cf. preceding. **B** *adjective* M20 Designating a leaf, sheet, fold, etc., that replaces another, or a slip that cancels text.

cancrizans *adjective, adverb, & noun* L18 **Medieval Latin** (present participle of *cancrizare* to walk backward, from Latin *cancer* crab). *Music* (Designating, pertaining to, in the manner of) a canon in which the theme or subject is repeated backward in the second part.

candelabrum *noun* plural **candelabra**, **candelabrums** (also **candelabra**, plural same, **candelabras**) E19 **Latin** (from *candela* candle). A large usually branched ornamental candlestick or lamp holder carrying several lights.

candida *noun* (also *Candida*) M20 **Modern Latin** (feminine of Latin *candidus* white). **1** M20 A yeastlike fungus of the genus *Candida*, especially *C. albicans*. **2** L20 *Medicine* and *Veterinary Medicine* Infection with candida, especially one causing vaginal or oral thrush; candidiasis.

canephora *noun* plural **canephorae** E17 **Latin** (*canephora* feminine, from Greek *kanēphoros*, from *kaneon* basket + *-phoros* carrying). In ancient Greece, each of the maidens who carried on their heads baskets bearing sacred things used at certain feasts; in *Architecture*, a caryatid representing or resembling such a maiden.

cannelloni *noun plural* M20 **Italian** (augmentative plural of *cannello* stalk). Rolls of pasta filled with meat or cheese and seasonings; an Italian dish consisting largely of this and usually a sauce.

cannelure *noun* M18 **French** (from *canneler* to groove, flute, from *canne* reed). A groove or fluting, especially around a bullet, etc.

cañon variant of CANYON.

cantabile *adverb, adjective, & noun* E18 **Italian** (= that can be sung). *Music* **A** *adverb & adjective* E18 In a smooth flowing style, as if singing. **B** *noun* M18 Cantabile style; a piece or movement in this style.

cantaloupe *noun* (also **cantaloup**) L18 **French**. A small round ribbed variety of melon, with orange flesh. Also called *rock melon*.

■ The French name is taken from *Cantaluppi*, the name of the place near Rome, where, on its introduction from Armenia, the melon was first grown in Europe.

cantata *noun* E18 **Italian** ((sc. *aria* air), feminine past participle of *cantare* to sing). *Music* An extended composition for one or more voices with instrumental accompaniment; originally, a narrative recitative or sequence of recitatives and ariettas, for solo voice; later, a choral work resembling a short oratorio.

cantatrice *noun* E19 **French and Italian** (from Latin *cantatrix*). A female professional singer.

cante hondo *noun phrase* (also **cante jondo**) M20 **Spanish** (= deep song). Flamenco singing, songs, of a predominantly mournful or tragic character.

canti fermi plural of CANTO FERMO.

cantilena *noun* M18 **Italian** (or Latin *cantilena*). *Music* A simple or sustained vocal melody, or an instrumental passage performed in a smooth lyrical style. Also, the (highest) melodic part in a composition.

cantina *noun* L19 **Spanish and Italian**. In Spain, Spanish-speaking countries, and the southwestern United States: a barroom, a saloon; in Italy: a wine shop.

canto *noun* plural **cantos** L16 **Italian** (literally, 'song', from Latin CANTUS). **1** L16 Each of the divisions of a long poem. **2** E17–E18 A song, a ballad. **3** E18 *Music* The upper part or melody in a composition.

canto fermo *noun phrase* plural **canti fermi** L16 **Italian** (translating medieval Latin CANTUS FIRMUS). *Music* Originally, an unadorned melody, plainsong; later *specifically* a melody used as a basis for counterpoint. Now also, an existing melody, taken as a basis for a new polyphonic composition.

canton *noun* E16 **Old and Modern French** (from Provençal from oblique case of Proto-Romance variant of Latin *cant(h)us*). A subdivision of a country; a small district; *specifically* one of the several states that form the Swiss confederation.

cantor *noun* M16 **Latin** (= singer, from *canere* to chant). **1** L19 An official who sings liturgical music and leads prayer in a synagogue, a HAZZAN. **2** M16 A person who leads or directs the singing of a choir or congregation in a church or cathedral; a precentor.

cantoris *adjective* M17 **Latin** (genitive of CANTOR). Of or pertaining to the north side of the choir of a church where the precentor usually sits; *Music* to be sung by the cantorial side in antiphonal singing (cf. DECANI).

cantus *noun* plural **cantus** L16 **Latin** (= song). *Early Music* A song, a melody, especially in church music. Also, the highest voice in a polyphonic song.

cantus firmus *noun phrase* plural **cantus firmi** M19 Medieval Latin (= firm song). *Music* CANTO FERMO.

canyon *noun* (also **cañon**) M19 Spanish (*cañón* tube, pipe, gun barrel, etc., augmentative of *caña* from Latin *canna* reed). A deep gorge, frequently with a stream at its bottom.

canzona *noun* L19 Italian (from next). (A musical setting of the words of) a canzone; an instrumental piece resembling a madrigal in character.

canzone *noun* plural **canzoni** L16 Italian (= song (corresponding to Old and Modern French *chanson*) from Latin *cantio(n-)* singing, from *cant-* past participle of *canere* to sing). An Italian or Provençal song or ballad; a style of lyric resembling a madrigal.

caoine *noun* E18 Irish (from *caoinim* I wail). An Irish funeral song accompanied by wailing in lamentation of the dead.

caoutchouc *noun & adjective* L18 French (from obsolete Spanish *cauchuc* from Quechua *kauchuk*). (Of) unvulcanized natural rubber.

capable de tout *adjective phrase* L19 French. Capable of anything; without scruple or restraint.

cap-à-pie *adverb* E16 Old French (*cap a pie* (Modern French *de pied en cap*)). From head to foot, fully (armed, ready, etc.). Now *archaic*.

capataz *noun* plural **capataces** E19 Spanish (irregular from Latin *caput* head). In Spain or Spanish-speaking America: an overseer, a superintendent, a boss.

capeador *noun* E20 Spanish (from *capear* to trick a bull with a cape, from *capa* cloak). *Bullfighting* A person who aids a bullfighter by distracting the bull with his cloak.

capitonné *adjective* L19 French (past participle of *capitonner* to upholster, quilt). Designating or characterized by a style of upholstery or embroidery in which the material is drawn in at intervals to present a quilted appearance.

capo *noun* plural **capos** M20 Italian (from Latin *caput* head). The head of a crime syndicate or one of its branches.

capo abbreviated form of CAPOTASTO.

capot *noun & verb* M17 French (perhaps from *capoter* dialectal variant of *chapoter* to castrate). *Piquet* **A** *noun* M17 The winning of all the tricks by one player; a score awarded for this. **B** *transitive verb* M17 Win all the tricks from.

■ Formerly stressed on the first syllable. *Capot* is the source of the German *kaputt*, from which the dated English slang KAPUT is taken.

capot *noun* L17 French (masculine form of CAPOTE). A long hooded cloak worn by soldiers, travelers, etc.

capotasto *noun* plural **capotastos** (also **capo tasto**) L19 Italian (literally, 'head stop': cf. TASTO). *Music* A movable bar attached to the fingerboard of a stringed instrument to make possible the simultaneous adjustment of the pitch of all the strings.

■ Generally known as a *capo*.

capote *noun* E19 French (diminutive of *cape* cape, cloak). **1 a** E19 A long hooded cloak worn by soldiers, travelers, etc. **b** M19 A long mantle worn by women. **2** E19 A bonnet with a soft crown and stiff projecting brim.

capouch variant of CAPUCHE.

cappuccino *noun* plural **cappuccinos** M20 Italian. (A cup of) coffee with milk, especially made with espresso coffee and topped with white foam.

capriccio *noun* plural **capriccios** E17 Italian. **1** E17–E19 A CAPRICE, a whim. **2** M17–M19 A sudden movement; a trick, a prank, a caper. **3** L17 A thing or work of lively fancy in art, etc.; *especially* a lively usually short musical composition, more or less free in form.

capriccioso *adverb* M18 Italian. *Music* (A direction:) in a free and impulsive style.

caprice *noun* M17 **French** (from Italian *capriccio*, literally, 'head with the hair standing on end', (hence) horror; later (by association with *capra* goat) sudden start, from *capo* head + *riccio* hedgehog, ultimately from Latin *(h)ericius* urchin). **1** M17 An unaccountable change of mind or conduct; a whim; a freakish fancy. **b** M17 Inclination or disposition to such changes, etc.; capriciousness. **2** E18 A CAPRICCIO.

capriole *noun & verb* L16 **French** ((now *cabriole*), from Italian *capriola*, from *capriolare* to leap, from *capriolo* roebuck, from Latin *capreolus* diminutive of *caper* goat). **A** *noun* **1** L16 A leap or caper, especially as made in dancing (cf. CABRIOLE 1). **2** *Equestrianism* L16 A trained horse's horizontal leap with the hind legs kicking vigorously. **B** *intransitive verb* L16 Perform a capriole; skip, leap, caper.

capuche *noun* (also **capouch**) L16 **French** ((now *capuce*) from Italian *cappuccio*). The hood of a cloak, *especially* that of a Capuchin cloak.

caput mortuum *noun phrase* M17 **Latin** (= dead head). **1** A death's head, a skull. Only in M17. **2** M17 *Alchemy* The residue remaining after distillation or sublimation. **3** E18 Worthless residue.

carabinero *noun* plural **carabineros** M19 **Spanish** (literally, 'carabineer'). A (Spanish) customs or revenue officer; a (Spanish) frontier guard.

carabiniere *noun* plural **carabinieri** M19 **Italian** (literally, 'carabineer'). An Italian soldier in a corps serving as a police force.

caracole *noun* (also **caracol**) E17 **French** (*caracol(e)* snail's shell, spiral). *Equestrianism* E17 A half turn or wheel to the right or left by a horse or rider. Formerly also, a series of such turns alternately to right and left.

■ The word was also formerly used in English for short periods in senses deriving directly from its basic French meanings: 'a spiral shell' (only E17) and in architectural contexts 'a helical staircase' (E18).

caracul variant of KARAKUL.

carafe *noun* L18 **French** (from Italian *caraffa*, of unknown origin). A glass bottle for water or wine at a table, in a bedroom, etc.

caramba *interjection* M19 **Spanish**. Expressive of surprise or dismay.

carambole *noun & intransitive verb* L18 **Spanish** (*carambola* (whence French *carambole* red ball in billiards), apparently from *bola* ball). (Make) a carom in billiards.

cara sposa *noun phrase* plural **care spose** L18 **Italian**. (One's) dear wife; a devoted wife. Cf. CARO SPOSO.

caravanserai *noun* (also **caravansary**, **caravansery**, and other variants) L16 **Persian** (*kārwānsarāy*, from *kārvān* (desert) caravan + SERAI). An Eastern inn with a large inner court where caravans rest.

carcinoma *noun* plural **carcinomas**, **carcinomata** E18 **Latin** (from Greek *karkinōma* from *karkinos* crab + suffix *-oma*). *Medicine* A cancer; now *specifically* a malignant tumor of epithelial origin.

care spose plural of CARA SPOSA.

caret *noun* L17 **Latin** (3rd person singular present indicative of *carere* to be without, lack). A mark (strictly ˆ) placed below a line of writing or printing, in a margin, etc., to show the place of an omission.

carezza variant of KAREZZA.

cargador *noun* plural **cargadores** E19 **Spanish** (from *cargo* cargo). In Spanish-speaking parts of the Americas: a porter.

caries *noun* L16 **Latin**. Decay of a tooth or bone.

carillon *noun* L18 **French** (alteration of Old French *car(e)ignon*, *quarregnon*, from Proto-Romance = peal of four bells). **1** L18 A set of bells sounded either from a keyboard or mechanically. **2** L18 A tune played on such bells. **3** E19 A musical instrument or part of an organ designed to imitate a peal of bells.

carioca *noun* M19 **Portuguese**. **1** M19 A native of Rio de Janeiro, Brazil. **2**

M20 A Brazilian dance resembling a samba; a piece of music for this dance.

cariole variant of CARRIOLE.

cari sposi plural of CARO SPOSO.

carissima *adjective* **M19 Italian** (superlative of *cara* dear). A term of endearment to a woman: dearest, darling.

carmagnole *noun* **L18 French. 1** L18 A popular song and round dance of the French Revolutionary period. **2** L18 A French revolutionary soldier; *transferred* an author of mischief.

■ In French, originally a style of jacket popular during the French Revolution, the name probably ultimately deriving from Carmagnola, a town in Piedmont.

carnet *noun* **E19 French. 1** E19 A notebook *rare*. **2** E20 A permit; *specifically* **(a)** one allowing a motorist to drive across a frontier; **(b)** one allowing use of some campsites.

caro sposo *noun phrase* plural **cari sposi** **L18 Italian.** (One's) dear husband; a devoted husband. Cf. CARA SPOSA.

carousel *noun* (also **carrousel**) **M17 French** (*carrousel* from Italian *carosello, garosello*). **1** M17 *History* A kind of tournament in which variously dressed companies of knights engaged in plays, chariot races, exercises, etc. **2** L17 A merry-go-round. **3** M20 A rotating delivery or conveyor system, *especially* one in an airport for the delivery of passengers' luggage.

carriole *noun* (also **cariole**) **M18 French** (from Italian *carriuola*, diminutive of *carro* car). **1** M18 A small open carriage for one; a covered light cart. Chiefly *historical*. **2** E19 A kind of sled used in Canada.

carrousel variant of CAROUSEL.

carte *noun* **LME French** (from Latin *c(h)arta* papyrus leaf, paper). **1** LME–M18 A charter, a document; an exposition; a chart, a diagram. **2** L15 A playing card; in *plural*, a game of cards. *Scottish*. **3** E19 A bill of fare. Cf. À LA CARTE. **4** M19 A CARTE-DE-VISITE.

carte blanche *noun phrase* plural **cartes blanches** **L17 French** (= blank paper). **1** L17 A blank sheet of paper to be filled in as a person wishes; *figurative* full discretionary power granted. **2** E19 *Cards* In piquet and bezique, a hand containing no face cards as dealt, and attracting a compensatory score.

■ The figurative use of sense 1 is now the one usually encountered.

carte-de-visite *noun* plural **cartes-de-visite** **M19 French** (= visiting card). A small photographic portrait mounted on a card. Now *archaic* or *historical*.

carte d'identité *noun phrase* plural **cartes d'identité** **E20 French.** An identity card.

carte du pays *noun phrase* plural **cartes du pays** **M18 French** (literally, 'map of the country'). (A statement of) the state of affairs.

cartel *noun* (branch I also **chartel**) **M16 French** (branch I from Italian *cartello* placard, challenge, diminutive of *carta* from Latin *c(h)arta*; branch II from German *Kartell* from French). **I 1** M16 A written challenge. In full *cartel of defiance*. Now *archaic* or *historical*. **2** L17 *History* A written agreement relating to the exchange or ransom of prisoners; an exchange or ransom of prisoners; (in full *cartel ship*) a ship commissioned for the exchange of prisoners. **3** L17 *generally* A paper or card bearing writing or printing. **II 4** L19 A combination between political parties to promote a mutual interest. **5** E20 A manufacturers' agreement or association formed to control marketing arrangements, regulate prices, etc.

cartes blanches, **cartes-de-visite**, etc., plural of CARTE BLANCHE, CARTE-DE-VISITE, etc.

cartonnage *noun* (also **cartonage**) **M19 French** (from *carton* cardboard (from Italian *cartone* augmentative of *carta*, from Latin *c(h)arta* paper) + *-age*). *Egyptology* A mummy case made of tightly fitting layers of linen or papyrus glued together.

carton-pierre *noun* **M19 French** (literally, 'cardboard (of) stone'). Papier mâché made to resemble stone or bronze.

cartouche *noun* E17 **French** (from Italian *cartoccio* from *carta* paper). **I 1a** E17 A case for containing propellant explosive, a cartridge. *obsolete* except *historical*. **b** E17–M18 A case of wood, pasteboard, etc., for cannon-balls. **II 2a** E17 *Architecture* A scroll-shaped ornament; a tablet representing a scroll with rolled-up ends or edges, with or without an inscription. **b** L18 A painting or drawing of a scroll with rolled-up ends, with or without a text; an ornate frame in the shape of such a scroll. **3** M19 *Egyptology* An elongated oval with a straight bar at the end containing the hieroglyphic names and titles of rulers.

casbah *noun* (also **kasbah**) M18 **French** (*casbah* from Maghribi pronunciation of Arab *ḳaṣaba* fortress). (The Arab quarter surrounding) a North African castle or fortress citadel.

cascara sagrada *noun phrase* L19 **Spanish** (*cáscara sagrada*, literally, 'sacred bark'). The bark of a California buckthorn, *Rhamnus purshiana*; an extract of this, used as a purgative.

■ Often shortened to *cascara*.

casha variant of KASHA.

casino *noun* plural **casinos** M18 **Italian** (diminutive of *casa* house, from Latin *casa* cottage). **1** M18 Originally, a public room used for social meetings; *especially* a public music or dancing saloon. Now, a building for gambling, often with other amenities. **2** M18 A summer house (*specifically* in Italy).

■ See also CASSINO, originally a variant of *casino*.

casque *noun* L17 **French** (from Spanish *casco*). **1** L17 A piece of armor to cover the head; a helmet. Now *historical* or *poetical*. **2** L18 *Zoology* A helmet-like structure, as in the cassowaries and hornbills.

cassareep *noun* M19 **Caribbean**. A thick brown syrup prepared by boiling down the juice of the cassava with sugar, spices, etc.

cassata *noun* E20 **Italian**. A Neapolitan ice cream containing fruit and nuts.

casse *noun* L19 **French** (from *casser* to break). Souring of certain wines, accompanied by the loss of color and the throwing of a sediment.

casserole *noun & verb* E18 **French** (extension of *cassole* diminutive of *casse* from Provençal *casa*, from late Latin *cattia* ladle, pan, from Greek *kuathion*, *kuatheion* diminutive of *kuathos* cup). **A** *noun* A covered heatproof vessel in which food is cooked and served (now also *casserole dish*, *pan*, etc.); (a dish of) food cooked in this. **B** *transitive verb* M20 Cook in a casserole.

cassette *noun* L18 **French** (diminutive of *casse*, *caisse* case). **1** L18 A casket. Now *rare*. **2** L19 A container for transporting photographic plates; a frame or holder for an X-ray plate or film. **3** M20 A container for a spool of magnetic tape, photographic film, etc., fashioned so as to be immediately usable on insertion into equipment designed for it; (now usually) such a container together with its tape, film, etc.; a video or audio magnetic recording on such a tape, etc. **4** L20 *Genetics* A block of genetic material that can be inserted or moved as a unit, *especially* one that is expressed only at one location.

cassino *noun* L18 **Italian** (variant of CASINO). A two-handed card game in which players match or combine cards exposed on the table with cards from their hands. Also, either of two high-scoring cards in this game, (*a*) *big cassino*, (now *rare*) *great cassino*, the ten of diamonds, (*b*) *little cassino*, the two of spades.

cassis *noun* L19 **French** (= blackcurrant, apparently from Latin *cassia*). A (frequently alcoholic) syrup made from blackcurrants and used to flavor drinks, etc.

cassolette *noun* (also **cassolet**) M17 **French** (from Provençal *casoleta* diminutive of *casola*, from *casa*; cf. CASSEROLE). **1** M17 A vessel in which perfumes are burned. **2** E19 A box with a perforated cover for diffusing the odor of perfume in it. **3** E19 A small casserole dish; (a dish of) food cooked in this.

cassone *noun* plural **cassones**, **cassoni** L19 **Italian** (augmentative of *cassa* chest). A large Italian coffer, especially to hold a bride's trousseau.

cassoulet *noun* M20 **French** (diminutive of dialect *cassolo* stew pan, tureen). A ragout of meat and beans.

castrato *noun* plural **castrati** M18 **Italian** (noun use of past participle of *castrare* to castrate). *History* An adult male singer castrated in boyhood so as to retain a soprano or alto voice.

castrum *noun* plural **castra** M19 **Latin**. A Roman encampment or fortress.

casus belli *noun phrase* M19 **Latin** (from *casus* case + *belli* genitive of *bellum* war). An act or situation justifying or precipitating war.

casus foederis *noun phrase* L18 **Latin** (from *casus* case + *foederis* genitive of *foedus* treaty). An event that, under the terms of a treaty of alliance, entitles one of the allies to help from the other(s).

catafalque *noun* (also (now *rare*) **catafalco**, plural **catafalco(e)s**) M17 **French** (from Italian *catafalco*, of unknown origin). **1** M17 A decorated structure fashioned so as to carry the coffin or effigy of a distinguished person during a funeral service or for a lying in state. **2** M19 A structure on which a coffin is drawn in procession.

catalogue raisonné *noun phrase* plural **catalogues raisonnés** L18 **French** (= reasoned catalog). A descriptive catalog with explanations or comments; *figurative* an exhaustive account.

catalysis *noun* plural **catalyses** M17 **Modern Latin** (from Greek *katalusis*, from *kataluein* to dissolve). **1** M–L17 Dissolution, destruction. **2** M19 *Chemistry* The action or effect of a substance in increasing the rate of a reaction without itself being consumed; an instance of this.

catamaran *noun* E17 **Tamil** (*kaṭṭumaram*, literally, 'tied wood'). **1** E17 A raft or float of logs tied side by side with the longest in the middle; a raft of two boats fastened side by side; a sailboat with two hulls side by side. **2** E19 *History* A naval weapon consisting of a floating chest packed with gunpowder. **3** M19 A quarrelsome woman. *colloquial.*

catastasis *noun* plural **catastases** M16 **Greek** (*katastasis* settling, appointment, from as *cata-* + *stasis*). The third part of the ancient drama, in which the action is heightened for the catastrophe.

catechesis *noun* plural **catecheses** M18 **ecclesiastical Latin** (from Greek *katēkhēsis* instruction by word of mouth, from *katēkhein*). **1** M18 Oral instruction given to catechumens; catechizing. **2** M18 A book for the instruction of catechumens.

catechumen *noun* LME **Old and Modern French** (*catéchumène* or ecclesiastical Latin *catechumenus* from Greek *katēkhoumenos* being instructed, present participle passive of *katēkhein*). A Christian convert under instruction before baptism. Also, a young Christian preparing for confirmation.

catharsis *noun* (in sense 2 also **katharsis**) plural **catharses** E19 **Modern Latin** (from Greek *katharsis*, from *kathairein* to cleanse, from *katharos* pure). **1** E19 *Medicine* Purgation. **2** M19 (A) purification of the emotions by vicarious experience, especially through drama, or, in psychotherapy, by abreaction.

■ In sense 2 from Aristotle's *Poetics*.

cathedra *noun* LME **Latin** (from Greek *kathedra* chair). A seat; *specifically* the chair of a bishop in his church; the episcopal see.

■ Most commonly in the phrase EX CATHEDRA.

catheter *noun* (also **katheter**) E17 **Late Latin** (*catheter* from Greek *kathetēr*, from *kathienai* to send or let down). *Medicine* A tube which can be passed into the bladder or other body cavity or canal to allow the draining of fluid.

cathexis *noun* E20 **Greek** (*kathexis* holding, retention). *Psychoanalysis* The concentration or accumulation of libidinal energy on a particular object.

■ A rendering of Freud's German term *(Libido)besetzung*.

caudillo *noun* plural **caudillos** M19 **Spanish** (from late Latin *capitellum* diminutive of *caput* head). In Spain and Spanish-speaking countries: a head of state, a military or political leader.

cause célèbre *noun phrase* plural **causes célèbres** M18 **French**. A notorious legal case; *generally* a controversy or scandal that attracts much attention.

causerie *noun* E19 **French** (from *causer* to talk). Informal (especially literary) talk; a chatty article in a magazine or journal.

causes célèbres plural of CAUSE CÉLÈBRE.

causeuse *noun* M19 **French** (from *causer* to talk). A small sofa for two people.

cavaliere servente *noun phrase* M18 **Italian** (literally, 'gentleman-in-waiting'). The lover or solicitous admirer of a (married) woman.

cavallard variant of CAVAYARD.

cavatina *noun* E19 **Italian**. *Music* A short simple song; a songlike piece of instrumental music, usually slow and emotional.

cavayard *noun* (also **cavallard**, **cavyyard**, and other variants) E19 **Spanish** (alteration of CABALLADA). A drove of horses or mules.

cave *noun & interjection* LME **Latin** (imperative singular of *cavere* to beware). **A** *noun* **1** LME–L15 A warning; an injunction. **2** E20 *keep cave*, act as a lookout. *school slang*. **B** M19 *interjection* As a warning cry: look out! *school slang*.

cavea *noun* plural **caveae** E17 **Latin** (= a hollow). *Roman Antiquities* The (concave) auditorium of a theater; a theater.

caveat *noun* M16 **Latin** (3rd person singular present subjunctive of *cavere* to beware). **1** M16 A warning, a proviso; *specifically* in *Law* a process or notice suspending or delaying proceedings. **2** L16–L17 A precaution.

■ Also formerly as a transitive verb (M17) in legal terminology or an intransitive verb (M17) in fencers' jargon meaning 'disengage'. Current verbal use is confined to the phrase CAVEAT EMPTOR.

caveat emptor *interjection* E16 **Latin**. (A maxim:) let the buyer beware!

■ A robust antique principle that the purchaser, rather than the seller, is responsible for making sure that the quality of the goods purchased is satisfactory. Frequently invoked in the context of horse-dealing—the earliest recorded use in English is in J. Fitzherbert's *A newe tracte . . . for all husbande men* (1523)—it fails to find much favor under modern consumer protection legislation.

cavy-yard variant of CAVAYARD.

cedilla *noun* (formerly (L16–M19) also **cerilla** L16 **Spanish** ((now *zedilla*), diminutive of *zeda* letter Z). The diacritical mark ¸ written under *c* to show that it is sibilant /s/ or /ts/, as before *a, o, u* in French and Portuguese and (formerly) Spanish; a similar mark under *c* and *s* indicating a manner of articulation in various other contexts, as distinguishing the voiceless from the voiced consonants in Turkish.

ceilidh *noun* L19 **Irish** (*céilidhe* (now *céilí*), Gaelic *cēilidh*, from Old Irish *céilide* visit, act of visiting, from *céile* companion). An informal gathering for (especially Scottish or Irish) folk music, dancing, song, etc.

ceinture *noun* LME **French** (from Latin *cinctura*, from *cinctus* past participle of *cingere* to gird). A girdle, a cincture.

■ Fell into disuse after the Middle English period, but was reintroduced in the early nineteenth century as part of the enthusiasm for all things Gothic and medieval.

celadon *noun & adjective* **M18 French** (*céladon*). **A** *noun* **1** M18 A pale grayish shade of green. **2** M19 A glaze of this color used on (especially Chinese) pottery or porcelain; ceramic ware thus glazed. **B** L19 *attributive* or as *adjective* Of this color; covered with this glaze.

■ From the name of the shepherd hero of D'Urfé's immensely popular pastoral romance *L'Astrée* (1607–27).

celebret *noun* **M19 Latin** (= let him celebrate, 3rd person singular present subjunctive of *celebrare* to celebrate). *Roman Catholic Church* A document granting permission by a bishop to a priest to celebrate mass in a particular parish.

celesta *noun* **L19 pseudo-Latin** (apparently based on French CÉLESTE). *Music* A small keyboard instrument in which hammers strike on steel plates, producing an ethereal bell-like sound.

celeste *noun* **L19 French** (*céleste* from Latin *caelestis* from *caelum* heaven). **1** L19 A stop on the organ and harmonium with a soft tremulous tone (French *voix céleste*). Also, a form of soft pedal on a piano. **2** M20 A CELESTA.

cella *noun* plural **cellae** **L17 Latin.** *Architecture* The internal section of a Greek or Roman temple housing the hidden cult image; a similar part of other ancient temples.

cembalo *noun* plural **cembalos** **M19 Italian** (abbreviation of CLAVICEMBALO). A harpsichord.

cenacle *noun* **LME Old and Modern French** (*cénacle* from Latin *cenaculum*, from *cena* dinner). **1** LME A dining room; *specifically* the room in which the Last Supper was held. **2** L19 A place where a discussion group, literary clique, etc., meets; the group itself.

cenobium variant of COENOBIUM.

cenote *noun* **M19 Yucatan Spanish** (from Maya *tzonot*). A natural underground reservoir of water, such as occurs in the limestone of Yucatan, Mexico.

census *noun* **E17 Latin** (from *censere* to assess). **1** E17–M19 A tax, a tribute; *especially* a poll tax. **2** M17 *History* The registration of citizens and their property in ancient Rome, usually for taxation purposes. **3** M18 An official enumeration of the population of a country, etc., or of a class of things, usually with statistics relating to them.

cento *noun* plural **centos** **E17 Latin** (literally, 'patchwork garment'). **1** E–M17 A piece of patchwork; a patchwork garment. **2** E17 A hodgepodge, a medley; *specifically* a composition made up of quotations from other authors.

centrifuge *adjective, noun, & verb* **E18 French** (from Modern Latin *centrifugus* centrifugal). **A** *adjective* E18–E19 Moving or tending to move away from the center, centrifugal. **B** *noun* L19 A centrifugal machine; *especially* a device for effecting separation, usually of one liquid from another or of a solid from a liquid, by rapid rotation. **C** E20 *transitive verb* Subject to centrifugal motion; separate by means of a centrifuge.

centum see PER CENTUM.

cep *noun* (also **cèpe**) **M19 French** (*cèpe* from Gascon *cep* tree trunk, mushroom, from Latin *cippus* stake). An edible mushroom, *Boletus edulis*, with a stout stalk and smooth brown cap.

cerebellum *noun* **M16 Latin** (diminutive of CEREBRUM). *Anatomy* The larger part of the hindbrain, responsible for the control of muscle tone and balance.

cerebrum *noun* **E17 Latin** (= brain). *Anatomy* The larger, anterior part of the brain, responsible for voluntary activity and mental processes.

cerilla obsolete variant of CEDILLA.

cerise *adjective & noun* **M19 French** (= cherry). (Of) a light clear red.

ceroon variant of SERON.

cervelat *noun* **E17 French** ((now *cervelas*) from Italian *cervellata* Milanese sausage). A kind of smoked pork sausage.

cervix *noun* plural **cervices** M18 **Latin.** *Anatomy* The neck; a part of an organ resembling or forming a neck; *specifically* the narrow passage forming the lower end of the uterus adjacent to the vagina.

c'est la guerre *interjection* F20 **French** (= that's war). (An expression of resignation:) that's the kind of thing that happens!

c'est la vie *interjection* E20 **French.** (An expression of resignation:) that's life!

cestui *noun* M16 **Anglo-Norman and Old French** (from Proto-Romance, from Latin *ecce* lo! + *iste* that (one), with element *-ui* as in *cui* dative of *quis* who). *Law* The person (who), he (who).

■ Only in the following legal phrases: *cestui que trust, cestui que use* the person for whose benefit something is given in trust to another; *cestui que vie* a person for whose lifetime an estate or interest in property is held by another.

cestus *noun 1* plural **cesti** M16 **Latin** (from Greek *kestos* noun use of participial adjective = stitched). A (bridal) belt or girdle for the waist, *especially* that of Aphrodite or Venus.

cestus *noun 2* plural same L17 **Latin** (*caestus*, from *caedere* to strike). *History* A covering for the hand made of thongs of bull hide loaded with metallic strips, used by boxers in ancient Rome.

ceteris paribus *adverb phrase* E17 **Modern Latin.** Other things being equal or unchanged.

ceviche variant of SEVICHE.

cha-cha *noun & verb* (also **cha-cha-cha** M20 **American Spanish. A** *noun* M20 A type of ballroom dance to a Latin American rhythm; a piece of music for this dance. **B** *transitive verb* M20 Perform this dance.

chacham variant of HAHAM.

chaconne *noun* L17 **French** (from Spanish *chacona*). A moderately slow musical composition on a ground bass, usually in triple time; a dance to this music.

chacun à son goût *interjection* L19 **French.** Everyone to his or her taste.

■ Also occasionally in the form usual in French: *à chacun son goût.*

chadar *noun* (also **chaddar**, **chador**, **chuddar**, and other variants) E17 **Urdu** (*chādar, chaddar* from Persian *čādar* sheet, veil). A large piece of material worn as a long shawl or cloak especially by Muslim women in the Indian subcontinent and Iran.

chaebol *noun* L20 **Korean.** In South Korea: a large business conglomerate comparable to the Japanese ZAIBATSU.

chagrin *noun & verb* M17 **French** (literally, 'rough skin', of unknown origin). **A** *noun* **1** M17–M19 Anxiety; melancholy. **2** E18 Vexation arising from disappointment or failure; acute annoyance. **B** also *transitive verb* M17 Affect with chagrin. Usually in *passive.*

■ The spelling *shagreen* of the noun is an obsolete (L17–M19) variant that is now used solely in senses that retain the literal French meaning, being applied to a kind of untanned leather with a rough granular surface (often dyed green) or to the rough scaly skin of sharks or rays especially as used for polishing.

chaîné *noun* M20 **French** (= linked). *Ballet* A quick step or turn from one foot to the other, or a series of these, performed in a line.

chaise *noun* M17 **French** (variant of *chaire* chair). **1** M17 A pleasure or traveling carriage, especially a light open one for one or two people. Chiefly *historical.* **2** M20 A CHAISE LONGUE.

chaise longue *noun phrase* plural **chaise longues**, **chaises longues** E19 **French** (= long chair). A kind of sofa with a backrest at only one end.

chaise percée *noun phrase* plural **chaises percées** M20 **French** (= pierced chair). A chair incorporating a chamber pot.

chaitya *noun* L19 **Sanskrit** (*caitya* (resembling) a funeral pile, mound, etc., from *citā* funeral mound). A Buddhist place or object of reverence.

chakra *noun* L18 **Sanskrit** (*cakra*; cf. Greek *kuklos* cycle). **1** L18 A thin knife-edged disk of steel formerly used as a weapon by Sikhs. **2** L19 A discus or mystic circle depicted in the hands of Hindu deities. **3** L19 *Yoga* Each of the centers of spiritual power in the human body. **4** M20 The circular emblem on the flag of the Indian Union.

chal *noun* M19 **Romany** (= person, fellow). A male Gypsy. Also *Romany chal*.

chalet *noun* L18 **Swiss French** (diminutive of Old French *chasel* farmstead from Proto-Romance derivative of Latin *casa* hut, cottage). A Swiss mountain cowherd's hut; a Swiss peasant's wooden cottage; a house with a widely overhanging roof; a small villa; a small house in a vacation camp, etc.

chalifa variant of KHALIFA.

challah *noun* L20 **Hebrew**. Jewish ceremonial bread for the Sabbath.

chalumeau *noun* plural **chalumeaux** E18 **French** (from late Latin *calamellus* diminutive of *calamus* reed). A musical pipe of reed or straw; an instrument having a reed mouthpiece, *especially* the forerunner of the clarinet. Also (in full *chalumeau register*), the lowest register of the clarinet.

chalutzim variant of HALUTZIM.

cham *noun* LME **French** (*cham, chan* from Turkic *kān* KHAN). A khan. Now only *transferred* and *figurative*, an autocrat, a dominant critic, etc.

■ The transferred use alludes to an expression of the Scottish author Tobias Smollett, who, in a letter to John Wilkes in 1759, referred to Samuel Johnson as the "great Cham of literature."

chambranle *noun* E18 **French**. *Architecture* An ornamental bordering around a door, window, or fireplace.

chambré *adjective* M20 **French** (past participle of *chambrer* to bring to room temperature, from Old French *chambre* from Latin *camera* room). Of wine: at room temperature. Usually *predicative*.

chametz variant of HAMETZ.

chamois *noun & adjective* (senses A2 and B2 also **shammy**) M16 **Old and Modern French** (probably ultimately from Swiss Proto-Romance; cf. Gallo-Latin *camox*). **A** *noun* M16 **1** A goat-like antelope, *Rupicapra rupicapra*, found in the mountains of Europe and Asia Minor. **2** L16 Soft pliable leather from the chamois or (now more usually) from sheep, goats, deer, etc.; a piece of this for polishing, etc. More fully *chamois leather*. **B** *attributive* or as *adjective*. **1** E17 Made of chamois leather. **2** M17 Of the color of chamois leather; yellowish brown.

champignon *noun* L16 **French** ((earlier *champaignon*), diminutive of *champagne*). A mushroom; a toadstool. Now *specifically* (*a*) the edible field mushroom *Agaricus campestris*; (*b*) an agaric, *Marismius oreades*, which often forms fairy rings.

champlevé *adjective & noun* M19 **French** (from *champ* field + *levé* raised). (Designating) enamelwork in which the colors in the pattern are set into hollows made in the surface of the metal base. Cf. CLOISONNÉ.

chancre *noun* L16 **French** (from Latin *cancer* crab). *Medicine* A painless ulcer, *especially* one occurring on the genitals and resulting from syphilis.

chandelier *noun* M17 **French** (from *chandelle* candle, from Latin *candela*). **1** M17 *Military* A wooden frame filled with fascines to form a traverse in sapping. **2** M18 A branched hanging support for several lights, originally candles.

changement *noun* M19 **French** (from *changer* to change). *Ballet* A jump during which the dancer changes the position of the feet. In full *changement de pieds* (literally, 'changing of feet').

chanson *noun* L15 **Old and Modern French** (from Latin *cantio* song). A French song.

chanson de geste *noun phrase* plural **chansons de geste** M19 **French** (= song of heroic deeds). Any of a group of medieval French epic poems dealing with chivalric and heroic subjects.

■ The earliest was the *Chanson de Roland*, written about 1100.

chansonette *noun* E19 **French**. A short song.

chansonnier *noun* L19 **French**. In France: a writer or performer of songs, especially of satirical songs in a cabaret; a collection of (French) songs.

chantage *noun* L19 **French**. Extortion of money by blackmail.

chanterelle *noun 1* E17 **French** (from *chanter* from Latin *cantare* frequentative of *canere* to sing). **1** A decoy bird. Only in E17. **2** L18 The highest-pitched string of a plucked or bowed musical instrument.

chanterelle *noun 2* (also **chantarelle**) L18 **French** (from Modern Latin *cantharellus* diminutive of *cantharus* from Greek *kantharos* drinking vessel). A yellow funnel-shaped edible fungus, *Cantharellus cibarius*.

chanteuse *noun* M19 **French**. A female singer of popular songs, originally in France.

chaparejos *noun plural* (also **chaparreras**) M19 **Mexican Spanish** (*chaparreras*, from *chaparra*, *chaparro* dwarf evergreen oak). Tough leather leggings worn over the pants by cowboys for protection against spiny vegetation.

■ *Chaparejos* is a later form than *chaparreras* and is probably influenced by Spanish *aparejo* 'equipment'. The abbreviation *chaps* has been commonly used from the late nineteenth century onward.

chaparral *noun* M19 **Spanish** (from as above). A thicket of dwarf evergreen oaks; dense tangled brushwood.

chaparreras variant of CHAPAREJOS.

chapatti *noun* (also **chapati**, **chupatti**, and other variants) E19 **Hindustani** (*capātī*, from *capānā* to flatten, roll out, ultimately from Dravidian). In Indian cooking: a small flat thin cake of coarse unleavened bread.

chapeau-bras *noun* plural **chapeaux-bras** M18 **French** (from *chapeau* (Old French *c(h)apel*, from Latin *cappellum* diminutive of *cappa* cap) hat + *bras* arm). A three-cornered flat silk hat able to be carried under the arm.

chapelle ardente *noun phrase* plural **chapelles ardentes** E19 **French** (= burning chapel). A chamber prepared for the lying-in-state of a distinguished person, and lit up with candles, torches, etc.

chaperon *noun & verb* (also **chaperone**) LME **Old and Modern French** (from *chape* cape, hood, ultimately from Latin *caput* head). **A** *noun* **1** LME A hood, a capital. *obsolete* except *historical*. **2** L17–L18 A small escutcheon placed especially on the forehead of a horse drawing a hearse. **3** E18 A person who ensures propriety, *especially* a married or older woman accompanying young unmarried people on social occasions. **B** L18 *transitive verb* Act as a chaperon to.

chappal *noun* (also **chappli**) L19 **Hindustani** (*cappal*, *caplī*). In the Indian subcontinent: a sandal, especially of leather.

chaprassi *noun* plural **chaprassi(e)s** (also **chuprassy**) E19 **Urdu** (*chaprāsī*, from *chaprās* official badge, from Persian *čaprāst*). In the Indian subcontinent: an attendant, a messenger, a household official.

charabanc *noun* (also **char-à-banc**) E19 **French** (*char-à-bancs* literally, 'carriage with seats'). A long and light vehicle with transverse seats looking forward; a tour bus. Now *archaic* or *jocular*.

charade *noun* L18 **French** (from Modern Provençal *charrado* conversation, from *charra* chatter, perhaps of imitative origin). **1** L18 A written or (now usually) acted clue from which a syllable of a word or a complete word is to be guessed. **b** M19 (in *plural* usually treated as *singular*) A game of guessing words from such clues. **2** L19 *figurative* An absurd pretense.

charcuterie *noun* M19 **French** (from *char* (modern *chair*) *cuite* cooked flesh). Cold cooked meats; a shop selling these; a (French) pork butcher's shop.

chargé *noun* M19 **French**. Abbreviation of CHARGÉ D'AFFAIRES.

chargé d'affaires *noun phrase* plural **chargés d'affaires** (also **chargé des affaires**) M18 **French** (= (a person) in charge of affairs). **1** M18 A minister who transacts diplomatic business during the temporary absence of an ambassador; a nation's representative at a minor foreign court or government. **2** L18 *generally* A person temporarily in charge.

charisma *noun* plural **charismata** M17 **ecclesiastical Latin** (from Greek *kharisma, -mat-*, from *kharis* favor, grace). **1** M17 *Christian Theology* A divinely conferred power or talent. **2** M20 A capacity to inspire devotion and enthusiasm; aura.

charivari *noun* M17 **French** (of unknown origin). A cacophonous mock serenade in derision of an unpopular person or in celebration of a marriage; marriage; a discordant medley of sounds, a hubbub.

■ The variant *shivaree* (M19) is mainly found in the United States.

charlotte *noun* L18 **French** (possibly the feminine name). A dessert made of stewed fruit with a casing or covering of bread, cookies, sponge cake, or breadcrumbs.

■ Usually with defining word, as in *apple charlotte, rhubarb charlotte*, etc. Cf. CHARLOTTE RUSSE.

charlotte russe *noun phrase* plural **charlottes russes, charlotte russes** M19 **French** (= Russian CHARLOTTE). A dessert with flavored custard or cream inside a molded sponge cake or ladyfingers casing.

charmeuse *noun* E20 **French** (feminine of *charmeur* charmer, from Old French *charme* charm, from Latin *carmen* song, incantation). A soft smooth silky dress fabric.

charoset(h) variants of HAROSETH.

charpoy *noun* M17 **Urdu** (*chārpāī* from Persian). In the Indian subcontinent: a light bedstead.

charqui *noun* E17 **American Spanish** (*charqui, charque* from Quechua *cc'arki*). Meat, especially beef, cut into thin slices and dried in the wind and sun.

■ English travelers to the New World in the seventeenth century apparently adopted the word from the Spanish, corrupting it in the process; from these corruptions the word *jerky* emerged (M19) to become the term widely used in North America. The South African equivalent is BILTONG; cf. PEMMICAN.

charro *noun* plural **charros** E20 **Mexican Spanish** (from Spanish = rustic). A Mexican cowboy, *especially* one elaborately dressed.

chartreuse *noun* E19 **French** (feminine of *Chartreux*). **1** E19 *Cooking* A dish turned out from a mold, of meat, vegetables, or (now more usually) of fruit enclosed in jelly, etc. **2** M19 A green or yellow liqueur of brandy and aromatic herbs, etc., originally made by the monks of La Grande Chartreuse, near Grenoble, France. **3** L19 An apple-green color.

chasid variant of HASID.

chasse *noun 1* LME **French** (*châsse* reliquary). A case for the relics of a saint.

chasse *noun 2* plural **chasses** M18 **French** (abbreviation of *chasse-café*, literally, 'chase-coffee'). A liqueur taken after coffee, tobacco, etc.; a chaser.

■ The full form *chasse-café* (E19) is now rare.

chassé *noun* E19 **French** (literally, 'chasing, chase'). A sliding step in which one foot displaces the other in dancing.

■ A mainly North American alteration is *sashay* (noun and verb), '(to perform) a *chassé* in square dancing'; as a verb *sashay* also has a general colloquial sense of 'to walk with an ostentatiously gliding or swinging step'.

chassé croisé *noun phrase* L19 **French** (literally, 'crossed chassé'). A dance movement comprising a double chassé causing partners to change position; *figurative* an elaborate reversal of position, especially a mix-up in which people trying to meet constantly miss one another.

chasseur *noun* M18 **French** (from *chasser* to hunt). **1** M18 *History* A soldier (especially French) equipped and trained for rapid movement. **2** M18 An attendant dressed in military style. Now *rare* or *obsolete*. **b** L19 A hotel messenger, especially in France. **3** L18 A huntsman.

■ The French equivalent of the German JÄGER.

chassid variant of HASID.

chassis *noun* plural same M17 **French** (*châssis* from Proto-Romance, from Latin *capsa* case). **1** M17–E18 A window frame, a sash. **2** M19 The sliding base frame of a mounted gun. **3** E20 The base frame of a motor vehicle, etc. **4** M20 A frame carrying radio, etc., equipment. **5** M20 The human or animal frame, the body. *slang*.

château *noun* plural **châteaux** M18 **French**. A large country house in France (formerly also elsewhere); *especially* one giving its name to wine made in its neighborhood.

■ Sometimes also used jocularly with the owner's name of an ostentatious or pretentious house anywhere, e.g., Château Jones.

Chateaubriand *noun* L19 **French**. A thick fillet of beefsteak, grilled and garnished with herbs, etc.

■ Called after François René, Vicomte de *Chateaubriand* (1768–1848), French writer and statesman. Also *Chateaubriand steak* or *steak à la Chateaubriand*.

chatelaine *noun* M19 **French** (*châtelaine* feminine of *châtelain*). **1** M19 A female castellan (*historical*); the mistress of a castle or (country) house. **2** M19 *History* A set of short chains attached to a woman's belt for carrying keys, a watch, a pencil, etc.

chaton *noun* L16 **French** (from German *Kasten* case (Old and Middle High German *kasto*)). The part of a finger ring in which a stone is set or on which a device is engraved.

chatoyant *noun & adjective* L18 **French** (present participle of *chatoyer* to shimmer). (Of) iridescent undulating luster.

■ Now *rare*.

chaud-froid *noun* L19 **French** (literally, 'hot-cold'). A dish of cold cooked meat or fish in a jelly or sauce.

chaukidar variant of CHOKIDAR.

chaussée *noun* E19 **French**. In France, Belgium, etc.: a causeway; a high road.

chaussure *noun* LME **French** (Anglo-Norman *chaucer* = Old French *chaucier* (modern *chaussure*), Provençal *causier* shoe; cf. medieval Latin *calceatura*). Footwear.

■ Formerly naturalized with the spelling *chawcer* and variants, but reintroduced as a borrowing from Modern French in the nineteenth century.

chayote *noun* L19 **Spanish** (from Nahnatl *chayotli*). A tropical American vine, *Sechium edule*, cultivated elsewhere for its fruit; the succulent fruit of this vine. Also called *chocho*.

chaz(z)an variants of HAZZAN.

chechia *noun* M19 **French** (*chéchia* from Maghribi pronunciation of Arabic *šāšiyya*, from Arabic *Šāš* Tashkent in Uzbekistan). A red felt cap worn in northwest Africa.

cheder variant of HEDER.

cheechako *noun* L19 **Chinook Jargon** (= newcomer). A recently arrived immigrant to the mining districts of Alaska or Canada; a greenhorn.

■ colloquial.

chee-chee variant of CHI-CHI.

chef *noun* E19 **French** (= head). A person (usually a man) who is (usually the chief) cook in a hotel, restaurant, etc.

■ Also in combinations such as *sous-chef* 'under-chef', COMMIS *chef*, etc.

chef d'école *noun phrase* plural **chefs d'école** M19 **French** (= head of school). The initiator or leader of a school or style of music, painting, literature, etc.

chef d'équipe *noun phrase* plural **chefs d'équipe** L20 **French** (= head of team; cf. ÉQUIPE). The manager of a sports team responsible for practical arrangements especially when traveling.

chef-d'œuvre *noun* plural **chefs-d'œuvre** E17 **French** (= chief (piece) of work). The greatest work of an artist, etc.; a masterpiece.

chef d'orchestre *noun phrase* plural **chefs d'orchestre** M19 **French** (= head of orchestra). The leader or conductor of an orchestra.

chela *noun* M19 **Hindustani** (*celā*). A disciple, a pupil, *specifically* in Hinduism.

chemin de fer *noun* L19 **French** (= railroad, literally, 'road of iron'). A form of baccarat.

chemise *noun* ME **Old and Modern French** (from late Latin *camisia* shirt, nightgown). **1** ME A garment for the upper body; *especially* a woman's loose-fitting undergarment or dress hanging straight from the shoulders. **2** E18 *History* A wall with which a bastion, etc., is lined as a fortification. **3** L19 *History* A loose covering for a book.

chemisette *noun* E19 **French** (diminutive of CHEMISE). **1** E19 A bodice, resembling the upper part of a chemise. **2** E19 A piece of muslin, lace, etc., used to fill in the open front of a woman's dress.

chenille *noun* M18 **French** (literally, 'hairy caterpillar', from Latin *canicula* diminutive of *canis* dog). Velvety cord with pile all around, used in trimming and bordering dresses and furniture.

cheongsam *noun* M20 **Chinese** (Cantonese (= Mandarin *chángshān*)). A Chinese woman's garment with a high neck and slit skirt.

cherchez la femme *interjection* L19 **French** (= look for the woman). The principle that there is certain to be a woman behind an untoward event.

■ A catchphrase of Alexandre Dumas *père* in *Les Mohicans de Paris* (1864).

chère amie *noun phrase* plural **chères amies** L18 **French** (literally, 'dear (woman) friend'). A female lover; a mistress.

cherem *noun* (also **herem**) E19 **Hebrew** (*ḥērem* from *ḥāram* devote, put under a curse). Excommunication from the Synagogue and the Jewish community.

cherimoya *noun* (also **chirimoya**) M18 **Spanish** (from Quechua, from *chiri* cold, refreshing + *muya* circle). (The pulpy edible fruit of) a small tree, *Annona cherimola*, native to the Andes of Peru and Ecuador.

cher maître *noun phrase* plural **chers maîtres** E20 **French** (literally, 'dear master'). (A flattering form of address to) a famous writer.

■ Often used ironically.

chernozem *noun* (also **chernosem**) M19 **Russian** (from *chërnyĭ* black + Slavonic base *zem-* (cf. Russian *zemlya*) earth). A dark, humus-rich, fertile soil characteristic of temperate or cool grassland.

■ Originally used of the soil of the Russian steppes, now generally for soils of this type.

chétif *adjective* E20 **French**. Puny, sickly, thin; miserable, wretched.

chetnik *noun* E20 **Serbo-Croat** (*četnik*, from *četa* band, troop). A guerrilla fighter in the Balkans; (*historical*) one of a royalist force led by General Draža Mihajlović in occupied Yugoslavia, 1941–5.

chevachee variant of CHEVAUCHÉE.

cheval *noun* plural **chevaux** L15 **French** (= horse, frame). Horse; frame.

■ Never independently naturalized in English, *cheval* occurs in the combination *cheval glass* (a tall glass set on a pivot in an upright frame) and in various phrases; see À CHEVAL, CHEVAL DE BATAILLE, CHEVAUX DE FRISE.

cheval de bataille *noun phrase* plural **chevaux de bataille** E19 **French** (literally, 'battle-horse'). An obsession, a pet subject; something made boring by repetition or overuse.

■ Native English equivalents are 'hobbyhorse' or 'warhorse', depending on context.

chevalet *noun* E19 **French** (diminutive of CHEVAL). **1** A trestle for a bridge. Only in E19. **2** L19 The bridge of a bowed musical instrument.

chevalier *noun* LME **Anglo-Norman** (*chevaler*, Old and Modern French *chevalier*, from medieval Latin *caballarius*, from Latin *caballus* horse). **1** LME *History* A horseman, *especially* a mounted knight. **2** M17 A chivalrous man, a gallant. **3** E18 A member of certain orders of knighthood, or of the French Legion of Honor, etc.

■ Sometimes in the phrase *chevalier sans peur et sans reproche* literally, 'a knight without fear or stain', a perfect gentleman; see also SANS PEUR.

chevauchée *noun* Also formerly written **chevachee** LME **French** (from Old French *chevauchiee* expedition on horseback, past participial formation on *chevauchier* (modern *chevaucher*) from Late Latin *caballicare* to ride, from *caballus* horse). *History* A mounted raid.

chevaux de frise *noun phrase* L17 **French** (literally, 'horses of Friesland'). Iron spikes closely set in wood, originally to repel cavalry; a similar device, often with the spikes rotating around a rod, now set along the tops of walls, fences, etc., to deter intruders.

■ The name is an ironic reference to the fact that the Frieslanders possessed no cavalry and relied upon such devices to beat off the cavalry of others. Although the phrase is plural in form it is often treated as singular.

chevelure *noun* LME **Old French** (*cheveleüre* (modern *chevelure*), from Latin *capillatura*, from *capillatus* haired, from *capillus* hair). **1** LME The hair of the head, a head of hair; (formerly) a wig. **2** L17 A halo around a star, etc.; a comet's coma.

chevet *noun* E19 **French** (= pillow). The apsidal termination of the east end of a church.

cheville *noun* L19 **French** (= peg, pin, plug). **1** L19 A meaningless or redundant word or phrase inserted to round off a sentence or complete a verse. **2** L19 A peg in a stringed musical instrument.

chevra variant of HEBRA.

chèvre *noun* M20 **French** (= goat, especially she-goat). French goat's-milk cheese.

chevron *noun* LME **Old and Modern French** (from Proto-Romance, from Latin *caper* goat; cf. Latin *capreoli* pair of rafters). **1** *Heraldry* LME A charge consisting of a bent bar of an inverted V shape. **b** E17 This shape used in decorative art, etc. **2** L16 A beam or rafters, *especially* in *plural*, the rafters of a roof that meet at an angle at the ridge. **3** E19 A badge in a V shape (whether inverted or not) on a uniform to denote rank and length of service; a V-shaped stripe.

chez, *before a vowel preposition* M18 **French** (from Old French *chiese* from Latin *casa* cottage). At the house or home of.

chiaroscuro *noun & adjective* M17 **Italian** (from *chiaro* clear, bright + *oscuro* dark, obscure). **A** *noun* plural **chiaroscuros**. **1** M17 A style of painting in which only light and shade are represented; black and white. **2** L17 The treatment or disposition of the light and shade, or brighter and darker masses, in a picture; an effect or contrast of light and shade in a picture or in nature. **3** E19 *figurative* The use of contrast in literature, etc. **B** M19 *attributively* or as *adjective* In chiaroscuro.

chiasmus *noun* plural **chiasmi** M17 **Modern Latin** (from Greek *khiasmos* from *khiazein* mark with a chi, from *khi* chi. **1** M17 *generally* A diagonal or crosswise arrangement. *rare.* **2** L19 *Rhetoric* The inversion in a second phrase or clause of the order of words in the first.

chibouk *noun* (also **chibouque**) E19 **French** ((*chibouque* from) Turkish *çubuk*, (earlier) *çıbık* tube, pipe). A long Turkish tobacco pipe.

chic *noun & adjective* M19 **French** (probably from German *Schick* skill). **A** *noun* M19 Stylishness; elegance in dress; skill, effectiveness. **B** *adjective* M19 Stylish, elegant.

chicane *noun* L17 **French** (from as next). **1** L17 Trickery or subterfuge in legal matters, chicanery. **2** L17–M18 An instance of chicanery; a subterfuge, a quibble. **3** L19 *Cards* A hand without trumps or without cards of one suit as dealt. **4** M20 An artificial barrier or obstacle, especially a sharp double bend, on an automobile racetrack.

chicane *verb* L17 **French** (*chicaner* to pursue at law, quibble, of unknown origin). **1** L17 *intransitive verb* Employ chicanery; quibble, cavil. **2** L18 *transitive verb* Quibble over; argue *away* by chicanery. *rare.* **3** M19 *transitive verb* Deceive by chicanery, cheat (*into, out of*, etc.).

chicano *noun & adjective* (also **Chicano**) M20 **Spanish** (alteration of *mejicano* Mexican, from *Méjico* Mexico). **A** *noun* M20 plural **chicanos** (feminine **chicana**) A North American of Mexican origin. **B** *adjective* M20 Of or pertaining to chicanos; Mexican American.

chicha *noun* E17 **American Spanish** (from Cuna). In South and Central America: a fermented liquor made from maize.

chicharron *noun* plural **chicharrones** M19 **American Spanish** (*chicharrón*). A piece of crackling, served as a delicacy in Mexico, parts of the southern United States, etc.

chichi *noun & adjective* E20 **French. A** *noun* E20 Showiness, fussiness; affectation; a frilly or showy thing. **B** *adjective* M20 Showy, frilly, fussy; affected.

chi-chi *adjective* (also **chee-chee**) L18 **Anglo-Indian** (perhaps from Hindustani *chī-chī* fie!). (Especially of a girl or woman) half caste, Eurasian; (of speech) characteristic of the English formerly spoken by some Eurasians in India.

■ Usually derogatory in application, *chi-chi* mimicks an affected expression supposed by the Europeans to be used by Eurasians.

chicken variant of CHIKAN.

chicle *noun* L19 **American Spanish** (from Nahuatl *tzictli*). The coagulated latex of the sapodilla, *Manilkara zapota*, and several related trees, which forms the basis of chewing gum.

chiffon *noun & adjective* M18 **French** (from *chiffe* rag). **A** *noun* **1** M18 In *plural* Trimmings or other adornments of women's dress. *archaic* **2** L19 A light diaphanous plain-woven fabric of silk, nylon, etc. **B** E20 *attributively* or as *adjective* Made of chiffon; light in weight.

chiffonier *noun* (also **chiffon(n)ière**) M18 **French** (*chiffonnier*, *chiffonière*, transferred use of CHIFFONNIER). A movable low cupboard with a sideboard top.

chiffonnade *noun* L19 **French**. A selection of shredded or finely cut vegetables, used especially as a garnish for soup.

chiffonnier *noun* M19 **French**. A collector of scraps, a ragpicker.

chignon *noun* L18 **French** (originally = nape of the neck, from Proto-Romance variant of Latin *catena* chain). A coil or mass of hair worn by women at the back of the head.

chikan *noun* (also **chicken**) L19 **Urdu** (*chikan* from Persian *čikin*). A type of hand embroidery of the Indian subcontinent.

chili *noun* (also **chile**, **chilli**) plural **chil(l)ies**, **chiles** E17 **Spanish** (*chile* from Nahuatl *chilli*). The (dried) red pod of the pepper *Capsicum annuum* var. *longum*, used in sauces, relishes, etc., and made into a hot cayenne; cayenne made from these dried pods. Also *chili pepper*.

chili con carne *noun phrase* (also **chile con carne**, **chilli con carne**) **M19 Spanish** (= chili with meat). A Mexican dish of ground beef, beans, and chili.

chili relleno *noun phrase* **Spanish** (= stuffed chili). A stuffed green pepper.

■ Sometimes abbreviated to *relleno* plural *rellenos* (E20).

chimera *noun* (also **chimaera**) **LME Latin** (*chimaera* from Greek *khimaira* she-goat, monster, from *khimaros* he-goat). **1** LME *Greek Mythology* A fire-breathing monster, with a lion's head, a goat's body, and a serpent's tail. **2** LME A grotesque monster represented in painting, etc. **3a** E16 A bogey, a horrible phantasm. **b** L16 A wild or fanciful conception. **c** M19 A thing of hybrid character. **4** E19 (Usually **chimaera**.) Any cartilaginous fish of the family Chimaeridae. **5** E20 *Biology* An organism whose cells are not all derived from the same zygote.

chin variant of TCHIN.

chinchilla *noun* **E17 Spanish** (probably from Aymara or Quechua). **I 1** E17 A South American rodent of the genus *Chinchilla*, with very soft gray fur. **2** L19 A cat of a silver-gray breed. **3** E20 A rabbit of a variety bred for its gray fur. **II 4** E19 The fur of the South American chinchilla or of the chinchilla rabbit.

chiné *noun & adjective* **M19 French** (past participle of *chiner*, from *Chine* China). (A fabric) given a mottled pattern of (supposedly) Chinese style by coloring the warp or weft threads, or both, before weaving.

chino *noun & adjective* **M20 American Spanish** (= toasted). **A** M20 *noun* plural **chinos** A cotton twill cloth, usually khaki-colored; in *plural*, pants made of this. **B** M20 *adjective* Of this cloth.

chinoiserie *noun* **L19 French** (from *chinois* Chinese + *-erie*). A Chinese or imitation Chinese artistic object, piece of furniture, etc.; the imitation of Chinese motifs in furniture, etc.

chipolata *noun* **L19 French** (from Italian *cipollata* dish of onions, from *cipolla* onion). In full *chipolata sausage*. A small (often spicy) sausage.

chipotle *noun* **L20 Mexican Spanish**. A kind of dried and smoked chili used in Mexican cooking.

chi-rho *noun* **M19 Greek** (twenty-second letter of the alphabet *chi* + seventeenth letter *rho*). A monogram representing the first two letters of Greek *Khristos* Christ.

■ The *chi-rho* was adopted in AD 312 by the Byzantine emperor Constantine the Great as a device for his military banners, following a vision in which he was told "By this sign you shall conquer." During the following centuries the *chi-rho* became ubiquitous in Christian art.

chirimoya variant of cherimoya.

chitarrone *noun* plural **chitarroni** **M18 Italian** (augmentative of *chitarra* guitar). A double-necked lute of great length, a theorbo.

chiton *noun* **E19 Greek** (*khitōn*; in sense 1 through Modern Latin *Chiton* genus name). **1** E19 A mollusk of the class Polyplacophora, characterized by a broad oval foot and a symmetrical dorsal shell composed of a series of eight overlapping plates. **2** M19 A long woolen tunic worn in ancient Greece.

chocolatier *noun* **L19 French** (from *chocolat* (or Spanish *chocolate* from Nahuatl *chocolatl* item of food made from caocao seeds)). A maker or seller of chocolate.

chokidar *noun* (also **chaukidar**) **E17 Urdu** (*chaukīdār*, from Hindustani *cauki* toll, police station + Urdu and Persian *-dār* keeper). In the Indian subcontinent; a watchman.

chola see CHOLO.

cholent *noun* **M20 Yiddish** (*tscholnt*; cf. SCHALET). A Jewish Sabbath dish of slowly baked meat and vegetables, prepared on a Friday and cooked overnight.

choli *noun* E20 **Hindustani** (*colī*). An Indian woman's short-sleeved bodice of a type worn under a SARI.

cholo *noun* (also **Cholo**; feminine **chola**) plural **cholos** M19 **American Spanish** (from *Chololián*, now *Cholula*, a district of Mexico). An Indian of Latin America; a mestizo; (frequently *derogatory*) a lower-class Mexican.

chometz variant of HAMETZ.

chop suey *noun* (also **chopsuey**) L19 **Chinese** ((Cantonese) *tsaâp suì* mixed bits). A Chinese dish of pieces of meat or chicken fried with rice, onions, etc., often made with leftover food.

choragus *noun* (also **choregus**) plural **choragi** E17 **Latin** (from Greek *khoragos*, *khorēgos*, from *khoros* chorus + *agein* to lead). Chiefly *Greek History* The leader of a chorus, or of any group; *specifically* at Athens, a person who defrayed the cost of bringing out a chorus.

chorea *noun* L17 **Latin** (from Greek *khoreia* dance). *Medicine* Jerky involuntary movements; a disease with symptoms of this kind.

chorizo *noun* plural **chorizos** M19 **Spanish**. A Spanish sausage of which the chief ingredient is pork.

chose jugée *noun phrase* plural **choses jugées** L19 **French**. A settled or decided matter; something it is idle to discuss.

chota *adjective* E19 **Anglo-Indian** (Hindustani *choṭā*). Small, little; younger, junior.

■ Occurs often in such phrases as *chota hazri* (a light early breakfast) and *chota peg* (a small drink of whiskey).

chott variant of SHOTT.

chou *noun* (also **choux**) plural **choux** E18 **French** (= cabbage, from Latin *caulis*). **1** E18 A small ball of pastry filled with cream, etc. **2** L19 A rosette or ornamental knot of ribbon, chiffon, etc., on a woman's hat or dress.

choucroute *noun* M19 **French** (from German dialect *Surkrut* SAUERKRAUT, assimilated to French CHOU). A kind of pickled cabbage.

chouette *noun* L19 **French** (literally, 'barn owl'). A player in a two-handed game (e.g., backgammon, piquet) who plays against a number of others successively or in combination, especially as a means of enabling three players to compete with one another.

chou moellier *noun phrase* E20 **French** (= marrow-filled cabbage). A kind of kale grown as fodder, marrow-stem. *Australia and New Zealand.*

choux see CHOU.

chow mein *noun phrase* L19 **Chinese** (*chăo miàn* fried noodles). A Chinese dish of fried noodles usually in a sauce with shredded meat and vegetables.

chroma *noun* L19 **Greek** (*khrōma* color). Purity or intensity as a color quality, especially in color television, etc.

chronique scandaleuse *noun phrase* plural **chroniques scandaleuses** M19 **French**. A compilation or body of gossip, scandal, etc.

chuddar variant of CHADAR.

chulo *noun* plural **chulos** L18 **Spanish**. *Bullfighting* A bullfighter's assistant.

chuño *noun* E17 **American Spanish** (from Quechua *ch'uñu*). (Flour prepared from) dried potatoes, as eaten by Andean Indians.

chupatti variant of CHAPATTI.

chuppah *noun* (also **chuppaha**) L19 **Hebrew** (*ḥuppāh* cover, canopy). A canopy beneath which Jewish marriage ceremonies are performed.

chuprassy variant of CHAPRASSI.

churinga *noun* (also **tjurunga**) plural **churingas**, same L19 **Aranda** (*tywerrenge*). Among Australian Aborigines, a sacred object, *specifically* an amulet.

churrasco *noun* L20 **South American Spanish** (probably from dialect *churrascar* to burn; cf. Spanish *soccarar* to scorch). A grilled dish, usually of meat.

chutzpah *noun* L19 **Yiddish** (from Aramaic *ḥuṣpā*). Shameless audacity, gall. *slang*.

chypre *noun* L19 **French** (= Cyprus, where perhaps originally made). A heavy perfume made from sandalwood.

ciabatta *noun* plural **ciabattas**, **ciabatte** L20 **Italian** ((dialect) literally, 'slipper' (from the shape of the loaf)). A type of moist aerated Italian bread made with olive oil; a loaf of this.

ciao *interjection* E20 **Italian** (dialectal alteration of *schiavo* (I am your) slave, from medieval Latin *sclavus* slave). Hello; goodbye.

■ A colloquial expression widespread in continental Europe, now also used as a casual greeting between English speakers.

cibol variant of CIBOULE.

ciborium *noun* plural **ciboria** M16 **Medieval Latin** (from Greek *kibōrion* cup-shaped seed vessel of the Egyptian water lily, a drinking cup made from this; sense 1 probably influenced by Latin *cibus* food). **1** M16 *Christian Church* A receptacle for the reservation of the Eucharist, shaped like a shrine, or a cup with an arched cover. **2** M18 *Architecture* A canopy; a canopied shrine.

ciboule *noun* (also **cibol**) M17 **French**. The Welsh onion, *Allium fistulosum*, which resembles a spring onion.

cicada *noun* LME **Latin** (*cicada*, *cicala*). Any of the family Cicadidae of large-winged homopteran insects, the males of which make shrill chirping sounds.

■ The Old Provençal name *cigala* (cf. French *cigale*) was the usual form in English during the seventeenth and eighteenth centuries.

cicatrice *noun* (also (especially *Medicine and Botany*) **cicatrix**) plural **cicatrices**, *especially Medicine and Botany* LME **Old and Modern French** (or Latin *cicatrix*, *cicatric-*). **1** LME The scar of a healed wound, burn, etc.; a scar on the bark of a tree. **b** E19 *Botany* A scar. **2** L16 A mark or impression resembling a scar.

cicerone *noun & verb* plural **ciceroni**, **cicerones** E18 **Italian** (from Latin name *Cicero*, *-onis*). **A** *noun* E18 A guide who understands and explains antiquities, etc.; any learned guide. **B** *transitive verb* L18 Act as a cicerone to.

■ Marcus Tullius Cicero (106–43 BC) was renowned for his learning, and it is surmised that English Grand Tourists dubbed the local Italian antiquaries who showed them around the sites *cicerones*, that is 'Ciceros'. The actual historical origin of the word is uncertain, as the earliest English use of *cicerone* (Addison was apparently the first, in 1726) antedates its appearance in Italian dictionaries.

cicisbeo *noun* plural **cicisbei**, **cicisbeos** E18 **Italian** (of unknown origin). A married (originally Italian) woman's male companion or lover.

ci-devant *adjective & adverb* E18 **French**. Former(ly).

■ Used with the person's earlier name or status.

cigala see under CICADA.

cilantro *noun* L20 **Spanish**. Coriander.

cilium *noun* plural **cilia** E18 **Latin**. **1** E18 An eyelash; (the edge of) an eyelid. **2** L18 A delicate hair like an eyelash, e.g., on the margin of a leaf, or the wing of an insect. **3** M19 A hairlike appendage, usually motile, that is found in numbers on the surfaces of some cells, and in many organisms is used in locomotion.

cimbalom *noun* (also **zimbalom**) L19 **Hungarian** (from Italian CYMBALO). A dulcimer.

cinéaste *noun* (also **cineast(e)**) E20 **French** (from *ciné* cine + *-aste* as in *enthousiaste* enthusiast). An enthusiast for or devotee of the cinema.

cinematheque *noun* (also **cinémathèque**) M20 **French** (*cinémathèque*, from *cinéma* cinema, after *bibliothèque* library). A library of movies; a (national) repository of old movies.

Also, a small movie theater showing artistic movies.

cinéma-vérité *noun* M20 **French.** (The making of) movies that avoid artificiality and have the appearance of real life.

ciné-vérité *noun* M20 **French.** CINÉMA-VÉRITÉ.

cinq-à-sept *noun* (also **cinq à sept**) L20 **French** (literally, 'five to seven'). A visit to a mistress or a brothel, traditionally made between five and seven p.m.

cinquecento *noun* M18 **Italian** (= five hundred). The sixteenth century in Italy; the Italian style of art of this period, with reversion to classical forms.

cipolin *noun* (also **cipollino**, plural **cipolinos**) L18 **French** (*cipolin* from Italian *cipollino*, from *cipolla* onion (Latin *cepa*); so called from the resemblance of its foliated structure to the coats of an onion). An Italian marble interfoliated with veins of talc, mica, quartz, etc., showing alternations of (especially white and green) colorings.

cippus *noun* plural **cippi** E18 **Latin** (= post, stake). *Architecture* A low column, usually bearing an inscription, used by the ancients as a landmark, funerary monument, etc.

■ Earlier (E17) in the sense of 'the stocks', but this sense does not seem to have survived into the eighteenth century.

circa *preposition* M19 **Latin.** About, approximately in or at (with dates, etc.).

■ Frequently in abbreviated form before a date: *c.* or *ca.*

circiter *preposition* L19 **Latin.** About, CIRCA.

■ Used with dates.

circulus vitiosus *noun phrase* plural **circuli vitiosi** E20 **Latin.** A vicious circle.

ciré *adjective & noun* E20 **French** (= waxed). (Fabric) with a smooth polished surface, obtained especially by heating and waxing.

cire perdue *noun phrase* L19 **French** (= lost wax). A method of casting bronze by pouring molten metal over a wax-surfaced core within a mold, to form a model in the space created by the melting and running out of wax.

cirque *noun* E17 **French** (from Latin *circus* circle, circus, corresponding to Greek *kirkos* ring, circle). **1** E17 Circus. **2** L17 A circle, a ring, a circlet. *literary.* **3** M19 *Physical Geography* A large bowl-shaped hollow of glacial origin at the head of a valley or on a mountainside.

cirrus *noun* (also **cirrhus**) plural **cirri** E18 **Latin** (= curl, fringe). **1** E18 A curl or tuft of hair. *rare.* **2** E18 *Botany* A tendril. **3** M18 *Zoology* A slender, filamentary appendage, e.g., the limb of a cirripede, a barbel of certain fishes. **4** E19 *Meteorology* A cloud type occurring at high altitude and having the appearance of wispy filamentous tufts.

cithara *noun* (also **kithara**) L18 **Latin** (from Greek *kithara*). An ancient Greek and Roman stringed musical instrument akin to the lyre, having two arms rising vertically from the soundbox.

civet *noun* E18 **French** (earlier *civé*, from *cive* chive). A highly seasoned stew of hare, venison, or other game.

clachan *noun* LME **Gaelic and Irish** (*clachán*). *In Scotland and Northern Ireland: a small village, a hamlet.*

clair-de-lune *noun* L19 **French** (literally, 'moonlight'). A soft white or pale blue-gray color; a Chinese porcelain glaze of this color.

clairschach *noun* (also **clarschach**) L15 **Irish** (*cláirseach*, Gaelic *clàrsach*). The traditional Celtic harp strung with wire.

clairvoyance *noun* M19 **French** (from as next). **1** M19 The supposed faculty of perceiving, as if by seeing, what is happening or exists out of sight. **2** M19 Keenness of mental perception: exceptional insight.

clairvoyant *adjective & noun* (occasionally feminine **clairvoyante**) L17 **French** (from *clair* clear + *voyant* present participial adjective of *voir* to see). **A** *adjective* **1** L17 Clear-sighted, perceptive. *rare.* **2** M19 Having or exercising the faculty of clairvoyance; pertaining to clairvoyance. **B** *noun* **1** L18 A clear-sighted person. *rare.* **2** M19 A person having the faculty of clairvoyance.

claque *noun* M19 **French** (from *claquer* to clap). A hired body of applauders; *transferred* a body of devoted or sycophantic followers.

claqueur *noun* M19 **French** (from *claquer* to clap). A member of a claque.

claro *noun* plural **claros** L19 **Spanish** (= light, clear). A light-colored cigar.

clarschach variant of CLAIRSCHACH.

classico *adjective* L20 **Italian.** Of an Italian wine: superior, in an established style of excellence.

■ Used after the name of a wine, as in *Bardolino classico.*

clave *noun* E20 **American Spanish** (from Spanish *clave* keystone, from Latin *clavis* key). *Music* Either of a pair of hardwood sticks used to make a hollow sound.

■ Usually in plural.

clavecin *noun* E19 **French** (from medieval Latin *clavicymbalum* from *clavis* key + *cymbalum* cymbal). A harpsichord, especially in or from France.

clavicembalo *noun* plural **clavicembalos** M18 **Italian** (from as CLAVECIN). A harpsichord, especially in or from Italy.

clementine *noun* E20 **French** (*clémentine*). A variety of tangerine grown especially in North Africa.

clepsydra *noun* plural **clepsydras, clepsydrae** LME **Latin** (from Greek *klepsudra,* from *kleps-* combining form of *kleptein* to steal + *hudōr* water). An instrument used in antiquity to measure time by the flow of water; a water clock.

cliché *noun* M19 **French** (noun use of past participle of *clicher* to stereotype, perhaps of imitative origin). **1** M19 *History* A metal stereotype or electrotype block. **2** L19 *figurative* A stereotyped expression, a hackneyed phrase or opinion; a stereotyped character, style, etc.

clientele *noun* (also **clientèle**) M16 **Latin and French** (either, directly from Latin *clientela,* from *cliens, -ntis* (earlier *cluens*) client, noun use of present participle of *cluere* to hear, obey; or, later, from French *clientèle* from Latin). **1** M16–L19 Clientship; patronage. **2** L16 A body of clients, a following; the customers (of a store); the patrons (of a theater, etc.); persons seeking the professional advice of a lawyer, architect, etc.

clique *noun* E18 **Old and Modern French** (from *cliquer* to make a noise, from Middle Dutch *klikken* to click). A small exclusive group; a coterie.

■ Possibly related to CLAQUE.

cloaca *noun* plural **cloacae, cloacas** L16 **Latin** (*cloaca, cluaca* related to *cluere* to cleanse). **1** L16 An underground conduit for drainage, a sewer. Also, a water closet. **2** M19 *Zoology* A common cavity for the release of digestive and urogenital products in birds, reptiles, amphibians, most fish, and monotremes.

clobiosh variant of KLABERJASS.

clochard *noun* M20 **French** (from *clocher* to limp). In France: a beggar, a vagrant.

cloche *noun* L19 **French** (= bell). **1** L19 A bell glass; a small translucent (especially glass) cover for forcing or protecting outdoor plants. **2** E20 A woman's close-fitting bell-shaped hat. In full *cloche hat.*

cloisonné *adjective & noun* M19 **French** (past participle of *cloisonner* to partition, from *cloison* division). More fully *cloisonné enamel.* (Designating) enamelwork or -ware in which the colors in the pattern are separated by thin strips of metal attached to the base. Cf. CHAMPLEVÉ.

cloqué *noun* (also Anglicized as **cloky**) E20 **French** (literally, 'blistered'). A fabric with an irregularly raised or embossed surface.

clou *noun* L19 **French** (literally, 'nail, stud'). The chief attraction, the point of greatest interest, the central idea.

cocasse *adjective* M19 **French**. Droll; ridiculous.

coccyx *noun* plural **coccyxes, coccyges** L16 **Latin** (from Greek *kokkux* (originally) cuckoo (from its resemblance (in humans) to a cuckoo's beak)). *Anatomy* The small triangular bone forming the lower end of the spinal column in humans and some apes; the analogous part in birds or other vertebrates.

coco-de-mer *noun* E19 **French** (= coco from the sea (as having been first known from the nuts found floating in the sea)). A tall palm tree *Lodoicea maldivica*, native to the Seychelles; its immense woody nut.

cocotte *noun* M19 **French** (sense 1 from a child's name for a hen; sense 2 from French *cocasse* from Latin *cucuma* cooking vessel). **1** M19 A fashionable prostitute. *archaic*. **2** E20 A small fireproof dish for cooking and serving an individual portion of food.

coda *noun* M18 **Italian** (from Latin *cauda* tail). **1** M18 *Music* An independent and often elaborate passage introduced after the end of the main part of a movement. **b** L19 *transferred* and *figurative* A concluding event, remark, literary passage, etc. **2** E20 *Ballet* The final section of a classical *pas de deux*; the concluding dance of a whole ballet.

codetta *noun* M19 **Italian** (diminutive of CODA). *Music* A short coda; a short passage connecting sections of a movement or fugue.

codex *noun* plural **codices** L16 **Latin** (*codex, codic-* block of wood, block split into leaves or tablets, book). **1** L16–M18 A legal code; *generally* a set of rules on any subject. **2** L18 A manuscript volume, especially of ancient texts. **3** M19 A collection of pharmaceutical descriptions of drugs, preparations, etc.

coenobium *noun* (also **cenobium**) plural **coenobia** E19 **ecclesiastical Latin** (from Greek *koinobion* community life, convent, from *koinos* common + *bion* life). **1** E19 A monastic house, a coenoby. **2** L19 *Biology* A cluster of unicellular organisms, e.g., green algae, that behaves as a colony.

cogida *noun* E20 **Spanish** (literally, 'a gathering of the harvest', noun use of feminine past participle of *coger* to seize, from Latin *colligare* to bind together). *Bullfighting* A tossing of a bullfighter by a bull.

cogito *noun* M19 **Latin** (= I think, 1st person present of *cogitare* to cogitate). *Philosophy* The principle establishing the existence of the thinker from the fact of his or her thinking or awareness.

■ The principle derives from the formula *cogito, ergo sum* 'I think (*or* I am thinking), therefore I am' of the French philosopher René Descartes (1596–1650).

cognitum *noun* plural **cognita** L19 **Latin** (neuter past participle of *cognoscere* to know). *Philosophy* An object of cognition.

cognomen *noun* plural **cognomens**, (earlier) **cognomina** E17 **Latin** (*cognomen* from as *co-* with + *(g)nomen* name). **1** E17 A surname; a nickname; *loosely* an appellation, a name. **2** L19 *Roman History* The third personal name of a Roman citizen (as Marcus Tullius *Cicero*); a fourth name or personal epithet (as Publius Cornelius Scipio *Africanus*).

cognoscente *noun* plural **cognoscenti** M18 **Italian** ((now *conoscente*), literally, 'a person who knows', Latinized form of *conoscente* from Latin *cognoscent-* present participial stem of *cognoscere* to know). A connoisseur; a discerning expert.

cohabitation *noun* LME **French**. **1** LME Living together; community of life. *archaic*. **2** M16 Living together as husband and wife, especially without legal marriage. **3** *Politics* L20 An alliance dictated by expediency between office-holders of differing political views (originally in France).

■ Fully naturalized in senses 1 and 2, the word in its general literal meaning, as used in Middle English, is now almost entirely superseded by the particular sense 2. As a recent introduction from the French political scene, sense 3 is often written in italics to differentiate it from sense 2 and is therefore accorded a version of the French pronunciation.

cohue *noun* M19 **French**. A mob, an unruly crowd.

coiffeur *noun* M19 **French** (from *coiffer* to dress the hair). A hairdresser.

coiffure *noun & verb* M17 **French** (*coiffe* from Old French *coife* headdress, from late Latin *cofia* helmet). **A** *noun* M17 The way the hair is arranged or (formerly) the head decorated or covered; a hairstyle, a headdress. **B** *transitive verb* E20 Dress or arrange hair, coif. Chiefly as *coiffured* participial adjective.

coitus *noun* M19 **Latin**. Copulation.

cojones *noun plural* M20 **Spanish** (plural of *cojón* testicle). Testicles; *figurative* courage, guts.

■ Colloquial, and in figurative use often euphemistic for 'balls'.

col *noun* M19 **French** (from Latin *collum* neck). **1** M19 A depression in the summit line of a mountain chain; a saddle between two peaks. **2** L19 *Meteorology* An area of lower pressure between two anticyclones.

collage *noun* E20 **French** (= gluing). An abstract form of art in which photographs, pieces of paper, string, matchsticks, etc., are placed in juxtaposition and glued to a surface; a work in this form; *figurative* a jumbled collection of impressions, events, styles, etc.

collectanea *noun* M17 **Latin** (*collectanea* neuter plural (from *collect-*, past participial stem of *colligere* to assemble) as used as adjective in *Dicta collectanea* of Caesar, and as noun in *Collectanea* of Solinus). As *plural*, passages, remarks, etc., collected from various sources. As *singular*, a miscellany.

collegium *noun* plural **collegia** L19 **Latin**. **1** L19 A society of amateurs for performing music, now *especially* one attached to a German or American university. In full *collegium musicum*, plural *collegia musica*. **2** E20 *History* (representing Russian *kollegiya*) An advisory or administrative board in Russia.

colloquium *noun* plural **colloquia**, **colloquiums** L16 **Latin** (from as *co(l)-* with + *loqui* to speak). **1** L16–M18 A conversation, a dialogue. **2** M19 A conference; *specifically* an academic conference or seminar.

colluvium *noun* M20 **Latin**. *Physical Geography* Material which accumulates at the foot of a steep slope.

colon *noun* E17 **French** (from Latin *colonus*). **1** E17 A husbandman. *rare*. **2** M20 *History* A colonial settler or farmer, especially in a French colony.

colophon *noun* E17 **Late Latin** (from Greek *kolophōn* summit, finishing touch). **1** E17 A crowning or finishing touch. *rare*. **2** L18 A statement, sometimes with a device, at the end of a manuscript or printed book, giving information about its authorship, production, etc. **b** M20 A publisher's or printer's imprint; *loosely* a publisher's device, especially on a title page.

coloratura *noun* M18 **Italian** (from late Latin *coloratura*, from *colorat-* past participial stem of *colorare* to color). **1** M18 Florid passages in vocal music, with runs, trills, etc.; the singing of these. **2** M20 A singer of coloratura, especially a soprano.

colossus *noun* plural **colossi colossuses** LME **Latin** (from Greek *kolossos* applied by Herodotus to the statues of Egyptian temples). **1** LME A statue of considerably more than life size. **2** E17 A gigantic or overawing person or thing; an empire, etc., personified as standing astride over dominions.

■ The Colossus of Rhodes, a gigantic statue of the Hellenistic period that is said to have straddled the harbor entrance on the island of Rhodes, was one of the Seven Wonders of the World.

colostrum *noun* (also (earlier) **colostra**) L16 **Latin**. The first milk of a mammal after giving birth.

colportage *noun* M19 **French** (from *colporter* to hawk, peddle (see next)). The work of a colporteur; the peddling of books, newspapers, bibles, etc.

colporteur *noun* L18 **French** (from *colporter*, probably alteration of *comporter* from Latin *comportare* transport, from as *com-* with + *portare* to carry). A peddler of books, newspapers, etc., *especially* one employed by a religious society to distribute bibles and other religious tracts.

columbarium *noun* plural **columbaria**, **columbariums** M18 **Latin** (*columbarium*, from *columba* dove + *-arium*). **1** M18 A vault or building with niches for the reception of cinerary urns; a niche in such a vault, etc. **2** E19 A pigeonhole; a columbary.

coma *noun 1* plural **comae** E17 **Latin** (from Greek *komē* hair of the head). **1** E17 *Botany* The top of a plant; *especially* a terminal tuft of bracts or leaves; a leafy crown of branches; a tuft of silky hairs at the end of some seeds. **2** M18 *Astronomy* The diffuse hazy region surrounding the nucleus of a comet. **3** M19 An optical aberration causing the image of an off-axis point to be flared, like a comet with a diverging tail; the flared image itself.

coma *noun 2* M17 **Modern Latin** (from Greek *kōma*, *kōmat-*, related to *koitē* bed, *keisthai* to lie down). *Medicine* A prolonged state of unconsciousness from which the patient cannot be roused. Also *figurative*.

comble *noun* M19 **French** (from Latin *cumulus* heap). A culminating point, a crowning touch.

comédie humaine plural **comédie humaines** L19 **French** (literally, 'human comedy'). The sum of human activities; a literary portrait of this.

■ The title given by Honoré de Balzac (1799–1850) to his series of novels on nineteenth-century French society.

comédie larmoyante plural **comédie larmoyantes** E19 **French** (literally, 'weeping comedy'). A sentimental, moralizing comedy.

■ Applied originally to the plays of P. C. Nivelle de La Chausée (1692–1754), which were very fashionable in eighteenth-century France.

comedienne *noun* (also **comédienne**) M19 **French** (feminine of *comédien* comedian). A female comedian.

comédie noire plural **comédie noires** M20 **French** (literally, 'black comedy'). A macabre or farcical rendering of a violent or tragic theme.

■ Now more common in English translation, 'black comedy', but cf. NOIR.

comes *noun* plural **comites** M18 **Latin** (= companion, from *com-* with + *ire* to go). *Music* An answering or imitating voice in a canon or fugue; the answer itself. Opposed to DUX sense 1.

commando *noun* plural **commandos** L18 **Portuguese** ((now *comando*), from *commandar* to command). **1** L18 A party, originally of Boers or burghers in South Africa, called out for military purposes, a militia; a unit of the Boer army made up of the militia of an electoral district; a raiding party, a raid; participation in such a raid. **2** M20 (A member of) a unit of British amphibious shock troops; (a member of) a similar unit elsewhere.

comme ci, comme ça *adverb & adjective phrase* M20 **French** (literally, 'like this like that'). So-so, middling(ly).

commedia dell'arte *noun phrase* L19 **Italian** (= comedy of art). The improvised popular comedy in Italian theaters between the sixteenth and eighteenth centuries with stock characters.

comme il faut *adverb & predicate adjective phrase* M18 **French** (literally, 'as it is necessary'). Proper(ly), correct(ly), as it should be (especially of behavior).

commendatore *noun* L19 **Italian.** A knight of an Italian order of chivalry.

commère *noun* E20 **French.** A female COMPÈRE.

commis *noun* L16 **French** (noun use of past participle of *commettre* to entrust). **1** L16–E19 A deputy, a clerk. **2** M20 A junior waiter or chef.

commissar *noun* LME **French** (*commissaire* from medieval Latin *commissarius* commissary; in sense 2 from Russian *komissar* from French). **1** LME–M18 A deputy, a delegate, a commissary. Chiefly *Scottish.* **2** E20 *History* The head of a government department in the former USSR; also *transferred,* a powerful official.

commissionaire *noun* (also **commissionnaire**) M17 **French** (*commissionnaire* from Latin *commissio(n-)* from *commiss-* past participial stem of *committere* to commit). **1** M17 A person entrusted with small commissions; a messenger. Now *rare.* **2** M19 A uniformed door attendant at a theater, hotel, office, etc.

■ The Corps of Commissionaires was founded in London in 1859 as an organization through which pensioned (originally wounded) soldiers could find light employment as messengers, porters, etc.

communard *noun* L19 **French.** A member of a commune; *especially* (**Communard**) an adherent of the Paris Commune (the socialist government March–May 1871); a communalist.

communautaire *adjective* L20 **French.** Attentive to or serving the best interests of the wider community (often with reference to the European Community).

communiqué *noun* M19 **French** (noun use of past participle of *communiquer* to communicate). An official communication; *especially* an official statement reporting on a meeting, conference, etc.

compactum *noun* E20 **Latin** (noun use of neuter of *compactus* past participle of *compingere* to put together). A structure or device intended to hold a number of articles; a container; *specifically* a wardrobe.

compadre *noun* M19 **Spanish** (= godfather, (hence) benefactor, friend). Companion, friend.

■ Often used as a form of address. The extension of meaning from 'godfather' to 'friend' is paralleled in the evolution of the native English word *gossip* from late Old English *godsibb* (from *god* God + *sib* kin) meaning a 'godparent' to mid-fourteenth-century *gossip* 'a familiar acquaintance'. (The usual modern sense of *gossip* follows from the restriction of the word to specifically *female friends,* and from there to mean the sort of talk enjoyed by women among themselves.)

compagnon de voyage *noun phrase* (also **compagnon du voyage**) plural **compagnons de voyage** M18 **French.** A traveling companion, a fellow traveler.

compendium *noun* plural **compendiums, compendia** L16 **Latin** (originally, 'profit, saving', from *compendere* to weigh together). **I 1** L16 A work presenting in brief the essential points of a subject; a digest, an epitome. **2** E17 *figurative* An embodiment in miniature. **3** M17–E19 Saving of labor, space, etc. **II 4** L19 An assortment, a varied collection. **5** L19 In full *compendium of games.* A box containing assorted table games. **b** E20 A package of stationery for letter writing.

compère *noun & verb* (also **compere**) M18 **French** (originally, 'godfather in relation to the actual parents', from medieval Latin *compater* from *com-* with + *pater* father). **A** *noun* **1** An elderly man who lavishes gifts on a younger woman. Only in M18. **2** E20 A person in a cabaret act, radio or television show, etc., who introduces the performers, comments on the turns, etc. **B** *transitive & intransitive verb* M20 Act as compère (to a show).

compluvium *noun* plural **compluvia** M19 **Latin** (from *compluere* to flow together). *Roman Antiquities* A square opening in the roof of the atrium, through which fell the rainwater collected from the roof.

compos mentis *adjective phrase* E17 **Latin**. In one's right mind, having control of one's mind, not mad. Cf. NON COMPOS MENTIS.

■ Usually used predicatively and sometimes shortened to *compos* (E19).

compote *noun* (also **compôte**) L17 **French** (Old French *composte* from Latin *compos(i)ta, compos(i)tum* noun use of feminine and neuter past participle of *componere* to place together, compound). **1** L17 (A dish of) fruit preserved or cooked in a syrup; a fruit salad, stewed fruit, especially with or in a syrup. **2** M18 A dish of stewed pigeon. **3** L19 A COMPOTIER.

compotier *noun* M18 **French** (from as preceding). A bowl-shaped dessert dish with a stem; a dish for stewed fruit, etc.

compte rendu *noun phrase* plural **comptes rendus** E19 **French** (= account rendered). A report, a review, a statement.

comptoir *noun* E18 **French**. A commercial agency or factory in a foreign country.

comte *noun* E17 **French**. A French nobleman corresponding in rank to an English earl.

comtesse *noun* E20 **French**. A French noblewoman corresponding in rank to an English countess.

con abbreviation of CONTRA.

con amore *adverb phrase* M18 **Italian** (= with love). With devotion or zeal; *Music* (a direction:) with tenderness.

con brio *adverb phrase* E19 **Italian**. *Music* (A direction:) with vigor. Also *figurative*.

conceptus *noun* M18 **Latin** (= conception, embryo, from *concept-* past participial stem of *concipere* to conceive). The product of conception in the uterus, especially in the early stages of pregnancy.

concertante *adjective & noun* plural of noun **concertanti** E18 **Italian** (participial adjective of *concertare* to bring into agreement or harmony). *Music* Formerly, (designating) those instrumental parts present throughout a piece of music. Now, (a piece of music) containing one or more solo parts (usually of less prominence or weight than in a concerto) playing with an orchestra; also, designating such a part.

concerti plural of CONCERTO.

concerti grossi plural of CONCERTO GROSSO.

concertino *noun* plural **concertinos** L18 **Italian** (diminutive of CONCERTO). *Music* **1** L18 A small or short concert. *rare*. **2** E19 The solo instrument(s) in a concerto. **3** L19 A simple or short concerto.

concerto *noun* plural **concertos, concerti** E18 **Italian** (from *concertare* to bring into agreement or harmony). *Music* Originally, a composition for various combinations of instruments. Now, a composition (in the classical form usually in three movements) for one, or sometimes more, solo instruments accompanied by orchestra.

concerto grosso *noun phrase* plural **concerti grossi** E18 **Italian** (= big concerto). *Music* A baroque concerto characterized by the use of a small group of solo instruments alternately with the full orchestra; a modern imitation of this.

concessionaire *noun* (also **concessionnaire**) M19 **French** (*concessionnaire*, from Latin *concessio(n)-* (from *concess-* past participial stem of *concedere* to concede) + *-aire*). The holder of a concession or grant, especially of the use of land or trading rights.

concierge *noun* M16 **French** (from Old French *cumcerges* etc. = medieval Latin *consergius*, probably ultimately from Latin *conservus* fellow slave). **1** M16 The warden of a house, castle, or prison; (the title of) a high official in France and other European countries, having custody of a royal palace, etc. *obsolete* except *historical*. **2** L17 A doorkeeper, porter, etc., for an apartment building or other building, especially in France. **3** A hotel employee whose job is to to assist guests in arranging tours, making theater and restaurant reservations, etc.

concordat *noun* E17 **French or Latin** (*concordatum* noun use of neuter past participle of *concordare* to agree on). An agreement, a compact; *especially* one between the Vatican and a secular government relating to matters of mutual interest.

concours d'élégance *noun phrase* plural same M20 **French** (= contest of elegance). A parade of motor vehicles in which prizes are awarded for the most elegant looking.

■ Sometimes shortened to *concours*, especially when used attributively.

conde *noun* (also **Conde**) M17 **Spanish** (from Latin *comes, comitis* companion). A Spanish count.

condominium *noun* E18 **Modern Latin** (from as *con-* with (others) + *dominium* rule). **1** E18 Joint control of a nation's affairs vested in two or more other nations. **2** M20 A set of apartments, group of cottages, etc., rented or bought by a group of people; a unit of property so held.

condor *noun* E17 **Spanish** (*cóndor* from Quechua *kuntur*). Either of two very large vultures, *Vultur gryphus*, native to the Andes of South America (more fully *Andean condor*), and *Gymnogyps californianus*, of the mountains of California (more fully *California condor*).

condottiere *noun* plural **condottieri** (also **condottiero**) L18 **Italian** (from *condotta* a contract, from feminine past participle of *condurre* to conduct, from as next). *History* A leader or member of a troop of mercenaries (originally and especially in Italy).

conférencier *noun* L19 **French**. A lecturer, a public speaker; a (leading) member of a conference; a compère.

confetti *noun* E19 **Italian** (plural of *confetto* comfit, bonbon). Colored paper shapes showered on the bride and bridegroom by the guests at a wedding. In Italy (the earlier sense), real or imitation bonbons thrown during carnival, etc.

■ Originally plural but now usually treated as singular.

confiture *noun* M16 **French** (Old French *confit*). A preparation of fruit preserved in sugar; a confection.

■ The word was a rare import from Old French in the Middle English period with the meaning of 'a preparation of drugs'. In its present sense the forms *confiture* and *comfiture* were both used until the form in *-n-* was readopted (E19) from Modern French.

confrater *noun* L16 **Medieval Latin**. A member of a brotherhood, especially of monks.

confrère *noun* LME **French** (Old French from medieval Latin CONFRATER). **1** LME–L A fellow member of a fraternity. **2** M18 A fellow member of a profession, scientific body, etc.

confrérie *noun* E19 **French** (from as preceding). A religious brotherhood; an association or group of people having similar interests, jobs, etc.

conga *noun & verb* M20 **American Spanish** (from Spanish feminine of *congo* of or pertaining to the Congo). **A** *noun* **1** M20 A Latin American dance usually performed by people in single file who take three steps forward and then kick. **2** M20 In full *conga drum*. A tall, narrow, low-toned drum that is beaten with the hands. **B** *intransitive verb* L20 (past tense and participle **conga'd**, **congaed**). Perform the conga.

congé *noun* (also (now *rare*) **congee**) LME **Old French** (*congié* (modern *congé*) from Latin *commeatus* passage, leave to pass, furlough, from *commeare* to go and come). **1** LME Permission (for any act). **2** LME Ceremonious leave-taking. **3** L15–L18 Formal permission to depart. **4** L16 A bow. *archaic*. **5** M19 (from Modern French) Unceremonious dismissal. Chiefly *jocular*.

con moto *adverb phrase* E19 **Italian** (= with movement). *Music* (A direction:) with spirited movement.

connoisseur *noun* E18 **French** ((now *connaisseur*), from Old French *conoiss-* present participial stem of *conoistre* (modern *connaître*) to know). A person with a thorough knowledge and critical judgment of a subject, especially one of the fine arts; an expert in any matter of taste, e.g., wines, foods.

■ Often followed by *of, in*.

conoscente *noun* plural **conoscenti** M18 **Italian**. COGNOSCENTE.

conquistador *noun* plural **conquistadors, conquistadores** M19 **Spanish**. A conqueror; *specifically* any of the Spanish conquerors of Mexico and Peru in the sixteenth century.

consensus *noun* M17 **Latin** (= agreement, from *consens-* past participial stem of *consentire* to assent). Agreement or unity of opinion, testimony, etc.; the majority view, a collective opinion; (an agreement by different parties to) a shared body of views.

conservatoire *noun* L18 **French** (from Italian CONSERVATORIO). An academy of music or other performing arts, especially in France or elsewhere in continental Europe.

■ Such an academy may also be called a CONSERVATORIO and CONSERVATORIUM in other parts of Europe (see below), while *conservatory* in this sense is chiefly North American.

conservatoria plural of CONSERVATORIUM.

conservatorio *noun* plural **conservatorios** L18 **Italian** (from late Latin *conservatorium* noun use of neuter of adjective *conservatorius* from *conservat-* past participial stem of *conservare* to conserve). An (Italian or Spanish) academy of music or other performing arts. Cf. CONSERVATOIRE, CONSERVATORIUM.

conservatorium *noun* plural **conservatoriums, conservatoria** M19 **German and Modern Latin** (from as CONSERVATORIO *noun*). An academy of music or other performing arts, especially in Germany, Austria, or Australia. Cf. CONSERVATOIRE, CONSERVATORIO.

consigne *noun* M19 **French** (from *consigner* to give instructions to a sentinel). **1** M19 An order given to a sentinel; a password. *rare*. **2** L19 In France, an office where luggage can be left for later retrieval, especially at a railroad station.

consolatio *noun* plural **consolationes** M20 **Latin**. A book, poem, etc., written to expound philosophical or religious themes as comfort for the misfortunes of life.

■ The much-translated *De Consolatione Philosophiae* of the Roman statesman Boethius (died AD 524) was the model for the *consolatio* genre in later European literature.

console *noun* M17 **French** (perhaps from *consolider* to consolidate). **1** M17 *Architecture* An ornamental flat-sided bracket or corbel, usually incorporating a volute at each end. **2** E19 A table supported by consoles, and either fixed to a wall or freestanding. In full *console table*. **3** L19 A cabinet containing the keyboards, stops, and pedals of an organ. **4** E20 A cabinet for audio equipment, a television set, etc. **5** M20 A cabinet or panel where switches, meters, and controls are grouped together.

consommé *noun* E19 **French** (noun use of past participle of *consommer* from Latin *consummare* to finish up). A clear soup, originally made by boiling meat slowly for a long time.

con sordino *adverb & adjective phrase* E19 **Italian**. *Music* (Played) with a mute or (*con sordini*) mutes.

consortium *noun* plural **consortia, consortiums** E19 **Latin** (from *consors, consort-* having an equal share with). **1** E19 Partnership, association. *rare*. **2** M19 *Law*. The companionship, affection, and assistance that each spouse in a marriage is entitled to receive from the other. **3** L19 An association of organizations or nations formed for commercial or financial purposes. **4** M20 A group; an assortment.

conspectus *noun* M19 **Latin** (from *conspectus* past participial stem of *conspicere* to view). **1** M19 A comprehensive mental survey. **2** M19 A summary, a synopsis.

consul *noun* LME **Latin** (related to *consulere* to take counsel). **1** LME *History* **a** A magistrate in ancient Rome. **b** E19 Each of the three chief magistrates of the French Republic, from 1799 to 1804, the first of whom was head of state. **2** L15 *History* A medieval earl or count. **3** E16–M18 A member of a council. **4** E16–L18 A foreign official or magistrate; *specifically* a representative head of the merchants of a particular nation resident in a foreign town. **5** M16 An agent appointed by a nation to reside in a foreign town to protect the interests of the nation's subjects and assist its commerce.

contadina *noun* plural **contadine** , **contadinas** E19 **Italian** (feminine of next). An Italian peasant girl or peasant woman.

contadino *noun* plural **contadini**, **contadinos** M17 **Italian** (from *contado* county, (peasant population of) agricultural area around a city). An Italian peasant or countryman.

conte *noun* L19 **French**. A short story; as a form of literary composition, *specifically* a medieval narrative tale.

contessa *noun* (also (especially in titles) **Contessa**) E19 **Italian** (from medieval Latin *comitissa*). An Italian countess.

conteur *noun* M19 **French** (from CONTE). A composer of *contes*; a narrator.

continua plural of CONTINUUM.

continuo *noun* plural **continuos** E18 **Italian** (= continuous). A figured bass, a thorough bass, (= BASSO CONTINUO); an accompaniment, usually for keyboard, improvised from this. Also, the instrument(s) playing this part.

continuum *noun* plural **continua** M17 **Latin** (noun use of neuter singular of Latin *continuus* continuous, unbroken). A continuous thing, quantity, or substance; a continuous series of elements passing into each other; *Mathematics* the set of real numbers.

contra *adverb, preposition, & noun* LME **Latin** (= against (adverb and preposition), ablative feminine of a comparative from *com, cum* with). **A** *adverb* LME On or to the contrary; contrariwise. Chiefly in *pro and con(tra)* 'for and against'. **B** *preposition* LME Against. **C** *noun* **1** LME The opposing or opposite (side); an opposing factor or argument. **2** (Also *Contra*.) L20 A counterrevolutionary in Nicaragua, *especially* one opposing the government.

■ Often in abbreviated form in the noun phrase *pros and cons* (the points for and against (something)).

contrabasso *noun* plural **contrabassos**, **contrabassi** E19 **Italian**. **1** E19 A double bass, a contrabass. **2** M19 (A part within) the octave below the normal (bass) range, a contrabass.

contrafactum *noun* plural **contrafacta** M20 **Modern Latin** (noun use of neuter past participle of medieval Latin *contrafacere* to counterfeit). *Early Music* A rearrangement of a vocal composition whereby the music is retained and the words altered.

contrafagotto *noun* plural **contrafagotti** L19 **Italian** (now *controfagotto*). Double bassoon.

contralto *noun & adjective* M18 **Italian** (from as *contra-* + ALTO). *Music* **A** *noun* (plural **contraltos**) M18 The lowest female voice or (formerly) highest adult male voice; a singer having such a voice; a part written for such a voice. **B** *adjective* M18 Possessing, belonging to, or written for a contralto voice.

contra mundum *adverb phrase* M18 **Latin**. Against the world; defying or opposing everyone.

contrapposto *noun* plural **contrapposti** E20 **Italian** (past participle of *contrapporre* from Latin *contraponere* to contrapose). In the visual arts, an arrangement of a figure in which the action of the arms and shoulders contrasts as strongly as possible with that of the hips and legs; a twisting of a figure on its own axis.

contra proferentem *adverb phrase* E20 **Latin.** *Law* Against the party that proposes or adduces a contract or a condition in a contract.

contrayerva *noun* M17 **Spanish** (literally, 'counter-herb', i.e., one used as an antidote, from *contra-* against + *yerva* (now *hierba*) herb). (The root of) any of several tropical American plants used medicinally (formerly against snakebites).

contre cœur variant of À CONTRECŒUR.

contrecoup *noun* M18 **French** (from *contre* against + *coup* blow). **1** M18 A repercussion, an adverse consequence. *rare.* **2** M19 *Medicine* An injury of a part (especially one side of the brain) resulting from a blow on the opposite side.

contredanse *noun* (also **contradance**) E19 **French** (alteration of *country dance* by association with *contre* against, opposite). A country dance, *especially* a social dance of which quadrille is a variant; a piece of music for such a dance.

contre-jour *noun* E20 **French** (from *contre* against + *jour* daylight). *Photography* Backlighting.

■ Usually attributive.

contretemps *noun* L17 **French** (originally 'motion out of time', from *contre* against + *temps* time). **1** L17 *Fencing* Originally, a thrust made at an inopportune moment or at the same time that one's opponent makes one. Now, a feint made with the intention of inducing a counterthrust. **2** E18 An unexpected or untoward occurrence, especially of an embarrassing kind; a hitch, a mishap. **b** M20 A disagreement, an argument, a dispute. *colloquial.* **3** E18 *Dancing* A (ballet) step danced on the offbeat. Also, an academic ballet step involving a partial crossing of the feet and a small jump from a knees-bent position.

convenance *noun* L15 **French** (from *convenir* from Latin *convenire* to agree with). **1** L15–L17 Agreement, concurrence. *rare.* **2** M19 Conventional propriety or usage; in *plural,* the proprieties.

conversazione *noun* plural **conversaziones, conversazioni** M18 **Italian** (= conversation). **1** M18 In Italy: an evening gathering for conversation and recreation. **2** L18–L19 An at-home. **3** L18 A social gathering for discussion of the arts, literature, etc.; an educational soirée.

conversus *noun* plural **conversi** L18 **Latin.** *History* A lay member of a monastery or convent, *especially* one entering monastic life as a mature person.

cooee *noun, interjection, & verb* (also **cooey**) L18 **Aboriginal. A** *noun & interjection* L18 (A call or cry) used as a signal to draw attention to the caller. **B** *intransitive verb* E19 Utter this call.

■ Chiefly Australia and New Zealand, imitative of a signal used by Aborigines and copied by settlers.

coon-can *noun* L19 **Spanish** (perhaps from *con quién?* with whom?). A card game of Mexican origin, for two players and ancestral to (gin) rummy. Formerly also, a form of this played with two decks each with two jokers.

coontie *noun* (also **coontah**) L18 **Seminole** (*kunti*). Any of several low-growing palmlike cycads of the genus *Zamia,* native to tropical and subtropical America; the arrowroot yielded by these plants.

copaiba *noun* (also **copaiva**) E17 **Portuguese** (*copaíba* (whence Spanish *copaiba*) from Tupi *copaiba,* Guarani *cupaiba*). A balsam of aromatic odor and acrid taste obtained from South American leguminous trees of the genus *Copaifera* and used in medicine and the arts. Formerly also, a tree yielding this.

copal *noun* L16 **Spanish** (from Nahuatl *copalli* incense). A hard translucent odoriferous resin obtained from various tropical trees and used to make a fine transparent varnish. Also *gum copal.*

coperta *noun* L19 **Italian** (= covering, from *coprire* from Latin *coperire, cooperire* to cover). A transparent lead glaze given as a final glaze to some majolica.

copita *noun* M19 **Spanish** (diminutive of *copa* from popular Latin *cuppa* cup). A tulip-shaped sherry glass of a type traditionally used in Spain; a glass of sherry.

copra *noun* L16 **Portuguese and Spanish** (from Malayalam *koppara*). Dried coconut kernels, from which oil is obtained.

copula *noun* E17 **Latin** (= connection, linking of words, from as *co-* + *apere* to fasten). **1** E17 *Logic* and *Grammar* A connecting word, esp. a part of the verb *be* connecting a subject and predicate. **2** M17 A connection, a link.

coq au vin *noun phrase* M20 **French** (literally, 'cock in wine'). Chicken cooked in wine.

coque *noun 1* E19 **French** (= shell). A loop, a looped bow. Now *specifically* a small loop of ribbon in the trimming of a woman's hat.

coque *noun 2* (also **coq**) E20 **French** (*coq* cock). A rooster's feather used in the trimming of a hat, etc. In full *coque feather*.

coquet *noun & adjective* L17 **French** (diminutive of *coq* cock; as adjective = forward, wanton, gallant). **A** *noun* L17 A man given to flirting or coquetry. **B** *adjective* L17 Coquettish.

■ The noun was formerly (L17–E19) both masculine and feminine; later the feminine became COQUETTE.

coquet *verb* (also **coquette**) L17 **French** (*coqueter*, from as preceding). **1** *intransitive & transitive verb* L17 with *it*. Of a woman, or (formerly) a man: flirt (*with*). **2** *transitive verb* Flirt with. Only in 18. **3** *intransitive verb* L18 Dally, trifle, or toy (*with* a matter, etc.)

coquette *noun & adjective* M17 **French** (feminine of COQUET (noun)). **A** *noun* **1** M17 A woman who trifles with men's affections; a woman given to flirting or coquetry. **2** M19 A crested hummingbird of the genus *Lophornis*. **B** *adjective* M18 COQUET (adjective).

coquillage *noun* M19 **French** (literally, 'shellfish'; see next). Decoration in the form of shells or shellfish, *especially* on furniture.

coquille *noun* L19 **French** (from medieval Latin from medieval Greek *kokhulia* plural of *kokhulion* for Greek *kogkhulion*, from *kogkhē* conch). (Scallop) shell.

coquina *noun* M19 **Spanish** (= shellfish, cockle, from Old Spanish *coca* from medieval Latin by-form of Latin *concha* shell). A soft white limestone composed of broken marine shells cemented together and used for building in the West Indies and Florida. Also *coquina rock, coquina stone*.

coquito *noun* plural **coquitos** M19 **Spanish** (diminutive of *coco* coconut). The Chilean wine palm, *Jubaea chilensis*, which yields palm honey and fiber. Also *coquito palm*.

coradgee variant of KORADJI.

corah *noun & adjective* E19 **Hindi** (*korā* new, unbleached). **A** *noun* E19 An Indian-pattern silk handkerchief. **B** *adjective* L19 Of silk: undyed.

coram *preposition* M16 **Latin**. Before, in the presence of.

■ Occurs in various archaic legal phrases used in English, such as CORAM JUDICE, *coram nobis* 'in our presence', *coram populo* 'in the presence of the people' (i.e., in public).

coram judice *adverb phrase* E17 **Latin** (= in the presence of a judge). In a properly constituted or an appropriate court of law.

cor anglais *noun phrase* L19 **French** (literally, 'English horn'). A musical instrument like an oboe but lower in pitch; a player of this. Also, an organ reed stop of similar quality.

corbeau *noun & adjective* E19 **French** (= crow, raven). In the drapery trade, (of) a dark green color verging on black.

corbeille *noun* E19 **French**. An elegant basket of flowers or fruit.

cordelle *noun & verb* **E16 French** (diminutive of *corde* rope, from Latin *chorda* from Greek *khordē* gut, string (of musical instrument)). **A** *noun* **1** E16–E17 A rope, especially on a ship. *Scottish.* **2** E19 A ship's towing line. **B** *transitive & intransitive verb* E19 Give a tow (to) with a cordelle.

cordillera *noun* **E18 Spanish** (from *cordilla* diminutive of *cuerda* from Latin *chorda* cord). Each of a series of parallel mountain ridges or chains, especially in the Andes; an extensive belt of mountains, valleys, etc., especially as a major continental feature.

cordon bleu *noun & adjective phrase* **M18 French** (*cordon* ribbon + *bleu* blue). **A** *noun* plural **cordons bleus.** M18 (A person having) a supreme distinction; *specifically* a first-class cook. **B** *adjective* M20 Of cooking: first-class.

■ In French history, a blue ribbon signified the highest order of chivalry under the Bourbon kings.

cordon sanitaire *noun phrase* plural **cordons sanitaires** **M19 French** (*cordon* ribbon, band + *sanitaire* sanitary). A guarded line placed between an area affected by disease and adjacent unaffected areas in order to prevent the infection from spreading. Also *figurative.*

■ Earlier (E19) simply *cordon.*

cordovan *adjective & noun* **L16 Spanish** (*cordován* (now *cordobán*) noun, *cordovano* adjective, from *Córdova* (now *Cordoba*) from Latin *Corduba* Córdoba). **A** *adjective* L16 Of or pertaining to the city of and province of Córdoba in Spain; made of cordovan. **B** *noun* L16 **1** A kind of pliable fine-grained leather used especially for shoes, made originally at Córdoba from goatskin and now from horsehide. **2** M17–E19 A skin of this leather.

cornada *noun* plural **cornadas** **M20 Spanish** (from *cuerno* from Latin *cornu* horn). *Bullfighting* The goring of a bullfighter by a bull; a wound so caused.

corniche *noun* **M19 French.** A road along the edge of a cliff; any coastal road with panoramic views. Also *corniche road.*

cornucopia *noun* **E16 Late Latin** (*cornucopia* from Latin *cornu copiae* horn of plenty (a mythical horn able to provide whatever is desired)). **1** E16 A goat's horn depicted as a horn of plenty, overflowing with flowers, fruit, and corn; an ornamental vessel or other representation of this. **2** E17 *figurative* An overflowing stock; an abundant source.

corps *noun* plural same **L16 French** (from Latin CORPUS body). **1** L16 A tactical division of an army; an organized body of troops assigned to a special duty or a particular kind of work (medical, ordnance, intelligence, etc.). See also ESPRIT DE CORPS. **2** M18 A body of people engaged (collectively or as individuals) in a particular activity. **3** L19 A students' society in a German university.

■ The first appearance of *corps* in English was in the phrase CORPS DE GARDE. It was apparently first used as an independent word by Addison in 1711 in the *Spectator* in a letter peppered with up-to-the-minute military jargon, which was largely the product of the Duke of Marlborough's campaigns in Europe. It was probably at first pronounced as the English word *corpse*, and Johnson's *Dictionary* (1755) gives *corps* and *corpse* as alternative spellings. The desirability of distinguishing between the two sorts of 'body' has ensured that the French pronunciation and spelling have been retained for the 'group of people' sense.

corps à corps *adverb phrase* **L19 French** (= body to body). In close, especially bodily, contact; *Fencing* the position of two fencers so close that their bodies are in contact.

corps de ballet *noun phrase* plural same **E19 French.** *Dance* The company of supporting dancers in a ballet.

corps de garde *noun phrase* plural same **L16 French.** A small body of soldiers set as a guard; the post they occupy, a guardhouse.

corps d'élite *noun phrase* plural same L19 **French**. A body of specially picked men; a select group.

corps de logis *noun phrase* plural same M17 **French** (literally, 'body of dwelling'). *Architecture* The main (part of a) building; the central block of a house.

corps diplomatique *noun phrase* plural **corps diplomatiques** L18 **French**. The body of ambassadors and their staff attached to a particular seat of government; the diplomatic corps.

corpus *noun* plural **corpora**, **corpuses** LME **Latin** (= body). **1** LME The body of a person or animal. Now *jocular*. **2** L17 *Anatomy* Any of various masses of tissue in the body that have a distinct structure or function. (Chiefly in technical terms such as *corpus callosum*, etc.) **3** E18 A body or collection of writing, knowledge, etc.; the whole body *of* a particular category of literature, etc. **b** M20 *specifically* A body of spoken or written material on which a linguistic analysis is based. **4** M19 Principal or capital, as opposed to interest or income. *archaic*. **5** M20 *Botany* The inner layers of cells in an apical meristem.

corral *noun & verb* L16 **Spanish and Old Portuguese** (*corral*, Portuguese *curral*: cf. KRAAL). **A** *noun* **1** L16 An enclosure for horses, cattle, etc. **2** M19 An enclosure in which to trap and capture wild animals. **3** M19 A defensive enclosure formed of wagons in an encampment. **B** *verb* inflected *-ll-*. **1** *transitive & intransitive verb* M19 Form (wagons) into a corral. **2** *transitive verb* M19 Shut up (as) in a corral, confine. **3** *transitive verb* M19 Obtain, get hold of. *colloquial*.

corrida *noun* L19 **Spanish** (literally, 'course (of bulls)'). A bullfight; bullfighting. In full *corrida de toros*.

corrigendum *noun* plural **corrigenda** E19 **Latin** (neuter gerundive of *corrigere* to correct). Something requiring correction, *specifically* in a book. In *plural especially* errors listed with the corrections alongside.

corroboree *noun* L18 **Aboriginal**. **A** *noun* **1** L18 A night-time dance of Australian Aborigines, which may be either festive or warlike; a song or chant for this. **2** L19 A noisy gathering; a disturbance.

corsetière *noun* M19 **French** (feminine of *corsetier*, from as Old French *cors* (modern *corps*) body + *-ière*). A woman who makes or fits corsets.

Corso *noun* (also **corso**) plural **Corsos** L17 **Italian** (= course, main street from Latin *cursus* course). In Italy and some other Mediterranean countries: a procession of carriages; a social promenade; a street given over to this, or where races, etc., were formerly held.

cortège *noun* M17 **French** (from Italian *corteggio*, from *corteggiare* to attend court, from *corte* court). A train of attendants; a procession of people, especially mourners.

cortex *noun* plural **cortices** LME **Latin** (= bark). **1** LME An outer layer of a part in an animal or plant; *specifically* (*Anatomy*) the outer layer of the cerebrum, composed of folded gray matter and playing an important role in consciousness; *Botany* a layer of plant tissue between the epidermis and the central vascular tissue. **2** M17–M18 *figurative* An outer shell or husk. **3** L17 The bark of a tree, or the peel or rind of a plant, as used medicinally; *specifically* cinchona bark.

cortile *noun* E18 **Italian** (derivative of *corte* court). An enclosed usually roofless and arcaded area within or attached to an Italian building.

corvée *noun* ME **Old and Modern French** (= Provençal *corroada* from Proto-Romance use as noun (sc. *opera* work) of Latin *corrogata* neuter plural past participle of *corrogare* to summon). A day's unpaid work required of a vassal by a feudal lord; forced labor exacted as a tax, *specifically* that on public roads in France before 1776; *figurative* an unpleasant duty, an onerous task.

corvette *noun* M17 **French** (ultimately diminutive of Middle and Modern Dutch *korf* basket, kind of ship). *History* **1** M17 Originally, a kind of small French vessel using both oars and sail. Later, a warship with a flush deck and one tier of guns. Now *historical.* **2** M20 An escort vessel smaller than a frigate used especially for protecting convoys against submarines in World War II.

coryphaeus *noun* plural **coryphaei** E17 **Latin** (from Greek *koruphaios* chief, chorus leader, from *koruphē* head, top). **1** E17 The leader of a chorus. **2** E17 The leader of a party, sect, school of thought, etc.

coryphée *noun* E19 **French** (from as preceding). A leading dancer of a CORPS DE BALLET.

coryza *noun* E16 **Latin** (from Greek *koruza* nasal mucus, catarrh). Acute catarrhal inflammation of the nose; *especially* the common cold.

Cosa Nostra *noun phrase* M20 **Italian** (= our thing). The American branch of the Mafia.

cosmos *noun* ME **Greek** (*kosmos* order, ornament, world). **1** ME The universe as an ordered whole. **2** M19 Harmony, order. **3** L19 An ordered system of ideas, etc.

costa *noun* (also **Costa**) M20 **Spanish** (= coast). A coast, *especially* one developed as a vacation resort.

■ On the pattern of genuine place names such as *Costa Brava* or *Costa del Sol,* jocular usage creates pseudo-Spanish names such as *Costa Geriatrica* (a seaside resort or area mainly populated by elderly people) or *Costa del Crime* (an area favored by criminals for enjoying their ill-gotten gains in luxury while remaining beyond the reach of extradition laws).

costumier *noun* M19 **French** (from *costumer* to costume). A person who makes or deals in costumes; *especially* a person who sells or hires out theatrical costumes and properties.

coteau *noun* plural **coteaus, coteaux** M19 **French** (= slope, hillside from Old French *costel,* from *coste* (modern *côte* rib, from Latin *costa*)). Any of various kinds of elevated geographical features, as a plateau, a divide between valleys, etc.

coterie *noun* E18 **French** ((in Old French = tenants holding land together), ultimately from Middle Low German *kote* cote, cottage). **1** E18 A small exclusive group with common interests; *especially* a select social group. **2** E19 A meeting of such a group.

cotillion *noun* (in sense 1 also **cotillon**) E18 **French** (*cotillon* petticoat, dance, diminutive of *cotte* coat). **1** E18 Any of several dances with elaborate steps and figures. **2** L19 A formal ball, *especially* one at which débutantes are presented.

cotta *noun* M19 **Italian** (from Proto-Romance, from Frankish, of unknown origin). *Christian Church* A short surplice.

cottage orné see under ORNÉ.

couac *noun* L19 **French** (imitative). *Music* A quacking sound made by bad blowing on the clarinet, oboe, or bassoon.

couchant *adjective* LME **Old and Modern French** (present participle of *coucher* to couch, lie down). **1** LME Especially of an animal: lying down. **2** E16 *Heraldry* Of an animal: lying on its belly with its head up, lodged. Usually *postpositive,* as in *lion couchant.*

couchee *noun* L17 **French** (*couché* variant of *coucher* lying down, going to bed, use as noun of *coucher* to couch). An evening reception.

■ The opposite of a LEVEE noun 1.

couchette *noun* E20 **French** (literally, 'little bed', diminutive of *couche*). A railroad car in which the seats convert into sleeping berths; such a berth.

coudé *adjective & noun* L19 **French** (past participle of *couder* to bend at right angles, from *coude* elbow from Latin *cubitum* cubit). (Of, pertaining to, or designating) a telescope in which the rays are bent to focus at a fixed point off the axis.

coulée *noun* (also **coulee**, (sense 1) **coulie**) E19 **French** (= (lava) flow, from Latin *colare* to filter, strain, (in Proto-Romance) flow, from *cōlum* strainer). **1** E19 (The bed of) an intermittent stream; a dry valley; a gulch or valley with steep sides. **2** M19 *Geology* A stream of molten or solidified lava.

couleur de rose *noun & adjective phrase* LME **French** (= rose color). **A** *noun phrase* LME Rose-color, pink; *figurative* optimism, cheerfulness. **B** *adjective phrase* L18 Rose-colored, pink; *figurative* optimistic, cheerful.

coulis *noun* L20 **French** (see next). A thin, flowing sauce.

coulisse *noun* E19 **French** (noun use of feminine of *coulis* sliding (from *coulisser* to slide); cf. *portcullis* literally, 'sliding door'). **1** E19 *Theater* Each of the side scenes of a stage; *singular* and (usually) in *plural*, the space between them, the wings. **2** M19 A groove in which a sluice gate or other movable partition slides up and down. **3** L19 The body of outside dealers on the Paris Bourse; similar dealers in other stock exchanges; the place where they deal. **4** E20 A corridor; *figurative* a place of informal discussion or negotiation.

couloir *noun* E19 **French** (= channel, from *couler* to pour, from Latin *colare* to filter). A steep gully on a mountainside.

coup *noun* LME **Old and Modern French** (from medieval Latin *colpus* from Latin *colaphus* from Greek *kolaphos* blow with the fist; in branch II reintroduced from French in figurative sense and also in a number of phrases (see below)). **I 1** LME–M16 A blow given or received in combat. **II 2** L18 A stroke or move that one makes; *especially* a notable or strikingly successful move. **b** M19 A COUP D'ÉTAT. **c** M19 *History* Among North American Indians: the act of touching an enemy, as a deed of bravery; the act of first touching an item of the enemy's in order to claim it. **3** L18 *Billiards* The direct pocketing of the cue ball, which is a foul stroke.

coup de fors *noun phrase* plural **coups de fors** M19 **French** (literally, 'stroke of force'). A sudden violent action.

coup de foudre *noun phrase* plural **coups de foudre** L18 **French** (literally, 'stroke of lightning'). A sudden unforeseen event; a revelation; love at first sight.

coup de grâce *noun phrase* plural **coups de grâce** L17 **French** (literally, 'stroke of grace'). A blow by which someone or something that has been mortally hurt is mercifully killed; *figurative* a decisive finishing stroke.

coup de main *noun phrase* plural **coups de main** M18 **French** (literally, 'stroke of hand'). Chiefly *Military* A sudden onslaught; a surprise attack.

coup d'état *noun phrase* plural **coups d'état**, **coup d'états** M17 **French** (literally, 'blow of state'). A violent or illegal change in government. Formerly also, any sudden and decisive stroke of national policy.

■ Now often abbreviated to *coup* in all but the most formal contexts.

coup de théâtre *noun phrase* plural **coups de théâtre** M18 **French** (literally, 'stroke of theater'). **1** A theatrical hit. **2** A sudden dramatic turn of events or action, *originally* in a play, now also *figurative*.

coup d'œil *noun phrase* M18 **French** (literally, 'stroke of eye'). A comprehensive glance; a general view; *Military* the faculty or action of rapidly assessing a position and sizing up its advantages, etc.

coupe *noun 1* L19 **French** (= goblet from medieval Latin *cuppa*). **1** L19 A shallow dish; a short-stemmed glass. **2** E20 A dessert of ice cream, fruit, etc., served in a glass coupe.

coupe *noun 2* E20 **French** (= felling, from *couper* to cut, slash). A periodic felling of trees; an area so cleared.

coupé *noun* (in sense 3b also **coupe**) E18 **French** (past participle of *couper* to cut; in branch II abbreviation of *car-*

rosse coupé, literally, 'cut carriage'). **I 1** E18 *Dancing* Formerly, *coupee*, a kind of bowing step. Now, a step in ballet in which one foot displaces another and weight is transferred to it. **2** L19 *Fencing* A movement of the sword similar to a disengage, but effected by drawing the sword along and over the point of the opponent's. **II 3a** M19 A four-wheeled carriage with a seat for two inside and an outside seat for the driver. Chiefly *historical*. **b** E20 An enclosed two-door automobile with two or four seats and (now) usually a sloping rear.

courante *noun* (also **courant**) L16 **French** (noun use of feminine present participle of *courir* to run). **1** L16 A court dance of the sixteenth and seventeenth centuries characterized by glides and light hops, a coranto. **2** L16 *Music* A piece of music for this dance; a piece of music in triple time, *especially* one which forms a movement of a suite.

courbette *noun* **M17 French** (from Italian *corvetta*). *Equestrianism* A leap in *haute école* in which a trained horse rears up and jumps forward on the hind legs without the forelegs' touching the ground.

coureur *noun* **E18 French** (= (wood-)runner). *History* A woodsman, trader, etc., of French origin in Canada and the northern United States. In full *coureur de bois*.

courge *noun* **M19 French** (= gourd from Old French *cohourde* from Latin *cucurbita*). A basket for holding live bait, towed behind a fishing boat.

courgette *noun* **M20 French** (from as preceding). A variety of squash, usually green. Also called ZUCCHINI.

course libre *noun phrase* plural **courses libres** **M20 French** (= free course). A bullfight, as in France, in which the bull is baited but not killed.

court bouillon *noun phrase* **M17 French** (from *court* short + BOUILLON). A stock made from wine, vegetables, etc., in which fish is boiled.

couscous *noun* (also **kouskous**, **couscoussou**) **E17 French** (from Arabic *kuskus*, *kuskusū* millet grain, probably of Berber origin). A spicy North African dish of crushed wheat or coarse flour steamed over broth, frequently with meat or fruit added; the granules of flour from which this dish is made.

couture *noun* **E20 French** (from Old French *cousture* sewing from late Latin *consutura*, from Latin *consutus* past participle of *consuere* to sew together). **1** Dressmaking; (the design and making of) fashionable garments, especially French ones. **2** Abbreviation of HAUTE COUTURE.

couvade *noun* **M19 French** (from *couver* to hatch from Latin *cubare* to lie). A custom in some cultures by which a man takes to his bed and goes through certain rituals when his wife bears a child.

■ Adopted in French in this sense (M19) owing to a misunderstanding of the expression *faire le couvade* 'to sit doing nothing' in earlier writers.

couverture *noun* **M20 French** (= covering). (A layer of) chocolate for coating candies and cakes.

couvre-pied *noun* (also **couvre-pieds**) **E19 French** (literally, 'cover foot', from *couvrir* to cover). A rug to cover the feet.

coyote *noun & verb* plural same, **coyotes** **M18 Mexican Spanish** (from Nahuatl *coyotl*). **A** *noun* M18 A small nocturnal wolflike animal, *Canis latrans*, of western North America, noted for its mournful howling. Also called *prairie wolf*. **B** *intransitive verb* M19 *Mining* Make a small lateral tunnel from a shaft, etc.

■ The sense of the verb refers to the small tunnels dug out by the coyote; in California the phrase *coyote diggings* described such lateral shafts.

cracovienne *noun* **M19 French** (feminine adjective from *Cracovie* Kraków (Cracow), a city in southern Poland). A lively Polish dance; a ballet dance in a Polish style. Also called *krakowiak*.

cranium *noun* plural **crania, craniums** LME **Medieval Latin** (from Greek *kranion* skull). **1** LME The bones enclosing the brain; the bones of the whole head, the skull. **2** M17 The head. *jocular.*

crannog *noun* E17 **Irish** (*crannóg*, Gaelic *crannag* wooden structure, from *crann* tree, beam). In Scotland and Ireland: an ancient fortified settlement constructed in a lake or marsh on an artificial island made from wood.

craquelure *noun* E20 **French**. A network of small cracks in the pigment or varnish on the surface of a painting.

crèche *noun* L18 **French** (from Old French *creche* wooden feeding rack for animals, from Proto-Romance from Germanic base related to *crib*). **1** L18 A model of the infant Jesus in the manger with attending figures, often displayed at Christmas. **2** M19 A day nursery for infants and young children.

■ *Crib* is now the more usual word for sense 1.

credenza *noun* L19 **Italian** (from medieval Latin *credentia* from Latin *credent-* present participial stem of *credere* to believe). A sideboard, a cupboard, a buffet.

credo *noun* plural **credos** ME **Latin** (*credo* I believe). **1** ME The Apostles' Creed, the Nicene Creed (from their first word). Now *especially* a musical setting of the Nicene Creed. **2** L16 *generally* A creed, a set of opinions or principles.

creese variant of KRIS.

crémaillère *noun* E19 **French** (formerly *cramaillère*, from *cramail* pot hanger, chimney hook). *Fortification* A zigzag or indented inside line of a parapet.

crème *noun* (also **crême**) E19 **French** (= cream). **1** E19 Cream; a cream, a custard. Used especially in names of desserts and liqueurs (see following entries). **2** M19 The CRÈME DE LA CRÈME.

crème brûlée *noun phrase* L19 **French** (literally, 'burnt cream'). A cream or custard dessert topped with caramelized sugar.

crème caramel *noun phrase* E20 **French**. A custard dessert topped with caramel. Cf. CRÈME RENVERSÉE.

■ Earlier (M19) as *crème au caramel*.

crème Chantilly *noun phrase* (also **crème chantilly**) E20 **French**. Whipped cream flavored with vanilla and sweetened.

■ Earlier (L19) as *crème à la Chantilly*. Chantilly is the name of a town in France, not far from Paris.

crème de cacao *noun phrase* M20 **French**. A chocolate-flavored liqueur.

crème de la crème *noun phrase* M19 **French** (literally, 'cream of the cream'). The pick of society; the elite in any field.

crème de menthe *noun phrase* E20 **French**. A peppermint-flavored liqueur.

crème de noyau *noun phrase* L19 **French**. An almond-flavored liqueur.

crème fraîche *noun phrase* (also **creme fraiche**) L20 **French**. *Cooking* Thick cream to which buttermilk, sour cream, or yogurt has been added.

crème renversée *noun phrase* E20 **French** (literally, 'inverted cream'). A custard made in a mold and then turned out, often with a caramel topping (*crème caramel renversée*).

cremona variant of CROMORNE.

creole *noun & adjective* (also (especially in strict use of sense A. 1 and corresponding uses of the adjective) **Creole**) E17 **French** (*créole*, earlier *criole* from Spanish *criollo* probably from Portuguese *crioulo* black born in Brazil, home-born slave, from *criar* to nurse, breed, from Latin *creare* to create). **A** *noun* **1** E17 A descendant of European settlers or (occasionally) of black slaves, in the West Indies or Central or South America; a descendant of French settlers in the southern United States, especially Louisiana. Also *loosely*, a person of mixed European and black descent. **2** L19 A former pidgin language that has developed into the sole or native language of a community. **B** *adjective* **1** M18 Of, pertaining to, or characteristic of a creole or creoles. **2** M18 Of a plant or animal: bred or grown in the West Indies but not of indigenous origin.

crêpe *noun & adjective* (also **crepe**) L18 **French** (earlier *crespe*, noun use of Old French *crespe* curled, frizzed, from Latin *crispus* curled). **A** *noun* **1** L18 A fine cotton or gauzelike fabric with a crinkled surface. **2** E20 A type of raw rubber rolled into thin sheets with a wrinkled surface, used for shoe soles, etc. More fully *crêpe rubber*. **3** E20 A very thin pancake. **B** *attributive* or as *adjective* Made of crêpe; resembling crêpe.

■ The Anglicized spelling *crape* was current in the seventeenth century in sense A.1, but later came to be restricted to a specific kind of black silk cloth used especially for mourning dresses and funereal drapes.

crêpe de Chine *noun phrase* L19 **French**. A fine crêpe of silk or similar fabric. Also called *China crêpe*.

crêpeline *noun* (also **crêpoline**) L19 **French** (diminutive of CRÊPE). A thin light dress material made of silk or silk and wool.

crêpe Suzette *noun phrase* plural **crêpes Suzette** E20 **French**. A thin dessert pancake served hot in a sauce that usually contains spirit or liqueur.

crépinette *noun* L19 **French** (diminutive of *crêpine* caul). A kind of flat sausage consisting of ground meat and savory stuffing wrapped in pieces of pork caul.

crêpoline variant of CRÊPELINE.

crépon *noun & adjective* L19 **French** (from as CRÊPE *noun & adjective*). (Made of) a fabric resembling crêpe, but heavier.

crepusculum *noun* (also Anglicized as **crepuscle**, **crepuscule**) LME **Latin** (related to *creper* dusky, dark). The period of half-dark at the beginning or end of the day; twilight, dusk.

crescendo *adverb, adjective, noun, & verb* L18 **Italian** (present participle of *crescere* to increase from Latin *crescere* to grow). **A** *adverb & adjective Music* L18 (A direction:) with a gradual increase in loudness. **B** *noun* plural **crescendos**, **crescendi**. **1** *Music* L18 A gradual increase in loudness; a passage (to be) played or sung with such an increase. **2** L18 A progressive increase in force or effect. **3** E20 A climax. **C** *intransitive verb* Increase gradually in loudness or intensity.

cresson *noun* M17 **French** (= cress). **1** In *plural* Cress. *rare* (only M17). **2** L19 A shade of green resembling that of watercress.

cretin *noun* L18 **French** (*crétin* from Swiss French *creitin*, *crestin* from Latin *Christianus*). **1** L18 *Medicine* A person afflicted with cretinism. **2** L19 A fool; a person who behaves stupidly.

cretonne *noun* L19 **French** (of unknown origin). A strong unglazed fabric printed on one or both sides with a (usually large floral) pattern, used for chair covers, curtains, etc.

crevasse *noun* E19 **French** (Old French *crevace*). **1** E19 A (usually deep) fissure or chasm in the ice of a glacier; *transferred* a deep crack or chasm. **2** E19 A breach in the bank or levee of a river, canal, etc.

criard *adjective* (also (French feminine) **criarde**) M19 **French**. Shrill; garish.

criblé *noun & adjective* L19 **French** (from Old French *crible* from popular Latin variant of Latin *cribrum* sieve). (Designating) a type of engraving with small punctures or depressions on a wood or metal ground. Cf. MANIÈRE CRIBLÉE.

■ The technique of using metalworkers' punches to create stippled areas on a printing plate was one of the earliest used in Renaissance metal engraving. The effect was to have patterns of white dots (likened to the holes of a sieve) against the black ground of the print.

cri de cœur *noun phrase* plural **cris de cœur** E20 French (= cry of or from the heart). An appeal in distress.

crime passionnel *noun phrase* plural **crimes passionnels** E20 French. A crime, especially murder, due to sexual jealousy.

criollo *noun & adjective* (also **Criollo**) plural of noun **criollos** L19 Spanish (= native to the locality). **1** L19 (Designating or pertaining to) a native of Spanish South or Central America, especially one of pure Spanish descent. **2** E20 (Designating) a cacao tree of a variety producing thin-shelled beans of high quality. **3** M20 (Designating) any of various South or Central American breeds of domestic animal, *especially* a small horse bred from native South American and Arab stock, or cattle of Spanish ancestry.

crise *noun* LME French. Crisis.

■ Formerly fully naturalized, it now occurs only in the following phrases or as an abbreviation of them.

crise de conscience *noun phrase* M20 French. A crisis of conscience.

crise de nerfs *noun phrase* (also **crise des nerfs**) E20 French (= crisis of nerves). An attack of nerves; a fit of hysterics.

critique *noun* Originally **critic** M17 French (ultimately from Greek *kritikē* (sc. *tekhnē*) the critical art, criticism). **1** M17 Criticism; *especially* the art of criticism. **2** M17 A criticism; *especially* a critical analysis, article, or essay.

crochet *noun & verb* M19 French (diminutive of *croc* with *-ch-* from *crochié, crochu* hooked). **A** *noun* M19 A kind of knitting done using a single hooked needle to form intertwined loops; knitted material made in this way. **B** *verb* **1** *transtitive verb* L19 Make in crochet. **2** *intransitive verb* L19 Do crochet work.

croisette *noun* L17 French (diminutive of *croix* cross). A small cross.

croissant *noun* L16 French. L19 A flaky pastry roll in the shape of a crescent.

■ Earlier (L16–L17) found as an occasional variant of *crescent*, especially with reference to the crescent moon, *croissant* is now solely used for the pastry roll.

cromlech *noun* L17 Welsh (from *crom* feminine of *crwm* bowed, arched + *llech* (flat) stone). A dolmen; any megalithic chamber tomb.

cromorne *noun* (also **cremona**) E18 French (from German KRUMMHORN). An organ reed stop, usually of 8-ft. pitch, suggestive of a krummhorn or (later) a clarinet in sound.

croque-monsieur *noun* M20 French. A toasted ham and cheese sandwich.

croquette *noun* E18 French (from *croquer* to crunch). A small ball or roll of vegetable, ground meat, or fish (to be) fried in breadcrumbs.

croquis *noun* plural same E19 French (from *croquer* to sketch). A rough draft; a sketch.

crostini *noun plural* L20 Italian. Snacks consisting of bread, usually toasted or fried, with a savory topping.

crotale *noun* M20 French (from Latin CROTALUM). A small tuned cymbal; a kind of castanet or clapper; a crotalum.

crotalum *noun* plural **crotala** L18 Latin (from Greek *krotalon*). *An ancient clapper or castanet the two halves of which were struck together with the finger and thumb.*

croupade *noun* M17 French (from Italian *groppata* (with assimilation to French *croupe* croup)). *Equestrianism* In *haute école* a single leap with the horse's hind legs brought up under the belly. Also, a high kick with the hind legs while the forelegs remain on the ground.

croupier *noun* **E18 French** ((originally a person who rides behind on a horse's croup), from *croupe* from Proto-Romance from Germanic base related to *crop*). **1** A person who stands behind a gambler to give support and advice. Only in E18. **2** M18 A person who rakes in and pays out the money or tokens at a gaming table. **3** L18 An assistant chairman sitting at the lower end of the table at a public dinner.

croustade *noun* **M19 French** (from Old French *crouste* (modern CROÛTE) or Italian *crostata* tart (from *crosta* crust)). A crisp piece of bread or pastry hollowed to receive a savory filling.

croûte *noun* **E20 French**. A crisp piece of toasted or fried bread; a croûton. See also EN CROÛTE.

croûton *noun* (also **crouton**) **E19 French** (from CROÛTE). A small piece of toasted or fried bread served with soup or as a garnish.

cru *noun & adjective* (also **crû**) **E19 French** (from *crû* past participle of *croître* grow). *Wine* (The grade or quality of wine produced in) a French vineyard or wine-producing region; (designating) French wine of a specified quality.

■ Often in phrases; see also CRU CLASSÉ, GRAND CRU, PREMIER CRU.

cru classé *noun phrase* plural **crus classés** **M20 French** (= classed growth). *Wine* A Bordeaux wine belonging to one of the highest official categories.

crudités *noun plural* **M20 French**. *Cooking* Assorted raw vegetables as an hors d'oeuvre.

crumhorn variant of KRUMMHORN.

crux *noun* plural **cruxes**, **cruces** **M17 Latin** (= cross). **1** M17 (A representation of) a cross. Chiefly in CRUX ANSATA. **2** E18 A difficult matter, a puzzle; the decisive point at issue; the central point. **3** M19 (Usually **Crux**) (The name of) the constellation of the Southern Cross.

crux ansata *noun phrase* plural **cruces ansatae** **M19 Latin** (= cross with a handle). An ANKH.

crwth *noun* **M19 Welsh** (cf. Gaelic *cruit* harp, violin, Irish *cruit* small harp, Old Irish *crot* harp, cithara). An old Celtic musical instrument with three, or later six, strings which was held against the chest and played by bowing and plucking.

■ Adopted earlier (ME) as *crowd*.

csardas *noun* (also **czardas**) plural same **M19 Hungarian** (*csárdás*, from *csárda* inn). A Hungarian dance usually having a slow start and a rapid wild finish, with many turns and leaps; a piece of music for this dance.

cuadrilla *noun* plural **cuadrillas** **M19 Spanish**. A company of people; *especially Bullfighting* A matador's team.

cuartel *noun* **M19 Spanish** (from *cuarta* quarter, from *cuarto* fourth, from Latin *quartus*). In Spain and Spanish-speaking countries: a military barracks.

cuesta *noun* **E19 Spanish** (= slope, from Latin *costa*). Originally, a steep slope that terminates a gently sloping plain; a plain in this configuration. Now (*Geography*), a ridge with a gentle slope on one side and a steep one on the other, a scarp and dip.

cui bono *interjection (interrogative), adjective & noun phrase* **E17 Latin** (= to whom (is it) a benefit?). **A** *interjection (interrogative)* E17 What is the purpose (of)? Who stands to gain (and so might be responsible)? **B** *adjective phrase* M18 Of or pertaining to the question *cui bono?* **C** *noun phrase* M19 The question *cui bono?*

cuir-ciselé *adjective* **M20 French** (= engraved leather). (Of a design on a leather binding) cut in relief with a pointed tool; having such a design.

cuisine *noun* **L18 French** (= kitchen, from Latin *coquina*, *cocina*, from *coquere* to cook). A culinary establishment; cooking as an art, especially as characteristic of a particular country or establishment. Cf. HAUTE CUISINE, NOUVELLE CUISINE.

cuivré *adverb & noun* M20 **French** (past participle of *cuivrer* to play with a brassy tone, from *cuivre* copper, from late Latin *cuprum*). *Music* (With) a harsh strident tone (in a brass instrument).

cul-de-sac *noun* plural **culs-de-sac, cul-de-sacs** M18 **French** (= sack bottom). **1** M18 *Anatomy* A vessel, tube, sac, etc., open only at one end; the closed end of such a vessel. **2** L18 A street, passage, etc., closed at one end; a blind alley; *Military* a position in which an army is hemmed in on all sides except behind.

culet *noun* (also (earlier) **collet**) L17 **French** (diminutive of *cul* bottom). **1** L17 The horizontal base of a diamond, formed by the blunting of a point, when the stone is cut as a brilliant. **2** M19 A piece of armor for protecting the hinder part of the body below the waist.

culmen *noun* M17 **Latin** (contraction of *columen* top, summit, etc). **1** M17 The top, the summit; *figurative* the acme, the culminating point. **2** M19 The upper ridge of a bird's bill.

culotte *noun* M19 **French** (= knee breeches; cf. SANSCULOTTE). **1** M19 Knee breeches. *rare*. **2** E20 *singular* and (usually) in *plural*. A woman's garment that hangs like a skirt but has separate legs, as in pants; a divided skirt. **3** E20 A fringe of soft hair on the back of the forelegs of some dogs.

culpa *noun* M19 **Latin**. *Law*. Neglect resulting in damage, negligence.

■ See also FELIX CULPA.

cultus *noun* M17 **Latin** (from past participial stem of *colere* to honor with worship). **1** Worship. *rare*. Only in M17. **2** M19 A system of religious worship or ritual; a cult.

cum *preposition* LME **Latin** (= with). **1** LME Combined with. Used in names of combined parishes (e.g., Horton-cum-Studley). **2** With. Chiefly in Latin phrases and English ones imitating them (e.g., cum dividend). **3** And also. Denoting a combined role or nature.

cum laude *adverb & adjective phrase* L19 **Latin** (= with praise). (Of a degree, diploma, etc.) with honors, with distinction.

■ Cf. MAGNA CUM LAUDE, SUMMA CUM LAUDE.

cumulus *noun* plural **cumuli** M17 **Latin**. **1** M17 A heap, a pile; an accumulation; the conical top of a heap. **2** E19 *Meteorology* (A cloud type consisting of) rounded masses of cloud heaped on each other and having a horizontal base at usually a low altitude. Also *cumulus cloud*.

cunnilingus *noun* L19 **Latin** (= a person who licks the vulva, from *cunnus* female external genitals + *lingere* to lick). Stimulation of a woman's genitals with the tongue.

cupidon *noun* (also **Cupidon**) E19 **French** (from Latin *Cupido* Cupid, the personification of desire, the god of love). A beautiful youth; a cupid, an Adonis.

■ *Cupid* or *cupid* has been the normal form since Late Middle English, and *cupidon* is chiefly poetic.

cupola *noun* M16 **Italian** (from late Latin *cupula* little cask, small burying vault, diminutive of *cupa* cask). **1** M16 A rounded vault or dome forming the roof of (part of) a building; *specifically* a small rounded dome forming or adorning a roof; the ceiling of a dome. **b** M17 Something likened to such a dome. **2** E18 A tall usually cylindrical furnace, open at the top and tapped at the bottom, for melting metal that is to be cast. Also *cupola furnace*. **3** E19 *Anatomy* The small dome-shaped end of the cochlear duct. **4** M19 A revolving dome for protecting mounted guns on a warship, etc. **5** E20 *Geology* A small dome-shaped projection on the top of a larger igneous intrusion.

curandero *noun* plural **curanderos** (feminine **curandera**) M20 **Spanish**

(from *curar* to cure, from Latin *curare*). In Spain and Latin America: a healer who uses folk remedies.

curare *noun* L18 **Spanish and Portuguese** (from Carib word represented also by *wourali*). A resinous bitter substance obtained from the bark and stems of various tropical and subtropical South American plants of the genus *Strychnos*, which paralyzes the motor nerves and was formerly used as an arrow poison by South American Indians and now in surgery, etc., to relax the muscles.

curé *noun* M17 **French** (from medieval Latin *curatus* a person who has a cure or charge (of a parish)). In France and French-speaking countries: a parish priest.

curettage *noun* L19 **French** (from as next). *Surgery* The scraping or cleaning of an internal surface of an organ or body cavity with a curette.

■ Often in the phrase *dilatation and curettage* (colloquially abbreviated *d&c*), a common operation on the uterus consisting of this.

curette *noun & verb* M18 **French** (from *curer* to take care of, clean, from Latin *curare* to heal). *Surgery* **A** *noun* M18 A small instrument resembling a scoop used to remove material by a scraping action, especially from the uterus. **B** L19 *transitive & intransitive verb* Scrape or clean with a curette.

curia *noun* (also in sense 3 **Curia**) plural **curiae**, **curias** E17 **Latin**. **1** E17 *History* Each of the ten divisions into which each of the three tribes of ancient Rome was divided; the senate of an ancient Italian town, as distinguished from that of Rome. **2** E18 A court of justice, counsel, or administration, especially of the Roman Catholic church or (*historical*) under the feudal system. **3** M19 *The Curia* Vatican tribunals, congregations, and other institutions through which the Pope directs the work of the Roman Catholic church; *the* government departments of the Vatican.

curiosa *noun plural* L19 **Latin** (*curiosa* neuter plural of *curiosus*). Curiosities, oddities; *specifically* erotic or pornographic books.

curiosa felicitas *noun phrase* M18 **Latin** (literally, 'careful felicity'). A studied appropriateness of expression.

■ The phrase is a quotation from Petronius (*Satyricon* cxviii).

currach *noun* (also **curragh**, **corrack**) LME **Irish** (Gaelic *curach* small boat, coracle). In Ireland and Scotland: a small boat made of slats or laths covered with watertight material (formerly hide, now usually tarred canvas).

curragh *noun* M17 **Irish** (*currach* marsh, Manx *curragh* moor, bog, fen). In Ireland and the Isle of Man: marshy waste ground.

currente calamo *adverb phrase* L18 **Modern Latin** (literally, 'with the pen running on'). Extempore; without deliberation or hesitation.

curriculum *noun* plural **curricula** E19 **Latin** (= running, course, race chariot, from *currere* to run). A course of study at a school, university, etc.; the subjects making up such a course.

curriculum vitae *noun phrase* plural **curricula vitae** E20 **Latin** (from as preceding + Latin *vitae* of life). A brief account of one's life or career, especially as required in an application for employment.

■ In job advertisements and colloquial contexts usually abbreviated to *c.v.*

cursillo *noun* plural **cursillos** M20 **Spanish** (literally, 'little course'). A short course of study, etc., *specifically* of intensive religious studies and exercises, originally for Roman Catholics in Spain.

cursor *noun* ME **Latin** (= runner, from *currere* to run). **1** ME–M17 A runner, a running messenger. **2** L16 A part of a mathematical or surveying instrument that can be slid back and forward; *specifically* the transparent slide with a fine line with which the readings on a slide rule are taken. **3** M20 A movable visual marker forming part of a computer or video display screen, showing where the next character to be keyed will appear.

cursus *noun* plural same, **cursuses** M18 **Latin** (= course, from *currere* to run). **1** M18 *Archaeology* A neolithic structure consisting of a long straight avenue, usually closed at the ends, formed by two earthen banks with a ditch on the outer side of each. **2** M19 A stated order of daily prayer or worship. **3** E20 One of the cadences that mark the ends of sentences and phrases, especially in Greek and Latin prose. **4** E20 Abbreviation of CURSUS HONORUM.

cursus honorum *noun phrase* plural same E20 **Latin** (= course of honors). An established hierarchy of positions through which a person may be promoted.

cuspidor *noun* **M18 Portuguese** (= spitter, from *cuspir* to spit, from Latin *conspuere*). A spittoon.

custos *noun* plural **custodes**, (originally) **custoses** LME **Latin**. A keeper, a guardian, a custodian.

■ Now chiefly in titles from Modern Latin, as in *custos rotulorum* (literally, 'keeper of the rolls'), a title given to the chief Justice of the Peace in an English county, who has nominal responsibility for the records of the commission of the peace in that county.

cutcha variant of KUTCHA.

cuvée *noun* **M19 French** (= vatful, from *cuve* from Latin *cupa* cask, vat). The contents of a vat of wine; a particular blend or batch of wine.

cuvette *noun* **L17 French** (diminutive of *cuve* vat). **1** L17 *Fortification* A trench along the middle of a dry ditch. **2** E18 A shallow vessel for holding liquid; a transparent vessel with flat sides for holding a spectrophotometric sample, etc. **3** M19 A large clay basin or crucible used in making plate glass. **4** E20 *Geology* A basin in which sedimentation is occurring or has occurred.

cwm *noun* **M19 Welsh** (= coomb). A bowl-shaped valley or hollow in (Welsh) mountains; *Physical Geography* A CIRQUE.

cyanosis *noun* plural **cyanoses** **M19 Modern Latin** (from Greek *kuanōsis* blueness). *Medicine* A blue discoloration of the skin due to deficient oxygenation of the blood.

cyma *noun* **M16 Modern Latin** (from Greek *kuma* billow, wave, wavy molding, from *kuein* to become pregnant). **1** M16 *Architecture* An ogee molding of a cornice. **2** E18 *Botany* A CYME.

cymatium *noun* plural **cymatia** **M16 Latin** (*cymatium* ogee, Ionic volute from Greek *kumation* diminutive of *kuma* CYMA). *Architecture* A CYMA.

cymbalo *noun* plural **cymbalos** **L19 Italian** (*cembalo*, *cimbalo* from Latin *cymbalum* cymbal; cf. CIMBALOM). A dulcimer.

cyme *noun* (in sense 1 also written **cime**) **E18 French** (*cyme*, *cime* summit, top, from popular form of Latin CYMA). **1** The unopened head of a plant. *rare*. Only in E18. **2** L18 *Botany* An inflorescence (frequently forming a more or less flat head) in which the primary axis bears a single flower which develops first, flowers of secondary and higher order axes developing successively later.

czar *noun* (also **tzar**; also (especially in titles) with capital initial) **M16 Russian** (*tsar'* Old Church Slavonic *cěsarĭ* ultimately representing Latin *Caesar*, probably through Germanic; the spelling with *cz-* is not Slavonic). **1** *History* (The title of) the former emperor of Russia; (the title of) certain other eastern European rulers. **2** M19 *transferred* A person with great authority or power; a despot.

czardas variant of CSARDAS.

czarevich *noun* (also **tsarevich**; also (especially in titles) with capital initial) **E18 Russian** (from as CZAR + patronymic *-evich*). *History* The eldest son of the former emperor of Russia; the (male) heir of a czar.

czarevna *noun* (also **tsarevna**; also (especially in titles) with capital initial) L19 **Russian.** *History* A daughter of a czar.

czarina *noun* (also **tsarina**; also (especially in titles) with capital initial) E18 **Italian and Spanish** (*tzarina (c)zarina*, French *tsarine, czarine*, from German *Zarin, Czarin* feminine of *Zar, Czar*). The wife of a czar; *History* (the title of) the former empress of Russia.

czaritsa *noun* (also **tsaritsa**; also (especially in titles) with capital initial) L17 **Russian.** *History* (The title of) the former empress of Russia.

D

da capo *adverb phrase* E18 **Italian** (= from the beginning). *Music* (A direction:) repeat from the beginning.

dacha *noun* (also **datcha**) M19 **Russian** (= grant of land). In Russia: a small country house or villa.

dacoit *noun* L18 **Hindustani** (*ḍakait*, from *ḍākā* gang robbery). A member of an Indian or Myanmar (Burmese) band of armed robbers.

dado *noun* plural **dados** M17 **Italian** (= die, cube, from Latin *datum*). *Architecture* **1** M17 The plain portion of a pedestal between the base and the cornice. **2** L18 The lower part of an interior wall when faced or colored differently from the upper part.

daemon *noun* (also formerly **demon**) M16 **Latin** (medieval Latin *demon*, Latin *daemon* from Greek *daimōn* divinity, genius). **1** *Greek Mythology* M16 A being of a nature between that of the gods and men, a spirit; the soul of a deceased person regarded as a minor divinity. **2** E17 An attendant or indwelling spirit; a DAIMON.

■ *Demon*, meaning specifically 'an evil spirit' or 'devil', was naturalized in Middle English, and this spelling was also occasionally used in Early Modern English in the senses above. However, the usefulness of being able to differentiate between an evil spirit and other morally neutral entities taken over from pagan classical religion ensured that the spelling *daemon* has survived in the latter senses. A similar consideration lay behind the later (M19) introduction of DAIMON.

dagesh *noun* M16 **Hebrew** (*dāḡeš*). *Hebrew Grammar* A point or dot placed within a Hebrew letter, denoting either that it is doubled or that it is not aspirated.

dagga *noun* L17 **Afrikaans** (from Nama *daχa*). In South Africa: Indian hemp used as a narcotic; any indigenous plant of the genus *Leonotis* that is similarly used.

dagoba *noun* E19 **Sinhalese** (*dāgaba* from Pali *dhātu-gabbha* receptacle for relics). A stupa or dome-shaped structure containing Buddhist relics.

daimon *noun* M19 **Greek** (*daimōn*). An attendant or indwelling spirit, one's genius.

■ The direct transliteration of the Greek is intended to evoke the pagan classical concept of the personal spirit, unencumbered by the nuances of the earlier usages of *d(a)emon*; see also DAEMON.

daimyo *noun* (also **daimio**) plural **daimyos** E18 **Japanese** (from *dai* great + *myō* name). *History* In feudal Japan:

any of the chief landowning nobles, vassals of the shogun.

dak *noun* (also **dawk**) **E18 Hindustani** (*ḍāk*). In the Indian subcontinent: originally, mail or transport by relays; now, postal service, delivery of letters, mail.

dal variant of DHAL.

dalles *noun plural* **L18 French** (plural of *dalle* conduit, tube, etc.). Rapids where a river is compressed into long narrow troughlike channels.

dal segno *adverb phrase* **L19 Italian** (= from the sign). *Music* (A direction:) go back to the point indicated by the sign (not the beginning). Cf. AL SEGNO.

dame de compagnie *noun phrase* plural **dames de compagnie** **L18 French** (literally, 'lady of company'). A paid female companion.

dame d'honneur *noun phrase* plural **dames d'honneur** **E19 French** (literally, 'lady of honor'). A maid of honor, a lady-in-waiting.

damna plural of DAMNUM.

damnatio memoriae *noun phrase* **M20 Latin** (= condemnation of the memory). The attempt to obliterate the memory of a dead person by erasing inscriptions mentioning him or her, destroying statues and memorials, etc.

damnosa hereditas *noun phrase* **M19 Latin** (= inheritance that causes loss). An inheritance, tradition, etc., bringing more burden than profit.

damnum *noun* plural **damna** **E19 Latin** (= hurt, harm, damage). *Law* A loss, a wrong.

dan *noun* **M20 Japanese**. Each of the (numbered) grades in the advanced level of proficiency in judo, karate, etc. (also *dan grade*; a person who has reached (a specified grade of) this level. Cf. KYU.

danse du ventre *noun phrase* plural **danses du ventre** **L19 French**. A belly dance.

danse macabre *noun phrase* plural **danses macabres** **L19 French**. The dance of death; a musical piece or passage representing or suggestive of this.

■ Earlier (LME) Anglicized as *dance (of) macabre* (cf. MACABRE). As an allegory, the Dance of Death (called TOTENTANZ in German-speaking areas) was very popular in the late Middle Ages. Medieval and Renaissance representations of it show Death in the form of a skeleton approaching young and old, rich and poor, powerful and obscure, and leading them all away in a dance to the grave; the most famous of these images is the series of 50 woodcuts by Hans Holbein the Younger designed in the early 1520s and published at Lyons in 1538.

danseur *noun* **E19 French** (from *danser* to dance). *Ballet* A male dancer.

danseur noble *noun phrase* plural **danseurs nobles** **M20 French** (from as *danseur* + *noble* noble). *Ballet* A male dancer as partner of a ballerina.

danseuse *noun* **E19 French**. A female dancer; a ballerina.

dariole *noun* **LME Old and Modern French**. **1** LME An individual sweet or savory dish of various kinds; now *specifically* one made in a dariole mold. **2** M19 A small metal mold shaped like a flowerpot and used for making such a dish. In full *dariole mold*.

darshan *noun* **E20 Hindi** (pronunciation of Sanskrit *darśana* sight, seeing, from *dṛś-* to see). In the Indian subcontinent, etc.: the opportunity or occasion of seeing a holy person or the image of a deity.

Dasein *noun* **M19 German** (from *dasein* to exist, from *da* there + *sein* to be). *Philosophy* In Hegelian terms, existence, determinate being; in existentialism, human existence, the being of a person in the world.

dashiki *noun* **M20 West African** (probably Yoruba from Hausa: cf. Krio *da(n)shiki*). A loose brightly colored West African shirt.

data *noun* **M17 Latin** (plural of DATUM). *plural and collective singular* **1** M17 Things given or granted; things known or assumed as facts, and made the basis of reasoning or calculation. **2** L19 Facts, especially numerical facts, collected together for reference or information. **3** M20 The quantities, characters, or symbols on which operations are performed by computers and other automatic equipment, and which may be stored and transmitted in the form of electrical signals, records on magnetic, optical, or mechanical recording media, etc.

datcha variant of DACHA.

datum *noun singular* plural **data** M18 Latin (neuter past participle of *dare* to give). A thing given or granted; a thing known or assumed as a fact, and made the basis of reasoning or calculation; a fixed starting point for a series of measurements, etc.

■ Now much more frequent in the plural DATA.

daube *noun* E18 French. A braised meat (usually beef) stew with wine, spices, etc.

dauphin *noun* (also **Dauphin**) LME French ((Old French *daulphin*), family name of the lords of Viennois or Dauphiné). **1** LME *History* (The title of) the eldest son of the King of France, from 1349 to 1830. **2** A dolphin. *rare*. Only in L16.

■ See also AD USUM DELPHINI.

dazibao *noun* plural same M20 Chinese (*dàzìbào*, from *dà* big + *zì* character + *bào* newspaper, poster). In the People's Republic of China: a wall poster written in large characters expressing an (especially political) opinion.

débâcle *noun* (also **debacle**) E19 French (from *débâcler* to unbar, from *dé-* + *bâcler* to bar). **1** E19 A breaking up of ice in a river; a sudden flood or rush of water carrying along debris. **2** M19 A sudden and ignominious collapse or defeat; a humiliating and embarrassing situation.

débat *noun* L19 French (= debate). A poetic discussion between persons, personifications, or abstractions, on a question of morality, politics, or love, common in medieval European literature.

debitage *noun* M20 French (*débitage* cutting of stone). *Archaeology* Waste material produced in the making of prehistoric stone implements.

débouché *noun* M18 French (from *déboucher* from *dé-* de- + *bouche* mouth (after synonymous Italian *sboccare*)). An opening where troops, etc. (may) emerge; *generally* an outlet.

debris *noun* (also **débris**) E18 French (*débris*, from *débriser* to break down, break up, from *dé-* + *briser* to break). The remains of anything broken down or destroyed (originally *in figurative use*, of institutions, nations, etc.); fragments, wreckage, ruins; accumulated waste matter; *Geology* fragmentary material accumulated from the breakdown of rocks, etc.

début *noun* (also **debut**) M18 French (from *débuter* to lead off). Entry into society; the first appearance in public of a performer, etc.

débutant *noun* (also **debutant**) E19 French (present participle of *débuter* to lead off). A male person making his début.

débutante *noun* (also **debutante**) E19 French (feminine of *débutant*: see preceding). **1** E19 A female performer, etc., making her début. **2** E19 A young woman making her social début; *loosely* a young woman in fashionable society.

decalage *noun* E20 French (*décalage* displacement, from *décaler* to displace). *Aeronautics* The difference in the angle of incidence between two airfoils on an airplane.

decani *adjective* M18 Latin (genitive of *decanus* dean). Of or pertaining to the south side of the choir of a church where the dean usually sits; *Music* to be sung by the decanal side in antiphonal singing (cf. CANTORIS).

decemvir *noun* LME Latin (singular of *decemviri*, originally *decem viri* ten men). **1** LME In *plural* A council or ruling body of ten. Originally and *espe-*

cially (*Roman History*) either of two bodies of magistrates appointed in 451 and 450 BC respectively. **2** E18 A member of such a body.

decennium *noun* plural **decennia, decenniums** L17 **Latin** (from *decennis*, from *decem* ten + *annus* year). A period of ten years, a decade.

déclassé *adjective & noun* (feminine **déclassée**) L19 **French** (past participle of *déclasser* to (re)move from a class). (A person who is) reduced or degraded in social class or status.

décolletage *noun* L19 **French** (from *décolleter* to expose the neck). **1** L19 The low-cut neckline of a woman's garment. **2** L19 Exposure of the neck and shoulders by such a neckline.

décolleté *adjective* (also **décolletée**) M19 **French** ((feminine *décolletée*), from *décolleter* to expose the neck, from *dé-* + *collet* collar of a dress, etc). Of a (woman's) garment: having a low-cut neckline. Of a woman: wearing a low-necked garment. Also *figurative*, daring, slightly improper.

décor *noun* (also **decor**) L19 **French** (from *décorer* to decorate). **1** L19 The scenery and furnishings of a theater stage; the set. **2** E20 (The overall effect of) the decoration and furnishings of a room, building, etc.

decorum *noun* M16 **Latin** (noun use of neuter singular of *decorus* seemly). **1** M16 Suitability of artistic or literary style to the subject; congruity, unity. **2** L16 Suitability to the dignity or circumstances of a person or occasion. *archaic*. **3** L16 Propriety of behavior or demeanor; seemliness; etiquette.

découpage *noun* M20 **French** (from *découper* to cut up, cut out). **1** M20 The decoration of a surface with cutout paper patterns or illustrations; an object so decorated. **2** M20 *Cinematography* The cutting or editing of a movie.

decrescendo *adverb, adjective, noun & intransitive verb* plural of noun **decrescendos** E19 **Italian** (present participle of *decrescere* to decrease). DIMINUENDO.

decretum *noun* plural **decreta** E17 **Latin**. A decree.

de facto *adverb & adjective phrase* E17 **Latin** (= of fact). (Existing, held, etc.) in fact, in reality; in actual existence, force, or possession, whether by right or not.

■ Often distinguished from DE JURE.

defluvium *noun* E19 **Latin** (*defluvium* loss by flowing or falling away). *Medicine* A complete shedding of hair, fingernails, etc., as a result of disease.

dégagé *adjective* (feminine **dégagée**) L17 **French** (past participial adjective of *dégager* to set free). Unconstrained, relaxed; detached, unconcerned.

degras *noun* (also **dégras**) L19 **French** (*dégras*, from *dégraisser* to remove grease from). **1** L19 A dark wax or grease obtained when fish oils are rubbed into hides and recovered, used in the dressing of leather; a preparation containing this or synthesized in imitation of it; moellon. **2** L19 Wool grease, wool fat; a crude mixture of wax and fats obtained by scouring wool or treating it with organic solvents.

dégringolade *noun* L19 **French** (from *dégringoler* to descend rapidly). A rapid descent or deterioration; decadence.

de haut en bas *adverb and adjective phrase* L17 **French** (= from above to below). Condescending(ly) or patronizing(ly).

dehors *preposition* E18 **French** (in Old French used as a preposition (Modern French as adverb and noun)). *Law* Outside of; not within the scope of.

Dei gratia *adverb phrase* E17 **Latin**. By the grace of God.

déjà entendu *noun phrase* (also **déjà-entendu**) M20 **French** (= already heard, after DÉJÀ VU). A feeling (correct or illusory) that one has already heard or understood the words, music, etc., currently under attention.

déjà lu *noun phrase* M20 **French** (= already read, after next). A feeling that one may have read the present passage, or one very like it, before.

déjà vu *noun phrase* E20 **French** (= already seen). **1** E20 *Psychology* The illusory feeling of having already experienced the present moment or situation. **2** M20 The (correct) impression that something similar has been previously experienced; tedious familiarity.

déjeuner *noun* L18 **French** (noun use of infinitive = to break one's fast). **1** L18 A morning meal (early or late) in France or elsewhere; breakfast or (usually) lunch. **2** L18 A set of cups, saucers, plates, etc., for serving breakfast, breakfast service.

■ *Petit déjeuner* is commonly used for 'breakfast'.

de jure *adverb & adjective phrase* M16 **Latin** (= of law). (Existing, held, etc.) rightfully, according to law.

■ Often distinguished from DE FACTO.

dekko *noun* plural **dekkos** L19 **Hindustani** (*dekho* polite imperative of *dekhnā* to look). A look.

■ Originally army slang. Although the word also existed (L19) as a transitive and intransitive verb, the verbal sense is usually expressed by *have* (or *take*) *a dekko*.

délassement *noun* E19 **French** (from *délasser* to relax, from *dé-* + *las* weary). Relaxation.

del credere *adjective, adverb, & noun phrase* L18 **Italian** (= of belief, of trust). *Commerce* (Subject or relating to) a selling agent's guarantee, for which a commission is charged, that the buyer is solvent.

délicatesse *noun* L17 **French** (from *délicat* delicate). Delicacy.

delicatessen *noun* L19 **German** (*Delikatessen* plural or Dutch *delicatessen* plural, from as preceding). **1** L19 Cooked meats, cheeses, and unusual or foreign prepared foods. **2** M20 A store, or a counter or department in a store, selling delicatessen.

■ Sense 2 is often abbreviated colloquially to *deli*, which in Australia has undergone an extension of meaning to 'a small shop open long hours and selling perishable goods, newspapers, etc.'

delirium *noun* plural **deliriums, deliria** M16 **Latin** (from *delirare* to deviate, be deranged, from *de-* + *lira* ridge between furrows). **1** M16 A disordered state of the mind resulting from disease, intoxication, etc., characterized by incoherent speech, hallucinations, restlessness, and often extreme excitement. **2** M17 Great excitement; ecstasy, rapturous frenzy.

delirium tremens *noun phrase* E19 **Modern Latin** (= trembling delirium, from as DELIRIUM + *tremens* present participial adjective of *tremere to shake). Delirium accompanied by tremors and terrifying illusions, usually as a symptom of withdrawal in cases of chronic alcoholism.*

■ A term invented by a Dr. T. Sutton in 1813 for a type of delirium that was worsened by bleeding but alleviated by opium; later medical writers established its modern sense.

delta *noun* ME **Latin** (from Greek). **1** ME The fourth letter (Δ, δ) of the Greek alphabet. **2** M16 A tract of alluvial land, often more or less triangular in shape, enclosed or traversed by the diverging mouths of a river; originally (*the Delta*) *specifically* that of the River Nile. **3** M17 A triangle; a triangular area or formation. Usually *attributive*, as in *delta connection* (*Electricity*) and *delta wing* (*Aeronautics*). **4** L18 Denoting the fourth in a numerical sequence: *attributive Science* (frequently written δ) as *Astronomy* (preceding the genitive of the Latin name of the constellation): the fourth brightest star in a constellation; (**b**) *delta rays*, rays of low penetrative power consisting of slow electrons released from atoms by other particles; (**c**) *delta rhythm, delta waves*, slow electrical activity of the unconscious brain. **5** E20 **Brit.** A fourth-class or poor mark in an examination, etc.

deluxe *adjective phrase* (also **de luxe**) E19 **French** (= of luxury). Luxurious, sumptuous; of a superior kind.

■ Used either postpositively or as a premodifier. Cf. POULE DE LUXE.

démarche *noun* M17 **French** (from *démarcher* to take steps, from *dé-* + *marcher* to march). A step, a proceeding; *especially* a diplomatic action or initiative.

déménagement *noun* L19 **French**. The removal of household possessions from one place to another; moving.

démenti *noun* L16 **French** (from *démentir* to contradict, from *dé-* from + *mentir* to lie). A contradiction, a denial; now *especially* an official denial of a published statement.

dementia *noun* L18 **Latin** (from *demens* insane, from *de-* + *mens* mind). **1** L18 *Psychiatry* Chronic mental and emotional deterioration caused by organic brain disease. **2** L19 Madness, folly.

demi-caractère *noun & adjective* L18 **French** (literally, 'half character'). *Ballet* **A** *noun* L18 A dance retaining the form of the character dance but executed with steps based on the classical technique. Also, a dancer of demi-caractères. **B** *adjective* E19 Of, pertaining to, or designating dancing of this kind.

demi-glace *noun* E20 **French** (literally, 'half-glaze'). *Cooking* A meat stock from which the liquid has been partially evaporated. In full *demi-glace sauce*.

demilune *noun & adjective* E18 **French** (literally, 'half-moon'). **A** *noun* **1** E18 *Fortification* An outwork resembling a bastion, with a crescent-shaped gorge. **2** M18 A half-moon, a crescent; a crescent-shaped body. **B** *adjective* L19 Crescent-shaped, semilunar.

demi-mondaine *noun* L19 **French** (from as next). A woman of the DEMI-MONDE.

demi-monde *noun* M19 **French** (literally, 'half world'). The class of women of doubtful reputation and social standing; the class of kept women or *loosely* of prostitutes; *transferred* any social group regarded as behaving with doubtful propriety or legality.

■ *Le Demi-monde* was the title of a novel (1855) by the younger Alexandre Dumas.

de minimis *adverb and adjective phrase* E17 **Latin** (= about the smallest things (*de* about + noun use of ablative plural of *minimus* least, smallest)). About petty details.

■ An elliptical use of the Latin legal tag *de minimis non curat lex* 'the law does not concern itself with petty matters', which is used as an injunction not to become overconcerned about trivia.

demi-pension *noun* M20 **French**. Originally in France and French-speaking countries: (the price of) bed, breakfast, and one other meal at a hotel, etc.; half board.

demi-saison *adjective* M18 **French** (literally, 'half season'). Of a style or fashion intermediate between that of the past and that of the coming season.

demi-sec *adjective* M20 **French** (literally, 'half-dry'). *Wine* Medium dry.

demitasse *noun* M19 **French** (literally, 'half-cup'). (The contents of) a small coffee cup.

demi-vierge *noun* E20 **French** (literally 'half-virgin'). A woman who behaves licentiously while remaining a virgin.

■ From the title of the novel *Les demi-vierges* (1874) by M. Prévost.

démodé *adjective* L19 **French** (past participle of *démoder* to send, go out of fashion, from *dé-* from + *mode* fashion). Out of fashion, unfashionable.

demoiselle *noun* E16 **French**. **1** E16 A young lady, a girl. *archaic*. **2** L17 A Eurasian and North African crane, *Anthropoides virgo*, with elongated black breast feathers and white neck plumes. Now usually more fully *demoiselle crane*. **3** M19 A dragonfly or (*es-*

pecially) a damselfly. **4** L19 A damselfish.

de mortuis *noun phrase* **Latin** (= about the dead). (An injunction not to speak ill) of the dead.

■ An elliptical form of the Latin saying *de mortuis nil nisi bonum* '(say) nothing but good of the dead'. The saying is traditionally ascribed to Chilon of Sparta, one of the sages of ancient Greece.

demos *noun* plural **demi** **L18 Greek** (*dēmos*). **1** L18 A district of ancient Attica, Greece; a deme. *rare.* **2** M19 (**Demos**) The common people of an ancient Greek state; (a personification of) the populace, especially in a democracy.

dengue *noun* (also **denga**) **E19 West Indian Spanish** (from Kiswahili *denga, dinga* (in full *kidingapopo*), identified with Spanish *dengue* fastidiousness, prudery, with reference to the stiffness of the neck and shoulders caused by the disease). A debilitating tropical viral disease. Also *dengue fever*.

dénigrement *noun* **L19 French.** Blackening of character, denigration.

de nos jours *postpositive adjective phrase* **E20 French** (= of our days). Of the present time; contemporary.

denouement *noun* (also **dénouement**) **M18 French** (from *dénouer* (earlier *desnouement* to untie, from *des, dé-* + *nouer* to knot). The unraveling of the complications of a plot, or of a confused situation or mystery; the final resolution of a play, novel, or other narrative.

de nouveau *adverb phrase* **L18 French** (= from new). Afresh, starting again from the beginning. Cf. next.

de novo *adverb phrase* **E17 Latin** (= from new). Starting again from the beginning.

deoch an doris *noun phrase* (also **doch an doris**) **M17 Gaelic** (*deoch an doruis* (Irish *deoch an dorais*) a drink at the door). In Scotland and Ireland: a drink taken at parting, a stirrup cup.

Deo gratias *interjection* **L16 Latin** (= (we give) thanks to God). Thanks be to God.

Deo volente *adverb phrase* **M18 Latin.** God willing; if nothing prevents it.

■ Abbreviated to *d.v.*

dépaysé *adjective* (feminine **dépaysée**) **E20 French** (= (removed) from one's own country). Removed from one's habitual surroundings.

depot *noun* (also (now *rare*) **depôt**) **L18 French** (*dépôt*, Old French *depost* from Latin *depositum* noun use of neuter past participle of *deponere* to place, put away). **1 a** L18–M19 The action or an act of depositing. *rare.* **b** M19 A deposit, a collection, a store. Now *specifically* (*transferred* from sense 4 below) a localized accumulation of a substance in the body. **2** L18 A military establishment at which stores are deposited, recruits or other troops assembled, etc.; *especially* a regimental headquarters. **3** L18 A place where goods, etc., are deposited or stored, often for later dispatch; a warehouse, an emporium. **b** M19 A place where vehicles, locomotives, etc., are housed and maintained and from which they are dispatched for service; a railroad or bus station. **4** E20 A site in the body at which a particular substance naturally concentrates or is deposited.

de profundis *noun & adverb phrase* **LME Latin** (= from the depths). **A** *noun* LME A psalm of penitence; *specifically* Psalm 130 (129 in the Vulgate); *generally* a cry of appeal from the depths (of sorrow, humiliation, etc.). **B** *adverb phrase* LME Out of the depths (of sorrow, etc.).

■ The initial words of Psalm 130 (129 in the Vulgate): "Out of the deep have I called unto thee O Lord" (Book of Common Prayer). *De Profundis* was the title of Oscar Wilde's posthumously published apologia written after being sentenced to a term of imprisonment in Reading Gaol, and modern use of the phrase often contains an unspoken allusion to Wilde's work.

déraciné *adjective & noun* (feminine **déracinée**) E20 **French** (= uprooted, past participial adjective of *déraciner*). **A** *adjective* E20 Uprooted from one's environment; displaced geographically or socially. **B** *noun* E20 A *déraciné* person.

derailleur *noun* M20 **French** (*dérailleur*, from *dérailler* to cause (a train) to run off the rails). A bicycle gear in which the ratio is changed by switching the line of the chain (while pedaling) so that it jumps to a different sprocket.

de rigueur *predicative adjective phrase* M19 **French** (literally, 'of strictness'). Required by custom or etiquette.

dernier *adjective* E17 **French** (from Old French *derrenier*, from *derrein* last). Last, ultimate, final.

■ Formerly fully naturalized, but now only in phrases (see below).

dernier cri *noun phrase* (also **le dernier cri**) L19 **French** (literally, '(the) last cry'). The very latest fashion.

dernier mot *noun phrase* (also **le dernier mot**) M19 **French**. The last word.

dernier ressort *noun phrase* (also **le dernier resort**) M17 **French**. A last refuge; *originally* the ultimate court of appeal.

derrière *noun* L18 **French** (= behind). The buttocks.

■ Usually only in jocular or colloquial use.

dervish *noun* L16 **Turkish** (*derviş* from Persian *darvīš* poor, a religious mendicant). A Muslim (*specifically* Sufi) religious man who has taken vows of poverty and austerity; *specifically* (more fully *dancing*, *whirling*, *howling*, etc., *dervish*) one whose order includes the practice of dancing, etc., as a spiritual exercise.

desaparecido *noun* plural **desaparecidos** L20 **Spanish** (= (one who has) disappeared). In Argentina: a person who disappeared during the period of military rule between 1976 and 1983, presumed killed by members of the armed services or the police; a child removed from his or her arrested parents and placed with another family without consent.

■ By extension, the word is now also applied to any persons who have vanished or been separated from their real families under totalitarian regimes in South America.

désaxé *adjective & adverb* E20 **French**. Of an automobile crankshaft: (set) out of line with the center of the cylinder.

descamisado *noun* plural **descamisados** M19 **Spanish** (= shirtless). *History* An extreme liberal in the Spanish Revolutionary War of 1820–23; *transferred* an impoverished revolutionary.

■ A similar sartorial deficiency gave rise to the earlier French Revolutionary equivalent, SANSCULOTTE.

déshabillé *noun* (also **deshabille**, **déshabille**, **dishabille**) L17 **French** (*déshabillé* noun use of past participle of *déshabiller* to undress). **1** L17 The state of being casually or only partially dressed. Chiefly in *in dishabille*, EN DÉSHABILLÉ. **2** L17 A garment or costume of a casual or informal style.

desideratum *noun* plural **desiderata** M17 **Latin** (noun use of neuter singular of past participle of *desiderare* to feel the lack of, desire). A thing for which desire is felt; a thing lacked and wanted, a requirement.

détente *noun* E20 **French** (= loosening, relaxation). The easing of strained relations, especially between nations.

détenu *noun* (also **detenu**) E19 **French** (noun use of past participle of *détenir* to detain). A detainee, now especially in the Indian subcontinent.

detour *noun & verb* (also **détour**) M18 **French** (*détour* change of direction, from *détourner* to turn away). **A** *noun* M18 A deviation from one's route, a roundabout way; a digression. **B** *verb* **1** *intransitive* M19 Make a detour. **2** *transitive* E20 Send by a detour. **3** *transitive* M20 Bypass, make a detour around.

détraqué *adjective & noun* (feminine **détraquée**) E20 **French** (past participial adjective of *détraquer* to put out of order, derange). **A** *adjective* E20 Deranged; crazy; psychopathic. **B** *noun* E20 A deranged person, a psychopath.

detritus *noun* L18 **Latin** (*detritus* rubbing away, from *deterere* to wear away; in sense 2 after French *détritus*). **1** L18–E19 Wearing away by rubbing; disintegration. **2** E19 Matter produced by detrition; *especially* material eroded or washed away, as gravel, sand, silt, etc. **3** M19 Debris of any kind.

de trop *adjective phrase* M18 **French** (literally, 'excessive'). Not wanted, unwelcome, in the way.

detur *noun* L18 **Latin** (= let there be given). Any of several prizes of books given annually at Harvard University.

■ *Detur* is the first word of the inscription accompanying these books.

deus absconditus *noun phrase* M20 **Latin** (= hidden god). *Theology* A divine being that is inaccessible to human perception.

■ Cf. Isaiah 45:15 "Verily thou art a God that hidest thyself, O God of Israel . . ."

deus ex machina *noun phrase* L17 **Modern Latin** (translation of Greek *theos ek mēkhanēs*, literally, 'god from the machinery'). A power, event, or person arriving in the nick of time to solve a difficulty; a providential (often rather contrived) interposition, especially in a novel or play.

■ The "machine" was originally the device by which deities were suspended above the stage in the theater in classical antiquity. The phrase is generally used in its entirety but also occurs abbreviated to *ex machina*, with another agent of providence substituted for *deus*.

deva *noun* E19 **Sanskrit** (= a god, (originally) a shining one). Any of a class of deities in Vedic mythology; any of the lower-level gods in Hinduism and Buddhism.

devadasi *noun* E19 **Sanskrit** (*devadāsī*, literally, 'female servant of a god' (cf. preceding)). A hereditary female dancer in a Hindu temple.

développé *noun* E20 **French** (noun use of past participle of *développer* to develop). A ballet movement in which one leg is raised and then fully extended.

dévot *noun* (feminine **dévote**) E18 **French** (noun use or adjective). A devotee; a devout person.

dey *noun* (also (especially in titles) **Dey**) M17 **French** (from Turkish *dayl* maternal uncle, used also as a courtesy title). *History* (The title of) any of the supreme rulers of Algiers, 1710–1830. Also, (the title of) the local ruler of Tunis or Tripoli under nominal Ottoman suzerainty.

dhal *noun* (also **dal**) L17 **Hindustani** (*dāl*). Split pulses (especially the seed of the pigeon pea, *Cajanus cajan*), a common ingredient in Indian cooking.

dhamma *noun* E20 **Pali** (from as *dharma*). Especially among Theravada Buddhists, DHARMA.

dhania *noun* E20 **Hindi** (*dhaniyā*). In Indian cooking: coriander.

dharma *noun* L18 **Sanskrit** (= something established, decree, custom; cf. DHAMMA). In *Hinduism*: social or caste custom, right behavior, law; justice, virtue; natural or essential state or function, nature. In *Buddhism*: universal truth or law, especially as proclaimed by Buddha.

dharmsala *noun* (also **dharmasala**) E19 **Sanskrit** (representing Hindustani pronunciation of Sanskrit *dharmaśālā*, from *dharma* + *śālā* house). In the Indian subcontinent: a building devoted to religious or charitable purposes, *especially* a rest house for travelers.

dhobi *noun* (also **dhoby**, **dhobie**) M19 **Hindustani** (*dhobī*, from *dhob* washing). In the Indian subcontinent: a washerman or washerwoman.

dhoti *noun* (also formerly **dhootie** and other variants) E17 **Hindustani**

(*dhotī*). A cloth worn by male Hindus, the ends being passed through the legs and tucked in at the waist.

dhow *noun* (also **dow**) L18 **Arabic** (*dāwa*, probably related to Marathi *ḍāw*). A lateen-rigged sailing vessel of the Arabian Sea, with one or two masts. Formerly also *loosely*, an Arab slaver or other vessel.

diable *interjection & noun* L16 **French** (from ecclesiastical Latin *diabolus* devil). **A** *interjection* L16 Expressing impatience, amazement, dismay, etc. **B** *noun* M19 (*le diable*) DIABOLO. Now *rare* or *obsolete*.

diable au corps *noun phrase* L19 **French** (literally, 'devil in the body'). Restless energy; a spirit of devilry.

diablerie *noun* (also **diablery**) M18 **French** (from as DIABLE). **1** M18 Dealings with the Devil; sorcery, witchcraft. **b** M19 *figurative* Mischievous fun, devilment. **2** E19 The mythology or lore of devils; a description or representation of devils. **3** M19 The realm of devils.

diabolo *noun* plural **diabolos** E20 **Italian** (from ecclesiastical Latin *diabolus* devil). A game in which a two-headed top is thrown up and caught on a string stretched between two sticks; the top used in this game.

diabolus in musica *noun phrase* M20 **Latin** (literally, 'the devil in music'). *Music* The interval of the diminished fifth.

■ So called because of its displeasing or unsettling effect.

diaeresis *noun* (also **dieresis**) plural **diaereses** L16 **Latin** (from Greek *diairesis* noun of action from *diairein* to take apart, divide). **1** L16 The division of one syllable into two, especially by the resolution of a diphthong into two simple vowels. **2** E17 The sign placed over a vowel to indicate that it is pronounced separately, as in *Brontë, naïve*. **3** M19 *Prosody* A break in a line where the end of a foot coincides with the end of a word.

diamanté *adjective & noun* E20 **French** (past participle of *diamanter* to set with diamonds, from *diamant* diamond). (Material) given a sparkling effect by means of artificial gems, powdered crystal, etc.

Diaspora *noun* (also **diaspora**) L19 **Greek** (from *diaspeirein* to disperse, scatter). The dispersion of Jews among the Gentile nations; all those Jews who live outside the biblical land of Israel; (the situation of) any body of people living outside their traditional homeland.

dibbuk variant of DYBBUK.

dictum *noun* plural **dicta**, **dictums** L16 **Latin**. **1** L16 A saying, an utterance; *especially* one that claims some authority, a pronouncement. **2** L18 *Law* An expression of opinion by a judge that is not essential to the decision and so has no binding authority as precedent. See also OBITER DICTUM. **3** E19 A common saying; a maxim.

didgeridoo *noun* (also **didjeridoo**, **didgeridu**) E20 **Aboriginal** (of imitative origin). A long tubular wooden musical instrument of the Australian Aborigines that is blown to produce a resonant sound.

dieresis variant of DIAERESIS.

dies irae *noun phrase* E19 **Latin** (= day of wrath). A thirteenth-century Latin hymn that was formerly an obligatory part of the requiem mass in the Roman Catholic church; a musical setting of this part of the mass; *hence* the Day of Judgment or *transferred* any day of reckoning.

■ The text of which *Dies irae* is the opening phrase is attributed to Thomas of Celano (*c.*1250).

dies non *noun phrase* E19 **Latin** (literally, 'a non day'). A day that does not count because there has been no (specific) activity or because it cannot be used for a particular purpose.

■ Used in its original legal sense, it is an abbreviated form of the following, but it is also applied in other contexts.

dies non juridicus *noun phrase* plural **dies non juridici** E17 **Latin** (literally, 'day not judicial'). *Law* A day on which no legal business is enacted.

differentia *noun* plural **differentiae** L17 **Latin**. A distinguishing mark or characteristic, *especially* (*Logic*) that distinguishing a species from others of the same genus.

difficile *adjective* **LME French** (from Latin *difficilis*, from *dif-* not + *facilis* easy). **1** LME–L17 Requiring physical or mental effort or skill. **2** L15–M17 Hard to understand; obscure. **3** M16 Of a person: not easy to get along with, stubborn, unaccommodating.

difficilior lectio *noun phrase* plural **difficiliores lectiones** E20 **Latin** (from the maxim *difficilior lectio potior* the harder reading is to be preferred). *Textual Criticism* The more difficult or unexpected of two variant readings and therefore the one that is less likely to be a copyist's error; (the principle of) giving preference to such a reading.

digamma *noun* L17 **Latin** (from Greek, from *di-* twice + *gamma* (from the shape of the letter, a GAMMA with a doubled cross stroke)). The sixth letter of the original Greek alphabet, probably equivalent to W, later disused.

digestif *noun* E20 **French**. Something that promotes good digestion, especially a drink taken after a meal.

diktat *noun* M20 **German** (from Latin *dictatum* use as noun of neuter past participle of *dictare* to dictate). **1** M20 A severe settlement, especially one imposed by a victorious nation on a defeated one. **2** M20 A dictate; a categorical assertion.

dilemma *noun* E16 **Latin** (from Greek *dilēmma*, from as *di-* twice + *lēmma* assumption, premise). **1** E16 In *Rhetoric*, a form of argument involving an opponent in choice between two (or more) alternatives, both equally unfavorable. In *Logic*, a syllogism with two conditional major premises and a disjunctive minor premise. **2** L16 A choice between two (or several) alternatives that are equally unfavorable; a position of doubt or perplexity.

dilettante *noun & adjective* plural **dilettanti**, **dilettantes** M18 **Italian** (noun use of verbal adjective from *dilettare* from Latin *delectare* to delight). **A** *noun* M18 A lover of the fine arts; a person who cultivates the arts as an amateur; a person who takes an interest in a subject merely as a pastime and without serious study, a dabbler. **B** *adjective* M18 Of, pertaining to, or characteristic of a dilettante; amateur.

■ The English use of the word is linked to the eighteenth-century British fashion for wealthy young aristocrats to travel to Italy on the so-called Grand Tour to study the remains of classical antiquity there and to purchase sculptures, coins, and other objects for their personal collections. In 1733–34 "some gentlemen who had travelled in Italy, desirous of encouraging, at home, a taste for those objects which had contributed so much to their entertainment abroad" founded the Society of Dilettanti. Despite Horace Walpole's unkind observation that the nominal qualification for membership of the Dilettanti was "having been in Italy, and the real one, being drunk", the society subsequently financed some major expeditions and publications and generally played a key role in developing British knowledge of the ancient world.

dilruba *noun* E20 **Hindustani** (*dilrubā* = robber of the heart). An Indian musical instrument with a long neck, three or four strings played with a bow, and several sympathetic strings.

diminuendo *noun, verb, adverb, & adjective* L18 **Italian** (= diminishing, present participle of *diminuire* from Latin *deminuere* to lessen). *Music* **A** *noun* L18 plural **diminuendos**, **diminuendi**. A gradual decrease in loudness; a passage (to be) played or sung with such a decrease. **B** *intransitive verb* L18 Become quieter; grow less. **C** *adverb & adjective* E19 (A direction:) with a gradual decrease in loudness.

dim sum *noun phrase* (also **dim sim** and other variants) plural **dim sum(s)** etc. M20 **Chinese** (Cantonese) (*tím sam*, from *tím* dot + *sam* heart). A Chinese snack consisting of different hot savory pastries.

dinanderie *noun* M19 **French** (from *Dinant* (formerly *Dinand*), a town near Liège, Belgium + *-erie*). Household and other utensils of brass (frequently embossed) made in late medieval times in and around Dinant; ornamental brassware from other parts, including India and the eastern Mediterranean region.

dinero *noun* plural **dineros** L17 **Spanish** (= coin, money from Latin *denarius* a silver coin). **1** *History* L17 A monetary unit in Spain and Peru, now disused. **2** M19 Money. *slang.*

Ding an sich *noun phrase* M19 **German** (= thing in itself). *Philosophy* A thing as it really is, apart from human observation or experience of it. Cf. NOUMENON.

diorama *noun* E19 **French** (from as Greek *dia* through + *orama* view (after *panorama*). **1** E19 A scenic painting, viewed through a peephole, in which changes in lighting, color, etc., are used to suggest different times of day, changes in weather, etc.; a building in which such paintings are exhibited. **2** E20 A small-scale tableau in which three-dimensional figures are shown against a painted background; a museum display of an animal, etc., in its natural setting; a scale model of an architectural project in its surroundings. **3** M20 *Cinematography* A small-scale set used in place of a full-scale one for special effects, animation, etc.

diploma *noun & verb* M17 **Latin** (from Greek = folded paper, from *diploun* to make double, fold, from *diploos* double). **A** *noun* plural **diplomas**, (*rare*) **diplomata**. **1** M17 A government paper, an official document; a charter; in *plural*, historical or literary muniments. **2** M17 A document conferring some honor, privilege, or license; a certificate of a university, college, or school degree or qualification; such a degree or qualification. **B** *transitive verb* M19 Award a diploma to. Chiefly as *diplomaed, diploma'd* participial adjective.

Directoire *noun & adjective* L18 **French** (from Late Latin *directorium* noun use of neuter singular of *directorius* from *director* person who directs). **A** *noun* L18 *History* The French Directory (1795–99). **B** *adjective* L19 Also **directoire**. Of, pertaining to, or resembling an extravagant style of fashion, decorative art, etc., prevalent at the time of the Directory and characterized especially by an imitation of Greek and Roman modes.

■ The adjective is often found in the phrase *directoire knickers* (women's knee-length underwear with elastic at the knee and waist).

dirigisme *noun* (also **dirigism**) M20 **French** (from *diriger* from Latin *dirigere* to direct). The policy of governmental direction and control in economic and social matters.

dirigiste *adjective & noun* M20 **French** (as preceding). (A proponent) of DIRIGISME.

dirndl *noun* M20 **German** (dialect, diminutive of *Dirne* girl). **1** M20 A dress in the style of Alpine peasant costume with a bodice and full skirt. **2** M20 A full skirt with a tight waistband. More fully *dirndl skirt*.

dis aliter visum *interjection* M20 **Latin.** The gods decided otherwise.

■ Quoted from Virgil *Aeneid* ii.428.

discobolus *noun* plural **discoboli** E18 **Latin** (from Greek *diskobolos*, from as *discus* + *-bolos* throwing, from *ballein* to throw). *Classical History* A discus thrower; a statue representing one in action.

discothèque *noun* (also **discotheque**) M20 **French** (originally = record library (after *bibliothèque*)). A place or event at which recorded pop music is played for dancing.

■ Now almost universally abbreviated to *disco*.

discus *noun* M17 **Latin** (from Greek *diskos*). **1** M17 A heavy thick-centered disk or plate thrown in ancient and modern athletic sports; the sporting event in which it is thrown. **2** L17–E18 Any disk or disk-shaped body.

diseuse *noun* L19 **French** (= talker, feminine of *diseur*, from *dire* to say). A female performer who specializes in monologue.

dishabille variant of DÉSHABILLÉ.

disinvoltura *noun* M19 **Italian** (from *disinvolto* unembarrassed, from *disinvolgere* to unwind). Self-assurance; lack of constraint.

disjecta membra *noun phrase plural* (also **disiecta membra**) E18 **Latin.** Scattered remains.

■ Alteration of Latin *disjecti membra poetae* 'limbs of a dismembered poet' (Horace *Satires* I.iv.62). The word order *membra disjecta* is apparently a later (M20) variant.

dissensus *noun* M20 **Latin** (= disagreement; or from *dis-* + *(con)sensus*). Widespread dissent; the reverse of consensus.

distingué *adjective* (feminine **distinguée**) E19 **French.** Having an air of distinction; having a distinguished appearance or manner.

distinguo *noun* plural **distinguos** L19 **Latin** (= I distinguish). A distinction in thought or reasoning.

distrait *adjective* (feminine **distraite**) LME **French** (from Old French *destrait* past participle of *destraire* from Latin *distrahere* to distract). **1** Only in LME. Distracted in mind. **2** LME–L16 Divided, separated. **3** M18 Absent-minded; not paying attention.

■ Sense 3 represents a reborrowing from French after *distrait* had become obsolete in English in its two earlier senses.

dithyramb *noun* (also in Latin form **dithyrambus**, plural **dithyrambi**) E17 **Latin** (*dithyrambus* from Greek *dithurambos*). **1** E17 An ancient Greek choric hymn, vehement and wild in character; a Bacchanalian song. **2** M17 A passionate or inflated poem, speech, or writing.

ditto *adjective, adverb, & noun* plural of noun **dittos** E17 **Italian** (dialect (Tuscan) variant of *detto* said, from Latin *dictus* past participle of *dicere* to say). **1** In or of the month already named; the aforesaid month. Only in 17. **2** L17 In the same way, similar(ly); the same; (the) aforesaid; (the same as, another of) what was mentioned above or previously. *colloquial* except in lists, etc. (where usually represented by dots or commas under the matter repeated). **b** *noun* L19 A symbol representing the word 'ditto'. Also *ditto mark*. **3** *noun* M18 Cloth of the same material. Chiefly in *suit of dittos*, a suit of clothes of the same material and color throughout. *archaic*. **4** *noun* L18 Something identical or similar; an exact resemblance; a repetition. **5** E20 (also **Ditto**) (Proprietary name for) a duplicator, a small offset press for copying.

diva *noun* L19 **Italian** (from Latin *diva* goddess). A distinguished female (especially operatic) singer; a prima donna.

divan *noun* L16 **French** (or Italian *divano*, from Turkish *dīvān* from Persian *dīvān* brochure, anthology, register, court, bench; cf. DOUANE). **1** L16 An oriental council of state; *specifically* (*historical*) the privy council of the Ottoman Empire. **b** E17 Any council. *archaic*. **2** L16 The hall where the Ottoman divan was held; an oriental court of justice or council chamber. **3** L17 In oriental countries: a room entirely open at one side toward a court, garden, river, etc. **4** E18 (Now the usual sense.) A couch or bed without a head- or footboard. Originally, a low bench or a raised part of a floor forming a long seat against the wall of a room. **5** E19 (A smoking room attached to) a cigar store. *archaic*. **6** E19 An anthology of poems in Persian or other oriental language; *specifically* a series of poems by one author, with rhymes usually running through the alphabet.

divertimento *noun* plural **divertimenti, divertimentos** M18 **Italian** (= diversion). **1** M18 An amusement. Long *rare*. **2** E19 *Music* A composition primarily for entertainment, *especially* a suite for a small group of instruments or a single instrument; a light orchestral piece.

divertissement *noun* E18 **French** (from *divertiss-* stem of *divertir* to divert). **1** A short ballet or other entertainment between acts or longer pieces. **b** L19 A DIVERTIMENTO sense 2. **2** E19 An entertainment.

divisi *adverb, adjective, & noun* M18 **Italian** (= divided, plural past participial adjective of *dividere* to divide). *Music* **A** *adverb & adjective* M18 (A direction:) with a section of players divided into two or more groups each playing a different part. **B** *noun* M20 (The use of) *divisi* playing or scoring.

divorcee *noun* (also (earlier) **divorcé**, feminine **divorcée**) E19 **French** (partly from *divorcé(e)* noun use of past participial adjective of *divorcer* to divorce, partly from *divorce* + *-ee* after the French). A divorced person.

dix-huitième *adjective & noun* E20 **French** (= eighteenth). (Of or pertaining to) the eighteenth century.

dixit *noun* L16 **Latin** (= he has said). An utterance or statement (quoted as) already made.

djellaba(h) variant of JELLABA.

djibba(h) variant of *jibba*; see JUBBA.

djinn see JINNEE.

Dobos Torte *noun phrase* (also **Dobos Torta, dobos torte**) plural **Dobos Torten** E20 **German** (*Dobostorte*, from J. C. *Dobós* (1847–1924), Hungarian pastry cook + *Torte* tart, pastry, cake; cf. Hungarian *dobostorta*). A rich cake made of alternate layers of sponge cake and chocolate or mocha cream, with a crisp caramel topping.

docent *noun* L19 **German** (*Docent, Dozent*, from Latin *docent-* present participial stem of *docere* to teach). **1** L19 Originally, a *Privatdozent* (formerly in German universities, a teacher paid by the students taught). Now, in certain universities and colleges, a member of the teaching faculty below professorial rank. **2** E20 A (usually voluntary) guide in a museum, art gallery, or zoo.

doch an doris variant of DEOCH AN DORIS.

doctorand *noun* (also in Latin form **doctorandus**, plural **doctorandi**) E20 **German** (from medieval Latin *doctorandus*). A candidate for a doctor's degree.

doctrinaire *noun & adjective* E19 **French** (from *doctrine* + *-aire*). **A** *noun* **1** E19 *History* In early nineteenth-century France, a member of a political movement that supported constitutional government and the reconciliation of the principles of authority and liberty. **2** M19 A person who tries to apply principle without allowance for circumstance; a pedantic theorist. **B** *adjective* M19 Pertaining to or of the character of a doctrinaire; determined to apply or promote a doctrine in all circumstances; theoretical and unpractical.

doek *noun* L18 **Afrikaans** (= cloth). In South Africa: a cloth, *especially* a headscarf.

dogana *noun* M17 **Italian**. In Italy (and Spain): a custom house; the customs.

dogaressa *noun* E19 **Italian** (irregular feminine of DOGE). *History* The wife of a doge.

doge *noun* M16 **French** ((monosyllabic) from Italian (disyllabic) from Venetian Italian *doze* ultimately from Latin *dux, duc-* leader). *History* The chief magistrate in the former republics of Venice and Genoa.

dogma *noun* plural **dogmas, dogmata** M16 **Late Latin** (from Greek *dogma, dogmat-* opinion, decree, from *dokein* to seem good, think). **1** M16 An opinion, a belief; *specifically* a tenet or doctrine authoritatively laid down, especially by a church or sect; an arrogant declaration of opinion. **2** L18 A whole body of doctrines or opinions, especially on religious matters, laid down authoritatively or assertively.

dojo *noun* plural **dojos** M20 **Japanese** (from *dō* way, pursuit + *-jō* a place). A room or hall in which judo or other martial arts are practiced; an area of padded mats for the same purpose.

dolce far niente *noun phrase* E19 **Italian** (= sweet doing nothing). Delightful idleness.

■ Also in the shortened form FAR NIENTE.

dolce vita *noun phrase* M20 **Italian** (= sweet life). A life of luxury, pleasure, and self-indulgence.

■ Frequently preceded by *the* or *la*.

doli capax *adjective phrase* L17 **Latin** (from *doli* genitive singular of *dolus* guile, fraud + *capax* capable). *Law* Capable of having the wrongful intention to commit a crime.

doli incapax *adjective phrase* L17 **Latin** (from as DOLI CAPAX). *Law* Not *doli capax*, especially because under fourteen years old.

dolman *noun* (in sense 1 also written (earlier) **doliman**) L16 **French** (in sense 1 from French *doliman*; in sense 2 from French *dolman* from German from Hungarian *dolmány*; both ultimately from Turkish *dolama(n)*). **1** L16 A long Turkish robe open in front and with narrow sleeves. **2** L19 A hussar's jacket worn with the sleeves hanging loose. **3** L19 A woman's mantle with dolman sleeves. **4** M20 A loose sleeve made in one piece with the body of a coat, etc. In full *dolman sleeve*.

dolmas *noun* plural **dolmades** (also **dolma**, plural **dolmas**) L17 **Modern Greek** (*ntolmas* from Turkish *dolma*, from *dolmak* to fill, be filled). In the cooking of Greece, Turkey, and other East European countries: a dish of seasoned chopped meat and rice enclosed in a vine leaf, cabbage, pepper, etc.

dolmen *noun* M19 **French** (perhaps from Cornish *tolmen* hole stone). A megalithic structure found especially in Britain and France, consisting of a large flat stone supported on stone slabs set vertically in the ground forming a burial chamber, probably originally covered by an earth mound.

dolmus *noun* M20 **Turkish** (*dolmuş* filled, (as noun) dolmus). In Turkey: a shared taxi.

dolus *noun* E17 **Latin**. *Law* Deceit; intentional damage. Cf. DOLI CAPAX.

dom *noun* M19 **German** (from Latin *domus* house). In Germany, Austria, and other German-speaking areas: a cathedral church.

domaine *noun* M20 **French**. A vineyard.

■ Often in the phrase *domaine-bottled*, indicating that the wine has been bottled at the estate where the grapes of which it is made were grown.

domine *noun* (also (especially as a title) **Domine**) M16 **Latin** (vocative of *dominus* lord, master; cf. DOMINEE, DOMINIE). **1** M16–L17 Lord, master; sir: used in respectful address to a clergyman or a member of one of the professions. **2** E17 DOMINIE sense 1. Now *rare* or *obsolete*. **3** M17 A member of the clergy, a pastor; *especially* a pastor of the Dutch Reformed church. (Cf. DOMINEE, DOMINIE 2). *archaic*.

dominee *noun* (also (especially as a title) **Dominee**) M20 **Afrikaans and Dutch** (from Latin DOMINE). In South Africa: a pastor of the Dutch Reformed church.

dominie *noun* L17 **Latin** (alternative form of DOMINE). **1** L17 A schoolmaster. Now chiefly *Scottish*. **2** L17 A pastor of the Dutch Reformed church; *(dialect)* any minister. **3** E19 A variety of large apple. More fully *dominie apple*.

dominium *noun* M18 **Latin**. *Law* Lordship, ownership, dominion.

■ Chiefly in the phrases *dominium directum* 'direct ownership' and *dominium utile* 'ownership of use', differentiating the rights of the owner and those of the tenant who has only the use of something.

domino *noun & interjection* L17 **French** (= hood worn by priests in winter (also in Spanish, = a masquerade garment), probably ultimately from Latin *dominus* lord, master, but unexplained). **A** *noun* plural **domino(e)s**. **1** L17 A garment worn to cover the head and shoulders; *specifically* a loose cloak with a mask for the upper part of the face, worn to conceal the identity at masquerades, etc. **2** M18 A person wearing a domino. **3** L18 Each of a set of small oblong pieces, usually 28 in number and marked with 0 to 6 dots in each half, used in various matching and trick-taking games; in *plural* (treated as *singular*) or *singular*, the game played with such pieces. **4** M19 Paper printed with a design from a woodblock and colored, used as wallpaper, etc. In full *domino paper*. **B** *interjection* M19 Notifying that one has matched up all one's dominoes; *transferred* notifying or registering the end of something.

■ The phrases *domino effect* and *domino theory*, much used in the mid–twentieth century, allude to what happens when a row of dominoes (sense 3) is stood on end and the first one pushed over, resulting in the speedy collapse of the remainder; in political terms this is what Western governments feared would happen, particularly in Southeast Asia but also in Africa, if one country became Communist-controlled.

don *noun* E16 **Spanish** ((in sense 1c Italian) from Latin *dominus* lord, master). **1** E16 (**Don**) Used as a title of respect preceding the forename of a Spanish man (originally one of high rank) or (formerly, *jocular*) preceding the name or designation of any man. **b** E17 A Spanish lord or gentleman. **c** M20 A high-ranking or powerful member of the Mafia. *slang*. **2** L16 A distinguished or skilled man; a man who is outstanding in some way. *archaic*. **3** M17 At British universities, especially Oxford and Cambridge: a head, fellow, or tutor of a college; a member of the teaching faculty.

donatio mortis causa *noun phrase* plural **donationes mortis causa** M17 **Latin** (= gift by reason of death). *Law* A (revocable) gift of personal property made in expectation of the donor's imminent death and taking effect thereafter.

doner kebab *noun phrase* M20 **Turkish** (*döner kebap*, from *döner* rotating + *kebap* KEBAB). A Turkish dish consisting of spiced lamb roasted on a vertical rotating spit and sliced thinly.

donga *noun* L19 **Nguni**. **1** L19 A ravine or watercourse with steep sides. *South Africa*. **2** E20 A broad shallow depression in the ground. *Australia*. **3** E20 A makeshift shelter; a temporary dwelling. *Australia*.

donnée *noun* (also **donné**) L19 **French** (feminine past participial adjective of *donner* to give). **1** L19 A subject, theme, or motif of a literary work. **2** L19 A datum, a given fact; a basic assumption.

dop *noun* L19 **Afrikaans** (of uncertain origin). **1** L19 In South Africa: brandy, especially of a cheap or inferior kind. In full *dop brandy*. **2** M20 A dram of liquor, especially of wine as given to farm laborers in the Cape Province of South Africa.

doppelgänger *noun* (also **doppelganger**) M19 **German** (literally, 'double-goer'). A supposed spectral likeness or double of a living person.

doppione *noun* plural **doppioni** M20 **Italian** (from *doppio* double). *Early Music* A double-bore woodwind instrument of the Italian Renaissance.

dormeuse *noun* M18 **French** (feminine of *dormeur*, literally, 'sleeper', from *dormir* to sleep). **1** A cap or hood worn in bed. Only in M18. **2** E19 A traveling carriage adapted for sleeping in; *obsolete* except *historical*. **3** M19 A kind of couch or settee.

dos-à-dos *adverb, noun, & adjective* (also **do-se-do, do-si-do**) M19 **French** (from *dos* back). **A** *adverb* M19 Back to back. **B** *noun* plural same. M19 A seat, carriage, etc., so constructed that the occupants sit back to back. *archaic*. **C** *adjective* M20 Designating binding or books in which two volumes are bound together facing in opposite directions and sharing a central board.

dot *noun* M19 **Old and Modern French** (from Latin *dos, dot-*). A dowry, particularly one from which only the interest or annual income was available to the husband.

dotaku *noun plural* (also **dōtaku**) E20 **Japanese.** Prehistoric Japanese bronze objects, shaped like bells and usually decorated with geometric or figurative designs.

douane *noun* M17 **French** (from Italian *do(g)ana* from Arabic *dīwān* office, from Old Persian *dīwān* DIVAN). A customhouse in France or other Mediterranean country.

douanier *noun* M18 **French** (from as preceding). A customs officer, *especially* one at a douane.

doublé *adjective* M19 **French** (past participle of *doubler* to line). Covered or lined *with*; (of a book) having a doublure; plated *with* precious metal.

double entendre *noun phrase* plural **double entendres** L17 **French** (now obsolete (modern *double entente*) = double understanding). A double meaning; an ambiguous expression; a phrase with two meanings, one usually indecent. Also, the use of such a meaning or phrase.

double entente *noun phrase* plural **doubles ententes** L19 **French.** A DOUBLE ENTENDRE.

doublure *noun* L19 **French** (= lining, from *doubler* to line). An ornamental lining, usually of leather, on the inside of a book cover.

douçaine *noun* M20 **French** (from *douce* sweet). *Early Music* A soft-toned reed instrument.

douce *adjective* ME **Old French** (*dous* (modern *doux*), feminine *douce* from Latin *dulcis* sweet). **1** ME Pleasant, sweet. (Formerly a stock epithet of France.) Now *Scottish* and *northern English (dialect)*. **2** E18 Quiet, sober, sedate. *Scottish* and *northern English (dialect)*.

douceur *noun* LME **French** (from Proto-Romance variant of Latin *dulcor* sweetness). **1** LME Originally, sweetness of manner, amiability, (of a person). Now, agreeableness, charm (chiefly in DOUCEUR DE VIVRE). **2** L17–E19 A complimentary speech or turn of phrase. **3** M18 A conciliatory present; a gratuity, a bribe. **4** L20 A tax benefit available to a person who sells a work of art by private treaty to a public collection rather than on the open market.

douceur de vivre *noun phrase* (also **douceur de (la) vie**) M20 **French** (literally, 'sweetness of living'). The pleasure or amenities of life.

douche *noun & verb* M18 **French** (from Italian *doccia* conduit pipe, from *docciare* to pour by drops, from Proto-Romance from Latin *ductus* duct). **A** *noun* M18 (The application of) a jet of (especially cold) liquid or air to a part of the body, as a form of bathing or for medicinal purposes; *specifically* the flushing of the vagina, as a contraceptive measure. Also, a syringe or similar device for producing such a jet. **B** *verb* **1** *transitive verb* M19 Administer a douche to. **2** *intransitive verb* M19 Take a douche; *specifically* take a vaginal douche, especially as a contraceptive measure.

dow variant of DHOW.

doyen *noun* L17 **French** (Old French *d(e)ien* from Late Latin *decanus* chief of a group of ten, from Latin *decem* ten, after *primanus* member of the first legion). The most senior or most prominent of a particular category or body of people.

■ Found as a rare borrowing from Old French in the Late Middle English period, with the sense of 'a leader or commander of ten', the word became obsolete after this period and was then reintroduced from Modern French in its modern sense. The English word *dean* (from Anglo-Norman *de(e)n*) is closely related.

doyenne *noun* M19 **French** (feminine of DOYEN). The most senior or prominent woman in a particular group or category of people, a female doyen.

dragée *noun* L17 **French** (Old French *dragie*, from medieval Latin *drageia*, *dragetum*, perhaps from Latin *tragemata* sweetmeats, from Greek). A candy consisting of a center covered with some coating, *especially* a sugared almond, etc., or a chocolate; a small silver-coated sugar ball for use in cake decoration; a candy used as a vehicle for a medicine or drug.

drageoir *noun* M19 **French** (from as preceding). A box for holding candies.

dramatis personae *noun plural* (frequently treated as *singular*) M18 **Latin** (= persons of the drama). The (list of) characters in a play; *figurative* the participants in an event, etc.

dramaturge *noun* (also **dramaturg**) M19 **French** (*dramaturge*, German *Dramaturg*, from Greek *dramatourgos*, from *dramat-* drama + *-ergos* worker). A dramatist; *specifically* a reader and literary editor, etc., to a permanent theatrical company.

Drang *noun* M19 **German**. Strong tendency, pressure; urge, strong desire.

■ Chiefly in phrases DRANG NACH OSTEN, STURM UND DRANG.

Drang nach Osten *noun phrase* E20 **German** (literally, 'drive toward the east'). *History* The German imperialist policy of eastward expansion; *transferred* any political or economic drive eastward.

dreidel *noun* (also **dreidl**) M20 **Yiddish** (*dreydl*, from Middle High German *dræ(je)n* (German *drehen*) to turn). A four-sided spinning top with a Hebrew letter on each side; a game played with this, especially at Hanukkah.

dressage *noun* M20 **French** (literally, 'training', from *dresser* to train, drill). The training of a horse in obedience and deportment; the execution by a horse of precise movements in response to its rider.

droit *noun* LME **Old and Modern French** (from Proto-Romance noun use of variant of Latin *directum* neuter of *directus* past participle of *dirigere* to direct, guide). **1** LME A right; a legal claim; something to which one has a legal claim; a due. **2** L15–M16 Law, right, justice; a law.

droit de seigneur *noun phrase* (also **droit du seigneur**) E19 **French** (literally, 'lord's right'). An alleged custom whereby a medieval feudal lord might have sexual intercourse with a vassal's bride on the latter's wedding night.

dromos *noun* plural **dromoi** M19 **Greek**. *Greek Antiquities* An avenue or entrance passage to an ancient temple, tomb, etc., often between rows of columns or statues.

droshky *noun* (also **drosky**) E19 **Russian** (*drozhki* plural, diminutive of *drogi* wagon, hearse, plural of *droga* center pole of a carriage). A low open horse-drawn carriage used especially in Russia; any horse-drawn passenger vehicle.

druzhina *noun* plural **druzhinas**, **druzhiny** L19 **Russian** (from *drug* friend + group suffix *-ina*). *History* **1** L19 The retinue or bodyguards of a Russian prince. **2** M20 In the former USSR: a military or police unit; *specifically* a detachment of volunteers assuming police powers.

duce *noun* (also **Duce**) E20 **Italian**. A leader.

■ *Il* (Italian = the) *Duce* was the title assumed by Benito Mussolini (1883–1945), creator and leader of the Fascist regime in Italy; hence *duce* in English usage generally has derogatory overtones.

duchesse *noun* (also **Duchesse**) L18 **French** (from medieval Latin *ducissa* feminine from Latin *dux* leader). **1** L18 A chaise longue consisting of two facing armchairs connected by a detachable footstool. **2** M19 A dressing table with a pivoting mirror. More fully *duchesse dressing chest*, *(dressing) table*. **3** L19 More fully *duchesse satin*, *satin duchesse*. A soft heavy kind of satin.

■ Also in several English phrases: e.g., *duchesse lace* (a kind of fine Brussels lace worked in large sprays); *duchesse potatoes* (mashed potatoes mixed with egg, molded into small cakes and baked or fried); *duchesse set* (lace mats for a dressing table); *duchesse sleeve* (a two-thirds-length sleeve with an elaborate trim).

duende *noun* E20 **Spanish.** **1** E20 A ghost, an evil spirit. **2** M20 Inspiration, magic.

duenna *noun* M17 **Spanish** (*dueña, duenna* from Latin *domina* lady, mistress). **1** M17 An older woman acting as governess and companion to one or more girls, especially within a Spanish family. **2** E18 A chaperon.

duettino *noun* plural **duettinos** M19 **Italian** (diminutive of next). A short duet.

duetto *noun* plural **duettos** E18 **Italian** (from Latin *duo* = two). *Music* A duet.

dulciana *noun* L18 **Medieval Latin** (from Latin *dulcis* sweet). *Music* A small-scaled, soft, open metal diapason usually of 8-ft. length and pitch.

dulia *noun* LME **Medieval Latin** (from Greek *douleia* servitude, from *doulos* slave). *Roman Catholic Church* The veneration properly given to saints and angels.

■ Cf. HYPERDULIA and LATRIA. Similar distinctions in degrees of veneration obtain in the Orthodox churches, *dulia* being the honor paid to icons as representative of the saints.

duma *noun* L19 **Russian.** *History* A Russian elective municipal council; *specifically* the elective legislative council of state of 1905–17; the Russian parliament.

dum casta *noun & adjective phrase* L19 **Latin** (abbreviation of *dum sola et casta vixerit* as long as she shall live alone and chaste). *Law* (Designating) a clause conferring on a woman a benefit that is to cease should she (re)marry or cease to lead a chaste life.

dummkopf *noun* (also **domcop**) E19 **German** (from *dumm* stupid + *Kopf* head; obsolete variant *domcop* from Dutch). A stupid person, a blockhead. *slang.*

duo *noun* plural **duos** L16 **Italian** ((whence also French) from Latin = two). **1** L16 *Music* A duet. **2** L19 Two people; a couple; *especially* a pair of entertainers.

duodecimo *noun & adjective* M17 **Latin** ((*in*) *duodecimo* in a twelfth (sc. of a sheet), from Latin *duodecimus* twelfth). **A** *noun* plural **duodecimos** M17 A size of book or paper in which each leaf is one-twelfth of a standard printing sheet. (Abbreviation *12mo.*) **B** L18 *attributive* or as *adjective* pertaining to a book of this size, in duodecimo; *figurative* diminutive.

duodenum *noun* LME **Medieval Latin** (*duodenum* (so called from its length = twelve fingers' breadth), from Latin *duodeni* distributive of *duodecim* twelve). *Anatomy* The first portion of the small intestine immediately beyond the stomach.

duomo *noun* (also (earlier) **domo**) plural **duomos, duomi** M16 **Italian.** An Italian cathedral.

durbar *noun* E17 **Urdu** (from Persian *darbār* court). **1** E17 A public levee held by an Indian ruler or by a British ruler in India. Also, the court of an Indian ruler. **2** E17 A hall or place of audience where durbars were held.

durchkomponiert *adjective* L19 **German** (from *durch* through + *komponiert* composed). *Music* (Of composition) having a formal design that does not rely on repeated sections; *especially* (of song) having different music for each stanza; through-composed.

du reste *adverb phrase* E19 **French** (literally, 'of the rest'). Besides, moreover.

durgah *noun* L18 **Persian** (*dargāh* royal court). In the Indian subcontinent: the tomb and shrine of a Muslim holy man.

du tout *adverb phrase* E19 **French** (abbreviation of PAS DU TOUT). Not at all; by no means.

duumvir *noun* plural **duumvirs**, in Latin form **duumviri** E17 **Latin** (singular from *duum virum* genitive plural of *duo viri* two men). In *Roman History*, either of a pair of coequal magistrates or officials; *generally* either of two people with joint authority, a coalition of two people.

duvet *noun* M18 **French** (= down) A thick soft quilt used instead of other bedclothes. Also called *continental quilt*, PLUMEAU.

dux *noun* plural **duces**, **duxes** M18 **Latin** (= leader). **1** M18 *Music* The subject of a fugue or canon; the leading voice or instrument in a fugue or canon. Opposed to COMES. **2** L18 The top pupil in a class or school. Chiefly in *Scotland, New Zealand*, and *South Africa*.

duxelles *noun* L19 **French** (Marquis *d'Uxelles*, seventeenth-century French nobleman). *Cooking* A mixture of finely chopped shallots, parsley, onions, and mushrooms, *especially* used to flavor a sauce.

d.v. abbreviation of DEO VOLENTE.

dybbuk *noun* (also **dibbuk**) plural **dybbukim**, **dybbuks** E20 **Yiddish** (*dibek* from Hebrew *dibbūq*, from *dābaq* to cling, cleave). In Jewish folklore, a malevolent wandering spirit that enters and possesses the body of a living person until exorcized.

dyspepsia *noun* E18 **Latin** (from Greek *duspepsia*, from *duspeptos* difficult of digestion, from *dus-* + *peptos* cooked, digested). Indigestion; abdominal pain or discomfort associated with taking food.

dysphoria *noun* M19 **Greek** (*dusphoria* malaise, discomfort, from *dusphoros* hard to bear, from *dus-* + *pherein* to bear). A state of unease or discomfort; *especially* an unpleasant state of mind marked by malaise, depression, or anxiety. Opposed to EUPHORIA.

dyspnoea *noun* (also **dyspnea**) M17 **Latin** (from Greek *duspnoia*, from *dus-* + *pnoē* breathing). *Medicine* Difficulty in breathing or shortness of breath, as a symptom of disease.

dystopia see UTOPIA.

eau *noun* plural **eaux** E19 **French**. Water.

■ Occurs in English only in various phrases, mainly the names of liquids used in medicine or perfumery (see following, also JET D'EAU, SALLE D'EAU).

eau-de-Cologne *noun* (also **eau de Cologne**) E19 **French**. A lightly scented perfume made mainly from alcohol and essential oils, originally produced at Cologne, Germany.

eau de Javel *noun phrase* (also **eau de Javelle**) E19 **French**. A solution of sodium or potassium hypochlorite, used as a bleach or disinfectant.

■ Also called *Javelle water*. Javel was a village just outside Paris, now a suburb, where this solution was first used.

eau-de-Nil *noun phrase* L19 **French** (literally, 'water of (the) Nile'). A pale greenish color (purportedly resembling the waters of the River Nile).

eau de toilette *noun phrase* E20 **French** (= toilet water). A dilute form of perfume.

eau-de-vie *noun phrase* (also **eau de vie**) M18 **French** (literally, 'water of life'). Brandy.

eau sucrée *noun phrase* E19 **French** (literally, 'sugared water'). Water with sugar dissolved in it.

ébauche *noun* E18 **French. 1** E18 A sketch; a rough-hewn sculpture; a first draft. **2** E20 A partly finished watch movement.

ébéniste *noun* E20 **French** (from *ébène* ebony). An ebonist; *specifically* a French cabinetmaker who veneers furniture (originally with ebony).

éboulement *noun* E19 **French** (from *ébouler* to crumble). A crumbling and falling of rock, etc.; a landslide.

écarté *noun* E19 **French** (past participle of *écarter* to discard, from *é-* + *carte* card). **1** E19 A card game for two people in which cards may be exchanged for others and those from the two to the six are excluded. **2** E20 *Ballet* A pose with one arm and one leg extended, the body being at an oblique angle to the audience.

ecce *interjection* LME **Latin.** Lo!; behold.

■ Especially in the following phrases.

Ecce Homo *interjection & noun phrase* E17 **Latin. A** *interjection* Behold the Man! **B** *noun phrase Art* A portrayal of Jesus wearing the crown of thorns.

■ The source is the Latin text of the account of the presentation of Jesus to the crowd after his trial by Pontius Pilate: "Then came Jesus forth, wearing the crown of thorns, and the purple robe. And Pilate saith unto them, Behold the man!" (John 19:5).

ecce signum *interjection* L16 **Latin.** Behold the sign!

echelon *noun* (also **echellon**) L18 **French** (*échelon*, from *échelle* ladder, from Latin *scala*). **1** L18 An arrangement of troops or equipment in parallel lines such that the end of each line is stepped somewhat sideways from that in front; *generally* a formation of people or things arranged, individually or in groups, in a similar stepwise fashion. Also *echelon arrangement*, *echelon formation*, etc. Cf. EN ÉCHELON. **2** E19 Each of the divisions of an echelon formation. **b** E19 Each of the subdivisions of the main supply service for troops in warfare. **3** M20 (A group of people occupying) a particular level in any organization.

echinus *noun* plural **echini** LME **Latin** (sense 1 from Greek *ekhinos* hedgehog, sea urchin; the origin of sense 2 (also in Latin and Greek) is unknown). **1** LME A sea urchin. Now *specifically* a member of the genus *E. chinus*, which includes the common edible sea urchin *E. esculentus*. **2** M16 *Architecture* An ovolo molding next below the abacus of a capital.

echt *adjective & adverb* E20 **German.** Authentic(ally), genuine(ly), typical(ly).

éclair *noun* M19 **French** (literally, 'lightning'). A small finger-shaped cake of choux pastry, filled with cream and iced, especially with chocolate icing.

éclaircissement *noun* M17 **French** (from *éclairciss-* lengthened stem of *éclaircir* to clear up, from as *ex-*, *clair* clear *-ment*). A clarification of what is obscure or misunderstood; an explanation.

éclat *noun* L17 **French** (from *éclater* to burst out). **1** L17 Radiance, dazzling effect (now only *figurative*); brilliant display. **2** L17–L19 Ostentation, publicity; public exposure, scandal; a sensation. **3** M18 Social distinction; celebrity, renown. **4** M18 Conspicuous success; universal acclamation. Chiefly as *with* (*great*, etc.) *éclat*.

écorché *noun* M19 **French** (past participle of *écorcher* to flay). *Art* An anatomical subject treated so as to display the musculature.

écossaise *noun* M19 **French** (feminine of *écossais* Scottish). (A dance to) a lively tune in duple time.

écrevisse *noun* M18 **French.** A crayfish.

ecru *adjective & noun* M19 **French** (*écru* raw, unbleached). (Of) the color of unbleached linen; light fawn.

ecuelle *noun* (also **écuelle**) M19 **French** (*écuelle* ultimately from Latin *scutella* small dish). **1** M19 A two-handled soup bowl. **2** L19 The process or apparatus by which oils are extracted from the peel of citrus fruit.

edema *noun* (also **oedema**) plural **edemata**, **edemas** LME **Late Latin** (from Greek *oidēma*, from *oidein* to swell). *Medicine* (A) local or general swelling produced by the accumulation of fluid in the body tissues or cavities; dropsy.

editio princeps *noun phrase* plural **editiones principes** E19 **Modern Latin** (from Latin *editio* publication + *princeps* first). The first printed edition of a book.

effendi *noun* E17 **Turkish** (*efendi* from Modern Greek *aphentē* vocative of *aphentēs* from Greek *authentēs* lord, master). A man of education or social standing in an eastern Mediterranean or Arab country. Frequently (usually *historical*) as a title of respect or courtesy in Turkey or (former) Turkish territory.

effluvium *noun* plural **effluvia**, **effluviums** M17 **Latin** (from *effluere*, from *ef-* + *fluere* to flow). **1** M17–E18 A flowing out. **2** M17 Chiefly *History*. An outflow or stream of imperceptible particles, especially as supposedly transmitting electrical or magnetic influence, etc. **3** M17 An (especially unpleasant) exhalation affecting the lungs or the sense of smell.

efreet variant of AFREET.

e.g. abbreviation of EXEMPLI GRATIA.

égalité *noun* L18 **French** (= equality, from *égal* from Latin *aequalis* equal). The condition of having equal rank, power, etc., with others.

■ Historically, as part of the rallying cry of the French Revolution: *Liberté, égalité, fraternité* 'Liberty, equality, brotherhood'.

églomisé *adjective & noun* L19 **French** (from *Glomy*, eighteenth-century Parisian picture framer). **A** *adjective* L19 Of glass: decorated on the back with engraved gold or silver leaf or paint. Frequently in VERRE ÉGLOMISÉ. **B** *noun* L19 (A panel of) verre églomisé.

ego *noun* plural **egos** E19 **Latin** (= I (pronoun)). **1** E19 *Metaphysics* Oneself, the conscious thinking subject. **2** L19 *Psychoanalysis* That part of the mind which has a sense of individuality and is most conscious of self. **3** L19 Self-esteem, self-importance.

eheu fugaces *interjection* M19 **Latin** (= alas, the fleeting (years are hurrying by)). An expression of regret for the rapidity with which life passes.

■ The words are from the opening line of one of Horace's *Odes* (II.xiv).

eid *noun* (also **id**) L17 **Arabic** (*'īd* festival, from Aramaic). A Muslim feast day; *specifically* that at the breaking of the fast at the end of Ramadan (cf. ID UL-FITR).

eidolon *noun* plural **eidola**, **eidolons** M17 **Greek** (*eidōlon*). **1** An emanation considered by atomic philosophers to constitute the visible image of an object. *rare*. Only in M17. **2** E19 A specter, a phantom. Also, an idealized image.

Einfühlung *noun* E20 **German** (from *ein-* into + *Fühlung* feeling, from *fühlen* to feel). Empathy.

eisteddfod *noun* plural **eisteddfods**, **eisteddfodau** E19 **Welsh** (= session). A congress of Welsh bards; a gathering for competitions in Welsh poetry, music, etc.

Eiswein *noun* M20 **German** (from *Eis* ice + *Wein* wine). Wine made from ripe grapes picked while covered with frost.

ejecta *noun plural* (treated as *plural* or *singular*) L19 **Latin** (neuter plural of past participle of *e(j)icere* to eject). **1** L19 Matter that is thrown out of a volcano or a star. **2** L19 Material discharged from the body, *especially* vomit.

■ An earlier (M19) synonym for sense 1 was *ejectamenta*.

ejido *noun* plural **ejidos** L19 **Mexican Spanish** (from Spanish = common land (on the road leading out of a village), from Latin *exitus* going out). In

Mexico: a cooperative farm; a piece of land farmed communally.

ek dum *adverb phrase* (also **ek dam**) L19 **Hindustani** (from *ek* one + Urdu *dam* breath). At once, immediately.

élan *noun* M19 **French**. Vivacity, vitality; energy arising from enthusiasm.

élan vital *noun phrase* E20 **French**. An intuitively perceived life force; any mysterious creative principle.

■ The French philosopher Henri Bergson (1859–1941) posited the *élan vital*, as opposed to inert matter, in *L'Evolution créatrice* (1907); as a philosophical concept it has frequently been attacked for its lack of content, but the phrase remains current in English in more general use.

élégante *noun* L18 **French** (feminine of *élégant* elegant). A fashionable woman.

elenchus *noun* plural **elenchi** M17 **Latin** (from Greek *elegkhos* argument of refutation). *Logic* A syllogism in refutation of a syllogistic conclusion; a logical refutation.

elephanta *noun* (also **elephanter**) E18 **Portuguese** (*elephante*, feminine *elephanta* from Proto-Romance variant of Latin *elephantus*, *elepha(n)s* from Greek *elephas*, elephant ivory, elephant). A violent storm at the end (or the beginning) of a monsoon.

elite *noun & adjective* (also **élite**) L18 **French** (noun use of feminine of obsolete past participle of *élire*, *eslire* from Proto-Romance variant of Latin *eligere* to elect). **A** *noun* **1** L18 The choice part, the best, (of society, a group of people, etc.); a select group or class. **2** E20 A size of type used on typewriters, having twelve characters to the inch. **B** *attributive adjective* M19 Of or belonging to an elite; exclusive.

El Niño *noun phrase* (also **el Niño**, **El Nino**) L19 **Spanish** (*El Niño* (*de Navidad*) the (Christmas) child, with reference to beginning in late December). Formerly, an annual warm southward current off northern Peru. Now, an irregularly occurring southward current in the equatorial Pacific Ocean, associated with weather changes and ecological damage; these associated phenomena.

éloge *noun* M16 **French** (from Latin *elogium* short saying or epitaph, altered from Greek *elegeia* elegy; apparently confused with *eulogium* eulogy). **1** M16–E19 A commendation; an encomium. **2** E18 A discourse in honor of a deceased person; *especially* that pronounced on a member of the French Academy by his successor.

Elysium *noun* L16 **Latin** (from Greek *Elusion* (sc. *pedion* plain)). **1** L16 *Classical Mythology* The home of the blessed after death. **2** L16 A place or state of perfect happiness.

email ombrant *noun phrase* (also **émail ombrant**) plural **email ombrants**, **émaux ombrants** L19 **French** (*émail ombrant*, from *émail* enamel + *ombrer* to shade). A form of decoration in which a colored glaze is laid over intagliated earthenware or porcelain to give a monochrome picture.

emakimono *noun* plural same M20 **Japanese** (from *e* painting, picture + *makimono* scroll). A Japanese scroll containing pictures representing a narrative; a pictorial MAKIMONO.

émaux ombrants plural of EMAIL OMBRANT.

embarcadero *noun* plural **embarcaderos** M19 **Spanish** (from *embarcar* to embark). A wharf, a quay.

embargo *noun & verb* (also formerly **imbargo**) E17 **Spanish** (from *embargar* to arrest, impede, from Proto-Romance, from Latin *in-* + *barra* bar). **A** *noun* plural **embargoes**. **1** E17 An order prohibiting ships from entering or leaving a country's ports, usually issued in anticipation of war. **2** M17 An official, usually temporary, prohibition of a particular commercial activity, or of trade in general, with another country. **3** L17 *generally* A prohibition, an impediment. **B** *transitive verb* **1** M17 Seize, confiscate; *specifi-*

cally seize, requisition, or impound (ships, freight, etc.) for the service of the state. **2** M18 Place (ships, trade, etc.) under an embargo.

embarras *noun* M17 **French.** Embarrassment.

■ Now in English only in phrases below.

embarras de choix *noun phrase* L19 **French** (literally, 'embarrassment of choice'). More choices than one knows what to do with.

embarras de richesse *noun phrase* (also **embarrass de richesses**) M18 **French** (literally, 'an embarrassment of riches'). More resources, pleasures, etc., than one knows what to do with.

■ *L'embarras des richesses* (1726) was the title of a work by the Abbé d'Allainval, and the earliest recorded use in English (1751) is in one of Lord Chesterfield's letters. *Richesse* as an independent noun is found earlier (ME–L17) with the meanings 'wealth' or 'richness' and also (L15) 'a group of martens', but it has long been archaic as an independent noun.

embolus *noun* plural **emboli** M17 **Latin** (= piston of a pump, from Greek *embolos* peg, stopper). **1** M17–M18 *Mechanical* Something inserted or moving in another; *especially* the piston of a syringe. **2** M19 *Medicine* The blood clot or other object or substance that causes embolism.

embonpoint *noun & adjective* L17 **French** (phrase *en bon point* in good condition). **A** *noun* L17 Plumpness. **B** *adjective* E19 Plump.

■ In quotation as euphemism for 'cleavage'.

embouchure *noun* M18 **French** (from *s'emboucher* reflexive, to discharge itself by a mouth, from *emboucher* put in or to the mouth, from as *em-* + *bouche* mouth). **1** M18 *Music* The manner in which a player's mouth and lips are placed when playing a woodwind or brass instrument. **b** M19 The mouthpiece of a musical instrument, especially of a flute. **2** L18 The mouth of a river; the opening of a valley onto a plain.

embourgeoisé *adjective* M20 **French** (past participle of *embourgeoiser* to make or become BOURGEOIS). Something that or someone who has been bourgeoisified.

embourgeoisement *noun* M20 **French** (from *embourgeoiser* to make or become BOURGEOIS). Bourgeoisification.

embrasure *noun* E18 **French** (from obsolete *embraser* (modern *ébraser*) to widen (a door or window opening), of unknown origin). **1** *Military* E18 An opening in a parapet that widens toward the exterior, made to fire a gun through. **2** M18 A slanting or beveling of the wall on either side of a door or window opening so as to form a recess; the area contained between such walls. **3** *Dentistry* M20 The angle between adjacent teeth where their two surfaces curve inward toward the line of contact.

embusqué *noun* E20 **French** (past participle of *embusquer* from Old French *embuschier* to ambush). A person who avoids military service by obtaining a job in a government office or the like.

emeritus *adjective* M18 **Latin** (past participle of *emereri* to earn (one's discharge) by service, from *e-* + *mereri* to deserve). Honorably discharged from service; (of a former officeholder, especially a professor) retired but allowed to retain his or her title as an honor.

■ Often postpositive.

émeute *noun* L18 **French** (from Old French *esmote*, from *esmeu* (modern *ému*) past participle of *esmovoir* (modern *émouvoir*), after *meute* crowd, uprising). A popular rising or disturbance.

emigré *noun & adjective* (also **émigré**) L18 **French** (*émigré*, past participle of *émigrer* from Latin *emigrare* to emigrate). **A** *noun* L18 Originally, a French emigrant, *especially* one from the Revolution of 1789–99. Now, any emigrant, *especially* a political exile. **B**

adjective E20 One who is an emigré; composed of emigrés.

emincé *noun* E20 French (noun use of past participle of *émincer* to slice thinly). A dish consisting of thinly sliced meat in sauce.

éminence grise *noun phrase* plural **éminences grises** M20 French (literally, 'gray eminence'). A person who exercises power or influence though holding no official position. Also, a confidential adviser.

■ Originally applied to the Capuchin Père Joseph, confidential agent of the French statesman Cardinal Richelieu (1585–1642).

emir *noun* L16 French (*émir* from Arabic *'amīr*). **1** L16 A male descendant of Muhammad. Now *rare*. **2** M17 A title of certain Muslim rulers; an Arab prince, governor, or commander.

empanada *noun* M20 Spanish (noun use of feminine past participle of *empanar* to bake or roll in pastry, from as *em-* + *pan* bread, from Latin *panis*). *Cooking* A turnover with a filling of meat, cheese, or vegetables.

empiecement *noun* L19 French (*empiècement*, from as *em-* + *piece* piece). A piece of material inserted in a garment for decoration.

emplacement *noun* E19 French (from as *em-* + *place* place). **1** E19 *Military* A defended or protected position where a gun or missile is placed ready for firing. **2** E19 Situation, position; *specifically* that of a building. **3** M19 The action of putting or settling into place.

employé *noun* (feminine **employée**) E19 French (past participial adjective of *employer* to employ). A person who works for an employer.

■ Now naturalized in the later (M19) form *employee*.

emporium *noun* plural **emporiums, emporia** L16 Latin (from Greek *emporion*, from *emporos* merchant, from as *em-* + verbal stem *por-*, *per-* to journey). **1** L16 A center of commerce; a market. **2** M19 A store, *especially* one that sells unusual or ornamental items.

empressé *adjective* (feminine **empressée**) M19 French (past participial adjective of *empresser* to urge, (reflexive) be eager, (in Old French) to press, crowd in). Eager, zealous; showing EMPRESSEMENT.

empressement *noun* E18 French (from *empresser* (see preceding)). Eagerness; effusive friendliness.

enamorata, enamorato variants of INAMORATA, INAMORATO.

en attendant *adverb phrase* M18 French. In the meantime, while waiting.

en avant *adverb & interjection phrase* E19 French. Forward, onward.

en beau *adverb phrase* E19 French. In a favorable manner; in the best light. Cf. EN NOIR.

en bloc *adverb & adjective phrase* M19 French (literally, 'as a block'). **A** *adverb phrase* M19 As a whole; collectively, all together. **B** *adjective phrase* E20 Performed or made *en bloc*.

en brosse *adverb & adjective phrase* E20 French (literally, 'as a brush'). (Of hair) cut short and bristly.

en cabochon *adverb phrase* E19 French. Of a gem: cut as a CABOCHON, with curved surfaces rather than facets.

enceinte *noun* E18 French (from Latin *incincta* feminine past participle of *incingere* to gird in). The main enclosure or enclosing wall of a fortified place.

enceinte *adjective* (also (in legal use) **ensient**) E17 French (from medieval Latin *incincta* ungirded, from Latin *in-* + *cincta* feminine past participle of *cingere* to gird). Of a woman: pregnant.

■ Now archaic or euphemistic.

enchaînement *noun* M19 French (literally = a chaining up, a concatenation). *Ballet* A sequence of steps.

enchilada *noun* M19 American Spanish (feminine of *enchilado* past participle of *enchilar* to season with chili). A usually meat-filled tortilla served with chili sauce.

enchiridion *noun* LME Late Latin (from Greek *egkheiridion*, from as *en-* +

kheir hand + diminutive suffix *-idion*). A handbook, a manual.

encierro *noun* plural **encierros** M19 **Spanish** (literally, 'shutting in', from *en-* (from as *in-*) + *cierre* shutting). The driving of bulls through the streets of a Spanish town from a corral to the bullring.

en clair *adverb & adjective phrase* L19 **French**. (Transmitted, written, etc.) in ordinary language, not in code or cipher; also *figurative*.

enclave *noun* M19 **French** (from Old and Modern French *enclaver* to enclose, from popular Latin *in-* + *clavis* key). **1** M19 A region belonging to a country but surrounded by another country as viewed by the latter. **2** M20 A culturally or socially distinct minority group in a society or place.

encoignure *noun* M19 **French** (from as *en-* + *coin* corner). A piece of usually ornamental furniture made with an angle to fit into a corner.

encomium *noun* plural **encomiums, encomia** L16 **Latin** (from Greek *egkōmion* eulogy, noun use of neuter of adjective (sc. *epos* speech), from as *en-* + *komos* revel). A formal or high-flown expression of praise; a panegyric.

■ Earlier (M16) Anglicized as *encomy*.

encore *interjection, noun & verb* E18 **French**. (= still, again). **A** *interjection* E18 Again! **B** *noun* M18 An audience's demand for an item to be performed again or for a further item after the program finale in a concert, etc. Also an item (to be) performed thus. **C** *transitive verb* M18 Call for a repetition.

■ The origin is uncertain. The Italian equivalent *ancora* 'still' was also formerly used (E18) but neither it nor *encore* occurs in this context in the original languages.

encourager les autres see POUR ENCOURAGER LES AUTRES.

en croûte *adverb & adjective phrase* L20 **French**. (Cooked) in a pastry crust.

en daube *adverb & adjective phrase* L20 **French** (cf. DAUBE). Stewed, braised.

en déshabillé *adjective & adverb phrase* (also Anglicized as **en déshabille, en dishabille**) L17 **French** (from preposition *en* + *déshabillé* dishabille). In a state of undress or of partial dress; casually dressed.

en échelon *adjective & adverb phrase* (also **en echelon**) E19 **French**. (Arranged) in an ECHELON.

en évidence *adverb phrase* E19 **French**. In or at the forefront; conspicuously.

en face *adverb phrase* M18 **French**. **1** M18 With the face to the front, facing forward. Cf. EN REGARD. **2** M20 *Bibliography* On the facing page.

en famille *adverb phrase* E18 **French**. At home, with one's family; as one of the family, informally.

enfant gâté *noun phrase* plural **enfants gâtés** E19 **French** (= spoiled child). A person given undue flattery or indulgence.

enfantillage *noun* E19 **Old and Modern French** (from Old French *enfantil* from Latin *infantilis* of an infant). A childish action or prank.

enfant terrible *noun phrase* plural **enfants terribles** M19 **French** (= terrible child). A person who causes embarrassment by ill-considered, or unorthodox behavior or speech; an unconventional person.

en fête *predicative adjective phrase* M19 **French**. Prepared for or engaged in celebration, especially of a holiday.

enfilade *noun & verb* E18 **French** (from *enfiler* to thread on a string, pierce or traverse from end to end, from as *en-* + *fil* thread). **A** *noun* **1** *Military* **a** The situation of a post such that it commands the whole length of a line. Only in E18. **b** L18 Gunfire directed along a line from end to end (also *enfilade fire*); an act of firing in this way. **2** E18 A suite of rooms with doorways in line with each other; a vista between rows of trees, etc. **B** *transitive verb* E18 *Military* Subject to enfilade; cover the whole length of (a target) with a gun or guns.

engagé *noun & adjective* E19 **French** (past participle of *engager* to engage). **A** *noun* E19 *History* A boatman hired by a fur trader or explorer; an engagee. **B** *adjective* M20 Of writers, artists, etc., or their works: showing social or political commitment.

en garçon *adverb phrase* E19 **French**. As or in the manner of a boy or a bachelor.

engobe *noun* M19 **French**. A mixture of white clay and water applied as a coating to pottery to cover the natural color or to provide a ground for decoration; a slip.

en grande tenue *adverb phrase* M19 **French**. In full dress, *especially* full military dress.

en grand seigneur *adverb phrase* E19 **French**. In the manner of a nobleman.

engrenage *noun* E20 **French** (literally, 'gearing', from *engrener* to feed corn into (a threshing machine), throw into gear). **1** E20 A set of circumstances that trap one; an organization or society regarded as full of snares. **2** M20 The process of preparing for effective joint action.

en gros *adverb phrase* E18 **French**. In general, in broad terms.

en l'air *adverb phrase* E18 **French** (= in the air). **1** E18 *Ballet* While leaping vertically. **2** E19 *Military* While unsupported.

en masse *adverb phrase* L18 **French**. In a mass; all together, as a group.

en noir *adverb phrase* M19 **French**. On the black side; in the worst light. Cf. EN BEAU.

ennui *noun* M18 **French** (from Latin *in odio* in *mihi in odio est* it is hateful to me). Mental weariness and dissatisfaction arising from lack of occupation or interest; boredom.

ennuyant *adjective* L18 **French** (present participle of *ennuyer*; see next). Something that gives rise to ennui; boring, tedious.

ennuyé *adjective* (feminine **ennuyée**) M18 **French** (past participial adjective of *ennuyer* to bore, from ENNUI). Affected with ennui; bored.

enosis *noun* M20 **Modern Greek** (*henōsis*, from *hena* one). Political union, *especially* that proposed between Greece and Cyprus.

en pantoufles *adverb phrase* E20 **French** (literally, 'in slippers'). Relaxed, off guard; in a free and easy manner or atmosphere.

en papillote see PAPILLOTE.

en passant *adverb phrase* E17 **French**. In passing, by the way.

en pension *adverb and adjective phrase* E19 **French**. Living as a boarder, in lodgings.

■ Formerly (L16 onward) Anglicized as *in* or *on pension*; cf. PENSION.

en permanence *adverb phrase* M19 **French**. Permanently.

en place *adverb phrase* E19 **French**. In place, in position.

en plein *adverb phrase* L19 **French** (= in full). *Gambling* Entirely on one number or side; with the whole of one's bet.

en plein air *adverb phrase* L19 **French**. In the open air.

■ Especially with reference to the working methods of the French Impressionist painters, as compared with their academic *confrères* who worked in studios and from posed models; cf. PLEIN AIR.

en poste *adverb phrase* M20 **French**. In an official diplomatic position (at a specified place).

en primeur *adverb & adjective phrase* L20 **French**. (Of vegetables) fresh, new; (of wine) young, especially before bottling. Cf. PRIMEUR.

en prince *adverb phrase* L17 **French**. Like a prince; in a princely or luxurious manner.

en principe *adverb phrase* E20 **French**. In principle.

en prise *adverb phrase* E19 **French**. *Chess* In a position to be taken.

enragé *adjective & noun* (also **enrage**) (feminine **enragée**) E18 **French** (past participle of *enrager* to enrage). **A** *ad-*

jective E18 Furiously angry. **B** *noun* L18 An enraged person; a fanatic.

en rapport *adjective phrase* **E19 French.** In (close and harmonious) relationship *(with)*; in harmony *(with)*. Cf. RAPPORT.

en regard *adverb phrase* **E20 French.** *Bibliography* On the facing page. Cf. EN FACE.

en règle *adverb phrase* **E19 French.** In order, according to form.

en retraite *adverb phrase* **M19 French.** In retirement.

en revanche *adverb phrase* **E19 French.** In return, as compensation; in revenge.

en route *adverb phrase* **L18 French.** On the way.

ens *noun* plural **entia** **M16 Late Latin** (*ens* noun use of present participle formed from *esse* to be, on the supposed analogy of *absens* absent, to translate Greek *on* noun use of present participle of *einai* to be). **1** M16 *Philosophy*, etc. Something that has existence; a being, an entity, as opposed to an attribute or quality. **2** L16–M18 The essence; the essential part.

■ Used in various phrases relating especially to Christian medieval theology and scholastic philosophy; thus *ens necessarium* (a necessarily existent being, i.e., God), *ens rationis* (a being having no existence outside the mind), *ens reale* (a being that exists independently of any finite mind), etc.

ensemble *noun* **M18 Old and Modern French** (from Proto-Romance from Latin *insimul*, from *in-* into, in + *simul* at the same time). **1** M18 (The parts of) a thing viewed as a whole. **2** E19 The unity of performance achieved by a group of artists. **b** E20 A group of stage artists who perform together; *especially* the supporting actors or dancers as opposed to the principals. **c** E20 A scene on stage in which the whole cast appears. **d** M20 A group of singers or musicians, especially soloists, who perform together. **3** E20 A set of (usually women's) clothes that harmonize and are worn together. **4** E20 *Science* A notional collection of systems of identical constitution but not necessarily in the same state.

■ Originally (LME) introduced in the adverbial sense of 'together, at the same time', which it retains in French, but this has long been rare in English. Sense 1 is found slightly earlier in the phrase TOUT ENSEMBLE.

ensient variant of ENCEINTE.

ensilage *noun & verb* **L19 French** (from *ensiler* from Spanish *ensilar*, from *en-* + *silo* silo). **A** *noun* **1** L19 The process of making silage. **2** L19 Silage. **B** *transitive verb* L19 Treat (fodder) by ensilage; turn into silage.

en suite *adverb, adjective, & noun phrase* (also (especially as adjective & noun phrase) **ensuite**) **L18 French. A** *adverb phrase* **1** L18 In agreement or harmony (*with*). Now *rare* or *obsolete*. **2** E19 In a row, with one room leading into another; as part of the same set of rooms. (Followed by *with*.) **b** M20 As part of the same set of objects. (Followed by *with*.) **B** *adjective phrase* M20 Of a room: that is en suite; forming part of the same set, immediately adjoining. **C** *noun phrase* L20 An en suite room, *especially*, an en suite bathroom.

■ The phrase is used frequently in Great Britain to describe accommodations.

entasis *noun* plural **entases** **M17 Modern Latin** (from Greek, from *enteinein* to strain). *Architecture* A slight bowing of the shaft of a column (introduced to correct the visual illusion of concavity).

entente *noun* **M19 French.** A friendly understanding, especially between nations; a group of nations sharing such an understanding.

entente cordiale *noun phrase* plural **ententes cordiales** **M19 French.** An entente, *specifically* (*historical*) that arrived at by France and Britain in 1904.

entia plural of ENS.

entourage *noun* **M19 French** (from *entourer* to surround, from *entour* surroundings, noun use of adverb = 'round about'). A group of people in attendance on or accompanying someone important. Also, surroundings, environment.

en tout cas *noun & adjective phrase* L19 **French** (= in any case or emergency). **A** *noun phrase* L19 A parasol that also serves as an umbrella. **B** *adjective & noun phrase* M20 (*En-Tout-Cas*) (Proprietary name designating) a hard tennis court.

entr'acte *noun* M19 **French** (now obsolete (modern *entracte*), from *entre* between + *acte* act). The intermission between two acts of a play; a performance or entertainment that takes place during an intermission.

entrain *noun* M19 **French**. Enthusiasm, animation.

en train *adverb phrase* L18 **French**. Afoot, underway; in or into the swing of something; occupied (*with*).

en travesti *adverb phrase* M20 **pseudo-French**. *Theater* In the dress of the opposite sex.

■ The phrase is not recorded in French, and represents the misunderstanding as a noun of French *travesti*, the past participle of *travestir* (from Italian *travestire*, from *trans* (a)cross + *vestire* to clothe).

entrechat *noun* L18 **French** (from Italian (*capriola*) *intrecciata* complicated (caper)). *Ballet* A leap in which a dancer strikes the heels together or crosses the feet a number of times while in the air.

entrecôte *noun* M19 **French** (literally = between rib). A boned steak cut off the sirloin. More fully *entrecôte steak*.

entredeux *noun* M19 **French** (literally = between two). An insertion of lace, linen, etc., in sewing.

entrée *noun* E18 **French**. **1** E18 *Music* **a** A piece of instrumental music, usually resembling a march, forming the first part of a suite or divertissement, or introducing a character, etc., on stage. **b** L18 A group of dances on one theme in seventeenth- and eighteenth-century French ballet; an act of a seventeenth- or eighteenth-century French opera ballet. **2** M18 The action or manner of entering. **b** E19 The entrance of the performers in a play, circus, or other large show. **3** M18 The privilege or right of entrance; admission, especially to an exclusive social or professional circle. **4** M18 A dish served between the fish course and the main meat course; the main dish of a meal.

entrée en matière *noun phrase* M20 **French** (literally, 'entry into the matter'). An opening remark or statement; the beginning of a literary work.

entremet *noun* plural **entremets** L15 **French** (*entremets*). **1** L15 In *plural*. Side dishes. **2** M18 *singular* and in *plural* (treated as *singular* or *plural*). A sweet dish; a dessert; *rare* a side dish.

entre nous *adverb phrase* L17 **French**. Between ourselves; in private.

entrepôt *noun* E18 **French** ((earlier *entrepost*, *entrepos*), from *entreposer* to store, from *entre* among + *poser* to place). **1** E18 A storehouse for the temporary deposit of freight, provisions, etc.; *rare* temporary deposit. **2** M18 A commercial center to which freight is brought for import and export, and for collection and distribution.

entrepreneur *noun* E19 **French** (from *entreprendre* to undertake). **1 a** E19 A director of a musical institution. **b** M19 A person who organizes entertainments, especially musical performances. **2** M19 A person who undertakes or controls a business or enterprise and bears the risk of profit or loss; a contractor who acts as an intermediary.

entresol *noun* (also **entersole**, **intersole**) E18 **French** (from Spanish *entresuelo*, from *entre* between + *suelo* story). A low story between the first floor and the second floor of a building; a mezzanine story.

Entscheidungsproblem *noun* M20 **German** (= decision problem). *Math-*

ematics and *Logic* The problem of finding a way to decide whether a formula or class of formulas is true or provable within a given system of axioms.

en ventre sa mère *adverb phrase* (also **en ventre sa mere**) L18 **French** (= in its mother's womb). *Law* In the uterus.

environs *noun plural* M17 **French** (plural of *environ* surrounding(s)). The district surrounding a place, especially an urban area. (Followed by *of*.)

envoy *noun* (also **envoi**) LME **Old and Modern French** (from *envoyer* to send, from phrase *en voie* on the way). The concluding part of a literary work, *especially* a short stanza concluding a ballade; *archaic* an author's concluding words, dedication, etc.; *generally* a conclusion.

eo ipso *adverb phrase* L17 **Latin** (ablative of *idipsum* the thing itself). By that very act (or quality); through that alone; thereby. Cf. IPSO FACTO.

eo nomine *adverb phrase* E17 **Latin** (ablative of *id nomen* that name). Under that name; that is so called; explicitly.

épatant *adjective* E20 **French** (present participial adjective of *épater* to flabbergast). Shocking (to conventional persons); daring.

épater *transitive verb* E20 **French** (= flabbergast). Startle, shock.

▪ Only used in the infinitive, especially in phrase below or English phrases based upon it.

épater les bourgeois *adverb phrase* (also **épater le bourgeois**) E20 **French** (= to amaze the bourgeois). To shock the narrow-minded or conventional.

▪ "Je les ai épatés, les bourgeois" is attributed to Alexandre Private d'Anglemont (d. 1859).

épaulement *noun* M19 **French** (see next). *Ballet* A stance in which one shoulder is turned forward and the other drawn back, with the head facing over the forward shoulder; correct positioning of the shoulders.

epaulette *noun* (also **epaulet**) L18 **French** (*épaulette* diminutive of *épaule* shoulder, from Latin *spatula*, (in Late Latin) shoulder blade). **1** L18 An ornamental shoulder piece worn on a military or other uniform, usually as a sign of rank. **b** E19 A military officer; a commission. **2** E19 A small shoulder plate on a suit of armor. **3** M19 A loop or tab on the shoulder of a coat; a piece of trimming on the shoulder of a dress, etc.

épée *noun* L19 **French** (= sword, from Old French *espee*). A sharp-pointed dueling sword used (blunted) for fencing; the art of fencing with this.

ephemera *noun* plural **ephemeras, ephemera** L17 **Medieval Latin** (from noun use of feminine of late Latin *ephemerus* from Greek *ephēmeros* lasting only one day). **1** Originally, a winged insect that lives only one day; an EPHEMERON. Now, a winged insect of the genus *Ephemera*, a mayfly. **2** M18 A person or thing of short-lived usefulness or interest.

ephemeris *noun* plural **ephemerides** E16 **Latin** (from Greek, from *ephēmeros* lasting only a day). A table or book of tables giving information about celestial bodies on a daily or regular basis over a particular period; an astronomical almanac.

ephemeron *noun* plural **ephemerons, ephemera** L16 **Greek** (neuter of *ephēmeros* lasting only one day). **1** L16 A winged insect that lives only one day or spends only one day in its winged form; cf. EPHEMERA 1. **2** L18 A short-lived person, institution, or production. **3** M20 As *ephemera (plural)*. Printed or written items intended for short-term use, as tickets, posters, etc.

épicerie *noun* E20 **French**. In France: a grocery store.

epigramme *noun* M18 **French** (*épigramme*, apparently a fanciful use of *épigramme* = epigram). *Cooking* A small piece of meat, usually lamb, served between the fish course and the main meat course.

epithalamium *noun* (also (earlier) **epithalamion**) plural **epithalamiums, epithalamions, epithalamia** L16 Latin (from Greek *epithalamion* noun use of neuter of *epithalamios* nuptial, from as *epi-* + *thalamos* bridal chamber). A song or poem in celebration of a wedding.

epitome *noun* (also (*non-standard*) **epitomy**) E16 Latin (from Greek *epitomē*, from *epitemnein* to cut into, cut short, from as *epi-* + *temnein* to cut). **1** E16 A summary or abstract of a written work; a condensed account. **2** E16 A thing that represents another in miniature; a person who or thing that embodies a quality, etc.; a typical example.

epode *noun* E17 French (*épode* or Latin *epodos* from Greek *epōidos*, from as *epi-* + *ōidē* ode). **1** E17 A Greek lyric poem composed of couplets in which a long line is followed by a shorter; a serious poem. **2** L17 The part of a Greek lyric ode following the strophe and antistrophe.

éponge *noun* E20 French (from Latin *spongia* sponge). Sponge cloth.

epos *noun* M19 Latin (from Greek = word, song, from *ep-* stem of *eipein* to say). **1** M19 Epic poetry; an epic poem; *especially* narrative poetry embodying a nation's conception of its past history. **2** M19 Something in real life regarded as a fit subject for an epic poem.

épris *adjective* (feminine **éprise**) L18 French (past participial adjective of (*(s')éprendre* to become attached or enamored, from as *es-* + Latin *prehendere* to seize). Enamored *(of)*; taken *with*.

epsilon *noun* E18 Greek (*e psilon*, literally, 'bare e', short e written ε). **1** E18 The fifth letter (E, ε) of the Greek alphabet; *Astronomy* (preceding the genitive of the Latin name of the constellation) the fifth brightest star in a constellation. **2** E20 Brit. An examiner's fifth-class mark; a person of low intelligence.

epyllion *noun* plural **epyllia**, L19 Greek (*epullion* diminutive of EPOS). A narrative poem resembling an epic in style or matter but of shorter extent.

équipe *noun* (also **equipe**) M20 French (= group, team, from as *équiper* to equip (cf. Anglo-Norman *eskipeson*, medieval Latin *eschipare* to man (a vessel)), probably from Old Norse *skipa* to man (a vessel), fit up, from *skip* ship). A motor racing stable; a team, especially of sports players.

equivoque *noun* (also **equivoke**) LME Old and Modern French (*équivoque* or late Latin *aequivocus*). **1** L16–M17 A thing that has the same name as something else. **2** E17 An expression capable of more than one meaning; a pun; wordplay, punning. **3** E19 The fact of having more than one meaning or interpretation; ambiguity.

■ Earlier (LME–M17) as an adjective meaning 'equivocal'.

erbswurst *noun* L19 German (from *Erbse* pea + *Wurst* sausage). *Cooking* Seasoned pease meal compressed into a sausage shape and used for making soup.

erg *noun* plural **areg** L19 French (from Arabic *'irḳ, 'erg*). An area of shifting desert sand dunes, especially in the Sahara.

ergo *adverb* LME Latin. Therefore.

■ Later (L16) there was also a noun sense of *ergo*, meaning 'a use or occurrence of *ergo*, as in a logical conclusion', but this sense has long been rare.

ergot *noun* L17 French (= cock's spur, from Old French *ar(i)got, argoz* of unknown origin). **1** L17 A disease of rye and certain other grasses in which the seeds become replaced by hard black sclerotia of a fungus, giving the appearance of a rooster's spur: a sclerotium, or sclerotia, of this kind; a fungus causing such a disease. **2** M19 (A preparation or extract of) the dried sclerotia of this fungus used medicinally for the alkaloids they contain, especially to induce contraction of the uterus. **3** L19 A small horny protrusion on the back of the fetlock of most horses.

erh hu *noun phrase* (also **erhu**) E20 **Chinese** (*èrhú*, from *èr* two + *hú* bowed instrument). A Chinese two-stringed musical instrument played with a bow.

Erlebnis *noun* plural **Erlebnisse** E20 **German** (literally, 'experience', from *leben* to live). A conscious experience undergone, as opposed to the content or the memory of one.

Eros *noun* plural **Erotes**, **Eroses** (also **eros**) L17 **Latin** (from Greek). **1** L17 Love; the god of love, Cupid; earthly or sexual love. **2** E20 In Freudian psychology: the urge for self-preservation and sexual pleasure.

errata *noun* L16 **Latin** (plural of ERRATUM). **I 1** L16 *plural* of ERRATUM. **II** *singular* plural **errata's**, **erratae**. **2** M17 A list of errors in a text.

erratum *noun* plural **errata** M16 **Latin** (= error, noun use of neuter past participle of *errare* to err). An error in a printed or written text; *especially* one noted in a list appended to a book or published in a subsequent issue of a journal.

ersatz *adjective & noun* L19 **German** (= compensation, replacement). **A** *adjective* L19 Made or used as a (usually inferior) substitute for something else. **B** *noun* L19 An ersatz thing.

eruv *noun* plural **eruvim** L20 **Hebrew**. An area marked out by a community of observant Jews within which they are allowed to move on the Sabbath without contravening the restrictions on Sabbath activity.

escargot *noun* L19 **French** (from Old French *escargol* from Provençal *escaragol*). A snail as an article of food.

escarole *noun* E20 **French** (from Italian *scar(i)ola* from late Latin *(e)scariola*, from Latin *escarius* used as food, from *esca*). A variety of endive with broad undivided leaves, used in salads.

esclandre *noun* M19 **French** (from ecclesiastical Latin *scandalum* scandal). Unpleasant notoriety; a scandal, a scene.

escopette *noun* E19 **Spanish** (*escopeta* (assimilated to French *escopette* from Italian) from Italian *schioppetto* diminutive of *schioppo* carbine, from medieval Latin *sclop(p)us* harquebus). A kind of carbine formerly used in Mexico and the southern United States. *History*.

escritoire *noun* L16 **Old French** (= study, writing box (modern *écritoire* writing desk) from medieval Latin SCRIPTORIUM). A writing desk with drawers, etc., a bureau.

esophagus *noun* (also **oesophagus**) LME **Medieval Latin** (*ysophagus*, *iso-* from Greek *oisophagos*, from obscure first element + (apparently) *-phagos* eating, eater; current spelling after modern Latin). *Anatomy* and *Zoology* The canal leading from the back of the mouth, through which food and drink pass to the stomach; the gullet.

esoterica *noun plural* E20 **Greek** (*esōterika* neuter plural of *esōterikos* esoteric). Items or publications intended only for the initiated or appropriate only to an inner circle; esoteric details.

espacement *noun* M19 **French** (from *espacer* to space out). **1** M19 The action of spacing, or of placing at suitable intervals. **2** M20 The distance at which trees or crops are set apart when planted.

espada *noun* plural **espadas** L19 **Spanish** (from Latin *spatha* sword). A matador.

■ Although introduced originally (E18) in its literal sense of 'a Spanish sword', the word did not achieve currency and was later reintroduced in its present sense.

espadrille *noun* L19 **French** (from Provençal *espardi(l)hos*, from *espart* esparto). A light canvas shoe with a braided fiber sole, originally worn in the Pyrenees; an ALPARGATA.

espagnole *noun* M19 **French** (literally, 'Spanish' (feminine), from Old French *espaignol*, *espaigneul*). A simple brown sauce. In full *espagnole sauce*.

espagnolette *noun* E19 **French** (from *espagnol* Spanish; see preceding). A kind of bolt used for fastening French windows, in which a single handle operates fasteners at the top and bottom of the window.

espalier *noun* M17 **French** (from Italian *spalliera*, from *spalla* shoulder, from Latin *spatula*, (in late Latin) shoulder blade). **1** M17 A fruit tree or ornamental shrub trained on a lattice or a framework of stakes. **2** A row of trees or shrubs trained in this way. Only in E18. **3** M18 A lattice or framework, or one of the stakes, on which a tree or shrub is trained.

esparto *noun* plural **espartos** M19 **Spanish** (from Latin *spartum* from Greek *sparton* rope). A tough grass, *Stipa tenacissima*, growing in Spain and North Africa and used in making paper. Also *esparto grass*.

espièglerie *noun* E19 **French** (from (*Ul*)*espiegle* frolicsome, from Dutch *Uilenspiegel* (= German *Eulenspiegel*), from *uil* owl + *spiegel* mirror, from Latin *speculum*). Mischievousness; roguishness.

■ Till Eulenspiegel was a mythical fourteenth-century German peasant whose exploits and practical jokes were recounted in a collection of satirical tales first published in the early sixteenth century. The English noun *owlglass* (M16) is also a translation of *Eulenspiegel*.

esplanade *noun* L16 **French** (from Italian *spianata* from feminine of Latin *explanatus* flattened, leveled, past participle of *explanare*). **1** L16 *Fortification* **a** The glacis of a counterscarp. Formerly, an area of flat ground on the top of a rampart. **b** E18 A level open space separating a citadel from the town that it commands. **2** L17 Any level open space, but *especially* one where the public may walk; a road along the seafront of a resort.

espressivo *adverb & adjective* L19 **Italian** (from Latin *expressus* distinctly presented, past participle of *exprimere* to express). *Music* (Performed) with expression of feeling.

espresso *noun* (also **expresso**) plural **espressos** M20 **Italian** ((*caffè*) *espresso*, from *espresso* squeezed, pressed out, from Latin *expressus* (see preceding)). **1** M20 Coffee made by forcing steam through ground coffee beans. **2** M20 A coffee bar, etc., where such coffee is sold. Also *espresso bar*, *espresso café*, etc.

esprit *noun* L16 **French** (from Latin *spiritus* spirit). Vivacity; wit.

esprit de corps *noun phrase* L18 **French**. Regard for the honor and interests of the group or organization to which one belongs; team spirit.

esprit de l'escalier *noun phrase* (also **esprit d'escalier**) E20 **French** (literally, 'wit of the staircase'). A clever remark or rejoinder that only occurs to one after the opportunity for making it is past.

■ The phrase was coined by the French *philosophe* Denis Diderot (1713–84) in *Paradoxe sur le Comédien*. The staircase was the one descending from the salon, and *esprit d'escalier* was the witty saying that came to mind only as one was departing down it.

esprit fort *noun phrase* plural **esprits forts** M18 **French** (= strong spirit). A strong-minded person, *especially* one who claims independence from conventional thinking on religious or philosophical topics.

esquisse *noun* M18 **French** (from Italian *schizzo*). A rough or preliminary sketch.

esraj *noun* E20 **Bengali** (*esrāj*). A three- or four-stringed Indian musical instrument with added sympathetic strings.

esse *noun* M16 **Latin** (use as noun of *esse* to be). Essential nature, essence, especially as opposed to BENE ESSE.

estacade *noun* E17 **French** (from Spanish *estacada*, from *estaca*, from Proto-Romance, from Germanic base of *stake*). A dike made of piles or stakes in water or marshy ground in order to impede an enemy.

estaminet *noun* plural **estaminets** E19 **French** (from Walloon *staminé* byre, from *stamo* pole to which a cow is tethered in a stall, probably from German *Stamm* stem, trunk). Originally, a café where smoking was allowed. Now, a small unpretentious café selling wine, beer, etc.

estancia *noun* M17 **Spanish** (literally, 'station' = Old French *estance* dwelling, from medieval Latin *stantia*, from Latin *stant-* present participial stem of *stare* to stand). A cattle ranch in Latin America or the southern United States.

estocada *noun* E20 **Spanish** (from *estoque* sword (from Old and Modern French *estoc*) short sword for thrusting + *-ada*). *Bullfighting* The sword thrust that finally kills the bull.

estouffade *noun* L19 **French** (from Italian *stuf(f)ata* past participle of *stufare* to stew, from *stufa* stove, from popular Latin, ultimately from Greek *tuphos* smoke). (A dish of) meat cooked very slowly in its own vapor.

estrade *noun* L17 **French** (from Spanish *estrado*, from Latin STRATUM, literally, 'something spread or laid down', neuter past participle of *sternere* to throw down). Originally, a slightly raised platform or dais for persons of rank to sit or recline on. Later, any dais.

■ The Spanish equivalent *strado* was an earlier introduction into English (L16) than *estrade* and was used with the same two senses, but is now rare.

estrog variant of ETROG.

estrus *noun* (also **oestrus**) L17 **Latin** (from Greek *oistros* gadfly, breeze, sting, frenzy). **1** L17 A parasitic insect; now *specifically* a biting fly of the genus *Oestrus* or the family Oestridae whose larvae are parasitic on various animals; a botfly. Now chiefly as modern Latin genus name. **2** E19 *figurative* A sharp stimulus; a passion, a frenzy. Now *rare*. **3** L19 *Zoology* and *Physiology* (The period of) a female animal's readiness to mate, accompanied by certain physiological changes; the rut, heat.

estufa *noun* M19 **Spanish** (corresponding to Old French *estuve* (modern *étuve*)). **1** M19 An underground chamber in which a fire is kept permanently alight, used as a place of assembly by the Pueblo Indians. **2** L19 A heated chamber in which Madeira is stored and matured.

et *conjunction* ME **Latin**. And.

■ In Modern English only in medieval and Modern Latin phrases; see ET AL., ET CETERA, etc.

eta *noun* LME **Greek** (*ēta*). **1** LME The seventh letter (H, η) of the Greek alphabet. **2** Frequently written (η). **a** L18 *attributive Astronomy* (Preceding the genitive of the Latin name of the constellation) denoting the seventh brightest star in a constellation. **b** M20 *Physics* A meson with zero isospin and spin and a mass of 549 MeV. In full *eta meson*.

etagere *noun* (also **étagère**) M19 **French** (*étagère*, from *étage* shelf, stage). A piece of furniture with a number of open shelves on which to display ornaments, etc.

et al. *adverb phrase 1* L19 **Latin** (*et* and + abbreviation of *alii, aliae, alia* masculine, feminine, and neuter plural of *alius* other). And others.

■ Often used in bibliographies in cases of works by several authors; the formula "Smith et al." avoids having to list all the authors' names in full.

et al. *adverb phrase 2* **Latin** (*et* and + abbreviation of ALIBI elsewhere). And elsewhere.

étalage *noun* E20 **French** (from *étaler* to display). A display, a show.

etamine *noun* (also **étamine**) E18 **French** (*étamine*). A lightweight open-weave fabric of coarse yarn, now usually cotton or worsted.

étang *noun* M19 **French** (from Old French *estanc*, ultimately from base of *stanch*, origin unknown). A shallow pool or small lake, especially one resulting from the blocking of streams by sand dunes along the French Mediterranean coast.

etatism *noun* (also **étatisme**) E20 **French** (*étatisme*, from *état* state). The extreme authority of the state over the individual citizen.

et cetera *adverb, noun, & verb* (also **etcetera**, **et caetera**) ME **Latin** (from *et* and + *cetera* the rest, neuter plural of *ceterus* remaining over). **A** *adverb* ME And the rest; and similar things; and so on; and the customary continuation. Also reduplicated. **B** *noun* **1** L16 (An instance of) the adverb *et cetera*. **2** L16 Something not mentioned explicitly for reasons of propriety. Formerly *specifically* (in *plural*) pants. **3** M17 A number of unspecified things or persons. **4** (In *plural*.) (The usual) additions, extras, sundries. **C** *verb* M19 Replacing a suppressed verb.

■ Often abbreviated to *etc* or *&c*.

ethos *noun* M19 **Greek** (*ēthos* nature, disposition). The characteristic spirit of a culture, era, community, institution, etc., as manifested in its attitudes, aspirations, customs, etc.; the character of an individual as represented by his or her values and beliefs; the prevalent tone of a literary work in this respect.

ethrog variant of ETROG.

etiquette *noun* M18 **French** (*étiquette* label, etiquette). The conventional rules of personal behavior in polite society; the prescribed ceremonial of a court; the formalities required in diplomatic intercourse; the order of procedure established by custom in the armed services, Parliament, etc.; the unwritten code restricting professional persons in what concerns the interests of their colleagues or the dignity of their profession.

■ Also formerly (M19) in the primary French sense of 'a label, ticket', but this is rare in English. The sense of 'a rule of etiquette', 'an observance prescribed by etiquette' was also briefly (L18–E19) current in English, generally in the plural. From the word's history in French it is not entirely clear how the transition between between the primary and secondary senses was effected, although the English colloquial expressions "just the ticket" and "not quite the ticket" (*ticket* here meaning 'the accepted (or needed) thing') suggest how it could have come about. Modern Romance languages have adapted the word from French in the secondary sense: Italian *etichetta*, Spanish *etiqueta*.

étourderie *noun* M18 **French** (from next). Thoughtlessness, carelessness; a thoughtless act, a blunder.

étourdi *adjective & noun* (feminine **étourdie**) L17 **French** (past participial adjective of *étourdir* to stun, make dizzy). (A person who is) thoughtless or irresponsible.

étrenne *noun* E19 **French** (from Old French *estreine* ultimately from Latin *strena*). A New Year's gift; a Christmas box.

etrier *noun* (also **étrier**) M20 **French** (*étrier* stirrup, etrier). *singular* and in *plural*. A short rope ladder with a few solid rungs, used by climbers.

etrog *noun* (also **ethrog**, **estrog**) plural **etrogs**, **etrogim** L19 **Hebrew** (*'etrōg*). A citron fruit as used ritually in the Jewish Feast of Tabernacles.

et seq. *noun phrase* plural **et seqq.** L19 **Latin** (*et* and + present participle of *sequi* to follow; abbreviation of *et sequentes* (Latin masculine and feminine plural of *sequens*) and *et sequentia* (neuter plural of *sequens*)). And following.

Et tu, Brute *interjection* L16 **Latin** (= and you, Brutus). (An expression of) reproach to a friend who has betrayed one's trust and gone over to the enemy.

■ The words spoken by Caesar in Shakespeare's *Julius Caesar* (III.i) when he sees his friend Brutus among his assassins. Another name is sometimes jocularly substituted for that of Brutus.

étude *noun* M19 **French** (= study). An instrumental piece, especially for the piano, that concentrates on a particular aspect of technique or allows a display of virtuosity.

etui *noun* (also **etwee**) E17 **French** (*étui*, Old French *estui* prison, from Old French *estuier* to shut up, keep, save). A small usually ornamental case for needles, etc. Formerly also, a case for surgical instruments.

euchre *noun & verb* E19 **German** (dialect *Jucker(spiel)*). **A** *noun* **1** E19 A card game for two to four players in which the highest cards are the joker (if used), the jack of trumps, and the other jack of the same color in a deck with the lower cards removed, the aim being to win at least three of the five tricks played. **2** M19 An instance of euchring or being euchred. **B** *transitive verb* **1** E19 Prevent (a bidder) from winning three or more tricks at euchre, thereby scoring points oneself. **2** M19 Cheat, trick, (*into, out of*); deceive, outwit. **3** M20 Exhaust; ruin, finish, do for, (a person). Usually in *passive*. *Australian*.

eudaimonia *noun* E20 **Greek** (from as *eudemon* from as *eu-* good + *daimōn* genius). *Philosophy* Happiness or well-being consisting in the full realization of human potential, *especially* (in Aristotle's ethics) in rational activity exhibiting excellence.

eunomia *noun* M19 **Greek** (from as *eu-* good + *-nomia* state of law). A political condition of good law well administered.

eupepsia *noun* E18 **Greek** (*eupepsia* digestibility, from *eupeptos*, from *eu-* good + *peptein* to digest). Good digestion; absence of indigestion.

euphoria *noun* L17 **Modern Latin** (from Greek, from *euphoros* borne well, healthy, from as *eu-* good + *pherein* to bear). Originally, a state of well-being, especially as produced in a sick person by a medicine. Now, a strong feeling of well-being, cheerfulness, and optimism, *especially* one based on overconfidence or overoptimism; a mood marked by this, as symptomatic of a mental illness or the influence of drugs.

eureka *interjection & noun* (also **Eureka**) E17 **Greek** (*heurēka*, 1st person singular perfect of *heuriskein* to find). **A** *interjection* E17 Expressive of exultation at a sudden discovery. **B** *noun* **1** M17 A cry of *eureka!* **2** M19 A fortunate discovery. **3** E20 (**Eureka**) (Proprietary name for) an alloy of copper and nickel used for electrical filament and resistance wire.

■ The exclamation supposedly uttered by the Sicilian Greek philosopher Archimedes (*c.*287–*c.*212 BC) when he hit upon a method of determining the purity of gold, an inspiration which, according to tradition, occurred to him as he was taking a bath.

euthanasia *noun* E17 **Greek** (from as *eu-* good + *thanatos* death). **1** E17 A gentle and easy death. **2** M18 A means of bringing about such a death (chiefly *in figurative use, of* something). **3** M19 The action of bringing about such a death, especially of a person who requests it as a release from incurable disease.

événement *noun* M20 **French** (= event, happening). Politically motivated civil disorder involving mass demonstrations.

■ Usually plural. The word became current in English with reference to the French strikes and student riots of 1968 and received a further boost from the wave of strikes and demonstrations in France in 1995, though it is no longer necessarily confined to the French political scene.

évolué *noun & adjective* M20 **French** (past participle of *évoluer* to evolve). (Characteristic of or designating) an African who has had a European education or has adopted European ways or attitudes.

Ewigkeit *noun* (also **ewigkeit**) L19 **German**. Eternity; infinity.

ex *noun & adjective* plural **exes**, **ex's** E19 **Latin** (from prefix *ex-* former(ly)). **A** *noun* E19 A person who formerly held a position, etc., denoted by the context; *specifically*, a former husband or wife. **B** *adjective* E19 Former; outdated.

ex *preposition* M19 **Latin** (= out of). **1** *Commerce* M19 Of stocks and shares: without, excluding. **2** Of freight: (sold) direct from (a ship, warehouse, etc.) **3** L19 Of an animal: out of (a specified dam).

exacta *noun* M20 **American Spanish** (*quiniela exacta* exact quinella). *Betting* A PERFECTA.

exalté *adjective & noun* (feminine **exaltée**) M19 **French** (past participial adjective of *exalter* to exalt, from as *ex-* up(ward) + *altus* high). (A person who is) elated or impassioned.

ex animo *adverb phrase* E17 **Latin** (= from the soul, from as *ex* (preposition) + *animo* ablative of *animus* soul). Heartily, sincerely.

ex ante *adjective & adverb phrase* M20 **Modern Latin** (from as *ex* (preposition) + *ante* before). Chiefly *Economics* **A** *adjective phrase* M20 Based on prior assumptions or expectations; predicted, prospective. **B** *adverb phrase* M20 Before the event, in advance, beforehand.

■ The opposite of EX POST.

ex cathedra *adverb & adjective* E17 **Latin** (= from the (teacher's) chair, from *ex* (preposition) + *cathedra* chair). **A** *adverb* E17 Authoritatively; as an official pronouncement; *especially* (*Roman Catholic Church*) with the full weight of the Pope's office as divinely appointed guardian of Christian faith and morals. **B** *adjective* E19 Authoritative, official; given *ex cathedra*; dogmatic.

excelsior *interjection & noun* (also **Excelsior**) L18 **Latin** (comparative of *excelsus* from *ex-* + *celsus* lofty). **A** L18 *interjection* Go higher! **B** *noun* **1** M19 Curled shavings of soft wood for stuffing, packing, etc. **2** L19 A person who or thing that reaches or aspires to reach higher. **3** E20 A very small size (3 points) of type.

exceptis excipiendis *adverb phrase* L19 **Late Latin** (from ablative plural of Latin *exceptus* past participle, and of *excipiendus* gerundive, of *excipere* to except). With appropriate exceptions.

excreta *noun plural* M19 **Latin** (noun use of neuter plural of *excretus* past participle of *excernere* to excrete). Waste matter discharged from the body; *especially* feces, urine.

excursus *noun* plural **excursuses**, **excursus** E19 **Latin** (= excursion, from *excurs-* past participial stem of *excurrere* to run out). **1** E19 A fuller treatment in an appendix of some point in the main text of a book, especially an edition of the classics. **2** M19 A digression within a narrative in which some point is discussed at length.

exeat *noun* E18 **Latin** (= let him or her go out, 3rd person singular present subjunctive of *exire* to go out). **1** E18 A permission for temporary absence from a college or other institution. **2** M18 A permission granted by a bishop to a priest to move to another diocese.

exedra *noun* (also **exhedra**) plural **exedrae** E18 **Latin** (from Greek, from as *ex-* + *hedra* seat). **1** E18 *Classical History* A hall or arcade with seats, attached to a palaestra or a private house and used for conversation. **b** M19 *generally* An apse, a recess, a large niche. **2** E18 A CATHEDRA.

exegesis *noun* plural **exegeses** E17 **Greek** (*exēgēsis*, from *exēgeisthai* to interpret). (An) exposition, especially of Scripture; an explanatory note or discourse.

exempla plural of EXEMPLUM.

exempli gratia *adverb phrase* M17 **Latin** (from genitive of *exemplum* example + ablative of *gratia* grace). For example; for instance.

■ Abbreviated to *e.g.*, *Exempli gratia* and its ubiquitous abbreviation have entirely superseded *exempli causa* (literally, 'by reason of example'), although the latter was the earlier (M16) in English.

exemplum *noun* plural **exempla** L19 **Latin.** An example; *especially* an illustrative or moralizing story.

exequatur *noun* E17 **Latin** (= let him or her perform, 3rd person singular present subjunctive of *exequi* to carry out, execute). **1** E17 *Roman Catholic*

Church A government's authorization for a bishop to exercise his office in its territory, or for any papal enactment to take effect there; a claim by a government that such authorization is required or can be withheld. **2** L18 An official recognition of a consul by a foreign government, authorizing him or her to exercise office.

exergue *noun* **L17 French** (from medieval Latin *exergum*, from Greek *ex-* + *ergon* work). *Numismatics* A small space on a coin or medal, usually on the reverse below the principal device, for the date, the engraver's initials, etc.; the inscription placed there.

exeunt *verb & noun* **L15 Latin** (3rd person plural present indicative of *exire* to go out). **A** *intransitive verb defective* (A stage direction:) (actors, or the characters whose names follow) leave the stage. Cf. EXIT. **B** A collective exit; a departure by more than one person.

■ Also in the phrase *exeunt omnes* 'all leave the stage' at the end of a scene or play.

ex gratia *adverb & adjective phrase* **M18 Latin** (from *ex* from + *gratia* grace). (Done, given, etc.) as a favor or without (especially legal) compulsion.

exhedra variant of EXEDRA.

ex hypothesi *adverb phrase* **E17 Modern Latin** (from Latin *ex* by + ablative of late Latin HYPOTHESIS). According to the hypothesis (made); supposedly.

exigeant *adjective* (feminine **exigeante**) **L18 French** (present participial adjective of *exiger* from Latin *exigere* to exact). Exacting, demanding.

exit *noun* **L16 Latin** (*exitus*; cf. EXIT (verb 1)). **1** L16 A departure of an actor, etc., from the stage during a scene; *figurative* a person's death. **2** M17 *generally* A departure from any place or situation. Also, freedom or opportunity to depart. **3** L17 A means of egress, especially from a public building; an outlet, a way out. **b** M20 A ramp or road where traffic can leave a highway, etc. **4** M20 *Cards* (especially *Bridge*) The action of deliberately losing the lead; a card enabling one to do this.

exit *verb 1 (intransitive) defective* **M16 Latin** (3rd person singular present indicative of *exire* to go out, from as *ex-* out + *ire* to go). (A stage direction:) (the last speaker, or the character whose name follows) leaves the stage. Cf. EXEUNT.

exit *verb 2* **E17 Latin** (from EXIT (noun)). **1** *intransitive verb* E17 Make one's exit or departure, especially from a stage; leave any place; *figurative* die. **2** *intransitive verb* M20 *Cards* (especially *Bridge*). Lose the lead deliberately. **3** *transitive verb* L20 Leave, get out of.

ex libris *noun* plural same (also **ex-libris**) **L19 Latin** (literally, 'out of the books *or* library (of —)'). An inscription, label, etc., indicating the owner of a book; *especially* a bookplate.

ex machina see DEUS EX MACHINA.

ex nihilo *adverb phrase* **L16 Latin**. Out of nothing.

exodus *noun* **OE ecclesiastical Latin** (*Exodus* from Greek *exodos*, from as *ex-* out + *hodos* way). **1** OE (*Exodus*) (The name of) the second book of the Bible, relating the release of the Israelites from their bondage in Egypt and their journey to Canaan. **2** E17 A departure, usually of many people; an emigration; *specifically* the departure of the Israelites from Egypt.

ex officio *adverb, adjective, & noun* **M16 Latin** (from *officium* duty, office). **A** *adverb* & (usually with hyphen) *adjective* M16 (That is such) by virtue of one's office. **B** *noun* E19 A person serving ex officio.

exordium *noun* plural **exordiums**, **exordia** **L16 Latin** (from *exordiri* to begin). The beginning of anything; *especially* the introductory part of a discourse or treatise.

exotica *noun plural* **L19 Latin** (neuter plural of *exoticus* exotic). Exotic things.

ex parte *adverb & adjective phrase* (as adjective frequently **ex-parte**) E17 **Latin** (= from a *or* the side). **A** *adverb phrase* **1** E17 Originally, on the part of. Now (*Law*), on behalf of. **2** L17 *Law* On behalf of or with reference to only one of the parties concerned (and without notice to the adverse party). **B** *adjective phrase* **1** L18 *Law* Of an application, injunction, deposition, etc.: made, issued, etc., by or for only one party in a case. **2** E19 Of a statement, etc.: one-sided, partial.

ex pede Herculem *adverb phrase* M17 **Latin** (= Hercules from his foot). Inferring the whole of something from an insignificant part.

■ The ancient Greek mathematician Pythagoras is supposed to have calculated the height of the hero Hercules from the size of his foot.

experimentum crucis *noun phrase* M17 **Modern Latin** (= crucial experiment). A decisive test showing which of several hypotheses is correct.

explication de texte *noun phrase* plural **explications de texte** M20 **French**. A detailed textual examination of a literary work; the making of such examinations.

explicit *noun* M17 **Late Latin** (either = here ends, 3rd person singular indicative of *explicare* to unfold (plural *expliciunt*); or abbreviation of *explicitus est liber* = the book is finished). The end; the conclusion.

■ Originally used by medieval scribes to denote the end of a Latin manuscript or work, *explicit* was sometimes also placed (ME–M19) at the end of an printed book, chapter, etc.

exposé *noun* (also **expose**) E19 **French** (past participle of *exposer* to set out, display). **1** E19 An orderly statement of facts. **2** E19 A showing up or revelation of something discreditable.

ex post *adjective & adverb phrase* M20 **Modern Latin** (from as preposition *ex* + Latin *post* after). Chiefly *Economics*. **A** *adjective phrase* M20 Based on past events or actual results; occurring afterward; actual rather than predicted; retrospective. **B** *adverb phrase* M20 After the event; retrospectively.

■ The opposite of EX ANTE.

ex post facto *adverb & adjective phrase* M17 **Latin** (erroneous division of Latin *ex postfacto* in the light of subsequent events, from *ex* from, out of + ablative of *postfactum* that which is done subsequently). **A** *adverb phrase* M17 After the event, after the fact; retrospectively. **B** *adjective phrase* L18 Done after another thing; *especially* (of a law) applied retrospectively.

expresso variant of ESPRESSO.

ex professo *adverb phrase* L16 **Latin** (from as preposition *ex* + ablative of *professus* noun use of past participial stem of *profiteri* to declare). By profession; professedly.

ex proprio motu *adverb phrase* L17 **Late Latin** (= by own motion). MOTU PROPRIO; *specifically* in *Law*, by decision of a court without anyone's application.

ex relatione *prepositional phrase* E17 **Latin**. *Law* By relation of; according to the report of, as reported by.

ex silentio *adverb phrase* E20 **Latin** (= from silence). By or from a lack of evidence to the contrary.

extempore *adverb, noun, & adjective* M16 **Latin** (*ex tempore* on the spur of the moment, from as preposition *ex* + *tempore* ablative of *tempus* time). **A** *adverb* **1** M16 Without premeditation or preparation; impromptu. (Now chiefly of speaking or of performing music.) **2** L16–M17 At once, immediately. **B** *noun* L16–E19 An unprepared improvised speech, composition, or performance. **C** *adjective* **1** E17 Of a speech, musical performance, etc.: spoken or done without preparation, especially without written notes. Of a speaker or performer: performing without preparation. **2** M17 Occasional; sudden, unprepared for. (Now only of personal actions, with some notion of sense 1.) **3** L17 Makeshift, contrived for the occasion.

extra dictionem *adverb phrase* E19 **Latin** (translation of Greek *exō tēs lexeōs* outside the wording). Of a logical fallacy: not arising from the wording used to express it.

■ A subdivision of logical fallacy noted by Aristotle in his *Sophistici Elenchi* (ch. 4); it is sometimes also called in Latin *in re* in the matter. Opposed to IN DICTIONE.

extrados *noun* L18 **French** (from Latin *extra* outside + French *dos* back). *Architecture* The upper or outer curve of an arch; *especially* the upper curve of the voussoirs that form the arch. Cf. INTRADOS.

extraordinaire *postpositive adjective* M20 **French.** Remarkable, outstanding; (of a person) unusually active or successful in a specified respect.

exuviae *noun plural* M17 **Latin** (= clothing stripped off, skins of animals, spoils, from *exuere* to divest oneself of). Cast-off skins, shells, or other shed outer parts of animals, whether recent or fossil; *specifically* (*Zoology*) sloughed skins; *figurative* remnants, remains.

ex vivo *adjective & adverb phrase* (also **ex-vivo**) L20 **Latin.** *Biology* (Performed, obtained, or occurring) outside a living organism.

■ Opposed to IN VIVO.

ex-voto *noun & adjective* plural of noun **ex-votos** L18 **Latin** (*ex voto* from *ex* out of, from + *voto* ablative singular of *votum* vow). (Designating) something offered in fulfillment of a vow previously taken.

ezan *noun* M18 **Persian and Turkish** (pronunciation of Arabic *'adān*). The Muslim call to prayer; the AZAN.

f abbreviation of FORTE *(musical direction).*

fabliau *noun* plural **fabliaux** E19 **French.** *Literature* A verse tale, often burlesque in character, from the early period of French poetry.

■ The word is also used to denote a similar verse tale of sex and trickery in medieval English, particularly the tales of the Miller, Reeve, Summoner, Merchant, and Shipman in Chaucer's *Canterbury Tales.*

façade d'honneur *noun phrase* plural **façades d'honneur** M20 **French.** *Architecture* The principal front of a building, esp. of a large formal building.

facetiae *noun plural* E16 **Latin** (plural of *facetia* jest). **1** E16 Witticisms; humorous sayings. **2** M19 *Bookselling* Pornography.

Fach *noun* (also **fach**) M19 **German** (= compartment, division, shelf). A line of business or work; a department of activity.

facia variant of FASCIA senses 4, 5.

faciendum *noun* plural **facienda** M19 **Latin** (= thing to be done, neuter gerundive of *facere* to make, do). *Philosophy* A thing that should be done.

facies *noun* plural same E17 **Latin** (= face). **1** L19 *Medicine* The appearance of the face, esp. when characteristic of a particular illness. **2** E18 *Science* A general aspect, appearance, or character. **b** M19 *Geology* The character of a rock formation. **c** E20 *Ecology* The characteristic set of species in a habitat.

facile princeps *adjective & noun phrase* M19 **Latin** (= easily first). (A person who is) easily first; the acknowledged chief or leader.

facilis descensus Averni *noun phrase* E17 **Latin** (= easy (is) the descent to Avernus). The descent to hell is easy.

■ A quotation from Virgil's *Aeneid* (vi.126); Avernus was the name of a deep lake near Puteoli in Italy, reputed to be one of the entrances to the underworld. The subsequent lines state that the difficulty lies in retracing one's steps to the upper air; hence *facilis descensus Averni* is a metaphor for the ease with which one can slide into bad ways, with the implication that it is very hard to recover. The phrase is sometimes abbreviated to simply *facilis descensus*.

façon de parler *noun phrase* plural **façons de parler** E19 **French** (= way of speaking). A manner of speaking; a mere phrase or formula.

façon de Venise *adjective & noun phrase* L20 **French** (= manner of Venice). (Designating) glassware made according to the technically demanding method and decorative style developed first in Venice during the later Middle Ages.

façonné *adjective & noun* (also **faconne**) L19 **French** (past participial adjective of *façonner* to fashion). (Designating) a fabric into which a design has been woven.

façons de parler plural of FAÇON DE PARLER.

factotum *noun* M16 **Medieval Latin** (from *fac* imperative of *facere* to do, make + *totum* the whole). A person who does all kinds of work; a servant or other employee who manages all the employer's affairs.

■ Originally in the now obsolete phrases *dominus factotum* or *magister factotum* (Latin = master) or *Johannes factotum* (Latin = John), now most often in the phrase *general factotum*.

fado *noun* plural **fados** E20 **Portuguese** (literally, 'fate'). A type of popular, frequently melancholy Portuguese song and dance, with a guitar accompaniment.

faena *noun* E20 **Spanish** (literally, 'task'). *Bullfighting* A series of passes made by a matador with cape and sword, preparatory to the kill.

faenza *noun* (also **Faenza**) M19 **Italian** (*Faenza*, city in the northern Italian province of Emilia-Romagna). (Designating) the type of decorated, tin-glazed pottery made in Faenza, especially between *c.*1450 and 1520. See also FAÏENCE.

fagotto *noun* plural **fagotti**, **fagottos** E18 **Italian**. A bassoon.

faïence *noun & adjective* (also **faience**, **fayence**) L17 **French** (from Faïence, Faenza). *Ceramics* (Designating) tin-glazed pottery (MAJOLICA), usually with elaborate and colorful painted decoration, of a type originally manufactured at the northern Italian town of Faenza; *generally*, any glazed ceramic. See also FAENZA.

faille *noun* M19 **French**. A ribbed silk fabric.

■ When originally introduced (M16) it denoted a kind of head covering worn by women.

fainéant *noun & adjective* (also **faineant**) E17 **French** (from *fait* 3rd person singular of *faire* to do + *néant* nothing). **A** *noun* E17 A person who does nothing; an idler. **B** *adjective* E19 Indolent, inactive.

fainéantise *noun* (also **faineantise**) E17 **French**. The state or quality of being a FAINÉANT; inactivity.

■ Also (L19) *fainéantism(e)*.

faisandé *adjective* E20 **French** (past participle of *faisander* hang (game) until it is high). Affected, artificial; piquant, improper.

fait accompli *noun phrase* plural **faits accomplis** M19 **French** (= accomplished fact). A thing done and irreversible before those affected know of it.

faits divers *noun phrase plural* L20 **French** (literally, 'sundry facts'). Short news items, usually trivial in character.

faja *noun* M19 **Spanish** (cf. FAJITA). A sash.

fajita *noun* plural **fajitas** L20 **Mexican Spanish** (literally, 'little belt'). *Cook-*

ing A small strip of grilled spiced beef or chicken; *plural* a dish made by rolling such strips of meat in a tortilla with vegetables, grated cheese, and other garnishings, topped with sour cream.

faki *noun* L16 **Arabic**. An expert in Islamic law; in parts of Africa, a teacher in a Koran school.

■ Not to be confused with FAKIR.

fakir *noun* (also formerly **faquir**) E17 **Arabic** (= poor (man); partly through French *faquir*). **1** E17 A Muslim or *loosely* Hindu religious mendicant or ascetic. **2** L19 A faker; a swindler (by popular etymology).

falafel *noun* (also **felafel**) plural same M20 **Arabic** (colloquial Egyptian). *Cooking* A small ball of spiced ground pulses (usually chickpeas), fried and typically eaten in bread.

falsetto *noun & adjective* L18 **Italian**. *Music* **A** *noun* L18 A voice pitched above its natural register; also, a person who sings in such a voice. **B** *attributive* or as *adjective* E19 Above the natural register; high-pitched.

falsobordone *noun* (also **falso bordone**) plural **falsobordoni** M18 **Italian** (from *falso* false + *bordone* BOURDON; cf. French FAUX-BOURDON). *Music* A technique of singing psalms in harmony, following simple chord progressions.

famille de robe *noun phrase* plural **familles de robe** M19 **French** (literally, 'family of the robe'). In France: a family with a legal tradition or one founded by a lawyer.

famille jaune *noun phrase* L19 **French** (literally, 'yellow family'). A type of Chinese enameled porcelain of which the predominant color is yellow, dating from the eighteenth century.

famille noire *noun phrase* L19 **French** (literally, 'black family'). A type of Chinese enameled porcelain of which the predominant color is black, dating from the eighteenth century.

famille rose *noun phrase* L19 **French** (literally, 'pink family'). A type of Chinese enameled porcelain of which the predominant color is pink, dating from the reign of Yongzheng (1723–35).

famille verte *noun phrase* L19 **French** (literally, 'green family'). A type of Chinese enameled porcelain of which the predominant color is green, dating from the reign of Kangxi (1662–1722).

famulus *noun* plural **famuli** L19 **Latin** (= servant). A servant, especially a youth attendant upon a scholar or magician.

fana *noun* M19 **Arabic** (= annihilation). *Islam* In Sufism, the obliteration of all human concerns and of consciousness of self and their replacement by pure consciousness of God.

fandango *noun* plural **fandangos** or **fandangoes** M18 **Spanish**. A lively Spanish dance for two in 3/4 or 6/8 time, usually accompanied by guitars and castanets; a piece of music for this dance.

fanfaronade *noun* (also **fanfaronnade**) M17 **French** (*fanfaronnade* from *fanfaron* a braggart). Ostentation; arrogant, swaggering talk; bluster.

fantaisiste *noun* E20 **French**. A person who indulges in extravagant fancies, especially an artist who creates elaborately fantastic works of art.

fantasia *noun* E18 **Italian**. A musical or other composition in which form is comparatively unimportant; a piece of music based on a familiar tune or tunes.

fantoccini *noun* L18 **Italian** (plural of *fantoccino*, diminutive of *fantoccio* puppet, from *fante* boy). **1** L18 *plural* Mechanically worked puppets; marionettes. **2** L18 *singular* A marionette show.

faquir variant of FAKIR.

farandole *noun* M19 **French** (from modern Provençal *farandoulo*). A lively Provençal communal dance, usually in 6/8 time; a piece of music for this dance.

farce *noun* E18 **French**. *Cooking* Forcemeat, stuffing.

■ In medieval cookbooks the word appears in the form *fars*. It was reintroduced into English in its modern form in Richard Bradley's *Family Dictionary* (1725), which was a translation of Chomel's *Dictionaire oeconomique*.

farceur *noun* (feminine **farceuse**) L17 **French**. **1** L17 A joker or buffoon; someone who is not to be taken seriously. **2** L19 A writer or actor of farces.

farci *adjective* M20 **French** (from *farcir* to stuff). *Cooking* Stuffed; filled with forcemeat.

■ Always used postpositively.

farfalle *noun plural* L20 **Italian** (plural of *farfalla* butterfly). Pasta in the form of butterflies.

farfel *noun* (also **farfal**, **ferfel**) plural same or **farfels** L19 **Yiddish** (*farfal, farfil, ferfel* (*plural*), from Middle High German *varveln* noodles, noodle soup). *Cooking* Ground or granulated noodle dough; in *plural* granules of this.

far niente *noun phrase* E19 **Italian** (= doing nothing). Idleness; DOLCE FAR NIENTE.

farouche *adjective* M18 **French** (ultimately from Latin *foras* out of doors). Unused to company; sullen, shy, ill at ease.

farrago *noun* plural **farragoes**, **farragos** M17 **Latin** (= mixed fodder for cattle, hence *figurative*, a medley). A jumble; a hodgepodge; a confused situation.

farrash *noun* (also **ferash**) E17 **Persian and Urdu** (*farrāš* from Arabic = a person who spreads out bedding, carpets, etc.). A servant in some Muslim countries, especially one who performs heavy domestic tasks.

farruca *noun* E20 **Spanish** (feminine of *farruco* Galician or Asturian, from *Farruco* pet form of male forename *Francisco*). A type of flamenco dance.

fartlek *noun* M20 **Swedish** (from *fart* speed + *lek* play). A method of training used by middle- and long-distance runners, alternating fast and slow work in a run across country.

fasces *noun plural* L16 **Latin** (plural of *fascis* bundle). **1** L16 In ancient Rome, rods tied in a bundle with an ax, carried before the leading magistrates as a symbol of power. **2** E17 (Emblems of) power or authority.

Fasching *noun* E20 **German**. In southern Germany and Austria: the carnival season extending from Epiphany to MARDI GRAS (Shrove Tuesday); a carnival.

fascia *noun* (also (senses 4, 5) **facia**) plural **fasciae**, **fascias** M16 **Latin** (= band, fillet, casing of a door, etc.). **1** M16 *Architecture* A horizontal band of wood, brick, etc., esp. as used in an architrave. **2** E18 Any object, or arrangement of objects, that gives the appearance of a stripe or band. **3** L18 *Anatomy* Connective tissue; a thin sheet of this enclosing a muscle or other organ. **4** E20 The board or strip over a storefront on which is written the trader's name and line of business. **5** E20 The instrument panel of a motor vehicle; dashboard.

fata morgana *noun* E19 **Italian** (= fairy Morgan (Morgan le Fay)). A kind of mirage often seen in the Strait of Messina between Italy and Sicily, formerly attributed to supernatural agency; an illusion.

■ According to the northern European Arthurian legends, Morgan le Fay was the sister of Britain's King Arthur and possessed magical powers. Her legend was taken to Sicily by the Normans when they conquered the island in the eleventh century.

fatwa *noun* (also **Fatwa**, **fetwa**, or **fatwah**) E17 **Arabic**. A ruling on a point of Islamic law given by a Muslim religious expert (MUFTI).

■ Although it was first used in English in the seventeenth century (in the form *fetfa*), the word came into general currency in the English-language media after February 1989, when Ayatollah Khomeini of Iran issued a *fatwa* condemning the Indian-born British writer Salman Rushdie and his publishers to death on account of Rushdie's novel *The Satanic Verses* (1988), which many Muslims held to be blasphemous and deeply objectionable in its treatment of the Koran. Because of the circumstances of the *fatwa* on Rushdie, the word is sometimes wrongly thought to mean 'a death sentence'. Since its revitalization in English, *fatwa* has moved far beyond its original Islamic context and is often used figuratively to indicate any strong denunciation.

faubourg *noun* L15 **French** (cf. medieval Latin *falsus burgus* not the city proper). A suburb, especially a suburb of Paris; formerly that part of a town or city lying just outside the walls.

fauna *noun* plural **faunae, faunas** L18 **Modern Latin** (application of *Fauna*, an ancient Italian rural goddess, sister of the god *Faunus*, who was equated with the Greek god Pan). **1** *collective singular and in plural* L18 The animals and animal life of a particular area, habitat, or epoch; cf. FLORA. **2** L19 A list of or treatise on these.

faute de mieux *adjective & adverb phrase* M18 **French.** (Used or done) only for want of a more satisfactory alternative.

fauteuil *noun* M18 **French.** An armchair; hence, any seat, especially one in a theater, resembling an armchair.

fauve *noun & adjective* (also **Fauve**) E20 **French** (literally, 'wild animal'). **A** *noun* E20 An adherent of fauvism, a style of painting notable for its use of brilliant color, originating in the early twentieth century with the work of Henri Matisse (1869–1954) and his followers; a fauvist(e). **B** *adjective* M20 Of or pertaining to fauvism(e) or fauvist(e)s.

■ The term was coined by the French art critic Louis Vauxcelles at the Autumn Salon in Paris in 1905, who, seeing a traditional Renaissance-type statue exhibited amid the works of Matisse and his adherents, exclaimed, "Donatello au milieu des fauves!"

fauvisme, fauviste see under FAUVE.

faux *adjective* L20 **French** (= false). *Fashion* and *Interior design* Imitation, fake.

■ Also *faux-* as first element in combinations, as in *faux-soul*, *faux-painted*, etc.

faux amis *noun phrase plural* M20 **French** (literally, 'false friends'). Pairs of words in two different languages (especially French and English) that appear the same but which have entirely different meanings.

■ The term derives from *Les Faux Amis ou les Trahisons du vocabulaire anglais*, the title of a book with a collection of such terms made in 1928 by M. Koessler and J. Derocquigny. An example is English *defiance* and French *défiance* 'distrust'.

faux bonhomme *noun phrase* (also **faux-bonhomme**) plural **faux bonshommes** E20 **French** (= false good-natured man). A malicious or devious person who pretends to be open-hearted and good-natured.

faux-bourdon *noun* L19 **French** (= faburden, literally, 'false hum'). A type of improvised polyphony, popular in England from the fifteenth to the mid–sixteenth century.

faux marbre *noun phrase* L20 **French** (= false marble). *Interior design* Fake marble; a finish imitating marble.

faux-naïf *noun & adjective* (also **faux-naif**) M20 **French** (from *faux* false + *naïf* ingenuous). **A** *noun* M20 A person who pretends to be naive. **B** *adjective* M20 Of a work of art, self-consciously or meretriciously simple; of a person, self-consciously artless.

faux pas *noun phrase* plural same L17 **French** (from *faux* false + *pas* step). An act that offends against social convention; an indiscreet remark or action; a slip.

favela *noun* M20 **Portuguese.** In Brazil: a shack or shanty.

■ Usually in plural *favelas* 'a slum'.

favelado *noun* M20 **Portuguese**. A person who lives in a FAVELA.

fazenda *noun* E19 **Portuguese**. In Portugal, Brazil, and Portuguese-speaking countries: a large farm or estate; the homestead belonging to such an estate.

■ The equivalent in Spanish-speaking countries is a HACIENDA.

fazendeiro *noun* E19 **Portuguese**. A person who owns or lives on a FAZENDA.

fec. abbreviation of FECIT.

fecit *verb & noun* 19 **Latin** (3rd person perfect singular of *facere* to make). *Art* (A statement:) he (or she) made (it).

■ Always preceded by a personal name, *fecit* is found inscribed on works of art. *Pinxit* 'he (or she) painted (it)' and *sculpsit* 'he (or she) sculpted (it)' are more specific alternatives. *Fecit* is sometimes abbreviated to *fec.*

fedai *noun* plural (in sense 1) same, **fedais**; (in sense 2) **fedayeen** L19 **Arabic** ((or Persian) = one who sacrifices his life for another, from *fada* ransom). **1** L19 An assassin belonging to the Muslim Ismaili sect. **2** M20 *(in plural)* Guerrillas in Arab Muslim countries, especially Arab guerrillas operating against the Israelis.

feijão *noun* M19 **Portuguese** (from Latin *phaseolus* bean). Any edible bean; especially a variety of haricot bean (*Phaseolus vulgaris*) used as a staple item of diet in Brazil.

feijoada *noun* M20 **Portuguese** (from FEIJÃO). A Brazilian stew made with black beans, pork, and sausage and served with rice.

feis *noun* (in sense 1 also **fes(s)**) plural **feiseanna** L18 **Irish** (= wedding feast, festival). **1** L18 An assembly of kings and chieftains, formerly believed to be a kind of early Celtic parliament. **2** L19 An Irish or Scottish arts festival, similar to the Welsh EISTEDDFOD.

felafel variant of FALAFEL.

feldgrau *noun & adjective* M20 **German** (= field gray). (Of) a dark gray; hence, a German soldier in a uniform of this color.

feldsher *noun* (also **feldscher**) L19 **Russian** (*fel'dsher* from German *Feldscher* a field surgeon). In Russia and the former USSR: a person with practical training in medicine and surgery, but lacking professional medical qualifications; an assistant to a physician or surgeon; a medical auxiliary.

felix culpa *noun phrase* M20 **Latin** (literally, 'happy fault'). *Theology* The Fall of Man through the sin of Adam understood as having the blessed outcome of the redemption of mankind by Jesus Christ; *transferred* any fault or disaster with ultimately beneficial consequences.

■ The phrase is taken from the Exultet, which forms part of the Roman Catholic liturgy for Holy Saturday (Easter Eve).

fellah *noun* plural **fellaheen**, **fellahin**, **fellahs** M18 **Arabic** (*fallah* colloquial plural *fallahin* tiller of the soil). A peasant in Egypt and other Arabic-speaking countries.

felo de se *noun phrase* plural **felones de se**, **felos de se** E17 **(Anglo-)Latin** (literally, 'felon of himself'). **1** E17 A person who commits suicide (formerly in the UK a criminal act) or intentionally brings about his or her own death. **2** L18 Suicide.

felsenmeer *noun* plural **felsenmeere** E20 **German** (literally, 'rock sea'). *Physical Geography* An expanse of angular, frost-riven rocks that may develop on level terrain in arctic or alpine climates; a boulder field.

felucca *noun* E17 **Italian** (*feluc(c)a* perhaps from an Arabic word via Spanish). A small sailing vessel with lateen sails and oars, formerly widely used in the Mediterranean area and still used on the River Nile.

feme covert *noun phrase* (also **femme couverte**) plural **femes coverts** M16 **Old French**. *Law* A married woman.

■ The technical spelling is *feme*, but the Modern French *femme* is also found.

feme sole *noun phrase* plural **femes soles** M16 Old French. *Law* An unmarried woman, especially a divorcée; *historical* a married woman who carries on a business in her own right, independently of her husband.

femme couverte see FEME COVERT.

femme de chambre *noun phrase* plural **femmes de chambre** M18 French (literally, 'woman of the (bed-)room'). **1** M18 A lady's maid. **2** E19 A chambermaid.

femme de ménage *noun phrase* (also **femme de menage**) plural **femmes de ménage** L19 French (literally, 'woman of the household'). A domestic help; a charwoman.

femme de trent ans *noun phrase* plural **femmes de trent ans** French (literally, 'a woman of thirty'). A woman who has passed the age at which romantic affairs are easily enjoyed.

■ The phrase alludes to the title of a novel published by Balzac in 1834.

femme du monde *noun phrase* plural **femmes du monde** L19 French. A woman of the world; a sophisticated woman.

femme fatale *noun phrase* plural **femmes fatales** E20 French (literally, 'fatal woman'). A dangerously or irresistibly attractive woman.

femme incomprise *noun phrase* plural **femmes incomprises** M19 French. A woman who is misunderstood or unappreciated.

femme savante *noun phrase* plural **femmes savantes** L19 French. A learned woman.

■ Usually with an implied derogatory allusion to Molière's play *Les Femmes savantes* (1672).

fenestella *noun* LME Latin (diminutive of *fenestra* window). **1** LME *Architecture* A small opening in a wall, especially one in the side of an altar that enables relics inside to be seen. **2** L18 A niche in an interior wall of a church, usually on the south side of the altar and containing the PISCINA.

feng-shui *noun* L18 Chinese (from *feng* wind + *shui* water). *Chinese Mythology* A system of spirit influences, both benign and malignant, that inhabit the natural features of the landscape; a kind of geomancy for dealing with these spirits, employed particularly when selecting the site for a dwelling or a grave.

ferae naturae *predicative & postpositive adjective & noun phrase* M17 Latin (= of wild nature). Chiefly *Law* Undomesticated or wild (animals).

ferash variant of FARRASH.

fer-de-lance *noun* plural **fers-de-lance**, **fer-de-lances** L19 French (= iron (head) of lance). A highly venomous tropical American pit viper, *Bothrops atrox*.

ferfel variant of FARFEL.

feria *noun* LME Latin (= holiday; in sense 2 through Spanish). **1** LME *Ecclesiastical* A weekday, especially one on which no festival falls. **2** M19 In Spain and Spanish-speaking countries: a fair.

fermata *noun* plural **fermatas**, **fermate** L19 Italian. *Music* (A sign indicating) an unspecified prolongation of a note or rest.

ferme ornée see under ORNÉ.

ferronnerie *noun & adjective* (also **ferronerie**) E20 French (= (wrought) ironwork). (Designating) decoration with motifs of arabesques and scrolls as used in wrought ironwork.

ferronnière *noun* (also **ferronière**) M19 French (literally, 'blacksmith's wife'; a frontlet). A piece of jewelry comprising a decorative chain worn around the head with a pendant on the center of the forehead; a frontlet.

■ The name derives from Leonardo da Vinci's portrait known as *La Belle Ferronnière*, which shows a woman wearing this sort of ornament.

fest *noun* (also **Fest**) M19 German (= festival). A special occasion; a celebration, a celebratory gathering.

■ Chiefly used as the second element in a combination, as in *filmfest*, *gabfest* (a gathering for talk; a conference), *glamfest* (= glamourfest), *songfest*, *talkfest*, etc.

festina lente *interjection & noun phrase* L17 Latin (= make haste slowly (imperative singular of *festinare* to hasten + *lente* slowly)). (An expression) urging caution; more haste, less speed!

■ According to Suetonius (*Life of Augustus Caesar* xxv), the Greek form of this tag was a favorite with Augustus with reference to military operations and the qualities he looked for in a commander.

Festschrift *noun* (also **festschrift**) plural **Festschriften**, **Festschrifts** E20 German (literally, 'celebration writing'). A volume of writings collected in honor of a scholar, usually presented to mark an occasion in his or her life.

feta *noun* (also **fetta**) M20 Modern Greek. A white salty ewe's milk cheese originally made in Greece.

fête *noun & verb* (also **fete**) LME French (from Old French *feste*). **A** *noun* **1** LME A festival, a fair. **2** L19 A sale or bazaar, often held out of doors, with the object of raising money for charity. **3** E19 A saint's day, a religious festival. **B** *transitive verb* E17 Entertain (a person) with a fête or feast, make much of (a person); give a fête in honor of.

fête champêtre *noun phrase* plural **fêtes champêtres** L18 French (= a rural fête). An outdoor or pastoral entertainment, a rural festival.

fête galante *noun phrase* plural **fêtes galantes** E20 French. A rural entertainment, especially as depicted in an eighteenth-century French genre of painting, a fête champêtre; a painting in this genre.

■ The subject matter of young ladies and gentlemen in elaborate or theatrical dress making music, flirting, and dancing in Arcadian surroundings is particularly associated with Jean Antoine Watteau (1684–1721).

fêtes champêtres, **fêtes galantes** plural of FÊTE CHAMPÊTRE, FÊTE GALANTE.

fetta variant of FETA.

fettucine *noun plural* (also **fettucine**) E20 Italian (plural of *fettuccina*, diminutive of *fetta* slice, ribbon). *Cooking* Pasta in the form of ribbons; an Italian dish consisting mainly of this, usually with a sauce.

fetus *noun* (also *Brit.* **foetus**) LME Latin (*fetus*, *foetus* pregnancy, giving birth, young offspring). An unborn viviparous animal in the uterus, especially an unborn human more than eight weeks after conception; an unhatched oviparous animal in the egg.

■ The American form *fetus* has etymological correctness on its side, but *foetus* is still in general use in British English.

fetwa variant of FATWA.

feu *adjective* E19 French. Of a person: deceased, late.

feu d'artifice *noun phrase* plural **feux d'artifice** L17 French (literally, 'fire of artifice'). A firework show; a firework.

feu de joie *noun phrase* plural **feux de joie** E17 French (literally, 'fire of joy'). **1** E18 A ceremonial or celebratory salute fired with rifles or other small arms. **2** M17 *figurative* A joyful occasion; a celebration.

feu follet *noun phrase* plural **feux follets** M19 French (literally, 'frolicsome fire'). A will-o'-the-wisp, an IGNIS FATUUS. Usually *figurative*.

feuillemorte *adjective* L16 French (= dead leaf). Of the color of a dead leaf; yellowish brown.

feuilleton *noun* M19 French (from *feuillet*, diminutive of *feuille* leaf). A section of a newspaper, etc., devoted to) fiction, criticism, light reading, etc.; an article or story suitable for or printed in that section.

fez *noun* plural **fezzes** E19 **Turkish** (*fes*, perhaps through French *fez*). A flat-topped conical brimless red hat with a tassel, worn by men in some Muslim countries.

■ Named after *Fez* (now *Fès*) in Morocco, once the principal place of manufacture, the fez was the national headgear of the Turks until the reforms of Kemal Atatürk in the 1920s.

ff abbreviation of FORTISSIMO *(musical direction)*.

fiancé *noun* (feminine **fiancée**) M19 **French** (from (Old) French *fiancer* to betroth). A man engaged to be married; the person to whom one is engaged.

fianchetto *noun & verb* M19 **Italian** (diminutive of *fianco* flank). *Chess* **A** *noun* plural **fianchettoes** M19 The development of a bishop by moving it one square to a long diagonal of the board. **B** *transitive verb* E20 Develop (a bishop) in this way.

fiasco *noun* plural **fiascos** M19 **Italian** (from phrase *far fiasco*, literally, 'make a bottle'). A complete and ignominious failure, originally of a theatrical or musical performance; an ignominious outcome.

■ The allusion in the Italian phrase is unexplained.

fiat *noun & verb* LME **Latin** (3rd person singular present subjunctive of *fieri* = let it be done, let there be made). **A** *noun* **1** LME A formal authorization for a proposed arrangement, etc.; generally, any authoritative pronouncement, decree. **2** L16 A command by which something is brought into being. **B** *transitive verb* M19 Sanction by (official) pronouncement.

■ In sense A.2 *fiat* is short for or an allusion to *fiat lux* = let there be light (Vulgate Genesis 1:3).

ficelle *noun* L19 **French** (= string). **1** L19 The off-white color of undyed string. **2** L19 A (stage) device, an artifice.

■ In sense 1 *ficelle* is used only attributively or in combination as *ficelle-color(ed)*.

fiche *noun* M20 **French** (short for *fiche de voyageur*). The registration form on which foreign guests must record details of passport, etc., when booking into a French hotel.

fichu *noun* M18 **French** (origin unknown). A triangular piece of lace or fine fabric worn by women around the neck or shoulders, and formerly also over the head.

fidalgo *noun* plural **fidalgos** M17 **Portuguese** (contraction of *filho de algo* son of something). A Portuguese nobleman.

■ The word is now obsolete except when used historically; cf. HIDALGO.

fides Punica *noun phrase* (also **Punica fides**) 19 **Latin** (literally, 'Punic faith'). Treachery.

■ The phrase *Punica fide* 'with Punic (i.e., Carthaginian) faith' occurs in Sallust *Jugurthine War* cviii. It is one of several tags expressing the deep Roman distrust of the Carthaginians, their deadly rivals for control of the Mediterranean world during the initial phase of Roman overseas expansion in the third and second centuries BC.

fidus Achates *noun phrase* L16 **Latin** (= faithful Achates). A trusted friend.

■ Quotation from Virgil *Aeneid* vi.158. Achates was the loyal and trusted companion of the poem's hero, Aeneas.

fiesta *noun* M19 **Spanish** (= feast). In Spain or Spanish America: a religious festival; *generally*, any festivity or holiday.

figura *noun* plural **figurae** M20 **Latin** (= figure). **1** M20 *Theology* A type of a person. **2** M20 In literary use, a person who represents a higher or supervening reality. **b** An act that is representative or symbolic.

figurant *noun* (feminine **figurante**) L18 **French** (present participial adjective of *figurer* to figure). A supernumerary actor with a walk-on role in a theatrical performance.

■ A *figurant* was originally a ballet dancer; in the context of ballet now the term usually denotes a nondancing performer with a supporting role.

filé *noun* M19 **French** (past participle of *filer* twist). Powdered or pounded sassafras leaves used to flavor and thicken soup, especially gumbo.

■ Earliest use in *gumbo filé*.

filet *noun* L19 **French** (= net). A kind of net or lace with a square mesh.

filet de boeuf *noun phrase* M19 **French**. *Cooking* A fillet of beef; a tenderloin.

filet mignon *noun phrase* plural **filet mignons** E20 **French** (= small fillet). *Cooking* A slice cut from the small end of a fillet of beef.

filioque *noun* (also **Filioque**) M19 **Latin** (= and from the Son). *Christian Church* The statement in the Nicene Creed that the Holy Spirit proceeds not only from God the Father but also from the Son.

■ *Filioque* appeared as an addition to the Creed in the Western church in the sixth century, possibly originating in Spain. It gradually became a source of contention between the theologians of Rome and Constantinople, since it was accepted in the West but rejected by the Eastern Orthodox churches. After the failure of attempts to resolve the issue in the period immediately before the conquest of Constantinople by the Ottoman Turks, it remains an issue between Eastern and Western Christendom.

filius nullius *noun phrase* plural **filii nullius** M20 **Latin** (= son of nobody). An illegitimate son whose paternity is unacknowledged.

fille de joie *noun phrase* plural **filles de joie** E18 **French** (literally, 'girl of pleasure'). A prostitute.

fillette *noun* M19 **French**. A young girl.

film noir *noun phrase* plural **films noirs** M20 **French** (literally, 'black film'). A genre of cinematographic film of a pessimistic, cynical, and somber character; a film of this type.

■ The typical *film noir* was a black-and-white Hollywood movie of the late 1940s or early 1950s with gloomy lighting, a menacing urban setting, and a fatalistic loner as the antihero. The phrase is sometimes abbreviated to simply *noir*, with examples of the revival of the genre in the 1990s being dubbed *neo noir*.

filo see PHYLLO.

fils *noun* L19 **French** (= the son). The son, the younger, junior.

■ *Fils* is appended to a name to distinguish between father and son of the same name; cf. PÈRE.

filtre *noun* M20 **French**. A filtering appliance for making coffee, which allows boiling water to pass through ground coffee beans into a cup or pot; coffee made by this method.

fin (de) see FIN DE SIÈCLE.

finale *noun* M18 **Italian** (noun use of adjective from Latin *finalis* from *finis* end). **1** M18 The closing section of a musical, operatic, or dramatic performance. **2** L18 The conclusion.

finca *noun* E20 **Spanish** (from *fincar* to cultivate). In Spain and Spanish America: a country estate; a ranch.

fin de guerre *noun & adjective phrase* **French** (= end of war). (Designating or characteristic of) the end of a war.

fin de saison *noun & adjective phrase* M20 **French** (= end of season). (Designating or characteristic of) the end of a season.

fin de siècle *noun phrase* (also **fin-de-siècle**) plural **fins de siècle** L19 **French** (= end of century). (Designating or characteristic of) the final years of a century, especially the nineteenth century; decadent. Also *attributive* or as *adjective phrase*.

■ 'Fin de' is sometimes used jocularly in combination with an English word to make a phrase modeled on *fin de siècle*.

fine *noun* E20 **French** (abbreviation of FINE CHAMPAGNE). (A) French brandy; specifically, FINE CHAMPAGNE.

fine champagne *noun phrase* M19 **French** (= fine (brandy from) Champagne). Old liqueur brandy from the Grande Champagne and Petite Champagne vineyards in the Charente, France; an example, glass, or drink of this.

■ The abbreviation FINE is also found in English.

fines herbes *noun phrase plural* M19 **French** (= fine herbs). Fresh mixed herbs (usually parsley, tarragon, chervil, and chives) chopped and used in cooking.

■ Frequently used in adjective phrase with *aux*, as in *omelette aux fines herbes*.

finesse *noun & verb* LME **French. A** *noun* **1** LME Clarity, purity (especially of metals). **2** M16 Delicacy of manipulation or discrimination; refinement. **3** M16 Artfulness; cunning. **4** An artful stratagem; a ruse, a trick. **b** M19 *Cards* An attempt to take a trick with a card lower than but not in sequence with a card of the same suit also held. **B** *verb* **1** M18 *Cards* **a** *intransitive* Attempt to take a trick by a finesse. **b** *transitive* Play (a card) in a finesse. **2** *intransitive* L18 Use artifice or stratagem. **b** *transitive* Achieve by stratagem; bring about or manage by artful handling.

Fingerspitzengefühl *noun* L20 **German** (= fingertip feeling). Intuition; tact, deftness in handling a task or situation.

finis *noun* LME **Latin** (= end). **1** LME At the end of a book: the end. **2** L17 The finish, the conclusion; the end of life, death.

■ In the Latin tag *finis coronat opus* 'the end crowns the work', *finis* is used in sense 2.

fino *noun* plural **finos** M19 **Spanish** (= fine *adjective*). A type of pale-colored dry sherry; an example, glass, or drink of this.

finocchio *noun* (also **finochio**) E18 **Italian** (from a popular Latin variant of *faeniculum* fennel). A form of fennel with swollen leaf bases eaten as a vegetable.

fiord variant of FJORD.

fioritura *noun* plural **fioriture** M19 **Italian** (from *fiorire* to flower). *Music* An elaboration or decoration of a melody.

firn *noun* M19 **German** ('(snow) of the previous year', from Old High German *firni* old, related to Old Saxon *fern* past, *forn* formerly, Old Norse *forn* ancient). The granular snow on the upper part of a glacier that is in the process of being compressed into ice. Also called NÉVÉ.

fiumara *noun* E19 **Italian**. (The dried bed of) a mountain torrent.

fjeld *noun* M19 **Norwegian** (Bokm°l) (from Old Norse *fjall*). A high barren rocky plateau, especially in Scandinavia.

fjord *noun* (also **fiord**) L17 **Norwegian**. A long, narrow, deep inlet of the sea between steep cliffs, as on the Norwegian coast.

fl. abbreviation of FLORUIT.

flacon *noun* E19 **French**. A small stoppered bottle, *especially* one used to contain perfume.

flagellum *noun* plural **flagella** E19 **Latin** (diminutive of *flagrum* scourge). **1** E19 A whip. **2** M19 *Biology* A motile whiplike projection from a cell; also, in botany, a runner, a creeping shoot.

flageolet *noun 1* M17 **French**. *Music* **1** M17 A small wind instrument resembling a recorder, having six principal holes, including two for the thumb, and sometimes keys. **2** M19 An organ stop having a tone similar to that of this wind instrument.

flageolet *noun 2* L19 **French** (ultimately from Latin *phaseolus* bean). *Cooking* A small kind of (especially French) kidney bean, dried and used in cassoulets. Also *flageolet bean*.

flagrante delicto *adverb phrase* E19 **Latin.** IN FLAGRANTE DELICTO.

flambé *adjective & verb* L19 **French** (past participle of *flamber* singe, pass through flame). **A** *adjective* **1** L19 (Of a copper-based glaze) iridescent from the effects of a special firing process; (of a type of Chinese porcelain) characterized by such a glaze. **2** E20 *Cooking* Of food, set alight after being drenched in brandy or other liquor and served while still flaming. **B** *transitive verb* M20 Drench (food) in liquor and set alight.

flambeau *noun* plural **flambeaus, flambeaux** M17 **French** (diminutive of *flambe*, from Latin *flammula*, diminutive of *flamma* flame). **1** M17 A flaming torch. **2** L19 A large (branched) candlestick.

flamenco *noun & adjective* plural **flamencos** L19 **Spanish** (= Fleming). (Designating or pertaining to) a style of music played (especially on a guitar) and sung by Spanish gypsies; (a song or dance) to music in this style.

flâneur *noun* (also **flaneur**) M19 **French** (from *flâner* to lounge, saunter idly). An idler.

flautando *noun & adverb* E19 **Italian** (present participle of *flautare* to play the flute). *Music* (A direction: with) a flutelike violin tone.

flautato *noun & adverb* M19 **Italian** (literally, 'fluted'). FLAUTANDO.

flautino *noun* plural **flautinos**; in sense 2 also **flautina** E18 **Italian** (diminutive of *flauto* flute). **1** E18 A small flute or flageolet. **2** M19 A gemshorn organ stop of 2-ft. length and pitch.

flauto *noun* plural **flauti, flautos** E18 **Italian** (= flute). **1** E18 Originally, a recorder; later, a flute; also, the part played by such an instrument. **2** L19 An organ stop of flute scale.

■ The *flauto piccolo* was likewise formerly a small recorder, now a PICCOLO. Another instrument sometimes known under its Italian name is the side-blown flute, the *flauto traverso*.

flebile *adjective* E17 **Italian** (from Latin *flebilis* that is to be wept for; plaintive). *Music* Mournful.

flèche *noun* (also **fleche**) ME **French** (= arrow). **1** E18 *Fortification* A work in communication with the covered way, placed at the salient angle of the GLACIS. **2** M19 *Architecture* A slender spire, often of wood and rising from a roof. **3** M19 Any of the twenty-four points on a backgammon board. **4** E20 *Fencing* A running attack. In full *flèche attack*.

■ First (ME only) in its original French sense; reintroduced in the specialist applications above.

fléchette *noun* (also **flechette**) E20 **French** (diminutive of *flèche* arrow). *Military* A missile resembling a dart, dropped from an aircraft.

fleur-de-coin *noun phrase* L19 **French** (= bloom of the minting die). *Numismatics* Mint or perfect condition of a coin.

fleur-de-lis *noun phrase* (also **fleur-de-lys**) plural **fleurs-de-lis** ME **French** (Old French *flour de lys*, literally, 'flower of the lily'). (The flower of) any of various plants of the iris family; hence, the heraldic lily composed of three petals bound together near their bases and traditionally supposed to have represented an iris, especially as used as a device on the former royal arms of France.

fleuron *noun* LME **French.** A decorative motif in the form of a stylized flower, used especially in printing, architecture, or coinage.

flic *noun* L19 **French.** A French police officer. *slang.*

flicflac *noun* M19 **French** (imitative of a succession of sharp sounds). *Ballet* A lashing movement of the leg related to the FOUETTÉ.

flor. abbreviation of FLORUIT.

flora *noun* plural **floras, florae** E16 **Latin** (*flos* flower, plural *flora*; *Flora*, an ancient Italian goddess of fertility and flowers). **1** E16 The personification of nature's power to produce flowers. **2** L18 A catalog of the plants of a given area, with descriptions. **3** L18 The plants or plant life of a particular area, habitat, or epoch; cf. FAUNA.

floreat *noun* **Latin** (= may he/she/it flourish (3rd person singular present subjunctive of *florere* to flourish)). The expressed wish that someone or something may thrive and prosper; hence, a thriving and prospering.

■ Often used as an interjection, followed by the name of a person, institution, etc., as in *Floreat Etona!* 'May Eton flourish!'

flore pleno *adjective phrase* **L19 Latin** (literally, 'with full flower'). Double-flowered.

■ Used after the names of certain garden flowers that exist in both single- and double-flowered versions.

florilegium *noun* plural **florilegia**, **florilegiums** **E17 Modern Latin** (literally, 'bouquet', from Latin *flori-* combining form of *flos* flower + *legere* to gather, translating Greek *anthologion* anthology). A collection of choice extracts from literature; an anthology.

floruit *noun* **M19 Latin** (= he/she/it flourished (3rd person singular perfect indicative of *florere* to flourish)). The period during which a person flourished; heyday, period of greatest activity or prosperity.

■ Often abbreviated to *fl.* or *flor.* and used in cases where a person's birth and death dates are unknown or uncertain.

flota *noun* **L17 Spanish** (= fleet). *History* The Spanish fleet that used regularly to cross the Atlantic during the colonial period to bring back the products of America and the West Indies.

flotilla *noun* **E18 Spanish** (diminutive of *flota* fleet). A small fleet; a fleet of small vessels.

flügelhorn *noun* (also **fluegelhorn**, **flugelhorn**, **flugel horn**) **M19 German** (*Flügelhorn*, from *Flügel* wing + *horn* horn). A brass wind instrument with a cup-shaped mouthpiece and a wide conical bore.

■ Also abbreviated to *flugel.*

focaccia *noun* plural **focacce** **L20 Italian**. Italian bread made with olive oil and sometimes herbs.

focus *noun & verb* plural **foci**, **focuses** **M17 Latin** (= domestic hearth). **A** *noun* **1** L17 *Physics* The adjustment (of a lens, the eye, etc.) to produce a well-defined image; the state of producing a well-defined image thus. **2** M18 The center of greatest interest, attraction, activity, or energy. **B** **1** *transitive verb* L18 Make converge to or as to a focus; bring into focus; concentrate *on.* **2** *intransitive verb* M19 Converge to or as to a focus; come into focus; concentrate *on.*

■ *Focus* was apparently first used in this Modern Latin sense by Kepler in his *Astronomia pars optica*, written in 1604, and it is conjectured that the technical sense of *focus* as 'the burning point of a lens or mirror' (which is easily derived from the literal one) was already current in technical Latin. It was introduced into English in similar technical contexts, first as a term in plane geometry by Hobbes, and then into physics by Boyle in its 'burning point' sense. The plural form *foci* is generally confined to the noun's more technical senses.

foetus see FETUS.

föhn *noun* (also **foehn**) **M19 German** (in Old High German *phonno*, Middle High German *foenne*, ultimately from Latin *(ventus) Favonius* mild west wind). **1** M19 A warm dry south wind that blows down valleys on the north side of the Alps. **2** L19 *Meteorology* A warm dry katabatic wind developing on the lee side of a mountain range as a result of air moving across the range. Also *föhn wind.*

foie gras *noun phrase* (also **foie-gras**) **E19 French**. Abbreviation of PÂTÉ DE FOIE GRAS.

folie *noun* **E19 French** (= madness). Mental illness, mania.

■ Now chiefly in names of pathological mental states (see following entries).

folie à deux *noun phrase* E20 French. An identical mental disorder or illusion affecting two closely associated people; *loosely* a shared act of folly between two people.

folie de grandeur *noun phrase* (also **folie des grandeurs**) L19 French. Delusions of grandeur or importance.

folie du doute *noun phrase* L19 French. Obsessive self-doubt.

fonctionnaire *noun* L20 French. In France: a national or local government employee; a civil servant.

fondant *noun* L19 French (noun use of present participle of *fondre* to melt). *Cooking* A candy made of a soft paste of flavored (and usually colored) sugar; such a paste used in candies and icings.

fondue *noun* M19 French (feminine past participle of *fondre*; cf. FONDANT). *Cooking* A dish of flavored melted cheese, a specialty in the Swiss Alpine region; any dish in which small pieces of food are cooked, usually at table, by being dipped into boiling oil or liquid.

fons et origo *noun phrase* E19 Latin. The source and origin *of*.

■ Earliest use is in the phrase *fons et origo mali* the source and origin of evil.

foo yong variant of FU YUNG.

force de frappe *noun phrase* plural **forces de frappe** M20 French. *Military* A striking force; especially, the French independent nuclear capability.

force majeure *noun phrase* L19 French (= superior strength). Irresistible force, overwhelming circumstances or opposition; in *Law* or *Commerce* an unforeseeable sequence of events excusing the fulfillment of a contract.

forma pauperis *noun phrase* L16 Latin (literally, 'the form of a poor person'). *Law* (The condition of) a poor person in respect of being able to bring a legal action without payment; *figuratively* humbly, in supplication.

■ Also frequently in *in forma pauperis* or *sub forma pauperis* as a poor person.

Formgeschichte *noun* E20 German (from *Form* form + *Geschichte* history). Textual analysis, especially of the Bible, by tracing the history of its content of proverbs, myths, and other forms; form criticism.

forte *noun 1* M17 French (use as noun of feminine of *fort* strong). **1** M17 *Fencing* The stronger part of a sword blade, from the hilt to the middle. **2** L17 The strong point of a person; the thing in which one excels.

■ The word entered English in its masculine form *fort*, but the feminine form *forte* was later substituted. The pronunciation of the word as one syllable follows this French form, but the modern pronunciation as two syllables (for-TAY) has been influenced by Italian *forte* (see next). Both are now considered standard.

forte *adverb, adjective, & noun 2* E18 Italian (= strong, loud, from Latin *fortis* strong). *Music* **A** *adverb & adjective* E18 (A direction:) loud(ly). **B** *noun* M18 A loud tone or passage.

■ As a direction, usually abbreviated to *f*.

forte-piano *noun, adverb, & adjective* M18 Italian. *Music* **A** *noun* M18 An early form of the pianoforte. **B** *adverb & adjective* L19 (A direction:) loud(ly) and then immediately soft(ly).

■ As a musical instrument often aphetized to PIANO (*noun* 2); as a musical direction, usually abbreviated to *fp*.

fortissimo *adverb, adjective, & noun* E18 Italian (superlative of FORTE loud(ly)). *Music* **A** *adverb & adjective* E18 (A direction:) very loud(ly). **B** *noun* plural **fortissimos, fortissimi** M19 A very loud tone or passage.

■ As direction, usually abbreviated to *ff*.

forum *noun* plural **forums**, **fora** LME **Latin** (related to *fores* (outside) door, originally an enclosure surrounding a house). **1** LME *Roman Antiquity* The public place or marketplace of a city; the place of assembly for judicial and civic business. **b** M18 A place of or meeting for public discussion; a periodical, etc., that provides an opportunity for conducting a debate. **2** L17 A court, a tribunal. Also *figurative*.

forzando *adverb & adjective* E19 **Italian** (from *forzare* to force). *Music* (A direction:) with force or emphasis; SFORZANDO.

foudroyant *adjective* M19 **French** (present participle of *foudroyer* to strike (as) with lightning, from *foudre* from Latin *fulgur* lightning). **1** M19 Thunderous, noisy. Also, dazzling. **2** L19 Of a disease, beginning suddenly and in a very severe form.

fouetté *noun* M19 **French** (past participle of *fouetter* to whip). *Ballet* A movement in which a dancer pivots on one *pointe* and executes a rapid whiplike movement with the lower part of free leg.

foulard *noun* M19 **French**. **1** M19 A lightweight printed or checked material of silk or silk and cotton. **2** L19 A headscarf or neckerchief made from this.

foulé *noun* L19 **French** (= pressed (cloth), past participle of *fouler* to full). A light woolen dress material with a fibrous appearance.

fourchette *noun* M18 **French**. **1** M18 Something forked or resembling a fork. **2** M19 A forked object, device, or instrument; the forked piece between two adjacent fingers of a glove. **3** L19 In any of several card games, a combination of cards immediately above and immediately below the card led.

fou rire *noun phrase* E20 **French** (literally, 'mad laughter'). (A fit of) wild or uncontrollable laughter.

fourreau *noun* plural **fourreaux** L19 **French** (literally, 'sheath, scabbard'). A close-fitting dress; an underskirt forming part of a dress.

foyer *noun* L18 **French** (= hearth, home, ultimately from Latin *focus* hearth). **1** L18 A center of activity; a focus. **2** M19 A large room in a theater, concert hall, etc., for the use of the audience during intermission; also, the entrance hall of a hotel or other public building.

■ Sense 1 is now uncommon, with *foyer* having been generally superseded by FOCUS in this sense.

fp abbreviation of FORTE-PIANO (musical direction).

fracas *noun* plural same E18 **French** (from *fracasser* from Italian *fracassare* to make an uproar). A disturbance, an uproar, a row.

Fraktur *noun* (also **fraktur**) L19 **German**. *Typography* A German style of black-letter type, the normal type used for printing German from the sixteenth to the mid–twentieth century.

framboise *noun & adjective* L16 **French** (ultimately from a conflation of Latin *fraga ambrosia* ambrosian strawberry). **A** *adjective* E20 Of raspberry color. **B** *noun* M20 A shade of pink; raspberry color.

■ *Framboise* in its original sense of 'raspberry' was current in English only in the sixteenth and seventeenth centuries.

franc fort *noun phrase* L20 **French** (= strong franc). *Economics* The French monetary policy devoted to maintaining the value of the French franc at a high level among international currencies.

franco *adjective & adverb* L19 **Italian** (*(porto) franco* free carriage). Of a foreign business transaction, free of any postal or delivery charge.

franc tireur *noun phrase* plural **francs tireurs** E19 **French** (= free shooter). An irregular soldier, a guerrilla fighter; *historically* a member of an irregular French light infantry corps.

franglais *noun* (also **Franglais**) M20 **French** (blend of *français* French + *anglais* English). A nonstandard version of the French language characterized by indiscriminate use of words and phrases taken from British and American English.

■ The problem, as perceived by the French, of their language being sullied by the influx of Anglo-Saxon words was aired under this name in R. Etiemble's *Parlez-vous Franglais* (1964). Despite various campaigns to exclude them, interlopers such as *le weekend* appear firmly entrenched and likely to remain.

frankfurter *noun* (also **frankfurt**) L19 **German** (*Frankfurter Wurst* Frankfurt sausage). A seasoned sausage made of smoked beef and pork, originally made at Frankfurt am Main in Germany.

frappé *adjective & noun* **M19 French** (past participle of *frapper* in the sense of 'to ice (drinks)'). **A** *adjective* M19 (Chiefly of wine) iced, chilled; (of a drink) served with crushed ice. **B** *noun* E20 A drink (especially coffee) served with crushed ice or partially frozen to a slushy consistency.

Frau *noun* (also **frau**) plural **Frauen**, **Fraus** **E19 German**. A German or Austrian woman.

■ Also used as a title, corresponding to *Mrs.*

Frauendienst *noun* **M20 German** (*frauen* women + *dienst* service). Exaggerated chivalry toward women.

■ The word derives from the medieval tradition of courtly love, specifically the title of the mid-thirteenth century *Frauendienst* of Ulrich von Lichtenstein (d. *c.*1275), in which the writer describes the extraordinary tasks required of him by his mistress.

Fräulein *noun* (also **fraulein**) L17 **German** (diminutive of FRAU). An unmarried German woman; a German governess.

■ Also used as a title, corresponding to *Miss.*

frazil *noun* **L19 Canadian French** (*frasil* = snow floating on water; cf. French *fraisil* cinders). Slush consisting of small ice crystals formed in water too turbulent to freeze solid. Also *frazil ice.*

fresco *noun & verb* **L16 Italian** (= cool, fresh). **A** *noun* plural **frescos, frescoes** L16 A method of painting by which watercolor is applied to damp, freshly laid plaster, so that the colors penetrate and become fixed as the plaster dries. **2** L17 A painting produced by this method. **B** *transitive verb* E19 Paint in fresco.

■ Earliest English use in the phrase *in fresco*, representing Italian *affresco* or *al fresco* 'on the fresh (plaster)'.

fresco buono *noun phrase* **M19 Italian** (= good fresco). FRESCO sense A. Also *buon fresco* (L19).

fresco secco *noun phrase* **M19 Italian** (= dry fresco). The process or technique of painting on dry plaster with colors mixed with water.

■ Sometimes abbreviated to *secco* (M19).

fricandeau *noun & verb* **E18 French**. **A** *noun* plural **fricandeaux** E18 *Cooking* (A slice of) veal or other meat fried or stewed and served with sauce; an escalope; a fricassee of veal. **B** *transitive verb* M18 Make into fricandeaux.

fricassee *noun & verb* **M16 French** (*fricassée* feminine past participle of *fricasser* to cut up and stew in sauce). **A** *noun* M16 *Cooking* Meat sliced and fried or stewed and served with sauce, especially a ragout of game. **B** *transitive verb* M17 Make a fricassee of.

frigidarium *noun* plural **frigidariums, frigidaria** **E18 Latin** (from *frigidus*, from *frigere* to be cold, from *frigus* cold). The room in Roman baths containing the final, cold bath.

frijoles *noun plural* **L16 Spanish** (plural of *frijol* bean, ultimately from Latin *phaseolus*). *Cooking* Especially in Mexico, a dish of beans.

frisé *adjective* **L19 French** (past participle of *friser* to curl). Of or designating a pile fabric with cut and uncut loops forming a pattern, chiefly used in upholstery.

frisée *noun* L20 **French** ((feminine) past participle of *friser* to curl). Curly endive.

■ Abbreviation of French *chicorée frisée.*

frisson *noun* L18 **French** (= shiver, thrill). An emotional thrill; a shiver of excitement.

frittata *noun* L20 **Italian**. An omelette.

fritto misto *noun phrase* E20 **Italian** (= mixed fry). *Cooking* A dish of mixed foods, especially seafood, deep-fried in batter.

froideur *noun* L20 **French** (from *froid* cold). Coldness; lack of warmth.

■ Only in figurative use.

fromage blanc *noun phrase* L20 **French** (= white cheese). *Cooking* A fresh soft white cheese.

fromage frais *noun phrase* L20 **French** (= fresh cheese). *Cooking* A soft curd cheese, often used as a basis for desserts.

■ In France this type of cheese is generally known as PETIT SUISSE.

fronde *noun* (usually **Fronde** in sense 1) L18 **French** (literally, 'sling'). **1** L18 *French History* A political party in France during the mid-seventeenth century, which initiated violent uprisings against the administration of Cardinal Mazarin during the minority of Louis XIV. **2** E19 *transferred* A malcontent or disaffected party; violent political opposition.

frondeur *noun* (usually **Frondeur** in sense 1) L18 **French** (from FRONDE). **1** L18 *French History* A participant in the Fronde. **2** M19 *transferred* A malcontent; a political rebel.

fronton *noun* L17 **French** (from Italian *frontone*, augmentative of *fronte* forehead; in sense 2 Spanish *frontón*). **1** L17 *Architecture* A pediment. **2** L19 A building in which pelota is played.

froom variant of FRUM.

frottage *noun* M20 **French** (= rubbing, friction). **1** M20 The practice of rubbing against or touching the (clothed) body of another person (usually in a crowd) as a means of obtaining sexual gratification. **2** M20 *Art* The technique or process of taking a rubbing from an uneven surface, such as grained wood, as a basis for a work of art.

frotteur *noun* L19 **French**. A person who indulges in FROTTAGE (sense 1).

frottola *noun* plural **frottole** M19 **Italian** (literally, 'fib, tall story'). *Music* A form of Italian comic or amorous song, especially from the fifteenth and sixteenth centuries.

frou-frou *noun* L19 **French** (imitative). A continuous soft rustling sound, esp. of skirts; hence, frills and frippery. *verb* E20 Move with a rustle of fabric. Also *attributive.*

fruits de mer *noun phrase* M20 **French** (= fruits of the sea). *Cooking* Seafood, especially a dish made up of mixed shellfish.

frum *adjective* (also **froom**) L19 **Yiddish** (from Middle High German *vrum* zealous; cf. German *fromm* pious). Pious, religious (used especially of an orthodox Jew).

frustum *noun* (also **frustrum**) plural **frustums**, **frusta** M17 **Latin** (= piece cut off). *Mathematics* The portion of a solid figure, such as a cone, that remains after the upper part has been cut off by a plane parallel to the base.

fuehrer variant of FÜHRER.

fugato *adverb, adjective, & noun* M19 **Italian** (= fugued, from *fuga* FUGUE). *Music* **A** *adverb & adjective* M19 In the fugue style, but not in strict or complete fugue form. **B** *noun* plural **fugatos** L19 A passage in this style.

fughetta *noun* L19 **Italian** (diminutive of *fuga* fugue). *Music* A short condensed fugue.

fugu *noun* M20 **Japanese**. A type of puffer fish, renowned as a Japanese delicacy.

fugue *noun* L16 **French** (or, its source, Italian *fuga*, from Latin *fuga* flight). **1** L16 *Music* A polyphonic composition in which a short melodic theme, the subject, is introduced by one part or voice, and successively taken up by the others and developed by their interweaving. **2** E20 *Psychiatry* A flight from or loss of awareness of one's own identity, sometimes involving wandering away from home, and often occurring as a reaction to shock or emotional distress.

führer *noun* (also **fuehrer**) **M20 German** (= leader). A (ruthless or tyrannical) leader; a dictator.

■ Hitler, in his role as leader of the Third Reich, is often alluded to under his assumed title of *the* (or) *die Führer*, and the transferred use of the word in English usually has strongly negative implications.

führerprinzip *noun* **M20 German** (literally, 'leader principle'). The doctrine that a FÜHRER has a right to command and the people a duty to obey.

■ Also partially Anglicized as *führer principle*.

fulcrum *noun* plural **fulcra**, **fulcrums** **L17 Latin** (= post or foot of couch, from base of *fulcire* to prop up, support). **1** A prop or support; now specifically, the point against which a lever is placed to get purchase or on which it turns or is supported. **2** L17 *figurative* The means by which or source from which influence, etc., is brought to bear.

functus officio *predicative adjective phrase* plural **functi officio** **M19 Latin** (= having discharged an office). *Law* Free from further obligations, having discharged its (or their) duty.

fungus *noun* plural **fungi funguses** **LME Latin** (probably from Greek *sphoggos*, *spoggos* sponge). **1** LME Any of a large division of organisms including mushrooms, that lack chlorophyll and grow on, or obtain nutrients from, organic matter. **b** M18 *figurative* Something growing or spreading rapidly. **2** L17 Soft or spongy diseased tissue. **3** E20 *slang* A growth of facial hair, a beard.

furioso *noun, adjective, & adverb* **M17 Italian** (from Latin *furiosus* enraged, furious). **A** *noun* plural **furiosos** M17 A furious person. **B** *adjective & adverb* E19 *Music* (A direction:) furious(ly), wild(ly).

furor (also *Brit.* **furore**) *noun* **L18 Italian** (from Latin *furor*, from *furere* to rage). **1** L18 Enthusiastic admiration; a craze. **2** M20 (An) uproar, (a) fuss.

furor academicus *noun phrase* **M20 Latin**. Academic frenzy; excessive excitement provoked by or over an intellectual issue.

furor poeticus *noun phrase* **E20 Latin**. Poetic frenzy; emotional overenthusiasm.

furor scribendi *noun phrase* **M19 Latin** (= frenzy of writing). An irresistible urge to write.

fusain *noun* **L19 French** (= spindle tree, charcoal). *Art* Artists' charcoal (made from the wood of the spindle tree); a charcoal drawing.

fusee *noun* **L16 French** (*fusée* spindleful, ultimately from Latin *fusus* spindle). **1** E17 *Horology* A conical pulley onto which a chain is wound so as to equalize the power of the mainspring in a mechanical watch or clock. **2** M17 A detonating device; a fuse. **3** M19 A large-headed match for lighting a cigar or pipe.

fuselage *noun* **E20 French** (from *fuseler* to shape like spindle, from *fuseau* spindle). The elongated body section of an aircraft in which the crew and passengers or cargo are carried.

fusillade *noun & verb* **E19 French** (from *fusiller* to shoot). **A** *noun* E19 (Wholesale slaughter by) a simultaneous or successive discharge of firearms; *figurative* a sustained barrage of criticism, etc. **B** *transitive verb* E19 Assault or shoot down with a fusillade.

fusilli *noun plural* **L20 Italian**. Pasta in the shape of small twists or spirals.

fustanella *noun* **M19 Italian** (from Modern Greek *phoustani*, *phoustanela*, Albanian *fustan*, probably from Italian *fustagno* fustian). A stiff white kilt formerly worn by men in Albania and Greece and still part of Greek ceremonial military dress.

futon *noun* (also **futong**) **L19 Japanese**. In Japan: a cotton-stuffed mattress rolled out over a mat on the floor for use as a bed; more generally, a low-slung Japanese-style bed or mattress.

■ The word has occurred in accounts of Japanese culture since the nineteenth century, but its introduction as a fashionable item of Western furniture dates from the 1980s. In modern Western furnishing the futon often includes a slatted wooden base capable of conversion into a seat by day.

fu yung *noun phrase* (also **foo yong**) M20 **Chinese** (Cantonese *foo yung*, literally, 'hibiscus'). *Cooking* A Chinese dish made with eggs mixed and cooked with vegetables and other ingredients.

gabelle *noun* LME **French** (from Italian *gabella* corresponding to Spanish *alcavala*). Chiefly *History* A tax, *especially* a foreign tax; *specifically* the salt tax imposed in France before the Revolution.

gabion *noun* M16 **French** (from Italian *gabbione* augmentative of *gabbia* cage). A cylinder of wicker or woven metal bands to be filled with earth or stones for use in engineering or (*historical*) fortification.

gaffe *noun* (also **gaff**) E20 **French**. A blunder, a clumsy or indiscreet act or remark.

gaga *adjective & noun* (also **ga-ga**) E20 **French**. **A** *adjective* E20 Senile; mad, crazy; foolish, fatuous. **B** *noun* M20 A senile or foolish person. *slang*.

gagaku *noun* M20 **Japanese** (from *ga* refined, graceful, noble + *gaku* music). A traditional type of (chiefly ceremonial) Japanese music.

gage d'amour *noun phrase* plural **gages d'amour** M18 **French**. A pledge of love; a love token.

gaieté de coeur *noun phrase* E18 **French**. Lightheartedness, playfulness.

gaijin *noun & adjective* M20 **Japanese** (contraction of *gaikoku-jin*, from *gaikaku* foreign country + *jin* person). **A** *noun* M20 plural same. In Japan: a foreigner, an alien. **B** M20 *attributive* or as *adjective* Foreign, alien (to the Japanese).

gala *noun* E17 **French** (or its source in Italian from Spanish from Old French *gale* merrymaking). **1** E17 Fine or showy dress. Now only in *in gala*. **2** E18–E19 Festivity, rejoicing. **3** M18 A festive occasion; a festival characterized by finery and display; a special theatrical or other performance.

galabiya *noun* (also **galabieh**, **gallabiya**, and many other variants) E18 **Arabic** (Egyptian variant of Arabic *jallābiyya*). A long loose garment worn in Arabic-speaking Mediterranean countries, especially in Egypt.

galant *adjective* L19 **French and German**. **1** L19 *Music* Designating or pertaining to a light and elegant style of eighteenth-century music. **2** L20 Courteous, attentive to women.

galanterie *noun* plural **galanteries**, (*in sense 1 also with German plural*) **galanterien** E20 **French** (or (sense 1) German). **1** E20 *Music* A light nonessential movement in an early eighteenth-century classical suite. **2** E20 Courtesy, politeness, especially to women.

■ *Galanterie* in its obsolete sense of 'splendor' or 'a display of magnificence' was introduced earlier (E17), but it did not displace the Anglicized form *gallantry* which was also formerly (L16–E19) used in this sense. The current senses represent a reintroduction.

galère *noun* M18 **French** (= galley). A coterie; a (usually undesirable) group of people; an unpleasant situation.

■ The primary literal sense of *galère* as 'a ship powered by oars' in which criminals were condemned to be rowers explains its use as a metaphor for a disagreeable situation or bad company. The figurative use is a reference to Molière's *Scapin* (II xi) "Que diable allait-il faire dans cette galère?"

galette *noun* L18 **French**. A broad thin cake usually of pastry.

Galgenhumor *noun* (also **galgenhumor**) E20 **German** (from *Galgen* gallows + *Humor* humor). Grim, ironic humor.

■ Also (E20) in the English form *gallows humor*.

galipot *noun* L18 **French** (*galipot, garipot*: cf. Provençal *garapot* pine tree resin). A kind of hardened turpentine formed on the stem of the cluster pine.

gallabiya variant of GALABIYA.

galleria *noun* L19 **Italian**. A shopping arcade in an Italian city or designed in imitation of one of these.

■ The idea of the shopping arcade on the Italian *galleria* principle became fashionable among urban architects in the English-speaking world during the 1960s, but the word *galleria* only became a fashionable synonym for 'arcade' in the 1980s. The term is also applied to small shops within a store.

gallinazo *noun* plural **gallinazos** M18 **Spanish** (from Latin *gallina* hen). In Latin America: a turkey buzzard or other vulture.

galop *noun* M19 **French**. A lively ballroom dance in 2/4 time; a piece of music for this dance.

galpon *noun* L19 **American Spanish** (*galpón* from Nahuatl *calpulli* large hall). A large building like a barn on a South American farm.

gamba *noun 1* (also **gambo**) L16 **Italian** (= leg; short for VIOLA DA GAMBA). **1** L16 A VIOLA DA GAMBA. **2** M19 An organ stop resembling a violin or cello in tone. Also *gamba stop*.

gamba *noun 2* M20 **Spanish**. A kind of shrimp, *Palaemon serratus*, as an article of food.

gamelan *noun* E19 **Javanese**. An Indonesian, especially Javanese or Balinese, orchestra consisting mainly of percussion instruments.

gamin *noun & adjective* M19 **French**. **A** *noun* M19 A street urchin, a waif; a streetwise or impudent child. **B** *adjective* M19 Of, pertaining to, resembling, or characteristic of a gamin.

gamine *noun & adjective* L19 **French**. **A** *noun* L19 A female gamin; a small, attractively informal, mischievous, or elfish young woman. **B** *adjective* E20 Of, pertaining to, resembling, or characteristic of a gamine.

gaminerie *noun* E20 **French**. The behavior or characteristics of a gamin or gamine.

gamma *noun* LME **Latin** (from Greek). **1** LME The third letter (Γ, γ) of the Greek alphabet. **2** E17–E19 *Music* Gamut. **3** L17 Denoting the third in a numerical sequence: *attributively Science* Frequently written γ, as in *Astronomy* (preceding the genitive of the Latin name of the constellation) denoting the third brightest star in a constellation; *Chemistry* denoting the third of a number of isomeric forms of a compound, or of allotropes of an element, etc.; *Physics* designating high-energy electromagnetic radiation that consists of photons of wavelengths shorter than those of X rays. **4** M20 *Brit.* A third-class mark in an examination, etc. **5** M19 The silver Y, *Plusia gamma*. More fully *gamma moth*. **6** E20 A unit of magnetic field strength equal to 10^{-5} oersted. **b** M20 A unit of mass equal to 10^{-6} gram. **7** E20 *Photography* and *Television* A measure of the contrast of an image compared with that of the scene represented.

gammadion *noun* M19 **Late Greek** (from GAMMA). An arrangement of shapes of capital gamma (Γ), especially of four, as a swastika or a hollow Greek cross.

ganbei *interjection* (also **kan-pei**) M20 **Chinese** (*gānbēi*, from *gān* empty, dry + *bēi* glass, cup). (A Chinese toast:) a call to drain one's glass.

ganbu *noun* (also **kanpu**) M20 **Chinese** (*gànbù*). In the People's Republic of China: an officeholder in a military or governmental organization; a CADRE.

gandharva *noun* (also **gandharba**) L18 **Sanskrit** (*gandharvās*; perhaps connected with Greek *kentauros* centaur). *Hindu Mythology* Any of a class of minor deities or genii of the sky, often represented as celestial musicians.

gandoura *noun* (also **gandourah**, **gandura(h)**) M19 **Arabic** (Algerian *gandūra*, variant of classical Arabic *kandūra*). A long loose gown worn mainly in the Near East and North Africa.

gangue *noun* E19 **French** (from German *Gang* way, course, vein or lode of metal). The valueless or unwanted components of an ore deposit.

ganja *noun* (also **ganga**) E19 **Hindi** (*gājā*). A strong preparation of marijuana, used chiefly for smoking.

ganosis *noun* E20 **Greek** (*ganōsis*, from *ganos* brightness, from *ganoun* to polish). The process of applying a wax polish to the white marble surface of a statue or occasionally to some other surface in order to give warmth to its appearance.

gaon *noun* plural **gaons**, **geonim** L18 **Hebrew** (*gā'ōn* excellence, pride). (An honorific for) a head of a Jewish academy in Babylonia, Palestine, Syria, or Egypt, from the sixth to the eleventh centuries. Later, especially in Spain, France, Italy, and Lithuania, an outstanding Talmudic scholar. Also *generally*, a genius, a prodigy.

garam masala *noun phrase* M20 **Urdu** (*garam maṣālā*). A spice mixture used in Indian cooking.

garbanzo *noun* plural **garbanzos** M18 **Spanish**. A chickpea.

garçon *noun* E17 **French**. A waiter, a male servant, especially in a French hotel or restaurant.

garconnière *noun* E20 **French**. A bachelor's set of rooms or apartment.

garde champêtre *noun phrase* plural **gardes champêtres** E19 **French** (literally, 'rural guard'). In France: a rural police officer; a gamekeeper.

gare *noun* M19 **French**. **1** M19 A dock basin on a river or canal. Also, a pier, a wharf. **2** L19 In France and French-speaking countries: a railroad station.

gare *intransitive verb (imperative)* M17 **French** (imperative of *garer* to shelter). Look out! Beware! Take care.

gargouillade *noun* M20 **French** (from *gargouiller* to bubble, gurgle). *Ballet* A series of steps in which the left leg describes two circular movements in the air, before the left foot is drawn up to the right knee.

garigue *noun* (also **garrigue**) L19 **French**. In the south of France: uncultivated land of a calcareous soil overgrown with low scrub; the vegetation found on such land.

garimpeiro *noun* M19 **Portuguese**. In Brazil: an independent prospector for diamonds, gold, etc.

garrigue variant of GARIGUE.

garrocha *noun* M19 **Spanish**. A goad, *especially* (in bullfighting) a short-pointed spear.

garuda *noun* L19 **Sanskrit** (*garuḍa*). *Indian Mythology* A fabulous bird, half eagle, half man, ridden by the god Vishnu.

garum *noun* L16 **Latin** (from Greek *garon*, earlier *garos*). *History* A sauce made from fermented fish, popular in ancient Rome; this sauce used as a medicine for horses.

gaseosa *noun* E20 **Spanish**. Soda; (a drink of) carbonated (mineral) water.

gaspacho variant of GAZPACHO.

Gastarbeiter *noun* plural **Gastarbeiters**, same M20 **German** (from *Gast* guest + *Arbeiter* worker). A person with temporary permission to work in another (especially western European) country.

Gasthaus *noun* plural **Gasthäuser** M19 **German** (from *Gast* guest + *Haus* house). A small inn or hotel in a German-speaking country.

Gasthof *noun* plural **gasthofs**, **Gasthöfe** M19 **German** (from *Gast* guest + *Hof* hotel, large house). A German hotel, usually larger than a GASTHAUS.

gateau *noun* (also **gâteau**) plural **gateaux**, **gateaus** M19 **French** (*gâteau* cake). A large rich cake, *especially* one with layers of cream or fruit eaten as a dessert.

■ The word also applies to other recipes, such as a *gâteau de riz* (= of rice) (M19) a rich rice dessert in the shape of a cake, or to meat or fish baked and served in the form of a cake (L19); both usages are now rare.

gauche *adjective* M18 **French** (literally, 'left(-handed)'). **1** M18 Lacking in tact or ease of manner, awkward, blundering; lacking in subtlety or skill, crude, unsophisticated. **2** L19 *Mathematics* Skew, not plane. *archaic*. **b** M20 *Chemistry* Of a molecular conformation: skew, having two groups staggered along a central axis by (about) 60 degrees.

gaucherie *noun* L18 **French** (from *gauche*; see preceding). Gauche or awkward manner; a gauche action.

gaucho *noun* plural **gauchos** E19 **American Spanish** (probably from Araucanian *kauču*). A mounted herdsman of the South American pampas, usually of mixed European and American Indian descent.

gavotte *noun* L17 **French** (from modern Provençal *gavoto*, from *Gavot* an inhabitant of the Alps). **1** L17 A medium-paced dance popular in the eighteenth century. **2** E18 A piece of music for this dance, composed in common time with each phrase beginning on the third beat of the bar; a piece of music in this rhythm, *especially* one that forms a movement of a suite.

gazette *noun & verb* (also **Gazette**) E17 **French** (or its source Italian *gazzetta*, originally Venetian *gazeta de la novità*, i.e., a 'halfpennyworth of news', so called because sold for a *gazeta*, a Venetian coin of small value). **A** *noun* **1** E17 Originally, a news sheet; a periodical publication giving an account of current events. Now, a newspaper, *especially* (the title of) the official newspaper of an organization or institution. **2** M17 *specifically* (The title of) an official journal in Britain containing lists of government appointments, bankruptcies, and other public notices; an official journal of any government. **B** *transitive verb* L17 Publish in a gazette. Usually in *passive*, be the subject of an announcement in an official gazette, *especially* be named as appointed *to* a post, command, etc.

gazon coupé *noun phrase* L20 **French** (= cut lawn, cut turf). A garden feature comprising an area of grass out of which a design is cut and filled with a contrasting material such as colored gravel.

gazpacho *noun* (also **gaspacho**) plural **gazpachos**, E19 **Spanish**. A Spanish soup made from tomatoes, peppers, cucumber, garlic, etc., and served cold.

Gebrauchsmusik *noun* M20 **German** (from *Gebrauch* use + *Musik* music). Music intended primarily for practical use and performance; *especially* music considered suitable for amateur groups and domestic playing.

Gedankenexperiment *noun* M20 **German** (from *Gedanken* thought + *Experiment* experiment). An experiment conducted in the imagination only; a thought experiment.

gefilte fish *noun phrase* (also **gefüllte fish**) L19 **Yiddish** (= stuffed fish, from *gefilte* inflected past participle of *filn* to fill). A dish either of stewed or baked stuffed fish or of fish cakes boiled in a fish or vegetable broth.

gelato *noun* (also) plural **gelati**, **gelatos** L20 **Italian**. An ice cream.

■ Originally in Italy and Italian-speaking countries and now also United States.

Gelehrte *noun* (also **Gelehrter**) plural **Gelehrten** M19 **German** (from *gelehrt* learned, *lehren* to instruct). A learned (German) person; a scholar; a savant.

Gemeinschaft *noun* M20 **German** (from *gemein* common, general + *-schaft* -ship). *Sociology* A form of social integration based on personal ties; community. Cf. GESELLSCHAFT.

gemshorn *noun* E19 **German** (literally, 'chamois horn'). *Music* A light-toned organ stop.

gemütlich *adjective* (also **gemutlich**) M19 **German**. Pleasant, cheerful; cozy, snug, homely; genial, good-natured.

Gemütlichkeit *noun* M19 **German** (cf. preceding). The quality of being *gemütlich*; geniality; coziness; cheerfulness.

gendarme *noun* plural **gendarmes**, (now *historical*) **gens d'armes** M16 **French** (a singular from the plural (now *historical*) *gens d'armes* men of arms). **1** M16 In the older French army, a horseman in full armor, having several others under his command; later, a mounted trooper, especially of the royal companies. Usually in *plural; obsolete* except *historical*. **2** L18 In France and French-speaking countries: a police officer; originally a member of a military force employed in policing. **b** E20 *generally* A police officer. *slang*.

gendarmerie *noun* (also **gendarmery**) M16 **French** (from *gendarme*; see preceding). **1** M16 *History* A body of cavalry, especially in the older French army. **2** L18 In France and French-speaking countries: a body of police officers, a police force. **b** M20 A police station.

gêne *noun* E19 **French** (from Old French *gehine* torture). Constraint, embarrassment, discomfort.

gêné *adjective* (feminine **gênée**) E19 **French** (past participial adjective of *gêner* to embarrass: related to preceding). Constrained, embarrassed, discomforted.

genera plural of GENUS.

generalia *noun plural* M19 **Latin** (neuter plural of *generalis* general). General principles.

generalissimo *noun* plural **generalissimos** E17 **Italian** (superlative of *generale* general). The commander of a combined military, naval, and air force, or of several armies.

genesis *noun* LOE **Latin** (from Greek = generation, creation, nativity, horoscope, from base of *gignesthai* to be born or produced). **1** LOE (**Genesis**) (The name of) the first book of the Bible. **2** E17 Origin, mode of formation or generation.

■ *Genesis* is the name given in the Septuagint to the first book of the Old Testament, dealing with the creation of the world; from there it was adopted by the Vulgate and vernacular Bibles. It was formerly (LME–M17) also an astrological term for 'nativity, horoscope'.

genie *noun* plural **genii**, **genis** M17 **French** (*génie* from Latin GENIUS). **1** M17–E18 A GENIUS (sense 1). **2** M18 A spirit or jinnee (in Arabian stories), especially one inhabiting a bottle, lamp, etc., and capable of granting wishes.

genitor *noun* LME **Latin** (*genitor* (Old French *géniteur*) from base of *gignere* to beget). **1** LME A male parent. **2** M20 *Anthropology* A person's biological as opposed to legal father.

■ Long archaic in the general sense 1, *genitor* in sense 2 was revived in the specific context of the distinction between biological and legal fatherhood; cf. PATER sense 3b.

genius *noun* plural **genii**, **geniuses** LME **Latin** (from base of *gignere* to beget, Greek *gignesthai* to be born, come into being). **1** LME The tutelary or attendant spirit in classical pagan belief allotted to every person at birth, or to a place, institution, etc. **b**

L16 Especially as *good* or *evil genius*. Either of the two mutually opposed spirits or angels supposed to attend each person. Hence a person who or thing which for good or bad powerfully influences another. **2** L16 A demon or spirit. **3 a** L16–E19 Characteristic disposition, bent, or inclination. **b** M17 Prevalent feeling, opinion, taste, or character (of a nation, age, etc.). **c** M17 The prevailing character or spirit, or characteristic method (of a law, language, etc.). **d** E19 The body of associations connected with or inspirations derived from a place; the GENIUS LOCI. **4** E17 Natural ability or tendency; attributes that fit a person for a particular activity. (Passing into sense 5.) **b** M17 Natural aptitude, talent, or inclination *for*, *to* (something). **5** M17 Inborn exalted intellectual power; instinctive and extraordinary imaginative, creative, or inventive capacity, frequently opposed to *talent*; a person having this.

genius loci *noun phrase* E17 **Latin** (= genius of the place). The presiding god or spirit of a place. Also = sense 3d above.

genizah *noun* (also **geniza**) L19 **Hebrew** (literally, 'a hiding, hiding place', from *gānaz* to set aside, hide). (The contents of) a storeroom for damaged, discarded, or heretical manuscripts and sacred relics, usually attached to a synagogue.

genre *noun* E19 **French** (= kind). Kind, type; *especially* a style or category of painting, novel, movie, etc., characterized by a particular form or purpose; *specifically* a style of painting depicting scenes of ordinary life.

gens *noun* plural **gentes** M19 **Latin** (from base of *gignere* to beget). **1** M19 In ancient Rome: a group of families with a supposed common origin, a common name, and common religious rites. Also, a similar group of families in other cultures. **2** L19 *Anthropology* A kinship group composed of people related through their male ancestors.

gens de la robe *noun phrase* (also **gens de robe**) L17 **French** (literally, 'folk of the long robe'). Lawyers.

genus *noun* plural **genera**, **genuses** M16 **Latin** (= birth, family, nation). **1** M16 *Logic* A class of things containing a number of subordinate classes (called species) with certain common attributes. **2** E17 *Biology* A basic taxonomic grouping ranking below family and subfamily. Formerly also used in the classification of minerals, chemical substances, etc. **b** M17 *generally* A category, a kind. **3** M18 In ancient Greek music, each of the three kinds of tetrachord.

georgette *noun & adjective* E20 **French** (from Mme *Georgette* de la Plante (flourished *c.*1900), French dressmaker). (Made of) a thin plain-woven crêpe dress material, usually of silk.

germen *noun* E17 **Latin** (= seed, sprout). **1** E17 The rudiment of an organism. Now only *figurative*. **2** E17–L18 A shoot, a sprout. **3** M18 *Botany* The rudiment of a seed vessel.

Gesamtkunstwerk *noun* plural **Gesamtkunstwerke** M20 **German** (from *gesamt* total + *Kunstwerk* work of art). An ideal work of art in which drama, music, and other performing arts are integrated and each is subservient to the whole.

Gesellschaft *noun* (also **gesellschaft**) L19 **German** (from *Gesell(e)* companion + *-schaft* -ship). *Sociology* A form of social integration based on impersonal ties; association. Cf. GEMEINSCHAFT.

gesso *noun* plural **gessoes** L16 **Italian** (from Latin GYPSUM; cf. YESO). Gypsum, plaster of Paris, now only as prepared for use in painting and sculpture; any white substance that can be mixed with water to make a ground.

gestalt *noun* (also **Gestalt**) E20 **German** (= form, shape). Chiefly *Psychology*. An integrated perceptual structure or unity conceived as functionally more than the sum of its parts.

Gestapo *noun* plural **Gestapos** M20 **German** (acronym, from *Ge*heime *Sta*ats*po*lizei Secret State Police). *History* (An officer of) the secret police of the Nazi regime in Germany; also *transferred*.

gett *noun* (also **get**) L19 **Hebrew**. A Jewish bill of divorce, in prescribed form; a divorce by such a bill.

gharana *noun* M20 **Hindustani** (*gharānā* family). *Indian Music* A school of players who practice a particular style of interpretation.

ghat *noun* (also **ghaut**) E17 **Hindustani** (*ghāṭ*). **1** E17 *The Ghats* Either of two mountain chains running parallel to the east and west coasts of southern India. **2** L17 In India: a mountain pass. **3** L18 In India: a flight of steps leading to a riverbank; a landing place. **4** L19 A level place at the top of a riverbank ghat where Hindus cremate their dead. In full *burning-ghat*.

ghazal *noun* (also **ghazel**) L18 **Persian** (from Arabic *ġazal*). A usually amatory Arabic, Turkish, Urdu, or (especially) Persian lyric poem or song characterized by a limited number of stanzas and the recurrence of the same rhyme.

ghazi *noun* (also (as a title) **Ghazi**) plural **ghazis** M18 **Arabic** (*al-ġāzī* active participle of *ġazā* to braid, invade, foray). In the Middle East: a champion, especially of Muslims against non-Muslims; a dedicated Muslim fighter. Frequently as an honorific title.

ghee *noun* (also **ghi**) M17 **Hindustani** (*ghī*, from Sanskrit *ghṛta* past participle of *ghṛ-* to sprinkle). Indian clarified butter made from the milk of a buffalo or cow.

gherao *noun & verb* M20 **Hindi** (from *ghernā* to surround, besiege). **A** *noun* M20 plural **gheraos**. In India and Pakistan: a form of protest or harassment in labor disputes whereby employers, etc., are prevented by workers from leaving the place of work until their claims have been granted. **B** *transitive verb* M20 Detain (a person) in this manner.

ghetto *noun & verb* E17 **Italian** (origin uncertain: perhaps abbreviation of Italian *borghetto* diminutive of *borgo* borough, or from Italian *getto* foundry, where the first ghetto established in Venice, in 1516, was situated). **A** *noun* plural **ghetto(e)s**. **1** E17 *History* The quarter in a city, originally in Italy, to which Jews were restricted. **2** L19 A densely populated slum area occupied by a minority group or groups, usually as a result of social or economic pressures; an isolated or segregated social group or area.

ghi variant of GHEE.

ghibli *noun* (also **gibli**, **qibli**) E19 **Arabic** (*ḳiblī* southern). A hot dry southerly wind of North Africa.

ghilgai variant of GILGAI.

giallo antico *noun & adjective phrase* M18 **Italian** (literally, 'ancient yellow'). (Made of) a rich yellow marble found among ruins in Italy, and used as a decoration.

gibber *noun* L18 **Aboriginal**. In Australia: a boulder, a (large) stone.

gibli variant of GHIBLI.

gigolo *noun* plural **gigolos** E20 **French** (formed as masculine of *gigole* dance-hall woman). A professional male dancing partner or escort; a (usually young) man supported by a (usually older) woman in return for his attentions.

gigot *noun* E16 **French** (diminutive of dialect *gigue* leg, from *giguer* to hop, jump, of unknown origin). **1** E16 A leg of mutton, etc. **2** M16–M17 A dish made from ground meat, a sausage. **3** E19 A leg-of-mutton sleeve. More fully *gigot sleeve*.

gigue *noun* L17 **French**. A lively piece of music in duple or triple time, often with dotted rhythms and forming the last movement of a suite; a jig.

gilet *noun* L19 **French**. A light often padded vest, usually worn for warmth by women.

gilgai *noun* (also **ghilgai**) M19 **Aboriginal** ((Kamilaroi) *gilgaay*). In Australia: a shallow depression between mounds or ridges, in which rainwater collects.

gimbri *noun* (also **gunibri**) L19 **Arabic** (dialectal variant of *ḳunbura* pomegranate). A small Moorish guitar; a player of this instrument.

ginseng *noun* M17 **Chinese** (*rénshēn* (Wade–Giles *jên shên*), from *rén* man + *shēn* kind of herb). **1** M17 A tuberous root credited, especially in the Far East, with valuable tonic properties. **2** L17 The source of this root, any of several plants of the genus *Panax* (family Araliaceae), with palmate leaves and umbels of small greenish flowers.

giocoso *adverb & adjective* E19 **Italian** (= merry). *Music* (A direction:) merr(il)y, joyous(ly).

girandole *noun* (also **girandola** in senses 1 and 2) M17 **French** (from Italian *girandola*, from *girare* from late Latin *gyrare* to gyrate). **I 1** M17 A kind of revolving firework; a discharge of rockets, etc., from a revolving wheel. **2** E19 A revolving jet of water; a series of jets in an ornamental fountain. **II 3** M18 A branched support for candles or other lights that either stands on a surface or projects from a wall. **4** E19 An earring, a pendant, *especially* one that has a large central stone surrounded by smaller ones.

girasol *noun* (also **girasole**) L16 **French** (or Italian *girasole*, from *girare* to gyrate + *sole* sun). **1** A sunflower. *rare*. Only in L16. **2** L16 A variety of opal that reflects a reddish glow, a fire opal.

giro *noun* plural **giri** L17 **Italian** (= round, circuit). A tour, a circuit; a turn.

girouette *noun* E19 **French**. A weathercock, weather vane.

gitana *noun* M19 **Spanish** (feminine of next). A female (Spanish) Gypsy.

gitano *noun* plural **gitanos** M19 **Spanish** (representation of popular Latin = Egyptian, from Latin *Aegyptus* Egypt + *-anus*). A male (Spanish) Gypsy.

gîte *noun* (also **gite**) L18 **French**. **1** L18 A stopping place, a lodging. Now *rare*. **2** M20 In France and French-speaking countries: a furnished vacation home, usually in a rural district.

Giuoco Piano *noun phrase* E19 **Italian** (= quiet game). *Chess* An initially quiet opening in chess.

gjetost *noun* E20 **Norwegian** (from *gjet*, *geit* goat + *ost* cheese). A Norwegian cheese made from goat's milk.

glacé *adjective & noun* M19 **French** (past participle of *glacer* to ice, give a gloss to, from *glace* ice). **A** *adjective* **1** M19 Of cloth, leather, etc.: smooth, highly polished, glossy. **2** L19 Of fruit: covered with icing or sugar. Of icing: made with confectioner's sugar and water. **B** *noun* M19 Glacé silk, glacé leather.

glacis *noun* plural same L17 **French** (from Old French *glacier* to slip, slide, from *glace* ice, from Proto-Romance alteration of Latin *glacies* ice). **1** L17 A gently sloping bank; *specifically* in *Fortification*, a natural or artificial bank sloping down from the covered way of a fort so as to expose attackers to the defenders' missiles, etc. **b** M20 *figurative* A zone or area acting as a protective barrier or buffer between two (potential) enemies. **2** L19 A sloping armor plate protecting an opening, etc., in a ship. In full *glacis plate*.

glaistig *noun* (also **glastick**) E20 **Gaelic**. A fairy with a variety of forms and characters, frequently appearing in the shape of a goat or as half woman, half goat, but also as a beautiful water sprite.

glasnost *noun* L20 **Russian** (*glasnost'* the fact of being public). In the former USSR: the policy or practice of more open consultative government and wider dissemination of information. Also *transferred*.

▪ *Glasnost* is an old Russian word, but its connotation of 'freedom of information' only evolved in the latter years of the Soviet regime. A debate on the subject started by the state newspaper *Izvestiya* in January 1985 was taken up by Mikhail Gorbachev in his speech in March the same year accepting the position of General Secretary of the Communist Party and expressing his commitment to reform. *Glasnost* was one of the key concepts in the Gorbachev reform program (see also PERESTROIKA), and English-speaking political commentators, finding that there was no English word exactly equivalent to *glasnost*, opted to use the Russian one. It became widely current in the late 1980s and was soon applied to mean 'openness', in particular 'openness in government', in a variety of situations quite outside its original context.

glastick variant of GLAISTIG.

glaucoma *noun* M17 **Greek** (*glaukōma*, from *glaukos* bluish green, bluish gray). *Medicine* An eye condition characterized by increased pressure within the eyeball and a gradual impairment or loss of sight.

Gleichschaltung *noun* (also **gleichschaltung**) M20 **German**. The standardization of political, economic, and cultural institutions in authoritarian nations.

glissade *noun & verb* M19 **French** (from *glisser* to slip, slide). **A** *noun* **1** M19 *Dancing* A step consisting of a glide or slide in any direction, usually a joining step. **2** M19 *Mountaineering* The action or an act of sliding down a steep slope especially of snow, usually on the feet with the support of an ice ax, etc. **B** *verb* **1** *intransitive & transitive verb* M19 *Dancing* Perform a glissade; progress by glissades. **2** M19 *Mountaineering* Slide down a steep slope especially of snow by means of a glissade.

glissando *noun* plural **glissandi, glissandos** L19 **Italian** (from French *glissant* present participle of *glisser* to slip, slide). *Music* A continuous slide of adjacent notes upward or downward.

glissé *noun* E20 **French** (past participle of *glisser* to slip, slide). *Ballet* A sliding step in which the flat of the foot is often used. More fully *pas glissé*.

globule *noun* M17 **French** (or Latin *globulus* diminutive of *globus* globe). **1** M17 A small spherical body or globe; a round drop (of liquid). **2** M19 A small pill.

glockenspiel *noun* E19 **German** (= bell play). *Music* 1 E19 An organ stop imitating the sound of bells. **2** M19 Any of several percussion instruments, *especially* (**a**) a series of tuned metal bars mounted on a horizontal frame; (**b**) a series of bells or metal bars in a lyre-shaped frame carried in marching bands (also *lyra glockenspiel*).

glögg *noun* (also **glugg**) E20 **Swedish**. A Scandinavian winter drink, consisting of hot sweetened red wine with brandy, almonds, raisins, and spices.

gloire *noun* M19 **French**. Glory; *specifically* the national glory and prestige of France. In full *la gloire*.

gloria *noun & adjective* (in sense 1 **Gloria**) ME **Latin** (= glory). **A** *noun* **1** ME Any of several Christian liturgical formulae, as *Gloria (Patri)* the doxology 'Glory be to the Father', *Gloria (tibi)* the response 'Glory be to thee', *Gloria (in excelsis)* the hymn 'Glory be to God on high', forming part of the Mass, etc. **b** L16 The music to which any of these is set. **2** L18 An aureole, a nimbus. **3** M19 In France: (a drink of) coffee mixed with brandy or rum. **4** L19 A closely woven fabric of silk and wool or cotton, etc.; a garment made of this. **B** *adjective* E20 Made of the fabric gloria.

gloriette *noun* M19 **French**. A highly decorated chamber in a castle or other building.

glugg variant of GLÖGG.

glühwein *noun* (also **gluhwein**) L19 **German** (from *glühen* to mull, glow + *wein* wine). Mulled wine.

gneiss *noun* (also (earlier) **kneiss**) M18 **German** (from Old High German *gneisto* (= Old English *gnāst*, Old Norse *gneisti*) spark). A foliated usually coarse-grained metamorphic rock in which bands of granular minerals alternate with bands of flaky or prismatic ones, and typically consisting of feldspar, quartz, and mica.

gnocchi *noun plural* L19 **Italian** (plural of *gnocco*, from *nocchio* knot in wood). Small dumplings made with flour, semolina, or potato.

gnomon *noun* M16 **French** (or Latin *gnomon*, from Greek *gnōmōn* inspector, indicator, carpenter's square). **1** M16 A pillar, rod, etc., that shows the time of day by casting its shadow on a marked surface; *especially* the pin or triangular plate of a sundial. **b** E17 A column, etc., used in observing the meridian altitude of the sun. **2** L16 *Geometry* The part of a parallelogram left after a similar parallelogram is taken away from one of its corners.

■ Various other technical and general uses are now no longer current.

gnosis *noun* plural **gnoses** L16 **Greek** (*gnōsis* investigation, knowledge, from *gno-* base of *gignōskein* to know). A special knowledge of spiritual mysteries; *specifically* in *Theology*, the redemptive knowledge that the Gnostics claimed to possess.

go *noun* L19 **Japanese**. A Japanese board game of territorial possession and capture. Cf. WEI CH'I.

gobang *noun* L19 **Japanese** (*goban* board for playing the game of go). A simplified form of the game of GO played on a board marked with squares, each player seeking to place five counters in a row.

godet *noun* ME **Old and Modern French**. **1** ME–E17 A drinking cup. **2** L19 A triangular piece of material inserted into a dress, glove, or other garment. **3** E20 A driven roller or wheel around which the filaments of any of various man-made fibers are drawn during manufacture.

goiter *noun* (also *Brit.* **goitre**) E17 **French** (either (i) from Old French *goitron* from Provençal from Proto-Romance, from Latin *guttur* throat, or (ii) back-formation from French *goitreux* goitered, from Latin adjective from *guttur*). *Medicine* A swelling of the neck due to enlargement of the thyroid gland, as caused by disease of the gland, iodine deficiency, etc.

goldwasser *noun* E20 **German** (= gold water). A liqueur containing particles of gold leaf, originally made at Gdańsk in Poland.

golem *noun* L19 **Yiddish** (*goylem* from Hebrew *gōlem* shapeless mass). A human figure of clay, etc., supernaturally brought to life; an automaton, a robot.

golgotha *noun* E17 **Late Latin** ((Vulgate), from Greek by metathesis from Aramaic *gōgoltâ*, perhaps under influence of Hebrew *gulgōleṯ* skull). A place of interment; a graveyard, a charnel house.

■ From the explanation in Matthew 27:33 and elsewhere of the name of the site of the Crucifixion as 'a place of a skull', wits at the universities of Oxford and Cambridge formerly (E18–E19) gave the nickname of Golgotha to the meeting place of the heads ('skulls') of university colleges or halls.

gompa *noun* E20 **Tibetan** (*gōn-pa*, *gōm-pa* a solitary place, a hermitage). A Tibetan temple or monastery.

gondola *noun* M16 **Italian** ((Venetian) from Rhaeto-Romance *gondolà* to rock). **1** M16 A light asymmetric flat-bottomed boat used on the Venetian canals, having a high pointed prow and stern and usually propelled by a single oar at the stern. **2** L17 A large light flat-bottomed riverboat; a lighter, used also as a gunboat. **3** M19 A car or nacelle attached to the underside of a dirigible or airship; something resembling this. **4** L19 An open railroad freight car with low sides. More fully *gondola car*, *gondola wagon*. **5** M20 A car attached to a ski lift. **6** M20 An island display counter in a self-service store.

gondolier *noun* E17 **French** (from Italian *gondoliere*, from GONDOLA). A person who rows a Venetian gondola.

gonfalonier *noun* L16 **French** (Old French *gonfanonier*). A standard-bearer; *specifically* (**a**) the Pope's standard-bearer; (**b**) *History* any of various officials or magistrates in the Italian city-states.

gonzo *adjective & noun* L20 **Italian** (= foolish, or perhaps Spanish *ganso* goose, fool). **A** *adjective* L20 Of, pertaining to, or designating a style of subjective journalism characterized by factual distortion and exaggerated rhetoric; *generally* bizarre, crazy. **B** *noun* plural **gonzos** L20 Gonzo journalism; a journalist writing in this style; *generally* a crazy or foolish person.

goombah *noun* (also **goombay**) L18 **West Indian creole** (cf. Kikongo [*n*]*kumbi* a kind of drum, Twi *gumbe* drum music). In the West Indies: any of various types of drum played with the fingers (rather than with sticks).

goonda *noun* (also **goondah**) E20 **Hindi** (*guṇḍā* rascal). In the Indian subcontinent: a hired bully.

goondie *noun* (also **gundy**) L19 **Aboriginal** ((Kamilaroi) *gunday* stringy bark). In Australia: an Aboriginal hut; a GUNYAH.

gooroo variant of GURU.

gopi *noun* (also **Gopi**) L18 **Sanskrit**. *Hindu Mythology* Any of the milkmaids of Brindavan, companions of Krishna.

gopura *noun* (also **gopuram**) M19 **Sanskrit** (*gopura* city gate, from *go* cow, cattle + *pura* city, quarter). In southern India: the great pyramidal tower over the entrance gate to a temple precinct.

Gorsedd *noun* L18 **Welsh** (= mound, throne, assembly). A meeting of Welsh bards and druids; *especially* the assembly that meets to announce the next Royal National Eisteddfod and at certain times during this festival.

Götterdämmerung *noun* E20 **German** (literally, 'twilight of the gods'). *Germanic mythology* The downfall of the gods; *generally* a cataclysmic collapse of a regime, institution, etc. Cf. RAGNAROK.

■ *Götterdämmerung* is the title of the final opera in Wagner's Ring cycle.

gouache *noun* L19 **French** (from Italian *guazzo*). A method of opaque watercolor painting, in which the pigments are bound by a glue to form a sort of paste; a painting executed in this way; the pigments thus used.

goujon *noun* L19 **Old and Modern French** (from Latin *gobio(n)-*, from *gobius* goby). **1** L19 The flathead catfish, *Pylodictis olivaris*. **2** M20 *Cooking* In *plural*. Narrow strips of fish, especially sole, or of chicken, usually for deep-frying.

goulash *noun* M19 **Hungarian** (*gulyás(hús)*, from *gulyás* herdsman + *hús* meat). **1** M19 A highly seasoned stew or ragout of meat and vegetables. **2** E20 *Bridge* A fresh deal of unshuffled cards, usually three or more at a time, after the hands have been thrown in without bidding.

gourmand *noun & adjective* (occasionally feminine **gourmande**) LME **Old and Modern French** (of unknown origin). **A** *noun* **1** LME A person who is overfond of eating; a glutton. **2** M18 A person who is fond of, or a judge of, good food; a GOURMET. **B** *adjective* M16 Gluttonous, greedy; fond of eating.

gourmet *noun & adjective* E19 **French** (formerly = wine merchant's assistant, wine taster, influenced in sense by GOURMAND). **A** *noun* E19 A connoisseur in eating and drinking; a judge of good food. **B** *attributive* or as *adjective* E20 Of the nature of a gourmet; of a kind or standard suitable for gourmets.

goût *noun* (also **gout**) L16 **French** (earlier *goust* from Latin *gustus* taste). **1** L16 Liking, relish, fondness (*for*). **2** E18 The ability to perceive and discriminate between flavors, smells, etc.; the faculty of aesthetic appreciation or judgment; (good) taste. **3** E18 Style or manner; *especially* a prevailing or fashionable style. **4** M18 Flavor, savor, taste.

goy *noun* plural **goyim**, **goys** M19 **Hebrew** (*gōy* people, nation). Among Jews: a non-Jew, a Gentile.

gradus *noun* M18 Latin (*gradus* step(s)). *History* A manual of classical prosody used in schools to help in writing Greek and Latin verse.

■ This category of schoolbook took its name from the title of a manual of Latin prosody, the *Gradus ad Parnassum* 'Step(s) to Parnassus', which appeared in England in many editions from the late seventeenth century onward and inspired a *Greek Gradus* and other imitations.

Graf *noun* M17 German. A German nobleman corresponding in rank to a European count or British earl.

■ Chiefly in titles. The feminine equivalent is *Gräfin*.

graffiti *transitive verb* L20 Italian (from plural of next). Apply graffiti to; write as graffiti.

graffito *noun* plural (frequently used as *singular*) **graffiti** M19 Italian (from *graffio* scratching). **1** M19 A drawing, writing, or scribbling on a wall, etc., originally *specific* on an ancient wall, as at Rome and Pompeii. Usually in *plural*. **2** L19 A method of decoration or design produced by scratching through a plaster layer to reveal a different color below.

gramdan *noun* M20 Sanskrit (*grāma* village + *dāna* gift). In India: the pooling by villagers of their land for the collective good, especially as advocated by Vinoba Bhave (1895–1982).

grand battement *noun phrase* plural **grands battements** M19 French. *Ballet* A BATTEMENT executed with the moving leg stretched out as it is raised.

grand coup plural **grands coups** E19 French. **1** E19 A bold or important stroke or effort. **2** L19 *Whist* and *Bridge* The deliberate disposal of a superfluous trump by ruffing a winning card from the opposite hand.

grand cru *noun & adjective phrase* plural **grands crus, grand crus** E20 French (= great growth). *Wine* (Designating) a wine of superior quality.

grande amoureuse plural **grandes amoureuses** E20 French. A passionate or amorous woman; a woman skilled in the arts of love.

grande dame plural **grandes dames** M18 French. A woman of high rank or eminence and dignified bearing.

grande horizontale *noun phrase* plural **grandes horizontales** L19 French. A courtesan or prostitute.

grande passion plural **grandes passions** E19 French (= grand passion). An overmastering passion for another person; an engrossing love affair.

grande sonnerie M20 French. *Horology* A system of chiming in which the hour and the quarter is struck each quarter on different toned bells.

grande tenue see EN GRANDE TENUE.

Grand Guignol *noun phrase* E20 French (= Great Punch). A dramatic entertainment in which short horrific or sensational pieces are played successively; a literary work with similar characteristics.

■ In France *Guignol* is a marionette drama equivalent to the English Punch and Judy show. *Grand Guignol* takes its name from a theater in Paris.

grandioso *adverb, adjective & noun* L19 Italian. *Music* **A** *adverb & adjective* L19 (A direction:) in a grand or imposing manner. **B** *noun* plural **grandiosi** L20 A movement or passage played in this way.

grand jeté *noun phrase* plural **grands jetés** M20 French. *Ballet* A JETÉ achieving a high elevation.

grand mal *noun phrase* L19 French (literally, 'great sickness'). General convulsive epilepsy, with loss of consciousness. Cf. PETIT MAL.

grand monarque plural **grands monarques** L17 French. A supreme and absolute ruler; *specifically* an epithet of Louis XIV of France (reigned 1643–1715).

grand monde E18 French. The BEAU MONDE.

Grand Prix *noun phrase* plural **Grands Prix** M19 **French** (= great prize). **1** M19 An international horse race for three-year-olds run annually in June at Longchamps, Paris. In full *Grand Prix de Paris.* **2** L19 The highest prize awarded in a competition or exhibition. **3** E20 Any of a series of motor or motorcycle races forming the World Championship, held in various countries under international rules. Also, a very important competitive event in various other sports.

grand seigneur plural **grands seigneurs** E17 **French.** A great nobleman.

grand siècle M19 **French** (literally, 'great century *or* age'). A classical or golden age; *especially* the reign of Louis XIV (1643–1715) in France.

granita *noun* plural **granite** M19 **Italian.** A coarse water ice or sherbet; a drink made with crushed ice.

gran turismo *noun & adjective phrase* M20 **Italian** (literally, 'great touring'). (Designating) a comfortable high-performance model of automobile.

■ Abbreviated to *GT.*

grappa *noun* L19 **Italian.** A brandy distilled from the refuse of grapes after winemaking.

graticule *noun* L19 **French** (from medieval Latin *graticula* for (also classical Latin) *craticula* small gridiron, diminutive of Latin *cratis* hurdle). **1** L19 A network of lines representing meridians and parallels, on which a map or plan can be represented. **2** E20 A series of fine lines or fibers incorporated in a telescope or other optical instrument as a measuring scale or an aid in locating objects; a plate, etc., bearing this.

gratin *noun* M17 **French** (from *gratter*, earlier *grater* to grate). **1** M17 A method of cooking, or a dish cooked, with a crisp brown crust, usually of grated cheese or breadcrumbs. Cf. AU GRATIN. **2** M20 The highest class of society.

■ For sense 2, cf. the English metaphorical phrase 'the upper crust'.

gratiné *noun & adjective* (also **gratinée**) E20 **French** (past participial adjective of *gratiner* to cook *au gratin*). *Cooking* (A dish) cooked with a crisp topping or stuffing of breadcrumbs or grated cheese.

gratis *adverb & adjective* LME **Latin** (*gratis* contraction of *gratiis* out of favor or kindness, ablative plural of *gratia* grace, favor). **A** *adverb* **1** LME Freely, for nothing, without return made or expected; without charge, cost, or pay. **2** L16–E19 Without a reason; gratuitously, unjustifiably. **B** *adjective* M17 Given or done for nothing; free; gratuitous.

graupel *noun* L19 **German.** *Meteorology* Soft hail, small snow pellets with a fragile ice crust.

gravadlax variant of GRAVLAX.

gravamen *noun* plural **gravamens**, **gravamina** E17 **Late Latin** (*gravamen* physical inconvenience, (in medieval Latin) grievance, from Latin *gravare* to weigh on, oppress, from *gravis* heavy, grave). **1** E17 In the Anglican church: a memorial from the Lower House of Convocation to the Upper House representing the existence of disorders and grievances within the church. **b** M17–L19 A formal complaint or accusation. **2** M17 A grievance. **3** M19 The essential or most serious part of an accusation; the part that bears most heavily on the accused.

gravida *noun* M20 **Latin** (noun use of feminine of *gravidus* gravid). *Medicine* A woman who is pregnant; (with preceding or following numeral) a woman who had had the specified number of pregnancies, including a present one.

gravitas *noun* E20 **Latin.** Solemn demeanor; seriousness.

gravlax *noun* (also **gravlaks**, **gravadlax**) M20 **Swedish** (from *grav* grave, trench +*lax* salmon (because the process was originally carried out in a hole in the ground)). Raw salmon cured with salt, spices, and especially dill.

grazioso *adjective & adverb* E19 **Italian** (= gracious, graceful). *Music* (A direction:) graceful(ly).

grecque *noun* M19 **French** (feminine of *grec* Greek). *Architecture* A Greek fret.

grège *adjective & noun* (also **greige**) E20 **French** (in *soie grège* raw silk, from Italian *greggio* raw, crude, unprocessed). (Of) a color between beige and gray.

grenadine *noun* L19 **French** ((*sirop de*) *grenadine* from *grenade* pomegranate). A cordial syrup made from pomegranates; a drink of this.

Grenzbegriff *noun* L19 **German** (from *Grenze* limit, boundary + *Begriff* concept). In Kantian philosophy, a concept showing the limitation of sense experience, a limiting concept; *generally* a conception of an unattained ideal.

grès *noun* L19 **French**. Stoneware.

■ Chiefly in *grès de Flandres*, Flemish ware.

grillade *noun* M17 **French** (from *griller* to cook on a grill). (A dish of) grilled food; a grill.

grimoire *noun* M19 **French** (alteration of *grammaire* grammar). A manual of black magic supposedly used to cast spells, invoke demons, etc.

gringo *noun & adjective* plural **gringos** M19 **Spanish** (= foreign, foreigner, gibberish). **A** *noun* M19 A (male) foreigner, especially American or British, in a Spanish-speaking country. **B** *adjective* L19 Of or pertaining to a gringo or gringos; foreign.

■ Usually derogatory.

griot *noun* E19 **French**. In North and West Africa: a member of a class of traveling poets, musicians, and folk historians; a praise singer.

grippe *noun* L18 **French**. Influenza.

grisaille *noun & adjective* M19 **French** (from *gris* gray). **A** *noun* M19 A method of painting in gray monochrome, used to represent objects in relief or to decorate stained glass; a stained-glass window or other work of this kind. **B** *adjective* M19 Executed in grisaille.

grisette *noun & adjective* E18 **French** (from *gris* gray). **A** *noun* **1** E18 A cheap gray dress fabric, formerly worn by working girls in France. **2** E18 A young working-class Frenchwoman. **B** *adjective* E18 Made of grisette.

grissino *noun* plural **grissini** M19 **Italian**. A long thin stick of crisp bread.

■ Usually in plural.

grognard *noun* E20 **French** (literally, 'grumbler'). A member of Napoleon's Old Guard; *transferred* a veteran soldier.

gros *noun* plural same M18 **French** (noun use of *gros* gross). **1** A heavy silk fabric (*gros du soie*). Only in M18. **2** L18 A silk fabric originally from or associated with a specified city, etc., as *gros de Londres*, *gros de Lyons*, *gros de Naples*, etc.

gros bleu *noun & adjective phrase* L19 **French** (= dark blue). (Of) a deep blue used to paint china.

grosgrain *noun & adjective* M19 **French**. (Made of) any of various heavy ribbed fabrics, especially silk or rayon.

gros point *noun phrase* M19 **French** (= large stitch). **1** M19 A type of lace, originally from Venice, worked in bold relief. More fully *gros point de Venise*. **2** M20 Any of various embroidery stitches worked over two or more horizontal and vertical threads of the canvas.

grosso modo *adverb phrase* M20 **Italian**. Roughly, approximately.

Grübelsucht *noun* L19 **German** (from *grübeln* to brood + *Sucht* mania). A form of obsession in which even the simplest facts are compulsively queried.

gruppetto *noun* plural **gruppetti**, **gruppettos** M19 **Italian** (diminutive of *gruppo* group). *Music* A melodic ornament consisting of a group of three, four, or five notes, comprising the principal note and the notes one degree above and below it; a turn.

GT abbreviation of GRAN TURISMO.

guaca, **guaco** variants of HUACA, HUACO.

guacamole *noun* (also **guacomole**) E20 **American Spanish** (from Nahuatl *ahuacamolli*, from *ahuacatl* avocado + *molli* sauce). A Mexican dish made from mashed avocados, onions, tomatoes, chilies, and seasoning.

guaiacum *noun* M16 **Modern Latin** (from Spanish *guayaco*, *guayacan*, from Taino *guayacan*). **1** M16 Any of various trees and shrubs of the genus *Guaiacum* native to the West Indies and tropical America. **2** M16 The hard very heavy wood of such a tree; lignum vitae. **3** M16 A resin obtained from such a tree, formerly used to treat gout and rheumatism, now as a flavoring; a drug prepared from it. Also more fully *gum guaiacum*.

guajira *noun* E20 **Cuban Spanish** (feminine of next). A Cuban song and dance tune whose rhythm shifts from 6/8 to 3/4 time.

guajiro *noun* plural **guajiros** M19 **Cuban Spanish** (= rustic, rural). A Cuban agricultural worker.

guano *noun* plural **guanos** E17 **Spanish** (or South American Spanish *huano*, from Quechua *huanu* dung). **1** E17 The excrement of seabirds as found especially on the islands off Peru and Chile and used as fertilizer. **2** M19 More fully *fish guano*. An artificial fertilizer resembling natural guano, *especially* one made from fish.

guaracha *noun* M19 **Spanish**. A lively Cuban song and dance in 3/4 and 6/8, or 2/4, time; a ballroom dance resembling this.

guarache variant of HUARACHE.

guarana *noun* M19 **Portuguese** (from Tupi *guaraná*). A Brazilian liana, *Paullinia cupana*, of the soapberry family; a paste prepared from the seeds of this shrub, used as a food or medicine and especially to make a drink resembling coffee.

guardia civil *noun phrase* plural **guardias civiles** M19 **Spanish** (= civil guard). (A member of) a police force in Spain organized on military lines.

guêpière *noun* M20 **French** (from *guêpe* wasp). A corset designed to emphasize the slenderness of the waist.

guéridon *noun* M19 **French**. A small ornamental table or stand, usually round, with a single central pedestal, and ornately carved.

guerrilla *noun & adjective* (also **guerilla**) E19 **Spanish** (diminutive of *guerra* war). **A** *noun* **1** E19 A person taking part in an irregular war waged by small bands operating independently (frequently against a stronger more organized force) with surprise attacks, etc. **2** E19 A war waged by guerrillas. Now *rare*. **B** E19 *attributive* or as *adjective* Of fighting: carried on by small irregular bands. Of a person: taking part in such fighting.

■ Introduced into France and England during the Peninsular War (1808–14), when the Spaniards fought such campaigns against the vastly superior invading forces of Napoleon.

gueule de bois *noun phrase* plural **gueules de bois** L20 **French** (literally, 'mouth of wood'). A hangover.

■ Colloquial in both French and English.

gueux *noun plural* E17 **French** (plural of *gueux* ragamuffin, beggar). *History* The Dutch nobles who in 1566 petitioned Margaret of Parma on behalf of Protestants; the Dutch and Flemish Protestant partisans who subsequently fought against Spain in the wars of the sixteenth century.

■ Four hundred nobles assembled in Brussels in April 1566 to present a petition to the Habsburg Governess of the Netherlands, Margaret of Parma, against the intolerant edicts being enforced by her administration in the provinces that she was ruling as deputy for her half brother, the Spanish king Philip II. The president of her council of finance, the Count of Berlaymont, contemptuously dismissed them as *gueux* 'beggars', a sobriquet gleefully seized upon by the disaffected Dutch, who transformed it into a rallying cry for the subsequent revolt against the Habsburgs.

gugelhupf *noun* (also **guglhupf**, **kugelhupf**) plural **gugelhupfe** L19 German (the form with *k* is from dialect). A light Austrian cake baked in a ring-shaped mold.

guichet *noun* M19 French. A wicket, a hatch; *especially* one through which tickets are sold.

guidon *noun* M16 French (from Italian *guidone*, from *guida* guide). **1** M16 A pennant narrowing to a point or fork at the free end, especially as used as the standard of a regiment or a troop of cavalry. **2** L16 An officer who carries a guidon.

guilloche *noun* M19 French (*guillochis* guilloche, or *guilloche* the tool used in making it). An architectural or metalwork ornament imitating braided or twisted ribbons.

guillotine *noun & verb* L18 French (from Joseph-Ignace *Guillotin* (1738–1814)). **A** *noun* **1** L18 An instrument for beheading consisting of a heavy blade with a diagonal cutting edge that is allowed to drop between two tall grooved uprights, used in France during the Revolution. **b** M19 *the guillotine* Execution by means of a guillotine. **2** M19 A surgical instrument with a blade that slides in a long groove. **3** L19 A machine with a long blade used for cutting paper, etc. **4** L19 A method used in a legislative assembly for preventing obstruction of a bill by fixing times at which its different parts must be voted on. **B** *transitive verb* **1** L18 Behead by means of a guillotine. **2** L19 Cut with a guillotine; *figuratively* cut short.

■ Guillotin suggested the use of this instrument as a means of capital punishment in 1789 on the grounds that executions should be as swift and painless as possible. Such devices had been in operation earlier in England, Scotland (where it was called a 'maiden'), Germany (called a *Diele* or *Hobel*), and Italy (called a *mannaia*), but by the eighteenth century they seem to have fallen out of use until Guillotin's recommendation aroused new interest. There was a period of experimentation using dead bodies, during which the machine was referred to as *La Petite Louison* or the *Louisette*, but after its first public use in April 1792 it speedily and universally became known as *la guillotine*.

guimpe *noun* (also **guimp**) M19 French. A high-necked CHEMISETTE; a blouse designed for wearing under a low-necked dress.

guipure *noun* M19 French (from *guiper* to cover with silk, wool, etc., from Germanic base meaning 'wind around'). A kind of openwork lace in which the motifs are connected by threads.

guiro *noun* L19 Spanish (= gourd). A gourd with an artificially serrated surface that gives a rasping sound when scraped with a stick, used (originally in Latin America) as a musical instrument.

gul *noun* E19 Persian. **1** E19 A flower; *especially* a rose. **2** E20 A large geometrical motif derived from the shape of the rose that forms part of the design of a Turkoman rug.

■ Sense 1 is poetical, as in the phrase *gardens of gul*.

Gulag *noun* (also **gulag**) M20 Russian (acronym, from Glavnoe upravlenie ispravitel'no-trudovykh *lag*ereĭ Chief Administration for Corrective Labor Camps). **1** M20 A department of the Soviet secret police that administered corrective labor camps and prisons between 1934 and 1955. *rare*. **2** L20 The Soviet network of labor camps; a camp or prison within it; *figurative* a coercive institution, an oppressive environment.

gundy variant of GOONDIE.

gung-ho *adjective* M20 Chinese (*gōnghé*, taken as 'work together'). Enthusiastic, eager.

■ Adopted as a slogan in World War II by the United States Marines.

gunibri variant of GIMBRI.

gunyah *noun* E19 Aboriginal. In Australia: an Aboriginal hut; a bush hut.

gurdwara *noun* E20 **Panjabi** (*gurduārā*, from Sanskrit GURU + *dvāra* door). A Sikh temple.

guru *noun* (also **gooroo**) E17 **Sanskrit** (*guru* elder, teacher). **1** E17 A (Hindu) spiritual teacher. **2** M20 Anyone looked up to as a source of wisdom or knowledge; an influential leader or pundit.

gusto *noun* plural **gusto(e)s** E17 **Italian** (from Latin *gustus* taste). Keen enjoyment displayed in action or speech, especially in eating or drinking; relish, zest.

■ Often in the phrase *with (great) gusto*. The other early (E17) sense of *gusto* as 'an individual fondness or preference' and the art critical sense (M17) of 'the style in which a work of art, etc., is executed' (especially in *great* or *grand gusto* (= Italian *gran gusto*)) are both now archaic.

gutta *noun* plural **guttae** LME **Latin** (= drop (of any liquid)). **1** LME–E18 Gum; gum resin, *especially* gamboge. **2** M16 *Architecture* Each of a row of usually conical projections resembling drops underneath the triglyph (and sometimes the mutule) of a Doric capital. **3** M16 *Pharmacology* and *Medicine* A drop of liquid. Now *rare* or *obsolete*. **4** E19 A roundish colored dot on an insect's wing, *especially* one of a light color.

gutta-percha *noun* M19 **Malay** (*getah perca*, from *getah* gum + *perca* strips of cloth (which it resembles); assimilated to GUTTA). **1** M19 The coagulated latex of certain Malaysian trees, a hard tough thermoplastic substance consisting chiefly of a hydrocarbon isomeric with rubber and now used especially in dentistry and for electrical insulation. **2** M19 Any of the trees, of the sapote family, that yield gutta-percha.

gymnasium *noun* plural **gymnasiums**, **gymnasia** L16 **Latin** (from Greek *gumnasion*, from *gumnazein* to exercise naked, from *gumnos* naked). **1** L16 A place, room, or building, equipped for gymnastics or for indoor sports. **2** L17 Formerly, a high school, college, or academy in Continental Europe. Now *specifically* in Germany and some other Continental countries, a school of the highest grade, preparing pupils for universities.

gypsum *noun & verb* LME **Latin** (from Greek *gupsos* chalk, gypsum). **A** *noun* LME Hydrated calcium sulfate, a soft mineral that occurs as colorless, white, or gray monoclinic prismatic crystals in many sedimentary rocks and is used for making plaster of Paris and as a fertilizer. **B** *transitive verb* E19 *Agriculture* Dress with gypsum.

gyro *noun* plural **gyros** L20 **Modern Greek** (*guros* turning). A sandwich of pita bread filled with slices of spiced meat cooked on a spit, tomatoes, onions, etc.

H

habanera *noun* L19 **Spanish** (short for *danza habanera* Havanan dance, feminine of *habanero* of Havana the capital of Cuba). A slow Cuban dance and song in duple time.

habeas corpora *noun phrase* LME **Latin** (= thou (shalt) have the bodies (sc. in court)). *Law* (now *historical*). A process formerly issued from the British Court of Common Pleas, directing the sheriff to compel the attendance of reluctant jurors.

habeas corpus *noun phrase* LME **Latin** (= thou (shalt) have the body (sc. in court)). *Law* A writ requiring a person to be brought before a judge or into a court; *specifically* such a writ requiring the investigation of the legitimacy of a person's detention, by which his or her release may be secured.

habitat *noun* L18 **Latin** (literally, 'it inhabits', 3rd person singular present of *habitare* to dwell in). **1** L18 The natural environment characteristically occupied by a particular organism; an area distinguished by the set of organisms that occupy it. Also, such areas collectively. **2** M19 *generally* One's dwelling place; a habitation; usual surroundings.

habitué *noun* E19 **French** (past participle of *habituer* from Latin *habituare* to frequent). A habitual visitor or resident (*of* a place).

habutai *noun* L19 **Japanese** (*habutae*). Fine soft silk of a type originally made in Japan. Also called *Japanese* (or *Jap*) *silk*.

háček *noun* M20 **Czech** (diminutive of *hák* hook). A diacritical mark (č) used chiefly in Baltic and Slavonic languages, especially to indicate various types of palatalization.

hacendado *noun* (also **haciendado**) plural **hacendados** M19 **Spanish**. The owner of a HACIENDA.

hachure *noun & verb* M19 **French** (from *hacher* to hatch). *Cartography* **A** *noun* M19 Any of a number of short lines of shading on a map running in the direction of a slope and indicating steepness by their closeness and thickness. Also *hachure line*. Usually in *plural*. **B** *transitive verb* M19 Shade (a map) with hachures.

hacienda *noun* M18 **Spanish** (from Latin *facienda* things to be done, from *facere* to do). In Spain and Spanish-speaking countries: an estate including a house; a large farm, a plantation; a rural factory.

haciendado variant of HACENDADO.

Hadith *noun* E18 **Arabic** (*ḥadīt* statement, tradition). The body of tradition concerning the sayings and doings of the prophet Muhammad, now considered to be second in authority to the Koran and to embody the Sunna; a single such saying.

hadj, hadji variants of HAJJ, HAJJI.

haff *noun* M19 **German** (from Middle and Modern Low German *haf* sea, corresponding to Old Norse *haf*, Old English *hæf* sea). A shallow freshwater lagoon found at a river mouth, especially on the Baltic coast.

hafiz *noun* M17 **Persian** (from Arabic *ḥāfiẓ* present participle of *ḥafiẓa* to guard, know by heart). A Muslim who knows the Koran by heart.

ha-ha *noun* (also **haw-haw**) E18 **French** (perhaps from the cry of surprise on discovering the obstacle). A ditch with a wall on its inner side below ground level, forming a boundary to a garden or park without interrupting the view from within.

haham *noun* (also **chacham** and other variants) L17 **Hebrew** (*ḥākām* wise). A person learned in Jewish law; a wise man; *specifically* among Sephardic Jews, a rabbi; the spiritual head of a Sephardic community.

haiku *noun* plural same, **haikus** L19 **Japanese** (abbreviation of *haikai no ku* unserious or comic verse). A short Japanese poem in three parts and usually having seventeen syllables; an English imitation of such a poem. Cf. HOKKU.

hajj *noun* (also **hadj, haj**) E18 **Arabic** ((*al-*) *ḥajj* (the Great) Pilgrimage). The pilgrimage to the Sacred Mosque at Mecca undertaken in the twelfth month of the Muslim year and constituting one of the religious duties of Islam.

hajji *noun* (also (feminine) **hajja**; **hadji**) E17 **Persian** (Turkish *ḥājjī*, *ḥājī* pilgrim, from as preceding). (The title given to) a person who has undertaken the hajj. Cf. ALHAJI.

haka *noun* M19 **Maori**. A ceremonial Maori dance accompanied by chanting.

■ Best known through its adoption by New Zealand international rugby teams as a pregame ritual.

hakama *noun* M19 **Japanese**. Japanese loose pants with many pleats in the front.

hakeem variant of HAKIM 2.

Hakenkreuz *noun* (also **hakenkreuz**) plural **Hakenkreuze** M20 **German** (from *Haken* hook + *Kreuz* cross). A swastika, especially as a Nazi symbol.

hakim *noun 1* E17 **Arabic** (*ḥākim* ruler, governor, judge from *ḥakama* to pass judgment). A judge, ruler, or governor in a Muslim country.

hakim *noun 2* (also **hakeem**) M17 **Arabic** (*ḥakīm* wise man, philosopher, physician, from as preceding). A physician in a Muslim country.

halal *adjective, verb, & noun* (also **hallal**) M19 **Arabic** (*ḥalāl* according to religious law). **A** *adjective* M19 Killed or prepared in the manner prescribed by Islamic law. **B** *transitive verb* M19 Kill (an animal) in this manner. **C** *noun* M20 An animal killed, or meat prepared, in this manner.

halcyon *noun & adjective* LME **Latin** (*(h)alcyon* from Greek *alkuōn* kingfisher (also *halkuōn* by association with *hals* sea and *kuōn* conceiving), related to Latin *alcedo* kingfisher). **A** *noun* **1** LME A bird said by the ancients to breed in a nest floating on the sea around the time of the winter solstice, and to charm the wind and waves so that the sea was calm for this purpose; *poetical* a kingfisher. **b** L18 Any of various brightly colored tropical kingfishers of the genus *Halcyon*. **2** M17–L18 Calm, quietude. **B** *adjective* **1** L16 Calm, peaceful; happy, prosperous, idyllic. **2** E17 Of or pertaining to the halcyon or kingfisher.

haldi *noun* (also **huldee**) M19 **Hindustani** (from Sanskrit *haridrā*). The plant *Curcuma longa*, of the ginger family, whose powdered tubers yield turmeric. Also, turmeric itself.

hallal variant of HALAL.

halling *noun* M19 **Norwegian** (from *Hallingdal* a valley in southern Norway). A Norwegian country dance in duple rhythm; a piece of music for this dance.

halma *noun* L19 **Greek** (= leap). A game played by two or four people on a checkerboard of 256 squares, with pieces advancing from one corner to the opposite corner by being moved over other pieces into vacant squares.

haltere *noun* plural **halteres** M16 **Greek** (*haltēres* plural (sense 1), from *hallesthai* to jump). **1** M16 In *plural*. Weights, like dumbbells, held in the hand to give an impetus in jumping. **2** E19 *Entomology* Either of the two knobbed filaments which in dipteran insects take the place of posterior wings. Also called *balancer, poiser*. Usually in *plural*.

halutzim *noun plural* (also **haluzim**, **chalutzim**) E20 **Hebrew** (*ḥălūṣīm*). *History* Jewish pioneers who entered Palestine from 1917 onward to build it up as a Jewish state.

halva *noun* (also **halvah**, (earlier) **hulwa**) M17 **Yiddish** (*hal(a)va*, modern Hebrew *ḥalbāh*, modern Greek *khalbas*, Turkish *helva*, etc., from) Arabic (and Persian) *ḥalwā* sweetmeat). A Middle Eastern sweet confection made of sesame flour and honey.

■ Later (M19) also found in its Arabic form *halawi*.

hamada variant of HAMMADA.

hamartia *noun* L18 **Greek** (= fault, failure, guilt). The fault or error leading to the destruction of the tragic hero or heroine of a play, novel, etc.

hamel *noun* M19 **Afrikaans** (= Dutch *hamel*, German *Hammel*, from Old High German *hamal* mutilated). In South Africa: a castrated ram, a wether.

hametz *noun* (also **chametz**, **chometz**) M19 **Hebrew** (*ḥāmēṣ*). Leaven or food mixed with leaven, prohibited during the Passover.

hammada *noun* (also **hamada**) M19 **Arabic** (*ḥammāda*). A flat rocky area of desert blown free of sand by the wind, typical of the Sahara.

hammam *noun* (also **hummum**) E17 **Turkish** (or its source Arabic *ḥammām* bath, from *ḥamma* to heat). An establishment where one may take a Turkish bath.

hamsin variant of KHAMSIN.

hamza *noun* E19 **Arabic** (literally, 'compression'). (A symbol in Arabic script representing) the glottal stop.

han variant of KHAN.

haneef variant of HANIF.

hanepoot *noun* L18 **Afrikaans** (from Dutch *haan* cock + *poot* foot). **1** L18 A variety of sweet muscat grape, grown in South Africa and used for making wine or raisins. **2** E19 The sweet white wine made from these grapes.

hangi *noun* M19 **Maori**. An earth oven in which food is cooked on heated stones; the food cooked in such an oven.

■ Chiefly New Zealand.

hanif *noun* (also **haneef**) M18 **Arabic** (*ḥanīf*, an epithet applied to Abraham in the Koran). Among Muslims, a follower of the original and true (monotheistic) religion.

haniwa *noun* plural same M20 **Japanese** (literally, 'rings of clay'). *Archaeology* A clay image based on a cylindrical shape of a type placed outside Japanese tombs of the fifth to seventh century.

Hanse *noun* (also **hanse**) ME **Middle Low German** (*hanshūs* and medieval Latin *hansa* from Old High German *hansa*, Middle and Modern High German *hanse* (whence Middle Low German *hanse*) Gothic *hansa* company, crowd, from Germanic, whence also Finnish *kansa* people, company). *History* **1** ME A merchant guild. **b** LME *specifically* (A merchant, citizen, or town of) the Hanseatic League. **2** ME A membership fee payable to a merchant guild; a trading fee imposed on nonmembers of the guild.

haoma variant of HOM.

hapax legomenon *noun phrase* plural **hapax legomena** M17 **Greek** (= (a thing) said only once). A word, form, etc., of which only one recorded instance is known.

■ Used in Greek characters until L19 and sometimes abbreviated *hapax*.

harai-goshi *noun* M20 **Japanese** (from *harai* sweep + *koshi* waist, hips). *Judo* A type of sweeping hip throw.

hara-kiri *noun* (also (corruptly) **hari-kiri**) M19 **Japanese** (from *hara* belly + *kiri* cutting). In Japan: a ritual form of suicide by disemboweling, formerly prescribed by a feudal superior to disgraced members of the samurai class as an alternative to execution. Also, suicide practiced voluntarily from a sense of shame, as a protest, etc.

haram *noun & adjective* E17 **Arabic** (*ḥarām* forbidden; cf. HAREM). **A** *noun* E17 A Muslim sacred place, forbidden to non-Muslims. **B** *adjective* E17 Of food; forbidden under Islamic law. Opposed to HALAL.

haras *noun* plural same ME **Old and Modern French** (of unknown origin). An enclosure or establishment in which horses are kept for breeding. Formerly, a herd of such horses.

harem *noun* M17 **Turkish and Arabic** (originally from Turkish *harem* from Arabic *ḥaram* (that which is) prohibited, (hence) sacred or inviolable place, sanctuary, women's apartments, wives, women; later also from Arabic *ḥarīm* with same meaning, both from *ḥaruma* to be prohibited or unlawful). **1** M17 Separate women's quarters in a Muslim house, designed for the privacy and seclusion of the occupants. **2** L18 The occupants of such quarters collectively; *specifically* a Muslim's wives and concubines. **b** L19 A group of female animals of a single species sharing a mate.

haricot *noun* M17 **French** (in sense 1 in *febves de haricot*, perhaps from Aztec *ayacotli*; in sense 2 Old French *hericoq, hericot (de mouton)*, probably related to *harigoter* to cut up). **1** M17 A leguminous plant, *Phaseolus vulgaris*, native to tropical America but having numerous widely cultivated varieties; the edible pod or seed of this plant; *especially* white varieties of the dried seed. More fully *haricot bean*. **2** M17 A ragout, especially of mutton or lamb.

hari-kiri variant of HARA-KIRI.

harka *noun* E20 **Moroccan Arabic** (*ḥarka*: cf. literary Arabic *ḥaraka* movement, action, military operation). A body of Moroccan irregular troops.

harmattan *noun* L17 **Twi** (*haramata*). A parching dusty land wind on the West African coast from December to February. Also *harmattan wind*.

haroseth *noun* (also **charoseth, haroset**) L19 **Hebrew** (*ḥărōseṯ* from *ḥeres* earthware). A mixture of apples, nuts, spices, etc., eaten at the Passover Seder service to symbolize the clay mixed by the Israelites during their slavery in Egypt.

hartal *noun* E20 **Hindustani** (*haṛtāl, hartāl*, for *haṭṭal*, literally, 'locking of shops' (Sanskrit *haṭṭa* shop, *tāla* lock, bolt)). In the Indian subcontinent: the organized closing of stores and offices as a mark of protest or as an act of mourning.

hashish *noun* L16 **Arabic** (*ḥašīš* dry herb, hay, powdered hemp leaves, intoxicant made from this). Cannabis.

hasid *noun* (also **cha(s)sid, hassid**, and with initial capital) plural **hasidim** E19 **Hebrew** (*ḥāsīd* pious, pietist). A member of a Jewish sect founded in the eighteenth century by Israel Baal Shem Tov and emphasizing joy in the service of God.

hasta la vista *interjection* M20 **Spanish**. In Spain: goodbye, *au revoir*.

hatha yoga *noun phrase* E20 **Sanskrit** (from *haṭha* force + *yoga*). A system of physical exercises and breathing control used in YOGA.

hatha yogi *noun phrase* M20 **Sanskrit** (from *haṭha* force + *yogi*). A person who practices HATHA YOGA.

hausfrau *noun* plural **hausfraus, hausfrauen** L18 **German** (from *Haus* house + *Frau* wife, woman). A (German) housewife; a person who embodies housewifely qualities.

hausmaler *noun* M20 **German** (from *Haus* house + *Maler* painter). A person who paints undecorated china at home or in a private workshop.

haute Bohème *noun phrase* E20 **French** (literally, 'high Bohemia'). A fast or upper-class Bohemian set of people.

■ The phrase was apparently coined by the English writer Maurice Baring in *Cat's Cradle* (1925) on the model of HAUTE BOURGEOISIE.

haute bourgeoisie *noun phrase* L19 **French** (literally, 'high bourgeoisie'). The upper middle class.

haute couture *noun phrase* E20 **French** (literally, 'high dressmaking'). High fashion; the leading dressmakers and fashion houses or their products collectively.

haute cuisine *noun phrase* E20 **French** (literally, 'high cooking'). High-class (French) cooking.

haute école *noun & adjective phrase* M19 **French** (literally, 'high school'). (Of or pertaining to) the more difficult feats of horsemanship, or *transferred* of music or other arts.

haute-luxe *adjective* M20 **French** (literally, 'high luxury'). Luxurious, opulent.

haute noblesse *noun phrase* L18 **French** (literally, 'high nobility'). The upper stratum of the aristocracy. Cf. PETITE NOBLESSE.

hauteur *noun* E17 **French** (from *haut* high). Haughtiness of manner.

haute vulgarisation *noun phrase* M20 **French** (literally, 'high vulgarization'). The popularization of abstruse or complex matters.

haut-goût *noun* M16 **French** (literally, 'high flavor'). **1** M16 A strong flavor or relish, seasoning (*literally* and *figuratively*). **2** M17–E19 A highly flavored or seasoned dish. **3** L17 A slightly rotten flavor; a taint.

haut monde *noun phrase* M19 French (literally, 'high world'). The fashionable world. Cf. BEAU MONDE.

haut-pas *noun* plural same LME French (literally, 'high step'). A dais raised one or more steps above the level of the rest of the floor.

haut-relief *noun* M19 French (literally, 'high relief'). ALTO-RELIEVO.

haut ton *noun phrase* E19 French (literally, 'high tone'). (People of) high fashion.

■ Now less common than just 'the TON' in the sense of 'fashionable society'.

havildar *noun* L17 Urdu (*hawildār* from Persian *ḥawāl(a)dār* charge holder, from *ḥawāl*, from Arabic *ḥawāl(a)* charge, assignment + Persian *hawāl(a)dār* holding, holder). An Indian noncommissioned officer equivalent to a sergeant.

haw-haw variant of HA-HA.

hazzan *noun* (also **chaz(z)an**, **hazan**) plural **hazzanim** M17 Hebrew (*ḥazzān* beadle, cantor, probably from Assyrian *hazannu* overseer or governor). A CANTOR in a synagogue.

Hebe *noun* E17 Greek (*hēbē* youthful beauty, *Hēbē* the Greek goddess of youth and spring, daughter of Zeus and Hera, and cupbearer of Olympus). **1** E17 A young woman resembling Hebe; a waitress. **2** M20 (**hebe**) Any of numerous New Zealand evergreen shrubs constituting the genus *Hebe* (formerly included in *Veronica*), with spikes of blue, white, mauve, etc., flowers.

hebra *noun* (also **chevra**) plural **hebras**, **hebroth** L19 Hebrew (*ḥebrāh* association, society). A small group formed by members of a Jewish community for religious and charitable purposes.

heder *noun* (also **cheder**) plural **hedarim**, **heders** L19 Hebrew (*ḥeder* room). A school for Jewish children in which Hebrew and religious knowledge are taught.

Heft *noun* plural **Hefte** L19 German. A number of sheets of paper fastened together to form a book; *specifically* a part of a serial publication, a fascicle.

hegemon *noun* E20 Greek (*hēgemōn* leader, from *hēgeisthai* to lead). A leading or paramount power; a dominant state or person.

hegira *noun* (also **Hegira**, **hejira**, **hijra**) L16 Medieval Latin (from Arabic *hijra* departure from one's home and friends, from *hajara* to separate, emigrate). **1** L16 The emigration of Muhammad from Mecca to Medina in 622; the Muslim era reckoned from this. **2** M18 Any exodus or departure.

■ The abbreviation AH (for *anno Hegirae*) is used in Islamic dates.

Heilsgeschichte *noun* M20 German. *Theology* Sacred history; *specifically* the history of the salvation of humankind by God; history seen as the working out of this salvation.

heimisch *adjective* M20 Yiddish (*heymish* domestic, homelike). In Jewish speech: homely, unpretentious.

Heimweh *noun* E18 German. Homesickness.

hejira variant of HEGIRA.

hélas *interjection* LME French (later form of *ha las*, *a las* alas). Expressing grief, sadness, regret, etc.

Heldentenor *noun* plural **Heldentenöre** E20 German (= hero tenor). A singer with a powerful tenor voice suited to heroic roles, especially in Wagnerian opera.

helix *noun* plural **helices**, **helixes** M16 Latin (*helix*, *helicis* from Greek *helix*). **1** M16 Chiefly *Architecture*. A spiral ornament, a volute; *specifically* each of the eight smaller volutes under the abacus of a Corinthian capital. **2** E17 An object of coiled form, either around an axis (like a corkscrew) or, less usually, in one plane (like a watchspring); *Geometry* a three-dimensional curve on a (notional) conical or cylindrical surface that becomes a straight line when the surface is unrolled into a plane. **3** L17 *Anatomy* The curved fold that forms the rim of the exterior ear. **4**

E19 *Zoology* Any spiral-shelled mollusk of the genus *Helix*.

helot *noun* L16 **Latin** (*Helotes* plural from Greek *Heilōtes* (plural of *Heilōs*), also *Hilotae* from Greek *Heilōtai* (plural of *Heilōtēs*): usually derived from *Helos* a town in Laconia whose inhabitants were enslaved). *Greek History* **1** L16 (*Helot*) A member of a class of serfs in ancient Sparta, intermediate in status between slaves and citizens. **2** E19 *transferred* and *figurative* A serf, a slave.

hendiadys *noun* L16 **Medieval Latin** (from Greek *hen dia duoin* 'one through two'). A figure of speech in which a single complex idea is expressed by two words usually connected by *and*.

■ An example of *hendiadys* is *nice and warm* for *nicely warm*.

herbarium *noun* L18 **Late Latin** (*herbarium*, noun use of adjective represented by Latin *herbarius* botanist, *herbaria* (sc. *ars*) botany). A collection of dried botanical specimens systematically arranged for reference. Also, a room or building housing such a collection.

herem variant of CHEREM.

hermandad *noun* plural **hermandades** M18 **Spanish** (= brotherhood). *History* In Spain: a resistance group against oppression by the nobility; *specifically* a voluntary organization later reorganized as regular national police.

heroon *noun* plural **heroa** (also (earlier) **heroum**) L18 **Latin** (*heroum* from Greek *hērōon*, from *hērōios* of a hero, from *hērōs* hero). Originally, a temple dedicated to a hero, often over his supposed tomb. Now, a sepulchral monument in the form of a small temple.

herpes *noun* LME **Latin** (= shingles, from Greek, literally, 'creeping', from *herpein* to creep). Originally, any skin disease characterized by the formation of groups of vesicles. Now, (infection with) any of a small group of viruses affecting the skin and nervous system.

Herrenvolk *noun* M20 **German** (= master race, from *Herren*, plural of *Herr*, from Old High German *hērro*, comparative of *hēr* exalted + *volk* race). The German nation, viewed (especially by the Nazis) as a race born to mastery; in extended usage, a group regarding itself as innately superior.

hetaera *noun* (also **hetaira**, plural **hetairas**, **hetairai**) plural **hetaeras**, **hetaerae** E19 **Greek** (*hetaira* feminine of *hetairos* companion). Especially in ancient Greece: a mistress, a concubine; a courtesan, a prostitute.

hetman *noun* M18 **Polish** (probably from German *Hauptmann* (earlier *Heubtman*) headman, captain). A Cossack military commander. Cf. ATAMAN.

Heurige *noun* (also **Heuriger**) plural **Heurigen** M20 **German** ((southern and Austrian) = new (wine); vintner's establishment). **1** M20 Especially in Austria: wine from the latest harvest. **2** M20 An establishment where such wine is served.

hexapla *noun* (also **hexaple**) E17 **Greek** ((*ta*) *hexapla* (title of Origen's work) neuter plural of *hexaplous* sixfold). A sixfold text in parallel columns, especially of the Old or New Testament.

hiatus *noun* plural same, **hiatuses** M16 **Latin** (= gaping, opening, from *hiare* to gape). **1** M16 A physical break in continuity; a gaping chasm; an opening, an aperture. *rare* in *general* sense. **b** L19 *Anatomy* Any of various natural openings or gaps. Usually with specifying word. **2** E17 A gap or break in continuity, especially in a series or an account; a missing link in a chain of events; *especially* in *Geology* (the time value of) a break or unconformity in the stratigraphic sequence. **b** M19 *Logic* A missing link in a chain of argument. **3** E18 *Grammar* and *Prosody* A break between two vowels that come together without an intervening consonant in successive words or syllables.

hibachi *noun* M19 **Japanese** (from *hi* fire + *bachi* bowl, pot). **1** M19 In Japan: a large earthenware pan or brazier in which charcoal is burned to provide indoor heating. **2** M20 A type of especially outdoor cooking apparatus similar to a barbecue.

hibakusha *noun* plural same M20 **Japanese** (from *hi* suffer + *baku* explosion + *sha* person). A survivor of an atomic explosion, *especially* in *plural*, the survivors of the atomic explosions at Hiroshima and Nagasaki in 1945.

hic jacet *noun phrase* E17 **Latin** (literally, 'here lies', the first two words of a Latin epitaph). An epitaph.

hidalgo *noun* plural **hidalgos** L16 **Spanish** (formerly also *hijo dalgo* contraction of *hijo de algo*, literally, 'son of something'; cf. FIDALGO). **1** L16 In Spain: a member of the lower nobility. **2** E19 *transferred* A person resembling a hidalgo; *specifically* one who is suited to be or aspires to be a member of the nobility.

hiera picra *noun phrase* LME **Medieval Latin** (from Greek, from *hiera* sacred (name of many medicines) + *pikra* feminine of *pikros* bitter). *Pharmacology* A purgative drug composed mainly of aloes and canella bark.

■ Also altered to *hickery-pickery*.

hijab *noun* L20 **Arabic**. The headscarf worn by Muslim women.

hijra variant of HEGIRA.

hilo *noun* plural **hilos** M19 **Spanish** (= thread, from Latin *filum*). A thin vein of ore.

hippocampus *noun* plural **hippocampi** L16 **Latin** (from Greek *hippokampos*, from *hippos* horse + *kampos* sea monster). **1** L16 A fish of the genus *Hippocampus*; a sea horse. **2** E17 A mythical sea monster, half horse and half fish or dolphin, represented as drawing the chariot of Neptune, etc.; a representation of this. **3** E18 *Anatomy* A swelling on the floor of each lateral ventricle of the brain.

hippodrome *noun & verb* L16 **Old and Modern French** (Latin *hippodromus* from Greek *hippodromos*, from *hippos* horse + *dromos* race, course). **A** *noun* **1** L16 In ancient Greece and Rome, a course for chariot or horse races. Also, a modern circus. **2** L19 (*Hippodrome*) (The name of) a theater used for various stage entertainments. **3** L19 A race or contest in which the result is prearranged or fixed. *slang*. **B** M19 *intransitive verb* Prearrange or fix the result of a race or contest. Chiefly as *hippodroming* verbal noun, *slang*.

hiragana *noun* (also **hirakana**) E19 **Japanese** (from *hira* plain + KANA). The form of kana normally used in Japanese, derived from the cursive style of writing. Cf. KATAKANA.

hochgeboren *noun & adjective* plural of noun same E20 **German**. (A person who is) highborn.

hogan *noun* L19 **Navajo**. An American Indian (especially Navajo) hut made from logs, earth, etc.

hoi polloi *noun phrase* M17 **Greek** (= the many). The majority, the masses; the rabble.

■ Frequently with *the* in English, unnecessarily duplicating the Greek definite article *hoi*.

hokku *noun* plural same, **hokkus** L19 **Japanese** (= 'opening verse (of a linked sequence of comic verses)'). A HAIKU.

hollandaise *noun & adjective* M19 **French** (feminine of *hollandais* Dutch, from *Hollande* Holland). (Designating) a sauce made with butter, egg yolks, vinegar or white wine, and lemon juice, usually served with fish.

hom *noun* (also **haoma**, **homa**) M19 **Persian** (obsolete *hōm* (modern *hūm*), Avestan *haoma* = Sanskrit *soma* SOMA). (The juice of) the sacred plant of the ancient Persians and Parsees.

hombre *noun* M19 Spanish (= man, from Latin *homo, homin-* human being). A man, especially a man of a specified type (tall, mean, tough, or the like). *slang.*

homme d'affaires *noun phrase* plural **hommes d'affaires** E18 French. A businessman, an agent.

homme moyen sensuel *noun phrase* (also **homme sensuel moyen**) E20 French. The average man; the man in the street.

homo *noun* plural **homos** L16 Latin (= man). **1** L16 A human being. **2** L18 (**Homo**) The genus to which human beings (HOMO SAPIENS) and certain of their fossil ancestors belong. Also with Latin specific epithets in names of (proposed) species, and with Latin or mock-Latin adjectives (in imitation of zoology nomenclature) in names intended to personify some aspects of human life or behavior.

homoeoteleuton *noun* (also **homoioteleuton**) L16 Late Latin (from Greek *homoioteleuton* (sc. *rhēma* word), from *homoios* like + *teleutē* ending). **1** L16 A rhetorical figure consisting in the use of a series of words with the same or similar endings. *rare.* **2** M19 (An error in copying caused by) the occurrence of similar endings in two neighboring words, lines, etc.

Homoiousion *noun* M19 ecclesiastical Greek (neuter of *homoiousios* of like essence, from *homoios* like, similar + *ousia* essence, substance). *Christian Theology The* doctrine that the first and second persons of the Trinity are of like but not identical essence or substance. Cf. HOMOOUSION.

Homoousion *noun* L18 ecclesiastical Greek (neuter of *homoousios*, from *homos* same + *ousia* essence, substance). *Christian Theology The* doctrine that the first and second persons of the Trinity are of identical essence or substance. Cf. HOMOIOUSION.

■ After a long period of theological and philosophical discussion in the early centuries of the Christian era, this view prevailed at the Council of Chalcedon in 451 against that of the Homoiousian party.

Homo sapiens *noun phrase* (also **homo sapiens**) E19 Modern Latin (= wise man). Modern human beings regarded as a species.

■ Term introduced in Linnaeus's *Systema Naturae* (10th edn. 1758), and thence into English via the translation of Linnaeus's book.

homunculus *noun* plural **homunculi** M17 Latin (diminutive of *homo* man). A diminutive person, a dwarf.

■ Formerly also applied to a fetus considered as a fully formed human being.

honcho *noun & verb* M20 Japanese (*hanchō* group leader). **A** *noun* M20 plural **honchos**. The leader of a small group or squad; a person who is in a position of power; a strong leader. **B** *transitive verb* M20 Oversee; be in charge of (a situation).

■ Chiefly North American slang.

honda *noun* (also **hondo**, plural **hondos**, **hondu**) L19 Spanish (probably from *hondón* eyelet, influenced by Spanish *honda* sling). The eye at the end of a lasso through which the rope passes to form a loop.

hong *noun* E18 Chinese (*háng*, (Cantonese) *hòhng* row, trade). **1** E18 In China: a series of rooms or buildings used as a warehouse, factory, etc., *especially* one of the foreign factories formerly maintained at Canton. Also in Hong Kong, a trading establishment. **2** L18 *History* The corporation of Chinese merchants at Canton who had a monopoly of trade with Europeans.

honnête homme *noun phrase* plural **honnêtes hommes** M17 French. A decent, cultivated man of the world.

honorarium *noun* plural **honorariums**, **honoraria** M17 Latin (*honorarium* gift made on being admitted to a position of honor, use as noun of neuter of *honorarius* honorary). A (voluntary) fee, especially for professional services nominally rendered without payment.

honoris causa *adverb phrase* E17 **Latin** (= for the sake of honor). As a mark of esteem, especially in reference to an honorary degree at a university.

hookah *noun* M18 **Urdu** (from Arabic *ḥuḳḳa* small box, container, pot, jar). A pipe of oriental origin for smoking tobacco, marijuana, etc., with a long flexible tube connected to a container of water, through which the smoke is drawn from the tobacco, etc.

hoopla *interjection & noun* (also **hoop-la**, **houp-la**) L19 **French** (*houp-là!*, from *houp* interjection + *là* there). **A** *interjection* L19 Accompanying or drawing attention to a quick or sudden movement. **B** *noun* L19 An exclamation of 'houp-la!'; *slang* a commotion, ballyhoo, noisy publicity, pretentious nonsense.

horae *noun* L19 **Latin** (*horae* plural of *hora* hour). A book of hours.

horchata *noun* (also **orchata**) M19 **Spanish**. An almond-flavored soft drink in Spain and Latin American countries.

horizontale *noun slang* L19 **French**. A prostitute. More fully GRANDE HORIZONTALE.

horme *noun* (also **hormé**) L17 **Greek** (*hormē* impulse). **1** L17 A passion, an impulse. *rare*. Only in L17. **2** E20 *Psychology* Vital or purposeful energy.

■ *Horme* was first used in English in the writings of the Cambridge Platonist philosopher Ralph Cudworth (1617–88) but did not achieve currency until its reintroduction as a term in Jungian psychology.

hornito *noun* plural **hornitos** M19 **American Spanish** (diminutive of *horno* (from Latin *furnus*) oven, furnace). *Geology* A driblet cone formed by successive ejections through a vent in a lava flow.

horresco referens L17 **Latin** (= I shudder to relate, from *horrescere* to stand on end (of hair) + *referens*, present participle of *referre* to relate). Expressing horror at a memory.

■ The expression comes from Virgil's *Aeneid* (ii. 204), at the point when the hero Aeneas is relating how giant sea serpents killed the priest Laocoon for attempting to warn the Trojans against taking the Greeks' wooden horse into their city.

horribile dictu *adverb phrase* M19 **Modern Latin** (by analogy with MIRABILE DICTU). Horrible to relate.

horror vacui *noun phrase* M19 **Modern Latin** (= the horror of a vacuum). (A) fear or dislike of leaving empty spaces in an artistic composition, etc.

hors concours *adverb & predicate adjective phrase* L19 **French** (= out of the competition). Not competing for a prize; *figurative* without a rival, in a class of its own.

■ Both the literal and the figurative senses are also present in modern French.

hors de combat *adverb & predicate adjective phrase* M18 **French** (= out of the fight). Out of the fight; out of the running; in an injured or disabled condition.

hors de question *adverb phrase* L20 **French**. Out of the question.

hors d'oeuvre *noun phrase* plural same, **hors d'oeuvres** M18 **French** (literally, 'outside the work'). An extra dish served as an appetizer before or (occasionally) during a meal; in *plural* also, (usually mixed) items of food served as such a dish. Also *figurative* a preliminary.

horst *noun* L19 **German** (= heap, mass). *Geology* A block of the earth's surface bounded by faults on some or all sides and raised relative to the surrounding land.

horti conclusi, **horti sicci** plurals of HORTUS CONCLUSUS, HORTUS SICCUS.

hortus conclusus *noun phrase* plural **horti conclusi** E17 **Latin** (= enclosed garden). **1** E17 An enclosed inviolate garden; frequently, in spiritual and exegetical tradition, as symbolic of the soul, the Christian church, or the virginity of Mary. **2** M19 A painting of the Madonna and Child in an enclosed garden.

hortus siccus *noun phrase* plural **horti sicci** L17 Latin (= dry garden). An arranged collection of dried plants; *figurative* a collection of uninteresting facts, etc.

hôtel de ville *noun phrase* plural **hôtels de ville** M18 French. In France and French-speaking countries: a town hall.

hôtel-Dieu *noun* plural **hôtels-Dieu** M17 French. In France and French-speaking countries: a hospital.

hôtel garni *noun phrase* plural **hôtels garnis** L18 French. In France and French-speaking countries: a lodging house providing bed and breakfast only; also, a furnished apartment.

hotelier *noun* E20 French (*hôtelier*). A person who owns or runs a hotel or group of hotels.

hotel particulier *noun phrase* plural **hotels particuliers** M20 French. In France and French-speaking countries: a large privately owned town house or apartment building.

hoummos, houmous variants of HUMMUS.

houp-la variant of HOOPLA.

houri *noun* M18 French (from Persian *ḥūrī* from Arabic *ḥūr* plural of *'aḥwar*, feminine *ḥawrā'* having eyes with marked contrast of white and black). Any of the virgins of the Muslim paradise, promised as wives to believers; *transferred* a voluptuously beautiful woman.

howdah *noun* L18 Urdu (*haudah* from Arabic *hawdaj* a litter carried by a camel). A seat for two or more, usually with a canopy, carried on an elephant's back.

huaca *noun* (also (earlier) **guaca**) E17 Spanish (*huaca, guaca* from Quechua *waca* god of the house). **1** E17 The all-pervading spirit thought by some Peruvian Indians to be disseminated through the whole world; any material object thought to be the abode of such a spirit. **2** M19 A prehistoric Peruvian tomb or temple.

huaco *noun* (also **guaco**) plural **huacos** M20 Spanish (alteration of preceding). In Peru, Bolivia, and Chile: a piece of ancient Indian pottery.

huarache *noun* (also **guarache**) L19 Mexican Spanish. A leather-thonged sandal, originally worn by Mexican Indians.

hubris *noun* (also **hybris**) L19 Greek. Presumption, insolence; pride, excessive self-confidence.

■ The earliest instance of *hubris* in a nonspecialist English text, a newspaper of 1884, refers to it as 'Academic slang' and defines it as 'a kind of high-flown insolence'. In its original context in ancient Greek literary texts it indicated insolence toward the gods, manifested either in spiritual pride or by behavior that flouted divine or social law; thus the arrogant and riotous conduct of Penelope's suitors in Homer's *Odyssey* is an instance of hubris that met its due when they were almost all slaughtered by the returned Odysseus. The spelling *hybris* is a slightly later (E20) alternative transliteration of the Greek; both transliterations are current, but *hubris* is marginally more common in general contexts.

huerta *noun* M19 Spanish. In Spain and Spanish-speaking countries: a piece of irrigated land; an orchard.

huevos rancheros *noun phrase* L20 (Mexican) Spanish. A Mexican dish of fried eggs served on tortillas with a spicy sauce.

hui *noun* M19 Maori and Hawaiian. In New Zealand: a large social or ceremonial gathering; in Hawaii: a formal club or association.

hula *noun & intransitive verb* (also **hula-hula**) E19 Hawaiian. (Perform) a Hawaiian dance with six basic steps and gestures symbolizing or imitating natural phenomena, historical events, etc.

hulan variant of UHLAN.

huldee variant of HALDI.

hulwa variant of HALVA.

hum *noun* E20 **Serbo-Croat.** *Physical Geography* A steep-sided hill, of roughly circular cross section, characteristic of karst topography. Cf. MOGOTE.

huma *noun* M19 **Persian and Urdu** (*humā* phoenix). A mythical bird similar to the phoenix, supposed to bring luck to any person over whom it hovers on its restless flights.

humanitas *noun* M20 **Latin.** Humanity.

hummum variant of HAMMAM.

hummus *noun* (also **hoummos, h(o)umous**) M20 **Arabic** (*ḥummuṣ*). Ground chickpeas mixed with tahini, garlic, and lemon juice, frequently served as an hors d'oeuvre or dip.

humus *noun* L18 **Latin** (= soil). The organic constituent of soil, formed by the decomposition of plant materials.

hybris variant of HUBRIS.

hydra *noun & adjective* LME **Old French** (((*h*)*ydre, idre* from) Latin *hydra* from Greek *hudra* water snake). **A** *noun* **1** LME *Greek Mythology* (also **Hydra**) A monster with many heads, which grew again as fast as they were cut off. **2** LME (usually **Hydra**) (The name of) a long faint constellation; the Sea Serpent. **3** L15 A thing or person likened to the mythological hydra in its baneful character, its multifarious aspects, or the difficulty of its extirpation. **4** M16 Any terrible serpent or reptile. *rhetorical.* **5** E17 A water snake. **6** L18 Any of several hydrozoans of the genus *Hydra* that live as solitary polyps attached to pond plants.

hydria *noun* plural **hydriae** ME **Old French** (*idr(i)e*, from Latin *hydria*, from Greek *hudria*). Formerly, a water pot. Now (*Archaeology*), a three-handled pitcher of ancient Greece.

hydrophobia *noun* LME **Late Latin** (*hydrophobia* from Greek *hudrophobia*, from *hudrophobos* water-fearing). **1** LME A strong aversion to or fear of water arising from the spasms that a rabid person suffers when attempting to drink; rabies itself. **2** M18 *generally* A fear or dislike of water; *figurative* madness.

hyle *noun* LME **Late Latin** (from Greek *hulē* wood, material, matter). Matter, substance; *specifically* the primordial matter of the universe.

hyperbaton *noun* M16 **Latin** (from Greek *huperbaton* overstepping, from *huperbainein*, from as *hyper-* beyond, over + *bainein* to walk). *Grammar* and *Rhetoric* A figure of speech in which the logical order of words or phrases is inverted, especially for the sake of emphasis.

hyperbole *noun* LME **Latin** (from Greek *huperbolē* excess, exaggeration, from as *hyper-* beyond, over + *ballein* to throw). A figure of speech consisting in exaggerated or extravagant statement, used to express strong feeling or produce a strong impression and not meant to be taken literally; an instance of this; *generally* overstatement.

hyperdulia *noun* M16 **Medieval Latin** (*hyperdulia*, from as *hyper-* beyond + *dulia*). *Roman Catholic Church* The veneration properly given to the Virgin Mary (higher than DULIA but less than LATRIA).

hypogeum *noun* (also **hypogaeum**) plural **hypog(a)ea** M17 **Latin** (*hypogeum, hypogaeum* from Greek *hupogeion, hupogaion* noun use of neuter singular of *hupogeios* underground). An underground chamber or vault.

hypostasis *noun* plural **hypostases** E16 **ecclesiastical Latin** (from Greek *hupostasis* sediment, foundation, subject matter, (later) substance, existence, essence, personality, from as *hypo-* below + *stasis* standing). **1** E16 *Theology* A person; *specifically* **a** the single person of Christ, as opposed to his two natures, human and divine; **b** each of the three persons of the Trinity. **2** M16 *Medicine* **a** A sediment, especially in urine. Long *rare* or *obsolete*. **b** M19 The accumulation of blood or other fluid in a dependent part of the body. **3 a** L16–E17 A base or foundation on which something abstract rests. **b** *Philosophy* E17 An underlying reality, substance, as opposed to attributes ("accidents") or as distinguished from what is unsubstantial. **c** L17 Essence, essential principle. **4** E20 *Genetics* (Back-formation from *hypostatic*.) Inhibition of the expression of a gene by another at a different locus. **5** M20 *Linguistics* The citing of a word, element, etc., as an example or model; the word, etc., so cited.

■ The Anglicized form *hypostasy* is rare.

hypothesis *noun* plural **hypotheses** L16 **Late Latin** (from Greek *hupothesis* foundation, base, from as *hypo-* + *thesis* placing). **1** L16 A proposition put forward merely as a basis for reasoning or argument, without any assumption of its truth. **2** L16–E18 A subordinate thesis forming part of a more general one; a particular case of a general proposition; a detailed statement. **3** E17 A supposition, an assumption; *especially* one made as a starting point for further investigation or research from known facts. **4** E17 A groundless assumption; a guess. **5** L18 An actual or possible situation considered as a basis for action.

hysterica passio *noun phrase* **E17 Latin** (feminine of *hystericus* (from Greek *husterikos* belonging to the uterus) + *passio* passion). Hysteria.

■ Hysteria was formerly held to be a disorder peculiar to women resulting from a disturbance of the uterus.

hysteron proteron *noun, adverb, & adjective phrase* **M16 Late Latin** (from Greek *husteron proteron* latter (put in place of) former). **A** *noun phrase* **1** M16 *Rhetoric* A figure of speech in which what should come last is put first. **2** L16 *generally* Position or arrangement of things in the reverse of their natural or rational order. **B** *adverb phrase* In a topsy-turvy way. Only in E17. **C** *adjective phrase* M17 Involving or employing hysteron proteron.

I

iambus *noun* plural **iambuses**, **iambi** L16 **Latin** (from Greek *iambos* iambus, lampoon, from *iaptein* to assail in words). *Prosody* A metrical foot consisting of one short followed by one long syllable or (in English, etc.) of one unstressed followed by one stressed syllable.

■ The meter known as the iambic trimeter was first used by the ancient Greek satirists, hence the connection with lampoons.

ibid *adverb* **M17 Latin** (abbreviation of next). IBIDEM.

ibidem *adverb* **M18 Latin** (= in the same place, from *ibi* there + demonstrative suffix *-dem*, as in *idem*, *tandem*, etc). In the same book, chapter, passage, etc.

■ The abbreviated form *ibid* is in more general use in bibliographies, etc.

ichor *noun* **M17 Greek** (*ikhōr*). **1** M17 Blood; a liquid likened to the blood of animals. Now *literary*. **2** M17 *Medicine* A watery discharge from a wound or sore. *archaic*. **3** L17 *Greek Mythology* A fluid supposed to flow like blood in the veins of the gods. **4** E20 *Geology* An emanation from magma supposed by some to cause granitization.

icon *noun* (also **ikon**) M16 **Latin** (from Greek *eikōn* likeness, image, similitude). **1** M16–L17 *Rhetoric* A simile. **2 a** L16–E18 A portrait, a picture; *especially* one of an animal or plant in a book of natural history. **b** M19 *Ecclesiastical* An image in traditional Byzantine style of Christ or a holy person that is used ceremonially and venerated in the Orthodox church. **c** L20 *Computing* A small symbolic picture on a computer or video display screen, *especially* one that may be selected with a cursor to exercise an option that it represents. **3** L16 A statue. **4** L16 A realistic description in writing. *rare*. **5** E20 *Philosophy* A sign with some factor in common with the object it represents.

iconostasis *noun* plural **iconostases** M19 **Modern Greek** (*eikonostasis*, from as *icono-* (combining form of) icon + *stasis*, literally, 'standing'). A screen separating the sanctuary or altar from the nave in most Orthodox churches and used to display icons.

id *noun* E20 **Latin** (= it, translating German *es*). *Psychoanalysis* The inherited instinctive impulses of the individual, forming part of the unconscious and, in Freudian theory, interacting in the psyche with the ego and the superego.

id al-fitr variant of ID UL-FITR.

idée fixe *noun phrase* plural **idées fixes** M19 **French** (= fixed idea). An idea that dominates the mind, an obsession.

idée reçue *noun phrase* plural **idées reçues** M20 **French** (= received idea). A generally accepted notion or opinion.

idem *noun & adverb* LME **Latin**. (In) the same author, work, etc.

idem sonans *noun & adjective phrase* M19 **Latin** (= sounding the same). *Law* chiefly *United States*. **A** *noun* M19 The occurrence in a document of a material word or name misspelled but having the sound of the word or name intended. **B** *adjective* M19 Homophonous *with*.

Identitätsphilosophie *noun* M19 **German** (= identity philosophy). *Philosophy* A system or doctrine that assumes the fundamental identity of spirit and nature.

id est *adverb phrase* L16 **Latin** (= that is). That is (to say).

■ Usually abbreviated to i.e.

idioticon *noun* M19 **German** (from Greek *idiōtikon* use as noun of neuter singular of *idiōtikos* uneducated). A dictionary, word list, etc., of words and phrases peculiar to a dialect, a particular group of people, etc.

idiot savant *noun phrase* plural **idiots savants** L20 **French** (= learned idiot). A person who in many respects is ignorant or uneducated, but who has an exceptional mastery of one subject or (usually mental) skill.

idolum *noun* plural **idola** E17 **Latin** (from Greek *eidōlon* idol). **1** E17 An image without substance; a phantom; a mental image, an idea. **2** M17 *Philosophy* (now *historical*) A false mental image.

id ul-fitr *noun* (also **id al-fitr**) M18 **Arabic** (*'īd al-fiṭr*; cf. EID). *Islam* The major festival to celebrate the ending of the Ramadan fast.

i.e. abbreviation of ID EST.

igloo *noun* (in sense 2 also **agloo, aglu**) M19 **Eskimo** ((Inuit) *iglu* house). **1** M19 An Eskimo dome-shaped hut, usually one built from blocks of snow. **b** *transferred* M20 Any similarly shaped building or structure used for storage, shelter, etc. **2** M19 A cavity in the snow above a seal's breathing hole.

ignis fatuus *noun phrase* plural **ignes fatui** M16 **Modern Latin** (= foolish fire, so called from its erratic flitting from place to place). **1** M16 A phosphorescent light seen hovering or floating over marshy ground, perhaps due to the combustion of methane; a will-o'-the-wisp. **2** L16 *figurative* A delusive guiding principle, hope, or aim.

ignoramus *noun* L16 **Latin** (= we do not know, (in legal use) we take no notice of (it)). **1** L16 The endorsement formerly made by a grand jury on an indictment that they rejected as not being backed by sufficient evidence. *obsolete* except *historical*. **2** E17 An ignorant person.

■ In sense 2 very probably from *Ignoramus*, a comedy by George Ruggle satirizing lawyers, produced before James I in 1615.

ignoratio elenchi *noun phrase* plural **ignorationes elenchi** L16 **Medieval Latin** (translation of Greek *hē tou elegkou agnoia* ignorance of the conditions of valid proof). A logical fallacy that consists in apparently refuting an opponent while actually disproving something not asserted; *generally* any argument which is irrelevant to its professed purpose.

ignotum per ignotius *noun phrase* LME **Late Latin** (literally, 'the unknown by means of the more unknown'). An explanation that is harder to understand than what it is meant to explain.

ihram *noun* E18 **Arabic** (*'iḥrām*, ultimately from *ḥarama* forbid; cf. HAREM). **1** E18 The sacred state into which a Muslim must enter before performing a pilgrimage, during which sexual intercourse, shaving, and several other actions are forbidden. **2** E18 The costume worn by a Muslim in this state, consisting of two lengths of seamless usually white fabric.

ikat *noun* M20 **Malay** (literally, 'tie, fasten'). (A fabric made using) an Indonesian technique of textile decoration in which warp or weft threads, or both, are tied at intervals and dyed before weaving.

ikebana *noun* E20 **Japanese**. The art of Japanese flower arrangement, with formal display according to strict rules.

ikon variant of ICON.

ilang-ilang variant of YLANG-YLANG.

illuminato *noun* (also **Illuminato**) usually in plural **illuminati** L16 **Italian** (= enlightened; plural partly from Latin *illuminati* plural of *illuminatus*, but in German context translating German *Illuminaten*). A member of any of various sects or societies claiming special enlightenment. Also *generally*, a person claiming special knowledge on any subject.

illuminé *noun* (also **Illuminé**) L18 **French** (= enlightened). An ILLUMINATO.

imago *noun* plural **imagines**, **imagos** L18 **Latin**. **1** L18 *Entomology* The final, fully developed form of an insect after passing through all stages of metamorphosis. **2** E20 *Psychoanalysis* An unconscious image of an archetype or of someone (especially a parent) that influences a person's behavior, etc.

imam *noun* E17 **Arabic** (*'imām* leader, from *'amma* to lead the way). **1** E17 The leader of prayers in a mosque. **2** M17 (**Imam**) (A title of) any of various Muslim leaders, especially one succeeding Muhammad as the leader of Shiite Islam.

imam bayildi *noun phrase* (also **Imam Bayildi**) M20 **Turkish** (*imam bayıldı*, literally, 'the imam fainted'). A dish, originating in Turkey, consisting of eggplant stuffed with a garlic-flavored onion-and-tomato mixture and cooked in oil.

■ Whether the *imam* fainted from pleasure and repletion or because he was overcome by horror at the cost of the dish seems to be a moot point.

imbrex *noun* plural **imbrices** M19 **Latin** (from *imber* rain shower). *Archaeology* A curved roof tile used to cover joints in a Roman tiled roof. Cf. TEGULA sense 2.

imbroglio *noun* (also **embroglio**) plural **imbroglios** M18 **Italian** (from *imbrogliare* to confuse, corresponding to French *embrouiller* to embroil). **1** M18 A confused heap. *archaic*. **2** E19 A state of great confusion; a complicated or difficult (especially political or dramatic) situation; a confused misunderstanding.

immortelle *noun* M19 **French** (from *fleur immortelle* everlasting flower). An everlasting flower, especially *Xeranthemum annuum.*

immram *noun* (also **imram**, **imrama**) plural **immra** L19 **Old Irish** (*imram* (modern *iomramh*), from *imm-rá* to row around). Any of various stories of fabulous sea voyages written in Ireland between the late eighth and eleventh centuries.

impair *adjective & noun* M19 **French** (= unequal, from negative *im-* un- + *pair* equal). **A** *adjective* **1** M19 Not paired; not forming one of a pair. **2** M20 *Roulette* Of or pertaining to an odd number or the odd numbers collectively. **B** *noun* M19 *Roulette* An odd number; the odd numbers collectively. Cf. PAIR.

■ In the early seventeenth century Shakespeare may have used *impair* in *Troilus and Cressida* in the sense of 'unfit, inferior', but the reading is doubtful.

impasse *noun* M19 **French** (from negative *im-* not + stem of *passer* to pass). **1** M19 A position from which there is no escape, a deadlock. **2** L19 *literal* A road, etc., without an outlet, a blind alley.

impasto *noun* L18 **Italian** (from *impastare*, from *im-* in + *pasta* paste). **1** L18 The action of painting by laying color on thickly; this manner of painting. **2** E20 *Ceramics* Enamel, etc., colors standing out in relief on a surface.

impayable *adjective* ME **French** (from as *im-* not + *payer* to pay). **1** Implacable, unappeasable. Only in ME. **2** L18 Impossible to pay or discharge. **3** E19 Priceless, invaluable; extraordinary, absurd.

impedimenta *noun plural* E17 **Latin**. Traveling equipment, especially of an army, etc.; encumbrances; bulky equipment in general.

imperium *noun* M17 **Latin**. Command; absolute power; supreme or imperial power; empire.

■ Used especially of the rule of the Roman emperors.

impetus *noun* M17 **Latin** (= assault, force, from *impetere* to assail). **1** M17 The force or energy with which a body moves; impulsion. **2** M17 *figurative* Moving force, (an) impulse, a stimulus.

impi *noun* M19 **Zulu**. Chiefly *South African History*. A body of Zulu warriors or armed tribesmen.

impluvium *noun* plural **impluvia** E19 **Latin** (from *impluere* to rain into). *Roman Antiquities* The square basin in the center of the atrium of a Roman house, which received rainwater from an opening in the roof.

imponderabilia *noun plural* E20 **Modern Latin** (neuter plural of *imponderabilis* that cannot be weighed). Imponderables, imponderable factors.

impresa *noun* L16 **Italian** (= undertaking, device, from Proto-Romance verb, from Latin *em-* on + *prendere* to take). **1** L16 An emblem, a device; *especially* one accompanied by a motto. **2** E17 A sentence accompanying an emblem; a motto, a maxim, a proverb. Long *rare*.

impresario *noun* plural **impresarios** M18 **Italian** (from as preceding). An organizer or sponsor of public entertainments; a manager of an operatic or a concert company.

imprévu *noun* M19 **French** (from as *im-* + *prévu* past participle of *prévoir* foresee). *The* unexpected, *the* unforeseen.

imprimatur *noun* M17 **Latin** (= let it be printed, 3rd person singular present subjunctive passive of *imprimere* to imprint). In the Roman Catholic church: an official license authorizing the printing of an ecclesiastical or religious work, etc.; *generally* official approval, an official sanction.

imprimatura *noun* M20 **Italian** (*imprimitura*). A usually colored transparent primer or glaze applied to an artist's canvas or panel.

impromptu *adverb, noun, adjective, & verb* M17 **French** (from Latin *in promptu* at hand, in readiness, from *promptus* readiness). **A** *adverb* M17

Without preparation; on the spur of the moment; extempore. **B** *noun* L17 Something composed, uttered, or done impromptu; an improvisation; *specifically* a musical composition having the character of an improvisation. **C** *adjective* M18 Composed, uttered, or done impromptu; improvised; makeshift. **D** *transitive and intransitive verb* E19 Improvise; extemporize.

imram(a) variants of IMMRAM.

imshi *transitive verb (imperative)* (also **imshee**) E20 **Arabic** ((from colloquial) *'mšī* imperative of *miši* to go). Go away!

■ Military slang, recorded (1916) during World War I as being used to street hawkers in Cairo by the Australasian Corps.

in absentia *adverb phrase* L19 **Latin**. In his, her, or their absence.

■ Almost always in a legal context modifying the verbs 'try' or 'convict'.

in abstracto *adverb phrase* E17 **Latin** (= in the abstract). As an abstract thing. Cf. IN CONCRETO.

inamorata *noun* (also **enamorata**) M17 **Italian** ((now *innamorata*), feminine of INAMORATO). A female lover.

inamorato *noun* (also **enamorato**) plural **inamoratos** L16 **Italian** (now *innamorato*, past participle of *innamorare* to fall in love with). A male lover.

in antis *adjective phrase* M19 **Latin**. *Classical Architecture* (Of columns) positioned between two antas; (of a building) having walls prolonged beyond the front, with terminating pilasters in line with columns of a façade.

in articulo mortis *adverb phrase* L16 **Latin** (= in the article of death). At the point or moment of death.

in camera *adverb phrase* E19 **Late Latin** (= in the chamber). In a judge's private chambers, not in open court; *generally* in secret or private session, not in public.

incipit *noun* L19 **Latin** (3rd person singular present indicative of *incipere* to begin). The opening words of a manuscript, a printed book (usually an early one), a chanted liturgical text, etc.

■ The word used by medieval scribes to indicate the beginning of a new treatise, poem, division, etc. Cf. EXPLICIT.

incisor *noun* L17 **Medieval Latin** (in *dens incisor* incisor tooth, from Latin, literally, 'cutter', from *incis-*, past participial stem of *incidere* to cut). A narrow-edged tooth adapted for cutting; in humans, any of the front four teeth in each jaw. Also *incisor tooth*.

incognita *noun plural* M19 **Latin** (neuter plural of *incognitus* unknown, from as INCOGNITO). Unknown things or places.

incognita *adjective & noun* L17 **Italian** (feminine of *incognito* unknown). **A** *adjective* L17 Of a woman: disguised; unknown. **B** *noun* E18 plural **incognitas**, **incognite**. A disguised or unknown woman, especially one's lover.

incognito *adjective, adverb, & noun* M17 **Italian** (from Latin *incognitus* unknown, from as *in-* un- + *cognitus*, past participle of *cognoscere* to know). **A** *adjective* M17 Of a person: concealed under a disguised or assumed identity; unknown. **B** *adverb* M17 Under a disguised or assumed identity. **C** *noun* plural **incognitos** **1** M17 A person who conceals his or her identity; an anonymous or unknown person. **2** E19 The condition of being unknown, anonymity; assumed or pretended identity.

incommunicado *adjective & adverb* (also in Spanish form **incomunicado**) M19 **Spanish** (*incomunicado* past participle of *incomunicar* to deprive of communication). **A** *adjective* M19 Having no means of communication with others; *especially* (of a prisoner) held in solitary confinement. **B** *adverb* M20 Without means of communication with others.

in concreto *adverb phrase* E17 **Latin**. As a concrete thing. Cf. IN ABSTRACTO.

inconnu *noun* (in sense 1 feminine **inconnue**, plural (in sense 1) **inconnu(e)s**, (in sense 2) same) E19

French (= unknown). **1** E19 An unknown person, a stranger. **2** E19 A predatory freshwater salmonid game fish, *Stenodus leucichthys*, of the Arctic. Originally *Canadian*.

in contumaciam *adverb phrase* L19 Latin. While in contempt of court.

in corpore *adjective & adverb phrase* E20 Latin (literally, 'in the body'). *Biology* IN VIVO.

incubus *noun* plural **incubuses, incubi** ME Late Latin (= Latin *incubo* nightmare, from *incubare* to lie on). **1** ME An evil spirit supposed to descend upon sleeping people and especially to have sexual intercourse with sleeping women. **2** M16 An oppressive nightmare; a person who or thing that oppresses or troubles like a nightmare.

incunabulum *noun* plural (earlier) **incunabula** E19 Latin (*incunabula* neuter plural swaddling clothes, cradle, from as *in-* in + *cunae* cradle). **1** E19 In *plural* The early stages of development of a thing. **2** M19 A book printed at an early date; *specifically* one printed before 1501.

indaba *noun* E19 Zulu (= discussion). **1** E19 A conference between or with members of southern African black peoples. **2** L20 A person's business, problem, or concern. *South African colloquial*.

indecorum *noun* L16 Latin (noun use of neuter singular of *indecorus* unseemly). **1** L16 An indecorous action or proceeding; an offense against recognized standards of behavior. **2** M17 The quality of being indecorous; lack of decorum; improper behavior.

index *noun* plural **indexes**, (especially *in technical use*) **indices** LME Latin (*index, indic-* forefinger, informer, etc., from base represented by *dicere* to say, Greek *deiknunai* to show). **1** LME The finger used in pointing, the forefinger. Now usually *index finger*. **b** L19 *Ornithology* The second (occasionally the first) digit of the manus in a bird's wing. **2** L16 A piece of wood, metal, etc., that serves as a pointer; *specifically* (in a scientific instrument) a pointer that moves along a graduated scale so as to show movements or quantities. **b** L16 The arm of a surveying instrument; an alidade. **3** L16 A thing that serves to point *to* a fact or conclusion; a sign or indication *of*. **4** L16 A list of things in (usually alphabetical) order; *especially* a list, usually at the end of a book, giving the names, topics, etc., mentioned in the book and the places where they occur. Formerly also, a table of contents. **5 a** L16–M19 *Music* A sign placed on the stave at the end of a page or line to indicate the position of the next note. **b** E18 *Typography* A hand-shaped symbol with a pointing finger used to draw attention to a note, etc. Also called *fist*. **6** L17 *Mathematics* A subscript or superscript symbol denoting some characteristic of a quantity or function, as the exponent in x^2, etc. **7** E19 A number or formula expressing a specific property, especially a ratio; *especially* in *Anatomy*, a formula expressing the ratio between two dimensions (especially of the skull). **8** L19 *Economics* (A number in) a scale relating (usually in the form of a percentage) the level of prices, wages, etc., at a particular time to those at a date taken as a base.

■ There are also a number of other specialist technical uses of *index* in mathematics, computing, and engineering. In sense 4 the Latin names of various types of index may be used: *index locorum* (index of the passages cited or discussed), *index nominum* (index of the names of people discussed), *index rerum* (index of the subjects and matters treated), *index verborum* (index of the significant words discussed).

index librorum prohibitorum *noun phrase* (also **Index Librorum Prohibitorum**) M17 Latin (= index of prohibited books). *Roman Catholic Church* The official list of books that Roman Catholics were forbidden to read.

■ The first *Index Librorum Prohibitorum* was published in 1564 as part of the Counter-Reformation program instituted at the Council of Trent, and the list was not abolished until 1966. It was also referred to simply as *the Index*.

indicium *noun* plural **indicia** E17 **Latin** (from as INDEX). An indication, a sign; a distinguishing mark. Usually in *plural*.

in dictione *adjective phrase* E19 **Latin** (translation of Greek *para tēn lexin* in relation to the wording). Of a logical fallacy: arising from the wording used to express it.

■ One of the subdivisions of logical fallacy noted by Aristotle in his *Sophistici Elenchi* (ch. 4), also sometimes referred to in Latin as *in voce* in the voice. Opposed to EXTRA DICTIONEM.

indumentum *noun* plural **indumenta** M19 **Latin** (= garment, from *induere* to put on). *Botany* The covering of hairs, scales, etc., on (part of) a plant, especially when dense.

induna *noun* M19 **Zulu** (from nominal prefix *in-* + *duna* councilor, headman, overseer, captain). **1** M19 A tribal councilor or headman among the Nguni peoples of southern Africa. **2** M20 *transferred* A person, especially a black person, in authority; a foreman.

inédit *noun* E20 **French** (cf. next). An unpublished work; *figurative* something secret or unrevealed.

inedita *noun plural* L19 **Modern Latin** (noun use of neuter plural of Latin *ineditus*, from *in-* not + *editus* past participle of *edere* to give out, edit). Unpublished writings.

inertia *noun* E18 **Latin** (= inactivity). **1** E18 *Physics* The property of a body, proportional to its mass, by virtue of which it continues in a state of rest or uniform straight motion in the absence of an external force. **b** L19 In other physical properties: the tendency to continue in some state, to resist change. **2** E19 *transferred* Inactivity; disinclination to act or exert oneself; sloth; apathy.

in esse *adjective phrase* L16 **Latin**. In actual existence.

■ Opposed to IN POSSE.

in excelsis *adverb phrase* LME **Latin** (= in the highest (places); cf. EXCELSIOR). In the highest.

■ Often in the phrase *Gloria in excelsis Deo* 'Glory to God in the highest!'

in extenso *adverb phrase* E19 **Latin** (from *in* in + *extenso* ablative of *extensus* past participle of *extendere* to stretch out). In full, at length.

in extremis *adverb phrase* M16 **Latin** (from *in* in + *extremis* ablative plural of *extremus* last, uttermost). At the point of death; in great difficulty; in a painful or awkward situation.

infanta *noun* L16 **Spanish** (Portuguese feminine of INFANTE). *History* A daughter of the king and queen of Spain or Portugal; *specifically* the eldest daughter who is not heir to the throne. Formerly also *generally*, a girl, a princess.

infante *noun* M16 **Spanish and Portuguese** (from Latin *infans, infant-* child). *History* A son of the king and queen of Spain or Portugal other than the heir to the throne; *specifically* the second son.

inferno *noun* plural **infernos** M19 **Italian** (from Christian Latin *infernus* below, subterranean). Hell; *transferred* a scene of horror or distress; *especially* a raging fire.

■ Reference to hell as *the inferno* is generally in allusion to Dante's *Divine Comedy*.

in fine *adverb phrase* M16 **Latin**. Finally, in short, to sum up.

infinitum *noun* L16 **Latin** (noun use of neuter of *infinitus* unlimited). Infinity; an infinitude, an endless amount or number.

■ Often in the phrase AD INFINITUM.

in flagrante *adverb phrase* E17 **Latin** (abbreviation of next or similar Latin phrase). In the very act. *colloquial*.

in flagrante delicto *adverb phrase* L18 **Latin** (= in the heat of the crime: cf. preceding). In the very act of committing an offense; *specifically* in the act of adultery or other sexual misconduct.

influenza *noun* M18 **Italian** (literally, 'influence', from medieval Latin *influentia* influence). A highly contagious viral infection of the lining of the trachea and bronchi, often epidemic, and usually marked by fever, weakness, muscular aches, coughing, and watery catarrh. Used loosely to refer to any acute respiratory infection accompanied by fever.

■ Generally abbreviated to *flu* in all but the most formal usage.

infra *adverb* L19 **Latin.** Later, further on (in a book or article); below.

infra dig *adjective phrase* E19 **Latin** (abbreviation of Latin *infra dignitatem* beneath (one's) dignity). Beneath the dignity of one's position; undignified. *colloquial.*

ingenium *noun* plural **ingenia** L19 **Latin** (= mind, intellect). Mental ability, talent; a person possessing this. Also, mental inclination, disposition.

ingénue *noun* (also **ingenue**) M19 **French** (feminine of *ingénu* ingenuous). An artless innocent young woman, especially as a stage role; an actress playing such a role.

ingesta *noun plural* E18 **Latin** (neuter plural of *ingestus* past participle of *ingerere* to carry in, pour in). Substances introduced into the body as nourishment; food and drink.

in infinitum *adverb phrase* M16 **Latin.** To infinity, without end.

■ Cf. AD INFINITUM.

injuria *noun* plural **injuriae** L19 **Latin.** *Law* An invasion of another's rights; an actionable wrong.

inkosi *noun* M19 **Nguni.** In South Africa: (the title of) a Zulu ruler, chief, or high official.

in limine *adverb phrase* E19 **Latin.** On the threshold; at the outset.

in loco parentis *prepositional phrase* E19 **Latin** (= in place of a parent). Assuming the responsibilities of a parent.

in medias res *adverb phrase* L18 **Latin.** Into the midst of things; *especially* into the middle of a narrative, without preamble.

in medio *adverb phrase* E17 **Latin.** In the middle; in an undecided state.

in memoriam *prepositional & noun phrase* M19 **Latin. A** *prepositional phrase* M19 To the memory of, in memory of. **B** *noun phrase* L19 A poem, notice, etc., in memory of a dead person.

■ The fashion for poems with this title was set by Tennyson's sequence of poems (1850), written in memory of his friend A. H. Hallam, who died in 1833.

in nomine *noun phrase* M17 **Latin** (= in the name (of)). An instrumental composition in fugal style (probably originally one set to a Latin text including the words *in nomine*); a free fugue in which the answer does not exactly correspond with the subject.

in nubibus *adverb & adjective phrase* L16 **Latin.** In the clouds; as yet unsettled; undecided; incapable of being carried out.

in nuce *adverb phrase* M19 **Latin.** In a nutshell; in a condensed form.

innuendo *adverb & noun* M16 **Latin** (= by nodding at, pointing to, intimating, ablative gerund of *innuere* to nod to, signify, from as *in-* + *nuere* to nod). **A** *adverb* M16 Meaning, that is to say, to wit, (especially in legal documents, introducing a parenthetical explanation of the precise reference of a preceding noun or pronoun). **B** *noun* plural **innuendo(e)s. 1** L17 A parenthetical explanation of, or construction put upon, a word or expression; *especially* in an action for libel or slander, the injurious meaning alleged to be conveyed by a word or expression not in itself actionable. **2** L17 An allusive or oblique remark, hint, or suggestion, usually disparaging; a remark with a (usually suggestive) double meaning; allusion, hinting, suggestion.

in ovo *adverb phrase* M19 **Latin** (= in the egg). In embryo. Also *figurative.*

in pari materia *adverb phrase* M19 **Latin.** In an equivalent case or position.

in partibus *adverb phrase* L17 **Latin** (*in partibus* (*infidelium*) in the regions (of the infidels)). *Roman Catholic Church* In full *in partibus infidelium.* In heretical territory (with reference to a titular bishop, etc., especially in a Muslim country).

in parvo *adverb phrase* E20 **Latin.** In little, in miniature, on a small scale.

in pectore *adverb phrase* M19 **Latin** (= in one's breast). Secretly; IN PETTO sense 1.

in perpetuum *adverb phrase* M17 **Latin.** For all time, in perpetuity.

in personam *adjective phrase* L18 **Latin** (= against a person). *Law* Made or availing against or affecting a specific person only; imposing a personal liability. Frequently *postpositive.* Cf. IN REM.

in petto *adverb phrase* L17 **Italian** (= in the breast). **1** L17 In contemplation; undisclosed, secretly (especially of the appointment of cardinals not named as such). **2** M19 (By confusion with *petty* (adjective)). In miniature, on a small scale; in short.

in pontificalibus *adverb phrase* LME **Latin.** In the full vestments of a cardinal, archbishop, etc.; in pontificals.

in posse *adjective phrase* L16 **Latin.** In the condition of being possible. Opposed to IN ESSE.

in potentia *adverb phrase* E17 **Latin.** In potentiality.

in propria persona *adverb phrase* M17 **Latin.** In one's own person.

in puris naturalibus *adverb phrase* E17 **Latin** (cf. PURIS NATURALIBUS). In one's natural state; stark naked.

in re *adverb, adjective, & preposition phrase* E17 **Latin. A** *adverb phrase* E17 In reality. **B** *adjective phrase* **1** M19 *Logic* EXTRA DICTIONEM. **2** L19 *Philosophy* Of a universal: existing only in the particulars that instantiate it. Cf. ANTE REM, POST REM. **C** *preposition phrase* L19 In the (legal) case of; with regard to. Cf. RE.

in rem *adjective phrase* M18 **Latin** (= against a thing). *Law* Made or availing against or affecting a thing, and therefore other people generally; imposing a general liability. Frequently *postpositive.* Cf. IN PERSONAM.

in rerum natura *adverb phrase* L16 **Latin.** In nature, in the physical world.

inro *noun* plural **inros**, same E17 **Japanese** (*inrō*, from *in* seal + *rō* basket). An ornamental box with compartments for seals, medicines, etc., formerly worn by Japanese on a girdle.

in saecula saeculorum *adverb phrase* L16 **Late Latin** (= to the ages of ages). To all eternity; forever.

in se *adverb phrase* M19 **Latin.** *Philosophy* In itself.

inselberg *noun* plural **inselbergs, inselberge** E20 **German** (from *Insel* island + *Berg* mountain). *Physical Geography* An isolated hill or mountain that rises abruptly from the surrounding landscape, especially from an arid plain.

inshallah *interjection* M19 **Arabic** (in *šā' Allāh*). If God wills it.

■ The Muslim equivalent of DEO VOLENTE.

insignia *noun* M17 **Latin** (plural of *insigne* mark, sign, badge of office, use as noun of neuter of *insignis* distinguished (as by a mark)). **1** *plural* M17 Badges or distinguishing marks (*of* office, honor, etc.); emblems (*of* a nation, person, etc.). **2** *singular* L18 (plural **insignias**) A badge or distinguishing mark (*of* office, honor, etc.); an emblem (*of* a nation, person, etc.). **3** L18 Usually as *plural.* Marks or tokens indicative of something.

in situ *adverb phrase* M18 **Latin.** In its (original) place; in position.

insomnia *noun* (also (earlier) **insomnie, insomnium**) E17 **Latin** (from *insomnis* sleepless (from as negative *in-* + *som-*

nus sleep)). Chronic inability to sleep; sleeplessness.

insouciance *noun* L18 **French** (from as next). Carefreeness, lack of concern.

insouciant *adjective* E19 **French** (from as negative *in-* + *souciant* present participle of *soucier* to care, from Latin *sollicitare* to disturb). Carefree, undisturbed.

inspan *transitive verb* E19 **Afrikaans** (from Dutch *inspannen*, from *in-* + *spannen* to span, fasten). **1** E19 Yoke (oxen, horses, etc.) in a team to a vehicle; harness (a wagon). **2** E20 *figurative* Persuade (a person) to give assistance or service; use as a makeshift. *South African.*

instanter *adverb* L17 **Latin**. Immediately, at once.

■ Now archaic or jocular.

in statu pupillari *adjective phrase* M19 **Latin**. Under guardianship; of junior status at a university; not having a master's degree.

in statu quo *adjective phrase* E17 **Latin**. In the same state as formerly. More fully *in statu quo ante.*

insurrecto *noun* plural **insurrectos** E20 **Spanish** (from Latin *insurrectus* past participle of *insurgere* to rise up). Especially in Spain and Spanish-speaking countries: an insurgent, a rebel; an insurrectionist.

intacta *adjective* M20 **Latin** (feminine of *intactus*, extracted from VIRGO INTACTA). Inviolate, unaffected; not spoiled or sullied.

intaglio *noun & verb* (also **intaglia**) M17 **Italian** (from *intagliare* to engrave). **A** *noun* plural **intaglios**. **1** M17 A figure or design incised or engraved; a cutting or engraving in a hard material. **2** M17 A thing ornamented with incised work; *especially* a precious stone having a figure or design cut on its surface. **b** E19 A mold of something to be cast or struck in relief. **3** M18 The process or art of engraving or carving in a hard material; printing in which the image is engraved or etched into a metal plate or cylinder so that it lies below the nonprinting areas. Also, the condition of being incised. **B** *transitive verb* M19 Engrave with a sunken pattern; execute in intaglio.

intarsia *noun* (in senses 1 and 2 also **intarsio**, plural **intarsios**) M19 **Italian** (*intarsio*). **1** M19 (A piece of) mosaic woodwork, especially made in fifteenth-century Italy; the art of making this. Also called *tarsia.* **2** M19 (A piece of) similar inlaid work in stone, metal, or glass. **3** M20 A method of knitting with a number of colors in which a separate length or ball of yarn is used for each area of color (as opposed to the different yarns being carried at the back of the work). Frequently *attributive.*

intelligentsia *noun* E20 **Russian** (*intelligentsiya*, from Polish *inteligencja*, from Latin *intelligentia* intelligence). The part of a nation (originally in prerevolutionary Russia) having aspirations to intellectual activity, a section of society regarded as possessing culture and political initiative; *plural* the members of this section of a nation or society, intellectuals.

intendant *noun* (also **intendent**) M17 **French** (from Latin *intendent-* present participial stem of *intendere* to direct, promote). **1** M17 Chiefly as the title of certain officials: a superintendent, a director; *especially* (in seventeenth- and eighteenth-century France) any of certain agents of the king appointed to supervise the administration of justice, finance, etc., in the provinces on behalf of central government. **2** L19 The administrator of an opera house or theater. Also, a musical director, a conductor.

inter alia *adverb phrase* M17 **Latin** (from *inter* among + *alia* accusative neuter plural of *alius* another). Among other things.

inter alios *adverb phrase* M17 **Latin** (from *inter* among + *alios* accusative masculine plural of *alius* another). Among other people.

interim *noun, adverb, & adjective* M16 **Latin** ((adverb), from *inter* between + adverbial ending *-im*). **A** *noun* **1** M16

Ecclesiastical History (usually *Interim*) A provisional arrangement for the adjustment of religious differences between the German Protestants and the Roman Catholic church in the mid–sixteenth century. **b** M16 *generally* A temporary or provisional arrangement. **2** L16–M17 A thing done in an interval; an interlude. **3** E17 An intervening time; *the* meantime. **4** M20 An interim dividend. **B** *adverb* L16 In the meantime; meanwhile. Now *rare*. **C** *adjective* E17 Done, made, provided, etc., in or for the meantime; provisional, temporary. Formerly (of time), intervening.

Interimsethik *noun* (also Anglicized as **interim-ethic**) E20 **German** (from as INTERIM + *Ethik* ethics). *Theology* The moral principles of Jesus interpreted as meant for people expecting the imminent end of the world; *transferred* a code of behavior for use in a specific temporary situation.

intermed(i)i plural of INTERMEDIO.

intermedia plural of INTERMEDIUM.

intermedio *noun* plural **intermed(i)i** L19 **Italian** (from as INTERMEDIUM). A musical interlude between the acts of a play or an opera. Cf. INTERMEZZO.

intermedium *noun* plural **intermedia**, **intermediums** L16 **Late Latin** (noun use of neuter singular of Latin *intermedius* intermediate). **1** L16 An intervening action or performance. Now only *specifically* (*Music*), an INTERMEDIO. **2** E17 An interval of time or space. Now *rare* or *obsolete*. **3** M17 An intermediate agent, an intermediary. **4** L19 *Zoology* (modern Latin *os intermedium*). In tetrapods: a carpal in the center of the wrist joint; a tarsal in the center of the ankle joint.

intermezzo *noun* plural **intermezzi**, **intermezzos** L18 **Italian** (from as INTERMEDIUM; cf. MEZZO). **1** L18 A short light dramatic, musical, or other performance inserted between the acts of a play or (formerly) an opera. **2** M19 A short connecting instrumental movement in an opera or other musical work; a similar piece performed independently; a short piece for a solo instrument.

internuncio *noun* plural **internuncios** M17 **Italian** (*internunzio* from Latin *internuntius*, from as *inter-* + *nuntius* messenger). **1** M17 A messenger between two parties; a go-between. **2** L17 An official papal representative or ambassador at a foreign court, ranking below a nuncio. **3** E18 *History* A minister representing a government (especially of Austria) at Constantinople (Istanbul).

inter partes *adjective phrase* E19 **Latin**. *Law* (Of an action) relevant only to the two parties in a particular case; (of a deed, etc.) made between two parties.

interreges plural of INTERREX.

interregnum *noun* plural **interregnums**, **interregna** L16 **Latin** (from as *inter-* between + *regnum* reign). **1** L16–L18 Temporary authority or rule exercised during a vacancy of the throne or a suspension of the normal government. **2** L16 An interval during which the normal government is suspended, especially during the period between the end of a monarch's rule and the accession of his or her successor; any period of cessation or suspension of rule, authority, etc. **3** M17 An interval, a pause, a break.

interrex *noun* plural **interreges** L16 **Latin** (from as *inter-* between + *rex* king). A person holding the supreme authority in a nation during an interregnum.

in terrorem *adverb & adjective phrase* E17 **Latin** (= into a state of terror). (Done) as a warning or to deter.

inter se *adverb phrase* M19 **Latin**. Between or among themselves.

interstitium *noun* plural **interstitiums**, **interstitia** L16 **Latin** (from *intersistere* to stand between). **1** L16–E18 An intervening (usually empty) space, an interstice. **b** L16–E18 An intervening space. **2** M20 *Anatomy* and *Zoology* The tissue or region lying between the principal cells, tissues, etc., of a part of the body.

inter vivos *adverb & adjective phrase* M19 **Latin.** (Made) between living people (especially of a gift as opposed to a legacy).

intifada *noun* L20 **Arabic** (*intifāḍa* shaking off). An uprising by Arabs; *specifically* that begun by Palestinians in 1987 against Israeli authority.

■ The word had earlier been current among Islamic groups, for instance in Lebanon, but only began to appear in English-language reports of events on the West Bank in the late 1980s.

intime *adjective* E17 **French** (from Latin *intimus* innermost). Intimate. Now only *specifically* friendly, familiar, cozy.

intimism *noun* (also **intimisme**) E20 **French** (*intimisme*, from as INTIME). A style of intimate domestic genre painting using impressionist techniques.

intimist *noun & adjective* (also **intimiste**) E20 **French** (from *intimisme*, from as INTIME). **A** *noun* E20 A painter following the principles of intimism. **B** *adjective* M20 Of or pertaining to intimism.

intombi *noun* E19 **Xhosa and Zulu.** In southern Africa: a young woman who has been ritually prepared for marriage.

intonaco *noun* (also **intonico**) plural **intonacos** E19 **Italian** (*intonico, intonaco*, from *intonicare* to cover with plaster, ultimately from Latin *tunica* coat, tunic). The final coating of plaster spread upon a wall or other surface, especially for fresco painting.

in toto *adverb phrase* L18 **Latin.** Completely, without exception; altogether, in all.

intrados *noun* L18 **French** (from as *intra-* inside + *dos* back). *Architecture* The lower or inner curve of an arch; *especially* the lower curve of the voussoirs that form the arch. Cf. EXTRADOS.

intra vires *adverb phrase* L19 **Latin** (= within the powers). Chiefly *Law.* Within the powers or legal authority (*of* a corporation or person).

■ Opposed to ULTRA VIRES.

intra vitam *adjective phrase* L19 **Latin.** *Biology* Taking place during life; while still living. Cf. IN VIVO.

intriguant *noun & adjective* (also **intrigant**) L18 **French** (present participle of *intriguer* to scheme). **A** *noun* L18 An intriguer. **B** *adjective* E19 Intriguing; scheming.

intriguante *noun* (also **intrigante**) E19 **French** (feminine of *intriguant*: see preceding). A woman who intrigues.

introit *noun* LME **Old and Modern French** (*introït* from Latin *introitus* entrance, from *introire* to enter, from as *intro-* + *ire* to go). **1** LME The action or an act of going in; (an) entrance. Long *rare.* **2** L15 *Ecclesiastical* An antiphon or psalm sung while the priest approaches the altar to celebrate the Eucharist. Also, the first two or three words of the office of a particular day.

introuvable *adjective* E19 **French** (from as negative *in-* + *trouver* to find). Unfindable, undiscoverable.

in utero *adverb & adjective phrase* E18 **Latin.** In the uterus; before birth.

in vacuo *adverb phrase* M17 **Latin.** In a vacuum.

invita Minerva *adverb phrase* L16 **Latin** (= Minerva (being) unwilling). When one is not in the mood; without inspiration.

■ Minerva was the Roman goddess of learning and patroness of arts and handicrafts, so her blessing was considered essential to enterprises in these fields.

in vitro *adjective & adverb phrase* L19 **Latin** (literally, 'in glass'). *Biology* (Performed, obtained, or occurring) in a test tube or elsewhere outside a living organism.

in vivo *adjective & adverb phrase* E20 **Latin.** *Biology* (Performed, obtained, or occurring) within a living organism.

■ Opposed to EX VIVO; cf. INTRA VITAM.

involucrum *noun* plural **involucra** L17 **Latin** (from *involvere* to involve). **1** L17 An outer covering, an envelope; a covering membrane. **2** M18 *Botany* A whorl or rosette of bracts surrounding an inflorescence or at the base of an umbel; an involucre.

inyanga *noun* M19 **Zulu**. In South Africa: a traditional herbalist and medicine man, sometimes acting as diviner or magician.

ion *noun* M19 **Greek** (neuter present participle of *ienai* to go). *Physics* and *Chemistry* Originally, either of the constituents that pass to the electrodes during electrolysis. Now *generally*, any individual atom, molecule, or group having a net electric charge (either positive or negative) due to loss or gain of one or more electrons.

iota *noun* LME **Greek** (*iōta*, of Phoenician origin; cf. Hebrew *yod*). **1** LME The ninth (and smallest) letter (Ι, ι) of the Greek alphabet. **2** M17 *figurative* The smallest or a very small part or quantity.

■ The English noun *jot* (from Latin *iota*) is a doublet of *iota* in sense 2.

ipecacuanha *noun* E17 **Portuguese** (from Tupi-Guarani *ipekaaguéne*, from *ipe* small + *kaa* leaves + *guíne* vomit). **1** E17 The root of *Cephaelis ipecacuanha*, a Brazilian plant of the madder family; an extract or preparation of this, formerly much used as an emetic and expectorant. Also, the plant itself. **2** E18 Any of various other plants with emetic roots; a preparation of such a root.

ippon *noun* M20 **Japanese**. A score of one full point in judo, karate, etc.

ipse dixit *noun* plural **ipse dixits** L16 **Latin** (literally, 'he himself said (it)', translation of Greek *autos epha*). An unproved assertion resting only on the authority of a speaker; a dogmatic statement; a dictum.

■ The Greek expression was used of their master's sayings by the followers of the sage Pythagoras.

ipsissima verba *noun phrase* E19 **Latin** (= the very words themselves). The precise words used by a writer or speaker.

ipso facto *adverb phrase* M16 **Latin**. By that very fact or act; by the fact itself; thereby. Cf. EO IPSO.

ipso jure *adverb phrase* L16 **Latin**. By the operation of the law itself.

irredenta *noun* plural **irredente**, **irredentas** E20 **Italian**. A region containing people ethnically related to the inhabitants of one nation but politically subject to another.

■ Also used postpositively as an adjective. Also in TERRA IRREDENTA.

isangoma variant of SANGOMA.

isba *noun* (also **izba**) L18 **Russia** (*izba* (related to Old High German *stuba* from the Germanic base of which modern English *stove* is also ultimately derived)). A Russian hut or log house.

isblink *noun* L18 **Swedish** (or from corresponding words in Danish, German, Dutch). A luminous appearance on the horizon caused by the reflection from ice.

■ Also in Anglicized form as *iceblink*.

ishan *noun* E20 **Arabic** (perhaps from Arabic dialect *īšān* from Persian *nīšān* mark). A prehistoric mound in Iraq.

isolato *noun* plural **isolati**, **isolatos** M19 **Italian**. An isolated person, an outcast.

item *adverb* LME **Latin** (= just so, similarly, moreover, from *ita* thus, so). Likewise, also.

■ Chiefly used to introduce and draw attention to a new statement, particular, or entry, especially in a list or formal document. From this is derived the fully Anglicized noun meaning 'an individual thing, article, or unit included in a set, list, computation, etc.'.

ius cogens, **ius gentium**, **ius naturae**, **ius primae noctis** variants of JUS COGENS, JUS GENTIUM, JUS NATURAE, JUS PRIMAE NOCTIS.

izar *noun* M19 **Arabic** (*'zār*). An enveloping outer garment worn by

Muslim women (and, in some countries, Muslim men). Also, the lower garment of the IHRAM (sense 2).

izba variant of ISBA.

izzat *noun* (also **izzut**) M19 **Persian** (Urdu *'izzat*, from Arabic *'izza* glory). Honor, reputation, credit, prestige.

J

jabot *noun* E19 **French** (= bird's crop, shirt frill, probably from a Proto-Romance base meaning 'crop, maw, gullet'). **1** E19 A frill on the front of a man's shirt, edging the opening. Now chiefly *historical*. **2** L19 An ornamental frill on a woman's bodice.

jacal *noun* M19 **Mexican Spanish** (from Nahuatl *xacalli* contraction of *xamitl calli* adobe house). A hut built of erect stakes filled in with wattle and mud, common in Mexico and the southwestern United States; an adobe house. Also, the material or method used in building such a hut.

j'accuse *noun* M20 **French** (= I accuse). An accusation, particularly one of injustice against an authority.

■ The opening words of Emile Zola's famous letter to the newspaper *L'Aurore* (January 13, 1898) denouncing the French military establishment for wrongly condemning the Jewish army officer Alfred Dreyfus for treason in 1894 and then attempting to suppress the facts that proved that a miscarriage of justice had taken place.

jacquard *adjective & noun* (also **Jacquard**) M19 **French**. **A** *adjective* **1** M19 Designating an attachment to a loom that enables the pattern in the cloth to be produced automatically by means of punched cards. **2** M19 Designating a fabric, article, or pattern made with the aid of this; of an intricate variegated design. **B** *noun* **1** M19 A jacquard fabric, pattern, or article. **2** L19 A jacquard attachment or loom.

■ The loom attachment is called after its inventor, Joseph-Marie Jacquard (1752–1834).

jacquerie *noun* E16 **Old and Modern French** (from male forename *Jacques*). A popular rising of the peasantry.

■ The original *jacquerie* was the revolt of the peasants of northern France against the nobles in 1357–58. *Jacques* was the former French name for a villein or peasant.

jadam *noun* E20 **Malay**. A type of silver or brass niello ware from the Malay peninsula and Sumatra, used especially for decorating belt buckles.

j'adoube *interjection* E19 **French** (from *je, j'* I + 1st person singular of *adouber* to repair, mend (ultimate origin unknown)). *Chess* Indicating that a player wishes to touch a piece without making a move.

jäger *noun* (also **jaeger**) L18 **German** (from *jagen* to hunt, pursue). **1** L18 Originally, a marksman in the German or Austrian infantry. Later, a member of a battalion of riflemen in these armies. Now, a member of a regiment using the name as an official title. **2** E19 A (German or Swiss) huntsman or hunter. **3** E19 An attendant wearing a huntsman's costume. Cf. CHASSEUR sense 2a.

■ *Yager* (or *yager rifle*) (E19), meaning 'a type of short-barreled large-bore rifle formerly used in the southern

United States', is apparently an Anglicized form of *Jäger*.

jai alai *noun phrase* E20 **Spanish** (from Basque *jai* festival + *alai* merry). The game of PELOTA.

jalap *noun* M17 **French** (from Spanish *jalapa*, in full *purga de Jalapa*, from *Jalapa, Xalapa* a Mexican city). **1** M17 A purgative drug obtained from the tuberous roots of a Mexican climbing plant, *Ipomoea purga*, and from certain other plants of the bindweed family. **2** L17 The plant yielding this drug; (with specifying word) any of certain other plants yielding a similar drug.

jalapeño *noun* plural **jalapeños** M20 **Mexican Spanish**. A very hot green chili pepper. Also *jalapeño pepper*.

jalebi *noun* M19 **Hindustani** (*jalebī*). An Indian candy made by frying a coil of batter and then soaking it in syrup.

jaleo *noun* M19 **Spanish** (literally, 'halloo'). Clapping to accompany Andalusian dancing; a lively Andalusian dance.

jalousie *noun* M18 **French** (literally, 'jealousy'; also, a type of blind or shutter). A blind or shutter made from a row of angled slats to exclude sun and rain and control the entry of air and light.

jambalaya *noun* L19 **Louisiana French** (from Provençal *jambalaia*). A dish composed of rice mixed with shrimp, chicken, sausage, etc.; *figurative* a mixture, a jumble.

janitor *noun* M16 **Latin** (from *janua* door, entrance). **1** M16 A doorkeeper, a porter; *historically* an ostler. **2** E18 A caretaker of a building, especially a school, responsible for its cleaning, heating, etc.

janken *noun* M20 **Japanese**. A children's game played by using the hands to represent one of three things, paper, scissors, or stone.

japonaiserie *noun* L19 **French**. Japanese characteristics or fashion; in *plural*, Japanese ornaments or knickknacks.

■ Cf. CHINOISERIE. The Anglicized form *Japanesery* also dates from the same period (L19) of enthusiasm for Japanese art and artifacts in the West.

jarabe *noun* (also **jarave**) M19 **American Spanish** (from Spanish = syrup). A Mexican pair dance in which the man dances the ZAPATEADO steps, performed especially as an exhibition dance in national costume.

jardinière *noun* M19 **French** (literally, 'female gardener'). **1** M19 An ornamental receptacle, pot, or stand for the display of growing or cut flowers. **2** M19 *Cooking* A garnish made with cooked vegetables.

jargonelle *noun* (also **jargonel**) L17 **French** (diminutive of *jargon* from Italian *giargone*, usually identified ultimately with zircon). An early-ripening (originally inferior) variety of pear.

jaspé *noun* M19 **French** (past participle of *jasper* to marble). Marbled, mottled, variegated.

jat *noun* (also **jati**) L19 **Hindustani** (*jāt*, *jāti* from Sanskrit *jāti* birth). In the Indian subcontinent: a caste, a tribe, a class.

jatha *noun* E20 **Punjabi and Hindustani** (*jāthā*). In the Indian subcontinent: an armed or organized band of Sikhs.

jati variant of JAT.

jaune *adjective* LME **French** (from Latin *galbinum* greenish yellow). Yellow.

■ Although formerly fully naturalized, *jaune* is now obsolete in English except in the names of pigments, such as *jaune brilliant* cadmium yellow.

jebel *noun* M19 **Arabic** (*jabal*, (colloquial) *jebel*, plural *jibāl*, mountain). In the Middle East and North Africa: a mountain, a range of hills.

■ Frequently in place names.

jehad variant of JIHAD.

jellaba *noun* (also **djellaba**, **jellabah**, **jelab**, and other variants) E19 **Arabic** ((Moroccan) *jellāb*(*a*), *jellābiyya*: cf. GALABIYA). A loose hooded long-sleeved usually woolen cloak of a kind worn originally by Arab men in North Africa.

je ne sais quoi *noun phrase* M17 **French** (literally, 'I do not know what'). An indefinable quality, something indescribable or inexpressible.

jet d'eau *noun* plural **jets d'eau** L17 **French** (= jet of water). An ornamental jet of water rising from a fountain or pipe; a fountain or pipe from which such a jet rises.

jeté *noun* M19 **French** (past participle (sc. *pas* step) of *jeter* to throw). *Ballet* A step in which a spring is made from one foot to land on the other, especially with one leg extended forward and the other backward. Cf. GRAND JETÉ.

jeté en tournant *noun phrase* plural **jetés en tournant** M20 **French**. *Ballet* A jeté executed with a turning movement. Also called *tour jeté*.

jeton *noun* (also in sense 1 **jetton**) M20 **Old and Modern French** (from *jeter* to cast up (accounts), calculate). **1** M20 A counter or token used to operate a slot machine. **2** M20 A metal disk used instead of a coin for insertion in a public telephone booth, especially in France.

jets d'eau plural of JET D'EAU.

jetton variant of JETON.

jeu *noun* plural **jeux** L18 **French** (from Latin *jocus* joke). Play, game.

■ In English occurs only in various phrases as below.

jeu de mots *noun phrase* plural **jeux de mots** M18 **French** (literally, 'play of words'). A play on words, a pun.

jeu de paume *noun phrase* L18 **French** (literally, 'game of the palm (of the hand)'). Tennis in its original form, played on an indoor court; a court where this is played.

jeu de société *noun phrase* plural **jeux de société** E19 **French** (literally, 'game of society'). A party game or amusement.

■ Used especially in the plural.

jeu d'esprit *noun phrase* plural **jeux d'esprit** E18 **French** (literally, 'game of wit'). A playful action in which some cleverness is displayed; (now usually) a humorous literary trifle.

jeune fille *noun & adjective phrase* M19 **French**. **A** *noun phrase* M19 plural **jeunes filles**. A young girl, an ingénue. **B** *attributive* or as *adjective phrase* L19 Characteristic of an ingénue.

jeune fille bien élevée *noun phrase* plural **jeunes filles bien élevées** L20 **French**. A young girl brought up in a genteel way.

jeune premier *noun phrase* plural **jeunes premiers** feminine **jeune première**) M19 **French** (literally, 'first young man (woman)'). An actor who plays the part of a principal lover or young hero (or heroine).

jeunes filles, jeunes filles bien élevées plurals of JEUNE FILLE, JEUNE FILLE BIEN ÉLEVÉE.

jeunes premiers plural of JEUNE PREMIER.

jeunesse *noun* L18 **French**. Young people; the young.

jeunesse dorée *noun phrase* M19 **French** (literally, 'gilded youth'). Young people of wealth and fashion.

■ The original *jeunesse dorée* was a group of fashionable counterrevolutionaries in France during the Revolution, following the fall of Robespierre.

jheel *noun* (also **jhil**) E19 **Hindi** (*jhīl*). In the Indian subcontinent: a (large) pool or lake left after a flood.

jibba variant of JUBBA.

jigotai *noun* M20 **Japanese** (from *ji* self + *go* defense + *tai* posture). A defensive posture in judo.

jihad *noun* (also **jehad**) M19 **Arabic** (*jihād*, literally, 'effort'). A holy war undertaken by Muslims against unbelievers or for the propagation of Islam; *transferred* a fervent campaign in some cause.

Jina *noun* E19 **Sanskrit** (*jina*). *Jainism* A great Jain teacher who has attained liberation from KARMA; a sculptured representation of such a teacher.

jinnee *noun* plural **jinn** (also **jinn**, **djinn**, plural **jinnees**, same) E19 **Arabic** (*jinnī* masculine singular, plural *jinn*). In Arabian stories and Muslim mythology: a spirit of an order lower than the angels, able to appear in human or animal form and to exercise supernatural influence.

jinricksha *noun* (also **jinrikisha**) L19 **Japanese** (*jin-riki-sha*, from *jin* man + *riki* strength, power + *sha* vehicle). A rickshaw.

jiu-jitsu, **jiu-jutsu** variants of JUJITSU.

jiva *noun* E19 **Sanskrit** (*jīva*). *Hindu and Jain Philosophy* The soul; the embodied self; the vital principle.

joie de vivre *noun phrase* L19 **French** (= joy of living). A feeling of healthy enjoyment of life; exuberance, high spirits.

jojoba *noun* E20 **Mexican Spanish**. A desert shrub, *Simmondsia chinensis* (family Simmondsiaceae), of Mexico and the southwestern United States, whose seeds yield an oil used as a lubricant and in cosmetics.

■ The word was familiar in the United States long before it became current in general English, which happened only from the mid 1970s onward, when its value as a substitute for sperm whale oil and its properties as an ingredient in cosmetics and soaps became more widely appreciated.

jolie laide *noun & adjective phrase* plural **jolies laides** L19 **French** (from feminine adjectives *jolie* pretty + *laide* ugly). (An) attractively or fascinatingly ugly (woman).

■ The masculine form *joli laid* is also occasionally found.

jong *noun* E17 **Afrikaans** (= young (man)). Formerly in South Africa, a term for a male servant of the class once designated as "Colored."

■ South African colloquial, used especially among young people.

jongleur *noun* L18 **French** (alteration of *jougleur* (Old French *jogleor* accusative of *joglere*) from Latin *joculator* jester). *History* An itinerant minstrel.

jornada *noun* plural **jornadas** M17 **Spanish** (= Italian *giornata*, French *journée* journey). **1** M17–M19 An act of a play; a book or canto of a poem. **2** E19 In Mexico, etc.: a day's journey; *specifically* one across a waterless desert tract with no place to halt.

joruri *noun* L19 **Japanese** (*jōruri*, from the name of a character in a popular recitation). **1** L19 A dramatic recitation to music, accompanying a Japanese puppet performance. **2** M20 Japanese puppet drama.

jota *noun* M19 **Spanish**. A northern Spanish folk dance performed by one or more couples in rapid triple time; a piece of music for this dance.

jotun *noun* M19 **Old Norse** (*jǫtunn* = Old English *eoten*, from Germanic). In Scandinavian mythology: a member of a supernatural race of giants.

joual *noun* M20 **Canadian French** (dialect form of French *cheval* horse). Demotic Canadian French characterized by nonstandard pronunciations and grammar, and influenced by English vocabulary and syntax.

jour *noun* LME **Old and Modern French** (from Latin *diurnum* neuter singular (used as noun in popular Latin) of *diurnus* diurnal). **1** LME–M16 A day. **2** M19 A kind of open stitch used in lacemaking. Usually in *plural*.

■ In sense 1 now occurs only in certain phrases used in English, e.g., BONHEUR DU JOUR, PLAT DU JOUR.

jubba *noun* (also **jibba(h)**, **jubbah**) M16 **Arabic** (whence also French JUPE). A type of long open cloth coat with wide sleeves, worn especially by Muslims.

jubilate *noun* (also **Jubilate**) ME **Latin** (imperative of *jubilare* to call, halloo, (in Christian writers) shout for joy). **1** ME Psalm 100 (90 in the Vulgate) used as a canticle; a musical setting of this. More fully *Jubilate Deo* (the first two words of this psalm). **2** M18 A call to rejoice; an outburst of joyous triumph.

Judenrat *noun* plural **Judenrate** M20 German (= Jewish council). A council representing a Jewish community in a locality controlled by the Germans during the war of 1939–45.

judenrein *adjective* M20 German (= free from Jews). Of a society, organization, etc., *specifically* in Nazi Germany: without Jewish members, out of which Jews have been expelled.

judo *noun* L19 Japanese (from *jū* gentle + *dō* way). A refined form of jujitsu using principles of movement and balance, practiced as a sport or a form of physical exercise.

juge d'instruction *noun phrase* plural **juges d'instruction** L19 French. In France: an examining magistrate, a police magistrate.

Jugendstil *noun & adjective* E20 German (from *Jugend* youth + *Stil* style). (Of, pertaining to, or designating) German ART NOUVEAU.

■ *Die Jugend* was the name of an influential German magazine started in 1896 in Munich.

jujitsu *noun* (also **ju-jitsu**, **jiu-jitsu**, **ju-jutsu**) L19 Japanese (*jūjutsu*, from *jū* gentle + *jutsu* skill). A Japanese system of unarmed combat using an opponent's strength and weight to his or her disadvantage, now also practiced as physical training. Cf. JUDO.

juju *noun* (also **ju-ju**) E17 West African (probably from French *joujou* plaything, reduplicated form from *jouer* to play from Latin *jocare*). A charm, amulet, or cult object used by some West African peoples; the supernatural force believed to be associated with such objects. Also, the system of observances associated with such objects.

jujube *noun* LME French (or medieval Latin *jujuba*, ultimately from Latin *zizyphum* from Greek *zizuphos*, *zizuphon* zizyphus (tree)). **1** LME An edible berry-like drupe, the fruit of various trees of the genus *Ziziphus*, of the buckthorn family. **b** M16 Any of the trees that produce this fruit, especially *Ziziphus jujuba*, extending from the Mediterranean to China, and *Z. lotus* of North Africa. Also *jujube tree*. **2** M19 A candy or confection made of gum arabic, gelatin, etc., originally one flavored with or tasting like this fruit.

jukskei *noun* E19 Afrikaans (from *juk* yoke + *skei* pin, peg). **1** E19 A wooden peg on an ox yoke. **2** M20 A game resembling quoits, originally played with yoke pins; the bottle-shaped peg used in this game.

juku *noun* L20 Japanese. In Japan: a cramming school.

julienne *adjective & noun* E18 French (from male forename *Jules* or *Julien*). **A** *adjective* **1** E18 Designating soup made of various vegetables (especially carrots), chopped and cooked in meat stock. **2** L19 Designating a small thin strip of a vegetable, etc.; (of a vegetable, etc.) cut into such strips; (of a dish or garnish) consisting of or containing such strips. **B** *noun* **1** M19 Julienne soup. **2** E20 A julienne strip; a dish of julienne vegetables, etc.

jumar *noun* M20 Origin unknown (originally Swiss). *Mountaineering* A clamp that when attached to a fixed rope automatically tightens when weight is applied and relaxes when it is removed, thus facilitating the climbing of the rope; a climb using such clips.

jumby *noun* (also **jumbie**) E19 Kikongo (*zumbi* fetish; cf. *zombie*). A ghost, an evil spirit. Chiefly *West Indies*.

jumelle *adjective* L15 French (feminine (masculine *jumeau*), from Latin *gemellus* diminutive of *geminus* twin). Twinned, paired; made or shaped in couples or pairs, double.

junker *noun* M16 German (earlier *Junkher(r)*, from Middle High German *junc* young + *herre* (modern *Herr*) lord). A young German noble; *specifically* a member of the reactionary party of the Prussian aristocracy who aimed to maintain the exclusive privileges of their class; a narrow-minded, overbearing (younger) member of the German aristocracy.

■ Obsolete except in historical contexts.

junta *noun* E17 **Spanish and Portuguese** (*junta* (whence French *junte*) from Italian *giunta* from Proto-Romance noun use of Latin *juncta* feminine past participle of *jungere* to join). **1** E17 A Spanish or Italian deliberative or administrative council or committee. **2** E18 *generally* A body of people combined for a common (especially political) purpose; a self-elected committee or council, a cabal. Now frequently *specifically*, a political or military clique or faction taking power after a revolution or *coup d'état*.

■ The alternative form *junto*, modeled on Spanish nouns in *-o*, has also been current in English in sense 2 from the same period and briefly (E–M18) in sense 1.

jupe *noun* ME **Old and Modern French** (from Arabic JUBBA). **1** ME A man's loose jacket, tunic, or jerkin. Now only *Scottish*. **2** E18–E20 A woman's jacket, gown, or bodice. In *plural* also, a kind of bodice or stays. *Scottish*. **3** E19 A woman's skirt.

jupon *noun* LME **Old French** (*juppon*, (also modern) *jupon*, from JUPE). *History* A close-fitting tunic or doublet; *especially* one worn under a hauberk, sometimes of thick material and padded. Also, a sleeveless surcoat worn outside armor, of rich material and emblazoned with arms.

jure divino *adverb phrase* L16 **Latin**. By divine right or authority.

jus *noun* M20 **French** (= juice). A thin broth or gravy.

jus cogens *noun phrase* (also **ius cogens**) L19 **Latin** (= compelling law). A principle of international law that cannot be set aside by agreement or acquiescence; a peremptory norm of general international law.

jus gentium *noun phrase* (also **ius gentium**) M16 **Latin** (= law of nations). International law.

jus naturae *noun phrase* (also **ius naturae**) M17 **Latin** (= law of nature). Natural law.

jus primae noctis *noun* (also **ius primae noctis**) L19 **Latin** (= right of the first night). DROIT DE SEIGNEUR.

jusqu'au bout *adverb phrase* E20 **French** (= up to the end). To the bitter end; until a conclusive victory has been gained.

■ The policy of *jusqu'auboutisme* applied originally in the context of World War I.

juste milieu *noun phrase* M19 **French** (literally, 'the right mean'). A happy medium, the golden mean; judicious moderation, especially in politics.

juvenilia *noun plural* E17 **Latin** (neuter plural of *juvenilis* juvenile). Literary or artistic works produced in an author's or artist's youth.

K

kabbalah *noun* (also **cabala**, **cabbala**, **kabbala**, and (in sense 1) with initial capital) E16 **Medieval Latin** (*cab(b)ala* from rabbinical Hebrew *qabbālāh* tradition, from *qibbēl* to receive, accept). **1** E16 The esoteric and mystical Jewish tradition, first transmitted orally, of which the Zohar (thirteenth century) is the basic text. **2** *generally* **a** M–L17 (An) oral tradition. **b** M17 (An) esoteric doctrine; (a) mystic interpretation; occult lore.

kabloona *noun* L18 **Eskimo** ((Inuit) *kabluna* big eyebrow). Among Canadian Eskimos: a person who is not an Eskimo; a white person.

kabuki *noun & adjective* L19 **Japanese** (originally (as verb) to act dissolutely; later interpreted as from *ka* song + *bu* dance + *ki* art, skill). (Of, pertaining to, or characteristic of) a traditional and popular form of Japanese drama with highly stylized song, mime, and dance, performed by male actors only.

kacha variant of KUTCHA.

kachina *noun* L19 **Hopi** (*kacína* supernatural, from Keresan). A deified ancestral spirit in North American Pueblo Indian mythology.

Kaddish *noun* E17 **Aramaic** (*qaddīš* holy). An ancient Jewish doxology regularly recited in the synagogue, including brief prayers for the welfare of Israel and concluding with a prayer for universal peace.

kadi variant of CADI.

kafenion *noun* M20 **Greek** (*kafeneio(n)*). A Greek coffeehouse.

kaffeeklatsch *noun* (also **Kaffeeklatsch**, **kaffee klatsch**, **kaffee-klatch**) L19 **German** (from *Kaffee* coffee + *Klatsch* gossip; cf. KLATCH). Gossip over coffee cups; a coffee party.

kaffiyeh variant of KEFFIYEH.

kaftan variant of CAFTAN.

kagoule variant of CAGOULE.

kagura *noun* L19 **Japanese**. A form of traditional sacred music and dance performed at Shinto festivals.

Kahal *noun* E20 **Hebrew** (*qāhāl* assembly, community). (The governing body of) any of the former localized Jewish communities in Europe.

kahuna *noun* L19 **Hawaiian**. In Hawaii: a priest, a wise man; a minister; a sorcerer.

kai *noun* M19 **Maori**. Food.

■ New Zealand colloquial. Also in reduplicated form *kaikai* or *kai-kai*, meaning the same or 'feasting'.

kaid *noun* (also *(archaic)* **caid**) E19 **Arabic** (*ḳā'id* leader). An ALCAIDE.

kaikai variant of KAI.

kain *noun* plural **kains**, same L18 **Malay**. In Malaysia and Indonesia: (a piece of) cloth, especially for use as clothing; a sarong.

■ Frequently with postpositive adjective.

kairos *noun* M20 **Greek** (= right or proper time). Fullness of time; the propitious moment, especially for decision or action.

■ The word became current in English through the writings of the German-born American theologian Paul Tillich (1886–1965).

Kaiser *noun* M19 **German** (in modern use and in this form; ultimately from Latin *Caesar*, but cf. Old English *cāsere*, Old Frisian *keisar*, Old Saxon *kēsur*, *kēsar*, Old Norse *keisari*, Gothic *kaisar*, Dutch *keizer*). (The title of) an emperor: *specifically* an Austrian or German emperor.

■ Current in various spellings from the OE period, the word in its modern form reflects a Bavarian spelling that supplanted the more usual *keiser* in the seventeenth century. Its use in modern English appears to be because it was the form favored by the nineteenth-century historian Thomas Carlyle.

k'ai shu *noun phrase* L19 **Chinese** (*kǎishu*, from *kǎi* model + *shū* write). The usual script used for the Chinese language, suitable for everyday purposes.

kaizen *noun* L20 **Japanese** (= improvement). Continuous improvement of working practices, personal efficiency, etc., as a business philosophy.

kakemono *noun* plural **kakemonos** L19 **Japanese** (from *kake-* hang + *mono* thing). A Japanese unframed wall picture, usually painted or inscribed on silk or paper.

kalimba *noun* M20 **Bantu**. A musical instrument played with the thumbs, consisting of metal strips mounted on a small hollow piece of wood.

kalpa *noun* L18 **Sanskrit**. In Indian cosmology: an eon, a great age of the world, a cycle of YUGAS; *specifically* in *Hinduism*, a period of 4,320 million years.

Kama Sutra *noun & adjective phrase* L19 **Sanskrit** (from *kāma* love, desire + *sūtra* SUTRA). **A** *noun phrase* L19 (The title of) an ancient Sanskrit treatise on the art of love and sexual technique; a sex manual. **B** *adjective phrase* M20 Sexually explicit; sensual.

kameez *noun* (also **kameeze**) E19 **Arabic** (*ḳamīṣ*, perhaps from late Latin *camisia* shirt, nightgown). A loose long-sleeved shirt or tunic worn, especially by Muslims, in the Indian subcontinent, and by some Muslims elsewhere. Cf. SHALWAR.

kamerad *interjection* E20 **German** (literally, 'comrade', from French *camerade, camarade*). (Expression used by a German-speaking soldier:) notifying to an enemy a wish to surrender.

■ The word was current between combatants in this situation during World War I and became a cliché of war movies.

kami *noun* plural same E17 **Japanese**. A Shinto god or deity. Also, the Japanese emperor.

kamikaze *noun & adjective* L19 **Japanese** (= divine wind, from as KAMI + *kaze* wind). **A** *noun* **1** L19 In Japanese tradition, the gale that destroyed the fleet of the invading Mongols in 1281. **2** M20 In World War II, (a crewman of) a Japanese aircraft, usually loaded with explosives, making a deliberate suicidal crash on an enemy target; a suicide pilot or plane; also *transferred*. **3** M20 *Surfing* A deliberately taken wipeout. **B** M20 *adjective* Of, pertaining to, or characteristic of a kamikaze; reckless, potentially self-destructive.

kana *noun* plural same E18 **Japanese**. (A character or syllabary in) Japanese syllabic writing. Cf. HIRAGANA, KATAKANA.

kanat variant of QANAT.

kanban *noun* L20 **Japanese** (= billboard, sign). **1** L20 A card used for ordering parts, etc., in a just-in-time manufacturing system evolved in Japan. **2** L20 A just-in-time manufacturing system in which parts, etc., are ordered on cards. In full *kanban system*.

kanga variant of KHANGA.

kanji *noun* plural same E20 **Japanese** (from *kan* Chinese + *ji* letter, character). (Any of) the set of borrowed and adapted Chinese ideographs used in the Japanese writing system. Cf. KANA.

kanoon *noun* E19 **Persian** (*ḳānūn* from Arabic, ultimately from Greek *kanōn*). A plucked musical instrument of the dulcimer or psaltery type, in the classic form with seventy-two strings, now with fifty to sixty.

kan-pei variant of GANBEI.

kanpu variant of GANBU.

kantele *noun* E20 **Finnish**. A form of zither used in Finland and the adjoining part of Russia.

kanzu *noun* E20 **Kiswahili**. A long white cotton or linen robe worn by East African men.

kaolin *noun* E18 **French** (from Chinese *gāolǐng*, literally 'high hill', a place in Jiangxi province where it is found). A fine white clay resulting from the decomposition of feldspar, used to make porcelain and china, as a filler in paper and textiles, and in medicinal adsorbents and poultices. Also (*Mineralogy*), any of a group of clay minerals that typically occur in such clay, *especially* kaolinite.

kapai *adjective & adverb* M19 **Maori** (*ka pai*). Good; well, fine.

■ New Zealand. Also used as interjection, expressing pleasure or approval.

kapellmeister *noun* M19 **German** (from *Kapelle* court orchestra, from medieval Latin *capella* chapel + *Meister* master). Chiefly *History* The leader or conductor of a court orchestra, an opera, a choir, etc.

kappa *noun* LME **Greek.** **1** LME The tenth letter (Κ, κ) of the Greek alphabet. **2** M20 *Biology* An infective and independently reproducing particle (now usually regarded as a commensal bacterium) that occurs within cells of some strains of the ciliate *Paramecium aurelia*. Also, such particles collectively.

kappie *noun* M19 **Afrikaans** (from Dutch *kapje* diminutive of *kap* hood). In South Africa: a sun bonnet with a large brim to protect the face.

kapu *adjective & noun* M20 **Hawaiian.** TABOO.

kaput *adjective* (also **kaputt**) L19 **German** (*kaputt* from French (*être*) *capot* (to be) without tricks in piquet, etc.; cf. CAPOT). Finished, worn out; dead, destroyed; rendered useless or unable to function; broken.

■ *Slang*. The allusion by an English writer in 1914 to *kaputt* as "the Germans' favourite word about their foe, meaning 'done'" (Duchess of Sutherland *Six Weeks at the War*) indicates the historical background to the word's entrance into the English-speaking consciousness.

karabiner *noun* M20 **German** (abbreviation of German *Karabiner-haken* spring-hook). A metal oval or D-shaped coupling link with a closure protected against accidental opening, used in mountaineering.

■ Often further contracted to *krab* in colloquial use.

karaburan *noun* E20 **Turkish** (from *kara* black + *buran* whirlwind). A hot dusty wind that blows in central Asia.

karakul *noun & adjective* (also **caracul**) M19 **Russian** (*karakul'*, from the name of an oasis in Uzbekistan and of two lakes in Tajikistan, apparently ultimately from Turkic). **A** *noun* **1** M19 (An animal of) a breed of sheep with a coarse wiry fleece. **2** L19 (Cloth or fur resembling) the glossy curled fleece of a young lamb of this breed. Also called *Persian lamb*. **B** L19 *attributive* or as *adjective* Of or pertaining to the karakul or karakul.

karamat variant of KRAMAT.

karana *noun* M20 **Sanskrit** (*karaṇa* action, posture). Any of the 108 basic postures in Indian dance.

karanga *noun* E20 **Maori.** A (Maori) ritual chant of welcome. *New Zealand.*

karaoke *noun* L20 **Japanese** (from *kara* empty + *oke* abbreviation of *ōkesutora* orchestra). A form of entertainment (originating in Japan) in which one or more people sing popular songs as soloists against prerecorded backing music; (in full *karaoke music*) such prerecorded backing music.

■ Introduced in both the United States and Britain during the 1980s, *karaoke* became hugely popular. The word is often used attributively, as in *karaoke bar*, an establishment in which the management provides the *karaoke machine* or jukebox that plays the backing music.

karate *noun* M20 **Japanese** (from *kara* empty + *te* hand). A Japanese system of unarmed combat using the hands and feet as weapons.

karezza *noun* (also **carezza**) L19 **Italian** (*carezza* caress). Sexual intercourse in which ejaculation is avoided.

karma *noun* E19 **Sanskrit** (*karman* action, effect, fate). Fate or destiny following as effect from cause.

■ *Karma* has specific meanings within the religions of the Indian subcontinent: in Buddhism and Hinduism, it is the sum of a person's actions, especially intentional actions, regarded as determining that person's future states of existence; in Jainism it is subtle physical matter that binds the soul as a result of bad actions.

karoshi *noun* L20 **Japanese.** Death through overwork.

kaross *noun* (also **kross**) M18 **Afrikaans** (*karos*, perhaps from Nama). A cloak or sleeveless jacket like a blanket made of hairy animal skins, worn by the indigenous peoples of southern Africa. Also, a rug of sewn skins used on a bed or on the floor.

Karren *noun plural* L19 **German.** *Physical Geography* The furrows or fissures of a KARRENFELD; terrain characterized by these. Cf. LAPIÉS.

Karrenfeld *noun* plural **Karrenfelder, Karrenfelds** L19 **German** (from preceding + *Feld* field). *Physical Geography* An area or landscape, usually of limestone bare of soil, that has been eroded by solution so as to have an extremely dissected surface with conspicuous furrows and fissures, often separated by knifelike ridges. Cf. LAPIÉS.

karst *noun* L19 **German** (*der Karst* (perhaps related to Slovene *Krâs*) a limestone plateau region in Slovenia). *Physical Geography* A kind of topography characteristic of areas of relatively soluble rock (usually limestone) and mainly underground drainage, marked by numerous abrupt ridges, gorges, fissures, swallow-holes, and caverns; a region dominated by such topography.

kasbah variant of CASBAH.

kasha *noun* (also (earlier) **casha**) E19 **Russian.** **1** E19 A porridge made from cooked buckwheat or other grains. **2** M20 A beige color resembling that of buckwheat groats.

Kashrut *noun* (also **Kashruth**) E20 **Hebrew** (= legitimacy (in religion), from as KOSHER *adjective*). The body of Jewish religious laws relating to the suitability of food, ritual objects, etc.; the observance of these laws.

kat variant of KHAT.

kata *noun* M20 **Japanese.** A system of basic exercises or postures and movements used to teach and improve the execution of techniques in judo and other martial arts.

katabothron see KATAVOTHRON.

katakana *noun* (also **katagana**) E18 **Japanese** (from *kata* side + KANA). An angular form of kana, used in modern Japanese mainly for writing words of foreign origin and for emphasis. Cf. HIRAGANA.

katavothron *noun* (also **catavothron, katabothron, katavothra**) plural **katavothra, katavothrai, katavothrons** E19 **Modern Greek** (*katabothra*, plural *katabothrai, katabothres*, from Greek *kata* down + *bothros* hole (*katavothron* representing modern Greek pronunciation, *katavothron* from misunderstanding singular as neuter plural)). A subterranean channel or deep hole formed by the action of water; a swallow-hole.

■ A feature of the landscape in certain parts of mainland Greece. In general use the word is now usually replaced by *swallow-hole*.

katel *noun* (also **kartel**) M19 **Afrikaans** (apparently from Portuguese *catel, catle* little bed, from Malay *katil* from Tamil *kaṭṭil* bedstead). A lightweight portable bed or hammock, used in an ox wagon.

■ South African. The Malay word *katil* is used in the Cape Malay community to denote the bier used in funeral ceremonies.

katharevousa *noun* E20 **Modern Greek** (*kathareuousa* feminine of *kathareuōn* present participle of Greek *kathareuein* to be pure, from *katharos* pure). The purist form of modern Greek.

■ At one time (but not since 1976), the archaizing literary version of Greek officially used by the state, as opposed to the popular and spoken demotic.

kathi *noun* M20 **Malay** (*kadi* from Arabic *ḳāḍī* CADI). A judge in Islamic law, who also functions as a registrar of Muslim marriages, divorces, etc.

katsuo *noun* E18 **Japanese.** A bonito, *Katsuwonus pelamis*, important as a food fish in Japan, fresh or dried.

katsura *noun* E20 **Japanese.** **1** E20 A type of Japanese wig worn mainly by women. **2** E20 A type of romantic Noh play with a woman as the central character. In full *katsuramono* (*mono* piece, play).

katzenjammer *noun* **M19 German** (from *Katzen* (combining form of *Katze* cat) + *Jammer* distress, wailing). **1** M19 A hangover; a severe headache. **2** L19 *transferred* and *figurative* Confusion, disorder; clamor, uproar.

■ *Colloquial.* The currency of the word has been promoted by the comic strip called *The Katzenjammer Kids*, first drawn in 1897 by Rudolph Dirks for the *New York Journal*.

kava *noun* **L18 Tongan.** A shrub, *Piper methysticum*, of the West Pacific islands; a narcotic fermented drink made especially in Fiji from its macerated roots. Cf. YANGGONA.

kavadi *noun* **M20 Tamil** (*kāvaṭi*). In Hindu religious practice, a decorated arch carried on the shoulders as an act of penance or in fulfillment of a vow. Also the festival at which this act is performed.

kayak *noun* **M18 Eskimo** ((Inuit) *qayaq*). **A** *noun* **1** M18 An Eskimo canoe, made of a framework of light wood covered with sealskins, and having a small watertight opening in the top to admit a single man. **2** M20 A small covered canoe modeled on this, used for touring or sport. **B** *intransitive verb* L19 Travel by kayak, paddle a kayak.

kazachoc *noun* (also **kozatchok** and other variants) **E20 Russian** (diminutive of *kazak* cossack). A Slavonic, chiefly Ukrainian, dance with a fast and usually quickening tempo, and employing the step PRISIADKA.

kebab *noun* (also (earlier) **cabob**) **L17 Arabic** (*kabāb* (perhaps ultimately from Persian), partly through Urdu, Persian, and Turkish). A dish consisting of pieces of meat (occasionally with vegetables) grilled or roasted on a skewer or spit.

■ The arrangement of the meat pieces on the skewer has given rise (L20) to the use of *kebab* for components of a similar polymer structure in physical chemistry.

kebaya *noun* (also (earlier) **cabaia** and other variants) **L16 Arabic** (*ḳabāya* representing colloquial pronunciation of *ḳbā'a* feminine of *ḳbā'* tunic, gown, shirt; in early use through Portuguese *cabaya* or Persian, in modern use through Malay *kebaya*). **1** L16 A light loose tunic of a type worn in Southeast Asia by women or (formerly) by men. **2** M20 A short tight-fitting long-sleeved jacket, together with a sarong the traditional dress of Malay and Indonesian women.

kef *noun* (in sense 1 also **kief**, **keif**; in sense 2 also **kif**) **E19 Arabic** (representing colloquial pronunciation of *kayf*). **1** E19 A state of drowsiness or dreamy intoxication produced by the use of cannabis, etc. Also, the enjoyment of idleness. **2** L19 In Morocco and Algeria: cannabis or some other substance smoked to produce dreamy intoxication.

keffiyeh *noun* (also **kaffiyeh**, **kuffiyeh** and other variants) **E19 Arabic** (*kūfiyya*, (colloquial) *keffiyya*). A kerchief worn as a headdress by Bedouin Arabs.

keftedes *noun plural* (also **keftedhes**) **E20 Modern Greek** (*kephtes*, plural *kephtedes* from Turkish *köfte* from Persian KOFTA). In Greek cooking, small meatballs made with herbs and onions.

kehilla *noun* plural **kehillot(h)** **L19 Yiddish** (*kĕhilĕ* from Hebrew *qĕhillāh* community). The Jewish community in a town or village.

keif variant of KEF.

keiretsu *noun* **L20 Japanese.** A group of closely associated Japanese business companies linked especially by cross-shareholding.

kelebe *noun* **M19 Greek** (*kelebē*). *Greek Antiquities* A wide-mouthed vessel with a broad flat rim and two handles connecting this to the body but not extending above the rim.

Kelim variant of KILIM.

keller *noun* (also **Keller**) **E20 German** (= cellar). A beer-cellar in Austria or Germany.

Kempeitai *noun* M20 Japanese (*kenpeitai*). The Japanese military secret service in the period 1931–45.

ken *noun* L19 Japanese. A Japanese game of forfeits played with the hands and with gestures.

kenaf *noun* L19 Persian (variant of *kanab* hemp). The brown fiber of the *Hibiscus cannabinus* plant used to make rope and coarse cloth; ambari hemp.

kendo *noun* E20 Japanese (from *ken* sword + *dō* way). A Japanese sport of fencing with two-handed bamboo staves.

kenosis *noun* L19 Greek (*kenōsis* an emptying). *Christian Theology* Christ's full or partial renunciation of his divine nature or powers in his Incarnation.

■ The reference is to the Greek New Testament text of Philippians 2:7 *heauton ekenōse*, literally, 'he emptied himself'.

kente *noun* (also **Kente**) M20 Twi (= cloth). In Ghana: a brightly colored banded material; a long garment made from this material, loosely draped on or worn around the shoulders and waist. More fully *kente cloth*.

kepi *noun* M19 French (*képi* from Swiss German *Käppi* diminutive of *Kappe* capital). A French military cap with a flat circular top that slopes toward the front and a horizontal peak.

kêrel *noun* (also **kerel**) L19 Afrikaans (from Dutch from Old High German *kar(a)l* man). A fellow, a young man; a boyfriend. *South African colloquial*.

kermes *noun* L16 French (*kermès* from Arabic *ḳirmiz* (= sense 2 below)). **1** L16 A small evergreen oak, *Quercus coccifera*, of the Mediterranean region. More fully *kermes oak*. **2** E17 (The dried bodies of) adult females of the scale insect *Kermes ilicis*, which form hard berry-like galls on the kermes oak, used to make dye and (formerly) medicines; the scarlet dye made from these.

kermesse *noun* L19 French (from as next). **1** L19 A KERMIS. **2** M20 *Cycling* A circuit race.

kermis *noun* (also **kirmess**) L16 Dutch (*kermis*, *kermisse*, from *kerk* church + *misse* mass). In the Low Countries, parts of Germany, etc.: an annual fair or carnival. Also, a similar fair or bazaar, usually for charitable purposes.

■ Originally a *kermis* was a mass held annually on the anniversary of the dedication of a church, when a fair was also held.

kernos *noun* plural **kernoi** E20 Greek. *Archaeology* An ancient Mediterranean and Near Eastern baked clay vessel having small cups around the rim or fixed in a circle to a central stem.

ketubah *noun* M19 Hebrew (*kĕtubbāh* written statement). A formal Jewish marriage contract that includes financial provisions for the wife in the event of the husband's death or of divorce.

khaddar *noun & adjective* (also **khadi**) E20 Punjabi (*khaddar*, Hindustani *khādar*, *khādī*). (Made of) handspun hand-woven cotton (or silk) cloth of the Indian subcontinent.

khaki *adjective & noun* M19 Urdu (*kākī* dust-colored, from *kāk* dust from Persian). **A** *adjective* M19 Dust-colored; dull brownish yellow. Also, made of khaki. **B** *noun* **1** M19 The dull brownish yellow color of this. **2** M19 A dull yellowish brown fabric, originally of stout twilled cotton, later also of wool, etc., used especially for army uniforms. **3** L19 A soldier dressed in khaki; *specifically* (*South African slang*) a British soldier in the Boer War of 1899–1902. **4** M20 In *plural* Khaki pants; khaki clothes.

khalifa *noun* (in sense 2 also **chalifa**) E18 Arabic (*ḳalīfa*). **1** E18 Chiefly *History* The chief civil and religious ruler of the Muslim community, a caliph. **2** M19 A Malay ceremony in which a dancer pierces his body with swords, originally as a demonstration of Islamic faith. *South African*.

khalsa *noun* (also **khalsah**) L18 Urdu (from Persian *kāl(i)ṣa* crown land, revenue department, from feminine of Arabic *kāliṣ* pure, free (from), belonging (to)). **1** L18 The governmental revenue department in a state in the Indian subcontinent. **2** L18 The fraternity of warriors into which Sikh males are initiated at puberty.

khamsin *noun* (also **hamsin**) L17 Arabic (*ḳamāsīn*, from *ḳamsīn*, *ḳamsūn* fifty (from the number of days on which it blows)). An oppressive hot southerly wind that blows in Egypt at intervals for about fifty days in March, April, and May, and fills the air with sand from the desert.

khan *noun* (also **han**) LME Persian (*ḳān*). A caravanserai.

khanga *noun* (also **kanga**) M20 Kiswahili. In East Africa: a fabric printed in various colors and designs with borders, used especially for women's clothing.

khanum *noun* M17 Persian (*kānum* from Turkish *hanim*, from *hān* lord + *-im* 1st person singular possessive suffix). In certain parts of the Middle East and the Indian subcontinent: a lady of high rank, *historically* the wife of a khan. Now also used as a polite form of address affixed to a Muslim woman's name.

khat *noun* (also **kat**, **qat**) M19 Arabic (*ḳāt*). A shrub, *Catha edulis*, of the spindle tree family, cultivated in Arabia for its leaves, which are chewed or infused as a stimulant; the narcotic drug obtained from these leaves.

khatun *noun* M19 Turkic (*katūn*, Persian *kātūn* perhaps from Sogdian *kwat'yn* queen). In certain parts of the Middle East: a lady of high rank; *historically* a queen. Also used as an honorific title affixed to a Muslim woman's name.

khidmutgar *noun* (also **khitmutgar**) M18 Urdu (from Persian *kidmatgār*, from Arabic *kidma(t)* service + Persian agent-suffix *-gār*). In the Indian subcontinent: a male servant who waits at table.

khoja *noun* E17 Turkish ((*hoca* from) Persian *kʷāja*). **1** E17 A teacher in a Muslim school; a Muslim scribe or clerk. **2** L19 (*Khoja*) A member of a Muslim sect found mainly in western India.

khutbah *noun* E19 Arabic (*kuṭba*). A form of sermon, consisting of homily and supplication, delivered in mosques before the midday Friday prayer, at the time of the two main Muslim festivals, and on other exceptional occasions.

ki *noun* M19 Hawaiian. A shrub of the agave family, *Cordyline fruticosa*, found in China and the Pacific islands, the fermented root of which yields an alcoholic drink.

kibbutz *noun* plural **kibbutzim**, (occasionally) **kibbutzes** M20 Modern Hebrew (*qibbūṣ* gathering). A collective (especially farming) settlement in Israel, owned communally by its members, and organized on cooperative principles.

kibbutznik *noun* M20 Yiddish (from as KIBBUTZ + Polish and Russian noun suffix *-nik* person connected with (something)). A member of a kibbutz.

kibitz *intransitive verb* E20 Yiddish (from German *kiebitzen*, from *Kiebitz* lapwing, pewit, interfering onlooker at cards). Look on at cards, or some other activity, especially offering unwanted advice. *slang.*

kiblah *noun* (also **qibla(h)**, **kibla**) M17 Arabic (*ḳibla* that which is opposite). **1** M17 (The direction of) the place to which Muslims must turn for prayer, now the Kaaba at Mecca. **2** L18 The MIHRAB on an oriental rug.

kiboko *noun* plural **kibokos** E20 Kiswahili (= hippopotamus). A strong heavy whip made of hippopotamus hide.

kiddush *noun* (also **Kiddush**) M18 Hebrew (*qiddūš* sanctification). A ceremony of prayer and blessing over wine, performed by the head of a Jewish household at the meal ushering in the Sabbath (on a Friday night) or a holy day or at the lunch preceding it.

kiddushin *noun* (also **Kiddushin**) L19 **Aramaic** (*qiddūshīn*). *Judaism* The section of the Mishnah dealing with betrothal and marriage. Also, the Jewish ceremony of betrothal; the gift given by a Jewish groom to effect a betrothal.

kief variant of KEF.

kielbasa *noun* M20 **Polish** (*kie^basa* sausage). A type of highly seasoned Polish sausage, usually containing garlic.

kierie *noun* (also (earlier) **kirri**) M18 **Nama**. A short club or knobbed stick used as a club or missile by indigenous peoples of South Africa.

■ The South African English word *knobkerrie*, by which this weapon is also known, is from Afrikaans *knop* knob + *kierie*.

kif variant of KEF.

kikoi *noun* M20 **Kiswahili**. In East Africa: a distinctive striped cloth with an end fringe, worn around the waist.

kilim *adjective & noun* (also **Kilim**, **Kelim**) L19 **Turkish** (*Kılım* from Persian *gelīm*). (Designating) a pileless woven carpet, rug, etc., made in Turkey, Kurdistan, and neighboring areas, and now a fashionable furnishing item in the West.

kimchi *noun* L19 **Korean**. A raw strongly flavored cabbage pickle, the Korean national dish.

kimono *noun & adjective* M17 **Japanese** (from *ki* wearing + *mono* thing). **A** *noun* M17 plural **kimonos**. A long Japanese robe with wide sleeves, tied with a sash. Now also, in Western countries, a garment (especially a robe) modeled on this. **B** *attributive* or as *adjective* E20 Resembling or characteristic of a kimono.

kinder, kirche, küche *noun phrase plural* L19 **German** (literally, 'children, church, kitchen'). The domestic and religious concerns traditionally regarded as appropriate for a woman.

■ Doubly discredited by its association with the Nazi ideal of womanhood and by the agenda of modern feminism, *kinder, kirche, küche* is now most frequently used ironically.

kindergarten *noun* M19 **German** (literally, 'children's garden'). **1** M19 A nursery school. **2** E20 *History* The group of young men with imperialist ideals recruited by Lord Milner, High Commissioner of South Africa, to help with reconstruction work after the second Boer War of 1899–1902.

■ The term *kindergarten* was coined in 1840 by Friedrich Fröbel (1782–1852) for a school for teaching young children according to his method of stimulating their intelligence by means of interesting objects, exercises with toys, games, singing, etc.

kinderspiel *noun* E20 **German** (literally, 'children's play'). A dramatic piece performed by children.

kinesis *noun* plural **kineses** E17 **Greek** (*kinēsis* movement). **1** E17 *generally* Motion; a kind of movement. *rare*. **2** E20 *Biology* An undirected movement of an organism that occurs in response to a particular kind of stimulus. **3** M20 *Zoology* Mobility of the bones of the skull, as in some birds and reptiles.

kippa *noun* (also **kipa(h)**, **kippah**) M20 **Modern Hebrew** (*kippāh*). A skullcap, usually of crocheted thread, worn by Orthodox male Jews.

kir *noun* (also **Kir**) M20 **French** (personal name). (Proprietary name for) a drink made from dry white wine and cassis.

■ Called after Canon Félix *Kir* (1876–1968), mayor of Dijon in France, who is said to have invented the recipe.

kirin *noun* (also **Kirin**) E18 **Japanese** (from as KYLIN). A mythical beast of composite form resembling a unicorn, frequently portrayed in Japanese pottery and art.

kirmess variant of KERMIS.

kirpan *noun* E20 **Punjabi and Hindustani** (*kirpān* from Sanskrit *kṛpāṇa* sword). The dagger or sword worn by Sikhs as a religious symbol.

kirri variant of KIERIE.

kirsch *noun* M19 **German** (abbreviation of *Kirsch(en)wasser* from *Kirsche* cherry + *Wasser* water). An alcoholic spirit distilled, chiefly in Germany and Switzerland, from the fermented juice of cherries.

■ Earlier (E19) in English in the fuller form *Kirschenwasser*.

kisan *noun* M20 **Hindustani** (*kisān* from Sanskrit *kṛṣāṇa* person who plows. In the Indian subcontinent: a peasant, an agricultural worker.

kishke *noun* (also **kishka**, **kishkeh**) M20 **Yiddish** (from Polish *kiszka* or Ukrainian *kishka*: cf. Russian *kishka*). **1** M20 Beef intestine casing stuffed with a savory filling. **2** M20 *singular* and in *plural* The guts. *slang*.

kismet *noun* E19 **Turkish** (*kısmet* from Arabic *ḳisma(t)* division, portion, lot, fate). Destiny, fate.

kissel *noun* E20 **Russian** (*kisel'*, from same base as *kislyĭ* sour). A dessert dish made from fruit juice or purée boiled with sugar and water and thickened with potato or cornstarch.

kist *noun* ME **Old Norse** (*kista*; cf. Dutch *kist*). **A** *noun* **1** ME A chest, a trunk, a coffer. **2** ME A coffin; *especially* a stone coffin, a sarcophagus. **b** M19 *Archaeology* A prehistoric burial chamber lined with stone slabs, a cist.

■ The early use of *kist*, mainly in the north of England and Scotland, derives from Old Norse, but its use in South African English in the sense of 'chest' or 'coffer' is derived through Dutch and Afrikaans.

Kitab *noun* L19 **Arabic** (*kitāb* piece of writing, record, book). The Koran. Also, among Muslims, the sacred book of any of certain other revealed religions, as Judaism or Christianity.

kithara variant of CITHARA.

kitsch *noun & adjective* (also **Kitsch**) E20 **German**. **A** *noun* E20 Art or artifacts perceived as being of poor quality, especially when garish or sentimental; these enjoyed in a perverse, ironic, or self-conscious way; the qualities associated with such art or artifacts. **B** *adjective* Of the nature of or pertaining to kitsch; garish, tasteless.

kittel *noun* L19 **Yiddish** ((German = overall, smock), from Middle High German *ki(e)tel* cotton or hempen outer garment). A white cotton or linen robe worn by orthodox Jews on certain holy days; such a robe used as a shroud.

kiva *noun* L19 **Hopi** (*kíva*). A chamber, built wholly or partly underground, used by male Pueblo Indians for religious rites, etc. Cf. ESTUFA.

klaberjass *noun* (also **clobiosh** and other variants) L19 **German** (from Dutch *klaverjas*). *Cards* A two-handed card game distantly related to bezique, in which points are scored for winning value cards in tricks and for declaring combinations.

klatch *noun* (also **Klatsch**) M20 **German** (*Klatsch* gossip). A social gathering. Cf. KAFFEEKLATSCH.

kletterschuh *noun* plural **kletterschuhe** E20 **German** (literally, 'climbing-shoe'). A cloth- or felt-soled light boot worn especially for rock climbing. Usually in *plural*.

klezmer *noun* plural same, **klezmorim** M20 **Yiddish** (contraction of Hebrew *kĕlēy zemer* musical instruments). A member of a group of musicians playing traditional eastern European Jewish music; this type of music (in full *klezmer music*).

klippe *noun* E20 **German** (= partly submerged or buried rock). *Geology* A part of a nappe that has become detached from its parent mass by sliding or by erosion of intervening parts.

klister *noun* M20 **Norwegian** (= paste). *Skiing* A soft wax for applying to the running surface of skis to facilitate movement, used especially when the temperature is above freezing.

klompie *noun* (also **klompje**) M19 **Afrikaans** (from Dutch *klompje* diminutive of *klomp* clump). **1** M19 A group, a cluster, especially of animals or of shrubs or trees. *South African colloquial.* **2** E20 A type of hard yellow brick, originally imported into South Africa from the Netherlands.

klonkie *noun* M20 **Afrikaans** (blend of *klein* small, *jong* boy + diminutive suffix *-kie*). In South Africa: a young black or Colored boy.

kloof *noun* M18 **Dutch** (= cleft). A deep valley, a ravine, a gorge. *South African.*

klops *noun* plural same **klopse** M20 **German**. A type of meatball or meat loaf.

klutz *noun & verb* (also **klotz**) M20 **Yiddish** (from German *Klotz* wooden block, from Middle High German *kloz*; cf. Old English *clot(t)*, whence modern English *clot* (in derogatory sense) stupid or awkward person). **A** *noun* M20 A clumsy awkward person, *especially* one considered socially inept; a fool. **B** *intransitive verb* L20 Followed by *about, around*: behave awkwardly or foolishly, move clumsily. *slang.*

knaidel *noun* (also **kneidel**) plural **knaidlach** M20 **Yiddish** (*kneydel* from Middle High German, German KNÖDEL). A type of dumpling eaten especially in Jewish households during Passover. Usually in *plural.*

knallgas *noun* L19 **German** (from *Knall* bang, detonation + *Gas* gas). *Chemistry* An explosive mixture of gases, especially one of two volumes of hydrogen with one of oxygen.

kneidel variant of KNAIDEL.

Kneipe *noun* plural **Kneipen, Kneipes** M19 **German**. In Germany: a lively social gathering of young people, especially students, in a bar or restaurant; a tavern, a bar.

knish *noun* M20 **Yiddish** (from Russian (also *knysh*) kind of bun or dumpling). A baked or fried dumpling made of flaky dough filled with chopped liver, potato, or cheese.

knödel *noun* (also **knoedel**) E19 **German**. In South Germany and Austria: a type of dumpling.

knout *noun* M17 **French** (from Russian *knut* from Old Norse *knútr* related to 'knot'). *History* A scourge or whip used in imperial Russia, often causing death.

ko *noun* plural **kos** M20 **Chinese** (*gē* (Wade–Giles *ko*) spear, lance). *Chinese Antiquities* A dagger, a halberd.

koan *noun* M20 **Japanese** (*kōan*, from Chinese *gōngàn* official business). *Zen Buddhism* A riddle without a solution, used to demonstrate the inadequacy of logical reasoning and provoke sudden enlightenment.

kobold *noun* M19 **German**. In German folklore, a familiar spirit, supposed to haunt houses and help the occupants; a brownie. Also, an underground spirit; a goblin, a gnome.

koeksister *noun* (also **koesister**) E20 **Afrikaans** (*koe(k)sister*, perhaps from *koek* cake + *sissen* sizzle). In South Africa: a plaited doughnut dipped in syrup, a traditional South African confection.

kofta *noun* L19 **Urdu and Persian** (*koftah* pounded meat). A kind of meat or fish rissole, popular in Eastern cooking.

kohl *noun* L18 **Arabic** (*kuḥl*). A powder, usually consisting of antimony sulfide or lead sulfide, used as eye makeup and as eye ointment, especially in Eastern countries.

kohlrabi *noun* E19 **German** (*Kohlrabi* from (with assimilation to *Kohl* cole) Italian *cauli* or *cavoli rape*, plural of *cavolo rapa* (whence French *chou-rave*), representing medieval Latin *caulorapa*). A variety of cabbage, *Brassica oleracea* var. *gongylodes*, with an edible turnip-shaped base to its stem.

koi *noun* plural same E18 **Japanese**. A carp (in Japan). Now *especially* a carp of a large ornamental variety bred in Japan. Also *koi carp.*

koine *noun* L19 **Greek** (*koinē* feminine singular of *koinos* common, ordinary). **1** L19 The common literary lan-guage of the Greeks from the close of classical Attic to the Byzantine era. **2** L19 *Linguistics* and *Philology* A language or dialect common to a wide area in which different languages or dialects are, or were, used locally; a lingua franca. **3** E20 A set of cultural or other attributes common to various groups.

koinonia *noun* E20 **Greek** (*koinōnia* communion, fellowship). *Theology* Christian fellowship or communion, with God or, more commonly, with fellow Christians.

kolach *noun* plural **kolache, kolaches** E20 **Czech** (*koláč*, from *kolo* wheel, circle). A small tart or pie popular in the Czech Republic and Slovakia, topped or filled with fruit.

kolkhoz *noun* plural same, **kolkhozes, kolkhozy** E20 **Russian** (from *kol(lektivnoe) khoz(yaĭstvo)* collective farm). In countries of the former USSR: a collective farm.

Kol Nidre *noun* L19 **Aramaic** (*kol nidrē* all the vows (the opening words of the prayer)). An Aramaic prayer annulling vows made before God, sung by Jews at the opening of the Day of Atonement service on the eve of Yom Kippur. Also, the service or the melody at or to which this prayer is sung.

kolo *noun* plural **kolos** L18 **Serbo-Croat** (= wheel). A Slavonic dance performed in a circle.

kombu *noun* L19 **Japanese**. A brown seaweed of the genus *Laminaria*, used in Japanese cooking, especially as a base for stock.

Kommers *noun* plural **Kommerse** M19 **German** (from Latin *commercium* communication). A social gathering of German students.

konak *noun* M19 **Turkish** (= halting place, inn). A large house, palace, or official residence, in Turkey or the former Ottoman Empire.

Konditorei *noun* plural same, **Konditoren** M20 **German** (from *Konditor* confectioner). Confectionery; a store selling confectionery or rich pastries.

konfyt *noun* M19 **Afrikaans** (= Dutch *konfijt*, probably from French *confiture*). Fruit preserved in sugar; preserve, jam. *South African*.

kop *noun* M19 **Afrikaans** (from Dutch *kop* head). **1** M19 A prominent hill or peak. Frequently in place names. *South African*. **2** E20 *Soccer* (*the Kop*) A high bank of terracing for standing spectators, usually supporting the home side, originally and especially at the field of the Liverpool Football Club; the spectators massed on such terracing.

■ In sense 2, also more fully *Spion Kop*, after a mountain in Natal that was the site of a battle in 1900 during the South African Boer War.

kopje variant of KOPPIE.

koppel *noun* L19 **Yiddish**. A skullcap worn by male Jews.

koppie *noun* (also **kopje**) M19 **Afrikaans** (from Dutch *kopje* diminutive of *kop* head; cf. KOP). In South Africa: a small hill, *especially* any of the flat-topped or pointed hillocks characteristic of the veld.

koradji *noun* (also (earlier) **coradgee** and other variants) L18 **Aboriginal**. In Australia: an Aboriginal medicine man.

kore *noun* E20 **Greek** (*korē* = maiden). *Greek Antiquities* A statue of a clothed young woman. Cf. KOUROS.

korero *noun* plural **koreros** E19 **Maori**. In New Zealand: talk, conversation, discussion; a conference.

korma *noun* L19 **Urdu** (*ḳormā, ḳormah* from Turkish *kavurma*). A mildly spiced Indian dish of meat or fish marinaded in yogurt or curds.

koro *noun* E19 **Japanese** (*kōro* incense pot, censer). An elaborate Japanese vase, usually of bronze, jade, or porcelain, in which incense is burned.

korrigan *noun* M19 **Breton** ((Vannes dialect) feminine of *korrig* gnome, diminutive of *korr* dwarf). In Breton folklore, a fairy or witch noted especially for stealing children.

kosher *adjective & noun* M19 **Hebrew** (*kāšēr* fit, proper). **A** *adjective* **1** M19 Of food: prepared according to the Jewish law. **2** L19 That sells or prepares such food; where such food is cooked or eaten. **3** L19 Correct, genuine, legitimate. *colloquial*. **B** *noun* **1** L19 *elliptical* Kosher food; a kosher shop. **2** M20 The Jewish law regarding food. Chiefly in *keep kosher*.

koto *noun* plural **kotos** L18 **Japanese**. A long Japanese zither, now usually having thirteen silk strings, usually played on the floor.

kotow variant of KOWTOW.

koumiss variant of KUMIS.

kouros *noun* plural **kouroi** E20 **Greek** (Ionic form of *koros* boy). *Greek Antiquities* A sculptured representation of a naked youth. Cf. KORE.

kowtow *noun & verb* (also **kotow**) E19 **Chinese** (*kētóu* (Wade–Giles *k'ot'ou*), from *kē* knock, strike + *tóu* head). **A** *noun* E19 The action or practice, formerly customary in China, of touching the ground with the forehead as a sign of extreme respect, submission, or worship; *figuratively* an act of obsequious respect. **B** *intransitive verb* M19 Perform the kowtow; *figurative* act in an obsequious manner.

kozatchok variant of KAZACHOC.

kraak porselein *noun phrase* (also **kraak porcelain**) M20 **Dutch** (from *kraak* carrack (the type of Portuguese ship from which the porcelain was first captured in 1603) + *porselein* porcelain). Blue and white Chinese porcelain of the Wan-li period (1573–1619) or later in the seventeenth century; a European imitation of this.

kraal *noun* M18 **Afrikaans** (from Portuguese *curral* from Nama). **1** M18 In southern Africa: a village of huts enclosed by a fence or stockade, and often having a central space for cattle, etc.; the community of such a village. **2** L18 In southern Africa: an enclosure for cattle or sheep, a stockade, a pen, a fold. **3** L19 In Sri Lanka (Ceylon): an enclosure into which wild elephants are driven; the process of capturing elephants by driving them into an enclosure.

krab see KARABINER.

kragdadig *adjective* (also (in attributive use) **kragdadige**) M20 **Afrikaans** (= Dutch *krachtdadig*). Forceful, vigorous in wielding power, unyielding. *South African*.

kraken *noun* M18 **Norwegian**. A mythical sea monster of enormous size, said to appear off the coast of Norway.

kramat *noun & adjective* (also **karamat**) L18 **Malay** (*keramat* (adjective) sacred, holy, (noun) holy place, holy person, from Arabic *karāma* miracle worked by a saint other than a prophet). **A** *noun* L18 A Muslim holy place or place of pilgrimage. **B** *adjective* M20 Sacred to Muslims.

krans *noun* (also **krantz**) L18 **Afrikaans** (from Dutch = coronet, chaplet from Old High German, Middle High German, German *Kranz* coronet, circle, encircling ring of mountains, from a base meaning 'ring'). In South Africa: a wall of rock encircling a mountain or summit; a precipitous or overhanging cliff above a river, valley, etc.

kraut *noun* M19 **German** (= vegetable, cabbage; cf. earlier SAUERKRAUT). **1** M19 Sauerkraut. **2** E20 (usually **Kraut**) A German, *especially* a German soldier. *derogatory slang*.

kremlin *noun* M17 **French** (from Russian *kreml'* citadel). A citadel or fortified enclosure within a Russian town or city, *especially* (*Kremlin*) that of Moscow; (*the Kremlin*) *the* government of the former USSR.

kreplach *noun plural* L19 **Yiddish** (*kreplech* plural of *krepel* from dialect German *Kräppel* fritter). Triangular noodles filled with chopped meat or cheese and served with soup.

kriegspiel *noun* L19 **German** (from *Krieg* war + *Spiel* game). **1** L19 A war game in which blocks representing troops, etc., are moved about on maps. **2** L19 A form of chess with an umpire and two players, in which each player plays at a separate board and has only limited information about the other's moves.

kril *noun* (also **krill**) plural same E20 **Norwegian** (*kril* small fish fry). A small shrimplike planktonic crustacean of the order Euphausiacea, important as food for fish, and for some whales and seals.

■ Chiefly used as collective plural.

krimmer *noun* (also **crimmer**) M19 **German** (from *Krim* (Russian *Krym*) Crimea). The gray or black furry fleece of young lambs from the Crimean area; a cloth resembling this. Cf. KARAKUL.

kris *noun* (also **creese**) L16 **Malay** (*keris*, partly through Dutch *kris*, German *Kris*, Spanish, Portuguese *cris*, French *criss*, etc.). A Malay or Indonesian dagger with a straight or wavy blade.

kross variant of KAROSS.

krug *noun* M19 **German**. In Germany and German-speaking countries: a beer mug, a tankard.

krummholz *noun* E20 **German** (= elfin-tree, literally, 'crooked wood'). A wood composed of dwarfed and deformed trees, such as is found in alpine regions, an elfin-wood.

krummhorn *noun* (also **crumhorn**) L17 **German** (from *krumm* crooked, curved + *Horn* horn). *Music* **1** L17 A medieval and Renaissance wind instrument with a double reed and a curved end. **2** L19 An organ reed stop, usually of 8-ft. pitch, suggestive of a krummhorn or clarinet in tone; a CROMORNE.

kuchen *noun* plural **kuchens** M19 **German** (= cake). In Germany or among German- or Yiddish-speaking people: a cake; *especially* a cake taken with coffee.

kudos *noun* L18 **Greek** (= praise, renown). Glory, renown. *colloquial.*

kudzu *noun* L19 **Japanese** (*kuzu*). A quick-growing, climbing leguminous plant, *Pueraria lobata*, originally of China and Japan, cultivated elsewhere for fodder, as an ornamental, and to prevent soil erosion; now common to southeastern United States. In full *kudzu vine*.

kuei *noun* M20 **Chinese** (*gŭi* (Wade–Giles *kūei*)). *Chinese Antiquities* A bronze food vessel, usually with two handles and often surmounted by animal heads.

kuffiyeh variant of KEFFIYEH.

kugel *noun* M19 **Yiddish** (= ball, from Middle High German *kugel(e)* ball, globe). In Jewish cooking: a kind of pudding; *especially* a savory pudding, usually of potatoes or other vegetables, served as a separate course or as a side dish.

kugelhupf variant of GUGELHUPF.

kukri *noun* E19 **Nepali** (*khukuri*). A curved knife broadening toward the point and usually with the sharp edge on the concave side, used by Gurkhas.

kula *noun* E20 **Melanesian**. In some Pacific communities, especially in the Trobriand Islands: an inter-island system of ceremonial exchange of items as a prelude to or concomitant of regular trading.

kulah *noun* E20 **Persian** (*kulāh* cap). A conical cap of felt or lambskin worn by Muslims in the Middle East.

kulak *noun* L19 **Russian** (literally, 'fist, tight-fisted person' from Turkic *ḳol* hand). Originally, a well-to-do Russian farmer or trader. Later, a peasant-proprietor working for his own profit in the Soviet Union.

Kultur *noun* (also **kultur**) E20 **German** (*Kultur* from Latin *cultura* or French *culture* culture). German civilization and culture.

■ Often used in the aftermath of the Nazi era in a derogatory sense to suggest authoritarianism and militarism but also used neutrally as a component in words such as those below.

Kulturgeschichte *noun* (also **kulturgeschichte**) L19 **German** (*Kultur* culture + *Geschichte* history). The history of the cultural development of a country; history of civilization.

Kulturkampf *noun* (also **kulturkampf**) L19 German (*Kultur* culture + *Kampf* struggle). The conflict in Germany (1872–87) between the government and the church for control of schools and ecclesiastical appointments; *transferred* a conflict of moral or social issues and ideas.

kulturny *adjective* M20 Russian (*kul'turnyĭ*, from *kul'tur* from Latin *cultura* or French *culture* culture). In countries of the former USSR: cultured, civilized; good mannered, well behaved. Cf. NEKULTURNY.

kumis *noun* (also **koumiss, kumiss**) L16 French (*koumis*, German *Kumiss*, Polish *kumys*, Russian *kumys* from Tartar *kumiz*). A fermented liquor prepared from mare's or other milk, used as a beverage and medicinally especially by central Asian nomadic tribes; a spirituous liquor distilled from this.

kumkum *noun* M20 Sanskrit (*kuṅkuma* saffron). A red powder used ceremonially, especially by Hindu women to make a small distinctive mark on the forehead; the mark so made.

kümmel *noun* M19 German (representative of Middle High German, Old High German *kumil* variant of *kumîn* cumin). A sweet liqueur flavored with caraway and cumin seeds.

kundalini *noun* L19 Sanskrit (*kuṇḍalinī* literally 'snake'). *Yoga* **1** L19 The latent (female) energy that lies coiled at the base of the spine. **2** M20 A type of meditation that aims to direct and release this energy. In full *Kundalini yoga*.

kung fu *noun* L19 Chinese (*gongfu* (Wade–Giles *kung fu*), from *gong* (*kung*) merit + *fu* master). The Chinese form of KARATE.

Kunstforscher *noun* plural same L19 Greek (from *Kunst* art + *Forscher* researcher). An art historian.

Kunstgeschichte *noun* L19 German (from *Kunst* art + *Geschichte* history). The history of art, art history.

Kunsthistoriker *noun* plural same M20 German (from *Kunst* art + *Historiker* historian). An art historian.

Künstlerroman *noun* plural **Künstlerromane** M20 German (from *Künstler* artist + *Roman* novel). A BILDUNGSROMAN about an artist.

Kunstprosa *noun* M20 German (from *Kunst* art + *Prosa* prose). Literary prose, ornate and stylized prose.

Kur *noun* plural **Kuren** L19 German (= a cure). A cure, a medicinal drinking of the waters at a spa in Germany or a German-speaking country; a spa.

kurgan *noun* L19 Russian (of Turkic origin: cf. Turkish *kurgan* castle, fortress). A prehistoric sepulchral tumulus or barrow such as is found in Siberia and central Asia.

Kurhaus *noun* plural **Kurhäuser** M19 German (from *Kur* cure + *Haus* house). In Germany and German-speaking countries: a building at a health resort where medicinal water is dispensed; a pump room.

kuri *noun* M19 Maori (= dog). In New Zealand: a Maori dog. Also, a mongrel; *slang* an unpleasant or disliked person.

Kurort *noun* plural **Kurorte** M19 German (from *Kur* cure + *Ort* place). In Germany and German-speaking countries: a health resort, a spa, a watering place.

kursaal *noun* plural **kursäle, kursaals**, M19 German (from as *Kur* cure + *Saal* hall, room). Especially in Germany and German-speaking countries: a public building at a health resort, provided for the use and entertainment of visitors.

kurta *noun* E20 Urdu and Persian (*kurtah*). A loose shirt or tunic worn by especially Hindu men and women.

kurtosis *noun* E20 Greek (*kurtōsis* a bulging, convexity, from *kurtos* bulging, convex). *Statistics* The degree of sharpness of the peak of a frequency distribution curve.

kuru *noun* M20 **New Guinea.** *Medicine* A fatal viral brain disease found among certain peoples of New Guinea.

■ *Kuru* was formerly of mainly anthropological interest as a disease found among peoples of New Guinea who practiced ritual cannibalism of human brain tissue. It became of interest to the wider medical establishment on account of its similarities to BSE (bovine spongiform encephalopathy) or *mad cow disease* which was identified in cattle in the UK in 1986. In 1990 it was discovered that cats could also contract the disease, maybe as the result of eating contaminated cattle brain or other tissue in pet foods, and the possibility that BSE could be transmitted to humans through cattle offal became the subject of urgent investigations.

kutcha *adjective & noun* (also **cutcha, kacha**) E19 **Hindustani** (*kaccā* raw, crude, uncooked). **A** *adjective* E19 In the Indian subcontinent: slight, makeshift, unfinished; built of dried mud. **B** *noun* M19 Dried mud used as a building material in the Indian subcontinent.

kuzushi *noun* M20 **Japanese.** *Judo* The fact or state of being unbalanced by one's opponent; a loss of the initiative.

kvass *noun* (also **kvas, quass**) M16 **Russian** (*kvas*). In Russia and some neighboring countries: a fermented beverage, low in alcohol, made from rye flour or bread with malt; rye beer.

kvell *intransitive verb* M20 **Yiddish** (*kveln* from German *quellen* gush, well up). Boast; feel proud or happy; gloat. *slang.*

kvetch *noun & verb* M20 **Yiddish** (as noun from Yiddish *kvetsh*, as verb from Yiddish *kvetshn*, from German *Quetsche* crusher, presser, *quetschen*, crush, press). **A** *noun* M20 An objectionable person; *specifically* someone who complains a great deal, a faultfinder. **B** *intransitive verb* M20 Complain, whine. Chiefly as *kvetching* verbal noun. *slang.*

kvutza *noun* E20 **Modern Hebrew** (*qěbhūṣāh* from Hebrew = group). In Israel: a communal and cooperative settlement, which, with others, may form a kibbutz.

kwai-lo *noun* M20 **Chinese** ((Cantonese) *(faan) kwaí ló*, literally, '(foreign) devil fellow'). In China, a foreigner, *especially* a European.

■ A derogatory Chinese expression for all non-Chinese.

kwashiorkor *noun* M20 **Ghanaian** (local name). A form of malnutrition caused by severe protein and energy deficiency, chiefly affecting young (especially newly weaned) children in tropical Africa, and producing apathy, edema, loss of pigmentation, diarrhea, and other symptoms.

kwela *noun* M20 **Afrikaans** (perhaps from Zulu *khwela* climb, mount). A popular dance, and its accompanying music, resembling jazz, of central and southern Africa.

kya *noun* E20 **Zulu** (*-khaya* place of abode). In South Africa, Zimbabwe, etc.: an African's hut; the living accommodations of an African servant.

kylin *noun* M19 **Chinese** (*qílín*, from *qí* male + *lín* female). A mythical animal of composite form figured on Chinese and Japanese pottery, a Chinese unicorn. Cf. KIRIN.

kylix *noun* (also **cylix**, plural **cylices**) plural **kylikes** M19 **Greek** (*kulix*). *Greek Antiquities* A shallow cup with a tall stem, a tazza.

kyogen *noun* plural same L19 **Japanese** (*kyōgen*). A comic interlude presented between performances of Noh plays.

Kyrie eleison *noun phrase* ME **Medieval Latin** (from Greek *Kuriē eleēson* Lord, have mercy). The words ("Lord, have mercy") of a short repeated invocation or response used in the Roman Catholic, Greek Orthodox, and Anglican churches, especially at the beginning of the Eucharist. Also, a musical setting of these words, especially as the first movement of a mass.

kyu *noun* M20 **Japanese** (*kyū* class). Each of the (numbered) grades of the less advanced level of proficiency in judo, karate, and other martial (or originally martial) arts, (also *kyu grade*); a person who has reached (a specified grade of) this level. Cf. DAN.

L

La *adjective* (*definite article*) (also **la**) M19 **French** (or Italian feminine definite article, from Latin *illa*, feminine of *ille* that). Used preceding the name of a prima donna, or (frequently *jocular* or *ironical*) the name of any woman.

laager *noun* M19 **Afrikaans** (= German *Lager*, Dutch *leger*). A camp, an encampment; *South African History* a Boer camp marked out and protected by a circle of wagons; *transferred* and *figurative* a defensive position, *especially* one protected by armored vehicles; an entrenched policy, viewpoint, etc., under attack from opponents.

▪ In its figurative sense *laager* was often used attributively in the phrase *laager mentality* to denote the intransigent defensiveness of Afrikaners in their dealings with the outside world during the apartheid era. The noun gave rise (L19) to both transitive and intransitive verbal uses of *laager*, sometimes followed by *up*.

laban *noun* (also **leban**, **leben**) L17 **Arabic** (= milk). A drink consisting of coagulated sour milk.

labarum *noun* E17 **Late Latin** (whence Byzantine Greek *labaron*). The imperial standard of Constantine the Great (306–337), with Christian symbols added to Roman military symbols; *generally* a symbolic banner.

labrys *noun* E20 **Greek** (*labrus*). *Greek Antiquities* The sacred double-headed ax of ancient Crete; a representation of this.

lac *noun* (also **lack**, (earlier) **lacca**) LME **Medieval Latin** (*lac*, *lac(c)a* from Portuguese *lac(c)a* from Hindustani *lākh*, Persian *lāk*). LME The dark red resinous incrustation secreted as a protective covering by the females of certain homopteran insects (especially *Laccifer lacca*) parasitic on Southeast Asian trees, used (especially in the Indian subcontinent) to make shellac and dye.

▪ Formerly (L16–E18) used also for the varnish made from lac or various other resinous wood varnishes (*lacquer*) and (L17–M18) for the crimson color or pigment derived from lac (*lake*).

lacet *noun* L19 **French** (= lace, hairpin bend). A hairpin bend in a road.

lachryma Christi *noun phrase* L17 **Modern Latin** (literally, 'Christ's tear(s)', in Italian *lagrima* (or *-me*) *di Cristo*). A white, red, or pink Italian wine originally from grapes grown near Mount Vesuvius, now also produced elsewhere in Italy.

lachsschinken *noun* E20 **German** (from *Lachs* salmon + *Schinken* ham). Cured and smoked loin of pork.

lacrimae rerum *noun* (also **lachrymae rerum**) E20 **Latin** (literally, 'tears (for the nature) of things'). The sadness of life; tears for the sorrows of life.

■ A quotation from Virgil's *Aeneid* (i.462). The etymologically incorrect spelling *lachrymae* is also frequent.

lacuna *noun* plural **lacunae**, **lacunas** M17 **Latin** (from *lacus* lake). **1** M17 A hiatus, a blank, a missing portion, especially in a manuscript or text. **2** E18 *in technical use* A gap, a depression; a space or cavity.

ladanum *noun* M16 **Latin** (*ladanum*, *ledanum* from Greek *ladanon*, *lēdanon*, from *lēdon* mastic). A gum resin that exudes from plants of the genus *Cistus*, much used in perfumery and for fumigation.

ladino *noun* E20 **Italian**. A large fast-growing variety of white clover (*Trifolium repens*), native to northern Italy and cultivated elsewhere, especially in the United States, as a fodder crop. In full *ladino clover*.

la dolce vita see DOLCE VITA.

l'affaire see AFFAIRE.

lager *noun* M19 **German** (*Lager-Bier* beer brewed for keeping, from *Lager* storehouse). A light kind of beer, originally German or Bohemian, that is stored to mature before use; a drink of this.

lagniappe *noun* M19 **Louisiana French**, from Spanish *la ñapa*. something given as a bonus or extra gift to what is purchased or earned; a tip.

lahar *noun* E20 **Javanese**. *Geology* A mud flow of volcanic ash mixed with water.

laissez-aller *noun* (also **laisser-aller**) E19 **French** (literally, 'allow to go'). Absence of restraint; unconstrained ease and freedom.

laissez-faire *noun* (also **laisser-faire**) E19 **French** (literally, 'allow to do'). Government abstention from interference in the actions of individuals, especially in commerce; *generally* noninterference or indifference.

■ The maxim *laissez faire et laissez passer* is associated particularly with the French free trade economists of the eighteenth century.

laissez-passer *noun* (also **laisser-passer**) E20 **French** (literally, 'allow to pass'). A permit to travel or to enter a particular place, a pass.

lakh *noun* (also **lac**) E17 **Hindustani** (*lākh* from Sanskrit *lakṣa* mark, token, 100,000). In the Indian subcontinent: one hundred thousand; occasionally, an indefinite large number.

lakoum, **lakum** variants of LOKUM.

lama *noun* M17 **Tibetan** (*bla-ma* (the *b* is silent)). A Buddhist religious teacher of Tibet or Mongolia.

lambada *noun* L20 **Brazilian Portuguese** (literally, 'beating, lashing'). A fast and erotic dance of Brazilian origin, in which couples dance with their stomachs touching each other; the music for this dance.

■ The *lambada*, danced in Brazil for many years, became a craze in the United States in the late 1980s, and media hype helped spread it to the United Kingdom and Australia. The speed and thoroughness with which this ethnic dance was marketed in the West gave rise to the coinage *lambadazation* for the whole process of taking up and marketing elements of ethnic culture for Western consumers.

lambda *noun* E17 **Greek**. **I 1** E17 The eleventh letter (Λ, λ) of the Greek alphabet. **II 2** M20 *Chemistry* A millionth of a liter. Usually written λ. **3** M20 *Nuclear Physics* A neutral hyperon (or its antiparticle) with a mass 2183 times that of the electron; originally also, any of several similar charged hyperons. Frequently written Λ. More fully *lambda particle*. **4** M20 *Microbiology* A bacteriophage originally isolated from *Escherichia coli*, used in genetic research. Frequently written λ.

lamdan *noun* E20 **Hebrew** (*lamdān*, literally, 'a person who has learned', from *lāmad* learn). A person learned in Jewish law; a Talmudic scholar.

lamé *noun & adjective* E20 **French** (from Old French *lame* from Latin *lamina*, *lamna* thin plate, especially of metal). (Made of) a brocaded fabric consisting of silk or other yarns interwoven with metallic threads.

lamento *noun* plural **lamenti** M20 **Italian.** *Music* An elegiac or mourning song; in Italian opera, a tragic aria.

lamentoso *adverb & adjective* L19 **Italian.** *Music* (A direction:) in a mournful style.

lamia *noun* plural **lamias, lamiae** LME **Latin** (from Greek = mythical monster, carnivorous fish). A mythical monster supposed to have the body of a woman, and to prey on human beings and suck the blood of children. Also, a witch, a she-demon.

lamina *noun* plural **laminae** M17 **Latin** (*la(m)mina*). A thin plate or layer of a metal or other material.

■ Also with technical senses in Anatomy and Biology, Botany (M18), Geology (M19), and Mathematics (M19).

lammergeyer *noun* (also **lammergeier**) E19 **German** (*Lämmergeier*, from *Lämmer* plural of *Lamm* lamb + *Geier* vulture). A long-winged, long-tailed vulture, *Gypaetus barbatus*, inhabiting lofty mountains in southern Europe, Asia, and Africa. Also called *bearded vulture*.

lammervanger *noun* M19 **Afrikaans** (from *lam* lamb + *vanger* catcher). In South Africa: an eagle, especially one believed to prey on lambs. Also, = preceding.

lanai *noun* (also (earlier) **ranai**) E19 **Hawaiian.** A porch or veranda, originally in Hawaii; a roofed structure with open sides near a house.

Land *noun* plural **Länder, Lands** E20 **German.** A semi-autonomous unit of local government in Germany and Austria.

landau *noun* M18 **German** (from *Landau* name of town in Germany, where first made). Chiefly *History* A four-wheeled horse-drawn carriage, with folding front and rear hoods enabling it to travel open, half-open, or closed. Also *landau carriage*.

lande *noun* L18 **French.** A tract of wild land, a moor, especially in southwest France.

Länder plural of LAND.

ländler *noun* L19 **German.** An Austrian peasant dance, similar to a slow waltz; a piece of music for this dance.

landnam *noun* M20 **Danish** (= occupation of land). *Archaeology* The clearance of forested land for (usually short-term) agricultural purposes; evidence of this provided by sudden changes in pollen spectra.

landrace *noun* M20 **Danish** (= national breed). A breed of large white pig, originally developed in Denmark; an animal of this breed.

landsknecht see LANSQUENET.

landsman *noun* plural **landsleit** M20 **Yiddish** (from Middle High German *lantsman, lantman* a native). Among Jews: a fellow Jew; a compatriot.

Landsturm *noun* plural **Landstürme** E19 **German** (literally, 'land storm'). *History* In Germany and German-speaking countries: a general levy in time of war; an auxiliary militia force.

Landwehr *noun* E19 **German** (literally, 'land defense'). *Military* In Germany and some other countries: that part of the organized land forces of which continuous service is required only in time of war; the army reserve.

langeleik *noun* plural **langeleiken** (also **langleik**) E20 **Norwegian.** An early Norwegian stringed instrument, resembling the zither.

langlauf *noun* (also **Langlauf**) E20 **German** (literally, 'long run'). Cross-country skiing; a cross-country skiing race.

langleik variant of LANGELEIK.

langosta *noun* L19 **Spanish** (from popular Latin alteration of Latin *locusta* locust). **1** L19 A locust. Now *rare* or *obsolete*. **2** E20 A LANGOUSTE.

langostino *noun* plural **langostinos** E20 **Spanish** (from as preceding). A LANGOUSTINE.

langouste *noun* M19 **French** (from Old Provençal *lagosta* from popular Latin alteration of Latin *locusta* locust). A lobster; *especially* the spiny lobster, *Palinurus vulgaris.*

langoustine *noun* M20 **French** (from as preceding). The Norway lobster, especially as food.

langue *noun* ME **French** (from Latin *lingua* tongue, language). **1** ME–M17 A language. *rare.* **2** L18 A national division or branch of a religious and military order. Long *rare* except *historical.* **3** E20 *Linguistics* A language viewed as an abstract system used by a speech community, in contrast to the actual linguistic behavior of individuals. Opposed to PAROLE sense 3.

langue de chat *noun phrase* plural **langues de chat** L19 **French** (literally, 'cat's tongue'). A long thin piece of chocolate; a long finger-shaped crisp cookie.

langue d'oc *noun phrase* E18 **Old and Modern French** (from as LANGUE + *de* of + *oc* yes (from Latin *hoc*)). The language of medieval France south of the Loire, generally characterized by the use of *oc* to mean 'yes', and the basis of modern Provençal. Cf. LANGUE D'OÏL.

langue d'oïl *noun phrase* (also **langue d'oui**) E18 **Old and Modern French** (from as LANGUE + *de* of + *oïl* (now *oui*) yes (from Latin *hoc ille*)). The language of medieval France north of the Loire, generally characterized by the use of *oïl* to mean 'yes', and the basis of standard modern French. Cf. LANGUE D'OC.

langues de chat plural of LANGUE DE CHAT.

lansquenet *noun* (also (in sense 1 now the usual form) **landsknecht**) E17 **French** (from German *Landsknecht*, from genitive of *Land* land + *Knecht* soldier). **1** E17 *History* A member of a class of mercenary soldiers in the German and other Continental armies in the sixteenth and seventeenth centuries. **2** L17 A gambling card game of German origin.

lanx *noun* plural **lances** LME **Latin.** *Antiquities* A large dish or bowl.

lapiés *noun plural* (also **lapies**) E20 **French** (dialectal *lapiaz, lapiés* (singular *lapié*) ultimately from Latin *lapis* stone). *Physical Geography* KARREN. Also (treated as *singular*) KARRENFELD.

lapillus *noun* plural **lapilli** M18 **Latin** (diminutive of *lapis* stone; in plural also from Italian *lapilli*, plural of *lapillo*). Originally, a small stone or pebble. Now (*Geology*), a fragment of rock or lava ejected from a volcano, *specifically* one between 2 and 64 mm in size. Usually in *plural.*

lapis *noun* LME **Latin.** **1** LME Stone; *specifically* the philosopher's stone. *rare* except in phrases. **2** E19 (Abbreviated form of) LAPIS LAZULI.

lapis lazuli *noun phrase* LME **Latin** (from Latin *lapis* stone + medieval Latin *lazuli* genitive of *lazulum*, varying with *lazur, lazurius*, from Persian *lāžward* lapis lazuli). A blue semiprecious stone composed chiefly of a sulfer-containing silicate of sodium and aluminum; *History* a pigment consisting of crushed grains of this, the original ultramarine; the color ultramarine.

lappa *noun* M20 **Hausa** (from Arabic *laffa* to wrap up, cover). In West Africa: a woman's shawl, wrap, or skirt.

lapsus *noun* plural same E17 **Latin.** A lapse, a slip, an error.

■ Chiefly in phrases below.

lapsus calami *noun phrase* L19 **Latin.** A slip of the pen.

lapsus linguae *noun phrase* M17 **Latin.** A slip of the tongue.

laquear *noun* plural **laquearia** E18 **Latin** (*laqueare* paneled ceiling). *Architecture* A ceiling consisting of paneled recessed compartments, with bands between the panels.

lar *noun* (in sense 1 also **Lar**) plural **lars, lares** L16 **Latin.** **1** L16 *Roman History* A household or ancestral god. Frequently in *plural*, the protective gods of a house; household gods; also, the home. Cf. PENATES. **2** E19 The common or white-handed gibbon, *Hyloba-*

tes lar, of Thailand and Malaysia. More fully *lar gibbon*.

■ The phrase *lares et penates* (or *lares and penates*) is used figuratively of those components of a household that the owner holds dearest; thus in 1775 Horace Walpole wrote in a letter "I am returned to my own Lares and Penates—to my dogs and cats".

lardon *noun* (also **lardoon**) **LME French** (from Old French *lard* bacon, from Latin *lar(i)dum* related to Greek *larinos* fat). *Cooking* A strip of bacon or pork inserted into other meat before cooking to give it flavor and keep it moist.

la recherche du temps perdu see RECHERCHE DU TEMPS PERDU.

lares plural of LAR.

largamente *adverb & adjective* **M19 Italian** (= broadly). *Music* (A direction:) in a slow dignified style.

largesse *noun* (also **largess**) **ME Old and Modern French** (from Proto-Romance, from Latin *largus* liberal in giving). **1** ME Liberality, generosity, munificence. Long *obsolete* except *historical*. **2** ME Liberal bestowal of gifts, especially by a person in a high position on some special occasion. **b** M16 An act of such giving; a free gift of money, etc. **3** LME–L16 Freedom, liberty.

larghetto *adverb, adjective, & noun* **E18 Italian** (diminutive of LARGO). MUSIC **A** ADVERB & ADJECTIVE E (A DIRECTION:) IN FAIRLY SLOW TIME. **B** NOUN PLURAL **LARGHETTOS** L A MOVEMENT OR PASSAGE (TO BE) PLAYED IN THIS WAY.

largo *adverb, adjective, & noun* **L17 Italian** (= broad). *Music* **A** *adverb & adjective* L17 (A direction:) in slow time and with a broad dignified treatment. **B** *noun* plural **largos** M18 A movement or passage (to be) played in this way.

larmoyant *adjective* **E19 French** (present participle of *larmoyer* to be tearful). Given to tears, lachrymose.

larnax *noun* plural **larnakes** **L19 Greek**. *Greek Antiquities* A chest, ossuary, urn, or coffin, usually of terracotta and frequently ornamented with designs.

larva *noun* plural **larvae** **M17 Latin** (= ghost, mask). **1** M17 A disembodied spirit; a ghost, a specter. *obsolete* except *historical*. **2** M18 An insect in a state of development (displaying little or no similarity to the adult) lasting from the time of its leaving the egg until its transformation into a pupa; a grub, a caterpillar. Also, an immature form in other animals that undergo some sort of metamorphosis, e.g., amphibians, tapeworms, etc.

larynx *noun* plural **larynges, larynxes** **L16 Modern Latin** (from Greek *larugx, larugg-*). *Anatomy* and *Zoology* A hollow cartilaginous and muscular organ forming the upper part of the trachea or windpipe, and holding the vocal cords in humans and most mammals.

lasagna *noun* (also **lasagne**) **M19 Italian** (plural of *lasagna*, ultimately from Latin *lasanum* chamber pot, perhaps also cooking pot). Pasta in the form of long wide strips; an Italian dish consisting largely of this, usually with a sauce.

lassi *noun* **L19 Hindustani** (*lassī*). In the Indian subcontinent: a drink made from a buttermilk or yogurt base with water.

lasya *noun* **M20 Sanskrit** (*lāsya*). A graceful Indian style of female dancing.

latex *noun* plural **latexes, latices** **M17 Latin** (= liquid, fluid). **1** M17–M18 *Medicine* Any of various body fluids. **2** M19 *Botany* A milky liquid found in many plants; *specifically* that of *Hevea brasiliensis* or other plants used to produce rubber. **3** M20 A dispersion in water of particles of a polymer that is formed during polymerization and is used to make paints, coatings, etc.

lathi *noun* (also **lathee**) **M19 Hindustani** (*lāṭhī*). *In the Indian subcontinent: a long heavy iron-bound stick, usually of bamboo, used as a weapon.*

latifundium *noun* plural **latifundia** **M19 Latin** (from *latus* broad + *fundus* landed estate; partly from Spanish *la-*

tifundio from Latin). A large landed estate or ranch, frequently worked by slaves or people of semiservile status; *especially* one in Spain or Latin America or in ancient Rome.

■ Now usually occurring in the plural, *latifundium* was originally (M17) Anglicized as *latifund*. Its opposite is a MINIFUNDIUM.

latigo *noun* plural **latigo(e)s** L19 **Spanish**. A strap for tightening a cinch.

Latino sine flexione *noun phrase* E20 **Latin** ((*Latino* ablative of adjective *Latinus* Latin) = in Latin without inflection). The language Interlingua, in which nouns are taken from the ablative case of Latin nouns.

latke *noun* E20 **Yiddish** (from Russian *latka* earthenware cooking vessel, (dialect) dish cooked in such a vessel). In Jewish cooking: a pancake, *especially* one made with grated potato.

latria *noun* E16 **Late Latin** (from Greek *latreia*, from *latreuein* to wait on, serve with prayer). *Roman Catholic Church* The highest form of worship, due to God alone; the veneration properly given to God. Cf. DULIA, HYPERDULIA.

latticinio *noun* Also written **latticino** M19 **Italian** (literally, 'dairy produce', from medieval Latin *lacticinium*). An opaque white glass used in threads to decorate clear Venetian glass.

laúd *noun* plural **laúdes** L19 **Spanish** (*laúd* from Arabic *al-'ūd*). A Spanish lute.

laudator temporis acti *noun phrase* plural **laudatores temporis acti** M18 **Latin** (= a praiser of times past). A person who holds up the past as a golden age.

■ *Laudator temporis acti se puero* 'a praiser of former times when he himself was a boy' is a quotation from a passage in Horace's *Ars Poetica* (173–74) on the tiresome traits that tend to accompany old age.

laulau *noun* M20 **Hawaiian** (reduplication of *lau* leaf). A portion of a Hawaiian dish of meat or fish wrapped in leaves and steamed or baked. Also, the wrapping of leaves for this dish.

laura *noun* (also **lavra**) E18 **Greek** (= lane, passage, alley). *Christian Church* A group of huts or cells inhabited by reclusive monks in Egypt and the Middle East. In the Orthodox church, a monastery consisting of separate cells; a large monastery.

lavabo *noun* plural **lavabo(e)s** M18 **Latin** (= I will wash). **1** M18 *Ecclesiastical* In the Eucharist, the ritual washing of a celebrant's hands at the offertory; also the small towel or the basin used for the washing. **2 a** L19 A washing trough used in some medieval monasteries. **b** E20 A washbasin. **c** M20 A lavatory; washroom.

lavage *noun & verb* L18 **French** (from *laver* to wash). **A** *noun* **1** L18 An act of washing, a wash. **2** L19 *Medicine* The irrigation of an organ, either to cleanse it or to allow its contents to be examined. **B** *transitive verb* M20 *Medicine* Cleanse, irrigate, (an organ).

lava-lava *noun* L19 **Samoan**. In Samoa and some other Pacific islands: a wraparound skirtlike garment worn by either sex.

lavaliere *noun* (also **lava(l)lière**, **lavalier**, **Lavaliere**) L19 **French** (proper name). **1** L19 Used *attributively* to designate any of various items of women's clothing in styles associated with the reign of Louis XIV of France. **2** E20 A pendant necklace. **3** M20 A loosely tied cravat. **4** M20 A small microphone worn hanging around the neck. Also *lavaliere microphone*.

■ Louise de *la Vallière* (1644–1710) was mistress to the French king Louis XIV. In French the most frequent context is *une cravate lavallière*.

lavolta *noun* L16 **Italian** (from *la* the + *volta* turn). *History* A lively dance for couples in 3/4 time, in which each partner lifts the other clear of the ground in turn.

lavra variant of LAURA.

layette *noun* M19 **French** (diminutive of Old French *laie* drawer, box, from

Middle Dutch *laege*). A set of clothing, toilet articles, and bedclothes for a newborn child.

lazaretto *noun* plural **lazarettos** M16 **Italian** (diminutive of LAZZARO). **1** M16 A hospital for diseased people, especially those with leprosy. **2** E17 A building or ship for quarantine. **3** E18 *Nautical* The after part of a ship's hold, used for stores.

■ Less common, but also used in all three senses, is the French word *lazaret* (E17 in sense 1), derived from the Italian.

lazzaro *noun* (also plural **lazzari**) M17 **Italian.** A LAZZARONE.

lazzarone *noun* plural **lazzaroni** L18 **Italian** (augmentative of LAZZARO). In Naples and other Italian cities: a person who subsists on the proceeds of odd jobs, an idler, a beggar.

leban, leben variants of LABAN.

Lebensform *noun* plural **Lebensformen** M20 **German** (literally, 'form of life'). A sphere of human social activity involving values; a style or aspect of life.

Lebenslust *noun* L19 **German.** Zest for life, *joie de vivre*.

lebensraum *noun* Also written **Lebensraum** E20 **German** (= living room). Space for living, room to exist and function freely; *specifically* territory which many German nationalists in the mid–twentieth century claimed was needed for the survival and healthy development of the nation.

■ Originally the biological concept of a space inhabited, or habitable, by a particular organism, *Lebensraum* was developed by the nineteenth-century German geographer Friedrich Ratzel to mean the space sufficient both for a people's material needs and for the evolution of its particular social and cultural identity. The concept was subsequently hijacked by the Nazis to justify the racist and expansionist policies of the Third Reich.

lebensspur, *noun* plural **lebensspuren** (also **Lebensspur**) M20 **German** (from *Leben* life + *Spur* trace, track). *Geology* A small track, burrow, cast, etc., left in sediment by a living organism; *especially* one preserved in fossil form in sedimentary rock, a trace fossil.

■ Usually in the plural, the term was apparently first used in German by O. Abel in 1912.

Lebenswelt *noun* plural **Lebenswelten** M20 **German.** *Philosophy* All the immediate experiences, activities, and contacts that make up the world of an individual, or of a corporate, life.

■ A term particularly associated with the German philosopher E. G. A. Husserl (1859–1938), it is often translated into English as 'life world'.

leberwurst *noun* M19 **German.** (A) liver sausage.

lebes *noun* M19 **Greek** (*lebēs*). *Greek Antiquities* A deep round-bottomed bowl for holding wine.

lechayim *interjection* (also **lechaim** and other variants) M20 **Hebrew** (*lĕ-ḥayyīm*). (A drinking toast:) to life!

lectio difficilior *noun phrase* plural **lectiones difficiliores** M20 **Latin.** (Word-order variant of) DIFFICILIOR LECTIO.

lector *noun* LME **Latin** (from *lect-* past participial stem of *legere* to read). **1** LME *Ecclesiastical* A person commissioned as, or ordained to the office of, a liturgical reader. **2** LME A person who reads; *specifically* a reader or lecturer in a college or university, now especially one in a Continental country, as Germany or France, or in a foreign country teaching his or her native language.

lectrice *noun* L19 **French** (from Latin *lectrix* feminine of Latin LECTOR). **1** L19 A woman engaged as an attendant or companion to read aloud. **2** M20 A female lecturer.

lecythus see LEKYTHOS.

lederhosen *noun plural* M20 **German** (from *Leder* leather + *Hosen* plural of *Hose* trouser). Leather shorts, especially as traditionally worn in Alpine regions of Bavaria, etc.

legato *adjective, adverb, & noun* M18 **Italian** (past participle of *legare* to bind, from Latin *ligare*). *Music* **A** *adjective & adverb* M18 (A direction:) smooth(ly) and connected(ly), with no breaks between successive notes. **B** *noun* L19 A legato style of performance; a piece or passage (to be) played legato.

legator *noun* M17 **Latin** (from *legat-* past participial stem of *legare* to bequeath). A person who gives something by will, a testator.

legerdemain *noun* LME **French** (*léger de main*, from *léger* light + *de* of + *main* hand). **1** LME Sleight of hand; juggling; conjuring. **2** M16 *transferred* and *figurative* Trickery, deception. **3** M16–M17 An instance of legerdemain.

leggiero *adjective & adverb* (also **leggero**) L19 **Italian.** *Music* (A direction:) light(ly) and graceful(ly).

legionnaire *noun* (also **legionaire**) E19 **French** (*légionnaire*, from *légion* legion). A member of a legion; *especially* (usually *Legionnaire*) a member of a named legion, as the American Legion, the Royal British Legion, or the French Foreign Legion.

legong *noun* E20 **Indonesian.** (A participant in) a stylized Balinese dance performed especially by young girls.

legume *noun* M17 **French** (*légume* from Latin *legumen*, from *legere* to gather: so called because the fruit may be gathered by hand). **1** M17 The fruit or edible portion of any leguminous plant (bean, pea, etc.) grown for food; any vegetable used as food. Usually in *plural*. **2** L17 A leguminous plant. **3** L18 The pod or seed vessel of a leguminous plant.

■ The Latin word *legumen* was used earlier (LME) in English and is found, though not so commonly, in all three senses above.

Lehrjahr *noun* plural **Lehrjahre** M19 **German** (from *lehr(en)* teach + *Jahr* years). A year of apprenticeship or learning.

■ Usually in the plural, the word is also often used figuratively for one's apprenticeship to life. Cf. WANDERJAHR.

lei *noun 1* M19 **Hawaiian.** A Polynesian garland made of flowers, feathers, shells, etc., often given as a symbol of affection.

lei *noun 2* E20 **Chinese** (*léi*). *Chinese Antiquities* An urn-shaped bronze wine vessel of the Shang period (*c.* 250 BC).

leitmotiv *noun* (also **leitmotif**) L19 **German** (from *leit-* leading + *Motiv* motive). **1** L19 *Music* A theme associated throughout a work with a particular person, situation, or sentiment. **2** L19 *generally* A recurrent idea or image in a literary work, etc.

lekach *noun* M20 **Yiddish.** A Jewish cake traditionally made with honey.

lekane *noun* E20 **Greek** (*lekanē* a bowl, a dish). *Greek Antiquities* A shallow bowl, usually with handles and a cover.

lekker *adjective* E20 **Afrikaans** (from Dutch (cf. German *lecker*) related to Dutch *likken* to lick). Pleasant, sweet, nice; good, excellent.

■ South African colloquial, used as a general term of approbation.

lekythos *noun* plural **lekythoi** M19 **Greek** (*lēkuthos*). *Greek Antiquities* A vase or flask with a narrow neck.

■ Also in the Late Latin form *lecythus* (M19).

lemma *noun* plural **lemmas**, **lemmata** L16 **Latin** (from Greek *lēmma*, plural *lēmmata*, something taken for granted or assumed, theme, argument, title, from base also of *lambanein* to take). **1** L16 An axiom or demonstrated proposition used in an argument or proof. **2** E17 The argument or subject of a literary work, prefixed as a heading. Also, a motto attached to a picture, etc. **3** M20 A word or phrase defined in a dictionary, glossed in a glossary, entered in a word list, etc.

lemur *noun* plural (in sense 1) **lemures**, (in sense 2) **lemurs** M16 **Modern Latin** (from Latin *lemures* (plural) shades of the dead). **1** M16 Chiefly *Roman Mythology* In *plural*, the spirits of the dead, ghosts. Now occasionally *singular*, a ghost. **2** L18 *Zoology* Any mammal of the prosimian family Lemuridae, comprising long-tailed, sharp-muzzled, arboreal animals found chiefly in Madagascar. Also, any related primate, as the indri and the loris.

lentamente *adverb* **M18 Italian** (from *lento* from Latin *lentus* slow). *Music* Slowly, in slow time.

lente *adjective* **M20 Latin** (= slowly). *Medicine* Of a substance, especially insulin: that is metabolized or absorbed gradually when introduced into the body.

lento *adverb & adjective* **E18 Italian. 1** *adverb & adjective* E18 *Music* (A direction:) in slow time, slower than adagio. **2** *adjective* M20 Pronounced more slowly than in normal speech.

leprechaun *noun* **E17 Irish** (*leipreachán* alteration of Middle Irish *luchrupán* alteration of Old Irish *luchorpán*, from *lu* small + *corp* body). In Irish folklore, a small, usually mischievous being of human form, often associated with shoemaking or buried treasure.

lèse-majesté *noun* (also **lese-majesty**) **LME French** (from Latin *laesa majestas* hurt or violated majesty (i.e., of the sovereign people), from *laesa* feminine past participle of *laedere* to injure, hurt, *majestas* majesty). **1** LME The insulting of a monarch or other ruler. Also, treason. **2** M17 *transferred* Presumptuous behavior, disrespect.

■ *Lese-* or *lèse-* is also used with other French or English words in jocular imitation of *lese-majesty* or *lèse-majesté*.

le tout *adjective phrase* **E20 French.** The whole of, everyone in, all, (a place).

■ Frequently used in a context of making fun of social pretensions. The word(s) defined by *le tout* may be French, on the analogy of *(le) tout Paris* all Paris (meaning 'Parisian society') or, in jocular use, more often English. Cf. TOUT.

lettre *noun* **E18 French** (from Latin *littera* letter of the alphabet, *(in plural)* epistle, document). A letter.

■ Occurs in English only in various phrases mainly designating styles of handwriting: e.g., *lettre bâtard* a kind of cursive Gothic script originating in France in the late Middle Ages (also known as *bastarda*), *lettre de forme* a kind of formal, angular handwriting on which some typefaces for early printed books were based (also known as *textura*), and *lettre de somme* a kind of rounded Gothic script originating in thirteenth-century Italy on which some typefaces for early printed books were based (also known as *rotunda*).

lettre de cachet *noun phrase* plural **lettres de cachet E18 French** (literally, 'letter of seal'). **1** *History* In France under the *ancien régime*, a warrant for the imprisonment of a person without trial at the pleasure of the monarch. **2** An (arbitrary) official order for imprisonment, exile, etc.

lettrisme *noun* (also in Anglicized form **lettrism**) **M20 French** (from as LETTRE). A movement in French art and literature characterized by a repudiation of meaning and the use of letters (sometimes invented) as isolated units.

levade *noun* **M20 French** (from *lever* to raise). A dressage movement (superseding the *pesade*) in which the horse raises its forequarters with the forelegs drawn up, and balances on its hind legs which are placed well forward under the body and deeply bent.

levee *noun 1* **L17 French** (*levé* variant of *lever* rising, noun use of *lever* to rise). **1 a** L17 *History* A reception of visitors on rising from bed; a morning assembly held by a person of distinction. **b** M18 *History* An afternoon assembly for men only held by (a representative of) the British monarch. **c** M18 A reception or assembly at any time of day. Now *archaic* except in *North America*. **2** The company assembled at a levee. Only in 18. **3** E18–

E19 The action of rising, *specifically* from one's bed.

■ The less fashionable evening equivalent of sense 1 was the COUCHEE.

levee *noun 2 & verb* E18 French (*levée* feminine of *levé* past participle of *lever* to raise). **A** *noun* **1** E18 An embankment to prevent the overflow of a river. **b** L19 *Physical Geography* A low broad ridge of sediment running alongside a river channel. Also, any similar natural embankment, as one formed by a mud flow, lava flow, or submarine current. **2** M19 A landing place, a pier, a quay. **B** *transitive verb* M19 Raise a levee or embankment along (a river) or in (a district). Also, shut or keep *off* by means of a levee.

levée en masse *noun phrase* plural **levées en masse** E19 French. A mass mobilization (originally in Revolutionary France) in response to the threat of invasion.

lever de rideau *noun phrase* plural **levers de rideau** M19 French (= curtain-raiser). A short opening piece before the main perfomance; a preliminary event.

lex domicilii *noun phrase* E19 Latin (= law of the domicile). *Law* The law of the country in which a person is domiciled, as determining the right to make a will, succeed to property, etc.

lex fori *noun phrase* E19 Latin (= law of the court). *Law* The law of the country in which an action is brought, as regulating procedure, evidence, execution of judgments, etc.

lexis *noun* M20 Greek (= a word, phrase, from *legein* to speak). **1** M20 The diction or wording, in contrast to other elements, of a piece of writing. **2** M20 *Linguistics* Items of lexical, as opposed especially to grammatical, meaning; the total word stock of a language. Also, the branch of knowledge that deals with words as lexical items.

lex loci *noun phrase* L18 Latin (= law of the place). *Law* The law of the country in which some event material to a case took place.

■ Frequently followed by a defining word or phrase, as in *lex loci contractus* the law of the country in which a contract was made or *lex loci delicti* the law of the country in which an offense was committed.

lex talionis *noun phrase* M17 Latin (from *lex* law + *talionis* genitive of *talio(n)* recompense). The (supposed) law of retaliation; the retributive theory of punishment, based on the Mosaic principle "an eye for an eye, a tooth for a tooth".

li *noun 1* L17 Chinese (*lǐ*). In Neo-Confucianism: correct observance of the rules governing behavior to others, regarded as needed to maintain a person's harmony with the moral principles of nature.

li *noun 2* plural same M20 Chinese (*lǐ*). *Chinese Antiquities* A bronze or pottery cooking vessel, with (usually three) hollow legs.

liaison *noun* M17 French (from *lier* to bind, from Latin *ligare*). **1** M17 *Cooking* A binding or thickening agent for sauces, consisting chiefly of the yolks of eggs. Formerly, the process of binding or thickening. **2** E19 An intimate relation or connection; *specifically* an illicit sexual relationship, especially between a man and a married woman. **3** E19 Communication and cooperation, original *specifically* between military forces or units, especially during a battle or campaign. **4** L19 *Phonetics* The pronunciation of a normally silent final consonant before a vowel (or mute *h*) beginning the following word, especially in French.

■ In sense 2 sometimes in the phrase *liaison dangereuse* (literally, 'dangerous acquaintance'), an allusion to the brilliant and scandalous epistolary novel *Les Liaisons dangereuses* (1782) by Pierre Laclos.

libero *noun* plural **liberi** M20 Italian (literally, 'free'). *Soccer* A defending player positioned near the goal, a sweeper.

liberum arbitrium *noun phrase* M17 **Latin** (= free judgment, free will). Full power to decide; freedom of action.

■ A quotation from Livy's history of Rome (iv.43.5).

libido *noun* E20 **Latin** (= desire, lust). *Psychoanalysis* Psychic drive or energy, *especially* that associated with the sexual instinct.

libretto *noun* plural **librettos, libretti** M18 **Italian** (diminutive of *libro* book). The text of an opera or other long vocal composition.

lidia *noun* L19 **Spanish** (literally, 'fight'). A bullfight, especially the earlier stages in which the CUADRILLA prepares the bull for the FAENA.

lidiador *noun* plural **lidiadores** L19 **Spanish**. A bullfighter.

lido *noun* plural **lidos** L17 **Italian** (= shore, beach, from Latin *litus*). A bathing beach; a resort; a public open-air swimming pool.

■ Originally specifically *the Lido*, a bathing beach near Venice.

lié *predicative adjective* M19 **French** (past participle of *lier* to bind). Connected (*with*), intimately acquainted (*with*).

liebchen *noun* (also **Liebchen**) L19 **German**. A person who is very dear to another; a sweetheart, a pet, a darling.

■ Frequently used as a term of endearment.

Liebestod *noun* (also **liebestod**) L19 **German** (literally, 'love's death'). An aria or a duet in an opera, etc., proclaiming the suicide of lovers; such a suicide.

liebling *noun* (also **Liebling**) M19 **German**. A sweetheart. Cf. LIEBCHEN.

lied *noun* plural **lieder** (also **Lied**) M19 **German**. A song; *especially* a song characteristic of the German Romantic period, usually for solo voice with piano accompaniment.

lien *noun* M16 **French** (from Old French *loien* from Latin *ligamen* bond, from *ligare* to tie). *Law* A right to retain possession of property belonging to another person until a debt due by that person is discharged.

■ Often in the expression *have a lien on (something)*, used both literally and figuratively.

lierne *noun* LME **French** (perhaps transferred use of *lierne* clematis, dialectal variant of *liane*). *Architecture* A short rib connecting the bosses and intersections of vaulting ribs.

lieu *noun* ME **French** (from Latin *locus* place). Place, stead.

■ Only in *in lieu* 'in the place, instead, (*of*)'.

lignum vitae *noun* L16 **Latin** (= wood of life). GUAIACUM (senses 1–3).

limaçon *noun* (also **limacon**) L16 **French** (= snail shell, spiral staircase, etc., from Old and modern French *limace* from Latin *limax, limac-* slug, snail). **1** A kind of spiral military maneuver. Only in L16. **2** L19 *Mathematics* A type of heart-shaped curve.

limbo *noun* plural **limbos** LME **Latin** (ablative singular of *limbus* edge, border (in medieval Latin, border of Hell), in phrases like *in limbo, e* (= out of) *limbo*). **1** LME *Christian Church* A region supposed in some beliefs to exist on the border of Hell as the abode of the just who died before Christ's coming and of unbaptized infants. **b** L16–M17 Hell, Hades. **2** L16 Prison, confinement. *slang*. **3** M17 An unfavorable place or condition, likened to limbo; *especially* a condition of neglect or oblivion to which people or things are consigned when regarded as superseded, useless, or absurd; an intermediate or indeterminate condition; a state of inaction or inattention pending some future event.

limes *noun* plural **limites** M16 **Latin** (= limit). Now *Archaeology* A boundary; *specifically* the boundary of the Roman Empire, especially in the north of Europe.

linctus *noun* L17 **Medieval Latin** ((classical Latin = licking, from *lingere* to lick), after late Latin *electuarium* electuary). A syrupy liquid medicine, now *especially* a soothing cough mixture.

linga *noun* (also **lingam**) E18 **Sanskrit** (*liṅga* sign, (sexual) characteristic; variant influenced by Tamil *iliṅkam*). A Hindu sacred object constituting a symbol of the god Siva, *specifically* (the representation of) a phallus.

ling chih *noun phrase* E20 **Chinese** (*língzhī* (Wade–Giles *ling chih*), from *ling* divine + *zhī* fungus). A motif on Chinese ceramic ware, especially a representation of the fungus *Polyporus lucidus*, symbolizing longevity or immortality.

lingerie *noun* M19 **French** (from *linge* linen). Originally, linen articles collectively; all the articles of linen, lace, etc., in a woman's wardrobe or trousseau. Now, women's underwear and nightclothes.

lingoa geral variant of LINGUA GERAL.

lingua franca *noun phrase* plural **lingua francas**, **lingue franche** L17 **Italian** (= Frankish tongue). A mixture of Italian with French, Greek, Arabic, Turkish, and Spanish, used in the Levant (now *historical*). Also, any language serving as a medium between different nations, etc., whose own languages are not the same; a system of communication providing mutual understanding.

■ 'Frank', in many local variants, was the word generally used by the inhabitants of the eastern Mediterranean region for a person of western or northern European origin—not only a Frenchman.

lingua geral *noun phrase* (also **lingoa geral**) M19 **Portuguese** (*língua geral* general language). A trade language based on Tupi and used as a LINGUA FRANCA in Brazil.

lingue franche plural of LINGUA FRANCA.

linguine *noun plural* M20 **Italian** (plural of *linguina* diminutive of *lingua* tongue, from Latin). Pasta in the form of tongue-shaped ribbons; an Italian dish consisting largely of this and usually a sauce.

Linzertorte *noun* plural **Linzertorten** E20 **German** (from *Linzer* adjective of the Austrian city *Linz* + *Torte* tart, pastry, cake). A kind of pastry with a jam filling, decorated on top with strips of pastry in a lattice pattern.

liqueur *noun* M18 **French** (= liquor). **1** M18 Any of various strong sweet alcoholic beverages flavored with aromatic substances, usually drunk after a meal. Also, a glass of such a drink. **2** E20 *elliptically* A liqueur glass; a liqueur chocolate.

lisse *noun & adjective* M19 **French** (= smooth (in *crêpe lisse*)). (Of) a kind of silk or cotton gauze.

lissoir *noun* E20 **French** (from *lisser* to smooth). *Archaeology* A smoothing, polishing tool.

literae humaniores *noun phrase* (also **litterae humaniores**) M18 **Latin** (= more humane letters). The humanities, secular learning as opposed to divinity; *especially* at Oxford University, the school or subject of Greek and Roman classical literature, philosophy, and ancient history.

■ Abbreviated as *lit. hum.*

litera scripta *noun phrase* M19 **Latin**. The written word.

literati *noun plural* E17 **Latin** (*lit(t)erati* plural of *lit(t)eratus* literate). Men of letters; the learned class as a whole.

literatim *adverb* M17 **Medieval Latin** (*lit(t)eratim*, from *lit(t)era* letter, after *gradatim* step by step; cf. VERBATIM). Letter for letter; literally.

literato *noun singular* (corresponding plural LITERATI) E18 **Italian** (*litterato* (now usually *letterati*) from as Latin *lit(t)eratus* literate). A member of the literati; a man of letters.

litotes *noun* L16 **Late Latin** (from Greek *litotēs*, from *litos* single, simple, meager). *Rhetoric* Ironical understatement, *specifically* in which an affirmative is expressed by the negative of the contrary.

■ Examples of this figure of speech are "no small amount" and "no mean feat". It is also called, less commonly, MEIOSIS.

litterae humaniores variant of LITERAE HUMANIORES.

littérateur *noun* E19 **French** (from Latin *litterator*). A writer of literary or critical works, a literary person.

litzendraht *noun* E20 **German** (from *Litze* braid, cord, lace, strand + *Draht* wire). Wire composed of many fine strands twisted together and individually insulated.

■ Also partially translated as Litz wire.

livraison *noun* E19 **French** (from Latin *liberatio(n-)* liberation). A part, number, or fascicle of a work published by installments.

livre de chevet *noun phrase* plural **livres de chevet** E20 **French** (literally, 'book of the bed-head'). A bedside book; a favorite book.

livre de circonstance *noun phrase* plural **livres de circonstance** M20 **French**. A book composed or adapted for the occasion.

llanero *noun* plural **llaneros** E19 **South American Spanish** (from next). An inhabitant of a llano.

llano *noun* plural **llanos** E17 **Spanish** (from Latin *planum* level ground). A level treeless plain in the southwestern United States and the northern parts of South America.

loa *noun* plural same, **loas** M20 **Haitian** (creole *lwa*, from Yoruba *oluwa* lord, owner). A god in the voodoo cult of Haiti.

lobo *noun* plural **lobos** M19 **Spanish** (from Latin *lupus* wolf). A large gray wolf of the southwestern United States. Also called *loafer* (*wolf*).

lobola *noun* (also **lobolo**) M19 **Bantu** (cf. Xhosa *lobola* to give a bride-price). The bride-price, usually in cattle, given by many grooms in southern Africa to the parent or guardian of the bride; the custom of paying such a bride-price.

locale *noun* (also **local**) L18 **French** (*local* (noun), respelled to indicate stress; cf. MORALE). A place, a locality, especially with reference to some event or circumstances connected with it; a venue.

loc. cit. *adverb phrase* M19 **Latin** (abbreviation of Latin *loco citato* or *locus citatus* (in) the place cited). In the book, etc., that has previously been quoted, in the passage already cited.

loch *noun* LME **Gaelic**. In Scotland: a lake; (more fully *sea loch*) an arm of the sea, especially when narrow or partially landlocked.

loci classici, **loci desperati**, etc., plurals of LOCUS CLASSICUS, LOCUS DESPERATUS, etc.

loco *noun & adjective* L19 **Spanish** (= insane). **A** *noun* plural **loco(e)s**. **1** L19 Any of several leguminous plants (chiefly species of *Astragalus*) found in the western and southwestern United States that cause loco disease when eaten by cattle, horses, etc. **2** L19 Loco disease.

loco citato see LOC. CIT.

locoum variant of LOKUM.

locum *noun 1* E20 **Latin** (abbreviation of medieval Latin *locum tenens* from Latin *locum* accusative of *locus* place + *tenens* present participle of *tenere* to hold). **1** E20 A person (especially a physician or priest) who undertakes the professional duties of someone else or stands in for someone else during his or her absence. **2** E20 The situation of a locum; a position as a locum.

■ *Locum tenens*, now entirely superseded in everyday English usage, antedated *locum* in both sense 1 (from M17) and sense 2 (from L19).

locum noun 2 variant of LOKUM.

locus *noun* plural **loci** E18 **Latin** (= place). **1** E18 A place, a site; a position, a point, especially in a text. **b** E20 *Genetics* A position on a chromosome at which a particular gene is located; a gene. **2** E18 *Mathematics* The curve or other figure composed of all the points that satisfy a particular equation or are generated by a point, line, or surface moving in accordance with defined conditions. **3** M18 A subject, a topic. **4** E20 LOCUS STANDI.

locus citatus see LOC. CIT.

locus classicus *noun phrase* plural **loci classici** M19 **Latin** (= classical place). A passage regarded as the principal authority on a subject or the origin of a quotation or saying; the best-known occurrence of an idea or theme.

locus desperatus *noun phrase* plural **loci desperati** E20 **Latin** (= hopeless place). A passage in a manuscript that is so corrupted it defies interpretation.

locus poenitentiae *noun phrase* plural **loci poenitentiae** M18 **Latin** (= place of penitence). A place of repentance; *Law* an opportunity for a person to withdraw from a commitment or contract, especially an illegal one, so long as some particular step has not been taken.

locus standi *noun phrase* plural **loci standi** E19 **Latin** (= place of standing). A recognized or identifiable status, especially in law; the right to be heard in a court of law.

loden *noun & adjective* (also **Loden**) E20 **German**. **A** *noun* **1** E20 A heavy waterproof woolen cloth. **2** M20 A coat or cloak made of this. **3** M20 A dark green color in which the cloth is often made. **B** *adjective* E20 Made of this cloth.

loess *noun* M19 **German** (*Löss* from Swiss German *lösch* loose, from *lösen* to loosen). *Geology* A fine yellowish gray loam composed of material transported by the wind during and after the glacial period which forms extensive deposits from north central Europe to eastern China, in the American Midwest, and elsewhere.

loge *noun* M18 **French**. **1 a** M18 A booth, a stall. **b** M20 A concierge's lodge. **2** M18 A box in a theater, opera house, etc.

loggia *noun* M18 **Italian** (= lodge). **1** M18 A gallery or arcade having one or both of its sides open to the air. **2** E20 An open-sided extension to a house, a veranda.

Logos *noun* L16 **Greek** (= account, relation, ratio, reason(ing), argument, discourse, saying, speech, word, related to *legein* to choose, collect, gather, say). **1** L16 *Philosophy* and *Christian Theology* The Word of God, the second person of the Trinity. **2** M17 A pervading cosmic idea or spirit of creativity or rationality.

■ Used in a mystic sense by Hellenistic and Neoplatonist philosophers, *Logos* entered Christian discourse primarily through its use in the opening passage of St. John's Gospel.

Lohan *noun* M19 **Chinese** (*luóhàn* (Wade–Giles *Lo-han*)). An ARHAT.

lokoum variant of LOKUM.

lokshen *noun plural* L19 **Yiddish** (plural of *loksh* noodle). Noodles (in Jewish cooking).

lokum *noun* (also **lokoum**, **loc(o)um**, **lakum**) E20 **Turkish** (abbreviation of Turkish RAHAT *lokum*). Turkish delight.

loma *noun* M19 **Spanish** (from *lomo* back, loin, ridge). In the southwestern United States: a broad-topped hill or ridge.

longeron *noun* E20 **French**. *Aeronautics* A frame member running lengthways along a fuselage.

longo intervallo *adverb phrase* L17 **Latin** (= at a distance). At some remove; in spite of the gulf between.

■ Virgil uses the phrase in the spatial sense (*Aeneid* v.320), but other Roman writers (e.g., Cicero) also used it in the temporal sense 'after a long time'.

longueur *noun* L18 **French** (= length). A lengthy or tedious passage of writing, music, etc.; a tedious stretch of time.

loofah *noun* (also **luffa**) L19 **Arabic** (*lūfa* the plant, *lūf* the species). A coarse sponge made from the bleached vascular system of the fruit of a tropical gourd, *Luffa aegyptiaca*, used to cleanse and scrub the skin. Also, the gourd itself.

loquitur *intransitive verb* M19 **Latin** (3rd person singular present of *loquor* to speak). Speaks.

■ Used with the speaker's name added, as a stage direction or to inform a reader. Abbreviated as *loq.*

lorgnette *noun* E19 **French** (from *lorgner* to squint, ogle). *singular* and in *plural* A pair of eyeglasses to be held in the hand, usually by a long handle. Also, a pair of opera glasses.

■ *Lorgnon(s)* (M19), meaning 'a single eyeglass' as well as the above, is somewhat less common.

louche *adjective* E19 **French** (= cross-eyed, squinting). Not straightforward. Now usually, dubious, shifty, disreputable.

loup *noun* M18 **French** (= wolf, from Latin *lupus*). **1** M18 The sea bass, *Dicentrachus labrax*, found off the western European coast and in the Mediterranean. **2** M19 A light mask or half mask for a woman's face.

■ In sense 2 the word was known earlier (L17) in the form *loo* or more fully *loo mask*.

loup-garou *noun* L16 **French** (from *loup* wolf + *garou* (from Old High German antecedent of Middle High German *werwolf*) werewolf). A werewolf.

luau *noun* M19 **Hawaiian** (*lū'au*). A Hawaiian party or feast usually accompanied by some form of entertainment.

lucus a non lucendo *noun phrase* E18 **Latin** (literally, 'a grove from its not shining', i.e., *lucus* (a grove) is derived from *lucere* (to shine) because there is no light there). A paradoxical or otherwise absurd derivation; something of which the qualities are the opposite of what its name suggests.

■ Also abbreviated *lucus a non*. The phrase is discussed by the Roman rhetorician Quintilian in his *Institutio Oratoria* (i.6.34).

ludo *noun* L19 **Latin** (= I play). A simple board game played with dice and counters.

lues *noun* M17 **Latin** (= plague). Syphilis (also more fully *lues venerea*). Formerly also, a plague, a pestilence.

■ *Lues* also appears in a modern Latin phrase apparently coined by Macaulay who in 1834 wrote in the *Edinburgh Review* of the *Lues Boswellianae* or "disease of admiration" that tends to afflict biographers writing uncritically about their subjects—as James Boswell did in his life of Dr. Johnson.

luffa variant of LOOFAH.

luftmensch *noun* (also **luftmensh**) plural **luftmens(c)hen** E20 **Yiddish** (*luftmensh*, from *luft* (German *Luft*) air + *mensh* (German *Mensch*) person). An impractical visionary.

luge *verb & noun* L19 **Swiss French. A** *intransitive verb* L19 Toboggan; ride or race on a luge. **B** *noun* E20 A light toboggan for one or two people usually ridden in a supine position; the sport in which these are raced.

lulav *noun* (also **lulab**) plural **lulavs, lulavim** L19 **Hebrew** (*lūlāḇ* branch). A palm branch traditionally carried at the Jewish festival of Succoth.

lumbago *noun* L17 **Latin** (*lumbago, lumbagino*, from *lumbus* loin). Rheumatic pain in the lower muscles of the back.

lumen siccum *noun phrase* E17 **Latin** (literally, 'dry light'). The objective light of rational knowledge or thought.

■ Francis Bacon characterized rational knowledge as *lumen siccum* in 1605 in his *Advancement of Learning* (II.f.48), and the metaphor has been in intermittent use, especially among English philosophers, since then.

lumpenproletariat *noun derogatory* E20 **German** (from *Lumpen* rag + PROLETARIAT). The poorest and least cohesive section of the proletariat, making no contribution to the workers' cause; the ignorantly contented lower orders of society uninterested in revolutionary advancement. *derogatory*.

■ Originally used by Karl Marx in *Die Klassenkämpfe in Frankreich* (1850).

lundum *noun* M20 **Portuguese.** A simple Portuguese song and dance originating from Africa, probably one of the sources from which the FADO developed.

lunette *noun* L16 **French** (diminutive of *lune* moon, from Latin *luna*). **1** L16 *Farriery* A semicircular horseshoe for the front of the hoof only. Also *lunette shoe.* **2** E17 *Architecture* **a** An arched aperture in a concave ceiling for the admission of light. **b** E18 A crescent-shaped or semicircular space in a ceiling, dome, etc., decorated with paintings or sculptures; a piece of decoration filling such a space. **3** M17 A blinker for a horse. **4** L17 In *plural* Eyeglasses. Now *rare.* **5** E18 *Fortification* A work larger than a redan, consisting of two faces forming a salient angle and two flanks. **6** L18 The figure or shape of a crescent moon. **7** M19 A watch glass (crystal) of flattened shape. Also *lunette (watch)glass.* **8** M19 In the guillotine, the circular hole that receives the neck of the victim. **9** M19 Any of the flues connecting a glass furnace and its arch. (Earlier in the form *linnet-hole.*) **10** M19 A crescent-shaped ornament. **11** L19 A ring or forked plate to or by which a field-gun carriage or other vehicle for towing is attached. **12** L19 *Roman Catholic Church* A circular case, fitting into an aperture in a monstrance, for holding the consecrated host. **13** M20 *Physical Geography* A broad shallow mound of windblown material along the leeward side of a lake or dry lake basin, especially in arid parts of Australia, and typically crescent-shaped with the concave edge along the lake shore.

lunula *noun* plural **lunulae** L16 **Latin** (diminutive of *luna* moon). **1** L16 *Geometry* A figure formed on a plane by arcs of two circles intersecting at two points, a lune. **2** E18 *Archaeology* A gold crescent-shaped neck ornament of the early Bronze Age. **3** E19 *Anatomy, Zoology*, and *Botany* A crescent-shaped mark or spot, *specifically* the pale area at the base of a fingernail, a lunule. **b** M19 *Anatomy* A crescent-shaped region of thin tissue on each side of the nodule on each cusp of a valve in the heart or aorta. **4** M19 *Conchology* The crescent-shaped depression in front of the umbo of a shell, a lunule.

lupara *noun* M20 **Italian** ((slang), from *lupa* she-wolf). A sawed-off shotgun as used by the Mafia.

lustrum *noun* plural **lustra, lustrums** L16 **Latin** (originally, a purificatory sacrifice after a quinquennial census, later also, a period of five years: ultimate origin unknown). A period of five years.

lusus *noun* plural same, **lususes** E17 **Latin** (*lusus naturae* a sport of nature). A freak of nature, an abnormal formation, a natural curiosity. In full *lusus naturae.*

luthier *noun* L19 **French** (from *luth* lute). A maker of stringed instruments, *specifically* of the violin family.

luxe *noun* M16 **French** (from Latin *luxus* luxury). (A) luxury. Cf. DELUXE.

lycée *noun* M19 **French** (from Latin LYCEUM). A state secondary school in France.

Lyceum *noun* L16 **Latin** (from Greek *Lukeion* (sc. *gumnasion* gymnasium) neuter of *Lukeios* epithet of Apollo (from whose neighboring temple the Lyceum was named)). **1** L16 The garden at Athens in which Aristotle taught his philosophy; Aristotelian philosophy and its adherents. **2** E19 A LYCÉE. **3** E19 *United States History* (**lyceum**) An institution in which popular lectures were delivered on literary and scientific subjects. **4** L19 *Theater* A theater near the Strand in London, England. Used *attributively* to denote a melodramatic performance or style, formerly characteristic of this theater.

Lyonnais *adjective* (feminine **Lyonnaise**) E19 **French** (from *Lyon* the name of a city in southeast France). Of, pertaining to, or characteristic of the city of Lyons (Lyon) or the former province of Lyonnais, in France; *specifically* (*Lyonnaise*) in *Cooking*, designating food, especially sliced potatoes, cooked with onions or with white wine and onion sauce.

maar *noun* plural **maars, maare** E19 **German** (dialect). **1** E19 (Usually **Maar**) A crater lake in the Eifel district of Germany. **2** L19 *Geology* A broad low-rimmed usually lake-filled volcanic crater of a kind exemplified by the Eifel Maars.

maas *noun* (also in Zulu form **amasi**) E19 **Afrikaans** (from Zulu (plural) *amasi* curdled milk). In South Africa: thick sour milk.

mabele *noun* E19 **Bantu** (cf. Zulu, Xhosa *ibele*, plural *amabele*). In South Africa: kaffir corn, *Sorghum bicolor* var. *caffrorum*; meal or porridge made from this.

macabre *adjective* M19 **French** (Old French *macabré* adjective (modern *macabre*), perhaps alteration of *Macabé* Maccabaeus, Maccabee, with reference to a miracle play containing the slaughter of the Maccabees). Grim, gruesome.

■ In early use perhaps regarded as a proper name and introduced into English as a noun; the earliest (LME) instance of the phrase *daunce of Machabree* is in the title of one of Lydgate's works, but this usage has long been obsolete. The modern adjectival sense likewise originated in the phrase *dance macabre*, an Anglicized version of the French DANSE MACABRE. The deaths of seven Jewish brothers and their mother, tortured to death for their religion under Hellenistic rule in the second century BC, are narrated in the Apocrypha (2 Maccabees 7); the Western Christian church honored them as martyrs, with a feast day celebrated on August 1.

macaroni *noun* plural **macaronies** L16 **Italian** (*mac(c)aroni*, later *maccheroni*, plural of *mac(c)arone, maccherone* from late Greek *makaria* barley food). **1** L16 Pasta in the form of tubes. **2** M18 A fop, a dandy. *obsolete* except *historical*. **3** E19 *History* A West Indian coin worth a quarter of a dollar or (later) one shilling. **4** M19 In full *macaroni penguin*. A penguin, *Eudyptes chrysolophus*, apparently so called from its orange crest. **5** M19 An Italian. *slang. derogatory*. **6** E20 Nonsense, meaningless talk. *slang* (chiefly *Australian*).

macchia *noun* E20 **Corsican Italian** (from Latin *macula* spot). **1** E20 MAQUIS vegetation. **2** *Art* In painting, a fleck or touch of paint.

macédoine *noun* E19 **French** (from *Macédoine* Macedonia, with reference to the diversity of peoples in the empire of Alexander the Great, King of Macedon). Mixed fruit or vegetables cut up into small pieces; *figurative* a medley, a mixture.

machair *noun* L17 **Gaelic**. In Scotland: a flat or low-lying coastal strip of arable or grassland; land of this nature.

mâche *noun* L17 **French**. Lamb's lettuce, corn salad.

■ Originally Anglicized (only in plural) in the now obsolete form of *maches*.

macher *noun* M20 **Yiddish** (from German = maker, doer). A man of importance, a bigwig; a braggart. Frequently *derogatory*.

machete *noun* (also **matchet** and other variants) L16 **Spanish** (from *macho* hammer, from Latin *marcus*). A broad and heavy knife or cutlass, used, especially in Central America and the West Indies, as a tool or a weapon.

■ *Machete* has gained general currency in English in the twentieth century, superseding the Anglicized *matchet* and the other variants.

machismo *noun* M20 **Mexican Spanish** (from as MACHO). The quality of being macho; male virility, masculine pride; a show of this.

macho *noun & adjective* E20 **Mexican Spanish** (= male animal or plant, (as adjective) masculine, vigorous). **A** *noun* plural **machos** **1** E20 A man; *specifically* an assertively vigorous man. **2** M20 MACHISMO. **B** *adjective* Ostentatiously masculine, virile.

■ Originally United States.

Macht-politik *noun* E20 **German** (from *Macht* power, strength + *Politik* policy, politics). Power politics; strength as a potential factor to use in gaining a desired result.

macramé *noun & adjective* M19 **Turkish** (*makrama* handkerchief, tablecloth, towel from Arabic *miḳrama* bed cover, bedspread). **A** *noun* M19 A fringe, trimming, or lace of knotted thread or cord; knotwork; the art of making this. **B** *attributive* or as *adjective* L19 Made of or by macramé.

macro *noun & adjective* M20 **Greek** (*makro-* combining form of *makros* large, long). **A** *noun* plural **macros**. **1** M20 *Computing* A macro-instruction. **2** M20 *Photography* Macrophotography; a macro lens. **B** *adjective* M20 Macroscopic, large-scale; overall, comprehensive; *Chemistry* of macroanalysis; *Photography* pertaining to or used in macrophotography.

■ An independent use of the combining form found in numerous English words derived from Greek, particularly in scientific terminology; cf. MEGA. *Macro* is frequently contrasted, either explicitly or implicitly, with MICRO.

macron *noun* M19 **Greek** (- neuter of *makros* long). A straight horizontal line (¯) written or printed over a vowel to indicate length or stress.

macula *noun* plural **maculae, maculas** LME **Latin. 1** LME Chiefly *Science* A spot, a stain; *Medicine* a permanent spot or stain in the skin. **2** M19 *Anatomy* Any of various structures that have the appearance of a spot.

■ The French word *macule* deriving from *macula* was also found in English in sense 1 (from L15).

Madame *noun* (also **madame, madam**) plural **Mesdames** ME **Old French. I 1** ME Madam, my lady. **II 2 a** M16 Used as a title (preceding the surname) of or as a respectful form of address to a French married woman or (more widely) a married woman of any nationality (corresponding to English *Mrs.*), or in literal renderings of French speech. **b** L16 *French History* (A title of) a female member of the French royal family, *specifically* the eldest daughter of the French king or the dauphin (cf. MADEMOISELLE 3). **c** M19 Used as a title (preceding a name) by a businesswoman, fortune-teller, etc., especially to imply skill and sophistication, or foreign origin. **3** L16–M18 A woman usually addressed or referred to as 'Madame'; a French married woman; a Frenchman's wife.

■ As a title, usually abbreviated to *Mme*. The plural *Mesdames* (abbreviation *Mmes*) is also used as the plural of *Mrs*. The usual Anglicized version *madam* has also been current since the Middle Ages and is most generally used as a respectful form of address to a woman, although it has also evolved some derogatory associations (e.g., 'a spoiled or affected woman' (L16), 'a female brothel-keeper' (L19)).

madeleine *noun* M19 **French** (probably from *Madeleine* Paulmier, nineteenth-century French pastry cook). A (kind of) small rich cake, in French cooking baked in a fluted pan, and in English cooking usually baked in an individual mold and decorated with coconut and jam.

Mademoiselle *noun* (also **mademoiselle**) plural **Mesdemoiselles, Mademoiselles** LME **Old French. 1** LME Used as a title (preceding a name) of or as a respectful form of address to an unmarried Frenchwoman or (more widely) an unmarried woman of any non-British nationality (corresponding to English *Miss*), or in literal renderings of French speech. Also used as a respectful form of address to a French governess or a female French teacher in an English-speaking school. **2** M17 A woman usually addressed or referred to as '*Mademoiselle*'; an unmarried Frenchwoman; a French governess. **3** L17 *French History* (A title of) the eldest daughter of the eldest brother (known as '*Monsieur*') of the French king. Later, (a title of) the French king's eldest daughter or (if he had no daughter) the unmarried princess most closely related to him (cf. MADAME 2b). **4** L19 A croaker (fish), *Bairdiella chrysoura*, of the southern United States. Also called *silver perch, yellowtail.*

■ As a title, usually abbreviated to *Mlle.*

madérisé *adjective* M20 **French** (past participle of *madériser*). Of wine: affected with the brown discoloration that afflicts white wines that have been stored too long or under unsuitable conditions.

Madonna *noun* (also **madonna**) L16 **Italian** (from *ma* old unstressed form of *mia* my (from Latin *mea*) + *donna* lady (from Latin *domina*)). **1 a** L16 Used as a respectful form of address to an Italian woman, or in literal renderings of Italian speech. **b** E17 An Italian woman. *rare.* **2** M17 The or *the* Virgin Mary; a picture or statue of the Virgin Mary. **3** M19 A hairstyle in which the hair is parted in the center and arranged smoothly on either side of the face, as in certain Italian representations of the Virgin Mary. More fully *Madonna braid.*

madrasah *noun* (also **medresseh** and other variants) M17 **Arabian** (*madrasa*, noun of place from *darasa* to study). A Muslim college.

madrigal *noun* L16 **Italian** (from medieval Latin *matricalis* mother: cf. medieval Latin *ecclesia matrix* mother church). **1** L16 A short lyrical love poem. **2** L16 *Music* A part-song for several voices, *specifically* one of a sixteenth- or seventeenth-century Italian style, arranged in elaborate counterpoint, and sung without instrumental accompaniment. Also, a fourteenth-century Italian pastoral song of several stanzas. **3** L16 *generally* A song, a ditty.

madrilene *noun* E20 **French** ((*consommé à la*) *madrilène*, of or pertaining to Madrid). A clear soup usually served cold.

maelstrom *noun* L17 **Early Modern Dutch** ((now *maalstroom*), from *maalen* to grind, whirl around + *stroom* stream, whence the Scandinavian forms (e.g., Swedish *malström*, Danish *malstrøm*)). **1** L17 A great whirlpool, originally one in the Arctic Ocean off the west coast of Norway, formerly supposed to suck in and destroy all vessels that ventured near it. **2** M19 *figurative* A state of turbulence or confusion.

maestoso *adverb, adjective, & noun* E18 **Italian** (= majestic, from *maestà* from Latin *majestas, majestatis* majesty). *Music* **A** *adverb & adjective* E18 (A direction:) majestic(ally). **B** *noun* plural **maestosos** L19 A majestic piece or movement.

maestrale *noun* M18 **Italian** (from Latin *magistralis* (sc. *ventus* wind) from *magister* master; cf. MISTRAL). Any of several mainly northwesterly winds that blow in the Mediterranean, especially a summer wind in the Adriatic, and a winter wind, milder than a mistral, in the west.

maestria *noun* L19 **Italian** (from Latin *magisterium*, from *magister* master). Skill, mastery.

maestro *noun* plural **maestri, maestros** E18 **Italian** (from Latin *magister* master). **1 a** E18 An expert in music; a great musical composer, teacher, or conductor. **b** M20 *transferred* A great performer or leader in any art, profession, etc. **2** E20 The MAESTRALE.

Mafia *noun* (also **mafia, maffia**) M19 **Italian** ((Sicilian) = bragging, specifically hostility toward the law and its upholders, frequently as manifested in vindictive crimes). **1** M19 *the Mafia*, an organized secret society of criminals, originating in Sicily but now operating internationally, especially in the United States. **2** M20 *generally* Any group regarded as exerting a secret and often sinister influence.

Mafioso *noun* plural **Mafiosi, Mafiosos** feminine **Mafiosa** (also **mafioso, maffioso**) L19 **Italian** (from as MAFIA). A member or supporter of the Mafia or a mafia.

Magen David *noun phrase* E20 **Hebrew** (literally, 'shield of David' (king of Israel from *c.*1000 BC)). The Star of David, a six-pointed figure consisting of two interlaced equilateral triangles, used as a Jewish and Israeli symbol.

magi plural of MAGUS.

magma *noun* LME **Latin** (from Greek, from base of *massein* to knead). **1** LME–M19 The dregs remaining after a semiliquid substance has been pressed or evaporated. **2** L17 A mixture of mineral or organic substances having the consistency of paste. Now *rare*. **3** M19 *Geology* A hot fluid or semifluid material beneath the crust of the earth or other planet, from which igneous rocks are formed by cooling and which erupts as lava.

Magna Carta *noun phrase* (also **Magna Charta**) L15 **Medieval Latin** (literally, 'great charter'). The charter of English personal and political liberty obtained from King John in 1215; *transferred* any similar document establishing rights.

magna cum laude *adverb & adjective phrase* L19 **Latin** (literally, 'with great praise'). With or of great distinction; *specifically* (of a degree, diploma, etc.) of a higher standard than the average (though not the highest).

■ Chiefly North American; cf. CUM LAUDE, SUMMA CUM LAUDE.

magna mater *noun phrase* plural **magnae matres** E18 **Latin** (literally, 'great mother'). A mother goddess; a fertility goddess.

magna opera see MAGNUM OPUS.

magnificat *noun* ME **Latin** (2nd person singular present indicative of *magnificare* to magnify. **1** ME (the *Magnificat*) A canticle forming part of the Christian liturgy at evensong and vespers, and comprising the hymn of the Virgin Mary in Luke 1:46–55 (in the Vulgate beginning *Magnificat anima mea Dominum*). Also, the music to which this is set. **2** E17 *transferred* A song of praise.

magnifico *noun* plural **magnifico(e)s** L16 **Italian** ((adjective) = magnificent). A magnate (originally a Venetian one); a grandee.

magnum *noun & adjective* L18 **Latin** (noun use of neuter singular of *magnus* large). **A** *noun* **1** L18 A bottle for wine, liquor, etc., twice the standard size, now usually containing 1.5 liters; the quantity of liquor held by such a bottle. **2** M20 (Also *Magnum*) A Magnum revolver or cartridge (see sense **B** below). **3** M20 *Zoology* The section of a bird's oviduct that secretes albumen. **B** *attributively* or as *adjective* **1** M20 (Also *Magnum*) Of a cartridge: adapted so as to be more powerful than its caliber suggests. Of a gun: designed to fire such cartridges. **2** L20 Large, oversized.

■ In the United States, senses A.2 and B.1 are proprietary names.

magnum opus *noun phrase* (also **opus magnum**) plural **magnum opuses, magna opera** L18 **Latin** (= great work). A great and usually large work of art, literature, etc.; *specifically* the most important work of an artist, writer, etc.

magus *noun* (also **Magus**) plural **magi** ME **Latin** (from Greek *magos* from Old Persian *maguš*). **1** ME *History* A member of an ancient Persian priestly caste; *transferred* a magician, a sorcerer. **2** LME *the (three) Magi*, the three 'wise men' from the East who brought gifts to the infant Jesus (Matthew 2:1), a representation of these.

maharaja *noun* (also **maharajah**, **maharaj**, **Maharaja**) L17 **Sanskrit** (*mahārājā*, from *mahā* great + *rājān* RAJA). (The title of) an Indian prince of high rank.

maharani *noun* (also **maharanee**, **Maharani**) M19 **Hindustani** (*mahārāṇī*, from Sanskrit *mahā* great + *rājñī* RANEE). (The title of) the wife or widow of a maharaja.

maharishi *noun* (also **Maharishi**) L18 **Sanskrit** (alteration of Sanskrit *maharṣi*, from *mahā* great + *ṛṣi* holy man). (The title of) a Hindu sage; *generally* (the title of) a popular leader of spiritual thought. Cf. GURU.

mahatma *noun* L19 **Sanskrit** *mahātman*, from *mahā* great + *ātman* soul). **1** L19 In the Esoteric Buddhism of members of the Theosophical Society: any of a class of people with preternatural powers, supposed to exist in the Indian subcontinent and Tibet; *transferred* a sage, an adept. **2** M20 (*Mahatma*) In the Indian subcontinent: (the title of) a revered person regarded with love and respect.

Mahdi *noun* E19 **Arabic** ((*al-*)*mahdī*, literally, 'he who is rightly guided', from passive participle of *hadā* to lead on the right way, guide aright). In Muslim belief: the restorer of religion and justice who will rule before the end of the world; a claimant of this title.

■ The *Mahdi* best known to history was Muhammad Ahmad of Dongola in Sudan who proclaimed himself such in 1881 and launched a political and revolutionary movement that overthrew the Turco-Egyptian regime.

mah-jongg *noun* (also **mah-jong**) E20 **Chinese** (dialect *ma jiang* sparrows). A game (originally Chinese) for four, played with 136 or 144 pieces called tiles, divided into five or six suits.

maillot *noun* L19 **French**. **1** L19 Tights. **2** E20 A tight-fitting, usually one-piece, swimsuit. **3** M20 A jersey, a top.

maiolica variant of MAJOLICA.

maison *noun* M16 **French**. In France and French-speaking countries: a house; now usually a business (especially a fashion) house or firm.

■ See phrases below and PÂTÉ MAISON.

maison clos *noun phrase* M20 **French** (literally, 'closed house'). A brothel.

maison de couture *noun phrase* E20 **French**. A fashion house.

maison de passe *noun phrase* (also **maison-de-passe**) M20 **French** (literally, 'house of passage'). A house to which prostitutes can take clients.

maison de santé *noun phrase* M19 **French** (literally, 'house of health'). A nursing home, *especially* one for the mentally ill.

maisonette *noun* L18 **French** (*maisonnette* diminutive of *maison* house). **1** L18 A small house. **2** E20 A part of a residential building that is occupied separately, usually on more than one floor.

maison tolérée *noun phrase* L19 **French** (literally, 'tolerated house'). A licensed brothel.

maître *noun* L19 **French** (literally, 'master'). The title of or form of address to a French lawyer.

■ Also with the sense of 'instructor' in the phrases MAÎTRE D'ARMES and MAÎTRE DE BALLET; see also CHER MAÎTRE, MAÎTRE D'HÔTEL.

maître d' *noun phrase* (also **maître de**) plural **maîtres d'**, **maîtres de** L19 **French** (colloquial abbreviation of MAÎTRE D'HÔTEL). The manager of a hotel dining room or restaurant, a headwaiter.

maître d'armes *noun phrase* L19 **French** (literally, 'master of arms'). A fencing instructor.

maître de ballet *noun phrase* E19 French. *Ballet* Originally, the composer of a ballet who superintended its production and performance; now, a trainer of ballet dancers.

maître d'hôtel *noun phrase* plural **maîtres d'hôtel** M16 French (literally, 'master of house'). **1** M16 A majordomo, a steward, a butler. **2** L19 A hotel manager. Now usually the manager of a hotel dining room or restaurant, a headwaiter.

maîtres d', maîtres d'armes, etc., plurals of MAÎTRE D', MAÎTRE D'ARMES, etc.

maîtresse en titre *noun phrase* (also **maîtresse-en-titre, maitresse en titre**) plural **maîtresses en titre** M19 French (literally, 'mistress in name'). An official or acknowledged mistress.

maîtresse femme *noun phrase* M19 French. A strong-willed or domineering woman.

maja *noun* M19 Spanish. In Spain and Spanish-speaking countries: a woman who dresses gaily.

■ Best known in English in the titles of two of Goya's paintings, the *Naked Maja* and the *Clothed Maja*. The equivalent male term *majo* (M19) is less common.

Majlis *noun* (also **majlis**) E19 Arabic (= place of session, from *jalasa* to be seated). An assembly for discussion, a council; *specifically* the Parliament of any of various North African or Middle Eastern countries, especially Iran. Also, a reception room.

majolica *noun & adjective* (also **maiolica**) M16 Italian (from the former name of the island of Majorca). **A** *noun* M16 A fine kind of Renaissance Italian earthenware with colored decoration on an opaque white glaze; any of various other kinds of glazed Italian ware. Also, a modern imitation of this. **B** *attributive* or as *adjective* M19 Made of majolica.

majuscule *adjective & noun* E18 French (from Latin *majuscula* (*littera*) diminutive of *major* major). **A** *adjective* **1** E18 *Typography* Of a letter: capital. *rare.* **2** M19 *Paleography* Of a letter: large (whether capital or uncial); pertaining to, of, or written in large lettering; designating or pertaining to a script having every letter bounded by the same two (imaginary) lines. **B** *noun* **1** E19 *Typography* A capital letter. *rare.* **2** M19 *Paleography* A large letter, whether capital or uncial; (a manuscript in) large lettering or majuscule script.

makai *adverb & adjective* M20 Hawaiian (from *ma* toward + *kai* the sea). In Hawaii: in the direction of the sea, seaward.

makimono *noun* plural same, **makimonos** L19 Japanese (= something rolled up, a scroll). A Japanese scroll containing a narrative, usually in pictures with explanatory writing, designed to be examined progressively from right to left as it is unrolled. Cf. EMAKIMONO.

malade imaginaire *noun phrase* plural **malades imaginaires** E19 French. A person with an imaginary illness.

■ After the title of a play by Molière (1673).

maladif *adjective* M19 French (from *malade* sick, ill, from Proto-Romance, from Latin *male* badly + *habitus*, past participle of *habere* to have, hold). Sickly.

maladresse *noun* E19 French (from *mal-* bad, ill + *adresse* skill, dexterity). Lack of dexterity or tact; awkwardness.

maladroit *adjective* L17 French (from *mal-* bad(ly) + *adroit* skillful). Lacking in adroitness or dexterity; awkward, bungling, clumsy.

mala fide *adverb & adjective phrase* E17 Latin (= with bad faith (ablative of next)). (Acting or done) in bad faith; insincere(ly), not genuine(ly).

mala fides *noun phrase* L17 Latin (= bad faith). Chiefly *Law* Bad faith, intent to deceive.

mala in se plural of MALUM IN SE.

malaise *noun* M18 French (from Old French *mal* bad, ill (from Latin *malus*) + *aise* ease). A condition of bodily discomfort, *especially* one without the development of specific disease; a feeling of uneasiness. Frequently *figurative.*

malapropos *adverb, adjective, & noun* (also **mal-à-propos** and other variants) M17 **French** (*mal à propos*, from *mal* ill + *à* to + *propos* purpose). **A** *adverb* M17 In an inopportune or awkward manner; at an inopportune or awkward time; inappropriately. **B** *adjective* E18 Inopportune, inappropriate. **C** *noun* M19 An inopportune or inappropriate thing.

malaria *noun* M18 **Italian** (*mal' aria* = *mala aria* bad air). Originally, an unwholesome condition of the atmosphere in hot countries due to the exhalations of marshes, to which fevers were ascribed. Now (also *malaria fever*), any of a class of intermittent and remittent febrile diseases formerly supposed to result from this cause, but now known to be due to infection with parasitic protozoans of the genus *Plasmodium*, transmitted by the bite of a mosquito of the genus *Anopheles*.

mal de mer *noun phrase* L18 **French**. Seasickness.

mal du siècle *noun phrase* E20 **French**. World-weariness, weariness of life, deep melancholy because of the condition of the world.

malebolge *noun* M19 **Italian** (*Malebolge*, from *male* feminine plural of *malo* evil + *bolge* plural of *bolgia* literally 'sack, bag'). A pool of filth; a hellish place or condition.

■ In literary use only. Malebolge was the name given in Dante's *Inferno* to the eighth circle in hell, consisting of ten rock-bound concentric circular trenches (see especially Canto xviii).

maleesh *interjection & noun* E20 **Arabic** (colloquial) (*mā 'alē-š* never mind). **A** *interjection* E20 No matter! never mind! **B** *noun* M20 Indifference, slackness.

mal élevé *adjective phrase* (feminine **mal élevée**) L19 **French** (= badly brought up). Bad-mannered, ill-bred.

mal-entendu *adjective & noun* E17 **French** (from *mal* ill + *entendu* past participle of *entendre* to hear, understand). **A** *adjective* Mistaken, misapprehended. Only in E17. **B** *noun* L18 A misunderstanding.

malerisch *adjective* M20 **German** (= painterly, from *Maler* painter). (Of painting) characterized more by the merging of colors than by a formal linear style; painterly.

■ A term used by Heinrich Wölfflin in his *Kunstgeschichtliche Grundbegriffe* (1915).

malgré *preposition* E16 **French**. In spite of, notwithstanding.

mallee *noun* M19 **Aboriginal**. Any of various low-growing eucalypts that have many slender stems rising from a large underground stock; scrub or thicket formed by such trees, typical of some arid parts of Australia.

malpais *noun* M19 **Spanish** (from *malo* bad + *país* country, region). Rugged or difficult country of volcanic origin.

malum in se *noun & adjective phrase* plural of noun **mala in se** E17 **Medieval Latin** (= bad in itself). (A thing) intrinsically evil or wicked (*especially in legal contexts*).

mal vu *adjective phrase* E20 **French** (literally, 'badly seen'). Held in low esteem, looked down on.

mamaloi *noun* plural **mamalois** L19 **Haitian** (creole *mamalwa*, from *mama* mother + *lwa* LOA). A voodoo priestess. Cf. PAPALOI.

mama-san *noun* plural **mama-sans** M20 **Japanese** (from *mama* mother + SAN). In Japan and the Far East: a woman in a position of authority, *specifically* one in charge of a geisha house; the mistress of a bar.

mambo *noun* plural **mambos** M20 **American Spanish** (probably from Haitian creole, from Yoruba, literally, 'to talk'). **1** M20 A kind of rumba, a ballroom dance of Latin American origin; a piece of music for this dance. **2** M20 A voodoo priestess.

mamzer *noun* (also **momser**, **momzer**) plural **mamzerim**, **mamzers** M16 **Late Latin** (from Hebrew *mamzēr*). A person conceived in a forbidden sexual union, especially as defined by rabbinical tradition.

■ In contemporary colloquial speech often used, like "bastard", as a term of abuse or familiarity.

mana *noun* M19 **Maori**. Power, authority, prestige; *Anthropology* an impersonal supernatural power that can be associated with people or with objects and which can be transmitted or inherited.

■ Originally New Zealand.

mañana *adverb & noun* M19 **Spanish** (= morning, tomorrow (in this sense from Old Spanish *cras mañana*, literally, 'tomorrow early') ultimately from Latin *mane* in the morning). Tomorrow, (on) the day after today; (in) the indefinite future (from the supposed easygoing procrastination of Spain and Spanish-speaking countries).

mancala *noun* M19 **Arabic** ((colloquial) *manḳala*, from *naḳala* to remove, take away). A board game for two players, originally Arabic but now common throughout Africa and Asia, played on a special board with rows of holes or hollows.

mancando *adjective & adverb* E19 **Italian** (= lacking, failing). *Music* (A direction:) becoming even softer, dying away.

mandala *noun* M19 **Sanskrit** (*máṇḍala* disk, circle). A symbolic circular figure, usually with symmetrical divisions and figures of deities, etc., in the center, used in Buddhism and other religions as a representation of the universe; *Jungian Psychology* an archetype of a similar circle, held to symbolize a striving for unity of self and completeness.

mandat *noun* M19 **French** (from Latin *mandatum* noun use of neuter past participle of *mandare* to command, enjoin, entrust, from *manus* hand). **1** M19 *History* A paper money issued by the revolutionary government of France from 1796 to 1797. **2** L19 In France: a money order.

mandolin *noun* (also (the usual form in sense 2) **mandoline**) E18 **French** (*mandoline* from Italian *mandolino* diminutive of *mandola*). **1** E18 A musical instrument of the lute kind having from four to six paired metal strings stretched on a deeply rounded body, usually played with a plectrum. **2** M20 A kitchen utensil fitted with cutting blades and used for slicing vegetables.

mandorla *noun* L19 **Italian** (= almond). An almond-shaped panel or decorative space in religious art.

manège *noun* (also **manege**) M17 **French** (from Italian *maneggio* from *maneggiare* from Proto-Romance from Latin *manus* hand). **1** M17 A riding school. **2** L18 The movements in which a horse is trained in a riding school; the art or practice of training and managing horses; horsemanship.

manes *noun* LME **Latin**. **1** LME *plural* The deified souls of dead ancestors (as beneficent spirits). **2** L17 *singular* The spirit or shade of a dead person, considered as an object of reverence or as demanding to be propitiated.

manga *noun 1* E19 **Spanish** (literally, 'sleeve', from Latin *manica*). A Mexican and Spanish-American cloak or poncho.

manga *noun 2* L20 **Japanese**. A Japanese comic book or strip.

mange-tout *noun* plural same, **mange-touts** E19 **French** (literally, 'eat-all'). A variety of pea of which the pods are eaten whole with the seeds they contain. Also *mange-tout pea*. Also called *sugar pea* or *sugar snap*.

manicotti *noun plural* M20 **Italian** (plural of *manicotto* sleeve, muff). Large tubular pasta shells; an Italian dish consisting largely of these and usually a sauce.

maniéré *adjective* M18 **French**. Affected or characterized by mannerism, mannered.

manière criblée *noun phrase* E20 **French**. CRIBLÉ engraving.

manifesto *noun* plural **manifestos, manifestoes** M17 **Italian** (from *manifestare* to show, display, from Latin *manifestus* from *manus* hand + *-festus* struck). A public declaration or proclamation; *especially* a printed declaration or explanation of policy (past, present, or future) issued by a monarch, government, political party or candidate, or any other individual or body of individuals of public relevance.

manna *noun* OE **Late Latin** (from Hellenistic Greek from Aramaic *mannā* from Hebrew *mān* corresponding to Arabic *mann* exudation of the tamarisk *Tamarix mannifera*). **I 1** OE The edible substance described as miraculously supplied to the Israelites in the wilderness (Exodus 16). **2** ME Spiritual nourishment, *especially* the Eucharist; something beneficial provided unexpectedly (frequently *manna from heaven*). **II 3** LME A sweet hardened flaky exudation obtained from the manna ash and used as a mild laxative. Also, a similar exudation from other plants and certain insects. **4** LME–M18 (A grain of) frankincense. **5** L17–E18 *Chemistry* A fine white precipitate. **6** L18 The seeds of the floating sweet-grass, *Glyceria fluitans*, used as food. In full *Polish manna*.

mannequin *noun* M18 **French** (from Dutch *manneken* diminutive of *man* man). **1** M18 A model of a human figure; an artist's lay figure; a dummy for the display of clothes, etc. **2** E20 A woman (or occasionally a man) employed by a dressmaker, costumier, etc., to display clothes by wearing them; a model.

mano *noun* plural **manos** E20 **Spanish** (= hand). *Anthropology* A primitive hand-held stone implement, used in the Americas for grinding cereals, etc.

mano a mano *foreign adjective, adverb, & noun phrase* (also **mano-a-mano**) L20 **Spanish** (= hand to hand). **A** *adjective & adverb phrase* L20 Hand to hand; one to one; face to face. **B** *noun phrase* L20 A confrontation, a duel.

manoir *noun* M19 **French**. A French manor house; a country house built in the style of a French manor house.

manqué *adjective* (feminine **manquée**) L18 **French** (past participial adjective of *manquer* to lack). **1** *postpositive* L18 That might have been but is not, that has missed being. **2** *predicative* L18 Defective, spoiled, missing, lacking.

manso *noun & adjective* plural **mansos** M19 **Spanish**. (A person who or animal which is) meek, tame, or cowardly.

■ Especially in the context of bull-fighting.

manta *noun* L17 **Spanish** (= blanket). **1** L17 In Spain and Spanish-speaking countries: a wrap, a cloak. **2** M18 A very large tropical ray of the genus *Manta* or the family Mobulidae. More fully *manta ray*. Also called *devilfish*.

mantelletta *noun* plural **mantellettas, mantellette** M19 **Italian** (probably from medieval Latin *mantelletum* from Latin *mantellum* mantle). *Roman Catholic Church* A sleeveless vestment reaching to the knees, worn by cardinals, bishops, and other high-ranking ecclesiastics.

mantilla *noun* E18 **Spanish** (diminutive of *manta* mantle). **1** E18 A light scarf, frequently of black lace, worn over the head and shoulders, especially by Spanish women. **2** M19 A small cape or mantle.

mantra *noun* (also (*rare*) **mantram**) L18 **Sanskrit** (literally, 'thought', from *man* to think). A sacred Hindu text or passage, *especially* one from the Vedas used as a prayer or incantation; in Hinduism and Buddhism, a holy name or word, for inward meditation; *transferred* and *figurative* a repeated phrase or sentence, a formula, a refrain.

manyatta *noun* E20 **Masai**. Among certain African peoples, especially the Masai: a group of huts forming a unit within a common fence.

manzanilla *noun* M19 **Spanish** (literally, 'camomile'). **1** M19 A kind of pale very dry sherry; a drink or glass of this. **2** E20 A variety of olive, distinguished by small thin-skinned fruit.

maquereau *noun* plural **maquereaux** L19 **French** (literally, 'mackerel'). A pimp.

■ Colloquial, also used as a term of abuse.

maquette *noun* E20 **French** (from Italian *macchietta* speck, diminutive of *macchia* spot, from *macchiare* to spot, from Latin *maculare* to stain). A small preliminary sketch or wax or clay model from which a sculpture is elaborated.

maquiladora *noun* L20 **Mexican Spanish** (from *maquilar* to assemble). A factory in Mexico run by a foreign company and exporting its products to the country of that company.

maquillage *noun* L19 **French** (from *maquiller* to make up one's face, from Old French *masquiller* to stain, alteration of *mascurer* to darken). Makeup, cosmetics; the application of this.

maquillé *adjective* (feminine **maquillée**) E20 **French**. Wearing cosmetics, made up.

maquis *noun* plural same M19 **French** (from as MACCHIA). **1** M19 The dense scrub characteristic of certain Mediterranean coastal regions, especially in Corsica. **2** M20 *History* (usually **Maquis**) A member of the French resistance movement during the German occupation (1940–45). **b** M20 A member of any resistance group or army.

■ The maquis scrub was the traditional hiding place for fugitives, hence the connection between senses 1 and 2.

maquisard *noun* M20 **French**. A member of the Maquis.

marabou *noun & adjective* (also **maribou**, **marabout**) E19 **French** (from Arabic *murābiṭ* holy man (see next), the stork being regarded as holy). **A** *noun* **1** E19 A tropical African stork, *Leptoptilus crumeniferus*. Also *marabou stork*. **2** E19 A tuft of soft white down from the wings or tail of this stork, used for trimming hats, etc.; *collectively* trimming made of this down. **3** M19 An exceptionally white kind of raw silk that can be dyed without first removing the natural gum and is used in crêpe weaving. **B** *adjective* E19 Made of marabou.

marabout *noun* E17 **French** (from Portuguese *marabuto* from Arabic *murābiṭ*, from *ribāṭ* frontier station, where merit could be acquired by combat against the infidel). **1** E17 A Muslim holy man or mystic, especially in North Africa. **2** M19 A shrine marking the burial place of a marabout.

maraca *noun* (also **maracca**) E17 **Portuguese** (*maracá* from Tupi *maráka*). A Latin American percussion instrument made from a hollow gourd or gourd-shaped container filled with beans, etc., and usually shaken in pairs. Usually in *plural*.

maranatha *adverb, noun, & interjection* (also **Maranatha**) LME **Greek** (from Aramaic *māran 'tā* our Lord has come, or *māranā tā* O Lord, come). **A** *adverb* LME In translations of 1 Corinthians 16:22: at the coming of the Lord. **B** *noun* M17 (By a misunderstanding of 1 Corinthians 16:22:) a portentously intensified anathema; a terrible curse. More fully *anathema maranatha*. **C** *interjection* L19 In the early church: expressing a deep longing for the coming of the Lord.

maraschino *noun* plural **maraschinos** L18 **Italian**. A strong sweet red liqueur distilled from the marasca cherry.

marc *noun* E17 **French** (from *marcher* to walk (originally, to tread, trample, ultimately from late Latin *marcus* hammer)). **1** E17 The refuse of processed grapes, etc. **2** M19 A brandy made from this. Also *marc brandy*.

marcato *adverb & adjective* M19 **Italian** (past participle of *marcare* to mark, accent, of Germanic origin). *Music* (With each note) emphasized.

Märchen *noun* plural same (also **märchen**) L19 **German** (= fairy tale from Middle High German *merechyn* short verse narrative, from Middle High German *mære* (Old High German *mārī*) news, famous, ultimately from Germanic). A folk tale, a fairy tale.

marcottage *noun* E20 **French** (= layering). *Horticulture* A method of propagating plants in which an incision is made below a joint or node and covered with a thick layer of moss, etc., into which new roots grow.

Mardi Gras *noun phrase* (also **Mardi gras**) L17 **French** (literally, 'fat Tuesday'). The last day beford Lent, celebrated in some places, as New Orleans and in some Roman Catholic countries, with a carnival; Shrove Tuesday; the last day of a carnival, etc., especially in France; *Australia* a carnival or fair at any time.

maréchaussée *noun* (also **Maréchaussée**) L18 **French** (from Old French *mareschaucie*). *History* A French military force under the command of a marshal. Now (*jocular* and *colloquial*), the French police, the gendarmerie.

mare clausum *noun phrase* plural **maria clausa** M17 **Latin** (= closed sea). A sea under the jurisdiction of a particular country.

■ The title of a work published in 1635 by the English jurist John Selden (1584–1654), in answer to Grotius (see MARE LIBERUM). The terms *mare clausum* and *mare liberum* both originated in the struggle between the Dutch and English maritime empires in the seventeenth century.

mare liberum *noun phrase* plural **maria libera** M17 **Latin** (= free sea). A sea open to all nations. Cf. MARE CLAUSUM.

■ The title of a treatise (1609) by Hugo Grotius (1583–1645), Dutch jurist.

maremma *noun* plural **maremme** M19 **Italian** (from Latin *maritima* feminine of *maritimus* maritime). In Italy: low marshy unhealthy country by the seashore; an area of this.

mariachi *noun* M20 **Mexican Spanish** (*mariache, mariachi*). An itinerant Mexican folk band (also *mariachi band*); a member of such a band.

maria clausa plural of MARE CLAUSUM.

mariage blanc *noun phrase* plural **mariages blancs** E20 **French** (literally, 'white marriage'). An unconsummated marriage.

mariage de convenance *noun phrase* plural **mariages de convenance** M19 **French**. A marriage of convenience.

maria libera plural of MARE LIBERUM.

maribou(t) variant of MARABOU.

mari complaisant *noun phrase* plural **maris complaisants** L19 **French**. A husband tolerant of his wife's adultery.

marijuana *noun* (also **marihuana**) L19 **American Spanish**. **1** L19 Cannabis, *especially* in a form for smoking. **2** E20 Indian hemp, cannabis plant.

marimba *noun* E18 **Congolese**. A kind of deep-toned xylophone, originating in Africa and consisting of wooden keys on a frame with a tuned resonator beneath each key.

marina *noun* E19 **Italian and Spanish** (feminine of *marino* from Latin *marinus* marine). A harbor, usually specially designed or located, with moorings for yachts and other small craft.

marinade *noun* E18 **French** (from Spanish *marinada*, from *marinar* to pickle in brine (= Italian *marinare*, French *mariner*), from *marino*, from Latin *marinus* marine). A flavoring and tenderizing mixture of wine, vinegar or other acidic liquid, with oil, herbs, spices, etc., in which meat, fish, etc., may be soaked before cooking; the meat, fish, etc., thus soaked.

marinara *adjective* M20 **Italian** (*alla marinara* sailor-fashion, from feminine of *marinero* seafaring). Designating a sauce made from tomatoes, onions, herbs, etc., usually served with pasta.

marinera *noun* E20 **Spanish** (feminine of *marinero* marine, seafaring). A lively South American dance. Also called *cueca*.

marionette *noun* E17 **French** (*marionnette*, from *Marion* diminutive of *Marie* Mary). A puppet with jointed limbs operated by strings.

maris complaisants plural of MARI COMPLAISANT.

marivaudage *noun* M18 **French** (from P. C. de *Marivaux* (1688–1763), French novelist and dramatist). Exaggeratedly sentimental or affected style, language, etc., characteristic of Marivaux.

marmite *noun* E19 **French. 1** E19 An earthenware cooking vessel. **2** E20 (also **Marmite**) (Proprietary name for) a savory extract made from fresh brewer's yeast, used especially in sandwiches and for flavoring.

marocain *noun & adjective* E20 **French** (from *Maroc* Morocco). **A** *noun* E20 (A garment made from) a crêpe fabric of silk or wool or both. **B** *adjective* L20 Made of marocain.

maror *noun* L19 **Hebrew** (*mārōr*). Bitter herbs eaten at the Passover Seder service as a reminder of the bitterness of the Israelites' captivity in Egypt.

marque *noun* E20 **French** (back-formation from *marquer* to mark or brand, alteration of Old French *merchier*, from *merc* limit, of Scandinavian origin (cf. Old High German *marc(h)a* mark)). A make or brand of something, especially a motor vehicle.

marquise *noun* E17 **French** (feminine of *marquis* marquess, from Old French *marchis* (later altered to *marquis* after Provençal *marques*, Spanish *marqués*) from Proto-Romance base of *march* border). **1** E17 (The title of) a marchioness in Continental Europe or (formerly) Britain. **2** E18 A variety of pear. **3a** L18 A marquee. Now *rare* or *obsolete*. **b** L19 A permanent canopy projecting over the entrance to a hotel, theater, etc. Also called *marquee*. **4** L19 A finger ring set with a pointed oval gem or cluster of gems. Also more fully *marquise ring*.

marquisette *noun & adjective* E20 **French** (diminutive of MARQUISE). (Of) a plain gauze dress fabric originally made from silk, later from cotton.

marron *noun* L16 **French**. A large and particularly sweet kind of chestnut.

■ Now chiefly in MARRON GLACÉ.

marron glacé *noun phrase* plural **marrons glacés** L19 **French**. A chestnut preserved in syrup as a candy.

martelé *adjective, adverb, & noun* L19 **French** (past participle of *marteler* to hammer). *Music* Martellato.

■ Used only with reference to bowed stringed instruments (cf. MARTELLATO).

martellato *adjective, adverb, & noun* L19 **Italian** (past participle of *martellare* to hammer). *Music* **A** *adjective & adverb* L19 (Played) with notes heavily accented and left before their full time has expired. **B** *noun* E20 Martellato playing.

martyrion *noun* (also in Latin form **martyrium**) plural of both **martyria** E18 **Greek**. A shrine, oratory, or church built in memory of a martyr; a building marking the place of a martyrdom or the site of a martyr's relics.

Marxisant *adjective* (also **marxisant**) M20 **French** (from *Marxiste* Marxist). Having Marxist leanings.

marzacotto *noun* plural **marzacottos** L19 **Italian**. A transparent glaze used by Italian majolica workers.

mas *noun* plural same E20 **Provençal**. A farm, house, or cottage in the south of France.

masa *noun* E20 **Spanish**. In Central and South American cuisine, a type of dough made from cornmeal and used to make tortillas, etc.

masala *noun* L18 **Urdu** (*maṣālaḥ* from Persian and Urdu *masāliḥ* from Arabic *maṣāliḥ*). Any of various spice mixtures ground into a paste or powder for use in Indian cooking; a dish flavored with this. Cf. GARAM MASALA.

mascara *noun & verb* L19 **Italian** (*mascara, maschera* mask). **A** *noun* L19 A cosmetic for darkening and coloring the eyelashes. **B** *transitive verb* M20 Put mascara on.

mascaron *noun* M17 **French** (from Italian *mascherone*, from *maschera* mask). *Decorative Arts* A grotesque face or mask.

mascarpone *noun* M20 **Italian.** A soft mild Italian cream cheese.

mashallah *interjection* E19 **Arabic** (*mā šā'llāh*). (This is) what God wills.

■ Used as an expression of praise or resignation.

masjid *noun* M19 **Arabic.** A mosque.

Masorah *noun* (also **Massorah, Masora**) E17 **Hebrew** (variant of *māsōreṯ* bond (Ezekiel 20:37), from *'āsar* to bind (later interpreted as 'tradition' as if from *māsar* to hand down)). The body of traditional information and comment relating to the text of the Hebrew Scriptures, compiled by Jewish scholars in the tenth century and earlier; the collection of critical notes in which this information is preserved.

massage *noun & verb* L19 **French** (from *masser* to apply massage to, perhaps from Portuguese *amassar* to knead). **A** *noun* **1** L19 The application (usually with the hands) of pressure and strain on the muscles and joints of the body by rubbing, kneading, etc., in order to stimulate their action and increase their suppleness; an instance or spell of such manipulation. **2** E20 *euphemistic* The services of prostitutes. Chiefly in *massage parlor*. **B** *transitive verb* **1** L19 Apply massage to; treat by means of massage. **b** L20 Rub (lotion, etc.) *into* by means of massage. **2** M20 Manipulate (data, figures, etc.), especially in order to give a more acceptable result.

massé *adjective & noun* L19 **French** (past participle of *masser* to play a massé stroke, from *masse* mace). *Billiards*, etc. (Designating) a stroke made with the cue more or less vertical, so as to impart extra swerve to the cue ball.

massecuite *noun* L19 **French** (literally, 'cooked mass'). The juice of sugar cane after concentration by boiling.

masseur *noun* (feminine **masseuse**) L19 **French** (from *masser* to apply massage to). A person who provides massage (professionally).

massif *noun* E16 **French** (noun use of *massif* massive). **1** E16 A block of building. Passing into *figurative* use of sense 2. **2** L19 A large mountain mass; a compact group of mountain heights. **3** L19 *Horticulture* A mass or clump of plants.

Massorah variant of MASORAH.

mastaba *noun* (also **mastabah**) E17 **Arabic** (*misṭaba, maṣ-*). **1** E17 In Islamic countries: a (stone) bench or seat attached to a house. **2** L19 *Archaeology* An ancient Egyptian flat-topped tomb, rectangular or square in plan and with sides sloping outward to the base. Also *mastaba tomb*.

mastika *noun* E20 **Modern Greek** (*mastikha*). A liquor flavored with mastic gum.

matador *noun* (also (especially senses 2, 3) **matadore**) L17 **Spanish** (from *matar* to kill). **1** L17 A bullfighter whose task is to kill the bull. **2** L17 In some card games (as quadrille, ombre, solo): any of the highest trumps so designated by the rules of the game. **3** M19 A domino game in which halves are matched so as to make a total of seven; any of the dominoes that have seven spots altogether, together with the double blank.

matchet variant of MACHETE.

maté *noun* E18 **Spanish** (*mate* from Quechua *mati*). **1** E18 A gourd, calabash, etc., in which the leaves of the shrub maté are infused. Also *maté cup*. **2** M18 (An infusion of) the leaves of a South American shrub, *Ilex paraguariensis*; the shrub itself. Also more fully *yerba maté*.

matelassé *noun & adjective* (also **matelasse**) L19 **French** (past participle of *matelasser* to quilt, from *matelas* mattress). **A** *noun* L19 A silk or wool fabric with a raised design. **B** *adjective* L19 Having a raised design like quilting.

matelot *noun* E20 **French** (= sailor). **1** E20 A sailor. *nautical slang.* **2** E20 A shade of blue.

matelote *noun* E18 **French** (from as preceding). A dish of fish, etc., served in a sauce of wine, onions, etc.

mater *noun* L16 **Latin** (literally, 'mother'). **1** L16 The thickest plate of an astrolabe. **2** M19 Mother.

■ Sense 2 is chiefly jocular or in school slang; cf. PATER.

Mater Dolorosa *noun phrase* plural **Matres Dolorosae** E19 **Medieval Latin** (literally, 'sorrowful mother'). (A title of) the Virgin Mary, as having a role in the Passion of Christ; a representation, in painting or sculpture, of the Virgin Mary sorrowing; *transferred* a woman resembling the sorrowful Virgin in appearance, manner, etc.

materfamilias *noun* M18 **Latin** (from MATER + *familias* old genitive of *familia* family). The female head of a family or household.

materia medica *noun phrase plural* L17 **Modern Latin** (translation of Greek *hulē iatrikē* healing material). The remedial substances used in the practice of medicine; (treated as *singular*) the branch of medicine that deals with their origins and properties.

materia prima *noun phrase* M16 **Latin** (= first matter). The primordial substance formerly considered to be the original material of the universe.

matériel *noun* E19 **French** (noun use of adjective). **1** E19 Available means or resources. Also (*rare*), technique. **2** E19 The equipment, supplies, etc., used in an army, navy, or business. Opposed to *personnel.*

matière *noun* E20 **French**. The quality an artist gives to the pigment used.

matinée *noun* (also **matinee**) M19 **French** (= morning, what occupies a morning, from *matin*). **1** M19 An afternoon performance at a theater, movie theater, or concert hall. **2** L19 A woman's lingerie jacket.

matje *noun* (also **matjes**) L19 **Dutch** (*maatjes*). A young herring, especially salted or pickled. More fully *matje herring.*

■ In the form *matie, mattie* or other variants the word was known much earlier (E18), chiefly in Scotland. The form with 'j' represents a reintroduction from Dutch.

matraca *noun* E20 **Spanish**. In Spain: a mechanical wooden rattle used instead of church bells on Good Friday.

Matres Dolorosae plural of MATER DOLOROSA.

matrix *noun* plural **matrixes, matrices** LME **Latin** (= breeding female, register, (in Late Latin) womb, from *mater, matr-* mother). **1** LME The uterus, the womb. *archaic* **2** M16 A place or medium in which something is bred, produced, or developed; a setting or environment in which a particular activity or process occurs or develops; a place or point of origin and growth. **3** L16 A mold in which something is cast or shaped. **4** M17 The rock material in which a fossil, gem, etc., is embedded.

■ *Matrix* has also been adopted as a specialist technical term in a whole range of disciplines including Anatomy and Zoology (M19), Botany (M19), Mathematics (M19), and Computing (M20).

matzo *noun* (also **matzah**) plural **matzos, matzoth** M19 **Yiddish** (*matse* from Hebrew *maṣṣāh*). (A wafer of) unleavened bread for Passover.

maudit *noun & adjective* M20 **French** (literally, 'cursed', from *maudire* to curse). **A** *noun* M20 A person who is cursed; a despicable or deeply unpleasant person. **B** *adjective* L20 Cursed; (of an artist, etc.) insufficiently appreciated, forgotten.

■ The adjective is usually postpositive. Cf. POÈTE MAUDIT.

Maulana *noun* M19 **Arabic** (*mawlānā* our master). (A title given to) a Muslim man revered for his religious learning or piety.

maulvi variant of MOULVI.

mau-mau *transitive verb* L20 **Kikuyu** (*Mau Mau*, a secret society dedicated to the expulsion of British settlers from Kenya in the 1950s). Terrorize, threaten. *slang.*

mausoleum *noun* plural **mausolea, mausoleums** LME **Latin** (from Greek *Mausōleion*, from *Mausōlos* Mausolos). **1** LME The magnificent tomb of Mausolus, King of Caria, erected in the 4th century BC at Halicarnassus by his queen Artemisia. **2** LME *generally* A large and magnificent place of burial.

mauvais *adjective* E18 **French.** Bad.

■ In English only in the following French phrases.

mauvais coucheur *noun phrase* plural **mauvais coucheurs** M20 **French** (literally, 'bad bedfellow'). A difficult, uncooperative, or unsociable person.

mauvaise foi *noun phrase* M20 **French.** Bad faith.

mauvaise langue *noun phrase* plural **mauvaises langues** L19 **French** (literally, 'bad tongue'). A venomous tongue; a scandalmonger.

mauvais pas *noun phrase* plural same E19 **French** (literally, 'bad step'). *Mountaineering* A place that is difficult or dangerous to negotiate.

mauvais quart d'heure *noun phrase* plural **mauvais quarts d'heure** M19 **French** (literally, 'bad quarter of an hour'). An unpleasant but brief period of time; an unnerving experience.

mauvais sujet *noun phrase* plural **mauvais sujets** L18 **French** (literally, 'bad subject'). A worthless person, a scoundrel.

maven *noun* M20 **Hebrew** (*mēbīn* understanding). An expert, a connoisseur.

mavrodaphne *noun* E20 **Modern Greek** (from late Greek *mauros* dark (Greek *amauros*) + *daphnē* laurel). A dark red sweet Greek wine; the grape from which this is made.

maxixe *noun* E20 **Portuguese.** A dance for couples, of Brazilian origin, resembling the polka and the local tango.

maya *noun* L18 **Sanskrit** (*māyā*, from *mā* create). In *Hindu Philosophy*, illusion, magic, the supernatural power wielded by gods and demons. In *Hindu and Buddhist Philosophy*, the power by which the universe becomes manifest, the illusion or appearance of the phenomenal world.

mayonnaise *noun* E19 **French** (also *magnonaise, mahonnaise*, perhaps feminine of *mahonnais* adjective, from *Mahon* capital of Minorca). A thick sauce consisting of yolk of egg beaten up with oil and vinegar and seasoned with salt, etc., used as a dressing especially for salad, eggs, cold meat, or fish; a dish (of meat, etc.) having this sauce as a dressing.

mazar *noun* E20 **Arabic** (*mazār* place visited, from *zāra* to visit). A Muslim tomb revered as a shrine.

mazel tov *interjection* M19 **Modern Hebrew** (*mazzāl ṭōb*, literally, 'good star', from Hebrew *mazzāl* star). Among Jews: good luck, congratulations.

mazout variant of MAZUT.

mazuma *noun* E20 **Yiddish** (from Hebrew *mĕzummān*, from *zimmēn* to prepare). Money, cash; *especially* betting money. *United States and Australian slang.*

mazurka *noun* E19 **French** (or from German *masurka* from Polish *mazurka* woman of the province Mazovia). **1** E19 A Polish dance in triple time, usually with a slide and hop. **2** M19 A piece of music for this dance or composed in its rhythm, usually with accentuation of the second or third beat.

mazut *noun* (also **mazout**) L19 **Russian.** A viscous liquid left as residue after the distillation of petroleum, used in Russia as a fuel oil and coarse lubricant.

mbira *noun* L19 **Bantu.** A musical instrument of southern Africa consisting of a set of keys or tongues attached to a resonator, which are plucked with the thumb and forefingers. Also called *sansa.*

mea culpa *interjection & noun phrase* LME **Latin** (literally, '(through) my own fault'). **A** *interjection* LME Acknowledging one's guilt or responsibility for an error. **B** *noun phrase* E19 An utterance of '*mea culpa*'; an acknowledgment of one's guilt or responsibility for an error.

■ Taken from the prayer of confession in the Latin liturgy of the church. Also sometimes *mea maxima culpa* '(through) my own great fault'. As an interjection, now often jocular.

mealie *noun* (also **mielie**) E19 **Afrikaans** (*mielie* from Portuguese *milho* maize, millet, from Latin *milium*). In South Africa: maize; a corncob (usually in *plural*).

mebos *noun* L18 **Afrikaans** (probably from Japanese *umeboshi* dried and salted plums). A South African confection made from dried flattened apricots, preserved in salt and sugar.

mecate *noun* M19 **Mexican Spanish** (from Nahuatl *mecatl*). A rope made of horsehair or of maguey fiber, used especially to tether or lead a horse.

méchant *adjective* (feminine **méchante**) E19 **French**. Malicious, spiteful.

médaillon *noun* E20 **French** (from Italian *medaglione*, augmentative of *medaglia* medal). A small, flat, round or oval cut of meat or fish.

■ The cognate *medallion*, in the sense of 'large medal', was established in English much earlier (M17).

media *noun* E20 **Latin** (plural of MEDIUM (noun)). **1** E20 *plural* and *collective singular* The main means of mass communication (also *mass media*), *especially* newspapers, radio, and television; the reporters, journalists, etc., working for organizations engaged in such communication. **2** E20 *singular* A means of mass communication, a MEDIUM.

medina *noun* (also **Medina**) E20 **Arabic** (literally, 'town'). The old Arab or non-European quarter of a North African town.

medium *noun & adjective* plural of noun **media, mediums** (see also MEDIA) L16 **Latin** (literally, 'middle, midst', medieval Latin 'means', noun use of *medius* mid). **A** *noun* **1** L16 A middle quality, degree, or condition; something intermediate in nature or degree. **2** L16 An intervening substance through which a force acts on objects at a distance or through which impressions are conveyed to the senses, as air, water, etc. **b** M19 A pervading or enveloping substance; the substance in which an organism lives or is cultured; *figurative* one's environment, one's usual social setting. **3** E17 An intermediate agency, instrument, or channel; a means; *specifically* a channel of mass communication, as newspapers, radio, television, etc. See also MEDIA. **4 a** E19 A person acting as an intermediary, a mediator. *rare*. **b** M19 (plural **mediums**) A person thought to be in contact with the spirits of the dead and to communicate between the living and the dead. **5** M19 A liquid substance with which a pigment is mixed for use in painting. Also, anything used as a raw material by an artist, etc.; a style or variety of art, as determined by the materials or artistic form used. **B** *adjective* **1** L17–E19 Average, mean. **2** E18 Intermediate between two or more degrees in size, character, amount, quality, etc.

■ There also are or have been numerous technical applications of the noun *medium*, as in Logic (L16–E19) 'the middle term of a syllogism', Geometry and Arithmetic (E17–E19) 'a mean; an average', and Photography (L19) 'a varnish used in retouching'.

medresseh variant of MADRASAH.

medusa *noun* (in sense 1 usually **Medusa**) plural **medusae, medusas** LME **Latin** (from Greek *Medousa* the only mortal one of the three Gorgons in Greek mythology, with snakes for hair and a gaze which turned any beholder to stone: in sense 2 originally as modern Latin genus name). **1** LME A terrifying or ugly woman, a gorgon. **2** M18 A jellyfish; *specifically* in *Zoology*, a coelenterate in the medusoid stage of its life cycle.

mee *noun* M20 **Chinese** (*miàn* (Wade–Giles *mien*) flour). A Chinese dish made with noodles and other ingredients, popular in Malaysia.

meerschaum *noun* L18 **German** (from *Meer* sea + *Schaum* foam, translation of Persian *kef-i-daryā* foam of sea, with reference to its frothiness). A tobacco pipe with a bowl made from speiolite or hydrated magnesium silicate occurring as a soft white or yellowish claylike mineral.

méfiance *noun* L19 **French**. Mistrust.

mega *adjective* L20 **Greek** (*mega-* combining form of *megas* great) Large, great. Also, brilliant, excellent.

■ Originating in the United States, this is an independent colloquial use of a combining form, similar to that of MACRO.

megaron *noun* L19 **Greek**. In ancient Greece: the great central hall of a type of house characteristic especially of the Mycenaean period.

Megillah *noun* (also **megillah**) M17 **Hebrew** (*mĕḡillāh*, literally, 'parchment roll, scroll'). **1** M17 Each of five books of the Hebrew Scriptures (the Song of Solomon, Ruth, Lamentations, Ecclesiastes, and Esther) appointed to be read on certain Jewish notable days; *especially* the Book of Esther, read at the festival of Purim. Also, a copy of all, or any, of these books. **2** M20 A long, tedious, or complicated story. Frequently in *a* or *the whole megillah*. *slang*.

meiosis *noun* plural **meioses**, M16 **Modern Latin** (from Greek *meiōsis*, from *meioun* to lessen, from *meiōn* less). **1** M16 *Rhetoric* **a** A figure of speech by which something is intentionally presented as smaller, less important, etc., than it really is. Now *rare*. **b** M17 LITOTES. **2** E20 *Biology* A particular kind of cell division.

mei ping *noun phrase* E20 **Chinese** (*méi píng* prunus vase). A kind of Chinese porcelain vase with a narrow neck designed to hold a single spray of flowers.

meisie *noun* L19 **Afrikaans** (from Dutch *meisje*). In South Africa: a girl, a young woman.

melamed *noun* L19 **Hebrew** (*mĕlammēḏ*). A teacher of elementary Hebrew.

melancholia *noun* L17 **late Latin** (from Greek *melankholia* from *melan-*, *melas* black + *kholē* bile). *Medicine* A pathological state of depression. Also (*generally*), melancholy, depression.

mélange *noun* M17 **French** (from *mêler* to mix). **1** M17 A mixture; a collection of heterogeneous items or elements, a medley. **2** L19 Yarn, especially woolen yarn, to which dye has been applied unevenly so as to leave some areas undyed; a fabric of such a yarn. **3** E20 Coffee made with sugar and whipped cream; a drink of this.

mêlée *noun* (also **melée**, **melee**) M17 **French** (from Old French *mellée* past participial adjective of *meller* variant of *mesler* to meddle; sense 2 probably a different word). **1** M17 A battle at close quarters, a hand-to-hand fight; a confused struggle or skirmish, especially involving many people; a crush, turmoil; a muddle. **2** E20 *collectively* Small diamonds less than about a carat in weight.

melisma *noun* plural **melismata**, **melismas** L19 **Greek** (literally, 'song'). *Music* Originally, a melodic tune, melodic music. Now, in singing, the prolongation of one syllable over a number of notes.

melktert *noun* M20 **Afrikaans** (from *melk* milk + *tert* tart, pie). In South Africa: a kind of open pie with a custard filling sprinkled with cinnamon.

melos *noun* M18 **Greek** (= song, music). *Music* Song, melody; *specifically* the succession of tones considered apart from rhythm; an uninterrupted flow of melody.

meltemi *noun* E20 **Modern Greek** (*meltémi*, Turkish *meltem*). A dry north wind blowing over the eastern Mediterranean region in summer; an Etesian wind.

melusine *noun & adjective* (also **Melusine**) E20 **French** (*mélusine*, perhaps connected with *Mélusine*, a fairy in French folklore). **A** *noun* E20 A silky long-haired felt, used for making hats. **B** *attributive* or as *adjective* M20 Made of this material.

membra disiecta, membra disjecta variants of DISJECTA MEMBRA.

membrillo *noun* E20 **Spanish** (= quince). A Spanish preserve of quinces.

membrum virile *noun phrase* M19 **Latin** (= male member). The penis. *Archaic* or *euphemistic*.

memento *noun* plural **memento(e)s** LME **Latin** (imperative of *meminisse* to remember). **1** LME *Christian Church* Either of the two prayers (beginning with *Memento*) in the canon of the Mass, in which the living and the dead are respectively commemorated; the commemoration of the living or the dead in these prayers. **2** L16 A reminder, warning, or hint as to future conduct or events. Now *especially* an object serving as such a reminder or warning. Cf. MEMENTO MORI, MEMENTO VIVERE. **3** M18 A reminder of a past event or condition, of an absent person, or something that once existed. Now *especially* an object kept as a memorial of some person or event, a souvenir.

memento mori *noun phrase* **Latin** (= remember that you have to die). A warning or reminder of death, *especially* a skull or other symbolic object.

memento vivere *noun phrase* E20 **Latin** (= remember that you have to live). A reminder of (the pleasures of) life.

■ Formed as the opposite of MEMENTO MORI.

memo abbreviation of MEMORANDUM.

memorabilia *noun plural* L18 **Latin** (noun use of neuter plural of *memorabilis* from *memorare* to bring to mind). **1** L18 Memorable or noteworthy things. **2** L19 Souvenirs.

memorandum *noun* plural **memoranda, memorandums** L15 **Latin** (neuter singular of *memorandus* gerundive of *memorare* to bring to mind, from *memor* mindful). **1** L15 A note to help the memory, a record of events or of observations on a particular subject, especially for future consideration or use. **2** L16 *Law* A writing or document summarizing or embodying the terms of a transaction, contract, agreement, establishment of a company, etc. **3** E17 A record of a money transaction. **4** M17 An informal diplomatic message, especially summarizing the state of a question or justifying a decision. **5** L19 An informal written communication of a kind conventionally not requiring a signature, as within a business or organization, usually written on paper headed 'Memorandum' or 'Memo'.

■ *Memorandum* was first introduced (LME) as an adjective meaning 'to be remembered' and placed at the beginning of a note of something to be remembered or a record (for future reference) of something done, but this usage is now confined to legal contexts. In sense 5 *memorandum* is now generally abbreviated to *memo*, which also functions attributively (as in *memo pad*) and as a transitive verb meaning 'to make a memorandum of'.

memoria technica *noun phrase* M18 **Modern Latin** ((= technical memory) represented Greek *to mnēmonikon tekhnēma*). A method of assisting the memory by artificial contrivances; a system of mnemonics, a mnemonic aid.

memsahib *noun* M19 **Anglo-Indian** (from *mem* representing a pronunciation of 'ma'am' + SAHIB). A European married woman as spoken of or to by Indians.

ménage *noun* (also **menage**) ME **French** (Old French *menaige, manaige* (modern *ménage*) from Proto-Romance, from Latin *mansio* station, abiding-place, from *mans-* past participial stem of *manere* to stay, remain). **1** ME A domestic establishment, a household. Formerly also, the members of a household. **b** M20 A sexual relationship; an affair. **2** E19 The management of a household, housekeeping. **3** E19 An insurance group or savings club of which every member pays in a fixed sum weekly; an arrangement for paying for goods by installments. *Scottish and northern dialect.*

■ In sense 1 also occasionally found in the phrases *ménage à deux* 'household of two' and *ménage à quatre* 'household of four', but by far the most frequent is MÉNAGE À TROIS. The related French word *menagerie* (introduced L17) meaning 'a collection of wild animals kept in cages' is now completely Anglicized in pronunciation.

ménage à trois *noun phrase* (also **ménage-à-trois**) L19 **French** (= household of three). An arrangement or relationship in which three people live together, usually consisting of a husband and wife and the lover of one of them.

menhaden *noun* L18 **Algonquian** (perhaps from a base meaning 'fertilize'). A fish of the herring family, *Brevoortia tyrannus*, of the Atlantic coast of North America, an important source of fish guano and oil.

menhir *noun* M19 **Breton** (*maen-hir* (*maen* stone, *hir* long) = Welsh *maen hir*, Cornish *mênhere*). *Archaeology* A single tall upright monumental stone, especially of prehistoric times.

meniscus *noun* plural **menisci** L17 **Modern Latin** (from Greek *mēniskos* crescent, diminutive of *mēnē* moon). **1** L17 A lens convex on one side and concave on the other; *especially* a convexo-concave lens (i.e., one thickest in the middle, with a crescent-shaped section). **2** E18 A crescent moon. *rare.* **3** E19 The convex or concave upper surface of a column of liquid in a tube, caused by surface tension or capillarity. **4** M19 *Anatomy* A disklike fibrocartilage situated between the articular surfaces of certain joints, as those of the wrist and knee. **5** L19 A figure in the form of a crescent.

meno *adverb* L19 **Italian.** *Music* Less.

■ Used in directions, as *meno mosso* 'less rapidly'.

menologium *noun* (also **menology**) plural **menologia, menologiums** E18 **Modern Latin** (from ecclesiastical Greek *mēnologion*, from *mēn* month + *logos* account). An ecclesiastical calendar of the months.

■ The English form *menology* was introduced earlier (E17), but the form *menologium* is used in parallel with it, in particular with reference to the Old English metrical church calendar first published in 1705. The Greek form is also used specifically to mean a calendar of the Orthodox church containing biographies of the saints in the order of the dates on which they are commemorated.

menorah *noun* L19 **Hebrew** (*mĕnōrāh* candlestick). A holy candelabrum with seven branches that was used in the temple in Jerusalem; a candelabrum having any number of branches, but usually eight, used in Jewish worship, especially during Hanukkah; a representation of either as a symbol of Judaism.

mensch *noun* M20 **Yiddish** (from German = person). A person of integrity or rectitude; a just, honest, or honorable person.

menses *noun plural* L16 **Latin** (plural of *mensis* month). The menstrual discharge. Also, the time of menstruation.

mens rea *noun phrase* M19 **Latin** (= guilty mind). *Law* The state of mind accompanying an illegal act that makes the act a crime; criminal state of mind.

mens sana in corpore sano *noun phrase* E17 **Latin.** A sound mind in a sound body, especially regarded as the ideal of education.

■ Also elliptical as *mens sana*.

mensur *noun* plural **mensuren**, **mensurs** E20 **German** (literally, 'measure'). Chiefly *History* In Germany: a fencing duel between students fought with partially blunted weapons.

mentor *noun* M18 **French** (from Latin *Mentor* from Greek *Mentōr* the guide and adviser of Odysseus's son Telemachus (probably chosen as a name as from base meaning 'remember, think, counsel')). An experienced and trusted adviser or guide; a teacher, a tutor.

menudo *noun* M20 **Mexican Spanish** (noun use of adjective = small from Latin *minutus* very small). A spicy Mexican soup made from tripe.

menus plaisirs *noun phrase plural* L17 **French** (= small pleasures). Simple pleasures; small personal expenses or gratifications; fanciful or trifling objects bought with pocket money.

mercado *noun* plural **mercados** M19 **Spanish** (from Latin *mercatus* market). In Spain and Spanish-speaking countries: a market.

merde *noun* M20 **French** (from Latin *merda*). Excrement, dung.

■ Also in slang use as an interjection, expressing annoyance, exasperation, surprise, etc. Cf. MOT DE CAMBRONNE.

merdeka *noun* M20 **Malay**. In Malaysia and Indonesia: freedom, independence.

mère *noun* M19 **French** (= mother). The mother, elder.

■ *Mère* is appended to a name especially to distinguish between a mother and daughter of the same name.

merengue *noun* (also **meringue**) M20 **American Spanish** (from Haitian creole *méringue* literally, 'meringue' from French). A dance of Dominican and Haitian origin, with alternating long and short stiff-legged steps; a piece of music for this dance, usually in duple and triple time.

meridional *adjective & noun* (also **meridianal**) LME **Old and Modern French** (*méridional* from late Latin *meridionalis*, irregularly from *meridies* after *septentrionalis* septentrional). **A** *adjective* **1** LME Of or pertaining to the south; situated in the south; southern, southerly. **b** M19 *specifically* Pertaining to or characteristic of the inhabitants of southern Europe. **2** LME–M19 Of or pertaining to the position of the sun at midday; pertaining to or characteristic of midday. **3** M16 Of, pertaining to, or aligned with a meridian. **4** M17 Of a marking or structure on a roundish body: lying in a plane with the axis of the body. **B** *noun* L16 A native or inhabitant of the south. Now *specifically* a native or inhabitant of the south of France.

meringue *noun* E18 **French** (of unknown origin). A confection made chiefly of sugar and whites of eggs whipped together and baked crisp; a small cake or shell of this, usually decorated or filled with cream.

merino *noun & adjective* plural of noun **merinos** L18 **Spanish** (of unknown origin). **1** L18 (Designating or pertaining to) a breed of sheep prized for the fineness of its wool, originating in Spain; (designating) a sheep of this breed. **b** E19 *pure merino*, (*i*) an early immigrant to Australia with no convict origins, a member of a leading family in Australian society, a person of fine breeding or good character; (*ii*) *attributively* first-class, well-bred, excellent. *Australian slang*. **2** E19 (Of) a soft fine material resembling cashmere, made of wool (originally merino wool) or wool and cotton. **b** M19 A garment, especially a dress or shawl, made of this. **3** L19 (Of) a fine woolen yarn used in the manufacture of hosiery and knitwear.

mesa *noun* M18 **Spanish** (= table, from Latin *mensa*). A high rocky tableland or plateau; a flat-topped hill with precipitous sides.

■ The earliest occurrences are in the names of particular plateaus or hills in the United States.

mésalliance *noun* L18 **French** (from *més-* mis- + *alliance* alliance). A marriage with a person thought to be of inferior social position; an unsuitable union.

■ The English form *misalliance* (M18) is also current for an inappropriate marital or sexual union, but it is also used more generally.

mes ami(e)s plural of MON AMI(E).

mescal *noun* **E18 Spanish** (*mezcal* from Nahuatl *mexcalli*). **1** E18 Any of several plants of the genus *Agave* found in Mexico and the southwestern United States, used as sources of fermented liquor, food, or fiber. **2** E19 A strong intoxicating spirit distilled from the fermented sap of the American aloe or allied species. Cf. TEQUILA. **3** L19 A small desert cactus, *Lophophora williamsii*, of Mexico and Texas; a preparation of this used as a hallucinogenic drug. Cf. PEYOTE.

Mesdames plural of MADAME.

Mesdemoiselles plural of MADEMOISELLE.

meseta *noun* **E20 Spanish** (diminutive of MESA). In Spain and Spanish-speaking countries: a plateau; specifically *the* high plateau of central Spain.

meshuga *adjective* (also **meshugga(h)** and other variants) **L19 Yiddish** (*meshuge* from Hebrew *měshuggā'*; cf. German *meschugge* crazy). Mad, crazy; stupid.

■ Slang. *Meshuga* is chiefly used predicatively, in contrast to MESHUGENER.

meshugaas *noun* (also **mishugas** and other variants) **E20 Yiddish** (from Hebrew *měshuggā'*: see MESHUGA). Madness, craziness; nonsense, foolishness. *slang.*

meshugener *attributive adjective & noun slang* (also **meshuggener**, **meshugenah**, and other variants) **E20 Yiddish** (from Hebrew *měshuggā'*: see MESHUGA). (A person who is) mad, crazy, or stupid.

■ Slang. It is a positional variant of *meshuga* in that it precedes its noun.

meshugga(h) variant of MESHUGA.

meshuggenah, **meshuggener** variants of MESHUGENER.

meshumad *noun* (also **meshummad**) plural **meshumadim** **L19 Yiddish** (from Hebrew *měšhummād*, literally, 'a person who is destroyed', or *měšu'mād* baptized, from Aramaic *'mad* to be baptized). An apostate from Judaism.

meson *noun* **E19 Spanish** (*mesón*). In Mexico or the southwestern United States: an inn or lodging house.

messa di voce *noun phrase* plural **messe di voce** **L18 Italian** (literally, 'placing of the voice'). In singing, a gradual crescendo and diminuendo on a long-held note.

messagerie *noun* **L18 French**. The transportation or delivery of freight, messages, or people; a conveyance for these. In *plural* also, freight, messages, or people for transportation or delivery.

messaline *noun & adjective* **E20 French**. (Made of) a soft lightweight and lustrous silk or rayon fabric.

messe di voce plural of MESSA DI VOCE.

Messiah *noun* (also **messiah**, (earlier) **Messias**) **ME Old and Modern French** (*Messie* from popular Latin *Messias* from Greek *Messias* from Aramaic *měšīḥā*, Hebrew *māšhīāḥ* anointed, from *māšhaḥ* to anoint). The promised deliverer of the Jewish nation prophesied in the Hebrew Scriptures; Jesus regarded as the savior of humankind. Also (*transferred*), an actual or expected liberator of an oppressed people or country, etc.; a leader or savior of a specified group, cause, etc.

■ The modern form *Messiah* was created by the Geneva translators of the Bible of 1560 as looking more Hebraic than *Messias*.

mestizo *noun & adjective* plural of noun **mestizos** (feminine **mestiza**) **L16 Spanish** (from Proto-Romance from Latin *mixtus* past participle of *miscere* to mix). **A** *noun* L16 A Spanish or Portuguese person with parents of different races, *specifically* one with a Spaniard as one parent and an American Indian as the other; *generally* any person of mixed blood. Also, a Central or South American Indian who has adopted European culture. **B** *attributive* or as *adjective* E17 That is a mestizo or mestiza.

mesto *adverb & adjective* E19 **Italian** (from Latin *maestus* sad). *Music* (A direction:) sad(ly), mournful(ly).

métairie *noun* E19 **French** (from as MÉTAYER). A farm held on the MÉTAYAGE system.

metamorphosis *noun* plural **metamorphoses** M16 **Latin** (from Greek *metamorphōsis*, from *metamorphoun* to transform, from as *meta-* + *morphē* a form). **1** M16 The action or process of changing in form, shape, or substance; *especially* transformation by supernatural means. **b** L16 A metamorphosed form. **2** M16 A complete change in appearance, circumstances, condition, or character. **3** M17 *Biology* Normal change of form of a living organism, part, or tissue; *specifically* the transformation that some animals undergo in the course of becoming adult (e.g., from tadpole to frog), in which there is a complete alteration of form and habit.

metanoia *noun* L19 **Greek** (from *metanoein* to change one's mind, repent). Penitence; reorientation of one's way of life, spiritual conversion.

metastasis *noun* plural **metastases** L16 **Late Latin** (from Greek = removal, change, from *methistanai* to remove, change). **1** L16 *Rhetoric* A rapid transition from one point to another. Long *rare*. **2** M17 *Medicine* The transference of a bodily function, pain, or disease, or of diseased matter, from one site to another; *specifically* the occurrence or development of secondary foci of disease at a distance from the primary site, as in many cancers.

metate *noun* E17 **American Spanish** (from Nahuatl *métatl*). In Central America: a flat or somewhat hollowed oblong stone on which grain, cocoa, etc., are ground by means of a smaller stone. Also *metate stone*.

metathesis *noun* plural **metatheses** L16 **Late Latin** (from Greek, from *metatithenai* transpose, change, from as *meta-* + *tithenai* to put, place). **1** L16 *Linguistics* The transposition of sounds or letters in a word; the result of such a transposition. Formerly also, the transposition of words. **2** L17–M19 *Medicine* Spread of a disease within the body, METASTASIS; movement of diseased matter to another part of the body. **3** E18 *generally* Change or reversal of condition. **4** L19 *Chemistry* (An) interchange of an atom or atoms between two different molecules; *especially* double decomposition.

métayage *noun* (also **metayage**) L19 **French** (from as MÉTAYER). A system of land tenure in Europe and the United States, in which the farmer pays the owner a proportion (usually half) of the produce as rent, and the owner normally provides the stock and seeds.

métayer *noun* L18 **French** (from medieval Latin *medietarius*, from *medietas* half). A farmer who holds land on the MÉTAYAGE system.

metempsychosis *noun* plural **metempsychoses** L16 **Late Latin** (from Greek *metempsukhōsis*, from as *meta-* + *en* in + *psukhē* soul). Transmigration of the soul; *especially* the passage of the soul of a person or animal at or after death into a new body of the same or a different species.

■ Belief in *metempsychosis* was a feature of the ancient sect of Pythagoreans and is also a tenet in some Eastern religions.

méthode champenoise *noun phrase* E20 **French** (literally, 'champagne method'). The method of introducing a sparkle into wine by allowing the last stage of fermentation to take place in the bottle; a sparkling wine made in this way.

Methodenstreit *noun* plural **Methodenstreite** M20 **German** (literally, 'methods struggle'). (A) discussion or dispute concerning the methodology of a field of study.

Methuselah *noun* (also **Methuselem**) LME **Hebrew** (*mĕtūšelaḥ*, a pre-Noachian patriarch, stated to have lived 969 years (Genesis 5:27)). **1** LME A very old person or thing, especially as a type or representation of extreme longevity. **2** M20 (Usually **methuselah**) A very large wine bottle, equivalent to eight ordinary bottles.

métier *noun* L18 French (from Proto-Romance alteration of Latin *ministerium* service, ministry, probably influenced by *mysterium* mystery). One's occupation or department of activity. Now usually, a field in which one has special skill or ability; one's forte.

metif *noun* E19 French (*métif*, alteration of *métis*: see METIS). A person with one white and one quarter black parent.

metis *Canadian noun* plural same (feminine **métisse**, *Canadian also*, plural **métisses**) E19 French (*métis* from Old French *mestis* from Proto-Romance, from Latin *mixtus* past participle of *miscere* to mix). A person of mixed descent; *especially* (in Canada) a person with one white and one American Indian parent.

metope *noun* M16 Latin (*metopa* from Greek *metopē*, from *meta* between + *opē* hole in a frieze for a beam-end). *Architecture* A square space between triglyphs in a Doric frieze.

metro *noun colloquial* (also **Metro**) plural **metros** E20 French (*métro* abbreviation of (*Chemin de Fer*) *Métropolitain* Metropolitan (Railroad)). A subway; an underground railroad system in a city, *especially* that in Paris.

metteur en scène *noun phrase* plural **metteurs en scène** E20 French (literally, 'a person who puts on the stage'; cf. MISE EN SCÈNE). A PRODUCER OF A PLAY; A DIRECTOR OF A MOVIE.

Mettwurst *noun* L19 German. A type of smoked German sausage.

meum *noun archaic* L16 Latin (neuter of *meus* mine). The principle that a person has sole rights to his or her own property and no rights to another's.

■ Chiefly in *meum and tuum*, '(the distinction between) what is mine or one's own and what is yours or another's'.

meunière *adjective* M19 French ((*à la*) *meunière*, literally, '(in the manner of) a miller's wife'). *Cooking* Especially of fish: cooked or served in lightly browned butter with lemon juice and parsley.

■ Usually postpositive, as in *trout meunière*.

mézair *noun* M18 French (from Italian *mezzaria* middle gait). *Horsemanship* A movement involving a series of levades with a short step between each.

meze *noun* (also **mezé**) plural same, **mezes** E20 Turkish (= snack, appetizer, from Persian *maza* to taste, relish). (Any of) a selection of hot and cold dishes served as an hors d'oeuvre in the Middle East and eastern Mediterranean region.

mezuza *noun* (also **mezuzah**) plural **mezuzoth** M17 Hebrew (*mĕzūzāh*, literally 'doorpost'). A piece of parchment inscribed with Pentateuchal texts enclosed in a case and attached to the doorpost of a Jewish house in fulfillment of religious law.

■ The practice is based upon the injunction in Deuteronomy 6:9.

mezzani *noun* L19 Italian (plural of *mezzano*: see next). Pasta in the form of medium-sized tubes; an Italian dish consisting largely of this and usually a sauce.

mezzanine *noun & adjective* E18 French (from Italian *mezzanino* diminutive of *mezzano* middle, medium, from Latin *medianus* median). **A** *noun* **1** E18 A low story between two others in a building, usually between the first floor and the floor above. **b** M19 *Theater* A floor beneath the stage, from which the traps are worked. **c** E20 The lowest gallery in a theater; a dress circle. **2** M18 A small window at the level of a mezzanine or attic. **B** *adjective* **1** M19 Designating an intermediate floor, story, etc. **2** L20 *Commerce* Designating unsecured, higher-yielding loans that are subordinate to bank loans and secured loans but rank above equity.

mezza voce *adverb, noun, & adjective phrase* L18 **Italian** (*mezza* feminine of *mezzo* middle, half, *voce* voice). *Music* (With) half of the possible vocal or instrumental power; restrained.

mezzo *adverb* M18 **Italian** (= middle, half, from Latin *medius* medium). *Music* (Qualifying a direction:) half, moderately, fairly.

mezzo noun abbreviation of MEZZO-SOPRANO.

mezzo-relievo *noun* (also **mezzo-rilievo**) plural **mezzo-relievos** L16 **Italian** (*mezzo* half + *relievo* relief). (A sculpture, molding, carving, etc., in) half-relief.

mezzo-soprano *noun & adjective* M18 **Italian** (*mezzo* middle + SOPRANO). *Music* **A** *noun* M18 plural **mezzo-sopranos**. A female voice intermediate in compass between soprano and contralto; a singer with such a voice; a part written for such a voice. **B** *adjective* E19 Designating, pertaining to, or intended for a mezzo-soprano.

■ In informal contexts often abbreviated to *mezzo*.

mezzo termine *noun phrase* plural **mezzo termini** M18 **Italian** (*mezzo* half, *termine* term). A middle term, measure, or period.

miasma *noun* plural **miasmas, miasmata** M17 **Greek** (*miasma(t-)* defilement, pollution, related to *miainein* to pollute). **1** M17 (An) infectious or noxious vapor, especially from putrescent organic matter, which pollutes the atmosphere. **2** M19 *figurative* A polluting, oppressive, or foreboding atmosphere; a polluting or oppressive influence.

micro *noun & adjective* M19 **Greek** (combining form *mikr-* from *mikros* small) **A** *noun* plural **micros**. **1** M19 *Entomology* A moth belonging to the Microlepidoptera. **2** M20 A miniskirt. **3** L20 A microcomputer; a microprocessor. **4** L20 A microwave oven. **B** *adjective* **1** E20 Microscopic; very small; small-scale; *Chemistry* of microanalysis. **2** M20 Microeconomic.

■ A colloquial, independent use of the combining form found in many English words derived from Greek and other sources, particularly in technical terminology; cf. MEGA. *Micro*, particularly in its chemical sense, is often contrasted, either explicitly or implicitly, with MACRO.

midinette *noun* E20 **French** (from *midi* midday + *dînette* light dinner). A French, especially a Parisian, shopgirl; *especially* a milliner's assistant.

mielie variant of MEALIE.

migma *noun* M20 **Greek** (= mixture). *Geology* (A) MAGMA containing solid material.

mignon *adjective & noun* (feminine **mignonne**) M16 **French**. **A** *adjective* M16 Delicately formed; prettily small or delicate. **B** *noun* E19 A pretty child or young person.

mignonette *noun* E18 **French** (*mignonnette* diminutive of MIGNON). **1** E18 A kind of light fine narrow pillow lace. Also *mignonette lace*. **2** L18 Any of several plants of the genus *Reseda*, with small greenish or whitish flowers; specifically *R. odorata*, cultivated for its fragrant flowers. **b** L19 A color resembling that of the flowers of the mignonette; grayish green or greenish white. **c** L19 A perfume derived from or resembling that of the flowers of the mignonette.

migraine *noun* LME **Old and Modern French** (from late Latin *hemicrania* from Greek *hēmikrania*, from *hēmi-* half + *kranion* skull). A recurrent throbbing headache, usually affecting one side of the head, often accompanied by nausea or disturbed vision; the illness or condition characterized by such headaches.

mihrab *noun* E19 **Arabic** (*miḥrāb*). **1** E19 A niche, chamber, or slab in a mosque, indicating the direction of Mecca. **2** E20 A niche motif on an oriental prayer rug, resembling the shape of a mihrab in a mosque.

mikva *noun* (also **mikvah, mikveh**) M19 **Yiddish** (*mikve* from Hebrew *miqweh*, literally, 'collection, mass, especially of water'). A bath in which certain

Jewish ritual purifications are performed; the action of taking such a bath.

miles gloriosus *noun* plural **milites gloriosi** E20 **Latin** (= boastful soldier). A vainglorious soldier who boasts about his military exploits.

■ *Miles gloriosus* is the title of a comedy by the Roman playwright Plautus (*c.*250–184 BC). The *miles gloriosus* became a stock character of Renaissance comedy—Shakespeare's Parolles in *All's Well That Ends Well* is an example—and the phrase generally occurs in literary contexts.

milieu *noun* plural **milieus, milieux** M19 **French** (from *mi* (from Latin *medius* mid) + *lieu* place). **1** M19 An environment; (especially social) surroundings. **2** M20 *transferred* A group of people with a shared (cultural) outlook; a social class or set. **b** L20 (also **Milieu**) In France: (a group or organization belonging to) the criminal underworld.

milites gloriosi plural of MILES GLORIOSUS.

militia *noun* L16 **Latin** (= military service, warfare, war, from *miles, milit-* soldier). **1** L16–L17 A system of military discipline, organization, and tactics; a manner or means of conducting warfare. **2** L16 A military force, a body of soldiers; *specifically* a military force raised from the civilian population, as distinguished from mercenaries or professional soldiers; an auxiliary military force drawn from the civilian population in order to supplement the regular forces in an emergency; *collectively* the members of such a militia. **3** L18 The body of people, usually men, legally liable to military service, without enlistment.

millefeuille *noun* L19 **French** (literally, 'a thousand leaves'). A rich confection of thin layers of puff pastry and a filling of jam, cream, etc.

millefiore *noun* M19 **Italian** (from *mille* thousand + *fiore* flowers). A kind of ornamental glass made by fusing together a number of glass rods of different sizes and colors and cutting the mass into sections that exhibit ornamental figures of varying pattern. Also *millefiore glass.*

mille-fleurs *noun* M19 **French** (literally, 'a thousand flowers'). **1** M19 A perfume distilled from flowers of different kinds. **2** E20 A pattern of flowers and leaves used in tapestry, on porcelain, etc.

■ Usually attributive.

millegrain *noun & adjective* (also **milligrain**) M20 **French** (*mille* thousand + *grain* grain). (Designating) a gem setting of beaded or crenellated metal.

millennium *noun* plural **millenniums, millennia** M17 **Modern Latin** (from Latin *mille* thousand, after BIENNIUM). **1** M17 A period of one thousand years. Also, a thousandth anniversary. **2** M17 *Christian Church* *The* period of one thousand years during which (according to one interpretation of Revelation 20:1–5) Christ will reign in person on earth. **3** E19 A period of peace, happiness, prosperity, and ideal government.

millet *noun* E20 **Turkish** (= nation, group of coreligionists, from Arabic *milla(t)* religion). *History* A part of the population of the Ottoman Empire that owed allegiance to a particular religious leader, especially a non-Muslim one.

milpa *noun* M19 **Mexican Spanish**. In Central America and Mexico: a small cultivated field, usually of corn.

mimbar *noun* (also **minbar**) M19 **Arabic** (*minbar*, from *nabara* to raise). A small set of steps in a mosque from which the KHUTBAH is delivered.

mimesis *noun* M16 **Greek** (*mimēsis*, from *mimeisthai* to imitate, from *mimos* mime). **1** M16 Chiefly *Rhetoric* Imitation of another person's words or actions. **b** M20 The representation of the real world in art, poetry, etc. **2** M19 *Biology* Mimicry by one organism of another. Now *rare*. **3** M20 *Sociology* The deliberate imitation of the behavior of one group of people by another as a factor in social change.

minaret *noun* L17 **French** (or Spanish *minarete*, Italian *minaretto*, from Turkish *minâre* from Arabic *manāra* lighthouse, minaret, from *nāra* to shine). **1** L17 A tall tower or turret connected with a mosque and surrounded by one or more projecting balconies from which a muezzin calls at hours of prayer. **2** M19 *transferred* An object or structure shaped like this.

minaudière *noun* E18 **French** (from *minauder* to simper, flirt, from *mine* mien). **1** E18–E19 A coquettish woman. **2** M20 A small handbag without a handle, a clutch bag.

minbar variant of MIMBAR.

minerval *noun* E17 **Latin** (from *Minerva* (earlier *Menerva*) the Roman goddess of handicrafts, wisdom (cf. Sanskrit *manasvin* wise), and later also of war, from earlier form related to Sanskrit *manas* mind, Greek *menos* courage, fury). A gift given in gratitude by a pupil to a teacher.

minestra *noun* L17 **Italian**. In Italy: soup, *especially* MINESTRONE.

minestrone *noun* L19 **Italian**. A thick soup containing vegetables, beans, and pasta.

mingei *noun* M20 **Japanese** (from *min* people + *gei* arts). Japanese folk art; traditional Japanese handicraft.

minifundium *noun* plural **minifundia** (also **minifundio**, plural **minifundios**) M20 **Modern Latin** (or Spanish *minifundio* smallholding: cf. LATIFUNDIUM). In Latin America: a small farm or property, *especially* one that is too small to support a single family. Usually in *plural*.

minimus *noun & adjective* L16 **Latin**. **A** *noun* plural **minimi**. L16 A very small or insignificant creature. **B** *adjective* L18 Designating the youngest of several pupils with the same surname or the last to enter a school.

■ As an adjective appended to a surname, the usage is found especially in British public (i.e., private) schools; thus the eldest and middle brothers of the three of which Smith *minimus* was the youngest would be known respectively as Smith *major* and Smith *minor*. Cf. PRIMUS.

Minnelied *noun* plural **Minnelieder** L19 **German** (from *Minne* love + *Lied* song). A love song written by a minnesinger, or in the style of the minnesingers.

Minnesinger *noun* (also **minnesinger**) E19 **German** (from *Minne* love + *Singer* (modern *Sänger*) singer). A German lyric poet or singer of the twelfth to fourteenth centuries.

minuetto *noun* plural **minuetti**, **minuettos** E18 **Italian**. A minuet.

minuterie *noun* M20 **French** (= clockwork, timing mechanism, from *minute* minute). (An electric light controlled by) a light switch incorporating a timing mechanism to turn it off automatically after a short time.

minutia *noun* plural **minutiae** M18 **Latin** (= smallness (in plural, trifles), from *minutus* small). A precise detail; a small or trivial matter or object.

■ Almost always used in the plural.

minyan *noun* plural **minyanim** M18 **Hebrew** (*minyān*, literally, 'count, reckoning'). The quorum of ten males over thirteen years of age required for traditional Jewish public worship.

mirabelle *noun* E18 **French**. **1** E18 (A fruit from) a European variety of plum tree. **2** M20 (A) liqueur distilled from mirabelles, especially those grown in Alsace, France.

mirabile dictu *interjection* M19 **Latin** (*mirabile* neuter of *mirabilis* wonderful + *dictu* supine of *dicere* to say). Wonderful to relate.

■ Generally used sarcastically.

mirabilia *noun plural* M20 **Latin** (noun use of neuter plural of *mirabilis* wonderful). Wonders, marvels, miracles.

mirador *noun* L17 **Spanish** (from *mirar* to look, observe). In Spain: a watchtower. Also, a turret or belvedere on the top of a Spanish house.

mirage *noun & adjective* E19 **French** (from *se mirer* to be reflected or mirrored, from Latin *mirare*). **A** *noun* **1** E19 An optical illusion caused by atmospheric conditions (usually the refraction of light in heated air); *especially* the false appearance of a distant sheet of water in a desert or on a hot road. Also, the appearance in the sky of a reflected image of a distant object, a wavelike appearance of warmed air just above the ground. **2** E19 *figuratively* An illusion, a fantasy. **3** E20 Any of various pale fashion colors; *especially* pale blue, gray, or turquoise. **B** *adjective* **1** E20 Resembling a mirage. **2** M20 Of a pale color, especially blue, gray, or turquoise.

mirepoix *noun* plural same L19 **French** (from the Duc de *Mirepoix* (1699–1757), French diplomat and general). *Cooking* A mixture of sautéed diced vegetables used in sauces, etc., or served as a separate dish.

mirliton *noun* E19 **French** (= reed pipe, of imitative origin). **1** E19 A musical instrument resembling a kazoo; any instrument in which a sound is given a nasal quality by means of a vibrating membrane. **2** E20 A CHAYOTE.

miscellanea *noun* L16 **Latin** (neuter plural of Latin *miscellaneus* from *miscellus* mixed). As *plural*, miscellaneous items, especially literary compositions, collected together. As *singular*, a miscellaneous collection, especially of literary compositions; a miscellany.

Mischsprache *noun* plural **Mischsprachen** M20 **German** (= mixed language). A language made up of elements of two or more languages.

mise au point *noun phrase* plural **mises au point** M20 **French**. A focusing or clarification of an obscure subject or problem.

mise-en-page *noun* plural **mises-en-page** E20 **French** (*mise en pages* page setting, imposition). The design of a printed page, etc., including the layout of text and illustrations. Also, the composition of a picture.

mise en scène *noun phrase* (also **mise-en-scène**) plural **mises en scène** M19 **French** (cf. METTEUR EN SCÈNE). M THE STAGING OF A PLAY; THE SCENERY AND PROPERTIES OF A STAGE PRODUCTION. L THE SETTING OR SURROUNDINGS OF AN EVENT OR ACTION.

misère *noun* E19 **French** (= poverty, misery). **1** E19 *Cards* A declaration by which the caller undertakes not to win any tricks. **2** L19 Misery; a miserable condition or circumstance.

miserere *noun* ME **Latin** (imperative singular of *misereri* to have pity, have mercy, from *miser* wretched). **1 a** ME Psalm 51 (50 in the Vulgate), beginning *Miserere mei Deus* 'Have mercy upon me, O God', one of the penitential psalms. **b** L18 A musical setting of this psalm. **2** E17 *transferred* A cry for mercy; a prayer in which mercy is sought. **3** L18 A misericord seat.

mises au point plural of MISE AU POINT.

mises-en-page, **mises en scène** plurals of MISE-EN-PAGE, MISE EN SCÈNE.

miso *noun* E18 **Japanese**. Paste made from fermented soybeans and barley or rice malt, used in Japanese cooking.

mistral *noun* E17 **French** (from Provençal from Latin *magistralis* (sc. *ventus* wind)). A strong cold northwest wind that blows through the Rhône valley and southern France into the Mediterranean, mainly in winter.

mit *preposition & adverb* L19 **German** (= with). With (me, us, etc.). *jocular* and *colloquial*.

Mitbestimmung *noun* M20 **German** (= codetermination). In Germany: the policy in industry of involving both workers and management in decision making.

Mitnagged *noun* plural **Mitnaggim** E20 **Hebrew** (*mitnaggēd* opponent). A religious opponent of the Hasidim; any Jew who is not a Hasid.

Mitsein *noun* M20 **German** (noun use of infinitive *mitsein*, from *mit* with + *sein* to be). *Philosophy* The concept of a person's being in its relationship with others.

Mittelschmerz *noun* L19 **German** (= middle pain). *Medicine* Pain in the lower abdomen regularly experienced by some women midway between successive menstrual periods and often thought to coincide with ovulation.

Mittelstand *noun* L20 **German** (= middle class). Something between extremes of size; middling size range.

mittimus *noun & verb* LME **Latin** (literally, 'we send', the first word of the writ in Latin). **A** *noun* **1** *Law* **a** LME–E18 A writ to transfer records from one court to another. **b** L16 A warrant committing a person to prison. **2** L16 A dismissal from office; a notice to quit.

■ Sense 2 is chiefly used colloquially and in dialect in *get one's mittimus*, that is, 'be dismissed'.

mitzvah *noun* plural **mitzvoth** M17 **Hebrew** (*miṣwāh* commandment). *Judaism* A precept; a duty, an obligation. Also, a good deed. Cf. BAR MITZVAH, BAT MITZVAH.

mixte *adjective & noun* L20 **French** (= mixed). (Designating) a bicycle or bicycle frame having no crossbar but instead two thin tubes running from the head of the steering column to either side of the rear axle.

Mizpah *adjective* L19 **Hebrew** (*Miṣpah* place name in ancient Palestine). Designating a ring, locket, etc., given as an expression or token of association or remembrance, originally and especially one with 'Mizpah' inscribed on it.

■ The allusion is to the cairn of stones made in token of the covenant between Jacob and Laban (Genesis 31:43–55), which was called Mizpah "for he said, The Lord watch between me and thee, when we are absent one from another" (verse 49).

moccasin *noun* E17 **Virginia Algonquian** (*mockasin*, and in other North American Indian languages). **1 a** E17 A kind of soft leather shoe, worn by North American Indians, trappers, etc. **b** L19 A soft informal shoe resembling this. **2** L18 A venomous North American snake, as water moccasin.

mochi *noun* plural same E17 **Japanese**. A cake made from glutinous rice, steamed and pounded.

modello *noun* plural **modelli**, **modellos** M20 **Italian**. A detailed sketch for a larger painting, prepared for a patron's approval. Also, a small model for a larger sculpture.

moderato *adverb* E18 **Italian** (= moderate). *Music* (A direction:) at a moderate pace or tempo.

moderne *adjective & noun* M20 **French** (= modern). (Designating or characterized by) a popularization of the art deco style marked by bright colors and austere geometric shapes, or (frequently *derogatory*) any ultramodern style.

Modernismus *noun* M20 **German** (= modernism). Modernism in architecture, art, etc.

■ Frequently derogatory.

modi plural of MODUS.

modicum *noun* L15 **Latin** (= little way, short time, neuter singular of *modicus* moderate, from *modus* mode). A small quantity or portion; a limited amount.

■ Usually followed by *of* in contexts in which *modicum* means 'a decent or necessary minimum amount'.

modiste *noun* M19 **French** (from *mode* fashion, mode). A person who makes, designs, or deals in articles of fashion; *especially* a fashionable milliner or dressmaker.

modulus *noun* plural **moduli**, **moduluses** M16 **Latin** (diminutive of *modus* mode). **1** M16–M17 *Architecture* A unit of length by which proportions are expressed. **2** *Mathematics* **a** M18 A number by which logarithms to one base must be multiplied in order to obtain the corresponding logarithms to another base. **b** M19 A constant multiplier, coefficient, or parameter. **c** M19 A measure of a quantity that depends on two or more other quantities. **d** M19 A number by which another number may be divided leaving a remainder. **3** E19 *Physics* and *Engineering* A numerical quantity representing some property of a substance, and equal to the ratio of the magnitude of a (usually mechanical) cause to the magnitude of its effect on the substance; *specifically* = modulus of elasticity.

modus *noun* plural **modi, moduses** L16 **Latin**. A mode; *especially* the way in which something is done; a mode or manner of operation.

■ Now chiefly in Latin phrases (see following entries) or used elliptically for MODUS OPERANDI.

modus operandi *noun phrase* M17 **Modern Latin** (= mode of operating). **1** M17 The way in which something operates. **2** L19 The way in which a person sets about a task.

modus vivendi *noun phrase* L19 **Modern Latin** (= mode of living). A way of living or coping; *especially* a working arrangement between parties in dispute pending a final settlement.

moellon *noun* L19 **French**. DEGRAS sense 1.

moeurs *noun plural* E20 **French** (from Latin MORES, plural of *mos* custom). The behavior, customs, or habits of a people or a group of people.

mofette *noun* E19 **French** (from Neapolitan Italian *mofetta* = Spanish *mofeta*). (An exhalation of gas from) a fumarole.

mofussil *noun & adjective* (also **Mofussil, mofusil**) L18 **Urdu** (*mufassil* from Persian and Urdu *mufassal* from Arabic *mufaṣṣal* passive participle of *faṣṣala* to divide, separate). **A** *noun* L18 In the Indian subcontinent: the rural localities of a district as distinguished from the chief station or the town. **B** *attributive* or as *adjective* Of the mofussil; remote, provincial.

mogote *noun* E20 **Spanish** (= hillock, heap, haystack). *Physical Geography* A steep-sided hill of roughly circular cross section characteristic of karst topography, especially in Cuba. Cf. HUM.

mohel *noun* M17 **Hebrew** (*mōhēl*). A Jew who performs the rite of circumcision.

moi *personal pronoun* L20 **French** (= me). Me; I, myself.

■ Since the late 1970s in jocular use as a pretentious reference to oneself. Chief popularizer of the expression was the character Miss Piggy in the television series *The Muppets*, the children's puppet show created by Jim Henson, and it was then also taken up by adult shows.

moire *noun* M17 **French** (later form of *mouaire* mohair). A watered fabric (originally mohair, now usually silk). Also *moire antique*.

moiré *adjective & noun* E19 **French** (past participle of *moirer* to give a watered appearance to, from as preceding). **A** *adjective* **1** E19 Of silk: watered. Also, (of metal, etc.) having a clouded appearance like watered silk. **2** M20 Designating or pertaining to a pattern of light and dark fringes observed when a pattern of lines, dots, etc., is visually superimposed on another similar pattern, or on an identical one slightly out of alignment with the first. **B** *noun* **1** E19 A variegated or clouded appearance like that of watered silk, especially as an ornamental finish applied to metal; a moiré pattern or effect. **2** M19 MOIRE.

moksha *noun* L18 **Sanskrit** (*mokṣa*, from *muc* to set free, release). *Hinduism* and *Jainism* The final release of the soul from a cycle of incarnations; the bliss so attained. Also called *mukti*.

mola *noun* M20 **Cuna**. A square of brightly colored appliquéd cloth worn as a blouse by Cuna Indian women of the San Blas Islands, Panama.

molcajete *noun* L20 **Mexican Spanish** (from Spanish *moler* to grind + *cajete* pot, bowl). A mortar for grinding spices and small seeds in.

mole *noun* M20 **Mexican Spanish** (from Nahuatl *molli* sauce, stew). A highly spiced Mexican sauce made chiefly from chili and chocolate, served with meat.

molleton *noun* L18 **French** (from *mollet* diminutive of *mol* soft). Swanskin (flannel).

moloch *noun* (in sense 1 usually **Moloch**) E17 **Late Latin** (from Greek *Molokh* from Hebrew *mōlek*, a Canaanite idol to whom children were sacrificed as burnt offerings (Leviticus 18:21), held to be alteration of *melek* king, by substitution of the vowels of *bōšet* shame). **1** E17 An object to which horrible sacrifices are made. **2** M19 A slow-moving spiny Australian lizard, *Moloch horridus*, of grotesque appearance. Also called *mountain devil, spiny lizard, thorny devil*. **3** L19 A forest monkey of tropical America, a dusky titi.

molossus *noun* plural **molossi** L16 **Latin** (= Greek *Molossos*). **1** L16 *Prosody* A metrical foot consisting of three long syllables. **2** E17 *History* A mastiff dog from the region of ancient Molossia, in northwestern Greece. More fully *molossus dog*.

molto *adverb* E19 **Italian** (from Latin *multus* much). *Music* Very.

■ Usually in directions modifying adjectives from Italian.

momentum *noun* plural **momenta** E17 **Latin**. **1** E17–M19 A turning motion. **2 a** L17 *Physics* The quantity of motion of a moving body, equal to the product of the mass and the velocity of the body. **b** L18 The effect of inertia in the continuance of motion; impetus gained by movement; *figuratively* strength or continuity derived from an initial effort. **3** *Mathematics* An infinitesimal increment. Only in M18. **4** M18–E19 Force of movement. **5** E19 An element of a complex conceptual identity, a moment.

mompei *noun plural* (also **mompe**) M20 **Japanese** (*monpe*). Baggy working pants worn in Japan.

momser, momzer variants of MAMZER.

monad *noun & adjective* (in sense 1 also (earlier) in Latin form **monas**, plural **monades** M16 **French** (*monade* or its source late Latin *monas, monad-* from Greek, from *monos* alone). **1** M16 (**Monad**) The Deity, God. **b** E17 The number one, unity; a unit. Now chiefly *Historical*, with reference to ancient Greek philosophy, in which the numbers were regarded as being generated from the unitary one. **2** M18 *Philosophy* Especially in the philosophy of Leibniz: an indivisible unit of being (as a soul, an atom); an absolutely simple entity. **3** M19 *Biology* A hypothetical simple organism, *especially* one assumed as the first term in the genealogy of living beings, or regarded as associated with others to form an animal or vegetable body.

mon ami *noun phrase* (also (feminine) **mon amie**) plural **mes amis** (feminine **mes amies**) L18 **French**. (As a form of address:) my friend.

monas see MONAD.

mon cher *noun phrase* L17 **French**. (As a form of address to a male:) my dear, my dear fellow.

mondain *noun & adjective* (feminine **mondaine**) L19 **French**. **A** *noun* L19 A worldly or fashionable person. Cf. DEMI-MONDAINE. **B** *adjective* L19 Of the fashionable world; worldly.

monde *noun* M18 **French** (= world). The world of fashionable or aristocratic people; such people collectively. Also, a person's particular circle or set.

■ Earlier in BEAU MONDE.

mondo *noun* plural **mondos** E20 **Japanese** (from *mon* asking + *dō* answering). An instructional technique of Zen Buddhism consisting of rapid dialogue of questions and answers between teacher and pupil.

mondo *adjective & adverb* M20 **Italian** (= world). **A** *adjective* **1** M20 Anarchic and tasteless. **2** L20 As an intensifier: considerable, much; huge. **B** *adverb* L20 Very, extremely.

■ Slang use of *mondo* derives ultimately from *Mondo Cane*, the title of an Italian movie (1961) showing bizarre behavior (released in 1963 in the English-speaking world as *A Dog's Life*). The movie gained a cult following and was imitated in similar titles such as *Mondo Bizarro* (1966). The adjectival and adverbial uses arose through the interpretation of, for instance, *mondo bizarro* as 'very bizarre'. In the 1980s *mondo* became simply an intensifier in American slang. It was used in this way by the children's comic book characters the Teenage Mutant Ninja Turtles in phrases such as *mondo cool* to express approval.

mondongo *noun* plural **mondongos** E17 **Spanish** (= tripe, blood sausage). A Latin American or West Indian dish composed of tripe.

monocoque *noun & adjective* E20 **French** (from *mono-* mono- + *coque* eggshell). **A** *noun* **1** E20 An aircraft fuselage or other structure having an outer covering in the form of a rigid load-bearing shell, usually without longerons or stringers. **2** M20 A motor vehicle underframe and body built as a single rigid structure (or in racing cars as a number of boxlike sections) throughout which the stresses are distributed. **B** *attributive* or as *adjective* E20 Designating or based on a structure of this type.

monosabio *noun* plural **monosabios** L19 **Spanish** (from *mono* monkey + *sabio* wise, trained). *Bullfighting* A picador's assistant in the ring.

monsoon *noun* L16 **Early Modern Dutch** (*monssoen* (modern *moesson*, influenced by French forms) from Portuguese *monção* (cf. Old Spanish *monzon*) from Arabic *mawsim* season, fixed period, from *wasama* to brand, mark). **1** L16 A seasonal wind that blows in southern Asia, especially in the Indian Ocean, approximately from the southwest from April to October (in full *southwest, summer, wet,* or *rainy monsoon*), and from the northeast from October to April (in full *northeast, winter,* or *dry monsoon*). **b** M18 The rainfall that accompanies the southwest or summer monsoon; the rainy season. **2** L17 Any wind that reverses its direction seasonally, as the temperature varies between two areas, especially between land and ocean.

mons pubis *noun phrase* L19 **Latin** (= mount of the pubes). *Anatomy* The rounded mass of fatty tissue on the lower abdomen, over the joint of the pubic bones; *especially* that of a female (= MONS VENERIS sense 2).

monstre sacré *noun phrase* plural **monstres sacrés** M20 **French** (literally, 'sacred monster'). A striking, eccentric, or controversial public figure.

mons Veneris *noun phrase* E17 **Latin** (= mount of Venus). **1** E17 *Palmistry* The ball of the thumb. **2** L17 *Anatomy* The rounded mass of fatty tissue on a female's lower abdomen, above the vulva. Cf. MONS PUBIS.

montage *noun* E20 **French** (from *monter* to mount). **1** E20 *Cinematography* and *Television* The selection and arrangement of separate sections of film as a consecutive whole; the blending (by superimposition) of separate shots to form a single picture; a sequence or picture resulting from such a process. **2** *generally* M20 The process or technique of producing a composite whole by combining several different pictures, pieces of music, or other elements, so that they blend with or into one another; the result of such a process.

montagnard *adjective & noun* M19 **French** (from *montagne* mountain). **A** *adjective* M19 Inhabiting a mountain region; of or pertaining to montagnards. **B** *noun* M20 A native or inhabitant of a mountain region; a highlander.

montagne russe *noun phrase* plural **montagnes russes** M19 **French** (literally, 'Russian mountain'). A switchback, a roller coaster. *Canadian.*

Montaña *noun* M19 **Spanish** (= mountain). In Spanish-American countries: a forest of considerable extent; *specifically* the forested eastern foothills of the Andes in Peru etc.

mont de piété *noun phrase* plural **monts de piété** M19 **French** (= mount of piety). A state pawnbroking organization in France providing loans to the poor at low rates of interest.

■ The term 'mount' for a financial institution was formerly (E17–M18) current in English. Cf. Italian MONTE DI PIETÀ.

monte *noun* (in branch I (especially sense 2) also **monty** E19 **Spanish** (= mountain, pile of cards left after dealing). **I 1** E19 A Spanish and Spanish-American gambling game usually played with a deck of forty cards. Also (in full *three-card monte*), a form of three-card trick. **2** L19 A certainty; *specifically* a horse considered a safe bet to win a race. *Australian and New Zealand colloquial.* **II 3** M19 In Spanish-American countries: a small wooded tract; (a region of) chaparral or scrub.

monte di pietà *noun phrase* plural **monti di pietà** M17 **Italian** (= mount of piety). A state pawnbroking organization in Italy providing loans to the poor at low rates of interest. Cf. French MONT DE PIÉTÉ.

montera *noun* (also (now *rare*) **montero**, plural **monteros**) E17 **Spanish** (from *montero* mountaineer, hunter, from *monte* mount). A Spanish cap, originally worn for hunting, with a spherical crown and flaps able to be drawn over the ears. Now usually *specifically*, the black hat worn by a bullfighter.

monti di pietà, **monts de piété** plurals of MONTE DI PIETÀ, MONT DE PIÉTÉ.

montuno *noun* plural **montunos** M20 **American Spanish** (= native to mountains, wild, untamed). **1** M20 A traditional male costume worn in Panama, consisting of white cotton short pants and an embroidered shirt. **2** M20 An improvised passage in a rumba.

mon vieux *noun phrase* L19 **French**. (As an affectionate form of address:) old friend, old man.

moolvi(e) variant of MOULVI.

moquette *noun* M19 **French** (perhaps from obsolete Italian *mocaiardo* mohair). A heavy piled fabric used for carpets and upholstery.

mor *noun* M20 **Danish** (= humus). *Soil Science* Humus forming a discrete layer on top of the soil with little mineral soil mixed with it, characteristic of coniferous forests and generally strongly acid.

moraine *noun* L18 **French** (from Savoyard Italian *morena*, from southern French *mor(re)* muzzle, snout, from Proto-Romance word). **1** L18 An area or bank of debris that a glacier or ice sheet has carried down and deposited; the material forming such a deposit. **2** E20 *Gardening* A bed made largely of stones covered with fine chippings, designed to produce suitable conditions for alpine plants.

morale *noun* M18 **French** (*moral*, respelled to indicate stress; cf. LOCALE). **1** M18 Morality; moral teaching. Now *rare*. **2** M19 The mental and emotional attitude of a group or individual with regard to confidence, willingness, hope, etc.; degree of contentment with one's lot or situation.

moratorium *noun* plural **moratoriums**, **moratoria** L19 **Modern Latin** (use as noun of neuter singular of late Latin *moratorius* that delays, from *morat-* past participial stem of *morari* to delay). **1** L19 *Law* A legal authorization to a debtor to postpone payment for a certain time; the period of such a postponement. **2** M20 A postponement or deliberate temporary suspension of some activity, etc.

morbidezza *noun* E17 **Italian** (from *morbido* morbid). **1** E17 *Painting* Lifelike delicacy in flesh tints. **2** L19 Delicacy, softness, especially in musical performance; sensibility, smoothness; sickliness.

morbilli *noun plural* M16 **Medieval Latin** (plural of *morbillus* pustule, spot characteristic of measles, diminutive of Latin *morbus* disease). *Medicine* (The spots characteristic of) measles.

morceau *noun* plural **morceaux** M18 **French** (Old French *morsel*, *morcel* diminutive of *mors* from Latin *morsus* bite, from *mors-* past participial stem of *mordere* to bite). A short literary or musical composition.

mordent *noun* E19 **German** (from Italian *mordente* use as noun of verbal adjective from *mordere* to bite, from Proto-Romance alteration of Latin *mordere*). *Music* An ornament consisting of the rapid alternation of the note written with the one immediately below it. Cf. PRALLTRILLER.

mordida *noun* M20 **Central American and Mexican Spanish**. In Mexico and Central America: a bribe, an illegal exaction.

mordoré *noun* L18 **French** (from Old French *More* (modern *Maure*) Moor + *doré* past participle of *dorer* to gild). A color between brown and red; russet.

more *noun* E17 **Latin** (ablative of *mos, mor-* custom). In the fashion *of*, according to the custom *of*.

■ Only in Latin adverbial phrases (see following entries).

more hispanico *adverb phrase* M20 **Latin**. In accordance with Spanish custom.

more majorum *adverb phrase* E17 **Latin** (*majorum*, genitive plural of *majores* ancestors). In traditional manner.

more meo *adverb phrase* E19 **Latin**. In my own fashion.

mores *noun plural* L19 **Latin** (plural of *mos* manner, custom). **1** L19 The acquired customs and moral assumptions that give cohesion to a community, social group, or period. Cf. O TEMPORA, O MORES. **2** E20 *Zoology* The habits, behavior, etc., of a group of animals of the same kind.

Moresca *noun* M19 **Italian** (feminine of *Moresco* from *Moro* Moor; cf. MORISCA). An Italian folk dance related to the English morris dance.

more suo *adverb phrase* M19 **Latin**. In his own fashion.

morgue *noun* M19 **French** (proper name of a Paris mortuary). **1** M19 A mortuary. **2a** E20 In a newspaper office, the collection of material assembled for the future obituaries of people still living. *colloquial*. **b** E20 A repository of cuttings, photographs, and information in a newspaper office, movie studio, etc. *colloquial*.

Morisca *noun* M20 **Spanish** (feminine of next; cf. MORESCA). A Spanish folk dance related to the English morris dance.

Morisco *adjective & noun* M16 **Spanish** (from *Moro* Moor). **A** *adjective* M16 Of or pertaining to the Moors; Moorish. **B** *noun* plural **Morisco(e)s**. **1** M16 A Moor, especially in Spain. **2** M16 Originally, a dance with Moorish elements and sharing some features with the morris dance. Now usually = MORISCA. **3** E18 Arabesque art, ornament, etc.

morituri te salutamus *interjection* (also **morituri te salutant** and other variants) E18 **Latin** (= we who are about to die salute you). *Roman History* The words addressed by gladiators to the Roman emperor as they entered the arena.

■ Quoted from Suetonius *Life of Claudius* xxi.6. Used allusively in English in many variant forms by people facing danger or difficulty.

moron *noun* E20 **Greek** (*mōron* neuter of *mōros* foolish). **1** E20 *Medicine* An adult with a mental age of between about eight and twelve. **2** E20 A stupid or slow-witted person; a fool. *colloquial*.

mortadella *noun* plural **mortadellas, mortadelle** E17 **Italian** (irregular from Latin *murtatum* (sausage) seasoned with myrtle berries). A large spiced pork sausage; Bologna sausage.

moscato *noun* plural **moscatos** E20 **Italian**. A sweet Italian dessert wine.

moshav *noun* plural **moshavim** M20 **Modern Hebrew** (*mōšāḇ* dwelling, colony). In Israel: a group of agricultural smallholdings worked partly on a cooperative and partly on an individual basis.

mosso *adverb* L19 **Italian** (past participle of *muovere* to move). *Music* (A direction:) rapidly, with animation.

mot *noun* L16 **French** (= word, saying, from Proto-Gallo-Romance alteration of popular Latin *muttum* related to Latin *muttire* to murmur; cf. MOTTO). **1** L16 Originally, a motto. Later (now *dialectal*) a word, an opinion. **2** E19 A witty saying. Cf. BON MOT.

motard *noun* M20 **French** (from *moto-* combining form of *moteur*). A member of the French motorcycle police.

mot de Cambronne *noun phrase* **French** (literally, 'Cambronne's word'). The French expletive *merde!*

■ The reputed reply of General Pierre Cambronne (1770–1842) when called upon to surrender at the Battle of Waterloo. The official version of what he said—*La garde meurt mais ne se rend pas* 'The Guard dies, but does not surrender'—seems to have been a happy journalistic invention, since the general himself denied saying it.

mot d'ordre *noun phrase* plural **mots d'ordres** M19 **French** (= word of command). A political slogan; a statement of policy; an oral directive.

motif *noun* M19 **French**. **1** M19 A distinctive, significant, or dominant idea or theme; *specifically* (**a**) *Art* a distinctive feature, subject, or structural principle in a composition or design; (**b**) in literature or folklore, a particular or recurrent event, situation, theme, character, etc.; (**c**) *Music* a figure, a leitmotiv. **2** L19 An ornamental design or piece of decoration; *specifically* (**a**) an ornament of lace, braid, etc., sewn separately on a garment; (**b**) an ornament on a vehicle identifying the maker, model, etc. **3** L19 A motivation, a basis, (for an idea, etc.).

motivi plural of MOTIVO.

motiviert *adjective* E19 **German**. Motivated.

motivo *noun* plural **motivi** M18 **Italian**. *Music* A motif.

mot juste *noun phrase* plural **mots justes** E20 **French** (= exact word). The precisely appropriate expression.

moto *noun* M18 **Italian**. *Music* Movement, pace.

■ In various musical directions; cf. CON MOTO.

moto perpetuo *noun phrase* plural **moti perpetui** L19 **Italian** (= perpetual motion). A rapid instrumental composition consisting mainly of notes of equal value.

motte *noun* L19 **French** (= mound). *Antiquities* A large man-made earthen mound with a flattened top, usually surmounted by a fort, castle, etc.

motto *noun* plural **mottos**, **mottoes** L16 **Italian** (from Proto-Gallo-Romance word whence also MOT). **1** L16 Originally, a sentence or phrase attached to an emblematical design to explain its significance. Later, a short sentence or phrase inscribed on an object, expressing a reflection or sentiment considered appropriate to its purpose or destination. Also, a maxim adopted as a rule of conduct. **b** E17 *Heraldry* A significant word or sentence usually placed on a scroll, either below an achievement of arms or above the crest. **c** M19 A verse or saying in a paper cracker, etc. **2** E18 A short quotation or epigram placed at the beginning of a book, chapter, etc.; an epigraph. **3** M19 A candy wrapped in fancy paper together with a saying or scrap of verse. Also *motto kiss*. **4** L19 *Music* A recurrent phrase having some symbolic significance.

motu proprio *adverb & noun phrase* E17 **Latin**. **A** *adverb phrase* E17 Of one's own volition, on one's own initiative, spontaneously. **B** *noun phrase* plural **motu proprios**. M19 An edict issued by the Pope personally to the Roman Catholic church, or to a part of it.

mouche *noun* L17 **French** (literally, 'a fly', from Latin *musca*). **1** L17 *History* A small black patch worn on the face as an ornament or to conceal a blemish. **2** M19 A natural mark on the face resembling such a patch; a beauty spot.

mouchette *noun* E20 **French**. *Architecture* A motif in curvilinear tracery shaped like a curved dagger.

moue *noun* M19 **French**. A pouting expression, a pout.

moujik variant of MUZHIK.

moulage *noun* E20 **French** (= molding, molded reproduction, from *mouler* to mold). A cast or impression of a (part of a) person or thing; the material used for or the process of making a cast or taking an impression.

moule *noun* L19 **French.** *Cooking* A mussel.

■ Usually in plural in names of dishes, as in *moules marinières*.

moulin *noun* M19 **French** (literally, 'mill'). **1** M19 A deep, nearly vertical shaft in a glacier, formed by falling water. Also called *glacier mill.* **2** M20 A type of kitchen utensil for grinding or puréeing food.

moulvi *noun* (also **maulvi**, **moolvi(e)**) E17 **Urdu** (*maulvī* from Arabic *mawlawī* judicial (used as noun), from *mawlā* mullah). A Muslim doctor of the law, an imam; *generally* (especially in the Indian subcontinent, used as a form of address to) a learned person or teacher.

mousaka variant of MOUSSAKA.

mousquetaire *noun & adjective* E18 **French** (= musketeer, from *mousquet* musket). **A** *noun* **1** E18 *History* A French musketeer. **2** L19 A glove with a long loose wrist. More fully *mousquetaire glove.* **B** *attributive* or as *adjective* M19 Of an article of clothing: in the style of that of a French musketeer.

moussaka *noun* (also **mousaka**) M20 **Turkish** (*musakka*, ultimately from Arabic *musakkā*; cf. modern Greek *mousakas*, Romanian *musaca*, Albanian, Bulgarian *musaka*, etc.). An eastern Mediterranean dish made with ground beef or lamb, eggplant, etc., with a cheese sauce.

mousse *noun* M19 **French** (= moss, froth). **1** M19 The aggregation of tiny bubbles in sparkling wine, as champagne, etc. **2** L19 *Cooking* A sweet or savory dish made from a purée or other base stiffened with whipped cream, gelatin, egg whites, etc., and usually served chilled. Frequently with specifying word. **3** M20 A brown emulsion of seawater and oil produced by the weathering of oil spills and resistant to dispersal; a mass of this substance. More fully *chocolate mousse.* **4** L20 *Hairdressing* A frothy preparation for applying to the hair to facilitate setting or coloring.

mousseline *noun* L17 **French. 1** L17 French muslin; a dress of this material. Also *mousseline-de-laine.* **2** M19 (A wineglass of) a very thin blown glassware with ornamentation resembling muslin or lace. More fully *mousseline glass.* **3** E20 *Cooking* A rich frothy sauce of seasoned or sweetened eggs or cream. More fully *mousseline sauce.* **b** E20 Any of various dishes with a light frothy texture and usually prepared by whipping or beating; a mousse.

mousseux *adjective & noun* E19 **French** (from as MOUSSE). **A** *adjective* E19 Of wine: sparkling. **B** *noun* M20 plural same. A sparkling wine, a VIN MOUSSEUX.

moustache variant of MUSTACHE.

mouton enragé *noun phrase* plural **moutons enragés** M20 **French** (literally, 'angry sheep'). A normally placid person who has become suddenly enraged or violent.

moutonné(e) see ROCHE MOUTONNÉE.

mouvementé *adjective* E20 **French.** Animated, agitated, bustling, full of variety; *specifically* (of music) lively.

moyen-âge *adjective* (also **moyen-age** and with capital initials) M19 **French** (= the Middle Ages). Of or pertaining to the Middle Ages, medieval.

moyen sensuel *adjective phrase* (also **moyen-sensuel**) E20 **French.** Of an average sensual and materialistic character.

■ Generally in the phrase HOMME MOYEN SENSUEL.

mozetta variant of MOZZETTA.

mozzarella *noun* E20 **Italian** (diminutive of *mozza* a kind of cheese, from *mozzare* to cut off). A white Italian cheese originally made in the Naples area from buffalo milk. More fully *mozzarella cheese.*

mozzetta *noun* (also **mozetta**) L18 **Italian** (aphetized from *almozzetta*, from medieval Latin *almucia* amice). *Roman Catholic Church* A short cape with a hood, worn by the Pope, cardinals, and some other ecclesiastics.

mu *noun* ME **Greek**. **1** ME The twelfth letter (Μ, μ) of the Greek alphabet. **2** L19 Plural same. One micrometer (micron). Usually denoted by μ. **3** E20 *Electronics* The amplification factor of a valve.

muchacha *noun* L19 **Spanish** (feminine of next). In Spain and Spanish-speaking countries: a girl, a young woman; a female servant.

muchacho *noun* plural **muchachos** L16 **Spanish**. In Spain and Spanish-speaking countries: a boy, a young man; a male servant.

mudra *noun* E19 **Sanskrit** (*mudrā* seal, sign, token). Any of a large number of symbolic hand gestures used in Hindu religious ceremonies and in Indian dance. Also, a movement or pose in yoga.

muesli *noun* M20 **Swiss German**. A dish, originating in Switzerland, consisting of a cereal (usually oats), fruit, nuts, etc., eaten with milk or cream, especially for breakfast.

muezzin *noun* L16 **Arabic** (dialectal variant of Arabic *mu'aḏḏin* active participle of *'aḏḏana* to call to prayer, from *'uḏn* ear). A Muslim crier who proclaims the hours of prayer from a minaret or the roof of a mosque.

mufti *noun* L16 **Arabic** (*muftī* active participle of *'aftā* to decide a point of law (related to FATWA)). A Muslim cleric or legal expert empowered to give rulings on religious matters; in the Ottoman Empire, a chief legal authority, especially of a large city (also *Grand Mufti*).

■ *Mufti* in the sense of 'plain or informal clothes worn by a person who has the right to wear a uniform of some kind' (E19) may be a facetious use of this word, but its origins are uncertain.

muguet *noun* L16 **French** (from medieval Latin *muscatum* musk-scented, from *muscus* musk). **1** L16–M17 Any of certain fragrant plants; *specifically* woodruff, *Galium odoratum*. **2** L16 Lily of the valley, *Convallaria majalis*; a scent made from or resembling it.

mukhtar *noun* E20 **Turkish** (*muhtar* from Arabic *muktār* passive participle of *iktāra* to choose, elect). In Turkey and some Arab countries: the head of the local government of a town or village; a minor provincial official.

mukti *noun* L18 **Sanskrit** (= release, from *muc* to set free, release). *Hinduism* and *Jainism* MOKSHA.

mulatta *noun* E17 **Spanish** (*mulata* feminine of *mulato* mulatto). A female mulatto.

mulatto *noun & adjective* plural **mulatto(e)s** L16 **Spanish and Portuguese** (*mulato* young mule, mulatto, irregularly from *mulo* mule). **A** *noun* L16 A person having one white and one black parent; a person of mixed white and black parentage. **B** *adjective* **1** E17 Of the color of the skin of a mulatto; tawny. **2** L17 That is a mulatto; of or pertaining to mulattos. **3** M18 Designating a kind of mid-brown fertile soil.

muleta *noun* M19 **Spanish**. *Bullfighting* A red cloth fixed to a stick used by a matador during the FAENA.

mulga *noun* M19 **Aboriginal**. **1** M19 Any of several small acacia, forming dense scrub in dry inland areas of Australia and sometimes used for fodder (also *mulga tree*); the land covered with such vegetation, (*colloquial*) the outback. **2** M19 A thing made of the wood of a mulga tree, *especially* a club or shield. **3** L19 A rumor, a message, a (false) report; *the* grapevine. In full *mulga wire*. *Australian slang*.

mullah *noun* E17 **Persian** (Urdu *mullā*, Turkish *molla* from Arabic *mawlā*). (A title given to) a Muslim learned in Islamic theology and sacred law.

multum in parvo *noun phrase* M18 **Latin** (= much in little). A great deal in a small compass.

mumpsimus *noun* M16 **pseudo-Latin** (erroneously for Latin *sumpsimus* in the passage in the Eucharistic service that runs *quod in ore sumpsimus* 'which we have taken into the mouth'). **1** M16 An obstinate adherent of old ways, in spite of clear evidence of their error; an ignorant and bigoted opponent of reform. Formerly also *loosely*, an old fogey. **2** M16 A traditional custom or notion obstinately adhered to although shown to be unreasonable.

■ The origin is Richard Pace's anecdote in *De Fructu* (1517) of an illiterate English priest who garbled the passage in the Mass quoted above by substituting the nonsense word *mumpsimus*. When corrected, he replied "I will not change my old mumpsimus for your new sumpsimus." Now only in literary use. Cf. SUMPSIMUS.

mu-mu variant of MUU-MUU.

mung *noun* E19 **Hindi** (*mūng*). (The seed of) either of two widely cultivated tropical legumes.

municipio *noun* plural **municipios** L19 **Spanish and Italian** (from Latin *municipium*). A Spanish, Latin American, or Italian municipality.

munshi *noun* (also **moonshee**) L18 **Persian and Urdu** (*munšī* from Arabic *munši'* writer, author, active participle of *'anša'a* to write (a book)). In the Indian subcontinent: a secretary, an assistant; a language teacher.

murex *noun* plural **murices**, **murexes** L16 **Latin** (perhaps related to Greek *muax* sea mussel). Any of various spiny-shelled predatory gastropod mollusks of the genus *Murex* and related genera, of tropical and temperate seas, from some of which the dye Tyrian purple was formerly obtained. Also *murex shell*.

murus gallicus *noun phrase* plural **muri gallici** M20 **Latin** (from *murus* wall + *gallicus* Gallic). *Archaeology* A type of late Iron Age Celtic fort having stone walls bound by horizontally placed wooden frames.

muscadel variant of MUSCATEL.

muscae *noun plural* M18 **Latin** (plural of *musca* fly). Chiefly *Medicine* Specks that appear to float before the eyes, frequently due to particles in the vitreous humor of the eye. In full *muscae volitantes* (present participle of *volitare* to fly about).

muscat *noun* M16 **Old and Modern French** (from Provençal (= Italian MOSCATO), from *musc* musk). **1** M16 MUSCATEL wine. In full *muscat wine*. **2** M17 Any of several varieties of grape with a musky taste or smell; a vine bearing a variety of such a grape. In full *muscat grape*. **3** M17–M18 A kind of peach or pear with a musky taste or smell.

muscatel *noun* (also **muscadel**) LME **Old French** (*muscadel*, *muscatel* (= Italian *moscatello*) from Provençal diminutive of MUSCAT). **1** LME (A) strong sweet wine made from the muscat or similar grape; a drink of this. **2** E16 A muscat grape. In full *muscatel grape*. **3** M16–M18 A variety of pear with a musky taste or smell. **4** M17 A raisin from the muscatel grape. In full *muscatel raisin*. Usually in *plural*.

museau *noun* plural **museaux** E19 **French** (colloquial, literally, 'muzzle, snout'). A person's face.

musée *noun* M17 **French** (from Latin *mus(a)eum* library, study, from Greek *mouseion* seat of the Muses). In France and French-speaking countries: a museum.

musette *noun* LME **Old and Modern French** (diminutive of *muse* bagpipe). **1** LME A kind of small bagpipe, *especially* a small French bagpipe of the eighteenth century with a soft tone. **2** E18 A soft pastoral air imitating the sound of the musette; a dance performed to such music. **3** E19 A reed stop in an organ producing a soft tone resembling that of the musette. **4** L19 A small and simple variety of oboe without a reed cap. **5** E20 A type of lightweight knapsack used especially by the military and by racing cyclists. More fully *musette bag*.

musica *noun* **Latin** (= music). Occurring in various phrases used in English, especially with reference to early music (see entries below).

musica ficta *noun phrase* E19 **Latin** (literally, 'feigned music'). (Early contrapuntal music characterized by) the introduction by a singer of conventional chromatically altered tones to avoid unacceptable intervals.

musica figurata *noun phrase* M18 Latin (literally, 'figured music'). **1** Contrapuntal music in which the different melodic strands move more or less independently. **2** M20 Plainsong with decorated melody.

musica plana *noun phrase* M20 Latin (literally, 'plain music'). Plainsong, canto fermo.

musica reservata *noun phrase* M20 Latin (literally, 'reserved music'). Early music characterized by clarity, balance, restraint, and expressiveness.

musicale *noun* L19 French ((*soirée*) *musicale* musical evening). A musical party; a concert, especially at a private address.

■ Cf. SOIRÉE MUSICALE.

musique concrète *noun phrase* M20 French (= concrete music). Electronic music constructed by the rearrangement of recorded natural sounds.

mustache *noun* (also **moustache**) L16 French (from Italian *mostaccio, mostacchio* from medieval Latin *mustacia*, ultimately from Greek *mustax, mustak-* upper lip, mustache). **1** L16 A (cultivated) growth of hair above the whole or either half (frequently in *plural*, especially in *pair of mustaches*) of a man's lip or extending from this on either side of the lip; a growth of hair above a woman's lip. Also, an artificial strip of hair worn in imitation of this. **2** E17 A growth of hairs or bristles, or a marking resembling a man's mustache, around the mouth of certain animals or birds.

mustafina *noun* E19 Spanish (apparently from *mustee*, abbreviation of Spanish MESTIZO). A person with one parent a mestizo and the other a white.

muta *intransitive verb* L19 Italian (imperative of *mutare* to change). *Music* (A direction:) change instrument or tuning.

mutatis mutandis *adverb phrase* L15 Latin (literally, 'things being changed that have to be changed'). Making the necessary changes; with due alteration of details.

mutato nomine *adverb phrase* E17 Latin. The name being changed, with a change of name or names.

■ Earliest in English as a quotation from Horace's *Satires* (I.i.69): *Quid rides? mutato nomine de te / Fabula narratur* 'Laughing are you? Just change the name and the tale is told about you'.

mutuel *noun* E20 French (abbreviation of PARI-MUTUEL). A totalizator, a *pari-mutuel*. Chiefly *North American*.

muu-muu *noun* (also **mu-mu**) E20 Hawaiian (*mu'u mu'u*, literally, 'cut off' from the original absence of a yoke). A woman's usually brightly colored and patterned loose-fitting dress, (as) worn in Hawaii.

muzhik *noun* (also **moujik**) M16 Russian. *History* A Russian peasant.

mystae plural of MYSTES.

mystagogue *noun* M16 French (Latin *mystagogus* from Greek *mustagōgos*, from *mustēs* MYSTES + *agōgos* leading, from *agein* to lead). In ancient Greece, a person who gave preparatory instruction to candidates for initiation into the Eleusinian or other mysteries; *generally* a person who introduces others to religious mysteries, a teacher of mystical doctrines, a creator or disseminator of mystical doctrines.

mysterioso *adjective* M20 Italian (= mysterious). *Music* Executed in a mysterious manner.

mysterium tremendum *noun phrase* E20 Latin (= tremendous mystery). A great or overwhelming mystery, *especially* the great or overwhelming mystery of God or of existence.

mystes *noun* plural **mystae** L17 Latin (from Greek *mustēs*). A person initiated into mysteries.

mystique *noun* L19 French. The atmosphere of mystery and veneration investing some doctrines, arts, professions, or people; a mysterious attraction; any professional skill or technique designed or able to mystify and impress the lay person.

mythoi plural of MYTHOS.

mythopoeia *noun* M20 **Greek** (*muthopoiia*). The creation of a myth or myths.

mythos *noun* plural **mythoi** M18 **Greek** (*muthos* myth). **1** M18 A traditional story, either wholly or partly fictitious, a myth; a body of myths. **2** M20 A traditional or recurrent narrative theme or pattern; a standard plot in literature.

■ *Mythos* and its Latin derivative *mythus* (E19), both now used solely in literary contexts, were current before the Anglicized *myth* (M19), which is now the form used in all general contexts for sense 1.

naan variant of NAN.

naartjie *noun* (also **naartje** and other variants) L18 **Afrikaans** (from Tamil *nārattai* citrus). In South Africa: a soft loose-skinned tangerine or mandarin orange.

naat *noun* M20 **Afrikaans** (= seam, from Dutch *naad*). An irregularity in the structure of a diamond caused by a change in direction in the grain; a diamond containing such an irregularity.

nabi *noun* plural (in sense 1) **nebiʿim**, (in sense 2) **nabis** (also **Nabi**) L19 **Hebrew** (*nābī* prophet). **1** L19 *Theology* A person inspired to speak the word of God; a prophet; *specifically* a prophetic writer of the Old Testament and Hebrew Scriptures. Also (in *plural*) = *the Prophets*. **2** M20 A member of a group of late nineteenth-century French post-impressionists following the artistic theories of the French painter Paul Gauguin (1848–1903).

nabla *noun* L19 **Greek** (= a kind of harp, probably of Semitic origin). *Mathematics* The symbolic differential operator in the shape of the inverted Greek capital letter delta Δ (hence often known under the abbreviation *del*).

nabob *noun* E17 **Portuguese** (*nababo* or Spanish *nabab* from Urdu *nawwāb*, *nawāb* deputy governor: cf. NAWAB). **1** E17 *History* (The title of) any of certain Muslim officials acting as deputy governors of provinces or districts in the Mughal Empire; a governor of an Indian town or district. **2** M18 A person of great wealth or (formerly) high rank; *specifically* a European returning from India with a large fortune acquired there.

nacarat *noun* M18 **French** (perhaps from Spanish and Portuguese *nacarado*, from *nacar* nacre). **1** M18 A bright orange red color. **2** M19 A fine linen fabric dyed in this color.

nacelle *noun* E20 **French** (from late Latin *navicella*, diminutive of Latin *navis* ship). **1** E20 The basket or car of a balloon or airship. **2** E20 Originally, the cockpit of an airplane. Now, a streamlined bulge on an aircraft's wing or fuselage enclosing an engine, etc. **3** M20 A similarly shaped structure on or in a motor vehicle.

■ In the core sense of 'a small boat', *nacelle* appears in Caxton's *Golden Legend* (1483), but it never achieved much currency in this sense, and seems not to have been used in English between the late fifteenth century and its modern reintroduction.

naches *noun* (also **nachas**) E20 **Yiddish** (*nakhes* from Hebrew *naḳat* contentment). A sense of pleasure or pride, especially at the achievements of one's children; joy, gratification.

Nachlass *noun* plural **Nachlasse**, **Nachlässe** M19 **German**. *singular* and (*rare*) in *plural*. Unpublished material left by an author after his or her death.

nacho *noun* plural **nachos** M20 (**Mexican**) **Spanish** (origin uncertain: perhaps from Mexican Spanish *Nacho* pet form of male forename *Ignacio*, but cf. Spanish *nacho* flat-nosed). A snack or appetizer consisting of fried tortilla chips covered in melted cheese, peppers, spices, etc.

■ Perhaps the invention of a Mexican chef, Ignacio Anaya, who worked in the Piedras Niegras area in the 1940s, the dish was originally found only in the northern Mexico–Texas area and did not spread much beyond there until the 1970s. Taken up by the fast-food chains in the 1980s, it is now a popular food item in Europe too. *Nacho* is always used in the plural except when attributive.

Nachschlag *noun* plural **Nachschläge** L19 **German** (from *nach* after + *Schlag* blow, note). *Music* A grace note taking its value from that of the note preceding it.

Nachtmaal variant of NAGMAAL.

Nacht und Nebel *noun phrase* M20 **German** (literally, 'night and fog'). A situation characterized by mystery or obscurity, especially as associated with Nazi Germany between 1941 and 1945.

nacre *noun* L16 **French** (probably ultimately of oriental origin). Mother-of-pearl.

nada *noun 1* E20 **Sanskrit** (*nāda* sound). *Hinduism* Inchoate or elemental sound considered as the source of all sounds and as a source of creation.

nada *noun 2* M20 **Spanish** (= nothing, from Latin (*res*) *nata* thing born, insignificant thing). Nothing; nothingness, nonexistence.

nadir *noun* LME **Old and Modern French** ((also Spanish, Italian) from Arabic *naẓīr* (*as-samt*) opposite (the zenith)). **1** LME–E18 *Astronomy* A point in the heavens diametrically opposite to some other point, especially to the sun. Followed by *of*, *to*. **2** L15 *Astronomy* The point of the heavens diametrically opposite to the zenith; the point directly below an observer. **3** L18 The lowest point (*of* something); the place or time of greatest depression or degradation.

naevus variant of NEVUS.

naga *noun* L18 **Sanskrit** (*nāga* serpent, snake). *Indian Mythology* A member of a race of semidivine creatures, half snake and half human, that are the genii of rain, rivers, etc.

nagana *noun* L19 **Zulu** (*nakane*). A disease of cattle, antelope, etc., in southern Africa, characterized by fever, lethargy, and edema caused by trypanosomes transmitted by tsetse flies.

Nagmaal *noun* (also (earlier) **Nachtmaal**) M19 **Afrikaans** (*nagmaal* (Dutch *nachtmaal*), from *nag* (Dutch *nacht*) night + *maal* meal). In South Africa: the usually quarterly celebration of the Eucharist in the Dutch Reformed church (an occasion of family reunions and celebration).

nahal *noun* M20 **Hebrew** (from initials of the name of the organization, *Nōʿar Ḥălūtzī Lōḥēm* Pioneer Military Youth). A military youth organization in Israel; an agricultural settlement manned by members of this organization.

naïf *adjective & noun* L16 **French** (see NAIVE). **A** *adjective* **1** L16 NAIVE sense 1. **b** M20 NAIVE sense 1b. **2** M–L17 Of a diamond: without an imperfection, flawless. *rare.* **B** *noun* L19 A naive person.

naive *adjective* (also **naïve**) M17 **Old and Modern French** (*naïve*, feminine of *naïf* from Latin *nativus* native; cf. NAÏF). **1** M17 Unaffected, unconsciously artless. Also, foolishly credulous, simple. **b** M20 Of art, etc.: straightforward in style, eschewing subtlety or conventional technique. **2** M20 *Biology* and *Psychology* Not having had a particular experience before, or been the subject of a particular experiment; lacking the knowledge to guess the purpose of an experiment; *especially* not having taken or received a particular drug. (Followed by *to*.)

naïveté *noun* L17 **French** (from as preceding). **1** L17 A naive action, remark, etc. **2** E18 The state or quality of being naive.

namaskar *noun* M20 **Hindi** (from Sanskrit *namaskāra*, from *namas* (see next) + *kāra* action). A traditional Hindu gesture of greeting made by bringing the palms together before the face or chest and bowing.

■ In Thailand a similar gesture is called *wai*.

namaste *noun, interjection, & verb* M20 **Hindi** (from Sanskrit *namas* bowing, obeisance + *te* dative of *tvam* you (singular)). **A** *noun* M20 A traditional Hindu greeting, a NAMASKAR. **B** *interjection* M20 Expressing respectful greeting (said when giving a namaskar). **C** *intransitive verb* M20 Give a namaskar.

nan *noun* (also **naan**) E20 **Persian and Urdu** (*nān*). In Indian cooking, a type of leavened bread cooked especially in a clay oven.

naos *noun* L18 **Greek** (= temple). (The inner cell or sanctuary of) a temple; also *Christian Church*, the main part of an Orthodox church where the congregation assembles (cf. BEMA, NARTHEX).

nappe *noun* L19 **French** (literally, 'tablecloth'). **1** L19 A sheet of water falling over a weir or similar surface. **2** E20 *Geology* A sheet of rock that has moved horizontally over neighboring strata, as a result of overthrusting or recumbent folding.

narcosis *noun* plural **narcoses** L17 **Greek** (*narkōsis*, from *narkoun* to make numb). *Medicine* The operation or effects of narcotics on the body; a state of insensibility or stupor, especially as induced by a drug; the production of this state. Also, therapeutic sleep artificially prolonged by the use of drugs.

narghile *noun* (also **narghileh**) M18 **Persian** (*nārgīl* coconut, hookah, from Sanskrit *nārikela* coconut; partly through French *nargileh*, *narguilé* from Turkish *nargile* from Persian *nārgīl*). A hookah.

narikin *noun* E20 **Japanese**. In Japan: a wealthy parvenu.

narod *noun* M20 **Russian**. In countries of the former USSR: the people; *specifically* the common people seen (in some ideologies) as the bearers of national culture.

■ The Narodnik movement was a type of socialism originating among the Russian intelligentsia in the nineteenth century that looked on the peasants and intelligentsia as revolutionary forces, rather than the urban working class. Supporters (*Narodniki*) endeavored to give political education to a community of rural or urban poor while sharing its living conditions.

narrischkeit *noun slang* L19 **Yiddish** (*naarishkeit*, *narrishkeit* from German *Närrischkeit*, from *närrisch* foolish, from *Narr* fool). Foolishness, nonsense.

narthex *noun* L17 **Latin** (from Greek *narthēx* giant fennel, stick, casket, narthex). An antechamber at the western end of some (especially early and Orthodox) churches, separate from the NAOS.

nasi *noun* L19 **Malay**. In Malaysian and Indonesian cooking: cooked rice.

naskhi *noun & adjective* (also **neskhi**) L18 **Arabic** (*naskī* (plural), from *na-*

saka to copy). (Designating) the standard Arabic script.

natatorium *noun* L19 **Late Latin** (noun use of *natatorius* of a swimmer). A swimming pool, *especially* an indoor swimming pool.

natura naturans *noun phrase* **E19 Latin** (Latin *natura* nature + medieval Latin *naturans* (present participle) creating, from *naturare). Philosophy* Nature as creative; the essential creative power or act. Cf. next.

natura naturata *noun phrase* **E19 Latin** (Latin *natura* nature + medieval Latin *naturata* (past participle) created, from *naturare*). *Philosophy* Nature as created; the natural phenomena and forces in which creation is manifested. Cf. preceding.

naturelle *adjective & noun* **L19 French** (feminine of *naturel* natural). (Of) a pale pink or beige color; skin-color(ed).

nature morte *noun phrase* plural **natures morte** **E20 French**. A still life.

■ Used as a descriptive term in French art since the eighteenth century.

Naturphilosophie *noun* **E19 German** (from *Natur* nature + *Philosophie* philosophy). The theory put forward, especially by Schelling (1775–1854) and other German philosophers, that there is an eternal and unchanging law of nature, proceeding from the absolute, from which all laws governing natural phenomena and forces derive.

naumachia *noun* plural **naumachiae**, **naumachias** **L16 Latin** (from Greek *naumakhia*, from *naus* ship + *makhē* fight). *Roman History* An imitation sea battle staged for entertainment; a place, especially a building enclosing a stretch of water, specially constructed for such a battle.

navarin *noun* **L19 French**. A casserole of mutton or lamb with (especially root) vegetables.

navarin printanier *noun phrase* plural **navarins printaniers** **E20 French** (= spring navarin). A navarin made with spring vegetables.

navette *noun* **E20 French** (= little boat, shuttle, from medieval Latin *naveta* diminutive of Latin *navis* ship). **1** E20 A cut of jewel in the shape of a pointed oval; a jewel cut in such a shape. **2** L20 A railroad truck designed to shuttle cars through a tunnel under the sea, *specifically* through the Channel Tunnel between England and France.

navicula *noun* plural **naviculae**, **naviculas** **M19 Latin** (diminutive of *navis* ship). *Ecclesiastical* An incense holder shaped like a boat.

nawab *noun* (also (as a title) **Nawab**) **M18 Urdu** (*nawāb* from Urdu, Persian *nawwāb* variant of *nuwwāb* plural (used as singular) of (Arabic) *nā'ib* deputy; cf. NABOB). (The title of) a governor or nobleman in the Indian subcontinent (*historical*); (the title of) a distinguished Muslim in the Indian subcontinent.

NB abbreviation of NOTA BENE.

né *adjective* **M20 French** (= born, masculine past participle of *naître* to be born). Born with the name, originally called: placed before the name by which a man was originally known.

■ Much more usual in the feminine NÉE.

nebbish *noun & adjective* (also **nebbich**) **L19 Yiddish** (*nebech* poor thing). **A** *noun* L19 A nobody, a nonentity, a submissive timid person. Also as *interjection*, expressing commiseration, dismay, etc. **B** *adjective* M20 Of a person: innocuous, ineffectual; timid, submissive. *colloquial*.

nebelwerfer *noun* **M20 German** (from *Nebel* mist, fog + *Werfer* thrower, mortar, from *werfen* to throw). A six-barreled rocket mortar used by the German forces in World War II.

nebula *noun* plural **nebulae**, **nebulas** **M17 Latin** (= mist, vapor). **1 a** M17 A film or clouded spot on or over the cornea of the eye. Now only *Medicine*. **b** M18 A cloud, (a) cloudlike appearance; an indistinct, insubstantial, or nebulous thing or *(figurative)* person. **2** E18 *Astronomy* A hazy or indistinct luminous area in the night sky representing a distant cluster of stars. Now usually *specifically*, a cloud of gas, dust, etc., in deep space.

nebulé *adjective* (also **nebuly**) M16 French (*nébulé* from medieval Latin *nebulatus* past participle of *nebulare* to cloud). **1** M16 *Heraldry* Of a particular wavy form, used to represent clouds. **2** M19 *Architecture* Of a molding: of a wavy form.

nécessaire *noun* E19 French. A small usually ornamental case for pencils, scissors, tweezers, etc.

necessarium *noun* plural **necessaria**, **necessariums** M19 Medieval Latin (noun use of neuter singular of *necessarius* (probably after accusative (*locum*) *necessarium* necessary (place)) from Latin *necessarius*). A privy, a toilet, especially in a monastic building.

necrosis *noun* plural **necroses** M17 Modern Latin (from Greek *nekrōsis* state of death, from *nekroun* to kill, mortify). *Medicine* and *Biology* The death or decay of (part of) an organ or tissue due to disease, injury, or deficiency of nutrients; mortification.

née *adjective* (also **nee**) M18 French (= born, feminine past participle of *naître* be born; cf. NÉ). **1** M18 Born with the name. **2** M20 *transferred* Formerly called.

■ Normally follows a woman's married name to indicate her family name before she married, as in "Julia Smith *née* Jones."

negligée *noun* (also **negligee**, **négligé**) M18 French (*négligé* past participle of *négliger* neglect). **1** M18 *History* A kind of loose gown worn by women in the eighteenth century. **2** M19 Informal, unceremonious, or incomplete attire. **3** E20 A shroud. **4** M20 A woman's light dressing gown, *especially* one of flimsy semitransparent fabric trimmed with ruffles, lace, etc.

négociant *noun* E20 French (= merchant (sc. *des vins*), from *négoce*, from Latin *negotium* business). A wine merchant.

Negritude *noun* (also **Négritude**, **negritude**) M20 French (*négritude* from Latin *nigritudo*, from *niger*, *nigr-* black). The quality or characteristic of being a Negro (black); affirmation of the value of black or African culture, identity, etc.

nekulturny *adjective* M20 Russian (*nekul'turnyĭ* uncivilized, from *ne-* not + KULTURNY). In countries of the former USSR: not having cultured manners, uncivilized, boorish.

nembutsu *noun* M20 Japanese (from *nen* thought + *butsu* Buddha). In Japanese Buddhism, the invocation and repetition of the name of the Buddha Amida for the purpose of salvation and spiritual unity; this invocation.

nem. con. *adverb phrase* L16 Latin (abbreviation of *nemine contradicente*). With no one contradicting.

■ *Nemine contradicente* (M17) is very seldom found in English.

nem. diss. *adverb phrase* L18 Latin (abbreviation of *nemine dissentiente*). With no one dissenting.

■ *Nemine dissentiente* is not used in English in its full form.

nemesis *noun* (also **Nemesis**) plural **nemeses** L16 Greek (= righteous indignation, personified as the goddess of retribution or vengeance, from *nemein* to deal out what is due, related to *nomos* custom, law). **1** L16 An agent of retribution; a person who avenges or punishes. **b** M20 A persistent tormentor; a long-standing rival or enemy. **2** L16 (An instance of) retributive justice.

nemine contradicente see NEM. CON.

nemine dissentiente see NEM. DISS.

nepenthes *noun* L16 Latin (from Greek *nēpenthes* neuter of *nēpenthēs* banishing pain (qualifying *pharmakon* drug), from *nē-* not + *penthos* grief). **1** L16 A drug mentioned in Homer's *Odyssey* (iv.221) as liberating the mind from grief or trouble; any drug or potion bringing welcome forgetfulness. Also, a plant yielding such a drug. **2** M18 Any of various frequently climbing pitcher plants of the genus *Nepenthes*, chiefly of Southeast Asia.

ne plus ultra *noun phrase* M17 **Latin** (= not further beyond). **1** M17 A prohibition of further advance or action; an impassable obstacle or limitation. **2** L17 The furthest limit reached or attainable; *especially* the point of highest attainment, the acme or highest point *of* a quality, etc.

■ The inscription imagined by the inhabitants of the ancient Mediterranean world to be on the Pillars of Hercules (Strait of Gibraltar), prohibiting further westward passage by ships.

neroli *noun* L17 **French** (*néroli*, from Italian *neroli* after an Italian princess of that name, to whom its discovery is attributed). An essential oil distilled from the flowers of the Seville orange and used in perfumery. Also *neroli oil, oil of neroli*.

neskhi variant of NASKHI.

netsuke *noun* plural **netsukes**, same. L19 **Japanese**. A small piece of ivory, wood, or other material, carved or otherwise decorated, formerly worn by Japanese on a cord suspending articles from a girdle.

Neue Sachlichkeit *noun phrase* E20 **German** (literally, 'new objectivity'). A movement in the fine arts, music, and literature, that developed in Germany during the 1920s and was characterized by realism and a deliberate rejection of romantic attitudes. Cf. SACHLICHKEIT.

neurosis *noun* plural **neuroses** M18 **Modern Latin** (from Greek *neuron* nerve). **1** M18 *Psychology* (A) mild mental illness, not attributable to organic disease, characterized by symptoms of stress such as anxiety, depression, obsessive behavior, hypochondria, etc., without loss of contact with reality. **2** E20 Any more or less specific anxiety or malaise experienced by an individual, group, nation, etc.

névé *noun* M19 **Swiss French** (from Latin *nix, niv-* snow). The crystalline or granular snow on the upper part of a glacier, that has not yet been compressed into ice. Also, a field or bed of this. Also called FIRN.

nevus *noun* (also **naevus**) plural **naevi** M19 **Latin**. *Medicine* A congenital reddish or brown mark or (usually) raised blemish on the skin, *especially* a hemangiona; a birthmark, a mole.

nexus *noun* plural same, **nexes** M17 **Latin** (from *nex-* past participial stem of *nectere* to bind). **1** M17 A connection; a bond, a link. **b** E20 *Grammar* A group of words (with or without a verb) expressing a predicative relation. **2** M19 A connected group or series; a network.

ngoma *noun* E20 **Kiswahili** ((also *goma*) drum, dance, music). In East Africa: a dance; a night of dancing.

nibbana *noun* E20 **Pali** (*nibbāna*, Sanskrit *nirvāṇa* nirvana). *Buddhism* NIRVANA.

niche *noun* E17 **Old and Modern French** (from Old French *nichier* (modern *nicher*) to make a nest, nestle, from Proto-Romance from Latin *nidus* nest). **1** E17 An artificially constructed wall recess; *specifically* a shallow ornamental recess for a statue, urn, etc. **b** M19 A natural hollow in a rock or hill. **c** E20 A MIHRAB motif on an oriental prayer rug. More fully *prayer niche*. **2** *figurative* **a** E18 A place or position suited to or intended for a person's capabilities, occupation, or status. **b** E18 A place of safety or retreat. **c** E20 *Ecology* A position or role taken by a kind of organism within its community. **d** M20 *Commerce* A position from which an opening in a market, etc., can be exploited; *especially* a specialized but profitable segment of a commercial market.

nicht wahr *interjection* E20 **German** (literally, 'not true'). Is it not true? Isn't that so?

Niçois *adjective* (feminine **Niçoise**) L19 **French** (= of Nice, a city in southern France). Of, pertaining to, or characteristic of Nice or its inhabitants;

specifically in *Cooking*, designating food, especially garnished with tomatoes, capers, anchovies, etc., characteristic of Nice or the surrounding region.

■ Generally postpositive, as in *salade Niçoise*.

niello *noun* plural **nielli**, **niellos** E19 **Italian** (from Latin *nigellus* diminutive of *niger* black). **1** A black composition of sulfer with silver, lead, or copper, for filling engraved designs on silver or other metals. **2** M19 (A specimen of) such ornamental work; an article decorated with niello. **3** M19 An impression on paper of a design to be filled with niello. **b** *transitive verb* M19 Inlay with niello. Chiefly as *nielloed* participial adjective.

nien hao *noun* plural same, **nien haos** L19 **Chinese** (*niánhào*, literally, 'reign year'). A title given to (part of) the reign of a Chinese emperor, used in imperial China as a system of dating. Also, a mark (signifying the reign of a particular emperor) used on Chinese pottery or porcelain to indicate an object's period of manufacture.

niente *noun, adverb, & adjective* E19 **Italian**. **A** *noun* E19 Nothing. **B** *adverb & adjective* E20 *Music* (A direction:) with gradual fading away of the sound or tone to nothing.

■ In nineteenth-century use the noun apparently existed in English only in the phrase (DOLCE) FAR NIENTE.

niet variant of NYET.

nihil obstat *noun phrase* M20 **Latin** (literally, 'nothing hinders' (the censor's formula of approval)). A certificate or statement recording that a work has been approved by the Roman Catholic church as free of doctrinal or moral error; a statement of official approval, authorization.

nil admirari *noun* M18 **Latin** (= to wonder at nothing). An attitude of imperturbability or indifference to the distractions of the outside world.

■ A stance advocated by the Roman poet Horace in the opening lines of one of his *Epistles* (I.vi.1): *nil admirari prope res est una . . . solaque quae possit facere et servare beatum* 'to wonder at nothing is just about the only way a man can become contented and remain so'.

nilas *noun* M20 **Russian**. Partly refrozen ice forming a thin flexible layer on the surface of water.

nil desperandum *interjection* E17 **Latin** (= no need to despair). Do not despair, never despair.

■ From Horace *Odes* I.vii.27: *nil desperandum Teucro duce et auspice Teucro*) 'no need to despair with Teucer as your leader and Teucer to protect you'.

nimbi plural of NIMBUS.

nimbu-pani *noun* M20 **Hindustani** (*nimbū* lime, lemon + *pānī* water). A drink of the Indian subcontinent consisting of lemon juice or lime juice with sugar and ice or water.

nimbus *noun* plural **nimbi**, **nimbuses** E17 **Latin** (= cloud, rain, aureole). **1** E17 A bright or luminous cloud or cloudlike formation investing a god, etc.; *transferred* a cloud of fine particles or other matter surrounding a person or thing. **2** E18 (A representation of) a halo surrounding the head of Jesus, a saint, etc. **3** E19 *Meteorology* A rain cloud. Now *rare*.

ninja *noun* plural same M20 **Japanese** (= spy). A person, especially a Japanese samurai, expert in NINJUTSU.

■ The word was little known in the West until the rise of interest in oriental martial arts in 1970s. *Ninjas* then began to play a role in fantasy and computer games but it was the huge popular and commercial success of the children's comic book characters the Teenage Mutant Ninja Turtles in the United States at the end of the 1980s that brought the word into a wider circulation.

ninjutsu *noun* M20 **Japanese** (from *nin* stealth, invisibility + *jutsu* art, science). The traditional Japanese technique of espionage, developed in feudal times for military purposes and subsequently used in the training of samurai.

Niño, el see EL NIÑO.

ninon *noun & adjective* E20 **French. A** *noun* E20 A lightweight dress fabric of silk, nylon, etc. **B** *attributive* or as *adjective* E20 Made of ninon.

nirvana *noun* **M19 Sanskrit** (*nirvāṇa* use as noun of past participle of *nirvā-* to be extinguished, from *nis-* out + *vā-* to blow). In *Buddhism*, the experience that comes to a person in life when greed, hatred, and delusion are extinguished and enlightenment gained; the release from the effects of KARMA and the cycle of death and rebirth that comes when an enlightened person dies. In *Hinduism* and *Jainism*, liberation of the soul from the effects of karma and from bodily existence. Also *figurative* a state of bliss, an ideal state.

nisei *noun* plural same **M20 Japanese** (from *ni-* second + *sei* generation). An American whose parents were immigrants from Japan. Cf. SANSEI.

nisi *postpositive adjective* **M19 Latin** (= unless). *Law* That takes effect only on certain conditions, not final.

■ Generally in the phrase *decree nisi* 'a provisional order for divorce that will be made absolute unless cause to the contrary can be shown within a fixed period'.

nitchevo *interjection & noun* **E20 Russian** (*nichego*). **A** *interjection* E20 In Russian: Never mind! It does not matter! **B** *noun* M20 The use of the word 'nitchevo'; an attitude of resignation or fatalism.

noblesse *noun* **ME Old and Modern French** (from Latin *nobilis*). **1** ME Noble birth or rank; nobility, nobleness. **2** L15 *The* nobility; a class of people of noble rank, now especially in a foreign country.

■ The most usual occurrence in English is of sense 1 in NOBLESSE OBLIGE; *petite noblesse* (sense 2) is used of the minor nobility of France.

noblesse oblige *noun phrase* **M19 French.** (The principle that) noble ancestry and privilege entail responsibility.

noceur *noun* E20 **French.** A reveler, a rake, a libertine; a person who stays up late at night.

nockerl *noun* plural **nockerln** **M19 Austrian German** (= little dumpling). A small light Austrian and Bavarian dumpling, made with a batter including eggs, and usually semolina.

■ A *Salzburger nockerl* is a sweetened version eaten as a dessert.

nocturne *noun* **M19 French. 1** M19 A musical composition of a dreamy character. **2** L19 A painting of a night scene, a night piece.

noel *noun* (also **noël**) **E19 French** (*noël*). A Christmas carol.

noema *noun* plural **noemata** **E20 Greek** (*noēma* thought). *Philosophy* An object of perception or thought, as opposed to a process or aspect of perceiving or thinking. Cf. NOESIS 3.

noesis *noun* plural **noeses** **L19 Greek** (*noēsis*, from *noein* to think, perceive). **1** L19 Mental capacity or action. *rare.* **2** L19 An intellectual view of the moral and physical world. *rare.* **3** M20 *Philosophy.* A process or aspect of perceiving or thinking, as opposed to an object of perception or thought. Cf. NOEMA.

nogaku *noun* **E20 Japanese** (*nōgaku*, from *nō* Noh + *gaku* music). Noh as a dramatic form or genre.

Noh *noun* (also **No**) **L19 Japanese** (*nō* (also = talent, accomplishment)). The traditional Japanese masked drama with dance and song, evolved from Shinto rites.

noia *noun* **M20 Italian** (ultimately from Latin *in odio*; cf. ENNUI). Boredom, weariness, ennui.

noir *adjective & noun* **LME French. 1** LME Black. **2** L18 Black as one of the two colors of divisions in rouge et noir and roulette. Earliest in *rouge et noir.*

■ Sense 1 is rare in English except in or with reference to the cinematic genre of FILM NOIR or, by extension, black humor in other media (see ROMAN NOIR). It occurs in its literal meaning in a few phrases such as *pinot noir* (a variety of black grape) and figuratively in EN NOIR.

noisette *noun* L19 French (diminutive of NOIX nut). A small round piece of meat.

noix *noun* plural same M19 French (literally, 'nut'; cf. NOISETTE). A piece of veal cut from the rump. Also *noix de veau.*

nolens volens *adverb phrase* L16 Latin (present participles of *nolo, nolle* to be unwilling, and *volo, velle* to be willing). Willing or unwilling, whether willing or not, willy-nilly.

noli me tangere *noun* LME Latin (= do not touch me). **1** LME *Medicine* An ulcerous condition attacking bone and soft tissues especially of the face: *specifically* lupus. Now *rare* or *obsolete.* **2** LME A person who or thing that must not be touched or interfered with. **3** M16–M18 *Botany* A balsam or impatiens the seed capsules of which burst open on a touch; *specifically Impatiens noli-tangere,* touch-me-not. **4** M17 A warning or prohibition against meddling or interference. **5** L17 A painting representing the appearance of Jesus to Mary Magdalen at the sepulcher (John 20:17).

■ The original injunction is the Vulgate version of the risen Christ's warning to Mary Magdalen when He appears to her outside the sepulcher (John 20:17).

nolle prosequi *noun* L17 Latin (= be unwilling to pursue). *Law* (Originally, now *United States*) the relinquishment by a plaintiff or prosecutor of part or all of his or her suit or prosecution; (later) a procedure by which the Attorney General can terminate criminal proceedings. Also, an entry of this in a court record.

■ Also abbreviated to *nolle* in the United States (L19).

nolo contendere *noun* L19 Latin (= I do not wish to contend). *United States Law* A plea by which a defendant in a criminal prosecution accepts conviction as in the case of a plea of guilty but does not admit guilt.

nom de guerre *noun phrase* plural **noms de guerre** L17 French (= war name). An assumed name under which a person fights or engages in some other action or enterprise.

nom de plume *noun phrase* plural **noms de plume** E19 pseudo-French (formed from *nom* name, *de* of, *plume* pen, after *nom de guerre*). An assumed name under which a person writes, a pen name.

nom de théâtre *noun phrase* plural **noms de théâtre** L19 French (= theater name). An assumed name under which a person performs on stage.

nomen dubium *noun phrase* plural **nomina dubia** E20 Latin (= doubtful name). *Taxonomy* A Latin name the correct application of which is vague or uncertain.

nomenklatura *noun* M20 Russian (from Latin *nomenclatura* list of names). In the former Soviet Union: a list of influential positions in government and industry to be filled by Party appointees; *collectively* the holders of these positions, the Soviet elite; also *transferred.*

nomen nudum *noun phrase* plural **nomina nuda** E20 Latin (= naked name). *Taxonomy* A Latin name that has no standing because it was not validly published.

nominata plural of NOMINATUM.

nominatim *adverb* M19 Latin (from *nomen, nomin-* name). Chiefly *Law* By name; particularly, expressly.

nominatum *noun* plural **nominata** M20 Latin (neuter of *nominatus*). The thing named by a sign or expression.

nominis umbra *noun phrase* M19 Latin (literally, 'the shadow or appearance of a name'). A name without substance; a thing that is not what the name implies.

■ The phrase comes from Lucan's *Pharsalia* (i. 135): *Stat magni nominis umbra* 'he stands the mere shadow of a mighty name'.

nomos *noun* M20 **Greek** (= usage, custom, law). *Theology* The law; the law of life.

noms de guerre, noms de plume, etc., plurals of NOM DE GUERRE, NOM DE PLUME, etc.

non *noun* L20 **French** (= no). In France and French-speaking countries: an utterance of 'non', an absolute refusal or veto.

nonchalance *noun* L17 **Old and Modern French** (see next). The state of being nonchalant; lack of enthusiasm or interest; casual indifference, unconcern.

nonchalant *adjective* M18 **Old and Modern French** (from *non* + *chalant* present participle of *chaloir* to be concerned). Calm and casual; lacking or showing no enthusiasm or interest.

non compos mentis *adjective phrase* E17 **Latin.** Not in one's right mind. Cf. COMPOS MENTIS.

■ Almost always predicative and often shortened to *non compos* (also E17).

non est *adjective phrase* L19 **Latin** (abbreviated from *non est inventus* he was not found). Nonexistent, absent.

■ *Non est inventus* (L15) was the legal name formerly given to a sheriff's statement in returning a writ, to the effect that the defendant was not to be found within the sheriff's jurisdiction.

non est factum *noun phrase* E17 **Latin** (= it was not done). *Law* A plea that a written agreement is invalid because the defendant was mistaken about its character when signing it. Long chiefly *United States*.

non nobis *interjection* E19 **Latin** (= not to us). Expressing humble gratitude or thanksgiving; disclaiming credit for a success or benefit.

■ In the Vulgate *Non nobis, Domine, non nobis* 'Not to us, O Lord, not to us' is part of a verse of Psalm 113; in the English Bible the words form the opening of Psalm 115.

non obstante *noun* (also **non-obstante**) LME **Medieval Latin** (*non obstante* not being in the way, from *non* not + *obstante* ablative present participle of *obstare* to be in the way (originally in ablative absolute, as *non obstante veredicto* notwithstanding the verdict)). **1** LME *History* A clause in a statute or letter patent, beginning 'non obstante', and conveying a dispensation from a monarch to perform an action despite any statute to the contrary. Also, a similar clause issued by the Pope. In full *clause of non-obstante*. **2** E17–M18 *generally* A dispensation from or relaxation of a law or rule (followed by *on, of, to*). Also, an exception to a rule.

nonpareil *adjective & noun* LME **French** (from *non-* + *pareil* like, equal, from popular Latin *pariculus* diminutive of Latin *par*). **A** *adjective* LME Having no equal; unrivaled, unique. **B** *noun* **1** L15 A person or thing having no equal; an unrivaled or unique person or thing. **2** M18 An old variety of apple. **3 a** M18 The painted bunting, *Passerina ciris*. **b** M18 The eastern rosella, *Platycercus eximius*. More fully *nonpareil parrot*. Chiefly *Australian*. **4** M18 Any of several attractively patterned moths.

■ Formerly also a size of type roughly equivalent to modern 6 point (L17) and a kind of candy (L17).

non placet *noun & verb phrase* (as verb also **non-placet**) L16 **Latin** (= it does not please). **A** *noun* L16 Originally, an expression of dissent or disapproval. Later, a negative vote in a university or church assembly. **B** *transitive verb* E19 Give a negative vote on (a proposition); reject (a measure).

■ A formula used especially in university and church assemblies in giving a negative vote on a proposition.

nonplus *noun & verb* L16 **Latin** (from *non plus* not more, no further). **A** *noun* L16 A state in which no more can be said or done; inability to proceed in speech or action; a state of perplexity; a standstill. Chiefly in *at a nonplus, bring* or *reduce to a nonplus*. **B** *transitive* *verb* L16 (inflected *-ss-*) Bring (a person, etc.) to a nonplus; perplex; make (a thing) ineffective or inoperative. Frequently as *nonplussed* participial adjective.

non plus ultra *noun phrase* L17 **Latin** (= not more beyond). A NE PLUS ULTRA, the highest point or culmination *of*.

non sequitur *noun* M16 **Latin** (literally, 'it does not follow'). An inference or conclusion not logically following from the premises; a response, remark, etc., not logically following from what has gone before.

■ Earliest in a rare and obsolete use (only LME) for part of the collar of a shirt, etc.; an unfastened collar.

nori *noun* L19 **Japanese**. Edible seaweed of the genus *Porphyra*, eaten especially by the Japanese either fresh or dried in sheets.

noria *noun* L18 **Spanish** (from Arabic *nāy'ūra*). Especially in Spain and the East: a device for raising water from a stream, etc., consisting of a chain of pots or buckets, revolving around a wheel driven by the water current.

norte *noun* M19 **Spanish** (= north). Any of the violent gales from the north prevailing in the Gulf of Mexico from September to March. Usually in *plural*.

norteamericano *noun & adjective* plural of noun **norteamericanos** (also **Norteamericano**, feminine **norteamericana**) E20 **Spanish and Portuguese** (from *norte* north + *americano* American). Especially in Latin America, (a native or inhabitant) of North America, a North American.

nosh *noun & verb* E20 **Yiddish** (cf. German *naschen* to nibble). **A** *noun* **1** E20 A restaurant; a snack bar. More fully *nosh bar, nosh house*. **2** M20 Food, a meal. **3** M20 A snack eaten between meals, a tidbit. **B** *transitive and intransitive verb* **1** M20 Nibble or eat (a snack); eat (food), especially heartily or greedily. **2** M20 Perform fellatio (with on). *slang*.

nostalgie de la boue *noun phrase* L19 **French** (literally, 'yearning for mud'). A desire for degradation and depravity.

nostos *noun* plural **nostoi** L19 **Greek**. A homecoming, a homeward journey, *specifically* of Odysseus and the other heroes from Troy. Also, an account of such a homecoming or homeward journey, especially as the conclusion of a literary work. *literary*.

■ *Nost(o)i* was the title of an ancient Greek poem, now lost, dealing with the homecomings of the Greek heroes after the Trojan War.

nostrum *noun* plural **nostrums**, **nostra** E17 **Latin** (neuter singular of *noster* our). **1** E17 A quack remedy, a patent medicine, *especially* one prepared by the person recommending it. **2** M18 A pet scheme, a favorite remedy, especially for bringing about social or political reform or improvement.

nota bene *verb phrase transitive & intransitive* (*imperative*) E18 **Latin** (from *nota* note + *bene* well). Mark well, observe particularly (usually drawing attention to a following qualification of what has preceded).

■ In general use in the abbreviated form *NB*.

notabilia *noun plural* M19 **Latin** (neuter plural of *notabilis* notable, after MEMORABILIA). Things worthy of note.

notes inégales *noun phrase plural* E20 **French** (literally, 'unequal notes'). *Music* In baroque music, notes performed by convention in a rhythm different from that shown in the score.

note verbale *noun phrase* plural **notes verbales** M19 **French** (literally, 'verbal note'). An unsigned diplomatic note, of the nature of a memorandum, written in the third person.

notitia *noun* E18 **Latin** (= knowledge, (in late Latin) list, account, etc., from *notus* known). **1** Knowledge, detailed information. *rare*. Only in E18. **2** L18

An account, a list; *specifically* a register or list of ecclesiastical sees or districts.

nougat *noun* (also (earlier) **nogat**) E19 **French** (from Provençal *nogat*, from *noga* nut, from Latin *nux*). (A candy made from) egg white sweetened with sugar or honey and mixed with nuts and sometimes pieces of fruit.

nouille *noun* M19 **French**. Noodle. Usually in *plural*.

noumenon *noun* plural **noumena** L18 **German** (from Greek, noun use of neuter present participle passive of *noien* to apprehend, conceive). An object of purely intellectual intuition, devoid of all phenomenal attributes.

■ Chiefly in the philosophy of Immanuel Kant (1724–1804); cf. DING AN SICH.

nous *noun* (also **nouse**) L17 **Greek**. **1** L17 *Greek Philosophy* Intuitive apprehension, intelligence; mind, intellect. **2** E18 Common sense, practical intelligence, gumption. *colloquial*.

nous autres *personal pronoun (1st plural)* M19 **French** (literally 'we others'). We as opposed to somebody or anybody else.

nouveau *adjective & noun* E20 **French** (= new). **A** *adjective* **1** E20 *Nouveau art* = ART NOUVEAU. **2** M20 Of a person: possessing recently acquired wealth, NOUVEAU RICHE; ostentatiously displaying such wealth. Of wealth, etc.: recently acquired. **b** L20 *Nouveau poor* = NOUVEAU PAUVRE. **3** L20 Modern, up to date. **B** *noun* plural **nouveaus, nouveaux**. **1** L20 A *nouveau riche*. Usually in *plural*. **2** L20 BEAUJOLAIS NOUVEAU. *colloquial*.

■ *Nouveau* seldom occurs independently in English, but is used elliptically and colloquially for such phrases as *Beaujolais nouveau*, etc., the context making plain the meaning intended.

nouveau pauvre *adjective & noun phrase* plural **nouveaux pauvres** M20 **French** (literally, 'new poor', after NOUVEAU RICHE). **A** *adjective* M20 Of a person: newly impoverished. **B** *noun* L20 A person who has recently become poor.

nouveau riche *noun & adjective phrase* plural **nouveaux riches** E19 **French** (literally, 'new rich'). **A** *noun* E19 A person who has recently acquired wealth, *especially* one who displays the fact ostentatiously or vulgarly. **B** *attributive* or as *adjective* L19 Of, pertaining to, or characteristic of a *nouveau riche*; that has recently acquired wealth.

nouveau roman *noun phrase* M20 **French** (literally, 'new novel'). A type of (especially French) novel characterized by precise descriptions of characters' mental states and absence of interpretation of or comment on them.

nouveaux plural of NOUVEAU.

nouveaux arrivés *noun phrase plural* L19 **French** (literally, 'new arrivals'). People who have recently acquired a higher financial and social standing.

nouveaux pauvres, nouveaux riches plurals of NOUVEAU PAUVRE, NOUVEAU RICHE.

nouvelle *noun* L17 **French**. A short fictitious narrative, a short novel, *especially* one dealing with a single situation or a single aspect of a character or characters.

nouvelle *adjective* L18 **French** (feminine of NOUVEAU; in sense 2 elliptical for NOUVELLE CUISINE). **1** L18 *generally* New, novel. Now *rare*. **2** L20 Of, pertaining to, or characteristic of *nouvelle cuisine*.

nouvelle cuisine *noun phrase* L20 **French** (literally, 'new cooking'). A style of (especially French) cooking that avoids traditional rich sauces and emphasizes the freshness of the ingredients and attractive presentation.

■ The fashion for *nouvelle cuisine* spread beyond France in the 1970s and early 1980s, and its characteristics of lightness, short cooking times, and small helpings continued to endear it to the healthy eating lobby. In the hands of pretentious practitioners, however, the fashionable extremes of artistic presentation and meagerness of quantity have incurred considerable ridicule.

nouvelles plural of NOUVELLE.

nouvelle vague *noun phrase* M20 **French** (literally, 'new wave'; cf. VAGUE). A new movement or trend; *specifically* that in filmmaking originating in France in the late 1950s.

nova *noun* plural **novae**, **novas** L19 **Latin** (feminine singular of *novus* new). *Astronomy* Originally, a new star or nebula. Now *specifically* a star whose brightness suddenly increases by several magnitudes, with violent ejection of gaseous material, and then decreases more or less gradually. Formerly also, a supernova.

■ The present astronomical term is a reintroduction, as *nova* was originally (L17) used in the rare and obsolete sense of 'a thick ring or roll of tobacco'.

novella *noun* E20 **Italian**. A short fictitious prose narrative, a short novel, a long short story.

■ The word was particularly applied to the tales in Boccaccio's *Decameron* and its Italian imitators before being transferred to a work in any language midway in length between a full-scale novel and a short story.

novena *noun* plural **novenae**, **novenas** M19 **Medieval Latin** (from *novem* nine, after Latin *novenarius* of nine days). *Roman Catholic Church* A devotion consisting of special prayers or services on nine successive days.

novi homines plural of NOVUS HOMO.

novillada *noun* plural **novilladas** L19 **Spanish** (from NOVILLO). A bullfight in which three-year-old bulls are fought by novice matadors.

novillero *noun* plural **novilleros** E20 **Spanish** (from NOVILLO). An apprentice matador who has fought only in NOVILLADAS.

novillo *noun* plural **novillos** M19 **Spanish** (from Latin *novellus* new). A young bull; *specifically* a fighting bull not more than three years old.

novio *noun* plural **novios** E20 **Spanish**. In Spain and Spanish-speaking countries: a boyfriend, a lover.

novus homo *noun phrase* plural **novi homines** L16 **Latin** (literally, 'new man'). A man who has recently risen to a position of importance from insignificance; an upstart.

■ In ancient Rome, the phrase was specifically applied to the first man in a particular family to rise to the office of a magistrate.

noxa *noun* plural **noxae** L19 **Latin** (= hurt, damage). *Medicine* A thing harmful to the body.

noyade *noun* plural **noyades** E19 **French** (from *noyer* to drown, from Latin *necare* kill without a weapon, (later) drown, from *nex*, *nec-* slaughter). An execution carried out by drowning, especially a mass one as in France in 1794.

noyau *noun* plural **noyaux** L18 **French** (earlier *noiel* kernel, from Proto-Romance noun use of neuter of late Latin *nucalis*, from *nux*, *nuc-* nut). **1** L18 A liqueur made of brandy flavored with the kernels of certain fruits. **2** E20 A type of candy similar to nougat.

nritta *noun* E20 **Sanskrit** (*nṛtta* dancing). A type of Indian dance with abstract patterns of movement and neutral facial expressions.

nritya *noun* L19 **Sanskrit** (*nṛtya* dance, mime). A type of Indian dance through which ideas or emotions are expressed.

nuance *noun & verb* L18 **French** (from *nuer* to show cloudlike variations in color, from *nue* cloud, from popular Latin variant of Latin *nubes*). **A** *noun* L18 A slight or subtle variation in or shade of meaning, expression, color, etc. **B** *transitive verb* L19 Give a nuance or nuances to.

nuancé *adjective* M20 **French** (from as preceding). Having or characterized by nuances.

nucleus *noun* plural **nuclei**, **nucleuses** E18 **Latin** (= nut, kernel, inner part, variant of *nuculeus*, from *nucula* diminutive of *nux*, *nuc-* nut). **1** E18 *Astronomy* The dense core of the head of a comet. **b** L18 A dense, usually bright, central part in a galaxy or nebula. **2** M18 The central part or thing around which others are grouped or collected; the center or kernel of an aggregate or mass; an initial part or collection of things to which others may be added.

■ Besides its initial astronomical sense, *nucleus* has acquired a large number of specialist senses in a variety of subject fields: Anatomy (E19), Archaeology (M19), Biology (M19), Chemistry (M19), Beekeeping (L19), Physics (E20), and Linguistics (E20).

nudnik *noun* (also **nudnick**) M20 **Yiddish** (from Russian *nudnyĭ* tedious, boring + noun suffix *-nik* person connected with (something)). A pestering, nagging, or irritating person; a bore. *slang*.

nuée ardente *noun phrase* plural **nuées ardentes** E20 **French** (literally, 'burning cloud'). *Geology* A hot dense cloud of ash and fragmented lava suspended in a mass of gas, typically ejected from the side of the dome of certain volcanoes and flowing downhill like an avalanche.

■ The phrase was introduced into formal vulcanology in 1903 by A. Lacroix, who subsequently observed (in *La Montagne Pelée et ses eruptions* (1904)) that the expression had earlier been in use among the inhabitants of San Jorge in the Azores. While Lacroix said that by *nuée ardente* he meant *brulant* 'burning' rather than *incandescent* 'glowing', the phrase is nonetheless usually rendered in English as 'glowing cloud'.

nugae *noun plural* E18 **Latin**. Trifles.

■ Chiefly in NUGAE DIFFICILES.

nugae difficiles *noun plural phrase* E18 **Latin** (= difficult trifles). *Philosophy* Matters of trifling importance occupying a disproportionate amount of time owing to their difficulty.

nuit blanche *noun phrase* plural **nuits blanches** M19 **French** (literally, 'white night'). A sleepless night.

nulla bona *noun phrase* E19 **Latin** (= no goods). The return made by a sheriff upon an execution when the party has no goods to be distrained.

nulli secundus *adjective phrase* (also **nulli secundum**) M19 **Latin**. Second to none.

numdah *noun* E19 **Urdu** (*namdā* from Persian *namad* felt, carpet, rug). **1** E19 In the Indian subcontinent and the Middle East: a kind of felt or coarse woolen cloth, frequently embroidered; a rug or carpet made from this (also *numdah rug*). **2** L19 A NUMNAH.

numen *noun* plural **numina** E17 **Latin** (related to *nuere* to nod, Greek *neuein* to incline the head). Divinity; a local or presiding god.

numéro *noun* plural **numéros** E20 **French**. A person or thing having a place in a series, a number. Also, a remarkable or strange person.

numero uno *noun phrase* plural **numero unos** L20 **Italian and Spanish** (= number one). The best or most important person.

numerus clausus *noun phrase* E20 **Latin** (literally, 'closed number'). A fixed maximum number of entrants admissible to an academic institution.

numina plural of NUMEN.

numnah *noun* M19 **Urdu** (*namdā* from Persian *namad* felt, carpet, rug; a variant of NUMDAH). A saddle cloth; a pad placed under a saddle to prevent soreness.

nunatak *noun* L19 **Eskimo** ((Greenlandic) *nunataq*). An isolated peak of rock projecting above a surface of inland ice or snow in Greenland, Norway, etc.

nunc dimittis *noun phrase* M16 **Latin** (= now you let (your servant) depart). **1** M16 A canticle forming part of the Christian liturgy at evensong and compline, comprising the song of Simeon in Luke 2:29–32 (in the Vulgate beginning *Nunc dimittis, Domine*). **2** L16 Permission to depart; dismissal.

nunchaku *noun* L20 **Japanese** (from Okinawa dialect). A Japanese martial arts weapon consisting of two hardwood sticks joined together by a strap, chain, etc. More fully *nunchaku stick*. Usually in *plural*.

nuncio *noun* plural **nuncios** E16 **Italian** (*nuncio, nuntio* (now *nunzio*) from Latin *nuncius, nuntius* messenger). **1** E16 *Roman Catholic Church* A papal ambassador to a foreign court or government. **2** E17 A person bearing a message; a messenger. **3** L17 *History* A member of the Polish diet.

nuntius *noun* plural **nuntii** E17 **Latin** (variant of *nuncius* messenger). A NUNCIO.

nuoc mam *noun phrase* E20 **Vietnamese**. A spicy Vietnamese fish sauce.

nuragh *noun* plural **nuraghi** E19 **Sardinian**. *Archaeology* A type of massive stone tower found in Sardinia, dating from the Bronze and Iron Ages. Cf. TALAYOT.

nux vomica *noun phrase* LME **Medieval Latin** (literally, 'emetic nut', from Latin *nux* nut + adjective from *vomere* to vomit). The highly poisonous seeds of the tree *Strychnos nux-vomica*, used as a major source of strychnine and in homeopathic remedies; this tree, a native of southern Asia.

nyet *adverb & noun* (also **niet**) E20 **Russian** (*net* no). **A** *adverb* E20 In Russian: no, *especially* expressing a blunt refusal. **B** *noun* E20 An utterance of 'nyet'.

nymphaeum *noun archaic* plural **nymphaea** (also **nympheum**, plural **nymphea**) L18 **Latin** (from Greek *numphaion, -eion* temple or shrine of the nymphs, neuter of *numphaios, -eios* sacred to the nymphs, from *numphē* nymph). *Classical Antiquities* A grotto or shrine dedicated to a nymph or nymphs; (a part of) a building built to represent this.

ob. abbreviation of OBIIT.

obbligato *adjective and noun* (also **obligato**) L18 **Italian** (= obliged, obligatory). *Music* **A** *adjective* L18 Indispensable; that cannot be omitted: designating a part or accompaniment forming an integral part of a composition, and the instrument on which it is played. **B** *noun* M19 plural **obbligatos**. An obbligato part or accompaniment, *especially* one of particular prominence in a piece.

obelus *noun* plural **obeli** LME **Latin** (= spit, critical obelus, from Greek *obelos*). A straight horizontal stroke (-), sometimes with a dot above and below (÷), used in ancient manuscripts to mark a word, passage, etc., especially as spurious. Also, a dagger-shaped reference mark (†) used in printed matter as a reference to a footnote, etc., and in some dictionaries to denote obsoleteness. Also called *obelisk*.

oberek *noun* M20 **Polish**. A lively Polish dance in triple time, related to the mazurka but usually faster.

obi *noun* E19 **Japanese** (= belt). A sash worn around the waist with Japanese clothing.

obiit *verb* **Latin**. He, she, or it died.

■ Frequently on epitaphs, followed by the date of death; also abbreviated to *ob*.

obiit sine prole *phrase* L19 **Latin**. He, she, or it died without offspring.

■ Frequently in genealogies, usually abbreviated to *ob.s.p.* or *o.s.p.*

obit *noun* LME **Old and Modern French** (from Latin *obitus* going down, setting, death, from *obit-* past participial stem of *obire* to perish, die (from *mortem obire* to meet death); in sense 3 partly abbreviation of *obituary*). **1** LME–L17 Departure from life, death, decease. **2 a** LME–E18 A ceremony performed at the burial of a deceased person; a funeral service. **b** LME *History* A ceremony (usually a mass) commemorating, or commending to God, a deceased person, especially a founder or benefactor of an institution on the anniversary of his or her death; an annual or other regular memorial service. **3** LME Originally, a record or notice of (the date of) a person's death. Later (*colloquial*), an obituary.

obiter *adverb, noun, & adjective* L16 **Latin** (originally two words, *ob itur* by the way). **A** *adverb* L16 By the way, in passing, incidentally. **B** *noun* E17 A thing said, done, or occurring by the way; an incidental matter. Also, an OBITER DICTUM. **C** *adjective* M18 Made or said by the way; incidental.

obiter dictum *noun phrase* plural **obiter dicta** E19 **Latin** (from as preceding + DICTUM). A judge's expression of opinion uttered in discussing a point of law or in giving judgment, but not essential to the decision and so without binding authority; *generally* an incidental remark.

objet *noun* M19 **French**. **1** M19 An object displayed as an ornament. **2** M19 A person forming the object of another's attentions or affection. *rare*.

objet d'art *noun phrase* plural **objets d'art** M19 **French** (literally, 'object of art'; cf. preceding). A small decorative object.

oblietjie *noun* L19 **Afrikaans** (from French *oublie* (from ecclesiastical Latin *oblata* use as noun of feminine of past participle of *offerre* to offer) + diminutive suffix *-tjie*). In South Africa: a rolled wafer-thin teacake.

obligato variant of OBBLIGATO.

oboe da caccia *noun phrase* plural **oboi da caccia** L19 **Italian** (literally, 'hunting oboe'). Chiefly *History* An obsolete type of tenor oboe with a pitch a fifth lower than the ordinary oboe.

oboe d'amore *noun phrase* plural **oboes d'amore, oboi d'amore** L19 **Italian** (literally, 'oboe of love'). A type of alto oboe with a pear-shaped bell and a pitch a minor third below that of the ordinary oboe, now used especially in baroque music.

oboi da caccia, oboi d'amore plurals of OBOE DA CACCIA, OBOE D'AMORE.

obscurum per obscurius *noun phrase* L19 **Late Latin** (literally, 'the obscure by the still more obscure'). An explanation that is more difficult to understand than that which it purports to explain. Cf. IGNOTUM PER IGNOTIUS.

ob.s.p. abbreviation of OBIIT SINE PROLE.

ocarina *noun* L19 **Italian** (from *oca* goose (with reference to its shape)). A simple wind instrument in the form of a hollow egg-shaped body with finger holes and a hole to blow at.

occupatio *noun* L16 **Latin**. *Rhetoric* (The device of making) mention of a thing by pretending to omit to mention it.

octapla *noun* (also **octaple**) L17 **Greek** (*oktapla* neuter plural of *oktaplous* eightfold, after HEXAPLA). A text consisting of eight versions in parallel columns, especially of the Old or New Testament.

octli *noun* M19 **Mexican Spanish**. PULQUE.

oculus *noun* plural **oculi** M19 **Latin** (= eye). *Architecture* A round or eyelike opening or design; *specifically* a circular window (especially in a church); the central boss of a volute; an opening at the apex of a dome.

■ Previously also in the phrases *oculus Christi* (literally, 'eye of Christ'), wild clary (a plant reputed to be good for the eyes) (LME–M17), and *oculus mundi* (literally, 'eye of the world') a white variety of opal, hydrophane (L17–L18).

odalisque *noun* L17 **French** (from Turkish *ōdalık*, from *ōda* chamber + *lık* suffix expressing function). A female slave or concubine in an Eastern harem, especially in the seraglio of the Sultan of Turkey (now *historical*); *transferred* an exotic sexually attractive woman.

odeon *noun* (also in sense 1 **odeion**; in sense 2 **Odeon**) M19 **Greek** (*ōdeion*; see ODEUM). **1** M19 An ODEUM. **2** M20 Any of a chain of large, lavish movie theaters in a chain built by Oscar Deutsch in the 1930s; *generally* a luxurious movie theater.

odeum *noun* plural **odeums**, **odea** E17 **French** (*odéum* or Latin *odeum* from Greek *ōideion* from *ōidē* Attic form of *aoidē* song, singing, from *aeidein* to sing). A building for the performance of vocal and instrumental music, especially among the ancient Greeks and Romans.

odium *noun* E17 **Latin** (= hatred, from *odi* I hate). The fact or state of being hated; general or widespread unpopularity or opprobrium.

oedema variant of EDEMA.

oeil-de-boeuf *noun* plural **oeils-de-boeuf** M18 **French** (literally, 'ox eye'). **1** M18 A small round window. **2** L18 A small vestibule or antechamber in a palace (*specifically* one in Versailles lighted by a small round window); *transferred* (a part of) a monarch's court.

■ Sense 1 appears later (M19) in English form as 'bull's-eye'.

oeil-de-perdrix *noun* M19 **French** (literally, 'partridge eye'). **1** M19 In French pottery and porcelain, a design of dotted circles, usually on a colored background, frequently used on Sèvres porcelain. Also *oeil-de-perdrix pattern*, etc. **b** L19 A similar design used as a ground in lace-making. **2** L19 Pink or pale red wine or champagne. In full *oeil-de-perdrix wine, champagne.*

oeils-de-boeuf plural of OEIL-DE-BOEUF.

oenochoe *noun* (also **oinochoe**) L19 **Greek** (*oinokhoē*, from *oeno-* combining form of *oinos* wine + *khoas, khoē* pouring). *Greek Antiquities* A vessel used for ladling wine from a bowl into a cup.

oesophagus variant of ESOPHAGUS.

oestrus variant of ESTRUS.

oeufs en cocotte *noun phrase plural* E20 **French** (= eggs in a cocotte). A French dish of eggs in butter baked and served in individual cocottes or ramekins.

œuvre *noun* (also **oeuvre**) L19 **French** (= work). A work of art, music, literature, etc.; the whole body of work produced by an artist, composer, etc. Cf. CHEF-D'ŒUVRE.

œvre de vulgarisation *noun phrase* (also **oeuvre de vulgarisation**) M20 **French** (= work of popularization). A work that attempts to make an academic or esoteric subject accessible to the general public.

officina *noun* plural **officinae** E19 **Latin** (= workshop, etc., contraction of *opificina*, from *opifex* workman). A workshop; a place of production (frequently *figurative*).

oficina *noun* L19 **Spanish** (from Latin OFFICINA). In Spanish-speaking South America or Mexico: a factory.

ogham *noun* (also **ogam**, **Ogham**) E18 **Old Irish** (*ogam*, *ogum* (genitive *oguim*), modern Irish *ogham*, plural **oghaim**, Gaelic *oghum*, connected with its mythical inventor *Ogma*). An ancient British and Irish system of writing using an alphabet of twenty or twenty-five characters; any of these characters, consisting of a line or stroke, or a group of two to five parallel strokes, arranged alongside or across a continuous line or the edge of a stone (usually in *plural*). Also, an inscription in this alphabet.

oinochoe variant of OENOCHOE.

ojime *noun* plural same, **ojimes** L19 **Japanese** (from *o* string + *shime* fastening, fastener). A bead or beadlike object, often very elaborate, used in Japan as a sliding fastener on the strings of a bag, pouch, or INRO.

ole *noun* M19 **Spanish.** A Spanish folk dance accompanied by castanets and singing.

olé *interjection & noun* E20 **Spanish. A** *interjection* E20 Bravo! **B** *noun* M20 A cry of '*olé!*'

olim *noun plural* M20 **Hebrew** (*'ōlīm* plural of *'ōleh* person who ascends). Jewish immigrants who settle in the state of Israel.

olim *adverb* M17 **Latin.** At one time; formerly.

olla *noun* plural **ollas**, (in sense 3) **ollae** E17 **Spanish** ((Portuguese *olha*) from Proto-Romance variant of Latin *olla* pot, jar; in sense 3, from Latin). **1** E17 In Spain and Spanish-speaking countries: an earthen jar or pot used for cooking, etc.; a dish of (especially stewed) meat and vegetables cooked in this. Cf. OLLA PODRIDA sense 1. **2** M19 In Spanish America: a large porous earthen jar for keeping drinking water cool by evaporation from its outer surface. **3** M19 An ancient cinerary urn.

■ *Olio* (M17) is an alteration of *olla* used in sense 1 and also figuratively for a hodgepodge, medley, or miscellany.

olla podrida *noun phrase* L16 **Spanish** (literally 'rotten pot', from as OLLA *noun* + *podrida* putrid). **1** L16 A highly spiced stew of various meats and vegetables, of Spanish and Portuguese origin; *generally* any dish containing a great variety of ingredients. **2** M17 *figurative* Any mixture of heterogeneous things or elements; a hodgepodge, a medley.

oloroso *noun* plural **olorosos** L19 **Spanish** (= fragrant). A heavy, dark, medium-sweet sherry; a glass of this.

olpe *noun* L19 **Greek** (*olpē*). *Greek Antiquities* A leather flask for oil, wine, etc. Also, a pear-shaped jug with a handle.

om *interjection & noun* L18 **Sanskrit** (*oṃ*, *om*, sometimes regarded as composed of three sounds, *a-u-m*, symbolizing the three major Hindu deities: see also OM MANI PADME HUM). *Hinduism and Tibetan Buddhism* **A** *interjection* L18 Used as a mantra or auspicious formula at the beginning of prayers, etc. **B** *noun* L19 An utterance of 'om'.

ombré *noun & adjective* L19 **French** (past participle of *ombrer* to shade). (A fabric or design) having gradual shading of color from light to dark.

ombrellino *noun* plural **ombrellini**, **ombrellinos** M19 **Italian.** *Roman Catholic Church* A small umbrella-like canopy held over the sacraments when they are moved from one place to another.

ombres chinoises *noun phrase plural* L18 **French** (= Chinese shadows). *History* A European version of Chinese shadow puppets, used in a pantomime or a galanty show.

ombudsman *noun* plural **ombudsmen** M20 **Swedish** (from *ombud* commissioner, agent, representing Old Norse *umboD* charge, commission, *umboDsmaDr* commissary, manager). An official appointed to investigate complaints by individuals against maladministration by public authorities; *especially* a British official of this kind (officially called the Parliamentary Commissioner for Administration), first appointed in 1967.

omega *noun* E16 **Greek** (*ō mega*, literally, 'great O', opposed to *o mikron* omicron). **1** E16 The last letter (Ω, ω) of the Greek alphabet, having originally the value of a long open *o*; *figurative* the last of a series; the last word, the final development. **2** M20 *Particle Physics* Either of two subatomic particles: *omega meson* and *omega minus*.

■ In the figurative use of sense 1, often in the phrase *the alpha and the omega* (see under ALPHA).

omertà *noun* L19 **Italian** (dialectal variant of *umiltà* humility). A code of silence observed by members or associates of the Mafia or (*trans-*

ferred) others engaged in clandestine activities.

■ The Italian sense of 'humility' originally referred to the Mafia code that enjoins submission of the group to its leader.

om mani padme hum *noun phrase & interjection* L18 **Sanskrit** (*Oṃ maṇipadme hūṃ* literally, 'oh (goddess) Manipadma', reinterpreted as 'oh jewel in the lotus', from *maṇi* jewel, *padma* lotus; cf. OM). *Tibetan Buddhism* (Used as) a mantra or auspicious formula in prayer and meditation.

omnium *noun* M18 **Latin** (literally, 'of all (things, sorts)', genitive plural of *omnis* all: cf. next). **1** *British Stock Exchange* **a** M18 *History* The total value of the stock and other interests offered by the government to each subscriber when raising a loan. **b** L19 Any combined stock the constituents of which can be dealt with separately. *colloquial.* **2** M18 The sum of what one values; one's all. **3** M19 A piece of furniture with open shelves for ornaments; a whatnot.

omnium gatherum *noun phrase* plural **omnium gatherums**, (*rare*) **omnium gathera** M16 **pseudo-Latin** (from Latin OMNIUM + English *gather*). A gathering or collection of all sorts of persons or things; a confused medley. *colloquial.*

omphalos *noun* M19 **Greek** (literally, 'navel'). **1** M19 *Greek Antiquities* **a** A boss on a shield, etc. **b** M19 A stone, in the temple of Apollo at Delphi, reputed to mark the central point of the earth. **2** M19 *figurative* A central point, a center.

on dit *noun* plural **on dits** E19 **French** (= they say). An item of gossip; something reported on hearsay.

onnagata *noun* plural same E20 **Japanese** (from *onna* woman + *kata* figure). In Japanese kabuki theater, a man who plays female roles. Also called *oyama.*

onomasticon *noun* E18 **Greek** (noun use (sc. *biblion* book) of neuter of *onomastikos* pertaining to naming, from *onoma* name). A vocabulary or alphabetic list of (especially personal) proper names. Also, a vocabulary of nouns; a general lexicon.

onomatopoeia *noun* L16 **Late Latin** (from Greek *onomatopoiia* making of words, from *onomatopoios*, from *onomato-* combining form of *onoma* name + *-poios* making, from *poiein* to make, create). **1** L16 The formation of a word by an imitation of the sound associated with the thing or action designated; the principle or practice of forming words by this process. **2** M19 A word formed by this process. **3** M19 *Rhetoric* The use of naturally suggestive language for rhetorical effect.

onus *noun* M17 **Latin** (= load, burden). A burden, a responsibility, a duty.

oom *noun* E19 **Afrikaans** (from Dutch *oom*). Uncle.

■ Frequently used by children or young people in South Africa as a respectful form of address to any older or elderly man.

oomiak variant of UMIAK.

op. abbreviation of OPUS.

op. cit. *noun & adverb phrase* L19 **Latin** (abbreviation of *opus citatum* the work quoted, or *opere citato* in the work quoted). (In) the work already quoted.

opera plural of OPUS.

opéra bouffe *noun phrase* plural **opéras bouffe(s)** L19 **French** (from as next). OPERA BUFFA; (an example of) French comic opera.

opera buffa *noun phrase* plural **operas buffa**, **opere buffe** E19 **Italian** (= comic opera). (Italian) comic opera, with dialogue in recitative and characters drawn from everyday life; an example of this.

opéra comique *noun phrase* plural **opéras comiques** M18 **French** (= comic opera). A type of opera (originally humorous, later romantic) characterized by spoken dialogue; an example of this.

opéras bouffe(s), **operas buffa**, etc., plurals of OPÉRA BOUFFE, OPERA BUFFA, etc.

opera seria *noun phrase* plural **operas seria**, **opere serie** L19 Italian (= serious opera). A type of opera prevalent in the eighteenth century, with elaborate arias and usually based on mythological themes; an example of this. Cf. TRAGÉDIE LYRIQUE.

opere buffe, **opere serie** plurals of OPERA BUFFA, OPERA SERIA.

operetta *noun* L18 Italian (diminutive of *opera*). A short, originally one-act, opera on a light or humorous theme.

■ *Opérette*, the French word derived from *operetta* and Anglicized as *operette*, is a more recent introduction (L19), but *operetta* remains the more generally used term.

opprobrium *noun* plural **opprobria** M17 Latin (= infamy, reproach, from *ob-* toward + *probrum* shameful deed, disgrace, use as noun of neuter of *probus* disgraceful). **1** M17 An occasion or cause of reproach; shameful conduct; something that brings disgrace. **2** L17 Disgrace attached to conduct considered shameful; the expression of this disgrace; shame, reproach.

optime *noun* M18 Latin (= best, very well, from *optime disputasti* you have disputed very well). In the mathematical honors examination (tripos) for the BA degree at Cambridge University, a student placed in the second or third division. Also (respectively) *senior, junior optime*.

optimum *noun & adjective* L19 Latin (noun use of neuter of *optimus* best). Originally *Biology*. **A** *noun* L19 The conditions most favorable for growth, reproduction, or other vital process; *generally* the best, a level, condition, etc., regarded as the best or most favorable. Opposed to PESSIMUM. **B** *adjective* L19 Best, most favorable, especially under a particular set of circumstances; optimal.

opus *noun* plural **opuses**, **opera** E18 Latin (= work). An artistic work, a composition; *especially* a musical composition or set of compositions as numbered among the works of a composer in order of publication.

■ In bibliographies and catalogs usually abbreviated to *op*. Cf. OP. CIT.

opus Alexandrinum *noun phrase* M19 Medieval Latin (literally, 'Alexandrian work'). A pavement mosaic work widely used in Byzantium in the ninth century and later in Italy, consisting of colored stone, glass, and semiprecious stones arranged in intricate geometric patterns.

opus anglicanum *noun phrase* (also **opus Anglicanum**) M19 Medieval Latin (literally, 'English work'). Fine pictorial embroidery produced in England in the Middle Ages and used especially on ecclesiastical vestments.

opus araneum *noun phrase* M19 Medieval Latin (literally, 'spider's work'). Darned netting; delicate embroidery done on a net and resembling a spider's web. Also called *spider-work*.

opus citatum see OP. CIT.

opus consutum *noun phrase* L19 Medieval Latin (literally, 'work sewn together'). APPLIQUÉ work.

opuscule *noun* plural **opuscules** (also in Latin form **opusculum**, plural **opuscula**) M17 Old and Modern French (from Latin *opusculum* diminutive of *opus* work). A minor (especially literary or musical) work.

opus Dei *noun phrase* L19 Medieval Latin. **1** L19 *Ecclesiastical* The work of God; *specifically* liturgical worship regarded as man's primary duty to God. **2** L19 (*Opus Dei*) A Roman Catholic organization of priests and lay people founded in Spain in 1928 with the aim of reestablishing Christian ideals in society.

opus magnum variant of MAGNUM OPUS.

opus sectile *noun phrase* M19 Latin (literally, 'cut work'). An originally Roman floor decoration made up of pieces shaped individually to fit the pattern or design, as distinct from mosaic which uses regularly shaped pieces.

opus signinum *noun phrase* M18 **Latin** (literally, 'work of Signia'). An originally Roman flooring material consisting of broken tiles, etc., mixed with lime mortar.

■ The town of Signia (now Segni) in Central Italy was famous for its tiles.

or *noun* LME **Old and Modern French** (ultimately from Latin *aurum* gold). Originally, gold. Later (*Heraldry*), the tincture gold or yellow in armorial bearings.

orangerie *noun* (also **orangery**) M17 **French** (from French *oranger* orange tree). A place, especially a special protective structure, where orange trees are cultivated.

orans *noun* E20 **Latin** (*orans, orantem* present participle of *orare* to pray). *Art* A representation of a person in a kneeling or praying position.

■ Often postpositive, as in *Virgin orans.*

oratio obliqua *noun phrase* M19 **Latin** (*oratio* speech + *obliqua* feminine of *obliquus* oblique). Indirect speech.

oratio recta *noun phrase* M19 **Latin** (from *oratio* speech + *recta* feminine of *rectus* straight, direct). Direct speech.

oratorio *noun* plural **oratorios** E18 **Italian** (from ecclesiastical Latin *oratorium* oratory). **1** E18 A semidramatic extended musical composition, usually based on a Scriptural theme, performed by a choir with soloists and a full orchestra, without costume, action, or scenery. **2** L19 The genre of musical composition or drama characterized by such a theme and such performance.

■ Originally (M17) in English in its more literal sense of 'a pulpit', but this is rare and became obsolete before its reintroduction in its modern senses, which derive from the musical services in the church of the Oratory of St. Philip Neri in Rome.

orchata variant of HORCHATA.

ordinaire abbreviation of VIN ORDINAIRE.

ordonnance *noun* M17 **French** (alteration of Old French *ordenance* after Old and Modern French *ordonner* to arrange). **1** M17 Systematic arrangement, especially of literary material or architectural parts; a plan or method of literary or artistic composition; an architectural order. **2** M18 In various European countries, especially France, an ordinance, a decree, a law. **3** M18 *French History* Any of those organized companies of men-at-arms who formed the beginnings of a standing army in France. In full *company of ordonnance.*

oregano *noun* L18 **Spanish and American Spanish** (variant of ORIGANUM). A seasoning prepared from the (usually dried) leaves of wild marjoram, *Origanum vulgare*, or, especially in Central and South America, of shrubs of the genus *Lippia*, especially *Lippia graveolens.*

ore rotundo *adverb phrase* E18 **Latin** (literally, 'with round mouth', from ablative of *os* mouth + ablative of *rotundus* round). With round, well-turned speech.

orfèvrerie *noun* ME **French** (from *orfèvre* from popular Latin *aurifabrum* worker in gold, goldsmith). Goldsmiths' work.

■ Formerly also the goldsmiths' quarter in London.

organon *noun* L16 **Greek** (= instrument, organ). **1** L16–E17 A bodily organ, especially as an instrument of the soul. **2** E17 An instrument of thought or knowledge; a means of reasoning; *specifically* a system of logical rules of investigation or demonstration.

■ The *Organon* is the collective title of the logical treatises of Aristotle.

orgeat *noun* LME **French** (from Provençal *orjat*, from *ordi* barley from Latin *hordeum*). A syrup or cooling drink made from barley (later from almonds) and orange-flower water.

orientalia *noun plural* E20 **Latin** (neuter plural of *orientalis* oriental). Things, especially books, relating to or characteristic of the Orient.

oriflamme *noun* LME **Old and Modern French** (*oriflambe, oriflamme*, in medieval Latin *auriflamma*, from *aurum* gold + *flamma* flame). **1** LME *History* The sacred red or orange red silk banner of St. Denis, given to early kings of France by the abbot of St. Denis on setting out for war. **2** E17 *transferred* and *figurative* **a** A banner, principle, ideal, etc., that serves as a rallying point in a struggle. **b** M19 A bright conspicuous object, color, etc.

origami *noun* M20 **Japanese** (from *oru, -ori* fold + *kami* paper). The Japanese art of folding paper into decorative shapes and objects. Also *figurative.*

origanum *noun* ME **Latin** (from Greek *origanon*, perhaps from *oros* mountain + *ganos* brightness, joy; cf. OREGANO). Any of various aromatic labiate plants of the genus *Origanum*, much grown as herbs; *especially* wild marjoram, *O. vulgare*.

orihon *noun* E20 **Japanese** (from *ori* fold + *hon* book). A book formed by folding a printed roll alternately backward and forward between the columns, and usually fastening it with cord down one side.

orlo *noun* plural **orlos** M17 **Italian** (= border, hem, etc., from Latin *ora* edge, border). *Architecture* **1** M17 The fillet under the ovolo of a capital. **2** E18 The plinth under the base of a column.

orné *adjective* (feminine **ornée**) L18 **French** (= ornate, past participle of *orner* from Latin *ornare* to adorn). Decorated, ornate.

■ Usually in English in the noun phrases *cottage orné* and *ferme ornée*. Despite its appearance, *cottage orné* ('a rural dwelling in the form of a cottage with a decorative appearance') is an Anglo-French hybrid, as *cottage* derives from Old English *cot*, via Anglo-Latin *cotagium* and Anglo-Norman *cotage*. *Cottage*, identified in the *Encyclopédie* in 1754 as a *mot anglais* was indeed borrowed into French in the nineteenth century, but the English phrase (L18) antedates this borrowing. A *ferme ornée* is 'a farm designed for aesthetic pleasure as well as practical purposes'.

orterde *noun* M20 **German** (from *Ort* place + *Erde* earth). *Soil Science* A dark sandy layer in soil containing redeposited materials from the upper layers, but not cemented into a hardpan. Cf. ORTSTEIN.

orthosis *noun* plural **orthoses** M20 **Greek** (*orthōsis* making straight, from *orthoun* to set straight). *Medicine* An artificial external device, as a brace or splint, serving to prevent or assist relative movement in the limbs or the spine.

ortolan *noun* M17 **French** (from Provençal = gardener, from Latin *hortulanus*, from *hortulus* diminutive of *hortus* garden). A bunting, *Emberiza hortulana*, found throughout much of the western Palaearctic, formerly esteemed as a delicacy (also *ortolan bunting*). Also (*United States* and *West Indies*, *rare*) any of certain other birds of similar gastronomic reputation.

■ Earlier (but only E16) in its original sense of 'gardener'.

ortstein *noun* E20 **German** (from *Ort* place + *Stein* stone). *Soil Science* A hardpan; *especially* an iron pan in a podzol. Cf. ORTERDE.

orzo *noun* L20 **Italian** (= barley). Pasta in the shape of grains of rice.

o.s.p. abbreviation of OBIIT SINE PROLE.

ossia *conjunction* L19 **Italian**. *Music* In directions: or, alternatively.

■ Indicating an alternative and usually easier way of playing a passage.

osso bucco *noun phrase* M20 **Italian** (= marrowbone). (An Italian dish of) shin of veal containing marrowbone stewed in wine with vegetables.

ostinato *adjective & noun* L19 **Italian** (= obstinate, persistent). *Music* **A** *adjective* L19 Recurring; frequently repeated. **B** *noun* E20 plural **ostinati**, **ostinatos**. A melodic phrase repeated through all or part of a piece.

Ostpolitik *noun* M20 **German** (from *Ost* east + *Politik* policy). *History* The foreign policy of a western country (*specifically* of the Federal Republic of Germany) with reference to the

Communist countries. Cf. WESTPOLITIK.

ostracon *noun* plural **ostraca** (also **ostrakon**, plural **ostraka**) L19 **Greek** (*ostrakon* hard shell, potsherd). *Archaeology* A potsherd used as a writing surface. Usually in *plural*.

o tempora, o mores! *interjection* M16 **Latin** (= o times, o manners!). What times, what ways!

■ Originally quoted from the Roman orator Cicero's impeachment of the conspirator Catiline (*In Catilinam* I.1) in 63 BC; now a general expression of alarm, contempt, amusement, etc., about behavior in contemporary society.

otium *noun* E18 **Latin**. Leisure, ease, idleness.

■ Chiefly in *otium cum dignitate* or *cum dignitate otium* 'dignified leisure', quoting from one of Cicero's letters *Ad Familiares* (I.ix.21).

ottava rima *noun* L18 **Italian** (= eighth rhyme). A stanza of eight lines, 11-syllabled in Italian, 10-syllabled in English, rhyming as *abababcc*.

ottocento *noun* (also **Ottocento**) E20 **Italian** (= eight hundred). The nineteenth century in Italy; the style of Italian art, architecture, music, etc., of this period.

ou *adjective & noun* M19 **Afrikaans** (from Dutch *oud* old). **A** *adjective* M19 Old, elder. **B** *noun* plural **ouens**, **ous** M20 A man, a fellow. Cf. OUTJIE.

■ In South African colloquial speech, frequently used in terms of affection or casual reference.

oubaas *noun* M19 **Afrikaans** (from OU + BAAS). A head of a family; an elderly man.

■ In South Africa, a colloquial form of address to an older man.

oubliette *noun* L18 **French** (from *oublier* to forget). A secret dungeon accessible only through a trapdoor.

oudstryder *noun* M20 **Afrikaans** (= ex-soldier). In South Africa: a veteran of the South African War (1899–1902) who fought on the side of the Boer republics; *generally* any war veteran.

oued see under WADI.

ouens plural of OU.

oukha variant of UKHA.

ouma *noun* E20 **Afrikaans** (= grandmother, from OU old + *ma* mother). A grandmother; an elderly woman.

■ In South Africa, chiefly as a respectful or affectionate form of address or reference.

oupa *noun* E20 **Afrikaans** (= grandfather, from OU old + *pa* father). A grandfather; an elderly man.

■ In South Africa, chiefly as a respectful or affectionate form of address or reference.

oursin *noun* E20 **French**. A sea urchin, *especially* an edible one.

outjie *noun* M20 **Afrikaans** (from as OU + diminutive suffix *-tjie*). A child, a little fellow.

■ In South African colloquial speech can also be used jocularly or derogatively of an adult.

outré *adjective* E18 **French** (past participle of *outrer* to exaggerate). Beyond the bounds of what is usual or proper; eccentric, unusual, out-of-the-way.

ouvert *noun* E20 **French** (= open). *Ballet* An open position of the feet.

ouvrier *noun* (feminine **ouvrière**) M19 **French**. In France: a manual or industrial worker; a laborer.

ouzo *noun* plural **ouzos** L19 **Modern Greek**. (A glass of) an aniseed-flavored spirit from Greece.

ova plural of OVUM.

ovolo *noun* plural **ovoli** M17 **Italian** (diminutive of *uovo*, *ovo* from Latin *ovum* egg). *Architecture* A rounded convex molding.

ovum *noun* plural **ova** E17 **Latin** (= egg). **1** E17 *Roman History* Any of a number of egg-shaped objects used in the circus to indicate the number of laps in a race. Usually in *plural*. **2** E18 *Biology* The female gamete or reproductive cell in animals; an egg, an egg cell. **b** M18 *Botany* Originally (*rare*), the ovule or seed of a plant. Now, the egg cell in the nucellus of an ovule. **3** E18 *Architecture* An egg-shaped ornament or carving.

oy *interjection* (also **oi**) L19 **Yiddish.** Used by Yiddish-speakers as an exclamation of dismay, grief, etc.

■ Also in *oy vay, oy vey* (Yiddish *vey* = woe).

oyama *noun* plural same **M20 Japanese.** An ONNAGATA.

oyer *noun* **LME Anglo-Norman** (= Old French *oïr*: see next). *Law* **1** LME The hearing of a case. **2** LME A criminal trial held under the commission of oyer and terminer. **3** E17 *History* The hearing of a document read in court, especially an instrument in writing pleaded by one party in a suit.

■ Sense 1 exists only in the phrase *oyer and terminer* (formerly also *oyer (and) determiner*) 'a commission authorizing a judge on circuit to hold courts'.

oyez *verb & noun* (also **oyes**) **LME Anglo-Norman** (Old French (also *oiez*) imperative plural of *oïr* (modern *ouïr*) from Latin *audire* to hear). **A** *intransitive verb* LME (*imperative*) Listen! **B** *noun* LME plural same **oyesses**. A call or cry of 'oyez!'.

■ Uttered (usually three times) by a public crier or a court officer to command silence and attention.

P

p.a. abbreviation of PER ANNUM.

pabulum *noun* **M17 Latin** (from stem of *pascere* to feed). **1** M17 Food, nutriment, especially for plants or animals or their tissues. **2** L17 That which feeds a fire. **3** M18 That which nourishes and sustains the mind or soul. **4** L20 Bland intellectual fare; an insipid or undemanding diet of words, entertainment, etc.

pace *preposition* **L18 Latin** (ablative singular of *pax* peace, as in *pace tua* by your leave). With due deference to (a person named).

■ Used especially as a courteous or ironical apology for a contradiction or difference of opinion. Normally italicized to distinguish it from the English verb or noun 'pace'.

pacha variant of PASHA.

pachalic variant of PASHALIC.

pachinko *noun* **M20 Japanese.** A variety of pinball popular in Japan.

pachisi *noun* (also **parcheesi, Pachisi**) **E19 Hindustani** (*pac(c.)īsī* (throw of) twenty-five (the highest in the game), ultimately from Sanskrit *pañcaviṃśati* twenty-five). A four-handed Indian board game with six cowries for dice.

pachuco *noun* plural **pachucos** **M20 Mexican Spanish** (literally, 'flashily dressed'). A juvenile delinquent of Mexican-American descent, especially in the Los Angeles area; *derogatory* any Mexican-American. Also the argot spoken by pachucos.

pacifico *noun* plural **pacificos** **L19 Spanish.** A person of peaceful character; *specifically* (*historical*) a native or inhabitant of Cuba or the Philippines who submitted without active opposition to Spanish occupation.

paco *noun* plural **pacos** **E17 Spanish** ((in sense 2 with reference to the brown and white color) from Quechua *pako* red, reddish yellow). **1** E17 An alpaca. **2** M19 *Mineralogy* An earthy brown oxide of iron, containing particles of silver.

padma *noun* M19 **Sanskrit** (= lotus). (The flower of) the lotus plant; an emblematic representation of this.

padmasana *noun* L19 **Sanskrit** (*padmāsana*, from *padma* lotus + *āsana* seat, posture). *Yoga* A bodily position with legs crossed and feet resting on the opposite thighs, said to resemble the flower of a lotus.

padre *noun* L16 **Italian** ((also Spanish, Portuguese) from Latin *pater, patr-* father). In Italy, Spain, Portugal, Latin America, and other areas of Spanish influence: (a title of) a Christian clergyman, especially a Roman Catholic priest. Now chiefly (*colloquial*), a chaplain in the armed services.

padrone *noun* plural **padrones**, **padroni** (feminine (especially in sense (b)) **padrona**, plural **padronas**, **padrone**) L17 **Italian**. A patron, a master; *specifically* (**a**) (now chiefly *United States colloquial*) an employer, a manager; *especially* an exploitative employer of unskilled immigrant workers; (**b**) the proprietor of an inn or hotel in Italy.

paedeia variant of PAIDEIA.

paella *noun* L19 **Catalan** (from Old French *paele* (modern *paêle*), from Latin *patella* pan, dish). A Spanish dish of rice, saffron, chicken, seafood, vegetables, etc., cooked and served in a large shallow pan.

pagoda *noun* L16 **Portuguese** (*pagode*, probably ultimately from Persian *butkada* idol temple, from *but* idol + *kada* habitation, alteration by association with Prakrit *bhagodī* divine, holy). **1** A Hindu or Buddhist temple or sacred building, usually in the form of a many-tiered tower with stories of diminishing size, each with an ornamented projecting roof, in China, India, Japan, and elsewhere in the Far East. **2** L18 An ornamental structure built in imitation of such a temple.

pagri variant of PUGGAREE.

pahit *noun* E20 **Malay** (= bitter). In Southeast Asia: gin and bitters. More fully *gin pahit*.

pahoehoe *noun* M19 **Hawaiian**. *Geology* Smooth, undulating or corded lava. Cf. AA.

paideia *noun* (also **paedeia**) M20 **Greek**. *Greek History* Education, upbringing; the ideal result of this; a society's culture.

pai-hua *noun* E20 **Chinese** (*báihuà* (Wade–Giles *pai-hua*), from *bái* white, clear, plain + *huà* language, speech). The standard written form of modern Chinese, based on the northern dialects, especially that of Peking (Beijing). Cf. PUTONGHUA.

paillette *noun* M19 **French** (diminutive of *paille* straw, chaff). **1** M19 A small piece of glittering foil, shell, etc., used to decorate a garment; a spangle. **2** L19 A decorative piece of colored foil or bright metal used in enamel painting.

pain *noun* LME **Old and Modern French** (from Latin *panis, pan-*). Bread, *specifically* in French bakery.

■ Formerly naturalized, it now occurs only in *pain perdu* (toasted stale bread, usually sweetened and flavored with cinnamon) and in names of specialty breads.

pair *noun & adjective* plural of noun same M19 **French** (= equal). *Roulette* (Of) an even number; (of) the even numbers collectively.

paisano *noun* plural **paisanos** M19 **Spanish** (= peasant, rustic). **1** M19 In Spain and Spanish-speaking areas, especially in the southwestern United States: a fellow countryman; a peasant. **2** L19 In Mexico and the southwestern United States: a roadrunner.

pakapoo *noun* (also **pakapu** and other variants) E20 **Chinese** (*bái gē piào* (Wade–Giles *pai ko p'iao*) literally, 'white pigeon ticket', perhaps referring to a Cantonese competition that involved releasing pigeons and predicting the distance they would fly and the numbers expected to return). A

Chinese form of lottery played with slips of paper marked with columns of characters.

■ Chiefly Australian, and in the phrase *like a pakapoo ticket*, meaning 'disordered, unintelligible'.

pak-choi *noun* M19 **Chinese** ((Cantonese) *paâk ts' oì* white vegetable: cf. PE-TSAI). Chinese cabbage.

pakeha *noun & adjective* E19 **Maori**. **A** *noun* E19 A white person (as opposed to a Maori). **B** *adjective* M19 Of, pertaining to, or designating a pakeha. *New Zealand.*

pakora *noun* M20 **Hindustani** (*pakoṛā* a dish of vegetables in gram flour). A savory Indian dish consisting of diced or chopped vegetables coated in batter and deep-fried.

pa-kua *noun* L19 **Chinese** (*bāguà* (Wade–Giles *pà-kua*), from *bā* eight + *guà* divinatory symbols). **1** L19 *Art* Any of various decorative and religious motifs incorporating the eight trigrams of *I Ching*; *specifically* an arrangement of these trigrams in a circle around the yin-yang symbol. **2** M20 A Chinese martial art in which fighters are arranged around a circle according to the trigram sequence in positions that they must defend.

palacio *noun* plural **palacios** M19 **Spanish** (from Latin *palatium*). In Spain and Spanish-speaking countries: a palace, a country seat, an imposing official building.

paladin *noun* L16 **French** (from Italian *paladino*, from Latin *palatinus* officer of the palace). Each of the twelve bravest and most famous warriors of Charlemagne's court. Also, a knight errant, a champion.

palaestra *noun* (also **palestra**) LME **Latin** (from Greek *palaistra*, from *palaiein* wrestle). *Classical History* **1** LME A place devoted to the public teaching and practice of wrestling and athletic competition. **2** LME Wrestling, athletic competition.

palais *noun* plural same E20 **French** (literally, 'palace') Abbreviation of PALAIS DE DANSE.

■ Frequently used attributively, as in *palais glide* a form of ballroom dance.

palais de danse *noun phrase* plural same E20 **French**. A public hall for dancing.

Palais Royal *adjective phrase* L19 **French** Designating a type of indelicate farce said to be typical of the Palais Royal theater, Paris.

palapa *noun* L20 **Mexican Spanish** (= (the leaves and branches of) the palm *Orbignya cohune*). A traditional Mexican shelter roofed with palm leaves or branches. Also, any structure imitating this, especially on a beach.

palatschinken *noun plural* E20 **Austrian German** (from Hungarian *palacsinta* from Proto-Romance *placinta* from Latin *placenta* cake). Austrian (stuffed) pancakes.

palazzo *noun & adjective* M17 **Italian** (from Latin *palatium* palace). **A** *noun* plural **palazzos**, (in sense 1) **palazzi**. **1** M17 A palatial mansion; a large imposing building. **2** L20 *singular* and (usually) in *plural* Loose wide-legged pants worn by women. **B** *attributive* or as *adjective* M20 Designating a loose wide-legged garment, outfit, etc.

palestra variant of PALAESTRA.

paletot *noun* M19 **French** (of unknown origin). A short loose outer garment, coat, or cloak. Also, a fitted jacket worn by women in the nineteenth century.

palette *noun* L18 **French**. **1** L18 A thin (oval) board or slab, usually with a hole for the thumb, on which an artist lays and mixes colors. **b** L19 *transferred* The range of colors used by a particular artist or in a particular picture. **c** M20 The range or variety of tonal or instrumental color in a musical piece, composer's work, etc.; the verbal range of a writer, etc. **d** L20 *Computing* In computer graphics, the range of colors or shapes available to the user. **2** M19 *Zoology* A disklike structure. **3** M20 A device used by the banker in certain card games to move cards and money.

pali *noun* E19 **Hawaiian.** In Hawaii: a steep cliff.

■ *The Pali* is a precipice on the island of Oahu.

palio *noun* L17 **Italian** (from Latin *pallium* covering, cover). A traditional horse race held in Italy, especially in Siena, every July and August. Also, the cloth or banner of velvet, silk, etc., given as the prize for winning this race.

paliotto *noun* plural **paliotti, paliottos** M20 **Italian.** The frontal painting on an altarpiece.

palladium *noun* plural **palladia** LME **Latin** (from Greek *palladion*, from *Pallas, Pallad-* epithet of the goddess Athena). **1** LME *Classical Mythology* An image of the goddess Pallas (Athena), in the citadel of Troy, on which the safety of the city was supposed to depend, later reputed to have been taken to Rome. **2** E17 *transferred* and *figurative* A thing on which the safety of a nation, institution, etc., is believed to depend; a safeguard.

pallium *noun* plural **pallia, palliums** ME **Latin** (= covering, mantle). **1** ME *Ecclesiastical* A woolen vestment conferred by the Pope on an archbishop in the Latin church, consisting of a narrow circular band placed around the shoulders with a short lappet hanging from front and back. Also (*transferred*), the office or dignity of an archbishop. **2** M16 *Antiquities* A man's large rectangular cloak, worn especially by Greek philosophical and religious teachers. **3a** L19 *Zoology* The mantle of a mollusk or brachiopod. **b** L19 *Anatomy* and *Zoology* The outer wall of the cerebrum.

pallone *noun* L19 **Italian** (augmentative of *palla* ball). An Italian game, partially resembling tennis, in which a large ball is struck with a cylindrical wooden guard, worn over the hand and wrist.

palmette *noun* M19 **French** (diminutive of *palme* palm leaf). *Archaeology* An ornament (in sculpture or painting) with radiating petals like a palm leaf.

palmier *noun* E20 **French** (literally, 'palm tree'). A small crisp cake shaped like a palm leaf, made from puff pastry and sugar.

palomino *noun* plural **palominos** E20 **American Spanish** (from Spanish from Latin *palumbinus* of or resembling a dove). **1** E20 A horse with light golden-brown coat and white or pale mane and tail. Also *palomino horse*. **2** M20 A pale golden brown color.

palsa *noun* M20 **Swedish** (*palse, pals* (plural *palsar*) from Finnish and Lappish *palsa*). A landform of subarctic regions, consisting of a mound or ridge of peat covered with vegetation and containing a core of frozen peat or mineral soil in which are numerous ice lenses.

pampas *noun plural*, also used as *singular* (also in singular form **pampa**) E18 **Spanish** (plural of *pampa* from Quechua = a plain). **1** E18 *plural* (treated as *singular* or *plural*). The extensive treeless plains of South America south of the Amazon. Also in *singular*, these plains considered collectively; any one of these plains. **2** L20 *plural* (treated as *singular*). A yellowy green color. Usually *attributive*.

pan *noun* E17 **Hindustani** (*pān* betel leaf, from Sanskrit *parṇa* feather, leaf). In the Indian subcontinent: the leaf of the betel, especially as used to enclose slices of areca nut mixed with lime for chewing; the mixture for chewing so formed.

p'an *noun* M20 **Chinese** (*pán*). *Chinese Antiquities* A kind of shallow dish-shaped ritual vessel.

panacea *noun* M16 **Latin** (from Greek *panakeia*, from *panakēs* all-healing, from *pan-* all + base of *akos* remedy). A remedy for all diseases; a thing for solving all difficulties or adopted in every case of difficulty.

panache *noun* M16 **French** (from Italian *pennacchio* from late Latin *pinnaculum* diminutive of *pinna* feather). **1** M16 A tuft or plume of feathers, especially as a headdress or a decoration for a helmet. Formerly also, a decoration like a plume of feathers, e.g., a tassel. **2** L19 Flamboyantly or stylishly confident behavior; a manner marked by this.

panada *noun* (also **panade**) L16 **Spanish** ((also Portuguese) = Italian *panata*, represented a Proto-Romance derivation of Latin *panis* bread). Bread boiled in water to a pulp and flavored. Also, a paste of flour, water, etc., used for thickening.

panatela *noun* M19 **American Spanish** (= long thin cookie, sponge cake from Spanish from Italian *panatello* small loaf, diminutive of *panata* (as PANADA)). **1** M19 A long slender cigar, *especially* one tapering at the sealed end. Also more fully *panatela cigar*. **2** M20 *transferred* A cigarette made of Central or South American marijuana. *slang.*

pancetta *noun* M20 **Italian** (diminutive of *pancio* belly from Proto-Romance word (whence also 'paunch')). Italian cured belly of pork.

panchshila *noun* M20 **Sanskrit** (*pañcaśīla*, from *pañca* five + *śīla* moral principle). The five principles of peaceful relations formulated between India and China (and, by extension, other Communist countries) and set out in the preamble of a treaty signed in April 1954.

pancratium *noun* (also in Greek form **pancration**) E17 **Latin** (from Greek *pagkration*, from *pan-* all + *kratos* strength). **1** E17 *Greek History* An athletic contest combining both wrestling and boxing. **2** M17 *Botany* Any of various bulbous African and Mediterranean plants; *especially* the sea daffodil, *P. maritimum*.

panem et circenses *noun phrase* L18 **Latin** (= bread and circuses). Government provision of popular entertainment and distribution of food to win popularity with the people.

■ Originally, the handouts and gladiatorial games provided by Roman statesmen and emperors in the Circus of ancient Rome to assuage the city's notoriously volatile populace.

panettone *noun* (also **panetone**) plural **panettoni** E20 **Italian** (from *panetto* cake, bar, diminutive of *pane* bread, from Latin *panis*). A rich Italian bread made with eggs, fruit, and butter.

panforte *noun* L19 **Italian** (from *pane* bread + *forte* strong). A hard spicy Sienese cake containing nuts, candied peel, and honey.

panga *noun 1* (also **ponga**) E20 **American Spanish**. A flat-bottomed boat with rising stem and stern used especially in Latin America.

panga *noun 2* M20 **Kiswahili**. In East Africa: a large knife used either as a tool or a weapon.

panier de crabes *noun phrase* plural **paniers de crabes** M20 **French** (literally, 'basket of crabs'). A competitive struggle.

panino *noun* plural **panini** M20 **Italian**. An Italian bread roll or sandwich.

panne *noun* L18 **French** (of unknown origin). A soft silk or rayon fabric with a flattened pile, resembling velvet. Also *panne velvet*.

panocha, **panoche** variants of PENUCHE.

pansala *noun* M19 **Sinhalese** (from *pan* leaf + *sala* dwelling) from Sanskrit *parṇaśālā*, Pali *pannasālā*). A Buddhist temple or monastery; the home of a Buddhist religious teacher.

panthea see SIGNUM PANTHEUM.

panzanella *noun* L20 **Italian**. Bread salad made with olive oil and chopped vegetables.

panzer *noun & adjective* (also **Panzer**) M20 **German** (= mail, coat of mail). **A** *noun* M20 (A member of) a German armored unit. Also, a German tank. **B** *attributive* or as *adjective* M20 Of, pertaining to, or designating a panzer; *transferred* heavily armored.

papabile *adjective & noun* (also (as adjective) **papabili**) M20 **Italian** (from *papa* Pope). **A** *adjective* M20 (Of a prelate) worthy of or eligible to be elected Pope; *generally* suitable for high office. **B** M20 *absolutely* as *noun* plural **papabili**. A prelate regarded as eligible to be elected Pope; *generally* one regarded as suitable for high office. Usually in *plural*.

papaloi *noun* plural **papalois**, same L19 **Haitian** (creole *papalwa*, from *papa* father + *lwa* LOA). A voodoo priest. Cf. MAMALOI.

paparazzo *noun* plural **paparazzi** M20 **Italian**. A (freelance) photographer who pursues celebrities in order to take their pictures.

paperasserie *noun* E20 **French**. Excessive official paperwork or routine; bureaucracy.

papeterie *noun* M19 **French** (= paper manufacture, stationer's store, writing case, from *papetier* paper maker). A (usually ornamental) case or box for paper and other writing materials.

papier collé *noun phrase* plural **papiers collés** M20 **French** (= glued paper). A collage made from paper; the use of paper for collage.

papier déchiré *noun phrase* plural **papiers déchirés** M20 **French** (= torn paper). Paper torn haphazardly for use in collage; a collage made of such paper.

papier mâché *noun & adjective phrase* M18 **French** (*papier* paper + *mâché* past participle of *mâcher* to chew, from Latin *masticare*). **A** *noun* M18 Material made from pulped paper; paper reduced to a pulp mixed with glue, etc., or (for fine work) sheets of paper pasted together, used for making molded boxes, jars, trays, etc. **B** *adjective* M18 Made of papier mâché.

papier poudré *noun phrase* plural **papiers poudrés** E20 **French** (= powdered paper). A paper impregnated with face powder.

papillote *noun* M18 **French**. **1** M18 A piece of paper used for twisting hair into curls. *obsolete* except *historical*. **2** E19 A usually greased paper wrapper in which a fillet, etc., of meat or fish is cooked.

■ Frequently in *en papillote*, in a paper wrapper.

pappardelle *noun plural* L20 **Italian**. Pasta made in wider strips than TAGLIATELLE and served especially with meat sauces.

paprika *noun & adjective* L19 **Hungarian**. **A** *noun* **1** L19 A condiment made from the dried ground fruits of certain (especially red) varieties of the sweet pepper, *Capsicum annuum*. **b** M20 The bright orange red color of this. **2** E20 Any of several European varieties of the sweet pepper bearing mildly flavored fruits. **B** *adjective* **1** M20 Of a dish: flavored with (especially the condiment) paprika. Often *postpositive*. **2** M20 Of the color of paprika.

papyrus *noun* plural **papyri** LME **Latin** (from Greek *papuros* paper reed, of unknown origin). **1** LME An aquatic plant of the sedge family, formerly abundant in Egypt and the source of the writing material papyrus. **2** E18 Material in the forms of fine strips of the stem of the papyrus plant, soaked in water, pressed together, and dried, to form a writing surface, used by the ancient Egyptians, Romans, etc. **3** E19 A manuscript or document written on this.

par *preposition* ME **Old and Modern French** (from Proto-Romance combination of Latin *per* through + *ad* to). Through, by.

■ Occurring in various phrases used in English: see PAR ÉMINENCE, PAR EXCELLENCE, PAR EXEMPLE.

parador *noun* plural **paradores**, **paradors** M19 **Spanish**. In Spain: a hotel owned and administered by the government. Formerly, any Spanish hotel or inn.

parados *noun* plural **paradoses** M19 **French** (from *para-* protector of + *dos* back). An elevation of earth behind a defended place as a protection against attack from the rear; the mound along the back of a trench.

paramo *noun* plural **paramos** M18 **Spanish** ((also Portuguese) *páramo* from Spanish Latin *paramus* bare plain). A high plateau in the tropical parts of South America, bare of trees and exposed to wind and thick cold fogs.

parang *noun* M19 **Malay**. A large heavy knife used in Malaysia for clearing vegetation, etc.

paraphernalia *noun plural* M17 **Medieval Latin** (noun use of neuter plural of *paraphernalis*, from Latin *parapherna* from Greek, from *para-* beside, beyond + *phernē* dowry). **1** M17 *History* Those articles of personal property that the law allowed a married woman to keep and deal with as her own, when most of her personal or movable property vested in her husband. **2** M18 Personal belongings, especially of dress or adornment; the miscellaneous objects that go to make up a thing or are associated with it; trappings, bits and pieces. Also treated as *singular*.

paratha *noun* M20 **Hindustani** (*parāṭhā*). In Indian cooking, a flat piece of unleavened bread fried in butter, ghee, etc., on a griddle.

paratonnerre *noun* E19 **French** (from *para-* protection against + *tonnerre* thunder). A lightning conductor.

parc fermé *noun phrase* (also **parc ferme**) M20 **French** (literally, 'enclosed area'). In motor sports, an enclosure or paddock used by vehicles before or after a race.

parcheesi variant of PACHISI.

par éminence *adverb phrase* L19 **French**. Preeminently.

parens patriae *noun phrase* M18 **Modern Latin** (literally, 'parent of the country'). *Law* The monarch, or any other authority, regarded as the legal protector of citizens unable to protect themselves.

parergon *noun* plural **parerga** E17 **Latin** (from Greek, from *para-* beyond, beside + *ergon* work). **1** E17–E18 An ornamental accessory or addition, especially in a painting; an embellishment. **2** E17 Subsidiary work or business, apart from one's ordinary employment. Also, a work, composition, etc., that is supplementary to or a by-product of a larger work.

par excellence *adverb phrase* L17 **French** (from Latin *per excellentiam* by virtue of excellence). Preeminently; supremely, above all.

par exemple *adverb phrase* M19 **French**. For example.

parfait *noun* L19 **French** (literally, 'perfect'). A rich iced dessert of whipped cream, eggs, etc. Also, a dessert consisting of layers of ice cream, fruit, syrup, whipped cream, etc., served in a tall glass.

parfleche *noun & adjective* E19 **Canadian French** (*parflèche*, from French *parer* ward off + *flèche* arrow). **A** *noun* E19 (A) depilated (especially buffalo's) hide dried by stretching on a frame; an article made from this. **B** *attributive* or as *adjective* M19 Made of parfleche.

parfumerie *noun* M19 **French**. A store (or a department in a store) that sells perfume. Also, a perfume factory.

pariah *noun* E17 **Tamil** (*paraiyar* plural of *paraiyan*, literally, 'hereditary drummer', from *parai* drum). **1** E17 Originally, a member of a very extensive low caste in southern India. Later, a member of a low caste or of no Hindu caste. *obsolete* except *historical*. **2** E19 *transferred* A member of a despised social class; an outcast. **3** E19 A half-wild stray dog. Also *pariah-dog* or *pye-dog*.

pari-mutuel *noun* L19 **French** (= mutual stake or wager). **1** L19 A form of betting in which those backing the first three places divide the losers' stakes. **2** E20 A booth for placing bets under this system; a totalizator.

■ Often abbreviated to MUTUEL.

pari passu *adverb phrase* M16 **Latin** (literally, 'with equal step'). With equal speed; side by side; simultaneously and equally. Also, on an equal footing, without preference.

parka *noun* L18 **Aleut** (from Russian = skin jacket). A long hooded skin jacket worn by Eskimos; a similar garment, usually of windproof fabric, worn especially by mountaineers.

parlando *adverb, adjective, & noun* L19 **Italian**. *Music* **A** *adverb & adjective*

L19 (A direction:) in an expressive or declamatory manner, as if speaking. **B** *noun* M20 plural **parlandos**, **parlandi** An expressive or declamatory passage or piece.

parlementaire *noun* E20 **French** (from *parlementer* to discuss terms, parley). A person deputed to parley with an enemy.

parloir *noun* E18 **French**. A conversation room in a monastery or convent; a parlor. Also, a similar room in a prison.

parmigiana *adjective* L19 **Italian** (feminine of *parmigiano* of or pertaining to the city and province of Parma in northern Italy). *Cooking* Made or served with Parmesan cheese.

▪ Chiefly used postpositively in names of dishes, as in *veal parmigiana*.

parnas *noun* (also **parnass**) plural **parnassim** M19 **Hebrew** (from Greek *pronous* provident). The lay leader of the congregation of a synagogue.

parochet *noun* (also **parocheth** and other variants) plural **parochot** L19 **Hebrew** (*pārōket* curtain; cf. Akkadian *parāku* to shut off). A richly decorated curtain that hangs in front of the Ark in a synagogue.

parole *noun & verb* L15 **Old and Modern French** (from Proto-Romance, from Latin *parabola* parable, from Greek *parabolē* comparison, analogy, proverb, from *paraballein* to put alongside, compare). **A** *noun* **1** L15 A person's word of honor; *specifically* (**a**) a prisoner of war's promise to abide by the specific terms of a conditional release; (**b**) a prisoner's promise of good behavior in return for release before the fulfillment of a custodial sentence. Also, the granting to or acceptance by a prisoner of a conditional release on the basis of such a promise; the system or practice of granting or accepting such a conditional release. **2** L18 *Military* The password used by an officer or inspector of the guard. **3** M20 *Linguistics* The actual linguistic behavior or performance of an individual, in contrast to the linguistic system. Opposed to LANGUE sense 3. **B** *transitive verb* M17 Put on parole; release on parole.

paroli *noun* E18 **French** (from Italian, from *paro* like, from Latin *par* equality). In a gambling card game (especially faro), the staking of double the sum previously staked.

paronomasia *noun* L16 **Latin** (from Greek, from as *para-* beside, beyond + *onomasia* naming). A play on words, a pun; punning.

parquet *noun* E19 **Old and Modern French** (= small marked-off space, etc., diminutive of *parc* park). **1** E19 A flooring, *especially* one composed of blocks of various woods arranged in a geometric pattern. Also *parquet floor*. **2** M19 (The front part of) the first floor of a theater or auditorium. **3** L19 In France and French-speaking countries: the branch of the administration of the law that deals with the prosecution of crime.

parroco *noun* plural **parrocos** M19 **Italian** (*parroco*, Spanish *párroco* = parish priest). In Italian- and Spanish-speaking countries: a priest, *especially* a parish priest.

parsemé *adjective* E19 **French** (past participle of *parsemer* to sprinkle, strew). Especially of a fabric, garment, etc.: decorated with embroidered motifs, beads, etc., sprinkled over a background.

▪ Usually postpositive.

pars pro toto *noun phrase* E18 **Latin**. A part taken as representative of the whole.

▪ Frequently attributive.

parterre *noun* E17 **French** (use as noun of *parterre* on or along the ground). **1** E17 A level space in a garden occupied by an ornamental arrangement of flower beds. **2** L17 A level space on which a house or village stands. **3** E18 The part of the first floor of the auditorium of a theater behind the orchestra; the part beneath the galleries; the occupants of this.

parti *noun* L18 **French** (= choice, from Old French *partie* part, share, team in a contest, from Proto-Romance noun use of Latin *partita* feminine past participle of *partiri* to part). A person (especially a man) considered in terms of eligibility for marriage on grounds of wealth, social status, etc.

partie *noun* L17 French (cf. PARTI). A match in a game; a game.

partie carrée *noun phrase* plural **parties carrées** M18 French (from as PARTI + *carrée* square). A party of four, especially comprising two men and two women.

partigiano *noun* (also **Partigiano**) plural **partigiani** M20 Italian (Tuscan). *History* A member of the Italian resistance during World War II, an Italian partisan.

parti pris *noun & adjective phrase* M19 French (literally, 'side taken', from as PARTI + *pris* past participle of *prendre* to take). **A** *noun phrase* M19 plural **partis pris** A preconceived view, a prejudice; bias. **B** *adjective phrase* E20 Prejudiced, biased; on the side of a particular party.

partita *noun* plural **partite, partitas** L19 Italian (feminine past participle of *partire* to divide from Latin *partiri* to part). *Music* A suite, *especially* one for a solo instrument or a chamber ensemble; a variation in early modern music.

partouse *noun* (also **partouze**) M20 French (from as *parti* party + pejorative slang suffix *-ouse*). **1** M20 A party at which there is indiscriminate and collective sexual activity. **2** L20 A nightclub, etc., noted for the licentiousness of its entertainment.

parure *noun* ME Old and Modern French (from *parer* to adorn, arrange, peel (fruit), from Latin *parare* to prepare). **1** ME–E16 An ornament for an alb or amice. **2** LME–L16 A paring, a peeling. **3** E19 A set of jewels or other ornaments intended to be worn together.

parvenu *noun & adjective* E19 French (noun use of past participle of *parvenir* to arrive from Latin *pervenire*, from *per-* through + *venire* to come). **A** *noun* E19 (feminine **parvenue**) A person of humble origin who has gained wealth or position and risen in society, *especially* one regarded as unfitted for the position achieved in this way, or as lacking the accomplishments appropriate to it; an upstart. **B** *adjective* E19 That has recently risen to wealth or position; resembling or characteristic of a parvenu.

pas *noun* plural same E18 French. **1** E18 The right of going first; precedence. **2** L18 A step in dancing; a kind of dance, especially in classical ballet.

■ In sense 2 chiefly with qualifying word or phrase.

pas ciseaux variant of PAS DE CISEAUX.

pas d'action *noun phrase* M20 French. *Ballet* A dance expressing a theme or narrative.

pas d'âne *noun* L19 French (literally, 'donkey's step'). *Fencing* Two rings below the cross-guard of some old swords for protecting the fingers.

pas de basque *noun phrase* E19 French. A dance step in three beats similar to a waltz step, but with a circular movement of the right leg on the second beat.

pas de bourrée *noun phrase* E20 French. A BOURRÉE step.

pas de chat *noun phrase* E20 French (literally, 'step of cat'). *Ballet* A springing step in which each foot in turn is raised to the opposite knee.

pas de cheval *noun phrase* E20 French (literally, 'step of horse'). *Ballet* A step in which a pawing movement is executed with one foot.

pas de ciseaux *noun phrase* (also **pas ciseaux**) L19 French (literally, 'step of scissors'). *Ballet* A jump in which the legs are opened wide apart in the air.

pas de deux *noun phrase* M18 French. A dance for two people, especially in classical ballet.

pas de quatre *noun phrase* L19 French. A dance for four people, especially in classical ballet.

pas de trois *noun phrase* M18 French. A dance for three people, especially in classical ballet.

pas devant *interjection* M20 **French** (= not in front of). Of a statement, action, etc.: not appropriate or proper for the present company.

■ *Pas devant* is an elliptical version of the warning expression *pas devant les enfants* 'not in front of the children'. The assumption is that the children will not understand a warning given in French. Other nouns are substituted, as appropriate, for *les enfants*.

pas du tout E19 **French**. Not at all.

pasear *intransitive verb & noun* M19 **Spanish** (= to take a walk; cf. PASEO). (Take) a walk. *slang* and *dialect*.

paseo *noun* plural **paseos** M19 **Spanish**. In Spain, Spanish-speaking parts of America, and the southwestern United States: a leisurely walk or stroll; a parade or procession, *especially* at a bullfight; also, a road, an avenue.

pasha *noun* (also **pacha**) M17 **Turkish** (*paşa*, from Persian *pād(i)šhāh*, Pahlavi *pati* lord + SHAH). *History* (The title of) a Turkish officer of high rank, as a military commander, provincial governor, etc.

pashalic *noun & adjective* (also **pachalic**) L17 **Turkish** (*paşalık*, from as PASHA + suffix indicating quality or condition -*lık*). *History* **A** *noun* L17 The jurisdiction of a pasha; the district governed by a pasha. **B** *adjective* M19 Of or pertaining to a pasha.

paskha *noun* (also **paska**) E20 **Russian** (= Easter). A rich Russian dessert made with curd cheese, dried fruit, nuts, spices, etc., set in a mold and traditionally eaten at Easter.

paso *noun* plural **pasos** E20 **Spanish**. An image or group of images representing Passion scenes, carried in procession as part of Holy Week observances in Spain.

paso doble *noun phrase* plural **paso dobles** E20 **Spanish** (= double step). A quick ballroom dance based on a Latin American style of marching; a piece of music for this dance, usually in 2/4 time.

pasquinade *noun & verb* (originally **pasquinadata**) L16 **Italian** (*pasquinata*, French *pasquinade*, from *Pasquin* the name of a statue in Rome on which abusive Latin verses were annually posted during the sixteenth century). **A** *noun* L16 A lampoon, a satire, originally one exhibited in a public place. **B** *transitive verb* L18 Satirize or libel in a pasquinade.

passacaglia *noun* M17 **Italian** (from Spanish *pasacalle*, from *pasar* to pass + *calle* street (originally often played in the streets)). A slow musical composition usually with a ground bass and in triple time; an early kind of dance to this music.

passacaille *noun* (also **passecaille**) E18 **French** (from Spanish *pasacalle*). A PASSACAGLIA.

passade *noun* M17 **French** (from Italian *passata* or Provençal *passada*, from medieval Latin *passare* to pass). **1** M17 *Horsemanship* A forward or backward turn performed on the spot. *rare*. **2** E19 A transitory love affair; a passing romance.

passe *noun* M19 **French** (from *passer* to pass). In roulette: the section of the cloth covering the numbers 19 to 36; a bet placed on this section.

passé *adjective & noun* (feminine **passée**) L18 **French** (past participial adjective of *passer* to pass). **A** *adjective* **1** L18 Past one's prime. *archaic*. **2** E19 No longer fashionable; out of date, behind the times. **B** *noun* M20 *Ballet* The transitional movement of the leg from one position to the next.

passecaille variant of PASSACAILLE.

passée see PASSÉ.

passeggiata *noun* plural **passeggiate** M20 **Italian**. A stroll, a promenade.

■ Usually referring to the evening stroll for relaxation and socializing habitually taken by citizens of many Mediterranean countries; the equivalent of the Greek *volta*.

passéisme *noun* M20 **French**. Adherence to and regard for the traditions and values of the past, especially in the arts.

passementerie *noun* E17 **French** (from *passement* from *passer* to pass; the connection with Spanish and Italian *passamano* (apparently from *passare* to pass + *mano* hand) and the reason for this name are both obscure). Decorative trimming consisting of gold or silver lace, gimp, or braid.

passe-partout *noun* L17 **French** (from *passer* to pass + *partout* everywhere). **1** L17 A thing that goes or provides a means of going everywhere; *specifically* a master-key. **2** M19 A frame or border into which a picture of suitable size may be inserted for display; a frame for displaying mounted photographs, etc., consisting of two sheets of transparent material (or one sheet with a card backing) stuck together at the edges with adhesive tape. Also, adhesive tape used in such framing.

pas seul *noun phrase* plural **pas seuls** E19 **French**. A dance for one person, especially in classical ballet.

passim *adverb & adjective* E19 **Latin** (literally, 'scatteredly', from *passus* scattered, past participle of *pandere* to spread out). Of an allusion or reference in a published work: (to be found) at various places throughout the text. Also *transferred* and *figurative*.

passus *noun* plural same L16 **Latin** (= step, pace). A section, division, or canto of a (medieval) story or poem.

pasta *noun* L19 **Italian** (from late Latin *pasta* a small square piece of medicinal preparation, from Greek *pastē*). **1** L19 A type of dough made from durum wheat flour and water and extruded or stamped into particular shapes (and often dried if not for immediate use). Also, an Italian dish consisting largely of this and usually a sauce. **2** L20 Marijuana. *slang*.

pasticcio *noun* plural **pasticcios** M18 **Italian** (= pie, pasty, from Proto-Romance, from late Latin *pasta* paste). A PASTICHE.

pastiche *noun & verb* L19 **French** (from as PASTICCIO). **A** *noun* L19 A medley of various things; *specifically* (**a**) a picture or a musical composition made up of pieces derived from or imitating various sources; (**b**) a literary or other work of art composed in the style of a well-known author, artist, etc. **B** *transitive & intransitive verb* M20 Copy or imitate the style of (an artist, author, etc.).

pasticheur *noun* E20 **French** (from PASTICHE). An artist who imitates the style of another artist.

pastiglia *noun* E20 **Italian** (= paste). Intricately molded gesso used in the decoration of furniture, caskets, etc., in Renaissance Italy.

pastille *noun* (also **pastil**) M17 **French** (from Latin *pastillus* little loaf or roll, lozenge, diminutive of *panis* loaf). **1** M17 A small pellet of aromatic paste burned as a perfume or as a fumigator, deodorizer, or disinfectant. **2** M17 A small, flat, usually round, candy, often coated with sugar and sometimes medicated; a lozenge. **b** E20 *Medicine* A small disk of barium platinocyanide whose gradual change of color when exposed to X rays was formerly used as an indication of the dose delivered.

pastis *noun* E20 **French**. (A drink of) a liqueur flavored with aniseed.

pastorale *noun* plural **pastorales**, **pastorali** E18 **Italian** (noun use of *pastorale* pastoral, from Latin *pastoralis* from *pastor* shepherd, from *past-* past participial stem of *pascere* to feed, graze). *Music* **1** E18 A slow instrumental composition in compound time, often with drone notes in the bass suggestive of a shepherd's bagpipes. **2** L19 A simple musical play with a rural subject.

pastoralia *noun plural* E18 **Latin** (neuter plural of *pastoralis* pastoral). Spiritual care or guidance as a subject of theological study; the duties of a pastor.

pastourelle *noun* L19 **French** (feminine of *pastoureau* shepherd). A medieval lyric whose theme is love for a shepherdess.

■ The Provençal or Portuguese word *pastorela* (L19) is also used.

pastrami *noun* M20 **Yiddish** (from Romanian *pastramă*, probably of Turkish origin). Highly seasoned smoked beef, usually, served in thin slices.

pata *noun* M20 **Sanskrit** (*paṭa*). Cloth, canvas; *especially* (an example of) an ancient form of Indian painting typically executed on a strip of cloth or scroll of canvas.

patchouli *noun* (also **patchouly**) M19 **Tamil** (*pacçuli*). **1** M19 Either of two Indo-Malayan labiate shrubs, *Pogostemon cablin* and *P. heyneanus*, whose leaves yield an essential oil much used in perfumery. **2** M19 Perfume prepared from this plant.

pâte *noun* M19 **French**. Paste.

■ Occurs in English with a defining word or phrase, usually indicating a substance or process.

pâte brisée *noun phrase* M19 **French** (literally, 'broken paste'). *Cooking* A type of sweet flaky pastry.

pâte de verre *noun phrase* E20 **French** (literally, 'paste of glass'). Powdered glass that has been fired a second time.

pâte dure *noun phrase* M19 **French** (literally, 'hard paste'). (Porcelain made from) hard clay.

pâte-sur-pâte *noun phrase* L19 **French** (literally, 'paste on paste'). A method of relief decoration formed by applying layers of white slip on unfired porcelain.

pâte tendre *noun phrase* M19 **French** (literally, 'tender paste'). (Porcelain made from) soft clay.

pâté *noun* E18 **French** (from Old French *pasté*). **1** E18 A pie, a pasty. Now *rare*. **2** L19 A rich paste or spread made from finely ground or pounded meat, fish, herbs, etc.

■ In sense 2 often with a qualifying word or phrase indicating a particular recipe, such as *rough pâté*, *Strasbourg pâté* (see also phrases below).

pâté de campagne *noun phrase* M20 **French** (= country pâté). A coarse pork and liver pâté.

pâté de foie gras *noun phrase* E19 **French**. A smooth rich pâté of fatted goose liver.

■ Originally a pie filled with this paste, also known as a 'Strasbourg pie'; now applied just to the filling served as a separate dish.

pâté en croûte *noun phrase* M20 **French**. Pâté baked in a pastry case.

pâté maison *noun phrase* M20 **French** (= house pâté). Pâté made to the recipe of a particular restaurant.

patella *noun* plural **patellae** (originally Anglicized as **patel**) L15 **Latin** (diminutive of PATERA). **1 a** *generally* A pan. Only in L15. **b** M19 *Archaeology* A small pan or shallow vessel, *especially* a Roman one. **2** L16 *Anatomy* The kneecap. **3** L17 A natural structure in the form of a shallow cup or pan. **4** L17 *Zoology* A univalve mollusk of the genus *Patella*, which includes the common limpet. Chiefly as modern Latin genus name.

pater *noun* ME **Latin**. **1** ME The Lord's Prayer, the PATERNOSTER. **2** E17–M19 An ecclesiastical or spiritual father. **3** E18 Father. Cf. MATER sense 2. Chiefly *jocular* and *school slang*. **b** M20 *Anthropology* A person's legal as opposed to biological father. Cf. GENITOR.

patera *noun* plural **paterae** M17 **Latin** (from *patere* to be open). **1** M17 *Roman Antiquities* A broad shallow dish used especially for pouring libations. **2** L18 *Architecture* An ornament resembling a shallow dish; any flat round ornament in bas-relief.

paterfamilias *noun* plural **patresfamilias** L15 **Latin** (from *pater* father + archaic genitive of *familia* family). **1** L15 A male head of a family or household. **2** M19 *Roman Law* The male head of a family or household having authority over its members. Also, any male legally independent and free from parental control.

paternoster *noun* OE **Latin** (*paternoster* literally, 'our father', the first two words of the Lord's Prayer in Latin). **1** OE The Lord's Prayer, especially in the Latin version. **b** ME A repetition or recital of this as an act of worship. **c**

LME *transferred* A form of words repeated as or like a prayer, imprecation, or charm. Also, a nonsensical or tedious recital. **2** ME Any of several special beads occurring at regular intervals in a rosary to indicate that a paternoster is to be said. Also, the whole rosary. **3** M19 A fishing line with hooks or weights attached at intervals. More fully *paternoster line*. **4** E20 An elevator consisting of a series of doorless compartments moving continuously on an endless belt. Also more fully *paternoster elevator* or *Brit. paternoster lift*.

patha patha *noun phrase* **M20 Xhosa** (*phathphatha* to feel with the hands). **1** M20 In South Africa: a sensuous black African dance; music for this dance. **2** L20 Sexual intercourse. *South African slang*.

pathos *noun* **L16 Greek** (= suffering, feeling, related to *paskhein* to suffer, *penthos* grief). **1** L16 A pathetic expression or utterance. *rare*. **2** M17 A quality in speech, writing, events, persons, etc., that excites pity or sadness; the power of stirring tender or melancholy emotion. **3** L17 Physical or mental suffering. *rare*.

patina *noun* **M18 Italian** (from Latin = shallow dish or pan). A usually green film produced by oxidation on the surface of old bronze; a similar alteration of the surface of coins, flint, etc. Also, a gloss on wooden furniture produced by age, polishing, etc; an acquired change in the appearance of a surface, *especially* one suggestive of age.

patio *noun* plural **patios** **E19 Spanish** (= court of a house). **1** E19 Originally, an inner court, open to the sky, in a Spanish or Spanish-American house. Now also, a usually roofless paved area adjoining and belonging to a house. **2** M19 *Mining* A yard or floor where ores are cleaned, sorted, or amalgamated.

patisserie *noun* (also **pâtisserie**) **L16 French** (*pâtisserie* from medieval Latin *pasticium*, from *pasta* paste). **1** L16 *singular* and in *plural* Articles of food made by a pastry cook, pastries collectively. **2** E20 A store that sells pastries.

patissier *noun* (also **pâtissier**, feminine **patissiere**, **patissière**) **E20 French**. A pastry cook.

patois *noun & adjective* **M17 Old and Modern French** (= rough speech, perhaps from Old French *patoier* to handle roughly, trample, from *patte* paw, of unknown origin). **A** *noun* plural same. **1** M17 A dialect (originally in France) of the common people in a particular area, differing fundamentally from the literary language; any non-standard local dialect. **2** L18 *transferred* A social dialect; jargon. **3** M20 The creole of the English-speaking Caribbean, especially Jamaica. **B** *attributive* or as *adjective* L18 Of, pertaining to, or of the nature of a patois.

patresfamilias plural of PATERFAMILIAS.

patria *noun* **E20 Latin**. One's native country; one's homeland.

patrin *noun* **M19 Romany**. A trail left by Gypsies, using arrangements of grass, leaves, twigs, etc., to indicate the direction taken.

patron *noun* **ME Old and Modern French** (from Latin *patronus* protector of clients, advocate, defender, from *pater*, *patr-* father). **1** LME The captain or master of a Mediterranean galley or coaster (now *rare* or *obsolete*); in North American waters, the captain or steersman of a longboat, barge, etc. **2** M16 A case for pistol cartridges; a cartridge. Now *obsolete* except *historical*. **3** E17–E18 A master or owner of slaves in countries bordering the eastern and southern Mediterranean. **4** M19 A manager or boss of a hacienda; in New Mexico, the master or head of a family. (From *Spanish*). **5** L19 The proprietor of an inn or restaurant, especially in France and Spain. Cf. Italian PADRONE.

■ The above senses represent only modern Romance uses. In these senses the pronunciation is with a soft *a* and accent on the second syllable, with the *o* pronounced "aw."

patronat *noun* **M20 French**. An organization of industrial employers in France; French employers collectively.

patronne *noun* L18 **French** (feminine of PATRON). A woman who is the owner, or the wife of the owner, of a business, especially a café, hotel, or restaurant.

patte *noun* L18 **French** (of unknown origin). **1** L18 A paw; *jocularly* a hand. Now only in PATTE DE VELOURS. **2** M19 A short band or strap sewn on a dress as a trimming, or used to fasten a coat, hold a belt in place, etc.

patte de velours *noun phrase* M19 **French** (= paw of velvet). A cat's paw with the claws retracted, as symbolic of ruthlessness or inflexibility hidden beneath apparent softness.

paupiette *noun* (originally **poupiets**) E18 **French** (perhaps from Italian *polpetta*, from Latin *pulpa* pulp). *Cooking* A long thin slice of fish, meat, etc., especially rolled and stuffed with a filling.

■ Usually in plural in names of dishes, as in *paupiettes de veau*. A dish of this sort is also sometimes called *alouettes sans tête* '(sky)larks without heads'. An alternative etymology perhaps connects with French *poupée* 'doll'; cf. the mincemeat dish called in modern Greek *koukla*, also meaning 'doll'.

pavane *noun* (also **pavan**) M16 **French** (probably from Italian dialect *pavana* feminine of *pavano* of Padua, from *Pavo* dialect name of Padua (Italian *Padova*)). **1** M16 *History* A grave and stately dance in slow duple time, performed in elaborate clothing and popular in the sixteenth century. **2** M16 A piece of music for this dance or in its rhythm.

pavé *noun* (also (earlier) Anglicized as **pave**) LME **French** (noun use of past participle of *paver* to pave). **1** LME A paved road or path. **2** L19 A setting of jewels placed close together so that no metal is visible.

pavillon *noun* L19 **French** (literally 'pavilion'). **1** L19 The bell-shaped mouth of a trumpet or similar musical instrument. **2** L19 A percussion instrument similar to a Turkish crescent, consisting of a stick having transverse brass plates from which hang a number of small bells that jingle. More fully *pavillon chinois* 'Chinese pavillon'. Also called *jingling Johnny*.

pax *noun* LME **Latin** (= peace). **1** LME *Ecclesiastical* (also **Pax**) The ceremonial exchange of greetings as part of a church service to signify Christian concord. **2** LME *Ecclesiastical History* A tablet of gold, silver, ivory, glass, etc., with a projecting handle, depicting the Crucifixion or other sacred subject, which was kissed by all participants at mass. Also called *osculatory*. **3** L15 Peace, tranquillity, concord; *especially* peace between nations. Cf. PAX ROMANA. **4** L18 A friend; good friends. *School slang*. **5** M19 As *interjection* A call for quiet or (a) truce. *school slang*.

pax Romana *noun phrase* L19 **Latin** (= Roman peace). The peace that existed between nationalities under the Roman Empire.

■ Originally from Pliny's *Natural History* (xxvii.3), *pax Romana* has been the model for other phrases with a Latin or modern Latin adjective referring to the dominant influence of a nation, empire, etc.

paysage *noun* E17 **French** (from *pays* country). (A representation of) a rural scene or landscape.

paysan *noun & adjective* E19 **French** (from Old French *païsant*, *païsent*, alteration of earlier *païsenc*, from *païs* (modern *pays*) country, from Proto-Romance alteration of Latin *pagus* rural district). **A** *noun* E19A peasant, a countryman, especially in France. **B** *adjective* L19 Of a style of art, dress, etc.: resembling that of peasants.

paysanne *noun* M18 **French** (feminine of PAYSAN). A peasant woman, a countrywoman, especially in France.

peag *noun* (also **peak**) M17 **American Indian.** WAMPUM.

péage *noun* (in sense 1 also **payage**) LME **Old and Modern French** (from medieval Latin *pedaticum*, from Latin *pes, ped-* foot; in sense 2 from modern French). **1** LME Toll paid for passing through a place or country. *obsolete* in *general* sense. **2** L20 Toll paid to travel on a French highway; a gate or barrier where this is paid.

peau-de-soie *noun* **M19 French** (literally, 'silk skin'). A close-woven heavy satin silk; an (especially rayon) imitation of this.

peau d'Espagne *noun phrase* (also **Peau d'Espagne**) **M19 French** (literally, 'skin of Spain'). **1** M19 Perfumed leather. **2** L19 A scent suggestive of the aroma of this leather.

peccadillo *noun* plural **peccadilloes, peccadillos** **L16 Spanish** (*pecadillo* diminutive of *pecado* sin). A small fault, a venial sin; a trifling offense.

peccavi *interjection & noun* **E16 Latin** (= I have sinned). **A** *interjection* E16 Acknowledging guilt. **B** *noun* L16 An acknowledgment or confession of guilt.

■ As an interjection, now usually jocular; cf. MEA CULPA.

pecorino *noun* **M20 Italian** (from *pecora* sheep). A hard Italian cheese made from ewe's milk.

pedregal *noun* **M19 Spanish** (from *piedra* stone, from Latin *petra*). In Mexico and the southwestern United States: a rocky tract, especially in a volcanic region; an old lava field.

peignoir *noun* **M19 French** (from *peigner* to comb). A woman's loose dressing gown or bathrobe.

peineta *noun* **M20 Spanish.** A woman's ornamental comb traditionally worn with a mantilla.

pelmeny *noun plural* **M20 Russian** (*pel'meni*). Small pasta cases stuffed with seasoned meat, etc., as a Russian dish.

pelota *noun* **E19 Spanish** (= ball, augmentative of *pella* from Latin *pila* ball). **1** E19 A Basque or Spanish ball game played in a walled court using basketlike wicker rackets attached to gloves. **2** E20 The ball used in pelota.

peloton *noun* **M20 French** (from *pelote* from Proto-Romance diminutive of Latin *pila* ball). *Cycling* The main field, group, or pack of cyclists in a race.

■ The original senses in which *peloton* was introduced (both E18) are now rare or obsolete: 'a small ball or pellet' and (its modern French sense) 'a platoon'.

pelouse *noun* **E20 French.** Especially in France: an area of grass; *specifically* a public enclosure at a racetrack.

pelta *noun* plural **peltae** (also Anglicized as **pelt**) **E17 Latin** (from Greek *peltē* a small light leather shield). **1** E17 *Classical Antiquities* A small light shield; a buckler. **2** M18 *Botany* Any of various shieldlike structures. **3** E20 An ornamental motif resembling a shield in architecture, metalwork, etc.

pelure *noun* **L19 French** (literally, 'peeling', from *peler* to peel). Especially *Philately.* A kind of very thin paper. Also *pelure paper.*

pelure d'oignon *noun & adjective phrase* **M20 French** (literally, 'onion peel'). **A** *noun phrase* M20 plural **pelures d'oignons** A tawny color characteristic of some aged red wines; a wine of this color. **B** *adjective phrase* M20 (Designating a wine) of this color.

pemmican *noun* **L18 Cree** (pimihkan, from *pimiy* grease). A lightweight, highly nutritious food of pounded dried meat mixed to a paste with melted fat and berries, used originally by North American Indians, now also by explorers, hikers, etc.

penates *noun plural* **E16 Latin** (*Penates* (plural), from *penus* provision of food, related to *penes* within). *Roman History* The protective gods of a house, especially of its storeroom; household gods. Cf. LAR.

■ Often in English in the phrase *lares and penates.*

penchant *noun* **L17 French** (noun use of present participle of *pencher* to incline, lean). An inclination, a (strong or habitual) liking.

penchée *adjective* **M20 French** (feminine of *penché* past participle of *pencher* to lean, incline). *Ballet* Especially of an arabesque: performed while leaning forward.

■ Usually postpositive.

pendeloque *adjective & noun* M19 **French** (from Old French *pendeler* to dangle). (A gem, especially a diamond) cut in the shape of a drop.

pendente lite *adverb phrase* E18 **Latin** (literally, 'with the lawsuit pending'). *Law* During the progress of a suit; during litigation.

penetralia *noun plural* M17 **Latin** (use as noun of *penetralia* neuter plural of *penetrālis* innermost). The innermost parts of a building, etc.; *especially* the sanctuary or innermost shrine of a temple; *figurative* secret parts, mysteries.

penne *noun plural* L20 **Italian** (literally, 'quills, pens'). Pasta in the form of short tubes cut diagonally at both ends.

pensée *noun* (also (in sense 1) **pensee**) LME **Old French** (*pensee*; in sense 2 reintroduced from French). **1** LME–L15 Thoughtfulness, anxiety, care; a thought, an idea. **2** L19 A poem or prose composition expressing a single thought or reflection. Also, an aphorism.

penseroso *noun & adjective* L18 **Italian** (obsolete form of *pensieroso*, from (obsolete) *pensiere* thought, from Provençal *pensier*, from Proto-Romance variant of Latin *pensare* to weigh, ponder, consider). **A** *noun* L18 plural **penserosos, penserosi** . (A person having) a brooding or melancholy character. **B** *adjective* E19 Pensive, brooding, melancholy.

■ John Milton's classic depiction of the melancholy character in his poem 'Il Penseroso' (1632) was responsible for the wider use of the word in English.

pensiero *noun* plural **pensieri** E20 **Italian**. **1** E20 A thought, an idea; an anxiety. **2** M20 *Art* A sketch.

pension *noun* M17 **French** (Old French *pension* from Latin *pensio(n-)* payment, rent, from *pens-* past participial stem of *pendere* to weigh, pay). A usually fixed-rate boardinghouse or (formerly) a boarding school in France or another European country. Cf. EN PENSION.

■ *Pension* was first introduced in the LME period and, with the pronunciation, is now wholly Anglicized in its numerous senses deriving from Old French and Latin, almost all of which contain the idea of 'a fixed regular payment'. The sense above was also formerly Anglicized.

pensionnaire *noun* L16 **French** (from medieval Latin *pensionarius*). **1** L16 A person receiving a pension; a pensioner, a paid retainer. *rare*. **2** L18 A person who boards in a French lodging house or institution, or with a French family.

pentathlon *noun* (also formerly in Latin form **pentathlum**) E17 **Greek** (from *penta-* five + *athlon* contest). **1** E17 *Classical History* An athletic contest in which competitors engaged in five different events (leaping, running, discus throwing, spear throwing, and wrestling). **2** E20 An athletic or sporting contest in which competitors engage in five different events (especially (in full *modern pentathlon*) fencing, shooting, swimming, riding, and cross-country running).

pentimento *noun* plural **pentimenti** E20 **Italian** (literally, 'repentance'). *Art* A visible trace of (an) earlier painting beneath a layer or layers of paint; (a) painting revealed by such traces.

penuche *noun* (also **panocha, panoche**, and other variants) M19 **American Spanish** (*panoche*). **1** M19 A kind of coarse brown sugar used in Mexico. **2** L19 A kind of candy resembling fudge, made with brown sugar, butter, milk or cream, and often nuts.

peon *noun* plural **peons**, (*in sense 3 also*) **peones** E17 **Portuguese and Spanish** (in sense 1 from Portuguese *peão*; in senses 2 and 3 from Spanish *peón* peasant, from medieval Latin *pedo(n-)* foot soldier). **I 1** E17 In the Indian subcontinent and Southeast Asia: a person of low rank; *specifically* (**a**) a foot soldier; (**b**) an orderly; (**c**) an office boy. **II 2** E19 A Spanish-American day laborer or farm worker, *especially* one in poor circumstances. Also (*historical*), a debtor held in servitude by a creditor, especially in the southern United States and Mexico. **3** M20 A BANDERILLERO.

peperoni variant of PEPPERONI.

peplos *noun* L18 **Greek.** *Greek Antiquities* A (usually rich) outer robe or shawl worn by women in ancient Greece, hanging in loose folds and sometimes drawn over the head; *specifically* the one woven for the statue of the goddess Athena at Athens, and carried in procession to her temple at the greater Panathenaea.

peplum *noun* L17 **Latin** (from Greek PEPLOS). **1** L17 A PEPLOS. **2** M19 Formerly, a kind of overskirt, in supposed imitation of the ancient peplum. Now also, a usually short flounce on a jacket, blouse, or tunic, hanging from the waist over a skirt; a jacket, etc., incorporating this.

pepperoni *noun* (also **peperoni**) M20 **Italian** (*peperone* chili, from *peper-*, *pepe* pepper, from Latin *piper* + augmentative suffix *-one*). Beef and pork sausage seasoned with pepper.

per *preposition* LME **Latin** (whence Old French and Italian *per*, French *par* through). **1** LME Through, by; by means of: (**a**) in Latin and modern Latin (also medieval Latin and Italian) phrases, as PER SE; (**b**) in Old French phrases and words derived therefrom. **2** M16 *Heraldry* In the direction of (a specified ordinary). **3** L16 By means of, by the instrumentality of; in accordance with (usually *as per*); *Law* as laid down by (a judge) in a specified case. **4** L16 For each, for every, as *per cent*, *per mil*, etc. **b** L19 With ellipsis of following noun: per hour, per cent, etc.

per accidens *adverb phrase* E16 **Modern Latin** (from as PER + Latin *accidens*, *accident-* present participial stem of *accidere* to happen). **1** E16 By virtue of some nonessential circumstance; contingently, indirectly. Opposed to PER SE. **2** L16 *Logic* By which the quantity of the proposition is changed from universal to particular in a conversion. Opposed to *simply*.

per annum *adverb phrase* E17 **Modern Latin** (from as PER + accusative of Latin *annus* year). For or in each year.

■ Abbreviated to *p.a.*

percale *noun* E17 **French** (in modern use, but origin unknown (= Spanish *percal*, Italian *percalle*)). Originally, a fabric imported from India in the seventeenth and eighteenth centuries. Later, a light fine cotton fabric without gloss.

per capita *adverb & adjective phrase* L17 **Modern Latin** (from as PER + accusative plural of Latin *caput* head). **A** *adverb phrase* **1** L17 *Law* (Divided, shared, etc.) equally among or by individuals, on an individual basis. Opposed to PER STIRPES. **2** E20 For each person or head of population. **B** *adjective phrase* M20 Possessed, performed, etc., by each person when averaged over a population, etc.

per centum *adverb phrase* M17 **Modern Latin** (Latinized form of *percent*). Percent.

■ Frequently in legal contexts. In everyday use the form is usually written as one word in American English (*percent*), although two words are preferred in British English (*per cent*).

perceptum *noun* plural **percepta** L19 **Latin** (neuter of *perceptus* past participle of *percipere* to perceive). An object of perception, a percept.

per contra *adverb & noun phrase* M16 **Italian.** **A** *adverb phrase* M16 On the opposite side (of an account, assessment, etc.); on the other hand. **B** *noun phrase* E19 The opposite side.

per diem *adverb, noun, & adjective phrase* E16 **Modern Latin** (from as PER + accusative of Latin *dies* day). **A** *adverb phrase* E16 For or in each day. **B** *noun phrase* E19 An amount or allowance of so much each day. **C** *adjective phrase* E19 Daily.

perdu *adjective* (also **perdue**) L16 **Old and Modern French** (past participle of *perdre* to lose, from Latin *perdere*). **A** *adjective* **1** L16–L17 Posted in, or designating, a sentinel's position that is so dangerous that death is almost inevitable. Only in *sentinel perdue, perdue sentinel.* **b** E–M17 Placed in a very hazardous situation; (of a case) desperate. **2** E17 Hidden and on the watch; lying in ambush. Chiefly in *lie, set, stand,* etc., *perdu.* **3** E18 Concealed, hidden; out of sight; disguised.

■ Also formerly a noun (E17–M18), meaning principally 'soldier(s) posted in a very hazardous situation', but now obsolete in all noun senses.

père *noun* E17 **French** (= father). **1** E17 Father: used in France and French-speaking countries as a title preceding the name of a priest. **2** E19 The father, senior.

■ *Père* in sense 2 is appended to a name to distinguish between a father and son of the same name. Cf. FILS; also in phrase *père et fils* 'father and son'.

père de famille *noun phrase* E19 **French.** A father of a family, a family man.

perestroika *noun* L20 **Russian** (*perestroĭka* restructuring). The reform of the economic and political system of the former USSR, first proposed by Leonid Brezhnev in 1979 and actively promoted under the leadership of Mikhail Gorbachev from 1985; *transferred* any program of fundamental reform.

perfecta *noun* L20 **American Spanish** (shortened from *quiniela perfecta* perfect quinella). *Betting* A bet in which the first and second finishers of a race must be predicted in the correct order.

perfecto *noun* plural **perfectos** L19 **Spanish** (= perfect). A large thick cigar tapered at each end.

perfide Albion *noun phrase* M19 **French** (= perfidious Albion). England (with reference to its alleged habitual treachery toward other nations); an (untrustworthy) Englishman.

pergola *noun* L17 **Italian** (from Latin *pergula* projecting roof, vine arbor, from *pergere* to come or go forward). An arbor or covered walk, formed of growing plants trained over trelliswork.

■ First (M17 only) in the sense of 'an elevated stand or balcony', but this never passed into general currency.

peri *noun* L18 **Persian** (*perī*). In Iranian mythology, one of a race of superhuman beings, originally represented as evil but subsequently as good and graceful; *transferred* a graceful or beautiful person.

peridot *noun* ME **Old French** (*peritot* (modern *peridot*) = medieval Latin *peridotus*, of unknown origin; in sense 2 readopted from French). **1** A green gemstone. Only in ME. **2** E18 Olivine (chrysolite), especially as used as gem.

periegesis *noun* plural **periegeses** E17 **Greek** (*periēgēsis* from *peri-* around + *hēgēsis*, from *hēgeisthai* to lead, guide). A description of a place or region.

per impossibile *adverb phrase* M19 **Latin.** As is impossible.

peripeteia *noun* (also **peripetia**) L16 **Greek** (ultimately from *peri-* around + stem *pet-* of *piptein* to fall). A sudden change of fortune or reverse of circumstances (fictional or real).

■ Used by Aristotle in his *Poetics* as a technical term for the sequence of events in the plot of a drama that, in the case of a tragic hero, takes the protagonist from happiness to misfortune.

periphrasis *noun* plural **periphrases** M16 **Latin** (from Greek, from *periphrazein*, from *peri-* + *phrazein* to declare). The figure of speech that consists in expressing a meaning by many or several words instead of by few or one; a roundabout way of speaking or writing; (a) circumlocution.

periplus *noun* L18 **Latin** (from Greek *periplous*, from *peri-* around + *plous* voyage). (A) circumnavigation; a voyage (or journey) around a coastline, etc.; a narrative of such a voyage.

peristyle *noun* E17 **French** (*péristyle* from Latin *peristylum* from Greek *peristulon* noun use of neuter of *peristulos* having pillars all around, from *peri-* + *stulos* column). *Architecture* **1** E17 A row of columns surrounding a building, court, cloister, etc.; the court, etc., surrounded by the columns. **2** L17 The columned porch of a church or other large building; a pillared veranda.

per mensem *adverb phrase* M17 **Modern Latin** (from as PER + accusative singular of Latin *mensis* month). For or in each month.

permis de séjour *noun phrase* plural same L19 **French**. Permission to stay in a country; a residence permit.

perpetuum mobile *noun phrase* L17 **Latin** (from *perpetuus* perpetual + *mobilis* movable, mobile, after PRIMUM MOBILE). **1** L17 Motion that continues forever; *specifically* that of a hypothetical machine that runs forever; such a machine. **2** L19 *Music* A MOTO PERPETUO.

perruquier *noun* M18 **French** (from *perruque* peruke). A person who makes, dresses, or sells wigs.

per se *adverb phrase* L16 **Latin**. By or in itself; intrinsically. Opposed to PER ACCIDENS 1.

persiennes *noun plural* M19 **French** (noun use of feminine plural of *persien* Persian). Window shutters or outside blinds made of light movable slats fastened horizontally in a frame.

persiflage *noun* M18 **French** (from *persifler* to banter, from as PER- + *siffler* to whistle). Light banter or raillery; frivolous talk.

persona *noun* plural **personas, personae** E20 **Latin** (originally = the mask worn by actors in ancient Greek and Roman drama). **1** E20 A character assumed by an author, performer, etc., in his or her writing, work, etc. **2** E20 An aspect of the personality as displayed to others. Cf. ANIMA.

persona designata *noun phrase* plural **personae designatae** L19 **Law Latin** (from as PERSONA + Latin *designata* feminine of *designatus* past participle of *designare* to mark out, elect). A person individually specified in a legal action, as opposed to one included in a category.

personae gratae, personae non gratae plurals of PERSONA GRATA, PERSONA NON GRATA.

persona grata *noun phrase* plural **personae gratae** L19 **Late Latin** (from as PERSONA + Latin *grata* feminine of *gratus* pleasing). A person, especially a diplomat, acceptable to certain others.

personalia *noun plural* E20 **Latin** (neuter plural of *personalis* personal). Personal matters; personal mementos.

persona non grata *noun phrase* plural **personae non gratae** E20 **Late Latin** (from as PERSONA GRATA + Latin *non* not). An unacceptable or unwelcome person.

personnel *noun* E19 **French** (noun use of adjective, as contrasted with MATÉRIEL). **1** E19 The body of people employed in an organization, etc., or engaged in a service or undertaking, especially a military one. Opposed to *matériel*. **2** M20 *specifically* The members of an orchestra or band. **3** M20 The department in an organization, etc., concerned with the appointment, welfare, records, etc., of employees. Also more fully *personnel department*.

per stirpes *adverb phrase* L17 **Modern Latin** (from as PER + accusative plural of Latin *stirps* family, stem). *Law* (Divided, shared, etc.) equally among the branches of a family (and then each share among the members of one branch). Opposed to PER CAPITA sense A.1.

pervenche *noun* L19 **French** (= periwinkle). A shade of light blue resembling the color of the flowers of the periwinkle. More fully *pervenche blue*.

peshmerga *noun* plural **peshmergas**, same M20 **Kurdish** (*pêshmerge* from *pêsh* before, in front of + *merg* death). A member of a Kurdish nationalist guerrilla organization.

pessimum *noun* M20 **Latin** (neuter singular of *pessimus* worst). The most unfavorable condition (original especially, in the habitat of an animal or plant). Frequently *attributive*. Opposed to OPTIMUM.

pesto *noun* M20 **Italian** (contraction of *pestato* past participle of *pestare* to pound, crush). A sauce of crushed basil, nuts (especially pine nuts), cheese, garlic, and olive oil, served with pasta and other foods. Cf. PISTOU.

pétanque *noun* M20 **French**. A game similar to BOULE noun 2 sense 2.

pétillant *adjective* L19 **French**. Sparkling, lively. Of wine: slightly sparkling.

petit *adjective* LME **French** (cf. feminine PETITE). Little, small.

■ Occurs in various phrases used in English, and until the seventeenth century was in common use alongside the English form *petty*.

petit battement *noun phrase* plural **petits battements** E20 **French**. *Ballet* A BATTEMENT executed with the moving leg bent.

petit beurre *noun phrase* plural **petits beurres** E20 **French**. A sweet butter cookie.

petit bourgeois *noun & adjective phrase* plural **petits bourgeois**; (feminine **petite bourgeoise**, plural **petites bourgeoises**) M19 **French** (literally, 'little citizen'). **A** *noun phrase* M19 A member of the lower middle classes; *derogatory* a person judged to have conventional or conservative attitudes. **B** *adjective phrase* L19 Pertaining to or characteristic of the PETITE BOURGEOISIE; lower middle class; conventional.

■ Also partially Anglicized (L19 onward) as *petty bourgeois*.

petite *adjective & noun* M16 **French** (feminine of PETIT). **A** *adjective* **1 a** M16–L17 Of a small size or importance. **b** L18 Of small stature. Now chiefly of a woman or girl. **c** E20 Designating a small size in women's clothing. **2** E18 The French (feminine) for 'little, small', occurring in various phrases used in English. **3** M20 *Microbiology* Designating mutant strains of yeast that are characterized by defective mitochondrial DNA and tend to form small colonies. **B** *noun* **1** M20 A petite woman or girl. **2** M20 A petite size in women's clothing. **3** M20 A petite strain of yeast.

petite amie *noun phrase* plural **petites amies** M20 **French** (= little (female) friend). A young mistress.

petite bourgeoise see PETIT BOURGEOIS.

petite bourgeoisie *noun phrase* E20 **French**. The lower middle classes collectively.

■ Also partially Anglicized (M19, but mainly 20) as *petty bourgeoisie*.

petite noblesse *noun phrase* L19 **French**. The lesser nobility in France. Cf. HAUTE NOBLESSE.

petites amies, **petites marmites**, etc., plurals of PETITE AMIE, PETITE MARMITE, etc.

petit four *noun phrase* plural **petits fours** L19 **French** (literally, 'little oven'). A small cake or cookie usually served with the coffee after a meal.

petitio principii *noun phrase* M16 **Latin** (= assuming a principle, from *petitio* laying claim to + genitive of PRINCIPIUM). *Logic* A fallacy in which a conclusion is taken for granted in a premise; begging the question.

petit-maître *noun phrase* plural **petits-maîtres** E18 **French** (literally, 'little master'). **1** E18 A dandy, a fop. **2** M19 An artist, writer, etc., of minor importance.

■ In sense 2 sometimes translated as *little masters* with reference to practitioners of the minor arts, such as the engravers of late medieval Germany.

petit mal *noun phrase* L19 **French** (literally, 'little sickness'). Mild epilepsy, with only momentary loss of consciousness. Cf. GRAND MAL.

petit marmite *noun phrase* plural **petits marmites** E20 **French**. Soup served in the (individual serving sized) MARMITE in which it has been cooked.

petit pain *noun phrase* plural **petits pains** M18 **French**. A small bread roll.

petit point *noun phrase* L19 **French**. **1** L19 Embroidery on canvas using small stitches. **2** L19 Tent stitch.

petit poussin *noun phrase* plural **petits poussins** E20 **French**. A young chicken for eating.

■ Now rare, being almost entirely superseded by POUSSIN.

petits battements, **petits beurres**, etc., plurals of PETIT BATTEMENT, PETIT BEURRE, etc.

petits chevaux *noun phrase plural* L19 **French** (literally, 'little horses'). A gambling game in which bets are placed on mechanical horses made to spin around a flag at the center of a special table.

petits fours, **petits pains** plurals of PETIT FOUR, PETIT PAIN.

petits pois *noun phrase plural* E19 **French** (literally, 'small peas'). Small young green peas.

petits poussins plural of PETIT POUSSIN.

petits soins *noun phrase plural* E19 **French**. Small attentions or services.

petit suisse *noun phrase* E20 **French**. A small round cream cheese. Cf. FROMAGE FRAIS.

petit tranchet *noun phrase* M20 **French** (= little knife). *Archaeology* A small stone artifact of mesolithic and neolithic cultures with the end made into a broad cutting edge.

petit verre *noun phrase* plural **petits verres** M19 **French**. A glass of liqueur.

pétrissage *noun* L19 **French** (from *pétrir, pétriss-* to knead). A kneading process used in massage.

pétroleur *noun* (feminine **pétroleuse**) L19 **French** (from *pétrole* gasoline). An arsonist who uses gasoline.

pe-tsai *noun* L18 **Chinese** ((Pekingese) *báicài* (Wade–Giles *pê ts'ai*), literally, 'white vegetable': cf. PAK-CHOI). A kind of Chinese cabbage, *Brassica pekinensis*, with leaves in a loose head, grown as a winter vegetable.

peyote *noun* M19 **American Spanish** (from Nahuatl *peyotl*). MESCAL sense 3.

phaeton *noun* L16 **French** (*phaéton* from Latin *Phaethon* from Greek *Phaethōn* (*phaethōn* shining), in Greek mythology the son of Helios and Clymene, who was allowed to drive the sun's chariot for a day, with disastrous results). **1** L16–M18 A rash or adventurous charioteer like Phaethon; any charioteer; a thing that, like Phaethon, sets the world on fire. **2** M18 Chiefly *History* A light four-wheeled open carriage, usually drawn by a pair of horses, and with one or two forward-facing seats. **3** E20 A touring car.

phallus *noun* plural **phalli**, **phalluses** E17 **Late Latin** (from Greek *phallos*). **1** E17 An image of the erect penis, symbolizing the generative power in nature; *specifically* that carried in solemn procession in the Dionysiac festivals in ancient Greece. **2** E20 The penis, especially as an organ of symbolic significance; an erect penis.

phantasma *noun* plural **phantasmas**, **phantasmata** L16 **Italian** (*fantasma* from Latin *phantasma* from Greek, from *phantazein* to make visible). An illusion, a vision, a dream; an apparition, a ghost.

pharmacopoeia *noun* (also **pharmacopeia**) E17 **Modern Latin** (from Greek *pharmakopoiia* art of preparing drugs, from *pharmakopoios* preparer of drugs, from *pharmaco-* combining form of *pharmakon* drug + *-poios* making, maker). **1** E17 A book containing a list of drugs with their effects and directions for their use (and, formerly, their preparation and identification); *specifically* such a book officially published and revised periodically. **2** E18 A collection or stock of drugs.

phenomenon *noun* (also **phaenomenon**, **phainomenon**) plural **phenomena**, also (*nonstandard*) used as singular, **phenomenas** L16 Late Latin (*phaenomenon* from Greek *phainomenon* noun use of neuter present participle passive of *phainein* to show, (in passive) be seen, appear). **1** L16 A fact or event that appears or is perceived by one of the senses or by the mind; *especially* one whose cause or explanation is in question. **2** L17 *Philosophy* An immediate object of perception (as distinguished from substance, or a thing in itself). **3** E18 A very notable, extraordinary, or exceptional fact or occurrence; *colloquial* a thing, person, or animal remarkable for some unusual quality.

Phi Beta Kappa *noun phrase* M19 Greek (from the initial letters *phi, beta, kappa*, of *philosophia biou kubernētēs* philosophy the guide of life). (A member of) an intercollegiate society to which distinguished (usually undergraduate) scholars may be elected as an honor. Frequently *attributive*.

philia *noun* M20 Greek. Amity, friendship, liking.

philosophe *noun* OE French (from Latin *philosophus* from Greek *philosophos* lover of wisdom, from *philo-* from *philein* to love + *sophos* wise). A (skeptical) philosopher, *specifically* a member of the French rationalist group associated with the production of the *Encyclopédie* in the mid–eighteenth century.

■ *Philosophe*, which was also occasionally found in Anglicized form as *philosoph*, appears in Old English in the general sense of *philosopher*, and during the Middle Ages the form *philosophe* was reinforced by Old French *philosophe* or *filosophe*. Since the Enlightenment, the word is mainly used in English for the French Encyclopedists or, derogatively, for those who emulate their skeptical stance or fall into similar errors.

philosophia perennis *noun phrase* M19 Latin (= perennial philosophy). A posited core of philosophical truths independent of and unaffected by time or place, frequently taken to be exemplified in the writings of Aristotle and St. Thomas Aquinas.

philosophia prima *noun phrase* E17 Latin (= first philosophy). (The branch of inquiry that deals with) the most general truths of philosophy; *specifically* (the branch of inquiry that deals with) the divine and the eternal.

phobia *noun* L18 Latin (independent use of the Latin suffix *-phobia* from Greek *-phobos* fearing, from *phobos* fear). (A) fear, (a) horror, (an) aversion; *especially* an abnormal and irrational fear or dread aroused by a particular object or circumstance.

■ *Phobia* as a suffix also appears in numerous abstract nouns, especially in modern coinages after the Greek denoting states in clinical psychology, such as AGORAPHOBIA, *arachnophobia* (E20) 'fear of spiders', etc., and in other (often jocular or nonce) formations such as *Anglophobia* (L18), *Francophobia* (L19), etc.

phyllo *noun* (also **filo**) M20 Modern Greek (*phullo* leaf). Dough that can be stretched into very thin sheets and layered; pastry made from this dough and used in sweet and savory pastries.

physique *noun* E19 French (noun use of adjective = physical). The form, size, and development of a person's body.

pi *noun* LME Greek (in sense 2 representative of initial letter of Greek *periphereia* periphery). **1** LME The sixteenth letter (Π, π) of the Greek alphabet. **2** E18 *Mathematics* The ratio of the circumference of a circle to its diameter. Usually written π.

■ More recently (E20) pi (generally written π or Π and used attributively) has also become part of the technical vocabulary of Electricity (as *pi-network*, etc.) and Physics and

Chemistry (as π electron or Π molecule).

piaffe *verb & noun* **M18 French** (*piaffer* to strut, make a show). *Horsemanship* **A** *intransitive verb* M18 Move (especially on the spot) with a high slow trotting step. **B** *noun* L19 An act of piaffing.

pianissimo *adverb, adjective, & noun* **E18 Italian** (superlative of PIANO). *Music* **A** *adverb & adjective* E18 (A direction:) very soft(ly). **B** *noun* L19 plural **pianissimos, pianissimi** A very soft passage.

■ As a musical direction abbreviated to *pp* or *ppp*.

piano *noun 1* plural **pianos, piani M18 Italian** (from Latin *planus* flat, (later of sound) soft, low). **1** M18 *Music* A soft or quiet passage. **2** M19 A story in an Italian building. Cf. PIANO NOBILE.

piano *noun 2* plural **pianos E19 Italian** (abbreviation of PIANOFORTE or aphetized from FORTE-PIANO). **1** E19 A large keyboard musical instrument having metal strings struck by hammers and stopped by dampers, with two or three pedals to regulate the volume or length of the notes. **2** M20 The playing of this instrument.

piano *adverb & adjective* **L17 Italian** (from Latin *planus* flat, (later of sound) soft, low). **1** *adverb & adjective* L17 *Music* (A direction:) soft(ly), quiet(ly). **2** *adjective* E19 Of a person: quiet, subdued.

■ As a musical direction usually abbreviated to *p*.

pianoforte *noun* **M18 Italian** (earlier *pian(o) e forte*, literally, 'soft and loud' (with reference to its capacity for gradation of tone); cf. FORTE-PIANO). A PIANO noun 2 sense 1.

piano nobile *noun* **L19 Italian** (from *piano* floor, story + *nobile* noble, great). *Architecture* The main (usually first-floor) story of a large house, containing the principal rooms.

piano piano *adverb phrase* (also (earlier) **pian piano**) **E17 Italian** (= softly, softly). In a quiet leisurely manner; little by little.

piazza *noun* **L16 Italian** (= French *place* (town) square). **1** L16 A public square or marketplace, *especially* one in an Italian town. Formerly also, any open space surrounded by buildings. **2 a** M17 A covered gallery or walk surrounding an open square; a single such gallery or walk in front of a building. Now *rare*. **b** E18 The veranda of a house.

pibroch *noun* **E18 Gaelic** (*pìobaireachd* the art of playing the bagpipe, from *pìobair* piper (from *pìob* pipe, from English *pipe*) + suffix of function *-achd*). A series of variations on a theme for the bagpipes, usually of a martial or funerary character.

picador *noun* **L18 Spanish** (from *picar* to prick, pierce). *Bullfighting* A person mounted on horseback who goads the bull with a lance.

picaresque *adjective & noun* **E19 French** (from Spanish *picaresco*, from *pícaro* roguish, knavish, (noun) rogue; cf. next). **A** *adjective* **1** E19 Of or pertaining to rogues, knaves, or urchins; *especially* (of a style of especially Spanish fiction) dealing with the episodic adventures of such characters. **2** M20 Drifting; wandering.

picaro *noun* plural **picaros E17 Spanish** (see PICARESQUE). A rogue, a scoundrel.

picayune *noun & adjective* **E19 French** (*picaillon* old copper coin of Piedmont, halfpence, cash from Provençal *picaioun*, of unknown origin). **A** *noun* E19 Originally (in the southern United States), a Spanish half-real, worth 6¼ cents. Now, a five-cent piece or other coin of small value; *colloquial* an insignificant or mean person or thing. **B** *adjective* E19 Mean, contemptible, insignificant. *colloquial*.

piccolo *noun & adjective* **M19 Italian** (= small). **A** *noun* plural **piccolos 1** M19 A small flute sounding an octave higher than the ordinary flute; a player on this in an orchestra, etc. **b** L19 An organ stop having the tone of a piccolo. **2** M19 A small upright piano. **3** E20 A waiter's assistant in a hotel, restaurant, etc.; a page at a hotel. **4** M20 A jukebox. *slang.* **B** *adjective* M19 Designating the highest-pitched member of a family of musical instruments.

pickelhaube *noun* plural **pickelhaubes, pickelhauben** L19 **German.** *History* A spiked helmet worn by German soldiers, especially before and during World War I.

picot *noun* E17 **French** (diminutive of *pic* peak, point, prick). Any of a series of small loops worked in lace or embroidery, used to form an ornamental edging, buttonhole, etc.

picotee *noun & adjective* E18 **French** (*picoté(e)* past participle of *picoter* to mark with points, prick, from as PICOT). **A** *noun* E18 A variety of carnation, having light petals marked or edged with a darker color. **B** *adjective* L19 Of a color, pattern, etc.: resembling that of the picotee.

picquet variant of PIQUET.

pièce à thèse *noun phrase* plural **pièces à thèse** M20 **French.** A play written with the aim of supporting a thesis or proposition. Also called *thesis play*.

pièce de circonstance *noun phrase* plural **pièces de circonstance** M19 **French.** A literary composition, theory, etc., arising out of a particular situation.

pièce de résistance *noun phrase* plural **pièces de résistance** L18 **French. 1** L18 The most important or outstanding item. **2** M19 The main dish of a meal.

pièce d'occasion *noun phrase* plural **pièces d'occasion** L19 **French.** A literary or musical work written for a special occasion.

pièce noire *noun phrase* plural **pièces noires** M20 **French** (literally, 'black play'). A play or movie with a tragic or macabre theme.

■ The phrase originated with French dramatist Jean Anouilh (1910–87); see PIÈCE ROSE.

pièce rose *noun phrase* plural **pièces roses** M20 **French** (literally, 'pink play'). A play or movie with a pleasantly entertaining theme; a comedy.

■ *Pièces roses* and *Pièces noires* were the titles given by Anouilh to collections of his plays published in 1942, roughly analogous to George Bernard Shaw's *Plays: Pleasant and Unpleasant*.

pièces à thèse, pièces de circonstance, etc., plurals of PIÈCE À THÈSE, PIÈCE DE CIRCONSTANCE, etc.

pied-à-terre *noun* plural **pieds-à-terre** E19 **French** (literally, 'foot to earth'). A small townhouse, apartment, or room used for short periods of residence; a home base.

pied d'éléphant *noun phrase* plural **pieds d'éléphant** M20 **French** (literally, 'elephant's foot'). A padded sack used to protect the lower part of the body on a bivouac when mountaineering, etc.

pied noir *noun phrase* plural **pieds noirs** M20 **French** (literally, 'black foot'). A person of European origin who lived in Algeria during French rule.

■ Competing explanations of the sobriquet are based either on the black shoes worn by Europeans but not by native Algerians or on the traditional employment of barefooted Algerians as stokers on French steamers.

pieds-à-terre, pieds d'éléphant, etc., plurals of PIED-À-TERRE, PIED D'ÉLÉPHANT, etc.

pierrette *noun* L19 **French** (feminine diminutive of *Pierre* Peter, corresponding to next). A female member of a company of pierrots.

pierrot *noun* (also **Pierrot**) M18 **French** (appellative use of pet form of *Pierre* Peter). A typical character in French pantomime. Now also, a musical entertainer with a whitened face and a loose white costume.

Pietà *noun* M17 **Italian** (from Latin *pietas* piety). A painting or sculpture representing the Virgin Mary holding the dead body of Jesus on her lap or in her arms.

pietas *noun* E20 **Latin**. An attitude of respect toward an ancestor, institution, etc.

pietra commessa *noun phrase* plural **pietre commesse** M17 **Italian** (literally, 'stone fitted together'). (An example of) mosaic work.

pietra dura *noun phrase* plural **pietre dure** E19 **Italian** (literally, 'hard stone'). Semiprecious stones; *singular* and in *plural*, mosaic work of such stones.

pietre commesse, **pietre dure** plurals of PIETRA COMMESSA, PIETRA DURA.

pignon *noun* E17 **French** (= Spanish *piñon*, Portuguese *pinhão*, all from late Latin derivation of Latin *pinea* pine cone). The edible seed of the stone pine, *Pinus pinea*, of southern Europe.

pikau *noun & verb* M19 **Maori**. **A** *noun* M19 A pack for carrying on the back, a knapsack. **B** *transitive verb* L19 Carry (a load or pack) on the back. *New Zealand.*

piki *noun* L19 **Hopi** (*pí:ki*). Maize-meal bread in the form of very thin sheets, made by the Hopi Indians of the south-western United States.

pilaf *noun* (also **pilaff**, **pilau**, **pilaw**, **pulao**, and other variants) E17 **Turkish** (*pilâv* cooked rice = Persian *pīlaw* boiled rice and meat). An Indian or Middle Eastern dish of rice (or occasionally other grain) cooked in stock with spices and often meat, fish, vegetables, etc.

pileus *noun* plural **pilei** M18 **Latin** (= felt cap). **1** M18 *Botany* The spore-bearing circular structure surmounting the stipe in a mushroom or toadstool, which has an undersurface composed of radiating plates or gills. Also called *cap*. **2** L18 *Classical Antiquities* L18 A felt cap without a brim.

pilón *noun* plural **pilones** L19 **Mexican Spanish** (from Spanish = sugar loaf, pillar, post). In Mexico and the southwestern United States: a small gift given to a customer making a purchase, etc.

pilotis *noun plural* M20 **French**. *Architecture* A series of columns or piles, used to raise the base of a building above ground level.

pilpul *noun* L19 **Hebrew** (from *pilpēl* to search, debate hotly). (An instance of) subtle or keen rabbinical disputation; *transferred* unprofitable argument, hair-splitting.

pimento *noun & adjective* L17 **Spanish** (PIMIENTO). **A** *noun* plural **pimentos** **1** Cayenne pepper. Only in L17. **2** L17 The spice allspice; (more fully *pimento tree*) the West Indian tree, *Pimenta dioica*, of the myrtle family, from which allspice is obtained. Now *West Indies*. **3** E20 A sweet (especially a red) pepper, a capsicum. **B** *adjective* M20 Pimento red.

pimiento *noun* plural **pimientos** (also written **pimienta**) M17 **Spanish** (from Latin *pigmentum* paint, color). **1** M17 PIMENTO sense 2. *West Indies*. **2** M19 PIMENTO sense 3.

pina colada *noun* (also **piña colada** E20 **South American Spanish** (literally, 'strained pineapple' from *piña* (Portuguese *pinha*) pineapple, (originally pine cone, from Latin *pinea* pine cone). A drink made with pineapple juice, rum, and coconut (milk).

pinard *noun* (also **Pinard**) E20 **French**. Rough red wine; *generally* any wine; a glass of this.

piñata *noun* L19 **Spanish** (= jug, pot). In Mexico and the southwestern United States: a decorated container filled with candies or small gifts, which is opened (especially by breaking) by a blindfolded person at a festive celebration.

pinax *noun* plural **pinaces** L17 **Latin** (from Greek = board, plank, tablet, picture). **1** L17 A tablet; a list inscribed on this; a catalog, an index. Now *rare* or *obsolete*. **2** M19 *Antiquities* A (painted or engraved) plate, platter, or dish.

pince-nez *noun* (treated as *singular* or *plural*) L19 **French** (from *pincer* to pinch + *nez* nose). A pair of eyeglasses kept in position by a spring clipping the nose rather than by earpieces.

pinetum *noun* plural **pineta**, M19 **Latin** (from *pinus* pine). A plantation or collection of pines or other conifers, for scientific or ornamental purposes.

pinga *noun* M20 **Portuguese** (literally, 'drop (of water)'). A raw white rum distilled from sugar cane in Brazil; a drink of this.

pingo *noun* plural **pingo(e)s** M20 **Eskimo** ((Inuit) *pinguq* NUNATAK). *Physical Geography* A persistent low conical or dome-shaped mound, often with a crater on top, formed in regions with thin or discontinuous permafrost; a round depression in temperate regions thought to be the remains of such a mound.

pinole *noun* M19 **American Spanish** (from Aztec *pinolli*). Parched cornstarch mixed with the flour of mesquite beans, sugar, and spice.

piñon *noun* plural **piñons**, **piñones** M19 **Spanish** (cf. French PIGNON). (The edible seed of) any of a group of small pines of southwestern North America. Also, the wood of these trees.

pinto *adjective & noun* plural **pintos** M19 **Spanish** (= painted, mottled, from Proto-Romance). **A** *adjective*. **1** M19 Of a horse: piebald; skewbald. **2** E20 *pinto bean*, a variety of kidney bean with mottled seeds, widely cultivated in Central America and the southwestern United States; the seed of this. **B** *noun* M19 A piebald horse.

■ With reference to horses, chiefly North American.

piob mhor *noun phrase* M19 **Gaelic** (*piob mhòr*, literally, 'big pipe'). A kind of bagpipes traditionally played in the Scottish Highlands.

piolet *noun* M19 **French** ((Savoy dialect) diminutive of *piolo*, apparently cognate with *pioche*, *pic* pickax). A two-headed ice ax used by mountaineers.

piperade *noun* M20 **French**. A dish originating in the Basque country, consisting of eggs scrambled with tomatoes and peppers.

pipette *noun & verb* (also **pipet**) M19 **French** (diminutive of *pipe* pipe). **A** *noun* M19 A frequently tubular device for transferring or measuring small quantities of a liquid or gas by means of aspiration and dispensation, used especially in scientific laboratories. **B** M19 *transitive verb* inflected *pipette*, **pipete**. Transfer, measure, draw *off* or *out*, (a liquid or gas) with a pipette.

pipkrake *noun* plural **pipkrakes**, **pipkraker** M20 **Swedish** ((dialect) from *pip* pipe + *krake* variant of *klake* frozen ground). *Physical Geography* An ice needle; needle ice.

piquant *adjective* (in senses 2 and 3 also **piquante**) E16 **French** (present participial adjective of *piquer* to prick, sting). **1** E16 Sharp or stinging to the feelings; severe, bitter. Long *archaic*. **2** M17 Of food, etc.: agreeably pungent, sharp-tasting, spicy; savory, appetizing. **3** M17 Pleasantly stimulating to the mind; racy, spicy; fascinating, charming.

pique *noun* M16 **French** (literally, 'pike', figuratively, 'cutting remark', from *piquer* to prick, pierce, sting, irritate, *se piquer* take offense, from Proto-Romance, origin uncertain). **1** M16 A quarrel or feeling of enmity between two or more people; ill feeling, animosity. **2** L16 (A feeling of) anger or resentment resulting from a slight or injury, especially to one's pride; offense taken.

■ Also early (M17) in English use as verb.

piqué *noun, adjective, & verb* (also **pique** M19 **French** (noun use of past participle of *piquer* to backstitch). **A** *noun* **1** M19 A stiff fabric woven in a strongly ribbed or raised pattern (originally in imitation of hand quilting); the raised pattern (characteristic) of such a fabric. **2** L19 Work inlaid with gold, etc., dots. **3** M20 *Ballet* A step directly on to the point of the leading foot without bending the knee. **B** *adjective* **1** M19 *Cooking* Larded. *rare*. **2** L19 Made of piqué; having the pattern of piqué. **3**

L19 Inlaid with gold, etc., dots. **4** *Ballet* E20 Stepping directly on to the point of the leading foot without bending the knee. **C** *transitive verb* M19 *Cooking* Lard.

piquet *noun* (also **picquet**) M17 **French** (of unknown origin). A card game for two players with a deck of 32 cards, the cards from the two to the six being excluded.

piqûre *noun* (also **piqure**) E20 **French** (from *piquer*; see PIQUE). A hypodermic injection; a puncture made in the skin by such an injection.

piranha *noun* M18 **Portuguese** (from Tupi *pirányе, piráya*, from *pirá* fish + *sainha* tooth). Any of several gregarious predatory freshwater fishes of South America, noted for their aggressiveness and voracity.

piri-piri *noun* M20 **Ronga** (= pepper). A sauce made with red peppers. Also *piri-piri sauce*.

pirog *noun* plural **pirogi**, **pirogen** M19 **Russian**. A large Russian pie. Cf. PIROSHKI.

pirogue *noun* E17 **French** (probably from Carib). A long narrow canoe. Also, any canoe or open boat.

piroshki *noun plural* (also **pirotchki**, **pirozhki**) E20 **Russian** (*pirozhki* plural of *pirozhok* diminutive of PIROG). Small Russian pastries or patties filled with meat, fish, rice, etc.

pirouette *noun & verb* M17 **French** (ultimate origin unknown). **A** *noun* **1** M17 *Horsemanship* A full circle made by pivoting on a hind leg while walking or cantering. **2** E18 An act of spinning around on one foot or on the points of the toes by a ballet dancer, etc.; *generally* a rapid whirl of the body. **3** L19 *Music* A form of mouthpiece used with a shawm, rackett, etc. **B** *intransitive verb* E19 Perform a pirouette. Cf. RACKETT

pirozhki variant of PIROSHKI.

pis aller *noun* L17 **French** (from *pis* worse + *aller* to go). The worst that can be or happen; a last resort.

piscina *noun* plural **piscinas**, **piscinae** L16 **Latin** (= fishpond, in medieval Latin in sense 2, from *piscis* fish). **1** L16 A fishpond. Also (*historical*), a pool or pond for bathing or swimming. **2** L18 *Ecclesiastical* A stone basin for draining water used in the Mass.

pisé *noun & adjective* (also **pisée**) L18 **French** (noun use of past participle of *piser* to beat, pound, stamp (earth), from Latin *pinsere*). **A** *noun* L18 A building material of stiff clay or earth, sometimes mixed with gravel, forced between boards that are removed as it hardens; building with this material. Also *pisé de terre* (= of earth). Also called *terre pisée*. **B** *attributive* or as *adjective* M19 Made with or using *pisé*.

pissaladière *noun* (also **pissaladiera**) M20 **French** (from Provençal *pissaladiero*, from *pissala* salt fish). A Provençal open pie similar to pizza, usually with onions, anchovies, and black olives.

pissoir *noun* E20 **French**. A public urinal, especially in France.

piste *noun* E18 **French** (= track, from Latin *pista* (sc. *via*) beaten track, from feminine past participle of *pinsere* to pound, stamp). **1** E18 A trail or track beaten by a horse or other animal; the track of a racetrack or training ground. **2** E20 The specially marked-out rectangular playing area in fencing. **3** E20 A specially prepared or marked slope or trail of compacted snow used as a ski-run.

pistou *noun* M20 **Provençal** (= Italian PESTO). A sauce or paste made from crushed basil, garlic, cheese, etc., used especially in Provençal dishes; a thick vegetable soup made with this.

pita *noun* (also **pitta**) M20 **Modern Greek** (*pētta, pit(t)a* bread, cake, pie; cf. Turkish *pide*, Aramaic *pittā* in similar sense). A flat unleavened bread of Mediterranean and Arab countries, which can be cut open to receive a filling.

pithos *noun* plural **pithoi** L19 **Greek**. *Archaeology* A large spherical wide-mouthed earthenware jar used for holding wine, oil, food, etc.

piton *noun* L19 **French** (= eye-bolt). **1** L19 *Mountaineering* A metal spike that is hammered into rock or ice and used to secure a rope through an eye at one end. **2** E20 A (steep-sided) volcanic peak, especially in the West Indies.

pitta variant of PITA.

più *adverb* E18 **Italian.** *Music* More.

▪ Used in directions, as in *più mosso* more animated(ly).

pizza *noun* L19 **Italian** (= pie). A flat usually round base of dough baked with a topping of tomatoes, cheese, meat, olives, etc.

pizzeria *noun* M20 **Italian.** A place where pizzas are made or sold.

pizzicato *noun, adjective, & adverb* M19 **Italian** (past participle of *pizzicare* to pinch, twitch, from *pizzare*, from Old and Modern Italian *pizza* point, edge). *Music* **A** *noun* plural **pizzicati**, **pizzicatos**. M19 A note or passage played on a violin, cello, etc., by plucking a string with the finger instead of bowing. **B** *adjective & adverb* L19 (Played) by plucking a string instead of bowing.

placebo *noun* plural **placebo(e)s** ME **Latin** (= I shall please or be acceptable (first word of Psalm 114:9), 1st person singular future indicative of *placere* to please). **1** ME *Roman Catholic Church* The vespers for the dead, from the initial word of the antiphon formerly used to open the office. **2** LME–L18 A flatterer, a sycophant. **3** L18 A pill, medicine, procedure, etc., prescribed more for the psychological benefit to the patient of being given a prescription than for any physiological effect. Also, a substance with no therapeutic effect used as a control in testing new drugs, etc.; a blank sample in a test.

place d'armes *noun phrase* plural **places d'armes** E18 **French** (= place of arms). An assembly point for troops, weapons, or ammunition; a parade ground; an arsenal.

placement *noun* M19 **French** (from *placer* to place, seat (guests)). The allocation of places to people at a dining table, etc. Also *place à table*.

▪ Also fully naturalized, with pronunciation, in the sense of 'the action or an act of placing or positioning a thing or person', especially '(a period of) attachment to a workplace or educational establishment other than one's own'.

places d'armes plural of PLACE D'ARMES.

placet *interjection & noun* **L16 Latin** (= it pleases, 3rd person singular present indicative of *placere* to please). **A** *interjection* L16 Expressing assent to a vote in a council or assembly of a university, church, etc. **B** *noun* L16 Assent or sanction (as) by an utterance of '*placet*'.

plafond *noun* M17 **French** (from *plat* flat + *fond* bottom). **1** M17 *Architecture* An ornately decorated ceiling, either flat or vaulted; painting or decoration on a ceiling. Also, a soffit. **2** M20 *Cards* An early form of contract bridge.

plage *noun* LME **Old French** (= region, (modern) beach (from Italian *piaggia*) from medieval Latin *plaga* open space). **1** LME–E17 A region, a district; a zone. **2** LME–M17 Each of the four principal directions or quarters of the compass; a direction, a side. **3** L19 A beach or promenade at a seaside resort, especially at a fashionable one; a seaside resort. **4** M20 *Astronomy* A bright region of the sun's chromosphere, usually associated with sunspots. Also *plage region*.

planche *noun* E20 **French** (literally, 'plank'). *Gymnastics* A position in which the body is held parallel to the ground, especially by the arms (as on the parallel bars, etc.).

planchette *noun* M19 **French** (diminutive of *planche* plank, (wooden) board). **1** M19 A small usually heart-shaped board, supported by two castors and a vertical pencil, which, when one or more people rest their fingers lightly on the board, supposedly writes automatic messages under spirit guidance. **2** M20 A small shallow dish used to hold a sample while its radioactivity is measured.

planctus *noun* plural same **E20 Latin** (= beating of the breast, lamentation). A medieval poem or song of lament.

plastique *noun* **L19 French** (noun use of adjective = plastic, from Latin *plasticus* from Greek *plastikos* from *plastos* past participle of *plassein* to mold, form). **1** L19 *Dance* Statuesque poses or slow graceful movements; the art or technique of performing these. **2** E20 A plastic substance used for modeling. **3** M20 Plastic explosive; a plastic bomb.

plastiqueur *noun* **M20 French** (from as PLASTIQUE). A person who plants or detonates a plastic bomb.

plat *noun* **M18 French**. A dish of food.

plat du jour *noun phrase* **E20 French** (= dish of the day). A dish specially featured on a restaurant's menu for a particular day.

plateau *noun & adjective* plural **plateaux**, **plateaus** **L18 French** (Old French *platel*, from *plat* wide, flat, from popular Latin, from Greek *platus* broad, flat). **A** *noun* **1** L18 *Physical Geography* An elevated tract of comparatively flat or level land; a tableland. **b** L19 *transferred* A more or less level portion of a graph or trace (originally, of the pulse) adjacent to a lower sloping portion; a stage, condition, or period when there is neither an increase nor a decrease in something. **2** L18 An ornamented tray or dish for table service. **B** E20 *attributive* or as *adjective* Of the nature of or pertaining to a plateau.

platteland *noun* **M20 Afrikaans** (from Dutch *plat* flat + *land* country). The remote rural inland part of South Africa.

■ In South Africa often used attributively with derogatory connotations of backwardness and reaction, as in 'platteland mentality'.

platzel *noun* **M20 Yiddish** (perhaps related to German *Plätzchen* fancy biscuit). A flat crisp bread roll.

playa *noun* **M19 Spanish** (= shore, beach, coast, from late Latin *plagia* open space). **1** M19 A flat area of silt or sand, free of vegetation and usually salty, lying at the bottom of a desert basin and dry except after rain; (more fully *playa lake*) a temporary lake formed in such an area. **2** M19 In Spain and Spanish-speaking countries: a beach. **3** L19 *Geography* Flat alluvial coastland.

plaza *noun* **L17 Spanish** (from Proto-Romance source of *place*). A marketplace, square, or open public space, originally in Spain and Spanish-speaking countries; (chiefly *North America*) a large paved area surrounded by or adjacent to buildings, especially as a feature of a shopping complex.

plectrum *noun* plural **plectrums**, **plectra** **LME Latin** (from Greek *plēktron* anything to strike with, from *plēssein* to strike). **1** LME Originally (*rare*), a device for tightening the strings of a harp. Now, a thin flat piece of horn, metal, plastic, etc., held in the hand and used to pluck the strings of a guitar, lyre, etc. Also, the corresponding mechanical part of a harpsichord, etc. **2** E19 *Anatomy* and *Zoology* A small process, a single thick bristle.

plein-air *adjective* **L19 French** (from EN PLEIN AIR (literally, 'in full air')). Designating a style or school of impressionist painting originating in France during the late 1860s, that sought to represent the transient effects of atmosphere and light by direct observation from nature. Also, designating a work painted out of doors or representing an outdoor scene and painted with a spontaneous technique.

■ Also as a noun phrase *plein air*.

plein-airisme *noun* **M20 French** (from as PLEIN-AIR). The theories and practices of the *plein-air* school of painters.

plein-airiste *noun* **L19 French** (from as PLEIN-AIR). A painter of the *plein-air* school.

plein jeu *adverb, adjective, & noun phrase* **M19 French** (= full play). *Music* **A** *adverb & adjective phrase* M19 (A direction:) with full power; *specifically* without reeds in organ playing. **B** *noun* M19 A type of mixture stop in an organ; music written for the full organ.

plenum *noun & adjective* L17 **Latin** (neuter of *plenus* full (sc. *spatium* space); in sense 2 later influenced by Russian *plenum* plenary session). **A** *noun* **1** L17 *Physics* A space completely filled with matter; *specifically* the whole of space regarded as being so filled. **b** L18 *transferred* A condition of fullness; a full place. **2** L18 A full assembly; a meeting of a legislative body, conference, association, etc., at which all the members are expected to be present; *specifically* a meeting of all the members of a Communist Party committee. **3** M20 (The air in) a plenum chamber in a ventilation system, etc. **B** *attributive* or as *adjective* E20 Pertaining to or designating an artificial ventilation system in which fresh air is forced into a building and drives out the stale air.

pleroma *noun* M18 **Greek** (*plērōma* that which fills, from *plēroun* to make full, from *plērēs* full). *Theology* **1** M18 In Gnosticism, the spiritual universe as the abode of God and of the totality of the divine powers and emanations. **2** E19 The totality of the Godhead that dwells in Christ; completeness, fullness (with allusion to Colossians 2:9).

plethora *noun* M16 **Late Latin** (from Greek *plēthōrē* fullness, repletion, from *plēthein* to be full). **1** M16 *Medicine* Originally a condition characterized by an excess of blood or a bodily humor; later, an excess of red blood cells. **2** E18 Overfullness, oversupply; a glut.

■ Sense 2 is now the only current sense, as sense 1, except in historical contexts, is rare or obsolete.

plié *noun* L19 **French** (past participle of *plier* to bend). *Ballet* A movement in which the knees are bent outward in line with the out-turned feet.

plique à jour *noun* L19 **French** (literally, 'braid that lets in the daylight'). A technique in enameling in which small areas of translucent enamel are fused into the spaces of a wire framework to give an effect similar to stained glass.

plissé *noun & adjective* L19 **French** (past participle of *plisser* to pleat). **A** *noun* L19 Originally, a piece of fabric shirred or gathered into narrow pleats; a gathering of pleats. Now usually, fabric with a wrinkled or puckered finish produced by chemical treatment. **B** *adjective* L19 Formed into small pleats; treated so as to give a wrinkled or puckered effect.

plombière *noun* M19 **French** (*Plombières*-les-Bains, a village in the Vosges department of eastern France). A kind of dessert made with ice cream and glacé fruits.

plongeur *noun* M20 **French** (from *plonger* to plunge, immerse in liquid). A person employed as a menial in a restaurant or hotel, especially to wash dishes.

■ The word entered English via George Orwell's account of menial labor in *Down and Out in Paris and London* (1933).

plumeau *noun* plural **plumeaux** L19 **French** (from *plume* from Latin *pluma* small soft feather). A duvet.

plus ça change *interjection & noun phrase* E20 **French** (shortened form of *plus ça change, plus c'est la même chose*). The more things change, the more they remain the same.

■ The observation was originally made by the French author and satirical journalist Alphonse Karr (1808–90) writing in *Les Guêpes* (January 1849).

Pluvius *adjective* E20 **Latin** (= rainy, causing or bringing rain). Designating the insurance of holidays, outdoor sports and events, etc., against disruption by bad weather.

■ Frequently in the phrase *Pluvius policy*.

p.m. abbreviation of POST MERIDIEM.

pneuma *noun* L19 **Greek** (= wind, breath, spirit, that which is blown or breathed, from *pneein, pnein* to blow, breathe). The spirit of a person, as opposed to the soul; the breath of life.

■ In Stoic and Epicurean philosophy the *pneuma* was a person's vital force or energy, but modern usage takes its cue from the New Testament distinction between the spirit and the soul or PSYCHE (cf. 1 Thessalonians 5.23).

poblador *noun* plural **pobladores** M20 **Spanish**. In Spanish America: a settler, a colonist; *specifically* a country person who moves to settle or squat in a town.

pochade *noun* L19 **French** (from *pocher* to sketch (roughly), blur). A rough, smudgy, or blurred sketch.

poché *noun* E20 **French** (noun use of past participle of *pocher* to sketch). *Architecture* Shading on an architectural plan representing the solid parts of a building; the use of such shading.

pochette *noun* L19 **French. 1** L19 A small violin, as used by French dancing masters. **2** E20 A small pocket. **3** E20 A handbag shaped like an envelope. Also *pochette bag*.

pochismo *noun* plural **pochismos** M20 **Mexican Spanish** (from as POCHO). A form of slang consisting of English words given a Mexican Spanish form or pronunciation; a word of this sort.

■ An example of a *pochismo* is *lonche* for 'lunch'.

pocho *noun & adjective* plural of noun **pochos** M20 **Mexican Spanish** (= Spanish *pocho* discolored, pale, faded). (Designating or pertaining to) a citizen of the United States of Mexican origin or a culturally Americanized Mexican. Often *derogatory*.

pochoir *noun* M20 **French** (= stencil). A process used in book illustration, especially for limited editions, in which a monochrome print is colored by hand, using a series of stencils; a print made by this process.

pococurante *noun & adjective* M18 **Italian** (from *poco* little + *curante* caring). **A** *noun* M18 A careless, indifferent, or nonchalant person. Now *rare*. **B** *adjective* E19 Caring little; careless, indifferent, nonchalant.

pocosin *noun* (also **poquosin**) M17 **Algonquian** (probably from Algonquian *poquosin*). In the southern United States: a tract of low swampy ground, usually wooded; a marsh, a swamp.

podium *noun* plural **podia**, (in branch I also) **podiums** M18 **Latin** (= elevated place, balcony from Greek *podion* diminutive of *pous, pod-* foot). **I 1** M18 A raised platform surrounding the arena in an ancient amphitheater. **2** L18 *Architecture* **a** A continuous projecting base or pedestal, a stylobate. **b** M20 A projecting lower structure around the base of a tower block. **3** M20 A raised platform or dais at the front of a hall or stage; *specifically* one occupied by the conductor of an orchestra. **II 4** M19 *Zoology* A foot; an organ acting as a foot.

podzol *noun* (also **podsol**) E20 **Russian** (from *pod-* under + *zola* ash; variant altered after *-sol* from Latin *solum* soil). *Soil Science* An acidic, generally infertile soil characterized by a white or gray subsurface layer resembling ash, and occurring especially under coniferous woods or heaths in moist, usually temperate climates.

poêlée *noun* M19 **French** (literally, 'panful', from *poêler* to cook in a pan). A broth or stock made with bacon and vegetables.

poète maudit *noun phrase* plural **poètes maudits** M20 **French** (literally, 'cursed poet'). A poet or other creative artist who is insufficiently appreciated by his or her contemporaries.

■ *Les Poètes maudits* (1884) was the title of a study of several such poets by the French Symbolist poet Paul Verlaine (1844–96).

poffertje *noun* (also **poffertjie**) L19 **Dutch** (*poffertje*, Afrikaans *poffertjie*, from French *pouffer* to blow up). A small light doughnut or fritter dusted with sugar, as made in the Low Countries and South Africa.

pogrom *noun & verb* E20 **Russian** (= devastation, from *gromit'* to destroy by violent means). **A** *noun* **1** E20 An organized massacre in Russia, originally and especially of Jews. **2** E20 *generally* An organized, officially tolerated, attack on any community or group. **B** *transitive verb* E20 Massacre or destroy in a pogrom.

poi *noun* E19 **Polynesian** (cf. POIPOI). A Hawaiian dish made from the fermented root of the taro. Also = POIPOI.

poilu *noun* E20 **French** (= hairy, virile, from Latin *pilus* hair). A soldier in the French army, *especially* one who fought in World War I.

■ Slang, alluding to the unkempt appearance.

point *noun* M17 **French** (= stitch). Needle-lace.

■ Chiefly in *point de* (or *d'*) (of), specifying a real or supposed place of manufacture, as *point d'Alençon, point d'Angleterre, point de France, point de Paris, point de Venise,* etc. Cf. PETIT POINT.

point d'appui *noun phrase* E19 **French** (= point of support). A fulcrum; a strategic point.

point de départ *noun phrase* E20 **French**. A point of departure.

point de repère *noun phrase* L19 **French**. A point of reference.

point d'orgue *noun phrase* L19 **French**. An organ point, a pedal point.

pointe *noun* M19 **French**. *Dancing* The tip of the toe. Also, a dance movement executed on the tips of the toes.

pointillé *adjective* E20 **French** (past participle of *pointiller* to mark with dots). Ornamented with designs engraved or drawn with a sharp-pointed tool or style.

pointillism *noun* (also **pointillisme**) E20 **French** (*pointillisme*, from *pointiller* to mark with dots, from *pointille* from Italian *puntiglio* diminutive of *punto* point). **1** E20 A technique of impressionist painting in which luminous effects are produced by tiny dots of various pure colors, which become blended in the viewer's eye. **2** M20 *Music* The breaking up of musical texture into thematic, rhythmic, and tonal fragments.

poipoi *noun* E19 **Polynesian** (reduplication of POI). A Polynesian dish made from fermented fruit, especially breadfruit.

poivrade *noun* L17 **French** (from *poivre* pepper). Pepper sauce.

polder *noun* E17 **Dutch** (from Middle Dutch *polre*). A piece of low-lying land reclaimed from the sea, a lake, etc., and protected by dikes, originally and especially in the Netherlands.

polenta *noun* OE **Latin** (in later use directly from Italian from Latin = pearl barley). Originally, pearl barley, (porridge made from) barley meal. Later, cornmeal as used in Italian cooking; a paste or dough made from this boiled and then often fried or baked.

policier *noun* L20 **French** (literally, 'detective novel'). A movie based on a police novel. Cf. ROMAN POLICIER.

polis *noun* plural **poleis** L19 **Greek** (= city). *History* A city-state, especially in ancient Greece; *specifically* such a state considered in its ideal form.

polisson *noun* M19 **French**. An urchin, a scamp; an ill-bred and uncouth person.

Politbureau *noun* (also **politburo**, plural **politburos**) E20 **Russian** (*politbyuro*, from *polit(icheskiĭ* political + *byuro* bureau). The highest policy-making committee of a Communist country or party, especially of the former USSR. Also *transferred* and *figurative*.

politesse *noun* E18 **French** (from Italian *politezza, pulitezza,* from *pulito* from Latin *politus* past participle of *polire* to smooth, polish). Formal politeness.

politique *noun* E17 **French** (use as noun of adjective = political). **1** *History* E17 A member or supporter of a French opportunist and moderate party, founded in *c.*1573, which regarded peace and reform as more important than the continuing civil war between Catholics and Huguenots. Also, an indifferentist, a temporizer. **2** M20 A political concept or doctrine; an expression of political ideas.

polka *noun & verb* M19 **German** (French from Czech, perhaps related to *Polka* feminine of *Polák* a Pole). **A** *noun* **1** M19 A lively dance of Bohemian origin in duple time. **2** M19 A piece of music for this dance or in its rhythm. **3** M19 A woman's tight-fitting jacket, usually knitted. Now *rare.* **B** *intransitive verb* M19 Dance the polka.

■ The nineteenth-century craze for the *polka* led to the word's being attached a variety of commercial articles; hence *polka dot* for a pattern of dots of uniform size and distribution.

pollo *noun* plural **pollos** M19 **Spanish** (Italian = chicken). *Cooking* Chicken, a chicken dish, *especially* one cooked in an Italian or (Mexican-)Spanish fashion.

polloi *noun* M20 **Greek** (= many). A crowd, a mob.

■ Slang, shortened from HOI POLLOI.

polonaise *noun, adjective, & verb* M18 **French** (noun use of feminine of *polonais* Polish, from medieval Latin *Polonia* Poland). **A** *noun* **1** M18 A slow dance of Polish origin, consisting chiefly of an intricate march or procession, in triple time; a piece of music for this dance or in its time or rhythm. **2** L18 A kind of dress or overdress, with the skirt open at the front and looped up at the back, originally resembling a garment worn by Polish women. **b** L19 A fabric made from a silk and cotton mixture. **3** L19 *Cooking* A dish cooked in a Polish style. **4** M20 A polonaise rug or carpet. **B** *adjective* **1** E20 Designating a kind of rug or carpet made in Persia during the sixteenth and seventeenth centuries, using silver and gold warp threads. **2** *Cooking* M20 Of a dish: cooked in a Polish style. **C** *intransitive verb* E19 Dance a polonaise; move in a stately manner.

polska *noun* L19 **Swedish** (from *Polsk* Polish). A processional Scandinavian folk dance of Polish origin, usually in 3/4 time; a piece of music for this dance.

poltergeist *noun* M19 **German** (from *poltern* to make a noise, create a disturbance + *Geist* ghost). A spirit believed to manifest itself by making noises and moving physical objects.

polynya *noun* (also **polynia**) M19 **Russian** (from base of *pole, polyana* field). A space of open water in the midst of ice, especially in Arctic seas.

pomade *noun & verb* M16 **French** (*pommade* from Italian *pomata* from modern Latin POMATUM). **A** *noun* M16 A scented ointment (in which apples were perhaps originally an ingredient) for the skin, now especially for the skin of the head and for the hair. **B** *transitive verb* L19 Anoint with pomade. Chiefly as *pomaded* participial adjective.

pomatum *noun & verb* M16 **Modern Latin** (from Latin *pomum* apple). **A** *noun* M16 Hair ointment, pomade. **B** *transitive verb* M17 Anoint with pomatum. Chiefly as *pomatumed* participial adjective.

pomme *noun* E20 **French** (short for POMME DE TERRE). *Cooking* A potato.

■ Chiefly plural and in phrases designating ways of cooking potatoes, as in *pommes Anna* (sliced, buttered potatoes baked in a casserole) and *pommes frites* (French fries).

pomme de terre *noun* plural **pommes de terre** E19 **French** (literally, 'apple of the earth'). *Cooking* A potato.

pompadour *noun & adjective* M18 **French** (Jeanne-Antoinette Poisson, Marquise de *Pompadour* (1721–64), mistress of Louis XV of France). **A** *noun* **1** M18 Any of various items of costume fashionable in the time of the Marquise de Pompadour or resembling these. **2** M18 A shade of crimson or pink; a fabric of this color. **3** M18 A South American cotinga with brilliant crimson-purple plumage. Also *pompadour cotinga.* **4a** L19 A style of dressing men's hair, in which it is combed back from the forehead without a parting. **b** L19 A style of arranging women's hair, in which it is turned back off the forehead in a roll, sometimes over a pad. **B** *attributive* or as *adjective* M18 (Of dress, furniture, etc.) in the style prevalent in the time of the Marquise de Pompadour; *specifically* (**a**) of a crimson color or fabric; (**b**) patterned with sprigs of (usually pink and blue) flowers on a white ground; (**c**) (of hair) arranged in a pompadour.

pompier *noun* M19 **French** (from *pompe* pump). **1** M19 In France, a fireman. **2** E20 An artist regarded as painting in an academic, imitative, vulgarly neoclassical style.

■ The designation of late nineteenth-century French academic artists as *pompiers* is probably based on their fondness for showing the Greek and Roman heroes in their pictures wearing helmets that put the viewer in mind of the helmets worn by Parisian firefighters.

pompon *noun* (also (in senses 2 and 3) **pompom**, (in sense 1) **pompoon**) M18 **French** (of unknown origin). **1** M18 A bunch of ribbon, feathers, flowers, silk threads, etc., formerly worn by women in the hair, or on the cap or dress. *obsolete* except *historical*. **2** M19 A variety of chrysanthemum, dahlia, or cabbage rose, bearing small globular flowers. **3** L19 An ornamental ball of wool, silk, ribbons, etc., on a woman's hat, a slipper, etc.; the round tuft on a sailor's cap, on the front of a shako, etc.

pomposo *adverb & noun* E19 **Italian** (from Latin *pomposus* from *pompa* solemn procession, from Greek *pompē* from *pempein* to send). **A** *adverb* E19 *Music* (A direction:) in a stately manner. **B** *noun* **1** M20 An affected, self-important person. **2** M20 *Music* A stately movement or passage.

poncho *noun* plural **ponchos** E18 **South American Spanish** (from Araucanian). A South American cloak made of a piece of cloth like a blanket with a slit in the middle for the head; any garment in this style.

poncif *noun* E20 **French** (literally, 'pounced design'). Stereotyped literary ideas, plot, character, etc.

pondok *noun* (also **pondokkie**) E19 **Afrikaans** (probably from Malay, ultimately from Arabic *funduq* hotel). A shack or shanty made of oddments of wood, corrugated iron, etc.; *transferred* a house, etc., in a poor state of repair. *South African*.

pons asinorum *noun phrase* M18 **Latin** (= bridge of asses). The fifth proposition of the first book of Euclid, so called from the difficulty beginners have in 'getting over' it.

ponticello *noun, adverb, & adjective* M18 **Italian** (= little bridge). *Music* **A** *noun* plural **ponticellos**. M18 The bridge of a stringed instrument. **B** *adverb & adjective* M19 (A direction:) with the bowing close to the bridge.

pontifex *noun* (also **Pontifex**) plural **pontifices** L16 **Latin** (from *pons, pontis* bridge + *-fex* from *facere* to make). **1** L16 *Roman History* A member of the principal college of priests in ancient Rome. **2** M17 The Pope.

pontificalia *noun plural* L16 **Latin** (noun use of neuter plural of *pontificalis* pontifical). The vestments and insignia of a bishop, cardinal, or abbot; pontificals.

pontil *noun* M19 **French** (apparently from Italian *pontello, puntello* diminutive of *punto* point). *Glassmaking* An iron rod used to hold or shape soft glass (also *pontil rod*). Also called *punty*.

pooja variant of PUJA.

poort *noun* L18 **Dutch** (*poort* gate, port). In South Africa: a narrow mountain pass, *especially* one cut by a stream or river.

popadam variant of POPPADAM.

popote *noun* E20 **French**. A French military kitchen or canteen.

poppadam *noun* (also **popadam**, **poppadom**, and other variants) E19 **Tamil** (*pappaṭam*, perhaps from *paruppa aṭam* lentil cake). A (flat cake of) thin crisp spiced bread usually eaten with curry or other Indian food.

poquosin variant of POCOSIN.

port-a-beul *noun* (also **puirt-a-beul**) plural **puirt-a-beul** E20 **Gaelic** (literally, 'music from mouth'). A quick lively tune of Lowland Scottish origin to which Gaelic words of a quick repetitive nature have been added.

portail *noun* L15 **French** (literally, 'façade of a church', alteration of Old French *portal* from medieval Latin *portale*). A door or gateway.

■ Confused with *portal* in both French and English.

portamento *noun* plural **portamenti** L18 **Italian** (literally, 'a carrying'). *Music* Gliding or moving from one note to another without a break in singing or in playing a trombone or a bowed stringed instrument, as a violin. Also, piano playing of a style between legato and staccato.

port-crayon *noun* (also **porte-crayon**) E18 **French** (*porte-crayon*, from *porte-* stem of *porter* to carry + *crayon* crayon). An instrument used to hold a crayon for drawing, usually a metal tube split at the end with a sliding ring so as to secure the crayon.

port de bras *noun phrase* plural **ports de bras** E20 **French** (literally, 'carriage of the arms'). *Ballet* The action or manner of moving and posing the arms; any of a series of exercises designed to develop graceful movement and disposition of the arms.

port de voix *noun* plural **ports de voix** M18 **French** (literally, 'carrying of the voice'). *Music* Originally, a kind of APPOGGIATURA. Now, a vocal PORTAMENTO.

porte-bouquet *noun* M19 **French** (from *porte-* stem of *porter* to carry + *bouquet* bouquet). A device for holding a bouquet.

porte-cochère *noun* (originally **port-cocher**; also **porte cochère**) L17 **French** (from *porte* port + *cochère* feminine adjective from *coche* coach). **1** L17 A gateway for carriages, leading into a courtyard. **2** L19 A covered area at the entrance to a building into which vehicles can be driven.

porte-crayon variant of PORT-CRAYON.

portée *noun* (also **portee**) L19 **French** (from *porter* to carry, from Latin *portare*). **1** L19 The importance or weight of a theory, an argument, etc.; the (far-reaching) consequences of an action or event. **2** E20 In handloom weaving, a specified number of threads grouped together to form the warp. **3** M20 *Military* A self-propelled vehicle on which an antitank gun can be mounted.

porte-monnaie *noun* M19 **French** (from *porte-* stem of *porter* to carry + *monnaie* money). A flat purse or pocketbook, especially of leather.

porteur *noun* M20 **French** (literally, 'a person who carries'). *Ballet* A male dancer whose role is (only) to lift and support a ballerina when she performs leaping or jumping movements.

portico *noun* plural **portico(e)s** E17 **Italian** (from Latin *porticus* porch). *Architecture* A formal entrance to a classical temple, church, or other building, consisting of columns at regular intervals supporting a roof often in the form of a pediment; a covered walkway in this style; a colonnade.

portière *noun* M19 **French** (from *porte* door). A curtain hung over a door or doorway, as a screen or for ornament, or to prevent drafts.

portmanteau *noun & adjective* M16 **French** (*portemanteau* from *porte-* stem of *porter* to carry + *manteau* mantle). **A** *noun* plural **portmanteaus, portmanteaux** **1** M16 A case or bag for carrying clothing, etc., when traveling, *especially* one made of stiff leather and hinged at the back so as to open into two equal parts. **2** E18 A rack or arrangement of pegs for hanging clothes on. Now *rare.* **B** *attributive* or as *adjective* L19 Of a word, expression, etc.: consisting of a blend, both in spelling and meaning, of two other words. Of a description, expression, etc.: of general or widespread application.

portrait parlé *noun phrase* plural **portraits parlés** E20 **French** (= spoken portrait). A detailed chiefly anthropometric description of a person's physical characteristics, especially of the type invented by Bertillon and used in the identification of criminals.

ports de bras, ports de voix plurals of PORT DE BRAS, PORT DE VOIX.

posada *noun* M18 **Spanish** (from *posar* to lodge). **1** M18 In Spain and Spanish-speaking countries: an inn or place of accommodations for travelers. **2** M20 In Mexico: each of a series of visits traditionally paid to different friends before Christmas, representing Mary and Joseph's search for a lodging in Bethlehem.

posaune *noun* plural **posaunen, posaunes** E18 **German** (ultimately from Old French *buisine* from Latin *buccina* trumpet). *Music* **1** E18 A trombone. **2** M19 An organ reed stop resembling a trombone in tone.

posé *adjective & noun* E18 **French** (past participle of *poser* to place, pose). **A** *adjective* **1** E18 *Heraldry* Of an animal: standing still. **2** M19 Composed, poised, self-possessed. **3** M20 *Ballet* Of a position: held, prolonged. **4** M20 Adopted as a pose. *rare.* **B** *noun* **1** E20 *Ballet* A movement in which a dancer steps with a straight leg on to the full or half point. **2** M20 *North American History* A resting place on a portage.

pose plastique *noun phrase* plural **poses plastiques** M19 **French** (literally, 'flexible pose'). A type of *tableau vivant*, usually one featuring near-naked women.

poseur *noun* (feminine **poseuse**) L19 **French** (from *poser* to pose). A person who poses for effect or attitudinizes; one who adopts an affected style or demeanor.

post-bellum *adjective* (also **Post-bellum, post-Bellum**) L19 **Latin** (from *post* after + *bellum* war). Existing, occurring, etc., after a (particular) war, especially the American Civil War. Opposed to ANTEBELLUM.

post coitum *adjective, adverb & noun phrase* E20 **Latin** (from *post* after + *coitum* accusative of COITUS). (Condition) following sexual intercourse; postcoital(ly) (state).

■ Used especially with reference to the saying *post coitum omne animal triste est* 'after sexual intercourse every animal is sad'. The saying itself is not known from classical Latin, although the idea can be traced back to passages in Aristotle and Pliny.

poste restante *adverb & noun phrase* M18 **French** (= letter(s) remaining). **1** *adverb & noun phrase* M18 (A direction written on a letter indicating that it is) to remain at the post office specified until called for by the addressee. **2** *noun* M19 The department in a post office where such letters are kept.

post eventum *adverb phrase* M19 **Latin** (= after the event). POST FACTUM.

post factum *adverb phrase* L17 **Latin** (= after the fact). After the event; with hindsight.

post festum *adverb phrase* L19 **Latin** (= after the festival). After the event.

post hoc *adverb & adjective phrase* M19 **Latin**. After this; after the event; consequent(ly).

■ Chiefly with reference to the fallacy *post hoc, ergo propter hoc* 'after this, therefore because of this'.

postiche *adjective & noun* (as adjective also (earlier) **postique**) E18 **French** (from Italian *posticcio* counterfeit, feigned). **A** *adjective* E18 Artificial; (of a decoration in architecture, etc.) added to a finished work, especially inappropriately or superfluously. *rare.* **B** *noun* **1** L19 An imitation substituted for the real thing; *especially* a piece of false hair worn as an adornment. **2** L19 Imitation, pretense. *rare.*

post meridiem *adjective & adverb phrase* M17 **Latin.** After midday; between noon and midnight.

■ Abbreviated to *p.m.*

postmortem *adverb, adjective, noun, & verb* (also **post-mortem**, (especially as adverb) **post mortem**) M18 **Latin. A** *adverb* M18 After death. **B** *adjective* M18 Taking place, formed, or done after death or (*colloquial*) after the conclusion of a matter (cf. sense C.2 below). **C** *noun* **1** M19 An examination of a body performed after death especially in order to determine the cause of death; an autopsy. **2** E20 An analysis or discussion conducted after the conclusion of a game, examination, or other event. *colloquial.* **D** *transitive verb* L19 Conduct a postmortem examination of.

postpartum *adjective & adverb* M19 **Latin** (*post partum* after childbirth). *Medicine* (Occurring, existing, etc.) after childbirth; postnatal(ly).

post rem *adjective & adverb phrase* E20 **Medieval Latin** (= after the thing). *Philosophy* Subsequent to the existence of something else; (of a universal) existing only as a mental concept or as an abstract word after the fact of being experienced from particulars. Cf. ANTE REM, IN RE.

postscriptum *noun* plural **postscripta** E16 **Latin** (noun use of neuter past participle of *postscribere* to write after, from *post* after + *scribere* to write). Additional matter appended to any text, a postscript.

potage *noun* ME **Old and Modern French** (literally, 'what is put in a pot', from *pot* pot). (A) soup, *especially* (a) thick (vegetable) soup.

■ Originally from Old French, the word was Anglicized in the form *pottage*; it was later reintroduced from French first in Scotland and later (M17) in England with reference to dishes of French provenance.

potager *noun* (also **potagère**) M17 **French** (in *(jardin) potager* (garden) for the kitchen). A kitchen garden.

■ The original sense of *potager* as 'one who makes pot(t)ages' is long obsolete. The seventeenth-century garden writer John Evelyn introduced the word with its present sense in the form *potagere*.

pot-au-feu *noun* plural **pot-au-feux** L18 **French** (literally, 'pot on the fire'). A large cooking pot of a kind common in France; the (traditional) soup cooked in this.

pot de chambre *noun phrase* plural **pots de chambre** L18 **French.** A chamber pot.

pot-et-fleur *noun* M20 **French** (literally, 'pot and flower'). A style of floral decoration using potted plants together with cut flowers.

potiche *noun* L19 **French.** A large (especially Chinese) porcelain jar or vase with a rounded bulging shape and a wide mouth, frequently having a lid.

potpourri *noun* (also **pot-pourri**) E17 **French** (literally, 'rotten pot', from *pot* pot + *pourri* past participle of *pourrir* to rot (translating Spanish OLLA PODRIDA)). **1** E17–E18 A stew made of different kinds of meat. **2** M18 Dried flower petals, leaves, etc., mixed with spices and kept in a jar or bowl to scent the air. Also, a container for holding this. **3** M19 *figurative* A medley, *especially* a musical or literary one.

potrero *noun* plural **potreros** M19 **Spanish** (from as next). **1** M19 In South America and the southwestern United States, a paddock or pasture for horses or cattle. **2** L19 In the southwestern United States, a narrow steep-sided plateau.

potro *noun* plural **potros** L19 **Spanish.** A colt, a pony.

pots de chambre plural of POT DE CHAMBRE.

poudre *noun* L18 **French** (= powder, earlier *pol(d)re* from Latin *pulvis, pulver-* dust). Light powdery snow. *Canadian.*

poudré *adjective* (feminine **poudrée**) E19 **French** (past participial adjective of *poudrer* to powder). Of the hair, a wig, etc.: powdered.

poudreuse *noun* E20 **French** (from as POUDRE). A lady's dressing table of a kind made in France in the time of Louis XV.

pouf *noun* (in sense 3 usually **pouffe**) E19 **French** (ultimately imitative). **1** E19 An elaborate female headdress fashionable in the late eighteenth century; (*History*) a high roll or pad of hair worn by women. **2** M19 *Dressmaking* A part of a dress gathered up to form a soft projecting mass of material. **3** L19 A large firm cushion with a stable base, used as a low seat or footstool. Also, a soft stuffed ottoman or couch.

poule *noun* E20 **French** (literally, 'hen'). A young woman, *especially* a promiscuous one. *slang.*

poule au pot *noun phrase* plural **poules au pot** L19 **French**. A boiled chicken.

poule de luxe *noun phrase* plural **poules de luxe** M20 **French** (= 'poule' of luxury). A prostitute.

poulet *noun* M19 **French**. **1** M19 A chicken; a chicken dish. **2** M19 A (neatly folded) billet-doux.

■ In sense 1 especially with reference to French cooking, usually with a qualifying adjective, as in *poulet Provençal* (Provençal chicken), *poulet rôti* (roast chicken), etc.

poulette *noun* E19 **French**. *Cooking* A (French) sauce made with butter, cream, and egg yolks. More fully *poulette sauce.*

poult-de-soie *noun & adjective* M19 **French** (alteration of *pou-de-soie* of unknown origin). (Made of) a fine corded silk or taffeta, usually colored.

poupée *noun* L18 **French** (= doll, puppet, wax figure). A figure used in making and displaying dresses, wigs, and other items of dress.

pourboire *noun* E19 **French** (literally, 'for drinking'). A gratuity, a tip.

pour encourager les autres *adverb phrase* E19 **French** (literally, 'to encourage the others'). As an example to others; to encourage others.

■ The source is a witticism of Voltaire's in *Candide* (1759) concerning the execution in 1757 of Admiral John Byng for failing to relieve Minorca when the island came under attack by the French in 1756: *Dans ce pays-ci il est bon de tuer de temps en temps un amiral pour encourager les autres* (In this country [sc. England] it is thought a good idea to kill an admiral from time to time to encourage the others).

pour le sport *adverb phrase* E20 **French**. For fun, amusement, or sport.

pourparler *noun* E18 **French** (noun use of Old French *po(u)rparler* discuss, from *po(u)r-* pro- + *parler* to speak). An informal discussion or conference preliminary to actual negotiation.

pour passer le temps *adverb phrase* L17 **French**. To pass the time; to amuse oneself.

pour rire *adjective & adverb phrase* L19 **French** (literally, 'in order to laugh'). (In a manner) that causes amusement or suggests jocular pretense; not serious(ly).

pourriture noble *noun phrase* E20 **French** (= noble rot). A common gray mold, *Botrytis cinerea*, as deliberately cultivated on grapes to perfect certain French and German wines and Tokay; the condition of being affected by this mold; noble rot.

pour-soi *noun* M20 **French** (literally, 'for itself, for oneself'). *Philosophy* In the thought of J.-P. Sartre, the spontaneous free being of consciousness; being for itself.

■ Contrasted with *en-soi* ((being) in itself) in Sartre's *L'Être et le néant* (1943).

pousada *noun* M20 **Portuguese** (literally, 'resting place', from *pausar* to rest). An inn or hotel in Portugal, *especially* one of a chain of hotels administered by the government.

pousse-café *noun* L19 **French** (literally, 'push coffee'). A glass of various liqueurs or cordials poured in successive layers, taken immediately after coffee.

poussin *noun* M20 **French**. A young chicken for eating.

■ Earlier in PETIT POUSSIN.

pou sto *noun* M19 **Greek** (*pou stō* where I may stand). A place to stand on, a standing place; *figuratively* a basis of operation.

■ *Dos moi pou stō kai kinō tēn gēn* (Give me a place where I may stand and I will move the earth), a saying attributed to the ancient Greek sage Archimedes (died *c.*212 BC).

powwow *noun & verb* (also **pow-wow**) E17 **Narragansett** (*powah, powwaw* shaman). **A** *noun* **1** E17 A North American Indian priest, sorcerer, or medicine man, a shaman. **b** M19 The art of a powwow, especially as used in healing. **2** E17 A North American Indian ceremony, *especially* one involving magic, feasting, and dancing. Also, a council or conference of or with Indians. **3** E19 *transferred* Any meeting for discussion; a conference, congress, or consultation, especially among friends or colleagues. Also, noisy bustle or activity. **B** *verb* **1** *intransitive verb* M17 Of North American Indians: practice powwow; hold a powwow. **2** *transitive verb* E18 Treat with powwow. **3** *intransitive verb* L18 *transferred* Confer, discuss, deliberate.

praecognitum *noun* plural **praecognita** E17 **Latin** (neuter past participle of *praecognoscere* to know beforehand). A thing known beforehand; *especially* a thing needed or assumed to be known in order to infer or ascertain something else. Usually in *plural*.

praenomen *noun* E17 **Latin** (= forename, from *prae* pre- + *nomen* name). An ancient Roman's first or personal name preceding the nomen and cognomen (as *Marcus* Tullius Cicero); *generally* a first name, a forename.

Praesidium variant of PRESIDIUM.

praetorium *noun* (also **pretorium**) plural **praetoria** E17 **Latin** (use as noun of adjective *praetorius* belonging to a praetor). *Roman History* **1** E17 The tent of the commanding general in a Roman camp; the space where this was placed. **2** E17 The court or palace of the governor of a Roman province; *transferred* an official building, *especially* the court or palace of an ancient king. **3** L17 The quarters of the praetorian guard in Rome.

Prägnanz *noun* E20 **German** (= conciseness, definiteness). *Psychology* In gestalt theory, the tendency of every perceptual or mental form to be integrated into a whole and become coherent and simple.

■ Also Anglicized as *pregnance* (M20).

praire *noun* E20 **French**. The European clam or the North American hardshell clam especially as an item of food.

praline *noun* E18 **French** (from Marshal de Plessis-*Praslin* (1598–1675), the French general whose cook invented the technique). A confection made by heating together chopped almonds or other nuts with sugar until the sugar liquefies and turns brown and then letting the mixture cool, used especially as a filling for chocolates.

pralltriller *noun* plural same, **pralltrillers** M19 **German** (from *prallen* to bounce + *Triller* trill). *Music* An ornament consisting of rapid alternation of the note written with the one immediately above it. Cf. MORDENT.

pratiquant *adjective* E20 **French**. Observant of religious duties or practices.

pratique *noun* E17 **Old and Modern French** (= practice, intercourse, corresponding to or from Italian *pratica* from medieval Latin *practica* noun use (sc. *ars* art) of *practicus* from Greek *praktikos* from *prattein* to do). Permission granted to a ship to use a port after quarantine or on showing a clean bill of health.

praxis *noun* L16 **Medieval Latin** (from Greek, from *prattein* to do). **1** **a** L16

Action, practice; *specifically* the practice of a technical subject or art, as opposed to or arising out of the theory of it. **b** L19 Habitual action, accepted practice, custom. **c** M20 In Marxism, the willed action by which a theory or philosophy becomes a practical social activity. **2** E17 An example or collection of examples used for practice in a subject, especially in grammar; a practical specimen.

précieux *noun & adjective* (feminine **précieuse**) **E18 French** (= precious). **A** *noun* E18 plural same. A person affecting an overrefined delicacy of language and taste. **B** *adjective* L18 Overrefined, affectedly fastidious in taste, etc.

■ Use of *précieux* (or *précieuse*) in English is under the influence of *Les Précieuses ridicules* (1659), Molière's famous comedy of manners satirizing the circle of people surrounding the Marquise de Rambouillet; thus the feminine form of the French noun and adjective was current in English earlier than the masculine (M20 and L19 respectively). The English word 'precious' as an adjective had long been in use (LME onward) in the sense of 'overrefined', 'affected'. However, as a noun (L16) it is used only as an endearment and the derogatory sense is confined to the French word.

precipitato *adjective & adverb* **L19 Italian.** *Music* (A direction:) in a hurried or headlong manner; (to be) played in this manner.

précis *noun & verb* **M18 French** (noun use of *précis*). **A** *noun* plural same . **1** M18 A summary or abstract, especially of a text or speech. **2** L19 The action or practice of précis writing. **B** *transitive verb* M19 Make a précis of; summarize.

predella *noun* **M19 Italian** (= stool). **1** M19 A step or platform on which an altar is placed, an altar step; a painting or sculpture on the vertical face of this. **2** M19 A raised shelf at the back of an altar; a painting or sculpture on the front of this, forming an appendage to an altarpiece above; any painting that is subsidiary to another painting.

premier cru *noun phrase* plural **premiers crus** **M19 French** (literally, 'first growth'). A wine of the best quality.

premier danseur *noun phrase* plural **premiers danseurs** **E19 French** (literally, 'first dancer'). A leading male dancer in a ballet company. Cf. PREMIÈRE DANSEUSE.

premiere *noun & adjective* (also **première**) **L19 French** (feminine of *premier*; as noun short for *première représentation* first representation). **A** *noun* L19 A first performance or showing of a play, movie, etc.; a first night. **B** *adjective* L19 First in order or importance; leading, foremost.

■ *Premiere* as a transitive and intransitive verb is a more recent (M20) development.

première danseuse *noun phrase* plural **premières danseuses** **E19 French** (feminine of PREMIER DANSEUR). A leading female dancer in a ballet company; a ballerina.

premiers crus, premiers danseurs plurals of PREMIER CRU, PREMIER DANSEUR.

pre-mortem *adjective & noun* **L19 Latin** (*prae mortem* before death). **A** *adjective* L19 Taking place or performed before death (opposed to *postmortem*). **B** *noun* L20 A discussion or analysis of a presumed future death. Chiefly *figurative.*

pré-salé *noun* **M19 French** (= salt meadow). In France: seashore meadow or marshland, *especially* one on which sheep are reared; the flesh of sheep reared on such a meadow.

presidio *noun* plural **presidios** **M18 Spanish** (from Latin *praesidium* garrison, fort). In Spain and Spanish America: a fort, a fortified settlement, a garrison town. Also, a Spanish penal settlement in a foreign country.

Presidium *noun* (also **Praesidium**) plural **Presidia, Presidiums** **E20 Russian** (*prezidium* from Latin *praesidium*). The presiding body or standing committee in a Communist organization, *especially* (*historical*) that in the Supreme Soviet.

prestissimo *adverb, adjective, & noun* E18 **Italian** (superlative of PRESTO). *Music* **A** *adverb & adjective* E18 (A direction:) very rapid(ly). **B** *noun* E20 plural **prestissimos, prestissimi** A very rapid movement or passage.

presto *adverb, interjection, noun, & adjective* L16 **Italian** (= quick, quickly, from late Latin *praestus* ready, for Latin *praesto* at hand). **A** *adverb & interjection* **1** L16 In various commands used by conjurors: quickly, at once. Also as *interjection*, announcing the climax of a trick or a surprising denouement. Frequently in *hey presto*. **2** L17 *Music* (A direction:) rapidly. **B** *noun* plural **prestos** **1** E17 An exclamation of 'presto!' **2** M19 *Music* A rapid movement or passage. **C** *attributive* or as *adjective* **1** M17 Originally, in readiness. Now, rapid, instantaneous; of the nature of a magical transformation. **2** M20 *Music* In a rapid tempo.

prêt-à-porter *adjective & noun* M20 **French**. **A** *adjective* M20 Of clothes: sold ready to wear. **B** *noun* M20 Ready-to-wear clothes.

pretorium variant of PRAETORIUM.

pretzel *noun* (also (now *rare* or *obsolete*) **bretzel**) M19 **German** (South German dialect form of *Brezel* from Old High German *brizzilla* (Italian *bracciello* usually taken as adaptation of medieval Latin *bracellus* bracelet). A hard salted bread usually in the form of a knot, eaten originally in Germany.

preux chevalier *noun phrase* L18 **French**. A gallant knight, *especially* a man who behaves chivalrously toward women.

■ The Old French adjective *preu*, from which the modern *preux* derives, was current in the Middle English period but became obsolete in the sixteenth century. Revived in the phrase *preux chevalier*, *preux* now exists in English only in this context.

Priapus *noun* (also **priapus**) plural **Priapi**, **Priapuses** LME **Latin** (from Greek *Priapos*, the Greek and Roman god of procreation whose symbol was the phallus, later adopted as a god of gardens). **1** LME A statue or image of the god Priapus, especially characterized by having large genitals. **2** L16 *transferred* (A representation of) the penis, especially when erect.

prie-dieu *noun* plural **prie-dieux** M18 **French** (literally, 'pray God'). A desk for prayer consisting of a kneeling surface and a narrow upright front surmounted by a ledge for books, etc. Also, (more fully *prie-dieu chair*) a chair with a low seat and a tall sloping back, used especially as a prayer seat or stool and fashionable in the mid–nineteenth century.

prima *noun* M18 **Italian** (feminine of PRIMO). A first or most important female; a prima donna, a prima ballerina.

prima ballerina *noun phrase* L19 **Italian** (from as PRIMA + BALLERINA). The principal female dancer in a ballet or ballet company; a ballerina of the highest accomplishment or rank.

prima donna *noun phrase* L18 **Italian** (from as PRIMA + *donna* lady). **1** L18 The principal female singer in an opera or opera company; a female opera singer of the highest accomplishment or rank. **2** M19 Originally, *transferred* a person of high standing in a particular field of activity. Now chiefly, a temperamentally self-important person.

prima facie *adverb & adjective phrase* L15 **Latin** (= at first sight, from feminine ablative of *primus* first and of *facies* face). **A** *adverb* L15 At first sight; from a first impression. **B** *adjective* E19 Arising at first sight; based on a first impression.

prima inter pares see PRIMUS INTER PARES.

prima materia *noun phrase* E20 **Latin** (literally, 'first matter'). A supposed formless primordial matter out of which the universe was created.

prima vista *adverb phrase* M19 **Italian** (literally, 'first sight'). *Music* At first sight.

primeur *noun* L19 **French** (= newness, something quite new, from as *prime* first). A new or early thing; *specifically* (**a**) in *plural*, fruit or vegetables grown to be available very early in the season; (**b**) new wine. Cf. EN PRIMEUR.

primo *adjective & noun* plural (in senses A.1, B) **primi**, (in sense B) **primos** M18 **Italian** (= first; cf. PRIMA). **A** *adjective* **1** M18 *Music* Of a musician, performer, role, etc.: principal, chief; of highest quality or importance. **2** L20 First-class, first-rate; of top quality. *slang*. **B** *noun* L18 *Music* (The pianist who plays) the upper part in a piano duet.

primum mobile *noun phrase* plural **primum mobiles** L15 **Medieval Latin** (literally, 'first moving thing', from Latin neuter of *primus* first + *mobilis* mobile). **1** L15 In the medieval version of the Ptolemaic system, an outermost sphere supposed to revolve around the earth in twenty-four hours, carrying with it the inner spheres. **2** E17 *transferred* An initiator of a course of action, events, etc.

primus *adjective* L16 **Latin** (= first). **1** L16 First, original, principal. Originally and chiefly in Latin phrases. **2** L18 Designating the first of several pupils with the same surname to enter a school. Cf. SECUNDUS, TERTIUS.

primus inter pares *adjective & noun phrase* (feminine **prima inter pares**) E19 **Latin**. (The) first among equals, (the) senior in a group.

princesse lointaine *noun phrase* plural **princesses lointaines** E20 **French** (literally, 'distant princess'). An idealized unattainable woman.

■ The title of a play (1895) by Edmond Rostand (1868–1918), based on the theme of the love of the twelfth-century troubadour poet Rudel for the Lady of Tripoli.

principium *noun* plural **principia** L16 **Latin** (from *princip-*). **1** L16 *Roman History* In *plural* The general's quarters in an army camp. **2** E17 A fundamental cause or basis of something; a principle.

■ In scholastic philosophy the *principium individuationis* ('principle of individuation') was the criterion by which any individual was uniquely distinguished from any other. In sense 2 *Principia* occurs as the abbreviated title of either of two major works by English philosophers: the *Philosophiae Naturalis Principia Mathematica* (1687) of Isaac Newton and the *Principia Mathematica* (1910–13) of Bertrand Russell and A. N. Whitehead.

printanier *adjective & noun* (feminine **printanière**) M19 **French** (literally, 'of springtime', from *printemps* spring, from Latin *primus* first + *tempus* time). (A soup) made from or garnished with spring vegetables.

prisiadka *noun* M20 **Russian** (*prisyadka*). A dance step in which a squatting male dancer kicks out each leg alternately to the front; the dance that uses this step. Cf. KAZACHOC.

prix fixe *noun phrase* L19 **French** (literally, 'fixed price'). A meal consisting of several courses served at a total fixed price. Cf. À LA CARTE.

pro *preposition, adverb, noun & adjective* LME **Latin** (= before, in front of, for, on behalf of, in return for). **A** *preposition* **1** LME For. In Latin phrases (cf. PRO BONO PUBLICO, PRO FORMA). **2** M19 In favor of. **B** *adverb* LME In favor (of a proposition, etc.). **C** *noun* **pros** LME A reason, argument, or arguer in favor of something. **D** *adjective* E18 Favorable, supportive.

■ As an adverb, chiefly in the phrase *pro and contra* or *pro and con* ('for and against'), and as a noun chiefly in the phrase *pros and cons* ('(the points) for and against').

problematique *noun* (also **problématique**) L20 **French**. The problematic area of a subject, etc.; *specifically* environmental and other global problems collectively.

■ Earlier in sociological terminology in Anglicized form *problematic* (M20).

pro bono publico *adverb & adjective phrase* E18 **Latin.** For the public good.

■ In colloquial use often shortened to *pro bono*. This has given rise, originally in United States usage, to the adjective *pro bono* (or *pro-bono*), designating legal work undertaken at no charge for a person unable to pay legal fees, also a lawyer who undertakes such work.

procédé *noun* L19 **French.** Manner of proceeding; a method, a procedure, a process.

procès-verbal *noun* plural **procès-verbaux** M17 **French.** A detailed written report of proceedings; minutes; an authenticated written statement of facts in support of a charge.

proconsul *noun* LME **Latin** (from earlier *pro consule* (person acting) for the consul). **1** LME *History* In the Roman Republic, an officer, usually an ex-consul, who acted as governor or military commander of a province; in the Roman Empire, the governor of a senatorial province. **2** L17 A governor of a modern dependency, colony, or province.

proferens *noun* plural **proferentes** M20 **Latin** (present participle of *proferre* to bring forth). *Law* The party that proposes or adduces a contract or a condition in a contract.

profil perdu *noun phrase* plural **profils perdus** M20 **French** (literally, 'lost profile'). A profile in which the head is more than half turned away from the onlooker.

profiterole *noun* L19 **French** (diminutive of *profit* profit). A small hollow case of choux pastry usually filled with cream and covered with chocolate sauce.

■ Earlier (E16–E18) evidence exists in English for the word in the sense of some kind of cooked food; the literal etymological sense of 'small gains', meaning the gratuities or tips that a servant can pick up, is attested in Cotgrave's French–English dictionary of 1611.

pro forma *adverb, adjective, & noun phrase* E16 **Latin. A** *adverb phrase* E16 As a matter of form. **B** *adjective phrase* M19 Done or produced as a matter of form; designating a model or standard document or form; *specifically* (of an invoice) sent in advance of goods supplied or with goods sent on approval. **C** *noun* plural **pro formas** E20 A pro forma invoice or form.

prognosis *noun* plural **prognoses** M17 **Late Latin** (from Greek *prognōsis*, from *progignōskein* to know beforehand, from *pro-* before + *gignōskein* to know). **1** M17 *Medicine* (A prediction of) the likely outcome of a disease (in general or in a particular case). **2** E18 *generally* (A) prognostication.

projet *noun* E19 **French** (from Latin from *projectum* from *project-* past participial stem of *pro(j)icere*) to throw out). A proposal or a draft, especially of a treaty.

prolegomenon *noun* plural **prolegomena** M17 **Latin** (from Greek, use as noun of neuter present participle of *prolegein* to say beforehand). A critical or discursive introduction prefaced to a literary work; *transferred* a preliminary remark; *figurative* an event, action, etc., serving as an introduction *to* something. Frequently in *plural* (treated as *singular* or *plural*).

proletariat *noun* M19 **French** (*prolétariat*, from Latin *proletarius* a Roman citizen of the lowest class, from *proles* offspring (since such citizens were considered capable of serving the state only by producing offspring)). **1** M19 The lowest class of any community, especially when regarded as uncultured. **2** M19 The working class(es); wage earners collectively.

proletkult *noun* (also **proletcult**) E20 **Russian** (contraction of *proletarskaya kul'tura* proletarian culture). Especially in the former USSR, (the advocacy of) cultural activities designed to reflect or encourage a purely proletarian ethos.

prominenti *noun plural* M20 **Italian** (plural of noun from *prominente* adjective, from Latin *prominent-* present participial stem of *prominere* to jut out). Prominent or eminent people; leading personages.

pronaos *noun* plural **pronaoi** E17 **Latin** (from Greek, from *pro-* before + NAOS). *Classical Antiquities* The space in front of the body of a temple, enclosed by a portico and projecting side walls. Also, a narthex.

prononcé *adjective* M19 **French** (past participle of *prononcer* to pronounce, from Latin *pronuntiare* to proclaim, narrate). Pronounced; strongly marked; conspicuous.

pronto *adverb 1 & adjective* M18 **Italian** (from Latin *promptus* prompt; cf. next). *Music* (A direction:) quick(ly), prompt(ly).

pronto *adverb 2* E20 **Spanish** (from Latin *promptus* prompt; cf. preceding). Quickly; promptly, at once.

■ Colloquial, originally United States.

pronunciamento *noun* plural **pronunciamentos** M19 **Spanish** (*pronunciamiento*, from *pronunciar* (from Latin *pronuntiare* to pronounce)). Especially in Spain and Spanish-speaking countries: a pronouncement, proclamation, or manifesto, *especially* a political one.

pro-nuncio *noun* M20 **Italian** (*pro-nunzio*, from *pro-* + *nunzio* nuncio). *Roman Catholic Church* A papal ambassador to a country that does not accord the Pope's ambassador automatic precedence over other ambassadors.

propaganda *noun* E18 **Italian** (from modern Latin *congregatio de propaganda fide* congregation for propagating the faith). **1** E18 *Roman Catholic Church* (Also **Propaganda**) A committee of cardinals responsible for foreign missions, founded in 1622 by Pope Gregory XV. Also more fully *Congregation* or *College of the Propaganda*. **2** L18 An organization or concerted movement for the propagation of a particular doctrine, practice, etc. Now *rare*. **3** E20 The systematic dissemination of doctrine, rumor, or selected information to propagate or promote a particular doctrine, view, practice, etc.; ideas, information, etc., disseminated thus (frequently *derogatory*).

proprium *noun* plural **propria** M16 **Latin** (noun use of neuter singular of *proprius* proper). **1** M16 *Logic* A non-essential characteristic common to all, and only, the members of a class, a property. **2** L18 Chiefly *Theology*. An essential attribute of something, a distinctive characteristic; essential nature, selfhood.

propugnaculum *noun* L18 **Latin**. A bulwark, a rampart; *figurative* a defense, a protection.

propylaeum *noun* plural **propylaea** E18 **Latin** (from Greek *propulaion* noun use of neuter of adjective *propulaios* before the gate, from *pro-* before + *pulē* gate). The entrance to a temple or other sacred enclosure; *specifically* (**Propylaeum**) *the* entrance to the Acropolis at Athens; *generally* a gateway, a porch.

■ The Greek word is represented in English in the form *propylon* (M19): both are current, although the Latin word is perhaps more common.

pro rata *adverb & adjective phrase* L16 **Latin** (= according to the rate). **A** *adverb* L16 In proportion, proportionally. **B** *adjective* M19 Proportional.

proscenium *noun* plural **prosceniums**, **proscenia** E17 **Latin** (from Greek *proskēnion*, from *pro-* before + *skēnē* scene). **1** E17 *Classical Antiquities* The performance area between the background and the orchestra of a theater; the stage. **b** E19 The part of the stage of a modern theater in front of the curtain. Frequently *attributive*. **2** *transferred* and *figurative* M17 The front, the foreground.

prosciutto *noun* M20 **Italian** (= ham). Italian cured ham, usually served raw and thinly sliced as an hors d'oeuvre.

prosit *interjection & noun* (also **prost**, (as noun) **Prosit**) M19 **German** (from Latin = may it benefit). (An utterance of the exclamation) wishing a person good health, success, etc., especially in drinking a toast.

prospectus *noun* M18 **Latin** (= view, prospect, noun use of past participle of *prospicere* to look forward). A printed document giving advance notification of the chief features of a forthcoming publication, issue of shares for a commercial enterprise, etc. Also, a brochure or pamphlet detailing the courses, facilities, etc., of an educational institution.

prosthesis *noun* plural **prostheses** M16 **Late Latin** (from Greek, from *prostithenai* to add, from *pros* to + *tithenai* to place). **1** M16 *Grammar* The addition of a letter or syllable at the beginning of a word. **2 a** E18 The branch of surgery that deals with artificial replacements for defective or absent parts of the body. Now *rare*. **b** E20 An artificial replacement for a part of the body.

protégé *noun* (feminine **protégée**) L18 **French** (past participial adjective of *protéger* from Latin *protegere* to protect). A person under the protection, care, or patronage of another, especially of a person of superior position or influence.

pro tem abbreviation of PRO TEMPORE.

pro tempore *adverb & adjective phrase* LME **Latin** (= for the time). **A** *adverb phrase* LME For the time being, temporarily. **B** *adjective phrase* M18 Temporary.

■ Also colloquially in abbreviated form *pro tem* (E19).

protocolaire *adjective* M20 **French** (from *protocole* protocol). Characterized by a strict regard for protocol; formal, ceremonial.

protome *noun* M18 **Greek** (*protomē* the foremost or upper part of a thing, from *protoenein* to cut off in front). Chiefly *Classical Antiquities*. A bust; a piece of sculpture representing the forepart of an animal.

proviso *noun* plural **proviso(e)s** LME **Latin** (neuter ablative singular of past participle of *providere* to provide, as in medieval Latin *proviso quod* (or *ut*) it being provided that). A clause in a legal or formal document, making some condition, stipulation, exception; or limitation, or on the observance of which the operation or validity of the instrument depends; *generally* a condition, a qualification, a stipulation, a provision.

provocateur *noun* E20 **French** (= provoker). A person who provokes a disturbance; an agitator. Cf. AGENT PROVOCATEUR.

provolone *noun* M20 **Italian** (from *provola* buffalo's milk cheese). An Italian smoked cheese, often made in a variety of shapes. Also *provolone cheese*.

prox. abbreviation of PROXIMO.

proxime accessit *noun phrase* L19 **Latin** (literally, '(he or she) came very near'). Second place in merit to the actual winner of a prize, scholarship, etc.; a person gaining this.

proximo *adjective* M19 **Latin** (= in the next (sc. *mense* month)). Chiefly *Commerce* Of next month.

■ Often abbreviated to *prox.*, it is used following the ordinal number denoting the day, as in *1st proximo*.

prunelle *noun* E20 **French** (literally, 'sloe', diminutive of *prune* ultimately from Latin *prunum* plum; cf. PRUNELLO). A French brandy-based liqueur flavored with sloes.

prunello *noun* plural **prunello(e)s** E17 **Italian** (alteration of obsolete Italian *prunella* diminutive of *pruna* (now *prugna*) plum, prune). Originally, a variety of plum or prune. Now, a fine kind of prune, *especially* one made from a greengage.

pruritus *noun* M17 **Latin** (from *prurire* to itch). Itching of the skin, with or (especially) without visible eruption.

■ Frequently with modern Latin specifying word.

pseudepigrapha *noun plural* L17 **Greek** (noun use of neuter plural of *pseudepigraphos* with false title, from *pseudo-* false + *epigraphein* to inscribe). Books or writings collectively wrongly titled or attributed; spurious writings; *specifically* Jewish writings ascribed to various biblical patriarchs and prophets but composed *c.*200 BC–AD 200.

pseudo *adjective & noun* LME **Greek** (independent use of *pseudo-* false). **A** *adjective* **1** LME False, counterfeit, pretended, spurious. **2** M20 Intellectually or socially pretentious; insincere, affected; meaningless. **B** *noun* plural **pseudo(e)s**. **1** LME–M19 A false person, a pretender. **2** M20 An intellectually or socially pretentious person; an insincere person. Abbreviated to *pseud (slang)*.

psi *noun* LME **Greek** (*psei*). **1** LME The twenty-third letter (Χ, ψ) of the Greek alphabet. **2** M20 Paranormal phenomena or faculties collectively; the psychic force supposed to be manifested by these. Frequently *attributive*, as *psi powers*, etc. **3** L20 *Nuclear Physics* A neutral, relatively long-lived strongly interacting particle, produced by high-energy collisions.

psyche *noun* M17 **Latin** (from Greek *psukhē* breath, life, soul, mind (also butterfly, moth), related to *psukhein* to breathe; in some uses with allusion to *Psukhē* Psyche, in Greek mythology the beloved of Eros (Cupid), the god of love). **I 1** M17 The soul, the spirit. Formerly also (*rare*), the animating principle of the universe. Now chiefly *historical*. **2** E20 The mind, especially in its spiritual, emotional, and motivational aspects; the collective mental or psychological characteristics of a nation, people, etc. **II 3** E19 (After Greek). A butterfly, a moth. *rare*. **III 4** M19 (Said to be after Raphael's painting of Psyche.) A cheval mirror. Also *psyche-glass*. *archaic*.

psychomachia *noun* (also occasionally Anglicized as **psychomachy**) E17 **Late Latin** ((title of a poem by Prudentius *c.* 400) from Greek *psukhē* psyche + *makhē* fight). Conflict of the soul; the battle between spirit and flesh, or virtue and vice.

psychopompos *noun* (also in English form **psychopomp**) M19 **Greek** (*psukhopompos*, from *psukhē* psyche + *pompos* conductor). A mythical conductor of souls to the place of the dead. Also, the spiritual guide of a (living) person's soul.

pteroma *noun* plural **pteromata** M19 **Latin** (from Greek *pterōma*). *Architecture* The space between the cella of a Greek temple and the surrounding colonnade (peristyle).

pubes *noun* plural same L16 **Latin** (= the pubic hair, the groin, the genitals). **1** L16 The pubic hair. Now *colloquial*. **2** L17 The lower part of the abdomen at the front of the pelvis, which becomes covered with hair from the time of puberty.

puchero *noun* plural **pucheros** M19 **Spanish** (= pot, from Latin *pultarius* cooking or drinking vessel, from *puls*, *pult-* a kind of thick porridge). **1** M19 A glazed earthenware cooking pot. *rare*. **2** M19 A Latin American stew of beef, sausage, bacon, and various vegetables.

pucka variant of PUKKA.

pudendum *noun* plural **pudenda** M17 **Latin** (*pudenda* noun use of neuter plural of *pudendus* gerundive of *pudere* to be ashamed). In *plural* and (occasionally) *singular*. The genitals, *especially* the female external genitals.

pudeur *noun* M20 **French** (from Latin PUDOR). A sense of shame or embarrassment, especially with regard to matters of a sexual or personal nature; modesty.

pudor *noun* E17 **Latin** (= shame, modesty, from *pudere* to be ashamed). Due sense of shame; bashfulness, modesty.

pueblo *noun & adjective* plural **pueblos** E19 **Spanish** (from Latin *populus* people). **A** *noun* **1** E19 A town or village in Latin America or the southwestern United States; *especially* an Indian settlement. **2** M19 (**Pueblo**) A member of the Pueblo Indians. **B** *attributive* or as *adjective* M19 Of or pertaining to a pueblo; (usually **Pueblo**) designating or pertaining to a group of North American Indians living in pueblos chiefly in New Mexico and Arizona.

puggaree *noun* (also **pagri**, **puggree**) M17 **Hindustani** (*pagṛī* turban). **1** M17 A turban, as worn in the Indian subcontinent. **2** M19 A thin scarf wound around the crown of a sun helmet or hat so that the ends of the scarf form a shade for the neck.

puisne *noun & adjective* L16 **Old French** ((modern *puîne*), from *puis* (from Latin *postea* afterward) + *né* (from Latin *natus* born)). **A** *noun* **1** L16–M17 A junior; an inferior; a novice. **2** E19 A puisne judge (see sense B.1 below). **B** *adjective* **1** E17 Younger, junior. Now *rare* or *obsolete* except in *Law*, denoting a judge of superior court lower in rank than a chief justice. **2** E17–L18 Small, insignificant, petty. **3** M17 Later, more recent, of subsequent date. Now chiefly in *puisne mortgage*.

puissance *noun* LME **Old and Modern French** (from Proto-Gallo-Romance from Latin *posse* to be able). **1** LME Power, strength, force, might; influence. Chiefly *archaic* and *poetical*. **b** M20 A show jumping competition testing a horse's ability to jump large obstacles. **2** LME–L16 An armed force. Also, a number or crowd of people.

puja *noun* (also **pooja**, **pujah**) L17 **Sanskrit** (*pūjā* worship). A Hindu religious ceremony or rite.

pukka *adjective* (also **pukkah**, **pucka**) L17 **Hindi** (*pakkā* cooked, ripe, substantial). **1** L17 Of full weight, full; genuine. **2** L18 Certain, reliable; authentic, true; proper, socially acceptable. **3** L18 Permanent; (of a building) solidly built. Cf. KUTCHA.

■ Originally Anglo-Indian, often in phrases such as *pukka sahib*, a true gentleman; now colloquial or slang. The spelling *pucka* was the one in most frequent use prior to the twentieth century. *Pukka* was also formerly used in noun and other adjectival senses that are now rare or obsolete.

pulao variant of PILAF.

pullus *noun* plural **pulli** L18 **Latin** (= young chick). A young bird or nestling prior to fledging (especially with reference to ringed birds and museum specimens).

pulperia *noun* E19 **American Spanish**. In Spanish-speaking America: a grocery; a tavern.

pulpitum *noun* M19 **Latin**. A stone screen in a church separating the choir from the nave, frequently surmounted by an organ loft.

pulque *noun* L17 **American Spanish** (from Nahuatl *puliúhki* decomposed). A Mexican and Central American fermented drink made from the sap of any of several agaves.

pulvino *noun* plural **pulvini**, **pulvinos** E20 **Italian** (from Latin *pulvinus* cushion, pillow). *Architecture* A dosseret resembling a cushion pressed down by a weight.

pumpernickel *noun* M18 **German** (transferred use of earlier sense 'lout', ultimate origin unknown). Dark German bread made from coarsely ground wholemeal rye.

puna *noun* E17 **American Spanish** (from Quechua). **1** E17 A high bleak plateau in the Peruvian Andes. **2** M19 Difficulty of breathing, nausea, etc., caused by climbing to high altitudes; mountain sickness.

punctum *noun* plural **puncta** L16 **Latin** (originally neuter of *punctus* past participle of *pungere* to prick). **1** L16 A point. *obsolete* except in phrases; cf. PUNCTUM INDIFFERENS. **2** M17 *Zoology*, *Botany*, *Medicine*, etc. A minute rounded speck, dot, or spot of color, or a small elevation or depression on a surface. **3** L18 *Anatomy* The orifice of either of the two lacrimal canals, at the corner of the eye. More fully *punctum lachrymale*. **4** M20 *Paleography* A punctuation mark consisting of a point in a medieval manuscript.

punctum indifferens *noun phrase* E20 **Latin** (= not differing point). A neutral point.

punctus *noun* plural **puncti** M20 **Latin** (see PUNCTUM). *Paleography* A punctuation mark in a medieval manuscript.

pundonor *noun* plural **pundonores** M17 **Spanish** (contraction of *punto de honor* point of honor). In Spain: (originally, with *plural*) a point of honor; (now) one's sense of honor, dignity, self-respect, pride.

Punica fides variant of FIDES PUNICA.

punkah *noun* (also **punka**) L17 **Hindustani** (*paṅkhā* fan, from Sanskrit *pakṣaka*, from *pakṣa* wing). In the Indian subcontinent: a large fan to cool a room, etc.; *specifically* (**a**) a large portable fan made especially from a palmyra leaf; (**b**) a large swinging cloth fan on a frame worked manually by a cord operated by a punkah-WALLAH or by electricity.

punto *noun* (in sense 3 also **ponto**) plural **puntos** L16 **Italian or Spanish** (= Latin *punctum* point). **1** L16–E18 A small point or detail; a particle, a jot. Also, a moment, an instant. **b** L16–M18 A small point of behavior, (a) punctilio. **2** L16–E17 *Fencing* A stroke or thrust with the point of the sword or foil. **3** L17 *Cards* In quadrille, the ace of trumps when trumps are either diamonds or hearts. **4** M19 *Lacemaking* Lace, embroidery. Only in phrases *punto a rilievo*, a type of lace worked in bold relief, and *punto in aria*, an early form of needlepoint lace originally made in Venice.

punto banco *noun phrase* L20 **Italian or Spanish** (probably from as PUNTO + BANCO). A form of baccarat.

purdah *noun* E19 **Persian and Urdu** (*parda* veil, curtain). **1** E19 In the Indian subcontinent and Southeast Asia, a curtain, a veil; *especially* one used to screen women from men or strangers. **2** M19 A system in certain Muslim and Hindu societies, especially in the Indian subcontinent, of screening women from men or strangers by means of a veil or curtain. **b** E20 *transferred* Seclusion; (medical) isolation or quarantine; secrecy. Chiefly in *in, into, out of, purdah*.

purée *noun & verb* E18 **Old and Modern French** (in form feminine past participle of *purer* from medieval Latin *purare* to refine (metal), from *purus* pure). **A** *noun* E18 A pulp of vegetables, fruit, etc., reduced to the consistency of cream. **B** *transitive verb* M20 Reduce (food) to a purée.

pur et simple *adjective phrase* M19 **French** (= pure and simple). Taken absolutely by itself, nothing short of.

■ Follows a noun, as does its much more common English equivalent 'pure and simple'.

puri *noun* M20 **Hindustani** (*pūrī* from Sanskrit *pūrikā*). In Indian cooking, a small round cake of unleavened wheat flour deep-fried in ghee or oil.

puris naturalibus *adverb phrase* E20 **Latin** (cf. earlier IN PURIS NATURALIBUS). In one's natural state; stark naked.

puro *noun* plural **puros** M19 **Spanish** (literally, 'pure'). In Spain and Spanish-speaking countries: a cigar.

pur sang *adjective & adverb phrase* M19 **French** (*pur-sang* thoroughbred animal, from *pur* pure + *sang* blood). Without admixture, genuine(ly).

purusha *noun* L18 **Sanskrit** (*puruṣa* literally 'man', plural 'mankind'; in Hindu mythology, a being sacrificed by the gods in order to create the universe). *Hinduism* The universal spirit or soul; spirit or consciousness as opposed to matter; *specifically* in Sankya philosophy, the active or animating principle (personified as male) which with the passive (female) principle produces the universe.

puta *noun* M20 **Spanish**. A prostitute, a slut. *slang*.

putonghua *noun* M20 **Chinese** (*pŭtōnghuà*, from *pŭtōng* common + *huà* spoken language; cf. PAI-HUA). The standard spoken form of modern Chinese, based on the northern dialects, especially that of Beijing.

putsch *noun* E20 **Swiss German** (= thrust, blow). **1** E20 An attempt at (political) revolution; a violent uprising. **2** M20 A sudden vigorous effort or campaign. *colloquial*.

putto *noun* plural **putti** M17 **Italian** (from Latin *putus* boy). A representation of a (boy) child, naked or in swaddling clothes, in (especially

Renaissance and baroque) art, a cherub, a cupid.

putz *noun* E20 **German** (= decoration, finery; in sense 2 from Yiddish). **1** E20 In Pennsylvanian Dutch homes, a representation of the Nativity scene traditionally placed under a Christmas tree. **2** M20 The penis. *slang.* **b** M20 A fool; a stupid or objectionable person. *slang.*

puy *noun* M19 **French** (= hill, from Latin PODIUM). A small extinct volcanic cone; originally and *specifically* any of those in the Auvergne, France.

qadi variant of CADI.

qanat *noun* (also **kanat**) M19 **Persian** (from Arabic *ḳanāt* reed, lance, pipe, channel). A gently sloping underground channel or tunnel, *especially* one constructed to lead water from the interior of a hill to a village below.

qat variant of KHAT.

QED abbreviation of QUOD ERAT DEMONSTRANDUM.

QEF abbreviation of QUOD ERAT FACIENDUM.

qibla(h) variants of KIBLAH.

qinghaosu *noun* L20 **Chinese** (*qīnghāosū*, from *qinghao* artemisia (plant) + suffix *-su* 'active principle'). *Medicine* A naturally occurring compound extracted from the Chinese plant *Artemisia annua* for use against malaria, artemisium.

■ Used for centuries against fever in traditional Chinese medicine, *qinghaosu* became an object of study by Western researchers seeking for a compound with which to treat strains of malaria that were resistant to standard antimalarial drugs.

qiviut *noun* M20 **Eskimo** ((Inuit) plural of *qiviuq*). The underwool of the musk ox; fiber made from this.

qq.v. see QUOD VIDE.

qua *adverb* M17 **Latin** (ablative singular feminine of *qui* who). In so far as; in the capacity of.

quadra *noun* M17 **Latin** (= a square). *Architecture* The plinth of a podium. Also, a platband, a fillet, *especially* one above or below the scotia in an Ionic base.

quadrennium *noun* (also (earlier) **quadriennium**) plural **quadrenniums**, **quadrennia** E19 **Latin** (*quadriennium*, from *quadri-* combining form of *quottuor* four + *annus* year). A period of four years.

quadriga *noun* plural **quadrigae** E17 **Latin** (singular form of plural *quadrigae* contraction of *quadrijugae*, from *quadri-* combining form of *quottuor* four + *jugum* yoke). *Roman Antiquities* A chariot drawn by four horses harnessed abreast; *especially* a representation of this in sculpture or on a coin.

quadrille *noun 1* M18 **French** (from Spanish *cuadrilla*, Italian *quadriglia* troop, company, from *cuadro*, *quadro* square). **1** M18 Each of four groups of riders taking part in a tournament or carousel; *generally* a riding display. **2** L18 A square dance usually performed by four couples and containing five figures, each of which is a complete dance in itself; a piece of music for such a dance.

quadrille *adjective & noun 2* (also **quadrillé**) L19 French *quadrillé*, from *quadrille* small square from Spanish *cuadrillo* square block). (Something, especially paper) marked with small squares.

quadrivium *noun* E19 Latin (= place where four ways meet, from *quadri-* combining form of *quottuor* four + *via* way). In the Middle Ages, the higher division of a course of study of seven sciences, comprising arithmetic, geometry, astronomy, and music. Cf. TRIVIUM.

quaere *verb & noun* (also (earlier) **quere**) M16 Latin (imperative singular of *quaerere* to inquire, seek). **1** *transitive verb* M16 (in *imperative* now also interpreted as *noun*) Ask, inquire, query. Chiefly and now only in *imperative* introducing a question. **2** *noun* L16 A question, a query.

quaesitum *noun* plural **quaesita** M18 Latin (neuter singular of *quaesitus* past participle of *quaerere* to inquire, seek). That which is sought; the answer to a problem.

quae vide plural of QUOD VIDE.

quai *noun* L19 French. **1** L19 A public street or path along the embankment of a stretch of navigable water, usually having buildings on the land side; *specifically* such a street on either bank of the Seine in Paris. **2** E20 The French Foreign Office. In full *Quai d'Orsay* (the quai on the south bank of the Seine where the French Foreign Office is situated).

quaich *noun* (also **quaigh**) M16 Gaelic (*cuach* cup, perhaps from *cua* hollow; cf. Latin *caucus* (Greek *kauka*), Welsh *caurg* bowl). In Scotland: a shallow cup, usually made of wooden staves hooped together and having two handles, but sometimes made of silver or fitted with a silver rim.

quand même *adverb phrase* E19 French. All the same, even so, nevertheless.

quanta see QUANTUM.

quantité négligeable *noun phrase* plural **quantités négligeables** L19 French (= negligible quantity). A factor of no account, something insignificant.

quantum *noun & adjective* M16 Latin (neuter of *quantus* how much). **A** *noun* plural **quanta**, **quantums**. **1** M16 Quantity; a quantity. Now *especially* in *Law*, an amount of or *of* money payable in damages, etc. **2** M17 One's (required or allowed) share or portion. **3** E20 *Physics* A discrete quantity of electromagnetic energy proportional in magnitude to the frequency of the radiation it represents. **b** M20 *transferred* and *figurative* A small discrete amount of anything. **4** M20 *Physiology* The unit quantity of acetylcholine that is released at a neuromuscular junction by each single synaptic vesicle, corresponding to a certain small voltage. **B** *attributive* or as *adjective* E20 *Physics*, etc. Involving quanta or quantum theory; quantized.

quantum meruit *noun phrase* M17 Latin (= as much as he has deserved). *Law* A reasonable sum of money to be paid for services rendered or work done, when the amount due is not stipulated in a legally enforceable contract.

quantum sufficit *adverb & noun phrase* L17 Latin. As much as suffices; (in) a sufficient quantity; (to) a sufficient extent.

quark *noun* M20 German (= curd(s), cottage or curd cheese). A low-fat soft cheese of German origin.

quartier *noun* E19 French (from Latin *quartarius* fourth part of a measure, from *quartus* fourth). A district or area, originally of a French city; *elliptical* for *Quartier Latin* the Latin Quarter of Paris on the left bank of the Seine, where students and artists live.

quasi in rem *adjective phrase* L19 Latin (literally, 'as if against a thing'). *United States Law* Brought against a person in respect of his or her interest in a property within the jurisdiction of the court. Frequently *postpositive*.

quatorze *noun* E18 **French** (from Latin *quattuordecim* fourteen). **1** E18 In piquet, a set of four aces, kings, queens, or jacks held by one player, scoring fourteen. **2** M20 In full *Quatorze Juillet*. In France, Bastille Day (July 14).

quatre-couleur *adjective* (also **quatre-couleurs**) M20 **French** (*quatre-couleurs*, from *quatre* four + *couleurs* colors). Of an *objet d'art*: made of or decorated with carved gold of several (especially four) different colors.

quatsch *noun* E20 **German**. Nonsense, rubbish.

■ Frequently used as an interjection.

quattrocento *noun & adjective* L19 **Italian** (= four hundred). **A** *noun* L19 The fifteenth century in Italy; the Italian style of art, architecture, etc., of this period. **B** *attributive* or as *adjective* E20 Of or pertaining to the quattrocento.

quebrada *noun* plural **quebradas** M19 **Spanish** (feminine of *quebrado* past participle of *quebrar* to break). A mountain stream or ravine in South America.

quel *adjective* plural **quels** (feminine **quelle**, plural **quelles**) L19 **French**. What (a) (with following noun).

■ Only in French phrases and in English phrases imitating them.

Quellenforschung *noun* M20 **German** (from *Quelle* source + *Forschung* research). The investigation of the sources of, or influences on, a literary work.

quenelle *noun* M19 **French** (of unknown origin). A seasoned ball or roll of meat or fish ground to a paste.

quere variant of QUAERE.

querencia *noun* M20 **Spanish** (= lair, haunt, home ground, from *querer* to desire, love). **1** M20 *Bullfighting* The part of the arena where the bull takes its stand. **2** M20 *figurative* A person's home ground, a refuge.

quesadilla *noun* plural **quesadillas** M20 **Spanish**. A tortilla stuffed with cheese (or occasionally other filling) and heated.

questionnaire *noun* L19 **French** (from *questionner* to question). A formulated series of questions by which information is sought from a selected group, usually for statistical analysis; a document containing these.

quête *noun* E20 **French** (= quest). The traditional act of begging for food or alms to the accompaniment of folk song.

quia timet *adverb & adjective phrase* E17 **Latin** (literally, 'because he or she fears'). *Law* **A** *adverb phrase* E17 So as to prevent a possible future injury. **B** *adjective phrase* L17 Of an injunction: brought for this purpose.

quiche *noun* M20 **French** (from Alsatian dialect *Küchen* (German *Kuchen* cake)). An open flan consisting of a pastry case filled with a savory mixture of milk, eggs, and other ingredients, and baked until firm.

quid *noun* L16 **Latin** (= what, anything, something, neuter singular of *quis* who, anyone, etc.; in sense 3 abbreviation of TERTIUM QUID). **1** A nicety in argument, a quibble. *rare*. Only in L16. **2** E17 The nature of something; that which a thing is. **3** E19 *United States History* A section formed within the Republican Party, 1805–11.

quid pro quo *noun phrase* M16 **Latin** (= something for something). **1** M16 A thing (originally a medicine) given or used in place of another; a substitute. **b** L17 The action or fact of substituting one thing for another. Also, a mistake or blunder arising from such substitution. **2** L16 An action performed or thing given in return or exchange for another.

quieta non movere *verb phrase* L18 **Latin** (literally, 'not to move settled things'). Let sleeping dogs lie.

quietus *noun* LME **Latin** (abbreviation of medieval Latin *quietus est*, literally, 'he is quit'). **1 a** LME An acquittance granted on payment of a debt; a receipt. Originally more fully *quietus est*. **b** L16–L18 A discharge or release from office or duty. **2** M16 *figurative* Death regarded as a release from life; something that causes death. **b** E19 A final settlement, an ending. **3** M18 (By association with *quiet*). A sedative, a salve; a state of quiet or repose, a lull.

quincaillerie *noun* L19 **French.** **1** L19 Metalwork; metal artifacts. *rare.* **2** M20 In France: a hardware store.

quinella *noun* (also (earlier) **quiniela**) E20 **American Spanish** (*quiniela*). A form of betting in which the punter must select the first two place-winners in a race, etc., not necessarily in the correct order.

quinquennium *noun* plural **quinquenniums, quinquennia** E17 **Latin** (from *quinque* five + *annus* year). **1** E17 A fifth anniversary. **2** M17 A period of five years.

quinta *noun* M18 **Spanish and Portuguese** (from *quinta parte* fifth part, originally the amount of a farm's produce paid as rent). In Spain, Portugal, and Latin America: a large house or villa in the country or on the outskirts of a town; a country estate; *specifically* a winegrowing estate in Portugal.

quipu *noun* (also **quipo**) E18 **Quechua** (*khípu* knot). An ancient Peruvian device for recording information, events, etc., consisting of variously colored cords arranged and knotted in different ways.

qui vive *noun phrase* L16 **French** (literally, '(long) live who?'). An alert or watchful state or condition. Chiefly in *on the qui vive*, on the alert or lookout.

■ Originating in a sentry's challenge to a person approaching his post in order to ascertain to whom that person is loyal.

quoad *preposition* E17 **Latin** (= so far as, as much as, as to, from *quo* where, whither + *ad* to). To the extent of, as regards, with respect to.

quod erat demonstrandum *noun phrase* M17 **Latin** (translating Greek *hoti edei deixai*). (Which is) what it was necessary to prove.

■ Generally abbreviated to QED and used to emphasize the clinching point in an argument or to conclude a mathematical proof. Like the less widely used QUOD ERAT FACIENDUM, the phrase and its use are derived from the Greek mathematician Euclid (early 3rd century BC).

quod erat faciendum *noun phrase* L17 **Latin** (translating *hoti edei poiein*). (Which is) what it was necessary to construct.

■ Abbreviated to QEF and appended to a geometrical proof.

quodlibet *noun* LME **Medieval Latin** (*quodlibet(um)* from Latin *quodlibet*, from *quod* what + *libet* it pleases). **1** LME *History* A question proposed as an exercise in philosophical or theological debate; a scholastic debate, thesis, or exercise. **2** E19 *Music* A lighthearted combination of several tunes; a medley.

quod vide *noun phrase* plural **quae vide** M18 **Latin** (*quod* which + imperative singular of *videre* to see). Which see.

■ Abbreviated to *q.v.* (plural *qq.v.*) and used to direct a reader to further information under the reference cited.

quondam *adverb, noun, & adjective* M16 **Latin** (= formerly). **A** *adverb* M16 At one time, formerly. *rare.* **B** *noun* M16 The former holder of an office or position; *derogatory* a person who has been deposed or ejected. **C** *adjective* L16 That once was or existed; former.

quorum *noun* LME **Latin** (literally, 'of whom (we wish that you be one, two, etc.)' in the wording of commissions for members of bodies, committees, etc.). **1** LME Originally, certain (usually eminent) justices of the peace whose presence was necessary to constitute a deciding body. Later *generally*, all justices collectively. **b** L16 *transferred* Distinguished or essential members of any body; a select company. **2** E17 A fixed minimum number of members whose presence is necessary to make the proceedings of an assembly, society, etc., valid.

quota *noun* E17 **Medieval Latin** (*quota* (sc. *pars*) how great (a part), feminine of *quotus*, from Latin *quot* how many). **1** E17 The share that an individual or group is obliged to contribute to a total; the minimum number or quantity of a particular product that under official regulations must be produced, exported, imported, etc. **b** M19 In a system of proportional representation, the minimum number of votes required to elect a candidate. **2** L17 The share of a total or the maximum number or quantity belonging, due, given, or permitted to an individual or group. **b** E20 The maximum number (of immigrants or imports) allowed to enter a country within a set period; (a) regulation imposing such a restriction on entry to a country. Also, the number of students allowed to enroll for a course, at a college, etc.

quot homines, tot sententiae *noun phrase & interjection* **M16 Latin.** (There are) as many opinions as (there are) men.

■ From the comedy *Phormio* (line 454) by the Roman playwright Plautus (died 184 BC).

quotum *noun* **M17 Latin** (neuter singular of *quotus*). A number or quantity considered in proportion to a larger number or amount of which it forms part; a quota.

q.v. abbreviation of QUOD VIDE.

rabat *noun* **M20 French** (= collar). A false shirtfront, a stock.

■ Earlier (L16–M17) a *rabat* (also called a *rabato*) was a stiff collar but the word has long been obsolete in this sense.

rabbi *noun* **LOE ecclesiastical Latin and Greek** (from Hebrew *rabbī* my master, from *rab* master). **1** LOE A Jewish scholar or teacher having authority on law and doctrine; now *specifically* one authorized by ordination to deal with questions of law and ritual and to perform certain functions. Also as a title of respect and form of address (usually with following personal name). **2** M16 *transferred* A person whose learning, authority, or status is comparable to that of a Jewish rabbi; *specifically* (*slang*) a senior official who exerts influence or patronage on behalf of a person.

■ The French word *rabbin* is now rare in English but was formerly used in both senses (sense 1 from L16, sense 2 M16–M17). The ending *-n* may be due to a Semitic plural form.

raccourci *noun* **M20 French** (noun use of past participle of *raccourcir* to shorten). *Ballet* A movement in which the toe is made to touch the bent knee of the other leg.

rackett *noun* (also **racket**, **ranket**) **L19 German** (*Rackett*, *Rankett*). *Music* A Renaissance wind instrument related to the oboe.

raclette *noun* **M20 French** (= small scraper). **1** M20 *Archaeology* A stone tool of the scraper type discovered in the valley of the Vézère in southwest France, dating from the early Magdalenian period. **2** M20 A dish of cheese melted before an open fire, scraped onto a plate, and served with potatoes.

racloir *noun* **L19 French** (= scraper). *Archaeology* A prehistoric flint instrument with one broad side shaped for scraping.

raconteur *noun* **E19 French** (from *raconter* to relate). A (usually skilled) teller of anecdotes.

raconteuse *noun* **M19 French** (feminine of RACONTEUR). A female teller of anecdotes.

radeau *noun* M18 **French** (from Provençal *radel*, from Latin diminutive of *ratis* raft). A raft; *specifically* (*Military*) a floating battery.

radicchio *noun* plural **radicchios** L20 **Italian** (= chicory). A variety of chicory from Italy, with reddish purple white-veined leaves.

radius *noun* plural **radii** L16 **Latin** (= staff, spoke, ray). **1** L16–M18 A straight object such as a staff or bar. **2** L16 *Anatomy* and *Zoology* One of the two bones of the forearm; the corresponding bone of a tetrapod's foreleg or a bird's wing. **3** E17 A straight line from the center of a circle or sphere to the circumference. **4** E18 Any of a set of lines, rods, spokes, etc., diverging from a point like the radii of a circle; a radiating part. **5** M19 A circular area of which the extent is measured by the length of the radius of the circle that bounds it.

radix *noun* plural **radices**, **radixes** L16 **Latin** (*radix*, *radic-* root of a plant). **1 a** L16–E18 *Mathematics* A root of a number. **b** L18 *Mathematics* and *Computing* The number from whose various powers a system of counting, logarithms, etc., proceeds, a base. **2** E17–L18 *Astrology* and *Astronomy* A fact used as a basis of calculation. **3** E17 A thing in which something originates; a source.

■ Sometimes in the phrase *radix malorum* 'the root of evil', with allusion to 1 Timothy 6:10 (Vulgate version). In the Bible it is 'love of money' (*cupiditas*) which is 'the root of all evil', while in popular use it is frequently just 'money'.

rafale *noun* E20 **French** (literally, 'gust of wind'). Repeated bursts of gunfire; a drumroll.

raffia *noun* (in sense 1 also **raphia**, (earliest) **rofia**) E18 **Malagasy**. **1** E18 A palm of the African genus *Raphia*, especially *R. farinifera* of Madagascar. **2** L19 The soft fiber from the leaves of such a palm, used as garden twine, in basketwork, etc.

raffiné *adjective* L19 **French**. Of manners or judgment: refined.

raga *noun* (also **rag**) L18 **Sanskrit** (*rāga* color, passion, melody). In Indian music: a pattern of notes used as a basis for melodies and improvisations; a piece of music based on a particular raga.

Ragnarok *noun* (also **Ragnarök**) L18 **Old Norse** (*ragnarœk*, *ragna-røkkr* (Icelandic *Ragnarök*), from *ragna* genitive of *regin* the gods + *rœk* destined end or (later) *røkr*, *røkkr* twilight). *Scandinavian Mythology* The destruction of the gods; *specifically* the defeat of gods and men by monsters in a final battle. Cf. GÖTTERDÄMMERUNG.

ragout *noun* M17 **French** (*ragoût*, from *ragoûter* to revive the taste of, from as GOÛT). **1** M17 A highly seasoned dish of meat cut into small pieces and stewed with vegetables. **2** L17–M18 A sauce, a relish.

rahat *noun* M19 **Turkish** (*rahat (lokum)* from Arabic *rāḥat* (*al-ḥulḳūm*) ease (of the throat); cf. LOKUM). Turkish delight. In full *rahat lokum*.

rais variant of REIS.

raison d'état *noun phrase* plural **raisons d'état** M19 **French** (= reason of state). A reason having to do with the security or interests of a nation.

raison d'être *noun* plural **raisons d'être** M19 **French** (= reason for being). A purpose or reason accounting for or justifying the existence of a thing.

raisonné *adjective* L18 **French** (past participle of *raisonner* to reason, from *raison* reason). Reasoned out, systematic. Chiefly in CATALOGUE RAISONNÉ.

raisonneur *noun* E20 **French** (literally 'a person who reasons or argues'). A character in a play, etc., who expresses the author's message or standpoint.

raisons d'état, **raisons d'être** plurals of RAISON D'ÉTAT, RAISON D'ÊTRE.

raita *noun* M20 **Hindustani** (*rāytā*). An Indian dish consisting of chopped vegetables (or fruit) in curd or yogurt.

raj *noun* E19 **Hindustani** (*rāj* from Sanskrit *rājya*; cf. RAJA). **1** E19 Sovereignty, rule; kingdom. **2** M19 *History* (*the Raj*) (The period of) British rule in the Indian subcontinent before 1947. In full *British Raj*.

raja *noun* (also **rajah**, (as a title) **Raja**) M16 **Sanskrit** (*rājan* king, from *rāj* to reign or rule; probably through Portuguese and related to Latin *rex, regis*, Old Irish *rí, ríg* king). *History* Originally, an Indian king or prince. Later also, a petty dignitary or noble in India; a Malay or Javanese ruler or chief.

raja yoga *noun phrase* L19 **Sanskrit** (from *rājan* king + YOGA). A form of yoga aimed at gaining control over the mind and emotions.

raki *noun* L17 **Turkish** (*rāqī* (now *rakı* whence also modern Greek *rhakē, rhaki*) brandy, liquor). Originally, an aromatic liquor made from grain spirit or grape juice in Greece, Turkey, and the Middle East. Now also, a liquor made from various other ingredients in eastern Europe and the Middle East; a drink of this.

rakshasa *noun* (also **raksasa**) M19 **Sanskrit** (*rākṣasa* demon). *Hindu Mythology* A malignant demon, *especially* any of a band at war with Rama and Hanuman; a representation of such a demon.

raku *noun & adjective* L19 **Japanese** (literally 'ease, relaxed state, enjoyment'). (Designating) a kind of usually lead-glazed Japanese pottery, often used as tea bowls and similar utensils.

rallentando *adverb, adjective, & noun* E19 **Italian** (present participle of *rallentare* to slow down). *Music* **A** *adverb & adjective* E19 (A direction:) with gradual decrease of speed. **B** *noun* M19 plural **rallentandos**, **rallentandi**. A gradual decrease of speed; a passage (to be) played with a gradual decrease of speed.

ramada *noun* M19 **Spanish**. An arbor, a porch.

rambutan *noun* (also **rambootan**) E18 **Malay** (from *rambut* hair, in reference to the covering of the fruit). A Malaysian tree, *Nephelium lappaceum* (family Sapindaceae); the fruit of this tree, resembling a lychee and covered with soft bright red spines or prickles.

ramen *noun* (treated as *singular* or *plural*) L20 **Japanese** (from Chinese *lā* to pull + *miàn* noodles). Quick-cooking Chinese noodles, usually served in a broth with meat and vegetables.

rancheria *noun* E17 **Spanish** (*ranchería*, from as RANCHO). In Spanish America and the western United States: a collection of Indian huts; a place or house where a number of rancheros live.

ranchero *noun* plural **rancheros** E19 **Spanish** (from as RANCHO). A rancher or ranchman, especially in Mexico.

ranchito *noun* plural **ranchitos** M19 **Spanish** (diminutive of RANCHO). In the western United States: a small ranch or farm.

rancho *noun* plural **ranchos** E19 **Spanish** (= a group of people who eat together). **1** E19 In Latin America: a hut, a hovel, a very simple building; a group of these, a small village; *especially* one put up to accommodate travelers. Later also, a roadhouse, an inn; a meal at such a place. **2** M19 In the western United States: a cattle farm, a ranch.

rancio *adjective & noun* M19 **Spanish** (literally, 'rancid', from Latin *rancidus* stinking). **A** *adjective* M19 Of wine: having the distinctive bouquet, nutty flavor, or tawny color characteristic of certain well-matured, fortified, or dessert wines. **B** *noun* M20 plural **rancios**. A rancio wine.

rand *noun* plural **rands**, (in sense 2 also) same M19 **Afrikaans** (from Dutch *rand* edge). **1** M19 In South Africa: a rocky ridge or area of high sloping ground, especially overlooking a river valley; *specifically* (*the Rand*), the Witwatersrand, the chief gold mining area of the Transvaal. **2** M20 The basic monetary unit of South Africa since 1961.

randkluft *noun* plural **randklufts**, **randklüfte** E20 **German** (literally, 'edge, crevice'). A crevasse between the head of a glacier and a surrounding rock wall.

randori *noun* E20 **Japanese** (from *ran* disorder + *tori* bout, participation). Free or informal judo practice.

ranee *noun* (also **rani**, (as a title) **Ranee**) L17 **Hindustani** (*rānī* from Prakrit from Sanskrit *rājñī* feminine of *rājan* RAJA). *History* A Hindu queen; a raja's wife or widow.

rangé *adjective* (feminine **rangée**) L19 **French** (past participial adjective of *ranger* to range). Of a person, lifestyle, etc.: orderly, regular, settled.

■ Earlier (L18) in dictionaries in a heraldic sense describing charges 'placed in a row' or 'set within a band', but this sense seems never to have gained wider circulation.

rangoli *noun* M20 **Marathi** (*rāngoḷī*). A Hindu symbolic design painted in colored powdered stone, rice, etc.

rani variant of RANEE.

ranz-des-vaches *noun* plural same L18 **Swiss French dialect** (from unknown first element + 'of the cows'). A melody played especially by Swiss cowherds, consisting of irregular phrases formed from the harmonic notes of the Alpine horn.

rapide *noun* E20 **French**. In France: an express train.

rapido *adverb, adjective, & noun* L19 **Italian**. **A** *adverb and adjective* L19 *Music* (A direction:) in rapid time. **B** *noun* M20 plural **rapidi**, **rapidos**. In Italy: an express train.

rappel *noun* M19 **French** (from *rappeler* to recall). **1** M19 A drumroll calling soldiers to arms. *rare*. **2** M20 *Mountaineering*. An abseil.

rapport *noun* M17 **French** (from *rapporter* to bring back). **1** M17 Relationship, *especially* a relationship characterized by harmonious accord. **2** M19 A posited state of deep spiritual, emotional, or mental connection between people.

■ Originally (M16) introduced in the sense of 'report' or 'talk', but this was never widely current and has been totally ousted by the current sense. Cf. EN RAPPORT.

rapportage *noun* E20 **French** (literally, 'tale-telling', influenced by *reportage*). The reporting or describing of events in writing; mere description, uncreative recounting.

rapporteur *noun* L18 **French** (from *rapporter* to bring back). A person who makes a report of the proceedings of a committee, etc., for a higher body.

■ Introduced earlier (but used only L15) from Old French in the general sense of 'a reporter, a recounter', *rapporteur* is now used in English only in the very specific sense above.

rapprochement *noun* E19 **French** (from *rapprocher* to bring closer together, from *re-* + *approcher* to approach). (An) establishment or resumption of harmonious relations, especially between foreign states.

raptus *noun* M19 **Latin**. **1** M19 A state of rapture. **2** M19 *Medicine* A sudden violent attack. Usually with modern Latin specifying word.

rara avis *noun phrase* plural **rarae aves** E17 **Latin** (= rare bird). **1** E17 A kind of person rarely encountered; an unusual or exceptional person. **2** L19 A rarity; an unusual or exceptional occurrence or thing.

rariora *noun plural* M19 **Latin** (neuter plural comparative of *rarus* rare *adjective*). Rare books.

rarissime *adjective* E20 **Latin** (literally, 'very rarely (sc. found)'). Extremely rare.

rasa *noun 1* (also **ras**) L18 **Sanskrit** (literally, 'juice, essence, flavor'). The mood or aesthetic impression of an artistic work.

rasa *noun 2* (also **ras**) E19 **Sanskrit** (*rāsa*). A traditional Indian dance (commemorating that) performed by Krishna and the gopis in Hindu mythology; a festival celebrating this.

rasant *adjective* (also **razant**) L17 **Old and Modern French** (present participle of *raser* to shave close). *Military* Of a line of defense: sweeping; long and curving (originally so that the shot would graze the target).

rasgado *noun* plural **rasgados** M19 **Spanish** (past participle of *rasgar* to strum, make a flourish). *Music* (An arpeggio produced by) the act of sweeping the strings of a guitar with the fingertips.

Raskolnik *noun* (also **raskolnik**) E18 **Russian** (*raskol'nik*, from *raskol* separation, schism + noun suffix *-nik* person connected with (something)). *Ecclesiastical History* A member of a Russian Orthodox group that refused to accept the liturgical reforms of the patriarch Nikon (1605–81); an Old Believer.

rassolnik *noun* (also **rasolnik**) E20 **Russian** (*rassol'nik* from *rassol* brine + *-nik*). A Russian soup of brine, salted dill cucumbers, and pickled vegetables, meat, or fish, served chilled.

rasta *noun* E20 **French**. Abbreviation of RASTAQUOUÈRE.

rastaquouère *noun & adjective* L19 **French** (from South American Spanish *rastacuero* tycoon in the hide trade, upstart). **A** *noun* L19 A person (especially from a Mediterranean or South American country) intruding into a particular social group and having an exaggerated manner or style of dress; a dashing but untrustworthy foreigner. **B** *attributive* or as *adjective* E20 Of, pertaining to, or characteristic of *rastaquouères*; of the nature of a *rastaquouère*.

ratafia *noun* L17 **French**. **1** L17 A liqueur flavored with almonds or kernels of peach, apricot, or cherry. **2** M19 A kind of small macaroon.

rataplan *noun* M19 **French** (of imitative origin). A drumming or beating noise; a tattoo.

ratatouille *noun* L19 **French** ((dialect) cf. French *touiller* to stir up). **1** A ragout. Only in L19. **2** M20 A vegetable dish of eggplant, zucchini, tomatoes, onions, and peppers fried and stewed in oil.

raté *adjective & noun* E20 **French**. **A** *adjective* E20 Ineffective; unsuccessful. **B** *noun* E20 A person who has failed in his or her vocation.

ratelier *noun* M17 **French** (*râtelier*). **1** A stand for arms. *rare*. Only in M17. **2** M19 A set of (especially false) teeth.

ratine *noun & adjective* (also **ratiné**) E20 **French** (*ratiné* past participle of *ratiner* to put a nap on (cloth), from *ratine* ratteen). (Made of) a plain-woven (usually cotton) fabric with a loose open weave and rough surface, used for linings, furniture covers, etc.

rauschpfeife *noun* plural **rauschpfeifen** L19 **German** (= reed pipe; cf. SCHREIERPFEIFE). *Music* **1** L19 A low-pitched mixture stop in an organ. **2** M20 A reed cap shawm of the Renaissance period.

ravalement *noun* M20 **French** (from *ravaler* to bring down, reduce). *Music* The action or an instance of modifying and extending the range of a keyboard instrument by rebuilding; an instrument modified in this way.

ravelin *noun* L16 **French** (from Italian *ravellina* (now *rivellino*), of unknown origin). *History* An outwork of fortifications, consisting of two faces forming a salient angle, constructed beyond the main ditch and in front of the curtain.

ravigote *noun* M19 **French** (from *ravigoter* to invigorate). A mixture of chopped chervil, chives, tarragon, and shallots, used to give piquancy to a sauce, as a base for a herb butter, etc.; a vinaigrette dressing containing capers and chopped hard-boiled egg flavored with such a mixture; a velouté sauce containing such a herb butter.

ravinement *noun* E20 **French** (from *raviner* to furrow). *Physical Geography* Erosion of ravines or gullies in soil or soft rock by running water. Also, an unconformity in river or shallow marine sediments caused by interruption of deposition by erosion.

ravioli *noun* M19 **Italian** (plural of *raviolo*). Pasta in the form of small square cases filled with ground meat, vegetables, etc.

ravissant *adjective* (also (feminine) **ravissante**) M17 **French** (present participial adjective of *ravir* (formerly) to seize, carry off, (now) to enchant). Ravishing, delightful.

■ Originally (ME–M16) used in English of an animal and reflecting the older French sense of *ravir*, hence 'ravening'; it also had a specific heraldic sense (E18) meaning 'in the half-raised posture of a wolf beginning to spring on its prey'.

rayah *noun* E19 **Turkish** (*râya* from Arabic *ra'āyā* plural of *ra'iyya(t)*). Under the Ottoman Empire, a non-Muslim subject of the Sultan of Turkey, liable to a poll tax.

rayonnant *adjective* (feminine **rayonnante**) E19 **French** (present participial adjective of *rayonner* to shine forth). Of a person: beaming, radiant.

razant variant of RASANT.

razet *noun* M20 **French** (from Provençal *raset*). *Bullfighting* In southern France, a contest in which teams compete to snatch a rosette from between the bull's horns.

razeteur *noun* M20 **French**. A member of a team competing in a *razet*.

razzia *noun* M19 **French** (from Algerian Arabic *ġāziya* raid, from Arabic *ġazā* to go forth to fight, make a raid). A raid, a foray; *specifically* (*historical*) a hostile Moorish incursion for purposes of conquest, plunder, capture of slaves, etc.

re *preposition* E18 **Latin** (ablative of *res* thing). In the matter of, concerning, about.

realia *noun plural* M20 **Late Latin** (noun use of neuter plural of *realis* real). **1** M20 Objects that may be used as teaching aids but were not made for the purpose. **2** M20 Real things, actual facts, especially as distinct from theories about them.

realpolitik *noun* E20 **German** (*real* real + *Politik* politics). Politics based on practical, rather than moral or ideological, considerations; practical politics.

Realpolitiker *noun* M20 **German**. A person who believes in, advocates, or practices REALPOLITIK.

reata variant of RIATA.

reb *noun* L19 **Yiddish** (from as REBBE). A traditional Jewish courtesy title used preceding a man's forename or surname.

rebab *noun* M18 **Arabic** (*rabāb*). A bowed or (occasionally) plucked stringed instrument of Arab origin, used especially in North Africa, the Middle East, and the Indian subcontinent.

rebbe *noun* L19 **Yiddish** (from Hebrew *rabbī* rabbi). A rabbi; *specifically* a Hasidic religious leader.

rebbitzin *noun* L19 **Yiddish** (feminine of REBBE). The wife of a rabbi.

rebec *noun* (also **rebeck**) LME **French** (alteration of Old French *rebebe, rubebe*). Chiefly *History* A medieval musical instrument with usually three strings and played with a bow; a player on this in an orchestra, etc.

reblochon *noun* E20 **French**. A soft French cheese made originally and chiefly in Savoy.

reboso variant of REBOZO.

rebours see À REBOURS.

rebozo *noun* (also **reboso**) plural **rebozos** E19 **Spanish**. A long scarf covering the head and shoulders, traditionally worn by Spanish-American women.

rebus *noun* E17 **French** (*rébus* from Latin *rebus* ablative plural of *res* thing). A representation of a word or phrase by pictures, symbols, arrangement of letters, etc., that suggest the word or phrase, or the syllables of which it is made up; *specifically* a device, often of heraldic appearance, suggesting the name of its bearer.

■ This usage originated in *De rebus quae geruntur* (literally, 'concerning the things that are taking place'), the title given in sixteenth-century Picardy to satirical pieces containing riddles in picture form.

rebus sic stantibus *noun & adverb phrase* E17 **Modern Latin** (literally, 'things standing thus'). *International Law* (According to) the principle that a treaty is subject to an implied condition that if circumstances are substantially different from those obtaining when it was concluded, then a party to the treaty is entitled to be released from it.

recado *noun* plural **recados** E17 **Spanish and Portuguese** (= gift, of unknown origin). **1** A present; a message of goodwill. Only in 17. **2** E19 A South American saddle or saddlecloth.

Récamier *noun & adjective* (also **récamier**) E20 **French** (from the name of Jeanne *Récamier* (1777–1849), society hostess, depicted reclining on a chaise longue in a famous portrait by Jacques Louis David). (Designating) a style of chaise longue.

réchaud *noun* E20 **French** (from *réchauffer* to reheat, warm up again). A dish in which food is warmed or kept warm.

réchauffé *noun & adjective* E19 **French** (past participle of *réchauffer* to reheat, from *re-* again + *échauffer* to warm (up), from Proto-Romance variation of Latin *cal(e)facere* to make warm, from *calere* to be warm + *facere* to make). **A** *noun* E19 A warmed-up dish; *figurative* a rehash. **B** *adjective* E20 (Of food) reheated; *figurative* rehashed.

recherché *adjective* L17 **French** (past participle of *rechercher* to seek out, look for). Carefully sought out; rare, exotic; far-fetched, obscure.

recherche du temps perdu *noun phrase* M20 **French** (*à la recherche du temps perdu*, literally, 'in search of the lost time', title of novel by Marcel Proust (1871–1922)). A narration or evocation of one's early life.

Rechtsstaat *noun* M20 **German** (from *Recht* right + genitive suffix *-s* + *Staat* state). A country in which the rule of law prevails.

récit *noun* L19 **French**. **1** L19 *Music* A passage or composition for a solo voice or instrument. Also, a division of the classical French organ. **2** M20 The narrative of a book as opposed to the dialogue; a book or passage consisting largely of this.

recitativo *noun* plural **recitativi, recitativos** M17 **Italian** (from Latin *recitat-* past participial stem of *recitare* to recite). *Music* A style of musical declamation between singing and ordinary speech; a passage in a musical score or libretto (intended to be) delivered in this style; (a) recitative.

■ *Recitativo* may be accompanied either by the full orchestra (*recitativo accompagnato* or *recitativo stromentato* (literally, 'instrumented')) or by continuo instruments only (*recitativo secco*).

réclame *noun* L19 **French** (from *réclamer* to ask for). (An) advertisement; self-publicity; public acclaim or notoriety.

récolte *noun* (also (earlier) **recolt**) L18 **French**. In France: a harvest, a crop.

recta plural of RECTUM.

recte *adverb* M19 **Latin** (literally, 'in a straight line, rightly'). Correctly.

■ Used when introducing a word or phrase as a correct version of that just given, as in "Jane Blundell *recte* Blunden".

recti plural of RECTUS.

rectius *adverb* M20 **Latin** (comparative of RECTE). More correctly: introducing a word or phrase as a more correct version of that just given.

recto *noun* plural **rectos** E19 **Latin** ((sc. *folio*) ablative of *rectus* right). The right-hand page of an open book; the front of a leaf in a manuscript or printed book, as opposed to the back or VERSO.

rectum *noun* plural **rectums, recta** M16 **Latin** (neuter of *rectus* straight, short for *intestinum rectum* straight gut). The final section of the large intestine leading to the anus.

rectus *noun* plural **recti** E18 **Latin** ((sc. *musculus* muscle) see preceding). **1** E18 *Anatomy* Any of several straight muscles, especially of the abdomen, thigh, neck, and eye. Frequently with modern Latin specifying word. Also *rectus muscle.* **2** M20 *Music* In a fugal composition, the version of a theme performed in the original, as opposed to the reversed or inverted, order.

recueil *noun* L15 **Old and Modern French** (from *recueillir* to gather up, from Latin *recolligere*, from as *re-* + *colligere* to collect). **1** L15 A literary compilation. **2** L15–L16 Reception, welcome; succor.

recueillement *noun* M19 **French** (from as RECUEIL). Serious concentration of thought.

reculer pour mieux sauter *noun phrase* E19 **French** (literally, 'to draw back in order to leap better'). The use of a withdrawal or setback as a basis for further advance or success.

redingote *noun* L18 **French** (from English *riding coat*). Originally, a man's double-breasted greatcoat with long plain skirts not cut away in the front. Now usually, a woman's long coat with a cutaway front or a contrasting piece on the front.

redivivus *postpositive adjective* (feminine **rediviva**; occasionally (earlier) Anglicized as **redivive**) L16 **Latin** (from *re-* again + *vivus* living, alive). Come back to life; reborn, renewed.

■ Always postpositive. The Latin form first appeared (L17) in book titles, e.g., R. Head's *Proteus redivivus: or the art of wheedling* (1675). Cf. REDUX.

redowa *noun* M19 **French** (or German, from Czech *rejdovák*, from *rejdovat* to turn or whirl around). A Bohemian folk dance; a ballroom dance in relatively quick triple time resembling this; a piece of music for such a dance.

reductio ad absurdum *noun phrase* M18 **Latin** (literally, 'reduction to the absurd'). *Logic* A method of proving the falsity of a premise by showing that the logical consequence is absurd.

reductio ad impossibile *noun phrase* M16 **Latin** (literally, 'reduction to the impossible'). A method of proving a proposition by drawing an absurd or impossible conclusion from its contradictory.

redux *adjective* L19 **Latin** (from *reducere* to bring back). **1** L19 *Medicine* Of crepitation, etc.: indicating the return of the lungs to a healthy state. Now *rare.* **2** L19 Brought back, revived, restored.

■ Usually postpositive and often in titles, from John Dryden's poem on the restoration of King Charles II *Astraea Redux* (1662) to John Updike's novel *Rabbit Redux* (1971); cf. REDIVIVUS.

Reeperbahn *noun* L20 **German** (a street in Hamburg, Germany, literally, 'rope walk', from *Reeper* rope-maker + *Bahn* road, way). (The principal street in) the red-light district of a city, etc.

referendum *noun* plural **referendums**, **referenda** M19 **Latin** (gerund or neuter gerundive of *referre* to refer). The process or principle of referring an important political question, e.g., a proposed constitutional change, to the entire electorate to be decided by a general vote; a vote taken by referendum.

reflet *noun* M19 **French**. Color due to reflection; luster, iridescence; *specifically* a metallic luster on pottery.

refugium *noun* plural **refugia** M20 **Latin** (= place of refuge). *Biology* A refuge, *specifically* one in which a species survived a period of glaciation.

reg *noun* E20 **Arabic** (colloquial). *Physical Geography* A desert plain covered with small rounded pebbles; a stony desert.

regalia *noun 1 plural and collective singular* M16 **Medieval Latin** (= royal residence, royal rights, noun use of neuter plural of *regalis* regal). **1** M16 Rights belonging to a king or queen; royal powers or privileges. **2** The emblems or insignia of royalty. Also *transferred*, the decorations or insignia of an order; any distinctive or elaborate clothes.

regalia *noun 2* E19 **Spanish** (= royal privilege). A Cuban or other large high-quality cigar.

regardant *adjective & noun* LME **Old and Modern French** ((also Anglo-Norman) present participle of *regarder* to look at). **1** LME *Heraldry* Usually of a lion: looking backward over the shoulder. Usually *postpositive*. **2** L16 Observant, watchful, contemplative.

■ In feudal usage also with reference to a serf attached to a manor, as in *villein regardant*.

regatta *noun* E17 **Italian** (Venetian dialect *regatta, rigatta, regata* a fight, a struggle, a contest). **1** E17 Any of certain boat races held on the Grand Canal in Venice. **2** L18 An organized series of boat or yacht races. **3** M19 A cotton fabric, usually made in twill; a striped garment made in this fabric.

régie *noun* L18 **French** (feminine past participle of *régir* to rule). In some European countries, a government department that controls an industry or service; *specifically* (*historical*) one with complete control of the importation, manufacture, and taxation of tobacco, salt, etc.

regime *noun* (also **régime**) L15 **French** (*régime* from Latin REGIMEN). **1** L15 A lifestyle adopted for health reasons; a REGIMEN 2. **2** L18 A method or system of rule or government; a system or institution having widespread influence or prevalence. Now frequently (usually *derogatory*), a particular government. **3** *Physical Geography* **a** M19 The condition of a watercourse with regard to changes in its form or bed; *especially* an equilibrium between erosion and deposition. **b** L19 The condition of a body of water with regard to the rates at which water enters and leaves it. **4** L19 *Science* and *Engineering* The set of conditions under which a system occurs or is maintained.

regimen *noun* LME **Latin** (from *regere* to rule). **1** LME The action of governing; government, rule. Later also, a particular system of government; a regime. *archaic*. **2** LME Chiefly *Medicine* A prescribed course of exercise, way of life, or diet, especially for the promotion or restoration of one's health. **3** M16 *Grammar* The government of one word by another; the relationship between one word and another dependent word. Now *rare*. **4** E19 *Physical Geography* REGIME sense 3a.

régisseur *noun* E19 **French**. *Theater* and *Ballet* A stage manager, an artistic director.

Regius *adjective* E17 **Latin** (= royal, from *rex, reg-* king). Designating (a professor holding) a university chair founded by a monarch or filled by Crown appointment.

reglement *noun* L16 **French** (*règlement, reiglement*, from Old and Modern French *regler, reigler* to rule, from late Latin *regulare* to regulate). **1** L16–M18 The action of regulating or controlling something. **2** M17 A regulation.

règlement de compte *noun phrase* L20 **French**. Settlement of an account; the settling of a score.

Reich *noun* plural **Reiche** E20 **German** (= kingdom, empire, state). Chiefly *History* The former German nation or commonwealth, *especially* the Third Reich (the Nazi regime 1933–45).

reine *noun* M19 **French** (= queen). *Cooking* Chiefly in *à la reine* (literally, 'in the fashion of a queen'), designating a dish prepared in some special way.

reinette *noun* LME **French** (*reinette, rainette*, perhaps from *raine* tree frog (from Latin *rana* frog), from the spots in certain varieties). Any of several eating apples of French origin, chiefly small and late-ripening, with dry skin and firm juicy flesh.

reis *noun* (also **rais**) L16 **Arabic** (*ra'īs* chief from *ra's* head). **1** L16 The captain of a boat or ship. **2** L17 A chief, a governor.

reja *noun* M19 **Spanish**. In Spain: a wrought-iron screen or grille used to protect windows, chapel tombs, etc.

relâche *noun* M19 **French.** A period of rest, an intermission; a break *from* something.

relais *noun* M20 **French.** In France: a café, a restaurant, sometimes also providing overnight accommodation.

relance *noun* L20 **French.** *Politics* A relaunch, a revival, especially of a policy.

relevé *noun* E19 **French** (= raised up). **1** E19 A course of a meal; a remove. *archaic.* **2** M20 *Ballet* A step in which the body is raised on half or full point. **3** M20 *Ecology* An enumeration of the species and environmental factors in a small stand of vegetation, taken as a sample of a wider area; the stand of vegetation itself.

relievo *noun* plural **relievos** (also **rilievo**) E17 **Italian** (*rilievo* from *rilevare* to raise, ultimately from Latin *relevare* to raise again). **1** A method of molding, carving, etc., in which the design stands out from the plane surface. Cf. ALTO-RELIEVO, BASSO-RELIEVO, MEZZO-RELIEVO. **2** The appearance of solidity given to a composition on a plane surface; *figurative* vividness or distinctness due to artistic presentation.

religieuse *noun* L17 **French** (feminine of next). **1** L17 A woman bound by religious vows; a nun. **2** M20 A confection consisting of two round cakes of choux pastry sandwiched together with cream and decorated with icing.

religieux *noun* plural same M17 **French.** A man bound by religious vows; a monk.

religioso *adverb & adjective* M19 **Italian** (= religious). *Music* (A direction:) with a devotional quality.

reliquiae *noun plural* M17 **Latin** (noun use of feminine plural of *reliquus* remaining, from as *re* + *liq-* stem of *linquere* to leave). Remains; *specifically* (**a**) *Geology* fossilized remains of animals or plants; (**b**) literary remains, unpublished or uncollected writings.

relleno abbreviation of CHILI RELLENO.

remanié *adjective* L19 **French** (past participle of *remanier* to rehandle, reshape). *Geology* Derived from an older stratum or structure.

remaniement *noun* E20 **French** (from as preceding). A rearrangement, a reconstruction.

remarque *noun* (also **remark**) L19 **French.** *Engraving* A distinguishing feature indicating the state of the plate, frequently taking the form of a sketch in the margin.

remboîtage *noun* M20 **French** (from *remboîter* to re-case (a book)). The action or an act of transferring a book into new binding, especially of superior quality.

remittitur *noun* L18 **Latin** (3rd person singular passive of *remittere* to remit). *Law* **1** L18 The remission of excessive damages awarded to a plaintiff; a formal statement of this. **2** L18 The action of sending the transcript of a case back from an appellate to a trial court; a formal notice of this.

remontoir *noun* (also **remontoire**) E19 **French** (from *remonter* to remount). *Horology* A device by which a uniform impulse is given to the pendulum or balance at regular intervals.

remora *noun* M16 **Latin** (= delay, hindrance, from *re-* + *mora* delay). **1** M16 Any of various slender marine fishes of the family Echeneidae, with the dorsal fin modified to form a large sucker for attachment to sharks, etc., formerly believed to hinder the progress of any sailing ship to which it attached itself. **2** E17 An obstacle, a hindrance, an impediment.

rémoulade *noun* (also **remoulade**) M19 **French** (from Italian *remolata,* of unknown origin). A salad dressing made with hard-boiled egg yolks, oil, vinegar, herbs, etc.

remplaçant *noun* (feminine **remplaçante**) M19 **French** (present participial adjective of *remplacer* to replace). A person who replaces another.

remskoen *noun* (also **riemskoen** and other variants) plural **remskoene** E19

Afrikaans (from Dutch *remschoen*, from *rem* brake + *schoen* shoe). *South African History* A wooden or metal shoe used to prevent a wheel from revolving; *figurative* an impediment to progress.

remuage *noun* E20 French (literally, 'moving about'). The periodic turning or shaking of bottled wine, especially champagne, to move sediment toward the cork.

remuda *noun* L19 American Spanish (from Spanish = exchange, replacement). A collection of saddle horses kept for remounts.

remueur *noun* E20 French (literally, 'mover'). A person who engages in REMUAGE.

Renaissance *noun* (also (especially in sense 2) **renaissance**) M19 French ((in specific use short for *renaissance des arts, renaissance des lettres*), from as *re-* + *naissance* birth from Latin *nascentia*, from *nasci* be born, or from French *naiss-* present stem of *naître* from Proto-Romance). **1 a** M19 The revival of art and literature under the influence of classical models between the fourteenth and sixteenth centuries, begun in Italy; the period of this movement. **b** M19 The style of art, architecture, etc., developed in and characteristic of this period. **2** L19 Any revival or period of significant improvement and new life in cultural, scientific, economic, or other areas of activity.

rendezvous *noun* (also **rendez-vous**) plural same L16 French (use as noun of imperative *rendez-vous* 'present yourselves', from *rendre* from Proto-Romance alteration of Latin *reddere* to give back). **1** *Military* **a** L16 A place appointed for the assembling of troops or armed forces. **b** E17 A place or port used or suitable for the assembling of a fleet or number of ships. Also, instructions concerning such a place. **2** L16 *generally* Any appointed or habitual meeting place. **3** E17 A meeting or assembly held by appointment or arrangement. Formerly also, a group of people thus assembled. **b** M–L17 An assemblage of things. **c** M20 The prearranged meeting in space between a spacecraft and another spacecraft or a celestial body; an instance of this.

rendu *adjective* M20 French (= rendered, delivered). Designating a price on imported goods that includes tariffs and delivery costs.

rendzina *noun* E20 Russian (from Polish *rędzina*). *Soil Science* A fertile lime-rich soil characterized by a dark friable humus-rich surface layer above a softer pale calcareous layer.

renga *noun* plural same, **rengas** L19 Japanese (from *ren* linking + *ga* from *ka* poetry). A Japanese poem consisting of a series of half-tanka contributed by different poets in turn.

renseignement *noun* M19 French. (A piece of) information. Also, a letter of introduction.

rente *noun* L19 French. Stock, *especially* French government stock; the interest or income accruing from such stock.

rentier *noun* M19 French (from RENTE). A person who makes an income from property or investment.

rentrée *noun* L19 French. A return, *especially* a return home after an annual vacation.

renvers *noun* plural same L19 French (from *renverser*, from as *re-* + *enverser* to overturn). *Horsemanship* A movement in which a horse walks parallel to a wall with its head and neck facing forward and its hindquarters curved toward the wall.

renversement *noun* E17 French (from as RENVERS). Originally, the action of reversing or inverting; the result of this. Now usually *specifically*, an airplane maneuver consisting of a half loop effected simultaneously with a half turn.

repêchage *noun* E20 French (from *repêcher*, literally, 'to fish out, rescue'). An extra contest, especially in rowing and cycling, in which the runners-up in the eliminating heats compete for a place in the final.

répétiteur *noun* M20 **French** (= tutor, coach). **1** M20 A person who teaches musicians and singers, especially opera singers, their parts. **2** M20 A person who supervises ballet rehearsals, etc.

réplique *noun* (also **replique**) L15 **French** (from *répliquer* from Latin *replicare* to unfold, (later) reply). A reply, a rejoinder.

■ Formerly fully Anglicized.

repoussé *adjective & noun* **M19 French** (past participle of *repousser*, from *re-* + *pousser* to push). **A** *adjective* M19 Of metalwork: raised into or ornamented in relief by means of hammering from the reverse side. **B** *noun* M19 Ornamental metalwork fashioned by the repoussé method; the process of hammering into relief.

repoussoir *noun* **L19 French** (from REPOUSSÉ). An object in the foreground of a painting serving to emphasize the principal figure or scene.

reprise *noun* **LME Old and Modern French** (noun use of past participle feminine of *reprendre* to take back, take again). **I 1** The fact of taking back something for one's own advantage; an amount taken back; loss, expense, cost. Only in LME. **2** LME A charge or payment falling due annually from a manor or estate. Usually in *plural*. **3a** M16–M18 Compensation. **b** M17–E18 The action of taking something by way of retaliation. **4** L17 A renewal or repetition of an action; a separate occasion of doing something. **II 5** E16 *Architecture* A return of moldings, etc., in an internal angle. **6a** E18 *Music* The repetition of the first theme of a movement after the close of the development. Formerly also, a refrain. **b** M20 *Linguistics* The repetition of a word or word group occurring in a preceding phrase. **c** M20 A repetition of a theatrical performance; a restaging or rewriting of a play; a replay. Also more widely, a further performance of any kind.

requiem *noun* **ME Latin** (accusative of *requies* rest, first word of the introit in the mass for the dead, *Requiem aeternam dona eis, Domine* Give them eternal rest, O Lord). **1** ME (frequently **Requiem**) *Roman Catholic Church* A special mass said or sung for the repose of the soul of a dead person. Also *mass of requiem, requiem mass*. **b** L18 A musical setting of a mass for the dead. **2** E17 Any dirge, solemn chant, etc., for the repose of the dead; *figurative* a memorial, a commemoration. **3** E17 Rest, peace, quiet; a period of this. Now *rare*.

requiescat *noun* **E19 Latin** (from *requiescat in pace* may he or she rest in peace). A wish for the repose of a dead person.

res *noun* plural same **E17 Latin** (= thing). A thing, a matter.

■ Originally in legal terminology and still chiefly in Latin legal phrases, e.g., *res communis* 'common property', *res integra* 'a matter that has not been covered', *res judicata* 'a matter that has been adjudicated', *res nullius* 'no one's property'. Used alone, *res* can now also have the more general senses of 'the condition of something; the matter in hand, the point at issue, the crux'.

res cogitans *noun phrase* **E20 Latin** (= thinking thing). *Philosophy* The concept of a human as a thinking being.

■ The concept originated with Descartes in his *Meditationes* (1641): *Sed quid igitur sum? res cogitans* 'But what therefore am I? A thinking being' (ii.23).

réseau *noun* plural **réseaux** (also **rézel**) **L16 French** (= net, web) **1** L16 A plain net ground used in lacemaking. **2** E20 A network, a grid, *especially* one superimposed as a reference marking on a photograph in astronomy, surveying, etc. **3** M20 A spy or intelligence network, especially in the French resistance movement during the German occupation (1940–45).

res extensa *noun phrase* plural **res extensae** **M20 Latin** (= extended thing). *Philosophy* A material thing considered as material substance.

res gestae *noun phrase plural* E17 **Latin** (= things done). (An account of) things done; (a person's) achievements; events in the past; in *Law* the facts of the case.

residentura *noun* M20 **Russian** (*rezidentura*). A group or organization of intelligence agents in a foreign country.

residuum *noun* plural **residua** L17 **Latin** (noun use of neuter of *residuus* remaining, from *residere* to reside). **1** L17 That which remains; a residue. **b** M19 The masses; the poor. **2** M18 *Law* The residue of an estate. **3** M18 *Chemistry*, etc. A substance left after combustion, evaporation, etc., a residue.

résistant *noun* M20 **French**. A member of the French Resistance movement in World War II.

res non verba *noun phrase plural* M20 **Latin** (= things not words). Action rather than talk.

■ Also as a motto, sometimes with the addition *crux non vis* 'the Cross not force'.

respondentia *noun* E18 **Modern Latin** (from *respondent-* present participial stem of Latin *respondere* from *re-* + *spondere* to pledge). A loan on the cargo of a vessel, to be repaid (with maritime interest) only if the freight arrives safely at its destination.

responsum *noun* plural **responsa** L19 **Latin** (= reply). A written reply by a rabbi or Talmudic scholar to an inquiry on some matter of Jewish law.

ressentiment *noun* M20 **German** (*Ressentiment* from French *ressentiment*, from *ressentir* to resent). *Social Psychology* A negative attitude toward society or authority arising from repressed hostility, feelings of inadequacy, etc.

■ The term is particularly associated with the philosophy of Friedrich Nietzsche (1844–1900).

restaurant *noun* E19 **French** (noun use of present participle of *restaurer* to restore). A public establishment where meals or refreshments may be obtained.

restaurateur *noun* L18 **French** (from *restaurer* to restore). A keeper of a restaurant.

restitutio in integrum *noun phrase* E18 **Latin** (= restoration to the uninjured state). *Law* Placement of an injured party in the situation that would have prevailed had no injury been sustained; restoration of the STATUS QUO ANTE.

résumé *noun* (also **resumé**, in sense 2 **resume**) E19 **French** (past participle of *résumer* to resume). **1** E19 A summary, an epitome. **2** M20 A summary, especially of a person's employment history; CURRICULUM VITAE.

resurgam *interjection* M17 **Latin** (literally, 'I shall rise again'). Proclaiming one's Christian faith in the resurrection of the dead. Usually *transferred* and *figurative*.

retable *noun* E19 **French** (*rétable*, *retable* from Spanish *retablo* from medieval Latin *retrotabulum*, from Latin *retro-* behind + *tabula* table). A frame enclosing painted or decorated panels or a shelf or ledge for ornaments, raised above the back of an altar.

retablo *noun* plural **retablos** M19 **Spanish** (see preceding). A RETABLE. Also, a votive picture displayed in a church.

retardataire *noun & adjective* E20 **French**. Chiefly *Art*. **A** *noun* E20 A work of art executed in the style of an earlier period. **B** *adjective* M20 Behind the times; characterized by the style of an earlier period.

retiarius *noun* plural **retiarii** M17 **Latin** (from *rete* net). *Roman History* A gladiator who fought using a net with which to entangle his adversary.

reticella *noun & adjective* M19 **Italian** (diminutive of *rete* net). **A** *noun* M19 A lacelike fabric with a characteristic geometric pattern produced especially in Venice from the fifteenth to the seventeenth century. **B** M20 *attributive* or as *adjective* Of, pertaining to, or characteristic of reticella.

reticello *noun* plural **reticelli** L19 **Italian** (from as preceding). A network of fine glass threads embedded in some Venetian glass. Also (more fully *reticello glass*), glass made with this type of decoration.

reticule *noun* E18 **French** (*réticule* from Latin *reticulum* diminutive of *rete* net). **1** E18 A grid of fine lines or threads set in the focal plane or eyepiece of an optical instrument, a reticle. **2** E19 A woman's small netted or other bag, especially with a drawstring, carried or worn to serve the purpose of a pocket.

retina *noun* LME **Medieval Latin** (from Latin *rete* net). The light-sensitive layer that lines much of the inside of the eyeball, in which nerve impulses are triggered and pass via the optic nerve to the brain where a visual image is formed.

retiré *noun* M20 **French** (past participle of *retirer* to withdraw). *Ballet* A movement in which one leg is raised at right angles to the body until the toe is in line with the knee of the supporting leg.

retornado *noun* plural **retornados** L20 **Portuguese** (from past participle of *retornar* to return). A Portuguese citizen returning to settle in Portugal after living in a Portuguese colony.

retraite *noun* M19 **French** (from Old French *retraite* retreat). **1** M19 Retirement, seclusion, retreat. **2** L19 *Military* The signal for retreating.

retroussage *noun* M20 **French** (from as *retroussé*: see next). In etching, the action of drawing a fine cloth across an inked plate to draw out some ink and smear it irregularly across the plate.

retroussé *adjective* E19 **French** (past participle of *retrousser* to turn up, from *re-* + *trousser* from Old French *trusser*, medieval Latin *trossare*, probably from late Latin *tors-* past participial stem of *torquere* to twist). Usually of the nose: turned up at the tip.

retsina *noun* E20 **Modern Greek** (from *retsini* from Greek *rētinē* pine resin). A Greek white wine flavored with resin.

réussi *adjective* M20 **French** (past participle of *réuss* to turn out, result, succeed). Fine, excellent, successful.

revanche *noun* M19 **French** (earlier *revenche*, from Old French *revencher* from late Latin *revindicare* to avenge, claim). Revenge; retaliation; *specifically* a nation's policy of seeking the return of lost territory.

■ The policy of *revanchisme* was particularly associated with France's determination to recover Alsace-Lorraine after losing the territory to Germany in the Franco-Prussian War of 1870, but in other contexts the word is now generally Anglicized as *revanchism*.

reveille *noun* (also (now *rare*) **reveillé**) M17 **French** (*réveillez* imperative plural of *réveiller* to awaken, from *ré-* + *veiller* from Latin *vigilare* to keep watch). A signal given in the morning, usually on a drum or bugle, to waken soldiers and indicate that it is time to rise; (the time of) the sounding of this signal.

réveillon *noun* E19 **French** (from *réveiller* (see preceding)). In France: a nighttime feast or celebration, originally one after midnight on Christmas morning.

revenant *noun & adjective* E19 **French** (present participle of *revenir* to return). **A** *noun* E19 A person who has returned, especially supposedly from the dead; a ghost. **B** *adjective* E20 Returned, especially supposedly from the dead.

reverdie *noun* M20 **French** (noun use of feminine past participle of *reverdir* to grow, turn green again). A medieval French song celebrating the return of spring.

reverie *noun* (also **revery**) ME **French** (in branch I from Old French *reverie* rejoicing, revelry, from *rever* to be delirious (modern *rêver* to dream), of unknown origin; in branch II from later French *resverie* (now *rêverie*)). **I 1** ME-

M16 Joy, delight; revelry; wantonness, wildness. *rare.* **II 2** E17 A fantastic, fanciful, or unpractical notion; a delusion. *archaic.* **3** M17 A fit of abstracted musing; a daydream. **b** L19 *Music* An instrumental composition suggestive of a dreamy or musing state. **4** M18 The fact, state, or condition of being lost in thought or engaged in musing.

revers *noun* plural same M19 French. A turned-back edge of a garment revealing the undersurface; the material covering such an edge. Usually *plural.*

revirement *noun* E20 French. An alteration of one's plans; a complete change of attitude or opinion.

revolte *noun* (also **révolté**, (feminine **révoltée**)) L19 French. A person who revolts; a rebel; a nonconformist.

revue *noun* L19 French (= review). A light theatrical entertainment consisting of a series of short (usually satirical) sketches, comic turns, songs, etc. Also, the genre comprising such entertainments.

rezident *noun* plural **rezidenty** M20 Russian. An intelligence agent in a foreign country.

rhagades *noun plural* OE Latin (from Greek, plural of *rhagas* fissure). *Medicine* Cracks, fissures, or thin scars in the skin, especially around the mouth or anus.

rho *noun* LME Greek (*rhō*). **1** LME The seventeenth letter (Ρ, ρ) of the Greek alphabet. **2** M20 *Statistics* A correlation coefficient. **3** M20 *Physics* A meson with isospin and spin of one and a mass of 770 MeV. In full *rho meson.*

rhodomontade variant of RODOMONTADE.

rhombus *noun* plural **rhombuses**, **rhombi** M16 Latin (from Greek *rhombos*). **1** M16 *Geometry* A plane figure having four equal sides and equal opposite angles (two acute and two obtuse); an oblique equilateral parallelogram. **2** E17 A lozenge-shaped object, part, marking, etc.

rhumba variant of RUMBA.

rhyton *noun* plural **rhytons**, **rhyta** M19 Greek (*rhuton* neuter of *rhutos* flowing, related to *rhein* to flow). *Greek Antiquities* A type of drinking vessel, often in the form of an animal's head, with one or more holes at the bottom through which liquid can flow.

ria *noun* L19 Spanish (*ría* estuary). *Physical Geography* A long narrow inlet of the sea formed by partial submergence of an unglaciated river valley.

Rialto *noun* (also **rialto**) M16 Italian (name of district of Venice in which the Exchange was situated). A market, an exchange.

riata *noun* (also **reata**) M19 Spanish (*reata*). A lariat.

richesse *noun* ME Old French (*richeise*, *richesce* (modern *richesse*), from *riche* rich). **1** ME–L17 *singular* and in *plural* Wealth; richness; riches. **2** L15 A number or group of martens.

■ Long archaic, but cf. EMBARRAS DE RICHESSE.

ricochet *noun* M18 French (= the skipping of a shot or of a flat stone on water, of unknown origin). Originally *Military* The action of a projectile, especially a bullet or shell, in rebounding at an angle off a surface or surfaces after being fired; a hit made after such a rebound.

ricordo *noun* plural **ricordi** E20 Italian (literally, 'memory'). A token of remembrance, a souvenir; *Art* a copy made by a painter of another's composition.

ricotta *noun* L19 Italian (= recooked, from Latin *recocta* feminine past participle of *recoquere*, from as *re-* + *coquere* cook). A kind of soft white unsalted Italian cheese. Also *ricotta cheese.*

rictus *noun* M18 Latin (literally, 'open mouth', from *rict-* past participial stem of *ringi* to gape). **1** M18 *Botany* The throat of a two-lipped corolla. **2** E19 The expanse or gape of the mouth, or of the beak or jaws of a bird, fish, etc.; *transferred* a fixed grin or grimace.

riegel *noun* E20 **German** (from Middle High German *rigel* crossbar, Old High German *rigil* bar). *Physical Geography* A low transverse ridge of resistant bedrock on the floor of a glacial valley, a rock bar.

riem *noun* E19 **Dutch** (from Middle Dutch *rieme*). A long strip or thong of dressed softened leather. *South African.*

riempie *noun & adjective* (also **riempje**) M19 **Dutch** (*riempje*, from as RIEM + Afrikaans diminutive suffix *-ie*). **A** *noun* M19 A fine narrow *riem* or leather thong. **B** E20 *attributive* or as *adjective* Of furniture: having a seat or bottom of crisscrossed fine narrow leather thongs, as a *riempie chair* (Afrikaans *riempiestoel*). *South African.*

rien ne va plus *interjection* (also **rien n'va plus**) L19 **French**. In roulette, the call made by the croupier while the wheel is spinning: no more bets!

rifacimento *noun* plural **rifacimenti** L18 **Italian** (from *rifacimento* stem of *rifare* to remake). A remodeling or recasting of a literary work.

rigadoon *noun* (also **rigaudon**) L17 **French** (*rigodon, rigaudon* said to be from *Rigaud* a dancing master who devised it). **1** L17 A lively dance for couples, in duple or quadruple time, of Provençal origin. **2** M18 A piece of music for this dance.

rigatoni *noun* M20 **Italian** (from *rigato* past participle of *rigare* to draw a line, make fluting, from *riga* a line). Pasta in the form of short hollow fluted tubes; an Italian dish consisting largely of this and usually a sauce.

rijsttafel *noun* L19 **Dutch** (from *rijst* rice + *tafel* table). A Southeast Asian meal consisting of a selection of different foods (such as eggs, meat, fish, fruit, curry, etc.) mixed with rice and served in separate dishes.

rikka *noun* L19 **Japanese** (literally, 'standing flowers', from *ritsu* stand + *ka* flower(s)). A traditional and formal style of Japanese flower arrangement, used especially to decorate Buddhist temples.

rillettes *noun* (treated as *singular* or *plural*) L19 **French**. Pâté made of ground pork, chicken, etc., seasoned and combined with fat.

rimaye *noun* E20 **French** (from Latin *rima* fissure + French collective suffix *-aye*). A BERGSCHRUND.

rimmon *noun* (also **rimon**) plural **rimmonim** M20 **Hebrew** (*rimmōn*, literally, 'pomegranate'). A pomegranate-shaped ornament or decorative cover for each of the bars at either end of a Jewish law scroll.

rinceau *noun* plural **rinceaux** L18 **French**. A molded, carved, or painted decoration on furniture etc., often in the form of scrolls or acanthus leaves.

rinderpest *noun* M19 **German** (from *Rinder* cattle (plural of *Rind*) + *Pest* plague). An infectious disease of ruminants, especially oxen; cattle plague.

rinforzando *adverb, adjective, & noun* E19 **Italian** (present participle of *rinforzare* to strengthen). *Music* **A** *adverb & adjective* E19 (A direction:) with a sudden stress or crescendo. **B** *noun* M19 plural **rinforzandos, rinforzandi** A sudden stress or crescendo made on a short phrase.

ripieno *adjective & noun* E18 **Italian** (from *ri-* re- + *pieno* full). *Music* **A** *attributive adjective* E18 Originally, supplementary, reinforcing. Now chiefly, of or pertaining to a ripieno. **B** *noun* M18 plural **ripienos, ripieni** Originally, a supplementary player or instrument. Now chiefly, the body of instruments accompanying the concertino in baroque concerto music.

riposte *noun* E18 **French** ((earlier *risposte*) from Italian *risposta* noun use of feminine past participle of *rispondere*, from Latin *respondere* from *re-* + *spondere* to pledge). **1** E18 *Fencing* A quick thrust given after parrying a lunge; a return thrust. **2** M19 A retaliatory action; a quick sharp reply or retort.

ripresa *noun* plural **riprese** M18 **Italian.** *Music* A repeat; a refrain.

ris de veau *noun phrase* E19 **French.** Sweetbread of veal prepared as a dish.

risoluto *adjective & adverb* M18 **Italian.** *Music* **A** *adjective* Resolved into a concord. Only in M18. **B** *adverb* M19 (A direction:) with resolution or emphasis.

Risorgimento *noun* plural **Risorgimenti, Risorgimentos** L19 **Italian** (= renewal, renaissance). **1** L19 *History* The movement that led to the unification of Italy as an independent nation in 1870. **2** M20 A revitalization or renewal of activity in any sphere.

risotto *noun* plural **risottos** M19 **Italian** (from *riso* rice). An Italian dish of rice cooked in stock with various other ingredients, as meat, onions, etc.

risqué *adjective* (feminine **risquée**) M19 **French** (past participle of *risquer* to risk). Slightly indecent, liable to shock slightly.

rissole *noun* E18 **French** (later form of Old French *ruissole* dialectal variant of *roisole, roussole* from Proto-Romance noun use of feminine of late Latin *russeolus* reddish, from Latin *russus* red). A ball or small cake of chopped meat, etc., coated with breadcrumbs, cooked by frying.

risus sardonicus *noun phrase* L17 **Modern Latin** (from Latin *risus* laugh (from *ridere* to laugh) + medieval or modern Latin *sardonicus* sardonic). *Medicine* An involuntary grinning expression resulting from chronic abnormal contraction of the facial muscles, as in tetanus.

ritardando *adverb, adjective, & noun* plural of noun **ritardandos, ritardandi** E19 **Italian** (present participle of *ritardare* to slow down). *Music* RALLENTANDO.

rite de passage *noun phrase* plural **rites de passage** E20 **French.** *Anthropology* A formal procedure or act marking the beginning of a new defined stage in a person's life, a rite of passage.

■ The phrase was coined by Arnold van Gennep in the title of his book *Les Rites de passage* (1909). In English use, the translation *rite of passage* appeared in the same year as van Gennep's book; the 1960 translators of *Les Rites de passage* suggested that *rites of transition* would have been a better rendering, but acknowledged that *rites of passage* had become too firmly established in general usage to dislodge. Although less frequent than the English version, *rite de passage* is still found.

ritenuto *adverb, adjective, & noun* E19 **Italian** (past participle of *ritenere* from Latin *retinere* to hold back). *Music* **A** *adverb & adjective* E19 (A direction:) with immediate reduction of speed, restrained, held back in tempo. **B** *noun* E19 plural **ritenuti, ritenutos** A ritenuto phrase or passage.

rites de passage plural of RITE DE PASSAGE.

ritornello *noun* plural **ritornellos, ritornelli** L17 **Italian** (diminutive of *ritorno* return). *Music* An instrumental refrain, interlude, or prelude, especially in a vocal work.

ritournelle *noun* M19 **French** (from as preceding). *Music* A RITORNELLO.

ritter *noun* E19 **German** (variant of *reiter* rider). A German or Austrian knight or mounted warrior; a member of the German or Austrian minor nobility.

■ Obsolete except in historical contexts.

riu variant of RYU.

riverain *adjective & noun* M19 **French** (from *rivière* river). **A** *adjective* M19 Riverine. **B** *noun* M19 A person who lives beside or near a river.

riviera *noun* (also **Riviera**) M18 **Italian** (= seashore, coast). A coastal region with a warm climate and popularity as a vacation resort, originally *specifically* one around Genoa in Italy, later also the Mediterranean coast from Marseilles in France to La Spezia in Italy.

rivière *noun* M19 **French.** **1** M19 *Needlework* A row of openwork. **2** L19 A necklace of diamonds or other gems, *especially* one consisting of more than one string.

riza *noun* E20 **Russian** (from Old Church Slavonic = garment). A metal shield or plaque framing the painted face and other features of a Russian icon, and engraved with the lines of the completed picture.

robe de chambre *noun phrase* plural **robes de chambre** M18 **French.** A dressing gown, a negligée.

robe de nuit *noun phrase* plural **robes de nuit** M19 **French.** A nightgown.

robe de style *noun phrase* plural **robes de style** E20 **French.** A woman's formal dress with a tight bodice and a long bouffant skirt.

robes de chambre, robes de nuit, etc., plurals of ROBE DE CHAMBRE, ROBE DE NUIT, etc.

rocaille *noun* M19 **French.** An artistic or architectural style of decoration characterized by ornate rock- and shellwork; a rococo style.

roche moutonnée *noun phrase* plural **roches moutonnées** M19 **French** (*roche* rock (from medieval Latin *rocca, rocha* of unknown origin) + *moutonnée* (from *mouton* sheep, from medieval Latin *multo(n-)*, probably of Gaulish origin). *Physical Geography* A bare rock outcrop that has been shaped by glacial erosion, characteristically smoothed and rounded by abrasion but often displaying one side that is rougher and steeper.

rococo *adjective & noun* M19 **French** (fanciful alteration of *rocaille* pebble- or shell-work from *roc* rock). **A** *adjective* **1** M19 Old-fashioned, antiquated. **2** M19 (Of furniture or architecture) of or characterized by an elaborately ornamental late baroque style of decoration prevalent in eighteenth-century Continental Europe, with asymmetrical patterns involving motifs, scrollwork, etc.; (of music, literature, etc.) highly ornamented, florid; *generally* extravagantly or excessively ornate. **B** *noun* M19 The rococo style of art, decoration, etc.

rodeo *noun* plural **rodeos** M19 **Spanish** (from *rodear* to go around, based on Latin *rotare* to rotate). **1** M19 A roundup of cattle for counting, inspecting, branding, etc.; a place where cattle are rounded up. **2** E20 A display or competition exhibiting the skills of riding broncos, roping calves, wrestling steers, etc. **b** E20 *transferred* A similar (usually competitive) exhibition of other skills, as motorcycle riding, fishing, etc.

rodomontade *noun, verb, & adjective* (also **rhodomontade**) E17 **French** (from Italian *rodomontada, rodomontata*, from *Rodomonte* the name of a boastful character in the Renaissance *Orlando* epics). **A** *noun* **1** E17 A brag, a boast; an extravagantly boastful or arrogant remark or speech. **2** M17 Boastful or inflated language or behavior; extravagant bragging. **B** *intransitive verb* L17 Boast, brag; rant. **C** *adjective* M18 Bragging, boastful; ranting.

roemer *noun* L19 **Dutch** (or German *Römer*). A type of decorated German or Dutch wineglass with knobs or prunts on the stem.

▪ The English *rummer* or *rummer glass* is cognate with *roemer* and its other Continental variants and has nothing to do with the liquor rum. The ultimate origin may be 'Roman glass'.

roesti *noun plural* (treated as *singular* or *plural*) (also **rösti**) **M20 Swiss German.** A Swiss dish of grated potatoes, formed into a pancake and fried.

rofia see RAFFIA.

rogan josh *noun phrase* (also **roghan josh**) **M20 Urdu** (*roġan još, rauġan-još* (preparation of mutton) stewed in ghee, from Urdu *roġan, rauġan* from Persian *rauġan* oil, ghee + Urdu, Persian *roġan još* act of braising or stewing). A dish of curried meat (usually lamb) cooked in a rich sauce.

rognon *noun* E19 **French.** **1** E19 A kidney, used as food. Usually in *plural.* **2** M20 *Mountaineering* A rounded outcrop of rock or stones surrounded by a glacier or an ice-field.

roi fainéant *noun phrase* plural **rois fainéants** M19 **French** (literally, 'sluggard king'; cf. FAINÉANT). Any person with merely nominal power.

■ Originally applied to any of the later Merovingian kings of France, whose power was merely nominal.

roi soleil *noun phrase* plural **rois soleils** L19 **French** (literally, 'sun king', (the heraldic device of) Louis XIV of France). A preeminent person or thing.

romaine *noun* E20 **French** (feminine of *romain* Roman). **1** E20 A cos lettuce. Also more fully *romaine lettuce.* **2** E20 Any of various crêpe fabrics.

■ *Romaine crêpe* (a proprietary name in the United States) is a semi-sheer crêpe fabric of silk, rayon, or acetate.

roman à clef *noun phrase* (also **roman-à-clef**) plural **romans à clef** L19 **French** (literally, 'novel with a key'). A novel in which actual people or events appear under fictitious names.

roman à thèse *noun phrase* plural **romans à thèse** M19 **French** (literally, 'novel with a thesis'). A novel that seeks to expound or promote a theory.

romancé *adjective* M20 **French** (from *romancer* to fictionalize). Especially of a biography: fictionalized, written in the form of a novel.

roman de geste *noun phrase* plural **romans de geste** M19 **French** (literally, 'romance of heroic deeds'). A CHANSON DE GESTE.

roman-fleuve *noun phrase* plural **romans-fleuves** M20 **French** (literally, 'river novel'). A novel featuring the leisurely description of the lives and members of a family; a sequence of self-contained novels.

romanità *noun* E20 **Italian** (from next). **1** E20 ROMANITAS. **2** M20 The spirit or influence of the central Roman Catholic authorities; acceptance of papal policy.

romanitas *noun* M20 **Late Latin** (from Latin *Romanus*). The spirit or ideals of ancient Rome.

roman noir *noun phrase* plural **romans noirs** M20 **French** (literally, 'black novel'). A Gothic novel, a thriller.

roman policier *noun phrase* plural **romans policiers** E20 **French.** A detective novel or story.

romanza *noun* M19 **Spanish** (or Italian, from popular Latin adverb formed on Latin *Romanicus* from *Romanus* Roman). *Music* A romantic song or melody; a lyrical piece of music; a romance.

Romanze *noun* plural **Romanzen** L19 **German** (literally, 'romance'). *Music* A composition of a tender or lyrical character; *specifically* a slow romantic instrumental piece or movement.

rondavel *noun* L19 **Afrikaans** (*rondawel*). A round tribal hut usually with a thatched conical roof. Also, a similar building used especially as a vacation cottage or an outbuilding on a farm. *South African.*

rond de cuir *noun phrase* plural **ronds de cuir** E20 **French** (literally, 'circle of leather'). A round leather cushion, often used on office chairs in France. Also *transferred,* a bureaucrat.

ronde *noun* M19 **French** (feminine of *rond* round). **1** M19 A style of script with gothic characteristics used in France from the eighteenth century; printing type imitating or based on this writing. **2** M20 A dance in which the participants move in a circle or ring. **3** M20 A round or course of talk, activity, etc.; *figurative* a treadmill.

rondeau *noun* plural **rondeaux** E16 **Old and Modern French** (later form of *rondel* from *rond* round). **1** E16 A poem of ten or thirteen lines with only two rhymes throughout and with the opening words used twice as a refrain. **2** L18 *Music* A RONDO sense 1.

rondelle *noun* M19 French (from *rond* round). A circular piece of something.

rondo *noun* plural **rondos** L18 Italian (from French RONDEAU). **1** L18 A piece of music with a recurring leading theme, often as the final movement of a concerto, sonata, etc. **2** M19 A game of chance played with balls on a table.

rond-point *noun* plural **ronds-points** L19 French (from *rond* round + *point* center). A circular space in a garden from which paths radiate; a traffic circle where roads converge.

ronds de cuir plural of ROND DE CUIR.

rongeur *noun* L19 French (= gnawing, a rodent, from *ronger* to gnaw). *Surgery* Strong surgical forceps with a biting action, used for removing small pieces from bone. Also *rongeur forceps*.

ronin *noun* plural same, **ronins** L19 Japanese. In feudal Japan: a lordless wandering samurai; an outlaw. Now also *transferred*, a Japanese student who has failed and is permitted to retake a university (entrance) examination.

rooinek *noun* L19 Afrikaans (from *rooi* red + *nek* neck). A British or English-speaking South African.

■ In derogatory or jocular use in South African slang, the term was especially associated with the British troops in South Africa during the Boer War (1899–1902).

roquette *noun* E20 French. A cruciferous plant eaten as a salad, rocket.

rosalia *noun* E19 Italian (female forename in *Rosalia, mia cara* title of an Italian song using this device). *Music* The repetition of a phrase or melody one note higher, with the retention of the same intervals and a consequent change of key.

rosé *noun & adjective* L19 French (= pink). (Designating) any light red or pink wine, colored by brief contact with red grape skins.

rosemaling *noun* M20 Norwegian (= rose painting). The art of painting (wooden objects) with flower motifs; flower motifs, especially painted on wood.

rosolio *noun* (also **rosoglio**) plural **rosolios** E19 Italian (variant of *rosoli*, from Latin *ros* dew + *solis* genitive of *sol* sun). A sweet cordial made especially in Italy from alcohol, raisins, sugar, rose petals, cloves, cinnamon, etc.

rosso antico *noun phrase* L18 Italian (literally, 'ancient red'). **1** L18 A red stoneware produced at Josiah Wedgwood's Staffordshire factories. **2** L19 A rich red Italian marble used for decoration.

rösti variant of ROESTI.

rostrum *noun* plural **rostra**, (*rare*) **rostrums** M16 Latin (= beak, beak-head, from *rodere* to gnaw). **1** M16 *Roman Antiquities* A platform or stand for speakers in the Forum of ancient Rome, decorated with the beak-heads of captured warships. **b** M18 *transferred* A platform, stage, stand, etc., especially for public speaking; *specifically* (**a**) a pulpit; (**b**) a conductor's platform facing the orchestra; (**c**) a platform for supporting a movie or television camera. **2** E17 *Roman Antiquities* A beak-like projection from the prow of a warship. **3** *Anatomy* and *Zoology* **a** M18 A beak, a snout; an anterior prolongation of the head, as in a weevil. **b** E19 A process or formation resembling a beak. **4** M19 *Botany* A beaklike process.

rota *noun* L17 Latin (= wheel). A rotational order of people, duties to be done; a list of these.

■ *Rota* occurs first (E17) as the name of the supreme court of the Roman Catholic church, then (M17) as the name of a political club. The above is the only sense generally used in English.

roti *noun* E20 Hindustani (*roṭī*). A type of unleavened bread originally from the Indian subcontinent.

rôti *noun & postpositive adjective* L18 French (from *rôtir* to roast). *Cooking* **A** *noun* L18 A dish or main course of roasted meat. **B** *postpositive adjective* M19 Of food: roasted.

rotisserie *noun* M19 **French** (*rôtisserie*, from *rôtir* to roast). **1** M19 A restaurant or store specializing in roasted or barbecued meat, etc. **2** M20 A type of roasting oven with a power-driven rotating spit. Also *rotisserie oven*.

rôtisseur *noun* M18 **French** (from *rôtir* to roast). A chef in charge of all roasting, and usually grilling and frying, in a restaurant, etc.

roué *noun* E19 **French** (noun use of past participle of *rouer* to break on the wheel (the punishment said to be deserved by such a person)). A debauchee, a rake.

rouge *noun & adjective* LME **Old and Modern French** (from Latin *rubeus* red). **A** *adjective* LME Red. *obsolete* except in certain heraldic contexts. **B** *noun* **1** The color red. *rare*. Only in LME. **2** M18 A red powder or cream used as a cosmetic to add color to the lips or especially the cheeks. **3** L18 Red as one of the two colors of divisions in rouge-et-noir and roulette. Earliest in ROUGE-ET-NOIR. **4** E19 A radical; a republican; a socialist. Now chiefly (*Canadian*), a member of the Quebec Liberal Party. **5** M19 Any of various metallic oxides, etc., used as polishing powders; *especially* (in full *jeweler's rouge*) a fine preparation of ferric oxide used as a metal polish. Usually with specifying word. **6** M20 French red wine.

rouge de fer *noun phrase* E20 **French** (literally, 'red of iron'). An orange red enamel used on Chinese porcelain, made from a ferric oxide base.

rouge-et-noir *noun phrase* L18 **French** (= red and black). A gambling game in which stakes are placed on a table marked with red and black diamonds.

rouge flambé *noun phrase* E20 **French**. A bright red Chinese porcelain glaze, made from copper oxide.

rouget *noun* L19 **French**. A red mullet, especially as used in cooking.

rouille *noun* M20 **French** (literally, 'rust'). A Provençal sauce made from pounded red chilies, garlic, breadcrumbs, etc., blended with stock, frequently added to bouillabaisse.

roulade *noun* E18 **French** (from *rouler* to roll). **1** E18 *Music* A florid passage of runs, etc., in solo vocal music, *especially* one sung to one syllable. **2** L19 Any of various dishes prepared by spreading a filling onto a base of meat, sponge, etc., which is then rolled up and frequently served sliced.

rouleau *noun* plural **rouleaux**, **rouleaus** L17 **French** (from *rôle*, originally, a roll or paper containing an actor's part). **1** L17 A cylindrical packet of gold coins. **b** M19 A stack of disk-shaped objects, especially red blood cells. **2** L18 A roll or a coil *of* something, especially hair. **3** E19 A turned tube or length of rolled fabric used as trimming or to form a belt on a garment, etc. **4** E20 A type of narrow-necked cylindrical vase originally made in China in the late seventeenth century. In full *rouleau vase*.

roulement *noun* E20 **French** (literally, 'roll, roster'). *Military* (A) movement of troops or equipment, especially from a reserve force to provide relief.

roulette *noun* M18 **French** (diminutive of *rouelle* wheel, from late Latin *rotella* diminutive of *rota* wheel). **1** *generally* A small wheel. *rare*. Only in M18. **2** M18 A gambling game in which a ball is dropped onto a revolving wheel with numbered compartments in the center of a table, players betting on (the color, height, or parity of) the number at which the ball comes to rest. **3** M19 A revolving toothed wheel; *specifically* (**a**) one for making dotted lines in etching and engraving; (**b**) one for perforating a sheet of paper.

■ Other senses are now rare or obsolete. A transferred use of sense 2 is in the phrase 'Russian roulette' (the act of bravado involving spinning the cylinder of a revolver, one chamber of which is loaded, and then pulling the trigger while pointing it at one's head); hence figuratively, *playing Russian roulette* means taking dangerous risks.

routier *noun* M17 **French** (from Old French *rute* from Proto-Romance noun use (sc. *via* way) of feminine of Latin *ruptus* past participle of *rumpere* to break). **1** M17 *History* A mariner's guide to sea routes, a rutter. **2** M19 *History* A member of any of numerous bands of mercenaries active in France during the later Middle Ages. **3** M20 In France: a long-distance truck driver.

routinier *noun* E19 **French**. A person who adheres to (a) routine; *especially* (*Music*) a conductor who performs in a mechanically correct but uninspiring way.

roux *noun* E19 **French** (= browned (sc. butter)). *Cooking* A blend of melted fat (especially butter) and flour used as a thickener in making sauces.

ruana *noun* M20 **American Spanish** (from Spanish (*manta*) *ruana*, literally, 'poor man's cloak', from *rúa* street, from late Latin *ruga* furrow, street, from Latin *ruga* wrinkle). A South American cape or poncho, worn especially in Colombia and Peru.

rubato *adjective & noun* L18 **Italian** (literally, 'robbed'). *Music* **A** *adjective* L18 *tempo rubato*, rubato. **B** *noun* plural **rubatos, rubati** L19 The action or practice of temporarily disregarding strict tempo during performance; an instance of this.

rubella *noun* L19 **Latin** (noun use of neuter plural of Latin *rubellus* reddish, from *rubeus* red). German measles.

ruche *noun* E19 **Old and Modern French** (from medieval Latin *rusca* tree bark, of Celtic origin). A frill of gathered ribbon, lace, etc., used especially as a trimming on a garment.

rucola *noun* L20 **Italian**. A vegetable the leaves of which are used for salads.

rumba *noun* (also **rhumba**) E20 **American Spanish**. An Afro-Cuban dance; a ballroom dance imitative of this, danced on the spot with a pronounced movement of the hips; the dance rhythm of this, usually in 2/4 time; a piece of music with this rhythm.

rusé *adjective* (feminine **rusée**) M18 **French**. Inclined to use ruses; deceitful, sly, cunning.

ruse de guerre *noun phrase* plural **ruses de guerre** E19 **French** (literally, 'ruse of war'). A stratagem intended to deceive an enemy in war; *transferred* a justifiable trick.

rusée see RUSÉ.

ruses de guerre plural of RUSE DE GUERRE.

rus in urbe *noun phrase* M18 **Latin** (literally, 'country in city'). An illusion of countryside created by a building, garden, etc., within a city; an urban building, etc., that has this effect.

rya *noun* M20 **Swedish**. A Scandinavian type of knotted pile rug. In full *rya rug*.

ryu *noun* (also **riu**) plural same L19 **Japanese** (*-ryū* school, style, system). Any Japanese school or style of art.

sabayon *noun* E20 **French** (from Italian *zabaione* variant of ZABAGLIONE). Zabaglione.

sabha *noun* E20 **Sanskrit** (*sabhā*). In the Indian subcontinent: an assembly; a council; a society.

■ Hence the *Lok Sabha* and the *Rajya Sabha* are respectively the lower and the upper houses of the Indian parliament.

sabi *noun* M20 **Japanese** (literally, 'loneliness'). In Japanese art, a quality of simple and mellow beauty expressing a mood of spiritual solitude recognized in Zen Buddhist philosophy. Cf. WABI.

sabkha *noun* (also **sebkha**) L19 **Arabic** (*sabḵa* a saline infiltration, salt flat). *Geography* An area of coastal flats subject to periodic flooding and evaporation, found especially in North Africa and Arabia.

sabot *noun* E17 **French** (from Old French *çabot* blend of *çavate* (modern SAVATE) and *bote* (modern *botte*) boot). **1 a** E17 A shoe made of a single piece of wood shaped and hollowed out to fit the foot. **b** M19 A heavy shoe with a thick wooden sole. **c** M20 A decorative metal foot-cover for a piece of wooden furniture. **2** *Military* **a** M19 A wooden disk attached to a spherical projectile to keep it in place in the bore when discharged. **b** M19 A metal cup or ring fixed to a conical projectile to make it conform to the grooves of the rifling. **c** M20 A device fitted inside the muzzle of a gun to hold the projectile to be fired. **3** M20 In baccarat and chemin de fer, a box for dealing the cards, a shoe. **4** M20 A small snub-nosed yacht. *Australian.*

sabotage *noun & verb* E20 **French** (from *saboter* to make a noise with sabots, execute badly, destroy, from as preceding). **A** *noun* E20 Deliberate damage to or destruction of property, especially in order to disrupt the production of goods or as a political or military act. **B** *transitive verb* E20 Commit sabotage on; destroy; make useless.

saboteur *noun* E20 **French** (from *saboter* (see SABOTAGE)). A person who commits sabotage.

sabra *noun* (also **Sabra**) M20 **Modern Hebrew** (*ṣabbār* or its source Arabic *ṣabr* prickly pear). A Jew born in the region of the modern nation of Israel.

sabreur *noun* M19 **French** (from *sabrer* to saber). **1** M19 A person, especially a cavalry soldier, who fights with a saber. **2** E20 A person who fences using a saber.

saccade *noun* E18 **French.** **1** E18 A jerking movement. Now *rare* except as passing into sense 2. **2** M20 A brief rapid movement of the eye from one position of rest to another, whether voluntary or involuntary.

Sachertorte *noun* plural **Sachertorten** E20 **German** (from Franz *Sacher* Viennese pastry chef, its creator + *Torte* tart, pastry, cake). A chocolate gateau with apricot jam filling and chocolate icing.

sachet *noun* L15 **Old and Modern French** (diminutive of *sac*). **1** A small carrying bag. *rare* Only in L15. **2 a** M19 A small scented bag, especially for holding handkerchiefs. **b** M19 (A small bag or packet containing) dry perfume for placing among clothing, etc. **3** E20 A small sealed bag or packet, now frequently of plastic, containing a small portion of a substance, especially shampoo.

Sachlichkeit *noun* M20 **German** (literally, 'objectivity'). Objectivism, realism. Also *specifically* NEUE SACHLICHKEIT.

sacro egoismo *noun phrase* M20 **Italian** (literally, 'sacred egoism'). Egocentric nationalism, especially in dealing with foreign nations.

■ Usually derogatory, the phrase was coined (1914) by the Italian statesman Antonio Salandra (1853–1931) who, on the outbreak of World War I, first proclaimed Italy's neutrality in defiance of treaty obligations to Germany and Austria-Hungary and then brought Italy into the war on the side of the Allies.

sacrum *noun* plural **sacrums, sacra** M18 **Latin** (short for late Latin *os sacrum*, translation of Greek *hieron osteon* sacred bone (from the belief that the soul resides in it)). *Anatomy* A triangular bone that is wedged between the two hip bones, forming the back of the pelvis and resulting from the fusing of (usually five) vertebrae.

sadhu *noun* (also **Sadhu**) M19 **Sanskrit** (*sādhu* adjective, good, (as noun) good man, holy man). *Hinduism* A holy man, a sage.

saeva indignatio *noun phrase* M19 **Latin** (literally, 'savage indignation'). An intense feeling of contemptuous anger at human folly.

■ The phrase is particularly associated with the satirist Jonathan Swift (1667–1745), appearing in the epitaph that he composed for his tomb in St. Patrick's, Dublin.

safari *noun, verb, & adjective* L19 **Kiswahili** (from Arabic *safar* journey, trip, tour). **A** *noun* **1** L19 A hunter's or traveler's party or caravan, especially in East Africa. **2** E20 A journey; a cross-country expedition on foot or in vehicles, originally and especially in East Africa, for hunting, tourism, or scientific investigation. Frequently in *on safari*. **B** *intransitive verb* E20 Go on safari. **C** *attributive* or as *adjective* L20 Sandy brown or beige; of the color of clothes traditionally worn on safari.

saga *noun* E18 **Old Norse** ((Icelandic); cf. Old English *sagu* (modern *saw*), German *Sage*). **1** E18 An Old Norse prose narrative of Iceland or Norway, *especially* one that recounts the traditional history of Icelandic families or of the kings of Norway. **b** *transferred* M19 A narrative regarded as having the traditional characteristics of the Icelandic sagas; a story of heroic achievement. Also, a novel or series of novels recounting the history of a family through several generations; *loosely* a long and complicated account of a series of events. **2** M19 (partly after German *Sage*) A story that has been handed down by oral tradition and added to or adapted in the course of time; historical or heroic legend.

sagamité *noun* M17 **French** (representing Cree *kisa:kamite:w*, literally, 'it is a hot liquid'). Gruel or porridge made from coarse hominy.

saganaki *noun* M20 **Modern Greek** (= small two-handled frying pan (traditionally used to prepare the dish)). A Greek dish consisting of breaded or floured cheese fried in butter, often with lemon juice, served as an appetizer.

sahib *noun* (also **saab**) L17 **Urdu** (through Persian from Arabic *ṣāḥib* friend, lord, master). **1** L17 An Englishman or other European as addressed or spoken of by Indians. **2** E20 *transferred* A gentleman; a person considered socially acceptable. See also PUKKA.

■ Anglo-Indian. Also as a title affixed to a person's name or office, as in *Malarao Sahib, the inspector sahib.*

sainfoin *noun* (also **sanfoin**) M17 **French** (*saintfoin* (modern *sainfoin*), originally 'lucerne', from modern Latin *sanctum foenum*, literally, 'holy hay', alteration of *sanum foenum* wholesome hay, which was based on Latin *herba medica* erroneous alteration of *herba Medica*, literally, 'Median grass', translation of Greek *Mēdikē poa*). A leguminous plant, *Onobrychis viciifolia*, with pinnate leaves and bright pink flowers in dense racemes, formerly much grown for fodder.

sais variant of SYCE.

sake *noun* (also **saké**, **saki**) L17 **Japanese**. A Japanese alcoholic drink made from fermented rice.

sakia *noun* L17 **Arabic** (*sāḳiya* noun use of feminine active participle of *saḳā* to irrigate). A machine for drawing water for irrigation, consisting of a large vertical wheel to which earthen pots are attached and moved by means of a horizontal wheel turned by oxen or asses.

salaam *noun* E17 **Arabic** (*salām* = Hebrew *šālōm*). **1** E17 An oriental greeting, meaning 'Peace', used chiefly in Muslim countries; a ceremonial obeisance sometimes accompanying this salutation, consisting in the Indian subcontinent of a low bow with the right palm on the forehead. **2** L18 In *plural* Respectful compliments.

salade niçoise *noun phrase* plural **salades niçoises** E20 **French** (= salad from Nice (in southern France)). A salad usually made from hard-boiled eggs, anchovies, black olives, tomatoes, etc.

saladero *noun* plural **saladeros** L19 **Spanish**. In Spain and Latin America: a slaughterhouse where meat is also prepared by drying or salting.

salades niçoises plural of SALADE NIÇOISE.

salami *noun* M19 **Italian** (plural of *salame*, representing popular Latin word from verb meaning 'to salt'). **1** M19 An original Italian variety of sausage, highly seasoned and often flavored with garlic. **2** L20 A way of carrying out a plan by means of a series of small or imperceptible steps; *specifically* computer fraud in which small amounts of money are transferred from numerous customer accounts into another account. In full *salami technique* or *salami tactics*.

salariat *noun* E20 **French** (from *salaire* salary, after *prolétariat* PROLETARIAT). *The* salaried class; salary earners collectively.

salaud *noun* M20 **French** (from *sale* dirty). As a term of abuse: a contemptible or objectionable person.

salep *noun* M18 **French** (from Turkish *sālep* from Arabic *ṯa'lab* fox, shortening of *kuṣā 't-ṯa'lab* orchid (literally, 'fox's testicles')). A starchy preparation of the dried tubers of various orchids, used in cooking and formerly as a tonic.

salina *noun* L16 **Spanish** (from medieval Latin = salt pit; in Latin only as plural *salinae* salt pans). A salt lake, spring, or marsh; a salt pan, a saltworks. Also (originally *Jamaican*), a low marshy area of land near the coast.

salle *noun* M18 **French**. A hall; a large room

■ Generally as an element in one of the following phrases, but also sometimes as the abbreviation of one of them.

salle-à-manger *noun phrase* M18 **French**. A dining hall, a dining room.

salle d'armes *noun phrase* L19 **French**. A fencing hall or school.

salle d'attente *noun* M19 **French**. A waiting room, especially at a station.

salle d'eau *noun phrase* M20 **French**. A washroom, a shower room.

salle de jeux *noun phrase* M20 **French**. A gambling house or room.

salle des pas perdus *noun phrase* M19 **French** (literally, 'hall of the lost footsteps'). A waiting hall at a court of law, station, etc.; a lobby.

salle privée *noun phrase* M20 **French**. A private gambling room in a casino.

salmi *noun* (also **salmis**) M18 **French** (abbreviation of French *salmigondis* salmagundi). A game stew with a rich sauce.

salon *noun & adjective* L17 **French** (from Italian *salone* augmentative of *sala* hall). **A** *noun* **1** L17 A reception room in a palace or large house, especially in France or other Continental country; a drawing room. **2** E19 *specifically* The reception room of a lady of fashion, especially in Paris; a social gathering of eminent people in such a room. **3** E20 An establishment in which the business of hairdresser, beautician, etc., is conducted.

salon des refusés *noun phrase* L19 **French** (= exhibition of rejected works). An exhibition ordered by Napoleon III in 1863 to display pictures rejected by the Salon; also *transferred.*

■ The Salon, the annual exhibition in Paris of painting, sculpture, etc., by living artists, was notoriously hostile to the works of impressionist artists.

salonnière *noun* (also **salonière**) E20 **French** (from as SALON). A woman who holds a salon; a society hostess.

salopette *noun* L20 **French.** *singular* and (usually) in *plural* Pants with a high waist and shoulder straps, worn especially as a skiing garment and as a Frenchman's overalls.

salpicon *noun* E18 **French** (from Spanish, from *salpicar* to sprinkle (with salt)). *Cooking* A stuffing for veal, beef, or mutton, also used as a garnish.

salsa *noun* M19 **Spanish** (= sauce; in sense 2 American Spanish). **1** M19 *Cooking* A sauce containing chilies and tomatoes. **2** L20 Contemporary dance music of Caribbean origin that incorporates jazz and rock elements; a dance to this music.

saltarello *noun* plural **saltarellos, saltarelli** L16 **Italian** (*salterello*, Spanish *salterelo* related to Italian *saltare*, Spanish *saltar* to leap, dance, from Latin *saltare*). **1** L16 The jack of a spinet or harpischord. *rare.* **2** E18 *History* An animated Italian and Spanish dance for a couple involving numerous sudden skips or jumps; a piece of music for this dance or in its rhythm.

salti plural of SALTO.

saltimbocca *noun* M20 **Italian** (from *saltare* to leap + *in* in, into + *bocca* mouth). *Cooking* A dish consisting of rolled pieces of veal and ham cooked with herbs.

salto *noun* plural **saltos**, (in sense 1) **salti** L19 **Italian** (= leap, from Latin *saltus*). **1** L19 *salto mortale* (= fatal leap), a daring or flying leap; *figurative* a risky step, an unjustified inference, a leap of faith. **2** L20 A somersault.

salumeria *noun* E20 **Italian** (= grocer's, or pork butcher's shop, from *salume* salted meat, from *sale* from Latin *sal* salt). A delicatessen.

salve *noun* LME **Latin** (= hail, greetings, imperative of *salvere* be well; in sense 1 from the opening words of the antiphon *salve regina* hail (holy) queen). **1** LME *Roman Catholic Church* (usually **Salve**) More fully *Salve Regina.* A popular Marian antiphon, now said or sung especially after compline. Also, a musical setting for this. **2** L16 An utterance of 'salve'; a greeting or salutation on meeting. Now *rare* or *obsolete.*

salvo *noun* plural **salvos** E17 **Latin** (ablative neuter singular of *salvus* safe, as in medieval Latin law phrases like *salvo jure* without prejudice to the right of (a specified person), etc.). **1** E17 A saving clause; a provision that a certain ordinance shall not be binding where it would interfere with a specified right or duty; a reservation, a qualification. (Followed by *of, for, to.*) **2** M17 A dishonest mental reservation; an evasion, an excuse. Now *rare.* **3** M17–L18 A solution of a difficulty, an answer to an objection. **4** M18 A thing intended to save a person's reputation or soothe offended pride or conscience.

sal volatile *noun phrase* M17 **Modern Latin** (= volatile salt). Ammonium carbonate, especially in the form of an aromatic solution in alcohol to be sniffed as a restorative in faintness, etc.; smelling salts.

salwar variant of SHALWAR.

samadhi *noun* L18 **Sanskrit** (*samādhi* contemplation, literally, 'a putting together, joining'). *Hinduism* and *Buddhism* **1** L18 The state of union with creation into which a perfected yogi or holy man is said to pass at the time of apparent death. **2** E19 A state of intense concentration induced by meditation, in which union with creation is attained; the last stage of yoga.

samba *noun* L19 **Portuguese** (of African origin). A Brazilian dance of African origin; a Latin American and ballroom dance imitative of this; a piece of music for this dance, usually in 2/4 or 4/4 time.

sambal *noun* E19 **Malay**. In Malayan and Indonesian cooking, a relish consisting of raw vegetables or fruit prepared with spices and vinegar.

sambar *noun* M20 **Tamil** (*cāmpār* from Marathi *sāmb(h)ar* from Sanskrit *sambhāra* collection, materials). In southern Indian cooking, a highly seasoned lentil and vegetable dish.

sambo *noun* M20 **Russian** (acronym, from *samo*zashchita *bez o*ruzhiya, literally, 'unarmed self-defense'). A type of wrestling resembling judo, originating in the former USSR. Also more fully *sambo wrestling*.

sambok variant of SJAMBOK.

samfu *noun* M20 **Chinese** ((Cantonese) *shaam foò*, from *shaam* coat + *foò* pants). A suit consisting of jacket and pants worn by Chinese women and occasionally men.

samisen *noun* (also **shamisen**) E17 **Japanese** (from Chinese *sānxián* (Wade–Giles *sān-hsien*), from *sān* three + *xián* string). A long-necked three-stringed Japanese lute, played with a plectrum. Cf. SAN-HSIEN.

samizdat *noun* (also **Samizdat**) M20 **Russian** (from *sam(o-* self + *izdat(el'stvo* publishing house). The clandestine or illegal copying and distribution of literature, especially in the former USSR; an underground press; a text or texts produced by this.

samosa *noun* M20 **Persian and Urdu** (*samosa(h)*). A triangular pastry fried in ghee or oil, containing spiced vegetables or meat.

samovar *noun* M19 **Russian** (from *samo-* self + *varit'* to boil). A Russian tea urn, with an internal heating device to keep the water at boiling point.

sampan *noun* E17 **Chinese** (*sānban* (Wade–Giles *san-pan*) boat, from *sān* three + *băn* board). A small boat used in the Far East, usually with a stern oar or stern oars.

samsara *noun* L19 **Sanskrit** (*saṃsāra* a wandering through). *Hinduism* and *Buddhism* The endless cycle of death and rebirth to which life in the material world is bound.

samskara *noun* E19 **Sanskrit** (*saṃskāra* preparation, a making perfect). **1** E19 *Hinduism* A purificatory ceremony or rite marking a stage or an event in life. **2** E19 *Buddhism* A mental impression, instinct, or memory.

samurai *noun & adjective* E18 **Japanese**. **A** *noun* E18 plural same. In feudal Japan, a member of a military caste, *especially* a member of the class of military retainers of the daimyos. Now also more widely, a Japanese army officer. **B** *attributive* or as *adjective* **1** L19 Of or pertaining to the samurai. **2** L20 *Samurai bond*, a bond in yen in the Japanese market, issued by a foreigner.

samyama *noun* E19 **Sanskrit** (*saṃyama* restraint, control of the senses). *Hinduism* and *Buddhism* Collectively, the three final stages of meditation in yoga, which lead to SAMADHI.

san *noun* L19 **Japanese** (contraction of more formal *sama*). In Japan: an honorific title used after a personal or family name as a mark of politeness. Also (*colloquially*), used after other names or titles (cf. MAMA-SAN).

sanatarium *noun* plural **sanataria**, **sanatariums** M19 **Modern Latin** (from as SANATORIUM). A SANATORIUM senses 1, 2.

sanatorium *noun* plural **sanatoriums**, **sanatoria** M19 **Modern Latin** (from *sanat-* past participial stem of *sanare* to heal). **1** M19 An establishment for the medical treatment and recuperation of invalids, especially convalescents or the chronically sick. **2** M19 A health resort. **3** M19 A room or building for sick people in a school, etc. Often abbreviated in school slang to *san*.

sanbenito *noun* plural **sanbenitos** M16 **Spanish** (*sambenito*, from *San Benito* St. Benedict, so called ironically from its resemblance to the Benedictine scapular). In the Spanish Inquisition, a yellow scapular-shaped garment, with a red St. Andrew's cross before and behind, worn by a confessed and penitent heretic. Also, a similar black garment with flames, devils, and other devices, worn by an impenitent confessed heretic at an auto-da-fé.

sancocho *noun* M20 **American Spanish** (from Spanish = half-cooked meal, from *sancochar* to parboil). In South America and the Caribbean: a rich soup or stew of meat, fish, and vegetables.

sancta plural of SANCTUM.

sancta sanctorum plural of SANCTUM SANCTORUM.

sancta simplicitas *interjection* M19 **Latin** (literally, 'holy simplicity'). Expressing astonishment at a person's naïveté.

■ These are said to have been the last words of the Bohemian religious reformer John Huss, burned at the stake in 1415, on seeing a simple peasant bringing wood to add to the fire.

sanctum *noun* plural **sanctums**, **sancta** L16 **Latin** (neuter of *sanctus* holy; cf. next). **1** L16 A sacred place or shrine in a temple or church. **2** E19 A place where a person can be alone and free from intrusion; a private room, study, etc.

sanctum sanctorum *noun phrase* plural **sancta sanctorum** LME **Latin** (neuter singular and neuter genitive plural of *sanctus* holy, translation of Hebrew *qōdeš haq-qŏdāšīm* holy of holies). **1** LME *Jewish Antiquities* The holy of holies in the Jewish Temple. **2** L16 A SANCTUM sense 1. **3** E18 A SANCTUM sense 2.

sanctus *noun* LME **Latin** (= holy, the first word of the hymn). *Christian Church* (also **Sanctus**) The hymn beginning *Sanctus, sanctus, sanctus* 'Holy, holy, holy', which forms the conclusion of the Eucharistic preface; a musical setting of this.

sandur *noun* plural **sandar**, **sandurs** (also **sandr**, plural same, **sandurs**) L19 **Icelandic** (*sandur*, plural *sandar*, (Old Norse *sandr*), sand). *Physical Geography* A broad, flat or gently sloping plain of glacial outwash.

sanfoin variant of SAINFOIN.

sang-de-boeuf *noun* L19 **French** (literally, 'ox's blood'). A deep red color found on old Chinese porcelain; (porcelain bearing) a ceramic glaze of this color.

Sängerfest *noun* (also **Saengerfest**) M19 **German** (from *Sänger* singer + FEST). A choral festival.

sang-froid *noun* M18 **French** (literally, 'cold blood'). Coolness, self-possession, especially in the face of danger or disturbing circumstances.

sangha *noun* M19 **Sanskrit** (*saṃgha*, from *sam* together + *han* to come in contact). *Buddhism* The Buddhist community, the Buddhist order of monks, nuns, and novices.

sanglier *noun* LME **Old French** (*sengler*, (also modern) *sanglier* from Latin *singularis* solitary, singular, used as noun in late Latin = a boar separated from the herd, in medieval Latin = wild boar). A wild boar. Formerly *specifically*, one that is fully grown.

sangoma *noun* (also **isangoma**) L19 **Nguni**. In southern Africa: a witch doctor, usually a woman, claiming supernatural powers of divination and healing.

sangre azul *noun phrase* M19 **Spanish** (= blue blood). The purity of blood claimed by certain ancient Castilian families, which professed to be free from Moorish or Jewish ancestry.

sangria *noun* (also **Sangria**) M20 **Spanish** (*sangría*, literally, 'bleeding'). A Spanish drink made of sweetened diluted red wine with spices and fruit.

san-hsien *noun* (also **sanxian**) M19 **Chinese** (*sānxián* (Wade–Giles *sān-hsien*), from *sān* three + *xián* string). *Music* A Chinese three-stringed lute. Cf. SAMISEN.

sannyasi *noun* (also **sanyasi**, **sannyasin**) E17 **Sanskrit** (*saṃnyāsī* nominative singular of *saṃnyāsin* laying aside, abandoning, ascetic, from *saṃ* together + *ni* down + *as* throw). A brahmin in the fourth stage of his life; a wandering Hindu fakir.

sanpaku *noun* M20 **Japanese** (literally, 'three white', from *san* three + *haku* white). Visibility of the white of the eye below the iris as well as on either side.

sans *preposition* ME **Old French** (*san*, *sanz* (modern *sans*), earlier *sen(s)* from Proto-Romance variation of Latin *sine* without, partly influenced by Latin *absentia* absence). Without.

■ Although formerly fully naturalized, *sans* is now, apart from use in heraldic terminology, mainly literary and often jocular—especially with reference to Shakespeare's line on second childhood: "Sans teeth, sans eyes, sans taste, sans everything" (*As You Like It* II.vii). It also occurs in a number of phrases borrowed from French.

sans blague *interjection* E20 **Old French** (literally, 'without joking'). You don't say! I don't believe it!

sans cérémonie *adverb phrase* M17 **Old French**. Unceremoniously; without the usual ceremony or formality.

sansculotte *noun* (also **sans culottes**) L18 **French** (from *sans* without + *culotte* knee breeches). **1** L18 *History* A lower-class Parisian republican in the French Revolution; *generally* an extreme republican or revolutionary. **2** E19 *transferred* A shabbily dressed person, a ragamuffin.

sansei *noun* plural same M20 **Japanese** (from *san* three, third + *sei* generation). An American whose grandparents were immigrants from Japan. Cf. NISEI.

sanserif variant of SANS SERIF.

sans façon *adverb phrase* L17 **Old French** (literally, 'without manner'). Without the customary formality; SANS CÉRÉMONIE.

sans-gêne *noun phrase* L19 **Old French** (literally, 'without embarrassment'). Disregard of the ordinary forms of civility or politeness.

sans pareil *adjective phrase* **Old French** (literally, 'not having its like'). Unique, unequaled.

■ Earlier (M18) current as a noun meaning 'smelling salts' or some other kind of perfume.

sans peur *adjective phrase* E19 **Old French**. Without fear, fearless.

■ Especially in the phrase *sans peur et sans reproche*, which was applied to the Chevalier de Bayard (1476–1524), a renowned soldier in the Italian wars of Charles VIII of France.

sans phrase *adjective phrase* E19 **Old French**. Without more words, without exceptions or qualifications.

■ After *La mort sans phrase* ('death, without more words'), the expression allegedly used by the Abbé Sieyès (1748–1836) in giving his vote for the execution of Louis XVI.

sans recours *noun phrase* L19 **Old French** (literally, 'without recourse'). *Law* An endorsement on a bill of exchange absolving the endorser or any other party from liability.

sans reproche *adjective phrase* M19 **Old French**. Without reproach, blameless.

■ Earlier (E19), and especially, in *sans peur et sans reproche*; cf. SANS PEUR.

sans serif *noun & adjective* (also **sanserif**) M19 **French** (apparently from SANS + *serif* cross stroke of a letter (origin uncertain, but possibly from Dutch *schreef* dash, line)). *Typography* **A** *noun* M19 A letterform, especially a typeface, without serifs. **B** *adjective* L19 Having no serifs.

santeria *noun* M20 Spanish (*santería*, literally, 'holiness, sanctity'). An Afro-Cuban religious cult with many Yoruba elements.

santero *noun* plural **santeros** M20 Spanish. **1** M20 In Mexico and Spanish-speaking areas of the southwestern United States: a maker of religious images. **2** M20 A priest of a religious cult, especially of *santeria*.

santir *noun* (also **santoor**, **santour**) M19 Arabic (*sanṭīr*, *sinṭīr*, *sanṭūr* (Persian *santūr*, Turkish *santur*), alteration of Greek *psaltērion* psaltery). A dulcimer of Arab and Persian origin.

santo *noun* plural **santos** M17 Spanish (or Italian). **1** M17 A SANTON sense 1. **2** M19 A wooden representation of a saint or other religious symbol from Mexico or the southwestern United States.

santon *noun* L16 French (from Spanish, from *santo* saint). **1** L16 A Muslim hermit or holy man, a marabout. Formerly also, a yogi, a Hindu ascetic. **2** E20 Chiefly in Provence: a figurine adorning a representation of the manger in which Jesus was laid.

santoor, **santour** variants of SANTIR.

san ts'ai *noun phrase* E20 Chinese (*sāncǎi* (Wade–Giles *sān-ts'ai*), from *sān* three + *cǎi* color). Chinese pottery, especially of the Tang dynasty, decorated in three colors; decoration in three enamel colors applied to pottery and porcelain.

sanyasi variant of SANNYASI.

saphir d'eau *noun* E19 French (literally 'sapphire of water'). An intense blue variety of cordierite occurring mainly in Sri Lanka; a water sapphire.

sarabande *noun* (also **saraband**) E17 French (from Spanish or Italian *zarabanda*). A slow and stately Spanish dance in triple time; a piece of music for this dance or in its rhythm.

sarang variant of SERANG.

sarangi *noun* M19 Sanskrit (*sāraṅgī*). An Indian bowed stringed instrument.

sarape variant of SERAPE.

sarcoma *noun* plural **sarcomas**, **sarcomata** M17 Modern Latin (from Greek *sarkōma*, from *sarkoun* to become fleshy, from *sarx*, *sark-* flesh). *Medicine* **1** M17–M18 A fleshy excrescence. **2** E19 A malignant tumor of connective or other non-epithelial tissue.

sarcophagus *noun* plural **sarcophagi** LME Latin (from Greek *sarkophagos* (adjective & noun), from *sarx*, *sark-* flesh + *-phagos* eating). **1** A stone coffin, *especially* one adorned with sculpture, an inscription, etc. **2** E17 *Greek Antiquities* A stone fabled to be able to consume the flesh of dead bodies deposited in it, and used for coffins. Now *rare*. **3** E17–M19 A flesh-eater; a cannibal. *rare*.

sardana *noun* E20 Catalan and Spanish. A Catalan dance performed to pipes and drum.

sari *noun* (also **saree**) L18 Hindi (*sāṛī* from Sanskrit *śāṭikā*). A traditional garment of Indian women, worn over a CHOLI and an underskirt, consisting of a length of cotton, silk, or other cloth wrapped around the waist and draped over one shoulder.

sarmale *noun plural* M20 Romanian. A Romanian dish of forcemeat and other ingredients wrapped in especially cabbage or vine leaves.

sarod *noun* M19 Urdu (from Persian *surod* song, melody). An Indian stringed musical instrument.

saron *noun* E19 Javanese. An Indonesian musical instrument, normally having seven bronze bars that are struck with a mallet.

sarong *noun* M19 Malay (literally, 'sheath, quiver'). A traditional skirt-like garment of the Malay archipelago, Java, and some Pacific islands, consisting of a long strip of (often striped) cloth worn tucked around the waist or under the armpits by both sexes; a woman's garment resembling this, worn especially on the beach.

sarsaparilla *noun* L16 **Spanish** (*zarzaparilla*, from *zarza* bramble + diminutive of Spanish *parra* vine, twining plant). **1** L16 Any of several tropical American kinds of smilax used medicinally; the dried root of such a plant, used to treat rheumatism, skin complaints, and formerly also syphilis. Also, a carbonated drink flavored with this root. **2** M19 Any of several plants of other genera that resemble sarsaparilla or have a root used similarly. Chiefly with specifying word.

sartage *noun* L19 **French** (from *sarter* to clear ground). The clearing of woodland by setting fire to trees.

sashimi *noun* L19 **Japanese** (from *sashi* pierce + *mi* flesh). A Japanese dish of slices of raw fish served with grated horseradish and soy sauce.

sassafras *noun* L16 **Spanish** (*sasafrás*, perhaps ultimately from Latin *saxifraga* saxifrage). **1** L16 A tree of the genus *Sassafras*, of the laurel family, especially *S. albidum* native to the eastern United States; also, the wood of this tree. **b** L16 The dried bark of this tree, used as a medicine and flavoring and for infusing. **c** M18 An oil extracted from (the bark of) the sassafras, used medicinally and in perfumery. In full *sassafras oil*, also *oil of sassafras*. **2** E19 Any of various similarly aromatic and medicinal trees of other genera and families; also, the wood or bark of such a tree.

sastruga *noun* (also **zastruga**) plural **sastrugi** M19 **German** (from Russian *zastruga* small ridge, furrow in snow, from *zastrugat'* to plane or smooth, from *strug* plane (the tool)). Any of a series of low irregular ridges formed on a level snow surface by wind erosion, often aligned parallel to the wind direction. Usually in *plural*.

satay *noun* (also **satai, saté**) M20 **Malay** (*satai, sate*, Indonesian *sate*; cf. SOSATIE). AN INDONESIAN AND MALAYSIAN DISH CONSISTING OF SMALL PIECES OF MEAT GRILLED ON A SKEWER AND USUALLY SERVED WITH A SPICED PEANUT SAUCE.

sati variant of SUTTEE.

satori *noun* E18 **Japanese** (= awakening). *Zen Buddhism* A sudden inner experience of enlightenment.

satranji *noun* (also **sitringee** and other variants) E17 **Persian and Urdu** (*šhaṭranjī* from Persian *šaṭranj* chess, ultimately from Sanskrit *caturaṅga* army, chess, with reference to the original checkered pattern). A carpet or floor rug made of colored cotton, now usually with a striped pattern.

satsuma, in sense 1 also *noun* (also (especially in sense 1) **Satsuma**) L19 **Japanese** (name of a province in the island of Kiusiu, Japan). **1** L19 A kind of cream-colored Japanese pottery. In full *Satsuma ware*. **2** L19 A variety of tangerine, originally from Japan, with a sharper taste and frequently seedless or with undeveloped seeds; the tree bearing this fruit.

Saturnalia *noun* (treated as *singular* or *plural*) (in sense 2 also **saturnalia**) L16 **Latin** (noun use of neuter plural of *Saturnalis* of or pertaining to *Saturnus* Saturn, the Roman god of agriculture and ruler of the gods until deposed by his son Jupiter). **1** L16 *Roman History* The festival of Saturn, held in mid December and characterized by general unrestrained merrymaking, the precursor of Christmas. **2** L18 *transferred* and *figurative* A period of unrestrained tumult and revelry; an orgy.

satyagraha *noun* E20 **Sanskrit** (*satyāgraha* force born of truth, from *satya* truth + *āgraha* pertinacity). **1** E20 *History* A policy of passive resistance to British rule in India formulated by M. K. Gandhi. **2** E20 *generally* Any policy of nonviolent resistance.

saucier *noun* M20 **French**. A sauce cook.

saucisson *noun* M17 **French** (augmentative of *saucisse* sausage). **1a** M17 A firework consisting of a tube packed with gunpowder. **b** E19 *History* A long tube packed with gunpowder, formerly used as a fuse for firing a mine. **2** E18 *Military* A large fascine. **3** M18 A large thick sausage.

saudade *noun* E20 **Portuguese**. Longing, melancholy, nostalgia, as a supposed characteristic of the Portuguese or Brazilian temperament.

sauerbraten *noun* L19 **German** (from *sauer* sour + *Braten* roast meat). A dish of German origin consisting of beef marinaded in vinegar with peppercorns, onions, and other seasonings and then cooked.

sauerkraut *noun* M17 **German** ((whence French *choucroute*), from *sauer* sour + *Kraut* vegetable, cabbage). Finely chopped pickled cabbage, a typical German dish.

■ In United States slang *Sauerkraut* was in use earlier (M19) as a derogatory word for 'a German' than its British equivalent KRAUT.

sauna *noun* L19 **Finnish**. A Finnish-style hot steam bath; a room or building in which such a bath is taken. Also *sauna bath*.

saut *noun* L19 **French** (= leap). **1** L19 *Saut Basque*, a dance of the French Basque provinces. **2** L19 *Ballet* A leap in dancing. Especially in *saut de Basque*, a leap made while turning, holding one leg straight and the other at right angles to the body.

sauté *noun, adjective, & verb* E19 **French** (past participle of *sauter* to leap). *Cooking* **A** *noun* E19 A dish cooked by frying quickly in a little hot fat. **B** *adjective* M19 Of meat, vegetables, etc.: fried quickly in a little hot fat. **C** *transitive verb* M19 (past tense and participle *sautéed, sautéd*) Fry (food) quickly in a little hot fat.

sautoir *noun* M20 **French** (Old French *saut(e)our, sau(l)toir* stirrup cord). A long necklace consisting of a fine gold chain usually set with jewels.

sauve qui peut *noun & verb phrase* E19 **French** (literally, 'save-who-can'). **A** *noun phrase* E19 A general stampede, a complete rout; panic, disorder. **B** *verb phrase intransitive* M20 Stampede or scatter in flight.

savannah *noun* (also **savanna**) M16 **Spanish** (*zavana, çavana*, (now *sabana*) from Taino *zavana*). **1** M16 Originally, a treeless plain, especially in tropical America. Now, an open grassy plain with few or no trees in a tropical or subtropical region; grassland or vegetation of this kind. **2** L17 A tract of low-lying damp or marshy ground.

savant *noun* E18 **French** (noun use of adjective, originally present participle of *savoir* to know). A learned person, *especially* a distinguished scientist.

savante *noun* M18 **French** (feminine of preceding). A learned (French) woman. Cf. FEMME SAVANTE.

savarin *noun* L19 **French** (Anthelme Brillat-*Savarin* (1755–1826), French gastronome). A light ring-shaped cake made with yeast and soaked in liqueur-flavored syrup.

savate *noun* M19 **French** (originally, a kind of shoe (cf. SABOT)). A form of boxing in which the feet and fists are used.

savoir *noun* E19 **French** (literally, 'know'). Knowledge.

■ Also used elliptically for SAVOIR FAIRE and SAVOIR VIVRE.

savoir faire *noun* (also **savoir-faire**) E19 **French** (literally, 'to know how to do'). The instinctive ability to act suitably in any situation; tact.

savoir vivre *noun* M18 **French** (literally, 'know how to live'). Knowledge of the world and the ways of society, ability to conduct oneself well; worldly wisdom, sophistication.

savonette *noun* E18 **French** ((now *savonnette*), diminutive of *savon* soap). Soap, especially in the form of a ball.

sayonara *interjection & noun* L19 **Japanese** (literally, 'if it be so'). (The Japanese word for) goodbye.

sayyid *noun* (also **saiyid**, **syed**, and other variants, **Sayyid**) M17 **Arabic** (= lord, prince). (A title of respect for) a Muslim claiming descent from Muhammad through Husain, the prophet's elder grandson.

■ In Muslim countries, also as a respectful form of address.

sc. abbreviation of SCILICET.

scaglia *noun* L18 **Italian** (= scale, chip of marble, from Germanic base from which modern English *scale* (noun)). *Geology* A dark fine-grained shale found in the Alps and Apennines.

scagliola *noun* L16 **Italian** (*scagli(u)ola* diminutive of SCAGLIA). **1** L16–L18 SCAGLIA. **2** M18 Plasterwork of Italian origin, designed to imitate marble and other kinds of stone.

scala mobile *noun phrase* L20 **Italian** (literally, 'moving stair, escalator'). In Italy: a system of wage indexation by which earnings are linked by a sliding scale to the retail price index.

scald variant of SKALD.

scaloppine *noun* (also **scallopini**) M20 **Italian** (plural of *scaloppina* diminutive of *scaloppa* escalope). A dish consisting of escalopes of meat (especially veal) sautéed or fried.

scampi *noun plural* (also treated as *singular*; in sense 1 singular **scampo**) E19 **Italian** (plural of *scampo*). **1** E19 large shrimp. Also (*rare*) *singular*, a shrimp. **2** M20 A dish of these shrimp, usually fried in garlic butter, breadcrumbs, or a sauce. Usually treated as *singular*.

■ In British English *scampi* refers to a Norway lobster or a dish of Norway lobsters.

scandalon variant of SKANDALON.

scarabaeus *noun* plural **scarabaei** L16 **Latin** (= beetle: cf. Greek *karabos* horned beetle). **1** L16 *Entomology* A scarabaeid beetle. Now only as modern Latin genus name. **2** L18 *Antiquities* An ancient Egyptian amulet or seal in the form of a beetle with symbols on its flat underside, a scarab.

scarpetti *noun plural* L19 **Italian** (plural of *scarpetto* small shoe, from *scarpa* shoe). Rope-soled shoes worn for rock climbing, especially in the North Italian Alps.

scenario *noun & verb* L19 **Italian** (from Latin *scena* scene). **A** *noun* plural **scenarios**. **1a** L19 A sketch or outline of the plot of a play, ballet, novel, etc., with details of the scenes and situations. **b** E20 *Cinematography* A movie script with all the details of scenes, stage directions, etc., necessary for shooting the movie. **2** M20 A description of an imagined situation or a postulated sequence of events; an outline of an intended course of action; *specifically* a scientific description or speculative model intended to account for observable facts. Also *loosely*, a situation, a sequence of events. **B** *transitive verb* M20 Make a scenario of (a book, idea, etc.); sketch *out*.

scène à faire *noun phrase* plural **scènes à faire** L19 **French** (literally, 'scene for action'). *Theatrical* The most important scene in a play or opera.

Schadenfreude *noun* (also **schadenfreude**) L19 **German** (from *Schaden* harm + *Freude* joy). Malicious enjoyment of another's misfortune.

schalet *noun* M20 **Yiddish** (*shalent*, *shalet* variant of *tsholnt* cholent). **1** M20 CHOLENT. **2** M20 A Jewish baked fruit dessert.

schappe *noun* L19 **German** (= silk waste). A fabric or yarn made from waste silk.

schema *noun* plural **schemata**, **schemas** L18 **German** (from Greek *skhēma*, *skhēmat-*). **1** L18 In Kantian philosophy, a rule or procedure of the imagination enabling the understanding to apply a concept, especially a category, to what is given in sense perception. **2** M19 *Ecclesiastical* A draft canon or decree for discussion. **3** L19 A schematic representation of something; a hypothetical outline or plan; a draft, a synopsis, a design. **4** E20 *Psychology* An (unconscious) organized mental model of something in terms of which new information can be interpreted or an appropriate response made.

schemozzle variant of SHEMOZZLE.

scherzando *adverb, adjective, & noun* E19 **Italian** (from *scherzare* to joke, from SCHERZO). *Music* **A** *adverb & adjective* E19 (A direction:) playful(ly). **B** *noun* L19 plural **scherzandos**, **scherzandi**. A movement or passage (to be) played playfully.

scherzo *noun* plural **scherzos, scherzi** M19 **Italian** (literally, 'sport, jest'). *Music* A vigorous, light, or playful composition, especially as a movement in a symphony or sonata.

schiacciato variant of STIACCIATO.

schiller *adjective & noun* E19 **German** (= play of colors). *Geology* **A** E19 *attributive adjective* Designating minerals or rocks having a shining surface. **B** *noun* M19 An iridescent luster, *specifically* that characteristic of certain minerals.

Schimpfwort *noun* plural **Schimpfwörter** M20 **German** (from *Schimpf* insult + *Wort* word). An insulting epithet, a term of abuse.

schinken *noun* M19 **German**. German ham.

schlag *noun* M20 **German** (abbreviation). **1** SCHLAGOBERS. **2** SCHLAGSAHNE.

Schlagobers *noun* M20 **German** ((dialect) from *schlagen* to beat + *Obers* cream). (Coffee with) whipped cream.

schlagsahne *noun* E20 **German** (from *schlagen* to beat + *Sahne* cream). Whipped cream.

Schlamperei *noun* M20 **German**. Indolent slovenliness, muddleheadedness.

■ In its original German context, used derogatorily to designate the supposed sloppiness of the south Germans and Austrians.

schlemiel *noun* (also **schlemihl, Shlemihl**) L19 **German** (*Shlemihl*). An awkward or clumsy person; a foolish or unlucky person. *colloquial*.

■ The word may ultimately be connected with the biblical *Shelumiel*, head of the tribe of Simeon (Numbers 1:6), who, according to the Talmud, came to an unfortunate end. Modern use of *schlemiel* is influenced by Adelbert von Chamisso's famous tale *Peter Schlemihls wundersame Geschichte* (1814), the eponymous hero of which sells his shadow.

schlenter *noun & adjective* (also (*Australia* and *New Zealand*) **slanter** and other variants) M19 **Afrikaans** (or Dutch possibly from Dutch *slenter* knavery, trick). **A** *noun* **1** M19 A trick. *Australian* and *New Zealand colloquial*. **2** L19 A counterfeit diamond. *South African*. **B** *adjective* L19 Dishonest, crooked; counterfeit, fake. *Australian, New Zealand,* and *South African colloquial*.

■ The history of this word is obscure; the likelihood is that the Australian and New Zealand usages derive from South African English, but the route of the borrowing is uncertain. In Australia and New Zealand the most common spelling is now *slanter*, presumably under the influence of *slant* (i.e., crooked).

schlep *noun 1* M20 **Yiddish** (abbreviation). A SCHLEPPER. *colloquial*.

schlep *noun 2* M20 **Yiddish** (probably from German *schleppen* to drag). A troublesome business, (a piece of) hard work. Chiefly *colloquial*.

schlep *verb* (also **schlepp**; inflected *-pp-*) E20 **Yiddish** (*shelpn* from German *schleppen* to drag). **1** *transitive verb* E20 Haul, carry, drag. **2** *intransitive verb* M20 Toil; move or go slowly or awkwardly. *colloquial*.

schlepper *noun* M20 **Yiddish** (as preceding). A person of little worth; a fool; a hanger-on. *colloquial*.

schlimazel *noun* (also **shlimazel, schlimazl**) M20 **Yiddish** (from Middle High German *slim* crooked + Hebrew *mazzāl* luck). A consistently unlucky and accident-prone person. Chiefly *colloquial*.

schlock *noun & adjective* E20 **Yiddish** (apparently from *shlak* apoplectic stroke, *shlog* wretch, untidy person, apoplectic stroke, from *shlogn* to strike). **A** *noun* E20 Cheap, shoddy, or defective goods; inferior material, trash. **B** *adjective* E20 Cheap, inferior, trashy.

■ Colloquial and chiefly North American.

schlong *noun* M20 **Yiddish** (*shlang*, from Middle High German *slange* (German *Schlange*) snake). The penis. Also, a contemptible person. *slang*.

schloss *noun* E19 **German.** A castle, *especially* one in Germany or Austria.

schlub variant of SHLUB.

schmaltz *noun & verb* M20 **Yiddish** (from German *Schmalz* dripping, lard). **A** *noun* **1** M20 Melted chicken fat. Chiefly in *schmaltz herring*, a form of pickled herring. **2** M20 Sentimentality, emotionalism; excessively sentimental music, writing, drama, etc. *colloquial.* **B** *transitive verb* M20 Impart a sentimental atmosphere to; play (music) in a sentimental manner. Frequently followed by *up. colloquial.*

schmatte variant of SHMATTE.

schmear, **schmeer** variants of SHMEAR.

schmelz *noun* M19 **German** (= enamel). Any of several varieties of decorative glass; *especially* one colored red with a metallic salt, used to flash white glass.

Schmelzglas *noun* M20 **German.** SCHMELZ.

Schmerz *noun* E20 **German** (= pain). Grief, sorrow, regret, pain.

schmierkäse *noun* E20 **German** (from *schmieren* to smear + *Käse* cheese). A soft cheese, *specifically* cottage cheese.

schmooze *noun* M20 **Yiddish** (*schmues* chat, gossip from Hebrew *šĕmū'ōṯ* plural of *šĕmū'āh* rumor. Chat; gossip; a long and intimate conversation. *colloquial.*

schmuck *noun* L19 **Yiddish** (*shmok* penis). A contemptible or objectionable person; an idiot.

■ Slang. *Schmo* (also **schmoe**) is a more recent (M20) alternative.

schmutz *noun* **M20 Yiddish or German.** Dirt, filth, rubbish. *slang.*

schnapps *noun* (also **schnaps**) E19 **German** (*Schnaps* dram of drink, liquor (especially gin) from Low German, Dutch *snaps* gulp, mouthful, from *snappen* to seize, snatch, snap). Any of various strong liquors resembling genever.

■ The Dutch, Danish, and Swedish word *snaps* (M19) is less common in English.

schnitzel *noun* M19 **German.** A veal cutlet.

■ Especially in *Wiener* (or *Vienna*) *schnitzel*, a veal cutlet coated with egg and breadcrumbs and fried.

schnook *noun* **M20 German or Yiddish** (perhaps from German *Schnucke* a small sheep, or Yiddish *shnuk* snout). A dupe, a sucker; a simpleton. *colloquial.*

schnorrer *noun* L19 **Yiddish** (variant of German *Schnurrer*, from *schnurren* (slang) go begging). Originally (*specifically*) a Jewish beggar. Now (*generally*), a beggar, a layabout, a scrounger.

schnozz *noun* M20 **Yiddish** (*shnoytz* from German *Schnauze* snout). The nose; a nostril.

■ Slang. The Yiddish diminutive form of *shnoytz*, *shnoytzl*, has given rise to *schnozzle* (M20), also a slang word for 'nose'.

schola cantorum *noun phrase* plural **scholae cantorum** L18 **Medieval Latin** (= school of singers). **1** L18 A choir school attached to a cathedral or monastery; originally, the papal choir at Rome, established by Gregory the Great (*c.*540–604). **2** E20 *generally* A group of singers. Frequently as the title of such a group.

scholium *noun* plural **scholia** M16 **Modern Latin** (from Greek *skholion* from *skholē* learned discussion). An explanatory note or comment, *especially* one made by an ancient commentator on a classical text.

■ Generally used in the plural, but in the singular the Greek ending *-ion* (L16) is also found.

schottische *noun* M19 **German** ((*der*) *Schottische*(*tanz*) (the) Scottish (dance)). **1** M19 A dance resembling a slow polka; a piece of music for this dance. **2** L19 (*Highland Schottische*) A lively dance resembling the Highland fling.

Schrecklichkeit *noun* (also **schrecklichkeit**) E20 **German** (= frightfulness). Originally *specific*, a deliberate military policy of terrorizing an enemy, especially the civilian population. Now *generally*, frightfulness, awfulness, an atmosphere of dread or fear.

schreierpfeife *noun* plural **schreierpfeifen** M20 **German** (literally, 'screamer pipe'; cf. RAUSCHPFEIFE). *Music* A kind of shawm used in the sixteenth and seventeenth centuries.

■ This instrument is also called a *schryari* (M20), a word the origin of which is uncertain but which may be related to *schreierpfeife*.

schrund *noun* L19 **German** (= cleft, crevice). A crevasse; *specifically* a BERGSCHRUND.

schtoom variant of SHTOOM.

Schuhplattler *noun* L19 **German** (from *Schuh* shoe + southern German dialect *Plattler* (from *platteln* to slap)). A lively Bavarian and Austrian folk dance, characterized by the slapping of the thighs and heels.

schuss *noun & verb* M20 **German** (literally, 'a shot'). **A** *noun* M20 A straight downhill run on skis; the slope on which such a run is executed. Also *transferred*, a rapid downward slide. **B** *verb* **1** *transitive verb* M20 Ski straight down (a slope, etc.); cover (a certain distance) by means of a schuss. **2** *intransitive verb* M20 Ski straight down a slope. Also *transferred*, move rapidly (especially downward).

schvartze, **schvartzer** see SCHWARTZE.

schwa *noun* (also **shwa**) L19 **German**. *Phonetics* The neutral central vowel sound &schwa., typically occurring in unstressed syllables, as the final syllable of 'sofa' and the first syllable of 'along'. Also, the symbol '&schwa.' representing this sound, as in the International Phonetic Alphabet. Also called SHEVA.

schwarm *noun* E20 **German**. An enthusiasm, a craze, an infatuation.

■ Followed by *for*.

schwärmerei *noun* plural **schwärmereien** M19 **German** (from *schwärmen* to swarm, display enthusiasm, rave). Enthusiastic or fervent devotion to a person or a cause; a juvenile attachment, especially to a person of the same sex; (an) infatuation, a crush.

schwartze *noun* (also **schvartze**, **schwartzer**, and other variants) M20 **Yiddish** (*shvartser* (masculine), *shvartse* (feminine), from *shvarts* black, from German *schwarz* from Old High German *swarz* from Germanic). A black person. *slang, generally derogatory*.

Schweinerei *noun* (also **schweinerei**) plural **Schweinereien** E20 **German** (literally, 'piggishness'). Obnoxious behavior, an instance of this; a repulsive incident or object, a scandal.

schwerpunkt *noun* M20 **German** (= center of gravity, focal point, from *schwer* hard, weighty + *Punkt* point). Focus, emphasis; strong point; area of concentrated (especially military) effort.

Schwung *noun* M20 **German** (literally, 'swinging motion'). Energy, verve, panache.

scilicet *adverb & noun* LME **Latin** (from *scire licet* one may understand or know; cf. VIDELICET). **A** *adverb* LME To wit; that is to say; namely. **B** *noun* M17 The word 'scilicet' or its equivalent, introducing a specifying clause.

■ As an adverb, used to introduce a word to be supplied or an explanation of an ambiguity and generally abbreviated to *scil.* or sc.

scintilla *noun* L17 **Latin**. A spark; a trace, a tiny piece or amount.

scirocco variant of SIROCCO.

scordatura *noun* plural **scordature** L19 **Italian** (from *scordare* to be out of tune). *Music* Alteration of the normal tuning of a stringed instrument so as to produce particular effects for certain pieces or passages; an instance of this.

scoria *noun* plural **scoriae**, (*rare*) **scorias** LME **Latin** (from Greek *skōria* refuse, from *skōr* dung). **1** LME The slag or dross remaining after the smelting out of a metal from its ore. **2** L18 *Geology*

Rough masses resembling clinker, formed by the cooling of volcanic ejecta, and of a light aerated texture.

scorzonera *noun* E17 **Italian** (from *scorzone* from Proto-Romance alteration of medieval Latin *curtio(n)-* poisonous snake, against whose venom the plant may have been regarded as an antidote). Any of various plants constituting the genus *Scorzonera*; especially *S. hispanica*, cultivated in Europe for its tapering purple brown root. Also, the root of *S. hispanica*, eaten as a vegetable.

scotia *noun* M16 **Latin** (from Greek *skotia* from *skotos* darkness (with reference to the dark shadow within the cavity)). *Architecture* A concave molding, especially at the base of a column; a casement.

scriptorium *noun* plural **scriptoria**, **scriptoriums** L18 **Medieval Latin** (from *script-* past participial stem of *scribere* to write). A room set apart for writing; *especially* a room in a monastery where manuscripts were copied.

scrutator *noun* L16 **Latin** (from *scrutat-* past participial stem of *scrutari*). **1** L16 A person who examines or investigates something or someone. **2** E17 A person whose official duty it is to examine or investigate something closely; *especially* a scrutineer at an election.

scungille *noun* plural **scungilli** M20 **Italian** (dialect *scunciglio*, probably alteration of Italian *conchiglia* seashell, shellfish). A mollusk, a conch; *especially* the meat of a mollusk eaten as a delicacy.

scuola *noun* plural **scuole** M19 **Italian** (= school). In Venice: any of the buildings in which the medieval religious confraternities or guilds used to meet, a guildhall; *History* any of these guilds.

sebkha variant of SABKHA.

sebum *noun* L19 **Modern Latin** (use of Latin *sebum* suet, grease, tallow). *Physiology* The oily secretion of the sebaceous glands that lubricates and protects the hair and skin.

sec *adjective & noun* ME **French** (from Latin *siccus*). Dry (wine); a drink of this.

secateur *noun* M19 **French** (*sécateur*, irregularly from Latin *secare* to cut + -*ateur*). *singular* and (usually) in *plural* A pair of pruning clippers with crossed blades, for use with one hand. Also *pair of secateurs*.

secco *noun & adjective* M19 **Italian** (from Latin *siccus* dry; in sense A.1 elliptical for *fresco secco*, literally, 'dry fresco'). **A** *noun* plural **seccos** **1** M19 The process or technique of painting on dry plaster with colors mixed with water. **2** M20 *Music* (A) RECITATIVO secco. **B** *adjective* L19 *Music* Of recitative: plain, lacking or having only sparse instrumental accompaniment.

secretaire *noun* L18 **French** (*secrétaire* from late Latin *secretarius* confidential officer, noun use of adjective from Latin *secretum* secret). A writing desk with drawers and pigeonholes; a bureau.

secretariat *noun* (also **Secretariat**) E19 **French** (*secrétariat* from medieval Latin *secretariatus*, from as SECRETAIRE). The official position of secretary; the place where a secretary works, preserves records, etc. Also, the administrative and executive department of a government or similar organization; such a department's staff or premises.

secret de Polichinelle *noun phrase* M19 **French** (= Punchinello's secret). An apparent secret that is generally known; an open secret.

secundus *adjective* E19 **Latin** (= second). Designating the second of two or more pupils of the same surname to enter the school. Cf. PRIMUS adjective 2, TERTIUS.

sederunt *noun* E17 **Latin** (= there were sitting (sc. the following persons), use as noun of 3rd person plural perfect indicative of *sedere* to sit). **1** E17 A sitting of a deliberative or judicial body, especially an ecclesiastical assembly. Also *generally* (now *rare*), a (period of) sitting, especially for discussion or talk. **2** E18 The list of people present at such a sitting. Also in *plural*, the people named on such a list.

sede vacante *adverb phrase* **LME Latin** (= the seat being vacant). *Ecclesiastical* During the vacancy of an episcopal see.

sedile *noun* plural **sedilia** **LME Latin** (= seat, from *sedere* to sit). **1** *generally* A seat. Only in LME. **2** L18 *Ecclesiastical* Each of a series of usually canopied and decorated stone seats, usually three in number, placed on or recessed into the south side of the choir near the altar for use by the clergy. Usually in *plural*.

segue *adverb, verb, & noun* **M18 Italian** (3rd person singular present indicative of *seguire* to follow). *Music* **A** *adverb* M18 (A direction:) proceed to the next movement without a break; continue with an indicated formula. **B** *intransitive verb* M20 Of a person or music: move without interruption from one (live or prerecorded) song or melody to another. Frequently followed by *into*. **C** *noun* M20 An uninterrupted transition from one song or melody to another.

Sehnsucht *noun* **M19 German**. Yearning, wistful longing.

seicento *noun* (also **Seicento**) **E20 Italian** (= six hundred). The seventeenth century in Italy; the Italian style of art, literature, etc., of this period.

seiche *noun* **M19 Swiss French** (perhaps from German *Seiche* sinking (of water)). *Physical Geography* A short-lived standing oscillation of a lake or other body of water (as a bay or basin of the sea), resembling a tide, caused especially by abrupt changes in atmospheric conditions or by small earth tremors.

seif *noun* (also **sif**) **E20 Arabic** (*sayf*, literally, 'sword'). *Physical Geography* A sand dune in the form of a long narrow ridge parallel to the direction of the prevailing wind. Also *seif dune*.

seigneur *noun* (also **Seigneur**) **L16 Old and Modern French** (from Latin *senior* comparative of *senex* old). Especially in France and Canada, a feudal lord, the lord of a manor, (chiefly *historical* except in the Channel Islands, *specifically* Sark). Now *generally*, a lord, a person exercising (feudal) authority.

seigneurie *noun* (also **seigneury**) **L17 French** ((Old French *seignorie*) from as preceding; cf. SIGNORIA). **1** L17 *History* Especially in France and Canada, a landed estate held by feudal tenure, the territory or domain of a seigneur. **2** L19 Especially in the Channel Islands and Canada, the residence or mansion of a seigneur.

Seilbahn *noun* **M20 German** (from *Seil* cable, rope + *Bahn* road, way). A cable railroad, an aerial cableway.

seiza *noun* **M20 Japanese** (from *sei* correct + *za* sitting). An upright kneeling position which is the Japanese traditional formal way of sitting and is used in meditation and as part of the preparation in martial arts.

séjour *noun* **M18 French** (from *séjourner* to sojourn). **1** M18 The action of staying or sojourning in a place. **2** M18 A place of sojourn or residence.

Sekt *noun* **E20 German**. A German sparkling white wine; a drink of this.

selon les règles *adverb phrase* **E19 French**. According to the rules (of polite society).

selva *noun* **M19 Spanish or Portuguese** (from Latin *silva* wood). *Physical Geography* (A tract of land covered by) dense equatorial forest, especially in the Amazon basin. Usually in *plural*.

semiosis *noun* (also **semeiosis**) **E20 Greek** (*sēmeiosis* (inference from) a sign, from *sēmeion* sign, from *sēma* sign, mark). The process of signification, especially in language or literature.

semis *noun* **E20 French** (literally, 'sowing', from *semer* to sow). A form of decoration used in bookbinding, in which small ornaments are repeated regularly.

sempervivum *noun* (formerly Anglicized as **sempervive**) **L16 Latin** (neuter of *sempervivus* ever-living). Any of various succulent plants constituting the genus Sempervivum, of the stonecrop family; *especially* the houseleek, *S. tectorum*.

semplice *adverb & adjective* **M18 Italian** (= simple). *Music* (A direction:) simply, simple.

sempre *adverb* **E19 Italian.** *Music* (A direction:) always, still, throughout.

senex *noun* plural **senes** **L19 Latin** (= old man). In literature (especially comedy), an old man as a stock figure.

senhor *noun* **L18 Portuguese** (from Latin *senior* comparative of *senex* old). Used as a title (preceding the surname or other designation) of or as a respectful form of address to a Portuguese or Brazilian man (corresponding to English *Mr.* or *Sir*); a Portuguese or Brazilian man.

senhora *noun* **E19 Portuguese** (feminine of SENHOR). Used as a title (preceding the surname or other designation) of or as a respectful form of address to a Portuguese or Brazilian woman, especially a married one (corresponding to English *Mrs.* or *madam*); such a woman.

senhorita *noun* **L19 Portuguese** (diminutive of preceding). Used as a title (preceding the surname or other designation) of or as a respectful form of address to a young especially unmarried Portuguese or Brazilian woman (corresponding to English *Miss*); such a woman.

sennachie *noun* (also **shenachie** and other variants) **LME Gaelic** (*seanachaidh* (= Old Irish *senchaid*), from *sean* old (Old Irish *sen*)). In Ireland and the Scottish Highlands: a professional recorder and reciter of family or traditional history and genealogy, attached to the household of a clan chieftain or person of noble rank. Now, a teller of traditional Gaelic heroic tales (chiefly in Scotland).

sennin *noun* (also **sennen**) plural same **L19 Japanese** (= wizard, sage, recluse, from Chinese *Xi'anren* immortal man). In oriental mythology (originally in Taoism): an elderly recluse who has achieved immortality through meditation and self-discipline; a human being with supernatural powers, a reclusive mystic or teacher.

señor *noun* plural **señores** **1** E17 **Spanish** (from Latin *senior* comparative of *senex* old). Used as a title (preceding the surname or other designation) of or as a respectful form of address to a Spanish or Spanish-speaking man (corresponding to English *Mr.* or *Sir*). **2** M19 A Spanish or Spanish-speaking man.

señora *noun* **L16 Spanish** (feminine of SEÑOR). Used as a title (preceding the surname or other designation) of or as a respectful form of address to a Spanish or Spanish-speaking woman, especially a married one (corresponding to English *Mrs.* or *madam*; such a woman.

señorita *noun* **E19 Spanish** (diminutive of preceding). **1** E19 Used as a title (preceding the surname or other designating) of or as a respectful form of address to a young especially unmarried Spanish or Spanish-speaking woman (corresponding to English *Miss*); such a woman. **2** L19 A small labroid fish, *Oxyjulis californica*, of the eastern Pacific. Also *señorita fish*.

señorito *noun* plural **señoritos** **E20 Spanish** (diminutive of SEÑOR). Used as a title (preceding the surname or other designation) or as a respectful form of address to a young man; a young man, *especially* (frequently *derogative*) a noble or rich one regarded as leading an ostentatious or frivolous existence.

sensei *noun* **L19 Japanese** (from *sen* previous + *sei* birth). In Japan: a teacher, an instructor, frequently of martial or other arts; a professor, a scholar.

sensibile *noun* plural **sensibilia** M19 **Latin** (neuter of *sensibilis* sensible). *Philosophy* The kind of thing that, if sensed, is a sense-datum.

sensibilité *noun* E20 **French.** Sensibility; sensitivity.

sensiblerie *noun* M20 **French.** Sentimentality; exaggerated or superficial sensitivity.

sensorium *noun* plural **sensoria, sensoriums** M17 **Late Latin** (from Latin *sens-* past participial stem of *sentire* to feel). The seat of sensation in the brain of humans and animals; the percipient center to which sensory impulses are transmitted by the nerves; the whole sensory apparatus (including the sensory nerves). Formerly also, the brain regarded as center of consciousness and nervous energy. Also *common sensorium.*

sensu lato *adverb & adjective phrase* M20 **Latin.** (Of a scientific, etc., term) In the broad sense. Opposite of SENSU STRICTO.

sensu stricto *adverb & adjective phrase* M19 **Latin** (= in the restricted sense). (Of a scientific, etc., term) Strictly speaking, in the narrow sense. Opposite of SENSU LATO.

■ Also latterly (M20) as STRICTO SENSU.

sententia *noun* plural **sententiae** E20 **Latin** (= mental feeling, opinion, philosophical judgment, from *sentire* to feel). A pithy or memorable saying, a maxim, an aphorism, an epigram; a thought, a reflection.

senza *preposition* E18 **Italian** (probably from Latin *absentia* absence, with influence of Latin *sine* without; cf. SANS). *Music* (In directions:) without.

separatum *noun* plural **separata** L19 **Latin** (noun use of neuter, singular of *separatus* past participle of *separare* to separate). An offprint.

sephira *noun* plural **sephiroth** M16 **Hebrew** (*sĕpīrāh* (plural *sĕpīrōt*), from *sāpar* to number). In the philosophy of the Jewish cabala, each of the ten hypostatized attributes or emanations surrounding the Infinite, by means of which the Infinite enters into relation with the finite. Usually in *plural.*

sepia *noun & adjective* LME **Latin** (from Greek *sēpia* cuttlefish; in sense 2 (as French *sépia*) probably immediately from Italian *seppia*). **A** *noun* **1** LME A cuttlefish. Now chiefly as modern Latin genus name. **2** E19 A rich brown pigment prepared from the black secretion of the cuttlefish, used in monochrome drawing and watercolor painting; the dark reddish brown color of this pigment. Also, a brown tint used in photography. **b** L19 The black secretion itself. **3** M19 *elliptical* A sepia photograph or drawing. **B** *adjective* E19 Of the color of sepia; drawn or tinted in sepia.

■ The adjective was also used as an euphemism in the 1940s in the United States to denote skin color among African Americans.

seppuku *noun* L19 **Japanese** (from *setsu* to cut + *fuku* abdomen). HARA-KIRI.

sepsis *noun* L19 **Greek** (*sēpsis*, from *sēpein* to make rotten). *Medicine* The state of being septic; blood poisoning, especially through infection of a wound.

septennium *noun* plural **septennia, septenniums** M19 **Late Latin** (for classical Latin *septuennium*, from Latin *septem* seven + *annus* year). A period of seven years.

septum *noun* plural **septa** M17 **Latin** ((also *saeptum*), from *sepire, saepire* to enclose, from *sepes, saepes* hedge). **1** M17 *generally* A partition; a dividing wall, layer, membrane, etc., especially in a living organism. **2** L17 *specifically* in *Anatomy* A thin layer of tissue forming a partition in a cavity, organ, etc. **3** E18 *Geology* A thin sheet of material filling a crack. **4** M20 *Electronics* A metal plate placed transversely across a waveguide and attached to the walls by conducting joints.

sequela *noun* plural **sequelae** L18 **Latin** (*sequel(l)ae*, from *sequi* to follow). **1**

L18 *Medicine* A disease or condition occurring as the result of a previous disease or condition. Usually in *plural*. **2** L19 A consequence or result.

sequin *noun* (in sense 1 also (earlier) **chequeen**) **L16 French** (from Italian *zecchino*, from *zecca* mint, from Arabic *sikka* a die for coining, a coin). **1** L16 *History* Any of various Italian and Turkish gold coins. **2** L19 A small shiny usually circular piece of material for attaching to garments as a decoration.

sequitur *noun* **M19 Latin** (= it follows). An inference or conclusion that follows logically from the premises; a logical deduction, a logical remark. Cf. NON SEQUITUR.

sera plural of SERUM.

serac *noun* **M19 Swiss French** (*sérac*, originally the name of a compact white cheese, probably from Latin *serum* whey). A pinnacle or ridge of ice on the surface of a glacier where crevasses intersect.

seraglio *noun* plural **seraglios** **L16 Italian** (*serraglio*, from Turkish *saray* palace, mansion, from Persian, with assimilation to Italian *serraglio* cage (from medieval Latin *serraculum* diminutive of Latin *sera* bolt)). **1** L16 A harem, *especially* one in a palace. **b** M17 The women of a harem. **c** M–L17 *generally* An enclosure; a place of confinement. **2** L16 *History* A Turkish palace, *especially* that of the Sultan in Istanbul.

serai *noun* **E17 Turkish** (*saray* palace, mansion, from Persian: cf. preceding). **1** E17 In various Southwest Asian countries: a building for the accommodation of travelers, a caravanserai. **2** E17 *History* A SERAGLIO sense 2.

serang *noun* (also **sarang**) **L18 Anglo-Indian** (Persian and Urdu *sar-hang* commander, from *sar* head + *hang* authority). **1** A headman among Lascars. **2** E20 A person in authority, a person in charge. More fully *head serang*. *Australian slang*.

serape *noun* (also **sarape**, **zarape**) **E19 Mexican Spanish**. A shawl or blanket worn as a cloak by Spanish-Americans.

serdab *noun* **M19 Arabic** (*sirdāb* cellar, underground vault; or directly from Persian *sardāb* grotto, cellar for ice, from *sard* cold + *āb* water). **1** M19 In the Middle East: a cellar, an underground chamber. **2** L19 *Egyptology* A secret passage or chamber in an ancient tomb.

serein *noun* **L19 Old and Modern French** (from Proto-Gallo-Romance, from Latin *serum* evening, noun use of *serus* late). *Meteorology* A fine rain (apparently) falling from a cloudless sky.

sereno *noun* plural **serenos** **L19 Spanish**. In Spain and Spanish-speaking parts of America: a night watchman.

seriatim *adverb & adjective* **L15 Medieval Latin** (from as Latin *series* chain, row, series (from *serere* to join, connect) + *-atim* after Latin *gradatim*, *literatim*). **A** *adverb* L15 One after another, one by one in succession. **B** *adjective* L19 Following one after the other. *rare*.

serin *noun* **M16 French** (= canary, of unknown origin). Originally, a canary. Now, any bird of the same genus, *especially* (more fully *serin finch*) *Serinus serinus*, a small yellow European finch.

seron *noun* (also **ceroon**, **seroon**) **M16 Spanish** (= hamper, crate (from *sera* large basket), partly through French *serron*). A bale or package (especially of tropical plant products) bound with hide.

serra *noun* **M19 Portuguese** (from Latin *serra* saw; cf. SIERRA). In Portuguese-speaking regions: a ridge of mountains or hills.

serré *adjective* **M19 French**. Tightly compact; *figurative* constricted by grief or emotion.

sertão *noun* plural **sertãos** **E19 Portuguese**. *Geography* An arid barren region of Brazil; the remote interior of Brazil.

serum *noun* plural **sera, serums** L17 **Latin** (= whey, watery fluid). **1** L17 Watery fluid, as a normal or pathological constituent of animal tissues; *specifically* the yellowish protein-rich liquid that separates from coagulated blood. **2** L19 *Medicine* The blood serum of an animal used as a therapeutic or diagnostic agent.

servante *noun* L19 **French** (= side table). An extra table or concealed shelf used in conjuring tricks.

serviette *noun* L15 **Old and Modern French** (= towel, napkin, from *servir* to serve). A table napkin, now *especially* a paper one.

sestina *noun* M19 **Italian** (from *sesto* from Latin *sextus* sixth). A form of rhymed or unrhymed poem of six stanzas of six lines and a concluding triplet in which the same six words at the line-ends occur in each stanza in six different sequences.

se-tenant *adjective* E20 **French** (literally, 'holding together'). *Philately* Of postage stamps, especially of different denominations or designs: joined together as when printed.

settecento *noun* E20 **Italian** (= seven hundred). The eighteenth century in Italy; the style of Italian art, architecture, music, etc., of this period.

sève *noun* M18 **French** (= sap). The quality and flavor appropriate to a specified wine; liveliness, savor.

seviche *noun* (also **ceviche**) M20 **South American Spanish** (*seviche, cebiche*). A South American dish of marinaded raw fish or seafood, usually garnished and served as an appetizer.

sévigné *noun* (also **sevigné**) E19 **French** (probably from Mme. de *Sévigné* (1626–96), French letter writer). *History* A kind of bandeau, especially for the hair; a jewel or ornament for decorating a headdress.

sevruga *noun* L16 **Russian** (*sevryuga*). (Caviar from) the sturgeon, of the Caspian and Black Seas.

Sezession *noun* plural **Sezessien** E20 **German.** *Art* A radical art movement that started in Vienna and was contemporaneous with and related to ART NOUVEAU; SEZESSIONSSTIL.

Sezessionsstil *noun* L20 **German.** *Art* The style of the SEZESSION.

sf abbreviation of SFORZANDO (*musical direction*).

sforzando *adjective, adverb, & noun* E19 **Italian** (present participle of *sforzare* to use force). *Music* **A** *adjective & adverb* E19 (A direction:) with special emphasis or sudden loudness. Abbreviated to *sf, sfz.* **B** *noun* M19 plural **sforzandi, sforzandos**. A note or group of notes specially emphasized; an increase in emphasis and loudness.

sforzato *adjective, adverb, & noun* plural of noun **sforzati, sforzatos** E19 **Italian** (past participle of *sforzare* to use force). *Music* SFORZANDO.

sfumato *adjective & noun* M19 **Italian** (past participle of *sfumare* to shade off, from *s-* ex- + *fumare* to smoke). *Painting* **A** *adjective* M19 Painted with or using indistinct outlines, depicting hazy forms. **B** *noun* E20 The technique of softening outlines and allowing tones and colors to shade gradually into one another; an indistinct outline or hazy form produced in this way.

sfz abbreviation of SFORZANDO (musical direction).

sgraffiato *noun* plural **sgraffiati** M19 **Italian** (past participle of *sgraffiare* to scratch away; see next). SGRAFFITO.

sgraffito *noun* plural **sgraffiti** M18 **Italian** (from *sgraffiare* to scratch away: *s-* representing Latin *ex-* ex- + (later) GRAFFITO). A form of decoration or design made by scratching through wet plaster on a wall or through slip on pottery to reveal a different color below.

shabti *noun* plural **shabtiu, shabtis** M19 **Egyptian** (*šbty*). *Egyptology* A USHABTI. Cf. SHAWABTI.

shabu-shabu *noun* L20 **Japanese.** A Japanese dish of pieces of thinly sliced beef or pork cooked quickly with vegetables in boiling water.

shadoof *noun* (also **shaduf**) M19 **Arabic** ((Egyptian) *šādūf*). A device consisting of a pivoted rod or pole with a bucket at one end and a counterbalancing weight at the other, used especially in Egypt for raising water.

shaganappi *noun & adjective* M18 **Ojibwa**. **A** *noun* M18 Thread, cord, or thong made from rawhide, rawhide cut into strips; a strip of rawhide. Also, a rough pony. **B** *adjective* E19 Made of a strip or strips of rawhide; *figurative* tough, rough; cheap, inferior, makeshift.

shagetz, **shagitz** variants of SHEGETZ.

shah *noun* (also (as title) **Shah**) M16 **Persian** (*šāh* from Old Persian *xšāya-Tiya* king). *History* (A title of) the monarch of Iran (Persia).

shahada *noun* L19 **Arabic** (*šahāda* testimony, evidence). The Muslim profession of faith.

■ The *shahada—Lā ilāha illā (A)llāh, Muḥammadun rasūl Allāh* 'there is no God but Allah, [and] Muhammad is the messenger of Allah'—forms part of the regular call to prayer.

shahid *noun* (also **shaheed**) L19 **Arabic** (*šahīd* witness, martyr). A Muslim martyr.

shaikh, **Shaikha** variants of SHEIKH, SHEIKHA.

shako *noun* plural **shakos** E19 **French** (*schako* from Hungarian *csákó* probably from German *Zacken* peak, point, spike). A cylindrical military hat with a peak and a plume or pompom.

shakudo *noun & adjective* M19 **Japanese** (from *shaku* red + *dō* copper). (Made of) a Japanese alloy of copper and gold.

shakuhachi *noun* L19 **Japanese**. An end-blown Japanese flute, made of bamboo.

shalom *interjection & noun* L19 **Hebrew** (*šālōm* peace). In Jewish society, used as a salutation at meeting or parting; an utterance of "shalom".

shalwar *noun* (also **salwar**, **shalvar**) E19 **Persian and Urdu** (*šalwār*). *singular* and in *plural* Loose pants worn in some South Asian countries and by some Muslims elsewhere, *especially* those worn by women together with a KAMEEZ.

■ Often in the combination *shalwar-kameez*, describing a woman's matching outfit.

shaman *noun* L17 **German** (*Schamane*, Russian *shaman* from Tungusian *šaman*). A priest among certain peoples of northern Asia, regarded as one with healing and magical powers and influence over the spirits who bring about good and evil; a healer among North American Indians, regarded as possessing magical powers. Now also, a person regarded as having powers of spiritual guidance and healing through direct access to and influence in the spirit world.

shamba *noun* L19 **Kiswahili**. In East Africa: a cultivated plot of ground. Also, a farm, a plantation.

shambok variant of SJAMBOK.

shamisen variant of SAMISEN.

shanachie variant of SENNACHIE.

shanti *interjection & noun* L19 **Sanskrit** (*śānti* peace, tranquillity). *Hinduism* (A prayer for) peace; peace be with you.

■ Usually repeated three times at the end of an Upanishad for the peace of the soul.

sharif *noun* (also **shareef**, **shereef**, **sherif**) L16 **Arabic** (*šarīf* noble, high-born). **1** L16 A descendant of Muhammad through his daughter Fatima. **2** E17 (frequently **Sharif**) (The title of) any of various Arab rulers, magistrates, or religious leaders; *specifically* (**a**) the ruler of Morocco; (**b**) the governor of Mecca.

sharifa *noun* (also **shereefa**, **sherifa**, **Sharifa**) E20 **Arabic** (*šarīfa* feminine of *šarīf* SHARIF). The wife of a Moroccan sharif.

shashlik *noun* E20 **Russian** (*shashlyk* from Crimean Turkish *şişlik* from *şiş* skewer; cf. SHISH KEBAB). An eastern European and Asian kebab of mutton and garnishings, frequently served on a skewer.

shauri *noun* plural **shauri(e)s** E20 **Kiswahili** (from Arabic *šūrā* consultation, deliberation, counsel). In East Africa: counsel, debate; a problem.

shawabti *noun* plural **shawabtiu, shawabtis** E20 **Egyptian** (*šwZbt(y)*, probably from *šwZb* persea wood, perhaps the original material). *Egyptology* An USHABTI. Cf. SHABTI.

shchi *noun* E19 **Russian.** A Russian cabbage soup.

shebeen *noun* L18 **Irish** ((Anglo-Irish form of) *síbín*, of unknown origin). An unlicensed establishment selling alcoholic liquor; a disreputable bar.

■ Originally meaning an illicit liquor outlet in Ireland, *shebeen* is now commonly used in South African English for a black-run establishment where alcohol is illegally brewed and sold.

shechita *noun* L19 **Hebrew** (*šěḥīṭāh*, from *šāḥaṭ* to slaughter). The method of slaughtering animals that fulfills the requirements of Jewish law.

sheesh kebab variant of SHISH KEBAB.

shegetz *noun* (also **shagetz**, **shagitz**) plural **shkotsim** E20 **Yiddish** (*sheygets*, *sheyhets* from Hebrew *sheqeṣ* detested thing; cf. SHIKSA). Among Jewish people, a Gentile boy; a Jewish boy not observing traditional Jewish behavior.

■ Originally and chiefly United States, and usually derogatory.

sheikh *noun* (also **shaikh**, **sheik**) L16 **Arabic** (ultimately from Arabic *šayk* sheikh, old man, elder, from *šāka* to be or grow old). **1a** L16 (also **Sheikh**) Originally, an Eastern governor, prince, or king. Later *especially*, a chief or head of an Arab family, people, or village. Also, a title of respect. **b** E20 A strong, romantic, or dashing male lover. **2** L16 A leader of a Muslim religious order or community; a great religious doctor or preacher; now *especially*, a saint with a localized cult. **3** L19 In the Indian subcontinent, a Hindu convert to Islam.

■ In sense 1b from *The Sheik*, a novel by E. M. Hull (1919) made into a movie (1921) starring Rudolph Valentino.

sheikha *noun* (also **Sheik(h)a**, **Shaikha**) M19 **Arabic** (*šayka*). An Arab lady of good family; the (chief) wife of a sheikh. Also, a title of respect.

shekel *noun* M16 **Hebrew** (*šeqel*, from *šāqal* to weigh). **1** *History* A unit of weight and silver coin used in the ancient Middle East. **2** In *plural* Money; riches. *colloquial.* **3** The basic unit of currency in modern Israel.

■ In sense 2 often in colloquial phrases such as *bringing* (or *raking*) *in the shekels* meaning 'making a lot of money quickly and easily'.

shemozzle *noun & verb slang* (also **schemozzle**) L19 **Yiddish** (probably from as SCHLIMAZEL). **A** *noun* L19 A muddle, a complicated situation; a quarrel, a brawl, a mêlée. **B** *intransitive verb* E20 Make one's escape, leave hastily.

shenachie variant of SENNACHIE.

shenzi *noun* E20 **Kiswahili.** In East Africa: an uncivilized African; a barbarian, a person outside one's cultural group. Chiefly *derogatory*.

sherbet *noun* E17 **Turkish** (*şerbet*, Persian *šerbet* from Arabic *šarba(t)* draft, drink, from *šariba* to drink). **1** E17 A cooling drink made of sweetened and diluted fruit juice, drunk especially in Arab countries. Now also, an effervescing drink made of sherbet powder (see sense 2). **2** M19 A flavored sweet powder containing bicarbonate of soda, tartaric acid, etc., eaten as a confection or used to make an effervescing drink. Also more fully *sherbet powder*. **3a** L19 A sorbet. **b** L19 (A glass of) alcoholic liquor, especially (*specifically* in *Australia*) beer. *slang.*

shereef, **shereefa** variants of SHARIF, SHARIFA.

sherif, **sherifa** variants of SHARIF, SHARIFA.

sherpa *noun, adjective, & verb* M19 **Tibetan** (*sharpa* inhabitant of an eastern country). **A** *noun* plural **sherpas**, same **1** M19 (*Sherpa*) A member of a Tibetan people inhabiting the southern slopes of the Himalayas, renowned for their skill in mountaineering. **2** M20 (*sherpa*) *transferred* and *figurative* A mountain guide or porter; an official making preparations for a summit conference. **B** E20 *attributive* or as *adjective* Of, pertaining to, or designating the Sherpas and their language. **C** L20 *intransitive verb* Act as or like a sherpa.

sheshbesh *noun* L20 **Turkish** (*şeşbeş*, from Persian *šaš* six + Turkish *beş* five). A variety of backgammon played in the Middle East.

sheva *noun* (also **shewa**) L16 **Hebrew** (*šĕwā'*, apparently arbitrary alteration of *šāw'* emptiness, vanity, spelled in German books *Schwa*, whence SCHWA). **1** L16 *Hebrew Grammar* The sign : placed under a consonant to express the absence of a following vowel sound, having in certain positions no sound (*quiescent sheva*) but in others sounding as a schwa &schwa. (*movable sheva*); the sound of movable sheva. **2** *Phonetics* E19 A SCHWA.

shiatsu *noun* M20 **Japanese** (literally, 'finger pressure'). A kind of therapy of Japanese origin, in which pressure is applied with the thumbs and palms to certain points of the body.

■ Imported under this name into the West in the 1960s, *shiatsu* has, since the late 1970s, become more generally referred to as *acupressure*.

shibboleth *noun* M17 **Hebrew** (*šibbōleṯ* ear of corn, stream in flood, used as a test of nationality for the difficulty for foreigners of pronouncing the *th* sound at the end of the word (see Judges 12:4–6)). **1** M17 A word used as a test for detecting people from another district or country by their pronunciation; a word or sound very difficult for foreigners to pronounce correctly. **b** M17 A peculiarity of pronunciation or accent indicative of a person's origin; the distinctive mode of speech of a profession, class, etc. **c** E19 A custom, habit, style of dressing, etc., distinguishing a particular class or group of people. **2** M17 A long-standing formula, idea, phrase, etc., held (especially unreflectingly) by or associated with a group, class, etc.; a catchword, a slogan; a taboo. Also, a received wisdom; a truism, a platitude.

shibui *adjective & noun* (also **shibu**) M20 **Japanese** (= astringent, from *shibu* an astringent substance). **A** M20 *adjective* Tasteful in a quiet, profound, or unostentatious way. **B** *noun* M20 Tastefulness, refinement; appreciation of elegant simplicity.

shidduch *noun* L19 **Yiddish** (from Hebrew *šiddūḵ* negotiation, especially of an arranged marriage). An arranged marriage, a (good) match.

shifta *noun* plural same, **shiftas** M20 **Somali** (*shúfto* bandit, from Amharic). A Somali bandit or guerrilla, operating mainly in northern Kenya.

shiitake *noun* L19 **Japanese** (from *shii* a kind of oak + *take* mushroom). An edible agaric (mushroom), *Lentinus edodes*, cultivated in Japan and China on logs of various oaks and allied trees. Also *shiitake mushroom*.

shikar *noun & verb* E17 **Persian and Urdu** (*šikār*). **A** *noun* E17 Hunting, shooting; game. **B** *verb* Inflected *-rr-*. **1** *intransitive verb* L19 Hunt animals for sport. **2** *transitive verb* L19 Hunt (animals).

■ Originating and used almost solely in the Indian subcontinent, the word often occurs in the phrase *on shikar* 'on a hunting expedition'.

shikari *noun* E19 **Urdu** (from Persian *šikārī*: see SHIKAR). In the Indian subcontinent: a hunter (either European or Indian); an expert guide or tracker.

shikhara *noun* (also **sikhara**) E19 **Sanskrit** (*śikhara* peak, spire). A pyramidal tower on a Hindu temple, sometimes having convexly curved sides.

shiksa *noun & adjective* L19 **Yiddish** (*shikse* from Hebrew *šiqṣāh* from *šeqeṣ* detested thing + feminine suffix -

āh). **A** *noun* L19 A Gentile girl or woman. **B** *attributive* or as *adjective* M20 Of a girl or woman: Gentile. *derogatory.*

shippo *noun & adjective* (also **shipo**) L19 **Japanese** (*shippō* seven precious things, from *shichi* seven + *hō* jewel). (Made of) Japanese cloisonné-enamel ware.

shisha *noun* (also **shi-sha** M20 **Urdu** (*šīša(h)*, Persian *šīša* glass, mirror). (Used *attributively* to designate) mirror-work and items connected with it.

shish kebab *noun* (also **sheesh kebab**) E20 **Turkish** (*şiş kebab*, from *şiş* skewer + *kebab* roast meat; cf. SHASHLIK). A dish consisting of pieces of marinated meat (usually lamb) and vegetables grilled and served on skewers.

shiva *noun* (also **shivah**) L19 **Hebrew** (*šib'āh* seven). *Judaism* A period of seven days' formal mourning for the dead, beginning immediately after the funeral. Frequently in *sit shiva*, observe this period.

shivaree variant of CHARIVARI.

shkotsim plural of SHEGETZ.

shlub *noun* (also **schlub**) M20 **Yiddish** (perhaps from Poland *ż^ób* blockhead). A worthless person, an oaf. *slang.*

shmatte *noun* (also **schmatte**) L20 **Yiddish** (*schmatte*, from Poland *szmata* rag). A rag; a garment, *especially* a ragged one. *colloquial.*

shmear *noun* (also **schmear, schmeer**) M20 **Yiddish** (*schmirn* to flatter, grease, smear: cf. German *schmieren* smear). Bribery, corruption, flattery.

■ Colloquial. Often in the phrase *the whole shmear* meaning 'everything (possible)'.

shochet *noun* plural **shochetim** L19 **Hebrew** (*šōḥēṭ* present participle of *šāḥaṭ* to slaughter). A person officially certified as competent to kill cattle and poultry in the manner prescribed by Jewish law.

shofar *noun* plural **shofroth** M19 **Hebrew** (*šōpār*, plural *šōpārōt*). A ram's-horn trumpet used in Jewish religious services and in biblical times as a war trumpet.

shogi *noun* M19 **Japanese** (*shōgi*). A Japanese board game resembling chess.

shogun *noun* E17 **Japanese** (*shōgun*, from Chinese *jiāng jūn* general). *History* Any of a succession of hereditary commanders-in-chief of the Japanese army, before 1868 the virtual rulers of Japan.

shomer *noun* plural **shomerim** E20 **Hebrew** (*šōmēr* watchman). **1** E20 A watchman, a guard, now especially in Israel. **2** E20 An inspector who verifies that food is prepared in accordance with Jewish religious laws.

shonda *noun* M20 **Yiddish** (*shande* from Middle High German *schande*). A disgrace. *colloquial.*

shosagoto *noun* plural same E20 **Japanese** (from *shosa* acting, conduct + *koto* matter, affair). In Japanese kabuki theater: a dance play, a mime performed to music.

shosha *noun* plural same L20 **Japanese** (*shōsha* business firm, from *shō* mercantile + *sha* society, company). A SOGO SHOSHA.

shott *noun* (also **chott**) L19 **Arabic** (*šaṭṭ* shore, strand; (in North Africa) salt lake; (in Iraq) waterway, river). A shallow brackish lake or marsh especially in Algeria and southern Tunisia, usually dry in summer and covered with saline deposits. Cf. SABKHA.

shoyu *noun* E18 **Japanese** (*shōyu* from Chinese *jiàngyóu* (Wade-Giles *chiang-yu*) from *jiàng* bean paste + *yóu* oil). A sauce made from fermented soybeans; soy sauce. Also *shoyu sauce.*

shrikhand *noun* M20 **Sanskrit** (*śrīkhaṇḍa* sandalwood). An Indian sweet dish made from curd, sugar, almonds, and spices.

shtetl *noun* plural **shtetlach, shtetls** M20 **Yiddish** (= little town, from German *Stadt* town). *History* A small Jewish town or village in eastern Europe.

shtibl *noun* (also **shtiebel**) plural **shtiblach** E20 **Yiddish** (diminutive of *shtub* room, house; cf. German dialect *Stüberl* small room). A small synagogue.

shtick *noun* (also **shtik**) M20 **Yiddish** (from German *Stück* piece, play). **1** M20 A (comedian's) stage routine; a joke; *transferred* a patter, a gimmick. **2** M20 A particular area of activity or interest. *slang*.

shtiebel variant of SHTIBL.

shtik variant of SHTICK.

shtoom *adjective & verb* (also **s(h)tumm, schtoom**) M20 **Yiddish** (from German *stumm* silent). **A** *adjective* M20 Silent, mute. Chiefly in *keep* (or *stay*) *shtoom*, refrain from disclosing information, etc. **B** *intransitive verb* M20 Become silent, shut *up*.

shufti *noun* (also **shufty**) M20 **Arabic** (from colloquial Arabic *šuftī* have you seen?, from *šāfa* to see). A look; a glance.

■ Especially in *take* (or *have*) *a shufti*. Originally military slang, but also more generally used in dated colloquial speech. The verbal use from which the noun derives is rare in English.

shul *noun* L19 **Yiddish** (from German *Schule* school). A synagogue.

shunga *noun* plural same M20 **Japanese** (from *shun* spring + *ga* picture). An example of Japanese erotic art.

shura *noun* M20 **Arabic** (*šūrā* consultation). The Islamic principle of (rule by) consultation; an Islamic consultative council.

shuriken *noun* L20 **Japanese** (*shuri-ken*, literally, 'dagger in the hand', from *shu* hand + *ri* inside + *ken* sword, blade). A weapon in the form of a star with projecting blades or points, used in some martial arts.

sic *adverb & noun* L19 **Latin** (= so, thus). **A** L19 *adverb* Used or spelled as written. **B** *noun* M20 An instance of using 'sic'.

■ As an adverb used parenthetically after a quoted word, etc., to call attention to an anomalous or erroneous form or to prevent the supposition of misquotation.

sic et non *noun phrase* E20 **Latin** (literally, 'yes and no'). *Theology* A method of argument used by medieval theologians, in which contradictory passages of scripture are presented without commentary in order to stimulate readers to resolve the contradictions themselves. Frequently *attributive*.

■ *Sic et non* was the title of a work by the twelfth-century French theologian and philosopher Peter Abelard, in which he employed this method, later imitated by other Scholastic philosophers.

Sicherheitsdienst *noun* M20 **German** (from *Sicherheit* security + *dienst* service). *History* The security branch of the Nazi Schutzstaffel (SS), set up in 1931–32. Abbreviated to *SD*.

siciliana *noun* plural **siciliane** (also **siciliano**, plural **sicilianos, siciliani**) E18 **Italian** (feminine of *Siciliano* Sicilian). *Music* A piece of music for a Sicilian peasant dance, resembling a slow jig; *transferred* a composition in 6/8 or 12/8 time, frequently in a minor key and evoking a pastoral mood.

sicilienne *noun* L19 **French** (feminine of *sicilien* Sicilian). **1** L19 A fine poplin of silk and wool. **2** L19 *Music* A SICILIANA.

siddha *noun* M19 **Sanskrit**. In Indian religions: a person who has attained perfection, a saint, a semi-divine being; *specifically* in *Jainism*, a perfected bodyless being freed from the cycle of rebirths.

Sieg Heil *noun phrase & interjection* M20 **German** (literally, 'Hail victory'). (An exclamation of) a victory salute used especially at a political rally originally during the Nazi regime in Germany.

sierozem *noun* M20 **Russian** (*serozëm*, from *seryĭ* gray + Slavonic base *zem-* (cf. Russian *zemlya*) earth, soil). *Soil Science* A soil, usually calcareous and humus-poor, characterized by a brownish gray surface and developed typically under mixed shrub vegetation in arid climates.

sierra *noun* plural **sierras** M16 **Spanish** (from Latin *serra* saw; cf. SERRA). A long mountain range rising in jagged peaks, especially in Spain and Latin America.

siesta *noun & verb* M17 **Spanish** (from Latin *sexta* (*hora*) sixth hour of the day). **A** *noun* M17 An afternoon rest or nap; *especially* one taken during the hottest hours of the day in a hot country. **B** *intransitive verb* M19 Take a siesta.

siffleur *noun* (feminine (sense 2) **si'ffleuse**) E18 **French** (from *siffler* to whistle). **1** E18 Any of various animals that make a whistling noise. **2** E19 A person who entertains professionally by whistling.

sigilla plural of SIGILLUM.

sigillata *noun* E20 **Latin** (= sealed). *Archaeology* TERRA SIGILLATA sense 3.

sigillum *noun* plural **sigilla** M17 **Late Latin** (= sign, trace, impress, (in medieval Latin) seal (classical Latin *sigilla* (plural) little images, seal), diminutive of Latin *signum* sign). **1** In *plural* Small human images. *rare*. Only in M17. **2** E20 *Roman Catholic Church* The seal of confession. **3** M20 A sign, a symbol; an abbreviation.

siglum *noun* plural **sigla** E18 **Late Latin** (*sigla* plural, perhaps for *singula* neuter plural of *singulus* single). A letter (especially an initial) or other symbol used as an abbreviation for a word, proper name, etc., in a printed text; *Bibliography* such a letter or symbol used to designate a particular version of a literary text.

sigma *noun* LME **Latin** (from Greek). **1** LME The eighteenth letter (Σ, σ, or, when final, ς), of the Greek alphabet represented in English by *S*, *s*. **2** E20 *Physics* and *Chemistry* **a** Used *attributively* to designate an electron, orbital, molecular state, etc., possessing zero angular momentum about an internuclear axis. **b** M20 *Particle Physics* Used (usually *attributive*), to denote each of a triplet of hyperons (and their antiparticles). **3** L20 *Biochemistry* A component of RNA polymerase that determines where transcription begins. In full *sigma factor*. **4** L20 *Statistics* A (unit of) standard deviation.

signa, **signa panthea** plurals of SIGNUM, SIGNUM PANTHEUM.

significacio *noun* (also **significatio**) plural **significaciones** M20 **Medieval Latin** (from Latin *significatio(n-)*). A parallel or second meaning not directly stated in a text; the deeper or implied meaning of an allegory, emblem, symbol, etc.

signor *noun* plural **signori** L16 **Italian** (reduced form of *signore*, from Latin *senior*). **1** L16 Used as a title (preceding the surname or other designation) of or as a respectful form of address to an Italian or Italian-speaking man (corresponding to English *Mr.* or *sir*). **b** L18 An Italian man, especially a singer. **2** L16 A man of distinction, rank, or authority; a gentleman or nobleman.

signora *noun* M17 **Italian** (feminine of SIGNORE). Used as a title (preceding the surname or other designation) of or as a respectful form of address to an Italian or Italian-speaking (especially married) woman (corresponding to English *Mrs.* or *madam*). Also, an Italian (especially married) woman.

signoria *noun* M16 **Italian** (from as SIGNOR). *History* The governing body of any of various medieval Italian republics, especially Venice.

signorina *noun* E19 **Italian** (diminutive of SIGNORA). Used as a title (used preceding the surname or other designation) of or as a respectful form of address to a young (especially unmarried) Italian or Italian-speaking woman (corresponding to English *Miss*). Also, a young (especially unmarried) Italian woman.

signum *noun* plural **signa** M19 **Latin**. A mark, a sign.

signum pantheum *noun phrase* plural **signa panthea** E18 **Latin** (= divine statue, from *signum* statue + *pantheus* from Greek *pantheios* dedicated to all the gods (from *pan-* all + *theios* divine)). *Classical Antiquities* A statue combining the figures, symbols, or attributes of several gods.

sikhara variant of SHIKHARA.

silenus *noun* (also **Silenus**) plural **sileni** E17 **Latin** (*Silenus* from Greek *Seilēnos* foster father of Bacchus and leader of the satyrs). *Greek Mythology* A wood-god, a satyr, *especially* one represented as a bearded old man with the tail and legs of a horse.

■ Earlier (L16) in the Anglicized form *silen*.

silhouette *noun & verb* L18 **French** (from Étienne de *Silhouette* (1709–67), French author and politician). **A** *noun* **1** L18 A portrait obtained by tracing the outline of a profile, head, or figure, especially by means of its shadow, and filling in the whole with black or cutting the shape out of black paper; a figure or picture drawn or printed in solid black. **b** *figuratively* E19 A brief verbal description of a person, etc. **2 a** M19 An object seen as a dark outline against a lighter background; a dark shadow of something. **b** E20 The contour or outline of a garment or a person's body. **B** *verb* **1** *transitive verb* L19 Represent in silhouette, throw up the outline of. Usually in *passive* (followed by *against, on*). **2** *intransitive verb* L19 Show up as a silhouette.

sillar *noun* M20 **Spanish**. *Geology* A kind of volcanic tuff.

silo *noun* plural **silos** M19 **Spanish** (from Latin *sirus* from Greek *siros* pit). **1** M19 A pit or underground chamber used for storing grain, roots, etc.; *specifically* one in which green crops are compressed and preserved for fodder as silage. Also, a cylindrical tower or other structure built above ground for the same purpose. **2** E20 *transferred* A large bin used for storing loose materials, etc. **3** M20 An underground structure in which a guided missile is stored and from which it may be fired.

silva variant of SYLVA.

simba *noun* E20 **Kiswahili**. A lion; *figurative* a warrior. Chiefly *East African*.

simchah *noun* M20 **Hebrew** (*śimḥāh* rejoicing). A Jewish private party or celebration.

simi *noun* M20 **Kiswahili** (*sime*). In East Africa: a large two-edged knife.

simoom *noun* (also **simoon**) L18 **Arabic** (*samūm*, from *samma* to poison). A hot dry dust-laden wind blowing at intervals in the African and Asian (especially Arabian) deserts.

simpatico *adjective* (feminine **simpatica**) M19 **Spanish** (*simpático*, from *simpatía*, or Italian *simpatico* from *simpatia*, both from Latin *sympathia* from Greek *sumpatheia* from *sumpathēs* having a fellow feeling). Pleasing, likable; congenial.

simplex *adjective & noun* L16 **Latin** (= single, variant of *simplus* simple, with second element as in *duplex, multiplex*, etc.). **A** *adjective* **1** L16 Composed of or characterized by a single part or structure. **2** *Telecommunications* and *Computing* L19 Designating a system, circuit, etc., along which signals can be sent in only one direction at a time. **3** *Genetics* E20 Of a polyploid individual: having the dominant allele of a particular gene represented once. **B** *noun* **1** L19 A word without an affix; a simple uncompounded word. **2** E20 *Geometry* The figure, in any given number of dimensions, that is bounded by the least possible number of hyperplanes (e.g., the simplex in two dimensions is a triangle). **3** M20 *Linguistics* In early transformational grammar, a basic or core sentence, a kernel sentence.

simplex munditiis *noun & adjective phrase* M18 **Latin** (literally, 'simple in your adornments'). **A** *noun phrase* M18 Beauty without adornment or ostentation. **B** *adjective phrase* L19 Unostentatiously beautiful.

■ A quotation from Horace *Odes* I.v.

simulacrum *noun* plural **simulacrums, simulacra** L16 **Latin** (from *simulare* to simulate). **1** L16 A material image or representation of a person or thing, *es-*

pecially a god. **2** E19 A thing having the appearance but not the substance or proper qualities of something; a deceptive imitation or substitute; a pretense.

simurg *noun* (also **simurgh**) L18 **Persian** (*sīmurġ*, from Pahlavi *sēn* eagle + *murġ* bird). *Iranian Mythology* A giant bird believed to have the power of speech and reasoning and to be of great age.

sindicato *noun* plural **sindicatos** M20 **Spanish** (= syndicate, labor union). In Spain and Spanish-speaking countries: a labor union.

sine die *adverb phrase* E17 **Latin** (= without day, from *sine* without + *die* ablative singular of *dies* day). With reference to adjourned business, etc.: without any day being appointed for resumption; indefinitely.

sine qua non *adjective & noun phrase* (also in Latin plural form **sine quibus non**, (chiefly *Scottish Law*) Latin masculine form **sine quo non**) E17 **Latin** ((*causa*) *sine qua non* literally, '(cause) without which not', from *sine* without + *qua* ablative singular feminine of *qui* which + *non* not). **A** *adjective phrase* E17 Indispensable, absolutely essential. Also *postpositive*. **B** *noun phrase* **1** E17 An indispensable person or thing; *especially* an essential condition or element. **2** L17 *Scottish Law* (*sine quo non*) A curator, a trustee, *archaic*.

sinfonia *noun* L18 **Italian** (from Latin *symphonia* instrumental harmony, voices in concert, from Greek *sumphōnia* from *sumphōnos* harmonious). *Music* **1** L18 In baroque music, an orchestral piece used as an introduction to an opera, cantata, or suite; an overture. **2** (*Sinfonia*) (The title of) a small symphony orchestra.

sinfonietta *noun* E20 **Italian** (diminutive of SINFONIA). *Music* **1** E20 A short or simple symphony. **2** E20 (*Sinfonietta*) A SINFONIA sense 2.

singerie *noun* E20 **French** (from *singe* monkey). A painting depicting monkeys in human roles and attitudes; a piece of porcelain decorated with such paintings; work done in this style.

Singspiel *noun* plural **Singspiele** L19 **German** (from *singen* to sing + *Spiel* play). *Music* A dramatic performance alternating between song and dialogue, popular especially in late eighteenth-century Germany; (a) comic opera.

sinopia *noun* plural **sinopie** M19 **Italian**. **1** M19 A red pigment containing sinopite or similar-colored minerals. **2** M20 *transferred* A preliminary rough sketch for a fresco, covered by the final work.

sinter *noun* L18 **German** (= cinder). **1** L18 A hard incrustation formed on rocks, etc., by precipitation from mineral waters. **2** E20 Material that has been coalesced into a solid or porous mass under the influence of heat or pressure without liquefaction, especially after compression in a shaped die.

sirocco *noun* (also **scirocco**) plural **siroccos** E17 **Italian** (*scirocco* ultimately from Spanish Arabic *šalūḳ*, *šulūḳ*, *šalūk* southeast wind, perhaps of Romance origin). **1** E17 A hot, oppressive, and often dusty or rainy wind that blows from the north coast of Africa over the Mediterranean and parts of southern Europe; *generally* any hot southerly wind. **2** *figurative* M19 A blighting influence; a fiery storm. **3** L19 A machine or oven for drying hops or tea leaves by means of a hot, moist current of air. Also more fully *sirocco drying-machine, sirocco oven*.

sirop *noun* L19 **French**. (A drink made from) a syrupy preparation of sweetened fruit juice.

sissonne *noun* E18 **French**. *Ballet* A jump in the air from fifth position, landing on one foot with the other leg extended.

sistrum *noun* plural **sistra**, **sistrums** LME **Latin** (from Greek *seistron*, from *seiein* to shake). A musical instrument of ancient Egyptian origin, consisting of a metal frame with transverse metal rods that rattled when the instrument was shaken.

sitar *noun* M19 **Persian and Urdu** (*sitār* from *sih* three + *tār* string). A stringed Indian musical instrument, resembling a lute, with a long neck and (usually) seven principal strings that the player plucks.

situla *noun* plural **situlae**, **situlas** L19 **Latin** (= bucket). *Archaeology* A vessel resembling a bucket in shape.

situs *noun* E18 **Latin**. **1** E18 Situation, position *rare*. **2** *Law* **a** E19 The place to which for purposes of legal jurisdiction or taxation a property belongs. **b** M20 A work site, *especially* (in full *common situs*) one occupied by two or more employers.

Sitzfleisch *noun* (also written **sitzfleisch**) E20 **German** (from *sitzen* to sit + *Fleisch* flesh). The ability to persist in or endure an activity.

Sitz im Leben *noun phrase* M20 **German** (literally, 'place in life'). *Theology* In biblical criticism, the determining circumstances in which a tradition developed.

sitzkrieg *noun* M20 **pseudo-German** (after BLITZKRIEG, as if from German *sitzen* to sit + *krieg* war). (A part of) a war marked by a (relative) absence of active hostilities.

sjambok *noun* (also **sambok**, **shambok**) L18 **Afrikaans** (from Malay *sambuk*, *chambuk* from Persian and Urdu *chābuk* horsewhip). In South Africa: a heavy whip made of rhinoceros or hippopotamus hide.

skald *noun* (also **scald**) M18 **Old Norse** (*skáld*, of unknown origin). *History* An (itinerant or court) oral poet, a bard, originally and especially in ancient Scandinavia.

skandalon *noun* (also **scandalon**) M20 **Greek**. *Theology* A stumbling block; a cause of offense; a scandal.

skat *noun* M19 **German** (from Italian *scarto* (= French *écart*) cards laid aside, from *scartare* to discard; cf. ÉCARTÉ). A three-handed card game with bidding for contract, originating in Germany; *collective* the two cards dealt to the table in this game.

skaz *noun* E20 **Russian**. First-person narrative in which the author assumes a persona.

skene *noun* L19 **Greek** (*skēnē* hut, tent). *Theater* In ancient Greek theater, a three-dimensional structure forming part of the stage or set and able to be decorated according to the current play's theme.

skepsel *noun* M19 **Afrikaans** (*skepsel*, Dutch *schepsel* creature, from *scheppen* to create). A creature, a villain, a rascal.

■ In South African colloquial speech frequently used as a derogatory and offensive form of address to a black or Colored person.

ski-joring *noun* (also **skikjøring**) E20 **Norwegian** (*skikjøring*, from *ski* ski + *kjøring* driving). A winter sport in which a skier is towed by a horse or vehicle.

skoff *noun* L18 **Afrikaans** (*skof* from Dutch *schoft* quarter of the day, each of the four meals of a day). A stage of a journey; a period of travel between outspans. Also, a period of work, a shift. *South African colloquial*.

slainte *interjection* E19 **Gaelic** (*slàinte* (*mhór*) = '(good) health'). Expressing good wishes, especially before drinking.

slalom *noun & verb* E20 **Norwegian** (*slalåm*, from *sla* sloping + *låm* track). **A** *noun* **1** E20 A downhill ski race on a zigzag course marked by artificial obstacles, usually flags, and descended singly by each competitor in turn. **2** M20 A similar obstacle race for canoeists, waterskiers, skateboarders, etc. **B** *intransitive verb* M20 Perform or compete in a slalom; make frequent sharp turns (as) in a slalom.

slivovitz *noun* (also **slivovic**) L19 **Serbo-Croat** (*šljivovica* from *šljiva* plum). A plum brandy made chiefly in Romania, Serbia, and neighboring countries.

smetana *noun* E20 **Russian** (from *smetat'* to sweep together, collect). Sour cream. Frequently in *smetana sauce*.

smørbrød *noun* M20 **Norwegian** (from *smøre* butter + *brød* bread: cf. next). In Norway: an open sandwich; food consisting of open sandwiches.

smorgasbord *noun* L19 **Swedish** (*smörgåsbord*, from *smörgås* (slice of) bread and butter (from *smör* butter, *gås* goose, lump of butter) + *bord* board, table). **1** L19 Open sandwiches served with delicacies as hors d'oeuvres or a buffet, originally and especially in Scandinavia. **2** M20 *figurative* A medley, a miscellany, a variety.

smørrebrød *noun* E20 **Danish** (from *smør* butter + *brød* bread: cf. preceding). In Denmark: an open sandwich; food consisting of open sandwiches.

smorzando *adverb, adjective, & noun* E19 **Italian** (present participle of *smorzare* to extinguish). *Music* **A** *adverb & adjective* E19 (A direction:) dying away. **B** *noun* E19 plural **smorzandos**, **smorzandi**. A smorzando passage.

snobisme *noun* E20 **French**. Snobbishness.

snoek *noun* plural same L18 **Dutch** (= pike). A long slender food fish of southern oceans, a barracouta. Chiefly *South African*.

soba *noun* (treated as *singular* or *plural*) L19 **Japanese**. Japanese noodles made from buckwheat flour.

sobornost *noun* M20 **Russian** (*sobornost'* conciliarism, catholicity). *Theology* A unity of people in a loving fellowship in which each member retains freedom and integrity without excessive individualism.

sobriquet *noun* M17 **French** (of unknown origin). An epithet, a nickname.

■ The older French form SOUBRIQUET is also found in English.

socle *noun* E18 **French** (from Italian *zoccolo* wooden shoe, socle, representing Latin *socculus* diminutive of *soccus* sock). A low plinth serving as a pedestal for a statue, column, vase, etc.

sogo shosha *noun phrase* plural same, **sogo shoshas** M20 **Japanese** (*sōgō shōsha*, from *sōgō* comprehensive + SHOSHA). A very large Japanese company that trades internationally in a wide range of goods and services.

soi-disant *adjective* (also **soi disant**) M18 **French** (from *soi* oneself + *disant* present participle of *dire* to say). **1** M18 Of a person: self-styled, would-be. **2** M19 Of a thing: so-called, pretended.

soigné *adjective* (feminine **soignée**) E19 **French** (past participial adjective of *soigner* to care for, from *soin* care). Meticulously dressed, prepared, or arranged; well-groomed.

soigneur *noun* L20 **French** (from *soigner* to care for). In cycling, a person who gives training, massage, and other assistance to a team.

soirée *noun* L18 **French** (from *soir* evening). An evening party, gathering, or social meeting, especially in a private house.

soirée dansante *noun phrase* plural **soirées dansantes** M19 **French** (from as SOIRÉE + *dansante* feminine of present participle of *danser* to dance). An evening party with dancing.

soirée musicale *noun phrase* plural **soirées musicales** M19 **French** (from as SOIRÉE + MUSICALE). An evening party to perform or listen to music.

soit *interjection* L19 **French** (3rd person singular present subjunctive of *être* be). So be it.

soixante-neuf *noun* L19 **French** (= sixty-nine, after the position of the couple involved). Sexual activity between two people involving mutual oral stimulation of the genitals; a position enabling this.

sokaiya *noun* plural same L20 **Japanese** (from *sōkai* general meeting + *-ya* dealer). A holder of shares in a company who tries to extort money from it by threatening to cause trouble for executives at a general meeting of the shareholders.

sola *adverb & adjective* M18 **Latin** (feminine of *solus* alone, or Italian, feminine of *solo* alone). **1** *adverb & predicate adjective* M18 Of a woman:

solitary; alone. **2** *adjective* M18 *Commerce* Of a bill of exchange: single (as opposed to one of a set).

solarium *noun* plural **solaria**, **solariums** M19 **Latin** (from *sol* sun). **1** M19 A sundial. Now *rare* or *obsolete*. **2a** A room, etc, usually with large areas of glass designed to maximize exposure to the sun's rays. **2b** M20 A room equipped with sun lamps for inducing an artificial suntan; an establishment providing sun lamps.

solatium *noun* plural **solatia** E19 **Latin**. A sum of money or other compensation given to a person to make up for loss, inconvenience, injured feelings, etc.; *specifically* in *Law*, such an amount awarded to a litigant over and above the actual loss.

sola topi see under TOPI.

solera *noun* **M19 Spanish** (literally, 'crossbeam, stone base' from *suelo* ground, floor, dregs, from Latin *solum* soil). **1** M19 A blend of sherry or Malaga wine produced by the Spanish solera system (see sense 3 below). Also *solera wine*. **2** M19 A wine cask, usually with a capacity of four hogsheads; a set of such casks arranged in tiers so as to produce wine by the solera system. **3** M20 (*solera system*) A method of producing wine, especially sherry and Madeira, whereby small amounts of younger wines stored in an upper tier of casks are systematically blended with the more mature wine in the casks below.

solfatara *noun* (also earlier **solfaterra**) **L18 Italian** (originally, a sulferous volcano near Naples, from Italian *solfo* sulfer. *Geology* A fumarole that emits sulferous gases, encrusting the edge with sulfer, etc. Cf. SOUFRIÈRE.

solfège *noun* **E20 French**. *Music* SOLFEGGIO. Also (*generally*), rudimentary musical instruction, especially using textless exercises for the voice.

solfeggio *noun* plural **solfeggi**, **solfeggios** **L18 Italian** (from *sol-fa* sol-fa). *Music* An exercise for the voice (formerly also for a musical instrument), using the sol-fa syllables. Also, solmization.

solidus *noun* plural **solidi** **ME Latin** (*solidus* solid used as noun; in branch I from Latin *solidus (nummus)* a gold coin). **I 1** ME *History* A gold coin of the later Roman Empire, originally worth about 25 denarii. Formerly also, in medieval England, a shilling. **2** L19 An oblique stroke formerly written to separate shillings from pence, and now used in writing fractions, to separate figures and letters, or to denote alternatives or ratios. Cf. VIRGULE sense 1. **II 3** E20 A line or surface in a binary or ternary phase diagram respectively, or a temperature (corresponding to a point on the line or surface), below which a mixture is entirely solid and above which it consists of solid and liquid in equilibrium.

solitaire *noun* **E18 French** (from Latin *solitarius* solitary). **1** E18 A person who lives in solitude; a recluse. **2** E18 (A ring with) a diamond or other gem set by itself. **3** M18 A card or board game for one player. **4** M18 *History* A man's loose necktie of black silk or broad ribbon. **5** L18 Either of two extinct flightless birds related to the dodo.

solod *noun* (also **soloth**) plural **solodi**, **soloti**, **solods** **E20 Russian** (*solod'* from *sol'* salt). *Soil Science* A type of soil derived from a SOLONETZ by leaching of saline or alkaline constituents, occurring in arid regions.

solonchak *noun* **E20 Russian** (= salt marsh, salt lake, from *sol'* salt). *Soil Science* A type of salty alkaline soil that has little or no structure, is typically pale in color, and occurs in poorly drained regions.

solonetz *noun* **E20 Russian** (*solonets* salt marsh, salt lake, from *sol'* salt). *Soil Science* A type of alkaline soil that is rich in carbonates, has a thin friable surface layer, and occurs in better-drained areas than a SOLONCHAK.

solus *adverb & adjective* **L16 Latin** (cf. SOLA). **1** *adverb & predicate adjective* L16 Of a male (occasionally a female) person: alone, by oneself. Frequently as a stage direction. **2** *adjective* **a** M20

Of an advertisement: standing alone on a page, etc.; dealing with one item only. Also, pertaining to such an advertisement. **b** M20 *Commerce* Of a gas station, etc.: selling the products of one company only. Also, of or pertaining to such an arrangement.

solyanka *noun* M20 **Russian**. A soup made of vegetables and meat or fish.

sol y sombra *noun* M20 **Spanish** (literally, 'sun and shade'). A drink of brandy mixed with anisette or gin.

soma *noun* L18 **Sanskrit**. A plant the juice of which was used in India to prepare an intoxicating liquor; the liquor itself, used in Vedic ritual. Cf. HOM.

■ In his novel *Brave New World* (1932), Aldous Huxley gave the name *soma* to the narcotic drug distributed by the government to keep people happy and acquiescent.

sombrero *noun* plural **sombreros** L16 **Spanish** (from *sombra* shade). **1** L16–E18 An oriental umbrella or parasol. **2** L18 A broad-brimmed hat of felt or other soft material, of a type common in Mexico and the southwestern United States.

sommelier *noun* E19 **French**. A wine waiter.

sommité *noun* M19 **French** (= summit, top, tip). A person of great eminence or influence.

son *noun* M20 **Spanish** (= sound). A slow Cuban dance and song in 2/4 time.

sonata *noun* L17 **Italian** (feminine past participle of *sonare* to sound). A musical composition for one or two instruments (one usually being the piano), usually in several movements with one (especially the first) or more in sonata form.

■ Varieties of *sonata* popular in the seventeenth and eighteenth centuries were the *sonata da camera* (literally, 'chamber sonata'), for one or more solo instruments and continuo and usually consisting of a suite of dance movements, and the *sonata da chiesa* (literally, 'church sonata'), likewise for one or more solo instruments and continuo, but usually consisting of four alternately slow and fast movements. Both phrases were introduced into English somewhat later (E19).

sonatina *noun* M18 **Italian** (diminutive of SONATA). A short or simple sonata.

sondage *noun* plural **sondages** M20 **French** (= sounding, borehole). *Archaeology* A trench dug to investigate the stratigraphy of a site.

sonde *noun* E20 **French** (= sounding line, sounding). **1** E20 A radiosonde or similar device that is sent aloft to transmit or record information on conditions in the atmosphere. Originally only in combination with specifying word, as *ballon-sonde*, etc. **2** M20 An instrument probe for transmitting information about its surroundings underground or under water.

son et lumière *noun phrase* plural **son et lumières** M20 **French** (literally, 'sound and light'). **1** M20 An entertainment using recorded sound and lighting effects, usually presented at night at a historic building or other site to give a dramatic narrative of its history. **2** M20 *figurative* Writing or behavior resembling a son et lumière presentation, especially in its dramatic qualities.

sons bouchés *noun plural* E20 **French** (literally, 'blocked sounds'). In horn-playing, notes stopped by the insertion of the hand into the bell of the instrument; a direction indicating this.

sopaipilla *noun* plural **sopaipillas** M20 **American Spanish** (diminutive of Spanish *sopaipa* a kind of sweet fritter). Especially in New Mexico, a deep-fried usually square pastry eaten with honey or sugar or as a bread.

sopra bianco *noun phrase* M19 **Italian** (elliptical for BIANCO SOPRA BIANCO). Bianco sopra bianco.

soprani see SOPRANO.

sopranino *noun & adjective* plural **sopraninos** E20 **Italian** (diminutive of

SOPRANO). (Designating) an instrument (usually wind) of higher pitch than a soprano instrument.

soprano *noun & adjective* **M18 Italian** (from *sopra* above, from Latin *supra*). **A** *noun* plural **sopranos**, **soprani**. **1** M18 The highest singing voice; the quality or range of this voice. **b** E19 A part for or sung by such a voice. **2** M18 A female or boy singer having such a voice; a person singing a soprano part. **b** L19 (The player of) an instrument of a high pitch, *specifically* of the highest pitch in a family. **B** *attributive* or as *adjective* M18 Of, pertaining to, or designating the highest singing voice or instrumental pitch.

sorbet *noun* **L16 French** (from Italian *sorbetto* from as SHERBET). Originally, an Eastern sherbet. Now usually, a frozen confection of water, sugar, and usually fruit flavoring.

sorbetière *noun* **M20 French** (from as SORBET). A domestic ice cream–making machine, in which the mixture is stirred as it is being frozen.

sordino *noun* plural **sordini** (also **sordine**) **L16 Italian** (from *sordo*, from Latin *surdus* deaf, mute). A mute for a wind or bowed instrument; a damper for a piano. Cf. CON SORDINO.

sortes *noun plural* also treated as *singular* **L16 Latin** (plural of *sors* lot, chance). Divination, or the seeking of guidance, by chance selection of a passage in a book.

■ The authorities traditionally consulted in this way are Virgil (in full *sortes Virgilianae*), Homer (in full *sortes Homericae*), and the Bible (in full *sortes Biblicae*).

sosatie *noun* **M19 Afrikaans** (ultimately from Malay *sesate*; cf. SATAY). In South Africa: marinated spiced meat grilled on a skewer.

soshi *noun* plural same **L19 Japanese** (*sōshi*, literally, 'strong man'). A mercenary political agitator.

sostenuto *adverb, adjective, & noun* **E18 Italian** (past participle of *sostenere* to sustain). *Music* **A** *adverb & adjective* E18 (A direction:) in a sustained or prolonged manner. **B** *noun* M18 plural **sostenutos**. A passage (to be) played in a sustained or prolonged manner. Also, a sustained sound or note.

sottise *noun* **L17 French** (from *sot* fool, from medieval Latin *sottus*). A foolish remark or action.

sottisier *noun* **E20 French** (from as SOTTISE). A collection or (especially) a written list of *sottises*.

sottoportico *noun* plural **sottoportichi**, **sottoporticos** (also **sottoportego**, plural **sottoportighi**, **sottoportigos**) **E20 Italian** (from *sotto* under + PORTICO). *Architecture* The passage formed by a portico.

sotto voce *adverb & adjective phrase* **M18 Italian** (*sotto* under + *voce* voice). **A** *adverb* M18 In an undertone or aside. **B** *adjective* E19 Uttered in an undertone; *transferred* muted, understated.

sou *noun* **L15 French** (singular form deduced from *sous*, *soux* plural of Old French *sout*, from Latin *solidus* (sc. *nummus* coin) noun use of *solidus* solid). *History* A French coin, formerly a twentieth of a livre, later a five-centime piece.

■ In English mainly used in one or other form of the colloquial expression *haven't a sou*, i.e., 'have absolutely no money at all'. Cf. SOU MARKEE.

Soubise *noun* **L18 French** (Charles de Rohan *Soubise* (1715–87), French general and courtier). **1** A kind of cravat. Only in L18. **2** E19 A white onion sauce. Also *sauce Soubise*.

soubresaut *noun* **M19 French**. **1** M19 A jumping motion seen in some liquids when boiling. Now *rare* or *obsolete*. **2** E20 *Ballet* A straight-legged jump from both feet with the toes pointed and feet together, one behind the other.

soubrette *noun* **M18 French** (from modern Provençal *soubreto* feminine of *soubret* coy, from *soubra* (Provençal *sobrar*) from Latin *superare* to be above). **1** M18 A maidservant or lady's maid as a character in a play or opera, *especially* one of a pert or coquettish character; an actress or singer playing the role of a pert or coquettish female in any light entertainment. **2** E19 A lady's maid; a maidservant.

soubriquet *noun* **E19 French** (older variant of *sobriquet*). A nickname, a SOBRIQUET.

souchong *noun* **M18 Chinese** ((Cantonese) *siú chúng* small sort). A fine black variety of China tea.

soucouyant *noun West Indies* (also **soucriant** and other variants) **M20 West Indian creole** (probably related to Fulah *sukunyadyo* sorcerer, witch). In eastern Caribbean folklore, a malignant witch believed to shed her skin by night and suck the blood of her victims.

soufflé *noun & adjective* **E19 French** (past participle of *souffler* from Latin *sufflare*, from *sub* under + *flare* to blow). **A** *noun* E19 A light spongy dish made by mixing egg yolks and other ingredients with stiffly beaten egg whites, usually baked in an oven until puffy. **B** *adjective* L19 Of ceramic ware: having liquid color applied by means of blowing.

souffrante *adjective* **E19 French** (feminine singular present participial adjective of *souffrir* to suffer). Of a woman: delicate; prone to illness, anxiety, or depression.

souffre-douleur *noun* **M19 French** (literally, 'to suffer sorrow'). A person who is in a subservient position and must listen to or share another's troubles; *specifically* a woman who acts as a paid companion to an older woman.

soufrière *noun* **M19 French** (from *soufre* sulfer. A SOLFATARA.

souk *noun* (also **suk**, **sukh**, **suq**) **E19 Arabic** (*sūḳ* market, probably through French *souk*). An Arab market or marketplace, a bazaar.

soukous *noun* **L20 African** (from French *secouer* to shake). Zairean popular dance music.

sou markee *noun* **M17 French** (*sou marqué*, literally, 'marked sou'). A small eighteenth-century French coin issued for the colonies and circulating especially in the West Indies and North America (*historical*); *generally* something of little value.

soupçon *noun* **M18 French** (from Old French *sous(s)peçon*, from medieval Latin *suspectio(n-)). A suspicion, a suggestion; a very small quantity, a trace.*

soupe *noun* **M18 French**. Soup, especially in French cooking.

■ Chiefly in phrases designating particular kinds of soup, as *soupe à l'oignon* onion soup.

soupirant *noun* **M19 French** (present participle of *soupirer* to sigh). A male admirer, a suitor.

souple *noun* **L19 French**. A fabric made of partially degummed silk. More fully *souple silk*.

sous- *prefix* **ME Old and Modern French** (*sous*, from Latin *subtus* under). Under-, sub-.

■ Used in words adopted from French such as *sous-chef*, *sous-lieutenant*, etc.

sous-entendu *noun* **M19 French**. Something implied or understood but not expressed.

sous vide *adjective & adverb phrase* **L20 French** (from *sous* under + *vide* vacuum). Of food: (prepared) by partial cooking followed by vacuum-sealing and chilling.

soutache *noun* **M19 French** (from Hungarian *sujtás*). A narrow flat ornamental braid used for decorative trimming. More fully *soutache braid*. Also called *Russia braid*.

soutane *noun* **M19 French** (from Italian *sottana*, from *sotto* from Latin *subtus* under). *Roman Catholic Church* A cassock, *especially* a cassock with scarf and cincture worn by a priest.

souteneur *noun* **E20 French** (= protector, from *soutenir* to sustain). A pimp.

soutenu *adjective & noun* M20 **French** (past participle of *soutenir* to sustain). *Ballet* **A** *adjective* M20 Of a movement: sustained, performed slowly. **B** *noun* M20. A sustained or slow movement; *especially* a complete turn on point or half point.

souterrain *noun* M18 **French** (from *sous* under + *terre* earth, after Latin *subterraneus*). Chiefly *Archaeology* An underground chamber or passage.

souvenir *noun* L18 **French** (noun use of verb = to remember, from Latin *subvenire* to come into the mind, from *sub-* + *venire* to come). **1** L18 A remembrance, a memory. Now *rare*. **2** L18 A token of remembrance; *especially* an article given or purchased as a reminder *of* a particular person, place, or event; a keepsake. **b** E19 *specifically* A usually illustrated publication designed to be purchased as a gift. **c** E20 In World War I, a bullet, a shell. *Military slang.*

souvlaki *noun* plural **souvlakia** M20 **Modern Greek** (*soublaki* from *soubla* skewer). A Greek dish of small pieces of meat grilled on a skewer.

sovkhoz *noun* plural same, **sovkhozes**, **sovkhozy** E20 **Russian** (from *sov(etskoe khoz(yaĭstvo* Soviet farm). A state-owned farm in countries of the former USSR.

soy *noun* (also **soya**) L17 **Dutch** (*soja* from Japanese *shōyu*; cf. SHOYU). Soy sauce.

■ Also used as short for *soybean*, the leguminous plant grown as a vegetable or for its protein-rich seeds that yield an edible oil.

spaghetti *noun* M19 **Italian** (plural of diminutive of *spago* string). **1** M19 Pasta in the form of long solid threads, between MACARONI and VERMICELLI in thickness. **2** M20 Complex roadways forming a multilevel junction, especially on a highway. In full *spaghetti junction. British colloquial.*

spaghettini *noun* M20 **Italian** (diminutive of preceding). Pasta in the form of strings of thin spaghetti.

Spätlese *noun* plural **Spätlesen**, **Spätleses** M20 **German** (from *spät* late + *Lese* picking, vintage). A white wine made (especially in Germany) from grapes picked later than the general harvest.

Spätzle *noun plural* L19 **German** ((dialect) literally, 'little sparrows'). Noodles of a type made in southern Germany.

spécialité *noun* (also **specialité**) M19 **French** (Old French *especialité* from late Latin *specialitas*, from Latin *specialis* special, particular). **1** M19 An article or service specially characteristic of, dealt in, or produced by, a particular place, firm, etc. **2** M19 An unusual or distinctive thing.

■ *Speciality* in the sense of 'the quality of being special, distinctive, or limited in some respect' was adopted from Old French in the late medieval period and quickly Anglicized, and the Anglicized version of *spécialité* (and of closely related *(e)specialté*) is used in most general senses. In sense 1, *spécialité* is often used in the phrase *spécialité de la maison* 'special(i)ty of the house', to mean a dish on which a particular restaurant prides itself.

specie *noun* E17 **Latin** (ablative singular of *species* kind, originally (M16) in phrase *in specie* in the real, precise, or actual form). Coin money as opposed to paper money. Frequently *attributive.*

spectrum *noun* plural **spectra**, **spectrums** E17 **Latin** (= image of a thing, apparition). **1** E17 An apparition, a specter. *archaic.* **2** L17 An image. *rare.* **3 a** L17 The colored band into which a beam of light is split by means of a prism or diffraction grating. **b** L19 (Any part of) the entire range of wavelengths of electromagnetic radiation. **c** L19 An actual or notional arrangement of the component parts of any phenomenon according to frequency, energy, mass, etc. **d** M20 *figurative* The entire or a wide range of something arranged by degree, quality, etc.

speculum *noun* plural **specula**, **speculums** LME **Latin** (from base of *specere* to look, see). **1** LME *Medicine* An instrument, usually of metal, used to dilate an orifice or canal in the body to allow inspection. **2** M17 Chiefly *Science* A mirror or reflector of glass or metal. **3** E19 *Ornithology* A bright patch of plumage on the wings of certain birds. **4** E20 An alloy of copper and tin in a ratio of around 2:1, formerly used to make mirrors for scientific instruments. Also more fully *speculum metal.*

spermaceti *noun* L15 **Medieval Latin** (from late Latin *sperma* (from Greek = sperm, seed, from base of *speirein* to sow) + *ceti* genitive of *cetus*, Greek *kētos* whale (from its appearance or the belief that it represents whale-spawn)). A soft white waxy substance used in the manufacture of candles, ointments, etc., found in the sperm whale and some other cetaceans, chiefly in a rounded organ in the head that focuses acoustic signals and aids control of buoyancy.

sphendone *noun* M19 **Greek** (*sphendonē*). *Archaeology* **1** M19 A headband or fillet shaped like a form of sling, worn by women in ancient Greece. **2** M19 An area composed of elongated sloping sides with a rounded end.

sphincter *noun* L16 **Latin** (from Greek *sphigktēr* band, contractile muscle, from *sphiggein* to draw tight). *Anatomy* A contractile muscular ring by which an orifice of the body is normally kept closed.

■ Often with modern Latin specifying word, as *sphincter ani* 'sphincter of the anus'.

sphinx *noun* plural **sphinxes**, **sphinges** LME **Latin** (from Greek *Sphigx*, *Sphigg-*, apparently from *sphiggein* to draw tight). **1** LME *Greek Mythology* (*Sphinx*) A hybrid monster, usually described as having a woman's head and a (winged) lion's body, that plagued the Greek city of Thebes until Oedipus solved its riddle. Also, any monster resembling this. **b** E17 *figurative* An inscrutable or enigmatic person or thing; a mystery. **2** L16 Any of several ancient Greek or (especially) Egyptian stone figures of a creature with a human or animal head and a lion's body. **3** M18 A moth of the genus *Sphinx*, or of the family Sphingidae, so called from the typical attitude of the caterpillar; a hawkmoth. Also *sphinx moth.*

spianato *adjective & adverb* L19 **Italian**. *Music* (Played) in a smooth, even, level-toned style.

spiccato *adjective, adverb, & noun* E18 **Italian** (= detailed, distinct). *Music* **A** *adjective & adverb* E18 (Played) in a staccato style performed by bouncing the bow on the strings of a violin, etc. **B** *noun* L19 Spiccato playing; a passage played in this style.

Spielraum *noun* plural **Spielräume** E20 **German** (from *Spiel* game, play + *Raum* room). *Philosophy* The range of possibilities within which the probability of an outcome or likelihood of a hypothesis is to be assessed.

spinto *noun & adjective* plural of noun **spintos** M20 **Italian** (past participle of *spingere* to push). *Music* (Designating) a lyric soprano or tenor voice of powerful dramatic quality; (designating) a singer with such a voice.

spirituel *adjective* (also **spirituelle**) L17 **French**. Highly refined and lively; witty.

spiritus rector *noun phrase* E20 **Latin**. A ruling or directing spirit.

sporran *noun* M18 **Gaelic** (*sporan* = Irish *sparán* purse, Middle Irish *sboran* from Latin *bursa* purse). A pouch or large purse usually made of leather or sealskin covered with fur and with ornamental tassels, etc., worn by a Scottish Highlander in front of the kilt.

sportif *adjective* M20 **French**. Sportive; active or interested in athletic sports; (of a garment) suitable for sports or informal wear.

Sprechgesang *noun* E20 **German** (literally, 'speech song'). *Music* A style of dramatic vocalization intermediate between speech and song.

Sprechstimme *noun* E20 **German** (literally, 'speech voice'). *Music* SPRECHGESANG.

sprezzatura *noun* M20 **Italian.** Ease of manner, studied carelessness, nonchalance, especially in art or literature.

springar *noun* M20 **Norwegian.** (A piece of music for) a Norwegian country dance in 3/4 time.

springbok *noun* (in sense 2 also **Springbok**, in sense 1 also Anglicized as **springbuck**) L18 **Afrikaans** (from Dutch *springen* to spring + *bok* goat, antelope). **1** L18 A common and gregarious southern African gazelle, characterized by the habit of leaping (pronking) when excited or disturbed. **2** E20 A South African.

▪ *Springboks* (often abbreviated to *Boks*) was formerly the name given to South African national sporting (especially rugby) teams.

spritzer *noun* M20 **German** (= a splash). A mixture of (usually white) wine and soda water; a drink or glass of this.

spritzig *adjective & noun* M20 **German** (from *spritzen* to squirt, splash). **A** *adjective* M20 Of wine: sparkling. **B** *noun* M20 Sparkle in wine.

spruit *noun* M19 **Dutch** (= sprout). In South Africa: a small watercourse that is usually dry except in the rainy season.

spumante *noun* E20 **Italian** (= sparkling). A sparkling white wine, especially from the Italian province of Asti (in full *Asti spumante*).

spumoni *noun* E20 **Italian** (*spumone*, from *spuma* foam). A rich dessert consisting of layered ice cream with candied fruits, nuts, and sometimes brandy.

spurlos *adjective* E20 **German** (= (sunk) without trace). (Sunk) without trace. Chiefly *figurative*, lost from sight, ruined. In full *spurlos versenkt*.

▪ The phrase became widely used in English as the result of the publication of a notorious secret telegram sent in May 1917 by the German minister in Buenos Aires, Count Luxburg, to Berlin, in which he recommended that Argentine shipping should either be turned back or sunk without trace.

sputa plural of SPUTUM.

sputnik *noun* (also **Sputnik**) M20 **Russian** (literally, 'traveling companion', from *s* with + *put'* way, journey + noun suffix *-nik* person connected with (something)). **1** M20 An unmanned artificial earth satellite, especially a Russian one; *specifically* each of a series of such satellites launched by the Soviet Union between 1957 and 1961. **2** M20 *Bridge* A take-out double of a suit overcall of one's partner's opening bid. In full *Sputnik double*.

sputum *noun* plural **sputa** L17 **Latin** (noun use of neuter past participle of *spuere* to spit). *Medicine* Thick mucus coughed up from the respiratory tract especially in certain diseases of the lungs, chest, or throat; a mass or quantity of this.

staccato *adjective, adverb, noun, & verb* E18 **Italian** (past participle of *staccare* aphetic from *distaccare* to detach). **A** *adjective & adverb* E18 With each note or sound sharply separated or detached from the next, with a clipped style. Opposed to LEGATO. **B** *noun* L18 A succession of disconnected notes or sounds; a staccato passage in music, etc.; staccato delivery, playing, or speech. **C** *transitive verb* E19 Play or utter in a staccato manner.

stadium *noun* plural **stadiums**; **stadia** LME **Latin** (from Greek *stadion*). **I 1** LME *Classical Antiquities* A unit of length, usually equal to 600 Greek or Roman feet, or one-eighth of a Roman mile (*c.*607 ft.). **2** E17 *Classical Antiquities* A course (originally a stadium in length) for footracing or chariot racing; a race on such a course. **3** M19 An athletic or sports field or arena with tiered seats or terraces for spectators. **II 4** M17 A stage of a process, disease, etc. **b** L19 *Zoology* An interval between molts in the growth of an insect, crustacean, etc. **5** M19 Any of various instruments for measuring distance; a levelling rod.

Stadthaus *noun* plural **Stadthauser** M19 **German** (from *Stadt* town + *Haus* house). A town hall in a German-speaking country.

■ The partially Anglicized form *stadthouse* derives either from *stadthaus* or from Dutch *stadhuis* and is used of a town hall in a German-speaking or (especially) a Dutch-speaking country.

staffage *noun* L19 **German** (pseudo-French form from *staffieren* to fit out, decorate, perhaps from Old French *estoffer*, from *estoffe* stuff). Accessory items in a painting, especially figures or animals in a landscape picture.

stagione *noun* plural **stagioni** M20 **Italian** (= season). An opera or ballet season, *especially* an opera season in which one work is performed on several occasions in a limited period with no change of cast.

stanza *noun* plural **stanzas**, (in sense 2 also) **stanze** L16 **Italian** (= standing, stopping place, room, strophe, from Proto-Romance, from Latin *stant-* present participial stem of *stare* to stand). **1** L16 A group of (usually between four and twelve) lines of verse occurring as the basic metrical unit of a song or poem consisting of a series of such groups; a verse. **2** M17 In Italy: an apartment, a chamber, a room; *specifically* a room in the Vatican (usually in *plural*). **3** M20 A half or other session of a game or sporting contest.

starets *noun* (also **startz**) plural **startsy**, **startzy**, E20 **Russian** (= (venerable) old man, elder). A spiritual leader or counselor in the Russian Orthodox church.

starover *noun* plural **starovery**, **starovers** E19 **Russian**. *Ecclesiastical History* An Old Believer, a RASKOLNIK.

startsy, **startz** see STARETS.

stasis *noun* plural **stases** M18 **Modern Latin** (from Greek, literally, 'standing, stoppage; party, faction', from *sta-* base of *histanai* to stand). **1** M18 *Medicine* A stagnation or stoppage of flow due usually to obstruction, as of the blood or lymph, or of the intestinal contents. **2** E20 *generally* Inactivity; stagnation; a state of equilibrium. **3** M20 *Psychoanalysis* The presence of high energy or excitement in the libido caused especially by repression and thought to produce neurosis. **4** M20 Party faction, civil strife.

status *noun* plural **statuses**, (*rare*) same L17 **Latin** (from *stat-* past participial stem of *stare* to stand). **1** *Medicine* **a** The crisis of a disease. *rare*. Only in L17. **b** L19 A state, a condition. Only with modern Latin specifying word (e.g., *status epilepticus* a condition in which epileptic fits follow one another without pause). **2** L18 Chiefly *Law* A person's standing or position such as determines his or her legal rights or limitations; condition in respect of marriage or celibacy, minority or majority, etc. **3** E19 Position or standing in society; rank, profession; relative importance; *specifically* (a) superior social, etc., position. Also *social status*. **4** M19 Condition or position of a thing, especially with regard to importance.

status quo *noun phrase* M19 **Latin** (= the state in which). The existing state of affairs.

status quo ante *noun phrase* L19 **Latin** (= the state in which before). The previously existing state of affairs.

stela *noun* plural **stelae** L18 **Latin** (from as STELE). *Antiquities* An upright slab or pillar, usually bearing a commemorative inscription or sculptured design and often serving as a gravestone.

stele *noun* plural **steles**, (especially in sense 1) **stelae** E19 **Greek** (*stēlē* standing block; cf. STELA). **1** E19 *Antiquities* A stela. Also *loosely*, any prepared surface on the face of a building, rock, etc., bearing an inscription. **2** L19 *Botany* The central core of the stem and root of a vascular plant.

stelline *noun plural* (also **stellini**) M20 **Italian** (from *stellina* diminutive of *stella* star). Small star-shaped pieces of pasta.

stelling *noun* M19 **Dutch** (from *stellen* to place). In Guyana and the Caribbean: a wooden pier or landing stage.

stemma *noun* plural **stemmata** M17 **Latin** (from Greek (= garland), from *stephein* to crown). **1a** M17 A recorded genealogy of a family, a family tree; a pedigree. **b** M20 A diagram representing a reconstruction of the interrelationships between surviving witnesses in the (especially manuscript) tradition of a text. **2** E19 *Zoology* In arthropods, a simple eye, an ocellus.

steppe *noun* L17 **Russian** (*step'*). Any of the vast level grassy usually treeless plains of Southeast Europe and Siberia. Also, any similar plain elsewhere.

stet *noun & verb* M18 **Latin** (3rd person singular present subjunctive of *stare* = let it stand). **A** *noun* M18 A direction in the margin of a proof sheet, etc., indicating that a correction or deletion should be ignored and that the original matter is to be retained. **B** *transitive verb* L19 (inflected *-tt*) Cancel the correction or deletion of; write 'stet' against (an accidental deletion, miscorrection, etc.).

stiacciato *noun* (also **schiacciato**) M19 **Italian** (*schiacciato, stiacciato* past participle of *schiacciare, stiacciare* to flatten). *Sculpture* Very low relief. Also more fully *stiacciato-relievo, relievo stiacciato*.

stifado *noun* plural **stifados** M20 **Modern Greek** (*stiphado* probably from Italian *stufato*). A Greek dish of meat stewed with onions and sometimes tomatoes.

stigma *noun* plural **stigmas, stigmata** L16 **Latin** (from Greek *stigma, stigmat-*, from base of *stizein* to prick). **1** L16 A mark made on the skin by pricking, cutting, or (especially) branding, as a sign of disgrace or subjection. **b** M17 (in *plural*) Marks resembling the wounds on Jesus' crucified body, said to have appeared on the bodies of certain saints, etc. **2a** E17 A mark or sign of disgrace or discredit, regarded as impressed on or carried by a person or thing. **b** M19 A visible or apparent characteristic indicative of some (especially undesirable or discreditable) quality, action, or circumstance (followed by *of*); *Medicine* a visible sign *of* a disease or condition. **3** M18 *Zoology* **a** A small external opening or pore. **b** E19 A natural spot or mark. **4** M18 *Botany* That part of the pistil in flowering plants that receives the pollen in impregnation.

stile antico *noun phrase* M20 **Italian** (= old style). *Music* The strict contrapuntal style of the sixteenth century, especially as exemplified in the works of Palestrina.

stile concitato *noun phrase* E20 **Italian** (= excited style). *Music* A baroque style developed by Monteverdi, emphasizing dramatic expression and excitement.

stile rappresentativo *noun phrase* L19 **Italian** (= representative style). *Music* The vocal style of recitative used by Italian musicians of the early seventeenth century.

stiletto *noun* E17 **Italian** (diminutive of *stilo* dagger, ultimately from Latin *stilus* stylus). **A** *noun* plural **stiletto(e)s**. **1** E17 A short dagger with a thick blade. **2** E19 A small pointed instrument for making eyelet holes. **3** M20 A very high tapering heel on a woman's shoe; a shoe with such a heel. In full *stiletto heel*.

Stimmung *noun* E20 **German**. Mood, spirit, atmosphere, feeling.

stimulus *noun* plural **stimuli** L17 **Latin** (= goad, spur, incentive, probably from base also of *stilus* stylus). **1** L17 A thing that provokes, increases, or quickens bodily activity. **b** L18 *generally* An agency or influence that rouses or spurs something or someone to action or quickens an activity or process; a spur, an incentive (followed by *to* an action, etc.) **c** L19 *Psychology* Any change or event that excites a nerve impulse and gives rise to a response or reaction. **2** L17 The effect or property of producing such a reaction; stimulation; an instance of this.

stoa *noun* plural **stoas**, **stoai** E17 **Greek**. **1** E17 (*the Stoa*) The great hall in ancient Athens in which the philosopher Zeno lectured; the Stoic school of philosophy. **2** L18 A portico, a roofed colonnade.

■ The followers of Zeno (335–263 BC) were accordingly called Stoics.

stoep *noun* **L18 Afrikaans** (from Dutch, related to *step*, from West Germanic; cf. STOOP). In South Africa: a raised platform or veranda running along the front and sometimes around the sides of a house.

stollen *noun* **E20 German**. A rich fruit loaf, often with nuts added.

stoop *noun* **M18 Dutch** (cf. STOEP). A small raised platform at the entrance door of a house; a set of steps approaching this; a small porch or veranda.

stoss *adjective* **L19 German** (= thrust, push). *Geology* Designating the side of an object that faces a flow of ice or water.

strabismus *noun* **L17 Modern Latin** (from Greek *strabismos*, from *strabizein* to squint, from *strabos* squinting). **1** L17 *Medicine* A disorder of the eye muscles resulting in an inability to direct the gaze of both eyes to the same object simultaneously; squinting, a squint. **2** M19 *figurative* Perversity of intellectual perception.

stracchino *noun* **M19 Italian**. A variety of soft cheese made in the north of Italy. In full *stracchino cheese*.

stracciatella *noun* **M20 Italian**. An Italian soup made with stock, eggs, and cheese.

strapontin *noun* **E20 French**. A tip-up seat, usually additional to the ordinary seating in a theater, taxi, etc., especially in France.

strata plural of STRATUM.

strath *noun* **M16 Gaelic** (*Scottish s(t)rath* = Old Irish *srath* (modern *sraith*)). A broad river valley bounded by hills or high ground. Formerly also, a stretch of flat land by the waterside.

stratum *noun* plural **strata** **L16 Modern Latin** (from Latin *stratum*, literally, 'something spread or laid down', neuter past participle of *sternere* to lay down, throw down). **1** L16 *generally* A quantity of a substance or material spread over a nearly horizontal surface to a more or less uniform thickness; *especially* each of two or more parallel layers or coats successively superposed one upon another. **2** L17 A bed of sedimentary rock, usually consisting of a series of layers of the same kind. **3** M18 *Anatomy* and *Biology* Each of a number of layers composing an animal or plant tissue or structure (frequently with modern Latin specifying word). Also *Ecology*, a layer of vegetation in a plant community. **4** L18 A region of the atmosphere, of the sea, or of a quantity of fluid, assumed for purposes of calculation to be bounded by horizontal planes. **5** E19 *figurative* **a** A portion of a body of institutions, a set of traditions, an artist's work, etc., originating from one historical period, or representing one stage of development or level of analysis. **b** M19 (Part of a population belonging to) a particular level or grade in social status, education, etc. **6** E20 *Statistics* Each of the groups into which a population is divided in the technique of stratified sampling.

strepitoso *adverb, adjective, & noun* **E19 Italian** (literally, 'noisy, loud'). *Music* **A** *adverb & adjective* E19 (A direction:) spirited(ly), boisterous(ly). **B** *noun* M20 A spirited or boisterous piece or passage.

stretta *noun* plural **strette**, **strettas** **L19 Italian** (feminine of STRETTO). *Music* A final passage played at a (gradually) faster tempo.

stretto *adverb & noun* **M18 Italian** (literally, 'narrow'). *Music* **A** *adverb* M18 (A direction:) with gradually increasing speed (especially in a final passage). **B** *noun* M19 A fugal device in which subject entries follow closely in succession.

streusel *noun* E20 **German** (from *streuen* to sprinkle). (A cake or pastry with) a crumbly topping or filling made from fat, flour, cinnamon, and sugar.

■ Chiefly North American and frequently attributive as in *streusel cake*.

stria *noun* plural **striae** M16 **Latin** (= furrow, grooving). **1** M16 *Architecture* A fillet between the flutes of a column, pilaster, etc. **2** L17 Chiefly *Science* A small groove, channel, or ridge; a narrow streak, stripe, or band of distinctive color, structure, or texture; *especially* each of two or more.

stricto sensu *adverb & adjective phrase* M20 **Latin** (= in the restricted sense). SENSU STRICTO.

striges *noun plural* M16 **Latin**. *Architecture* The fillets of a fluted column.

■ Deriving from the writings of the Roman architectural authority Vitruvius (*c.*50–26 BC), *striges* is perhaps a misreading of *striae* (see STRIA) or *strigae* 'row, strip'.

stringendo *adverb, adjective, & noun* M19 **Italian** (present participle of *stringere* to press, squeeze, bind together, from Latin *stringere* to bind). *Music* **A** *adverb & adjective* M19 (A direction:) with increasing speed and excitement. **B** *noun* M20 plural **stringendos**, **stringendi**. An increase of speed and excitement; a passage (to be) played with such an increase.

strophe *noun* plural **strophes**, **strophae** E17 **Greek** (*strophē* (whence late Latin *stropha*), literally, 'turning', from *stroph-* ablaut variant of base of *strephein* to turn). Originally, a movement from right to left in Greek choruses and dances, answered by an ANTISTROPHE; the lines of choral song recited during this movement. Also (*Prosody*), a metrically structured section of a usually Greek choral ode or lyric verse, the structure of which is repeated in an antistrophe. More widely, a group of lines forming a section of a lyric poem.

strudel *noun* L19 **German** (literally, 'eddy, whirlpool'). A confection of thin layers of flaky pastry rolled up around a usually fruit filling and baked.

Stube *noun* plural **Stuben** M20 **German** (= room). A BIERSTUBE.

stucco *noun* plural **stuccoes** L16 **Italian** (ultimately from Germanic). **1a** L16 A fine plaster, especially made from gypsum and pulverized marble, for covering walls, ceilings, etc., and making cornices and other architectural decorations. **b** M18 A coarse plaster or calcareous cement especially for covering a rough exterior surface to give the appearance of stone. **c** M19 Plaster of Paris. **2** L17 The process of ornamenting walls, ceilings, etc., with stucco; work or ornamentation produced by this process. **b** L20 A building plastered with stucco.

studiolo *noun* plural **studioli** E20 **Italian** (= small study). In Italy: a private study hung with paintings.

studium generale *noun phrase* plural **studia generalia** M19 **Latin** (*studium* zeal, application (to learning) + neuter singular of *generalis* general). *History* In the Middle Ages, a university attended by students from outside as well as within its own locality.

stupa *noun* L19 **Sanskrit** (*stūpa*). A round usually domed structure erected as a Buddhist shrine.

Sturm und Drang *noun phrase* M19 **German** (literally, 'storm and stress'). (The period of) a radical movement in German literature in the late 1770s characterized by the violent expression of emotion and the rejection of neoclassical literary norms; *transferred* (a period of) emotion, stress, or turbulence.

■ *Sturm und Drang* was the title of a 1776 play by Friedrich Maximilian Klinger (1752–1831).

stylus *noun* plural **styli**, **styluses** E18 **Latin** (erroneous spelling of Latin *stilus* writing implement (influenced by the spelling of Greek *stulos* column)). **1** E18 *Botany* A projection of the ovary bearing the stigma. Now *rare*. **2** E19 An ancient implement for incising letters on wax. **3** M19 *Zoology*

A small slender pointed process or part. **4** L19 A tracing point used to produce a written record in a chart recorder, telegraph receiver, etc. **b** L19 A hard (especially diamond or sapphire) point following a groove in a record and transmitting the recorded sound for reproduction; a similar point used to make such a groove when producing a record; a needle.

■ Senses 1–3 are also found in the English form *style*.

subbotnik *noun* plural **subbotniki, subbotniks** E20 **Russian** (from *subbota* Saturday + noun suffix *-nik* person connected with (something)). In countries of the former USSR: the practice or an act of working voluntarily on a Saturday, for the benefit of the national economy.

subgum *noun* (also **sub gum, sup gum**) E20 **Chinese** ((Cantonese) *shâp kám*, from *shâp* mixed + *kám* brocade). A Chinese dish of mixed vegetables, as water chestnuts, mushrooms, bean sprouts, etc.

subito *adverb* E18 **Italian.** *Music* (A direction:) suddenly, quickly.

sub judice *adjective phrase* E17 **Latin** (literally, 'under a judge'). *Law* Under the consideration of a judge or court and therefore prohibited from public discussion elsewhere.

sub rosa *adjective & adverb phrase* M17 **Latin** (literally, 'under the rose'). Of communication, consultation, etc.: (given, told, etc.) in secrecy or confidence.

■ The concept of the rose as a symbol of confidentiality or secrecy may have originated in Germany and is enshrined in the German phrase *unter der rose* (cf. Early Modern Dutch *onder de roose*).

sub silentio *adverb phrase* E17 **Latin** (literally, 'under silence'). In silence, without remark.

sub specie aeternitatis *adverb phrase* L19 **Latin** (literally, 'under the aspect of eternity'). Viewed in relation to the eternal; in a universal perspective.

■ In Spinoza's *Ethices* (*Posthuma Opera* (1677) V.xxix.254). The opposite of SUB SPECIE TEMPORIS.

sub specie temporis *adverb phrase* L19 **Latin** (literally 'under the aspect of time'). Viewed in relation to time rather than eternity.

substratum *noun* plural **substrata,** (*rare*) **substratums** M17 **Modern Latin** (noun use of neuter past participle of Latin *substernere*, from *sub-* under + *sternere* to lay down, throw down). **1** M17 *Metaphysics* That which is regarded as supporting attributes or accidents; the substance in which qualities inhere. **2** M17 An underlying layer or substance; the basis or foundation of a structure, condition, activity, etc. **3** M18 An underlayer of soil or earth. **4** E20 *Linguistics* Elements or features of a language identified as being relics of, or due to the influence of, an earlier extinct language.

sub verbo *adverb phrase* E20 **Latin.** SUB VOCE.

sub voce *adverb phrase* M19 **Latin.** (As a direction in a text:) under the word or heading given; SUB VERBO.

■ Abbreviated to *s.v.*

succah *noun* **succoth** L19 **Hebrew** (*sukkāh*, literally, 'hut'). Any of the booths in which a practicing Jew spends part of the feast of Tabernacles (Succoth).

succedaneum *noun* plural **succedanea, succedaneums** E17 **Modern Latin** (neuter singular of Latin *succedaneus* from *succedere* to come close after). **1** E17 A thing that takes the place of another; a substitute; *specifically* a medicine or drug substituted for another. (Followed by *for, of, to.*) **2** M–L18 A remedy, a cure.

succès d'estime *noun phrase* M19 **French** (= success of opinion or regard). A critical as opposed to a popular or commercial success.

succès de scandale *noun phrase* L19 **French** (= success of scandal). Success due to notoriety or scandalous character.

succès fou *noun phrase* L19 French (= mad success). A success marked by wild enthusiasm.

succi plural of SUCCUS.

succuba *noun* plural **succubae** L16 Late Latin (= prostitute, from *succubare* from *sub-* under + *cubare* to lie). A SUCCUBUS.

succubus *noun* plural **succubi** LME Medieval Latin (masculine form (with feminine meaning) corresponding to SUCCUBA, after INCUBUS). **1** LME A demon in female form supposed to have sexual intercourse with sleeping men. **b** E17 *generally* A demon, an evil spirit. **2** E17 A prostitute, a whore. *archaic* and *derogatory*.

succus *noun* plural **succi** L18 Latin. A juice; a fluid secretion in an animal or plant.

sucrier *noun* M19 French (from *sucre* sugar). A sugar bowl, usually made of porcelain and with a cover.

sudarium *noun* plural **sudaria** E17 Latin (from *sudor* sweat). **1** E17 A cloth for wiping the face. **2** E17 A cloth with a likeness of Christ's face on it, a veronica. **3** M19 Chiefly *Roman Antiquities* A steam or hot air bath.

sudd *noun* L19 Arabic (= obstruction, dam, from *sadda* to obstruct, block, congest). **1** L19 An area of floating vegetation that impedes navigation on the White Nile. **2** L19 *transferred* A temporary dam across a river.

suede *noun & adjective* (also **suède**) M17 French (*Suède* Sweden). **A** *noun* M17 Leather, originally especially kidskin, with the flesh side rubbed to make a velvety nap; a shoe or other article made of this. **B** *attributive or as adjective* L19 Made of suede.

■ The French phrase *gants de Suède* 'gloves of Sweden' was misunderstood as referring to the material rather than to the country of origin.

suggestio falsi *noun phrase* plural **suggestiones falsi** E19 Modern Latin (literally, 'suggestion of what is false'). A misrepresentation of the truth whereby something incorrect is implied to be true.

■ Often in contexts with the associated verbal stratagem of SUPPRESSIO VERI.

suiboku *noun* E20 Japanese (literally, 'liquid ink', from *sui* water + *boku* ink stick). A style of Japanese painting, using black ink on a white surface and characterized by bold brushwork and subtle tones.

sui generis *adjective phrase* L18 Latin. Of its own kind; peculiar, unique.

sui juris *adjective phrase* E17 Latin (literally, 'of one's own right'). *Law* **1** E17 *Roman History* Of the status of a person who was not subject to paternal authority. **2** L17 Of full age and capacity.

suite *noun* L17 French. **1** L17 A set of people in attendance; a retinue. **2** E18 A succession, a series; a set of things belonging together. **3** E18 *specifically* **a** A set of rooms in a hotel, etc., for use by one person or group of people. **b** M18 *Music* Originally, a set or series of lessons, etc. Later, a set of instrumental compositions, in dance style, to be played in succession; a set of selected pieces from an opera, ballet, etc., arranged to be played as one instrumental work. **c** E19 A set of furniture, especially a sofa and armchairs, of the same design. **d** M19 *Geology* A group of associated minerals, rocks, or fossils, especially from the same place; an associated sequence of strata, etc., that is repeated at different localities.

suk, sukh variants of SOUK.

sukiya *noun* E20 Japanese (literally, 'room of fantasy, room of refined taste'). **1** E20 A room in which the tea ceremony is held, a teahouse. **2** M20 *Architecture* A style of Japanese architecture inspired by a certain type of tea-house, characterized by functionality of design and the use of wood and other natural materials. Frequently *attributive*.

sukiyaki *noun* E20 Japanese. A Japanese dish consisting of thin slices of beef fried with vegetables in sugar, stock, and soy sauce.

sultan *noun* M16 **French** (or medieval Latin *sultanus*, from Arabic *sulṭān* power, ruler). **1** M16 The monarch or chief ruler of a Muslim country. **b** M17 An absolute ruler; a despot, a tyrant. **2** M17 A plant of the Near East grown for its sweet-scented purple, pink, white, or yellow flowers. Originally more fully *sultan's flower*; now usually *sweet sultan*. **3** M19 A small white-crested variety of domestic fowl, originally brought from Turkey.

sultana *noun* L16 **Italian** (feminine of *sultano* sultan). **1** L16 A wife or concubine of a sultan; the queen mother or any other woman of a sultan's family. **2** E18 A mistress, a concubine. **3** E18 A Turkish warship. *obsolete* except *historical*. **4** M19 Any of various gallinules, *especially* the purple gallinule. Now *rare*. **5** M19 A kind of small seedless raisin used in desserts, cakes, etc. **6** M20 The plant Busy Lizzie, *Impatiens walleriana*.

sulu *noun* M19 **Fijian**. In Fiji: a length of cotton or other light fabric wrapped about the body as a sarong; a type of sarong worn from the waist by men and full-length by women; a similar fashion garment worn by women.

sumi *noun* E20 **Japanese** (= ink, blacking). A carbon-based pigment used for painting and writing.

summa *noun & adverb* plural **summae**, **summa(e)s** LME **Latin**. **1** LME–L18 A sum total. **2** L15–E16 The quantity or number *of* something. **3** E18 A treatise, a manual; a compendium of knowledge. **4** L20 A degree SUMMA CUM LAUDE.

summa bona plural of SUMMUM BONUM.

summa cum laude *adverb & adjective phrase* L19 **Latin** (literally, 'with the highest praise'). With or of highest distinction; *specifically* (of a degree, diploma, etc.) of the highest standard.

■ Cf. CUM LAUDE, MAGNA CUM LAUDE.

summae see SUMMA.

summa genera plural of SUMMUM GENUS.

summum bonum *noun phrase* plural **summa bona** M16 **Latin** (= highest good). The chief or a supreme good; *specifically* (*Ethics*) the highest good as the end or determining principle in an ethical system.

summum genus *noun* plural **summa genera** L16 **Latin** (= highest kind). The highest or most comprehensive class in a classification; *specifically* (*Logic*) a genus not considered as a species of a higher genus.

summum jus *noun* L16 **Latin** (= highest law). The utmost rigor of the law, extreme severity.

sumo *noun* plural **sumos**, same L19 **Japanese** (*sūmo*). A Japanese form of heavyweight wrestling in which a wrestler wins a bout by forcing his opponent outside a circle or making him touch the ground with any part of the body except the soles of the feet. Also, a sumo wrestler.

sumotori *noun* L20 **Japanese** (*sūmotori*, from as preceding + *tori* taking). A sumo wrestler.

sumpsimus *noun* M16 **Latin** (1st person plural perfect indicative of *sumere* to take). A correct expression taking the place of an incorrect but popular one.

■ Cf. MUMPSIMUS. The expressions usually occur together in contexts contrasting obtuse conservatism with a more enlightened attitude.

sunyata *noun* E20 **Sanskrit** (*śūnyatā* emptiness, from *śūnya* empty, void). *Buddhism* The doctrine that phenomena are devoid of an immutable or determinate intrinsic nature, often regarded as a means of gaining an intuition of ultimate reality.

superficies *noun* plural same M16 **Latin** (from *super-* above + *facies* face). **1** M16 *Geometry* A magnitude of two dimensions, having only length and breadth; a surface. **2 a** L16 The outer surface of an object. **b** E17 A surface layer. Now *rare*. **3a** L16–L18 A thing likened to a surface; the outward form or aspect. **b** L16 The outward appearance as distinct from the real nature. **4** M17 Superficial area or extent. **5** M19 *Roman Law* A structure in or on the surface of a piece of land that is so closely connected with it as to form part of it.

suppositum *noun* plural **supposita** M17 **Medieval Latin** (noun use of neuter singular of *suppositus* past participle of *supponere* to place under). **1** M17 *Metaphysics* A being that subsists by itself, an individual thing or person; occasionally, a being in relation to its attributes. Long *rare* or *obsolete*. **2** M19 *Logic* An assumption.

suppressio veri *noun phrase* plural **suppressiones veri** M18 **Modern Latin** (literally, 'suppression of what is true'). A misrepresentation of the truth by concealing facts that ought to be made known.

■ In use often linked with SUGGESTIO FALSI.

supra *adverb & adjective* E16 **Latin**. **A** *adverb* **1** E16 Earlier in a book or article; above. Cf. UT SUPRA. **2** L16–L18 In addition, besides. **B** *adjective* L16–L18 Additional, extra.

suprême *noun* E19 **French**. A rich cream sauce; a dish of especially chicken breasts cooked in this sauce.

■ Latterly (M20) often Anglicized as *supreme*, as in *chicken supreme*.

supremo *noun* plural **supremos** M20 **Spanish** ((*generalísimo*) *supremo* supreme general). **1** M20 A supreme leader or ruler. **2** M20 *transferred* A person in overall charge of something.

■ *Supremo* was the nickname given to Earl Mountbatten of Burma during his time as Supreme Allied Commander, Southeast Asia.

suq variant of SOUK.

sura *noun* E17 **Arabic** (*sūra*, (with definite article) *as-sūra*, probably from Syriac *ṣūrṭā* scripture). Any of the sections of the Koran.

■ *Sura* (M17) supplanted the now obsolete form *assura* (incorporating the Arabic definite article), in which the word was first used in English.

surah *noun & adjective* L19 **French** (representing French pronunciation of *Surat* a port in India). (Of) a soft twilled silk fabric.

surbahar *noun* L19 **Bengali** (*surbāhār*). A mellow-toned Indian stringed instrument, a bass sitar.

surimono *noun* plural same L19 **Japanese** (from *suri* printing + *mono* thing). A print; *specifically* a small Japanese color print used to convey greetings or to mark a special occasion.

sur place *adverb phrase* E20 **French**. **1** E20 At the place in question; on the spot. **2** M20 *Ballet* Without leaving the place where one has been standing.

Sursum corda *noun phrase* M16 **Latin** (from *sursum* upward + *corda* plural of *cor* heart). *Christian Church* In Latin Eucharistic liturgies, the words addressed by the celebrant to the congregation at the beginning of the Eucharistic Prayer; in English rites, the corresponding versicle, 'Lift up your hearts'.

surveillant *noun & adjective* (also (feminine) **surveillante**) E19 **French** ((noun use of) present participle of *surveiller* to watch over, from as *sur-* over + *veiller* to keep watch, from Latin *vigilare*). **A** *noun* **1** E19 A person who exercises surveillance. **2** M19 A teacher on nonteaching duty. **B** *adjective* M19 Exercising surveillance.

■ The corresponding noun *surveillance* (E19) is now fully Anglicized.

sushi *noun* L19 **Japanese**. A Japanese dish consisting of rolls of cold boiled rice flavored with vinegar and garnished with raw fish.

susurrus *noun* LME **Latin** (= a whisper, humming, muttering, of imitative origin). **1** Malicious whispering. Only in LME. **2** E19 A low soft whispering or rustling sound.

■ Only in literary use.

sutra *noun* E19 **Sanskrit** (*sūtra* thread, string, rule). **1** E19 In Sanskrit literature, a rule or aphorism, or a set of these, on grammar, or Hindu law or philosophy, expressed with maximum brevity. **2** L19 A Buddhist scripture, usually doctrinal in content. Also, the Jain scriptures.

suttee *noun* (also **sati**) L18 **Sanskrit** (*satī* faithful wife, feminine of *sat* good). Chiefly *History* **1** L18 A Hindu widow who immolates herself on her husband's funeral pyre. **2** E19 The immolation of a Hindu widow in this way.

suzuribako *noun* plural same **M20 Japanese** (from *suzuri* slab for ink + *hako* box). A box, often of finely wrought lacquerwork, for holding Japanese writing implements.

s.v. abbreviation of SUB VOCE.

svelte *adjective* **E19 French** (from Italian *svelto*). **1** E19 Slender, willowy. **2** E20 *transferred* Elegant, graceful.

swami *noun* (also **swamy**) **L18 Sanskrit** (*svāmin*, nominative *svāmī*, master, prince). **1** L18 A Hindu image or temple. **2** E20 A male Hindu religious teacher.

swart gevaar *noun phrase* **M20 Afrikaans** (literally, 'black peril', from Dutch *zwart* black + *gevaar* danger). The threat to the Western way of life and white supremacy in South Africa believed by some to be posed by the blacks. *South African*.

swastika *noun* **L19 Sanskrit** (*svastika* from *svasti* well-being, luck, from *su* good + *asti* being). **1** L19 An ancient symbol in the form of a cross with equal arms with a limb of the same length projecting at right angles from the end of each arm, all in the same direction and (usually) clockwise. **2** M20 This symbol (with clockwise projecting limbs) used as the emblem of the German and other Nazi parties; a HAKENKREUZ. Also, a flag bearing this emblem.

syce *noun* (also **sais**) **M17 Persian and Urdu** (*sā'is* from Arabic). In parts of Africa and Asia, and especially in the Indian subcontinent: a groom, a servant who attends to horses, drives carriages, etc.; a chauffeur. Also, an attendant following on foot a mounted rider or a carriage.

sylva *noun* (also **silva**) plural **sylvae**, **sylvas** **M17 Latin** (*silva* a wood, woodland (misspelled *sylva* after synonymous Greek *hulē* wood); in sense 2, after the title (*Silvae*) of Statius' collection of occasional poems). **1** M17 A treatise on forest trees; (a descriptive catalog of) the trees of a particular region. Cf. FLORA sense 2. **2** M17–L18 A collection of pieces, especially of poems.

■ The spelling *sylva* in English treatises on arboriculture is a tribute to the authority of John Evelyn's *Sylva; or a discourse of Forest Trees and the propagation of timber* (1664), which for many years remained the standard English text in its field.

symbiosis *noun* plural **symbioses** **E17 Modern Latin** (from Greek *sumbiōsis* a living together, from *sumbioun* to live together, from *sumbios* (adjective) living together, (noun) companion, partner, from *sym* together + *bios* life). **1** E17 Living together, communal living. *rare*. **2** L19 *Biology* An interaction between two dissimilar organisms living in close physical association; *especially* one in which each benefits the other. **3** E20 *transferred* and *figurative* A relationship or association of mutual advantage between people, organizations, etc.

sympathique *adjective* **M19 French**. Of a thing, a place, etc.: agreeable, to one's taste, suitable. Of a person: likable, in tune with or responsive to one's personality or moods.

sympathisch *adjective* **E20 German**. SYMPATHIQUE.

symposium *noun* plural **symposia**, **symposiums** **L16 Latin** (from Greek *sumposion*, from *sumpotēs* fellow drinker, from *sym-* together + *potēs* drinker). **1** L16 A drinking party; a convivial meeting, *especially* (*historical*) one held by the ancient Greeks for drinking, conversation, philosophical discussion, etc.; *History* an account of such a meeting or the conversation at it. **2a** L18 A meeting or conference for the discussion of a particular subject; a collection of opinions delivered or a series of articles contributed at such a meeting or conference. **b** L19 A collection of essays or papers on various aspects of a particular subject by a number of contributors.

syncope *noun* LME **Late Latin** (from Greek *sugkopē*, from *sun-* with + *kop-* stem of *koptein* to strike, cut off). **1** LME Fainting; temporary loss of consciousness caused by an insufficient flow of blood to the brain, frequently due to blood loss, shock, long standing, overheating, etc. **2** M16 Shortening of a word by omission of one or more syllables or letters in the middle; a word so shortened. **3** M17–L18 *Music* Syncopation. **4** M17 *generally* A cutting short of something; sudden cessation or interruption. *rare.*

synecdoche *noun* LME **Latin** (from Greek *sunekdokhē*, from *sunekdekhesthai*, literally, 'to take with something else', from *sun-* with + *ekdekhesthai* take, take up). *Grammar* and *Rhetoric* A figure of speech in which a more inclusive term is used for a less inclusive one or vice versa, as a whole for a part or a part for a whole.

synthesis *noun* plural **syntheses** LME **Latin** (from Greek *sunthesis*, from *suntithenai*, from *sun-* with + *tithenai* to put, place). **I 1** *Grammar* **a** Apposition. Only in LME. **b** E17–E18 The construction of a sentence according to sense, in violation of strict syntax. **II 2** E17 *Logic* and *Philosophy* **a** The action of proceeding in thought from causes to effects, or from laws or principles to their consequences. **3** E18 *Medicine* The joining of divided parts in surgery. Now *rare* or *obsolete*. **4** M18 *Chemistry* Formation of a compound by combination of its elements or constituents. **b** M19 *Physics* Production of white or other compound light by combination of its constituent colors, or of a complex musical sound by combination of its component simple tones. **5** M19 *Linguistics* The tendency of a language to mark categories by inflections rather than by (groups of) distinct words. Also, the process of making compound and derivative words. **6** M19 *generally* The action or an act of putting together parts or elements to make up a complex whole. Also, a complex whole made up of a number of united parts or elements. **III 7** E17 *Roman Antiquities* A loose flowing robe worn at meals and festivities.

■ Sense 2 also occurs in specialized uses in Kantian and Hegelian philosophy.

système D *noun phrase* L20 **French** (contraction of *système débrouillard* (or *système débrouiller*), literally, 'resourceful system'). A policy or practice for coping with difficult circumstances.

■ Apparently originating in France as a response to conditions during World War II, the phrase returned to currency during the French public transport strikes of 1995.

taal *noun* (also **Taal**) L19 **Dutch** (= language, speech, from Middle Dutch *tāle* = Old English *talu* tale). Afrikaans.

■ In colloquial South African English *die* (or *the*) *taal* is often a mildly contemptuous way of referring to Afrikaans.

tabac *noun* E20 **French**. In French-speaking countries: a tobacco shop.

tabbouleh *noun* M20 **Arabic** (*tabbūla*). A Syrian and Lebanese salad made with bulgur, parsley, onion, mint, lemon juice, oil, and spices.

tabi *noun* plural same **tabis** E17 **Japanese.** A thick-soled Japanese ankle sock with a separate stall for the big toe.

tabla *noun* M19 **Persian and Urdu** (*tabla(h)*, Hindustani *tablā* from Arabic *ṭabl*). A pair of small hand drums of unequal size used in Indian music; the smaller of these drums.

tableau *noun* plural **tableaux** L17 **French** (from Old French *tablel* diminutive of *table* from Latin *tabula* plank, tablet, list). **1** L17 A picture; *figurative* a picturesque presentation or description. **2** L18 A table, a schedule; an official list. **b** M20 *Mathematics* In full *simplex tableau*. A table displaying the constraints in problems of the type soluble by the simplex method. **3 a** E19 A group of people, etc., forming a picturesque scene. **b** E19 A TABLEAU VIVANT. **c** M19 *Theater* A motionless representation of the action at some (especially critical) stage in a play; a stage direction for this. Also (*transferred*), the sudden creation of a striking or dramatic situation. **4** L19 *Cards* The arrangement of the cards as laid out in a game of solitaire.

tableau vivant *noun* plural **tableaux vivants** E19 **French** (literally, 'living picture'). A silent and motionless representation of a character, scene, incident, etc., by a person or group of people; *transferred* a picturesque actual scene.

table d'hôte *noun phrase* E17 **French** (= host's table). Originally, a common table for guests at a hotel or eating house. Now usually, a meal at a hotel, restaurant, etc., consisting of a set menu at a fixed price.

tablier *noun* (in sense 1 also (earlier) **tabler**) ME **Old and Modern French** (ultimately from Latin *tabula* plank, tablet, list). **1** ME–L15 A backgammon board or chessboard. Also, backgammon. **2** M19 *History* A part of a woman's dress resembling an apron; the front of a skirt having the form of an apron. **3** L19 *Anthropology* An extension of the labia minora characteristic of Khoisan women.

taboo *adjective & noun* (also **tabu**, (chiefly *New Zealand*) **tapu**) L18 **Tongan** (*tabu*). **A** *adjective* **1** L18 Set apart for or consecrated to a special use or purpose; forbidden to general use or to a particular person or class of people; sacred; forbidden. **2** E19 *transferred* and *figurative* Especially of a word, topic, or activity: avoided or prohibited, especially by social custom. **B** *noun* L18 The putting of a person or thing under temporary or permanent prohibition or interdict, especially as a social custom; the fact or condition of being taboo; a customary prohibition or interdict. **2** M19 *transferred* and *figurative* Prohibition or interdiction of the use or practice of anything; ostracism; *specifically* a prohibition of the use of certain words, topics, etc., especially in social conversation.

tabouret *noun* M17 **French** (diminutive of Old French *tabor* (also *tanbor*, *tamb(o)ur*), apparently of oriental origin; cf. Persian *tabīra*, *tabūrāk* drum). **1** M17 A low backless seat or stool for one person. **2** E20 A small table, especially one used as a stand for houseplants; a bedside table.

tabula gratulatoria **Late Latin** (*tabula* list + feminine of *gratulatorius* congratulatory). L20 A list in a FESTSCHRIFT of the people and institutions who have subscribed to the publication.

tabula rasa *noun phrase* **Latin** (literally, 'scraped tablet'). A tablet from which the writing has been erased, ready to be written on again; a blank tablet; *figurative* a clean slate; a mind having no innate ideas (as in some views of the human mind at birth).

tac-au-tac *noun* E20 **French** (literally, 'clash for clash', from *tac* (imitative)). *Fencing* A parry combined with a riposte.

tacenda *noun plural* M19 **Latin** (plural of *tacendum*, noun use of neuter of gerundive of *tacere* to be silent). Things to be passed over in silence; matters not to be mentioned or made public, *especially* those of an embarrassing nature.

tacet *adverb & noun* E18 **Latin** (= is silent, from *tacere* to be silent). *Music* **A** *adverb* E18 (A direction:) be silent for a time; pause. **B** *noun* L18 A pause.

tache *noun* ME **Old French** (*teche*, (also modern) *tache*, ultimately from Frankish = a token). **1 a** ME A spot, a blotch, a blot. *obsolete* except *Scottish*. **b** L19 *Medicine* A blemish on the skin, an organ, etc. Usually with French specifying word. **c** *Art* M20 A dab or dash of color. **2** *figurative* **a** ME–E17 A moral spot or blemish. **b** E17 An imputation of fault or disgrace; a stain or blot on one's character. *Scottish*. **3** LME A distinctive mark, quality, or habit. *obsolete* except *dialect*.

taco *noun* plural **tacos** M20 **Mexican Spanish**. A Mexican dish comprising a tortilla or cornmeal pancake rolled or folded and filled with various mixtures, such as seasoned ground beef, chicken, beans, etc.

taedium vitae *noun phrase* M18 **Latin** (*taedium* weariness, disgust + *vitae* genitive of *vita* life). Weariness of life; extreme ennui or inertia, often as a pathological state with a tendency to suicide.

tae kwon do *noun phrase* M20 **Korean** (literally, 'art of hand and foot fighting'). A modern Korean system of unarmed combat developed chiefly in the mid–twentieth century, combining elements of KARATE, ancient Korean martial art, and KUNG FU, differing from karate in its wide range of kicking techniques and its emphasis on different methods of breaking objects.

taele variant of TJAELE.

taenia *noun* (also **tenia**) plural **taeniae**, **taenias** M16 **Latin** (from Greek *tainia* band, fillet, ribbon). **1** M16 *Architecture* A fillet or band between a Doric architrave and frieze. **2** E18 *Zoology* A tapeworm. Now only as modern Latin genus name. **3** M19 *Greek Antiquities* A headband, ribbon, or fillet. **4** L19 *Anatomy* A ribbonlike structure. Usually with specifying word.

Tafelmusik *noun* L19 **German** (literally, 'table music'). **1** L19 Music so printed as to enable the same page to be read by two or more people seated on opposite sides of a table. **2** L19 Music intended to be performed at a banquet or a convivial meal, especially popular in the eighteenth century.

Tafelwein *noun* L20 **German** (literally, 'table wine'). Ordinary German wine of mediocre quality, suitable for drinking with a meal.

tafia *noun* M18 **French** (from West Indian creole, alteration of RATAFIA). In the West Indies: a liquor resembling rum distilled from the lower grades of molasses, refuse brown sugar, etc.

tafone *noun* plural **tafoni** M20 **Corsican** (dialect *tafóne* hole, hollow). *Geology* A shallow rounded cavity in rock produced by weathering. Usually in *plural*.

tagliarini *noun* M19 **Italian** (*taglierini* plural, from *tagliare* to cut). Pasta made in very narrow strips.

tagliatelle *noun* L19 **Italian** (from *tagliare* to cut; cf. preceding). Pasta made in narrow strips.

tahina *noun* (also **tahini**) M20 **Modern Greek** (*takhini* from Arabic *ṭaḥīnā* from *ṭaḥana* to grind, crush, pulverize). A Middle Eastern paste or sauce made from sesame seeds.

T'ai Chi *noun* M18 **Chinese** (*tàijí* (Wade–Giles *t'ai chi*), from *tài* extreme + *jí* limit). **1** M18 In Taoism and Neo-Confucianism, the ultimate point, constituting both source and limit, of the life force. Also, the symbol representing this. **2** M20 A Chinese martial art and system of calisthenics consisting of sequences of very slow controlled movements, believed to have been devised by a Taoist priest in the Song dynasty (960–1279). In full *T'ai Chi Ch'uan* (Chinese *quán* fist).

taiga *noun* L19 **Russian** (*taĭga* from Mongolian). The swampy coniferous forest of high northern latitudes, *especially* that between the tundra and steppes of Siberia.

taiglach variant of TEIGLACH.

taihoa *interjection* M19 **Maori.** Wait a bit; by and by; presently. *New Zealand.*

taiko *noun* plural same, **taikos** L19 **Japanese.** A Japanese drum; *specifically* any of a class of barrel-shaped drums.

taille *noun* M16 **French** (from Old French *taillier* (modern *tailler*) from Proto-Romance (medieval Latin *talliare*) from Latin *talea* rod, twig, cutting). **1** M16 In France, a tax levied on the common people. *obsolete* except *historical.* **2** M17 Cut, shape, form; shape of the bust from the shoulders to the waist; figure, build. **3** M19 *Music* (now *historical*). The register of a tenor or similar voice; an instrument of this register.

taille-douce *noun* M17 **French** (= soft cutting, from TAILLE + *douce* soft). Engraving on a metal plate with a graver or burin as opposed to a drypoint or etching needle.

tailleur *noun* E20 **French** (from TAILLE). A woman's tailor-made suit.

taipan *noun* M19 **Chinese** ((Cantonese) *daaihbāan*). Originally, a foreign merchant or businessman in China. Now *especially*, the head of a foreign business in China.

taisch *noun* (also **taish**) L18 **Gaelic** (*taibhse* from Old Irish *taidbse* phantasm). In Scottish folklore, the apparition of a living person who is about to die; *generally* something perceived by second sight.

takamakie *noun* (also **takamakiye** and other variants) E20 **Japanese.** Decorative Japanese lacquerwork done in relief, especially in gold.

takhaar *noun* plural **takhare, takhaars** L19 **Afrikaans** (from Dutch *tak* branch + *haar* hair). In South Africa: an unkempt, unsophisticated person, especially from a rural area. *colloquial* and *derogatory.*

takht *noun* L20 **Persian** (*takt*). In Eastern countries: a sofa, a bed.

talak *noun* (also **talaq**) L18 **Arabic** (*ṭalaḳ*, from *ṭalaḳat, ṭaluḳat* be repudiated). In Islamic law: divorce, especially by the husband's verbal repudiation of his wife in the presence of witnesses.

talaq variant of TALAK.

talaria *noun plural* L16 **Latin** (neuter plural of *talaris* from *talus* ankle). *Roman Mythology* Winged sandals or small wings attached to the ankles of some gods and goddesses, especially Mercury.

talayot *noun* L19 **Catalan** (*talaiot* small watchtower, from Arabic (Muslim Spain) *ṭāli'āt* plural of *ṭāli'a* watchtower). *Archaeology* A Bronze Age stone tower characteristic of the Balearic Islands, usually circular with a large central pillar supporting the roof. Cf. NURAGH.

taleggio *noun* L20 **Italian.** A rinded semi-soft cheese.

talik *noun* M20 **Russian** (from *tayat'* to melt). *Physical Geography* An area of unfrozen ground surrounded by permafrost.

talio *noun* E17 **Latin.** (A) retaliation.

tallith *noun* E17 **Hebrew** (rabbinical Hebrew *ṭallīt*, from biblical Hebrew *ṭillel* to cover). The shawl with fringed corners traditionally worn by male Jews at prayer.

talus *noun* plural **taluses** M17 **French** (of unknown origin). **1** M17 A slope; *specifically* (*Fortification*) the sloping side of a wall or earthwork. **2** M19 *Geology* A scree slope, consisting of material that has fallen from the face of the cliff above. **b** *generally* M19 The slope of a mountain, hill, or iceberg. Now *rare.*

tamagotchi *noun* (also **Tamagotchi, tamagocchi**) L20 **Japanese** (= lovable egg). (Proprietary name for) a small, portable electronic device that can be programmed to mimic the demands for food, attention, etc. of a pet bird or animal.

tamale *noun* L17 **Mexican Spanish** (*tamal*, plural *tamales*, from Nahuatl *tamalli*). A Mexican dish of seasoned meat and maize flour steamed or baked in maize husks.

tamari *noun* L20 **Japanese.** A Japanese variety of rich wheat-free soy sauce. Also *tamari sauce.*

tamasha *noun* (also (earlier) **tomasha**) E17 **Persian and Urdu** (*tamāšā* (for *tamāšī*) walking about for amusement, entertainment, from Arabic *tamāšā* walk about together, from *mašā* walk). **1** E17 In the Indian subcontinent: an entertainment, a show, a spectacle, a public function. **2** L19 A fuss, a commotion. *colloquial.*

tambour *noun* L15 **French** (Old French *tabor* (also *tanbor, tamb(o)ur*), apparently of oriental origin (cf. Persian *tabīra, tabūrāk* drum), spelling perhaps influenced by Arabic *ṭunbūr* a kind of lute or lyre). **1** L15 A drum; now *especially* a small drum with a deep tone. **2** E18 *Architecture* **a** The part of a Corinthian or composite capital around which the foliage and volutes are arranged, a bell. **b** E18 Any of the courses forming the shaft of a cylindrical column. **c** E18 A lobby with a ceiling and folding doors serving to obviate drafts, especially in a church porch. **d** E19 A wall of circular plan, as one supporting a dome or surrounded by a colonnade. **3** E18 A projecting part of the main wall of a tennis or fives court, with a sloping end face. **4 a** A circular frame formed of one hoop fitting inside another, in which fabric is held taut for embroidering. **b** M19 Material embroidered or embroidery done using such a frame. **5** M19 *Military* A small redan defending an entrance or passage. **6** L19 *Medicine* A stretched membrane forming part of an instrument for recording arterial pulsations, respiratory movements, etc., by slight changes in air pressure. **7** M20 A sliding flexible shutter or door on a desk, cabinet, etc., made of strips of wood attached to a canvas backing.

tameletjie *noun* M19 **Afrikaans** (perhaps from *tabletje* small cake). In South Africa: (a piece of) hard toffee often containing almonds or pine nuts. Now also, a candy consisting of a roll of compressed and sweetened dried fruit (also more fully *tameletjie roll*).

tandoor *noun* (also (in sense 1 usually) **tandour**, and other variants) **M17 French or Urdu** (sense 1 from French *tandour* from Turkish *tandır* variant of Persian, Arabic *tannūr* oven, furnace; sense 2 from Urdu, *tandūr*, Persian *tanūr* ultimately from Arabic *tannūr*). **1** M17 A square table with a brazier under it, around which people sit for warmth in cold weather in Persia, Turkey, and adjacent countries. Now *rare.* **2** M19 A clay oven of a kind used originally in northern India and Pakistan; a shop selling food cooked in such an oven.

tandoori *adjective & noun* **M20 Persian and Urdu** (from *tandūr*: see preceding). **A** *adjective* M20 Designating, pertaining to, or using a style of Indian cooking based on the use of a tandoor. **B** *noun* M20 Tandoori cooking or food; a tandoori dish.

tandour see TANDOOR.

tanga *noun* **E20 Portuguese** (ultimately of Bantu origin). **1** E20 *Anthropology* A triangular loincloth or pubic covering worn by indigenous peoples in tropical America. **2** L20 A very brief bikini made of triangles of material connected by thin ties.

tango *noun & verb* plural **tangos**, (now *rare*) **tangoes** **L19 American Spanish** (perhaps of African origin). **A** *noun* **1** L19 A kind of Spanish flamenco dance. **2** L19 A syncopated ballroom dance in 2/4 or 4/4 time, of South American origin, characterized by slow gliding movements and abrupt pauses; a piece of music intended to accompany or in the rhythm of this dance. **B** *intransitive verb* E20 Dance a tango.

tanka *noun* plural same, **tankas** **L19 Japanese** (from *tan* short + *ka* song). A Japanese poem consisting of thirty-one syllables in five lines, the first and third lines having five and the others seven syllables. Also called *uta.*

tant bien que mal *adverb phrase* **M18 French** (literally, 'as well as badly').

With indifferent success; moderately well, after a fashion.

tant mieux *interjection* M18 **French**. So much the better. Cf. TANT PIS.

tanto *adverb* L19 **Italian** (from Latin *tantum* so much). *Music* So, so much.

■ Used to modify adjectives from Italian, as in *allegro non tanto*, meaning 'fast, but not too much so'.

tant pis *interjection* L18 **French**. So much the worse. Cf. TANT MIEUX.

tantra *noun* (also **Tantra**) L18 **Sanskrit** (= loom, warp, groundwork, system, doctrine). **1** L18 Any of a class of Hindu or Buddhist religious writings of the late medieval period, often of a magical, erotic, or mystical nature. **2** M20 Tantrism.

tapa *noun* M20 **Spanish** (literally, 'cover, lid'). In a bar or café, especially one providing Spanish food, a savory snack to accompany a glass of wine.

■ Usually in plural *tapas*, which is often treated as singular.

tapadero *noun* plural **tapaderos** (also **tapadera**) M19 **Spanish** (= cover, lid, stopper, from *tapar* to stop up, cover). In the western United States: a leather hood for the front of a stirrup, to hold and protect the foot especially when riding through brush.

tapénade *noun* M20 **French** (from Provençal *tapeno*). A Provençal dish, usually served as an hors d'oeuvre, made mainly from black olives, capers, and anchovies.

tapette *noun & adjective* M20 **French** ((slang) = pederast, homosexual, from *taper* hit, tap). **A** *noun* M20. A passive male homosexual; an effeminate man. **B** *adjective* M20 Of a man: effeminate; like a *tapette*.

tapia *noun* M18 **Spanish** (= mud wall). Clay or mud puddled, compressed, and dried, as a material for walls.

tapis *noun* plural same L15 **French** (= carpet, tablecloth, from Old French *tapiz* (also modern *tapis*) from late Latin *tapetium* from Greek *tapētion* diminutive of *tapēs*, *tapēt-* tapestry). A cloth, especially of a decorated oriental fabric of a type exported to France in the eighteenth century, worked with artistic designs in colors, used as a curtain, tablecloth, etc.; a tapestry.

■ The phrase *(up)on the tapis* (L17) meaning 'under discussion (*or* consideration)', is a partial translation of French *sur le tapis* (literally, 'on the tablecloth'), also occasionally used in English.

tapis vert *noun phrase* plural **tapis verts** M20 **French** (= green carpet). A long strip of grass.

tapotement *noun* L19 **French** (from *tapoter* to tap). A percussive technique used in massage, consisting of hacking, clapping, and pounding actions.

taqueria *noun* L20 **Mexican Spanish** (from TACO). A restaurant specializing in tacos.

taqueté *adjective* M20 **French** (from *taquet* wedge, peg). *Ballet* Designating or pertaining to a style of pointwork accentuated with quick precise short steps.

tarantella *noun* (also **tarantelle**) L18 **Italian** (diminutive of *Taranto* (Latin *Tarentum*), a town in southern Italy: popularly associated with *tarantola* tarantula). **1** L18 A rapid whirling South Italian dance popular since the fifteenth century, when it was supposed to be the most effective cure for tarantism. **2** M19 A piece of music for such a dance or composed in its triplet rhythm, with abrupt transitions from the major to the minor.

tarboosh *noun* (also **tarbush**) E18 **Arabic** ((Egyptian) *ṭarbūš* from Ottoman Turkish *terpōş*, Turkish *tarbuş* from Persian *sarpūš*, from *sar* head + *pūš* cover). A cap similar to a fez, usually of red felt with a tassel at the top, worn by Muslim men either alone or as part of a turban.

targa *adjective & noun* L20 **Italian** (= plate, shield; the name of a model of Porsche automobile (introduced in 1965) with a detachable hood (see below), probably after the *Targa Florio* (= Florio Shield), a motor time-trial held annually in Sicily). **A** *adjective* L20 Designating a type of detachable roof hood or paneling on a convertible sports car, *especially* one that when removed leaves a central roll bar for passenger safety. **B** *noun* L20 A car having this feature.

tarkashi *noun* **L19 Urdu** ((and Persian) *tār-kašī*, literally, 'wire drawing'). Especially in the Indian subcontinent: the craft of inlaying wood with brass wire; the artifacts so produced.

tarot *noun* **L16 French** (from Italian *tarocchi* plural of *tarocco*, of unknown origin). **1** L16 In *singular* or *plural* Any of various games played with a deck of tarot cards (see sense 2). **2** L19 Any of a deck of 78 playing cards having five suits, the last of which is a set of permanent trumps, first used in Italy in the fifteenth century and now also used for fortune-telling. Also, any of the trump cards in such a deck. Also *tarot card*.

tarsia *noun* **L17 Italian.** INTARSIA.

tartine *noun* **E19 French** (from *tarte* tart). A slice of (usually toasted) bread spread with butter or jam.

tasajo *noun* **L18 Spanish** (= slice of dried meat, of unknown origin). Buffalo meat cut into strips and dried in the sun.

■ The synonymous *tasso* is perhaps a derivation from *tasajo*, but cf. Louisiana French *tasseau* (jerked beef).

tastevin *noun* **M20 French** (*tastevin*, *tâte-vin* wine taster). A small shallow (especially silver) cup for tasting wines, of a type used in France. Also (**Tastevin**), a member of a French order or guild of wine tasters.

tasto *noun* plural **tastos** **M18 Italian** (= touch, key). *Music* A key of a piano or other keyboard instrument; the fingerboard of a stringed instrument.

tatami *noun* **E17 Japanese.** **1** E17 A rush-covered straw mat forming the standard floor covering in Japan. Also *tatami mat*. **2** E20 A standard unit in room measurement in Japan, approximately six feet by three feet.

tathata *noun* **M20 Pali** (*tathatā* true state of things, from *tathā* in that manner, so). *Buddhism* The ultimate nature of all things, as expressed in phenomena but inexpressible in language.

tâtonnement *noun* **M19 French** (from *tâtonner* feel one's way, proceed cautiously). Experimentation, tentative procedure; an instance of this.

tau *noun* (also **taw**) **ME Greek** (from Hebrew *tāw* final letter of Hebrew alphabet). **1** ME The nineteenth (originally the final) letter (Τ, τ) of the Greek alphabet, corresponding in form to the letter T. **2** ME A T-shaped mark, sign, or object; *specifically* (**a**) the sign of the cross as made with the hand; (**b**) (more fully *tau cross*) a cross in which the transverse piece surmounts the upright piece (also called *St Anthony's cross*); (**c**) An ANKH; (**d**) a T-shaped pastoral staff. (more fully *tau staff*) **3** M20 *Particle Physics* Frequently written τ. **a** A meson that decays into three pions, now identified as a kaon. **b** L20 An unstable heavy charged lepton. Also *tau lepton*, *tau particle*.

taula *noun* **L19 Catalan** (from Latin *tabula* table). *Archaeology* A megalithic Bronze Age structure found on Minorca, consisting of two slabs forming a T-shaped column, frequently enclosed by a horseshoe-shaped wall.

taupe *noun & adjective* **E20 French** (from Latin *talpa* mole). (Of) a brownish shade of gray resembling the color of moleskin.

taverna *noun* **E20 Modern Greek** (from Latin *taberna* tavern). A Greek eating house.

taxe de séjour *noun phrase* plural **taxes de séjour** **E20 French** (literally, 'tax of visit'). In France and French-speaking countries: a tax imposed on visitors to spas or tourist resorts.

tazia *noun* E19 **Arabic** (*ta'ziya* consolation, mourning). *Islam* **1** E19 A representation, often made of paper and elaborately decorated, of the tomb of Husain (grandson of Muhammad) carried in procession during Muharram. **2** L19 A play commemorating the suffering and death of Husain, performed especially on the anniversary of the event each year.

tazza *noun* plural **tazze**, **tazzas** E19 **Italian** (from Arabic *ṭasa*). A shallow ornamental wine cup or vase, *especially* one mounted on a foot.

tchin *noun* (also **chin**) M19 **Russian** (*chin* = rank). Rank; person or persons of quality.

tchotchke *noun* (also **tsatske**) M20 **Yiddish** (from Slavonic: cf. Russian *tsatska*). A trinket; *transferred* a pretty girl or woman. *colloquial.*

te *noun* L19 **Chinese** (*dé* virtue (Wade–Giles *te*)). (In Taoism) the essence of Tao inherent in all beings; (in Confucianism and in extended use) moral virtue.

tecbir variant of TEKBIR.

tedesco *noun & adjective* plural **tedeschi** E19 **Italian** (= German, from medieval Latin *theodiscus*, ultimately from Germanic base of *Dutch*). (An instance of) German influence in Italian art or literature; showing such influence.

Te Deum *noun phrase* OE **Latin**. **1** OE An ancient Latin hymn of praise beginning *Te deum laudamus* 'We praise you, O God', sung as an expression of thanksgiving on special occasions, and sung or recited regularly at Roman Catholic matins and (in translation) at Anglican matins. **2** L17 A recital of this; any (public) expression of thanksgiving or exultation. **3** M19 A musical setting of this hymn.

teepee variant of TEPEE.

tefillin *noun plural* E17 **Aramaic** (*tĕpillīn* prayers). Jewish phylacteries; the texts inscribed on these.

tegula *noun* plural **tegulae** E19 **Latin** (= tile, from *tegere* to cover). **1** E19 *Entomology* A small scalelike sclerite covering the base of the forewing in the orders Lepidoptera, Hymenoptera, Diptera, etc. **2** L19 *Archaeology* A flat roof tile, used especially in Roman roofs. Cf. IMBREX.

teiglach *noun plural* (also **taiglach** and other variants) E20 **Yiddish** (*teiglekh* plural of *teigl* dough pellet, from *teig* dough, ultimately from Old High German *teic* from Germanic from Indo-European base meaning 'smear, knead'). A Jewish confection made of pellets of dough boiled in honey.

tekbir *noun* (also **tecbir**) E18 **Arabic** (*tekbīr*, colloquial pronunciation of *takbīr* to proclaim the greatness of, from base also of *kabīr* great, *'akbar* greater, greatest). A cry of *Allāhu 'akbar* 'Allah is most great', uttered by Muslims.

tekke *noun* M17 **Turkish** (*tekke*, Arabic *takiyya*, Persian *takya* place of repose, pillow, abode of a dervish or fakir, perhaps ultimately from Arabic *ittaka'a* to lean on). A monastery of dervishes, especially in Ottoman Turkey.

telamon *noun* plural **telamones** E17 **Latin** (*telamones* (plural) from Greek *telamōnes* plural of *Telamōn* Telamon, a mythical hero). *Architecture* A male figure used as a pillar to support an entablature or other structure.

■ The female equivalent is a *caryatid.*

téléphérique *noun* (also **teleferic**, **téléférique**, **telepherique**) E20 **French** (Italian *teleferica*, from Greek *tēle-* far + *pherein* to carry). A cableway.

telos *noun* plural **teloi** M16 **Greek** (= end). **1** M16 FINIS sense 1. *rare.* **2** L19 End, purpose, (an) ultimate object or aim.

tel quel *adjective phrase* L19 **French**. Just as it is; without improvement or modification.

temblor *noun* L19 **American Spanish**. An earthquake. *Southwestern United States.*

temenos *noun* plural **temene** E19 **Greek** (from stem of *temnein* to cut off, sever). Chiefly *Archaeology* A piece of ground surrounding or adjacent to a temple; a sacred enclosure or precinct.

temmoku *noun* (also **tenmoku**) L19 **Japanese** (from Chinese *tiān mù* eye of heaven). A type of Chinese porcelain or stoneware with lustrous black or dark brown glaze; the glaze used on such porcelain or stoneware.

témoignage *noun* M20 **French** (from *témoigner* to bear witness). Testimony, witness; *especially* testimony regarding the character or beliefs of a person.

tempeh *noun* M20 **Indonesian** (*tempe*). An Indonesian dish made by deep-frying fermented soybeans.

tempera *noun* M19 **Italian** (in *pingere a tempera* paint in distemper). A method of painting using especially an emulsion, e.g., of pigment with egg, especially as a fine art technique on canvas. Also, the emulsion, etc., used in this method.

tempête *noun* L19 **French**. A country dance popular in England in the late nineteenth century; a piece of music for this dance.

tempi plural of TEMPO.

tempietto *noun* plural **tempietti** L19 **Italian** (literally, 'little temple'). A small usually circular building resembling a miniature temple.

tempo *noun* plural **tempi, tempos** M17 **Italian** (from Latin *tempus* time). **1** M17 The timing of an attack in fencing so that one's opponent is within reach. *rare*. **2** L17 *Music* Relative speed or rate of movement; pace; time; *specifically* the (especially characteristic) speed at which music for a dance, etc., is or should be played. **3** L19 The rate of motion or activity (*of* someone or something).

tempo giusto *noun phrase* M18 **Italian** (literally, 'strict time'). The speed at which a particular style of music is or should be played.

temporale *noun* M19 **Spanish** (*temporal* storm, spell of rainy weather). A weather condition on the Pacific coast of Central America consisting of strong southwest winds bringing heavy rain.

tempo rubato *noun phrase* L18 **Italian** (literally, 'stolen time'). Cf. RUBATO.

temps *noun* plural same L19 **French** (literally, 'time'). *Ballet* **1** L19 A movement in which there is no transfer of weight from one foot to the other. **2** E20 A movement forming one part of a step.

temps perdu *noun phrase* M20 **French** (literally, 'time lost'). The past, contemplated with nostalgia and a sense of irretrievability. Cf. RECHERCHE DU TEMPS PERDU.

tempura *noun* E20 **Japanese** (probably from Portuguese *tempêro* seasoning). A Japanese dish consisting of shellfish or whitefish and often vegetables, fried in batter.

temura *noun* (also **temurah**) E20 **Hebrew** (*tĕmūrāh* exchange). A cabalistic method of interpreting the Hebrew scriptures by the systematic replacement of the letters of a word with other letters.

tendenz *noun* L19 **German** (from English *tendence* or French *tendance*). Drift or aim of a story; purpose of a novel, etc.

Tendenzroman *noun* M19 **German** (TENDENZ + *Roman* novel). A novel with a purpose; a ROMAN À THÈSE.

tendido *noun* plural **tendidos** M19 **Spanish** (past participle of *tender* to stretch). An open tier of seats above the barrera in a bullring.

tendresse *noun* LME **French** (from *tendre* tender). (A) fondness, (an) affection.

tendu *adjective* E20 **French** (past participle of *tendre* to stretch). *Ballet* Stretched out or held tautly.

tenebroso *noun & adjective* L19 **Italian** (= dark, from Latin *tenebrosus* dark, gloomy). **A** *noun* L19 plural **tenebrosi** A member of a group of early seventeenth-century Italian painters influenced by Caravaggio, whose work is characterized by dramatic contrasts of light and shade. **B** *adjective* L19 Designating the style of this group of painters.

tenendum *noun* E17 **Latin** (literally, 'to be held' neuter gerundive of *tenere* to hold). *Law* (now *historical* except *United States*) That part of a deed defining the tenure by which the things granted are to be held.

tenet *noun* L16 **Latin** (literally, 'he holds', 3rd person present singular of *tenere* to hold). A doctrine, dogma, principle, or opinion, in religion, philosophy, politics, etc., held by a group or person. Also *loosely*, any opinion held.

■ Since E18 has entirely superseded the earlier form *tenent* (M16).

teniente *noun* L18 **Spanish**. A lieutenant.

tenmoku variant of TEMMOKU.

tenore *noun* M18 **Italian**. An adult male voice intermediate between a bass and countertenor or alto, a tenor voice; a singer having such a voice.

tenore di forza *noun phrase* L19 **Italian** (literally, 'tenor of power'). A singer with a powerful tenor voice.

tenore di grazia *noun phrase* L19 **Italian** (literally, 'tenor of grace'). A light or lyric tenor.

tenore robusto *noun phrase* L19 **Italian** (= strong tenor). A dramatic tenor.

tenorino *noun* plural **tenorini** M19 **Italian** (diminutive of TENORE). A high tenor.

tenue *noun* E19 **French** (noun use of feminine past participle of *tenir* to hold, keep). Deportment, bearing; propriety, manners; dress.

tenuto *adverb, adjective & noun* M18 **Italian** (past participle of *tenere* to hold). *Music* **A** *adverb & adjective* M18 (A direction:) giving the note its full time value; sustained(ly). Abbreviated to *ten.* **B** *noun* M20 plural **tenutos, tenuti** A note or chord played tenuto.

teocalli *noun* E17 **American Spanish** (from Nahuatl *teo:kalli*, from *teo:tl* god + *kalli* house). An ancient Mexican or Central American place of worship, usually consisting of a truncated pyramid surmounted by a temple.

tepache *noun* E20 **Mexican Spanish** (from Nahuatl *tepiatl*). Any of several Mexican drinks of varying degrees of fermentation, typically made with pineapple, water, and brown sugar.

tepee *noun* (also **teepee, tipi**) M18 **Sioux** (*tʰípi* dwelling). A conical tent of the North American Indians, made of skins, cloth, canvas, etc., stretched over a frame of poles fastened together at the top. Now also, a structure imitating or resembling such a tent.

tephra *noun* M20 **Greek** (= ashes). *Geology* Dust and rock fragments that have been ejected into the air by a volcanic eruption.

tepidarium *noun* plural **tepidaria** E19 **Latin**. In an ancient Roman bath, the warm room between the frigidarium and the caldarium. Also, a similar room in a Turkish bath.

teppan-yaki *noun* L20 **Japanese** (from *teppan* steel plate + *yaki* fry). A Japanese dish of meat, fish, or both, fried with vegetables on a hot steel plate forming the center of the dining table.

tequila *noun* M19 **Mexican Spanish** (from the name of a town producing the drink). A Mexican spirit made by distilling the fermented sap of a maguey, *Agave tequilana*. Cf. MESCAL sense 2.

terai *noun* L19 **Hindustani** (*tarāī* marshy lowlands). A wide-brimmed felt hat with a double-layered crown and a vent, worn by travelers, etc., in subtropical regions. In full *terai hat*.

■ The *terai* is a belt of marshy jungle lying between the southern foothills of the Himalayas and the plains.

tercet *noun* L16 **French** (from Italian *terzetto*, from *terzo* from Latin *tertius* third). *Prosody* A set or group of three lines rhyming together, or bound by double or triple rhyme with the adjacent triplet or triplets.

tercio *noun* plural **tercios** (in sense 1 also **tertio**) L16 **Spanish** (Italian *tertio*, *terzo*, Portuguese *têrço* a regiment, from Latin *tertium* a third). **1** L16 A regiment of Spanish (or, formerly, Italian) infantry, originally of the sixteenth and seventeenth centuries. Also *generally*, a body of infantry forming a main division of an army. **2** M20 Each of the three parts of a bullfight. **b** M20 Each of the three concentric circular areas into which a bullring is considered to be divided.

teriyaki *noun* M20 **Japanese** (from *teri* gloss, luster + *yaki* grill). A Japanese dish consisting of fish or meat marinated in soy sauce and grilled.

terminus ad quem *noun phrase* M16 **Latin** (= end to which; cf. TERMINUS A QUO). The finishing point of an argument, policy, period, etc.

terminus ante quem *noun phrase* M20 **Latin** (= end before which). The finishing point of a period, the latest possible date for something.

■ Also elliptically as *terminus ante*.

terminus a quo *noun phrase* M16 **Latin** (= end from which). The starting point of an argument, policy, period, etc.

■ Like TERMINUS AD QUEM, originally part of the technical vocabulary of the thirteenth-century scholastic philosophers (Albertus Magnus, Thomas Aquinas, etc.).

terminus post quem *noun phrase* M20 **Latin** (= end after which). The starting point of a period, the earliest possible date for something.

■ Also elliptically as *terminus post*.

terra alba *noun phrase* E20 **Latin** (*terra* earth + feminine of *albus* white). Any of various white earths, as pipe clay, kaolin, etc.; now *specifically* white pulverized gypsum used in the manufacture of paper, paint, etc.

terra cognita *noun phrase* M20 **Latin** (*terra* land + feminine of *cognitus* known). *figurative* Familiar territory. Opposite of TERRA INCOGNITA.

terra-cotta *noun & adjective* (also **terra cotta**, **terracotta**) E18 **Italian** (*terra cotta* baked earth from Latin *terra cocta*). **A** *noun* **1** E18 Hard unglazed usually brownish red earthenware, used chiefly for decorative tiles and bricks and in modeling. **b** E19 A statuette or figurine made of this substance. **2** L19 The typical brownish red color of this earthenware. **B** *attributive* or as *adjective* M19 Of or pertaining to terra-cotta; made of terra-cotta; of the typical color of terra-cotta, brownish red.

terrae filius *noun phrase* plural **terrae filii** L16 **Latin** (= a son of the earth, a man of unknown origin). **1** L16 A person of doubtful or obscure parentage. **2** M17 At Oxford University, an orator who made a humorous and satirical speech during the public defense of candidates' theses. *obsolete* except *historical*.

terra firma *noun phrase* M17 **Latin** (= firm land). **1** M17–E18 A mainland or continent, as distinct from an island, etc. **2** L17 The land as distinguished from the sea; dry land; firm ground. **3** L17–E18 Landed estate; land. *jocular* and *colloquial*.

■ Originally (E17) in English as the name of the territories on the Italian mainland that were subject to the state of Venice. Then later (M18–E19) used for the northern coastland of South America (Colombia), as distinguished from the West Indies. Also, the isthmus of Panama. Sense 2 is now the only one in common use.

terraglia *noun* M19 **Italian** (= earthenware, china, from Latin *terra* earth). *Ceramics* An Italian cream-colored earthenware.

terra ignota *noun phrase* E20 **Latin** (*terra* land + feminine of *ignotus* unknown). TERRA INCOGNITA.

terra incognita *noun phrase* E17 **Latin** (= unknown land). An unknown or unexplored territory, land, or region; *figurative* an unknown or unexplored area of study, knowledge, or experience.

■ Frequently without article.

terrain vague *noun phrase* E20 **French** (colloquial, literally 'waste ground'). Wasteland, no man's land; a gray area.

terra irredenta *noun phrase* M20 **Italian.** IRREDENTA.

terra rosa *noun phrase* L19 **Italian** (literally, 'rose-colored earth'). A light red pigment produced from iron oxide and used in oil and watercolor painting; the light red color of this pigment, similar to Venetian red.

terra rossa *noun phrase* L19 **Italian** (*terra* earth + feminine of *rosso* red). *Soil Science* A reddish soil occurring on limestone in Mediterranean climates.

terra sigillata *noun phrase* LME **Medieval Latin** (= sealed earth). **1** LME An astringent bole, of fatty consistency and reddish color, originally obtained from the Aegean island of Lemnos, formerly valued as a medicine and antidote. *obsolete* except *historical.* **2** M16–E17 Red pigment; raddle. **3** E20 *Archaeology* A type of fine Roman earthenware, especially Samian ware, made from this or a similar earth from the first century BC to the third century AD in Gaul (also Italy and Germany), usually red in color and sometimes decorated with stamped figures or patterns. **b** M20 A ware made in imitation of this.

terrasse *noun* L19 **French.** Originally in France, a flat, paved area outside a building, especially a café, where people sit to take refreshments.

terrazzo *noun* plural **terrazzos** E20 **Italian** (= terrace, balcony). A flooring material made of chips of marble or granite set in concrete and polished to give a smooth surface.

terre-à-terre *adjective & adverb phrase* E18 **French** (from Italian *terra a terra* level with the ground). *Ballet* Of a step or manner of dancing: in which the feet remain on or close to the ground. Also *transferred,* without elevation of style; down-to-earth, realistic; pedestrian, unimaginative.

terre cuite *noun phrase* M19 **French** (literally, 'baked (cooked) earth'). TERRACOTTA sense 1.

terre pisée *noun phrase* M20 **French** (literally, 'beaten earth'). PISÉ.

terreplein *noun* L16 **French** (*terre-plein* from Italian *terrapieno,* from *terrapienare* to fill with earth, from *terra* earth + *pieno* (from Latin *plenus*) full). **1** L16 Originally, a talus or sloping bank of earth behind a wall or rampart. Later, the surface of a rampart behind a parapet. **2** M17 The level base (above, on, or below the natural surface of the ground) on which a battery of guns is mounted in field fortifications. Also, the natural surface of the ground around a fortification.

terre-verte *noun* M17 **French** (= green earth). A soft green earth of varying composition used as a pigment, *especially* a variety of glauconite obtained from Italy, Cyprus, and France; the color of this pigment, a soft grayish green.

terribilità *noun* (also **terribiltà**) L19 **Italian.** **1** L19 *Art* Awesomeness or emotional intensity of conception and execution in an artist or work of art; originally a quality attributed to Michelangelo by his contemporaries. **2** M20 *generally* Terrifying or awesome quality.

terrine *noun* E18 **French** (= large earthenware pot, feminine of Old French *terrin* earthen, from Latin *terra* earth). **1** E18 Originally a tureen. Now, an earthenware or similar fireproof vessel, *especially* one in which a terrine or pâté is cooked or sold. **2** E18 Originally, a dish of meat, game, poultry, etc., stewed in a tureen or covered earthenware vessel. Now, a kind of pâté, usually coarse-textured, cooked in and often served from a terrine or earthenware vessel.

terroir *noun* L20 **French** (= soil). *Viticulture* The soil and other local conditions especially as seen as giving a particular character to a wine.

tertium comparationis *noun phrase* E20 **Latin** (= the third element in comparison). The factor that links or is the common ground between two elements in comparison.

tertium quid *noun phrase* E18 **Late Latin** (translation of Greek *triton ti* some third thing). Something indefinite or left undefined related in some way to two definite or known things, but distinct from both.

tertius *adjective* E19 **Latin** (= third). Designating the youngest (in age or standing) of three people, especially pupils, with the same surname.

■ Appended to a surname and used especially in British public (i.e., private) schools. Cf. PRIMUS adjective 2, SECUNDUS.

tertius gaudens *noun phrase* L19 **Latin** (from *tertius* third + *gaudens* present participle of *gaudere* rejoice). A third party benefiting by the conflict or estrangement of two others.

terza rima *noun phrase* E19 **Italian** (= third rhyme). *Prosody* A form of iambic verse of Italian origin, consisting of triplets in which the middle line of each triplet rhymes with the first and third of the next.

■ Best known as the meter of Dante's *Divina Commedia*.

terzetto *noun* plural **terzettos, terzetti** E18 **Italian.** *Music* A vocal or (occasionally) instrumental trio.

tessera *noun* plural **tesserae** M17 **Latin** (from Greek, neuter of *tesseres* variant of *tessares* four). **1a** M17 *Classical Antiquities* A small quadrilateral tablet of wood, bone, etc., used as a token, tally, ticket, etc. **b** M17 *figurative* A distinguishing sign or token; a watchword. **2** L18 A small square block of marble, glass, tile, etc., used in mosaic. **3** E20 *Zoology* Each of the plates of an armadillo's carapace.

tessitura *noun* L19 **Italian.** *Music* The range within which most tones of a voice part or melody lie.

teste *noun & preposition* LME **Latin** (ablative of *testis* witness, in the formula of authentication *teste meipso*, literally, 'I myself being a witness'). **A** *noun* LME *Law* (now *historical*). Originally, the final clause in a royal writ naming the person who authenticates the monarch's seal. Later, the concluding part of any duly attested writ, giving the date and place of issue. **B** *preposition* M19 On the authority or testimony of (a specified person).

testimonium *noun* plural **testimonia** L17 **Latin** (from *testis* witness). **1** L17 A letter testifying to the suitability of a candidate for holy orders; a certificate of proficiency awarded by a university, college, etc. **2** M19 *Law* A concluding part of a document stating the manner of its execution. In full *testimonium clause.*

testo *noun* plural **testi** E18 **Italian** (from Latin *textus* text). *Music* **1** E18 The words of a song; the libretto of an opera; the text or theme of a composition. **2** M20 The narrator in an oratorio or similar work.

tête-à-tête *noun, adverb, adjective, & verb* (also **tête à tête**) L17 **French** (literally, 'head to head'). **A** *noun* **1** L17 A private conversation or interview, especially between two people. **2** M19 An S-shaped sofa, enabling two people to sit face to face. **B** *adverb* E18 Together in private; face to face. **C** *attributive* or as *adjective* E18 Private, confidential; involving or attended by only two people. **D** *intransitive verb* M19 Engage in private conversation (*with* another person).

tête-bêche : *noun & adjective* L19 **French** (from *tête* head + *bêche* (reduced from *béchevet*), literally, 'double bed-head'). *Philately* (A postage stamp) printed upside down relative to the next stamp in the same row or column.

tête de boeuf *adjective phrase* L19 **French** (literally, 'ox's head'). *Embroidery* Designating an embroidery stitch involving two slanting stitches in the form of a V.

tête de cuvée *noun phrase* plural **têtes de cuvées** E20 **French** (literally, 'head of the vatful'). (Wine from) a vineyard producing the best wine in the locality of a village.

tête de nègre *adjective phrase* E20 **French** (literally, 'negro's head'). Of a dark brown color approaching black.

tête montée *adjective & noun phrase* E19 **French** (literally, 'excited head'). **A** *adjective phrase* E19 Overexcited, agitated, worked up. **B** *noun phrase* M19 Such a state of mind.

têtes de cuvées plural of TÊTE DE CUVÉE.

textura *noun & adjective* E20 **German** ((also *Textur*) from Latin *textura* texture). (Designating or pertaining to) any of a group of typefaces first used in the earliest printed books, distinguished by narrow, angular letters and a strong vertical emphasis. Also, (designating or pertaining to) the formal manuscript hand on which these typefaces were based.

textus receptus *noun* plural same M19 **Latin** (literally, 'received text' (medieval Latin *textus* the Gospel)). A text accepted as authoritative; *specifically* (usually with capital initials) the received text of the Greek New Testament.

thali *noun* M20 **Hindustani** (*thālī* from Sanskrit *sthālī*). A metal platter or flat dish on which Indian food is served; an Indian meal comprising a selection of assorted dishes, especially served on such a platter.

thalweg *noun* (also **talweg**) M19 **German** (from *thal* (now *Tal*) valley + *Weg* way). *Physical Geography* The line of fastest descent from any point on land; *especially* one connecting the deepest points along a river channel or the lowest points along a valley floor.

theatrum mundi *noun phrase* M16 **Latin** (literally, 'theater of the world'). The world thought of as a theatrical presentation of all aspects of human life.

thé complet *noun phrase* plural **thés complets** M20 **French** (literally, 'complete tea'). A light meal including tea and usually bread and cake. Cf. CAFÉ COMPLET.

thé dansant *noun phrase* plural **thés dansants** E19 **French** (literally, 'dancing tea'). An afternoon entertainment at which there is dancing and tea is served.

thermae *noun plural* M16 **Latin** (from Greek *thermai* hot baths). *Classical Antiquities* Public baths.

■ The Anglicized singular form, *therm*, is seldom found.

thesaurus *noun* plural **thesauri, thesauruses** L16 **Latin** (from Greek *thesauros* store, treasure, storehouse). **1** L16 A dictionary; an encyclopedia. **b** M19 A collection of words arranged in lists or groups according to sense. Also, a dictionary of synonyms (and occasionally of antonyms). **c** M20 A classified list of terms, especially keywords, in a particular field, for use in indexing and information retrieval. **2** E19 A treasury, especially of a temple.

thesis *noun* plural **theses** LME **Late Latin** (from Greek = putting, placing; a proposition, an affirmation, from *the-* base of *tithenai* to put, place). **I 1** LME The syllable or part of a metrical foot that is unstressed (originally, *Classical Prosody*, by lowered pitch or volume); the stressed beat in barred music. Opposed to ARSIS. **II 2** L16 A proposition laid down or stated, *especially* one maintained or put forward as a premise in an argument, or to be proved; a statement, an assertion, a tenet. **3** L16 A dissertation to maintain and prove a thesis or proposition; *especially* one written or submitted by a candidate as the sole or principal requirement for a university degree.

theta *noun* LME **Greek** (*thēta*). **1** LME The eighth letter (Θ, θ) of the Greek alphabet, also used in transliterating other languages. Also, the phonetic symbol θ, used *specifically* in the International Phonetic Alphabet to represent a voiceless dental fricative. **2** M20 *Chemistry* Used *attributively* to designate the temperature of a polymer solution at which it behaves ideally as regards its osmotic pressure (also θ, Θ *temperature*), and the conditions, solvent, etc., associated with such behavior. **3** M20 *Particle Physics* A meson that decays into two pions, now identified as a kaon. Also *theta meson*, *θ-meson*.

■ In a transferred use of sense 1, *theta* is a sign of doom or a death sentence, in allusion to the custom of using θ as standing for *thanatos* 'death' on the ballots used in voting on a sentence of life or death in ancient Greece.

tholos *noun* plural **tholoi** (also (especially in sense 1) **tholus**, plural **tholi**) **M17 Latin** (*tholus*, Greek *tholos*). **1** M17 *Architecture* A circular domed building or structure; a dome, a cupola. **2** L19 *Greek Antiquities* A dome-shaped tomb, especially of the Mycenaean period. Also *tholos tomb*.

thorax *noun* plural **thoraces**, **thoraxes** **LME Latin** (from Greek *thōrax*, *thōrak-*). **1** LME *Anatomy* and *Zoology* The part of the body of a mammal between the neck and the abdomen; the chest. Also, the corresponding part of a bird, reptile, amphibian, or fish. **2** M18 *Zoology* The middle section of the body of an arthropod, between the head and the abdomen. **3** M19 *Greek Antiquities* A breastplate, a cuirass.

threnos plural **threnoi** **E17 Greek** (*thrēnos* funeral lament). A song of lamentation; a dirge, a threnody.

■ The Anglicized form *threne* (cf. Old French *thrène*) was in use earlier (LME), but is now chiefly poetic. *Threnos* was the heading given by Shakespeare to the lament in his *Phoenix and Turtle* (1601), but in modern usage it is generally used with reference to a ritualized funeral lamentation as practiced in the ancient Mediterranean world.

Thule *noun* **OE Latin** (*Thule*, *Thyle* from Greek *Thoulē*, *Thulē*, of unknown origin; in sense 2, from *Thule* (now Dundas), a settlement in Northwest Greenland). **1a** OE *Antiquities* A land (variously conjectured to be the Shetland Islands, Iceland, or part of Denmark or Norway) to the north of Britain, believed by ancient Greek and Roman geographers to be the most northerly region in the world. **b** L18 *transferred* ULTIMA THULE. **2** E20 *Archaeology* A prehistoric Eskimo culture. Frequently *attributive*.

Thummim *noun* **M16 Hebrew** (*tummīm* plural of *tōm* completeness). One of the two objects of a now unknown nature worn on the breastplate of a Jewish high priest (Exodus 28:30). Chiefly in *Urim and Thummim*. See URIM.

thuringer *noun* **M20 German** (*Thüringer Wurst* Thuringian sausage). A mildly seasoned summer sausage.

thyrsus *noun* plural **thyrsi** **L16 Latin** (from Greek *thursos* stalk of a plant, Bacchic staff). **1** L16 *Classical Antiquities* A staff or spear tipped with an ornament like a pine cone, carried by Bacchus and his followers. **2** E18 *Botany* Any of several forms of inflorescence.

tian *noun* **M20 Provençal** (ultimately from Greek *tēganon* frying pan, saucepan). A large oval earthenware cooking pot traditionally used in Provence; a dish of finely chopped vegetables cooked in olive oil and then baked *au gratin*.

tiara *noun* **M16 Latin** (from Greek, partly through Italian). **1** M16 *History* Any of various headdresses formerly worn in (the region of) ancient Persia. **2** M17 A richly ornamental three-crowned diadem formerly worn by popes; *figurative* the office of pope. Also more fully *triple tiara*. **b** L18 *Heraldry* A charge in the form of a triple crown, representing the papal tiara. **3** E18 A woman's (usually jeweled) ornamental coronet or headband worn on the front of the hair. **4** M19 The headdress of the Jewish high priest.

tic *noun* **E19 French** (from Italian *ticchio*). **1** E19 (A disorder characterized by) a repeated habitual spasmodic twitching of one or more muscles, especially of the face, largely involuntary and accentuated under stress. **2** E19 TIC DOULOUREUX. **3** L19 A whim, a spontaneous reaction, an idiosyncrasy.

tic douloureux *noun phrase* E19 **French** (= painful tic). Trigeminal neuralgia, in which spasms of pain are frequently accompanied by twitching of the facial muscles.

tiens *interjection* M20 **French** (imperative singular of *tenir* hold). Expressing surprise.

tienta *noun* E20 **Spanish** (literally, 'probe'). In Spain: an occasion at which young bulls are tested for qualities suitable for stud and fighting bulls.

tiercé *noun* (also **tierce**) M20 **French** (past participle of Old and Modern French *tiercer* to divide into three parts). Especially in France, a method of betting requiring the first three horses in a race to be named in the correct order; a horse race at which this method prevails.

tierceron *noun* M19 **French** (from *tiers* third). *Architecture* A subordinate rib springing from the point of intersection of two main ribs of a vault.

tiers état *noun phrase* L18 **French**. Chiefly *History* The Third Estate, the commons in the National Assembly of pre-Revolutionary France.

tiers monde *noun phrase* M20 **French**. The Third World; the developing nations.

tignon *noun* L19 **Louisiana French** (from French *tigne* dialectal variant of *teigne* moth). A handkerchief worn as a turban headdress especially in Louisiana by Creole women.

tika *noun* (also **tikka**) L19 **Hindustani** (*ṭīkā*, Punjabi *ṭikkā*). Among Hindus, a mark on the forehead (especially of a woman) indicating caste, status, etc., or worn by both sexes as an ornament. Also *tika dot, mark*. Cf. TILAK.

tiki *noun* L18 **Maori** (= image). A large wooden or small ornamental greenstone image of an ancestor or any human figure.

tikka *noun* M20 **Punjabi** (*ṭikkā*). *Indian Cooking* (A dish of) small pieces of meat or vegetable marinaded in spices and cooked on a skewer. Frequently with qualifying word, as *chicken tikka, lamb tikka*.

tilak *noun* L19 **Sanskrit** (*tilaka*). Among Hindus, a mark or large symbol on the forehead indicating caste, status, etc., or worn as an ornament. Cf. TIKA.

tilde *noun* M19 **Spanish** (from (with metathesis) Latin *titulus* title). **1** M19 The diacritical mark ˜ placed in Spanish above *n* to indicate the palatalized sound, as in *señor*; a similar mark in Portuguese above *a* and *o* and in some phonetic transcriptions to indicate nasality. **b** M20 *Paleography* and *Printing* The diacritical mark ˜ placed above a letter to indicate contraction of a following *n* or *m*. **2** M20 This mark used as a symbol in mathematics and logic, chiefly to indicate negation.

tilleul *noun & adjective* M16 **French** (from Latin diminutive form from *tilia* linden). **A** *noun* **1** M16 A lime or linden tree. **2** L19 A pale yellowish green color. Also *tilleul green*. **B** *adjective* L19 Of a pale yellowish green color.

tilma *noun* M19 **Mexican Spanish** (from Nahuatl *tílmatli*). A simple cloak or blanket secured with a knot, worn by Mexican Indians.

timbale *noun* E19 **French** (in sense 3, perhaps from Spanish *timbal*, plural *timbales* of same origin). **1** E19 A drum-shaped dish made of finely ground meat, fish, etc., cooked in a pastry crust or a mold. Also (in full *timbale mold*), the mold or crust in which this dish is served. **2** M19 *Entomology* A membrane that forms part of the sound-producing organ in various insects, as the cicada. **3** E20 In *plural* Two single-headed drums played as a pair with drumsticks.

tinaja *noun* plural **tinajas** L16 **Spanish** (augmentative of *tina, tino* vat from Latin *tina*). **1** L16 In Spain: a large earthenware jar for holding wine, oil, olives, or salted fish or meat. In parts of Latin America: such a jar used for storing water. **2** M19 In the southwestern United States: a rock hollow where water is retained; any temporary or intermittent pool.

t'ing *noun* M19 **Chinese** (*tíng* (Wade–Giles *t'ing*)). In China: a small open pavilion used as a place to rest or view the landscape.

tinnitus *noun* M19 **Latin** (from *tinnire* to ring, tinkle, of imitative origin). *Medicine* A sensation of ringing or buzzing in the ears.

tinto *noun* L16 **Spanish** (= tinted, dark colored). A sweet deep red wine. Now also *generally*, (a drink of) any red wine.

tiorba *noun* plural **tiorbe** M20 **Italian**. A theorbo.

tipi variant of TEPEE.

tirade *noun & verb* E19 **French** (from Italian *tirata* volley, from *tirare* Proto-Romance verb meaning 'draw'). **A** *noun* **1** E19 A long vehement speech on some subject; a declamation, a denunciation. **2** E19 A passage of a poem dealing with a single theme or idea. **3** L19 *Music* An ornamental run or flourish filling an interval between two notes. **B** *intransitive verb* L19 Utter or write a tirade; declaim vehemently.

tirage *noun* L19 **French** (= drawing, bringing out, printing, from *tirer* to draw). A reprint of a book from the same type; an impression.

tirailleur *noun* L18 **French** (from *tirailler* to fire in skirmishing order, from *tirer* to draw, shoot). *French History* Any of a body of skirmishers employed in the French Revolutionary War in 1792; a skirmisher, a sharpshooter.

tiramisu *noun* L20 **Italian** (from phrase *tira mi sù* pick me up). An Italian dessert consisting of layers of sponge cake soaked in coffee and brandy or liqueur with powdered chocolate and mascarpone cheese.

tiro, tirocinium variants of TYRO, TYROCINIUM.

tisane *noun* LME **Old and Modern French** (*tisane*, also formerly *ptisane*, from Latin *(p)tisana* from Greek *ptisanē* peeled barley, barley water, related to *ptissein* to peel). A wholesome or medicinal drink or infusion, originally *specifically* made with barley; now (*especially*), an herbal tea.

titer *noun* (also **titre**) M19 **French**. **1** M19 Originally, the fineness of gold or silver. Now (*Chemistry*), the concentration of a solution as determined by titration; *Medicine* the concentration of an antibody, as measured by the extent to which it can be diluted before ceasing to give a positive reaction with antigen. **2** L19 *Chemistry* The highest temperature reached during controlled crystallization of free insoluble fatty acids in an oil.

titulus *noun* plural **tituli** E20 **Latin**. An inscription on or over something; *especially* the inscription on the Cross.

ti-tzu *noun* L19 **Chinese** (*dízi* (Wade–Giles *ti-tzu*)). *Music* A Chinese bamboo transverse flute.

tjaele *noun* (also **taele**) E20 **Swedish** (*tjäle* ice in frozen ground). A frozen surface at the base of the active layer in a periglacial environment, which moves downward as thaw occurs. Frequently *attributive*.

tjurunga variant of CHURINGA.

tmesis *noun* plural **tmeses** M16 **Greek** (*tmēsis* cutting, from *temnein* to cut). *Grammar* and *Rhetoric* The separation of the elements of a compound word by the interposition of another word or words.

toccata *noun* E18 **Italian** (noun use of feminine past participle of *toccare* to touch). *Music* A composition for a keyboard instrument, intended to exhibit the performer's touch and technique and having the air of an improvisation. Also, a fanfare for brass instruments.

toccatina *noun* M18 **Italian** (diminutive of TOCCATA). *Music* A short toccata.

tochis variant of TOKUS.

tofu *noun* L18 **Japanese** (*tōfu* from Chinese *dòufu*, from *dòu* beans + *fŭ* rot, turn sour). A curd made from mashed soybeans; bean curd.

toga *noun* E17 **Latin** (related to *tegere* to cover). **1** E17 *Roman History* A loose flowing outer garment worn by a Roman citizen, made of a single piece of cloth and covering the whole body apart from the right arm. **2** M18 *transferred* and *figurative* A robe of office; a professional gown; a mantle of responsibility, etc.

togidashi *noun & adjective* L19 **Japanese** (from *togu* whet, grind + *dasu* produce, let appear). (Made of) a kind of Japanese lacquer in which gold or silver designs are overlaid with several coats of lacquer that are then rubbed and ground down, revealing the underlying design as if floating below the lacquer surface.

togt *noun* M19 **Afrikaans** (from Dutch *tocht* expedition, journey). **1** A trading expedition or venture. Only in M19. **2** E20 In South Africa: casual labor, hired for a specific job.

tohu-bohu *noun* E17 **Hebrew** (*thōhū wabhōhū* emptiness and desolation (Genesis 1:2)). That which is empty and formless; chaos; utter confusion.

toile *noun* LME **French**. **1 a** LME–L16 Cloth; cloth or canvas used for painting on. *rare*. **b** E20 A painting on canvas. **2** L18 Any of various linen or cotton fabrics. Frequently with French specifying word(s), as in *toile de Jouy*. **3** M20 A reproduction of a fashion garment made up in muslin or other cheap material so that fitting alterations or copies can be made.

toison d'or *noun phrase* E17 **French** (= fleece of gold). *Heraldry* and *Greek Mythology* The Golden Fleece.

tokamak *noun* M20 **Russian** (from *to*roidal'naya *ka*mera s *mag*nitnym polem, toroidal chamber with magnetic field). *Physics* A toroidal apparatus for producing controlled fusion reactions in a hot plasma, in which the controlling magnetic field is the sum of a toroidal field and a poloidal field.

tokoloshe *noun* M19 **Sesotho** (*thokolosi*, *t(h)koloshi*, Xhosa *uThikoloshe*, Zulu *utokoloshe*). In southern African folklore, a mischievous and lascivious hairy manlike creature of short stature.

tokus *noun* (also **tochis**, **tuchis**) E20 **Yiddish** (*tokhes* from Hebrew *tahat* beneath). The buttocks; the anus. *slang*.

toldo *noun* plural **toldos** M19 **Spanish** (= awning, canopy, penthouse). **1** M19 In Spanish-speaking countries: a canopy. **2** M19 A South American Indian tent, hut, or other simple dwelling.

tole *noun & adjective* (also **tôle**) M20 **French** (*tôle* sheet iron, from dialect *taule* table, from Latin *tabula* a flat board). **A** *noun* M20 Enameled or lacquered tin-plated sheet iron used for making decorative metalwork. Also *tôle peinte*. **B** *attributive* or as *adjective* M20 Made of tole.

tolkach *noun* plural **tolkachi** M20 **Russian** (from *tolkat'* to push, jostle). In countries of the former USSR: a person who negotiates difficulties or arranges things, a fixer.

toman *noun* E19 **Gaelic** (diminutive of *tom* hill). A hillock; a mound, *especially* one formed of glacial moraine.

tomatillo *noun* L20 **Mexican Spanish** (= small tomato). A small green berry used in Mexican cooking.

tombac *noun* E17 **French** (from Portuguese *tambaca* from Malay *tembaga* copper, brass, perhaps from Sanskrit *tāmraka* copper; cf. TUMBAGA). *Metallurgy* A brittle brass alloy originally produced in Indochina, containing from 72 to 99 per cent of copper and from 1 to 28 per cent of zinc, used in the east for gongs and bells, and in the west for cheap jewelry, etc. Also called *red brass*.

tombarolo *noun* plural **tombaroli** L20 **Italian** (from *tomba* tomb, grave). A grave robber.

tombola *noun* L19 **French** (or Italian, from Italian *tombolare* to turn a somersault, tumble). A kind of lottery with tickets usually drawn from a turning drum-shaped container, especially at a carnival or fair.

tombolo *noun* plural **tombolos** L19 **Italian** (= sand dune). *Physical Ge-*

ography A bar of shingle, sand, etc., joining an island to the mainland.

tomme *noun* M20 **French**. Any of various cheeses made in Savoy, a region of southeast France.

ton *noun* M18 **French** (from Latin *tonus* tone). **1** M18 *The* fashion, *the* vogue; fashionableness, style. **2** M18 Fashionable people collectively; the fashionable world. Treated as *singular* or *plural*. Cf. HAUT TON.

tonadilla *noun* plural **tonadillas** M19 **Spanish** (diminutive of *tonada* tune, song). A light operatic interlude performed originally as an intermezzo but later independently.

tondi plural of TONDO.

tondino *noun* plural **tondini** E18 **Italian** (diminutive of TONDO). **1** E18 *Architecture* A round molding resembling a ring. **2** L19 *Ceramics* A majolica plate with a wide flat rim and deep center.

tondo *noun* plural **tondi**, **tondos** L19 **Italian** (= a round, a circle, a compass, shortened from *rotondo* round). An easel painting of circular form; a carving in relief within a circular space.

tong *noun* L19 **Chinese** ((Cantonese) *t'ōng* (= Mandarin *táng*) hall, meeting place). An association or secret society of Chinese in the United States, originally formed as a benevolent or protective society but frequently associated with underworld criminal activity.

tonneau *noun* plural **tonneaus**, in sense 1 also **tonneaux** L18 **French** (= barrel, cask). **1** L18 A unit of capacity for French (especially Bordeaux) wine, usually equal to 900 liters (198 gallons). **2** E20 The rounded rear body of some vintage automobiles (originally with the door at the back); the rear part of a car with front and rear compartments, or of an open car or carriage. Also, a car having a tonneau.

tonnelle *noun* M19 **French** (= tunnel). An arbor.

tontine *noun & adjective* M18 **French** (from Lorenzo *Tonti* (1630–95), Neapolitan banker, who started such a scheme to raise government loans in France around 1653). **A** *noun* **1** M18 A financial scheme by which subscribers to a loan or common fund each receive an annuity for life, the amount increasing as each dies, till the last survivor enjoys the whole income. Also, the share or right of each subscriber in such a scheme; the subscribers collectively; the fund so established. **2** L19 A scheme for life insurance in which the beneficiaries are those who survive and maintain a policy to the end of a given period. **B** *attributive* or as *adjective* L18 Of, pertaining to, or of the nature of a tontine.

tonto *noun & adjective* L20 **Spanish**. **A** *noun* L20 plural **tontos**. A foolish or stupid person. **B** *adjective* L20 Foolish, crazy; mad. *colloquial*.

topi *noun* (also **topee**) M19 **Anglo-Indian** (Hindustani *ṭopī* hat). A hat; *specifically* a pith helmet, a sola topi.

■ *Sola topi* has no etymological connection with the sun or *solar*, but refers to the tropical Asian swamp plants (Bengali *solā*, Hindustani *śolā*) from the lightweight pith of which the sun helmets were made.

topinambour *noun* (also (earlier) **topinambou**) M17 **French** (*topinambou*, now *topinambour*, from Portuguese *tupinambo(r)* alteration of *tupinamba* (sc. *batata* potato)). The Jerusalem artichoke, *Helianthus tuberosus*.

topos *noun* plural **topoi** M20 **Greek**. A traditional theme in a literary composition; a rhetorical or literary formula.

toque *noun* E16 **French** (corresponding obscurely to Italian *tocca*, *tocco*, Spanish *toca*, Portuguese *touca* cap, woman's headdress, of unknown origin). **1** E16 Originally, a type of hat with a full pouched crown and a narrow, closely turned-up brim, fashionable among both sexes in the sixteenth century. Now, a small hat without a projecting brim, or with a very small or closely turned-up brim. **b** E19 *His-*

tory A pad used in hairdressing to give additional height. *rare.* **2** L19 A TUQUE. *Canadian.* **3** M20 A tall white hat with a full pouched crown, worn by chefs.

torana *noun* L19 **Sanskrit** (*toraṇa* gate, arched portal). In the Indian subcontinent: a sacred Buddhist gateway, consisting of a pair of uprights with one or more (usually three) crosspieces and elaborate carving.

torc variant of TORQUE.

torchère *noun* E20 **French** (from Old and Modern French *torche* torch, from Proto-Romance, from Latin *torqua* variant of *torques* necklace, wreath, from *torquere* to twist). A tall ornamental flat-topped stand for a candlestick.

torchon *noun* M19 **French** (= duster, dishcloth, from *torcher* to wipe). A coarse loose-textured kind of bobbin lace with geometrical designs. In full *torchon lace.*

toreador *noun* plural **toreadors, toreadores** E17 **Spanish** (from *torear* to fight bulls, from TORO). A bullfighter, *especially* one on horseback. Cf. TORERO.

torero *noun* plural **toreros** E18 **Spanish** (from TORO). A bullfighter, *especially* one on foot. Cf. TOREADOR.

tori plural of TORUS.

torii *noun* plural same E18 **Japanese** (from *tori* bird + *i* sit, perch). A ceremonial gateway of a Japanese Shinto shrine, with two uprights and two crosspieces.

toril *noun* plural **toriles** L19 **Spanish.** *Bullfighting* Any of a series of pens confining the bull before a fight, *especially* the last pen leading to the ring.

toro *noun* plural **toros** M17 **Spanish** (from Latin *taurus* bull). A bull used in bullfighting.

torque *noun* (also **torc**) M19 **French** (from Latin *torques* necklace, wreath, from *torquere* to twist). *History* A neck ornament formed from a twisted band of (usually precious) metal, worn especially by the ancient Celts.

torsade *noun* L19 **French** (from Latin *tors-* past participial stem of *torquere* to twist). A decorative twisted braid, ribbon, etc., used as trimming; an artificial plait of hair.

Torschlusspanik *noun* M20 **German** (= last-minute panic (literally, 'shut door (or gate) panic')). A sense of alarm or anxiety at the passing of life's opportunities, said to be experienced in middle age.

torso *noun* plural **torsos** L18 **Italian** (= stalk, stump, trunk of a statue, from as THYRSUS). **1** L18 The trunk of a statue, without or considered independently of head and limbs. Also, the trunk of the human body. **2** E19 *figurative* An incomplete or mutilated thing.

torte *noun* plural **tortes, torten** M18 **German** (*Torte* tart, pastry, cake, from Italian *torta* from late Latin; cf. TOURTE). An elaborate sweet cake or tart.

■ Originally (ME–M16) used in English in the sense of 'round loaf of bread', probably deriving directly from late Latin *torta* meaning 'round loaf or cake', but the sense derived from German is now the only one current. Cf. LINZERTORTE, SACHERTORTE.

tortellini *noun plural* M20 **Italian** (plural of *tortellino* diminutive of *tortello* small cake, fritter). Small squares of pasta stuffed with meat, cheese, etc., rolled and shaped into rings; an Italian dish consisting largely of this and usually a sauce.

torticollis *noun* E19 **Modern Latin** (from Latin *tortus* crooked, twisted + *collum* neck). *Medicine* A condition in which the head is persistently or intermittently turned or twisted to one side.

tortilla *noun* L17 **Spanish** (diminutive of *torta* cake, from late Latin; see TORTE). Especially in Mexican cooking, a thin round cake made with either cornmeal or wheat flour and frequently filled with meat, cheese, beans, etc. Also, in Spanish cooking, a thick flat omelette frequently eaten cold in wedges.

tortillon *noun* L19 French (from *tortiller* to twist, twirl). An instrument with tapered ends used for softening the edges of a drawing and for making tints uniform, a stump.

torus *noun* plural **tori**, **toruses** M16 Latin (= swelling, bolster, round molding). **1** M16 *Architecture* A large convex molding, especially at the base of a column. **2** E19 *Botany* The receptacle of a flower. **3** L19 *Zoology* A protuberant part or organ; *Anatomy* a smooth rounded ridge. **4** L19 *Geometry* Originally, a surface or solid generated by the revolution of a circle or other conic about any axis. Now *specifically* a surface or solid generated by the circular motion of a circle about an axis outside itself but lying in its plane; a solid ring of circular cross section; a body topologically equivalent to this, having one hole in it but not necessarily circular in form or cross section.

tostada *noun* (also **tostado**, plural **tostados**) M20 Spanish (past participle of *tostar* to toast). A deep-fried cornmeal pancake topped with a seasoned mixture of beans, ground meat, and vegetables.

Totentanz *noun* plural **Totentänze** L18 German (literally, 'death dance'). A representation of Death leading people of all ranks in a dance toward the grave; the Dance of Death. Cf. DANSE MACABRE.

totidem verbis *adverb phrase* M17 Latin. In so many words.

toties quoties *adverb phrase* LME Latin (= so often as often). As often as something happens or occasion demands.

toto *noun* plural **totos** E20 Kiswahili (*mtoto* offspring, child). In East Africa: a child; a baby; a young animal; a young servant.

toto caelo *adverb phrase* L17 Latin (literally, 'by the whole heaven'). Entirely, utterly.

tot siens *interjection & noun* M20 Afrikaans (*tot (weer)siens* until we meet again, from Dutch *tot* until + *zien* see). In South Africa: (goodbye) until we meet again; an utterance of this.

touché *interjection* E20 French (past participle of *toucher* to touch). **1** E20 *Fencing* Expressing acknowledgment of a hit by one's opponent. **2** E20 Expressing good-humored acknowledgment of a valid point or justified accusation made by another person.

toughra variant of TUGHRA.

toujours gai *adverb* E18 French. Always cheerful, cheerful under all circumstances.

■ Now generally with reference to its use as the slogan of mehitabel the cat in Don Marquis' *archy and mehitabel* (1927).

toujours perdrix *adverb* E18 French (literally, 'always partridge'). (Implying that one can have) too much of a good thing.

toupet *noun* E18 French. A patch of false hair or a small wig to cover a bald spot.

■ Originally, a curl or artificial lock of hair worn on the top of the head, especially as part of a wig, or a wig or natural hair dressed to create such a topknot. Formerly also, a wearer of a toupee or topknot, hence a fashionable person.

tourbillion *noun* (also (especially in sense 3) **tourbillon**) L15 French (*tourbillon* from Old French *torbeillon*, from Latin *turbellae* bustle, stir, blended with *turbo* whirlwind). **1** L15 A whirlwind, a whirling storm. Now usually *transferred* and *figurative*, a vortex, a whirl; an eddy, a whirlpool. **2** M18 A kind of firework that spins as it rises. **3** L19 *Watchmaking* A revolving carriage in which the escapement is fitted to counteract position errors.

tour de force *noun phrase* plural **tours de force** E19 French. A feat of strength or skill; an impressive achievement or performance.

tour d'horizon *noun phrase* plural **tours d'horizon** M20 French (literally, 'tour of the horizon'). An extensive tour. Chiefly *figurative*, a broad general survey.

tour jeté see JETÉ EN TOURNANT.

tourmente *noun* M19 French. A whirling storm or eddy of snow.

tournasin *noun* M19 French (*tournas(s)in*, from *tournas(s)er* to turn pottery on a wheel, from *tourner* to turn). A knife or spatula used to remove partially dried excess slip from decorated pottery.

tournedos *noun* plural same L19 French (from *tourner* to turn + *dos* back). A small round thick cut from a fillet of beef, with a surrounding strip of fat.

tournee *noun* (also **tournée**) L18 French. A round, a circuit, a tour.

tournette *noun* E20 French (from *tourner* to turn). *Archaeology* A rotating disk resembling a simple form of potter's wheel.

tourniquet *noun* L17 French (perhaps alteration of Old French *tournicle* variant of *tounicle, tunicle* coat of mail, tunicle, by association with *tourner* to turn). A device for stopping or slowing the flow of blood through an artery by compression.

tournure *noun* M18 French (from Old French *torneure* from popular Latin *tornatura*, from Latin *tornare* to turn). **1** M18 Graceful manner or bearing, deportment. **2** E19 The turning of a phrase, mode of expression. *rare*. **3** E19 The contour or shape of a limb, etc. **4** M19 *History* A bustle. Also, a kind of corset.

tours de force, tours d'horizon plurals of TOUR DE FORCE, TOUR D'HORIZON.

tourte *noun* M17 French (from late Latin *torta* round loaf, cake; cf. TORTE). A pie, a tart, a flan.

tourtière *noun* M20 French (from as TOURTE). **1** M20 A kind of meat pie traditionally eaten at Christmas in Canada. **2** M20 A pan or round baking sheet for tarts and pies.

tout *adjective, noun, & adverb* E18 French. All, everything; quite entirely.

■ Mainly in following phrases, but see also LE TOUT, which may be shortened to *tout*, with similar high society connotations, as in *tout Paris* 'all Paris'.

tout au contraire *adverb phrase* E18 French. Quite the contrary. Cf. AU CONTRAIRE.

tout compris *adverb & adjective phrase* E18 French. All included, inclusive.

tout court *adverb phrase* E18 French. In short, simply, without qualification or addition.

tout de suite *adverb phrase* E18 French. At once, immediately.

tout ensemble *noun phrase* E18 French (from TOUT + ENSEMBLE *noun*). (The parts of) a thing viewed as a whole.

■ Independent use of *ensemble* in this sense is slightly later (M18).

tout le monde *noun phrase* E18 French. All the world, everyone.

tout Paris see under LE TOUT, TOUT.

tou ts'ai *noun & adjective* M20 Chinese (*dǒucǎi* (Wade–Giles *tou ts'ai*), literally, 'contrasting colors'). *Ceramics* (Designating) a kind of Chinese porcelain delicately decorated with a blue underglaze overlaid with colored enamels, developed in the reign of Ch'êng Hua (1465–87); (of or designating) this style of decoration.

tout seul *adverb phrase* E18 French. Quite alone, on one's own.

tout simple *adverb phrase* M20 French. Quite simply, just that.

tovarish *noun* (also **tovarich**) E20 Russian (*tovarishch* from Turkic, perhaps Tatar). In the former USSR: comrade.

■ Frequently as a form of address.

tracasserie *noun* M17 French (from *tracasser* to bustle, worry oneself). A state of disturbance or annoyance; a fuss; a petty quarrel.

■ Usually in plural.

tragédie lyrique *noun phrase* plural **tragédies lyriques** E20 French (literally, 'lyric tragedy'). A type of serious French opera of the seventeenth and eighteenth centuries making use of tragic mythological or epic subjects; an example of this. Cf. OPERA SERIA.

tragédienne *noun* M19 **French** (feminine of *tragédien* tragedian). A tragic actress.

tragédies lyriques plural of TRAGÉDIE LYRIQUE.

tragedietta *noun* L19 **Italian** (from *tragedia* tragedy). A slight or short tragedy; a dramatic sketch of tragic character.

trahison des clercs *noun phrase* M20 **French** (literally, 'the treachery of the clerks'). A compromise of intellectual integrity or betrayal of standards by writers, artists, and thinkers.

■ From *La Trahison des Clercs*, the title of a work by Julien Benda (1927).

traineau *noun* plural **traineaux** M17 **French** (*traîneau*, from *traîner*). A sled, a sleigh, *especially* one drawn by one or more horses or dogs over snow or ice.

trait d'union *noun phrase* plural **traits d'union** E20 **French** (literally, 'hyphen'). A link or point of contact between or among otherwise unconnected characteristics or parties.

traiteur *noun* M18 **French** (from *traiter* to treat, supply with food for money). Originally, (a person running) a restaurant in France, Italy, etc., supplying or sending out meals to order. Now, a caterer; (a person who runs) a delicatessen selling prepared meals.

traits d'union plural of TRAIT D'UNION.

trajet *noun* M18 **French** (from Latin *trajectus* place for crossing). **1** M18 A crossing, a passage. **2** M19 The course of a nerve, blood vessel, etc. *rare*.

tramontana *adjective & noun* ME **Italian** (*tramontana* north wind, polestar, *tramontani* dwellers beyond the mountains, from Latin *transmontanus*, from *trans-* across + *mons, mont-* mount). **A** *noun* **1** ME–M17 The polestar (originally so called because visible beyond the Alps from Italy); *figurative* a guiding star. **2** L16 A person living or originating from beyond the mountains, especially the Alps as seen from Italy; (especially from the Italian point of view) a foreigner. **3** E17 In the Mediterranean and especially in Italy, the north wind (as coming from beyond the Alps). More widely, a cold wind from across a mountain range. **B** *adjective* **1** L16 Living, situated, or originating from beyond the mountains, especially the Alps as seen from Italy. Also (especially from the Italian point of view), foreign; barbarous. **2** E18 Of wind: coming across or from beyond the mountains (especially the Alps).

tranche *noun* or L15 **Old and Modern French** (from *trancher* to cut, ultimately from Latin *truncare*). **1** L15 A cutting, a cut; a piece cut off, a slice. **2** M20 Chiefly *Economics* A portion of something, especially of income; an installment of a loan; a block of shares or of government stock.

tranche de vie *noun phrase* M20 **French** (literally, 'slice of life'). A representation of daily life, especially in literature or painting.

tranchet *noun* M19 **French** (from *trancher* to cut: cf. TRANCHE). **1** A cobbler's knife. Only in M19. **2** L19 *Archaeology* A chisel-shaped flint implement of some mesolithic and neolithic cultures.

tranchette *noun* L20 **French** (from as TRANCHE). *Economics* A small tranche; *especially* a limited issue of government stocks.

tranquillo *adverb, adjective, & noun* M19 **Italian** (from Latin *tranquillus*). *Music* **A** *adverb & adjective* M19 (A direction:) in a tranquil style or tempo; tranquil(ly). **B** *noun* M19 plural **tranquillos**, **tranquilli**. A movement or piece in a tranquil style or tempo.

transire *noun* L16 **Latin** (= to go across). *Law* A customs permit for the passage of goods.

trapezium *noun* plural **trapezia**, **trapeziums** L16 **Late Latin** (from Greek *trapezion* from *trapeza* table). **1** *Geometry* **a** L16 Any quadrilateral that is not a parallelogram. Now *rare*. **b** L17 A quadrilateral having only one pair of opposite sides parallel; a trapezoid.

Chiefly *Brit.* **c** L18 An irregular quadrilateral having neither pair of opposite sides parallel. Now chiefly *North American.* **2** M19 *Anatomy* and *Zoology* The first distal carpal bone of the wrist; the corresponding bone in other mammals. Also *trapezium bone.* **3** M19 *Astronomy* An asterism in the form of a trapezium; *specifically* the multiple star T Orionis in the Great Nebula of Orion.

■ Confusion can arise because American English and British English reverse the senses for *trapezium*and *trapezoid.* For sense **1 b** above, American English uses *trapezoid;* for sense **1 c**, American English uses *trapezium.*

trapiche *noun* M17 **American Spanish** (from Latin *trapetum* oil press). A sugar cane mill.

trapunto *noun* E20 **Italian** (noun use of past participle of *trapungere* to embroider). A kind of quilting in which the design is padded by pulling or cutting the threads of the underlying fabric to insert stuffing.

trascinando *adverb & adjective* L19 **Italian** (present participle of *trascinare* to drag, pull). *Music* RALLENTANDO *adverb & adjective.*

trasformismo *noun* E20 **Italian** (from *trasformare* to change, transform). In Italy: a system of shifting political alliances to form a stable administration or a workable policy.

trauma *noun* plural **traumas**, **traumata** L17 **Greek** (= wound). **1** L17 *Medicine* Originally, physical wound. Now, external or internal injury; a state or condition resulting from this, e.g. shock. **2** L19 *Psychoanalysis* and *Psychiatry* A psychic injury, especially one caused by emotional shock; a state or condition resulting from this. **3** L20 *generally* Distress; (a) disturbance.

travaux préparatoires *noun phrase plural* M20 **French** (literally, 'preparatory works'). *Law* Drafts, records of discussions, etc., relating to legislation or a treaty under consideration.

travers *noun* plural same L19 **French** (*pied de travers* foot askew, from *travers* breadth, irregularity, from *traverser* to traverse). *Horsemanship* A movement in which a horse walks parallel to a wall with its head and neck facing forward and its hindquarters curved out from the wall.

traverso *noun* plural **traversos** E19 **Italian.** *Music* A transverse flute.

travois *noun* plural same M19 **North American French** (alteration of French *travail*). A traditional North American Indian vehicle consisting of two joined poles pulled by a horse, etc.

trebuchet *noun* (also **trebucket**) ME **Old and Modern French** (*trébuchet* (medieval Latin *trebuchetum, trabuchetum*), from *trébucher* to overturn, overthrow, stumble, fall, ultimately from *tra-, tres-* (from Latin *trans-* expressing displacement) + *buc* trunk (of the body), bulk, from Frankish *būk* belly). **1** ME *History* A medieval military machine used in siege warfare for hurling heavy stones and other missiles. **2** M16 A small delicately poised balance or pair of scales. **3** M17 *History* A ducking stool.

trecento *noun* M19 **Italian** (= three hundred). The fourteenth century as a period of Italian art, architecture, literature, etc.; the style of the art, etc., of this period.

tre corde *adverb & adjective phrase* M20 **Italian** (= three strings). (A direction in music for the piano:) with release of the soft pedal; (to be) played with such release. Cf. UNA CORDA.

trefa *noun & adjective* (also **trifa**, **tref**, and other variants) M19 **Hebrew** (*ṭĕrēphāh* flesh of an animal torn or mauled, from *ṭāraf* to tear, rend). **A** *noun* M19 Meat forbidden to Jews because of coming from an animal not slaughtered according to Jewish law; *generally* any food that is not kosher. **B** *attributive* or as *adjective* M19 Of food: not prepared according to Jewish law, forbidden to Jews, not kosher.

treff *noun* M20 **German** (*Treff* meeting(-place), *Treffpunkt* rendezvous, from *treffen* to meet, strike). In espionage, a secret meeting or meeting place, especially for the transfer of goods or information. *slang.*

treillage *noun* L17 **French** (from Old French *treille* from Latin *trichila* arbor, bower). A trellis; trelliswork.

trek *noun* **M19 Afrikaans** (from Dutch *trekken* to pull). **1** M19 Travel by ox wagon; a journey, especially an organized migration or expedition, made in this way; a stage of such a journey. *South African,* chiefly *historical.* **2** L19 *generally* A long and arduous journey or expedition, *especially* one made on foot or by inconvenient means.

tremblement *noun* L17 **French. 1** L17 A tremor; the act of trembling. **2** L17 A cause of trembling; a terror. *rare.* **3** L19 *Music* A trill.

trembleuse *noun* **M19 French** (feminine of *trembleur* trembler). A cup having a saucer with a well into which it fits. More fully *trembleuse cup.*

tremendum *noun* **E20 Latin** (neuter of *tremendus* fearful, terrible, from *tremere* to tremble). Elliptical form of MYSTERIUM TREMENDUM.

tremie *noun* **E20 French** (*trémie* from Old French *tremuie* (mill-)hopper, from Latin *trimodia* a three-peck measure, from *tri-* three + *modius* peck). *Engineering* A movable metal tube, widening at its upper end into a large hopper, for depositing concrete under water.

tremolando *noun, adverb, & adjective* **M19 Italian** (present participle of *tremolare* to tremble). *Music* **A** *noun* M19 plural **tremolandos, tremolandi** A TREMOLO senses 1, 2a. **B** *adverb & adjective* M19 (A direction:) with tremolo.

tremolant *noun* **M19 German** (from Italian *tremolante* tremulant). A TREMOLO sense 2a.

tremolo *noun, adjective, & adverb* **M18 Italian** (from Latin *tremulus* from *tremere* to tremble). *Music* **A** *noun* plural **tremolos 1** M18 A tremulous or vibrating effect produced on musical instruments or in singing by rapid reiteration of a single note (especially on a stringed instrument) or rapid alternation between two notes. Cf. VIBRATO. **2a** M19 A mechanical device fitted in an organ to produce such an effect; a tremulant. Also *tremolo stop.* **b** M20 A device, especially a lever, fitted to an electric guitar to produce a similar effect (also *tremolo arm*); an electrical device of similar effect in an amplifier, etc. **B** *adjective & adverb* L19 (A musical direction:) with tremolo.

trente-et-quarante *noun* L17 **French** (literally, 'thirty-and-forty'). = ROUGE-ET-NOIR.

très *adverb* **E19 French.** Very.

■ Colloquial, usually with reference to a fashionable or modishly superior quality.

triage *noun & verb* **E18 Old and Modern French** (from *trier* to sort out). **A** *noun* **1** E18 The action of sorting samples of a commodity according to quality. **2** M20 *Medicine* The assignment of degrees of urgency of need in order to decide the order of treatment of a large number of injured or ill patients. **b** L20 *generally* Prioritization. **B** *transitive & intransitive verb* L20 Assign a degree of urgency of need to (a casualty); separate *out* by triage.

tribade *noun* **E17 French** (or its source Latin *tribas, tribad-* from Greek *tribas,* from *tribein* to rub). A lesbian.

triclinium *noun* plural **triclinia** M17 **Latin** (from Greek *triklinion* diminutive of *triklinos* dining room with three couches, from *tri-* combining form of *treis* three + *klinē* couch, bed). *Roman Antiquities* A couch, running around three sides of a table, on which to recline at meals. Also, a dining room.

tricorn *adjective & noun* (also **tricorne**) **M18 French** (*tricorne* or Latin *tricornis* three-horned, from *tri-* combining form of *tris* three + *cornu* horn). **A** *noun* **1** M18 An imaginary creature with three horns. **2** L19 A hat with the brim turned up on three sides. **B** *adjective* M19 Having three horns; (of a cocked hat) having the brim turned up on three sides.

tricot *noun* L18 **French** (from *tricoter* to knit). A fine warp knitted fabric made of a natural or man-made fiber, produced in any of various designs.

tricoteuse *noun* M19 **French** (from *tricoter* knit). **1** M19 *History* A woman who, during the French Revolution, sat and knitted at meetings of the Convention or at executions by guillotine. **2** M20 A small table with a gallery used for sewing.

tric-trac *noun* L17 **French** (from the clicking sound made by the pieces in the playing of the game). Chiefly *History* A form of backgammon.

triduo *noun* plural **triduos** M19 **Italian and Spanish** (from Latin TRIDUUM). *Roman Catholic Church* A three days' prayer or festal celebration.

triduum *noun* E18 **Latin** (noun use of adjective (sc. *spatium* space), from *tri-* combining form of *tres* three + *dies* day). A period of three days; *especially* (*Roman Catholic Church*) the last three days of Lent.

triennium *noun* plural **trienniums, triennia** M19 **Latin** (from *tri-* combining form of *tres* three + *annus* year). A space or period of three years.

trifa variant of TREFA.

triforium *noun* plural **triforia** E18 **(Anglo-)Latin** (of unknown origin). *Architecture* A gallery or arcade above the arches at the sides of the nave, choir, and sometimes transepts of some large churches, originally *specifically* of Canterbury Cathedral.

Trinkhalle *noun* L19 **German** (literally, 'drinking hall'). In German-speaking countries: a place at a spa where medicinal water is dispensed for drinking; a pump room. Also, an establishment at which liquor is served.

trio *noun* E18 **Italian** (from Latin *tres, tria* three, after DUO). **1** *Music* **a** E18 A composition for three voices or instruments. Also, a group or company of three performers. **b** M19 The central section of a minuet, scherzo, or march, frequently in a different key and style from the preceding and following main division. **2** L18 A group or set of three things or people.

tripot *noun* M19 **French**. In France: a gaming house, a gambling den.

tripotage *noun* L18 **French**. Underhand dealings, intrigue.

triptyque E20 **French**. A customs permit (originally in three sections) serving as a passport for a motor vehicle.

triquetra *noun* plural **triquetrae, triquetras** L16 **Latin** (feminine of *triquetrus* three-cornered). Originally, a triangle. Now *specifically* a symmetrical triangular ornament formed of three interlaced arcs or lobes.

triste *adjective* (originally Anglicized as **trist**) LME **Old and Modern French** (from Latin *tristis* sad). **1** LME Feeling or expressing sorrow; sad, melancholy; causing sorrow, lamentable. **2** M18 Not lively or cheerful; dull, dreary.

tristesse *noun* LME **Old French** (*tristesce* (modern *tristesse*) from Latin *tristitia*, from *tristis* sad). Sadness, sorrow; melancholy.

tristeza *noun* E20 **Portuguese** (and Spanish) literally, 'sadness', cognate with preceding). **1** E20 *Veterinary Medicine* In South America: Texas fever of cattle. Now *rare*. **2** M20 *Agriculture* A viral disease affecting some citrus plants, causing yellowing of the leaves, stunting, and death.

triumvir *noun* plural **triumvirs, triumviri** LME **Latin** (from *triumviri* plural, back-formation from *trium virorum* genitive plural of *tres viri* three men). **1** LME *Roman History* Each of three public officers forming a committee overseeing any of the administrative departments. Also *specifically*, each member of the first or second triumvirate. **2** E17 *transferred* In *plural* Any group of three persons or things in a joint position of power or authority.

trivia *noun plural* E20 **Modern Latin** (plural of TRIVIUM, influenced in sense by *trivial*). Trivialities, trifles; *specifi-*

cally unimportant factual information (as) used in the game of Trivial Pursuit.

trivium *noun* E19 **Latin** (= place where three ways meet, from *tri-* combining form of *tres* three + *via* way). *History* In the Middle Ages, the lower division of a university course of study, comprising grammar, rhetoric, and logic. Cf. QUADRIVIUM.

trochilus *noun* M16 **Latin** (apparently from Greek *trokhilos*, from *trekhein* to run). *Architecture* A SCOTIA.

Trockenbeerenauslese *noun* (also **trockenbeerenauslese**) plural **Trockenbeerenauslesen**, **Trockenbeerenausleses** M20 **German** (from *trocken* dry + as BEERENAUSLESE). A sweet white wine of superior quality made (especially in Germany) from selected individual grapes picked later than the general harvest and affected by noble rot.

troika *noun* M19 **Russian** (*troĭka*, from *troe* a set of three). **1** M19 A Russian vehicle drawn by three horses abreast; the team of horses for such a vehicle. **2** M20 A group of three people or things working together, especially in an administrative or managerial capacity.

trombenik *noun* M20 **Yiddish** (from *tromba* trumpet, horn + noun suffix -*nik* person connected with (something)). A boaster, a bragger; an idle or dissolute person. *slang*.

trompe l'oeil *noun phrase* plural **trompe l'oeils** L19 **French** (literally, 'deceives the eye'). Deception of the eye; (an) optical illusion; *especially* a painting or object intended to give an illusion of reality.

tronc *noun* E20 **French** (= collecting box). In a hotel or restaurant, a common fund into which tips and service charges are paid for distribution to the staff.

troppo *adverb* E20 **Italian**. *Music* (In directions:) too much.

■ Especially in adverb phrase *ma non troppo* 'but not too much'.

trotteur *noun* E20 **French** (from as next). *History* An ankle-length skirt, usually flared at the back for ease of walking.

trottoir *noun* L18 **French** (from *trotter* to trot). Especially in France and French-speaking countries: a sidewalk.

troubadour *noun* E18 **French** (from Provençal *trobador* (= Old French *troveor*), from *trobar* (= Old French *trover*) to find, compose in verse, invent, ultimate origin unknown; cf. TROUVÈRE). **1** E18 *History* Any of a class of French medieval lyric poets composing and singing in Provençal especially on the themes of chivalry and courtly love, living in southern France, eastern Spain, and northern Italy between the eleventh and thirteenth centuries. **2** E19 A person who composes or sings verses.

■ The northern French equivalent of the *troubadour* was the TROUVÈRE.

trousseau *noun* plural **trousseaus**, **trousseaux** M19 **French** (from Old French *troussel* diminutive of *trousse* truss). The clothes, etc., collected by a bride in preparation for her marriage.

■ Originally (ME) in the sense of 'a bundle or package', later 'a bunch', but long rare or obsolete with this meaning. Old French *troussel* in this sense was also represented in English as *trussell* (LME only).

trouvaille *noun* M19 **French** (from *trouver* to find). A lucky find; a windfall.

trouvère *noun* (also **trouveur**) L18 **French** (Old French (*trovere* (modern *trouvère*, *trouveur*) from *troveor*, from *trover* (modern *trouver* to find) to compose in verse, invent, find, ultimate origin unknown; cf. TROUBADOUR). *History* Any of a class of French medieval epic poets composing especially *chansons de geste* and fabliaux, living in northern France between the eleventh and fourteenth centuries.

truite au bleu *noun phrase* M20 **French** (literally, 'trout in the blue'). A dish consisting of trout cooked with vinegar, which turns the fish blue.

■ Also earlier (E20) as *truite bleue*, literally, 'blue trout'.

trullo *noun* plural **trulli** E20 **Italian**. In Apulia in southern Italy: a small round house built of stone, with a conical roof.

trumeau *noun* plural **trumeaux** L19 **French** (literally, 'calf of the leg'). **1** L19 A pier glass. Also *trumeau mirror*. **2** L19 *Architecture* A section of wall or a pillar between two openings, *especially* a pillar supporting the middle of the tympanum of a church doorway.

tsaddik *noun* (also **tzaddik**) plural **tsaddikim**, **tsaddiks** L19 **Hebrew** (*ṣaddīq* just, righteous). In Judaism, a man of exemplary righteousness; a Hasidic spiritual leader or sage.

tsar variant of CZAR.

tsarevich variant of CZAREVICH.

tsarevna variant of CZAREVNA.

tsarina variant of CZARINA.

tsaritsa variant of CZARITSA.

tsatske variant of TCHOTCHKE.

tsimmes variant of TZIMMES.

tsipouro *noun* M20 **Modern Greek**. A rough Greek liquor resembling RAKI, sometimes flavored with mastic gum.

tsitsith *noun* (treated as *singular* or *plural*) (also **tzitzit(h)**) L17 **Hebrew** (*ṣīṣīt*). The tassels on the corners of the Jewish tallith or prayer shawl. Also, (the tassels on each corner of) a small tasseled rectangular garment with a large hole in the middle, worn under the shirt by orthodox male Jews.

tsores *noun plural* E20 **Yiddish** (plural of *tsore* trouble, woe, from Hebrew *ṣārāh*). Troubles, worries; (treated as *singular*) trouble, worry. *colloquial*.

tsotsi *noun* M20 **Bantu** (perhaps from Nguni *-tsotsa* dress in exaggerated clothing). In South Africa: a hoodlum, *especially* a member of an African street gang wearing clothing of exaggerated cut.

tsuba *noun* plural same, **tsubas** L19 **Japanese**. A Japanese sword-guard.

tsugi ashi *noun phrase* M20 **Japanese** (from *tsugi* next, following + *ashi* foot). *Judo* A method of moving in which the same foot always leads rather than both feet alternating. Also in other martial arts.

tsuica *noun* (also **tuica**) E20 **Romanian** (*tuică*). A Romanian plum brandy.

tsukemono *noun* L19 **Japanese** (from *tsukeru* pickle + *mono* thing). A Japanese side dish of pickled vegetables, usually served with rice.

tsunami *noun* plural **tsunamis**, same L19 **Japanese** (from *tsu* harbor + *nami* wave). A long high undulation or series of undulations of the surface of the sea caused by an earthquake or similar underwater disturbance, traveling at great speed and in shallow waters often building up enough height and force to flood the land.

tsutsumu *noun* L20 **Japanese** (= wrap). The Japanese art of wrapping items in an attractive and appropriate way.

tuan *noun* L18 **Malay**. In Malaysia and Indonesia: a master, a lord. Also used as a respectful form of address corresponding to *Mr.* or *sir*.

tuchis variant of TOKUS.

tufa *noun* L18 **Italian** (obsolete local variant of *tufo*, from late Latin *tofus*). *Geology* Originally, a friable porous stone formed of consolidated, often stratified material; tuff, tophus. Now usually *specifically*, a soft porous calcium carbonate rock formed by deposition around mineral springs.

tughra *noun* (also **toughra**, **tugra**) M19 **Turkish** (*tuğra*). *History* A Turkish ornamental monogram incorporating the name and title of the sultan.

tuica variant of TSUICA.

tuile *noun* (in sense 1 also **tuille**) LME **French** (or from Old French *tieule* from Latin *tegula* tile). **1** LME *History* In medieval armor, any of two or more steel plates hanging below or forming the lowest part of the tasses, and covering the front of the thighs. **2** M20 A thin curved cookie, usually made with almonds.

tule *noun* M19 **Spanish** (from Nahuatl *tollin, tullin*). Either of two species of bulrush, *Scirpus lacustris* and *S. acutus*, abundant in flooded marshy areas in southwestern North America, especially in California; an area of low-lying ground in the United States dominated by such a plant.

■ The plural, *tules*, has given rise to the Canadian word *toolies* (M20) meaning 'the backwoods'.

tulle *noun & adjective* E19 **French** (*Tulle*, a town in south-west France where originally made). **A 1** E19 A fine soft silk bobbinet used for women's dresses, veils, etc. **2** M20 *tulle gras* (= fatty), a gauze dressing for the skin impregnated with petroleum jelly. **B** *attributive* or as *adjective* M19 Made of tulle.

tumbaga *noun* (also **tombaga, tumbago**, plural **tumbagos**) E17 **Spanish** (from Malay *tembaga* copper, brass). **1** E17–L18 TOMBAC. **2** M20 Chiefly *Archaeology* An alloy of gold and copper commonly used in pre-Columbian South and Central America.

tu-mo *noun* L20 **Chinese** (*dū mài* (Wade–Giles *tu mai*)). In Chinese medical theory, the chief passage through which vital energy circulates, located in the spine.

tumulus *noun* plural **tumuli** LME **Latin** (related to *tumere* to swell). An ancient sepulchral mound, a barrow.

tundra *noun* L16 **Lappish**. A vast, nearly level, treeless Arctic region usually with a marshy surface and underlying permafrost.

tunku *noun* (also (especially in titles) **Tunku**) L18 **Malay**. A male title of rank in certain states of Western Malaysia; prince.

tupik *noun* M19 **Eskimo** ((Inuit) *tupiq*). A hut or tent of skins used by Eskimos as a summer residence. Also called *summer lodge*.

tuque *noun* L19 **Canadian French** (from French *toque*). In Canada: a close-fitting knitted cap, *especially* a knitted stocking cap sealed at both ends, one end being tucked into the other to form a cap.

tu quoque *noun phrase* L17 **Latin** (literally, 'thou also' = English slang 'you're another'). An argument that consists of turning an accusation back on the accuser.

turba *noun* plural **turbae** L19 **Latin** (= crowd). *Music* The chorus in passion plays and other religious oratorios in which crowds participate in the action.

turbeh *noun* L17 **Turkish** (*türbe* from Arabic *turba* tomb). A small building, resembling a mosque, erected over the tomb of a Muslim, especially a person of sanctity or rank.

turlough *noun* L17 **Irish** (*turloch*, from *tur* dry + *loch* lake). In Ireland: a low-lying area on limestone that becomes flooded in wet weather through the welling up of groundwater from the rock.

turnverein *noun* M19 **German** (from *turnen* to do gymnastic exercises + *Verein* society, club). A gymnastics club, originally for German immigrants.

turron *noun* plural **turrones, turrons** E20 **Spanish** (*turrón*). A kind of Spanish confectionery resembling nougat, made from almonds and honey; a piece of this.

tusche *noun* L19 **German** (back-formation from *tuschen* from French *toucher* to touch). A greasy black composition, in liquid form or to be mixed with liquids, used for making lithographic drawings; lithographic drawing ink.

tutoyer *transitive verb* inflected **tutoy-**, past tense also written **tutoyered** L17 **French** (from the singular pronoun *tu, toi, te*). In French, address with the singular and more familiar pronoun *tu, toi, te* rather than the plural and more formal *vous*; *generally* treat or address with familiarity.

tutti-frutti *noun* (also (especially sense 2) **Tutti-frutti** and as two words) **M19 Italian** (= all fruits). **1** M19 A confection of mixed fruits; *specifically* a mixture of chopped preserved fruits, nuts, etc., used to flavor ice cream; ice cream so flavored. **2** M19 (Proprietary name for) a chewing gum with a mixed fruit flavoring.

tutti quanti *noun phrase* L18 **Italian**. Everyone, everything; all the people or things of this or that kind.

tutu *noun* E20 **French** (childish alteration of *cucu* diminutive of *cul* buttocks). *Ballet* A skirt made up of layers of stiffened frills that stand out from the dancer's legs (*classic tutu*) or extend to mid-calf (*romantic tutu*).

tuyère *noun* (also **tuyere**, **twyer**) L18 **French** (from *tuyau* pipe). *Metallurgy* A nozzle through which the air is forced into a forge or furnace.

tvorog *noun* E20 **Russian**. A soft Russian cheese similar to cottage or curd cheese.

tycoon *noun* M19 **Japanese** (*taikun* great lord or prince, from Chinese *dà* great + *jūn* prince). **1** M19 *History* A title applied by foreigners to the shogun of Japan in power between 1854 and 1868. **2** M19 A business magnate.

tympanum *noun* plural **tympanums**, **tympana** E16 **Latin** (from Greek *tumpanon* drum, from nasalized variant of base of *tuptein* to strike). **1** *Medicine* Severe distension of the abdomen by gas in the intestine, tympanites. *rare*. Only in E16. **2** E17 *Anatomy* and *Zoology* The tympanic membrane or eardrum. Also, a membrane in any animal that is thought to form part of a hearing organ. **b** L19 *Ornithology* Either of the two inflatable air sacs at the sides of the neck in certain birds, such as grouse. *rare*. **3** M17 *Architecture* **a** The die or dado of a pedestal. **b** L17 A vertical recessed area within a pediment; a similar area over a door between the lintel and the arch; a carving on this. **4** L17 A drum, *especially* a hand drum of ancient Greece and Rome. *archaic*. **5** L19 A kind of wheel (originally drum-shaped) with curved radial partitions, used for raising water from a stream.

typhoon *noun* L16 **Portuguese** (partly from Portuguese *tufão* from Urdu *ṭūfān* hurricane, tornado, from Arabic, perhaps from Greek *tuphōn*; partly from Chinese dialect *tai fung* big wind, from Chinese *dà* big + *fēng* wind). A violent storm occurring in or around the Indian subcontinent; *especially* a tropical cyclone occurring in the region of the Indian or western Pacific oceans.

tyro *noun* (also **tiro**) plural **tyro(e)s** LME **Latin** (= young soldier, recruit). A beginner, a learner, a novice.

tyrocinium *noun* (also **tirocinium**) plural **tyrocinia** E17 **Latin** (= first military service on campaign, young troops, from preceding). **1** E17 First experience of anything; training, apprenticeship; *transferred* inexperience, rawness. **2** M17 A band of novices or recruits.

tzatziki *noun* M20 **Modern Greek** (from Turkish *cacık*). A Greek side dish made with yogurt, cucumber, garlic, and usually mint.

tzedaka *noun* (also **tzedakah**) M20 **Hebrew** (*ṣĕḏāqāh* righteousness). The obligation to help fellow Jews; *generally* charity.

tzigane *noun & adjective* M18 **French** (from Hungarian *czigany*, *cigány*). **A** *noun* M18 A Hungarian Gypsy. **B** *adjective* L19 That is a tzigane; consisting of tziganes; characteristic of the tziganes or especially their music.

tzimmes *noun* (also **tsimmes**, **tzimmis** and other variants) plural same L19 **Yiddish** (*tsimes*, of unknown origin). A Jewish stew of sweetened vegetables or vegetables and fruit, sometimes with meat; *figurative* a fuss, a confusion.

tzitzit(h) variant of TSITSITH.

U

U-bahn *noun* M20 **German** (from *U* (abbreviation of *Untergrund*) underground + *Bahn* railroad). In Germany and Austria: the underground railroad in various major cities; the subway.

über alles *adjective & adverb phrase* M20 **German** (from *über* over + *alles* all). Above all else.

■ Generally used with implicit reference to the opening words of the German national anthem *Deutschland über alles*, misunderstood to mean 'Germany supreme'.

Überfremdung *noun* M20 **German** (from *überfremden* to give foreign character to (from *über* over + *fremd* foreign)). The admission or presence of too many foreigners.

■ Used particularly by right-wing politicians in Switzerland protesting against immigrant workers.

überhaupt *adverb* L19 **German** (from *über* over + *Haupt* head, (in compounds) main). In general, (taken) as a whole; par excellence.

Übermensch *noun* plural **Übermenschen** L19 **German** (back-formation from *übermenschlich* superhuman, from *über* over + *menschlich* human, from *Mensch* person). The highest type of human being, superman.

■ The concept was important in the philosophy of Friedrich Nietzsche (1844–1900), from whom George Bernard Shaw borrowed it for his comedy *Man and Superman* (1903). It—and its opposite UNTERMENSCH—subsequently became part of the vocabulary of the Nazi ideology of the master race. In English translations of Nietzsche, Übermensch is often translated as 'Overman', thus sidestepping the cartoon associations of 'Superman'. In jocular use *über* may be attached to an English noun.

uberrima fides *noun phrase* M19 **Latin.** *Law* The utmost good faith.

ubi sunt *adjective phrase* E20 **Latin** (= 'where are', the opening words or refrain of certain medieval Latin works). *Literary Criticism* Designating or characterizing a literary theme or passage lamenting the mutability of things.

uchiwa *noun* L19 **Japanese.** A flat Japanese fan that does not fold.

udon *noun* E20 **Japanese.** In Japanese cooking: a thick strip of pasta made from wheat flour; pasta in this form.

uhlan *noun* (also **hulan**) M18 **French** (*uhlan*, German *U(h)lan* from Polish *ułan*, *hułan* from Turkish *oğlan* youth, servant). *History* A type of cavalryman or lancer in certain European armies, especially that of Poland or (later) Germany.

uhuru *noun* (also **Uhuru**) M20 **Kiswahili** (= freedom). National independence of an African country, *specifically* Kenya.

Uitlander *noun* L19 **Afrikaans** (from Dutch *uit* out + *land* land). In South Africa: a foreigner, an alien; *specifically* a British person who went to South Africa before the Boer War of 1899–1902.

ujamaa *noun* M20 **Kiswahili** (= consanguinity, brotherhood, from *jamaa* family, from Arabic *jamā'a* group (of people), community). A kind of socialism introduced in Tanzania by President Nyerere in the 1960s, in which self-help village cooperatives were established.

ukase *noun* E18 **Russian** (*ukaz* ordinance, edict, from *ukazat'* show, order, decree). **1** E18 A decree or edict, having legal force, issued by the czarist Russian government. **2** E19 *generally* Any proclamation or decree; an order, an arbitrary command.

ukeke *noun* L19 **Hawaiian** (*'ūkēkē*). A Hawaiian stringed instrument consisting of a strip of wood with two or three strings that are played with the fingers and mouth.

ukelele variant of UKULELE.

ukemi *noun* M20 **Japanese** (from *uke* person held or thrown + *mi* body). *Judo* The art of falling safely.

ukha *noun* (also **oukha**) E20 **Russian.** A Russian fish soup.

uki *noun* E20 **Japanese** (= floating). *Judo* Used in the names of various techniques involving a controlled throw in which the opponent's feet and body leave the ground.

ukiyo-e *noun* L19 **Japanese** (from *ukiyo* fleeting world (from *uku* float, go by fleetingly + *yo* world) + *e* picture). A Japanese art form in which everyday subjects are treated simply in woodblock prints or paintings; a work in this art form.

ukulele *noun* (also **ukelele**) L19 **Hawaiian** (literally, 'jumping flea'). A small four-stringed guitar originating in Hawaii but developed from an earlier Portuguese instrument.

■ Colloquially abbreviated to *uke.*

ulema *noun* (also **ulama**) L17 **Arabic** (Turkish, Persian) (*'ulamā'*, plural of *'ālim*, *'alīm* learned, from *'alima* to have (religious) knowledge). **1** L17 *collectively* or in *plural* The members of a Muslim society or country who are recognized as having specialist knowledge of Islamic sacred law and theology. **2** M19 A person who belongs to a *ulema.*

ulpan *noun* plural **ulpanim** M20 **Modern Hebrew** (*ulpān*, from Aramaic *allēp* to teach). An intensive course in the Hebrew language, originally for immigrants to the state of Israel; a center providing such a course; *transferred* any intensive language course.

ult. abbreviation of ULTIMO.

ultima ratio *noun phrase* M19 **Latin.** The final sanction.

ultimata plural of ULTIMATUM.

ultima Thule *noun phrase* (also **ultima thule**) L18 **Latin** (= farthest Thule). The type of the extreme limit of travel and discovery; *figurative* the highest or uttermost point or degree attained or attainable, the (lowest) limit, the nadir. Cf. THULE.

ultimatum *noun* plural **ultimatums, ultimata** M18 **Latin** (noun use of neuter of late Latin *ultimatus* in the medieval Latin senses 'final, completed'). **1** M18 The final terms presented by one party in a dispute, etc., to another, the rejection of which could cause a breakdown in relations, a declaration of war, an end of cooperation, etc. **2** M18 The final point, the extreme limit; an ultimate end or aim. (Followed by *of.*) **3** M19 A primary element beyond which advance or analysis is impossible; something fundamental.

ultimo *adjective* L16 **Latin** ((sc. *die* or *mense*) ablative singular masculine of *ultimus* last, final). **1** L16–L17 Designating the last day (of a specified month). **2** E17 Of last month. Frequently written *ult.*, *ulto.*

ultra *adjective & noun* E19 **Latin** (independent use of *ultra-* lying beyond). **A** *adjective* **1** E19 Of a person or party: holding extreme views in politics or other matters of opinion. **2** E19 Going beyond what is normal or ordinary; excessive, extreme. **B** *noun* **1** E19 A person holding extreme views. **2** L20 A long-distance run of great length. *colloquial.*

■ Originally introduced as an abbreviation for French *ultra-royaliste*, referring to a political party in early nineteenth-century France.

ultra crepidam *preposition* L19 **Latin.** On matters beyond a person's knowledge.

ultra vires *adverb phrase* L18 **Latin** (= beyond the powers). Chiefly *Law*. Beyond the powers or legal authority of a corporation or person.

■ Opposed to INTRA VIRES.

ultreya *noun* M20 **Spanish** (apparently recalling the medieval cry (*E*)*ultreya* 'onward!', 'forward!' in the hymn sung by pilgrims to Compostela). *Roman Catholic Church* A regular discussion group held by participants in a CURSILLO.

umbilicus *noun* plural **umbilici**, **umbilicuses** L17 **Latin** (from base of UMBO, related to Greek *omphalos* and Indo-European base of navel). **1** L17 *Anatomy* A navel. **b** M19 *Botany* The scar on a seed marking its separation from the placenta; the hilum. Now *rare*. **2** *Mathematics* A focus of an ellipse. Only in E18. **b** M19 An umbilical point. **3** E19 *Biology* A small usually central depression or hole suggestive of a navel.

umbo *noun* plural **umbones**, **umbos** E18 **Latin** (= shield boss, knob). **1** E18 The boss of a shield. **2** M18 A rounded or conical projection or knob, especially in the center of a rounded natural structure.

umbra *noun* plural **umbras**, **umbrae** L16 **Latin**. **1** L16 A phantom, a ghost. **2** M17 A shadow; *especially* (*Astronomy*) the shadow cast by the moon or earth during an eclipse. **3** An inseparable companion, a hanger-on.

umfaan *noun* M19 **Zulu** (*umFana* small boy). In South Africa: a young African boy, *especially* one employed in domestic service.

umfundisi *noun* E19 **Xhosa and Zulu** (*umFundisi*). In South Africa: a teacher, a minister, a missionary. Also used as a respectful form of address.

umiak *noun* (also **umiaq**, **oomiak**) M18 **Eskimo** ((Inuit) *umiaq*). A large Eskimo canoe with a wooden frame covered in skins, *especially* one paddled by women.

umlaut *noun* M19 **German** (from *um-* about + *Laut* sound). **1** M19 *Philology* Vowel change arising historically by partial assimilation to an adjacent sound, usually a vowel or semivowel in a following syllable (often now lost), as in German *Mann*, *Männer*, or English *man*, *men*. Also called (*vowel*) *mutation*. **2** M20 A diacritical sign (¨) placed over a vowel, especially in Germanic languages, to indicate such a change.

umma *noun* L19 **Arabic** (= people, community, nation). The Muslim community, originally founded by Muhammad at Medina, comprising individuals bound to one another predominantly by religious ties.

umrah *noun* E19 **Arabic** (*'umra*). *Islam* A lesser pilgrimage to Mecca made independently of or at the same time as the HAJJ, and consisting of a number of devotional rituals performed within the city.

Umwelt *noun* plural **Umwelten** M20 **German** (= environment). The outer world as it affects and is perceived by the organisms inhabiting it; the environment.

una corda *adverb & adjective phrase* M19 **Italian** (= one string). *Music* (A direction:) using the soft pedal of the piano.

una voce *adverb phrase* M16 **Latin** (*una* ablative singular feminine of *unus* one + *voce* ablative singular of *vox* voice). With one voice; unanimously.

unberufen *interjection* M19 **German** (= unauthorized, gratuitous). Touch wood! (to avert ill luck).

unda maris *noun phrase* E19 **Latin** (literally, 'wave of the sea'). *Music* A type of organ stop, usually consisting of two ranks of pipes, one of which is tuned slightly sharp or flat, together producing a slowly undulating tone.

Unding *noun* M20 **German** (= absurdity). A nonexistent thing, a vague abstraction, a concept having no properties.

und so weiter *adverb phrase* L19 **German**. And so forth.

unheimlich *adjective* L19 **German**. Uncanny, weird.

unicum *noun* plural **unica** L19 **Latin** (neuter singular of *unicus* unique). A unique example, specimen, or thing.

Untergang *noun* M20 **German** (= decline, downfall). An irreversible decline, especially leading to the destruction of culture or civilization.

■ Often used with implicit allusion to Oswald Spengler's *Der Untergang des Abendlandes* (1918), translated as *The Decline of the West.*

Untermensch *noun* plural **Untermenschen** M20 **German.** Especially in Nazi Germany, a person regarded or classified as racially inferior.

unum necessarium *noun phrase* M20 **Modern Latin** (from (Vulgate) Latin *unum est necessarium* one thing is necessary (Luke 10:42)). The one or only necessary thing, the essential element.

uomo universale *noun phrase* plural **uomini universali** M20 **Italian** (literally, 'universal man'). A man who excels in the major fields of learning and action. Also called *Renaissance man.*

upsara variant of APSARA.

upsilon *noun* M17 **Greek** (*u psilon* simple or slender u, from *psilos* slender, with reference to the need to distinguish upsilon from the diphthong οι, with which upsilon shared a pronunciation in late Greek). **1** M17 The twentieth letter (Υ, υ) of the Greek alphabet. **2** L20 *Particle Physics* A meson with a mass of about 9.4 GeV. Also *upsilon particle.*

ur- M19 **German** (combining form). Forming words with the sense 'primitive, original, earliest'.

uraeus *noun* plural **uraei** M19 **Modern Latin** (from Greek *ouraios* (perhaps from *oura* tail), representing Egyptian word for 'cobra'). *Egyptian Antiquities* A representation of the sacred asp or snake, symbolizing supreme power, especially worn on the head-dresses of ancient Egyptian divinities and sovereigns.

urbi et orbi *adverb phrase* M19 **Latin.** (Of a papal proclamation, etc.) to the city (of Rome) and to the world; *transferred* for general information or acceptance, to everyone.

urbs *noun* M20 **Latin** (= city). The city, especially as a symbol of harsh or busy modern life.

Urfirnis *noun & adjective* E20 **German** (from UR- + *firnis* varnish, veneer). *Greek Archaeology* (Designating) an early form of Greek pottery characterized by the use of dark lustrous paint.

Urheimat *noun* M20 **German** (from UR- + *Heimat* home, homeland). The place of origin of a people or language.

Urim *noun* M16 **Hebrew** (*'ūrīm* plural of *'ōr*). One of the two objects of a now unknown nature worn on the breastplate of a Jewish high priest. Chiefly in *Urim and Thummim.* Cf. THUMMIM.

urinoir *noun* M20 **French.** In France: a public urinal.

urlar *noun* L19 **Gaelic** (*ùrlar* ground, floor). *Music* The ground theme in a pibroch.

urs *noun* M19 **Arabic** (*'urs*, literally, 'wedding, wedding feast'). Especially in the Indian subcontinent: a ceremony celebrating the anniversary of the death of a Muslim saint.

Ursprache *noun* plural **Ursprachen** E20 **German** (from UR- + *Sprache* speech). A hypothetical early language from which actual languages are derived, a proto-language.

Urtext *noun* plural **Urtexte** M20 **German** (from UR- + *Text* text (ultimately from Latin *textus*)). An original or the earliest version of a text.

ushabti *noun* plural **ushabtiu, ushabtis** L19 **Egyptian** (*wšbty* answerer, replacing *šwbt(y)* SHAWABTI). *Egyptology* A figurine of a dead person, made of faience, stone, wood, etc., and placed with the body in the tomb to substitute for the dead person in any work required in the afterlife. Also *ushabti figure.*

usine *noun* L18 French (= factory, (in early use) water mill). **1** Material used or suitable for a furnace or foundry. Only in L18. **2** M19 A factory; *especially* a West Indian sugar factory.

usque ad nauseam earlier variant of AD NAUSEAM.

uti possidetis *noun phrase* L17 Late Latin (= as you possess). *Law* A principle whereby property or territory not expressly disposed of in a treaty remains in the hands of the party holding it at the end of hostilities.

utopia *noun* (also **Utopia**) M16 Modern Latin (= no-place, from Greek *ou* not + *topos* place). **1** M16 An imaginary place or state of things considered to be perfect; a condition of (ideal) social perfection. **2** M18 An impossibly ideal scheme, especially for social improvement.

■ The origin of the name and of all subsequent *utopias* was the political fable *Utopia* (1516) written in Latin by Sir Thomas More (1477–1535) and translated into English in 1551. The antithesis of a *utopia* is a *dystopia* (modern Latin from Greek *dys-* bad + *topos*), a nightmare society of the kind depicted in, for example, Aldous Huxley's *Brave New World* (1932). The word *dystopia* (M19) was coined originally by J. S. Mill but it has only gained currency since the mid-twentieth century, especially in sociological contexts.

ut supra *adverb phrase* LME Latin (from *ut* as + *supra* above). In a book, etc.: as previously, as before, as above. Frequently abbreviated *ut sup.*

uvala *noun* E20 Serbo-Croat (= hollow, depression). *Physical Geography* A large depression in the ground surface occurring in karstic regions, resulting from the collapse of an underground watercourse.

v. abbreviation of VERSUS.

vaaljapie *noun* M20 Afrikaans (literally, 'tawny Jake', from Dutch *vaal* pale + *japie* diminutive of male forename *Jaap* from *Jakob* Jacob). In South Africa: rough young wine, cheap or inferior wine.

va banque *interjection* M20 French (literally, 'go bank'). In baccarat: expressing a player's willingness to bet against the banker's whole stake. Cf. BANCO.

vacherin *noun* M20 French. **1** M20 A soft French or Swiss cheese made from cow's milk. **2** M20 A dessert of a meringue shell filled with whipped cream, fruit, etc.

vade-mecum *noun* E17 French (from modern Latin noun use of Latin *vade mecum* go with me). **1** E17 A small book or manual carried on one's person for ready reference; a handbook, a guidebook. **2** M17 Anything useful commonly carried about or kept available for use by a person.

vae victis *interjection & noun* E17 Latin (= woe to the conquered). (A cry noting or calling for) the humiliation of the vanquished by their conquerors.

■ *Vae* was formerly (M16–M17) used on its own as a denunciation, calling down a curse on someone. *Vae victis* is a quotation from Livy (V. xlviii.9) and is chiefly used as an interjection.

vagantes *noun plural* E20 Latin (nominative plural of *vagans* present participle of *vagari* to wander). Itinerant medieval scholar monks.

vagitus *noun* M17 Latin (from *vagire* to wail). A cry, a wail, *specifically* that of a newborn child.

vague *noun* M20 French (literally, 'wave'). A movement, a trend. Cf. NOUVELLE VAGUE.

vahana *noun* (also **vahan**) E19 Sanskrit (*vāhana*, literally, 'conveyance'). *Indian Mythology* The mount or vehicle of a god.

vahine *noun* M20 Tahitian (cf. WAHINE). A Tahitian woman or wife.

vajra *noun* L18 Sanskrit. *Hinduism* and *Buddhism* (A representation of) a thunderbolt or mythical weapon, *especially* one wielded by the god Indra.

vale *interjection & noun* M16 Latin (imperative singular of *valere* to be well). **A** *interjection* M16 Farewell. Cf. AVE ATQUE VALE. **B** *noun* L16 A written or spoken farewell.

valet *noun & verb* L15 Old and Modern French ((also *vaslet, varlet* varlet), ultimately related to *vassal* from medieval Latin *vassallus* manservant, retainer). **A** *noun* **1** L15 *Military* A footman acting as attendant or servant to a horseman. Now *rare* or *obsolete*. **2** M16 A man's personal (usually male) attendant, responsible for his or her master's clothes, appearance, etc. Now also, a hotel employee performing similar duties for guests. **3** M20 A rack on which clothing may be hung to retain its shape. **B** *verb* **1** *transitive & intransitive verb* M19 Act as a valet (to). **2** *transitive verb* M20 Look after (clothes, etc.). **3** *transitive verb* L20 Clean (a motor vehicle).

valeta variant of VELETA.

valet-de-chambre *noun* plural **valets-de-chambre** M17 French (literally 'chamber valet'). A VALET (noun) sense 2.

Valhalla *noun* L17 Modern Latin (from Old Norse *Valhall-, Valhǫll*, from *valr* those slain in battle (= Old English *wæl*, Old Saxon, Old High German *wal*) + *hǫll* hall). **1** L17 In Scandinavian mythology, the hall in which the souls of those who have died in battle feast with Odin for eternity. **2** M19 *transferred* and *figurative* A place or sphere assigned to a person or thing worthy of special honor. Also, paradise; a place or state of perfect bliss.

valise *noun* E17 French (from Italian *valigia* corresponding to medieval Latin *valesia*, of unknown origin). **1** E17 A traveling case or portmanteau, now usually made of leather and of a size suitable for carrying by hand, formerly also for strapping to a horse's saddle. **2** M19 *Military* A soldier's cloth or leather kitbag.

vallum *noun* E17 Latin (collectively from *vallus* stake, palisade). **1** E17 A defensive wall or rampart of earth, sods, or stone; *especially* one constructed by the Romans in northern England and central Scotland. **2** E19 *Archaeology* A palisaded bank or rampart, formed of the earth dug up from the ditch or fosse around a Roman military camp.

valse *noun* L18 French (from German *Walzer* waltz). A waltz; a piece of music for this dance or in its rhythm.

valuta *noun* L19 Italian (= value). The value of one currency in respect of its exchange rate with another; a currency considered in this way.

Vanitas *noun* (also **vanitas**) E20 Latin (= vanity). *Art* A still life painting of a seventeenth-century Dutch genre incorporating symbols of mortality or mutability.

vanitas vanitatum *noun phrase* M16 Late Latin (= vanity of vanities). Futility.

■ Quotation from the Vulgate version of Ecclesiastes 1:2, often as an exclamation of disillusionment or pessimism.

vaporetto *noun* plural **vaporetti, vaporettos** E20 Italian (= small steamboat, diminutive of *vapore* from Latin *vapor* steam). In Venice: a canal boat (originally a steamboat, now a motorboat) used for public transport.

vaquero *noun* plural **vaqueros** E19 Spanish (from *vaca* cow; cf. Portuguese *vaqueiro*). In Spanish-speaking parts of America: a cowboy, a cowherd; a cattle driver.

■ *Buckaroo*, a now archaic term used (from E19) for a 'cowboy', was an alteration of *vaquero*.

vardo *noun* plural **vardos** (also **varda**) E19 **Romany**. A wagon. Now *specifically* a Gypsy wagon or trailer. Originally *slang*.

vargueño *noun* E20 **Spanish** (*bargueño*, *vargueño* adjective of Bargas, a village near Toledo, the former place of manufacture). A kind of cabinet made in Spain in the sixteenth and seventeenth centuries, with numerous small compartments and drawers behind a fall-front that opens out to form a writing surface.

varia lectio *noun phrase* plural **variae lectiones** M17 **Latin**. A variant reading in a text.

variorum *noun & adjective* E18 **Latin** (literally, 'of various (people)', genitive plural of *varius* various, especially in phrase *editio cum notis variorum* edition with the notes of various (commentators)). **A** *noun* **1 a** E18 An edition, especially of the complete works of a classical author, containing the notes of various commentators or editors. Also *variorum edition*. **b** M20 An edition, usually of an author's complete works, containing variant readings from manuscripts or earlier editions. Also *variorum edition*. **2** L18 Variation; (a) novelty; a source of variety. Also, an unnecessary decoration or flourish. *Scottish*. **B** *attributive* or as *adjective* E18 Of, pertaining to, or designating a variorum; (of matter in a book, etc.) obtained or collected from various sources. Also, (of a reading in a text) variant.

varna *noun* M19 **Sanskrit** (*varṇa*, literally, 'appearance, aspect, color'). Each of the four original castes of Hindu society; the system or basis of this division.

varve *noun* E20 **Swedish** (= layer, turn). *Physical Geography* A pair of thin layers of clay and silt of contrasting color and texture that represent the deposit of a single year (summer and winter) in still water at some time in the past (especially in a lake formed by a retreating ice sheet).

Vaterland *noun* M19 **German**. Germany as the fatherland.

vates *noun* E17 **Latin** (= seer, poet, related to Greek *ouateis* (plural) ovate, representing a Gaulish word). A poet, *especially* one divinely inspired; a prophet-poet.

vaudeville *noun* M18 **French** (earlier *vau* (plural *vaux*) *de ville*, *vau de vire*, and in full *chanson du Vau de Vire* song of the valley of Vire (in Normandy, northwest France)). **1** M18 A satirical or topical song; *specifically* one sung on the stage. Now *rare*. **2** E19 A light stage play or comedy with interspersed songs. Also, such plays as a genre; variety theater, music hall. Frequently *attributive*.

vedette *noun* L17 **French** (from Italian *vedetta*, alteration (after *vedere* to see) of southern Italian *veletta*, perhaps from Spanish *vela* watch, from *velar* to keep watch, from Latin *vigilare*). **1** L17 *Military* A mounted sentry placed in advance of an army's outposts to observe the movements of the enemy; a scout. **2** L19 In full *vedette boat*. A small vessel used for scouting purposes in naval warfare. Also *generally*, a small motor launch or patrol boat. **3** M20 A leading star of stage or screen.

veduta *noun* plural **vedute** E20 **Italian** (= a view, from *vedere* to see). In Italian art: a detailed, factually accurate landscape, usually a townscape showing buildings of interest.

veena *noun* (also **vina**) L18 **Sanskrit and Hindi** (*vīṇā*). *In the Indian subcontinent: a plucked musical instrument with a gourd at one or either end of a fretted fingerboard and seven strings.*

vega *noun* M17 **Spanish and Catalan** (*vega* = Portuguese *veiga*). **1** M17 In Spain and Spanish America: an extensive, usually fertile and grass-covered, plain or valley. **2** L19 In Cuba: a tobacco field.

veilleuse *noun* E19 **French**. A small and usually highly decorated night-light or night-lamp. Also, a small decorative bedside food warmer, usually with an enclosed burner under a bowl or teapot, and made of pottery or porcelain so as to give out some light.

veld *noun* (also **veldt**) L18 **Afrikaans** (from Dutch = field). Unenclosed country; open grassland.

■ South African; frequently with specifying word, as in *bushveld*, *sandveld*.

veldskoen *noun* E19 **Afrikaans** (= field shoe, ultimately by assimilation to VELD of earlier *velschoen*, from *fel* skin, + *schoen* shoe). Formerly, a light shoe made of untanned hide. Now, a strong but usually soft leather or suede boot or shoe for walking, etc.

veldt variant of VELD.

veleta *noun* (also **valeta**) E20 **Spanish** (= weather vane). An old-time round dance for couples in triple time, faster than a waltz and with partners side by side.

velours *noun* (also **velour**) E18 **French** (= velvet, from Old French *velour*, *velous* from Latin *villosus* hairy, from *villus* hair). **1** E18 A silk or velvet pad for smoothing hats. **2** L18 Any of various plush or pile fabrics similar to velvet and used for hats, garments, upholstery, etc.

■ Cf. PATTE DE VELOURS. The French phrase *velours croché* 'hooked velvet' has given rise to the proprietary name Velcro (M20) for a form of fastening widely used for fabrics, consisting of two strips of nylon with complementary meshed and hooked surfaces that adhere to each other when pressed together.

velouté *noun* M19 **French** (= velvety). A rich white sauce made with chicken, veal, or fish stock, and often thickened with cream and egg yolks. More fully *velouté sauce*.

vendange *noun* M18 **Old and Modern French** (cf. VENDEMMIA, VENDIMIA). In France: the grape harvest; the vintage or grapes harvested; a particular vintage of wine.

vendangeur *noun* L19 **French**. In France: a grape picker.

vendemmia *noun* plural **vendemmie** E19 **Italian** (from Latin *vindemia*; cf. VENDANGE, VENDIMIA). In Italy: the grape harvest; the vintage or grapes harvested; a particular vintage of wine.

vendetta *noun* M19 **Italian** (from Latin *vindicta* vengeance). **1** M19 A blood feud in which the family of a murdered person seeks vengeance on the murderer or the murderer's family, especially as customary in Corsica and Sicily. **2** M19 A similar blood feud, or prosecution of private revenge. Also, a prolonged bitter quarrel with or campaign against a person, etc.

vendeuse *noun* E20 **French** (from *vendre* to sell). A saleswoman; *specifically* one employed in a fashion house.

vendimia *noun* M20 **Spanish** (from Latin *vindemia*; cf. VENDANGE, VENDEMMIA). In Spain: the grape harvest; the vintage or grapes harvested; a particular vintage of wine. Also, a festival celebrating the vintage.

vendue *noun* L17 **Dutch** (*vendu*, *vendue* from Old and Modern French (now dialect) *vendue* sale, from *vendre* to sell). A public sale; an auction. *United States* and *West Indies*.

veni, vidi, vici *interjection* L16 **Latin**. I came, I saw, I conquered.

■ According to the ancient biographer Plutarch, the words in which Julius Caesar reported his victory at Zela over Pharnaces, king of Pontus in Asia Minor, in 47 BC. Used with reference to any swift and overwhelming success.

venire *noun* M17 **Latin** (= to come). **1** M17 *Law* (now *historical*) Elliptically for VENIRE FACIAS sense 1. **2** M20 *United States Law* A panel of people available for jury service.

venire facias *noun phrase* LME **Latin** (literally, 'to make or cause to come').

Law **1** LME A judicial writ directing a sheriff to summon a jury. Now *historical* except *United States*. **2** LME–M18 A writ issuing a summons to appear before a court.

ventre à terre *adverb phrase* M19 **French** (literally, 'belly to the ground'). **1** M19 Of an animal, especially a horse: represented in a painting, etc., with legs stretched out in line with the belly; moving at full speed. **2** M20 Lying on the stomach; prone.

venue *noun* ME **Old and Modern French** (noun use of feminine past participle of *venir* to come, from Latin *venire*). **1** ME A sally in order to assault someone, an attack. *rare*. Only in ME. **2** *Law* (now *historical*) The locality within which a cause must be tried. **b** The scene of a real or supposed action or event. **c** An appointed meeting place, especially for a performance, sporting event, or competition; a rendezvous.

■ Also formerly in sense 1 with now obsolete uses in fencing terminology.

vera causa *noun phrase* M19 **Latin** (= real cause). *Philosophy* A true cause that brings about an effect as a minimum independent agency.

vera copula *noun phrase* M19 **Latin** (= true union). *Law* Sexual intercourse with erection and penetration.

veranda *noun* (also **verandah**; **viranda**, **virando**) E18 **Hindustani** (*varaṇḍā* from Portuguese *varanda* railing, balustrade, balcony, of unknown origin). **1** E18 A usually roofed open portico or gallery extending along a wall of a house or building. **2** M19 A roof or canopy extending over the sidewalk outside a store or business establishment. *Australia* and *New Zealand*.

verbatim *adverb, adjective, & noun* L15 **Medieval Latin** (from Latin *verbum* word; cf. LITERATIM). **A** *adverb* **1** L15 Word for word; in exactly the same words. **2** E16–M17 In so many words; exactly, precisely. **B** *adjective* M18 Corresponding with or following an original word for word. **C** *noun* L19 A full or word-for-word report of a speech, etc.

verboten *adjective* E20 **German**. Forbidden, not allowed.

verbum sapienti *interjection* E19 **Latin** (*verbum sapienti sat est* a word is sufficient for a wise person). A word to the wise (implying that any further explanation or comment is unnecessary or inadvisable).

■ The expression in its full form is virtually never found; by far the most common variant is *verb. sap.* (E19), but *verbum sap.* or *verbum sat* 'a word (is) enough' (M17) are also used.

verd-antique *noun & adjective* M18 **French** (*verd* (now *vert*) green + *antique* antique). **A** **1** M18 An ornamental variety of marble, consisting chiefly of serpentine mixed with calcite and dolomite. **2** M19 A greenish patina or incrustation on brass or copper; verdigris. **3** M19 Greenstone. More fully *oriental verd-antique, verd-antique porphyry*. **B** *attributive* or as *adjective* E19 Made or consisting of verd-antique.

verde antico *noun phrase* M18 **Italian**. VERD-ANTIQUE sense 1.

Verfremdung *noun* M20 **German**. Chiefly *Theater* Distancing, alienation, especially of a theatrical audience.

■ Also *Verfremdungseffekt* (= alienation effect). The term was coined by the German dramatist and theatrical producer Bertolt Brecht (1898–1956) for his theory of theatrical alienation.

verglas *noun* E19 **French** (from *verre* glass + *glas* (now *glace*) ice). A glassy coating of ice formed on the ground or an exposed surface by rain freezing on impact or the refreezing of thawed ice.

verismo *noun* E20 **Italian**. Realism or naturalism in the arts, especially with reference to late nineteenth-century Italian opera.

vérité *noun* M20 **French** (= truth). Realism or naturalism, especially in movies, radio, and television; documentary method. Cf. CINÉMA-VÉRITÉ.

verkrampte *adjective & noun* (also (as predicate adjective) **verkramp**) M20 **Afrikaans** (= narrow, cramped). **A** *adjective* M20 Politically or socially conservative or reactionary, especially in racial matters. **B** *noun* M20 Such a conservative or reactionary person.

■ Originally used in South Africa of politicians on the conservative wing of the Nationalist Party, but now more generally of any diehard reactionary, especially a hardline segregationist Afrikaner. The word often appears in contexts in which it is explicitly or implicitly contrasted with VERLIGTE.

verligte *adjective & noun* (also (as predicate adjective) **verlig**) M20 **Afrikaans** (= enlightened). **A** *adjective* M20 Progressive, enlightened, especially in racial matters. **B** *noun* M20 Such a progressive or enlightened person.

■ In South Africa, the opposite of VERKRAMPTE.

vermicelli *noun* M17 **Italian** (plural of *vermicello* diminutive of *verme* worm, from Latin *vermis*). Pasta in the form of long slender threads, often added to soups. Now also (*transferred*), shreds of chocolate used as cake decoration, etc.

vernaccia *noun* E19 **Italian**. A strong (usually dry white) wine produced in the San Gimignano area of Italy and in Sardinia; the grape from which this is made.

vernis martin *noun & adjective phrase* L19 **French** (from *vernis* varnish + family name *Martin* of French brothers noted for using the lacquer). **A** *noun phrase* L19 A lacquer or varnish imitating oriental lacquer, used in the eighteenth century. **B** *adjective phrase* L19 Finished in vernis martin.

vernissage *noun* E20 **French** (literally, 'varnishing'). Originally, a day before an exhibition of paintings on which exhibitors could retouch and varnish pictures already hung. Now usually, a private view of paintings before public exhibition.

veronique *postpositive adjective* also **Véronique** E20 **French** (*Véronique* Veronica). *Cooking* Designating a dish, especially of fish or chicken, prepared or garnished with grapes.

verre églomisé *noun phrase* E20 **French** (*verre* glass + ÉGLOMISÉ). Glass decorated with a layer of engraved gold.

versant *noun* M19 **French** (noun use of present participle of *verser* from Latin *versare* to turn to and fro). The slope, side, or descent of a mountain or mountain chain; the general slope of an area or region.

vers de société *noun phrase* L18 **French** (literally, 'verse of society'). Verse treating topics provided by polite society in a light, often witty style.

vers d'occasion *noun phrase* M19 **French**. Light verse written for a special occasion.

vers libre *noun phrase* plural **vers libres** E20 **French** (literally, 'free verse'). Unrhymed verse that disregards the traditional rules of prosody; an example of this.

verso *noun* plural **versos** M19 **Latin** (*verso* (sc. *folio*) = (the leaf) being turned, ablative singular neuter of *versus* past participle of *vertere* to turn). **1** M19 The left-hand page of an open book; the back of a leaf in a manuscript or printed book, as opposed to the front or RECTO. **2** L19 The reverse side, especially of a coin or medal.

Versöhnung *noun* plural **Versöhnungen** M19 **German** (= conciliation, propitiation). A reconciliation of opposites.

Verstandesmensch *noun* plural **Verstandesmenschen** L19 **German**. A matter-of-fact person; a realist.

Verstehen *noun* M20 **German** (= understanding, comprehension). (The use of empathy in) the sociological or historical understanding of human action and behavior.

versus *preposition* LME **Medieval Latin** (use of Latin *versus* toward, in sense of *adversus* against). Against, in opposition to.

■ Used especially in legal or sporting contexts, where it is generally abbreviated *v.* or *vs.*, as in *Rovers v. Wolves.*

vertex *noun* plural **vertices**, **vertexes** LME **Latin** (= whirl, vortex, crown of the head, highest point, from *vertere* to turn). **1** LME *Anatomy* and *Zoology* The crown or top of the head or skull. **b** E19 *Entomology* The top of the head of an insect. **2** L16 *Geometry* The point opposite to the base of a (plane or solid) figure; the point in a curve or surface at which the axis meets it; an angular point of a triangle, polygon, etc. **b** E18 *Optics* The point where the optical axis intersects the surface of a lens. **c** L19 *Astronomy* The point on the limb of a celestial object where it is intersected by a circle passing through the zenith and the center of the object. Now also, the point to which a group of stars appears to converge, or from which a shower of meteors appears to radiate. **d** M20 *Mathematics* A junction of two or more lines in a network or graph; a node. **3** M17 The point in the sky directly above a given place; the zenith. **4** M17 The top or highest point of a thing.

vertigo *noun* LME **Latin** ((stem *vertigin-*) = whirling about, giddiness, from *vertere* to turn). **1** LME *Medicine* A sensation of whirling motion, tending to result in a loss of balance and sometimes of consciousness; giddiness, dizziness. **2** M17 *figurative* A disordered state of mind or things.

vertu variant of VIRTU.

vesica *noun* M17 **Latin** (= bladder, blister). **1** M17 *Anatomy* A bladder. Usually with Latin specifying word. *rare.* **2** E19 Elliptical for VESICA PISCIS.

vesica piscis *noun phrase* (also **vesica piscium**) E19 **Latin** (= fish's (or fishes') bladder). A pointed oval figure used as an architectural feature and as an aureole enclosing figures of Christ, the Virgin, etc., in medieval painting and sculpture.

■ The origin of the name is uncertain; one nineteenth-century writer objected that it was not a bladder belonging to a fish but a bladder which, when filled, would be in the shape of a fish. Another attributed the invention of the term to the German artist Albrecht Dürer (1471–1528).

vespasienne *noun* E20 **French** (abbreviation of *colonne vespasienne* Vespasian column). In France: a public toilet.

■ The allusion is to the Roman emperor Vespasian, who introduced a tax on public toilets.

vestigium *noun* plural **vestigia** M17 **Latin**. A vestige, a trace. Usually followed by *of.*

veto *noun & verb* E17 **Latin** (= I forbid, used by Roman tribunes of the people to oppose measures of the Senate or actions of the magistrates). **A** *noun* E17 plural **vetoes** A prohibition of a proposed or intended act, especially a legislative enactment; the right or power of preventing an act in this way. Frequently in *apply, place,* or *put a veto on* or *to.* **B** *transitive verb* E18 Put a veto on (a measure, etc.), refuse consent to, forbid authoritatively; refuse to admit or accept (a person).

ve-tsin *noun* M20 **Chinese** (*wèijīng*, from *wèi* taste, ingredient + *jīng* refined, essence, extract). Monosodium glutamate, as used in Chinese cooking.

veuve *noun* L18 **French**. In France: a widow.

■ Frequently as a title prefixed to a woman's surname and perhaps most familiar as part of a proprietary name of a brand of champagne: *Veuve Clicquot.*

vexata quaestio *noun phrase* plural **vexatae quaestiones** E19 **Latin**. A vexed question.

vexillum *noun* plural **vexilla** E18 **Latin** (= flag, banner, from *vex-*, *vect-*, *vehere* to carry, convey). **1** E18 *Roman History* A military standard or banner; a body of soldiers grouped under this. **b** L19 *Ecclesiastical* A small piece of linen or silk attached to the upper part of a crozier. **2** E18 *Botany* The standard or large uppermost petal of a papilionaceous flower. **3** M19 *Ornithology* The vane of a feather.

via *preposition* L18 **Latin** (ablative singular of *via* way). **1** L18 By way of; by a route passing through or over. **2** M20 By means of; with the aid of.

via affirmativa *noun phrase* M19 **Modern Latin** (= affirmative way). *Theology* The approach to God through positive statements about his nature. Cf. VIA NEGATIVA.

Via Crucis *noun phrase* M19 **Latin** (= way of the cross). The route followed by Christ to Calvary; *Christian Church* the Way of the Cross as a series of devotions or, *especially* in the Roman Catholic church, a series of "stations" or shrines set around a church interior for devotion and meditation; *figurative* an extremely painful experience requiring strength or courage to bear.

Via Dolorosa *noun phrase* L19 **Latin** (literally, 'sorrowing way'). **1** L19 The route believed to have been taken by Christ through Jerusalem to Calvary. **2** E20 *figurative* A prolonged ordeal.

via media *noun phrase* M19 **Latin** A middle way; an intermediate course, a compromise.

via negativa *noun phrase* M19 **Modern Latin** (= negative way). *Theology* The approach to God believing no positive statements can be made about his nature; *transferred* a way of denial.

viaticum *noun* plural **viatica** (formerly also Anglicized as **viatic**) M16 **Latin** (noun use of neuter of *viaticus* pertaining to a road or journey, from *via* road). **1** M16 *Christian Church* The Eucharist as administered to a person near or in danger of death. **2** L16 A supply or official allowance of money for a journey: traveling expenses. **b** M17 A supply of food for a journey.

vibrato *adverb & noun* M19 **Italian** (past participle of *vibrare* vibrate). *Music* **A** *adverb* M19 With a rapid slight variation in pitch. **B** *noun* L19 plural **vibratos** A rapid slight variation in pitch in the singing or playing of a note. Cf. TREMOLO noun 1.

vice anglais *noun phrase* M20 **French** (literally, 'English vice'). A vice considered characteristic of the English; *especially* the use of corporal punishment for sexual stimulation.

vicereine *noun* E19 **French** (from *vice-* vice- + *reine* queen). The wife of a viceroy. Also, a female viceroy.

vice versa *adverb phrase* E17 **Latin** (literally, 'the position being reversed', from as *vice* ablative of *vix* change, place, stead + *versa* ablative feminine singular of *versus* past participle of *vertere* to turn). With a reversal of the order of terms or conditions mentioned; contrariwise, conversely.

vichyssoise *noun* M20 **French** (*crême vichyssoise glacée*, literally, 'iced cream soup of Vichy'). A soup made with potatoes, leeks, and cream, and usually served cold.

victor ludorum *noun phrase* E20 **Latin** (= victor of the games). The overall champion in a sports competition, especially at a school or college; the sports competition itself.

vicuña *noun* (also **vicugna**, **vicuna**) E17 **Spanish** (from Quechua *wikúña*). **1** E17 A hoofed mammal of the high Andes, *Vicugna vicugna*, which is related to the llama and guanaco and has a fine silky coat used for textile fabrics. **2** M19 A fine fabric made from the wool of the vicuña (also more fully *vicuña cloth*). Also, a garment made of this fabric.

vicus *noun* plural **vici** M19 **Latin** (= village, group of dwellings). *Archaeology* In the Roman Empire, a village, a settlement; *specifically* the smallest unit of ancient Roman municipal administration, consisting of a village, part of a town, etc. Also, a medieval European township.

vide *transitive verb* (*imperative*) M16 **Latin** (imperative singular of *videre* to see). See, refer to, consult.

■ Used as a direction in a text referring the reader to a specified passage, work, etc., for fuller or further information. Also abbreviated to *vid.*

videlicet *adverb & noun* LME **Latin** (from *vide-* stem of *videre* to see + *licet* it is permissible; cf. SCILICET). **A** *adverb* LME Usually introducing an amplification or explanation of a previous statement or word; that is to say, namely. **B** *noun* M17 The word 'videlicet' introducing an explanation or amplification, especially in a legal document.

■ Frequently abbreviated to *viz(.)* (M16), the z representing the usual medieval Latin symbol of contraction for *-et*.

vidimus *noun* LME **Latin** (= we have seen, from *videre* to see). **1** LME A copy of a document bearing an attestation of its authenticity or accuracy. **b** M19 An inspection of accounts.

vie de Bohème *noun phrase* L19 **French**. A Bohemian way of life.

vie de château *noun phrase* E20 **French**. The way of life of a large country house; aristocratic social life.

vie d'intérieur *noun phrase* L19 **French**. Private or domestic life.

vie en rose *noun phrase* M20 **French**. A life seen through rose-colored glasses.

■ A phrase popularized by the French singer Edith Piaf (1915–63), one of whose songs was called "La Vie en rose".

vie intérieure *noun phrase* E20 **French**. One's inner life, the life of the spirit.

vie intime *noun phrase* L19 **French**. The intimate private life of a person.

vie romancée *noun phrase plural* **vies romancées** M20 **French**. A fictionalized biography.

vi et armis *adverb phrase* E17 **Latin** (= with force and arms). Violently, forcibly, by compulsion; *specifically* in *Law* (now *historical*), with unlawful violence.

vieux jeu *noun & adjective* plural of noun **vieux jeux** L19 **French** (literally, 'old game'). (Something or someone) old-fashioned, outmoded, passé.

vieux marcheur plural **vieux marcheurs** E20 **French** (literally, 'old campaigner'). An elderly womanizer.

■ From the title of a play *Le Vieux Marcheur* (1909) by Henri Lavedon.

vieux rose *noun & adjective* L19 **French**. (Of) a deep pink color, old rose.

viga *noun* M19 **Spanish**. A rough-hewn roof beam or rafter, especially in a Pueblo building.

vigia *noun* M19 **Portuguese** (= lookout, from *vigiar*, from Latin *vigilia* wakefulness, from *vigil* awake, alert). A warning on a sea chart to denote a reported but as yet unverified danger.

vigilante *noun* M19 **Spanish** (from Latin *vigilant-* present participial stem of *vigilare* to keep awake). A member of a vigilance committee; any person executing summary justice in the absence or breakdown of legally constituted law enforcement bodies. Now also, a member of a self-appointed group undertaking law enforcement but without legal authority, operating in addition to an existing police force to protect property, etc., within a localized area.

vigneron *noun* LME **French** (from *vigne* vine). A person who cultivates grapevines; a vine grower.

vignette *noun & verb* LME **Old and Modern French** (diminutive of *vigne* vine). **A** *noun* **1** LME A usually small decorative design or illustration on a blank space in a book, etc., especially at the beginning or end of a chapter or on the title page; *specifically* one not enclosed in a border, or with the edges shading off into the surrounding paper. **2** LME *Architecture* A carved decoration representing the trailing tendrils, branches, or leaves of a vine. **3** M19 A photographic portrait showing only the head or the head and shoulders and with the edges gradually shading into the background. **4** L19 A brief descriptive account, anecdote, or essay; a character sketch; a short evocative episode in a play, etc. **B** *transitive verb* **1** M19 Make a vignette of; *specifically* produce (a photograph) in the style of a vignette by softening away or shading off the edges of the subject. **2** M20 *Optics* Cause vignetting of an image.

vignoble *noun* L15 **Old and Modern French** (from popular Latin, from Latin *vinea* vineyard). A vineyard.

vihara *noun* L17 **Sanskrit** (*vihāra*). A Buddhist monastery or nunnery.

villa *noun* E17 **Italian and Latin** (partly from Latin *villa* country house, farm, partly from Italian *villa* from Latin). **1** E17 *Roman Antiquities* A large country house with an estate. Now, a country residence; *specifically* a rented or privately owned vacation home, especially abroad. **2** M18 A detached or semidetached house in a suburban or residential district.

■ In sense 2 often in proper names, as *Villa Ariadne*.

villancico *noun* plural **villancicos** E19 **Spanish** (diminutive of *villano* peasant, rustic, from medieval Latin *villanus* villager, from Latin *villa* villa (sense 1)). *Music* A form of Spanish and Portuguese song consisting of short stanzas separated by a refrain, originally a kind of folk song but later used in sacred music; now *especially* a Christmas carol.

villanella *noun* plural **villanelle**, **villanellas** L16 **Italian** (see next). *Music* A form of Italian part-song having a rustic character and a vigorous rhythm.

villanelle *noun* L16 **French** (from Italian *villanella* feminine of *villanello* rural, rustic, from *villano* peasant, rustic, from medieval Latin *villanus* villager, from Latin *villa* villa (sense 1)). **1** L16–L17 *Music* A VILLANELLA. **2** L19 A usually pastoral or lyric poem consisting normally of five three-line stanzas and a final quatrain, with only two rhymes throughout and some lines repeated.

ville *noun* M19 **French** (= town). A town, a village.

■ Colloquial, chiefly United States, where *-ville* occurs in the names of many towns (e.g., *Louisville*). Hence used jocularly as a suffix to form the name of a fictitious place that epitomizes the quality concerned.

villeggiatura *noun* plural **villeggiature** M18 **Italian** (from *villeggiare* to live at a villa or in the country, from *villa* villa). Residence at a country villa or in the country, especially in Italy; a vacation spent in this way.

ville lumière *noun* E20 **French** (= town or city of light(s)). A brightly lit city or town; an exciting modern city or town; *specifically* (*la Ville Lumière*), Paris.

vim *noun* M19 **Latin** (probably from *vim* accusative singular of *vis* strength, energy). Vigor, energy, spirit.

vimana *noun* M19 **Sanskrit**. In the Indian subcontinent: the central tower enclosing the shrine in a temple; *Mythology* a heavenly chariot.

vin *noun* L17 **French**. French wine.

vina variant of VEENA.

vinaigrette *noun* LME **French** (from *vinaigre* vinegar). **1** A stew, sauce, or other dish made with vinegar. Only in LME. **b** A condiment prepared with vinegar. Only in L17. **2** L17 *History* A small two-wheeled carriage drawn or pushed by people, formerly used in France. **3** E19 A small ornamental bottle or box for holding a sponge saturated with smelling salts, etc. **4** L19 A salad dressing of oil and wine vinegar with seasoning. Also more fully *vinaigrette dressing*, *vinaigrette sauce*.

vin blanc *noun phrase* L18 **French**. White wine.

vin compris *noun phrase* L19 **French**. Wine included in the price of a meal or other entertainment.

vin cuit *noun phrase* M19 **French** (literally 'cooked or boiled wine'). **1** M19 Grape juice boiled to a syrup and used to fortify or sweeten other wine. Cf. VINO COTTO. **2** M20 A sweet aperitif wine.

vinculum *noun* plural **vincula** M17 **Latin** (from *vincire* to bind). **1** M17 A bond, a tie. Chiefly *figurative*. **2** E18 *Mathematics* A horizontal line over two or more terms, denoting that they are to be treated as a unit in the following operation. **3** M19 *Anatomy* A connecting band or bandlike structure; *especially* a narrow tendon.

vindaloo *noun* L19 **Portuguese** (probably from Portuguese *vin d'alho* wine and garlic sauce, from *vinho* wine + *alho* garlic). A highly spiced hot Indian curry dish made with meat, fish, or poultry. Also *vindaloo curry*.

vin de paille *noun phrase* M19 **French** (= straw wine). Wine made from grapes that have been dried on straw mats before being pressed.

vin de table *noun phrase* M20 **French.** Wine suitable for drinking with a meal, usually one that is not fortified or sparkling.

■ The English phrase *table wine* (L17) is also used, especially of non-French wines; the German equivalent is TAFELWEIN.

vin d'honneur *noun phrase* E20 **French.** A wine formally offered in honor of a person or persons; the reception at which the wine is offered.

vin doux (naturel) *noun phrase* M20 **French** (literally, 'sweet (natural)'). A sweet fortified wine.

vin du pays *noun phrase* L18 **French** (literally, 'wine of the country'). A local wine.

vin fou *noun phrase* M19 **French** (literally, 'mad wine'). A white or rosé sparkling wine from the Jura.

vin gris *noun phrase* M19 **French** (literally, 'gray wine'). A rosé wine of eastern France.

vingt-et-un *noun* Also written **vingt-un** L18 **French** (= twenty-one). The card game pontoon.

vinho *noun* M19 **Portuguese.** Portuguese wine.

vinho branco *noun phrase* M19 **Portuguese.** White wine.

vinho corrente *noun phrase* L20 **Portuguese** (literally, 'common wine'). Cheap wine equivalent to VIN ORDINAIRE.

vinho da casa *noun phrase* M20 **Portuguese** (literally, 'wine of the house'). House wine.

vinho de consumo *noun phrase* L20 **Portuguese** (literally, 'wine for consumption'). VINHO CORRENTE.

vinho tinto *noun phrase* M19 **Portuguese.** Red wine.

vinho verde *noun phrase* M20 **Portuguese** (literally, 'green wine'). Young wine not allowed to mature.

vin jaune *noun phrase* M19 **French** (literally, 'yellow wine'). A yellowish wine from the Jura region of eastern France.

vin mousseux *noun phrase* L18 **French.** A sparkling wine. Also called MOUSSEUX.

vino *noun* L17 **Spanish and Italian** (= wine). **1** L17 Spanish or Italian wine. **2** E20 An alcoholic liquor distilled from nipa palm sap drunk in the Philippines. **3** E20 Wine, especially of an inferior kind. *colloquial*, often *jocular*.

vino blanco *noun phrase* L20 **Spanish.** White wine.

vino corriente *noun phrase* M20 **Spanish** (literally, 'common wine'). Cheap wine equivalent to VIN ORDINAIRE.

vino cotto *noun phrase* M19 **Italian** (literally 'cooked wine'). Grape juice boiled to a syrup and used to fortify or sweeten other wine, especially marsala. Cf. VIN CUIT.

■ The opposite is *vino crudo* (literally, 'raw wine') or 'wine in its natural state'. The distinction is first mentioned in English by the seventeenth-century English botanist John Ray: "The boil'd wine, which they call *Vin Cotto*, seemed to us much stronger than the wine unboil'd, which they call *Vin Crudo*" (*Observations . . .*, 1673).

vino de color *noun phrase* M19 **Spanish.** A rich sweet wine, used in the blending of sherry and other fortified wines.

vino de pasto *noun phrase* L19 **Spanish** (literally, 'pasture wine'). **1** L19 A pale and fairly dry sherry. **2** M20 A table wine for everyday consumption.

vino dolce *noun phrase* E20 **Italian**. Sweet Italian wine.

vino dulce *noun phrase* E20 **Spanish**. Sweet Spanish wine.

vino maestro *noun phrase* E20 **Spanish** (literally, 'master wine'). A sweet and strong wine used to fortify or sweeten other wines.

vino nero *noun phrase* M20 **Italian** (literally, 'black wine'). Dark red wine.

vin ordinaire *noun phrase* E19 **French** (literally, 'ordinary wine'). Simple (usually red) table wine for everyday use.

■ Also referred to elliptically as ORDINAIRE (M19).

vino rosso *noun phrase* M20 **Italian**. Red wine.

vino santo *noun phrase* L17 **Italian** (literally, 'holy wine'). VINSANTO.

vino secco *noun phrase* E20 **Italian**. Dry wine.

vino tierno *noun phrase* E20 **Spanish** (literally, 'tender'). Wine made from partially dried grapes, used especially for fortifying malaga.

vino tinto *noun phrase* L17 **Spanish**. Red wine.

vin rosé *noun phrase* M20 **French**. Rosé wine.

vin rouge *noun phrase* E20 **French**. Red wine.

vinsanto *noun* M20 **Italian** (from *vino santo* holy wine). A sweet white Italian dessert wine.

viola bastarda *noun phrase* E18 **Italian** (literally, 'bastard viol'). *Music* A bass viol tuned and played according to a system of tablature. Also called *lyra viol*.

viola da braccio *noun phrase* M19 **Italian** (literally, 'viol of the arm'). Any member of the violin family, as opposed to a viola da gamba; *specifically* a viol corresponding to the modern viola.

viola da gamba *noun phrase* (also (earlier) **viol da gamba**) L16 **Italian** (literally, 'leg viol'). **1** L16 A viol held between the player's legs, *especially* one corresponding to the modern cello. **2** M19 An organ stop resembling this instrument in tone.

viola d'amore *noun phrase* E18 **Italian** (literally, 'viol of love'). A kind of tenor viol usually having sympathetic strings and no frets.

violetta *noun* plural **violette** M18 **Italian** (diminutive of *viola* viola). *Music* A small viol.

violette de Parme *noun phrase* plural **violettes de Parme** E20 **French**. Any of various cultivated violets with double, scented, usually light purple flowers, used for perfume or crystallized for food decoration; a Parma violet.

violon *noun* M16 **French**. **1** M16–E17 A violin. Also, a violinist. **2** M19 A kind of organ stop resembling a double bass in tone.

violoncello *noun* E18 **Italian** (diminutive of *violone*). **1** E18 A cello. **b** M19 A cellist. **2** L19 An organ stop similar in tone to a cello.

violon d'Ingres *noun phrase* plural **violons d'Ingres** M20 **French** (literally, 'Ingres' violin'). An interest or activity other than that for which a person is best known; an occasional pastime.

■ The allusion is to the French painter J.-A.-D. Ingres (1780–1867), who was a keen amateur violinist and said to have been more proud of his violin playing than of his highly acclaimed pictures.

virage *noun* M20 **French**. A hairpin bend; a sharp turn made in negotiating such a bend.

virago *noun & adjective* LME **Latin** (from *vir* man). **A** *noun* plural **viragos**. **1** LME A woman of masculine strength or spirit; a female warrior, an amazon. *archaic*. **2** LME A domineering woman; a fierce or abusive woman. **B** *adjective* L16 That is a virago; of or pertaining to a virago or viragos.

■ Earlier (OE–L16) meaning 'woman', but only in biblical allusions with reference to the name given by Adam to Eve.

vires plural of VIS.

virga *noun* plural **virgae** E20 **Latin** (= rod). **1** E20 *Music* (A symbol designating) a note used in plainsong. **2** M20 *Meteorology, singular* and in *plural* Streaks of precipitation that appear to hang from the undersurface of a cloud and usually evaporate before reaching the ground.

virgo intacta *noun phrase* E18 **Latin** (literally, 'untouched virgin'). Chiefly *Law* A girl or woman who has never had sexual intercourse.

virgule *noun* M19 **French** (= comma, from Latin *virgula* diminutive of *virga* rod). **1** M19 A slanting or upright line used especially in medieval manuscripts to mark a caesura, or as a punctuation mark equivalent to a comma. Now also a SOLIDUS sense 2. **2** L19 *Watchmaking* A type of escapement in which the teeth of the wheel have the shape of a comma. More fully *virgule escapement*.

virtu *noun* (also **vertu**, **virtù**) E18 **Italian** (*virtù* virtue; the form *vertu* altered as if from French). **1** E18 A love of or interest in works of art; a knowledge of or expertise in the fine arts; the fine arts as a subject of study or interest. **2** M18 *collective* Objects of art; curios. **3** M20 The strength or worth inherent in a person or thing; *especially* inherent moral worth or virtue.

virtuoso *noun & adjective* E17 **Italian** (= learned, skillful, from late Latin *virtuosus*). **A** *noun* plural **virtuosi**, **virtuosos** **1** E17–L18 A person who has a general interest in arts and sciences, or who pursues special investigations in one or more of these; a learned person. **2** M17 A person who has a special knowledge of or interest in the fine arts; a connoisseur, *especially* a person pursuing these interests in a dilettante manner. **3** M18 A person who has special knowledge or skill in the technique of a fine art, especially music. Also, a person with outstanding technical skill in any sphere. **B** *attributive* or as *adjective* M17 Of or pertaining to a virtuoso; displaying the skills of a virtuoso; characterized by virtuosity.

virtute officii *adverb phrase* E19 **Latin.** *Law* By virtue of (one's) office.

vis *noun* plural **vires** E17 **Latin. 1** E17 Strength, force, energy, vigor. **2** L20 *Law* In *plural* Legal validity; legal authority or power.

■ Chiefly now in various phrases; in the legal sense *vires* occurs earlier in INTRA VIRES and ULTRA VIRES.

visa *noun* M19 **French** (from Latin = things seen, neuter plural of past participle of *videre* to see). An endorsement on a passport, etc., indicating that it has been examined and found correct, especially as permitting the holder to enter or leave a country.

vis a fronte *noun phrase* E19 **Latin.** A force operating from in front, as in attraction or suction. Opposite of VIS A TERGO.

visagiste *noun* (also **visagist**) M20 **French.** A makeup artist.

vis a tergo *noun phrase* E19 **Latin.** A force operating from behind; a propulsive force. Opposite of VIS A FRONTE.

vis-à-vis *noun, preposition & adverb* M18 **Old and Modern French** (literally, 'face to face', from Old French *vis* visage + *à* to + *vis*). **A** *noun* plural same. **1** M18 A light horse-drawn carriage for two people sitting face to face. *obsolete* except *historical*. **2** M18 A person or thing facing or situated opposite to another, especially in certain dances. **b** E20 A counterpart, an opposite number. Also, a social partner. **3** M19 A face-to-face meeting. **B** *preposition* M18 Regarding, in relation to. Also, opposite to, face to face with. **C** *adverb* E19 Opposite; facing one another.

vis comica *noun phrase* M18 **Latin.** Humorous energy; comic force or effect.

visibilia *noun plural* M20 **Latin** (neuter plural of *visibilis* visible). Visible things; visual images.

vis inertiae *noun phrase* E18 **Latin.** *Mechanics* The resistance offered by matter to any force tending to alter its state of rest or motion; *transferred* a tendency to remain inactive or unprogressive.

visitant *noun & adjective* L16 **French** (present participle of *visiter* to visit, or Latin *visitant-* present participial stem of *visitare*). **A** *noun* **1** L16 A person who visits a place, another person, etc.; a visitor, now *especially* a supernatural one. **2** M18 A thing that affects or comes to a person, especially for a temporary period. **3** L18 A migratory bird or animal that frequents a certain locality only at particular times of year. **B** *adjective* M17 Of the nature of a visitant.

visite de digestion *noun phrase* E20 **French** (literally, 'visit of digestion'). A formal call paid in return for hospitality received, especially after a dinner party.

vis major *noun phrase* E17 **Latin.** *Law* Overpowering force, especially of nature (used as a reason for damage done to, or loss of, property).

vis medicatrix naturae *noun phrase* E19 **Latin.** The healing power of nature.

vista *noun* M17 **Italian** (= view). **1** M17 A view, a prospect, *especially* one seen through an avenue of trees or other long narrow opening. **2** L17 A long narrow opening, especially one created deliberately in a wood, etc., through which a view may be obtained, or in itself affording a pleasant prospect. **b** E18 An open corridor or long passage in or through a large building; an interior portion of a building affording a continuous view. **3** L17 *figurative* A broad prospect or vision presented to the imagination; a mental view, in prospect or retrospect, of an extensive period of time or series of events, experiences, etc.

vis viva *noun phrase* L18 **Latin.** *Mechanics* The operative force of a moving or acting body, equal to the mass of the body multiplied by the square of its velocity.

vita *noun* M20 **Latin** (= life). **1** M20 A biography, a life history, *especially* a short Latin biography of a saint. **2** M20 A CURRICULUM VITAE.

vita nuova *noun phrase* M20 **Italian** (= new life). A fresh start or new direction in life, especially after some powerful emotional experience.

■ With allusion to the title of a work by Dante describing his love for Beatrice.

vitello tonnato *noun phrase* M20 **Italian** (from *vitello* veal + *tonno* tuna). An Italian dish consisting of roast or poached veal served cold in a tuna and anchovy mayonnaise.

viva *noun 1 & interjection* M17 **Italian** (= live!, 3rd person singular present subjunctive of *vivere* to live, from Latin). (A cry or cheer) wishing long life and prosperity to or expressing approval of an admired person or thing: hurrah! long live! Cf. VIVAT, VIVE (interjection).

viva *noun 2 & verb* L19 **Latin** (abbreviation of VIVA VOCE). **A** *noun* L19 A VIVA VOCE examination. **B** *transitive verb* L19 past tense *vivaed, viva'd.* Subject to a viva voce examination, examine orally.

vivandier *noun* (feminine **vivandière**) L16 **French.** *History* In the French and other Continental European armies, a supplier of provisions to troops in the field.

vivarium *noun* plural **vivaria, vivariums** E17 **Latin** (= warren, fishpond, noun use of *vivarius* from *vivus* alive, from *vivere* to live). **1** E17 A place for keeping living animals, especially fish, for food; a fishpond. *obsolete* except *historical.* **2** L17 A structure used for keeping animals under conditions approximating to the natural conditions, for observation or study.

vivat *interjection & noun* L16 **Latin** (= may he or she live, 3rd person singular present subjunctive of *vivere* to live). (A cry or cheer) wishing long life and prosperity to or expressing approval of an admired person or thing: hurrah! long live! Cf. VIVA, VIVE.

viva voce *adverb, adjective, & noun phrase* M16 **Medieval Latin** (literally, 'by or with the living voice'). **A** *adverb phrase* M16 Orally rather than in writing. **B** *adjective phrase* **1** E17 Expressed in speech rather than writing, spoken. **2** E19 Of an examination: conducted orally; *specifically* of a supplementary oral examination following a written one. **C** *noun phrase* M19 A viva voce examination.

■ In the noun sense frequently abbreviated to VIVA (noun 2).

vive *interjection* L16 **French** (= may he, she, or it live, from *vivre* from Latin *vivere* live). Wishing long life and prosperity to or expressing approval of an admired person or thing; long live! Cf. VIVA (interjection), VIVAT.

vive la bagatelle *interjection* M18 **French** (literally, 'success to frivolity or nonsense'). Expressing a carefree attitude to life.

vive la différence *interjection* M20 **French**. Expressing approval of the difference between the sexes.

■ In jocular use; also transferred.

viveur *noun* M19 **French** (= a living person). A person who lives a fashionable and social life. Cf. BON VIVEUR.

vivier *noun* LME **Old and Modern French**. A fishpond; a tank for storing live fish, etc.

viz. abbreviation of VIDELICET.

vlakte *noun* L18 **Afrikaans** (from Dutch). In South Africa: an extent of flat open country; a plain. Frequently in *plural*.

vlei *noun* L18 **Afrikaans** (from Dutch *vallei* valley). **1** L18 In South Africa: a shallow pool of water; a piece of low-lying ground covered with water during the rainy season. **2** L19 A swamp. *local*.

vobla *noun* (also **wobla**) M20 **Russian**. Dried and smoked roach eaten in Russia as a delicacy.

voce di gola *noun phrase* L19 **Italian** (literally, 'throat voice'). *Music* A throaty or guttural voice.

voce di petto *noun phrase* M18 **Italian** (literally, 'chest voice'). *Music* The chest register.

voce di testa *noun phrase* M18 **Italian** (literally, 'head voice'). *Music* The head register; formerly also, the falsetto voice.

vodka *noun* E19 **Russian** (diminutive of *voda* water). A colorless alcoholic spirit made especially in Russia by distillation of grain, etc.; a glass or drink of this.

voetganger *noun* E19 **Afrikaans** (from Dutch = pedestrian, from *voet* foot + *ganger* goer). **1** E19 A locust in its immature wingless stage. **2** E20 A pedestrian. Also (*colloquial*), an infantryman. *South African*.

voetsek *interjection & verb* (also **voetsak**) M19 **Afrikaans** (*voe(r)tsek*, from Dutch *voort zeg ik* be off I say). **A** *interjection* M19 Especially to a dog: go away!, off you go! **B** *verb* **1** *transitive verb* L19 Chase (a dog) away. **2** *intransitive verb* M20 Leave, go away. *South African*.

voeu *noun* plural **voeux** E20 **French** (= vow, wish). A nonmandatory recommendation made by an international conference.

vogue la galère *interjection* M18 **French** (literally, 'let the galley be rowed'). Let's get on with it! Let's give it a go!

voilà *transitive & intransitive verb* (*imperative & impersonal*) (also **voila**) M18 **French** (from imperative of *voir* see + *lá* there). There is, are, etc.; see there.

■ Also as an interjection: 'there it is!', 'there you are!'

voilà tout *interjection* E19 **French**. That's all! That's it! There is nothing more to do or say.

voile *noun & adjective* L19 **French** (= veil). **A** *noun* L19 A lightweight open-texture material of cotton, wool, silk, or acetate, used especially for blouses and dresses. **B** *attributive* or as *adjective* L19 Made of voile.

voir dire *noun* (also **voire dire**) L17 Law French (from Old French *voir* true, truth + *dire* to say). *Law* A preliminary examination by a judge or counsel of the competence of a witness or (occasionally) a juror; an oath taken by such a witness. Also, an investigation into the truth or admissibility of evidence, held during a trial.

voix céleste *noun phrase* plural **voix célestes** L19 French (= heavenly voice). An organ stop having an 8-ft. pitch, with 2 pipes to each note, tuned slightly apart, producing an undulating tone traditionally regarded as reminiscent of celestial voices. Also called *vox angelica*.

volage *adjective* LME Old and Modern French (from Latin *volaticus* winged, inconstant). Giddy, foolish; fickle, inconstant.

■ Formerly fully naturalized; now in literary use, reintroduced from modern French.

volante *noun 1* L18 Spanish (from present participle of *volar* to fly, from Latin *volare* to fly). A horse-drawn carriage or wagon, especially of a two-wheeled covered type, used in Cuba and formerly in other Spanish-speaking countries.

volante *noun 2* L19 Italian (= flying). *Music* The rapid execution of a series of notes in singing or playing; *especially* in violin playing, a bowing technique in which the bow bounces from the string in a slurred staccato.

vol-au-vent *noun* E19 French (literally, 'flight in the wind'). A (usually small and round) flat-bottomed case of puff pastry filled with chopped meat, fish, egg, etc., in sauce.

volens *adjective* L19 Latin (present participle of *velle* to be willing). *Law* Consenting to the risk of injury. Cf. NOLENS VOLENS.

volet *noun* M19 Old and Modern French (literally, 'shutter', from *voler* from Latin *volare* to fly). Each of the wings or side compartments of a triptych. Also called *volant*.

volk *noun* (also (German) **Volk**) L19 Afrikaans (from Dutch or German = nation, people). **1** L19 The Afrikaner people. Also (frequently *derogatory*), the Colored employees of a white (especially Afrikaner) master collectively. *South African*. **2** M20 The German people (especially with reference to Nazi ideology).

Völkerwanderung *noun* plural **Völkerwanderungen** M20 German (from *Völker* nations + *Wanderung* migration). A migration of peoples; *specifically* that of Germanic and Slavonic peoples into and across Europe from the second to the eleventh centuries.

völkisch *adjective* M20 German. Populist, nationalist, racialist.

volksgeist *noun* (also **Volksgeist**) M20 German. The spirit or genius that marks the thought or feeling of a nation or people.

volkslied *noun* plural **volkslieder** (also **Volkslied**) M19 German (or Afrikaans (from Dutch)). **1** M19 A German folk song; a song or other piece of music in the style of German folk songs. **2** L19 A national anthem; *specifically* (*historical*) that of the nineteenth-century Transvaal Republic. Also, a South African folk song.

volta *noun* L16 Italian (= turn; cf. VOLTE). The LAVOLTA.

volte *noun* L16 French (from Italian *volta* turn, noun use of feminine past participle of *volgere* to turn, from Latin *volvere* to roll). **1** L16–E17 The LAVOLTA. **2** L17 *Fencing* (now *historical*) A sudden jump or other movement to avoid a thrust. **3** E18 *Horsemanship* A small circle of determined size (proposed with a radius equal to the length of a horse); a movement by a horse sideways around the point of such a circle. **4** E20 (A) complete change. *rare*.

volte-face *noun* E19 French (from Italian *voltafaccia*, from *voltare* to turn (ultimately from frequentative of Latin *volvere* to roll) + *faccia* (ultimately from Latin *facies*) face). The act or an instance of turning so as to face in the opposite direction. Chiefly *figurative*, a complete change of attitude, opinion, or position in an argument.

volupté *noun* E18 **French**. Voluptuousness.

volute *noun* (also (earlier) in Latin form **voluta**, plural **volutae**) M16 **French** (Latin *voluta* noun use of feminine of *volutus* past participle of *volvere* to roll, to wrap). **1** M16 *Architecture* A spiral scroll characteristic of Ionic capitals and also used in Corinthian and composite capitals. **2** M18 A spiral part or object; a convolution. **3** M18 (A shell of) any of numerous gastropod mollusks of the family Volutidae.

vomitorium *noun* plural **vomitoria** M18 **Late Latin** (noun use of neuter of Latin *vomitorius* vomitory). *Roman Antiquities* **1** M18 A passage or opening in an amphitheater or theater, leading to or from the seats. Usually in *plural*. **2** E20 A room allegedly for vomiting deliberately during feasts, to make way for other food.

voorloper *noun* M19 **Afrikaans** (from *voor-* before + *loop* to run). In South Africa: the leader of a span of oxen, usually a young African or Colored boy.

Voortrekker *noun* L19 **Afrikaans** (from *voor-* before + *trekken* to trek). *South African History* A Boer pioneer, *especially* one who took part in the Great Trek from Cape Colony *c.*1835.

vorlage *noun* plural **vorlages**, **vorlagen** M20 **German**. **1** M20 *Skiing* A position in which the skier leans forward without lifting the heels from the skis. **b** M20 In *plural* Skiing pants. **2** M20 An original version of a manuscript from which a copy is produced.

vorlaufer *noun* M20 **German** (*Vorläufer*, from *vorlaufen* run on ahead). A skier who travels a course before a race to establish that it is within the capacity of the competitors.

Vorspiel *noun* plural **Vorspiele** L19 **German** (from *vor* before + *Spiel* play). *Music* A prelude.

Vorstellung *noun* (also **vorstellung**) plural **Vorstellen** E19 **German**. *Philosophy* and *Psychology* An idea, a mental picture.

vortex *noun* plural **vortexes vortices** M17 **Latin** ((variant of VERTEX) an eddy of water, wind, or flame, from *vortere*, *vertere* to turn). **1 a** M17 In Cartesian theory: any of the rapidly revolving collections of fine particles supposed to fill all space. Usually in *plural*. **b** M19 *Physics* A rapid motion of particles around an axis; a whirl of atoms, fluid, or vapor. **2** M17 A violent eddy of the air; a cyclone. Also, an eddying mass of fire. **3** E18 A swirling mass of water; a whirlpool. **4** *figurative* **a** M18 A whirl or constant round of frenetic activity, rapid change, etc. **b** L18 A place or state into which people or things are irresistibly drawn. **5** E20 *The Vortex* A group of modernist British artists (*c.*1914–15).

voulu *adjective* L19 **French** (past participle of *vouloir* to will, wish). Lacking in spontaneity; contrived.

voussoir *noun* ME **Old French** (*vausoir*, *vaussoir*, etc. (modern *voussoir*) from popular Latin *volsorium* ultimately from Latin *vols-* past participial stem of *volvere* to roll, to turn). Each of the wedge-shaped or tapered stones, bricks, etc., forming an arch or vaulting.

vox angelica *noun phrase* M19 **Latin** (= angelic voice). A VOIX CÉLESTE.

vox humana *noun phrase* E18 **Latin** (= human voice). An organ reed stop, having an 8-ft. pitch, producing a tone supposedly resembling the human voice.

vox nihili *noun phrase* L19 **Latin** (literally, 'voice of nothing'). A worthless or meaningless word, *especially* one produced by a scribal or printer's error.

vox populi *noun phrase* M19 **Latin** (= voice of the people). Expressed general opinion; common talk or rumor.

■ In colloquial use abbreviated to *vox pop* (M20), usually (but not always) with derogatory connotations of 'uninformed opinion, as expressed in the media by members of the public'. The Latin tag from which the phrase derives, *vox populi, vox Dei* 'the voice of the people is the voice of God' has been cited or alluded to in English from the fifteenth century.

voyagé *noun & adjective* M20 **French** (past participle of *voyager* to travel). *Ballet* (Designating) a movement in which the pose is held during progression.

voyant *noun* M20 **French** (from as next). A visionary; a seer.

voyant *adjective* E20 **French** (present participial adjective of *voir* to see). Showy, gaudy, flashy.

voyeur *noun* E20 **French** (from *voir* to see). A person who obtains sexual satisfaction from covert observation of the sexual organs or actions of others. Also (*transferred*) a powerless or passive spectator.

voyou *noun* E20 **French**. A street urchin; a lout, a hooligan.

vozhd *noun* M20 **Russian** (*vozhd'*). A leader, a person in supreme authority; *specifically* (*historical*) Stalin.

vrai réseau *noun phrase* plural **vrais réseaux** M19 **French** (= true net). A fine net ground used in making handmade (especially Brussels) lace. Cf. RÉSEAU sense 1.

vraisemblable *adjective* M19 **French** (from *vrai* true + *semblable* like). Believable, plausible.

vraisemblance *noun* E19 **French** (from *vrai* true + *semblance* likeness). **1** E19 Verisimilitude. **2** M19 A representation *of* a person or thing.

vrais réseaux plural of VRAI RÉSEAU.

vrouw *noun* (also **vrow**) E17 **Dutch** (= German *Frau*). A woman, a wife; *especially* one of Dutch origin. Chiefly *South African*.

vue d'ensemble *noun phrase* plural **vues d'ensemble** M19 **French**. A general view of matters; an overview.

vulgarisateur *noun* M20 **French** (from *vulgariser* to popularize, vulgarize). A popularizer, a vulgarizer.

vulgarisation *noun* M20 **French**. Vulgarization. Cf. HAUTE VULGARISATION.

Wabenzi *noun plural* (also **Wa-Benzi**) M20 **African languages** (invented to resemble the name of an African people: from human plural prefix *wa-* + Mercedes-*Benz*). In Africa: black politicians, civil servants, entrepreneurs, etc., whose status is marked by their ownership or use of a Mercedes-Benz or similar luxury car.

wabi *noun* M20 **Japanese** (literally, 'solitude'). In Japanese art, a quality of simple and serene beauty of a slightly austere or melancholy kind expressing a mood of spiritual solitude recognized in Zen Buddhist philosophy. Cf. SABI.

wadi *noun* (also **wady**) plural **wadis, wadies** E17 **Arabic** (*wādī* valley, riverbed). In certain Arabic-speaking countries, a rocky watercourse that is dry except during the rainy season; the stream running through such a watercourse.

■ French *oued*, a later (M19) introduction, represents the same Arabic word. *Oued* now mainly occurs in English with reference to place names in Francophone North African territories.

wagon-lit *noun* plural **wagon-lits, wagons-lits** L19 **French** (from *wagon* railroad coach + *lit* bed). A sleeping car on a train in Continental Europe.

wagon-restaurant *noun* plural **wagons-restaurants** E20 **French** (from *wagon* railroad coach + *restaurant*). A dining car on a train in Continental Europe.

wahala *noun* L20 **Hausa**. In Nigeria: trouble, inconvenience; fuss, bother.

wahine *noun* L18 **Maori** (cf. VAHINE). **1** L18 In New Zealand: a Maori woman or wife. **2** M19 In Polynesia: a VAHINE. **3** M20 A girl surfer. *surfing slang*.

wai see under NAMASKAR.

waka *noun 1* E19 **Maori**. In New Zealand: a Maori canoe.

waka *noun 2* **M20 Japanese**. **1** M20 A form of classic Japanese lyrical poetry developed from ancient traditional ballads. **2** M20 A TANKA.

wakame *noun* L20 **Japanese**. An edible Japanese seaweed.

wakf *noun* (also **waqf**) M19 **Arabic** (*waqf* stoppage, immobilization (sc. of ownership of property), from *waqafa* to stop, come to a standstill). In Islamic countries, endowment or settlement of property under which the proceeds are to be devoted to a religious or charitable purpose; land or property endowed in this way.

waldhorn *noun* M19 **German**. A French horn. Also, a natural valveless horn.

Waldsterben *noun* L20 **German** (from *Wald* wood, forest + *Sterben* dying, death). *Ecology* Disease and death in forest trees and vegetation as a result of atmospheric pollution.

■ The term has been current in English since about 1983, originally with reference to dieback through environmental causes affecting Germany's forest trees, but now applied to the same phenomenon elsewhere.

wallah *noun* (also **walla**) L18 **Hindi** (-*vālā* suffix expressing relation, from Sanskrit *pālaka* keeper). **1** L18 A person, formerly usually a servant, concerned with or in charge of a usually specified thing, task, etc. Chiefly as second element of combination. **2** M19 An Indian civil servant appointed by competitive examination. More fully *competition-wallah*. **3** M20 Any functionary doing a routine administrative job; a civil servant, a bureaucrat.

■ The Hindi suffix was commonly apprehended by Europeans as a noun with the sense 'man, fellow'; in Anglo-Indian speech it was used chiefly as the second element in combinations such as *box-wallah* ('an itinerant Indian peddler'). *Wallah* is now only used colloquially with a derogatory suggestion of 'an office-bound functionary' and generally (harking back to the Anglo-Indian usage) with a defining word.

Walpurgisnacht *noun* E19 **German** (genitive of *Walpurga* (name) + *Nacht* night). The eve of May Day, marked (according to German folklore and especially Goethe's *Faust*) by a witches' sabbath or a feast of the powers of darkness; *transferred* an orgiastic celebration or party.

■ St. Walpurga (or Walburga) was an eighth-century Anglo-Saxon nun who became abbess of Heidenheim in Germany. May Day marks the occasion of the translation of her bodily remains to Eichstätt, where her shrine became a pilgrimage center. The connection with the powers of darkness has nothing to do with the saintly abbess but is a fortuitous association with pagan festivities formerly celebrated on that date.

wampum *noun* M17 **Algonquian** (*wampumpeag* (from *wap* white + *umpe* string + plural suffix -*ag*) abbreviated on the erroneous analysis of the word as *wampum* + *peag*). **1** M17 Chiefly *History*. Beads made from the ends of shells rubbed down, polished, and threaded on strings, worn by North American Indians as decoration or (formerly) used as money or for mnemonic or symbolic purposes. **2** L19 *generally* Money. *slang.*

wamus *noun* E19 **Dutch** (probably from Dutch *wammes* contraction of *wambuis* from Old French *wambois* gambeson, tunic). In southern and western United States: a warm knitted jacket resembling a cardigan.

Wanderjahr *noun* plural **Wanderjahre** L19 **German** (*wander* wander + *Jahr* year). A year of wandering or travel, especially one undertaken by a young person.

■ Formerly a period of travel by an apprentice to improve his skill and broaden his experience; cf. LEHRJAHR. Also occurs in English form *wander-year* (L19).

wanderlust *noun* E20 **German.** An eagerness or fondness for wandering or traveling.

Wandervogel *noun* plural **Wandervögel** E20 **German** (literally, 'bird of passage'). A member of a German youth organization founded at the end of the nineteenth century for the promotion of outdoor activities (especially hiking) and folk culture; *transferred* a rambler, a hiker.

waqf variant of WAKF.

wasabi *noun* E20 **Japanese.** A cruciferous plant, *Eutrema wasabi*, whose thick green root is used in Japanese cooking, usually ground as an accompaniment to raw fish.

washi *noun* L20 **Japanese.** Japanese paper; *specifically* a thin handmade variety used to make lantern shades, kites, etc.

wat *noun* M19 **Thai** (from Sanskrit *vāṭa* enclosure). In Thailand or Cambodia (Kampuchea): a Buddhist monastery or temple.

wayang *noun* E19 **Javanese** (*wajang, wayang*). In Indonesia and Malaysia: a theatrical performance employing puppets or human dancers; *specifically* a Javanese and Balinese shadow puppet play (also *wayang kulit* (Javanese = skin, leather)).

wazir *noun* E18 **Arabic** (*wazīr* helper). *History* A high government official, especially in the Ottoman empire; a vizier.

wedeln *noun* (also **wedel**) M20 **German** (see next). *Skiing* A technique using a swaying movement of the hips to make a series of short parallel turns.

wedeln *intransitive verb* (also **wedel**) M20 **German** (literally, 'wag (the tail)'). *Skiing* Use the wedeln technique. Also, perform a similar movement on a skateboard.

Wehmut *noun* E20 **German.** Sadness, melancholy, wistfulness, nostalgia.

Wehrmacht *noun* M20 **German** (literally, 'defense force'). *History* The German armed forces, especially the army, between 1921 and 1945.

Wehrwirtschaft *noun* M20 **German** (from *Wehr* defense + *Wirtschaft* economy). The principle or policy of directing a nation's economic activity toward preparation for or support of a war effort, especially as applied in Germany in the 1930s.

wei ch'i *noun* L19 **Chinese** (*wéiqí* (Wade–Giles *wei-ch'i*), from *wei* to surround + *qí* (*ch'i*) chess). A traditional Chinese board game of territorial possession and capture. Cf. GO.

weiner variant of WIENER.

weinkraut *noun* M20 **German** (from *Wein* wine + *Kraut* cabbage). Pickled cabbage cooked with white wine and apples.

Weinstube *noun* plural **Weinstuben, Weinstubes** L19 **German** (from *Wein*, wine + *Stube* room). A small German wine bar or tavern. Cf. BIERSTUBE.

Wein, Weib, und Gesang *noun phrase* L19 **German.** Wine, woman, and song.

Weisswurst *noun* M20 **German** (from *weiss* white + *Wurst* sausage). (A) whitish German sausage made chiefly of veal.

Weltanschauung *noun* plural **Weltanschauungen, Weltanschauungs** M19

German (from *Welt* world + *Anschauung* perception). A particular philosophy or view of life; the worldview of an individual or group.

Weltbild *noun* M20 German (from *Welt* world + *Bild* picture). WELTANSCHAUUNG.

Weltliteratur *noun* (also **Weltlitteratur**) E20 German (from *Welt* world + *Literatur* literature). A literature of all nations and peoples; universal literature.

Weltpolitik *noun* E20 German (from *Welt* world + *Politik* politics). International politics; a particular country's policy toward the world at large.

Weltschmerz *noun* L19 German (from *Welt* world + *Schmerz* pain). A weary or pessimistic feeling about life; an apathetic or vaguely yearning attitude.

Weltstadt *noun* plural **Weltstädte** L19 German (from *Welt* world + *Stadt* town). A city of international importance or cosmopolitan character; a cosmopolis.

wendigo variant of WINDIGO.

wen jen *noun phrase plural* M20 Chinese (*wénrén* man of letters, from *wén* writing + *rén* (Wade–Giles *jên*) man). Chinese men of letters.

wen-yen *noun* (also **wenyen**, **wenyan**) M20 Chinese (*wényán*, from *wén* writing + *yán* speech, words). The traditional literary language or style of China, now superseded by PAI-HUA.

wertfrei *adjective* E20 German (from *Wert* worth + *frei* free). Free of value judgments; morally neutral.

■ In sociological contexts often in English translation as *value-free*; cf. WERTFREIHEIT.

Wertfreiheit *noun* M20 German (from as preceding + *-heit* -hood). The quality of being *wertfrei*.

■ *Wertfreiheit* (also frequently in English 'value-freedom'), was recommended by the German sociologist Max Weber (1864–1920) as an ideal to which sociologists should aspire in that they should not allow their own values to influence their judgments on the people and institutions they study.

Westpolitik *noun* L20 German (from *West* west + *Politik* policy: cf. OSTPOLITIK). *History* In European politics, a policy of establishing or developing diplomatic and trading relations with Western nations, especially formerly on the part of Communist countries.

whare *noun* E19 Maori. In New Zealand: a (Maori) house or hut; *generally* a hut, a shed, *specifically* one on a sheep station, where the workers sleep or eat.

wickiup *noun* (also **wickyup**) M19 Algonquian ((Menominee *wikiop*), perhaps a variant of *wikiwam* wigwam). A rough hut consisting of a frame covered with brushwood, used by nomadic peoples in the west and southwest of the United States; *colloquial* any small hut or shanty.

wiederkom *noun* (also **wiederkomm**, **Wiederkomm**) L19 French (*vidrecome* goblet, ultimately from German *wiederkommen* to return, come again). A tall cylindrical German drinking vessel made of (usually colored or painted) glass.

wiener *noun* (in sense 2 also **weiner**) L19 German (adjective from *Wien* Vienna). **I** *attributive* **1** L19 Used *attributively* to designate things from or associated with Vienna. **II 2** E20 *Elliptically* for WIENERWURST.

weiner schnitzel see under SCHNITZEL.

wienerwurst *noun* L19 German. Viennese sausage.

wili *noun* (also **willi**) M20 German or French (from Serbo-Croat *víla* nymph, fairy). *Mythology* In Slavonic and eastern German legends, a spirit of a betrothed girl who has died from grief at being jilted by her lover (used especially with reference to the ballet *Giselle*).

wiliwili *noun* L19 Hawaiian. A coral tree, *Erythrina tahitensis*, of Hawaii and Tahiti, that bears clusters of orange flowers; the wood of this tree, used to make surfboards.

willi variant of WILI.

willy-willy *noun* L19 **Aboriginal**. In Northwest Australia: a cyclone or dust storm.

windigo *noun* (also **wendigo**) plural **windigo(e)s** E18 **Ojibwa** (*wintiko*). In the folklore of the northern Algonquian Indians, a cannibalistic giant, the transformation of a person who has eaten human flesh.

Wirtschaft *noun* M19 **German** (in sense 2 abbreviation of *Gastwirtschaft* hotel). **1** M19 (Domestic) economy, housekeeping. **2** E20 A hostelry, inn.

Wirtschaftswunder *noun* (also **Wirtschaftwunder**) M20 **German** (*Wirtschaft* economy + *Wunder* miracle). The economic recovery of West Germany after World War II. Also *transferred*.

Wissenschaft *noun* M19 **German**. (The systematic pursuit of) knowledge, science; learning, scholarship.

witblits *noun* (also **witblitz**) M20 **Afrikaans** (from *wit* white + *blits* lightning). In South Africa: home-brewed brandy, a strong and colorless raw spirit.

witdoek *noun* plural **witdoeke**, **witdoeks** L20 **Afrikaans** (from *wit* white + DOEK). In South Africa: a member of a largely black conservative vigilante movement operating in the townships around Cape Town, identifiable by the wearing of a white cloth or scarf about the head. Usually in *plural*.

witloof *noun* L19 **Dutch** (literally, 'white leaf'). A variety of chicory grown for blanching, with broad leaves and midribs.

wobla variant of VOBLA.

wok *noun* M20 **Chinese** (Cantonese). A large bowl-shaped frying pan used in especially Chinese cooking.

■ The *wok*, introduced into Western kitchens in the 1970s, rapidly became a standard item of kitchen equipment.

wongi *noun* E20 **Aboriginal**. A talk, a chat; a speech. *Australian slang*.

wonton *noun* (also **won ton**) M20 **Chinese** ((Cantonese) *wān t'ān*). In Chinese cooking, (a dish consisting of) a small round dumpling or roll with a savory filling (especially of ground pork), often eaten boiled in soup.

woonerf *noun* plural **woonerfs**, **woonerven** L20 **Dutch** (from *woon-* residential (from *wonen* to live) + *erf* ground, premises). A road in a residential area, in which a number of devices are employed to create a safer environment by reducing and slowing the flow of traffic.

Wunderkammer *noun* L20 **German** (from *Wunder* wonder + *Kammer* chamber). A chamber or cabinet of wonders; *historical* a place exhibiting the collection of a connoisseur of curiosities.

wunderkind *noun* (also **Wunderkind**) plural **wunderkinds**, **wunderkinder** L19 **German** (from *Wunder* wonder + *Kind* child). **1** L19 A highly talented child; a child prodigy, especially in music. **2** M20 A person who achieves remarkable success at an early age. *colloquial*.

wurst *noun* M19 **German**. Sausage, especially of the German or Austrian type; a German or Austrian sausage.

wushu *noun* L20 **Chinese** (*wǔshù*, from *wǔ* military + *shù* technique, art). The Chinese martial arts.

wu ts'ai *noun* E20 **Chinese** (*wǔcǎi* (Wade–Giles *wu ts'ai*), from *wǔ* five + *cǎi* color). Polychrome; polychrome decoration in enamels applied to porcelain; porcelain with polychrome decoration.

XYZ

xenodochium *noun* plural **xenodochia** (also *xenodochion*) M16 **Late Latin** (from Late Greek from as *xeno-* stranger + *deskhesthai* to receive). *History* A house of reception for strangers and pilgrims, especially in a monastery.

xoanon *noun* plural **xoana** E18 **Greek** (related to *xein* to carve). Chiefly *Greek Antiquities* A primitive simply carved image of a deity, originally of wood, and often said to have fallen from heaven.

xystus *noun* plural **xysti** (also Anglicized as **xyst**) M17 **Latin** (from Greek *xustos* smooth, from *xuein* to scrape). *Classical Antiquities* A long covered portico or court used by ancient Greek athletes for exercises. Also, an open colonnade or terrace walk planted with trees and used by the Romans for recreation and conversation.

yabba *noun* L19 **Twi** (*ayawá* earthen vessel, dish). In Jamaica: a large wooden or earthenware vessel used for cooking or storage.

yacca, yacker variants of YAKKA.

yad *noun* E20 **Hebrew** (*yād*, literally, 'hand'). *Judaism* A pointer used by a reader of the Torah in a synagogue to follow the text, usually in the form of a rod terminating in a hand with an outstretched index finger.

yager see under JÄGER.

yagna variant of YAJNA.

yahrzeit *noun* M19 **Yiddish** (from Middle High German *jarzît* anniversary, from Old High German *jar* (German *Jahr*) year + *zît* (German *Zeit*) time). *Judaism* The anniversary of the death of a person, especially a parent.

yajna *noun* (also **yagna**) E19 **Sanskrit** (*yajña* worship, sacrifice). In Hinduism, a sacrificial rite with a specific objective, often involving the burning of substantial offerings.

yakitori *noun* M20 **Japanese** (from *yaki* toasting, grilling + *tori* bird). A Japanese dish consisting of pieces of chicken grilled on a skewer.

yakka *noun* (also **yacca, yacker**) L19 **Aboriginal**. Work, toil.

■ Australian slang, especially in the phrase *hard yakka*.

yaksha *noun* L18 **Sanskrit** (*yakṣa*). *Indian Mythology* (A statue or carving of) any of a class of demigods or nature spirits often serving as tutelary guardians.

yakuza *noun* plural same M20 **Japanese** (from *ya* eight + *ku* nine + *za* three, with reference to the worst kind of hand in a gambling game). A Japanese gangster or racketeer. Usually *plural* meaning such gangsters, etc., collectively.

yang *noun & adjective* L17 **Chinese** (*yáng* sun, positive, male genitals). **A** *noun* L17 In Chinese philosophy, the male or active principle of the two opposing forces of the universe. Cf. YIN. **B** *attributive* or as *adjective* L17 That represents yang; masculine.

yang ch'in *noun phrase* L19 **Chinese** (*yángqín*, from *yáng* high-sounding, foreign + *qín* (Wade–Giles *ch'in*) musical instrument, zither). A Chinese dulcimer.

yanggona *noun* (also **yaqona**) M19 **Fijian** (*yaqona*). KAVA.

yantra *noun* L19 **Sanskrit** (= device or mechanism for holding or fastening, from *yam* to hold, support). A geometrical diagram used as an aid to meditation in tantric worship; any object used similarly.

yaourt see under YOGURT.

yaqona variant of YANGGONA.

yarmulke *noun* (also **yarmulka**) E20 **Yiddish** (*yarmolke*, from Polish *jarmulka* cap, probably from Turkish *yağmurluk* raincoat, cape, from *yağmur* rain). A skullcap worn by male Jews.

yashmak *noun* M19 **Arabic** (*yašmaḳ* from Turkish *yaşmak* noun use of *yaşmak* to hide oneself). A veil concealing the face below the eyes, worn by Muslim women in public.

yataghan *noun* (also **ataghan**) E19 **Turkish** (*yatağan*). Chiefly *History* In Muslim countries, a sword or long dagger having a handle without a guard and often a double-curved blade.

yenta *noun* (also **yente**) E20 **Yiddish** (originally a personal name). A gossip, a busybody; a noisy, vulgar person; a scolding woman, a shrew. *colloquial.*

yentz *transitive verb* M20 **Yiddish** (from *yentzen* to copulate). Cheat, swindle. *slang.*

yerba *noun* E19 **Spanish** (= herb). MATÉ sense 2. More fully *yerba maté.*

yeshiva *noun* plural **yeshivas**, **yeshivot(h)** M19 **Hebrew** (*yĕšībāh*, from *yāšhab* to sit). An Orthodox Jewish college or seminary; a Talmudic academy.

yeso *noun* (also **yesso**) M16 **Spanish** (from Latin *gypsum*; cf. GESSO). Gypsum, plaster of Paris; *especially* gypsum-rich dust used to control acidity during the making of sherry.

yeti *noun* M20 **Tibetan** (*yeh-teh* little manlike animal). A creature said to resemble a large ape, whose tracks have supposedly been found in snow on the Himalayan mountains. Also called *Abominable Snowman.*

yé-yé *adjective & noun* M20 **French** (representing *yeah-yeah* reduplication of *yeah*, common in popular songs of the 1960s). **A** *adjective* M20 Designating or pertaining to a style of popular music, dress, etc., typical of the 1960s, especially in France; associated with or enthusiastic about this or subsequent forms of popular optimistic youth culture. **B** *noun* M20 A person associated with the yé-yé style. Also, rock or pop music.

yichus *noun* E20 **Yiddish** (from Hebrew *yiḥūs* pedigree). Social status, prestige. Chiefly *colloquial.*

yin *noun & adjective* L17 **Chinese** (*yīn* shade, feminine, the moon). **A** *noun* L17 In Chinese philosophy, the female or negative principle of the two opposing forces of the universe. Cf. YANG. **B** *attributive* or as *adjective* M20 That represents yin; feminine.

ying ch'ing *adjective & noun phrase* E20 **Chinese** (*yǐngqīng* (Wade–Giles *ying ch'ing*) literally, 'shadowy blue'). (Designating) a type of Chinese porcelain with a bluish white glaze produced in Jiangxi and other provinces, chiefly during the Song dynasty.

ylang-ylang *noun* (also **ilang-ilang**) L19 **Tagalog** (*ilang-ílang*). A tree of tropical Asia, *Cananga odorata*, with fragrant greenish yellow flowers from which a perfume is distilled; the perfume obtained from this tree.

yoga *noun* L18 **Sanskrit** (literally, 'union'). In Hindu philosophy, union of the self with the supreme being; a system of ascetic practice, meditation, etc., designed to achieve this.

■ Frequently specifically HATHA YOGA.

yogi *noun* (in sense 1 also **yogin**) E17 **Sanskrit** (*yogin*, nominative singular *yogī*, from YOGA). **1** E17 A person practicing, or proficient in, yoga. **2** E20 YOGA.

yogini *noun* L18 **Sanskrit** (*yoginī* feminine *yogin* yogi). **1** L18 *Hindu Mythology* A female demon, *especially* one of a group attendant on Durga or Siva. **2** M20 A female yogi.

yogurt *noun* (also **yoghurt**) E17 **Turkish** (*yoğurt*). A semisolid, somewhat sour foodstuff, now often fruit-flavored, made from milk curdled by the addition of certain bacteria; a carton of this substance.

■ The spelling *yaourt* (E19) as a representation of the pronunciation of *yoğurt* is now rare or obsolete.

yokozuna *noun* M20 **Japanese** (from *yoko* crosswise + *tsuna* rope (originally a kind of belt presented to the champion)). A grand champion sumo wrestler.

yom tov *noun phrase* M19 **Yiddish** (from Hebrew *yōm* day + *ṭōb* good). A Jewish holiday or holy day.

yoni *noun* L18 **Sanskrit**. Chiefly *Hinduism* A figure or representation of the female genitals as a sacred symbol or object.

yordim *noun plural* L20 **Hebrew** (plural of *yored* person who descends). Emigrants from the state of Israel.

yorgan *noun* E20 **Turkish**. A Turkish quilt.

yourt variant of YURT.

yuan *noun* (also **Yuan**) plural same E20 **Chinese** (*yuàn* courtyard). In China: any of several government departments.

yüeh ch'in *noun* M19 **Chinese** (*yuèqín* (Wade–Giles *yüeh-ch'in*) literally, 'moon guitar'). A Chinese lute with four strings and a flat circular body.

yuga *noun* (also **yug**) L18 **Sanskrit** (*yuga* yoke, an age of the world). In Hindu cosmology, each of four periods, each shorter than and inferior to its predecessor, together totaling 4,320,000 years. Cf. KALPA.

yugen *noun* E20 **Japanese** (from *jū* faint, distant + *gen* dark, unfathomable). In traditional Japanese court culture and Noh plays, a hidden quality of graceful beauty or mystery; profound aestheticism.

yukata *noun* E19 **Japanese** (from *yu* hot water, bath + *kata*(*bira*) light kimono). A light cotton kimono, frequently with stencil designs, worn after a bath, or as a housecoat.

yurt *noun* (also **yourt**) L18 **Russian** (*yurta* (through French *yourte* or German *Jurte*) from Turkic *jurt*). A circular tent of felt, skins, etc., on a collapsible framework, used by nomads in Mongolia and Siberia. Also, a semi-subterranean hut, usually of wood covered with earth or turf.

zabaglione *noun* L19 **Italian** (perhaps ultimately from late Latin *sabaia* an Illyrian drink). A dessert consisting of egg yolks, sugar, and (usually Marsala) wine, whipped to a frothy texture over a gentle heat and served either hot or cold. Cf. SABAYON.

zabuton *noun* L19 **Japanese** (from *za* sitting, seat + *buton* variant of FUTON). A flat floor cushion for sitting or kneeling on.

zaftig *adjective* (also **zoftig**) M20 **Yiddish** (from German *saftig* juicy). Of a woman: plump, having a full rounded figure. *colloquial*.

zaguan *noun* M19 **Spanish** (*zaguán* = vestibule, hall, from Arabic *'ustuwān*, perhaps ultimately from Greek *stoa* porch). In South and Central America and in the south-western United States: a passage running from the front door to the central patio of houses.

zaibatsu *noun* plural same M20 **Japanese** (from *zai* wealth + *batsu* clique). *Commerce* Originally, a Japanese capitalist organization usually based on a single family having controlling interests in a variety of companies. Now, (the members of) a Japanese business cartel or conglomerate.

zaikai *noun* M20 **Japanese** (from *zai* wealth + *kai* world). In Japan: (the elite who control) the world of business and high finance.

zaitech *noun* L20 **Japanese** (= financial engineering). Playing the money and stock markets as a business practice to enhance a company's profitability.

zakat *noun* E19 **Persian and Urdu** (*zakā(t)*, Turkish *zekât*, from Arabic *zakā(t)* almsgiving). An obligatory payment made annually under Islamic law on certain kinds of property and used for charitable and religious objects.

zakuska *noun* (also **zakouska**) plural **zakuskas**, **zakuski** L19 **Russian** (usually as plural *zakuski*). An hors d'oeuvre.

zamarra *noun* M19 **Spanish**. In Spain: a kind of sheepskin jacket.

zampogna *noun* M18 **Italian** (from (late) Latin *symphonia*). *Music* A traditional mouth-blown bagpipe of southern Italy having two chanters and two drones. Also, any of various other woodwind instruments.

zapateado *noun* plural **zapateados** M19 **Spanish** (from *zapato* shoe). **1** M19 A flamenco dance involving complex syncopated stamping of the heels and toes in imitation of castanets. **2** M20 Dancing or footwork of this kind.

zarape variant of SERAPE.

zarda *noun* L19 **Persian and Urdu** (*zardah*, from Persian *zard* yellow). A Persian and Indian sweet dish consisting of rice cooked with saffron and often almonds and raisins or sultanas.

zareba *noun* (also **zereba**, **zariba**, **zeriba**) M19 **Arabic** (*zarība* pen or enclosure for cattle). **1** M19 In Sudan and neighboring countries: (a camp fortified by) a fence, usually made of thorn trees, for defense against enemies or wild animals. **2** L19 *transferred* and *figurative* A defensive force or barrier.

zari *noun* M20 **Persian and Urdu** (*zarī*, from Persian *zar* gold). Indian gold and silver brocade; *colloquial* a sari decorated with this.

zariba variant of ZAREBA.

zarzuela *noun* L19 **Spanish**. **1** L19 A traditional form of operetta in Spain, with spoken dialogue, songs, and dances. **2** M20 A Spanish dish consisting of various kinds of seafood cooked in a rich sauce.

zastruga variant of SASTRUGA.

zawiya *noun* (also **zawiyeh**) M19 **Arabic** (*zāwiya* corner, prayer room). In North Africa: a Sufi religious community's mosque, especially when containing the shrine of a holy person.

zazen *noun* E18 **Japanese** (from *za* sitting, a seat + *zen* Zen). Zen meditation.

zearat variant of ZIARAT.

zeitgeber *noun* plural same, **zeitgebers** M20 **German** (from *Zeit* time + *Geber* giver). *Physiology* A rhythmically occurring event, especially in the environment, that acts as a cue in the regulation of certain biological rhythms in an organism.

Zeitgeist *noun* M19 **German** (from *Zeit* time + *Geist* spirit). The spirit of the age; the trend of thought or feeling in a period, especially as reflected in its literature, art, etc.

zek *noun* M20 **Russian** (representing pronunciation of *z/k*, abbreviation of *zaklyuchënnyĭ* prisoner). In countries of the former USSR: a person held in a prison or forced labor camp.

zemstvo *noun* plural **zemstvos**, **zemstva** M19 **Russian** (from *zem'* (now *zemlya*) land). *History* Any of the elected district or provincial councils set up in Russia by Alexander II in 1864 as part of his reforms.

Zen *noun* E18 **Japanese** (from Chinese *chán* quietude, from Sanskrit *dhyāna* meditation). A school of Mahayana Buddhism emphasizing meditation and personal awareness.

■ Also more fully *Zen Buddhism*. Influential in Japanese life from the thirteenth century onward, *Zen* became significantly fashionable in the West during the 1960s.

zenana *noun* M18 **Persian and Urdu** (*zanānah*, from *zan* woman). **1** M18 In the Indian subcontinent: the part of a house in which high-caste women are or were secluded. **2** E20 A light quilted thin fabric used for women's dresses.

zendo *noun* plural **zendos** M20 **Japanese** (*zendō*, from ZEN + *dō* hall). A place for Zen Buddhist meditation and study.

zeppole *noun* plural **zeppoli** M20 **Italian**. A kind of doughnut.

zereba, zeriba variants of ZAREBA.

zeugma *noun* LME **Latin** (from Greek, literally, 'yoking', from *zeugnunai* to yoke, related to *zugon* a yoke). A rhetorical figure by which a single word is made to refer to two or more words in a sentence, especially when applying to them in different senses.

ziarat *noun* (also **zearat**) L18 **Urdu** (from Persian *ziyārat* from Arabic *ziyāra(t)* visit, pilgrimage). A Muslim pilgrimage to a shrine.

zibeline *noun* L16 **French** (of Slavonic origin). **1** L16 The sable. Now *rare* or *obsolete*. **b** M19 The fur of this animal. **2** L19 A soft smooth woolen material with a long nap pressed flat, used especially for women's coats. Also *zibeline cloth*.

zibib *noun* M19 **Arabic** (*zabīb* (Egyptian Arabic *zibīb*) dried grapes, raisins). A strong colorless spirit made in Egypt from raisins.

Zigeuner *noun* plural same (feminine **Zigeunerin**, plural **Zigeunerinnen**) M19 **German**. A Gypsy.

zingana *noun* E18 **Italian**. **1** E18 (*Zingana*) A Gypsy girl or woman. *rare*. **2** M20 Striped wood furnished by various African trees; zebrano.

Zingaro *noun & adjective* (also **zingaro**) E17 **Italian**. **A** *noun* E17 plural **zingari** (feminine **zingara**, plural **zingare**). A Gypsy. **B** *attributive* or as *adjective* L18 Of or pertaining to Gypsies.

zita *noun* plural **zite**, **ziti** M19 **Italian**. Pasta in the form of tubes resembling large macaroni.

zocalo *noun* plural **zocalos** L19 **Spanish** (*zócalo*). In Mexico: a public square, a plaza.

zoco *noun* plural **zocos** L19 **Spanish** (from Arabic *sūķ* souk). In Spain and North Africa: a souk; a marketplace.

zoftig variant of ZAFTIG.

zollverein *noun* M19 **German** (from *Zoll* toll + *Verein* union). *History* A union of nations with a uniform rate of customs duties from other countries and free trade within the union; *specifically* that between states of the German Empire in the nineteenth century.

zombie *noun & verb* E19 **Bantu** (cf. JUMBY). **A** *noun* **1** E19 Originally, a snake deity in voodoo cults of or deriving from West Africa and Haiti. Now (especially in the West Indies and southern United States), a soulless corpse said to have been revived by witchcraft. **2** M20 A dull, apathetic, unresponsive, or unthinkingly acquiescent person. *colloquial*. **3** M20 In World War II, a man conscripted for home defense. *Canadian military slang (derogatory)*. **4** M20 A long mixed drink consisting of several kinds of rum, liqueur, and fruit juice. **B** *transitive verb* M20 *zombie out*. Exhaust; disorient.

zoppa *adjective & adverb* M18 **Italian** (feminine of *zoppo* limping). *Music* In a syncopated rhythm, especially one in which the second quaver of a 2/4 bar is accented.

■ Frequently in the phrase *alla zoppa*.

zori *noun* plural **zoris**, same E19 **Japanese** (*zōri*, from *sō* grass, (rice) straw + *ri* footwear, sole). A Japanese sandal, having a simple thong between the toes and a flat sole originally of straw but now often of rubber, felt, etc.

Zouave *noun* M19 **French** (from Kabyle *Zouaoua* name of a tribe). **1** M19 A member of a body of light infantry in the French army, originally formed of Algerian Kabyles, and long retaining the original oriental uniform. **b** M19 *History* More fully *Papal* or *Pontifical Zouave*. A member of a corps of French soldiers formed in Rome for the defense of the pope between 1860 and 1871. **c** M19 *History* A member of any of several volunteer regiments of Union troops in the American Civil War that adopted the name and in part the uniform of the French Zouaves. **2** M19 A garment resembling part of the Zouave uniform; *specifically* **a** *History* (in full *Zouave jacket, bodice*) a woman's short embroidered jacket or bodice, with or without sleeves; **b** in *plural*, pegtop pants, as worn by men in the late nineteenth century and women in the late twentieth century (also *Zouave trousers, pants*); **c** a wide loose skirt with a looped or tucked up hemline (also *Zouave skirt*).

zouk *noun* L20 **French** (apparently from Antillean creole *zouk* to party, possibly influenced by United States slang *juke* (or *jook*) to have a good time). An exuberant style of popular music originating in Guadeloupe in the Lesser Antilles.

■ Developed in Paris as a style of Antillean popular music intended to hold its own against Western pop and disco music, *zouk* was popularized in France during the 1980s by the group called Kassav, and began to feature on the British and American music scene at the end of the decade.

zucchetto *noun* plural **zucchettos** (also **zucchetta**) M19 **Italian** (*zucchetta* diminutive of *zucca* gourd, head). The skullcap worn by Roman Catholic ecclesiastics, black for priests, purple for bishops, red for cardinals, and white for the Pope.

zucchini *noun plural* (also **zucchinis**) E20 **Italian** (plural of *zucchino* small squash, courgette, diminutive of *zucca* gourd). A green variety of smooth-skinned summer squash.

■ Chiefly in North America and Australia; in Britain *courgettes* is the usual word.

zufolo *noun* (also **zuffolo**) plural **zufoli** E18 **Italian**. *Music* A flageolet, a small flute or whistle.

Zugunruhe *noun* M20 **German**. *Ornithology* Migratory restlessness; the migratory drive in birds.

zugzwang *noun* E20 **German** (from *Zug* move + *Zwang* compulsion, obligation). *Chess* A position in which a player must move but cannot do so without disadvantage; the obligation to make a move even when disadvantageous.

■ Frequently in *in zugzwang*.

zuppa di pesce *noun phrase* M20 **Italian**. Fish soup.

zuppa inglese *noun phrase* M20 **Italian** (= English soup). A rich Italian dessert resembling trifle.

zurla *noun* plural **zurle** M20 **Serbo-Croat** (*sûrla*, from (as) next). *Music* A kind of shawm introduced to the Balkans from the Middle East by Gypsies.

zurna *noun* L19 **Turkish** (from Persian *surnā* festival pipe). *Music* A kind of shawm found in Turkey, Arabic-speaking countries, and various neighboring regions.

zut *interjection* E20 **French**. Expressing irritation, contempt, impatience, etc.

■ Also *zut alors!*, in which *alors* acts as an intensifier.

zwieback *noun* L19 **German** (= twice-bake). A (sweet) rusk or cracker made by baking a small loaf, and then toasting slices until they are dry and crisp.

zwischenzug *noun* M20 **German** (from *zwischen* intermediate + *Zug* move). *Chess* A move interposed in a sequence of play in such a way as to alter the outcome.

The History of English

1. Fifteen centuries of English cannot easily be summarized, so this account is intended to pick out features on the landscape of language rather than to describe the scene in detail. This may afford some perspective on the information given in the dictionary, and help to make more sense of the strange and often unpredictable ways in which words seem to behave.

Origins

2.1 English belongs to the Indo-European family of languages, a vast group with many branches, thought to be derived from a common ancestor-language called Proto-Indo-European. The words we use in English are derived from a wide range of sources, mostly within this family. The earliest sources are Germanic, Norse, and Romanic; later, they are the languages of Europe more generally; and most recently, with developments in such areas as medicine, electronics, computers, and communications, they have been worldwide.

2.2 It is difficult to be sure exactly what we mean by an "English" word. Most obviously, words are English if they can be traced back to the Anglo-Saxons, Germanic peoples who settled in Britain from the fifth century and eventually established several kingdoms together corresponding roughly to present-day England. From this time are derived many common words such as *eat, drink, speak, work, house, door, man, woman, husband, wife.* The Anglo Saxons displaced the Celtic peoples, whose speech survives in Scottish and Irish Gaelic, in Welsh, and in the local languages of two extremities of the British Isles, Manx (in the Isle of Man) and Cornish (in Cornwall, a county in southwestern England). Little Celtic influence remains in English, except in names of places such as *Brecon, Carlisle,* and *London,* and in many river names, such as *Avon, Thames,* and *Trent.* This fact may be attributed to a lack of cultural interaction, the Celts being forced back into the fringes of the British Isles by the Anglo-Saxon invaders.

3. Anglo-Saxon Britain continued to have contact with the Roman Empire, of which Britain had formerly been a part, and with Latin, which was the official language throughout the Empire and survived as a language of ritual (and for a time also of learning and communication) in the Western Christian Church. Christi-

anity was brought to England with the mission of St. Augustine in AD 597. The Christianized Anglo-Saxons built churches and monasteries, and there were considerable advances in art and learning. At this time English was enriched by words from Latin, many of which are still in use, such as *angel, disciple, martyr,* and *shrine.* Other words came from Latin via the Germanic languages, for example *copper, mint* (in the sense of coinage), *pound, sack,* and *title,* and others were ultimately of more remote origin, for example *camel* (Semitic) and *shampoo* (Hindi).

4.1 The next important influence on the vocabulary of English came from the Danish and other Scandinavian invaders of the ninth and tenth centuries, collectively called Vikings. They occupied much of the eastern portion of England, and under Cnut (Canute) ruled the whole country for a time. The Danes had much more contact with the Anglo-Saxons than did the Celts, and their period of occupation has left its mark in the number of Scandinavian (Old Norse) words taken into English. Because Old Norse was also a Germanic language (of a different branch from English) many words were similar to the Anglo-Saxon ones, and it is difficult to establish the extent of the Old Norse influence. However, a number of Norse words are identifiable and are still in use, such as *call, take,* and *law,* names of parts of the body such as *leg,* and other basic words such as *egg, root,* and *window.*

4.2 In the Saxon kingdom of Wessex, King Alfred (reigned 871–899) and his successors did much to keep English alive by using it (rather than Latin) as the language of education and learning; by the tenth century there was a considerable amount of English prose and verse literature. Saxon and Danish kingdoms existed side by side for several generations, and there was much linguistic interaction. One very important effect on English was the gradual disappearance of many word endings, or inflections, leading to a simpler grammar. This was partly because the stems of English and Norse words were often very close in form (for example, *stāacn* and *steinn,* meaning 'stone'), and only the inflections differed as an impediment to mutual understanding. So other forms such as *stāne, stānes,* etc., began to be simplified and, eventually, eliminated. The process continued for hundreds of years into Middle English (see below).

The Norman Conquest

5. In 1066 William of Normandy defeated the English king, Harold, at the Battle of Hastings; he was crowned King of England

on Christmas Day. The arrival of the French-speaking Normans as a ruling nobility brought a transforming Romance influence on the language. The Romance languages (chiefly French, Italian, Spanish, Portuguese, and Romanian) have their roots in the spoken or "vulgar" Latin (*vulgar* here meaning 'of the (common) people') that continued in use until about AD 600. For two hundred years after the Norman Conquest, French (in its regional Norman form) was the language of the aristocracy, the law courts, and the Church hierarchy in England. Gradually the Normans were integrated into English society, and by the reign of Henry II (1154–1189) many of the aristocracy spoke English. During these years many French words were adopted into English. Some were connected with law and government, such as *justice*, *council*, and *tax*, and some were abstract terms such as *liberty*, *charity*, and *conflict*. The Normans also had an important effect on the spelling of English words. The combination of letters *cw*, for example, was standardized in the Norman manner to *qu-*, so that *cwēn* became *queen* and *cwic* became *quik* (later *quick*).

6. This mixture of conquering peoples and their languages—Germanic, Scandinavian, and Romance—had a decisive effect on the forms of words in modern English. The three elements make up the basic stock of English vocabulary, and different practices of putting sounds into writing are reflected in each. The different grammatical characteristics of each element can be seen in the structure and endings of many words. Many of the variable endings such as *-ant* and *-ent*, *-er* and *-or*, *-able* and *-ible* exist because the Latin words on which they are based belonged to different classes of verbs and nouns, each of which had a different ending. For example, *important* comes from the Latin verb *portare*, meaning 'to carry' (which belongs to one verb class or conjugation) while *repellent* comes from the Latin verb *pellere*, meaning 'to drive' (which belongs to another). *Capable* comes from a Latin word ending in *-abilis*, while *sensible* comes from one ending in *-ibilis*, and so on.

Middle English

7. Middle English, as the English of *c.* 1100–1500 is called, emerged as the spoken and written form of the language under these influences. The use of French diminished, especially after King John (reigned 1199–1216) lost possession of Normandy in 1204, severing an important Anglo-French link. Many Anglo-Saxon words continued in use, while others disappeared alto-

gether: for example, *niman* was replaced by the Old Norse (Scandinavian) *taka* (meaning 'take'), and the Old English *sige* was replaced by a word derived from Old French, *victory*. Other Old English words that disappeared are *ādl* (disease), *lof* (praise), and *lyft* (air: compare German *Luft*). Sometimes new and old words continued in use side by side, in some cases on a roughly equal footing, and in others with a distinction in meaning (as with *doom* and *judgment*, and *stench* and *smell*). This has produced pairs of words which are both in use today, such as *shut* and *close*, and *buy* and *purchase*, in which the second word of each pair is Romance in origin. Sometimes an even larger overlap was produced, as when *commence* (from the French) was added to the existing Old English *begin* and *start*. (The original meaning of *start* was 'leap,' 'move suddenly,' which is still current though no longer the main sense.)

8. Hundreds of the Romance words were short, simple words that would now be distinguished with difficulty from Old English words if their origin were not known: for example, *bar*, *cry*, *fool*, *mean*, *pity*, *stuff*, *touch*, and *tender*. Others, such as *commence* and *purchase*, have more formal connotations. The result was a mixture of types of words, a feature of modern English. For many meanings we now have a choice of less and more formal words, the more formal ones used only in very specific circumstances. For example, the word *vendor* is used instead of *seller* only in commercial contexts. Many technical words derived from or ultimately from Latin, such as *estop* and *usucaption*, survive only in legal contexts, to the great confusion of the layperson.

Printing

9. There was much regional variation in the spelling and pronunciation of Middle English, although a good measure of uniformity was imposed by the development of printing from the fifteenth century. This uniformity was based as much on practical considerations of the printing process as on what seemed most "correct" or suitable. It became common practice, for example, to add a final *e* to words to fill a line of print. The printers—many of them foreign—used rules from their own languages, especially Dutch and Flemish, when setting English into type. William Caxton, the first English printer (1422–1491), exercised an important but not always beneficial influence. The unnecessary insertion of *h* in *ghost*, for example, is due to Caxton (who learned the business of printing on the Continent), and the change had its effect on

other words such as *ghastly* and (perhaps) *ghetto*. In general, Caxton used the form of English prevalent in the southeast of England, although the East Midland dialect was the more extensive. This choice, together with the importance of London as the English capital, gave the dialect of southeastern England a significance and influence that survives to the present day.

Pronunciation

10. At roughly the same time as the early development of printing, the pronunciation of English was also undergoing major changes. The main change, which began in the fourteenth century during the lifetime of the poet Chaucer (1340?–1400), was in the pronunciation of vowel sounds. The so-called "great vowel shift" resulted in the reduction of the number of words that are pronounced with the vowel sound in long vowels (*deed* as distinct from *dead*). It also affected the pronunciation of other vowels: the word *life*, for example, was once pronounced as we now pronounce *leaf*, and *name* was pronounced as two syllables to rhyme with *comma*. In many cases, as with *name*, the form of the word did not change; this accounts for many of the "silent" vowels at the ends of words. The result of these developments was a growing difference between what was spoken and what was written.

The Renaissance

11. The rediscovery in Europe of the culture and history of the ancient Greek and Roman worlds exercised a further Romanizing influence on English. This began at the end of the Middle Ages and blossomed in the European Renaissance of the fifteenth to seventeenth centuries. Scholarship flourished, and the language used by scholars and writers was Latin. During the Renaissance words such as *arena*, *dexterity*, *excision*, *genius*, *habitual*, *malignant*, *specimen*, and *stimulus* came into use in English. They are familiar and useful words but their origins sometimes make them awkward to handle, as, for example, when we use *arena*, *genius*, and *stimulus* in the plural. There was also a tendency in the Renaissance to try to emphasize the Greek or Latin origins of words when writing them. This accounts for the *b* in *debt* (the earlier English word was *det*; in Latin it is *debitum*), the *l* in *fault* (earlier *faut*; the Latin source is *fallere*), the *s* in *isle* (earlier *ile*; *insula* in Latin), and the *p* in *receipt* (earlier *receit*; *recepta* in Latin). Some words that had gone out of use were reintroduced, usually with changed mean-

ings, for example *artificial*, *disk* (originally the same as *dish*), and *fastidious*.

Later Influences

12.1 In recent times English speakers have come into contact with people from other parts of the world, through trade, international relations, and improved communications generally. This contact has produced a rich supply of new words. India, where the British first had major dealings in the seventeenth century, is the source of words such as *bungalow*, *jodhpurs*, and *khaki*. Examples from other parts of the world are *harem* and *mufti* (from Arabic), *bazaar* (from Persian), *kiosk* (from Turkish), *ukulele* (from Hawaiian), *futon* (from Japanese), and *anorak* (from Eskimo). From European countries we have acquired *balcony* (from Italian), *envelope* (from French), and *yacht* (from Dutch).

12.2 Thousands of such words, though not English in the Germanic sense, are regarded as fully absorbed into English. In addition, there are many unnaturalized words and phrases that are used in English contexts but are generally regarded as "foreign," and are conventionally printed in italics to distinguish them when used in an English context. Very many of these are French, for example *accouchement* (childbirth), *bagarre* (a scuffle), *bonhomie* (geniality), *flânerie* (idleness), and *rangé* (domesticated), but other languages are represented, as with *echt* (genuine) and *Macht-politik* (power politics) from German, and *mañana* (tomorrow) from Spanish.

13.1 Usage often recognizes the difficulties of absorbing words from various sources by assimilating them into familiar forms. The word *picturesque*, which came into use in the eighteenth century, is a compromise between its French source *pittoresque* and the existing Middle English word *picture*, to which it is obviously related. The English word *cockroach* is a conversion of its Spanish source word *cucaracha* into a pair of familiar words, *cock* (a bird) and *roach* (a fish). Cockroaches have nothing to do with cocks or roaches, and the association is simply a matter of linguistic convenience.

13.2 Problems of inflection arise with words taken from other languages. The ending *-i* in particular is very unnatural in English, and usage varies between *-is* and *-ies* for the plural. A similar difficulty occurs with the many adopted nouns ending in *-o*, some of which come from the Italian (*solo*), some from Spanish (*armadillo*), and some from Latin (*hero*); here usage varies between *-os* and *-oes*. Verbs often need special treatment, as *bivouac* (from French, and before that probably from Swiss German), which needs a *k* in the past tense (*bivouacked*, not *bivouaced*, which might be mispronounced), and *ski* (from Norwegian, where usage allows both *ski'd* and *skied* as past forms).

Dictionaries

14.1 One obvious consequence of the development of printing in the fifteenth century was that it allowed the language to be recorded in glossaries and dictionaries, and this might be expected to have had a considerable effect on the way words were used and spelled. However, listing all the words in the language systematically in alphabetical order with their spellings and meanings is a relatively recent idea. There was nothing of the sort in Shakespeare's time, for example. In 1580, when Shakespeare was sixteen, a schoolmaster named William Bullokar published a manual for the "ease, speed, and perfect reading and writing of English," and he called for the writing of an English dictionary. Such a dictionary, the work of Robert Cawdrey (another schoolmaster), was not published until 1604. Like the dictionaries that followed in quick succession (including John (son of William) Bullokar's *English Expositor*), its purpose was described as being for the understanding of "hard words." It was not until the eighteenth century that dictionaries systematically listed all the words in general use at the time regardless of how "easy" or "hard" they were; the most notable of these were compiled by Nathaniel Bailey (1721) and, especially, Samuel Johnson (1755). They were partly a response to a call, expressed by Swift, Pope, Addison, and other writers, for the language to be fixed and stabilized, and for the establishment of an English Academy to monitor it. None of these hopes as such were realized, but the dictionaries played an important role in setting the form and senses of English words. Noah Webster's American dictionaries set new standards for spelling and concision, starting with his edition in 1828.

14.2 The systematic investigation and recording of words in all their aspects and on a historical basis is represented in the *Oxford English Dictionary*, begun by the Scottish schoolmaster James A. H. Murray in 1879 as the *New English Dictionary on Historical Principles*. This work describes historically the spelling, inflection, origin, and meaning of words, and is supported by citations from printed literature and other sources of evidence from Old English to the present day. A new edition integrating the original dictionary and its *Supplement* (1972–1986) appeared in 1989. Because of its depth of scholarship, the *Oxford English Dictionary* forms a major basis of all English dictionaries produced since it was first published. Smaller desktop, college, and other abridged dictionaries that aim at recording the main vocabulary in current use began to appear early the twentieth century and in recent years the number has grown remarkably.

14.3 Unlike French, which is guided by the rulings of the *Académie Française*, English is not monitored by any single authority; established usage is the principal criterion. One result of this is that English tolerates many more alternative spellings than other languages. The alternatives are based on patterns of word formation and variation in the different languages through which they have passed before reaching ours.

English Worldwide

15. English is now used all over the world; as a result, there are many varieties of English, with varying accents, vocabulary, and usage, as in South Africa, India, Australia, New Zealand, Canada, and elsewhere. These varieties have an equal claim to be regarded as "English" and, although learners of English may look to British and American English as the two poles of an English-speaking world, it is very important that dictionaries should take account of other varieties of English, especially as it affects that in use elsewhere. The process is a strengthening and enriching one, and is the mark of a living and flourishing language.

Further Reading

16. Those who are interested in exploring further will find a host of books on the history and development of English. Good general accounts are A. C. Baugh and T. Cable, *A History of the English Language* (4th ed., New Jersey, 1993) and B. M. H. Strang, *A History of English* (London, 1970). At a more popular level, and more up to date on recent trends, are R. W. Burchfield, *The English Language* (Oxford, 1985) and R. McCrum *et al.*, *The Story of English* (New York, 1993). *The Oxford Companion to the English Language* (ed. T. McArthur, New York and Oxford, 1996) contains much that will interest those who want to know more about the English of today and its place among the languages of the world.